Cognitive Modeling

Cognitive Modeling

edited by Thad A. Polk and Colleen M. Seifert

A Bradford Book

The MIT Press
Cambridge, Massachusetts
London, England

This book was set in Palatino in 3B2 by Asco Typesetters, Hong Kong and was printed and bound in the United States of America.

Library of Congress Cataloging-in-Publication Data

Cognitive modeling / edited by Thad A. Polk and Colleen M. Seifert.
    p.   cm.
"A Bradford book."
Includes bibliographical references and index.
ISBN 0-262-16198-2 (alk. paper) — ISBN 0-262-66116-0 (pbk. : alk. paper)
1. Cognition. 2. Cognitive science. I. Polk, Thad A. II. Seifert, Colleen M.
BF311 .C55175 2001
153—dc21   2001018325

Contents

Preface   xi
Sources   xix

Part I
Architectures and Approaches   1

A. Symbolic Models   3

Construction Integration   4

Chapter 1
The Role of Knowledge in Discourse Comprehension: A Construction–
Integration Model   5
Walter A. Kintsch

ACT   48

Chapter 2
ACT: A Simple Theory of Complex Cognition   49
John R. Anderson

Soar   69

Chapter 3
A Preliminary Analysis of the Soar Architecture as a Basis for General
Intelligence   71
Paul S. Rosenbloom, John E. Laird, Allen Newell, and Robert McCarl

EPIC   99

Chapter 4
Adaptive Executive Control: Flexible Multiple-Task Performance without
Pervasive Immutable Response-Selection Bottlenecks   101
*David E. Meyer, David E. Kieras, Erick Lauber, Eric H. Schumacher, Jennifer Glass,
Eileen Zurbriggen, Leon Gmeindl, and Dana Apfelblat*

CAPS   129

Chapter 5
A Capacity Theory of Comprehension: Individual Differences in Working
Memory   131
Marcel A. Just and Patricia A. Carpenter

B. Neural Network Models   179

Neural Networks   180

Chapter 6
How Neural Networks Learn from Experience   181
Geoffrey E. Hinton

Hopfield Networks   196

Chapter 7
The Hopfield Model   197
John Hertz, Anders Krogh, and Richard G. Palmer

Back Propagation   212

Chapter 8
Learning Representations by Back-Propagating Errors   213
David E. Rumelhart, Geoffrey E. Hinton, and Ronald J. Williams

Supervised Learning   221

Chapter 9
Forward Models: Supervised Learning with a Distal Teacher   223
Michael I. Jordan and David E. Rumelhart

Recurrent Networks   256

Chapter 10
Finding Structure in Time   257
Jeffrey L. Elman

Adaptive Resonance Theory   288

Chapter 11
A Self-Organizing Neural Network for Supervised Learning, Recognition, and
Prediction   289
Gail A. Carpenter and Stephen Grossberg

Optimality Theory   315

Chapter 12
Optimality: From Neural Networks to Universal Grammar   317
Alan Prince and Paul Smolensky

Part II
Case Studies in Cognitive Modeling   335

Perceptual Recognition   336

Chapter 13
Dynamic Binding in a Neural Network for Shape Recognition   337
John E. Hummel and Irving Biederman

Executive Processes   375

Chapter 14
Context, Cortex, and Dopamine: A Connectionist Approach to Behavior and
Biology in Schizophrenia   377
Jonathan D. Cohen and David Servan-Schreiber

Attentional Neglect   422

Chapter 15
The End of the Line for a Brain-Damaged Model of Unilateral Neglect   423
Michael C. Mozer, Peter W. Halligan, and John C. Marshall

List Memory   461

Chapter 16
An Integrated Theory of List Memory   463
John R. Anderson, Dan Bothell, Christian Lebiere, and Michael Matessa

Memory and Learning   497

Chapter 17
Why There Are Complementary Learning Systems in the Hippocampus and
Neocortex: Insights from the Successes and Failures of Connectionist Models
of Learning and Memory   499
James L. McClelland, Bruce L. McNaughton, and Randall C. O'Reilly

Category Learning   535

Chapter 18
ALCOVE: An Exemplar-Based Connectionist Model of Category
Learning   537
John K. Kruschke

Procedural Learning   576

Chapter 19
How People Learn to Skip Steps   577
Stephen B. Blessing and John R. Anderson

Conceptual Learning   621

Chapter 20
Acquisition of Children's Addition Strategies: A Model of Impasse-Free,
Knowledge-Level Learning   623
Randolph M. Jones and Kurt VanLehn

Language Learning   647

Chapter 21
Learning from a Connectionist Model of the Acquisition of the English Past
Tense   649
Kim Plunkett and Virginia A. Marchman

Learning Words   660

Chapter 22
Acquiring the Mapping from Meaning to Sounds   661
Garrison W. Cottrell and Kim Plunkett

Reading Words   690

Chapter 23
Understanding Normal and Impaired Word Reading: Computational
Principles in Quasi-Regular Domains   691
David C. Plaut, James L. McClelland, Mark S. Seidenberg, and Karalyn Patterson

Producing Language   747

Chapter 24
Language Production and Serial Order: A Functional Analysis and a
Model   749
Gary S. Dell, Lisa K. Burger, and William R. Svec

Understanding Language   795

Chapter 25
Interference in Short-Term Memory: The Magical Number Two (or Three) in
Sentence Processing   797
Richard L. Lewis

Processing Similarity   815

Chapter 26
Similarity, Interactive Activation, and Mapping: An Overview   817
Robert L. Goldstone and Douglas L. Medin

Mapping Analogies   848

Chapter 27
Analogical Mapping by Constraint Satisfaction   849
Keith J. Holyoak and Paul Thagard

Retrieving Analogies   910

Chapter 28
MAC/FAC: A Model of Similarity-Based Retrieval   911
Kenneth D. Forbus, Dedre Gentner, and Keith Law

Representing Structure   941

Chapter 29
Distributed Representations of Structure: A Theory of Analogical Access and Mapping   943
John E. Hummel and Keith J. Holyoak

Retrieving Structure   986

Chapter 30
Case-Based Learning: Predictive Features in Indexing   987
Colleen M. Seifert, Kristian J. Hammond, Hollyn M. Johnson, Timothy M. Converse, Thomas F. McDougal, and Scott W. VanderStoep

Inductive Reasoning   1008

Chapter 31
Feature-Based Induction   1009
Steven A. Sloman

Deductive Reasoning   1043

Chapter 32
Deduction as Verbal Reasoning   1045
Thad A. Polk and Allen Newell

Task Performance   1083

Chapter 33
Project Ernestine: Validating a GOMS Analysis for Predicting and Explaining Real-World Task Performance   1085
Wayne D. Gray, Bonnie E. John, and Michael E. Atwood

Part III
Issues in Cognitive Modeling   1115

Connectionist vs. Symbolic Models   1116

Chapter 34
Connectionism and the Problem of Systematicity (Continued): Why
Smolensky's Solution *Still* Doesn't Work   1117
Jerry Fodor

Theory vs. Modeling   1129

Chapter 35
Networks and Theories: The Place of Connectionism in Cognitive
Science   1131
Michael McCloskey

Computation in the Brain   1147

Chapter 36
Neuropsychological Inference with an Interactive Brain: A Critique of the
"Locality" Assumption   1149
Martha J. Farah

Mind vs. World   1191

Chapter 37
Is Human Cognition Adaptive?   1193
John. R. Anderson

Generality vs. Specificity of Models   1229

Chapter 38
Précis of *Unified Theories of Cognition*   1231
Allen Newell

Contributors   1261
Index   1267

Preface

Computational modeling has played a central role in cognitive science since its inception and yet, in our view, there is currently no single source that provides a representative introduction to computational models of human cognition. This book is meant to provide such an introduction.

We became aware of the need for such a book when we set out to teach a cognitive modeling course to our students in psychology, computer science, and other areas of cognitive science. Our goals were for the students learn about:

- some of the major approaches and architectures used in cognitive modeling (both neural network approaches and symbolic approaches);
- specific computational models of a variety of different cognitive processes, ranging from low-level cognitive processes (e.g., attention and memory) to higher-level cognitive processes (e.g., language and reasoning); and
- some of the major theoretical issues in the field.

In short, we wanted to provide our students with an overview of the methods, theories, and controversies in the field of cognitive modeling as a whole.

It will come as no surprise to researchers in the field that our search for a book that achieves these goals was unsuccessful. Cognitive modeling encompasses a variety of modeling approaches and cognitive domains, and no single researcher has expertise in all of them. Previous books in the field tend to reflect this specialization by highlighting work from a particular theoretical perspective. In particular, there are a number of excellent introductions to neural network modeling (e.g., Anderson, 1995; Holyoak and Barnden, 1994; Hertz, Krogh, and Palmer, 1991; Levine, 1991; and Rumelhart and McClelland, 1986, to name only a few) and similarly, there are excellent books reviewing symbolic approaches to cognition (cf. Chipman and Meyrowitz, 1993; Klahr and Kotovsky, 1989; VanLehn, 1991). But our search for a book that gathered the diverse perspectives of the field as a whole into a single source came up empty.

Of course, we still had to teach the class! So, after an extensive search of the literature, we put together a list of original articles in the field that we hoped would satisfy the goals we had set forth. We did not completely succeed the first time around; in fact, we substantially revised the list many times in order to make it more representative, coherent, and accessible to students. Eventually, the course went well enough that we thought our collection could be of value to others in the cognitive science community. We therefore decided to publish it as a resource for those designing their own modeling courses, interested in comparing competing approaches, or seeking their own introduction to the field of cognitive modeling.

Choosing a Format

As instructors, we felt that reading original journal articles, rather than a textbook, is key to developing an appreciation of research in cognitive modeling. Whether you are already a modeler, seek to become one, or simply want to comprehend the results of modeling projects, we believe one must "muck around" in the detailed descriptions only available in technical journals. These papers have also benefited from the peer review process, and so have achieved some level of completeness and accuracy in description. And because they are published in journal outlets where multiple perspectives appear, they also tend to include some background framework for how the piece fits into the field as a whole.

Of course, a collection of reprinted journal articles also lacks a single narrative voice that connects the pieces together and provides a single perspective on the whole. While this is often valuable, we feel commentary from a single set of authors is the wrong approach for this type of collection. The cutting edge of science in cognitive modeling involves controversy; that is, there is no single voice that represents "the right" perspective regarding which approaches will succeed, which issues are most important, and which articles will prove in the end to be the key to future development in the field. We expect that no two researchers in cognitive modeling would agree in their assessments; in fact, the two of us experienced many differences of opinion during our own editing process for this book.

Selecting the Studies

A literature search for articles on cognitive modeling demonstrates a burgeoning industry over the past fifteen years. Given the rapid pace of change in this field, where innovations take place continually and new approaches are propagated, there is a wealth of publications representing important technical and theoretical developments. Work in computational modeling has matured to provide new and interesting findings published within the past ten years. For each finding, there are also ongoing interactions in print among scientists from differing approaches.

From this vast reservoir of information, we had to select only a tiny subset of papers to include in this collection. The size was limited by the pragmatic constraints from the publisher regarding length, and the pedagogical constraints of covering the material within a semester-length course. To assist us in dramatically limiting the number of articles included, we adopted a number of specific selection criteria.

Content of Articles
To select articles for inclusion, we focused on those addressing a phenomenon involving human cognition. Thus, we did not include many excellent papers that addressed other types of phenomena from a computational perspective. For example, successful computer models of neural processing, qualitative physics, adaptive systems, complex social interactions, machine learning, and tutoring were excluded because their claims did not address cognition per se. A related criterion was that most of the papers selected should simulate real empirical data form human subjects. In particular, we did not include many excellent models in artificial intelligence that simulate cognitive processing but are not tightly constrained by detailed empirical data from studies with humans. In addition, we favored articles that included a fully implemented computational model; that is, simulations were run and performance results were available. We therefore excluded most mathematical models and non-formal approaches. Finally, the articles had to represent an original contribution to the field as demonstrated by its publication in a peer-reviewed journal. Because journal editors evaluate articles for their unique contributions, we preferred them to books or chapters from edited volumes.

Role in the Field
Even with these constraints, there are still hundreds of interesting articles to choose from. To narrow the list, we focused on the role of the article within the broader field of cognitive modeling. Our goal was to represent each of the major perspectives in some form in the book, and to include papers that addressed a very broad range of cognitive domains.

Thus, some papers were selected because they are particularly representative of a major paradigm in the field. Often, a single article covering a particular paradigm was not available, or the sources that were available were too long, or too dated, to include. We tried to ensure that papers from many prominent researchers from all of the major paradigms are included. This served our intent to make the selection as a whole represent the wide variety of alternative approaches in the field.

At the same time, we chose to maximize the diversity of cognitive domains included in the collection. In particular, our goal was not to choose the 40–50 *best* papers in cognitive modeling, but rather to illustrate how modeling has been applied in a variety of different domains. In some cases, this meant choosing a less well-known paper over a better-known paper if it also addressed a novel topic.

Pragmatic Issues

We also struggled with more pragmatic concerns that limited the selection of articles in this collection. We noted that several existing volumes include the "citation classics" that originated the area of cognitive modeling (for example, Collins and Smith, 1988). However, there are few collections including exemplars of current research in the central paradigm. Consequently, we favored more recent articles to the older classics, including only three published before 1990.

Second, we attended to the writing style of the article, and favored those written in a more accessible style. In journals focused on a particular field, little introductory material is typically provided for a reader outside the field. In other journals appealing to a broad audience (for example, *Psychological Review* or *Cognitive Science*), the writing style may tend to address a broader audience. We hoped these papers would be accessible to readers new to the field (especially to students). In addition, we tried to limit the length of articles so that a focus was maintained on a single model and empirical data used in comparison. As a result, nearly half of the articles appearing have been excerpted from their original presentation length, many by their authors. This step also serves to balance the length of readings across topics.

Unfortunately, we also ran into difficulties with copyright clearances, and the cost of reprinting articles from particular outlets. The cost of reprinting articles was also problematic for the "coursepack" version we created initially (reproduction for individual students through a copy service). But by far, the most influential constraint applied to our selection process was space: We were allowed only 700 journal pages to represent a booming literature. This severe space limitation led us to prefer shorter papers over longer ones, and to come to blows over the exclusion of true favorites.

Of course, each and every person in the field of cognitive modeling will have a very different opinion about the articles that should be selected for such a volume. Undoubtedly, our own backgrounds, preferences, and expertise (or, more likely, ignorance!) biased the selection of papers substantially. We suspect that readers will know at least one paper, and probably many more, that they think absolutely *must* be included in a volume like this one, but was not. Despite inevitable differences of opinion (or, if you prefer, ridiculous oversights!), we hope the care and consideration we put into the selection process will be evident to you. Most importantly, we hope this collection will serve as a useful resource for the cognitive modeling community.

Organizing the Approaches

The resulting selections are organized in this volume in three major sections.

In Part I, we included articles covering most of the major computational modeling approaches we could identify. Collectively, these articles constitute a comprehensive overview of current architectures. In the first group, symbolic models implemented as production systems are presented. These papers summarize very large-scale, detailed architectures that are currently in use to model a wide variety of cognitive processes. In the second group, neural network paradigms are presented in a series of shorter papers tracing the development of connectionist systems. These papers illustrate innovations in network modeling that are assumed in current connectionist models of phenomena. We have included a number of papers describing some of the better known symbolic architectures (Soar, ACT-R, EPIC, etc.) as well as some neural network architectures that are commonly used in cognitive modeling (back-propagation networks, recurrent networks, Hopfield networks, ART, etc.). Along with the dominant symbolic and neural network paradigms presented here, we include examples of interesting new architectures developed in those traditions. The goal in this section of the book is to provide a foundation of the major approaches to modeling.

These diverse architectures are then demonstrated "in action" in Part II of the collection. The second, and largest, section of the book includes a series of case studies that present a computational model in a specific cognitive domain. Each paper addresses a research topic through a model and comparison to human experimental data. The articles are organized in a loosely bottom-up order, starting with models that address lower cognitive processes (e.g., perception, memory) and moving toward models that address higher cognitive processes (e.g., language, reasoning). These articles were chosen to represent the breadth of topics studied in the field, including a wide range of substantive problems. This section demonstrates how the differing architectures of Part I are being used in studies of specific cognitive phenomena.

The papers in the third and final section of the book address a few of the major issues and controversies in the field of cognitive modeling. Should computational models be thought of as theories? Is the architecture of cognition symbolic or subsymbolic? How is the world reflected in the mind? These and other questions are raised in articles by some of the major figures in cognitive science. These short commentaries provide examples of how to interpret and critique the contributions of cognitive models. We find our own students very eager to engage in debates based on the arguments presented here.

Designing Courses of Study

In our experience, this organization works extremely well in the classroom. The articles in the first section provide a foundation for understanding the specific case studies presented in the second section. Familiarity with these specific cognitive models allows students to better appreciate the conceptual issues raised by the commentaries in the third section.

When we teach this course, we typically have students discuss one or occasionally two papers in each class. We have intentionally included more papers than can be comfortably addressed in one semester so that instructors can have some flexibility in choosing the specific papers that are covered. For example, it is possible to teach a course that is geared mainly toward symbolic modeling or to teach one that is geared mainly toward neural network modeling simply by choosing the appropriate papers in each of the first two sections. Consequently, within this organizing framework, we have identified alternative paths that provide a coherent focus for a specific course. We feel the collection offers the most variety by combining and comparing the variety of approaches across topics. This is the approach we have adopted in teaching our own students.

In teaching the course ourselves, we have found that letting the students lead the discussions can be very educational for them. We therefore allow students to preview the articles and to select those for which they would like to lead discussion (sometimes in pairs). Because the research topics are so wide-ranging, we find students are able to identify at least one related to their own research interests.

We hope the organization of the collection will assist other instructors in adapting the volume for their courses. In addition to allowing flexibility in choosing the specific papers for the class to read, many instructors will want to supplement this volume with other papers from the literature. Each of the articles reprinted here includes a reference section that can be used as pointers to other related articles and authors. For one specific example of a course based on this book, please see "http://www.umich.edu/~tpolk/psych808".

Acknowledgments

First and foremost, we would like to thank all the authors who graciously agreed to have their articles reprinted in this volume. Many of these authors were also kind enough to excerpt their own articles in order to satisfy the space constraints, and others were willing to trust us to do the excerpting. We will be the first to acknowledge that the excerpts do not always do justice to the original papers (and we apologize in advance for any confusions resulting from our attempts to shorten their masterpieces). We hope these failings are mitigated by the resulting broader coverage of the field.

We would also like to thank our editor at The MIT Press, Amy Brand. Throughout the process, she was both savvy and helpful (and, when necessary, tough!). Most of all, however, she was extremely patient with a project that took significantly longer than we initially anticipated. Thanks, too, to Amy Yeager for her help with the production process. Senior editorial assistant Mel Goldsipe patiently shepherded us through the final months of production; she and designer Chryseis Fox deserve much credit for the book's final form.

We are grateful for the resources provided by the University of Michigan and its psychology department, especially for Mary Mohrbach's help in the early stages. Thanks also to Rita Wood at Grade A Notes, Inc.

Last, but not least, thanks to our friends and family (especially Zeke Montalvo, and Norma, Sarah, and Rachel Polk) who promised to love us whether or not we ever finished this book.

References

Anderson, J. A. (1995). *An introduction to neural networks*. Cambridge, MA: MIT Press.

Barnden, J. A., and Holyoak, K. J. (1994). *Analogy, metaphor, and reminding: Advances in connectionist and neural computation theory (v. 3)*. Norwood, NJ: Ablex.

Chipman, S. F., and Meyrowitz, A. L. (1993). *Foundations of knowledge acquisition*. Boston, MA: Kluwer.

Collins, A., and Smith, E. E. (1988). *Readings in cognitive science: A perspective from psychology and artificial intelligence*. San Mateo, CA: Morgan Kaufmann.

Hertz, J., Krogh, A., and Palmer, R. G. (1991). *Introduction to the theory of neural computation*. Redwood City, CA: Addison-Wesley.

Holyoak, K. J., and Barnden, J. A. (1994). *Analogical connections: Advances in connectionist and neural computation theory (v. 2)*. Norwood, NJ: Ablex.

Levine, D. S. (1991). *Introduction to neural and cognitive modeling*. Hillsdale, NJ: L. Erlbaum Associates.

Klahr, D., and Kotovsky, K. (1989). *Complex information processing: The impact of Herbert A. Simon*. Hillsdale, NJ: L. Erlbaum Associates.

Rumelhart, D. E., McClelland, J. L., and The PDP Research Group. (1986). *Parallel distributed processing: Explorations in the microstructure of cognition*. Cambridge, MA: MIT Press.

VanLehn, K. (1991). *Architectures for intelligence: The Twenty-Second Carnegie Symposium on Cognition*. Hillsdale, NJ: L. Erlbaum Associates.

Sources

The editors and The MIT Press acknowledge with thanks permission granted to reproduce in this volume the following materials previously published elsewhere. Every effort has been made to secure the appropriate permissions, but if any have been inadvertently overlooked, please contact the publisher to make the necessary arrangements.

Kinstch, W. A. "The role of knowledge in discourse comprehension: A construction integration model," *Psychological Review, 95(2)*, 1988, © 1988 by the American Psychological Association, reprinted by permission of the author and the publisher.

Anderson, J. R. "ACT: A simple theory of complex cognition," *American Psychologist, 51(4)*, 1996, © 1996 by the American Psychological Association, reprinted by permission of the author and the publisher.

Rosenbloom, P. S., Laird, J. E., Newell, A., and McCarl, R. Excerpt from "A preliminary analysis of the Soar architecture as a basis for general intelligence," *Artificial Intelligence, 47*, 1991, © 1991 by Elsevier Science, Ltd., reprinted by permission of the first two authors and the publisher.

Meyer, D. E., Kieras, D. E., Lauber, E., Schumacher, E. H., Glass, J., Zurbriggen, E., Gmeidel, L., and Apfelblat, D. "Adaptive executive control: Flexible multiple-task performance without pervasive immutable response-selection bottlenecks," *Acta Psychologica, 90(1–3)*, 1995, © 1995 by Elsevier Science, Ltd., reprinted by permission of the first author and the publisher.

Just, M. A., and Carpenter, P. A. Excerpt from "A capacity theory of comprehension: Individual differences in working memory," *Psychological Review, 99(1)*, 1992, © 1992 by the American Psychological Association, reprinted by permission of the authors and the publisher.

Hinton, G. E. "How neural networks learn from experience," *Scientific American, 267(3)*, 1992, © 1992 by Scientific American, Inc., reprinted by permission of the author and the publisher.

Hertz, J., Krogh, A., and Palmer, R. G. "The Hopfield Model," chapter 2 of *Introduction to the Theory of Neural Computation*, 1991 © 1991 by Addison-Wesley Pub., reprinted by permission of the authors and the publisher.

Rumelhart, D. E., Hinton, G. E., and Williams, R. J. "Learning representations by back-propagating errors," *Nature, 323(6088)*, 1986, © 1986 by Nature, Inc., reprinted by permission of the second author and the publisher.

Jordan, M. I., and Rumelhart, D. E. (1992). Excerpt from "Forward models: Supervised learning with a distal teacher," *Cognitive Science, 16(3)*, 1992, © 1992 by the Cognitive Science Society, Inc., reprinted by permission of the authors and the society.

Elman, J. L. "Finding structure in time," *Cognitive Science, 14(2)*, 1990, © 1990 by the Cognitive Science Society, Inc., reprinted by permission of the author and the society.

Carpenter, G. A., and Grossberg, S. "A self-organizing neural network for supervised learning, recognition, and prediction," *IEEE Communications Magazine, 30*, 1992, © 1992 by IEEE, reprinted by permission of the authors and the society.

Prince, A., and Smolensky, P. "Optimality: From neural networks to universal grammar," *Science*, *275(5306)*, 1997, © 1997 by Science, Inc., reprinted by permission of the authors and the publisher.

Hummel, J. E., and Biederman, I. Excerpt from "Dynamic binding in a neural network for shape recognition," *Psychological Review*, *99(3)*, 1992, © 1992 by the American Psychological Association, reprinted by permission of the first author and the publisher.

Cohen, J. D., and Servan-Schreiber, D. Excerpt from "Context, cortex, and dopamine: A connectionist approach to behavior and biology in Schizophrenia," *Psychological Review*, *99(1)*, 1992, © 1992 by the American Psychological Association, reprinted by permission of the first author and the publisher.

Mozer, M. C., Halligan, P. W., and Marshall, J. C. "The end of the line for a brain-damaged model of unilateral neglect," *Journal of Cognitive Neuroscience*, *9(2)*, 1997, © 1997 by the MIT Press, reprinted by permission of the first author and the publisher.

Anderson, J. R., Bothell, D., Lebiere, C., and Matessa, M. Excerpt from "An integrated theory of list memory," *Journal of Memory and Language*, *38*, 1998, © 1998 by the American Psychological Association, reprinted by permission of the first author and the publisher.

McClelland, J. L., McNaughton, B. L., and O'Reilly, R. C. Excerpt from "Why there are complementary learning systems in the hippocampus and neocortex: Insights from the successes and failures of connectionist models of learning and memory," *Psychological Review*, *102(3)*, 1995, © 1995 by the American Psychological Association, reprinted by permission of the first author and the publisher.

Kruschke, J. K. Excerpt from "ALCOVE: An exemplar-based connectionist model of category learning," *Psychological Review*, *99(1)*, 1992, © 1992 by the American Psychological Association, reprinted by permission of the author and the publisher.

Blessing, S. B., and Anderson, J. R. "How people learn to skip steps," *Journal of Experimental Psychology: Learning, Memory, & Cognition*, *22(3)*, 1996, © 1996 by the American Psychological Association, reprinted by permission of the author and the publisher.

Jones, R. M., and VanLehn, K. "Acquisition of children's addition strategies: A model of impasse-free knowledge-level learning," *Machine Learning*, *16(1–2)*, 1994, © 1994 by Kluwer, reprinted by permission of the authors and the publisher.

Plunkett, K., and Marchman, V. A. "Learning from a connectionist model of the acquisition of the English past tense," *Cognition*, *61(3)*, 1996, © 1996 by Elsevier Science, Ltd., reprinted by permission of the first author and the publisher.

Cottrell, G. W., and Plunkett, K. Excerpt from "Acquiring the mapping from meaning to sounds," *Connection Science: Journal of Neural Computing, Artificial Intelligence & Cognitive Research*, *6(4)*, 1994, © 1994 by Carfax, Inc., reprinted by permission of the authors and the publisher.

Plaut, D., McClelland, J. L., Seidenberg, M. S., and Patterson, K. Excerpt from "Understanding normal and impaired word reading: Computational principles in quasi-regular domains," *Psychological Review*, *103(1)*, 1996, © 1996 by the American Psychological Association, reprinted by permission of the first author and the publisher.

Dell, G. S., Burger, L. K., and Svec, W. R. Excerpt from "Language production and serial order: A functional analysis and a model," *Psychological Review*, *104(1)*, 1997, © 1997 by the American Psychological Association, reprinted by permission of the first author and the publisher.

Lewis, R. L. "Interference in short-term memory: The magical number two (or three) in sentence processing," *Journal of Psycholinguistic Research*, *25(1)*, 1996, © 1996 by Plenum, Inc., reprinted by permission of the author and the publisher.

Goldstone, R. L., and Medin, D. L. Excerpt from "Interactive activation, similarity, and mapping: An overview," in K. J. Holyoak & J. Barnden (Eds), *Advances in Connectionist and Neural Computation Theory, Vol. 2: Analogical Connections*, 1994, © 1994 by Ablex Press, Inc., reprinted by permission of the authors and the publisher.

Holyoak, K. J., and Thagard, P. "Analogical mapping by constraint satisfaction," *Cognitive Science*, *13*, 1989, © 1989 by the Cognitive Science Society, Inc., reprinted by permission of the authors and the society.

Forbus, K. D., Gentner, D., and Law, K. Excerpt from "MAC/FAC: A model of similarity-based retrieval," *Cognitive Science*, *19(2)*, 1995, © 1995 by the Cognitive Science Society, Inc., reprinted by permission of the first two authors and the society.

Hummel, J. E., and Holyoak, K. J. (1997). Excerpt from "Distributed representations of structure: A theory of analogical access and mapping," *Psychological Review, 104(3)*, 1997, © 1997 by the American Psychological Association, reprinted by permission of the author and the publisher.

Seifert, C. M., Hammond, K. J., Johnson, H. M., Converse, T. M., MacDougal, T. F., and Vander-Stoep, S. W. "Case-based learning: Predictive features in indexing," *Machine Learning*, *16*, 1994, © 1994 by Kluwer, reprinted by permission of the first author and the publisher.

Sloman, S. A. Excerpt from "Feature-based induction," *Cognitive Psychology*, *25(2)*, 1993, © 1993 by Academic Press, Inc., reprinted by permission of the author and the publisher.

Polk, T. A., and Newell, A. Excerpt from "Deduction as verbal reasoning," *Psychological Review*, *102(3)*, 1995, © 1995 by the American Psychological Association, reprinted by permission of the author and the publisher.

Gray, W. D., John, B. E., and Atwood, M. E. Excerpt from "Project Ernestine: Validating a GOMS analysis for predicting and explaining real-world task performance," *Human-Computer Interaction*, *8(3)*, 1993, © 1993 by Lawrence Erlbaum Associates, Inc., reprinted by permission of the first two authors and the publisher.

Fodor, J. "Connectionism and the problem of systematicity (continued): Why Smolensky's solution *still* doesn't work," chapter 10 of *In Critical Condition: Polemical essays on cognitive science and the philosophy of mind*, 1998, © 1998 by MIT Press, reprinted by permission of the author and the publisher.

McCloskey, M. "Networks and theories: The place of connectionism in cognitive science," *Psychological Science*, *2(6)*, 1991, © 1991 by Blackwell Publishers, reprinted by permission of the author and the publisher.

Farah, M. J. "Neuropsychological inference with an interactive brain: A critique of the locality assumption," *Behavioral and Brain Sciences*, *17(1)*, 1994, © 1994 by Cambridge University Press, reprinted by permission of the author and the publisher.

Anderson, J. R. "Is human cognition adaptive?" *Behavioral and Brain Sciences*, *14(3)*, 1991, © 1991 by Cambridge University Press, reprinted by permission of the author and the publisher.

Newell, A. "Precis of *Unified Theories of Cognition*," *Behavioral & Brain Sciences*, *15(3)*, 1992, © 1992 by Cambridge University Press, reprinted by permission of the publisher.

Part I

Architectures and Approaches

A. *Symbolic Models*

Construction Integration

Chapter 1

The Role of Knowledge in Discourse Comprehension: A Construction–Integration Model

Walter A. Kintsch

Discourse comprehension, from the viewpoint of a computational theory, involves constructing a representation of a discourse upon which various computations can be performed, the outcomes of which are commonly taken as evidence for comprehension. Thus, after comprehending a text, one might reasonably expect to be able to answer questions about it, recall or summarize it, verify statements about it, paraphrase it, and so on.

To achieve these goals, current theories use representations with several mutually constraining layers. Thus, there is typically a linguistic level of representation, conceptual levels to represent both the local and global meaning and structure of a text (e.g., the micro- and macrostructure, constituting the *text base* in van Dijk & Kintsch, 1983), and a level at which the text itself has lost its individuality and its information content has become integrated into some larger structure (e.g., van Dijk & Kintsch's situation model).

Many different processes are involved in constructing these representations. To mention just a few, there is word identification, where, say, a written word like *bank* must somehow provide access to what we know about banks, money, and overdrafts. There is a parser that turns phrases like *the old men and women* into propositions such as AND[OLD[MEN],OLD[WOMEN]]. There is an inference mechanism that concludes from the phrase *The hikers saw the bear* that they were scared. There are macro-operators that extract the gist of a passage. There are processes that generate spatial imagery from a verbal description of a place.

It is one thing for a theorist to provide some formal description (e.g., a simulation model) for how such processes can occur and for what the computational steps were that led to a particular word identification, inference, or situation model. It is quite another to control construction processes in such a way that at each point in the process exactly the right step is taken. Part of the problem has to do with the characteristic ambiguity of language: How do we make sure that we access the financial meaning of *bank*, and not the meaning of *riverbank*? Why did we parse *the old men and women* as we did—maybe the women were not old at all. Why did we infer that the hikers were scared rather than that they had their eyes open, or a myriad of other irrelevancies?

Of all the many ways macro-operators could be applied, how did we get just the right sequence to reach a plausible gist without making the wrong generalizations? The number of possible alternative steps is distressingly large in constructing discourse representations, and without firm guidance, a computational model could not function properly for long. That is where knowledge comes in.

General knowledge about words, syntax, the world, spatial relations—in short, general knowledge about anything—constrains the construction of discourse representations at all levels. Indeed, this is what makes it possible to construct these representations. There is a striking unanimity among current theories about how this is done.

Our conceptions about knowledge use in discourse comprehension are dominated by the notions of top-down effects and expectation-driven processing. Knowledge provides part of the context within which a discourse is interpreted. The context is thought of as a kind of filter through which people perceive the world. At the level of word recognition and parsing, it lets through only the appropriate meaning of an ambiguous word or phrase and suppresses the inappropriate one. Through semantic priming, the feature counter of the logogen for *bank as a financial institution* will be incremented and will reach its threshold before that of *riverbank* in the right context (Morton, 1969). Parsing a sentence is often thought of as predicting each successive constituent from those already analyzed on the basis of syntactic rules (Winograd, 1983). Scripts, frames, and schemata constrain the inferences an understander makes (as in Schank & Abelson, 1977), thereby preventing the process from being swamped in a flood of irrelevancies and redundancies. Arithmetic strategies generate just the right hypothesis in solving a word problem and preclude the wrong ones (Kintsch & Greeno, 1985). In a word, knowledge makes understanding processes smart: It keeps them on the right track and avoids exploring blind alleys. People understand correctly because they sort of know what is going to come. This program of research is well expressed by the following quotation from Schank (1978, p. 94), which served as a motto for Sharkey's (1986) model of text comprehension:

> We would claim that in natural language understanding, a simple rule is followed. Analysis proceeds in a top-down predictive manner. Understanding is expectation based. It is only when the expectations are useless or wrong that bottom-up processing begins.

Empirically, this position is questionable: Even fluent readers densely sample the words of a text, as indicated by their eye fixations (Just & Carpenter, 1980), making the bottom-up mode appear the rule rather than the exception. Computationally, it is not an easy idea to make work. It is difficult to make a system smart enough so that it will make the right decisions, yet keep it flexible enough so that it will perform well in a broad range of situations. On the one hand, one needs to make sure that exactly the right thing (word meaning, proposition, inference) will be constructed; for that purpose one needs powerful, smart rules that react sensitively to subtle cues. On the other hand, humans comprehend well in ever-changing contexts and adapt easily to new and unforeseen situations; for that purpose one needs robust and general construction rules. Scripts and frames, as they were first conceived, are simply not workable: If they are powerful enough, they are too inflexible, and if they are general enough, they fail in their constraining function. This dilemma has long been recognized (e.g., Schank, 1982; van Dijk & Kintsch, 1983), and efforts have been undertaken to make expectation-driven processes sufficiently flexible (e.g., Schank's memory organization packets, or MOPs). In this article, an alternative solution to this problem will be explored.

Construction of Discourse Representations

The traditional approach to modeling knowledge use in comprehension has been to design powerful rules to ensure that the right elements are generated in the right context. The problem is that it is very difficult to design a production system powerful enough to yield the right results but flexible enough to work in an environment characterized by almost infinite variability. The approach taken here is to design a much weaker production system that generates a whole set of elements. These rules need to be just powerful enough so that the right element is likely to be among those generated, even though others will also be generated that are irrelevant or outright inappropriate. An integration process will then be used to strengthen the contextually appropriate elements and inhibit unrelated and inappropriate ones. Weak productions can operate in many different contexts because they do not have to yield precise outputs; on the other hand, a context-sensitive integration process is then required to select among the outputs generated. The integration phase is the price the model pays for the necessary flexibility in the construction process.

The model proposed here has been termed a *construction–integration* model to emphasize its most salient feature. It combines a construction process in which a text base is constructed from the linguistic input as well as from the comprehender's knowledge base, with an integration phase, in which this text base is integrated into a coherent whole. The knowledge base is conceptualized as an associative network. The construction process is modeled as a production system. Indeed, it is a generalization of the production system used in earlier work, such as the simulation-of-comprehension processes developed by Fletcher (1985) and Dellarosa (1986) after the model of Kintsch and Greeno (1985). The main difference is that instead of precise inference rules, sloppy ones are used, resulting in an incoherent, potentially contradictory output. However, this output structure is itself in the form of an associative net, which can be shaped into a coherent text base via relaxation procedures in the connectionist manner (e.g., Rumelhart & McClelland, 1986). Thus, the model represents a symbiosis of production systems and connectionist approaches.[1]

Certain limitations of the present article are worth noting at this point, for it does not offer a solution to all the problems in discourse understanding. Thus, it is not primarily concerned with the specific strategies (or rules) for the construction of text propositions or inferencing. Instead, it relies in this respect on what is available in the literature as well as on whatever future researchers will be able to come up with. The only point it makes is that whatever these strategies or rules are, they will be easier to formulate within the present framework, which allows them to be both weaker and more general. Thus, one need not worry about constructing just the right inference, but can be content with a much sloppier rule. Sometimes, of course, even the latter type of rule may be hard to come by, whereas in other cases (e.g., in the word problems discussed later) promiscuous hypothesis generation is straightforward (while selecting just the right one can be tricky).

Knowledge Representation
The process of constructing a discourse representation relies heavily on knowledge. To understand how it operates, one must first have an idea of how the to-be-used knowledge is organized. Typically, theorists have tried to create knowledge structures to support smart processes: semantic nets, frames, scripts, and schemata. As has been argued elsewhere (Kintsch, 1989), such fixed structures are too inflexible and cannot adapt readily enough to the demands imposed by the ever-changing context of the environment. Instead, a minimally organized knowledge system is assumed here in which structure is not prestored, but generated in the context of the task for which it is needed. An associative net with positive as well as negative interconnections serves this purpose.

Knowledge is represented as an associative net, the nodes of which are concepts or propositions.[2] The nodes in this net are interconnected. Connections among nodes have a strength value, which may be positive, zero, or negative, ranging from 1 to −1. Nodes consist of a head plus a number of slots for arguments. Thus, the nodes of the knowledge net are formally equivalent to the propositions used to represent texts (e.g., Kintsch, 1974).[3] The slot specifies the nature of the relation between the head and the argument. Slots may represent attributes, parts, cases of verbs, or arguments of functions. they need not be named, but may be named if the relation is a common one (such as the cases of verb frames). The arguments of a proposition are concepts or other propositions. The number of arguments in a proposition may vary from one to some small number. Examples of common types of nodes in the knowledge net are (a) MARY, (b) CAKE, (c) SWEET[CAKE], (d) BAKE[agent:MARY,object:CAKE], (e) CONSEQUENCE [condition:NOT[WATCH[agent:MARY,object:CAKE],effect:BURN[object:CAKE]]].   Examples A and B are lexical nodes that have associated with them perceptual procedures that identify certain patterns in the environment—either the objects themselves or the written or spoken words, such as MARY and CAKE, respectively. In the following I shall not deal with these perceptual procedures explicitly. The semantic and associative relations into which MARY and CAKE enter, which constitute a part of the general knowledge net, are the focus of interest here. MARY and CAKE appear as arguments in Examples C through E in various roles (the agent and object slots, etc.).

There are two ways of looking at the list of propositions in Examples A through E. On the one hand, it could be considered simply as a portion of a general knowledge network, whereas on the other hand, it could be considered the propositional base of a (brief) discourse, in which a particular Mary bakes and burns a particular cake.[4] Thus, the elements of which knowledge nets and text bases are constructed are the same. Indeed, as will be detailed later, text bases are formed by selecting, modifying, and rearranging propositional elements from the knowledge net. However, text bases are not part of the knowledge net, but separate structures with their own properties.

Concepts are not defined in a knowledge net, but their meaning can be constructed from their position in the net. The immediate associates and semantic neighbors of a node constitute its core meaning. Its complete and full meaning, however, can be obtained only by exploring its relations to all the other nodes in the net. Meaning must be created. As a first step one could add all propositions in the net directly related to a node to obtain what Mudersbach (1982) termed the first level of meaning; then all propositions directly related to the propositions at the first level can be added to form a second level, and so on, until the whole knowledge net is involved. Note, however, that such a construction is a theoretical exercise without direct psychological correspondence. It is not possible to deal with the whole, huge knowledge net at once. Instead, at any moment only a tiny fraction of the net can be activated, and only those propositions of the net that are actually activated can affect the meaning of a given concept. Thus, the meaning of a concept is always situation specific and context dependent. It is necessarily incomplete and unstable: Additional nodes could always be added to the activated subnet constituting the momentary meaning of a concept, but at the cost of losing some of the already activated nodes.[5]

The notion of an associative net is not unfamiliar, but it is usually thought of as relating concepts only, not propositional nodes. Two extremely simple examples will illustrate the nature of such an associative net. First, consider the representation of the homonym BANK in an associative net. Positive connections are indicated by arrows, negative ones by circles. Asterisks indicate further, unspecified nodes. Of course, each of the concepts and propositions shown in figure 1.1 participate in the general knowledge net beyond the single connection shown here. As a second example, consider the proposition BAKE[agent:PERSON, object:CAKE] (see figure 1.2). Once again, only a fragment of the complete network is shown, just to illustrate certain types of connections.

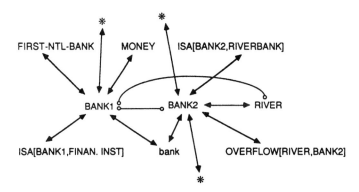

Figure 1.1
A fragment of the associative net for BANK. (Positive connections are indicated by arrows, negative ones by circles; asterisks indicate further, unnamed nodes.)

Representing knowledge in a propositional network has several advantages. Primarily, it provides a common format for the knowledge base and for the mental representation of discourse. Furthermore, we have by now considerable experience working with propositional structures, whereas other forms of representation are less well understood (e.g., the spatial-imagery and linear structures of Anderson, 1983; the mental models of Johnson-Laird, 1983; or whatever the appropriate representation in the affective system might be, as in Zajonc, 1980). However, the decision to use a propositional representation does not imply that all other forms of knowledge are to be considered unimportant or nonexistent. It would be desirable to expand the model to include nonpropositional representations, but one would first have to learn how to operate with such forms of representation.

Construction Processes
The steps in constructing a text base according to the construction–integration model involve: (a) forming the concepts and propositions directly corresponding to the linguistic input; (b) elaborating each of these elements by selecting a small number of its most closely associated neighbors from the general knowledge net; (c) inferring certain additional propositions; and (d) assigning connection strengths to all pairs of elements that have been created.

The result is an initial, enriched, but incoherent and possibly contradictory text base, which is then subjected to an integration process to form a coherent structure.

In Step A of this process, a propositional representation of the text is constructed from a parsed linguistic input, such as the words of a text with suitable syntactic annotations, and from a knowledge system as envisioned earlier. Note

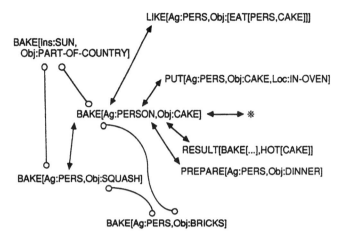

Figure 1.2
A fragment of the associative net for BAKE.

that the parser itself is not a part of the present model. The basic process of proposition building has been described in van Dijk and Kintsch (1983, chapter 4) and Kintsch (1985). I will illustrate it here with some simple examples. Consider the sentence *Mary bakes a cake.* The parser output needed is *Mary* (agent of BAKE) *bakes* (predicate) *a cake* (object of BAKE). *Mary, bake,* and *cake* activate their corresponding lexical nodes, and MARY and CAKE are assigned the roles of agent and object in the BAKE proposition. As was suggested in figure 1.2, BAKE requires a PERSON as agent, hence a test is made whether MARY is a person. This may either involve a search through the knowledge net for the proposition ISA[MARY,PERSON] or, should that search prove unsuccessful, an attempt to infer this proposition (e.g., the net may contain only propositions to the effect that MARY is a name and that persons have names; exactly how such problem-solving activity occurs within an associative net will not be considered here).

The present model, however, differs in a significant way from my earlier conceptions: It does not require that the right, and only the right, proposition always be formed. Instead, the construction rules for building propositions can be weakened, allowing for the formation of incomplete or "wrong" propositions. Proposition building is on-line, and frequently, all the relevant information for building just the right one is not available on-line, leading to false starts or incompleted attempts. In the aforementioned example, this has no interesting consequences; for example, if in response to the phrase *Mary bakes* ... the proposition BAKE[MARY,$]—the dollar sign indicates an unfilled slot—is formed, it will simply be replaced by the complete proposition when the rest of the sentence is processed. However, consider an example discussed by Frazier and Rayner (1982): *The linguists knew the solution of the problem would not be easy.* Here, the on-line construction of propositions is not so simple. First, the proposition KNOW[LINGUISTS,[MARY,$] is formed. Then, by the strategy of minimal attachment, the subsequent noun phrase is interpreted as the object of KNOW, yielding KNOW[LINGUISTS,SOLUTION]. The final verb phrase, however, requires a subject, so [NOT[EASY[SOLUTION]]] is constructed. As Frazier and Rayner pointed out, this does not involve a reinterpretation of the sentence. Subjects do not go back, noting in some way that *solution of the problem* had been attached to the wrong proposition, and repair this error. Instead, the incorrectly formed KNOW proposition somehow just disappears; the description of the integration process that follows shows how.

A third example of proposition building, involving pronoun identification, will be discussed here. There exists good psychological evidence that pronouns may activate more than one possible referent (e.g., Frederiksen, 1981). Thus, in *The lawyer discussed the case with the judge. He said "I shall send the defendant to prison."* the following propositions would be formed: DISCUSS[LAWYER,JUDGE, CASE]; SAY[LAWYER,[SEND[LAWYER,DEFENDANT,PRISON]]]; and SAY[JUDGE,[SEND [JUDGE,DEFENDANT,PRISON]]]. Eventually, of course, the right interpretation comes to dominate the wrong one, as will be shown shortly.

In Step B of the construction process, each concept or proposition that has been formed in Step A serves as a cue for the retrieval of associated nodes in the knowledge net. The retrieval process itself is modeled after well-known theories that have been developed and tested in the memory literature (Raaijmakers & Shiffrin, 1981). Suppose that node i in the knowledge net is positively associated with n other nodes in the net. Let $s(i, j)$ be the associative strength between nodes i and j. Then the probability that the retrieval cue j will retrieve node j is

$$P(j|i) = \frac{S(i, j)}{\sum_{h=1}^{n} s(i,h)} \tag{1}$$

Note that each concept or proposition in the text base serves as an independent retrieval cue, hence the particularly simple form of the retrieval process. (An intersection search would be required if the items in the text base acted as a compound cue.) On each retrieval attempt, an item among the associates of i is selected according to Equation 1. A sampling-with-replacement process is assumed so that dominant associates may be retrieved more than once. The number of retrieval attempts with item i as the cue is assumed to be fixed and is a parameter of the model, k. In the examples that follow, k was chosen to be 2 or 3, mostly to reduce the complexity of these examples. However, one may speculate that the most realistic value of k would not be much higher, perhaps between 5 and 7.

Consider some simple examples.

1.   Suppose the word *bank* is presented as part of a text. It will activate the lexical nodes BANK1 (financial institution) as well as BANK2 (riverbank), plus some of their associates; for example, the construction process might pick from figure 1.1: BANK1, MONEY, FIRST-NATIONAL-BANK, BANK2, RIVER, OVERFLOW[RIVER,BANK2].

2.   Suppose the sentence *Lucy persuaded Mary to bake a cake* is presented as part of a text. The parser should provide a phrase structure tree as output, from which the proposition PERSUADE[LUCY,MARY,BAKE[MARY,CAKE]] is constructed. Each text proposition activates propositions closely related to it in the general knowledge net, regardless of the discourse context. For instance, in the case of BAKE[MARY,CAKE] we might thus obtain LIKE[MARY, EAT[MARY,CAKE]], PUT[MARY,CAKE,IN-OVEN], RESULT[BAKE[MARY,CAKE],HOT [CAKE]], PREPARE[MARY,DINNER]. These propositions are all closely associated with baking a cake (figure 1.2). Note, however, that elaborating the text base in this way is not just a question of retrieving associated propositions from the knowledge net. The arguments of these retrieved propositions must be treated as variables that are to be bound to the values specified by the retrieval cue. Thus, because MARY is the agent of the text proposition, MARY is made the agent in the knowledge propositions it brings into the text representation, instead of PERSON in figure 1.2. Similarly, although the informality of the present notation hides this, CAKE now is the particular one MARY bakes, not the generic one in figure 1.2. These knowledge propositions function as potential inferences. Out of context there is no way of determining which of them are relevant: Maybe Mary really likes to eat cake, but perhaps she is in the process of cooking dinner, in which case PREPARE[MARY,DINNER] might become a macroproposition (what van Dijk, 1980, calls a *construction*). But it is also possible that next she will burn her fingers when she takes the cake out of the oven, making HOT, which plays no role at all in the other contexts, the relevant inference. At this point, the construction process lacks guidance and intelligence; it simply produces potential inferences, in the hope that some of them might turn out to be useful.

3.   In the third example, if the proposition SEND[LAWYER,DEFENDANT, PRISON] has been formed, the knowledge net contributes nothing, because one presumably does not know anything about lawyers sending defendants to prison. (Of course, LAWYER,DEFENDANT, and PRISON would each be associatively elaborated separately.) If, however, JUDGE rather than LAWYER were the agent of SEND, the elaboration process would contribute the information that this implies that the judge is sentencing the defendant and so forth.

Step C in the construction process, the generation of additional inferences, is necessary because not all inferences that are required for comprehension will, in general, be obtained by the random elaboration mechanism described earlier. In some cases more focused problem-solving activity is necessary to generate the desired inferences. Exactly how this is to be done is, however, beyond the scope of this article. I merely wish to point out here that in addition to the undirected elaboration which results from Step B of the construction process, there is still a need for controlled, specific inferences. Two types of such inferences are of particular importance in comprehension. Bridging inferences (Haviland & Clark, 1974; Kintsch, 1974) are necessary whenever the text base being constructed is incoherent (i.e., whenever either the original text base itself or the elaborated text base remains incoherent by the criteria discussed in van Dijk and Kintsch, 1983, chapter 5). Second, macropropositions have to be inferred (as discussed in general terms in chapter 6 of van Dijk & Kintsch, 1983, and operationalized as a production system by Turner, McCutchen, & Kintsch, 1986). Macropropositions are also elaborated associatively, as described in Step B for micropropositions.

What has been constructed so far is a set of propositions containing the (micro)propositions directly derived from the text, a randomly selected set of associates for each of these, the macropropositions generated from the text, and their associates. The final Step D of the construction process involves the specification of the interconnections between all of these elements. There are two ways in which elements are interconnected. (a) The propositions directly derived from the text (hence referred to as "text propositions") are positively interconnected with strength values proportional to their proximity in the text base. Specific realizations of this principle are described in the discussion of figure 1.4. (b) If propositions i and j are connected in the general knowledge net with the strength value $s(i, j)$, $-1 < s(i, j) < 1$, and if i and j become members of a text base, the strength of their connection in the text base is $s(i, j)$. In other words, propositions in the text base inherit their interconnections from the general knowledge net. Strength values are additive, up to a maximum of 1, in those cases in which an inherited strength value combines with a text-base-determined connection.

Consider, for instance, the portion of a network that is generated when the word *bank* activates both BANK1 and BANK2, as well as the associations MONEY and RIVER. A possible pattern of connections is shown in figure 1.3, where for simplicity, connection strengths have been limited to $\pm.5$ or 1. Alternatively, the graph shown in figure 1.3 can be expressed in matrix form as shown in table 1.1. BANK1 is associated with MONEY, BANK2 with RIVER, but inhibitory connections exist between MONEY and BANK2 and between RIVER and BANK1.

An example of text propositions that are interconnected via their positions in the text base is shown in figure 1.4. LUCY is connected most strongly to WEED[LUCY,GARDEN], and least strongly to VEGETABLE[GARDEN]. Although there

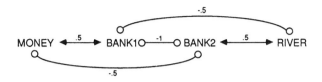

Figure 1.3
Connections between BANK1 and BANK2 and their associates.

Table 1.1
Connectivity matrix for the graph shown in figure 1.3

Proposition	1	2	3	4
1. MONEY	—	0.5	−0.5	0.0
2. BANK1	0.5	—	−1.0	−0.5
3. BANK2	−0.5	−1.0	—	0.5
4. RIVER	0.0	−0.5	0.5	—

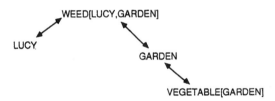

Figure 1.4
The text base for *Lucy weeded the vegetable garden.*

are many possible ways to assign numerical connection strengths to express this pattern of connectivity, the one chosen here results in the matrix shown in table 1.2.

Inferences inherit positive and negative interconnections from the general knowledge net, as seen in figure 1.5. The result of the construction process is, therefore, a network expressable as a connectivity matrix, consisting of all the lexical nodes accessed, all the propositions that have been formed, plus all the inferences and elaborations that were made at both the local and global level and their interconnections.

Integration
The network that has been constructed so far is not yet a suitable text representation. It was carelessly constructed and is therefore incoherent and inconsistent. At all levels of the representation, components associated with the text elements were included without regard to the discourse context, and many

Table 1.2
Connectivity matrix for the graph shown in figure 1.4

Proposition	1	2	3	4
1. LUCY	—	0.9	0.7	0.4
2. WEED	0.9	—	0.9	0.7
3. GARDEN	0.7	0.9	—	0.9
4. VEGETABLE	0.4	0.7	0.9	—

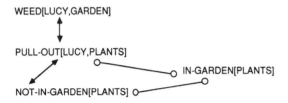

Figure 1.5
Inferences generated from WEED[LUCY, GARDEN] and their connections.

of them are inappropriate. An integration process in the connectionist manner can be used to exclude these unwanted elements from the text representation (e.g., see Rumelhart & McClelland, 1986, and Waltz & Pollack, 1985, for discourse).

Text comprehension is assumed to be organized in cycles, roughly corresponding to short sentences or phrases (for further detail, see Kintsch & van Dijk, 1978; Miller & Kintsch, 1980). In each cycle a new net is constructed, including whatever is carried over in the short-term buffer from the previous cycle.[6] Once the net is constructed, the integration process takes over: Activation is spread around until the system stabilizes. More specific, an activation vector representing the initial activation values of all nodes in the net is postmultiplied repeatedly with the connectivity matrix. After each multiplication the activation values are renormalized: Negative values are set to zero, and each of the positive activation values is divided by the sum of all activation values, so that the total activation on each cycles remains at a value of one (e.g., Rumelhart & McClelland, 1986). Usually, the system finds a stable state fairly rapidly; if the integration process fails, however, new constructions are added to the net, and integration is attempted again. Thus, there is a basic, automatic construction-plus-integration process that normally is sufficient for comprehension. This process is more like perception than problem solving, but when it fails, rather extensive problem-solving activity might be required to bring it back on track. These processes will not be considered further here.

The result of the integration process is a new activation vector, indicating high activation values for some of the nodes in the net and low or zero values

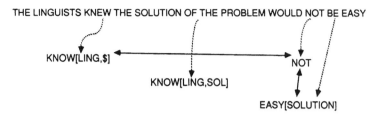

Figure 1.6
The strategic construction of a text base: SOLUTION-OF-THE-PROBLEM is first assigned to KNOW, then to EASY. (The dollar sign is a placeholder.)

Table 1.3
Connectivity matrix for the graph shown in figure 1.6

Proposition	1	2	3	4
1. KNOW[$]	—	0.9	0.7	0.9
2. KNOW[SOL]	0.9	—	−1.0	0.0
3. EASY	0.7	−1.0	—	0.9
4. NOT	0.9	0.0	0.91	—

for many others. The highly activated nodes constitute the discourse representation formed on each processing cycle. In principle, it includes information at many levels: lexical nodes, text propositions, knowledge-based elaborations (i.e., various types of inferences), as well as macropropositions.

A few simple examples will illustrate what is at issue here. Consider *Lucy persuaded Mary to bake a cake*, which was discussed earlier. The PERSUADE proposition will pull in related knowledge items, just as was shown for BAKE. However, out of context the integration process will not yield any striking results. In the context of *Lucy made tomato soup and sauteed some porkchops with herbs. She set the table and persuaded Mary to bake a cake*, the integration process has very different results: PREPARE[LUCY,DINNER] emerges as the dominant proposition (macroproposition) because most of the other propositions in the text base contribute to its activation value. That the cake was hot, or that she put it into the oven, disappears from the representation with activation values around zero.

Next, consider the example just discussed, where a perfectly good propositional strategy led to a wrong result. for *The linguists knew the solution of the problem would not be easy*, the text base that was constructed is shown in figure 1.6. It corresponds to the connectivity matrix exhibited in table 1.3 if connection strengths are assigned as in table 1.2. (KNOW[SOLUTION] and NOT[EASY] are connected positively via KNOW[$] but negatively via EASY, which adds up to 0.) The activation vector (.25, .25, .25, .25) corresponding to the assumption that all text

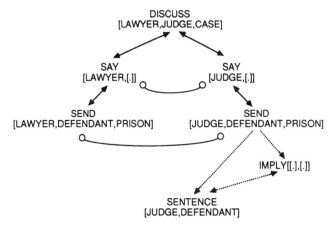

Figure 1.7
The strategic construction of a text base: The pronoun *he* is identified with two potential, mutually exclusive referents. (Instead of writing out whole propositions, the abbreviation [.] is used for the arguments of a proposition when they can be readily inferred.)

propositions are equally activated initially is repeatedly multiplied with this matrix, renormalizing the obtained activation values after each multiplication as described earlier. To decide when the activation vector has stabilized, the following criterion was established: A stable state is reached when the average change in the activation values after a multiplication is less than .001. Although this is an arbitrary criterion, even large changes (by one order of magnitude in either direction) make only minor differences in the final activation values obtained in this and many other cases. In the present case, this criterion is reached after 10 operations, yielding the final activation vector (.325, .000, .325, .350)—that is, the wrong KNOW[LINGUISTS,SOLUTION], which does not fit into the text base, has been deactivated. The integration process similarly resolves the problem of multiple pronoun referents. For *The lawyer discussed the case with the judge. He said "I shall send the defendant to prison,"* propositions were constructed for both lawyer and judge as referents of *he*. However, the process of associative elaboration generated some additional information for SEND[JUDGE, DEFENDANT,PRISON], but not for SEND[LAWYER,DEFENDANT,PRISON]. The resulting text base is shown in figure 1.7. To obtain the corresponding connectivity matrix (see table 1.4), connection strengths among text base propositions were assigned as in table 1.2, and among associates as in table 1.3 (other assignments result in different numerical values for the final activation vector, but its pattern remains the same as long as the essential features of the matrix are preserved—for example, which connections are positive, negative, and zero). Assume an initial activation vector of (.25, .25, .25, .25, .25, 0, 0), reflecting the fact that only the text propositions themselves are activated initially. After 19 multiplications

Table 1.4
Connectivity matrix for the graph shown in figure 1.7

Proposition	1	2	3	4	5	6	7
1. DISC	—	0.9	0.9	0.7	0.7	0.0	0.0
2. SAY[LAWYER]	0.9	—	−1.0	0.9	0.0	0.0	0.0
3. SAY[JUDGE]	0.9	−1.0	—	0.0	0.9	0.0	0.0
4. SEND[LAWYER]	0.7	0.9	0.0	—	−1.0	0.0	0.0
5. SEND[JUDGE]	0.7	0.0	0.9	−1.0	—	0.5	0.5
6. IMPLY	0.0	0.0	0.0	0.0	0.5	—	0.5
7. SENT	0.0	0.0	0.0	0.0	0.5	0.5	—

with the connectivity matrix, the two propositions in which *he* had been identified as the *lawyer* have activation values of 0, whereas the corresponding *judge*
propositions have activation values of .261 and .283, respectively. Just a little
knowledge was enough to choose the correct referent.

After this general description of the construction-plus-activation model, two
specific applications will be discussed in more detail: how words are identified
in a discourse context, and how a propositional text base and situation model
are constructed when comprehension depends heavily on activating a rich
knowledge set. For that purpose, arithmetic word problems were chosen as the
example, because the knowledge that needs to be activated is particularly well
defined in that domain, and unambiguous criteria of understanding exist—a
solution is either right or wrong. The purpose of these examples is twofold: to
show how the general framework proposed can be elaborated into specific
models in these experimental situations, and to compare the performance of
these models with empirical observations and experimental results as a first test
of the psychological adequacy of these models.

Word Identification in Discourse

The first problem to be considered in detail is how knowledge is used in understanding the meaning of words in a discourse. The previously sketched
model implies that word meanings have to be created anew in each context,
that this is initially strictly a bottom-up process with context having its effects in
the integration phase, and that this construction-plus-integration process takes
time, with different factors influencing successive phases of the process.

Context effects in word recognition are ubiquitous in the experimental literature, and the explanation of these context effects has been a primary goal of
theories of word recognition. Typically, it is taken for granted in these theories
that because context influences word recognition, contextual factors interact
with the perceptual processes. Context effects are said to be top-down and

expectation driven and are said to facilitate (or sometimes interfere with) the perceptual analysis. Similar ideas were once current in related fields, such as the "New Look" in perception (Bruner & Postman, 1949) and the filter theory of attention (Broadbent, 1958). People perceive what they expect or want, attention filters out the irrelevant. Some words are recognized because the context favors them; others are not because the context inhibits them. How these top-down effects of context are realized differs in detail among theories, but all the most influential current theories postulate interactive processes in which contextually expected words are favored. In the logogen model (Morton, 1969, 1979), context primes semantic features that enter into the feature counter of a logogen and therefore strengthen that logogen. In Forster's search model (Forster, 1976), perceptual analysis defines a candidate set that is then searched by semantic relations or by word frequency. In Becker's verification model (Becker, 1976), both a set of sensory candidates and a set of semantic candidates are created, with the latter being verified first. In the cohort model of Marslen-Wilson and Welsh (1978), context is used to exclude members of the cohort from the very beginning. Norris (1986) has recently reviewed these models and pointed out that they all involve some sort of priming mechanism through which context effects are mediated.

The model of how knowledge is used in discourse suggests a fundamentally different approach. Following earlier work by Kintsch and Mross (1985) and Norris (1986), the present model is neither interactive, nor does it involve priming. As these authors have argued, word identification is not simply a matter of lexical access. Rather, it is a complex process that responds to different influences at different stages. These stages, however, are merely convenient verbal labels. In fact, processing is continuous, and there is significant temporal overlap between the different subprocesses defining these stages. In the first stage (which was termed *sense activation* by Kintsch & Mross, 1985), the number of word candidates consistent with the perceptual input is progressively reduced through perceptual feature analysis. As in Forster or Becker, a set of sensory candidates is created through perceptual analysis, but its size decreases as the analysis progresses. This process rapidly reduces the number of word candidates to some manageable number, but not necessarily to one. At this point (probably at about 50 ms, see Fischler & Goodman, 1978), the semantic context comes into play. Some small number of lexical nodes has now been selected, each one activating a few of its strongest semantic or associative neighbors in the knowledge network. If there is a node whose associates fit into whatever context is present, it will be taken as the meaning of the to-be-identified word. What fits is determined by the integration process sketched earlier. This is the *sense-selection* stage of Kintsch and Mross.

Note that if the perceptual analysis had been allowed to continue for a sufficient period of time, for most words it would have yielded a result eventually by itself, and probably the same one. It is just that the association check helped to shortcut this process. With homonyms, however, the association check plays a crucial role: Perceptual analysis alone cannot decide which meaning of *bank* to select in any given context.

Sense selection by means of an association check is the very first of a possibly very long series of contextual plausibility checks (Norris's term). It comes first because the associative/semantic context of a lexical node can be computed rapidly. As more information about the context becomes available, the sentence and discourse meaning begin to emerge, and more and deeper plausibility checks can be performed as long as there still is time. This is the *sense-elaboration* phase, in which the meaning of a word is contextually explored and elaborated. However, once a response has been made in a recognition experiment, or once the process moves on in a discourse, elaboration is terminated. Thus, word meanings are usually identified long before complex inferences are made in comprehending a discourse.

At this point, a "meaning" has been constructed for the word in this particular context. It consists of the lexical node that has been activated (the contextually inappropriate nodes that had been activated have by now been deactivated through the various context checks), the associative and semantic neighbors of that node, the sentence and discourse context in which the word participated, and some inferences and elaborations that were produced in the course of the various plausibility checks that explored the role of that word in the given context.

What do we need to make such a model of word identification work? We shall disregard the perceptual analysis and take for granted that a certain number of appropriate lexical nodes has been activated (e.g., multiple semantic nodes for a homonym). We then need to compute the sentences and phrases in which the word in question participates, or more accurately, the propositions in which the corresponding concept token (for which the lexical node serves as the type) plays a role. Finally, we need to construct inferences and elaborations when necessary.

A model of word recognition that thus far is identical with the one favored here has recently been developed by Norris (1986). Norris called it the "checking model" and compares and contrasts it with the other extant models of word recognition in the literature. In Norris's model, the plausibility of word candidates in any given context is evaluated. The recognition criterion for contextually plausible words is lowered and that for implausible words is increased. By manipulating criterion bias in this way, Norris accounted for a wide range of observations from threshold and other types of recognition experiments.

Instead of equating plausibility with criterion bias, a different mechanism—integration—is used here. This mechanism has the great advantage of being applicable not only at the wordrecognition level (which is what Norris was concerned with), but it is equally suited to modeling knowledge integration at higher levels.

When a word is perceived, one or more lexical nodes are accessed, and some of their neighboring nodes that are closely related associatively or semantically are also activated. Similarly, when a proposition is constructed, a number of associatively and semantically related propositions are also constructed. Both related concepts and related propositions serve to determine the plausibility of the core words and propositions. A richly interconnected structure is thus formed, through which activation can spread, so that positively interconnected items strengthen each other, while unrelated items drop out and inconsistent items become inhibited. Or, said differently, implausible items will be suppressed, whereas plausible ones support each other—at the level of word recognition as well as of textual integration.

Time Course of Activation of Words in a Discourse Context
The model of word recognition just outlined is consistent with a great deal of experimental data. Norris (1986) has reviewed the word recognition literature in great detail and shown that his checking model accounts for the rich empirical findings in that area better than any of its competitors. The construction–integration model is closely related to Norris's model. On the one hand, it is more specific in that it proposes computational procedures by means of which Norris's "plausibility check" could actually be achieved, whereas on the other hand it replaces Norris's shift in criterion bias with the computationally more feasible integration mechanism. It appears likely that the present model can handle all the data the checking model accounts for, in just the same way and for just the same reasons as the checking model. There is, however, another part of the literature on word recognition that is not discussed in Norris (1986): the work on word identification in discourse. The empirical findings in this area are also in good agreement with the construction–integration model.

In a lexical decision task, the subject sees a string of letters and must decide as quickly as possible whether it forms an English word. If a target word is preceded by a closely related word, the response to the target word is speeded up (on the order of 20 to 40 ms) in comparison with unrelated control words. This priming effect has been well documented for some time and is obtained in list contexts (e.g., Meyer & Schvaneveldt, 1971) as well as in discourse contexts (e.g., Swinney, 1979). However, the discourse context is actually irrelevant to the priming effect. What matters is merely the associative relation between the prime word and the target word. As has been shown repeatedly (Kintsch & Mross, 1985; Swinney, 1979; Till, Mross, & Kintsch, 1988; also equivalent results obtained with a naming task by Seidenberg, Tanenhaus, Leiman, & Bienkowsky, 1982), homonyms will prime strong associates of both their meanings, irrespective of the discourse context and in spite of the fact that the context-inappropriate meaning of the homonym never enters consciousness. Furthermore, context appropriate inferences that are not associatively related to a priming word are not responded to any faster than unrelated control words. However, all of this depends on the amount of time allowed for the processing of the priming word. If the target word closely follows the priming word, so that the processing of the prime is still in its initial stages, the results are as already described. However, if there is enough time for more complete processing of the priming word in its discourse context, quite different results are observed. In this case, context-appropriate associates are still primed, but inappropriate associates no longer are, whereas context-appropriate inferences now become strongly primed. This time course of knowledge activation can be described in more detail by some illustrative experimental results.

In the study by Till et al. (1988), subjects read sentences like *The towns-people were amazed to find that all the buildings had collapsed except the mint*. After the priming word *mint* they were given a lexical decision task, with the target word being either *money*, *candy*, or *earthquake*. That is, the target was a context-appropriate associate of the prime (*money*), a context-inappropriate associate (*candy*), or a topical inference word (*earthquake*), respectively. In addition, the interval between the presentation of the prime and the target word (stimulus-onset asynchrony, or SOA) was varied from 200 ms to 1500 ms. In the first case, the prime could only be incompletely processed; with an SOA of 500 ms, a somewhat deeper processing of the prime was possible before a response had to be given to the target word; and with 1,000 ms, extensive processing of both the prime word and its discourse context was possible. The data are shown in figure 1.8. To keep this presentation simple, figure 1.8 shows the average

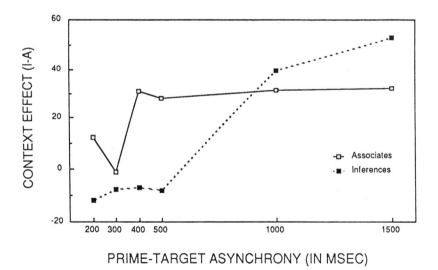

Figure 1.8
Context effects as indexed by the reaction time difference to context inappropriate and appropriate associates as a function of processing time, after Till, Mross, and Kintsch (1988).

priming effects observed in the three experiments of Till et al. for SOAs of 200, 300, 400, 500, 1,000, and 1,500 ms. The value shown for associates at 200 ms, for instance, is the difference between the mean reaction time for context-inappropriate and context-appropriate associates at that prime–target asynchrony. It is the average of two such values obtained in two different experiments (showing the data separately for each experiment merely complicates the picture without changing its essential features). The value for inferences, similarly, is based on the difference between topic words and unrelated control words. The purpose of figure 1.8 is, therefore, merely to give an impression of the over-all shape of the results of this study (for more detailed analyses, the original article must be consulted).

Targets that are contextually appropriate associates of the priming word are primed at all four SOAs. Contextually inappropriate targets, however, are primed only when the priming word is still in its initial processing stages; by 400 ms inappropriate associates are no longer activated. Topical inferences are primed only if there is ample time, more than 500 ms, for the processing of the prime and its discourse context. This observation implies that the topic was not inferred immediately as soon as the relevant information became available, but was left for the sentence wrap-up period. Till et al.'s sentences were written in such a way that the topic could have been inferred before the last word in the sentence. This, however, is not what happened: Topics were inferred only after the whole sentence was read, requiring more than 500 ms of processing time. Thus, the full contextual meaning of the prime required about 1 s to emerge.

Data like these suggest that the initial activation of lexical knowledge is independent of the discourse context. What matters is only the (relatively fixed and stable) associative/semantic context of each word by itself. This stage of sense activation, however, is quickly followed by a process of sense selection in which the discourse context becomes effective: By 500 ms, context-inappropriate associates are deactivated (see also Seidenberg et al., 1982, and Swinney, 1979). If given more time, context effects grow even stronger: By 1,000 ms, contextually appropriate inference words are strongly and reliably primed even in the absence of associative connections (similarly for recognition, see McKoon & Ratcliff, 1986).

Clearly, this pattern of results is in excellent agreement qualitatively with the model of knowledge use in discourse presented earlier. Right after a word is perceived, it activates its whole associative neighborhood in a context-independent way, with the consequence that strong associates of a word are likely to be represented in working memory and hence will be primed in a lexical decision task, whether they are context appropriate or not. The knowledge-integration process then results in the deactivation of material that does not fit into the overall discourse context (such as context-inappropriate associates). Note that in order to disambiguate words on-line, the integration phase cannot be delayed until the end of a processing cycle; word senses are disambiguated before that. In the model, therefore, as soon as a text proposition is constructed and its associates have been generated, they will be integrated into whatever context exists at that time in working memory. Thus, each processing cycle involves many integrations, and the single integration operation performed at the end of each cycle in many of the examples discussed here is merely a simplification, adopted whenever one is not concerned with the on-line generation of word meanings. Finally, contextual inferences should require the most time to become activated on the average because although they sometimes result from the initial knowledge sampling, in other cases repeated sampling or, further, strategic elaboration might be required.

Earlier, an example was given of one of the texts used in the Till et al. (1988) study. The predictions of the model will be illustrated by means of this example. The aforementioned text (*The townspeople were amazed to find that all the buildings had collapsed except the mint*) has the following propositional representation:

1. TOWNSPEOPLE
2. AMAZED[TOWNSPEOPLE,P3]
3. COLLAPSE[P4]
4. ALL-BUT[BUILDING,MINT]
5. BUILDING
6. MINT

Connection strengths of .9, .7, .4, and 0 were assigned to text propositions one, two, three, or more steps apart in the text base (e.g., P1 is two steps away from P3, connected via P2). Next, each text proposition was allowed to access at random two of its neighbors in the long-term associative net. This process was simulated by having an informant provide free associations to phrases based on each of these six propositions. For instance, the phrase *all buildings but the mint* elicited the associations *many buildings* and *mint is a building*. Of course, MONEY and CANDY were chosen as the associates of MINT. Each text proposition was connected by a value of .5 to its associates, yielding an 18×18 connectivity matrix. Activation was then allowed to spread from the text propositions to the knowledge elaborations. Specifically, an initial activation vector with $1/6$'s corresponding to the text propositions and zeros otherwise was multiplied with the connectivity matrix until the pattern of activation stabilized. As a result, text propositions achieved activation values between .0987 and .1612, depending on how closely they were tied into the text base, and the knowledge elaborations had much lower activation values, between .0142 and .0239, with both MONEY and CANDY having a value of .0186. Thus, at this stage of processing, MONEY and CANDY are equally activated.

Activation continues to spread, however, and differences begin to emerge among the activation values for the various knowledge elaborations that have been added to the text base. The reason for this is that the knowledge elaborations are connected not only to the text propositions that had pulled them into the net but also to other text propositions as well as to each other. To approximate these interrelations, a connection value of .5 was assigned to any two propositions sharing a common argument. Because the homophone *mint* contributed associations to the subnet that refers to both of its senses, an inhibiting connection of −.5 was assigned to MINT/CANDY and BUILDING, whereas CANDY and MONEY themselves were connected by a −1. Continued multiplication of the activation vector with this connectivity matrix yielded a stable pattern (average change <.001) after 11 operations. At this point text propositions had activation values ranging between .1091 and .0584. Several of the knowledge elaborations reached values in this range, for example, .0742 for both ISA[MINT,BUILDING] and MONEY and .0708 for KILL[BUILDING, TOWNSPEOPLE], whereas others had faded away by this time; for example, MAN, which entered the subnet as an associate of TOWNSPEOPLE, had an activation value of .0070 and, most significantly, .0000 for CANDY. This stage of processing corresponds to the 400- and 500-ms points in figure 1.8: MINT is now clearly embedded in its context as a kind of building, and the inappropriate association CANDY is no longer activated.

The next processing stage involves the construction of a topical inference—what is the sentence about? While the exact operations involved in the construction of such inferences are beyond the scope of this article, van Dijk and Kintsch (1983, chapter 6) have discussed some of the mechanisms involved, such as a strategy of looking for causal explanations, which is what actual subjects appear to use predominantly in the following case. If given enough time, the modal response of human readers is that the sentence is about an earthquake that destroyed a town. Thus, the (empirically determined) propositions EARTHQUAKE and CAUSE[EARTHQUAKE,P3] were added to the text base and connected with the text-base propositions from which they were derived by a value of .5. The two new propositions were given initial activation values of zero, and the integration process was resumed; that is, activation now spread from the previously stabilized subnet into the newly constructed part of the net. Nine more integration cycles were required before the expanded net stabilized. As one would expect, the two new inferences did not alter the pattern of activation much, but both of them became fairly strongly activated (thereby diminishing activation values in the already existing portion of the net). The topical inferences EARTHQUAKE and CAUSE[EARTHQUAKE,P3] ended up with activation values of .0463 and .0546, respectively, among the most strongly activated inferences in the net. At this point, the process appears to coincide with the time interval between 1,000 and 1,500 ms shown in figure 1.8.

The construction–integration model thus accounts for the data in figure 1.8 by means of an intricate interplay between construction and integration phases: the construction of the text base and the context-free, associative knowledge elaboration during the first 350 ms of processing; the establishment of a coherent text base, which appears to be complete by 400 ms; and finally, an inference phase, involving new construction and new integration and requiring more than 500 ms of processing under the conditions of the Till et al. study. The model does not account for the time values cited here, but it describes a processing sequence in accordance with the empirically determined time sequence.

In many models of word identification, the problem is thought to be "How do we get from a certain (acoustic or visual) stimulus pattern to the place in the mental lexicon where the meaning of this word is stored?" In the present model, word identification is much more deeply embedded into the process of discourse understanding. The lexical node itself provides just one entry point into the comprehender's long-term memory store of knowledge and experiences, and what eventually becomes activated from that store depends on the discourse context. In conceptions of the lexicon like that of Mudersbach's (1982), the meaning of a word is given by its "neighborhood" in the associative network into which it is embedded. Neighborhoods may be defined narrowly or broadly (nodes one link away vs. nodes several links away). In the present model, the meaning of a word is also given by its neighborhood—narrowly or broadly defined—not in the long-term memory net as a whole, but in the subnet that has been constructed as the mental representation of the discourse of which the word is a part. Because that representation changes as processing proceeds, word meanings change with it.

Figure 1.9 depicts the changing meaning of MINT in our example. MINT is directly linked to nine propositions in the network; indirectly it is linked to the whole net, of course. If one takes as its contextual meaning only its immediate neighbors, one finds at the beginning of processing mostly closely related propositions from the text base plus three weakly activated knowledge elaborations that in part do not fit into the context at all (CANDY). At the end of the process, however, the context-inappropriate association has dropped out, other inferences have been added, and the activation is more evenly distributed among text propositions and knowledge elaborations. Thus, textual information becomes part of the contextual meaning of a word, in contrast to most traditional conceptions of "meaning."

This example is, of course, no more than an illustration. Parameters in our calculations could be changed. For example, more than just two associates could be sampled initially in the process of knowledge elaboration. In this case the neighborhood of MINT would contain many more knowledge elaborations than are shown in figure 1.9, where there is a strong predominance of text propositions. Not enough is known at present to set some of these parameters with confidence. But figure 1.9 does reflect certain aspects of the data correctly: the equal initial activation of MONEY and CANDY, the later emergence of the topical inference EARTHQUAKE. Although much more research is needed to produce a more adequate picture of how the contextual meaning of words is

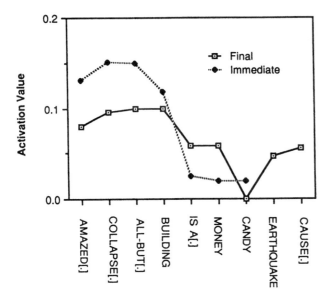

Figure 1.9
The changing meaning of MINT. (The activation values of all propositions directly connected to MINT at the beginning and at the end of the process. The [.] notation is used as an abbreviation for the arguments of a proposition.)

constructed during discourse comprehension, here is a technique that at least may help us to do so.

Arithmetic Word Problems

How children understand and solve simple word arithmetic problems provides an excellent domain to try out the construction-plus-integration model. Unlike with many other types of discourse, there are clear-cut criteria for when a problem is solved correctly, and the formal knowledge of arithmetic that is necessary for its solution is easily defined. However, word problems, like all other texts, share the ambiguity and fuzziness of all natural language. Not only formal, arithmetic knowledge is involved in understanding these problems, but all kinds of linguistic and situational knowledge. What makes word problems hard—and interesting—are often not their formal properties, but the way a problem is expressed linguistically and the way formal arithmetic relations map into the situations being described. Thus, word problems are ideal from the standpoint of knowledge integration because it is precisely the integration of formal arithmetic knowledge and linguistic and situational understanding that is at issue here.

Another reason for choosing the domain of word problems is that there already exist alternative formal models of how children solve simple word arithmetic problems (Briars & Larkin, 1984; Kintsch & Greeno, 1985). Specifically, the work of Kintsch and Greeno will be taken as a starting point here. Their model represents a union of the work on problem solving in arithmetic by Riley, Greeno, and Heller (1983) on the one hand, and that on discourse understanding by van Dijk and Kintsch (1983) on the other. Kintsch and Greeno (1985) added to the discourse-comprehension strategies of the van Dijk and Kintsch model some special purpose strategies for solving word arithmetic problems, which they named the *arithmetic strategies*. For instance, if the model encounters a quantity proposition, such as "six marbles," it forms a set and tries to fill in the various slots of the set schema: what the objects are, the cardinality of the set, a specification of the objects (e.g., that the marbles are owned by Fred), and the relation between the present set and other sets in the problem (the six marbles were given to Fred by Tom, which might identify them as a "transfer set"). Thus, the Kintsch and Greeno model for word problems builds a text base in quite the same way as in the van Dijk and Kintsch general theory of text comprehension, but it then forms a very specialized situation or problem model in terms of sets of objects and their interrelations. It solves a problem by recognizing a particular pattern of relations among sets (such as TRANSFER-IN or SUPERSET) and then using a stored-solution procedure appropriate to that case.[7] Thus, in terms of the foregoing discussion about knowledge use in discourse, the Kintsch and Greeno model is a "smart" model: Production rules are formulated in such a way that in each situation exactly the right arithmetic strategy is fired.

The Kintsch and Greeno model of solving arithmetic word problems is useful in several ways. The model identifies different classes of errors, such as errors caused by a lack of arithmetic knowledge, errors caused by linguistic misunderstandings, and errors that do not reflect a lack of knowledge at all but result from resource limitations. Certain formulations of word problems overload the resources of the comprehender, especially short-term memory, leading to a breakdown in processing. As Kintsch and Greeno have shown, within each arithmetic problem type there exists a strong correlation between the frequency of errors made in solving the problem and the memory load imposed by it, even though there are no differences within problem types in either the arithmetic or linguistic knowledge required for solution.

The model distinguishes between linguistic and arithmetic errors and helps us to investigate to what extent errors made by second- and third-grade pupils are caused by a failure to understand properly the text of the word problem, rather than by a faulty knowledge of arithmetic (e.g., Dellarosa, 1986; Dellarosa, Kintsch, Reusser, & Weimer, 1988; Kintsch, 1987). If certain linguistic misunderstandings about the meanings of such key words as *have more than*, *have altogether*, or *some* are built into the knowledge base of the model, the model produces a pattern of wrong answers and misrecall of the problem statements that strikingly parallels some of the main types of errors that experimental subjects make. This is a good example of how much can be achieved even with the use of knowledge-poor representations in studies of discourse processing. The Kintsch and Greeno model knows about arithmetic (its arithmetic strategies), and it knows about the meaning of words (its lexicon; a *semantic net* in Dellarosa, 1986). However, it has no general world knowledge that would allow it to understand the situation described in a word problem. It merely picks out the crucial arithmetic information from the discourse and builds a propositional text base for it. This is good enough for some purposes (e.g., the investigation of resource limitations or linguistic factors in understanding as mentioned earlier, or to predict recall, summarization, or readability as in Kintsch & van Dijk, 1978, and related work), but it is not good enough for other purposes.

The limits of this approach are illustrated by a well-known observation: If a word problem is embedded into a concrete, familiar situation or action context, it is much easier to solve than when the same problem is expressed abstractly (e.g., Dellarosa et al., 1988; Hudson, 1983). Thus, *Five birds saw three worms on the ground, and each bird tried to get a worm. How many birds didn't get a worm?* is easy for first graders, but *There are five red marbles and three green marbles. How many more red marbles are there than green marbles?* is very hard, even though the two problems are equivalent in form.

The Kintsch and Greeno model does not account for this difference. What is needed is a model in which all knowledge relevant to the understanding of a word problem becomes integrated into a representation that is sensitive to arithmetic as well as to situational information. In the model to be described shortly, this is achieved by forming many different hypotheses about the arithmetic relations in the problem, instead of only a single one, and then by looking for information in the text in support of each hypothesis. Thus, situational and arithmetic information can combine in forming the problem interpretation.

Arithmetic Strategies
Arithmetic knowledge forms a special subset of a person's general knowledge network. Sets of objects can be represented by a propositional schema with the slots object, specification, quantity, and role (i.e., their relation to other sets)—equivalent to the set schema of Kintsch and Greeno (1985). Superordinate schemata can be similarly defined. Thus, a TRANSFER-IN schema can be set up with slots for a START, TRANSFER-IN, and RESULT SET. With each such superordinate schema, various arithmetic procedures (such as the counting strategies of Kintsch & Greeno, 1985) can be associated.

Arithmetic knowledge is used in the same way as general world knowledge. That is, propositions that represent various hypotheses about the arithmetic structure of a word problem are constructed as the text of the word problem is read and become part of the subnet. Several possible arithmetic hypotheses are constructed at each point, and whatever evidence in the text favors one or the other of these hypotheses is connected positively to it.

The strategies required for solving arithmetic word problems have been described in Kintsch and Greeno (1985) and Kintsch (1984) and have been incorporated into the computer simulation of Dellarosa (1986). However, they are used here in a different way. In the aforementioned works, the intent was to circumscribe the conditions under which each strategy is applied so accurately that only the correct one is fired in each word problem. Here, strategies fire promiscuously whenever they are supported, however weakly, by the text, and it is left for the integration process to weed out what is not wanted, just as all sorts of general knowledge propositions are activated that later turn out to be useless. A problem is solved when the right superordinate schema is more strongly activated than its alternatives, which then triggers the desired arithmetic procedures.

Three forms of arithmetic strategies need to be considered. There are strategies that form arithmetic hypotheses about sets, strategies that determine the nature of the connections between various text propositions and these hypotheses, and strategies that form superordinate arithmetic schemata on the basis of which arithmetic calculations can be performed.

1. Hypotheses about sets are propositions of the form SET-[object:X, specification:Y,quantity:Z,role:W], where X refers to an object, such as TULIP; Y is one or more other text propositions, specifying X further—for example, PAST[LOCATION[TULIP,IN-GARDEN]]; Z is a quantity proposition with X as argument—for example, FOURTEEN[TULIP]; and W indicates the role of the set in some superschema, such as WHOLE or PART.

2. Whenever a quantity proposition is encountered in the text base, possible arithmetic hypotheses derivable from it are constructed (e.g., two otherwise identical propositions with the roles WHOLE and PART). Propositions in the text base that provide evidence for any of these alternatives are then connected positively to it. Key words can be used for this purpose, as in Kintsch and Greeno (1985): collection terms such as *altogether* indicate WHOLE sets; *give/take, of these*, and *have more/less than* indicate PART sets. In addition, general world knowledge about situations and actions is used to determine what is a WHOLE and what are its PARTS. The strategies involved have been described in Kintsch (1984): restricted subsets, conjunction, and time-ordered possession/location.

Restricted subsets If the specification of one set is more general than that of another, the former is assigned the role of WHOLE and the latter that of PART. Examples are LARGE-WINDOW, SMALL-WINDOW versus WINDOW, or ON-UPPER-SHELF, ON-LOWER-SHELF versus ON-SHELF.

Conjunction If the object or specification of one set consists of the conjunction of the objects or specification of two other sets, the former is the WHOLE and the others the PARTS. This conjunction may be explicit as in

YESTERDAY, TODAY, and YESTERDAY&TODAY, or implicit, as in TEDDYBEAR, DOLL, and TOY.

Time-ordered possession/location If the specification slots of three sets contain either HAVE[agent,object] or LOCATION[object,place], or the negations of these propositions, as well as information to establish a temporal order, WHOLE and PART roles can be assigned to the three sets according to the resulting patterns. For instance, if the specifications of three sets are TIME1[HAVE,JOE,P[MARBLES]]; TIME2[GIVE,JOE,TOM,Q[MARBLES]], which implies TIME2[NOT[HAVE,JOE,Q[MARBLES]]]; and TIME3[HAVE[JOE,Z[MARBLES]]], SET1 is indicated as the WHOLE set.

3. The PART–WHOLE schema is the only arithmetic superschema to be considered in the examples that follow, though various TRANSFER and COMPARISON schemata could have been treated in the same way, as in Kintsch and Greeno (1985). Three hypotheses can be formed about the PART–WHOLE schema, depending on whether the first, second, or third of the sets formed is to be considered the WHOLE set. (Note that the order in which the sets were formed in the word problem, not their true temporal order, is at issue here.) Thus, a proposition with the head PPW, which is simply a mnemonic for PART–PART–WHOLE, expresses the hypothesis that the problem is a PART–WHOLE problem with the third set as the WHOLE: PPW[role[SET1,PART],role[SET2,PART],role[SET3,WHOLE]]. Associated with this schema is the equation $Q1 + Q2 = Q3$, where Qi is the quantity of the i-th set, as well as procedures to solve this equation, depending on which of the quantities happens to be unknown.

Examples and Issues

Three examples will be analyzed here to show how the model understands, or fails to understand, as the case may be, arithmetic word problems. To see how these examples work, it is necessary to present at least the first one in sufficient detail. This problem is intended simply as an illustration of the basic mechanisms of the model—nothing much of interest happens with respect to the arithmetic, and textually, the only thing of significance is that a simple inference is formed, which, however, is crucial for the understanding of the problem. Two more examples, which will not be presented in as much detail, will serve as illustrations of how the model can account for some wellknown facts about word-problem solving that alternative models (Briars & Larkin, 1984; Kintsch & Greeno, 1985) do not handle readily.

Inferences

Manolita tried to weed her father's garden. "You sure weeded it," said Mr. Mundoza. "There were fourteen tulips in the garden and now there are only six." How many tulips did she pull out by mistake?

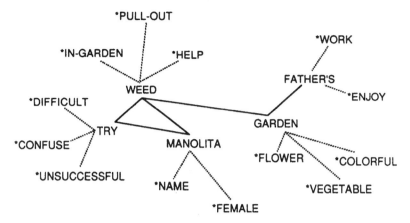

Figure 1.10
The elaborated text base for the first sentence of the Manolita problem. (Each proposition is indicated by a single word. Text propositions are connected by solid lines, their associates by broken lines. Associates are marked with an asterisk.)

This problem, modified from the "Thinking Stories" of Willoughby, Bereiter, Hilton, and Rubinstein (1981), requires for its solution the application of one of the LOCATION strategies: There were so many tulips in the garden, then some were pulled out, and now so many are left. A simple, knowledge-based inference becomes necessary: that the tulips that were pulled out are no longer in the garden. The knowledge-activation mechanism of the present model readily supplies this inference, and the problem will be solved successfully.

The model processes this problem in three cycles, which includes the first sentence, the statement by Mr. Mundoza, and the question sentence. The first sentence simply sets up a context and is not directly relevant to the arithmetic. In figure 1.10, the way the model understands this sentence is indicated, albeit in abbreviated form. The propositions constructed from the sentence itself are (P1) MANOLITA, (P2) GARDEN, (P3) TRY[MANOLITA,P4], (P4) WEED[MANOLITA, GARDEN], (P5) FATHER'S[GARDEN]. Only the first terms of these propositions are shown in figure 1.10. Also shown in figure 1.10 are the propositions that were added to the text base through the process of associative-knowledge elaboration (they are marked with an asterisk and, once again, abbreviated: *NAME stands for ISA[MANOLITA,NAME], etc.). Because no simulation of a general knowledge network is available, or even conceivable, the process of knowledge elaboration must be approximated empirically. An informal procedure was adopted for this purpose: Three persons were asked to provide free associations to phrases corresponding to P1 through P5 (as well as to corresponding phrases from the remaining two sentences of this word problem), and the responses generated by at least two persons were considered as the top associates of each

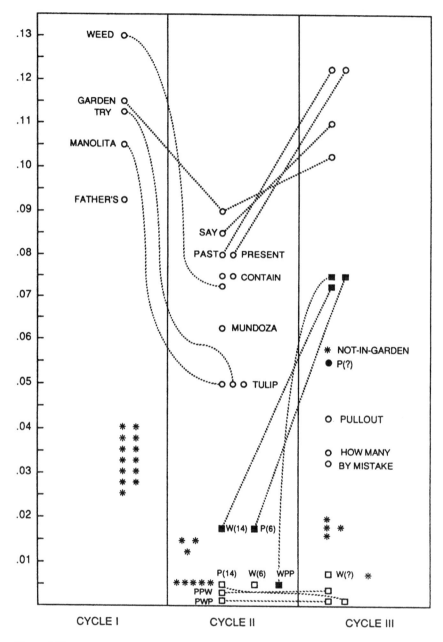

Figure 1.11
The result of the integration process for the three sentences in the Manolita problem. (Propositions
are indicated by single words; inferences are marked by an asterisk; their arrangement in the figure
is approximate. The ordinate shows the activation values of each proposition after the process has
stabilized. Propositions carried over from one processing cycle to the next are connected by arrows.)

proposition in the general knowledge net (up to a maximum of three associations per proposition).

The text base shown in figure 1.10 serves as a basis for deriving a connectivity matrix, using the principles illustrated earlier in tables 1.1 and 1.2: Text propositions are connected depending on their proximity in the text base, each text proposition is connected to its associates by a value of .5, and knowledge derived propositions are interconnected by the same value if they share an argument, or by −.5 if different word senses are involved (this does not occur in the present example).

An initial activation vector consisting of .2 s for the five propositions directly derived from the text, followed by 13 zeros for the propositions generated from the knowledge net, was then repeatedly updated by multiplying it with the connectivity matrix until the activation values stabilized, as in the examples discussed previously. In the present case, activation levels stabilize after 10 iterations. The resulting pattern of activation is shown in the first panel of figure 1.11. WEED[MANOLITA,GARDEN], whose centrality in the text base is apparent in the graphical representation, has the highest activation value, and the other text-derived propositions also have fairly high activation values. Knowledge-derived propositions are considerably less activated. The four most strongly activated propositions (P1 through P4) are retained in the short-term buffer and enter the second processing cycle.

The second processing cycle is shown in figure 1.12. The four propositions held over in the short-term memory buffer from Cycle 1 are joined by 9 new text propositions and 11 associated propositions from the knowledge base. (Because of lack of space, the latter are indicated only by asterisks.) The quantity propositions FOURTEEN[TULIP] and SIX[TULIP] generate four arithmetic hypotheses: that the 14 tulips that were in the garden in the past are, respectively, a PART or WHOLE set, and that the 6 tulips now in the garden are a PART or WHOLE set. What the reader knows about weeding gardens provides the crucial information that discriminates among these hypotheses: The tulips before the garden was weeded are the WHOLE set, and only a PART is left after the weeding. This knowledge is expressed in the connectivity matrix by connecting PAST with WHOLE[14], and PRESENT with PART[6].

The last three propositions that enter the subnet are the superordinate arithmetic hypotheses PPW, PWP, and WPP. They receive support from their corresponding first-order arithmetic hypotheses. Thus, whatever strength each arithmetic hypothesis gathers from the text is fed into the superordinate arithmetic schemata consistent with it. These schemata are mutually exclusive and inhibit each other with connection values of −1. Note that only at this final level is inhibition among arithmetic hypotheses used: The hypotheses that a particular set of objects plays the role of WHOLE or PART set are also mutually exclusive, but they are not allowed to inhibit each other; they merely collect more or less positive evidence, which they then transmit to the superordinate stage where a selection among alternatives is made.

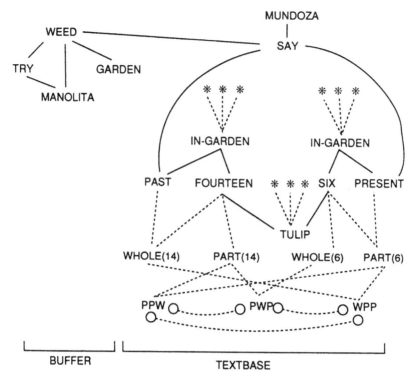

Figure 1.12
The elaborated text base for the second sentence of the Manolita problem. (Four propositions were carried over from the previous cycle in the short-term memory buffer. Solid lines connect text propositions, broken lines inferences; nonarithmetic inferences are indicated by asterisks only.)

The resulting connectivity matrix then becomes the multiplier of the activation-state vector for the 28 propositions participating in this second processing cycle. Initially, these activation values are positive for the text-derived propositions, and zero otherwise, except for the propositions carried over in the buffer, which retain the activation values they reached in the last cycle. In this case, the activation vector stabilizes already after seven operations. The results are shown in the second panel of figure 1.11. (If the activation process is extended to twice the number of cycles, the activation values for the arithmetic hypotheses, measured to four decimal places, do not change at all.) All text-derived propositions remain strongly activated, while none of the textual inferences (e.g., MUNDOZA is a NAME of a MALE, TULIPS are FLOWERS, RED, and GROW-IN-HOLLAND) reach a high level of activation. This is intuitively quite plausible. As far as the arithmetic is concerned, the problem is at this point understood correctly and practically solved: WHOLE[14] is more strongly activated than its alternative, PART[14]. Similarly, PART[6] is stronger than

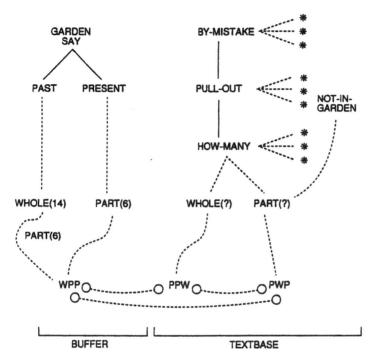

Figure 1.13
The elaborated text base for the third sentence of the Manolita problem.

WHOLE[6]. The correct hypothesis, WPP, is the most strongly activated of the three alternative superschemata.

Note that the text propositions and inferences are, in general, much more strongly activated than the arithmetic hypotheses. Therefore, the activation values of the latter must be considered separately, relative to each other, rather than in relation to the text propositions when it comes to selecting propositions to be maintained in the short-term memory buffer. This imbalance is required for the model to work. If the arithmetic hypotheses are weighted more heavily, they draw the activation away from the text itself, and the system cannot stabilize: It will flip-flop between alternative, mutually contradictory arithmetic schemata. The arithmetic hypotheses have to be anchored in a stable text representation.

For the third and final sentence, the short-term memory buffer needs to carry over both text propositions to establish textual coherence and arithmetic hypotheses to take advantage of the understanding of the problem that has been achieved so far. It has been assumed here that the four strongest text propositions as well as the four strongest arithmetic hypotheses are carried over in the buffer, as shown in figure 1.13. (There are, of course, other plausible alternatives.) The three text propositions generated on the basis of this sentence bring with them into the net six knowledge propositions, one of which is NOT[CONTAIN[GARDEN,TULIP]], which turns out to be crucial for the solution of the problem. In addition, new hypotheses about the question set are formed, and the schemata PPW and PWP, which were lost after the second cycle, are reconstructed. Because the child knows about weeding gardens, the tulips that were pulled out are identified as a part of those that were in the garden in the beginning. Hence, a connection that favors the PART hypothesis over the WHOLE hypothesis is formed between the inference NOT[CONTAIN[GARDEN,TULIP]] and PART[?]. It completes the pattern that is the condition for the use of a LOCATION strategy: some tulips at one place in the past, then some not there, now some are left.

The new net requires 43 operations to stabilize. The knowledge-based inference NOT[CONTAIN[GARDEN,TULIP]] achieves an activation level above the range of the text propositions (figure 1.11, third panel). The picture is completely clear as far as the arithmetic is concerned: All the correct hypotheses are strongly activated, and all incorrect alternatives have low or zero activation values.

The final steps in the solution of the problem are procedural. From information associated with the WPP pattern the equation $14 = 6 + ?$ is generated, which is then used to obtain the correct answer. A lot of mountains had to be moved to achieve a very simple result!

The Manolita problem was solved without problem solving. The basic comprehension operations were sufficient; that is, it produced the inference that the pulled-out tulips are not in the garden, which was required for the application of the LOCATION strategy. However, this is not always the case. In many, not necessarily difficult, problems, more focused problem-solving operations are required because the random-inference generation process described earlier fails to generate the required inference. Consider the following "thinking problem":

> Mrs. Nosho was telling Mark about the two huge aquariums she kept when she was a little girl. "There were 30 fish in one and 40 fish in the other, so you can tell how many fish I had." How many fish did Mrs. Nosho have?

In a simulation run of this problem the model failed because it did not come up with the transitive inference HAVE[X,Y]&CONTAIN[Y,Z] implies HAVE[X,Z]. At this point, the process needs to go into a problem-solving mode in which the information in the text is elaborated in a more focused manner than is possible with the automatic-comprehension mechanisms discussed here.

Context Effects
Problems embedded into a familiar situational context are much easier to solve than problems that must be solved without this situational support (e.g., Hudson, 1983). Thus, birds catching worms present a concrete, understandable situation that makes it clear what is the whole and what are the parts, whereas

abstract, ill-constrained problems do not. All depends on whether the right arithmetic strategy is used; the situation is of no help.

In the worm-and-bird problem, the text provides a situational constraint for the interpretation of the problem that has very little to do with arithmetic per se. It is the knowledge about birds eating worms that matters. The birds trying to catch the worm are understood as the WHOLE set, with the birds catching worms as one PART, and the birds unable to get a worm as the other PART. This understanding was achieved not because a certain key phrase, like *how many more*, was parsed correctly but on the basis of general world knowledge. If there are birds, some of whom catch and some of whom do not catch a worm, what is the WHOLE set and what are the PARTS is given by general world knowledge that is not specific to arithmetic. The arithmetic can hardly go wrong here because the well-known situation guarantees the right interpretation of the problem. It is this aspect that the present model deals with most effectively.

Context, however, does not always facilitate problem solution, it may also interfere with it. Consider this typical school problem, with its highly impoverished context:

> Fred has four Chevies and three Fords. (a) How many cars does he have altogether? (b) How many more Chevies does he have than Fords?

Context is no help with this problem; it must be solved on the basis of specialized arithmetic strategies, on the basis of the key words *have altogether* for Question A and *have more than* for Question B. Of course, children are much more familiar with the former (e.g., Riley et al., 1983), but if the right strategies are available, both problems will be solved. In the model, too, the *altogether* in Question A will be connected with the HOW-MANY/WHOLE hypothesis, and the *have more than* will be connected with the HOW-MANY/PART hypothesis in Question B, and both questions will be answered equally well. After the first sentence, PART and WHOLE hypotheses are established for both the Chevies and the Fords, but there is not much to distinguish them; the superordinate schemata PPW, PWP, and WPP are only weakly activated and hardly differentiated. Question A, on the other hand, correctly activates the PPW hypothesis, and Question B yields the WPP result. Thus, if the arithmetic knowledge is available, it makes very little difference which question follows the problem statement.

In contrast, if the problem is only slightly contextualized, the model can be biased in favor of one of the questions, and actually fails when it gets the wrong one. Suppose, the foregoing problem is changed to read

> Fred has a nice collection of antique cars. Four of his cars are Chevies, and three are Fords.

Collection, like some, is constructed as a quantity proposition, and hence PART and WHOLE hypotheses for a set of cars with unspecified quantity are established in the first processing cycle. They are both activated equally, however, at this point. This changes dramatically with the second sentence: The *four Chevies* and *three Fords* are both identified as PART sets because of the phrase *of his*. In consequence, the model begins to favor the WPP hypotheses. When it receives Question A, the WPP hypothesis is decisively strengthened, and the problem is solved correctly. On the other hand, if it is given Question B, the model becomes confused between the WPP and PWP hypotheses, which are both equally activated, and fails to solve the problem.

Thus, we have here an example where the problem context interferes with the solution of a problem. It biases the problem in favor of one particular interpretation, so that when another interpretation is required, the whole process fails. It is important, however, to analyze exactly why the model failed to answer Question B correctly: After processing the second sentence, it was so strongly convinced that the *four Chevies* and *three Fords* were both PART sets that it did not carry over the corresponding WHOLE set hypotheses and therefore had no way of using the information in the *have-more-than* question in support of the CHEVIES/WHOLE hypothesis. Thus, rather special circumstances prevented the model from answering Question B. In slightly different circumstances, it could have done so: (a) if the buffer were large enough, the CHEVY/WHOLE hypothesis would not have been lost, or (b) if the model had been allowed to reread the problem statement.

Question Specificity
The final example illustrates some different aspects of word-problem solving; namely the complex role that redundant specifications of sets may have. On the one hand, overspecifying a set can be helpful because it provides more than one way to refer to it. On the other hand, redundant specifications increase the length of the text and thus the likelihood that some important piece of information is no longer in active memory when it is required. In the following problem, three versions of the question are possible:

> Joe had a collection of nine marbles. He started his collection with some beautiful red marbles. Then Lucy added six pink marbles to his collection as a present. (a) How many beautiful red marbles did he start his collection with? (b) How many marbles did he start his collection with? (c) How many beautiful red marbles did he have?

The first processing cycle results in undifferentiated hypotheses about the nine marbles. The set constructed in the second cycle, on the other hand, is clearly a PART set, as is the one constructed in the third cycle. Indeed, at the end of the third cycle, the model understands the problem essentially correctly, with the WPP schema greatly exceeding alternative hypotheses in activation value. To understand what happens next, it is necessary to know which text propositions were maintained in the buffer at the end of the third cycle: Only propositions from the third sentence are carried over, while the propositions from the second sentence are no longer held in active memory at this point. This has non-trivial consequences when the question is asked. In Versions A and B everything is all right, because the question itself identifies the question set as a PART set—*starting a collection* serves this function, just as it did in Sentence 2. Version C of the question, on the other hand, does not yield a correct solution. The question itself does not indicate the role of the question set, and there is no information from the second sentence still available in active memory that would help to identify its role either; because there are already several strong PART hypotheses around, the model tends toward the hypothesis that the question set has the role of a WHOLE; the PWP schema thus becomes more activated than the correct WPP schema.

However, this is far from an unequivocal prediction of failure for Version C of the question. With a slightly larger buffer, or with a little less irrelevant material intervening (*pink marbles, as a present*), the critical information from the second sentence could have been maintained in the buffer and used to solve the problem. Or even more obviously, the problem solver could reread the problem or perform a reinstatement search (Kintsch & van Dijk, 1978; Miller & Kintsch, 1980) to activate the required information from long-term memory. Rather the prediction is that children, like the model, would have more trouble with Question C, and fail more frequently, than with either A or B.

Thus, the more specific the question the better. But how irrelevant or redundant material will affect the difficulty of a word problem is a more complex story. It may be quite harmless, or may even facilitate problem solving, if the question exploits a redundancy in the specification of a set. But it may be a source of difficulty and even a cause of failure when the question is asked in an unhelpful way. The present model has the flexibility to handle these complex effects of context: Many small effects are allowed to add up and pull the model one way or another. The "smart" models of Kintsch and Greeno (1985) and Briars and Larkin (1984) have no ready way to cope with these subtle contextual demands: Either the right strategy is used or not.

Discussion

How people recall relevant knowledge when they read a text is reminiscent of another experimental paradigm that has been studied extensively in psychological laboratories: how people recall lists of words. A widely used explanation for the recall of word lists is based on the generation–recognition principle. Some words are recalled directly, perhaps from a short-term memory buffer, and these words are then used to generate other semantically or contextually related, plausible recall candidates. Words that have actually appeared in the to-be-learned list will be recognized among these candidates and recalled, whereas intrusions will tend to be rejected. Generation–recognition theories have had their detractors, and in their most primitive form they are certainly inadequate to account for the more complex phenomena of list recall. However, sophisticated versions of this theory are widely accepted now. Almost every current model of list recall includes a generation/retrieval as well as a recognition/editing stage.

The model of knowledge use in discourse comprehension proposed here has two analogous stages: First, a propositional network must be constructed, and then it must be edited or integrated. The way the construction process is thought of here is a straight extension of previous work on discourse processing. The words and phrases that make up a discourse are the raw material from which a mental representation of the meaning of that discourse is constructed. This mental representation takes the form of a propositional text base. Text bases combine two sources of information: the text itself and knowledge—knowledge about language as well as knowledge about the world. To construct even a single proposition, an appropriate frame must be retrieved from one's store of knowledge, and its slots must be filled in the way indicated by the text. The novel aspect of the present model is that the role of knowledge is greatly expanded in this process. Previously, one could think of the text base—to put it crudely—as a translation into "propositionaleese" of the sentences in the text. Now, the text base becomes a much richer structure than before. Not only does it contain the propositions directly derivable from the text, but also each of these propositions brings with it a number of other propositions that are closely connected to it in the general knowledge net. Thus, propositions are constructed just as before (e.g., van Dijk & Kintsch, 1983); yet where previously a single proposition was formed, a whole cluster is generated now.

Crucial in the present model is how this cluster of propositions is obtained: by a context-free process of activation of the closest neighbors of the original text-derived proposition in the general knowledge net. Of course, such a process will inevitably activate a lot of material that is irrelevant for any given context and, indeed, inconsistent with it. However, the price that has to be paid for promiscuity is not very high: The resulting text base is a connectionist net in which further spreading activation processes rapidly take care of inconsistencies and irrelevancies. What is gained by this dumb and seemingly wasteful process of random knowledge activation is flexibility and context sensitivity. The research on knowledge activation in psychology, as well as the experience with artificial intelligence systems, suggests that it is very difficult to activate knowledge intelligently. Prediction or expectation-based systems that use frames or scripts do not adapt easily to new contexts; prestructured knowledge hardly ever is exactly in the form that is needed. The construction–integration scheme proposed here may turn out to be more successful in this respect.

The general framework sketched earlier could be extended and elaborated in various ways as more experience with it is obtained. It might prove necessary, for instance, to resort to greater formalization in the propositional notation used here. However, until it becomes quite clear what the gains of greater formalization would be, a robust, easy-to-use system is to be preferred, even at the cost of some imprecision.

Perhaps more important might be elaborations of the knowledge-sampling mechanism. As presented here, each text-derived proposition activates its own strongest associates. It might be worthwhile to explore schemes whereby pairs or clusters of propositions activate their strongest joint associates.

Similarly, other criteria for stabilizing a network might be explored. For instance, networks might be made to maximize some statistic like harmony, as in Smolensky (1986). This might have considerable advantages. For instance, it is not always possible now to compare different networks in terms of how fast they reach equilibrium, because the number of cycles required depends strongly on the number of nodes in the network. In addition, at present there is no really satisfactory way to tell how good an equilibrium a process achieves. In the word arithmetic problems, all one can tell is whether the right hypothesis is more strongly activated than its competitors, but comparisons of the size of that difference across problems are problematic.

Constructive processes other than the ones explored here will need to be considered. For word arithmetic problems, the most important constructions involved the arithmetic hypotheses. The construction of macropropositions could be neglected, mostly because the word problems were short ones and their macrostructure played no role in the problem-solving process.[8] For many other types of text, construction rules to form successive layers of abstractions and generalizations, as described by Turner et al. (1986), would be of primary interest. The macrostructure of a text could thus be made an integral part of a text base rather than a separate component, as it is presently treated.

Thus, there are a great many rules necessary to make the construction–integration model work for proposition building, assigning references and coreferences, bridging inferences, forming macrostructures, elaborating knowledge, and so on. Some of these construction rules are reasonably well worked out at this point, others are available within restricted domains, but many problems remain as yet unsolved. Thus, some of the same problems are encountered here as in conventional expectationdriven, top-down models of comprehension—but with one difference: Weaker, more general rules can be used here because these rules need not be fine-tuned to an ever-changing context. Whatever rules are still needed ought to be easier to work out within the construction–integration framework.

In van Dijk and Kintsch (1983), an important distinction was made between text bases and situation models. The former correspond to the propositional representation of a text, both at the level of the micro- and macrostructure. The latter correspond to a representation of the text that is integrated with other knowledge. Thus, in terms of the present model, the integrated text base—after irrelevant and inconsistent information has been deactivated and important knowledge elements have been absorbed—is a kind of situation model. The qualifying phrase "a kind of" is needed because text bases, integrated or not, are always propositional, whereas van Dijk and Kintsch specifically left open the possibility that situation models may be nonpropositional (e.g., Perrig & Kintsch, 1985). Situation models, under certain circumstances, may thus be like Johnson-Laird's (1983) mental models.[9]

The theory of knowledge use in discourse comprehension has been presented here at two levels: first, it is presented in terms of a general computational mechanism, at the level of what Pylyshyn (1985) called the "cognitive virtual machine"; and second, as a particular model that specifies how this mechanism is used in word identification in discourse and in understanding and solving word problems. The function of the model is primarily explanatory. Certain phenomena can now be interpreted within the framework of the model; for example, why a particular formulation of a word problem is especially hard or easy. Unlike less complex theories, however, there is no direct link between explanation and prediction in the present case. Unqualified experimental predictions are hard to come by in a model as complex as the present one. At best, one might predict that a particular problem should be a difficult one, but that might mean several different things at the empirical level: that the solution fails, that a particular error occurs, that extra memory resources are required, that a reinstatement search will occur, that the problem must be read twice, and so forth. Even if we knew precisely what the "knowledge-use virtual machine" was like, our ability to make precise experimental predictions that are testable in conventional ways would still be severely limited. That, however, is not to say that such theories are without empirical consequences. Although we cannot predict particular events, predictions concerning classes of events are quite feasible (e.g., the different ways people might have trouble with word problems). Furthermore, our new-found understanding of why and how certain things happen can have important consequences for how certain texts are created in the first place or for instructional practices designed to help people with particular comprehension tasks.

Notes

This research was supported by Grant MH 15872 from the National Institute of Mental Health. The work on word arithmetic problems was supported by Grant BNS 8741 from the National Science Foundation.

1. Conceivably, a purer connectionist model might be constructed. In the present model, an associative knowledge net is used to build a text-base net, which is then integrated. McClelland (1985) has put forth the idea of a connection information distributor, which is a subnetwork in which the units are not dedicated and connections are not hardwired. Instead, this subnetwork is programmable by inputs from the central network where the knowledge that controls processing in the subnetwork is stored. One could say that the production rules in the present model have the function of programming such a subnetwork.

2. Formally, concepts and propositions can be treated alike (e.g., Anderson, 1980).

3. This use of the term *proposition* differs from the standard one in logic. Furthermore, not all authors who use comparable semantic units in their analyses use the same term. For instance, Dik (1980) talked about *predicates* and *terms* combining to form *predications*. Wilensky (1986) used *relation* and *aspectuals*. In spite of this terminological disarray and the possibility of confusion with the meaning of proposition in logic, *proposition* appears to be the most widely accepted term and will be retained here.

4. The extreme informality of this notation is chosen for ease of exposition. Frequently, of course, a more precise formalism is needed. It is fairly straightforward to elaborate the present informal notation whenever that is the case. For example, in the computer simulation of word problem solving by Dellarosa (1986), the LOOPS language provides a ready-made type-token distinction. There seems to be no reason, however, to burden a general discussion like the present one with a cumbersome, formal notation when it is not needed.

5. As with *proposition*, this is a nonstandard use of the term's meaning. Meaning is used here as shorthand for the momentary, subject- and situation-specific activated semantic and experiential context of a concept. Clearly, this is not what many people have in mind when they speak about the meaning of a word—though it is a conception of meaning quite appropriate for a psychological processing model.

6. That integration occurs at the end of each processing cycle is proposed here merely as a simplifying assumption. Although there is clearly something going on at the end of sentences (e.g., Aaronson & Scarborough, 1977), integration does not need to wait for a sentence boundary (see the evidence for the "immediacy assumption"; Just & Carpenter, 1980; Sanford & Garrod, 1981). It would be quite possible to apply the relaxation procedure outlined here repeatedly in each cycle, as propositions are being constructed. This would allow for the disambiguation of word senses before the end of a cycle. Because inferences and macropropositions are usually not available before the end of a processing cycle, end-of-cycle integration plays an especially important role.

7. Computer simulations of this model have been developed by Fletcher (1985) and Dellarosa (1986) and are available from the author.

8. Longer problems in which the macrostructure does play a role have been investigated by Dellarosa et al. (1988). Depending on whether a word problem establishes a theme of competition or cooperation between two protagonists, *compare* or *combine* problems will be solved most easily.

9. Unlike the representation of the text itself—the text base, which is always propositional—situation models may have a different representation format, although this possibility was not considered in the present article. Both text bases and situation models are mental models of one kind or another in the sense of Gentner and Stevens (1983), though not necessarily in the more restrictive sense of Johnson-Laird (1983).

References

Aaronson, D., & Scarborough, H. S. (1977). Performance theories for sentence coding: Some quantitative models. *Journal of Verbal Learning and Verbal Behavior, 16*, 277–303.

Anderson, J. R. (1980). Concepts, propositions, and schemata: What are the cognitive units? *Nebraska Symposium on Motivation, 28*, 121–162.

Anderson, J. R. (1983). *The architecture of cognition.* Cambridge: Harvard University Press.

Becker, C. A. (1976). Semantic context and word frequency effects in visual word recognition. *Journal of Experimental Psychology: Human Perception and Performance, 2*, 556–566.

Briars, D., & Larkin, J. H. (1984). An integrated model of skill in solving elementary word problems. *Cognition and Instruction, 1*, 245–296.

Broadbent, D. A. (1958). *Perception and communication.* New York: Pergamon Press.

Bruner, J. S., & Postman, L. (1949). Perception, cognition, and behavior. *Journal of Personality, 18*, 15–31.

Dellarosa, O. (1986). A computer simulation of children's arithmetic word problem solving. *Behavior Research Methods, Instruments, & Computers, 18*, 147–154.

Dellarosa, D., Kintsch, W., Reusser, K., & Weimer, R. (1988). The role of understanding in solving word problems. *Cognitive Psychology, 20*, 405–438.

Dik, S. C. (1980). *Studies in functional grammar*. London: Academic Press.

Fischler, I., & Goodman, G. O. (1978). Latency of associative activation in memory. *Journal of Experimental Psychology: Human Perception and Performance, 4*, 455–470.

Fletcher, C. R. (1985). Understanding and solving arithmetic word problems: A computer simulation. *Behavior Research Methods, Instruments, and Computers, 17*, 565–571.

Forster, K. I. (1976). Accessing the mental lexicon. In R. J. Wales & E. C. T. Walker (Eds.), *New approaches to language mechanisms* (pp. 257–287). Amsterdam: North-Holland.

Frazier, L., & Rayner, K. (1982). Making and correcting errors during sentence comprehension: Eye movements in the analysis of structurally ambiguous sentences. *Cognitive Psychology, 14*, 178–210.

Frederiksen, J. R. (1981). Understanding anaphora: Rules used by readers in assigning pronominal referents. *Discourse Processes, 4*, 323–347.

Gentner, D., & Stevens, A. L. (1983). *Mental models*. Hillsdale, NJ: Erlbaum.

Haviland, S. E., & Clark, H. H. (1974). What's new? Acquiring new information as a process in comprehension. *Journal of Verbal Learning and Verbal Behavior, 13*, 512–521.

Hudson, T. (1983). Correspondences and numerical differences between disjoint sets. *Child Development, 54*, 84–90.

Johnson-Laird, P. N. (1983). *Mental models*. Cambridge: Harvard University Press.

Just, M. A., & Carpenter, P. A. (1980). A theory of reading: From eye fixation to comprehension. *Psychological Review, 87*, 329–354.

Kintsch, W. (1974). *The representation of meaning in memory*. Hillsdale, NJ: Erlbaum.

Kintsch, W. (1984). *Strategies for solving word arithmetic problems: Extensions of the Kintsch & Greeno Model* (Technical Report No. 133). Boulder: Institute of Cognitive Science, University of Colorado.

Kintsch, W. (1985). Text processing: A psychological model. In T. A. van Dijk (Ed.), *Handbook of discourse analysis* (Vol. 2, pp. 231–243). London: Academic Press.

Kintsch, W. (1987). Understanding word problems: Linguistic factors in problem solving. In M. Nagao (Ed.), *Language and artificial intelligence* (pp. 197–208). Amsterdam: North Holland.

Kintsch, W. (1989). The representation of knowledge and the use of knowledge in discourse comprehension. In C. Graumann & R. Dietrich (Ed.), *Language in the social context*. Amsterdam: Elsevier.

Kintsch, W., & van Dijk, T. A. (1978). Towards a model of text comprehension and production. *Psychological Review, 85*, 363–394.

Kintsch, W., & Greeno, J. G. (1985). Understanding and solving word arithmetic problems. *Psychological Review, 92*, 109–129.

Kintsch, W., & Mross, E. F. (1985). Context effects in word identification. *Journal of Memory and Language, 24*, 336–349.

Marslen-Wilson, W. D., & Welsh, A. (1978). Processing interactions and lexical access during word recognition in continuous speech. *Cognition, 10*, 29–63.

McClelland, J. L. (1985). Putting knowledge in its place: A scheme for programming parallel processing structures on the fly. *Cognitive Science, 9*, 113–146.

McKoon, G., & Ratcliff, R. (1986). Inferences about predictable events. *Journal of Experimental Psychology: Learning, Memory, and Cognition, 12*, 82–91.

Meyer, D. E., & Schvaneveldt, R. W. (1971). Facilitation in recognizing pairs of words: Evidence of a dependence between retrieval operations. *Journal of Experimental Psychology, 90*, 227–234.

Miller, J. R., & Kintsch, W. (1980). Readability and recall of short prose passages: A theoretical analysis. *Journal of Experimental Psychology: Human Learning and Memory, 6*, 335–354.

Morton, J. (1969). Interaction of information in word recognition. *Psychological Review, 76*, 165–178.

Morton, J. (1979). Word recognition. In J. Moron & J. C. Marshall (Eds.), *Psycholinguistics, Series 2: Structures and processes* (pp. 107–156). London: Paul Elek.

Mudersbach, K. (1982). Hol-Atomismus als Vereinheitlichung von Atomismus und Holismus. In *Proceedings of the 7th International Wittgenstein Symposium* (pp. 347–349). Wien: Hoelder-Pichler-Tempsky.

Norris, D. (1986). Word recognition: Context effects without priming. *Cognition, 22*, 93–136.

Perrig, W., & Kintsch, W. (1985). Propositional and situational representations of text. *Journal of Memory and Language, 24*, 503–518.

Pylyshyn, Z. W. (1985). *Computation and cognition*. Cambridge: MIT Press.

Raaijmakers, J. G., & Shiffrin, R. M. (1981). A theory of probabilistic search of associative memory. *Psychological Review, 88*, 93–134.

Riley, M. S., Greeno, J. G., & Heller, J. I. (1983). Development of children's problem solving ability in arithmetic. In H. P. Ginsburg (Ed.), *The development of mathematical thinking* (pp. 153–196). New York: Academic Press.

Rumelhart, D. E., & McClelland, J. L. (1986). *Parallel distributed processing. Explorations in the microstructure of cognition. Vol. 1: Foundations*. Cambridge: MIT Press.

Sanford, A. J., & Garrod, S. C. (1981). *Understanding written language*. New York: Wiley.

Schank, R. C. (1978). Predictive understanding. In R. N. Campbell & P. T. Smith (Eds.), *Recent advances in the psychology of language—Formal and experimental approaches* (pp. 91–101). New York: Plenum Press.

Schank, R. C. (1982). *Dynamic memory*. New York: Cambridge University Press.

Schank, R. C., & Abelson, R. P. (1977). *Scripts, plans, goals, and understanding*. Hillsdale, NJ: Erlbaum.

Seidenberg, M. S., Tanenhaus, M. K., Leiman, J. M., & Bienkowsky, M. (1982). Automatic access of the meaning of ambiguous words in context: Some limitations of knowledge-based processing. *Cognitive Psychology, 14*, 489–537.

Sharkey, N. E. (1986). A model of knowledge-based expectations in text comprehension. In J. A. Galambos, R. P. Abelson, & J. B. Black (Eds.), *Knowledge structures* (pp. 49–70). Hillsdale, NJ: Erlbaum.

Smolensky, P. (1986). Information processing in dynamical systems: Foundations of Harmony Theory. In D. E. Rumelhart & J. L. McClelland, *Parallel distributed processing. Explorations in the microstructure of cognition. Vol. 1: Foundations* (pp. 194–281). Cambridge: MIT Press.

Swinney, D. A. (1979). Lexical access during sentence comprehension: (Re)Consideration of context effects. *Journal of Verbal Learning and Verbal Behavior, 18*, 523–534.

Till, R., Mross, E. F., & Kintsch, W. (1988). Time course of priming for associate and inference words in a discourse context. *Memory & Cognition, 16*, 283–298.

Turner, A. A., McCutchen, D., & Kintsch, W. (1986). *The generation of macropropositions during comprehension*. Paper presented at the meeting of the Psychonomic Society, New Orleans.

van Dijk, T. A. (1980). *Macrostructures*. Hillsdale, NJ: Erlbaum.

van Dijk, T. A., & Kintsch, W. (1983). *Strategies of discourse comprehension*. New York: Academic Press.

Waltz, D. L., & Pollack, J. B. (1985). Massively parallel parsing: A strongly interactive model of natural language interpretation. *Cognitive Science, 9*, 51–74.

Wilensky, R. (1986). *Some problems and proposals for knowledge representation* (Tech. Rep. No. UCB/CSD 86/294). Berkeley: Computer Science Division, University of California.

Willoughby, S. S., Bereiter, C., Hilton, P., & Rubinstein, J. H. (1981). *Heal math: Thinking stories book. Level 2*. La Salle, IL: Open Court.

Winograd, T. (1983). *Language as a cognitive process. Volume I: Syntax*. Reading, MA: Addison-Wesley.

Zajonc, R. B. (1980). Feeling and thinking: Preferences need no inferences. *American Psychologist, 35*, 151–175.

ACT

Chapter 2

ACT: A Simple Theory of Complex Cognition

John R. Anderson

The designation of our species as *homo sapiens* reflects the fact that there is something special about human cognition—that it achieves a kind of intelligence not even approximated in other species. One can point to marks of that intelligence in many domains. Much of my research has been in the area of mathematics and computer programming, fields in which the capacity to come up with abstract solutions to problems is one ability that is frequently cited with almost mystical awe. A good example of this is the ability to write recursive programs.

Consider writing a function to calculate the factorial of a number. The factorial of a number can be described to someone as the result you get when you multiply all the positive integers up to that number. For instance,

$$\text{factorial}(5) = 5 \times 4 \times 3 \times 2 \times 1 = 120$$

In addition (it might appear by arbitrary convention), the factorial of zero is defined to be 1. In writing a recursive program to calculate the factorial for any number N, one defines factorial in terms of itself. Below is what such a program might look like:

$$\text{factorial}(N) = 1 \qquad\qquad\qquad \text{if } N = 0$$
$$= \text{factorial}(N - 1) \times N \quad \text{if } N > 0.$$

The first part of the specification, $\text{factorial}(0) = 1$, is just stating part of the definition of factorial. But the second recursive specification seems mysterious to many and appears all the more mysterious that anyone can go from the concrete illustration to such an abstract statement. It certainly seems like the kind of cognitive act that we are unlikely to see from any other species.

We have studied extensively how people write recursive programs (e.g., Anderson, Farrell, & Sauers, 1984; Pirolli & Anderson, 1985). To test our understanding of the process, we have developed computer simulations that are themselves capable of writing recursive programs in the same way humans do. Underlying this skill are about 500 knowledge units called *production rules*. For instance, one of these production rules for programming recursion, which might apply in the midst of the problem solving, is

    IF the goal is to identify the recursive relationship in a function with a
number argument
THEN set as subgoals to
1. Find the value of the function for some N
2. Find the value of the function for $N - 1$
3. Try to identify the relationship between the two answers.

Thus, in the case above, this might lead to finding that factorial$(5) = 120$
(Step 1), factorial$(4) = 24$ (Step 2), and that factorial $(N) =$ factorial $(N - 1) \times N$
(Step 3).

    We (e.g., Anderson, Boyle, Corbett, & Lewis, 1990; Anderson, Corbett,
Koedinger, & Pelletier, 1995; Anderson & Reiser, 1985) have created computer-
based instructional systems, called *intelligent tutors*, for teaching cognitive skills
based on this kind of production-rule analysis. By basing instruction on such
rules, we have been able to increase students' rate of learning by a factor of 3.
Moreover, within our tutors we have been able to track the learning of such
rules and have found that they improve gradually with practice, as illustrated
in figure 2.1. Our evidence indicates that underlying the complex, mystical skill
of recursive programming is about 500 rules like the one above, and that each
rule follows a simple learning curve like figure 2.1.

    This illustrates the major claim of this article: All that there is to intelligence is
the simple accrual and tuning of many small units of knowledge that in total
produce complex cognition. The whole is no more than the sum of its parts, but
it has a lot of parts.

    The credibility of this claim has to turn on whether we can establish in detail
how the claim is realized in specific instances of complex cognition. The goal of
the ACT theory, which is the topic of this article, has been to establish the
details of this claim. It has been concerned with three principal issues: How are
these units of knowledge represented, how are they acquired, and how are they
deployed in cognition?

    The ACT theory has origins in the human associative memory (HAM) theory
of human memory (Anderson & Bower, 1973), which attempted to develop a
theory of how memories were represented and how those representations
mediated behavior that was observed in memory experiments. It became apparent that this theory only dealt with some aspects of knowledge; Anderson
(1976) proposed a distinction between declarative knowledge, which HAM
dealt with, and procedural knowledge, which HAM did not deal with. Bor-
rowing ideas from Newell (1972, 1973), it was proposed that procedural
knowledge was implemented by production rules. A production-system model
called ACTE was proposed to embody this joint procedural–declarative theory.
After 7 years of working with variants of that system, we were able to develop
a theory called ACT* (Anderson, 1983) that embodied a set of neurally plausible
assumptions about how such a system might be implemented and also psy-

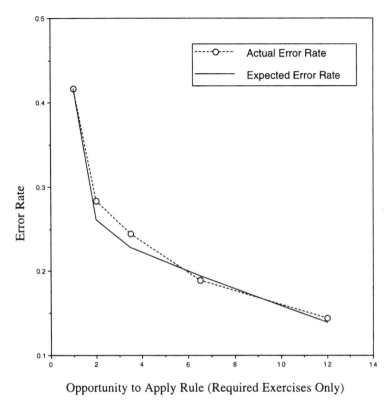

Opportunity to Apply Rule (Required Exercises Only)

Figure 2.1
Mean Actual Error Rate and Expected Error Rate across Successive Rule Applications. Note: From "Student Modeling in the ACT Programming Tutor," by A. T. Corbett, J. R. Anderson, and A. T. O'Brien, 1995, in P. Nichols, S. Chipman, and B. Brennan, *Cognitively Diagnostic Assessment*, Hillsdale, NJ: Erlbaum. Copyright 1995 by Erlbaum. Reprinted by permission.

chologically plausible assumptions about how production rules might be acquired. That system remained with us for 10 years, but a new system called ACT-R was then put forward by Anderson (1993b). Reflecting technical developments in the past decade, this system now serves as a computer simulation tool for a small research community. The key insight of this version of the system is that the acquisition and deployment processes are tuned to give adaptive performance given the statistical structure of the environment. It is the ACT-R system that we will describe.

Representational Assumptions

Declarative and procedural knowledge are intimately connected in the ACT-R theory. Production rules embody procedural knowledge, and their conditions and actions are defined in terms of declarative structures. A specific production rule can only apply when that rule's conditions are satisfied by the knowledge currently available in declarative memory. The actions that a production rule can take include creating new declarative structures.

Declarative knowledge in ACT-R is represented in terms of chunks (Miller, 1956; Servan-Schreiber, 1991) that are schema-like structures, consisting of an isa pointer specifying their category and some number of additional pointers encoding their contents. Figure 2.2 is a graphical display of a chunk encoding the addition fact that $3 + 4 = 7$. This chunk can also be represented textually:

fact3 + 4
    isa   addition-fact
    addend1   three
    addend2   four
    sum   seven

Procedural knowledge, such as mathematical problem-solving skill, is represented by productions. Production rules in ACT-R respond to the existence of specific goals and often involve the creation of subgoals. For instance, suppose a child was at the point illustrated below in the solution of a multicolumn addition problem:

  531
+248
    9

Focused on the tens column, the following production rule might apply from the simulation of multicolumn addition (Anderson, 1993b):

IF the goal is too add $n1$ and $n2$ in a column and $n1 + n2 = n3$
THEN set as a subgoal to write $n3$ in that column

This production rule specifies in its condition the goal of working on the tens column and involves a retrieval of a declarative chunk like the one illustrated in figure 2.2. In its action, it creates a subgoal that might involve things like processing a carry. The subgoal structure assumed in the ACT-R production system imposes this strong abstract, hierarchical structure on behavior. As argued elsewhere (Anderson, 1993a), this abstract, hierarchical structure is an important part of what sets human cognition apart from that of other species.

Much of the recent effort in the ACT-R theory has gone into detailed analyses of specific problem-solving tasks. One of these involves equation solving by college students (e.g., Anderson, Reder, & Lebiere, 1996). We have collected data on how they scan equations, including the amount of time spent on each symbol in the equation.[1] Figure 2.3 presents a detailed simulation of the solution of equations like $X + 4 + 3 = 13$, plus the average scanning times of par-

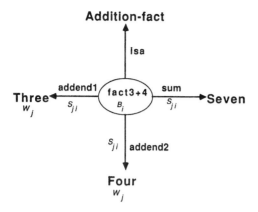

Figure 2.2
Network Representation of an ACT-R Chunk.

ticipants solving problems of this form (mixed in with many other types of equations in the same experiment). As can be seen in Parts a–c of that figure, the first three symbols are processed to create a chunk structure of the form x + 4. In the model, there is one production responsible for processing each type of symbol. The actual times for the first three symbols are given in Parts a–c of figure 2.3. They are on the order of 400 milliseconds, which we take as representing approximately 300 milliseconds to implement the scanning and encoding of the symbol and 100 milliseconds for the production to create the augmentation to the representation.[2]

The next symbol to be encoded, the +, takes about 500 milliseconds to process in Part d. As can be seen, it involves two productions, one to create a higher level chunk structure and another to encode the plus into that structure. The extra 100 milliseconds (over the encoding time for previous symbols) reflect the time for the extra production. The next symbol to be encoded (the 3) takes approximately 550 milliseconds to process (see Part e of figure 2.3), reflecting again two productions but this time also retrieval of the fact $4 + 3 = 7$. The mental representation of the equation at this point is collapsed into x + 7. The = sign is next processed in Part f of figure 2.3. It takes a particularly short time. We think this reflects the strategy of some participants of just skipping over that symbol. The final symbol comes in (see Part g of figure 2.3) and leads to a long latency reflecting seven productions that need to apply to transform the equation and the execution of the motor response of typing the number key.

The example in figure 2.3 is supposed to reflect the relative detail in which we have to analyze human cognition in ACT-R to come up with faithful models.

(a) Looking at the X
IF the goal is to solve an equation
and a variable has been read
and there are no arguments
THEN store it as the 1st argument.

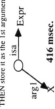

416 msec.

(b) Looking at the +
IF the goal is to solve an equation
and an operator has been read
and there is no operator stored
THEN store it as the operator.

387 msec.

(c) Looking at the 4
IF the goal is to solve an equation
and a number has been read
and there is no 2nd argument
THEN store it as the 2nd argument.

405 msec.

(d) Looking at the +
IF the goal is to solve an equation
and expression arg1 op arg2 is stored
and another operator is read
THEN make this expression the first argument

IF the goal is to solve an equation
and an operator has been read
and there is no operator stored
THEN store it as the first operator

495 msec.

(e) Looking at the 3
IF the goal is to solve an equation
and a number has been read
and there is no second argument
THEN store it as the second argument

IF the goal is to solve an equation
and the current expression is
(arg + n1) + n2
and n1 + n2 = n3
THEN make the current expression
arg + n3

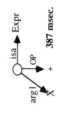

544 msec.

(f) Looking at the =
IF the goal is to solve an equation
and an equals has been read
THEN make the current structure
the left hand side

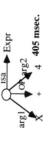

329 msec.

(g) Looking at the 13
IF the goal is to solve an equation
and a number has been read
and there is nothing yet on the
          right-hand side
THEN make that the right hand side

IF the goal is to solve an equation
and there are no more terms in the equation
THEN make the subgoal to transform the equation

IF the goal is to transform an equation
and the equation is of the form
          arg + n1 = n2
THEN make the equation arg + n1 - n1 = n2 - n1

IF the goal is to transform an equation
and the equation has n1-n1
THEN delete n1-n1.

IF the goal is to transform an equation
and the equation has n1-n2
and n2-n3 = n1
THEN replace n1-n2 by n3.

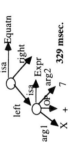

IF the goal is to transform an equation
and the equation is of the form
          X = n
THEN pop the goal with answer of n

IF the goal is to solve an equation
and the answer is n
Then type n and pop the goal   1519 msec

Figure 2.3
Steps in Solving the Equation $x + 4 + 3 = 13$. Note: Each panel represents a fixation and gives the average time for that fixation. The production rules are English renditions of the actual ACT-R production rules.

The simulation is capable of solving the same problems as the participants. It can actually interact with the same experimental software as the participants, execute the same scanning actions, read the same computer screen, and execute the same motor responses with very similar timing (Anderson, Matessa, & Douglass, 1995). When I say, "The whole is no more than the sum of its parts but it has a lot of parts," these are the parts I have in mind. These parts are the productions rules and the chunk structures that represent long-term knowledge and the evolving understanding of the problem.

Knowledge units like these are capable of giving relatively accurate simulations of human behavior in tasks such as these. However, the very success of such simulations only makes salient the two other questions that the ACT-R theory must address, which are how did the prior knowledge (productions and long-term chunks) come to exist in the first place and how is it, if the mind is composed of a great many of these knowledge units, that the appropriate ones usually come to mind in a particular problem-solving context? These are the questions of knowledge acquisition and knowledge deployment.

Knowledge Acquisition

A theory of knowledge acquisition must address both the issue of the origins of the chunks and of the origins of production rules. Let us first consider the origin of chunks. As the production rules in figure 2.3 illustrate, chunks can be created by the actions of production rules. However, as we will see shortly, production rules originate from the encodings of chunks. To avoid circularity in the theory we also need an independent source for the origin of the chunks. That independent source involves encoding from the environment. Thus, in the terms of Anderson and Bower (1973), ACT-R is fundamentally a *sensationalist* theory in that its knowledge structures result from environmental encodings.

We have only developed our ideas about environmental encodings of knowledge with respect to the visual modality (Anderson, Matessa, & Douglass, 1995). In this area, it is assumed that the perceptual system has parsed the visual array into objects and has associated a set of features with each object. ACT-R can move its attention over the visual array and recognize objects. We have embedded within ACT-R a theory that might be seen as a synthesis of the spotlight metaphor of Posner (1980), the feature-synthesis model of Treisman (Treisman & Sato, 1990), and the attentional model of Wolfe (1994). Features within the spotlight can be synthesized into recognized objects. Once synthesized, the objects are then available as chunks in ACT's working memory for further processing. In ACT-R the calls for shifts of attention are controlled by explicit firings of production rules.

The outputs of the visual module are working memory elements called chunks in ACT-R. The following is a potential chunk encoding of the letter H:

```
object
  isa H
  left-vertical    bar1
  right-vertical   bar2
  horizontal       bar3
```

We assume that before the recognition of the object, these features (the bars) are available as parts of an object but that the object itself is not recognized. In general, we assume that the system can respond to the appearance of a feature anywhere in the visual field. However, the system cannot respond to the conjunction of features that define a pattern until it has moved its attention to that part of the visual field and recognized the pattern of features. Thus, there is a correspondence between this model and the feature synthesis model of Treisman (Treisman & Sato, 1990).

A basic assumption is that the process of recognizing a visual pattern from a set of features is identical to the process of categorizing an object given a set of features. We have adapted the Anderson and Matessa (1992) rational analysis of categorization to provide a mechanism for assigning a category (such as H) to a particular configuration of features. This is the mechanism within ACT-R for translating stimulus features from the environment into chunks like the ones above that can be processed by the higher level production system.

With the environmental origins of chunks specified, we can now turn to the issue of the origins of production rules. Production rules specify the transformations of chunks, and we assume that they are encoded from examples of such transformations in the environment. Thus, a student might encounter the following example in instruction:

$$3x + 7 = 13$$

$$3x = 6$$

and encode that the second structure is dependent on the first. What the learner must do is find some mapping between the two structures. The default assumption is that identical structures directly map. In this case, it is assumed the $3x$ in the first equation maps onto the $3x$ in the second equation. This leaves the issue of how to relate the 7 and 13 to the 6. ACT-R looks for some chunk structure to make this mapping. In this case, it will find a chunk encoding that $7 + 6 = 13$. Completing the mapping ACT-R will form a production rule to map one structure onto the other:

> IF the goal is to solve an equation of the form
> $arg + n1 = n3$
>   and $n1 + n2 = n3$
> THEN make the goal to solve an equation of the form $arg = n2$

This approach takes a very strong view on instruction. This view is that one fundamentally learns to solve problems by mimicking examples of solutions. This is certainly consistent with the substantial literature showing that examples are as good as or better than abstract instruction that tells students what to do (e.g., Cheng, Holyoak, Nisbett, & Oliver, 1986; Fong, Krantz, & Nisbett, 1986; Reed & Actor, 1991). Historically, learning by imitation was given bad press as cognitive psychology broke away from behaviorism (e.g., Fodor, Bever, & Garrett, 1974). However, these criticisms assumed a very impoverished computational sense of what is meant by imitation.

It certainly is the case that abstract instruction does have some effect on learning. There are two major functions for abstract instruction in the ACT-R theory. On the one hand, it can provide or make salient the right chunks (such as $7 + 6 = 13$ in the example above) that are needed to bridge the transformations. It is basically this that offers the sophistication to the kind of imitation practiced in ACT-R. Second, instruction can take the form of specifying a sequence of subgoals to solve a task (as one finds in instruction manuals). In this case, assuming the person already knows how to achieve such subgoals, instruction offers the learner a way to create an example of such a problem solution from which they can then learn production rules like the one above.

The most striking thing about the ACT-R theory of knowledge acquisition is how simple it is. One encodes chunks from the environment and makes modest inferences about the rules underlying the transformations involved in examples of problem solving. There are no great leaps of insight in which large bodies of knowledge are reorganized. The theory implies that acquiring competence is very much a labor-intensive business in which one must acquire one-by-one all the knowledge components. This flies very much in the face of current educational fashion but, as Anderson, Reder, and Simon (1995) have argued and documented, this educational fashion is having a very deleterious effect on education. We need to recognize and respect the effort that goes into acquiring competence (Ericcson, Krampe, & TescheRomer, 1993). However, it would be misrepresenting the matter to say that competence is just a matter of getting all the knowledge units right. There is the very serious matter of deploying the right units at the right time, which brings us to the third aspect of the ACT-R theory.

Knowledge Deployment

The human mind must contain an enormous amount of knowledge. Actually quantifying how much knowledge we have is difficult (Landauer, 1986), but we have hundreds of experiences every day, which implies millions of memories over a lifetime. Estimates of the rules required to achieve mathematical competence are in the thousands and to achieve linguistic competence in the tens of thousands. All this knowledge creates a serious problem. How does one select the appropriate knowledge in a particular context? Artificial intelligence systems have run into this problem in serious ways. Expert systems gain power with increased knowledge, but with increases in knowledge these systems have become slower and slower to the point where they can become ineffective. The question is how to quickly identify the relevant knowledge.

Using the rational analysis developed in Anderson (1990), ACT-R has developed a two-pass solution for knowledge deployment. An initial parallel activation process identifies the knowledge structures (chunks and productions) that are most likely to be useful in the context, and then those knowledge structures determine performance as illustrated in our earlier example of the equation solving. The equation solving can proceed smoothly only because of this background activity of making the relevant knowledge available for performance.

Rational analysis posits that knowledge is made available according to its odds of being used in a particular context. Activation processes implicitly perform a Bayesian inference in calculating these odds. According to the odds form of the basic Bayesian formula, the posterior odds of a hypothesis being true given some evidence are

$$\frac{P(H|E)}{P(\bar{H}|E)} = \frac{P(H)}{P(\bar{H})} * \frac{P(E|H)}{P(E|\bar{H})}$$

Posterior-odds = Prior-odds ∗ Likelihood-ratio

or, transformed into log terms,

Log(posterior odds) = Log(Prior odds) + Log(Likelihood ratio).

Activation in ACT-R theory reflects its log posterior odds of being appropriate in the current context. This is calculated as a sum of the log odds that the item has been useful in the past (log prior odds) plus an estimate that it will be useful given the current context (log likelihood ratio). Thus, the ACT-R claim is that the mind keeps track of general usefulness and combines this with contextual appropriateness to make some inference about what knowledge to make available in the current context. The basic equation is

Activation-Level = Base-level + Contextual-Priming,

where *activation-level* reflects implicitly posterior odds, *base-level* reflects prior odds, and the *contextual-priming* reflects the likelihood ratio. We will illustrate this in three domains—memory, categorization, and problem solving.

Memory
Schooler (1993) did an analysis of how history and context combine to determine the relevance of particular information. For instance, he looked at headlines in the *New York Times*, noting how frequently particular items occurred. In

the time period he was considering, the word *AIDS* had a 1.8% probability of appearing in a headline on any particular day. However, if the word *virus* also appeared in a headline, the probability of *AIDS* in that day's headlines rose to 75%. Similarly, he looked at caregiver speech to children in the Child Language Data Exchange System (CHILDES; Mac Whinney & Snow, 1990) database. As an example from this database, he found that there was only a 0.9% probability of the word *play* occurring in any particular utterance. On the other hand, if the word *game* also appeared in that utterance, the probability of *play* increased to 45%. Basically, the presence of a high associate serves to increase the likelihood ratio for that item.

Schooler (1993) also examined what factors determined the prior odds of an item. One factor was the time since the word last occurred. As the time increased, the odds went down of the word occurring in the next unit of time. This temporal factor serves as the prior odds component of the Bayesian formula. Schooler examined how these two factors combined in his *New York Times* database and the child-language database. The results are displayed in figure 2.4. Parts (a) and (b) show that both the presence of a high associate ("strong context" in figure 2.4) and the time since last appearance ("retention" in figure 2.4) affect the probability of occurrence in the critical unit of time. It might appear from parts (a) and (b) of figure 2.4 that the time factor has a larger effect in the presence of a high associate. However, if one converts the odds scale to log odds and the time scale to log time (see Anderson & Schooler, 1991, for the justification) we get the functions in parts (c) and (d) of figure 2.4. Those figures show parallel linear functions representing the additivity that we would expect given the Bayesian log formula above.

The interesting question is whether human memory is similarly sensitive to these factors. Schooler (1993) did an experiment in which he asked participants to complete word fragments, and he manipulated whether the fragments were in the presence of a high associate or not as well the time since the target word had been seen. The data are displayed in log–log form in figure 2.5. They once again show parallel linear functions, implying that human memory is combining information about prior odds and likelihood ratio in the appropriate Bayesian fashion and is making items available as a function of their posterior probability.[3] Schooler's demonstration is one of the clearest and most compelling demonstrations of the way the mind tunes access to knowledge to reflect the statistical structure of the environment.

The statistical structure is represented in ACT-R by making the activation of a chunk structure, like the one in figure 2.2, a function of activation received from the various elements in the environment plus a base-level activation. The momentary activation of chunk **i** in ACT-R is

$$\mathbf{A_i} = \mathbf{B_i} + \sum_j \mathbf{W_j S_{ji}},$$

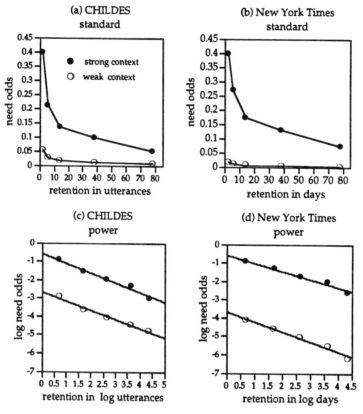

Figure 2.4

Probability of a Word Occurring. Note: (a) The probability of a word occurring in the next utterance as a function of the number of utterances since its last occurrence; (b) the probability of a word occurring in the day's headlines as a function of the number of days since its last occurrence. Separate functions are plotted for probability in the presence of high and low associates. Parts (c) and (d) replot this data probability to log odds and time to log time. From "Memory and the Statistical Structure of the Environment," by L. J. Schooler, 1993, p. 58, unpublished doctoral dissertation. Reprinted by permission. CHILDES = Child Language Data Exchange System.

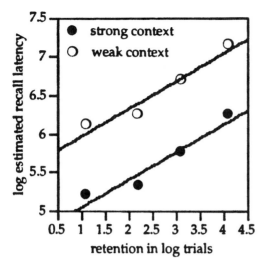

Figure 2.5
Log Latency to Complete a Word Fragment as a Function of Time Since the Word Was Seen.

where B_i is the base-level activation of chunk i, W_j is the weighting of contextual chunk j, and S_{ji} is the strength of association between chunk j and chunk i. For example, if *three* and *four* were chunks in an addition problem, they would be the contextual chunks (the j's) priming the availability of the relevant fact (the i) that $3 + 4 = 7$.

Categorization
Figure 2.6 plots some data from Gluck and Bower (1988) in a way the data are not often represented. Gluck and Bower had participants classify patients as having a rare or a common disease given a set of symptoms. Gluck and Bower manipulated what was in effect the likelihood ratio of those symptoms given the disease. Figure 2.6a plots the probability of the diagnosis of each disease as a function of the log likelihood ratio. It shows that participants are sensitive to both base rates of the disease and to the likelihood ratio of those symptoms for that disease. There has been considerable interest in the categorization literature in participants' failure to respond to base rates, but figure 2.6 clearly illustrates that they are often very sensitive. Figure 2.6b plots the same data with a transformation of the choice probability into log odds. It shows that participants are perfectly tuned to the likelihood ratios, showing slopes of 1.

Figure 2.7 shows the categorization network that we have built into ACT-R to produce categorization data such as those of Gluck and Bower (1988). Various features in chunks spread activation to various categories according to the likelihood of that feature given the category. Categories have base-level activa-

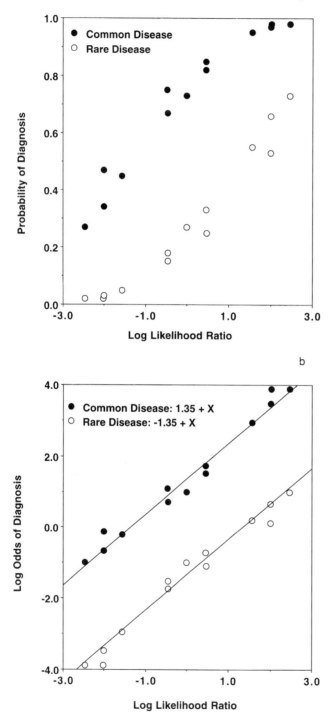

Figure 2.6
Probability of Diagnosis.

tions to reflect their prior frequencies. The resulting activations reflect the log posterior probability of the category. The most active category is chosen to classify the stimulus.

Problem Solving

In her dissertation on strategy selection in problem solving, Lovett (1994) developed what she called the *building sticks task* that is illustrated in figure 2.8. Participants are told that their task is to construct a target stick, and they are given various sticks to work with. They can either choose to start with a stick smaller than the target stick and add further sticks to build up to the desired length (called the *undershoot* operator) or to start with a stick longer than the target and cut off pieces equal to various sticks (called the *overshoot* operator). This task is an analog to the Luchins waterjug problem (Luchins, 1942). Participants show a strong tendency to select the stick that gets them closest to their goal. In terms of production rules, it is competition between two alternative productions:

Overshoot
>   IF the goal is to solve the building sticks task
>   and there is no current stick
>   and there is a stick larger than the goal
>   THEN add the stick
>   and set a subgoal to subtract from it.

Undershoot
>   IF the goal is to solve the building sticks task
>   and there is no current stick
>   and there is a stick smaller than the goal
>   THEN add the stick
>   and set a subgoal to add to it.

Lovett (1994) gave participants experience such that one of the two operators was more successful. Figure 2.9 shows their tendency to use the more successful operator before and after this experience as a function of the bias toward the operator (determined by how close the stick gets one to the goal relative to the alternative sticks). There are clear effects of both factors. Moreover, Lovett was able to model these data by assuming that participants were combining their experience with the operators (serving as prior odds) with the effect of distance to goal (serving as likelihood ratio). In the domain of question-answering strategies, Reder (1987, 1988) had earlier shown a similar combination of information about overall strategy success with strategy appropriateness.

ACT-R estimates the log odds that a production calling for an operator will be successful according to the formula

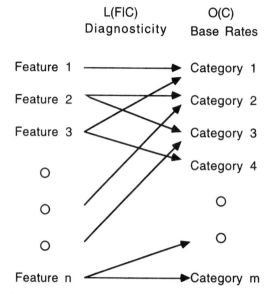

Note. The stimulus features spread activation to various categories as a function of their diagnosticity. L(F|C) are the log likelihood ratios and the O(C) are the log prior odds of the categories.

Figure 2.7
The Categorization Network Used to Classify Stimuli.

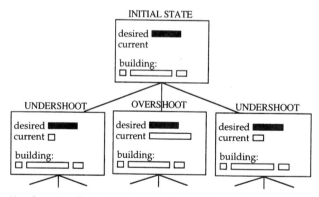

Note. From ''The Effects of History of Experience and Current Context on Problem Solving,'' by M. C. Lovett, 1994, p. 38, unpublished doctoral dissertation. Reprinted by permission.

Figure 2.8
Initial and Successor States in the Building Sticks Task.

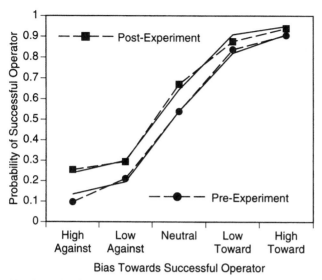

Figure 2.9
Probability of Using an Operator as a Function of the Bias Towards That Operator Both Before and After Experiencing Success with That Operator.

Log Odds(Operator) = Log(Prior Odds) + Context Appropriateness,

where the prior odds reflect the past history of success and context appropriateness reflects how close the operator takes one to the goal. When multiple productions apply, ACT-R selects the production with the highest expected gain.

Summary

Whether it is selecting what memory to retrieve, what category to place an object in, or what strategy to use, participants and ACT-R are sensitive to both prior information and information about appropriateness to the situation at hand. Although it is hardly a conscious process, people seem to combine this information in a way that is often optimal from a Bayesian perspective. It is this capacity that enables people to have the right knowledge at their fingertips most of the time. Although Bayesian inference is nonintuitive and often people's conscious judgments do not accord with it (even when their behavior does—see figures 2.5, 2.6, and 2.8), it is really a very simple mechanism. Thus, we achieve great adaptiveness in knowledge deployment by simple statistical inference.

The Metaphor of Simon's Ant

In *The Sciences of the Artificial*, Simon (1981) described a situation in which an ant produced a very complex path across the terrain of a beach. A person observing only the path itself might be inclined to ascribe a great deal of intelligence to the ant. However, it turned out that the complexity of the path is really produced by the complexity of the terrain over which the ant was navigating. As Simon wrote, "An ant, viewed as a behaving system, is quite simple. The apparent complexity of its behavior over time is largely a reflection of the complexity of the environment in which it finds itself" (p. 64). Simon argued that human cognition is much the same—a few relatively simple mechanisms responding to the complexity of the knowledge that is stored in the mind. In Simon's analogy, the complex behavior of the ant maps onto human cognition, the ant's navigating mechanisms map onto basic cognitive mechanisms, and the complexity of the beach maps onto the complexity of human knowledge.

ACT-R fully endorses Simon's (1981) analogy but also carries it one degree further in analyzing the complexity of the knowledge we as humans possess. In this application of the analogy, the complex behavior of the ant maps onto the knowledge we have acquired, the ant's navigating mechanisms maps onto our relatively simple learning processes, and the complexity of the beach maps onto the complexity of our environment. Under this analysis, complex human cognition is just a simple reflection, once removed, of its environment, even as the ant's navigation is directly a simple reflection of its environment.

In a nutshell, ACT-R implies that declarative knowledge is a fairly direct encoding of things in our environment; procedural knowledge is a fairly direct encoding of observed transformations; and the two types of knowledge are tuned in to their application by encoding the statistics of knowledge use in the environment. What distinguishes human cognition from the cognition of other species is the amount of such knowledge and overall cognitive architecture in which this is deployed (particularly the ability for organizing behavior according to complex goal structures).

Notes

A version of this article was originally presented as part of an Award for Distinguished Scientific Contributions address at the 103rd Annual Convention of the American Psychological Association, New York, NY, August 1995.
Author's note. This research was supported by Grant ONR N0014-90-J-1489 from the Office of Naval Research and Grant SBR 94-21332 from the National Science Foundation.
   I would like to thank Marsha Lovett and Lynne Reder for their comments on the article.
   Correspondence concerning this article should be addressed to John R. Anderson, Department of Psychology, Carnegie Mellon University, Pittsburgh, PA 15213. For more information on the ACT theory, consult the ACT-R home page on the World Wide Web: http://sands.psy.cmu.edu.
1. This involves a scheme wherein participants must point at the part of the equation that they want to read next.

2. Although our data strongly constrain the processing, there remain a number of arbitrary decisions about how to represent the equation that could have been made differently.
3. These linear functions on a log scale imply that latency is a power function of delay on an untransformed scale. See Rubin and Wenzel (1994) for a discussion.

References

Anderson, J. R. (1976). *Language, memory, and thought*. Hillsdale, NJ: Erlbaum.

Anderson, J. R. (1983). *The architecture of cognition*. Cambridge, MA: Harvard University Press.

Anderson, J. R. (1990). *The adaptive character of thought*. Hillsdale, NJ: Erlbaum.

Anderson, J. R. (1993a). Problem solving and learning. *American Psychologist, 48,* 35–44.

Anderson, J. R. (1993b). *Rules of the mind*. Hillsdale, NJ: Erlbaum.

Anderson, J. R., & Bower, G. H. (1973). *Human associative memory*. Washington, DC: Winston and Sons.

Anderson, J. R., Boyle, C. F., Corbett, A., & Lewis, M. W. (1990). Cognitive modelling and intelligent tutoring. *Artificial Intelligence, 42,* 7–49.

Anderson, J. R., Corbett, A. T., Koedinger, K., & Pelletier, R. (1995). Cognitive tutors: Lessons learned. *The Journal of Learning Sciences, 4,* 167–207.

Anderson, J. R., Farrell, R., & Sauers, R. (1984). Learning to program in LISP. *Cognitive Science, 8,* 87–130.

Anderson, J. R., & Matessa, M. (1992). Explorations of an incremental, Bayesian algorithm for categorization. *Machine Learning, 9,* 275–308.

Anderson, J. R., Matessa, M., & Douglass, S. (1995). The ACT-R theory of visual attention. In *Proceedings of the Seventeenth Annual Cognitive Science Society,* 61–65.

Anderson, J. R., Reder, L. M., & Lebiere, C. (1996). Working memory: Activation limitations on retrieval. *Cognitive Psychology, 30,* 221–256.

Anderson, J. R., Reder, L. M., & Simon, H. A. (1995). *Applications and misapplications of cognitive psychology to mathematics education.* Manuscript submitted for publication.

Anderson, J. R., & Reiser, B. J. (1985). The LISP tutor. *Byte, 10,* 159–175.

Anderson, J. R., & Schooler, L. J. (1991). Reflections of the environment in memory. *Psychological Science, 2,* 396–408.

Cheng, P. W., Holyoak, K. J., Nisbett, R. E., & Oliver, L. M. (1986). Pragmatic versus syntactic approaches to training deductive reasoning. *Cognitive Psychology, 18,* 293–328.

Corbett, A. T., Anderson, J. R., & O'Brien, A. T. (1995). Student modeling in the ACT Programming Tutor. In P. Nichols, S. Chipman, & B. Brennan (Eds.), *Cognitively diagnostic assessment* (pp. 19–41). Hillsdale, NJ: Erlbaum.

Ericcson, K. A., Krampe, R. T., & Tesche-Romer, C. (1993). The role of deliberate practice in the acquisition of expert performance. *Psychological Review, 100,* 363–406.

Fodor, J. A., Bever, T. G., & Garrett, M. F. (1974). *The psychology of language*. New York: McGraw-Hill.

Fong, G. T., Krantz, D. H., & Nisbett, R. E. (1986). Effects of statistical training on thinking about everyday problems. *Cognitive Psychology, 18,* 253–292.

Gluck, M. A., & Bower, G. H. (1988). From conditioning to category learning: An adaptive network model. *Journal of Experimental Psychology: General, 117,* 227–247.

Landauer, T. K. (1986). How much do people remember? Some estimates of the quantity of learned information in long-term memory. *Cognitive Science, 10,* 477–493.

Lovett, M. C. (1994). *The effects of history of experience and current context on problem solving*. Unpublished doctoral dissertation, Carnegie Mellon University, Pittsburgh, PA.

Luchins, A. S. (1942). Mechanization in problem solving. *Psychological Monographs, 54* (Whole No. 248).

MacWhinney, B., & Snow, C. (1990). The child language data exchange system: An update. *Journal of Child Language, 17*, 457–472.

Miller, G. A. (1956). The magical number seven, plus or minus two: Some limits on our capacity for processing information. *Psychological Review, 63*, 81–97.

Newell, A. (1972). A theoretical exploration of mechanisms for coding the stimulus. In A. W. Melton & E. Martin (Eds.), *Coding processes in human memory* (pp. 373–434). Washington, DC: Winston.

Newell, A. (1973). Production systems: Models of control structures. In W. G. Chase (Ed.), *Visual information processing* (pp. 463–526). New York: Academic Press.

Pirolli, P. L., & Anderson, J. R. (1985). The acquisition of skill in the domain of programming recursion. *Canadian Journal of Psychology, 39*, 240–272.

Posner, M. I. (1980). Orienting of attention. *Quarterly Journal of Experimental Psychology, 32*, 3–25.

Reder, L. M. (1987). Strategy selection in questions answering. *Cognitive Psychology, 19*, 90–138.

Reder, L. M. (1988). Strategic control of retrieval strategies. In G. H. Bower (Ed.), *The psychology of learning and motivation* (pp. 227–259). New York: Academic Press.

Reed, S. K., & Actor, C. A. (1991). Use of examples and procedures in problem solving. *Journal of Experimental Psychology: Learning, Memory, & Cognition, 17*, 753–766.

Rubin, D. D., & Wenzel, A. E. (1994, November). *100 years of forgetting: A quantitative description of retention.* Paper presented at the 35th Annual Meeting of the Psychonomics Society, St. Louis, MO.

Schooler, L. J. (1993). *Memory and the statistical structure of the environment.* Unpublished doctoral dissertation, Carnegie Mellon University, Pittsburgh, PA.

Servan-Schreiber, E. (1991). *The competitive chunking theory: Models of perception, learning, and memory.* Unpublished doctoral dissertation, Carnegie Mellon University, Pittsburgh, PA.

Simon, H. A. (1981). *The sciences of the artificial* (2nd ed.). Cambridge, MA: MIT Press.

Treisman, A. M., & Sato, S. (1990). Conjunction search revisited. *Journal of Experimental Psychology: Human Perception and Performance, 16*, 459–478.

Wolfe, J. M. (1994). Guided search 2.0: A revised model of visual search. *Psychonomic Bulletin & Review, 1*, 202–238.

Soar

Chapter 3

A Preliminary Analysis of the Soar Architecture as a Basis for General Intelligence

Paul S. Rosenbloom, John E. Laird, Allen Newell, and Robert McCarl

---

Introduction

The central scientific problem of artificial intelligence (AI) is to understand what constitutes intelligent action and what processing organizations are capable of such action. Human intelligence—which stands before us like a holy grail—shows to first observation what can only be termed *general intelligence*. A single human exhibits a bewildering diversity of intelligent behavior. The types of goals that humans can set for themselves or accept from the environment seem boundless. Further observation, of course, shows limits to this capacity in any individual—problems range from easy to hard, and problems can always be found that are too hard to be solved. But the general point is still compelling.

Work in AI has already contributed substantially to our knowledge of what functions are required to produce general intelligence. There is substantial, though certainly not unanimous, agreement about some functions that need to be supported: symbols and goal structures, for example. Less agreement exists about what mechanisms are appropriate to support these functions, in large part because such matters depend strongly on the rest of the system and on cost-benefit tradeoffs. Much of this work has been done under the rubric of AI tools and languages, rather than AI systems themselves. However, it takes only a slight shift of viewpoint to change from what is an aid for the programmer to what is structure for the intelligent system itself. Not all features survive this transformation, but enough do to make the development of AI languages as much substantive research as tool building. These proposals provide substantial ground on which to build.

The Soar project has been building on this foundation in an attempt to understand the functionality required to support general intelligence. Our current understanding is embodied in the Soar architecture [21, 25]. This article represents an attempt at describing and analyzing the structure of the Soar system. We will take a particular point of view—the description of Soar as a hierarchy of levels—in an attempt to bring coherence to this discussion.

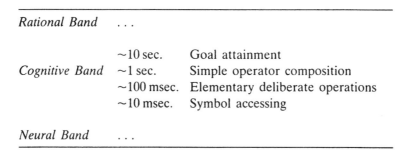

Rational Band	. . .	
	~10 sec.	Goal attainment
Cognitive Band	~1 sec.	Simple operator composition
	~100 msec.	Elementary deliberate operations
	~10 msec.	Symbol accessing
Neural Band	. . .	

Figure 3.1
Partial hierarchy of time scales in human cognition.

The idea of analyzing systems in terms of multiple levels of description is a familiar one in computer science. In one version, computer systems are described as a sequence of levels that starts at the bottom with the device level and works up through the circuit level, the logic level, and then one or more program levels. Each level provides a description of the system at some level of abstraction. The sequence is built up by defining each higher level in terms of the structure provided at the lower levels. This idea has also recently been used to analyze human cognition in terms of levels of description [37]. Each level corresponds to a particular time scale, such as ~100 msec. and ~1 sec., with a new level occurring for each new order of magnitude. The four levels between ~10 msec. and ~10 sec. comprise the cognitive band (Fig. 3.1). The lowest cognitive level—at ~10 msec.—is the symbol-accessing level, where the knowledge referred to by symbols is retrievable. The second cognitive level—at ~100 msec.—is the level at which elementary deliberate operations occur; that is, the level at which encoded knowledge is brought to bear, and the most elementary choices are made. The third and fourth cognitive levels—at ~1 sec. and ~10 sec.—are the simple-operator-composition and goal-attainment levels. At these levels, sequences of deliberations can be composed to achieve goals. Above the cognitive band is the rational band, at which the system can be described as being goal oriented, knowledge-based, and strongly adaptive. Below the cognitive band is the neural band.

In Section 2 we describe Soar as a sequence of three cognitive levels: the memory level, at which symbol accessing occurs; the decision level, at which elementary deliberate operations occur; and the goal level, at which goals are set and achieved via sequences of decisions. The goal level is an amalgamation of the top two cognitive levels from the analysis of human cognition.

In this description we will often have call to describe mechanisms that are built into the architecture of Soar. The architecture consists of all of the fixed structure of the Soar system. According to the levels analysis, the correct view to be taken of this fixed structure is that it comprises the set of mechanisms provided by the levels underneath the cognitive band. For human cognition this is the neural band. For artificial cognition, this may be a connectionist band, though it need not be. This view notwithstanding, it should be remembered that it is the Soar architecture which is primary in our research. The use of the levels viewpoint is simply an attempt at imposing a particular, hopefully illuminating, theoretical structure on top of the existing architecture.

In the remainder of this paper we describe the methodological assumptions underlying Soar, the structure of Soar, and a set of preliminary analyses of Soar as an architecture for general intelligence.

1 Methodological Assumptions

The development of Soar is driven by four methodological assumptions. It is not expected that these assumptions will be shared by all researchers in the field. However, the assumptions do help explain why the Soar system and project have the shapes that they do.

The first assumption is the utility of focusing on the cognitive band, as opposed to the neural or rational bands. This is a view that has traditionally been shared by a large segment of the cognitive science community; it is not, however, shared by the connectionist community, which focuses on the neural band (plus the lower levels of the cognitive band), or by the logicist and expert-systems communities, which focus on the rational band. This assumption is not meant to be exclusionary, as a complete understanding of general intelligence requires the understanding of all of these descriptive bands.[1] Instead the assumption is that there is important work to be done by focusing on the cognitive band. One reason is that, as just mentioned, a complete model of general intelligence will require a model of the cognitive band. A second reason is that an understanding of the cognitive band can constrain models of the neural and rational bands. A third, more applied reason, is that a model of the cognitive band is required in order to be able to build practical intelligent systems. Neural-band models need the higher levels of organization that are provided by the cognitive band in order to reach complex task performance. Rational-band models need the heuristic adequacy provided by the cognitive band in order to be computationally feasible. A fourth reason is that there is a wealth of both psychological and AI data about the cognitive band that can be used as the basis for elucidating the structure of its levels. This data can help us understand what type of symbolic architecture is required to support general intelligence.

The second assumption is that general intelligence can most usefully be studied by not making a distinction between human and artificial intelligence. The advantage of this assumption is that it allows wider ranges of research methodologies and data to be brought to bear to mutually constrain the structure of the system. Our research methodology includes a mixture of experimental data, theoretical justifications, and comparative studies in both artificial intelligence and cognitive psychology. Human experiments provide data about performance universals and limitations that may reflect the structure of the architecture. For example, the ubiquitous power law of practice—the time to perform a task is a power-law function of the number of times the task has been performed—was used to generate a model of human practice [38, 54], which was later converted into a proposal for a general artificial learning mechanism [26, 27, 60]. Artificial experiments—the application of implemented systems to a variety of tasks requiring intelligence—provide sufficiency feedback about the mechanisms embodied in the architecture and their interactions [15, 50, 59, 61, 70]. Theoretical justifications attempt to provide an abstract analysis of the requirements of intelligence, and of how various architectural mechanisms fulfill those requirements [37, 39, 48, 53, 55]. Comparative studies, pitting one system against another, provide an evaluation of how well the respective systems perform, as well as insight about how the capabilities of one of the systems can be incorporated in the other [6, 49].

The third assumption is that the architecture should consist of a small set of orthogonal mechanisms. All intelligent behaviors should involve all, or nearly all, of these basic mechanisms. This assumption biases the development of Soar strongly in the direction of uniformity and simplicity, and away from modularity [10] and toolkit approaches. When attempting to achieve a new functionality in Soar, the first step is to determine in what ways the existing mechanisms can already provide the functionality. This can force the development of new solutions to old problems, and reveal new connections—through the common underlying mechanisms—among previously distinct capabilities [52]. Only if there is no appropriate way to achieve the new functionality are new mechanisms considered.

The fourth assumption is that architectures should be pushed to the extreme to evaluate how much of general intelligence they can cover. A serious attempt at evaluating the coverage of an architecture involves a long-term commitment by an extensive research group. Much of the research involves the apparently mundane activity of replicating classical results within the architecture. Sometimes these demonstrations will by necessity be strict replications, but often the architecture will reveal novel approaches, provide a deeper understanding of the result and its relationship to other results, or provide the means of going beyond what was done in the classical work. As these results accumulate over time, along with other more novel results, the system gradually approaches the ultimate goal of general intelligence.

2 Structure of Soar

In this section we build up much of Soar's structure in levels, starting at the bottom with memory and proceeding up to decisions and goals. We then describe how learning and perceptual-motor behavior fit into this picture, and wrap up with a discussion of the default knowledge that has been incorporated into the system.

2.1 Level 1: Memory

A general intelligence requires a memory with a large capacity for the storage of knowledge. A variety of types of knowledge must be stored, including declarative knowledge (facts about the world, including facts about actions that can be performed), procedural knowledge (facts about how to perform actions, and control knowledge about which actions to perform when), and episodic knowledge (which actions were done when). Any particular task will require some subset of the knowledge stored in the memory. Memory access is the process by which this subset is retrieved for use in task performance.

The lowest level of the Soar architecture is the level at which these memory phenomena occur. All of Soar's long-term knowledge is stored in a single production memory. Whether a piece of knowledge represents procedural, declarative, or episodic knowledge, it is stored in one or more productions. Each production is a condition-action structure that performs its actions when its conditions are met. Memory access consists of the execution of these productions. During the execution of a production, variables in its actions are instantiated with values. Action variables that existed in the conditions are instantiated with the values bound in the conditions. Action variables that did not exist in the conditions act as generators of new symbols.

The result of memory access is the retrieval of information into a global working memory. The working memory is a temporary memory that contains all of Soar's short-term processing context. Working memory consists of an interrelated set of objects with attribute-value pairs. For example, an object representing a green cat named Fred might look like (object o025 ^name fred ^type cat ^color green). The symbol o025 is the identifier of the object, a short-term symbol for the object that exists only as long as the object is in working memory. Objects are related by using the identifiers of some objects as attributes and values of other objects.

There is one special type of working memory structure, the preference. Preferences encode control knowledge about the acceptability and desirability of actions, according to a fixed semantics of preference types. Acceptability preferences determine which actions should be considered as candidates. Desirability preferences define a partial ordering on the candidate actions. For example, a better (or alternatively, worse) preference can be used to represent the knowledge that one action is more (or less) desirable than another action, and a best (or worst) preference can be used to represent the knowledge that an action is at least as good (or as bad) as every other action.

In a traditional production-system architecture, each production is a problem-solving operator (see, for example, [41]). The right-hand side of the production represents some action to be performed, and the left-hand side represents the preconditions for correct application of the action (plus possibly some desirability conditions). One consequence of this view of productions is that the productions must also be the locus of behavioral control. If productions are going to act, it must be possible to control which one executes at each moment; a process known as conflict resolution. In a logic architecture, each production is a logical implication. The meaning of such a production is that if the left-hand side (the antecedent) is true, then so is the right-hand side (the consequent).[2] Soar's productions are neither operators nor implications. Instead, Soar's productions perform (parallel) memory retrieval. Each production is a retrieval structure for an item in long-term memory. The right-hand side of the rule represents a long-term datum, and the left-hand side represents the situations in which it is appropriate to retrieve that datum into working memory. The traditional production-system and logic notions of action, control, and truth are not directly applicable to Soar's productions. All control in Soar is performed at the decision level. Thus, there is no conflict resolution process in the Soar production system, and all productions execute in parallel. This all flows directly from the production system being a long-term memory. Soar separates the retrieval of long-term information from the control of which act to perform next.

Of course it is possible to encode knowledge of operators and logical implications in the production memory. For example, the knowledge about how to implement a typical operator can be stored procedurally as a set of productions which retrieve the state resulting from the operator's application. The productions' conditions determine when the state is to be retrieved—for example, when the operator is being applied and its preconditions are met. An alternative way to store operator implementation knowledge is declaratively as a set of structures that are completely contained in the actions of one or more productions. The structures describe not only the results of the operator, but also its preconditions. The productions' conditions determine when to retrieve this declarative operator description into working memory. A retrieved operator description must be interpreted by other productions to actually have an affect.

In general, there are these two distinct ways to encode knowledge in the production memory: procedurally and declaratively. If the knowledge is procedurally encoded, then the execution of the production reflects the knowledge, but does not actually retrieve it into working memory—it only retrieves the structures encoded in the actions. On the other hand, if a piece of knowledge is encoded declaratively in the actions of a production, then it is retrievable in its entirety. This distinction between procedural and declarative *encodings* of knowledge is distinct from whether the knowledge is declarative (represents facts about the world) or procedural (represents facts about procedures). Moreover, each production can be viewed in either way, either as a procedure which implicitly represents conditional information, or as the indexed storage of declarative structures.

2.2 Level 2: Decisions

In addition to a memory, a general intelligence requires the ability to generate and/or select a course of action that is responsive to the current situation. The second level of the Soar architecture, the decision level, is the level at which this processing is performed. The decision level is based on the memory level plus an architecturally provided, fixed, decision procedure. The decision level proceeds in a two phase elaborate-decide cycle. During elaboration, the memory is accessed repeatedly, in parallel, until quiescence is reached; that is, until no more productions can execute. This results in the retrieval into working memory of all of the accessible knowledge that is relevant to the current decision. This may include a variety of types of information, but of most direct relevance here is knowledge about actions that can be performed and preference knowledge about what actions are acceptable and desirable. After quiescence has occurred, the decision procedure selects one of the retrieved actions based on the preferences that were retrieved into working memory and their fixed semantics.

The decision level is open both with respect to the consideration of arbitrary actions, and with respect to the utilization of arbitrary knowledge in making a selection. This openness allows Soar to behave in both plan-following and reactive fashions. Soar is following a plan when a decision is primarily based on previously generated knowledge about what to do. Soar is being reactive when a decision is based primarily on knowledge about the current situation (as reflected in the working memory).

2.3 Level 3: Goals

In addition to being able to make decisions, a general intelligence must also be able to direct this behavior towards some end; that is, it must be able to set and work towards goals. The third level of the Soar architecture, the goal level, is the level at which goals are processed. This level is based on the decision level. Goals are set whenever a decision cannot be made; that is, when the decision procedure reaches an impasse. Impasses occur when there are no alternatives that can be selected (*no-change* and *rejection* impasses) or when there are multiple alternatives that can be selected, but insufficient discriminating preferences exist to allow a choice to be made among them (*tie* and *conflict* impasses). Whenever an impasse occurs, the architecture generates the goal of resolving the impasse. Along with this goal, a new *performance context* is created. The creation of a new context allows decisions to continue to be made in the service of achieving the goal of resolving the impasse—nothing can be done in the original context because it is at an impasse. If an impasse now occurs in this subgoal, another new subgoal and performance context are created. This leads to a goal (and context) stack in which the top-level goal is to perform some task, and lower-level goals are to resolve impasses in problem solving. A subgoal is terminated when either its impasse is resolved, or some higher impasse in the stack is resolved (making the subgoal superfluous).

In Soar, all symbolic goal-oriented tasks are formulated in problem spaces. A problem space consists of a set of states and a set of operators. The states represent situations, and the operators represent actions which when applied to states yield other states. Each performance context consists of a goal, plus roles for a problem state, a state, and an operator. Problem solving is driven by decisions that result in the selection of problem spaces, states, and operators for their respective context roles. Given a goal, a problem space should be selected in which goal achievement can be pursued. Then an initial state should be selected that represents the initial situation. Then an operator should be selected for application to the initial state. Then another state should be selected (most likely the result of applying the operator to the previous state). This process continues until a sequence of operators has been discovered that transforms the initial state into a state in which the goal has been achieved. One subtle consequence of the use of problem spaces is that each one implicitly defines a set of constraints on how the task is to be performed. For example, if the Eight Puzzle is attempted in a problem space containing only a slide-tile operator, all solution paths maintain the constraint that the tiles are never picked up off of the board. Thus, such conditions need not be tested for explicitly in desired states.

Each problem solving decision—the selection of a problem space, a state, or an operator—is based on the knowledge accessible in the production memory. If the knowledge is both correct and sufficient, Soar exhibits highly controlled behavior; at each decision point the right alternative is selected. Such behavior is accurately described as being algorithmic or knowledge-intensive. However, for a general intelligence faced with a broad array of unpredictable tasks, situations will arise—inevitably and indeed frequently—in which the accessible knowledge is either incorrect or insufficient. It is possible that correct decisions will fortuitously be made, but it is more likely that either incorrect decisions will be made or that impasses will occur. Under such circumstances search is the likely outcome. If an incorrect decision is made, the system must eventually recover and get itself back on a path to the goal, for example, by backtracking. If instead an impasse occurs, the system must execute a sequence of problem space operators in the resulting subgoal to find (or generate) the information that will allow a decision to be made. This processing may itself be highly algorithmic, if enough control knowledge is available to uniquely determine what to do, or it may involve a large amount of further search.

As described earlier, operator implementation knowledge can be represented procedurally in the production memory, enabling operator implementation to be performed directly by memory retrieval. When the operator is selected, a set of productions execute that collectively build up the representation of the result state by combining data from long-term memory and the previous state. This type of implementation is comparable to the conventional implementation of an operator as a fixed piece of code. However, if operator implementation knowledge is stored declaratively, or if no operator implementation knowledge is stored, then a subgoal occurs, and the operator must be implemented by the execution of a sequence of problem space operators in the subgoal. If a declarative description of the to-be-implemented operator is available, then these lower operators may implement the operator by interpreting its declarative description (as was demonstrated in work on task acquisition in Soar [60]). Otherwise the operator can be implemented by decomposing it into a set of simpler operators for which operator implementation knowledge is available, or which can in turn be decomposed further.

When an operator is implemented in a subgoal, the combination of the operator and the subgoal correspond to the type of deliberately created subgoal common in AI problem solvers. The operator specifies a task to be performed, while the subgoal indicates that accomplishing the task should be treated as a goal for further problem solving. In complex problems, like computer configuration, it is common for there to be complex high-level operators, such as Configure-computer, which are implemented by selecting problem spaces in which they can be decomposed into simpler tasks. Many of the traditional goal management issues—such as conjunction, conflict, and selection—show up as operator management issues in Soar. For example, a set of conjunctive subgoals can be ordered by ordering operators that later lead to impasses (and subgoals).

As described in [53], a subgoal not only represents a subtask to be performed, but it also represents an introspective act that allows unlimited amounts of meta-level problem-space processing to be performed. The entire working memory—the goal stack and all information linked to it—is available for examination and augmentation in a subgoal. At any time a production can examine and augment any part of the goal stack. Likewise, a decision can be made at any time for any of the goals in the hierarchy. This allows subgoal problem solving to analyze the situation that led to the impasse, and even to change the subgoal, should it be appropriate. One not uncommon occurrence is for information to be generated within a subgoal that, instead of satisfying the subgoal, causes the subgoal to become irrelevant and consequently to disappear. Processing tends to focus on the bottom-most goal because all of the others have reached impasses. However, the processing is completely opportunistic, so that when appropriate information becomes available at a higher level, processing at that level continues immediately and all lower subgoals are terminated.

2.4 Learning

All learning occurs by the acquisition of chunks—productions that summarize the problem solving that occurs in subgoals [27]. The actions of a chunk represent the knowledge generated during the subgoal; that is, the results of the subgoal. The conditions of the chunk represent an access path to this knowledge, consisting of those elements of the parent goals upon which the results depended. The results of the subgoal are determined by finding the elements generated in the subgoal that are available for use in subgoals—an element is a result of a subgoal precisely because it is available to processes outside of the subgoal. The access path is computed by analyzing the traces of the productions that fired in the subgoal—each production trace effectively states that its actions depended on its conditions. This dependency analysis yields a set of conditions that have been implicitly generalized to ignore irrelevant aspects of the situation. The resulting generality allows chunks to transfer to situations other than the one in which it was learned. The primary system-wide effect of chunking is to move Soar along the space-time trade-off by allowing relevantly similar future decisions to be based on direct retrieval of information from memory rather than on problem solving within a subgoal. If the chunk is used, an impasse will not occur, because the required information is already available.

Care must be taken to not confuse the power of chunking as a learning mechanism with the power of Soar as a learning system. Chunking is a simple goal-based, dependency-tracing, caching scheme, analogous to explanation-based learning [4, 35, 49] and a variety of other schemes [54]. What allows Soar to exhibit a wide variety of learning behaviors are the variations in the types of subgoals that are chunked; the types of problem solving, in conjunction with the types and sources of knowledge, used in the subgoals; and the ways the chunks are used in later problem solving. The role that a chunk will play is determined by the type of subgoal for which it was learned. State-no-change, operator-tie, and operator-no-change subgoals lead respectively to state augmentation, operator selection, and operator implementation productions. The content of a chunk is determined by the types of problem solving and knowledge used in the subgoal. A chunk can lead to skill acquisition if it is used as a more efficient means of generating an already generatable result. A chunk can lead to knowledge acquisition (or knowledge level learning [5]) if it is used to make old/new judgments; that is, to distinguish what has been learned from what has not been learned [51, 52, 55].

2.5 Perception and Motor Control

One of the most recent functional additions to the Soar architecture is a perceptual-motor interface [72, 73]. All perceptual and motor behavior is mediated through working memory; specifically, through the state in the top problem solving context. Each distinct perceptual field has a designated attribute of this state to which it adds its information. Likewise, each distinct motor field has a designated attribute of the state from which it takes its commands. The perceptual and motor systems are autonomous with respect to each other and the cognitive system.

Encoding and decoding productions can be used to convert between the high-level structures used by the cognitive system, and the low-level structures used by the perceptual and motor systems. These productions are like ordinary productions, except that they examine only the perceptual and motor fields, and not any of the rest of the context stack. This autonomy from the context stack is critical, because it allows the decision procedure to proceed without waiting for quiescence among the encoding and decoding productions, which may never happen in a rapidly changing environment.

2.6 Default Knowledge

Soar has a set of productions (55 in all) that provide default responses to each of the possible impasses that can arise, and thus prevent the system from dropping into a bottomless pit in which it generates an unbounded number of content-free performance contexts. Figure 3.2 shows the default production that allows the system to continue if it has no idea how to resolve a conflict impasse among a set of operators. When the production executes, it rejects all of the conflicting operators. This allows another candidate operator to be selected, if there is one, or for a different impasse to arise if there are no additional candidates. This default response, as with all of them, can be overridden by additional knowledge if it is available.

One large part of the default knowledge (10 productions) is responsible for setting up operator subgoaling as the default response to no-change impasses on operators. That is, it attempts to find some other state in the problem space to which the selected operators can be applied. This is accomplished by generating acceptable and worst preferences in the subgoal for the parent problem space. If another problem space is suggested, possibly for implementing the operator, it will be selected. Otherwise, the selection of the parent problem space in the subgoal enables operator subgoaling. A sequence of operators is then applied in the subgoal until a state is generated that satisfies the preconditions of an operator higher in the goal stack.

Another large part of the default knowledge (33 productions) is responsible for setting up lookahead search as the default response to tie impasses. This is accomplished by generating acceptable and worst preferences for the *selection* problem space. The selection problem space consists of operators that evaluate the tied alternatives. Based on the evaluations produced by these operators, default productions create preferences that break the tie and resolve the impasse. In order to apply the evaluation operators, domain knowledge must exist

---

If there is an impasse because of an operator conflict
    and there are no candidate problem spaces available
then reject the conflicting operators.

Figure 3.2
A default production.

that can create an evaluation. If no such knowledge is available, a second impasse arises—a no-change on the evaluation operator. As mentioned earlier, the default response to an operator no-change impasse is to perform operator subgoaling. However, for a no-change impasse on an evaluation operator this is overridden and a lookahead search is performed instead. The results of the lookahead search are used to evaluate the tied alternatives.

As Soar is developed, it is expected that more and more knowledge will be included as part of the basic system about how to deal with a variety of situations. For example, one area on which we are currently working is the provision of Soar with a basic arithmetical capability, including problem spaces for addition, multiplication, subtraction, division, and comparison. One way of looking at the existing default knowledge is as the tip of this large iceberg of background knowledge. However, another way to look at the default knowledge is as part of the architecture itself. Some of the default knowledge—how much is still unclear—must be innate rather than learned. The rest of the system's knowledge, such as the arithmetic spaces, should then be learnable from there.

3 Analysis of Soar

There are a variety of analyses that could be performed for Soar. In this section we take our cue from the issues provided by the organizers of the 1987 Workshop on the Foundations of Artificial Intelligence [13]. We examine the set of tasks that are natural for Soar, the sources of its power, and its scope and limits.

3.1 Natural Tasks

What does it mean for a task to be natural for an architecture? To answer this question we first must understand what a task is, and then what it means for such a task to be natural. By "task" we will mean any identifiable function, whether externally specified, or completely internal to the system. Computer configuration and maneuvering through an obstacle course are both tasks, and so are inheritance and skill acquisition. One way to define the idea of naturalness for a combination of a task and architecture is to say that a task is natural for an architecture if the task can be performed within the architecture without adding an extra level of interpretation within the software. This definition is appealing because it allows a distinction to be made between the tasks that the architecture can perform directly and those that can be done, but for which the architecture does not provide direct support. However, applying this definition is not without its problems. One problem is that, for any particular task, it is possible to replace the combination of an interpreter and its interpreted structures with a procedure that has the same effect. Some forms of learning—chunking, for example—do exactly this, by compiling interpreted structures into the structure of the interpreter. This has the effect of converting an unnatural task implementation into a natural one. Such a capability causes problems for the definition of naturalness—naturalness cannot be a fixed property of the combination of a task and an architecture—but it is actually a point is favor of architectures that can do such learning.

A second problem is that in a system that is itself built up in levels, as is Soar, different tasks will be performed at different levels. In Soar, tasks can be performed directly by the architecture, by memory retrieval, by a decision, or by goal-based problem solving. A task is implemented at a particular level if that level and all lower levels are involved, but the higher levels are not. For example, consider the task of inheritance. Inheritance is not directly implemented by the Soar architecture, but it can be implemented at the memory level by the firing of productions. This implementation involves the memory level plus the architecture (which implements the memory level), but not the decision or goal levels. Alternatively, inheritance could be implemented at the decision level, or even higher up at goal level. As the level of implementation increases, performance becomes more interpretive, but the model of computation explicitly includes all of these levels as natural for the system.

One way out of this problem is to have pre-theoretic notions about the level at which a particular task ought to be performable. The system is then natural for the task if it can be performed at that level, and unnatural if it must be implemented at a higher level. If, for example, the way inheritance works should be a function of the knowledge in the system, then the natural level for the capability is at the memory level (or higher).

In the remainder of this section we describe the major types of tasks that appear to us to be natural in Soar. Lacking any fundamental ways of partitioning the set of all tasks into principled categories, we will use a categorization based on four of the major functional capabilities of Soar: search-based tasks, knowledge-based tasks, learning tasks, and robotic tasks. The naturalness judgments for these task types are always based on assumptions about the natural level of implementation for a variety of subtasks within each type of task. We will try to be as clear as possible about the levels at which the subtasks are being performed, so that others may also be able to make these judgments for themselves.

3.1.1 Search-Based Tasks   Soar performs search in two qualitatively different ways: within context and across context. Within-context search occurs when Soar "knows" what to do at every step, and thus selects a sequence of operators and states without going into a subgoal. If it needs to backtrack in within-context search, and the states in the problem space are internal (rather than states of the outside world), it can do so by reselecting a previously visited state. Within-context search corresponds to doing the task, without lookahead, and recovering if anything goes wrong. Across-context search occurs when the system doesn't know what to do, and impasses arise. Successive states in the search show up in successively lower contexts. Backtracking occurs by terminating subgoals. Across-context search corresponds to lookahead search, hypothetical scenario generation, or simulation.

Various versions of Soar have been demonstrated to be able to perform over 30 different search methods [20, 24, 25]. Soar can also exhibit hybrid methods—such as a combination of hill-climbing and depth-first search or of operator subgoaling and depth-first search—and use different search methods for different problem spaces within the same problem.

Search methods are represented in Soar as method increments—productions that contain a small chunk of knowledge about some aspect of a task and its action consequences. For example, a method increment might include knowledge about how to compute an evaluation function for a task, along with the knowledge that states with better evaluations should be preferred. Such an increment leads to a form of hill climbing. Other increments lead to other search methods. Combinations of increments lead to mixed methods.

The basic search abilities of making choices and generating subgoals are provided by the architecture. Individual method increments are at the memory level, but control occurs at the decision level, where the results of all of the method increments can be integrated into a single choice. Some search knowledge, such as the selection problem space, exists at the goal level.

3.1.2 Knowledge-Based Tasks   Knowledge-based tasks are represented in Soar as a collection of interacting problem spaces (as are all symbolic goal-oriented tasks). Each problem space is responsible for a part of the task. Problem spaces interact according to the different goal-subgoal relationships that can exist in Soar. Within each problem space, the knowledge is further decomposed into a set of problem space components, such as goal testing, state initialization, and operator proposal [74]. These components, along with additional communication constructs, can then be encoded directly as productions, or can be described in a high-level problem space language called TAQL [74], which is then compiled down into productions. Within this overall problem space organization, other forms of organization—such as object hierarchies with inheritance—are implementable at the memory level by multiple memory accesses. Task performance is represented at the goal level as search in problem spaces.

Several knowledge-based tasks have been implemented in Soar, including the R1-Soar computer configuration system [50], the Cypress-Soar and Designer-Soar algorithm design systems [59, 61], the Neomycin-Soar medical diagnosis system [70], and the Merl-Soar job-shop scheduling system [15].

These five knowledge-based systems cover a variety of forms of both construction and classification tasks. Construction tasks involve assembling an object from pieces. R1-Soar—in which the task is to construct a computer configuration—is a good example of a construction task. Classification tasks involve selecting from among a set of objects. Neomycin-Soar—in which the task is to diagnose an illness—is a good example of a classification task.[3] In their simplest forms, both construction and classification occur at the decision level. In fact, they both occur to some extent within every decision in Soar—alternatives must be assembled in working-memory and then selected. These capabilities can require trivial amounts of processing, as when an object is constructed by instantiating and retrieving it from memory. They can also involve arbitrary amounts of problem solving and knowledge, as when the process of operator-implementation (or, equivalently, state-construction) is performed via problem solving in a subgoal.

3.1.3 Learning Tasks   The architecture directly supports a form of experiential learning in which chunking compiles goal-level problem solving into memory-level productions. Execution of the productions should have the same effect as the problem solving would have had, just more quickly. The varieties of subgoals for which chunks are learned lead to varieties in types of productions learned: problem space creation and selection; state creation and selection; and operator creation, selection, and execution. An alternative classification for this same set of behaviors is that it covers procedural, episodic and declarative knowledge [55]. The variations in goal outcomes lead to both learning from success and learning from failure. The ability to learn about all subgoal results leads to learning about important intermediate results, in addition to learning about goal success and failure. The implicit generalization of chunks leads to transfer of learned knowledge to other subtasks within the same problem (within-trial transfer), other instances of the same problem (across-trial transfer), and other problems (across-task transfer). Variations in the types of problems performed in Soar lead to chunking in knowledge-based tasks, search-based, and robotic tasks. Variations in sources of knowledge lead to learning from both internal and external knowledge sources. A summary of many of the types of learning that have so far been demonstrated in Soar can be found in [60].

The apparent naturalness of these various forms of learning depends primarily on the appropriateness of the required problem solving. Towards the natural end of the spectrum is the acquisition of operator selection productions, in which the problem solving consists simply of a search with the set of operators for which selection knowledge is to be learned. Towards the unnatural end of the spectrum is the acquisition of new declarative knowledge from the outside environment. Many systems employ a simple store command for such learning, effectively placing the capability at the memory level. In Soar, the capability is situated two levels further up, at the goal level. This occurs because the knowledge must be stored by chunking, which can only happen if the knowledge is used in subgoal-based problem solving. The naturalness of this learning in Soar thus depends on whether this extra level of interpretation is appropriate or not. It turns out that the problem solving that enables declarative learning in Soar takes the form of an understanding process that relates the new knowledge to what is already known. The chunking of this understanding process yields the chunks that encode the new knowledge. If it is assumed that new knowledge should always be understood to be learned, then Soar's approach starts to look more natural, and verbatim storage starts to look more inappropriate.

3.1.4 Robotic Tasks   Robotic tasks are performed in Soar via its perceptual-motor interface. Sensors autonomously generate working memory structures representing what is being sensed, and motor systems autonomously take commands from working memory and execute them. The work on robotics in Soar is still very much in its infancy; however, in Robo-Soar [29], Soar has been successfully hooked up to the combination of a camera and a Puma arm, and then applied to several simple blocks-world tasks.[4] Low-level software converts the camera signal into information about the positions, orientations and identifying characteristics of the blocks. This perceptual information is then input to working memory, and further interpreted by encoding productions. Decoding productions convert the high-level robot commands generated by the cognitive system to the low-level commands that are directly understood by the controller for the robot arm. These low-level commands are then executed through Soar's motor interface.

Given a set of operators which generate motor commands, and knowledge about how to simulate the operators and about the expected positions of blocks following the actions, Robo-Soar is able to successfully solve simple blocks-world problems and to learn from its own behavior and from externally provided advice. It also can make use of a general scheme for recovering from incorrect knowledge [22] to recover when the unexpected occurs—such as when the system fails in its attempt to pick up a triangular prism—and to learn to avoid the failure in the future. Robo-Soar thus mixes planning (lookahead search with chunking), plan execution and monitoring, reactivity, and error recovery (with replanning). This performance depends on all of the major components of the architecture, plus general background knowledge—such as how to do lookahead search and how to recover from errors—and specific problem spaces for the task.

3.2 Where the Power Resides

Soar's power and flexibility arise from at least four identifiable sources. The first source of power is the universality of the architecture. While it may seem that this should go without saying, it is in fact a crucial factor, and thus important to mention explicitly. Universality provides the primitive capability to perform any computable task, but does not by itself explain why Soar is more appropriate than any other universal architecture for knowledge-based, search-based, learning, and robotic tasks.

The second source of power is the uniformity of the architecture. Having only one type of long-term memory structure allows a single, relatively simple, learning mechanism to behave as a general learning mechanism. Having only one type of task representation (problem spaces) allows Soar to move continuously from one extreme of brute-force search to the other extreme of knowledge-intensive (or procedural) behavior without having to make any representational decisions. Having only one type of decision procedure allows a single, relatively simple, subgoal mechanism to generate all of the types of subgoals needed by the system.

The traditional downside of uniformity is weakness and inefficiency. If instead the system were built up as a set of specialized modules or agents, as proposed in [10, 33], then each of the modules could be optimized for its own narrow task. Our approach to this issue in Soar has been to go strongly with uniformity—for all of the benefits listed above—but to achieve efficiency (power) through the addition of knowledge. This knowledge can either be added by hand (programming) or by chunking.

The third source of power is the specific mechanisms incorporated into the architecture. The production memory provides pattern-directed access to large amounts of knowledge; provides the ability to use strong problem solving methods; and provides a memory structure with a small-grained modularity. The working memory allows global access to processing state. The decision procedure provides an open control loop that can react immediately to new situations and knowledge; contributes to the modularity of the memory by allowing memory access to proceed in an uncontrolled fashion (conflict resolution was a major source of nonmodularity in earlier production systems); provides a flexible control language (preferences); and provides a notion of impasse that is used as the basis for the generation of subgoals. Subgoals focus the system's resources on situations where the accessible knowledge is inadequate; and allow flexible meta-level processing. Problem spaces separate control from action, allowing them (control and action) to be reasoned about independently; provide a constrained context within which the search for a desired state can occur; provide the ability to use weak problem solving methods; and provide for straightforward responses to uncertainty and error (search and backtracking). Chunking acquires long-term knowledge from experience; compiles interpreted procedures into non-interpreted ones; and provides generalization and transfer. The perceptual-motor system provides the ability to observe and affect the external world in parallel with the cognitive activity.

The fourth source of power is the interaction effects that result from the integration of all of the capabilities within a single system. The most compelling results generated so far come about from these interactions. One example comes from the mixture of weak methods, strong methods, and learning that is found in systems like R1-Soar. Strong methods are based on having knowledge about what to do at each step. Because strong methods tend to be efficient and to produce high-quality solutions, they should be used whenever possible. Weak methods are based on searching to make up for a lack of knowledge about what should be done. Such methods contribute robustness and scope by providing the system with a fall-back approach for situations in which the available strong methods do not work. Learning results in the addition of knowledge, turning weak methods into strong ones. For example, in R1-Soar it was demonstrated how computer configuration could be cast as a search problem, how strong methods (knowledge) could be used to reduce search, how weak methods (subgoals and search) could be used to make up for a lack of knowledge, and how learning could add knowledge as the result of search.

Another interesting interaction effect comes from work on abstraction planning, in which a difficult problem is solved by first learning a plan for an abstract version of the problem, and then using the abstract plan to aid in finding a plan for the full problem [40, 56, 69, 68]. Chunking helps the abstraction planning process by recording the abstract plan as a set of operator-selection productions, and by acquiring other productions that reduce the amount of search required in generating a plan. Abstraction helps the learning process by allowing chunks to be learned more quickly—abstract searches tend to be shorter than normal ones. Abstraction also helps learning by enabling chunks to be more general than they would otherwise be—the chunks ignore the details that were abstracted away—thus allowing more transfer and potentially decreasing the cost of matching the chunks (because there are now fewer conditions).

3.3 Scope and Limits

The original work on Soar demonstrated its capabilities as a general problem solver that could use any of the weak methods when appropriate, across a wide range of tasks. Later, we came to understand how to use Soar as the basis for knowledge-based systems, and how to incorporate appropriate learning and perceptual-motor capabilities into the architecture. These developments increased Soar's scope considerably beyond its origins as a weak-method problem solver. Our ultimate goal has always been to develop the system to the point where its scope includes everything required of a general intelligence. In this section we examine how far Soar has come from its relatively limited initial demonstrations towards its relatively unlimited goal. This discussion is divided up according to the major components of the Soar architecture, as presented in Section 2: memory, decisions, goals, learning, and perception and motor control.

3.3.1 Level 1: Memory   The scope of Soar's memory level can be evaluated in terms of the amount of knowledge that can be stored, the types of knowledge that can be represented, and the organization of the knowledge.

AMOUNT OF KNOWLEDGE   Using current technology, Soar's production memory can support the storage of thousands of independent chunks of knowledge. The size is primarily limited by the cost of processing larger numbers of productions. Faster machines, improved match algorithms and parallel implementations [12, 64, 65] may raise this effective limit by several orders of magnitude over the next few years.

TYPES OF KNOWLEDGE   The representation of procedural and propositional declarative knowledge is well developed in Soar. However, we don't have well worked-out approaches to many other knowledge representation problems, such as the representation of quantified, uncertain, temporal, and episodic knowledge. The critical question is whether architectural support is required to adequately represent these types of knowledge, or whether such knowledge can be adequately treated as additional objects and/or attributes. Preliminary work on quantified [42] and episodic [55] knowledge is looking promising.

MEMORY ORGANIZATION   An issue which often gets raised with respect to the organization of Soar's memory, and with respect to the organization of production memories in general, is the apparent lack of a higher-order memory organization. There are no scripts [58], frames [32], or schemas [1] to tie fragments of related memory together. Nor are there any obvious hierarchical structures which limit what sets of knowledge will be retrieved at any point in time. However, Soar's memory does have an organization, which is derived from the structure of productions, objects, and working memory (especially the context hierarchy).

What corresponds to a schema in Soar is an object, or a structured collection of objects. Such a structure can be stored entirely in the actions of a single production, or it can be stored in a piecemeal fashion across multiple productions. If multiple productions are used, the schema as a unit only comes into existence when the pieces are all retrieved contemporaneously into working memory. The advantage of this approach is that it allows novel schemas to be created from fragments of separately learned ones. The disadvantage is that it may not be possible to determine whether a set of fragments all originated from a single schema.

What corresponds to a hierarchy of retrieval contexts in Soar are the production conditions. Each combination of conditions implicitly defines a retrieval context, with a hierarchical structure induced by the subset relationship among the combinations. The contents of working memory determines which retrieval contexts are currently in force. For example, problem spaces are used extensively as retrieval contexts. Whenever there is a problem solving context that has a particular problem space selected within it, productions that test for other problem space names are not eligible to fire in that context. This approach has worked quite well for procedural knowledge, where it is clear when the knowledge is needed. We have just begun to work on appropriate organizational schemes for episodic and declarative knowledge, where it is much less clear when the knowledge should be retrieved. Our initial approach has been based on the incremental construction, via chunking, of multiproduction discrimination networks [52, 55]. Though this work is too premature for a thorough evaluation in the context of Soar, the effectiveness of discrimination networks in systems like Epam [7] and Cyrus [18] bodes well.

3.3.2 Level 2: Decisions   The scope of Soar's decision level can be evaluated in terms of its speed, the knowledge brought to bear, and the language of control.

SPEED   Soar currently runs at approximately 10 decisions/second on current workstations such as a Sun4/280. This is adequate for most of the types of tasks we currently implement, but is too slow for tasks requiring large amounts of search or very large knowledge bases (the number of decisions per second would get even smaller than it is now). The principal bottleneck is the speed of memory access, which is a function of two factors: the cost of processing individually expensive productions (the *expensive chunks* problem) [66], and the cost of processing a large number of productions (the *average growth effect* problem) [63]. We now have a solution to the problem of expensive chunks which can guarantee that all productions will be cheap—the match cost of a production is at worst linear in the number of conditions [67]—and are working on other potential solutions. Parallelism looks to be an effective solution to the average growth effect problem [63].

BRINGING KNOWLEDGE TO BEAR   Iterated, parallel, indexed access to the contents of long-term memory has proven to be an effective means of bringing knowledge to bear on the decision process. The limited power provided by this process is offset by the ability to use subgoals when the accessible knowledge is inadequate. The issue of devising good assess paths for episodic and declarative knowledge is also relevant here.

CONTROL LANGUAGE   Preferences have proven to be a flexible means of specifying a partial order among contending objects. However, we cannot yet state with certainty that the set of preference types embodied in Soar is complete with respect to all the types of information which ultimately may need to be communicated to the decision procedure.

3.3.3 Level 3: Goals   The scope of Soar's goal level can be evaluated in terms of the types of goals that can be generated and the types of problem solving that can be performed in goals. Soar's subgoaling mechanism has been demonstrated to be able to create subgoals for all of the types of difficulties that can arise in problem solving in problem spaces [20]. This leaves three areas open. The first area is how top-level goals are generated; that is, how the top-level task is picked. Currently this is done by the programmer, but a general intelligence must clearly have grounds—that is, motivations—for selecting tasks on its own. The second area is how goal interactions are handled. Goal interactions show up in Soar as operator interactions, and are normally dealt with by adding explicit knowledge to avoid them, or by backtracking (with learning) when they happen. It is not yet clear the extent to which Soar could easily make use of more sophisticated approaches, such as non-linear planning [2]. The third area is the sufficiency of impasse-driven subgoaling as a means for determining when meta-level processing is needed. Two of the activities that might fall under this area are goal tests and monitoring. Both of these activities can be performed at the memory or decision level, but when they are complicated activities it may be necessary to perform them by problem solving at the goal level. Either activity can be called for explicitly by selecting a "monitor" or "goal-test" operator, which can then lead to the generation of a subgoal. However, goals for these tasks do not arise automatically, without deliberation. Should they? It is not completely clear.

The scope of the problem solving that can be performed in goals can itself be evaluated in terms of whether problem spaces cover all of the types of performance required, the limits on the ability of subgoal-based problem solving to access and modify aspects of the system, and whether parallelism is possible. These points are addressed in the next three paragraphs.

PROBLEM SPACE SCOPE   Problem spaces are a very general performance model. They have been hypothesized to underlie all human, symbolic, goal-oriented behavior [36]. The breadth of tasks that have so far been represented in problem spaces over the whole field of AI attests to this generality. One way of pushing this evaluation further is to ask how well problem spaces account for the types of problem solving performed by two of the principal competing paradigms: planning [2] and case-based reasoning [19].[5] Both of these paradigms involve the creation (or retrieval) and use of a data structure that represents a sequence of actions. In planning, the data structure represents the sequence of actions that the system expects to use for the current problem. In case-based reasoning, the data structure represents the sequence of actions used on some previous, presumably related, problem. In both, the data structure is used to decide what sequence of actions to perform in the current problem. Soar straightforwardly performs procedural analogues of these two processes. When it performs a lookahead search to determine what operator to apply to a particular state, it acquires (by chunking) a set of search control productions which collectively tell it which operator should be applied to each subsequent state. This set of chunks forms a procedural plan for the current problem. When a search control chunk transfers between tasks, a form of procedural case-based reasoning is occurring.

Simple forms of declarative planning and case-based reasoning have also been demonstrated in Soar in the context of an expert system that designs floor systems [46]. When this system discovers, via lookahead search, a sequence of operators that achieves a goal, it creates a declarative structure representing the sequence and returns it as a subgoal result (plan creation). This plan can then be used interpretively to guide performance on the immediate problem (plan following). The plan can also be retrieved during later problems and used to guide the selection of operators (case-based reasoning). This research does not demonstrate the variety of operations one could conceivably use to modify a partial or complete plan, but it does demonstrate the basics.

META-LEVEL ACCESS   Subgoal-based problem solving has access to all of the information in working memory—including the goal stack, problem spaces, states, operators, preferences, and other facts that have been retrieved or generated—plus any of the other knowledge in long-term memory that it can access. It does not have direct access to the productions, or to any of the data structures internal to the architecture. Nonetheless, it should be able to indirectly examine the contents of any productions that were acquired by chunking, which in the long run should be just about all of them. The idea is to reconstruct the contents of the production by going down into a subgoal and retracing the problem solving that was done when the chunk was learned. In this way it should be possible to determine what knowledge the production cached. This idea has not yet been explicitly demonstrated in Soar, but research on the recovery from incorrect knowledge has used a closely related approach [22].

The effects of problem solving are limited to the addition of information to working memory. Deletion of working memory elements is accomplished by a garbage collector provided by the architecture. Productions are added by chunking, rather than by problem solving, and are never deleted by the system. The limitation on production creation—that it only occurs via chunking—is dealt with by varying the nature of the problem solving over which chunking occurs [55]. The limitation on production deletion is dealt with by learning new productions which overcome the effects of old ones [22].

PARALLELISM   Two principal sources of parallelism in Soar are at the memory level: production match and execution. On each cycle of elaboration, all productions are matched in parallel to the working memory, and then all of the successful instantiations are executed in parallel. This lets tasks that can be performed at the memory level proceed in parallel, but not so for decision-level and goal-level tasks.

Another principal source of parallelism is provided by the motor systems. All motor systems behave in parallel with respect to each other, and with respect to the cognitive system. This enables one form of task-level parallelism in which non-interfering external tasks can be performed in parallel. To enable further research on task-level parallelism, we have added the experimental ability to simultaneously select multiple problem space operators within a single problem solving context. Each of these operators can then proceed to execute in parallel, yielding parallel subgoals, and ultimately an entire tree of problem solving contexts in which all of the branches are being processed in parallel. We do not yet have enough experience with this capability to evaluate its scope and limits.

Despite all of these forms of parallelism embodied in Soar, most implementations of the architecture have been on serial machines, with the parallelism being simulated. However, there is an active research effort to implement Soar on parallel computers. A parallelized version of the production match has been successfully implemented on an Encore Multimax, which has a small number (2–20) of large-grained processors [65], and unsuccessfully implemented on a Connection Machine [14], which has a large number (16 K–64 K) of small-grained processors [9]. The Connection Machine implementation failed primarily because a complete parallelization of the current match algorithm can lead to exponential space requirements. Research on restricted match algorithms may fix this problem in the future. Work is also in progress towards implementing Soar on message-passing computers [64].

3.3.4 Learning   In [60] we broke down the problem of evaluating the scope of Soar's learning capabilities into four parts: when can the architecture learn; from what can the architecture learn; what can the architecture learn; and when can the architecture apply learned knowledge. These points are discussed in Section 3.1, and need not be elaborated further here.

One important additional issue is whether Soar acquires knowledge that is at the appropriate level of generalization or specialization. Chunking provides a level of generality that is determined by a combination of the representation used and the problem solving performed. Under varying circumstances, this can lead to both overgeneralization [28] and overspecialization. The acquisition of overgeneral knowledge implies that the system must be able to recover from any errors caused by its use. One solution to this problem that has been implemented in Soar involves detecting that a performance error has occurred, determining what should have been done instead, and acquiring a new chunk which leads to correct performance in the future [22]. This is accomplished without examining or modifying the overgeneral production; instead it goes back down into the subgoals for which the overgeneral productions were learned.

One way to deal with overspecialization is to patch the resulting knowledge gaps with additional knowledge. This is what Soar does constantly—if a production is overspecialized, it doesn't fire in circumstances when it should, causing an impasse to occur, and providing the opportunity to learn an additional chunk that covers the missing case (plus possibly other cases). Another way to deal with overspecialized knowledge is to work towards acquiring more general productions. A standard approach is to induce general rules from a sequence of positive and negative examples [34, 44]. This form of generalization must occur in Soar by search in problem spaces, and though there has been some initial work on doing this [47, 57], we have not yet provided Soar with a set of problem spaces that will allow it to generate appropriate generalizations from a variety of sets of examples. So, Soar cannot yet be described as a system of choice for doing induction from multiple examples. On the other hand, Soar does generalize quite naturally and effectively when abstraction occurs [68]. The learned rules reflect whatever abstraction was made during problem solving.

Learning behaviors that have not yet been attempted in Soar include the construction of a model of the environment from experimentation in it [45], scientific discovery and theory formation [30], and conceptual clustering [8].

3.3.5 Perception and Motor Control   The scope of Soar's perception and motor control can be evaluated in terms of both its low-level I/O mechanisms and its high-level language capabilities. Both of these capabilities are quite new, so the evaluation must be even more tentative than for the preceding components.

At the low-level, Soar can be hooked up to multiple perceptual modalities (and multiple fields within each modality) and can control multiple effectors. The critical low-level aspects of perception and motor control are currently done in a standard procedural language outside of the cognitive system. The resulting system appears to be an effective testbed for research on high-level aspects of perception and motor-control. It also appears to be an effective test-bed for research on the interactions of perception and motor control with other cognitive capabilities, such as memory, problem solving, and learning. However, it does finesse many of the hard issues in perception and motor control, such as selective attention, shape determination, object identification, and temporal coordination. Work is actively in progress on selective attention [71].

At the high end of I/O capabilities is the processing of natural language. An early attempt to implement a semantic grammar parser in Soar was only a limited success [43]. It worked, but did not appear to be the right long-term solution to language understanding in Soar. More recent work on NL-Soar has focused on the incremental construction of a model of the situation by applying comprehension operators to each incoming word [31]. Comprehension operators iteratively augment and refine the situation model, setting up expectations for the part of the utterance still to be seen, and satisfying earlier expectations. As a side effect of constructing the situation model, an utterance model is constructed to represent the linguistic structure of the sentence. This approach to language understanding has been successfully applied to acquiring task-specific problem spaces for three immediate reasoning tasks: relational reasoning [17], categorical syllogisms, and sentence verification [3]. It has also been used to process the input for these tasks as they are performed. Though NL-Soar is still far from providing a general linguistic capability, the approach has proven promising.

4 Conclusion

In this article we have taken a step towards providing an analysis of the Soar architecture as a basis for general intelligence. In order to increase understanding of the structure of the architecture, we have provided a theoretical framework within which the architecture can be described, and a discussion of methodological assumptions underlying the project and the system. In order to facilitate comparisons between the capabilities of the current version of Soar and the capabilities required to achieve its ultimate goal as an architecture for general intelligence, we have described the natural tasks for the architecture, the sources of its power, and its scope and limits. If this article has succeeded, it should be clear that progress has been made, but that more work is still required. This applies equally to the tasks of developing Soar and analyzing it.

Acknowledgement

This research was sponsored by the Defense Advanced Research Projects Agency (DOD) under contract N00039-86-C-0133 and by the Sloan Foundation. Computer facilities were partially provided by NIH grant RR-00785 to Sumex-Aim. The views and conclusions contained in this document are those of the authors and should not be interpreted as representing the official policies, either expressed or implied, of the Defense Advanced Research Projects Agency, the US Government, the Sloan Foundation, or the National Institutes of Health.

We would like to thank Beth Adelson, David Kirsh, and David McAllester for their helpful comments on an earlier draft of this chapter.

Notes

1. Investigations of the relationship of Soar to the neural and rational bands can be found in [37, 48, 55].
2. The directionality of the implication is reversed in logic programming languages such as Prolog, but the point still holds.
3. In a related development, as part of an effort to map the Generic Task approach to expert system construction onto Soar, the Generic Task for classification by establish-refine has been implemented in Soar as a general problem space [16].
4. The work on Robo-Soar has been done in the newest major release of Soar (version 5) [23, 62], which differs in a number of interesting ways from the earlier versions upon which the rest of the results in this article are based.
5. The work on Robo-Soar also reveals Soar's potential to exhibit reactive planning [11]. The current version of Soar still has problems with raw speed and with the unbounded nature of the production match (the expensive chunks problem), but it is expected that these problems will be solved in the near future.

References

[1] F. C. Bartlett, *Remembering: A Study in Experimental and Social Psychology* (Cambridge University Press, Cambridge, England, 1932).
[2] D. Chapman, Planning for conjunctive goals, *Artif. Intell.* 32 (1987) 333–377.
[3] H. H. Clark and W. G. Chase, On the process of comparing sentences against pictures, *Cogn. Psychol.* 3 (1972) 472–517.
[4] G. DeJong and R. J. Mooney, Explanation-based learning: an alternative view, *Mach. Learn.* 1 (1986) 145–176.

[5] T. G. Dietterich, Learning at the knowledge level, *Mach. Learn.* 1 (1986) 287–315.

[6] O. Etzioni and T. M. Mitchell, A comparative analysis of chunking and decision analytic control, in: *Proceedings AAAI Spring Symposium on Limited Rationality and AI,* Stanford, CA (1989).

[7] E. A. Feigenbaum and H. A. Simon, Epam-like models of recognition and learning, *Cogn. Sci.* 8 (1984) 305–336.

[8] D. H. Fisher and P. Langley, Approaches to conceptual clustering, in: *Proceedings IJCAI-85,* Los Angeles, CA (1985) 691–697.

[9] R. Flynn, Placing Soar on the connection machine, Prepared for and distributed at the AAAI Mini-Symposium "How Can Slow Components Think So Fast" (1988).

[10] J. A. Fodor, *The Modularity of Mind* (Bradford Books/MIT Press, Cambridge, MA, 1983).

[11] M. P. Georgeff and A. L. Lansky, Reactive reasoning and planning, in: *Proceedings AAAI-87,* Seattle, WA (1987) 677–682.

[12] A. Gupta and M. Tambe, Suitability of message passing computers for implementing production systems, in: *Proceedings AAAI-88,* St. Paul, MN (1988) 687–692.

[13] C. Hewitt and D. Kirsh, Personal communication (1987).

[14] W. D. Hillis, *The Connection Machine* (MIT Press, Cambridge, MA, 1985).

[15] W. Hsu, M. Prietula and D. Steier, Merl-Soar: applying Soar to scheduling, in: *Proceedings Workshop on Artificial Intelligence Simulation, AAAI-88,* St. Paul, MN (1988) 81–84.

[16] T. R. Johnson, J. W. Smith Jr and B. Chandrasekaran, Generic Tasks and Soar, in: *Working Notes AAAI Spring Symposium on Knowledge System Development Tools and Languages,* Stanford, CA (1989) 25–28.

[17] P. N. Johnson-Laird, Reasoning by rule or model? in: *Proceedings 10th Annual Conference of the Cognitive Science Society,* Montreal, Que. (1988) 765–771.

[18] J. L. Kolodner, Maintaining order in a dynamic long-term memory, *Cogn. Sci.* 7 (1983) 243–280.

[19] J. L. Kolodner, ed., *Proceedings DARPA Workshop on Case-Based Reasoning,* Clearwater Beach, FL (1988).

[20] J. E. Laird, Universal subgoaling, Ph.D. thesis, Carnegie-Mellon University, Pittsburgh, PA (1983); also in: J. E. Laird, P. S. Rosenbloom and A. Newell, *Universal Subgoaling and Chunking: The Automatic Generation and Learning of Goal Hierarchies* (Kluwer, Hingham, MA, 1986).

[21] J. E. Laird, Soar user's manual (version 4), Tech. Rept. ISL-15, Xerox Palo Alto Research Center, Palo Alto, CA (1986).

[22] J. E. Laird, Recovery from incorrect knowledge in Soar, in: *Proceedings AAAI-88,* St. Paul, MN (1988) 618–623.

[23] J. E. Laird and K. A. McMahon, Destructive state modification in Soar, Draft V, Department of EECS, University of Michigan, Ann Arbor, MI (1989).

[24] J. E. Laird and A. Newell, A universal weak method, Tech. Rept. 83–141, Department of Computer Science, Carnegie-Mellon University, Pittsburgh, PA (1983).

[25] J. E. Laird, A. Newell and P. S. Rosenbloom, SOAR: an architecture for general intelligence, *Artif. Intell.* 33 (1987) 1–64.

[26] J. E. Laird, P. S. Rosenbloom and A. Newell, Towards chunking as a general learning mechanism, in: *Proceedings AAAI-84,* Austin, TX (1984) 188–192.

[27] J. E. Laird, P. S. Rosenbloom and A. Newell, Chunking in Soar: the anatomy of a general learning mechanism, *Mach. Learn.* 1 (1986) 11–46.

[28] J. E. Laird, P. S. Rosenbloom and A. Newell, Overgeneralization during knowledge compilation in Soar, in: T. G. Dietterich, ed., *Proceedings Workshop on Knowledge Compilation,* Otter Crest, OR (1986).

[29] J. E. Laird, E. S. Yager, C. M. Tuck and M. Hucka, Learning in tele-autonomous systems using Soar, in: *Proceedings NASA Conference on Space Telerobotics,* Pasadena, CA (1989).

[30] P. Langley, H. A. Simon, G. L. Bradshaw and J. M. Zytkow, *Scientific Discovery: Computational Explorations of the Creative Processes* (MIT Press, Cambridge, MA, 1987).

[31] R. L. Lewis, A. Newell and T. A. Polk, Toward a Soar theory of taking instructions for immediate reasoning tasks, in: *Proceedings 11th Annual Conference of the Cognitive Science Society*, Ann Arbor, MI (1989).

[32] M. Minsky, A framework for the representation of knowledge, in: P. Winston, ed., *The Psychology of Computer Vision* (McGraw-Hill, New York, 1975).

[33] M. Minsky, *The Society of Mind* (Simon and Schuster, New York, 1986).

[34] T. M. Mitchell, Generalization as search, *Artif. Intell.* 18 (1982) 203–226.

[35] T. M. Mitchell, R. M. Keller and S. T. Kedar-Cabelli, Explanation-based generalization: a unifying view, *Mach. Learn.* 1 (1986) 47–80.

[36] A. Newell, Reasoning, problem solving and decision processes: the problem space as a fundamental category, in: R. Nickerson, ed., *Attention and performance* 8 (Erlbaum, Hillsdale, NJ, 1980).

[37] A. Newell, *Unified Theories of Cognition* (Harvard University Press, Cambridge, MA, 1990).

[38] A. Newell and P. S. Rosenbloom Mechanisms of skill acquisition and the law of practice, in: J. R. Anderson, ed., *Cognitive Skills and Their Acquisition* (Erlbaum, Hillsdale, NJ, 1981) 1–55.

[39] A. Newell, P. S. Rosenbloom and J. E. Laird, Symbolic architectures for cognition, in: M. I. Posner, ed., *Foundations of Cognitive Science* (Bradford Books/MIT Press, Cambridge, MA, 1989).

[40] A. Newell and H. A. Simon, *Human Problem Solving* (Prentice-Hall, Englewood Cliffs, NJ, 1972).

[41] N. J. Nilsson, *Principles of Artificial Intelligence* (Tioga, Palo Alto, CA, 1980).

[42] T. A. Polk and A. Newell, Modeling human syllogistic reasoning in Soar, in: *Proceedings 10th Annual Conference of the Cognitive Science Society*, Montreal, Que. (1988) 181–187.

[43] L. Powell, Parsing the picnic problem with a Soar3 implementation of Dypar-1, Department of Computer Science, Carnegie-Mellon University, Pittsburgh, PA (1984).

[44] J. R. Quinlan, Induction of decision trees, *Mach. Learn.* 1 (1986) 81–106.

[45] S. Rajamoney, G. F. DeJong, and B. Faltings, Towards a model of conceptual knowledge acquisition through directed experimentation, in: *Proceedings IJCAI-85*, Los Angeles, CA (1985) 688–690.

[46] Y. Reich, Learning plans as a weak method for design, Department of Civil Engineering, Carnegie-Mellon University, Pittsburgh, PA (1988).

[47] P. S. Rosenbloom, Beyond generalization as search: towards a unified framework for the acquisition of new knowledge, in: G. F. DeJong, ed., *Proceedings AAAI Symposium on Explanation-Based Learning*, Stanford, CA (1988) 17–21.

[48] P. S. Rosenbloom, A symbolic goal-oriented perspective on connectionism and Soar, in: R. Pfeifer, Z. Schreter, F. Fogelman-Soulie and L. Steels, eds., *Connectionism in Perspective* (Elsevier, Amsterdam, 1989).

[49] P. S. Rosenbloom and J. E. Laird., Mapping explanation-based generalization onto Soar, in: *Proceedings AAAI-86*, Philadelphia, PA (1986) 561–567.

[50] P. S. Rosenbloom, J. E. Laird, J. McDermott, A. Newell and E. Orciuch, R1-Soar: an experiment in knowledge-intensive programming in a problem-solving architecture, *IEEE Trans. Pattern Anal. Mach. Intell.* 7 (1985) 561–569.

[51] P. S. Rosenbloom, J. E. Laird and A. Newell, Knowledge level leaning in Soar, in: *Proceedings AAAI-87*, Seattle, WA (1987) 499–504.

[52] P. S. Rosenbloom, J. E. Laird and A. Newell, The chunking of skill and knowledge, in: B. A. G. Elsendoorn and H. Bouma, eds., *Working Models of Human Perception* (Academic Press, London, 1988) 391–410.

[53] P. S. Rosenbloom, J. E. Laird and A. Newell, Meta-levels in Soar, in: P. Maes and D. Nardi, eds., *Meta-Level Architectures and Reflection* (North-Holland, Amsterdam, 1988) 227–240.

[54] P. S. Rosenbloom and A. Newell, The chunking of goal hierarchies: a generalized model of practice, in: R. S. Michalski, J. G. Carbonnell and T. M. Mitchell, eds., *Machine Learning: An Artificial Intelligence Approach* 2 (Morgan Kaufmann, Los Altos, CA, 1986) 247–288.

[55] P. S. Rosenbloom, A. Newell and J. E. Laird, Towards the knowledge level in Soar: the role of the architecture in the use of knowledge, in: K. VanLehn, ed., *Architectures for Intelligence* (Erlbaum, Hillsdale, NJ, 1990).

[56] E. D. Sacerdoti, Planning in a hierarchy of abstraction spaces, *Artif. Intell.* 5 (1974) 115–135.

[57] R. H. Saul, A. Soar2 implementation of version-space inductive learning, Department of Computer Science, Carnegie-Mellon University, Pittsburgh, PA (1984).

[58] R. Schank and R. Ableson, *Scripts, Plans, Goals and Understanding* (Erlbaum, Hillsdale, NJ, 1977).

[59] D. Steier, Cypress-Soar: a case study in search and learning in algorithm design, in: *Proceedings IJCAI-87*, Milan, Italy (1987) 327–330.

[60] D. M. Steier, J. E. Laird, A. Newell, P. S. Rosenbloom, R. Flynn, A Golding, T. A. Polk, O. G. Shivers, A. Unruh and G. R. Yost, Varieties of learning in Soar: 1987, in: P. Langley, ed., *Proceedings Fourth International Workshop on Machine Learning*, Irvine, CA (1987) 300–311.

[61] D. M. Steier and A. Newell, Integrating multiple sources of knowledge in Designer-Soar: an automatic algorithm designer, in: *Proceedings AAAI-88*, St. Paul, MN (1988) 8–13.

[62] K. R. Swedlow and D. M. Steier, Soar 5.0 user's manual, School of Computer Science, Carnegie Mellon University, Pittsburgh, PA (1989).

[63] M. Tambe, Speculations on the computational effects of chunking, Department of Computer Science, Carnegie Mellon University, Pittsburgh, PA (1988).

[64] M. Tambe, A. Acharya and A. Gupta, Implementation of production systems on message passing computers: Simulation results and analysis, Tech. Rept. CMU-CS-89-129, School of Computer Science, Carnegie Mellon University, Pittsburgh, PA (1989).

[65] M. Tambe, D. Kalp, A. Gupta, C. L. Forgy, B. Milnes and A. Newell, Soar/PSM-E: Investigating match parallelism in a learning production system, in: *Proceedings ACM/SIGPLAN Symposium on Parallel Programming: Experience with Applications, Languages, and Systems* (1988) 146–161.

[66] M. Tambe and A. Newell, Some chunks are expensive, in: J. Laird, ed., *Proceedings Fifth International Conference on Machine Learning* Ann Arbor, MI (1988) 451–458.

[67] M. Tambe and P. S. Rosenbloom, Eliminating expensive chunks by restricting expressiveness, in: *Proceedings IJCAI-89*, Detroit, MI (1989).

[68] A. Unruh and P. S. Rosenbloom, Abstraction in problem solving and learning, in: *Proceedings IJCAI-89*, Detroit, MI (1989).

[69] A. Unruh, P. S. Rosenbloom and J. E. Laird, Dynamic abstraction problem solving in Soar, in: *Proceedings Third Annual Aerospace Applications of Artificial Intelligence Conference*, Dayton, OH (1987) 245–256.

[70] R. Washington and P. S. Rosenbloom, Applying problem solving and learning to diagnosis, Department of Computer Science, Stanford University, CA (1988).

[71] M. Wiesmeyer, Personal communication (1988).

[72] M. Wiesmeyer, Soar I/O reference manual, version 2, Department of EECS, University of Michigan, Ann Arbor, MI (1988).

[73] M. Wiesmeyer, New and improved Soar IO, Department of EECS, University of Michigan, Ann Arbor, MI (1989).

[74] G. R. Yost and A. Newell, A problem space approach to expert system specification, in: *Proceedings IJCAI-89*, Detroit, MI (1989).

EPIC

Chapter 4

Adaptive Executive Control: Flexible Multiple-Task Performance without Pervasive Immutable Response-Selection Bottlenecks

David E. Meyer, David E. Kieras, Erick Lauber,
Eric H. Schumacher, Jennifer Glass, Eileen Zurbriggen,
Leon Gmeindl, and Dana Apfelblat

---

1 Introduction

Traditionally, it has been hypothesized that a pervasive immutable cognitive response-selection bottleneck (RSB) exists in the human information-processing system (for comprehensive reviews, see Meyer and Kieras, 1995; Pashler, 1994). According to the RSB hypothesis, there is a stage of processing that selects responses to stimuli for various tasks, and that only has enough capacity to accommodate one stimulus at a time. Thus, if two tasks (e.g., saying words in response to auditory tones, and pressing keys in response to visual letters) must be performed simultaneously, then even when different stimulus and response modalities are involved, the selection of a response for one task will supposedly have to wait until response selection for the other is completed. Theorists have typically attributed such delays to permanent "hardware" characteristics of central limited capacity decision mechanisms (Craik, 1948; Davis, 1957; De Jong, 1993; McCann and Johnston, 1992; Pashler, 1984, 1989, 1990, 1993; Pashler and Johnston, 1989; Ruthruff et al., 1995; Schweickert et al., 1992; Smith, 1967; Van Selst and Jolicoeur, 1993; Vince, 1949; Welford, 1952, 1959, 1967).

Assuming that it is valid, the RSB hypothesis has major implications for conceptualizing discrete and continuous information processing. These implications concern not only multiple-task but also single-task performance. Given a pervasive response-selection bottleneck, many individual tasks could appear to be performed through discrete processing stages that accomplish perceptual encoding, response selection, and movement production in a strict step-by-step fashion (cf. Luce, 1986; Meyer et al., 1988; Miller, 1988; Sanders, 1980; Sternberg, 1969; Townsend and Ashby, 1983). For example, suppose a task involves stimuli that have several orthogonal perceptual dimensions (e.g., shapes and sizes of visual objects). Also, suppose stimulus values on each perceptual dimension (e.g., round and square for shape; small and large for size) must be converted to values on other response dimensions (e.g., left and right hands; index and middle fingers). Then making responses to these stimuli may necessarily entail discrete substages, if there is a response-selection bottleneck. In particular, the start of selecting a correct response finger on the basis of an output from a relatively slow perceptual size-identification process might have to wait until the selection of a correct response hand on the basis of a faster shape-identification process has been completed (cf. Miller, 1982; Osman et al., 1992). Essentially, a response-selection bottleneck could limit the extent to which selections of response values along different dimensions can occur simultaneously.

Analyses of discrete and continuous information processing should therefore take the RSB hypothesis very seriously. Depending on whether or not there is a pervasive response-selection bottleneck, more or less constraint would be placed on what mental operations may temporally overlap each other and exploit their partial outputs. With these stipulations in mind, the remainder of this article has five parts. First, we survey some attractive features of the traditional RSB hypothesis. Second, strong arguments are made against taking the validity of this hypothesis for granted. Third, an alternative theoretical framework (Kieras and Meyer, 1994; Meyer and Kieras, 1992, 1994, 1995) is described, in which some components of the human information-processing system have substantially more capacity and flexibility than the RSB hypothesis allows. Fourth, using our framework, precise computational models are applied to account for results from representative studies of multiple-task performance. Fifth, we consider what the present theory implies about future research on discrete versus continuous information processing in a Brave New World without pervasive immutable response-selection bottlenecks.

2 Attractive Features of the RSB Hypothesis

Several features of the traditional RSB hypothesis have made it especially attractive. Among them are conceptual simplicity, predictive precision, intuitive appeal, and authoritative endorsement. Compared to alternatives such as general capacity theory (Moray, 1967; Kahneman, 1973; McLeod, 1978; Gottsdanker, 1980) and multiple-resource theory (Navon and Gopher, 1979; Wickens, 1984), the RSB hypothesis involves relatively few assumptions and yields more precise quantitative predictions about certain aspects of multiple-task performance. These assumptions and predictions are consistent with some expert intuitions about the nature of human attention and the mental processes that mediate it. As William James (1890, p. 409) rhetorically remarked: "how many ideas or things can we attend to at once ... the answer is, not easily more than one ... there must be a rapid oscillation of the mind from one idea to the next, with no consequent gain of time." When translated to modern information-processing concepts, James' answer is what might be expected in terms of a pervasive response-selection bottleneck (Norman, 1969).

2.1 Psychological Refractory-Period Procedure

Moreover, extensive behavioral evidence has been obtained to support the RSB hypothesis. A major source of this evidence is the psychological refractory-period procedure (Bertelson, 1966; Kantowitz, 1974; Pashler, 1994; Smith, 1967; Welford, 1967). On each trial of the PRP procedure, a warning signal is followed by a stimulus for the first of two tasks. In response to it, a subject must react quickly and accurately. Soon after the Task 1 stimulus, there is a stimulus for the second task. The time between the two stimuli is the stimulus-onset asynchrony (SOA). In response to the Task 2 stimulus, the subject must again react quickly and accurately. However, instructions for the PRP procedure typically state that regardless of the SOA, Task 1 should have higher priority than Task 2; subjects may also be required to make the Task 1 response first (e.g., Pashler, 1984; Pashler and Johnston, 1989). RTs are then measured to determine how much Task 1 interferes with Task 2.

2.2 Representative PRP Results

Some idealized representative results from the PRP procedure appear in Figure 4.1. Here mean RTs for both Tasks 1 and 2 are plotted versus the SOA as a function of Task 2 response-selection difficulty (easy or hard), which can be varied by manipulating factors like S–R compatibility and S–R numerosity in Task 2 (Becker, 1976; Hawkins et al., 1979; Karlin and Kestenbaum, 1968; McCann and Johnston, 1992). As Figure 4.1 indicates, such manipulations may produce patterns of data that are consistent with a response-selection bottleneck.

Constant Mean Task 1 RTs   A first salient aspect of Figure 4.1 is that mean Task 1 RTs are affected by neither the SOA nor Task 2 difficulty. This conforms nicely to the RSB hypothesis. If Task 1 stimuli come first at each SOA, then presumably they always enter the response-selection bottleneck before Task 2 stimuli, and the bottleneck's all-or-none "admissions policy" precludes Task 2 from competing with Task 1 for the limited processing capacity therein. Satisfying this implication, many PRP studies have yielded essentially constant mean Task 1 RTs (Davis, 1957; Hawkins et al., 1979; Karlin and Kestenbaum, 1968; McCann and Johnston, 1992; Pashler, 1990; Pashler and Johnston, 1989; Welford, 1959).

Elevated Task 2 RTs at Short SOAs   Second, the mean Task 2 RTs are higher at short SOAs in Figure 4.1. This elevation, called the *PRP effect*, follows directly from the RSB hypothesis. When the SOA is short, response selection for Task 2 supposedly waits while the Task 1 stimulus passes through the bottleneck and is converted to a Task 1 response. As a result, the concomitant extra delay should raise mean Task 2 RTs above their single-task baseline. Virtually all past studies will the PRP procedure have yielded such increases (Pashler, 1994).

PRP Curves With −1 Slopes   In Figure 4.1, however, mean Task 2 RTs gradually decrease as the SOA increases, forming so-called *PRP curves*. Specifically, under

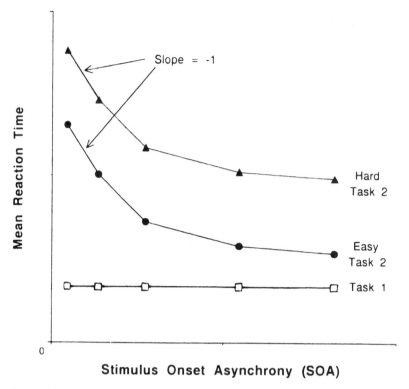

Figure 4.1
Idealized representative results from the PRP procedure.

the RSB hypothesis, the slopes of these curves should equal −1 at short SOAs. This is because each increment of the SOA, starting from zero, produces an equal opposite decrement in how long a Task 2 stimulus must wait to enter the response-selection bottleneck. Subsequently, once the SOA becomes long enough to yield some trials with no delay in Task 2, the PRP curves should become correspondingly shallower, bottoming out with a slope of zero at very long SOAs. Satisfying these additional expectations, PRP studies have typically manifested curves whose slopes range from −1 to 0 (e.g., Davis, 1957; Hawkins et al., 1979; Karlin and Kestenbaum, 1968; McCann and Johnston, 1992; Pashler, 1990; Pashler and Johnston, 1989; Welford, 1959).

Parallel PRP Curves   Another quantitative property implied by the RSB hypothesis is that the SOA and response-selection difficulty for Task 2 should affect mean Task 2 RTs additively. Thus, as in Figure 4.1, PRP curves ought to be "parallel" (i.e., vertically equidistant) when the difficulty of Task 2 response selection varies across conditions. This is because regardless of the SOA, each

Task 2 RT depends directly on how long response selection takes for Task 2 after the Task 1 stimulus has passed through the bottleneck (Karlin and Kestenbaum, 1968; Keele, 1973; McCann and Johnston, 1992; Pashler, 1984; Pashler and Johnston, 1989; Schvaneveldt, 1969). Such additivity and parallelism have been obtained in several PRP studies, even when Tasks 1 and 2 involve neither the same stimulus nor response modalities (Becker, 1976; McCann and Johnston, 1992; Pashler, 1984; Pashler and Johnston, 1989; Ruthruff et al., 1995; Van Selst and Jolicoeur, 1993). Of course, this would be expected if between-task interference occurs at a central cognitive level rather than merely at peripheral perceptual-motor levels.

Other Relevant Findings   PRP effects are also robust in other respects. Typically, they persist with extended practice. Even after thousands of practice trials on the PRP procedure, subjects still produce elevated Task 2 RTs at short SOAs (Gottsdanker and Stelmach, 1971; Karlin and Kestenbaum, 1968). Again, this is expected from the RSB hypothesis, which assumes that the response-selection bottleneck is an immutable "hardware" component of the human information-processing system.

3 Arguments Against the RSB Hypothesis

Nevertheless, various arguments can be made against the traditional RSB hypothesis. For example, its assumptions seem neurophysiologically implausible. Contrary to them, information processing in the brain is "massively parallel" and "distributed" throughout components of many interconnected neural networks (Anderson and Hinton, 1981; Rumelhart and McClelland, 1986). There are no obvious brain sites that constitute immutable response-selection bottlenecks of the sort to which PRP effects and other multiple-task performance decrements have been attributed (Allport, 1980, 1987; Neumann, 1987).

A second related concern is that the RSB hypothesis lacks computational flexibility. It provides little accommodation for executive control processes that allocate available system resources efficiently and adaptively to different ongoing tasks. Task scheduling through an immutable response-selection bottleneck has been assumed to happen simply on a first-come first-serve basis, whereby secondary tasks are completely blocked from access to essential resources during extended periods of time. Any performer who suffers from such rigidity would have great difficulty adapting successfully to major changes in task priorities and increased or decreased knowledge about impending environmental stimuli (Allport, 1980, 1987; Neumann, 1987).

Because of its unrealistic limitations, the RSB hypothesis seems inconsistent with results from many multiple-task situations (Wickens, 1984). An immutable response-selection bottleneck does not even account fully for data from the standard PRP procedure. Instead, it has become gradually but compellingly evident that subjects can and do produce systematic patterns of RTs different than those in Figure 4.1, extending well beyond the scope of the RSB hypothesis (Meyer and Kieras, 1992, 1994, 1995).

3.1 Divergent PRP Curves

One observed RT pattern for which the RSB hypothesis cannot account very well involves divergent PRP curves. Such divergence occurs when the difficulty of selecting Task 2 responses affects mean Task 2 RTs less at short SOAs than at long SOAs, yielding a positive SOA-by-difficulty interaction. For example, consider the left panel of Figure 4.2, which shows mean Task 2 RTs (solid curves) from a PRP study by Hawkins et al. (1979), who manipulated response-selection difficulty by varying the number of S–R pairs in Task 2. Here the Task 2 difficulty effect is only about 25 msec at the shortest SOA, whereas it is nearly 200 msec at the longest SOA.[1] Reliable positive interactions like this have also been reported by several other investigators (e.g., Ivry et al., 1994, 1995; Karlin and Kestenbaum, 1968; Lauber et al., 1994).

A plausible interpretation of these results is that: (1) at short SOAs, response selection for Task 2 occurs independently and simultaneously with response

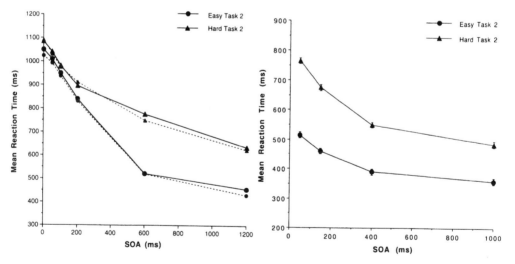

Figure 4.2

Left panel: divergent PRP curves obtained by Hawkins et al. (1979) with an auditory-manual Task 1 and a visual-manual Task 2. The solid functions represent mean Task 2 RT's observed when response selection for Task 2 was "easy" (large circles) or "hard" (large triangles). Each observed mean RT has a standard error of approximately 10 msec. Dashed functions (small circles and triangles) represent simulated mean Task 2 RT's from the SRD model to be discussed later (Fig. 7). Right panel: convergent PRP curves obtained by Ivry et al. (1995, 1995, Exp. 2) with a visual-manual Task 1 and a visual-manual Task 2. Mean Task 2 RT's plus-or-minus one standard error (based on the SOA-by-difficulty-by-subject interaction) are shown.

selection for Task 1; (2) progress on Task 2 pauses temporarily before initiation of its response movement, letting Task 1 finish first, as required by instructions for the PRP procedure; and (3) the slack introduced by this pause aborbs the effects of response-selection difficulty on Task 2 when the SOA is short. Keele (1973) and others have discussed how the latter sequence of events could yield the type of positive interaction in Figure 4.2 (left panel), whereas temporally separate response selection stages for Tasks 1 and 2 would not. Consequently, the absence of strict additivity between the effects of SOA and Task 2 response-selection difficulty raises compelling doubts about the existence of a pervasive immutable response-selection bottleneck.

3.2 Convergent PRP Curves

Another complementary RT pattern for which the RSB hypothesis cannot account very well involves convergent PRP curves. Such convergence occurs when the difficulty of selecting Task 2 responses affects mean Task 2 RTs more at short SOAs than at long SOAs, yielding a negative SOA-by-difficulty inter-action. Several cases like this have been reported recently (e.g., Ivry et al., 1994, 1995; Lauber et al., 1994).[2] For example, consider the right panel of Figure 4.2. Here mean Task 2 RTs are plotted from a PRP study by Ivry et al. (1994, 1995, Exp. 2), who manipulated response-selection difficulty by varying the spatial S–R compatibility in Task 2. At the shortest SOA, the difficulty effect on mean Task 2 RT is nearly 300 msec, whereas at the longest SOA, it is less than 200 msec, forming a substantial negative SOA-by-difficulty interaction. Given this pattern, Ivry et al. (1995) attributed their results to "resource sharing strategies." In contrast, the RSB hypothesis offers no simple satisfying answers for why, across various experiments, PRP curves sometimes converge or diverge as a function of SOA and Task 2 response-selection difficulty.

3.3 Slopes Steeper than −1

The plausibility of a pervasive immutable response-selection bottleneck is likewise reduced by carefully examining the slopes that PRP curves sometimes have. For example, consider the left panel of Figure 4.3, which shows mean Task 2 RTs from a study by Lauber et al. (1994, Exp. 2). These data were obtained under conditions similar to those of Hawkins et al. (1979), except that the present Task 1 had more S–R pairs (viz., four instead of two). This change yielded "parallel" (i.e., vertically equidistant) average PRP curves with approximately additive effects of SOA and Task 2 difficulty, as the RSB hypothesis predicts. However, over their two shortest SOAs, Lauber et al. (1994, Exp. 2) found that the PRP curves in Figure 4.3 had extremely negative slopes (almost −1.4 on average) that were reliably steeper than −1. Such extreme steepness was also found by Hawkins et al. (1979) in some of their conditions. Why and how might this happen? In reply, the RSB hypothesis again has no ready answer. As mentioned before, it implies that the slopes of PRP curves should be −1 or shallower (cf. Figure 4.1).

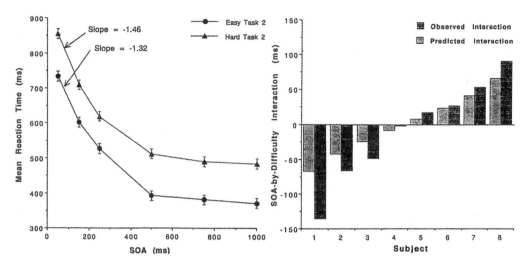

Figure 4.3
Left panel: "parallel" (i.e., vertically equidistant) average PRP curves obtained by Lauber et al. (1994, Exp. 2) with an auditory-manual Task 1 and a visual-manual Task 2. Mean Task 2 RT's plus-or-minus one standard error (based on the SOA-by-difficulty-by-subject interaction) are shown. Right panel: observed and predicted interactions between effects of SOA and response-selection difficulty on mean Task 2 RT's for eight subjects whose average PRP curves appear in the left panel. Nearly all of the dark vertical bars (observed interactions) are more extreme (RMS error = 29 ms; $p < 0.05$) than the light vertical bars (predicated interactions), which comes from the RSB hypothesis.

3.4 Systematic Individual Differences

Other implications of the RSB hypothesis may be refuted by comparing PRP curves from different subjects. If everyone has an immutable response-selection bottleneck, then each subject in an experiment should produce the same qualitative pattern of mean Task 2 RTs. Nevertheless, occasional checks for such homogeneity have instead revealed striking systematic individual differences (e.g., Ivry et al., 1994, 1995; Lauber et al., 1994).

For example, consider the right panel of Figure 4.3. Here we have plotted observed interactions between the effects of SOA and response-selection difficulty on mean Task 2 RTs for each of eight subjects who contributed to the average PRP curves of Figure 4.3's left panel. Across the horizontal axis of Figure 4.3's right panel, these subjects are ordered according to the magnitudes and signs of their SOA-by-difficulty interactions. On the vertical axis, a zero interaction indicates that a subject produced equal Task 2 difficulty effects at the shortest and longest SOAs, consistent with "parallel" PRP curves. A positive interaction indicates that the subject's PRP curves diverged as the SOA increased, and a negative interaction indicates that they converged. The dark vertical bars show how positive or negative each subject's interaction was. Three subjects had marked negative interactions (dark vertical bars extending downward) and convergent PRP curves. One subject had a near-zero interaction and virtually "parallel" PRP curves. Four other subjects had various degrees of positive interaction (dark vertical bars extending upward) and divergent PRP curves.

In contrast, the light vertical bars of Figure 4.3 (right panel) represent what the RSB hypothesis predicts for a sample of eight such subjects. These predictions were obtained by assuming that each subject belongs to a homogeneous population whose members all have theoretically additive effects of SOA and Task 2 response-selection difficulty. With this assumption, we estimated the distribution from which the subjects' observed interactions should come, given how much between-trial variance there was in each subject's data. Thus, if every subject had a response-selection bottleneck, then the light bars ought to match the dark bars closely.

However, this expected equivalence did not occur. A large majority (i.e., 7/8) of the dark vertical bars in Figure 4.3 (right panel) are longer than the light bars paired with them, revealing interactions consistently more extreme than the RSB hypothesis predicts. Our results instead suggest that there are two (or more) distinct subgroups of subjects, including some (e.g., Subject 1) who produce significantly convergent PRP curves and others (e.g., Subject 8) who produce significantly divergent PRP curves. Such individual differences reinforce two conclusions: people do not have immutable response-selection bottlenecks; other mechanisms—whose parameters depend on personal predilections—are the source of observed PRP effects.

3.5 Effects of Special Training

Finally, consistent with the preceding conclusions, some studies have revealed that subjects' PRP curves can be modified predictably through special types of training (e.g., Koch, 1993, 1994; Lauber et al., 1994; Sanders, 1964). Such results affirm that whatever the source of the PRP effect, it is certainly not "immutable." For example, during another study by Lauber et al. (1994, Exp. 3), additional subjects were tested under the same PRP procedure that yielded the data in Figure 4.3. However, they received special preliminary training before the PRP procedure began. This training, which followed the suggestions by Gopher (1993) about how to optimize multiple-task performance, required concurrent auditory-manual and visual-manual tasks to be performed as quickly as possible with equally high priority and relaxed constraints on the order of the tasks' stimuli and responses. As a result, subjects were strongly encouraged to overlap their response-selection processes for the two tasks. After this training finished, subjects then entered the standard PRP procedure.

Figure 4.4 (left panel) shows average Task 2 PRP curves that Lauber et al. (1994, Exp. 3) thereby obtained. Unlike before (cf. Figure 4.3, left panel), these new curves diverge substantially. At the shortest SOA, Task 2 response-selection difficulty has relatively little effect on mean Task 2 RTs, whereas at the

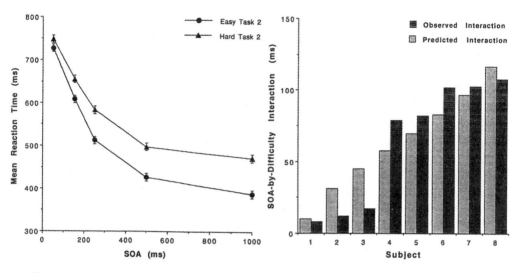

Figure 4.4
Left panel: divergent average PRP curves obtained by Lauer et al. (1994, Exp. 3) after subjects re-ceived special preliminary training that encouraged concurrent response-selection forn an auditory-manual Task 1 and a visual-manual Task 2. Mean Task 2 RT's plus-or-minus one standard error (based on the SOA-by-difficulty-by-subject interaction) are shown. Right panel: observed and pre-dicted positive interactions (RMS error = 17 ms) between effects of SOA and response-selection difficulty on man Task 2 RT's for eight subjects who contributed to the average PRP curves in the left panel. The predicted interactions (light vertical bars) assume that these subjects belong to a single homogeneous population whose members produce different amounts of observed positive interaction (dark vertical bars) only because of inherent between-trial variability in their RT's.

longest SOA, there is still a substantial difficulty effect. Furthermore, during the PRP procedure, all of the subjects who received special training produced some positive interaction between the effects of SOA and Task 2 difficulty (Figure 4.4, right panel). This latter outcome, combined with other prior ones (Figures 4.2 and 4.3), seems rather problematic for the RSB hypothesis.

4 A New Theoretical Framework

If a pervasive immutable response-selection bottleneck does not mediate the PRP effect, then what is the effect's true source? As hinted already, an answer may be found in the instructions for the standard PRP procedure (Meyer and Kieras, 1992, 1994, 1995; Koch, 1993, 1994). They typically request that Task 1 receive absolute priority. For example, in Pashler and Johnston's (1989) study, subjects were told that they *"should respond as rapidly as possible to the first stim-ulus,"* and *"the experimenter emphasized the importance of making the first response as promptly as possible."* Similarly, in a study by Pashler (1984, Exp. 1, p. 365), subjects were instructed that *"the first stimulus must be responded to before the second."* Because of such constraints, people may postpone completing Task 2 at short SOAs even though they have the potential capacity to perform concurrent tasks with no between-task interference. To satisfy the PRP procedure's instructions, perhaps optional temporary bottlenecks are programmed at one or more stages of processing for Task 2, deferring Task 2 responses until Task 1 has finished. If so, then the magnitudes of PRP effects and the forms of PRP curves may be under strategic control, and this could account for many of the phenomena (e.g., Figure 4.2 through 4) that seem antithetical to the traditional RSB hypothesis. Given these possibilities, we have therefore begun to develop a new theoretical framework for describing and predicting human multiple-task performance through detailed executive computation models (Kieras and Meyer, 1994; Meyer and Kieras, 1992, 1994, 1995).

4.1 Basic Assumptions

The first basic assumption of our framework is that in some respects, people have substantial cognitive capacity for performing multiple concurrent tasks. More precisely, we assume that various task procedures can be executed simultaneously with distinct sets of production rules (cf. Anderson, 1976, 1983; Newell, 1973a). For example, while driving a car, a person may also be able to talk on a cellular telephone because the production rules used respectively for driving and conversing are distinct and applied in parallel. According to the present framework, there is no immutable decision or response-selection bottleneck for executing task procedures at a central cognitive level.

Instead, we attribute decrements in multiple-task performance to other sources such as limited peripheral sensory and motor mechanisms, which cause "structural interference" (cf. Kahneman, 1973). For example, while making phone calls in a car, most drivers cannot keep their eyes simultaneously on the phone dial and the road, nor can they keep both hands on the steering wheel and hold the telephone. Perhaps it is these sensory-motor constraints—not limited cognitive capacity—that restrict people's ability to drive safely and make phone calls at the same time.

We also assume that conflicts caused by sensory-motor constraints can be alleviated by properly scheduling the tasks at hand. In particular, concurrent tasks may be scheduled by efficient flexible executive processes that help people obey instructions about relative task priorities. For example, when a driver sees a highway exit, his or her executive processes may end a phone call so that both hands can be put on the steering wheel to take the exit safely.

Of course, not all of our assumptions are entirely new. Some theorists have already begun to describe the functions of executive control in human multiple-task performance (Baddeley, 1986; Duncan, 1986; Logan, 1985; McLeod, 1977; Neisser, 1967; Newell, 1973b; Norman and Shallice, 1986; Shallice, 1972). By characterizing the nature of executive processes more precisely, and by implementing them in the framework of a detailed system architecture, we take further steps toward a comprehensive theory that supplants the traditional RSB hypothesis.

4.2 The EPIC Architecture

To embody our basic assumptions, we have developed the EPIC (Executive-Process/Interactive-Control) architecture, which is intended to have many of the same basic properties as the human information-processing system (Kieras and Meyer, 1994; Meyer and Kieras, 1992, 1994, 1995). EPIC may be viewed as a conceptual neighbor of other previously proposed architectures such as the Model Human Processor (Card et al., 1983), ACT * (Anderson, 1983), and SOAR (Laird et al., 1987). Figure 4.5 shows EPIC's major components. Among them are specific modules devoted to perceptual, cognitive, and motor processing. The perceptual processors include ones for vision, audition, and touch. The

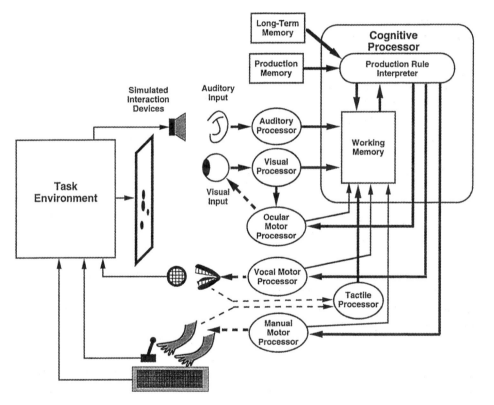

Figure 4.5
A schematic diagram of the EPIC (Executive-Process/Interactive-Control) architecture and the virtual task environment with which its components interact during computational simulations of human multiple-task performance.

motor processors include ones for manual, articulatory, and ocular action. Each module has software routines, written in the LISP programming language, that send and receive symbolic information to and from other parts of the overall system. Inputs to EPIC's perceptual processors come from simulated sensors (eyes, ears, etc.) that monitor external display devices (CRT screen, headphones, etc.) in a virtual task environment (e.g., the PRP procedure); outputs by EPIC's motor processors go to simulated effectors (hands, mouth, etc.) that operate the environment's external recording devices (keyboard, joystick, voice key, etc.). Constructing models based on EPIC involves programming its cognitive processor to interact with the task environment through the architecture's perceptual and motor processors.

Perceptual Processors During task performance, EPIC's perceptual processors detect and identify stimuli (printed alphanumeric characters, geometric objects, auditory tones, speech, etc.) that occur in the virtual task environment, depositing their symbolic representations in working memory. Consistent with previous empirical research (e.g., Pashler, 1989), each perceptual processor is assumed to operate asynchronously, in parallel with other components of the architecture. The times taken for stimulus detection and identification are task-dependent parameters, whose values we estimate from current data or past literature.

Cognitive Processor EPIC's cognitive processor has no immutable decision or response-selection bottleneck per se. Instead, it relies on three major subcomponents that enable a high degree of parallel processing. These subcomponents include an on-line declarative working memory, production memory, and production-rule interpreter that together implement sets of instructions whereby individual tasks are coordinated and performed simultaneously.

Working memory is assumed to contain various types of information, including (1) symbolic identities of external stimuli sent through EPIC's perceptual processors; (2) symbolic identities of selected responses waiting for transmission to EPIC's motor processor; (3) task goals; (4) sequential control flags; and (5) symbolic notes about the status of other system components (e.g., current motor-processor states). With this information, which evolves systematically over time, performance of each task may proceed efficiently from start to finish.

According to our assumptions, skilled performance is achieved by applying rules stored in EPIC's production memory. These rules, like those postulated by some other theorists (e.g., Anderson, 1976, 1983; Newell, 1973a), have the form "If X THEN Y", where "X" refers to the current contents of working memory, and "Y" refers to actions that the cognitive processor executes. For example, during a primary auditory-manual choice-reaction task, the following rule might be used to instruct EPIC's manual motor processor that it should prepare and produce a keypress by the left index finger in response to an 800 Hz tone:

```
IF
  ((GOAL DO TASK 1)
   (STEP DO CHECK FOR TONE 800)
   (AUDITORY TONE 800 ON)
   (STRATEGY TASK 1 RESPONSE MOVEMENT IS IMMEDIATE))
THEN
  ((SEND-TO-MOTOR (MANUAL PRESS LEFT INDEX))
   (ADD (TASK 1 RESPONSE UNDERWAY))
   (ADD (STEP WAIT FOR TASK 1 RESPONSE COMPLETION))
   (DEL (STEP DO CHECK FOR TONE 800))
   (DEL (AUDITORY TONE 800 ON))).
```

The actions of this rule, which not only instructs the manual motor processor but also adds and deletes specified symbolic items in working memory, would be executed whenever working memory contains all of the items in the rule's conditions. For each task that a person has learned to perform skillfully, there would be a set of such rules stored in EPIC's production memory. Also, complementing these task-rule sets, production memory is assumed to contain sets of executive-process rules that manage the contents of working memory, and that coordinate performance depending on task instructions and perceptual-motor constraints.

Task and executive rules in EPIC's production memory are tested and applied by the production-rule interpreter of EPIC's cognitive processor, using the Parsimonious Production System (PPS; Covrigaru and Kieras, 1987). Under PPS, the interpreter operates through a series of processing cycles, whose durations are assumed to have a mean length of 50 msec.[3] At the start of each cycle, the interpreter tests the conditions of all rules in production memory, determining which ones match the current contents of working memory. At the end of each cycle, for every rule whose conditions are completely matched by the current contents of working memory, all of the rule's actions are executed by the cognitive processor.

We assume that there is no limit on how many production rules can have their conditions tested and actions executed during any particular processing cycle. Also, the cycle durations do not depend on the number of rules involved. It is in this respect that EPIC's cognitive processor has no bottleneck per se. Through appropriate sets of task rules, the cognitive processor may simultaneously select responses and do other operations for multiple concurrent tasks, without between-task interference at this "central" level. Our computational models of multiple-task performance avoid conflicts among the actions of task rules at peripheral perceptual and motor levels by including executive-process rules that help coordinate and schedule tasks harmoniously.

Motor Processors   Upon receiving instructions from the cognitive processor, EPIC's motor processors convert symbolic identities of selected responses to specific features that desired overt movements should have. For example, a manual movement might have features that specify the style, hand, and finger (e.g., PRESS, LEFT, INDEX) to be used. We assume that the features for a response movement are prepared serially, with each feature adding a mean increment of 50 msec to the total movement-production time (cf. Rosenbaum, 1980). Under certain conditions, some features for anticipated response movements may be prepared in advance, if their identities are partially known beforehand. After all of the features for a response movement have been prepared, it is produced overtly through a final initiation step that likewise adds a mean increment of 50 msec. Because the motor preparation and initiation of overt movements are architecturally separate from the prior selection of symbolic response identities, EPIC enables precise control over the flow of information through its components. While response selection may occur simultaneously for multiple concurrent tasks, the production of distinct movements may be temporally staggered, depending on prevalent task instructions and available resources at the motor level.

As indicated already (Figure 4.5), EPIC includes distinct motor processors for manual, vocal, and ocular action. Each of these motor processors is assumed to operate in parallel with the others. We also assume, however, that each motor processor only has the capacity to prepare and initiate one response movement at a time. Thus, at the motor level, there are explicit peripheral bottlenecks in EPIC (cf. Ivry et al., 1994, 1995; Keele, 1973).

An especially relevant instance of this concerns manual movements. Based on results reported previously about manual movement production (e.g., McLeod, 1977), EPIC has only one motor processor devoted to preparing and initiating movements by the two (i.e., right and left) hands. Thus, for multiple manual tasks, substantial between-task interference is possible at the peripheral motor level. Such interference must be avoided through judicious executive control.

4.3 Adaptive Executive-Control Models

Within the framework of the EPIC architecture, we have formulated a class of adaptive executive-control (AEC) models to characterize performance in the PRP procedure. Our AEC models incorporate executive processes that flexibly control the extent to which progress on a secondary task overlaps with a primary task. Figure 4.6 illustrates how this control is achieved.

According to this view, performance of each task goes through several steps, including stimulus identification, response selection, and movement production, consistent with discrete stage models (Sternberg, 1969; Sanders, 1980). Furthermore, there is assumed to be an executive process that coordinates Tasks 1 and 2. Its supervisory functions include (1) enabling the primary and secondary tasks to proceed at the start of each trial; (2) specifying a Task 2 lockout point; (3) specifying a Task 1 unlocking event; (4) waiting for the Task 1

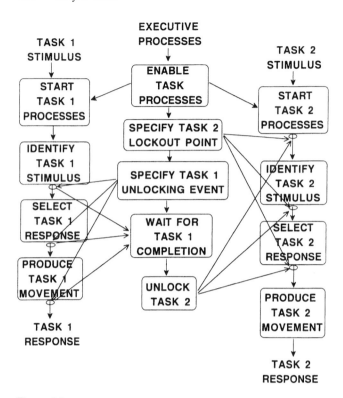

Figure 4.6
Component processes for the class of adaptive executive-control (AEC) models whereby the tasks of the PRP procedure may be flexibly coordinated.

unlocking event to occur; and (5) unlocking Task 2 processes so that they may be completed.

Task 2 Lockout Points   By definition, the Task 2 lockout point is a point during the course of Task 2 such that when it has been reached, further processing for Task 2 stops until Task 1 enters a "done" state. There are at least three potential alternative Task 2 lockout points (Figure 4.6, right-side ovals), which are located respectively before the start of stimulus identification, response selection, and movement production for Task 2. Depending on whether the executive process specifies a pre-movement, pre-selection, or pre-identification lockout point, progress on Task 2 would overlap more or less with Task 1.

Task 1 Unlocking Events   The extent of such overlap is also influenced by the specification of a Task 1 unlocking event. By definition, this is an event during the course of Task 1 such that when it occurs, Task 1 is deemed to be "done," and the executive process permits processing for Task 2 to continue beyond the Task 2 lockout point. There are several potential alternative Task 1 unlocking events (Figure 4.6, left-side ovals); Task 1 may be deemed "done" immediately after either its stimulus-identification, response-selection, or movement-production stage finishes. Again, depending on whether the executive process specifies a post-identification, post-selection, or post-movement unlocking event, progress on Task 2 would overlap more or less with Task 1.

Executive Production Rules   At the start of each trial, our AEC models' executive process specifies a particular Task 2 lockout point and Task 1 unlocking event by putting their designations in working memory. For example, the following executive production rule enables a post-response-selection lockout point for Task 2 and a post-movement-initiation unlocking event for Task 1:

```
IF
  ((GOAL DO PRP PROCEDURE)
   (STRATEGY AUDITORY-MANUAL TASK 1)
   (STRATEGY VISUAL-MANUAL TASK 2)
   (VISUAL FIXATION POINT DETECTED)
   (NOT (TRIAL UNDERWAY)))
THEN
  ((SEND-TO-MOTOR MANUAL RESET)
   (DEL (VISUAL FIXATION POINT DETECTED))
   (ADD (TRIAL UNDERWAY))
   (ADD (GOAL DO TASK 1))
   (ADD (GOAL DO TASK 2))
   (ADD (STRATEGY TASK 2 RESPONSE MOVEMENT IS DEFERRED))
   (ADD (STRATEGY UNLOCK ON MOTOR-SIGNAL MANUAL STARTED
   LEFT))
   (ADD (STEP WAIT FOR TASK 1 DONE)))).
```

Subsequently, when EPIC's manual motor processor informs the cognitive processor that the Task 1 response movement (a left-hand key press) has been initiated, the following executive production rule unlocks Task 2 and lets it finish:

```
IF
  ((GOAL DO PRP PROCEDURE)
   (STRATEGY AUDITORY-MANUAL TASK 1)
   (STRATEGY VISUAL-MANUAL TASK 2)
   (STEP WAIT-FOR TASK 1 DONE))
   (TASK 1 DONE)
THEN
  ((DEL (STEP WAIT-FOR TASK 1 DONE))
   (DEL (TASK 1 DONE))
   (DEL (STRATEGY TASK 2 RESPONSE MOVEMENT IS DEFERRED))
   (ADD (STRATEGY TASK 2 RESPONSE MOVEMENT IS IMMEDIATE))
   (ADD (STEP WAIT-FOR TASK 2 DONE)))).
```

As a result, response-selection but not movement-production stages for the two tasks could overlap. Other executive production rules may enable different lockout points and unlocking events instead of those just illustrated, regulating the amount of overlap that actually occurs.

Particular AEC Models   Overall, the class of AEC models includes many particular cases. For each possible combination of Task 2 lockout point and Task 1 unlocking event, there is a different set of executive production rules that can implement this combination, achieving a certain discretionary amount of temporal overlap between the two tasks. Which executive process is used under what circumstances may vary with task instructions, strategic goals, perceptual-motor requirements, and past experience.

In particular, one of our AEC models can mimic a response-selection bottleneck. Its executive process does this by specifying a pre-selection lockout point for Task 2 and a post-selection unlocking event for Task 1, thereby precluding response selection during Task 2 until Task 1 response selection has finished. Within EPIC's framework, however, such specifications are neither obligatory nor immutable, contrary to the traditional RSB hypothesis. An optional response-selection bottleneck may, but need not, be imposed when the situation encourages making extremely sure that Task 2 responses never precede Task 1 responses.

Other particular AEC models can mimic additional types of bottleneck. For example, Keele (1973) has hypothesized that a movement-initiation bottleneck rather than a response-selection bottleneck exists in the human information-processing system. Consistent with this hypothesis, an executive process may defer Task 2 movement initiation by specifying a post-selection/pre-movement lockout point for Task 2 and a post motor-initiation unlocking event for Task 1. Again, however, such specifications are neither obligatory nor immutable in EPIC. An optional movement-initiation bottleneck may, but need not, be imposed when the situation encourages producing Task 2 responses as quickly as possible after Task 1 finishes.

5 Qualitative Accounts of PRP Phenomena

Unified qualitative accounts for a variety of PRP phenomena, including many beyond the scope of the traditional RSB hypothesis, are provided by the EPIC architecture and its AEC models.

PRP Effect   In terms of our theoretical framework, elevated Task 2 RTs at short SOAs result mainly from having to satisfy task instructions for the PRP procedure. Due to these instructions, Task 2 cannot proceed freely from start to finish along with Task 1, because doing so might yield premature Task 2 responses when Task 1 is relatively hard and the SOA is short. Thus, executive processes for the PRP procedure must, out of strategic necessity, specify some intermediate unlocking event and lockout point for Tasks 1 and 2 respectively, delaying overt Task 2 responses enough that they never precede Task 1 responses. Recently, Koch (1993, 1994) has offered an independent account of the PRP effect that is similar to ours, thereby reinforcing some of the present article's main premises.

Diverse Forms of PRP Curves   Given the adjustability of their lockout points and unlocking events, our AEC models likewise imply that PRP curves may have diverse forms. If the executive process adopts a pre-selection lockout point for Task 2, then it can yield "parallel" (i.e., vertically equidistant) PRP curves of mean Task 2 RTs as in Figure 4.1. This would seem especially plausible when Task 1 is relatively difficult and has a high probability of finishing after Task 2 at short SOAs unless the executive process strongly intervenes. In contrast, if Task 1 is relatively easy and encourages a more ambitious strategy that needs to guard less against premature Task 2 responses, then the executive process may adopt a post-selection lockout point for Task 2, thereby producing divergent PRP curves like those in the left panels of Figures 4.2 and 4.4 (Meyer and Kieras, 1992, 1994, 1995).

Convergent PRP curves (e.g., Figure 4.2, right panel) are also accommodated naturally by our AEC models (Meyer and Kieras, 1995). Suppose that at the start of each trial, the unlocking event and lockout point specified for Tasks 1 and 2, respectively, depend on the anticipated difficulty of response selection in Task 2. Also, suppose that the specified Task 2 lockout point is a relatively earlier one when Task 2 will be difficult than when it will be easy, whereas the Task 1 unlocking event is a relatively later one. Then less overlap may occur between Tasks 1 and 2 at short SOAs in the difficult Task 2 condition than in the easy Task 2 condition, causing the difficult Task 2 to manifest a larger PRP effect than does the easy Task 2. Combined with the main effect of Task 2 difficulty at long SOAs, this difference between PRP effects in the easy and difficult Task 2 conditions would yield a pair of converging PRP curves. A possible rationale for such difficulty-dependent task scheduling is that, although not necessary under EPIC, it may seem to help preclude a difficult Task 2 from interfering more with Task 1 than does an easy Task 2.

Slopes Steeper than −1   Similarly, our AEC models account for PRP curves whose slopes are steeper than −1. Suppose that at the start of each trial, the executive process specifies an initial cautious unlocking event and lockout point for Tasks 1 and 2, respectively. Also, suppose that after the Task 1 stimulus has arrived, no Task 2 stimulus is detected during a subsequent period of time (i.e., the SOA is somewhat greater than zero). Then the executive process may modify the Task 2 lockout point and/or Task 1 unlocking event by updating their designations in working memory, because Task 1 now has a better chance of finishing first without much further delay in Task 2. Specifically, the executive process could make the modified Task 2 lockout point be later and/or Task 1 unlocking event be earlier than they were before, using what we call *progressive unlocking* (Meyer and Kieras, 1995). With progressive unlocking, mean Task

2 RTs at intermediate SOAs would be less than when the lockout point and unlocking event are static throughout each trial. The extra RT reduction, combined with the usual RT decrement caused by increasing the SOA, therefore yields PRP curves whose slopes are steeper than −1, as in Figure 4.3 (left panel). Indeed, such extreme steepness may be a hallmark of sophisticated executive processes that are sensitive to rapidly evolving contingencies in multiple-task performance.

Individual Differences   Of course, if people have such executive control, then individual differences might occur in their patterns of PRP curves. Depending on personal factors, different subjects may be inclined to adopt different Task 2 lockout points and Task 1 unlocking events. If so, then this would yield mixtures of diverging, parallel, and converging PRP curves, as some investigators have reported (e.g., Ivry et al., 1994, 1995; Lauber et al., 1994). Furthermore, the curves produced by any particular individual might change from one set of conditions to another, depending on how each condition meshes with the subject's predilections.

Training Effects   Yet despite these individual differences, our AEC models also imply that executive processes can be shaped and homogenized through proper experience. If Task 2 lockout points and Task 1 unlocking events are adjustable, then certain types of training should induce more overlap between primary and secondary tasks. For example, subjects might come to adopt more optimal executive processes when responses must be produced rapidly in an unconstrained rather than constrained order (Koch, 1993, 1994; Lauber et al., 1994; cf. Pashler, 1990). Consequently, upon later transfer to the standard PRP procedure, PRP curves may embody a pattern that is similar across subjects and indicative of concurrent response selection (e.g., Figure 4.4). Moreover, if there are no constraints on the order in which subjects must make their responses, then the PRP effect may virtually disappear (Koch, 1993, 1994), consistent with EPIC's capacity to select and execute multiple responses simultaneously.

6 Computational Simulations of Quantitative PRP Data

Additional justification of present claims is provided by computational simulations that account quantitatively for data from the PRP procedure (Meyer and Kieras, 1992, 1994, 1995). Our simulations to data are based on one instructive member of the AEC class. We call it the strategic response-deferment (SRD) model.

6.1 Strategic Response-Deferment Model
Figure 4.7 shows the SRD model's executive process, which starts each trial of the PRP procedure by putting Tasks 1 and 2 in "immediate" and "deferred" mode, respectively. While Task 2 is in deferred mode, the identities of Task 2 responses may be selected and sent to working memory, but Task 2 response

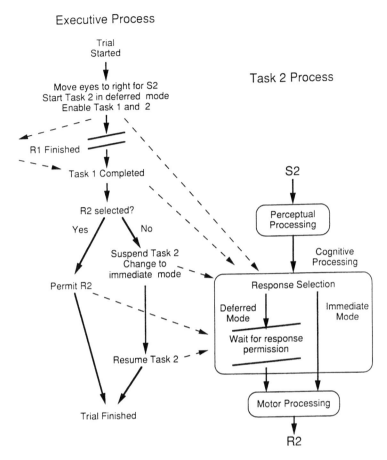

Figure 4.7
Flowchart for executive and Task 2 processes under the strategic response-deferment model.

movements are not produced by EPIC's motor processors. This constraint is imposed by assigning a post-selection/pre-motor lockout point to Task 2. Putting Task 1 in immediate mode lets its responses be selected and sent directly to their motor processor. When the Task 1 unlocking event occurs (e.g., the Task 1 response movement is initiated), the executive process temporarily suspends Task 2 (i.e., withdraws "GOAL DO TASK 2" from working memory) and shifts it to immediate mode, after which Task 2 is resumed again (i.e., "GOAL DO TASK 2" is reinserted in working memory). Following this transition, previously selected Task 2 responses are sent directly from working memory to their motor processor. If response selection has not yet finished for Task 2 before it enters the immediate mode, then Task 2 production rules may both select and send Task 2 responses to their motor processor. Because response selection for Task 2 is suspended briefly during the transition from deferred to immediate mode, the SRD model has a flexible combination of temporary "soft" movement-initiation and response-selection bottlenecks (cf. De Jong, 1993; Kantowitz, 1974; Keele, 1973).[4]

6.2 Simulations With the SRD Model

With the SRD model, we have successfully simulated quantitative data from many representative PRP studies (e.g., Hawkins et al., 1979; Karlin and Kestenbaum, 1968; McCann and Johnston, 1992; Pashler, 1990), confirming the utility of the EPIC architecture and the validity of our present theoretical claims (Meyer and Kieras, 1992, 1994, 1995).

PRP Study by Hawkins et al. (1979)   One PRP study that has provided us with extensive relevant data is by Hawkins et al. (1979). In part of this study, subjects performed an auditory-vocal Task 1 (saying words in response to two alternative tones) and an easy or hard visual-manual Task 2 (pressing keys in response to either two or eight alternative printed digits). A comparison between Hawkins et al.'s empirical mean RTs from these conditions and simulated mean RTs from the SRD model appears in Figure 4.8 (left panel, solid vs. dashed curves).

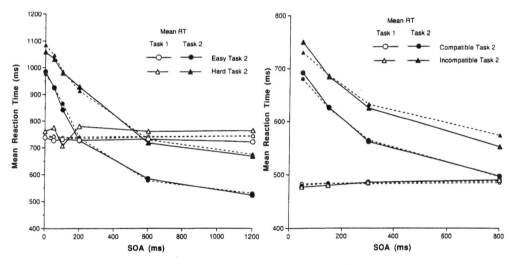

Figure 4.8

Left panel: goodness-of-fit between simulated mean RT's (small symbols on dashed curves) from the SRD model and empirical mean RT's (large symbols on solid curves) from Hawkins et al.'s (1979) PRP study with an auditory-vocal Task 1 and a visual-manual Task 2. Filled circles and triangles represent Task 2 RT's when response-selection was respectively easy or hard; unfilled circles and triangles represent corresponding Task 1 RT's. Right panel: goodness-of-fit between simulated mean RT's from the SRD model and empirical mean RT's from McCann and Johnston's (1992, Exp. 2) PRP study.

As this graph indicates, the SRD model accounts well ($R^2 = 0.99$) for the positive interaction that Hawkins et al. (1979) found between SOA and response-selection difficulty in Task 2, which yielded divergent PRP curves. This follows because the model's executive process lets response selection proceed simultaneously for Tasks 1 and 2 at short SOAs, so the difficulty effect on Task 2 is absorbed by waiting for the Task 1 unlocking event. With optional progressive unlocking (Meyer and Kieras, 1995), the executive process accurately reproduces a slope significantly steeper than −1, which occurred in the PRP curve at short SOAs when Task 2 was relatively easy (Figure 4.8, left panel). Our simulations of other data from Hawkins et al.'s (1979) study also produced good fits (e.g., see Figure 4.2, left panel, solid vs. dashed curves).[5]

PRP Study by McCann and Johnston (1992)   In addition, the SRD model accounts well for data from studies that have yielded "parallel" (i.e., vertically equidistant) rather than divergent PRP curves. For example, consider the right panel of Figure 4.8, which shows some of McCann and Johnston's (1992, Exp. 2) data. Here the effects of SOA and response-selection difficulty on empirical mean Task 2 RTs (solid curves) are additive. Similarly, simulated mean Task 2 RTs (dashed curves) produced by the SRD model manifest such additivity ($R^2 = 0.99$).

The latter pattern can be understood more fully in terms of how McCann and Johnston's (1992, Exp. 2) subjects were tested. During the PRP procedure, they performed an auditory-vocal Task 1 (saying words in response to tones) together with an easy or hard visual-manual Task 2 (pressing keys in response to horizontal arrows or printed letters). On each trial, a relatively small Task 2 stimulus was displayed several degrees to the right or left of a central visual fixation point. Subjects could not predict beforehand exactly where the Task 2 stimulus would be located. Following the SOA, eye movements presumably had to be made for stimulus identification in Task 2. This requirement— which is mimicked by the SRD model—probably created a temporary peripheral perceptual bottleneck that precluded Task 2 response selection from overlapping with response selection for Task 1. Because Task 1 was relatively easy, subjects may have already finished it and entered the unlocking phase of the SRD model (Figure 4.7) before the Task 2 stimulus identity became available for response selection (Meyer and Kieras, 1994, 1995).

More generally, this interpretation raises an important meta-theoretical point. Results (e.g., "parallel" PRP curves) that are superficially consistent with the traditional RSB hypothesis may actually have much subtler sources. Thus, future interpretation of data from the standard PRP procedure and other multiple-task paradigms should take such subtleties more fully into account.

7 Conclusion

In conclusion, our discourse on the RSB hypothesis, PRP procedure, EPIC architecture, and AEC/SRD models has potentially significant implications for characterizing discrete versus continuous human information processing. If the present theoretical claims are valid, then people's performance may entail a variety of concurrent discrete perceptual-motor and cognitive processes that provide symbolic partial outputs to each other. We therefore concur with at least some of the assumptions made by Miller's (1982, 1988) asynchronous discrete-coding model, under which stimulus identification and response selection overlap temporally, producing quantized intermediate outputs about relevant stimulus and response features, respectively. Furthermore, it now appears that when two or more tasks do not logically conflict, sets of production rules for them may be used simultaneously as if procedural cognitive processes have multiple channels rather than a single-channel response-selection bottleneck.

Another lesson from our research is that even in very elementary situations, sophisticated executive processes play a crucial role. For any task, there are many alternative paths from stimulus input to response output in the human information-processing system. The path that is actually taken, and the extent to which processing may seem "discrete" or "continuous," can depend on control strategies that subjects adopt. Future research on discrete versus continuous processing should take these strategies more fully into account. This may be facilitated by formulating a comprehensive system architecture and detailed computational models. An important role of such models will be to help specify how working memory is judiciously used so that procedural cognitive processes may interact effectively with limited-capacity peripheral perceptual-motor components.

Of course, now is not the first occasion on which human-performance theorists have needed to radically change their world view. More than fifty years ago, for example, a dominant model in sensory psychophysics was high-threshold theory (HTT). Analogous to the traditional RSB hypothesis, HTT claimed that people detect simple sensory stimuli (e.g., lights, tones, etc.) through a discrete all-or-none threshold mechanism. In order for a stimulus to be detected and reported, its subjective intensity supposedly had to exceed an absolute level within this mechanism. Because of the assumed threshold's rigidity, little or no accommodation was provided by HTT for subjects' possible judgment strategies. As a result, many problematic aspects of psychophysical data went unexplained. Then, however, statistical signal-detection theory (SDT) emerged on the scene, reconciling phenomena that had previously bedeviled HTT (Tanner and Swets, 1954).

Unlike HTT, this new framework assumed no discrete absolute high threshold; instead, SDT attributed subjects' detection performance to stochastic processes that involve a continuum of sensory states and adjustable decision criteria. According to SDT, people set their decision criteria strategically to achieve various combinations of stimulus "hits" and noise "correct rejections," depending on prevailing reward schemes. The adjustable decision criteria of

SDT have much the same spirit as the flexible lockout points and unlocking events of our AEC models for the PRP procedure. As in our AEC models, a key insight of SDT has been that even the seemingly most elementary human performance—for example, detection of sensory stimuli—is governed by sophisticated programmable executive processes rather than just rigid peripheral mechanisms. Perhaps keeping this historical precedent in mind will help smooth the entry of human-performance theory into a Brave New World without pervasive immutable response-selection bottlenecks.

Acknowledgements

We gratefully acknowledge helpful comments, suggestions, and criticisms from Bert Mulder, Andries Sanders, and our many other colleagues. Financial support has been provided by the U.S. Office of Naval Research through grant N00014-92-J-1173 to the University of Michigan.

Notes

1. Mean Task 1 RTs equalled slightly more than 600 ms and were not affected very much by either the SOA or Task 2 response-selection difficulty (Hawkins et al., 1979).
2. Converging PRP curves may occur even when there are very little effects of SOA and/or Task 2 response-selection difficulty on mean Task 1 RTs (Lauber et al., 1994).
3. During actual runs, the cognitive processor's cycle durations are sampled from a distribution whose standard deviation is typically 10 ms (i.e., 20% of the 50 ms mean), introducing realistic stochastic variation into simulated RT data (Kieras and Meyer, 1994; Meyer and Kieras, 1992, 1994, 1995).
4. Unlike the movement-initiation bottleneck hypothesis of Keele (1973) and the multiple-bottleneck hypothesis of De Jong (1993), however, the SRD model assumes that these bottlenecks are optional—not immutable—ones programmed by the executive process to efficiently satisfy instructions of the PRP procedure.
5. Across these different conditions, the number of variable parameter values used by the SRD model was markedly less than the number of reliable one-degree-of-freedom contrasts between mean RTs in Hawkins et al.'s data (Meyer and Kieras, 1995).

References

Allport, D. A., 1980. 'Attention and performance'. In: G. L. Claxton (ed.), Cognitive psychology: New directions (pp. 112–153). London: Routledge and Kegan Paul.

Allport, D. A., 1987. 'Selection-for-action: Some behavioral and neurophysiological considerations of attention and action'. In: H. Heuer and A. F. Sanders (eds.), Perspectives on perception and action (pp. 395–419). Hillsdale, NJ: Erlbaum.

Anderson, J. R., 1976. Language, memory, and thought. Hillsdale, NJ: Erlbaum.

Anderson, J. R., 1983. The architecture of cognition. Cambridge, MA: Harvard University Press.

Anderson, J. A. and G. E. Hinton, 1981. 'Models of information processing in the brain'. In: G. E. Hinton and J. A. Anderson (eds.), Parallel models of associative memory. Hillsdale, NJ: Erlbaum.

Baddeley, A. D., 1986. Working memory. Oxford: Oxford University Press.

Becker, C. A., 1976. Allocation of attention during visual word recognition. Journal of Experimental Psychology: Human Perception and Performance 2, 556–566.

Bertelson, P., 1966. Central intermittency 20 years later. Quarterly Journal of Experimental Psychology 18, 153–164.

Card, S. K., T. P. Moran and A. Newell, 1983. The psychology of human–computer interaction. Hillsdale, NJ: Erlbaum.

Covrigaru, A. and D. E. Kieras, 1987. PPS: A parsimonious production system. Tech. Rep. No. 26, TR-87/ONR-26. Ann Arbor, MI: University of Michigan, Technical Communication Program.

Craik, K. J. W., 1948. Theory of the human operator in control systems: II. Man as an element in a control system. British Journal of Psychology 38, 142–148.

Davis, R., 1957. The human operator as a single-channel information system. Quarterly Journal of Experimental Psychology 9, 119–129.

De Jong, R., 1993. Multiple bottlenecks in overlapping task performance. Journal of Experimental Psychology: Human Perception and Performance 19, 965–980.

Duncan, J., 1986. Disorganization of behaviour after frontal lobe damage. Cognitive Neuropsychology 3, 271–290.

Gopher, D., 1993. 'Attentional control: Acquisition and execution of attentional strategies'. In: D. E. Meyer and S. Kornblum (eds.), Attention and performance XIV. Synergies in experimental psychology, artificial intelligence, and cognitive neuroscience. Cambridge, MA: MIT Press.

Gottsdanker, R., 1980. 'The ubiquitous role of preparation'. In: G. E. Stelmach and J. Requin (eds.), Tutorials in motor behavior (pp. 315–371). Amsterdam: North-Holland.

Gottsdanker, R. and G. E. Stelmach, 1971. The persistence of psychological refractoriness. Journal of Motor Behavior 3, 301–312.

Hawkins, H. L., E. Rodriguez and G. M. Reicher, 1979. Is time-sharing a general ability? ONR Technical Report No. 3, University of Oregon, Eugene, OR.

Ivry, R. B., E. A. Franz, A. Kingstone and J. C. Johnston, 1994 (November). The PRP effect in a split-brain patient: Response uncoupling despite normal interference. Paper presented at the meeting of the Psychonomic Society, St. Louis, MO.

Ivry, R. B., E. A. Franz, A. Kingstone and J. C. Johnston, 1995. The PRP effect following callosotomy: Residual interference despite uncoupling of lateralized response codes. Manuscript submitted for publication.

James, W., 1890. The principles of psychology. New York: Holt.

Kahneman, D., 1973. Attention and effort. Englewood Cliffs, NJ: Prentice-Hall.

Kantowitz, B. H., 1974. 'Double stimulation'. In: B. H. Kantowitz (ed.), Human information processing: Tutorials in performance and cognition (pp. 83–131). Hillsdale, NJ: Erlbaum.

Karlin, L. and R. Kestenbaum, 1968. Effects of number of alternatives on the psychological refractory period. Quarterly Journal of Experimental Psychology 20, 67–178.

Keele, S. W., 1973. Attention and human performance. Pacific Palisades, CA: Goodyear.

Kieras, D. E. and D. E. Meyer, 1994. The EPIC architecture for modeling human information-processing and performance: A brief introduction. Technical Report TR-94/ONR-EPIC-1, University of Michigan, Ann Arbor.

Koch, R., 1993. Die psychologische Refraktärperiode. Doctoral dissertation, University of Bielefeld, Bielefeld, Germany.

Koch, R., 1994 (December). Hick's Law and the psychological refractory period. Paper presented at the KNAW Symposium on Discrete versus Continuous Information Processing, Amsterdam, The Netherlands.

Laird, J. E., A. Newell and P. S. Rosenbloom, 1987. SOAR: An architecture for general intelligence. Artificial Intelligence 33, 1–64.

Lauber E. J., E. H. Schumacher, J. Glass, E. Zurbriggen, D. E. Kieras and D. E. Meyer, 1994 (November). Adaptive PRP effects: Evidence of flexible attention to action. Paper presented at the meeting of the Psychonomic Society, St. Louis, MO.

Logan, G., 1985. Executive control of thought and action. Acta Psychologica 60, 193–210.

Luce, R. D., 1986. Response times: Their role in inferring elementary mental organization. New York: Oxford University Press.

McCann, R. S. and J. C. Johnston, 1992. Locus of the single-channel bottleneck in dual-task performance. Journal of Experimental Psychology: Human Perception and Performance 18, 471–484.

McLeod, P. D., 1977. A dual task response modality effect: Support for multiprocessor models of attention. Quarterly Journal of Experimental Psychology 29, 651–667.

McLeod, P., 1978. Parallel processing and the psychological refractory period. Acta Psychologica 41, 381–396.

Meyer, D. E. and D. E. Kieras, 1992 (November). The PRP effect: Central bottleneck, perceptual-motor limitations, or task strategies? Paper presented at the meeting of the Psychonomic Society, St. Louis, MO.

Meyer, D. E. and D. E. Kieras, 1994. EPIC computational models of psychological refractory-period effects in human multiple-task performance. Technical Report TR-94/ONR-EPIC-2, University of Michigan, Ann Arbor.

Meyer, D. E. and D. E. Kieras, 1995. A computational theory of human multiple-task performance: The EPIC architecture and strategic response-deferment model. Psychological Review, in press.

Meyer, D. E., A. M. Osman, D. E. Irwin and S. Yantis, 1988. Modern mental chronometry. Biological Psychology 26, 3–67.

Miller, J., 1982. Discrete versus continuous stage models of human information processing: In search of partial output. Journal of Experimental Psychology: Human Perception and Performance 8, 273–296.

Miller, J., 1988. Discrete and continuous models of human information processing: Theoretical distinctions and empirical results. Acta Psychologica 67, 191–257.

Moray, N., 1967. Where is capacity limited? A survey and a model. Acta Psychologica 27, 84–92.

Navon, D. and D. Gopher, 1979. One the economy of the human-processing system. Psychological Review 86, 214–255.

Neisser, U., 1967. Cognitive psychology. Englewood Cliffs, NJ: Prentice Hall.

Neumann, O., 1987. 'Beyond capacity: A functional view of attention'. In: H. Heuer and A. F. Sanders (eds.), Perspectives on perception and action (pp. 361–394). Hillsdale, NJ: Erlbaum.

Newell, A., 1973a. 'Production systems: Models of control structures'. In: W. G. Chase (ed.), Visual information processing (pp. 463–526). New York: Academic Press.

Newell, A., 1973b. 'You can't play 20 questions with nature and win'. In: W. G. Chase (ed.), Visual information processing (pp. 283–308). New York: Academic Press.

Norman, D. A., 1969. Memory and attention: An introduction to human information processing. New York: Wiley.

Norman, D. A. and T. Shallice, 1986. 'Attention to action: Willed and automatic control of behavior'. In: R. J. Davidson, G. E. Schwartz and D. Shapiro (eds.), Consciousness and self-regulation, Vol. 4. New York: Plenum Press.

Osman, A. M., T. R. Bashore, M. G. H. Coles, E. Donchin and D. E. Meyer, 1992. On the transmission of partial information: Inferences from movement-related brain potentials. Journal of Experimental Psychology: Human Perception and Performance 18, 217–232.

Pashler, H., 1984. Processing stages in overlapping tasks: Evidence for a central bottleneck. Journal of Experimental Psychology: Human Perception and Performance 10, 358–377.

Pashler, H., 1989. Dissociations and dependencies between speed and accuracy: Evidence for a two component theory of divided attention in simple tasks. Cognitive Psychology 21, 469–514.

Pashler, H., 1990. Do response modality effects support multiprocessor models of divided attention? Journal of Experimental Psychology: Human Perception and Performance 16, 826–842.

Pashler, H., 1993. 'Dual-task interference and elementary mental mechanisms'. In: D. E. Meyer and S. Kornblum (eds.), Attention and performance XIV. Synergies in experimental psychology, artificial intelligence, and cognitive neuroscience (pp. 245–264). Cambridge, MA: MIT Press.

Pashler, H., 1994. Dual-task interference in simple tasks: Data and theory. Psychological Bulletin 116, 220–244.

Pashler, H. and J. C. Johnston, 1989. Chronometric evidence of central postponement in temporally overlapping tasks. Quarterly Journal of Experimental Psychology 41A, 19–45.

Rosenbaum, D. A., 1980. Human movement initiation: Specification of arm, direction, and extent. Journal of Experimental Psychology: General 109, 475–495.

Rumelhart, D. E. and J. L. McClelland (eds.), 1986. Parallel distributed processing. Cambridge, MA: MIT Press.

Ruthruff, E., J. O. Miller and T. Lachmann, 1995. Does mental rotation require central mechanisms? Journal of Experimental Psychology: Human Perception and Performance, in press.

Sanders, A. F., 1964. Selective strategies in the assimilation of successively presented signals. Quarterly Journal of Experimental Psychology 16, 368–372.

Sanders, A. F., 1980. 'Stage analysis of reaction processes'. In: G. E. Stelmach and J. Requin (eds.), Tutorials in motor behavior (pp. 331–354). Amsterdam: North-Holland.

Schvaneveldt, R. W., 1969. Effects of complexity in simultaneous reaction time tasks. Journal of Experimental Psychology 81, 289–296.

Schweickert, R., A. Dutta, C. Sangsup and R. W. Proctor, 1992 (November). Scheduling processes using working memory. Paper presented at the meeting of the Psychonomic Society, St. Louis, MO.

Shallice, T., 1972. Dual functions of consciousness. Psychological Review 79, 383–393.

Smith, M. C., 1967. Theories of the psychological refractory period. Psychological Bulletin 67, 202–213.

Sternberg, S., 1969. On the discovery of processing stages: Some extensions of Donders' method. Acta Psychologica 30, 276–315.

Tanner, W. P., Jr. and J. A. Swets, 1954. A decision-making theory of visual detection. Psychological Review 61, 401–409.

Townsend, J. T. and F. G. Ashby, 1983. Stochastic modeling of elementary psychological processes. Cambridge: Cambridge University Press.

Van Selst, M. and P. Jolicoeur, 1993 (November). A response-selection account of the effect of number of alternatives on dual-task processing. Paper presented at the meeting of the Psychonomic Society, Washington, DC.

Vince, M. A., 1949. Rapid response sequences and the psychological refractory period. British Journal of Psychology 40, 23–40.

Welford, A. T., 1952. The "psychological refractory period" and the timing of high speed performance—A review and a theory. British Journal of Psychology 43, 2–19.

Welford, A. T., 1959. Evidence of a single-channel decision mechanism limiting performance in a serial reaction task. Quarterly Journal of Experimental Psychology 2, 193–210.

Welford, A. T., 1967. Single channel operation in the brain. Acta Psychologica 27, 5–22.

Wickens, C. D., 1984. 'Processing resources in attention'. In: R. Parasuraman, J. Beatty and R. Davies (eds.), Varieties of attention (pp. 63–101). New York: Wiley.

CAPS

Chapter 5

A Capacity Theory of Comprehension: Individual Differences in Working Memory

Marcel A. Just and Patricia A. Carpenter

Working memory plays a central role in all forms of complex thinking, such as reasoning, problem solving, and language comprehension. However, its function in language comprehension is especially evident because comprehension entails processing a sequence of symbols that is produced and perceived over time. Working memory plays a critical role in storing the intermediate and final products of a reader's or listener's computations as she or he constructs and integrates ideas from the stream of successive words in a text or spoken discourse. In addition to its role in storage, working memory can also be viewed as the pool of operational resources that perform the symbolic computations and thereby generate the intermediate and final products. In this chapter, we examine how the human cognitive capacity accommodates or fails to accommodate the transient computational and storage demands that occur in language comprehension. We also explain the differences among individuals in their comprehension performance in terms of their working memory capacity. The major thesis is that cognitive capacity constrains comprehension, and it constrains comprehension more for some people than for others.

This chapter begins with a general outline of a capacity theory of language comprehension. In the second section we use the capacity theory to account for several phenomena relating individual differences in language processing to working memory capacity. In the third section we describe a computer simulation model that instantiates the capacity theory. In the final section we discuss the implications of capacity theory for other aspects of cognition besides language comprehension.

Most recent conceptions of working memory extend its function beyond storage to encompass the actual computations themselves. The computations are symbolic manipulations that are at the heart of human thinking—such operations as comparison, retrieval, and logical and numerical operations. Of particular relevance are the processes that perform language comprehension. These processes, in combination with the storage resources, constitute working memory for language.

Construing working memory as an arena of computation was first advocated by Baddeley and Hitch (1974; Baddeley, 1986; Hitch & Baddeley, 1976), who constructed tasks that pitted the storage and processing aspects of comprehension against each other. They found that the ability to understand individual sentences rapidly and accurately decreased when listeners also had to encode several digits and later recall them. The trading relation between storage and processing suggested that the two functions were drawing on a common pool of resources. Thus, there are both conceptual and empirical reasons to express the dual roles of working memory within a single system.

It is important to point out the differences between our theory and Baddeley's (1986) conception of working memory. In our theory, working memory for language refers to a set of processes and resources that perform language comprehension. In Baddeley's theory, working memory has two components. One component consists of modality-specific storage systems, including the *articulatory loop*, a speech-based rehearsal buffer of fixed duration. The second component is the *central executive*. The central executive is the component that Baddeley addressed least in his empirical research and specified least in his theory; indeed, Baddeley termed the central executive "the area of residual ignorance" in his model (1986, p. 225). The working memory in our theory corresponds approximately to the part of the central executive in Baddeley's theory that deals with language comprehension. The working memory in our theory does not include modality-specific buffers, such as the articulatory loop.

Overview of the Theory

A major purpose of this article is to present a theoretical integration of the storage and processing functions of working memory in language comprehension. We present a computational theory in which both storage and processing are fueled by the same commodity: activation. In this framework, capacity can be expressed as the maximum amount of activation available in working memory to support either of the two functions.

In our theory, each representational element has an associated activation level. An element can represent a word, phrase, proposition, grammatical structure, thematic structure, object in the external world, and so on. The use of the activation level construct here is similar to its widespread use in other cognitive models, both symbolic (e.g., Anderson, 1983) and connectionist (e.g., McClelland & Rumelhart, 1988). During comprehension, information becomes activated by virtue of being encoded from written or spoken text, generated by a computation, or retrieved from long-term memory. As long as an element's activation level is above some minimum threshold value, that element is considered part of working memory, and consequently, it is available to be operated on by various processes. However, if the total amount of activation that is available to the system is less than the amount required to perform a comprehension task, then some of the activation that is maintaining old elements will be deallocated, producing a kind of forgetting by displacement. Thus, representations constructed early in a sentence may be forgotten by the time they are needed later on in the sentence, if enough computational activity has intervened. The activation is used not just for information maintenance—it is also the commodity that underlies computation. The computations are performed within a production system architecture in which productions manipulate symbols by modifying their activation levels. The most common manipulation occurs when a production increases the activation level of one of its action elements. Elements are added or deleted by changing their activation level appropriately.

The computations that are involved in language comprehension also can be expressed as manipulations of activation, as they typically are in connectionist models of comprehension (e.g., Cottrell, 1989; St. John & McClelland, 1990; Waltz & Pollack, 1985). In the current model, a production rule propagates activation from one element to another. The production has the source element as a condition, and the destination element as the action. The same production rule can fire repeatedly over successive cycles, reiteratively incrementing (or otherwise modifying) the target element's activation level, usually until it reaches some threshold. Consider an example in which the encounter with a grammatical subject of a sentence generates an expectation that a verb will occur. A proposition representing a grammatical subject is a source of activation for the proposition that a verb will be encountered. Thus, the rule-based processing typical of a symbolic system works in concert with the graded activation typical of a connectionist system.

Many of the processes underlying comprehension are assumed to occur in parallel. Thus, at the same time that the comprehender develops the expectation of encountering a verb, she or he could also be calculating other syntactic, semantic, and pragmatic features of the sentence. The theory proposes that all enabled processes can execute simultaneously, and generate partial products concurrently. However, if the number of processes (productions) is large or, more precisely, if the amount of activation they try to propagate would exceed the capacity, then their attempts at propagation are scaled back to a level that keeps the total activation within the maximum bound.

The trading relation between storage and processing occurs under an allocation scheme that takes effect when the activation maximum is about to be exceeded. Briefly, if the activation propagation on a given cycle of production firings would exceed the activation maximum, then both the activation propagated and the activation used for maintenance are scaled back proportionally to their current use. This scheme is analogous to imposing an across-the-board percentage budget cut if the spending quota (the amount of activation) is about to be exceeded. The scaling back of the activation propagated will increase the number of cycles required to bring an element to threshold, effectively slowing down the computation. The scheme implies that when the task demands are high (either because of storage or computational needs), then processing will slow down and some partial results may be forgotten. In sum, the time course and content of language processing within this system depends on the capacity for storage and computation. When the task demands exceed the available resources, both storage and computational functions are degraded. We call this theory *capacity constrained comprehension*.

Processing of Sentences in Context
Because a text can contain an indefinitely large number of sentences whose storage could eventually consume any finite capacity, there must be counter-vailing mechanisms that reduce the storage demands. Some of these mecha-nisms selectively retain representations of only the most recent and most central clauses in an activated form, while dampening the activation level of other propositions from earlier sentences (Glanzer, Fischer, & Dorfman, 1984; Kintsch & vanDijk, 1978; vanDijk & Kintsch, 1983). Moreover, analogous mechanisms may selectively retain only the most relevant aspects of world knowledge in an activated form, while dampening the activation level of other knowledge that might be initially activated by the reading of the text (Kintsch, 1988). Storage demands are also minimized through the immediacy of pro-cessing, the tendency to semantically interpret each new word or phrase as far as possible when the word is first encountered, in contrast to a wait-and-see strategy that imposes additional storage demands (Carpenter & Just, 1983; Just & Carpenter, 1980). Finally, some lower levels of the hierarchical representa-tions of language may be deactivated after suitable, higher level structures have been formed.

Processing a sequence of sentences with a finite working memory capacity is possible not only because the storage demands can be limited, but also because the context can provide some processing benefits. The stored context might facilitate the processing of the ensuing sentence by preactivating some con-cepts, relations, and schemas relevant to its comprehension (Sanford & Garrod, 1981; Sharkey & Mitchell, 1985).

In a later section of this article, we instantiate some parts of the theory in a computer simulation. The simulation is built using an architecture, called CAPS, that is a hybrid of a production system and an activation-based con-nectionist system. The new simulation is a modification of a computational model of the processing of successive words of a text during reading called READER (Thibadeau, Just, & Carpenter, 1982). The modified model reflects the assumption that comprehension processes are capacity constrained. Hence, the name for the new model is CC READER (Capacity Constrained READER). It is a conventional production system in its use of productions, a working memory, and the recognize–act governance of the flow of control. It is connectionist in that the productions reiteratively propagate activation from source elements to target elements, and all the productions that are satisfied on a given cycle can fire in parallel.

The constraint on capacity is imposed by limiting the total amount of activation that the system has available for maintaining elements in working memory and for propagating activation to other elements in the course of processing. Moreover, as we will describe below, the simulation's account of individual differences in working memory capacity for language is that subjects differ in the maximum amount of activation that they have available. Thus, the total amount of activation in the new CAPS system can express the conjoint constraint as well as any trade-offs that are made between storage and processing.

Individual Differences in Working Memory Capacity
A central thesis of this article is that the nature of a person's language comprehension depends on his or her working memory capacity. We will describe a number of recently uncovered systematic individual differences in reading comprehension that are related to working memory capacity for language. We propose that individuals vary in the amount of activation they have available for meeting the computational and storage demands of language processing. This conceptualization predicts quantitative differences among individuals in the speed and accuracy with which they comprehend language. In addition, it is capable of accounting for some qualitative differences among readers that we have observed.

We have described capacity as though it were an energy source that some people have more of than other people have. According to an analogy proposed by Kahneman (1973) in explaining his capacity theory of attention, a person with a larger memory capacity for language may be able to draw on a larger supply of resources, like a homeowner who can draw on more amperes of current than a neighbor, and can thus generate more units of cooling or heating. However, another account of individual differences is in terms of the efficiency of mental processes. To return to the electrical analogy, it may be that some homeowners have more efficient electrical appliances than others (appliances being the counterparts of mental processes), allowing them to do more with the current, such as produce more units. We can designate these as the *total capacity explanation* and the *processing efficiency explanation*. The two explanations are mutually compatible and the experiments described here do not attempt to discriminate between them.

Effects of Capacity Constraints

In this section, we present new data and summarize existing research supporting the hypothesis that comprehension is constrained by working memory capacity. We address five capacity-related issues: (a) the influence of pragmatic cues on syntactic processes; (b) the time course of comprehending a complex syntactic embedding; (c) the maintenance of two representations of a syntactic ambiguity; (d) the effect of an external memory load on sentence comprehension processes; and (e) the ability to track long-distance dependencies within and between sentences. The intention is to examine how individual differences in working memory capacity constrain comprehension, producing both qualitative and quantitative performance differences. Before dealing with these five issues, we will describe the measurement of working memory capacity.

Assessing Working Memory Capacity
To assess individual differences in working memory capacity for language, we have used the *Reading Span* task (Daneman & Carpenter, 1980), which was devised to simultaneously draw on the processing and storage resources of working memory. The task requires subjects to read a set of unrelated sentences, such as: "When at last his eyes opened, there was no gleam of triumph, no shade of anger"; "The taxi turned up Michigan Avenue where they had a clear view of the lake." After reading these two sentences, the subject tries to recall the final word of each sentence, in this case, "anger" and "lake." The test determines the maximum number of sentences per set for which the subject can recall all of the final words. The largest set size for which the subject successfully recalls all of the final words for at least three of five sets is defined as his or her *reading span*. If the subject is correct on only two of the five set, she or he is assigned a span that is intermediate between that size and the next lower one. Among college students, reading spans typically vary from 2 to 5.5 for sentences of this type. In most of the studies described below, *high span* individuals have spans of four words or more, *medium span* individuals have spans of three or three and a half words, and *low span* individuals are those with spans of less than three words. The label of *low span* is relative to our sample; our low span subjects are in the top half of the distribution of verbal ability in standardized tests such as the Scholastic Aptitude Test (SAT).

The Reading Span task measure correlates highly with certain aspects of reading comprehension, such as the verbal SAT, with these correlations lying between .5 and .6 in various experiments (Daneman & Carpenter, 1980; Masson & Miller, 1983). The correlation between reading span and particular comprehension skills is even higher. For example, the ability to answer a factual question about a passage correlates between .7 and .9 with reading span in various studies. For easy texts, low span subjects read only marginally slower than high span subjects, but on particularly difficult portions of a text, low span subjects tend to be substantially slower than high span subjects. In contrast to the strong relation between reading span and various comprehension indices, passive short-term memory span performance (e.g., recalling a list of digits or unrelated words) is not significantly correlated with reading comprehension (Perfetti & Goldman, 1976).[1]

Modularity of Syntactic Processing
Capacity constraints have the potential of creating boundaries between different types of processes when the total processing resources are insufficient to

permit direct interaction between different processes. Interaction between processes, like other forms of computation, requires operational resources, such as storage of partial products and communication from one process to another. In the absence of resources sufficient to support interaction, two processes that have the requisite interconnectivity may fail to interact; that is, they may fail to influence each other's ongoing computations. But the boundaries created by capacity constraints are outcomes of resource limitations, and not of architectural barriers.

Capacity constraints thus provide an interesting new perspective on the controversy concerning the modularity of language processing (Fodor, 1983; Garfield, 1989). A cognitive module is defined as a fast, domain-specific set of processes that is mandatory and informationally encapsulated. The interesting conjecture offered by Fodor is that the syntactic level of language processing is performed by a cognitive module. We propose that the postulated modularity of syntactic processing may be better explained as a capacity constraint that sometimes imposes informational encapsulation.

Informational encapsulation is the single most distinguishing property of a cognitive module. It refers to a module's activities and outputs being uninfluenced by certain classes of information that may exist elsewhere in the system. One of Fodor's (1983) examples of encapsulation is that when you push your eyeball with your finger you see motion, even though another part of your cognitive system has the information that the motion is not real. The information about the finger movement is apparently not available to or not used by the processes that interpret input from the retina. These perceptual interpretation processes are in some sense encapsulated from the finger motion information. Fodor also considered the syntactic processing of language to constitute a module that is encapsulated from nonsyntactic information. Fodor said "as things stand I know of *no* convincing evidence that syntactic parsing is ever guided by the subject's appreciation of pragmatic context or of 'real world' background" (p. 78). The rationale that Fodor offered for encapsulation is that input systems have to operate rapidly (without allocating time to consider all possible relevant information) and veridically, somewhat like a reflex.

The theory we propose reinterprets syntactic encapsulation as an issue of capacity rather than of architecture. According to our view, people with small working memories for language may not have the capacity to entertain (keep activated and propagate additional activation from) nonsyntactic information during the syntactic computations, or at least not to the degree that the nonsyntactic information can influence the syntactic processing. In this view, the syntactic processing of a person with a small working memory is encapsulated only by virtue of a capacity constraint, not an architectural constraint. Individuals with a large working memory capacity may be more able to keep both syntactic and nonsyntactic information activated, and hence their syntactic processing would be more likely to be influenced by the nonsyntactic information. Thus, some people's syntactic processing might seem more modular than others. The degree of modularity would depend on working memory capacity for language, not on some structural separation between modules. But any variation in modularity across subjects destroys the value of the concept of modularity. To replace it, we offer the concept of capacity for interaction, which can differ among individuals.

First, we briefly summarize the previous and new empirical findings, and then we report them in more detail. The empirical support for our position comes from a study in which we examined individual differences in encapsulation of syntactic processing. The study used a task that had previously provided the strongest support for the modularity of syntax (Ferreira & Clifton, 1986). Ferreira and Clifton constructed a task in which the reader could avoid being led down a garden path only by making immediate use of nonsyntactic information. Their surprising result was that readers were led down the garden path, despite the presence of prior disambiguating information about the proper resolution of a syntactic ambiguity. That disambiguating information was nonsyntactic, so its lack of influence on the syntactic processing was attributed to the encapsulation of the syntactic module. We repeated that experiment, separating subjects of different reading spans, and replicated Ferreira and Clifton's result in the case of the low span subjects. However, just as our theory predicted, the high span subjects did take the nonsyntactic information into account in initially interpreting the syntactic ambiguity. In effect, the syntactic processing of the high span subjects was not modular, but interactive.

Ferreira and Clifton (1986) examined the reading time on sentences like Sentence 1, "The evidence examined by the lawyer shocked the jury"; and Sentence 2, "The defendant examined by the lawyer shocked the jury." Because these sentences omit the complementizers and the verb ("who was" or "that was") of the relative clauses, the sentences are called *reduced relative clauses*. The initial part of Sentence 2 "The defendant examined" is temporarily ambiguous between the main verb interpretation (which could have continued as "The defendant examined the courtroom") and the eventually correct interpretation as a relative clause. The study varied whether or not a pragmatic cue, the animacy of the head noun, signalled the correct interpretation of the initial ambiguous portion of the sentences. In Sentence 1, the initial noun is inanimate and, consequently, an implausible agent of the following verb. If the pragmatic information concerning inanimacy influences the parsing decision, readers should be more likely to interpret the verb as a reduced relative verb than as a main verb. Moreover, they might expect that an agent will be specified later in the sentence. When an agentive phrase, such as "by the lawyer," occurs, it should be no surprise and it should present no particular processing difficulty. In contrast, in Sentence 2, "the defendant" is a plausible agent of the verb "examined." Consequently, readers are likely to interpret the verb as a main verb, and begin their trip down the garden path. The subsequent agentive phrase is inconsistent with the main verb interpretation, so the encounter with the *by* phrase should present a processing difficulty. The garden path effect can be measured by comparing the reading time on "by the lawyer" in sentences like 1 and 2, to determine whether or not the inanimacy of the noun "evidence" alleviates any of the surprise on the encounter with the *by* phrase.

The striking result that Ferreira and Clifton (1986) obtained was that readers still spent a long time on the *by* phrase when the head noun of the sentence was inanimate. This result suggested that readers were led down the garden path. In fact, the first-pass reading times on the *by* phrase (as indicated in eye fixation data) were no shorter in the sentences containing an inanimate head noun than in sentences with an animate head noun. In other words, the inanimacy of a head noun like "evidence" appeared not to penetrate the syntactic analysis of the verb "examined." Ferreira and Clifton concluded that the lack of effect of inanimacy occurred because syntactic analysis is a modular cognitive process that is informationally encapsulated. They reasoned that even if there were information available to influence the syntactic analysis, that kind of information would not be used on the first pass of the syntactic processing because syntactic processing, according to theories like Fodor's (1983), is impermeable to other sources of information.

Our experiment was similar to Ferreira and Clifton's (1986) in most respects, except that the data were separated for subjects of different reading spans—40 high span readers (spans of 4.0 or higher) and 40 low span readers (spans of 2.5 or lower). In addition, we improved some of the stimulus sentences so that the grammatical subject could not be interpreted as an instrument.

While the subject read sentences on a graphics monitor, his or her eye fixations were recorded using an ISCAN Model RK-426 Pupil/Corneal Tracking System, and a VAXstation 3200 computed the point of regard every 16.7 ms. Each screen display consisted of a neutral, introductory sentence, followed by the target sentence, followed by a true–false comprehension question that the reader answered by pressing one of two buttons.

The primary analysis focused on the first-pass reading times on the *by* phrase and on the initial verb and the main verb of the target sentence. Subsequent analyses examined any reading beyond a first pass (typically regressions back to the *by* phrase). The analysis used only trials in which the subject fixated on the first verb for at least 150 ms, and then on the *by* phrase for at least 150 ms.

The main result was a difference between the high and low span subjects in their reaction to an inanimate noun. Inanimacy decreased the first-pass reading time on the *by* phrase for high span subjects, but not for the low span subjects. This result suggests that high span readers were sensitive to the pragmatic cue during the first-pass syntactic analysis. In the case of the reduced relative clauses, the presence of an inanimate noun reduced the first-pass reading time on the *by* phrase by 75 ms for the high span subjects, but did not reduce it for the low span subjects, as shown in the bottom right side of Figure 5.1. Similarly, in the case of the unreduced relative clauses, the presence of an inanimate noun

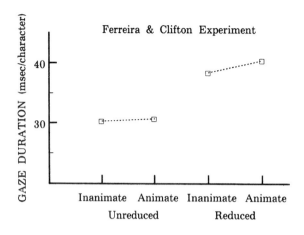

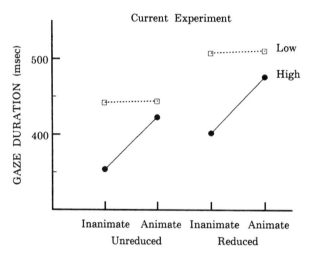

Figure 5.1

First-pass reading times on *by* phrase for the untested subjects of Ferreira and Clifton (1986) on the top and for hligh and low span subjects in the present study on the bottom. (The slope for the high span subjects between the inanimate and animate conditions indicates that their processing is faster if the grammatical subject of the sentence is inanimate; in contrast, the lack of difference between the inanimate and animate conditions indicates a negligible influence for Ferreira and Clifton's subjects and the low span subjects in the present experiment.)

reduced the first-pass reading time on the *by* phrase by 69 ms for the high span subjects, but did not reduce it for the low span subjects. This pattern produced a reliable interaction of animacy and span group, $F(1, 66) = 5.36$, $p < .025$, $MS_e = 15.487$. The results for the low span group parallel those of Ferreira and Clifton (1986); their data were reported as reading time per character and they are plotted in the top part of Figure 5.1.

Not surprisingly, the first-pass reading time on the *by* phrase was shorter (by 58 ms on average) for both span groups if the relative clause was not reduced, $F(1, 66) = 14.13$, $p < .01$, $MS_e = 16.334$. There was no interaction between span group and reduction. Taken together, these results suggest that the two groups of subjects make similar use of the explicit syntactic cue (i.e., the expanded relative clause), whereas only the high span subjects make use of the pragmatic cue of inanimacy.

Averaged over all four conditions, the high span subjects had marginally shorter first-pass reading times on the *by* phrase (by 62 ms), $F(1, 66) = 3.76$, $p < .06$, $MS_e = 70.308$.

This pattern of results is most easily explained in terms of a capacity difference between the two groups of subjects, such that only the high span subjects have the capacity to take the pragmatic information into account. The modularity explanation does not fit this pattern of results, unless one postulated that the syntactic processing of low span subjects is modular, and the syntactic processing of high span subjects is interactive. But modularity was construed as a hypothesis about a universal functional architecture, a construal that is violated by a finding of individual differences. In contrast, the capacity constrained comprehension model simply postulates that interaction requires capacity, so only those subjects with greater capacity have the resources to support interaction. The specific interaction in this case is the ability to represent, maintain, and use the inanimacy cue during the processing of the syntactic information.

The general pattern of results can be viewed from another useful perspective—the effects of various cues to sentence structure. One cue to the complex relative clause structure is the complementizer and auxiliary verb ("that was") that occur in the unreduced relative clause. This is a reliable and valid cue used by both high and low span subjects; when this cue is present, the reading times on the first verb and on the *by* phrase are shorter than if it is absent. The inanimacy of the head noun is another cue, which indicates that the head noun will not be the agent of the verb, but will instead occupy some other thematic role in the main clause and in any subordinate clauses. Only the high span subjects use this cue in their first-pass reading; their reading time on the first verb and on the *by* phrase is shorter if the inanimacy cue is present and longer if it is absent. In the case of the high span subjects, the two cues make approximately additive contributions to performance. The low span subjects show no effect of the inanimacy cue on the first-pass reading of the *by* phrase, indicating the insensitivity of their syntactic parsing process to this cue, as predicted by Ferreira and Clifton's (1986) instantiation of the syntactic modularity hypothesis. Completely unpredicted by the modularity hypothesis, but predicted by the capacity constrained comprehension model, is the high span subjects' use of this cue. Thus the syntactic encapsulation that some subjects exhibit is better explained in terms of a capacity constraint. The results contradict the view that syntactic processing is informationally encapsulated by an architectural barrier.

Processing Complex Embeddings
Capacity constraints, as measured by working memory capacity, should produce quantitative differences among individuals in the time course and accuracy of their processing. Moreover, these quantitative differences should be most apparent when the sentence or task is particularly capacity demanding. Several recent studies have obtained the predicted quantitative differences, that is, high span readers were both faster and more accurate in their comprehension of difficult sentences (King & Just, 1991). These studies demonstrated that much of the quantitative difference that results from working memory capacity can be localized to those portions of the sentence that are particularly capacity demanding.

The processing demands imposed by object-relative sentences provide a way to examine how working memory constrains the comprehension of normal (albeit difficult) sentences. The model predicts that each person's working memory capacity will determine how difficult each sentence type will be for him or her. All readers should find the object-relative sentences more difficult to comprehend than subject-relative sentences; more important for the thesis of this article, readers with lower capacity should have relatively more difficulty with object-relative sentences. King and Just (1991) measured the word-by-word reading times as subjects read sentences containing either an object-relative or subject-relative clause and then answered a question to assess the accuracy of their interpretation.

The results confirmed several important predictions of the theory, as shown in Figure 5.2. First, there were large individual differences in reading times, and these differences were primarily localized to the object-relative sentences which are shown on the right-hand panel of the figure. The fact that the intergroup differences were larger on the more demanding object-relative sentences suggests that working memory constraints are manifested primarily when processing demands exceed capacity. Second, the word-by-word reading times localized the processing difficulty of object-relative clauses to the point at which the critical syntactic information becomes available. All three groups of subjects showed a selective increase in reading time at the verb of the embedded relative clause ("attacked") and at the verb of the main clause ("admitted"). The increase was larger for subjects with smaller spans, so the three curves diverge in the right-hand panel of Figure 5.2 precisely at the location where the processing load is at its peak.

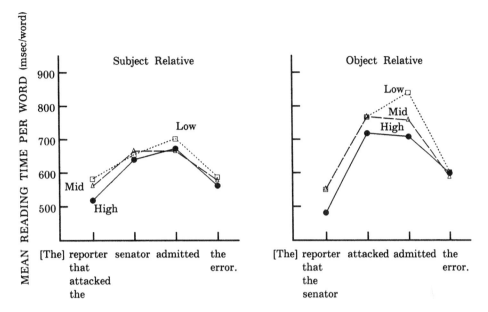

Figure 5.2

Reading time per word for successive areas of subject- and object-relative sentences, for high, medium (Mid), and low span subjects/(The differences among the span groups are larger for the more difficult object-relative construction, which is the more complex sentence. The differences are particularly large at the verbs, which are points of processing difficulty that are expected to stress working memory capacity. The readings times for parenthesized workds are not included in the plotted points.)

   The subjects with lower spans not only took longer to read the more complex sentences, but their comprehension accuracy was also poorer than that of higher span subjects. The accuracy of the low span subjects in answering true–false comprehension questions, such as "The senator admitted the error," was 64%, compared with 85% for the high span subjects (mid-span subjects' comprehension was 83%). The combination of reading time and comprehension-accuracy results shows that readers with lower reading spans have poorer comprehension, even though they may spend considerably more time processing in the syntactically critical area of the sentence. These results demonstrate systematic and localized individual differences in the comprehension of difficult syntactic structures, differences that are modulated by working memory capacity.

   The near absence of differences among the groups for undemanding sentences suggests that performance differences cannot be entirely attributed to the speed of some particular operation, a hypothesis that underlay much of the interesting research on individual differences in cognition in the 1970s (e.g.,

Hunt, Lunneborg, & Lewis, 1975). For example, suppose that the individual differences in reading times were due only to differences in the speed of lexical access. Then there should be a substantial reading time difference between high span and low span subjects even on the syntactically simpler sentences, which in this particular experiment happen to contain exactly the same words as the more complex sentences. But the large reading time differences occurred only on the more complex object-relative sentences, showing that the speed of lexical access cannot be more than a minor component of the individual differences.

Age-Related Differences
Syntactic constructions that make large demands on the working memory capacity of college students are the very types of constructions that produce age-related performance decrements in elderly people. One reason that working memory is implicated in the age-related changes is that the performance decrements are not general, nor do they appear to be attributed to the loss of some specific linguistic computation. For example, older adults (65–79 years of age) show relatively greater deficits than do younger adults when they must make an inference that requires integrating information across sentences (Cohen, 1979). Making the inference requires the storage of information from previous sentences concurrently with the processing of ensuing sentences, placing a large demand on working memory. The deficit is not general, because the older subjects have much less of a disadvantage when the comprehension test probes for verbatim information from the stimulus sentence.

Working memory was directly implicated in age-related changes in a task that required subjects to repeat sentences of various syntactic types (Kemper, 1986). Elderly adults (aged 70–89) were impaired (compared with young adults aged 30–49) at imitating sentences whose syntax made large demands on working memory. The elderly adults had particular difficulty in imitating sentences containing a long sentence-initial embedded clause, as in "The cookies that I baked yesterday for my grandchildren were delicious." They correctly imitated them only 6% of the time, as compared with 84% for the younger adults. The elderly adults also had some difficulty imitating a sentence containing a long sentence-final embedded clause (42% correct). By contrast, the elderly adults had no difficulty in imitating sentences with short embedded clauses. The age-related decline in the ability to imitate sentences is largest in cases in which the processing of the main syntactic constituent is interrupted by the processing of a long embedded constituent. This type of construction requires that the initial portion of the main constituent be retained in working memory while the embedded constituent is processed under the memory load, and then the stored portion must be made accessible again when its final portion is being processed. In addition to this age-related difference in imitation performance, Kemper found a corresponding age-related difference in spontaneous production (Kemper, 1988; Kynette & Kemper, 1986).

Thus, the decline in language performance in the elderly is focused on sentences whose syntax makes large demands on working memory. In general, the individual operations of language processing show little evidence of decline with age when the total processing load is small. However, at times of high demand, the total performance does decline, indicating an age-related decrease in the overall working memory capacity for language.

Syntactic Ambiguity: Single Versus Multiple Representations
Another facet of language that could generate demand for additional resources is syntactic ambiguity, particularly in the absence of a preceding context that selects among the possible interpretations. If comprehenders were to represent more than one interpretation of an ambiguity during the portion of a sentence that is ambiguous, this would clearly demand additional capacity. However, the existing data and the corresponding theories are in disagreement about the processing of syntactic ambiguities. A comprehender encountering an ambiguity might select a single interpretation (Frazier, 1978; Just & Carpenter, 1987; Marcus, 1980), or she or he might retain two alternative interpretations until some later disambiguating information is provided (Gorrell, 1987; Kurtzman, 1985). These two schemes for dealing with syntactic ambiguity have been posed as opposing (and mutually exclusive) alternatives. However, in a series of experiments, we found that both positions could be reconciled by postulating individual differences in the degree to which multiple representations are maintained for a syntactic ambiguity (MacDonald, Just, & Carpenter, 1992).

In the model we advance, multiple representations are initially constructed by all comprehenders on first encountering the syntactic ambiguity. Each of the multiple representations is assumed to have an activation level proportional to its frequency, its syntactic complexity, and its pragmatic plausibility. The important new postulate of our theory is that the working memory capacity of the comprehender influences the duration (i.e., intervening text) over which multiple syntactic representations can be maintained. A low span reader does not have sufficient capacity to maintain the two interpretations, and soon abandons the less preferred interpretation, which results in a single-interpretation scheme. In contrast, a high span reader will be able to maintain two interpretations for some period.

The full set of results is too long to present here, because it includes reading times and comprehension rates on unambiguous sentences and two resolutions of ambiguous sentences (see MacDonald, Just, & Carpenter, 1992, for details). However, we can present the critical data that support the central claim, which makes an unintuitive prediction. In the survey of capacity effects presented above, a greater capacity produces better performance in all ways that have been measured; the high span readers did not have to trade anything measurable away to read difficult sentences faster and comprehend them better. However, maintaining the multiple interpretations of a syntactic ambiguity is so demanding that it produces a performance deficit, which is shown only by the high span readers.

The critical data do not concern tricky garden path sentences, but on the contrary, they concern the most common syntactic structures in English, such as Sentence 7: "The experienced soldiers warned about the dangers before the midnight raid." This sentence is temporarily ambiguous, as can be demonstrated by considering an alternative resolution, such as Sentence 8: "The experienced soldiers warned about the dangers conducted the midnight raid." The syntactic ambiguity involves the interpretation of "warned" as either a main verb or as a past participle in a reduced relative construction. In Sentence 7 this ambiguity is resolved with the period at the end of the sentence.

The surprising result is that only high span subjects show any effect of the ambiguity in Sentence 7, as evaluated by comparison with the processing time on a control, unambiguous sentence that contains exactly the same words, except for the verb, such as Sentence 9: "The experienced soldiers spoke about the dangers before the midnight raid." Sentence 9 is unambiguous because the verb "spoke" can only be interpreted as a main verb and not as a past participle. For high span subjects, ambiguous sentences like Sentence 7 take longer than their unambiguous counterparts, particularly near or at the end of the sentence, where the ambiguity is resolved. In contrast, low span subjects show a small and generally unreliable effect of the ambiguity. Furthermore, in terms of absolute reading times, the high span subjects take longer than the low spans on reading ambiguous sentences, but not on unambiguous ones like Sentence 9. The reading time differences between the temporarily ambiguous main verb sentences and their unambiguous controls are shown in Figure 5.3. The sentences were presented in a self-paced, word-by-word, moving window paradigm. In the case of the main verb sentences, the three regions for which the reading time differences are plotted are indicated with brackets for the sample sentence:

"The experienced soldiers

[warned about the dangers] [before the midnight] [raid.]"

Region: 1   2   3

Precisely the same words (with the exception of the verbs) enter into each region for both the ambiguous and unambiguous conditions. Across a series of experiments, the high span readers showed a reliable ambiguity effect at and near the end of the sentence. These results strongly support the contention that high span subjects are maintaining two representations of the syntactic ambiguity, and they pay a concomitant price of slowing down their processing.

We have already commented on one remarkable facet of the results, namely that high span subjects pay a measurable price for maintaining two interpretations. The other remarkable facet is that sentences like Sentence 7, "The

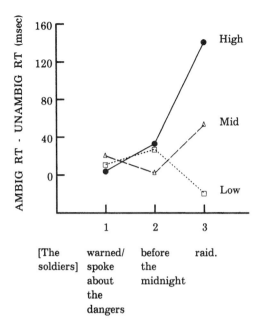

[The   warned/   before   raid.
soldiers] spoke   the
          about   midnight
          the
          dangers

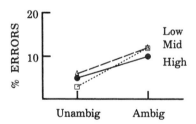

Figure 5.3
The differences between the ambiguous (AMBIG) and unambiguous (UNAMBIG) sentences in the average reading time (RT) per word for three regions of the sentences for the high, medium (Mid), and low span subjects. (The high span subjects take additional time on sentences with structurally ambiguous verbs, such as "warned," than those with unambiguous verbs, such as "spoke." This result is consistent with the hypothesis that high span subjects maintain the ambiguity in working memory for a longer period than do medium or low span subjects. The error rates are indicated in the bottom panel.)

experienced soldiers warned about the dangers before the midnight raid," are not garden path sentences. Even though the sentence is temporarily ambiguous, it is ultimately given the more frequent resolution, that "warned" turns out to be the main verb of the sentence. The high span readers have not been led down a garden path. They represented an alternative, less likely path as they walked down the main path. The low span subjects also have not been led down the garden path. They represented just one alternative, and it turned out to be the correct one. They maintained only one interpretation, and thus did not have to pay any significant costs due to the sentence's temporary ambiguity. However, even high span readers do not hold onto multiple interpretations indefinitely; the ambiguity effect for these subjects can also be eliminated if the ambiguous region is greatly lengthened.

Extrinsic Memory Load
The availability of working memory resources has often been experimentally manipulated through the introduction of an extrinsic memory load, such as a series of words or digits that are to be retained during comprehension. The extrinsic load could consume resources simply by virtue of being maintained in working memory or by virtue of rehearsal and recoding processes that compete for resources (Klapp, Marshburn, & Lester, 1983). As the extrinsic load increases, one or more facets of performance degrades, such as the reading rate or the ability to recall the load items (Baddeley & Lewis, reported in Baddeley, 1986; Baddeley, Eldridge, Lewis, & Thomson, 1984).

The maintenance of an extrinsic load interferes with sentence comprehension, which suggests that they compete for the same resources. An extrinsic load condition was included in the syntactic complexity experiment described earlier (King & Just, 1991), involving sentences with subject-relative and object-relative clauses, such as "The reporter that the senator attacked admitted the error." When the subjects were required to retain one or two unrelated words while reading the sentence, their ability to answer a subsequent comprehension question was less than in a condition in which there was no extrinsic load.

Figure 5.4 shows the comprehension accuracy of the high and low span subjects when there was no additional load, compared with a condition in which the subjects were maintaining either one or two words. A comparison of the overall performance for the two panels confirms that, as expected, accuracy is generally higher for the subject-relative sentences (left-hand panel) than for the linguistically more complex object-relative sentences (right-hand panel). The accuracy is particularly impaired for the low span readers, who have less capacity for the complex computations entailed in processing the object relatives. Indeed, King and Just (1991) found that half of the low span subjects had comprehension rates for the object-relative sentences that were indistinguishable from chance (66% in this study). Given the low level of comprehension in the absence of a load, the extrinsic load only slightly decreases comprehension

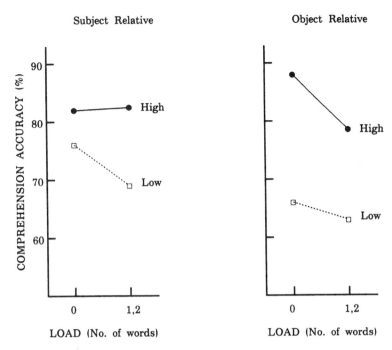

Figure 5.4
Comprehension accuracy for subject-relative and object-relative sentences in the absence or presence of an extrinsic memory load for high and low span reading groups. (Comprehension accuracy is lower for the low span subjects, for the more complex object-relative clause sentences, and when subjects are simultaneously retaining a load.)

accuracy. The effect of the load is much more apparent for the high span subjects who, in the absence of a load, have sufficient capacity to comprehend the object-relative sentences with much greater accuracy than the low span subjects. In sum, comprehension accuracy decreases both when there is less capacity because of a subject variable (as in the span contrast), because of additional linguistic complexity (as in the contrast between the two sentence types), or because of an additional extrinsic memory load (as in the contrast between a load of 0 words and 1 or 2 words). Such data are consistent with the hypothesis that some aspect of maintaining an extrinsic load competes for the resources used in the comprehension process.

Not only does load maintenance interfere with comprehension, but comprehension can reciprocally interfere with the maintenance of an extrinsic load. This effect was demonstrated in a modified version of the Reading Span task. The sentence-final words in this task constitute a concurrent load because the words from previous sentences must be maintained during comprehension of the current sentence. Thus, it is possible to manipulate the complexity of

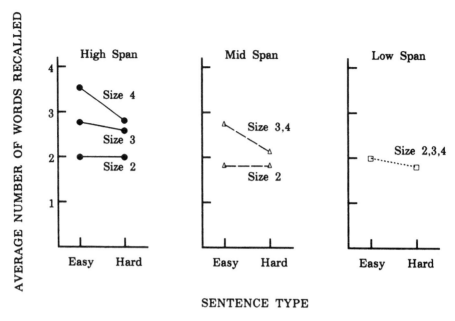

Figure 5.5
The average number of load words that are recalled after a subject reads a sent of sentences that are either hard, because they contain difficult vocabulary, or easy. (Recall primarily decreases when the subject is at or near his or her capacity and the sentence is hard.)

the sentences and examine its effect on recalling the sentence-final words. If the sentences in the set are linguistically more difficult, then the recall of the sentence-final words decreases (Carpenter & Just, 1989). The easy sentences (e.g., Sentence 11: "I thought the gift would be a nice surprise, but he thought it was very strange") primarily differed from the more difficult sentences (e.g., Sentence 12: "Citizens divulged that dispatching their first born was a traumatic event to face") in the presence of more common and concrete words, as well as in syntactic complexity. The subjects, all college students, were given sets of two, three, or four sentences to read and then asked to recall the sentence-final words.

The number of sentence-final words recalled was generally lower if the subjects had read a set of difficult sentences than if they had read easy sentences. This was particularly the case if the number of sentence-final words exceeded the reader's span, as assessed by the Reading Span task. The pattern of recall results, shown in Figure 5.5, demonstrates that the processing of difficult sentences interferes with the ability to retain and recall an extrinsic load, particularly if the subjects are operating close to their working memory capacity limit.

Distance Effects

An intrinsic part of language comprehension is the ability to interrelate information that comes from different constituents, such as clauses or sentences. Consequently, there is a need to retain information over time and intervening computations. Working memory provides the resources to store information from preceding constituents while simultaneously providing the computational resources to process ensuing constituents. The greater the distance between the two constituents to be related, the larger the probability of error and the longer the duration of the integration processes (e.g., Chang, 1980; Jarvella, 1971).

Text Distance Effects   A text distance effect has been found with a variety of constructions and relations. For example, sentences that contain pronouns take longer to read if other clauses or sentences intervene between the sentence and the earlier referent, presumably because of increased time to search for the referent (Clark & Sengul, 1979). Sentences that contain a term referring to a member (e.g., trombonist) of a category that is specified earlier (e.g., musician) take less time to read if the sentences are successive than if one or more sentences intervene between the sentence containing the superordinate term and the one containing the subordinate (Carpenter & Just, 1977; Lesgold, Roth, & Curtis, 1979). Similar distance effects have been found for sentences that are related by causality (Keenan, Baillet, & Brown, 1984), as well as pronominal reference, adverbial reference, and connectives (Fischer & Glanzer, 1986; Glanzer, Dorfman, & Kaplan, 1981; Glanzer et al., 1984). These distance effects have been interpreted as suggesting that comprehension involves representing the relation between the current phrase or clause and earlier information (Just & Carpenter, 1980; Kintsch & vanDijk, 1978). This relating takes less time if the earlier, relevant information is still available in working memory. In contrast, if the earlier, relevant information is no longer activated, then the relating process will require either searches of long-term memory and more constructive inferences, or there will be a failure to relate the new information to the earlier information.

Readers with larger working memory capacities are able to maintain more information in an activated state, and hence are better at interconstituent integration, as will be described below. In particular, there is a strong relation between a subject's reading span and the text distance over which he or she can successfully find an antecedent for a pronoun (Daneman & Carpenter, 1980). This result was found in two experiments that manipulated the number of sentences that intervened between the last mention of the referent and the pronoun. Readers with larger reading spans were more accurate at answering comprehension questions that asked the identity of the person referred to by the pronoun. More precisely, the maximal distance across which a reader could correctly assign the pronoun was well predicted by his or her reading span, as shown in Figure 5.6. One explanation that can be ruled out is that higher span

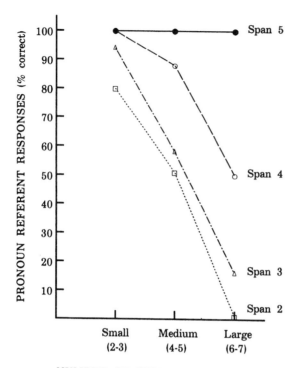

Figure 5.6
Correct interpretation of a pronoun as a function of its distance from the proceeding anaphoric reference for high, medium, and low span reading groups. (The subjects with the highest span [5 words] have no difficulty interpreting a pronoun, even if its referent occurred six or seven sentences before. By contrast, the subjects with the lowest span [2 words] cannot interpret such pronouns and are only moderately successful if the referent occurred two or three sentences earlier.)

readers are simply more skilled at selecting important referents for storage. If this were the only factor operating, then the performance should not decline monotonically with distance. Intervening text that does not reinstate a referent causes forgetting, with more forgetting by low span than high span subjects. Thus, working memory capacity and individual differences in this capacity are clearly implicated in the integration processes that are used in constructing a coherent referential representation of the text.

Summary of Results
Across these five aspects of comprehension, we have described qualitative differences among readers (in the permeability of their syntactic processing to pragmatic information, and in their representing one versus two interpretations

of a syntactic ambiguity) as well as quantitative differences (in the time course of comprehension and in the accuracy of comprehension). Comprehension performance generally declines with an intrinsic memory load (such as retaining information across successive sentences of a text) or an extrinsic one, with greater declines for lower span readers. Reading slows down at just that point in a sentence that introduces a computational demand, and slows down more for low span than high span subjects. Although lower span readers typically show a disadvantage compared with high span readers in both reading time and errors, there are also situations in which high span readers show an apparent disadvantage in the costs associated with maintaining two representations of a syntactic ambiguity. The constraints on every person's capacity limit the open-ended facets of comprehension, so that a reader or listener cannot generate every possible forward inference, represent every interpretation of every ambiguity, or take into consideration every potentially relevant cue to an interpretation.

Simulation Model

To examine the theoretical sufficiency of the capacity hypothesis, we have simulated aspects of the experiments described above using the CAPS architecture, which is a hybrid of a production system and a connectionist system. As in a connectionist system, activation is propagated from source (condition) elements to target (action) elements, but the propagation is performed by the productions. The productions can operate in parallel with each other and propagate activation reiteratively over several processing cycles, until the target element reaches some threshold. The constraint on capacity is imposed by limiting the total amount of activation that the system has available for maintaining elements in working memory and for propagating activation to other elements in the course of processing. Before describing how the activation constraint is applied, we will describe some of the key properties of CAPS/READER.

1. Associated with each working memory element is a real number called its activation level, which represents the element's strength. An element satisfies a production's condition side only if its activation level lies above some threshold specified by the production or by convention.
2. Most working memory elements are propositions of the form (concept :relation concept) or (concept [implicit :isa] concept). These elements can form a network.
3. Production firings direct the flow of activation from one working memory element (called the *source*) multiplied by a factor (called the *weight*) to another working memory element (called the *target*).
4. One processing cycle is defined as the matching of all productions against working memory and the consequent parallel firing of all satisfied productions.

5. Long-term knowledge consists of a declarative database separate from working memory.

One unconventional aspect of the parser, which we call CC READER, is that the number of processing cycles that it takes to process each word depends on the amount of activation that is available. If activation is plentiful, then a given production may be able to activate its action elements to threshold in a single cycle. But if storage or processing demands conjointly exceed the activation maximum, then the production would increment the activation level of its action elements rather gradually, until the level reached threshold. For example, in a conventional production system parser, there might be a production like, "If the word *the* occurs in a sentence, then a noun phrase is beginning at that word." In CC READER, the corresponding production would be, "If the word *the* occurs in a sentence, then increment the activation level of the proposition stating that a noun phrase is beginning at that word." If there were a shortage of activation, then the CC READER production would fire reiteratively over several cycles until the proposition's activation level reached a threshold. CC READER's smaller grain size of processing permits evidence (activation) for a particular result to accumulate gradually, with potential for input from several sources.

The constraint on the total amount of activation in the system conjointly limits how much activation can be propagated per cycle and how many elements can be maintained in working memory. Given a certain maximum on the amount of activation that is available, there are many points along an iso-activation curve that can be adopted. At one extreme, the brunt of an activation shortage could be borne by the storage function, so that at times of peak demand there would be a lot of forgetting of partial and final products in working memory, but processing (particularly the time it takes to compute something) would remain unchanged. At the other extreme, the brunt could be borne by the processing function, so that at times of peak demand, processing would slow down but there would be no forgetting. Limiting the amount of activation available per cycle slows down processing by requiring more cycles of propagation to raise an element's activation to a given level. The current implementation chooses an intermediate point in this trading relation. Any shortfall of activation is assessed against both the storage and processing, in proportion to the amount of activation they are currently consuming. For example, if the quota is a total of 36 units of activation, and the old elements are consuming 32 for maintenance, and the current processing cycle requires 16 for propagation (for a total budget request of 48 units), then the shortfall of 12 units is assessed proportionally. Thus, maintenance and storage each receive 36/48 or 3/4 of their need, or 24 units of activation for maintenance and 12 for propagation by the productions. The effect of exceeding the quota is both forgetting and a slowing down of the processing. In this scheme, the degree of constraint on processing (e.g, comprehension) depends on the maintenance demands of the moment, and vice versa.

There are several implications of this scheme. First, decrementing the activation levels of old elements is a form of continuous forgetting by displacement. This is unlike conventional displacement models, which posit one element displacing another from a limited number of storage locations. In contrast, this model posits that the activation that is used to maintain old elements is drawn away by the action of the productions' incrementing the activation levels of other elements. Thus, when the activation demands exceed the constraint, there will be gradual forgetting of old information (or old partial products) with each new cycle of processing that exceeds the activation quota. Second, when the number of partial products is small (e.g., early in a task) then the forgetting due to displacement will be less than when there are many partial products (e.g., late in a task that requires storage of partial products). Furthermore, the constraint does not apply until the demand for activation exceeds the quota. Thus the effects of the constraint will arise at different times for different people. The manifestation of the constraint is some combination of forgetting (decrease in activation of old elements) and a slowdown of processing (more cycles of activation will be required for an element's activation level to reach a given threshold).

CC READER deals primarily with the syntactic level of processing of sentences containing embedded clauses. The motivation for this focus is that many of the new results we have recently obtained on individual differences and capacity constraints pertain to the syntactic level of processing. We do not mean to imply that the syntactic level is in any sense the most important or central level of language understanding, even though it plays a central role in the reported experiments and hence in this simulation model. The model also involves some semantic analysis (assigning case roles) and lexical access (activating word meanings to threshold). CC READER parses only single sentences. As a matter of expedience, we have not inserted a referential level of processing, so that the model does not construct a referential representation of what it reads, and hence has no way of relating one sentence to another. The main goal of the simulation model is to demonstrate the sufficiency of a psychologically plausible understanding system whose performance varies under different capacity constraints. The variation in the model's performance is intended to resemble the variation among individuals of different capacities and the variation within individuals comprehending under different processing loads.

As CC READER parses a sentence word by word, it incrementally constructs a representation of the sentence that is sufficient for answering *wh-* and *yes–no* questions. Moreover, the parser simulates the real-time processing profiles of high or low span subjects (depending on its activation quota) as they read the successive words of the various sentences. For example, in the case of syntactic ambiguities, the parser performs either like a high span or a low span subject,

Table 5.1
Categories of productions in CC Reader

Category	Number	Subcategory
Initialization	3	Initializing system and getting next word
Lexical access	3	Accessing lexicon
Syntactic parsing	10	Parsing noun phrases
	16	Parsing verb phrases
	7	Handling transitions between subjects, predicates, and direct objects
	12	Handling embedded clauses
Semantic analysis	6	Handling verb voice and agent–patient assignment

depending on how much activation it has available to propagate per cycle. Thus it demonstrates the sufficiency of our theoretical account, including the capacity constrained individual differences.

The parser consists of 57 productions which may be sorted into four categories (initialization, lexical access, syntactic parsing, semantic analysis). The syntactic productions can be further subdivided, as indicated in Table 5.1. Some of the categorizations are somewhat arbitrary, because some productions perform functions that fall under two or more of the above categories. A brief description of the function of the productions follows.

One production initializes the entire system before a sentence is read, and a second production reinitializes before each new word of the sentence is input. A third production, which roughly corresponds to the perceptual encoding of a word form, fetches the next word of the sentence when all the processing of the preceding word is completed (i.e., when all of the new propositions engendered by the preceding word have been activated to their target level).

Lexical Access
When the next word in the sentence is fetched, then one of the lexical access productions inserts a token (a copy) of the corresponding lexical entry from the lexicon into working memory, as well as inserting a flag indicating that lexical access is taking place. The lexicon, a database that is considered a part of long-term memory, contains information about words, such as their possible parts of speech. The base activation level of an entry in the lexicon is proportional to the logarithm of the corresponding word's normative frequency in the language; when a lexical entry is copied into working memory, it is given an initial activation level equal to its parent activation level in the lexicon.

A second production reiteratively increments that token's activation level until it reaches a threshold. Because the initial activation level is proportional to the logarithm of the word's frequency, the number of iterations required to activate the entry to threshold is logarithmically related to word frequency, replicating the word frequency effect in human gaze durations (Carpenter & Just, 1983). A paraphrase of this production is "If you are doing lexical access of the current word, then propagate a fixed increment of activation to the corresponding word token." A third production removes the lexical access flag when the token's activation level reaches a threshold.

Syntactic Parsing

These productions implement a connectionist, activationbased parser. The grammar that the parser uses is conventional (largely adapted from Winograd, 1983), and fairly limited, with a focus on handling embedded clauses that modify the sentence subject. Figure 5.7 graphically depicts some of the main parsing paths that are taken in the processing of the sentences in some of the experiments described in this article.

The grammar and the productions that operate on it can be usefully compared to an augmented transition network (ATN), another procedure for parsing sentences. In an ATN, the nodes correspond to syntactic constituents and the arcs linking the nodes correspond to the syntactic and sequential properties of constituents. An ATN's syntactic parsing of a sentence consists of tracing a single path through the network, moving from one node to the next by choosing the arc whose conditions are satisfied by the next word or words. Although the current grammar resembles an ATN, there are several important differences between them. First, in CC READER's grammar, more than one arc can be traversed when leaving a node because two interpretations may be maintained concurrently if capacity permits. Second, traversing an arc can require several iterations of an action (to activate the next node to threshold), rather than a one-shot arc traversal. Third, nonsyntactic information can influence a syntactic decision if capacity permits.

The main syntactic constituents that CC READER parses include noun phrases, verb phrases, prepositional phrases, and clauses. Its general goal at the syntactic level is to recognize instances of these types of constituents, the transitions among them, and the relations among them. In addition, the syntactic productions attempt to recognize which of the constituents make up the subjects and predicates of clauses.

When the beginning of a new constituent is encountered, the goal of constructing a representation of that constituent is created. Similarly, if one constituent indicates that a mating constituent will be forthcoming (e.g., the presence of a subject indicates that a predicate will be encountered), then the goal of representing the mate will be activated. The activation level to which a goal is initially incremented is proportional to its a priori importance, so that an important goal is not likely to be completely forgotten even if the activation constraint applies. For example, the goal of representing a subject or a predicate of a clause, which might have to be maintained during the processing of many intervening words, is activated to a high level because of its importance in the

A. SENTENCE GRAMMAR

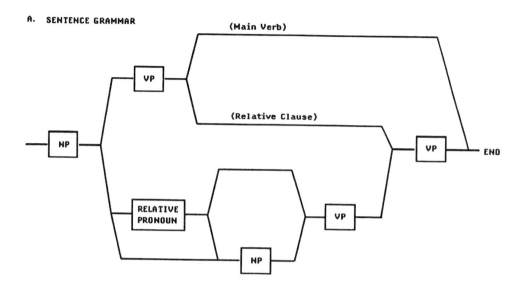

B. VERB PHRASE NETWORK

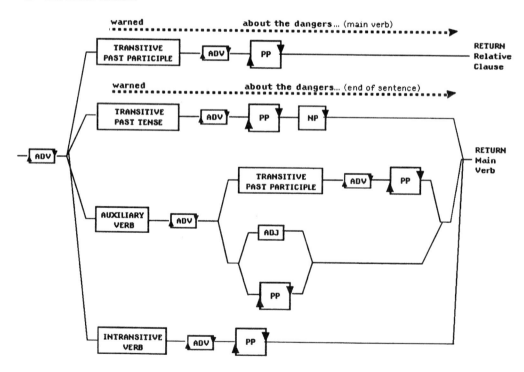

syntactic representation of a sentence. In contrast, the goal of representing a syntactically less crucial constituent, such as a prepositional phrase, is given a lower activational level.

The activation of a constituent is incremented to its target level over cycles by using a form of the delta rule used in McClelland's (1979) cascade model. Each activation increment is an increasing function of the difference of the proposition's current level and its target level. Thus, early increments are large, but as the difference between current and target activation levels decreases, the size of the increments also decreases.

Semantic Analysis

These productions do a limited case role analysis, focusing on agents and recipients of actions as they occur in active or passive clauses. For example, one of the productions can be paraphrased as "If you see a prepositional phrase starting with *by* containing an animate head noun, and modifying a passive verb, then activate the proposition that the head noun of the prepositional phrase is the agent of the verb." These case-role productions operate in collaboration with those that determine which constituents are the subjects and predicates.

CC READER is fairly word oriented, using word boundaries to segment its major processing episodes. As each ensuing word of a sentence is encoded, all the enabled productions continue to fire until they have all run their course. Then the next word is encoded, and so on. This scheme uses immediacy of processing in that the interpretation of each new word proceeds as far as possible when the word is first encountered. The notable exception to immediacy occurs in the processing of syntactic ambiguity under conditions of high capacity, as described.

The performance of CC READER can be compared to that of human subjects in a number of the situations that bear on the processing of syntactic complexity, syntactic ambiguity, and syntactic modularity (permeability to nonsyntactic information). The parsing model generally performs very much like the human subjects. It slows down in similar places, and has similar error distributions. The model's most novel property is that its performance changes with its activation maximum, and the model's variation in performance mirrors the differences between low and high span subjects. In the simulations described later, CC READER is given a low activation quota (constant across the three studies)

Figure 5.7
The sentence grammar, on the top, and the verb phrase network, on the bottom, that are used by the syntactic productions. (The ambiguity between main verb sentence and the reduced relative clause sentence is indicated in the verb phrase network by indicating that the phrase "warned about the dangers" is compatible with two branches of the network. VP = verb phrase; NP = noun phrase; ADV = adverb; PP = prepositional phrase; ADJ = adjective.)

to simulate low span subjects, and a high activation quota (again constant across the three studies) to simulate high span subjects.

Syntactic Ambiguity

The total amount of activation that is available determines whether CC READER will maintain one or two interpretations in the ambiguous region of a syntactic ambiguity. First consider the case of the model processing a fragment, like "The experienced soldiers warned ... ," under a high activation maximum (simulating a high capacity reader). Both representations of the syntactic ambiguity are activated when the ambiguity is first encountered, each with an activation level proportional to its relative normative frequency. The two interpretations of the fragment correspond to two alternative paths (indicated by dashed lines) in the grammar depicted in Figure 5.7, namely the two upper paths in the verb phrase network. In the case of a verb form like "warned," which can be either a transitive past participle or a transitive past tense, both representations are activated. However, the past tense interpretation is activated to a higher level than the past participle, by virtue of the former's higher normative frequency. As subsequent words of the sentence are encountered, they are interpreted in terms of both paths, as long as they fit both paths. In effect, the high capacity permits some degree of nonimmediacy, as the model is permitted to wait and see which of the two interpretations turns out to be correct. Recall that the disambiguation in the case of the main verb sentences used in the experiment is the end of the sentence. When the disambiguation is encountered, it fits only one path in the grammar. At that point, extra cycles relative to the unambiguous case are consumed in incrementing the activation level of the appropriate representation while deactivating the inappropriate interpretation. If the verb is unambiguous (e.g., "spoke"), then only one path (the second from the top in the verb phrase network) is followed.

Initially, the simulation of the low span subjects (low maximum activation) resembles the high span simulation, in that both interpretations are represented. However, in the case of the low maximum, the supply of activation is inadequate to maintain the secondary interpretation for more than one or two words beyond the ambiguity, so its activation level declines to a level below which it no longer satisfies the condition sides of productions. In the absence of a competing interpretation, the supply of activation is adequate to continue to process the main verb interpretation without further effect of the ambiguity up to and including the end of the sentence.

Thus, in the case of the low span simulation, there is little or no difference in the number of cycles per word between ambiguous and unambiguous sentences, either in the ambiguous region or at the encounter with the disambiguation, as shown in Figure 5.8. CC READER simulates the difference between processing ambiguous and unambiguous sentences by low and high span subjects, depending on its activation maximum.

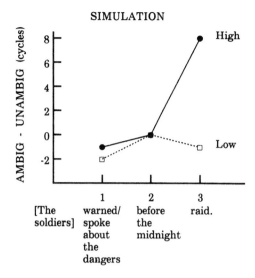

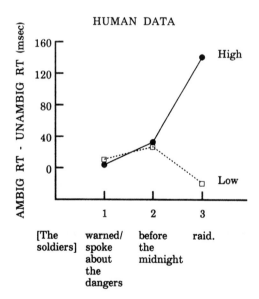

Figure 5.8
The top graph presents the difference in the number of cycles needed to process the ambiguous (AMBIG) and unambiguous (UNAMBIG) sentences when the simulation, CC READER, is operating with more working memory capacity, to simulate the high span subjects, or less, to simulate the low span readers. (The bottom graph presents the human data for comparison with the simulation. RT = reading time.)

Syntactic Complexity

In processing a center-embedded sentence, CC READER's performance profile (the number of cycles spent on each of the four sentence regions) resembles that of the human subjects in several respects, as shown in Figure 5.9. The most important similarity is that the model spends more time in the demanding regions if its activation maximum is smaller than if it is greater, simulating low and high span subjects respectively. Furthermore, the model's cycles (as a function of its activation maximum) differ more in the demanding regions of the sentence than in the undemanding regions, as is the case for the human subjects of different capacities. Additional points of similarity are that the model spends more cycles on the main verb and on the last word of the subordinate clause than on other parts of the sentence, and that like the subjects, the model takes longer on object relatives than on subject relatives.

Each of the effects in the model's performance can be explained in terms of the demand for activation and the consequences of the demand not being met. For example, the reason that the model takes extra time at the two verbs of object-relative sentences is that more productions fire during the computations on the verb than at other points in the sentences, because the verbs are grammatically related to a large number of other constituents, such as subjects and direct objects. The larger number of productions invoked at the verbs than at other points in the sentence demand extra activation, and moreover the activation pool is likely to have depleted somewhat by the time the sixth or seventh word of the sentence is encountered. Thus the productions that operate on the verbs require more cycles to accomplish their function. In the case of the object-relative sentences, the agent–patient computations that occur at the second verb require that a new agent be associated with the embedded clause, putting another additional demand on activation. The activation shortage is exacerbated in the case of the low span simulation, which has a smaller activation maximum. The words that follow the verbs evoke fewer productions, so even though the activation maximum applies during their firing, they complete their execution in a smaller number of cycles (compared with the verb processing), and the high–low difference becomes smaller.

In summary, a simulation that varies the amount of activation available for simultaneously computing and maintaining information accounts for the reading time differences between high and low span subjects dealing with syntactic complexity provided by center-embedded clauses.

Pragmatic Influence on Syntactic Processing

The simulation demonstrates how the contribution of a pragmatic cue to syntactic analysis depends on an adequate supply of activation. First consider the simulation of the high span subjects (in which the activation maximum is relatively high) in processing the sentences containing reduced relative clauses. The inanimacy information encoded with the subject noun (e.g., "evidence") is still

SIMULATION

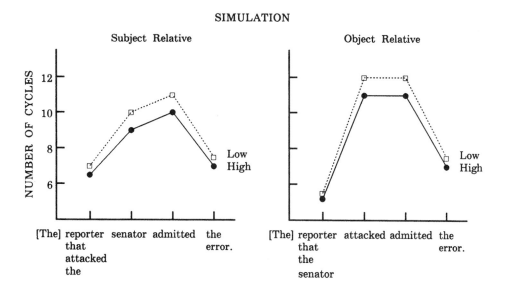

HUMAN DATA

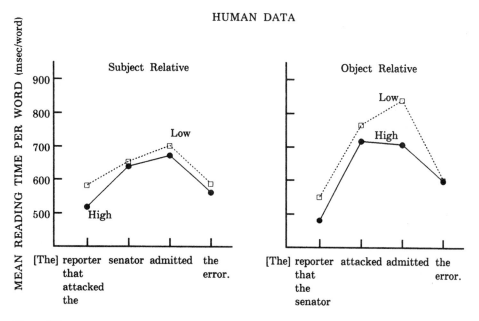

Figure 5.9

The number of cycles expended on various parts of the subject-relative sentences (on the left) and object-relative sentences (on the right) when the simulation, CC READER, is operating with more or less working memory capacity. (The bottom graph presents the human data for comparison with the simulation.)

in an activated state when the verb is being processed, and this information is used to select between the two interpretations of the verb (past tense vs. past participle) that are initially activated. The inanimacy of the subject noun favors the selection of the past participle and the deactivation of the past tense interpretation. From that point on, the sentence fragment is no longer ambiguous, so only one interpretation is maintained and it is the appropriate one. There is no unexpected resolution of an ambiguity at the *by* phrase for the high-capacity simulation that has been provided with the pragmatic cue.

Consider the case with an animate subject noun (e.g., "defendant"), which provides no information to resolve the ambiguity of the verb. Because the high span simulation has adequate capacity, both interpretations of the sentence fragment can be maintained in an activated state. But, as previously described, there is a cost associated with maintaining two interpretations, and this cost is incurred primarily at the disambiguation at the *by* phrase. Thus the number of cycles spent on the *by* phrase is greater in the animate reduced than in the inanimate reduced condition, as shown by the solid line in the right-hand side of the upper panel of Figure 5.10. Human high span subjects behaved similarly, as shown in the bottom panel of Figure 5.10.

Now consider the simulation of the low span subjects in processing the sentences with reduced relative clauses. Even if the subject noun is inanimate, the activation shortfall prevents the inanimacy information from being maintained long enough to be of use in disambiguating the verb. Furthermore, there is inadequate activation to maintain both interpretations of the verb, so only the more frequent main verb interpretation is maintained. The encounter with the *by* phrase reveals the inconsistency with the main verb representation, requiring a cycle-consuming reparsing of the ambiguous verb. So the number of cycles consumed on the *by* phrase is relatively large in the inanimate reduced condition. Similarly, the number is equally large in the animate reduced condition (in which there is no inanimacy cue), as shown by the dashed line in the right-hand side of the upper panel of Figure 5.10. The human low span subjects behaved similarly, as shown by the dashed line in the bottom panel of Figure 5.10.

The simulation model also provides a reasonable fit to the processing of the unreduced sentences, in both the high span and low span cases. The simulation of the low span subjects accurately predicts the absence of an inanimacy effect in the unreduced condition, and a lower cycle count than in the reduced conditions, as shown by the dashed lines in the left-hand sides of Figure 5.10. The simulation of the high span subjects benefits from the inanimacy information even in the unreduced condition, as do the human high span subjects.

Explorations of the Model
In this section, we will describe two aspects of the simulation model in more detail: (a) the total amount of activation being consumed after the processing

SIMULATION

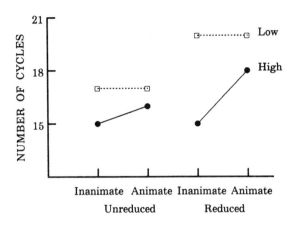

HUMAN DATA

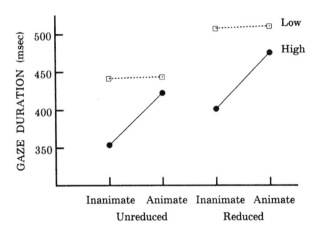

Figure 5.10
The number of cycles expended on the *by* phrase for sentences containing inanimate and animate grammatical subjects when the simulation is operating with more or less working memory capacity. (The bottom graph presents the human data for comparison with the simulation.)

of each successive word of a sentence, and (b) the consequences of alternative allocation schemes when the demands exceed the supply of activation.

Activation Consumption Over Time   In addition to the number of cycles spent on each word of a sentence, CC READER offers another index of resource consumption—the total amount of activation being consumed at the completion of each word of a sentence. In the simulation runs we have done, each sentence was treated as text initial, as though working memory were previously unused. Thus, the processing began with some total amount of available activation, a quota that differed for the simulations of low, medium, and high capacity subjects. Then, as each successive word was read, some of the total activation was consumed by the partial and final products that were generated in processing that word. These products are part of the orthographic, lexical, semantic, and syntactic representation of the word and sentence. A more complete model would also generate a referential level of representation.

In general, the total amount of activation that is consumed increases as the successive words of the sentence are processed, up to the point at which the maximum activation is reached, as shown in Table 5.2. The table shows the activation consumption of a simulation of a low capacity subject (using an activation maximum of 29 units) and a high capacity subject (53 units). Once the consumption reaches the maximum level (the quota), the consumption generally remains at the maximum throughout the rest of the sentence. The higher the maximum capacity, the later in the sentence the maximum consumption is reached.

The time course of the consumption has a number of potentially interesting implications. First, any sentence that is long enough or complex enough can bring a reader to his or her maximum consumption. Second, the partial products from a completed sentence must be purged if the processing of an ensuing sentence is to start out at a consumption level far below the maximum. Presumably, any such purging would spare the highest levels of representation.

One counterintuitive prediction of the model is that under some circumstances, a preceding context could slow the processing of an ensuing sentence, particularly in the case of a low capacity subject. These circumstances would arise if the costs (in terms of consumption of activation) of storing some of the representation of the preceding context outweighed the benefits. As we pointed

Table 5.2
Total consumption of activation after successive words of a sentence

Reading capacity	Units of activation consumed								
	The	reporter	that	the	senator	attacked	admitted	the	error.
Low	9.2	16.2	16.3	29.0	29.0	29.0	29.0	29.0	29.0
High	9.2	16.2	16.3	31.0	38.1	53.0	53.0	53.0	53.0

out in the introduction, the costs may be minimized by mechanisms that select only the most central and most recent propositions for retention while deactivating less central propositions. The benefits are that the preceding context could preactivate relevant concepts that facilitate the integration of the new sentence. If the costs outweigh the benefits, then the processing of an ensuing sentence could be slower when it is preceded by a supporting context sentence.

Alternative Allocation Schemes   The simulation results described above were obtained with a budget allocation scheme that was evenhanded when the activation demands exceeded the supply. That is, both processing and storage demands were scaled back by the same proportion to stay within the maximum activation limit, imposing an across-the-board budget cut. We will now briefly describe two other allocation schemes that were explored. One scheme favors processing, charging less of the projected activation deficit against the processing demands and charging more against the storage demands. Thus, if the activation quota is about to be exceeded, the amount of activation that is propagated by a production is only slightly less than it would be otherwise, but the activation levels of old elements are decremented more severely. The second scheme favors storage. If the activation quota is about to be exceeded, the amount of activation that is propagated by a production is substantially less than it would be otherwise, but the activation levels of old elements are decremented only slightly. These two schemes are implemented by changing the value of a bias parameter in the model. These two budget allocation schemes, as well as the evenhanded one used in the main simulation, come into play only when the quota is reached, so they do not make any difference early in a text-initial sentence.

The allocation scheme that favors processing makes the processing faster after the quota is reached; that is, fewer cycles are spent per word relative to the evenhanded allocation scheme. This is because there is more activation available to propagate on each cycle, requiring fewer cycles to increment an element's activation to a given level. An occasional negative consequence of this scheme is that an important intermediate product can be forgotten, especially if the maximum quota is a low one to begin with. If this occurs, the parser essentially fails to complete any processing that is dependent on the forgotten intermediate product.

The allocation scheme that favors storage makes the processing slower after the quota is reached; that is, more cycles are spent per word. The favoring of storage means that, relative to an evenhanded scheme, more elements can be maintained in an activated state, or that a similar number of elements can be maintained in a more activated state. If this scheme were applied to the processing of the syntactically ambiguous sentences, then the representations of both interpretations would be maintained for a longer time than with an evenhanded allocation.

These different schemes, in combination with a quota that is intermediate between the high and low, suggest a mechanism for a trading relation between speed and accuracy of processing, in which accuracy refers to maintaining and later using partial products appropriately. If the activation quota is intermediate, then an evenhanded allocation scheme produces performance that is intermediate between the performance with the high and low quotas. The biased allocations schemes applied to the intermediate quota can produce less predictable results. Favoring processing can make the processing as fast as high-quota, evenhanded allocation, at the expense of an occasional comprehension error resulting from the forgetting of an important partial product. Favoring storage can make the processing as slow as in the low-quota, evenhanded allocation situation, but the probability of errors due to forgetting is lower. Thus, the allocation bias parameter of the model provides a possible mechanism for a trading relation between speed and accuracy.

In summary, the simulations capture the critical empirical phenomena in several experiments related to individual differences in working memory. Although the fit of the simulations is imperfect, it nevertheless demonstrates how the same basic comprehension strategy can produce different kinds of performance when different amounts of resources are available.

General Discussion

A capacity theory shifts the scientific schema within which cognition is studied to focus on the intensity and dynamics of thought in addition to its structural aspects. This focus provides the basis of our account of individual differences in comprehension, and it also provides a new perspective on a number of issues. In this section, we will discuss three of them: (a) the implications of the capacity theory for cognitive theories in areas other than language; (b) the implications of capacity theory for resource allocation policy and processing efficiency differences; and (c) a comparison of the present analysis of individual differences to other approaches.

Dynamics of Cognition
A capacity theory deals centrally with the resources underlying thought. Like a structural theory, it assumes an underlying architecture, which in this case consists of a working memory, procedural knowledge (in the form of productions), and declarative knowledge (stored in a declarative knowledge base and in productions). The capacity theory further encompasses the dynamic aspects of processing and storage in this architecture, reflecting the moment-to-moment modulation in the resource demands. To account for the performance differences among individuals, the new theory proposes a dynamic allocation of a constrained capacity. Individual differences in the amount of capacity to be allocated or resultant differences in allocation policy can account for systematic

differences in performance without postulating differences in the underlying architecture.

The capacity theory turned out to have a surprising implication for functional system architecture: The degree of interaction between subsystems (modules) may be dependent on capacity. Interaction between modules has previously been viewed as being either architecturally permitted or not permitted. Capacity theory makes the useful point that architectural permission may be a necessary condition for interaction between subsystems, but it is not sufficient. Like every other aspect of cognitive processing, interaction requires resources, and in the absence of the resource, the interaction cannot occur, even if it is architecturally permitted. Thus, the question of whether a module of a system is autonomous or interactive may depend on the capacity to sustain the interaction.

More generally, the term *architecture* calls forth an analogy to the design of a house, with an emphasis on the partitioning of a larger structure into functionally distinguishable modules, such as kitchens and sleeping areas, and traffic patterns among them. In contrast, a focus on resource-dependent activity calls forth an analogy to a dynamic system, such as a river. Even though a river can sometimes be partitioned, the partitions are not its main features. Rather, the main features are the flow and the hydraulic structures, such as a waterfall or a standing wave or a whirlpool, which are influenced by the variation in the river's volume. Although both waterfalls and standing waves have the appearance of permanent attributes, they differ in that waterfalls are fairly permanent consequences of basic structure, whereas standing waves are transient attributes that can come and go with changes in the flow. To fully characterize a river, it is necessary to provide some account of its dynamics, and it is not sufficient to specify only its structure, as an aerial photograph might. A capacity theory of language provides some of the beginnings of a theory of cognitive dynamics.

Other Cognitive Domains   The implications of capacity theory may be examined in cognitive domains other than language, such as problem solving, complex decision making, and higher visual information processing. These domains seem amenable to analysis within a capacity theory because, like language, they involve sequential symbol manipulation.

One implication of capacity theory is that some of the performance differences among individuals within a task domain will be explained in large part in terms of working memory capacity. When the task demands are high enough to strain capacity, individuals with a smaller working memory capacity should be less able to perform computations quickly or store intermediate products. Some of these implications have recently been confirmed in the area of complex problem solving, specifically in solving the problems in the Raven Progressive Matrices Test. Subjects with lower scores in the Raven test were less able to store intermediate goals, as indicated in an independent task, and as indicated by their disadvantage on Raven test items that required the storage of a large number of subgoals and partial solutions (Carpenter, Just, & Shell, 1990).

A related implication is that within any task domain large performance differences among individuals will emerge, primarily when the task demands consume sufficient capacity to exhaust some subjects' resources. In the domain of language comprehension, capacity limitations are more evident when the linguistic construction is more complex or when there is an extrinsic load, as we have described. The current research extends this approach beyond finding larger individual differences in harder tasks, to finding larger individual differences in the harder parts of a single task. For example, within a given reading task, the reading times vary with the transient demand as the reader progresses through a sentence. Similarly, capacity use in other domains should vary with the ongoing computational and storage demands. Researchers in the domains of perception, motor control, and problem solving have shown that more capacity is required for more difficult tasks (e.g., Hirst, Spelke, Reaves, Caharack, & Neisser, 1980; Norman & Bobrow, 1975; Schneider & Shiffrin, 1977; Shallice, 1982). The research reported in this article suggests that individual differences could be used as an avenue for examining the effects of capacity constraints within tasks in these domains as well.

A third implication of capacity theory is that there is an intensity dimension of thought, in addition to the correctness and speed dimensions. Moreover, the intensity of thought varies in magnitude throughout the performance of a given task. Phenomenologically, one can feel oneself being more or less engaged in one's thought processes, or feel more or less concentration of thought. More objectively, pupillometry studies (Ahern & Beatty, 1979; Beatty, 1982) and physiological studies of glucose metabolism (Haier et al., 1988) have confirmed that these measures of intensity are sensibly related to the subject and task characteristics. For example, the pupillometry results indicate that the effort expended is greater if the subject is less skilled (as indicated by psychometric scores) or the task is more difficult (e.g., varying in arithmetic difficulty). Similarly, the glucose metabolism studies indicate that less skilled subjects expend greater effort at solving difficult problems from the Raven test. These findings are consistent with the hypothesis that individuals differ systematically in the effort that they have to expend to perform a task and that different tasks consume different amounts of resources in several domains besides language comprehension.

A fourth implication of the theory is specific to the domain of attention, the birthplace of capacity theory. In particular, Kahneman's (1973) capacity theory of attention laid a foundation for most of its successors, including the comprehension theory described in this article. Capacity theories of attention account for performance decrements that occur when the resource demands of the task exceed the available supply (Navon & Gopher, 1979; Wickens, 1984). Because detailed capacity theories of attention already exist, they are able to immediately benefit from the specific proposal made in the comprehension theory, that capacity be defined in terms of the activation available for information maintenance and computation. Attention theories often refer to some underlying commodity that enables performance, usually labeling it *capacity* or *resources* but failing to specify its nature (Navon, 1984). The activation definition provided by the current theory sharpens the concept of resources and their allocation, and may ultimately provide better accounts of capacity constraints in the types of situations addressed by theories of attention.

Finally, the theory implies that in areas besides language processing, interactions between component processes in a complex task will occur only if they are architecturally permissible and if there are adequate resources to support the interaction. Admittedly, language is the domain in which modules of processing are most frequently postulated. Nevertheless, it is often possible to decompose the performance of a complex task into subprocesses whose interaction can be usefully examined from this new perspective.

One Capacity or Many Capacities?   In this analysis of working memory capacity for language, we have assumed that there is a single capacity that encompasses various facets of language comprehension processing, including lexical access, syntactic analysis, and referential processing. This assumption is supported by several results. Perhaps the most important is the finding that comprehension deteriorated similarly when the demand on capacity was increased by a diversity of factors, including a syntactic embedding, a syntactic ambiguity, or the presence of additional sentences between a noun and a subsequent pronominal reference to it. In addition, the presence of an extrinsic load degraded comprehension similarly to a syntactic complexity (a center-embedded clause), suggesting that both effects occurred because of processes that drew on shared resources. The results of the animacy study, in which pragmatic information influenced the syntactic analysis for high span subjects, suggest that syntactic processing draws on the same capacity that supports the maintenance and use of pragmatic information. Finally, the Reading Span task measure correlated with comprehension performance across all of the various studies, implying that a common capacity (the one measured in the Reading Span test) mediated performance in all of the studies, regardless of whether a syntactic or a pragmatic factor was manipulated to increase the processing demand. The total set of results is most easily explained by a common capacity that underlies language comprehension.

Although the results from comprehension tasks indicate a common working memory capacity for language comprehension, it would be incorrect to assume that all language processes draw on a single capacity. In particular, there is evidence that language production may draw on somewhat different resources. Individual differences in a word-generation task (generating an appropriate completion for an incomplete sentence) do not correlate with individual differences in the Reading Span task after motor production speed has been partialled out (Daneman & Green, 1986). Another locale in which comprehension and production are distinguished is in language development. In a longitudinal study of language development in children, separate clusters of production and comprehension skills developed with different time courses, again supporting the suggestion that these are different types of skills (Bates, Bretherton, & Snyder, 1988).

In tasks that do not involve any overt language use at all (such as arithmetic or spatial tasks), the required resources overlap only partially with those used in language comprehension. Performance in the reading span task is sometimes positively correlated with nonlanguage tasks, but the correlations are generally much lower than with language comprehension tasks (Baddeley et al., 1985; Daneman & Tardif, 1987), indicating that only a subset of the resources is shared across diverse tasks (but see Turner & Engle, 1989, for an alternative view).

In sum, we cannot conclude that the working memory capacity used for language comprehension is the single cognitive capacity. Rather, it is likely that there is a large set of processing resources, only a subset of which is used for a given task domain. It remains to be seen whether a capacity theory within a domain other than language will be equally effective.

Resource Allocation and Processing Efficiency
The capacity theory also helps to crystallize a number of questions for which we cannot offer definitive answers, but which nevertheless benefit by being considered within this theoretical framework. In this section, we will describe two such issues: resource allocation and the role of processing efficiency.

Resource Allocation Schemes   The different performance characteristics of individuals as a function of their working memory capacity indicate the existence of an implicit allocation policy when demands exceed capacity. If the demand for resources exceeds supply, what factors influence the allocation of activation? We have already briefly explored the consequences of allocation schemes that favor storage or favor processing, but we have not discussed the question of whether some processes might be favored over others. For example, those processes that are less demanding of resources might be favored at time of inadequate resource supply. The less demanding processes include lower level processes (e.g., perceptual recognition) and automatic processes. In contrast, the higher level processes in comprehension, such as those that construct the referential level of representation in the case of a syntactic ambiguity, may be not executed or not executed fully in times of inadequate resource supply.

Processes that require a greater variety of inputs also may be less likely to be executed than those that require only one type of input. For example, if one of the inputs to the process is not yet computed because it depends on other intermediate products, then this process will be less likely to be executed to completion before a deadline is reached. Such a mechanism may account for the lack of effect of pragmatic information on first-pass syntactic processing in low span subjects. Thus, even in a parallel system, interactive processes might be subject to capacity constraints more than noninteractive processes. These general allocation heuristics account for the present studies and suggest that language comprehension may be a useful domain in which to study the issue that arises in other domains when the person's resources cannot meet the task's demands.

Total Capacity and Efficiency   As we discussed earlier, the individual differences reported here may reflect differences in total capacity, differences in processing efficiency, or both. Choosing between these two explanations of individual differences is not necessarily a matter of deciding which one is correct, but rather of deciding which one best accounts for a phenomenon, given some assumptions about total capacity and processing efficiency. One assumption is that capacity limitations affect performance only if the resource demands of the task exceed the available supply. One consequence of the assumption is that individual differences should be most evident during periods of high demand. If individuals differ in the amount of available activation, then performance differences should be more apparent if the task's demands exceed the available resources of lower ability subjects. Consistent with this assumption, our studies documented that performance differences among college student readers of different working memory capacities are smaller when the comprehension task is easy, and larger when it is demanding.

A second assumption is that changes in total capacity affect the execution of a wide range of processes in a wide range of tasks. Consequently, the types of generalized performance changes induced by fatigue, extreme age, or concentration can usually be interpreted as consequences of changes in total capacity. In contrast, a change in processing efficiency is assumed to be more specific to a particular process. Thus, changes in the efficiency of a process are often assumed to result from practice or some instructional intervention. Indeed, intensive practice in several simple tasks, such as Stroop-type tasks, induces large changes in the speed of responding that are typically interpreted in terms of changes in efficiency of underlying processes (Cohen, Dunbar, & McClelland, 1990; Schneider & Shiffrin, 1977). Intensive practice in reading might similarly induce greater efficiency in some component processes of comprehension; the time spent in out-of-school reading is correlated with reading skill in fifth-grade students, accounting for approximately 9% of the variance in one study (Anderson, Wilson, & Fielding, 1988). Total capacity is assumed to be less susceptible to such intervention. Although it is possible to explain practice effects in terms of a change in total capacity, the explanation would have to be more complex. In order to increase total capacity, the practice would have to recruit more activation or additional processes and structures, quite apart from producing any efficiency gain in the originally targeted processes.

The total capacity and processing efficiency accounts are not mutually exclusive. Like the particle–wave duality that is used to explain the nature of light, total capacity and process efficiency may conjointly explain differences in effective working memory among individuals. However, we believe that the new phenomena reported here are better explained in terms of total capacity than process efficiency.

The theory of capacity constrained comprehension not only provides an account of individual differences, but also suggests an important new perspective to complement the structural analysis that has dominated much of recent analyses of cognitive architecture. It also serves to bring language comprehension closer to the analysis of other types of cognition.

Notes

This work was supported in part by National Institute of Mental Health Grant MH 29617 and Research Scientist Development Awards MH-00661 and MH-00662 as well as a grant from the Andrew W. Mellon Foundation.

Sashank Varma played an important role in developing the capacity constrained interpreter and CC READER. We are also grateful to Jay McClelland, Maryellen MacDonald, Chuck Clifton, Mike Masson, Marilyn Turner, and Jonathan King for their constructive comments on earlier drafts of the manuscript.
1. The lack of correlation between the standard digit span task and reading comprehension indicates that the standard digit span task does not draw on the same resources as those used in most language comprehension tasks. The source of individual differences in standard span tasks is not clear (Lyon, 1977). One possibility is that such differences primarily reflect individual differences in the phonological store and the articulatory loop, an internal auditory–articulatory rehearsal process of fixed duration (Baddeley, 1986). The involvement of the articulatory loop in digit span performance has been implicated by cross-linguistic studies; in particular, the smaller digit span associated with the Welsh language has been attributed to the fact that Welsh vowels are longer and so Welsh digits take longer to subvocally rehearse than English digits (Ellis & Hennelley, 1980). Moreover, neuropsychological data suggest that impairments in digit span are not necessarily correlated with impaired language comprehension; some patients with very severely impaired digit span have relatively preserved sentence comprehension (Shallice, 1988). These neuropsychological data also support a dissociation between the standard digit span task and the mechanisms that are used in normal sentence comprehension.

References

Ahern, S., & Beatty, J. (1979). Pupillary responses during information processing vary with Scholastic Aptitude Test scores. *Science, 205*, 1289–1292.

Anderson, J. R. (1983). *The architecture of cognition*. Cambridge, MA: Harvard University Press.

Anderson, R. C., Wilson, P. T., & Fielding, L. G. (1988). Growth in reading and how children spend their time outside of school. *Reading Research Quarterly, 23*, 285–303.

Baddeley, A. D. (1986). *Working memory*. New York: Oxford University Press.

Baddeley, A. D., Eldridge, M., Lewis, V., & Thomson, N. (1984). Attention and retrieval from long-term memory. *Journal of Experimental Psychology: General, 113*, 518–540.

Baddeley, A. D., & Hitch, G. (1974). Working memory. In G. H. Bower (Ed.), *The psychology of learning and motivation* (Vol. 8, pp. 47–89). San Diego, CA: Academic Press.

Baddeley, A. D., Logie, R., Nimmo-Smith, I., & Brereton, N. (1985). Components of fluent reading. *Journal of Memory and Language, 24,* 119–131.

Bates, E., Bretherton, I., & Snyder, L. (1988). *From first words to grammar: Individual differences and dissociable mechanisms.* Cambridge, England: Cambridge University Press.

Beatty, J. (1982). Task-evoked pupillary responses, processing load, and the structure of processing resources. *Psychological Bulletin, 91,* 276–292.

Carpenter, P. A., & Just, M. A. (1977). Integrative processes in comprehension. In D. LaBerge & J. Samuels (Eds.), *Basic processes in reading: Perception and comprehension* (pp. 217–241). Hillsdale, NJ: Erlbaum.

Carpenter, P. A., & Just, M. A. (1983). What your eyes do while your mind is reading. In K. Rayner (Ed.), *Eye movements in reading: Perceptual and language processes* (pp. 275–307). San Diego, CA: Academic Press.

Carpenter, P. A., & Just, M. A. (1989). The role of working memory in language comprehension. In D. Klahr & K. Kotovsky (Eds.), *Complex information processing: The impact of Herbert A. Simon* (pp. 31–68). Hillsdale, NJ: Erlbaum.

Carpenter, P. A., Just, M. A., & Shell, P. (1990). What one intelligence test measures: A theoretical account of the processing in the Raven Progressive Matrices Test. *Psychological Review, 97,* 404–431.

Chang, F. R. (1980). Active memory processes in visual sentence comprehension: Clause effects and pronominal reference. *Memory & Cognition, 8,* 58–64.

Clark, H. H., & Sengul, C. J. (1979). In search of referents for nouns and pronouns. *Memory & Cognition, 7,* 35–41.

Cohen, G. (1979). Language comprehension in old age. *Cognitive Psychology, 11,* 412–429.

Cohen, J. D., Dunbar, K., & McClelland, J. L. (1990). On the control of automatic processes: A parallel distributed processing account of the Stroop effect. *Psychological Review, 97,* 332–361.

Cottrell, G. W. (1989). *A connectionist approach to word sense disambiguation.* London: Pitman.

Daneman, M., & Carpenter, P. A. (1980). Individual differences in working memory and reading. *Journal of Verbal Learning and Verbal Behavior, 19,* 450–466.

Daneman, M., & Green, I. (1986). Individual differences in comprehending and producing words in context. *Journal of Memory and Language, 25,* 1–18.

Daneman, M., & Tardif, T. (1987). Working memory and reading skill re-examined. In M. Coltheart (Ed.), *Attention and performance XII* (pp. 491–508). London: Erlbaum.

Ellis, N. C., & Hennelley, R. A. (1980). A bilingual word-length effect: Implications for intelligence testing and the relative ease of mental calculation in Welsh and English. *British Journal of Psychology, 71,* 43–52.

Ferreira, F., & Clifton, C. (1986). The independence of syntactic processing. *Journal of Memory and Language, 25,* 348–368.

Fischer, B., & Glanzer, M. (1986). Short-term storage and the processing of cohesion during reading. *The Quarterly Journal of Experimental Psychology, 38A,* 431–460.

Fodor, J. A. (1983). *The modularity of mind.* Cambridge, MA: Bradford.

Frazier, L. (1978). *On comprehending sentences: Syntactic parsing strategies.* Bloomington: Indiana University Linguistics Club.

Gernsbacher, M. A., Varner, K. R., & Faust, M. (1990). Investigating differences in general comprehension skill. *Journal of Experimental Psychology: Learning, Memory, and Cognition, 16,* 430–445.

Glanzer, M., Dorfman, D., & Kaplan, B. (1981). Short-term storage in the processing of text. *Journal of Verbal Learning and Verbal Behavior, 20,* 656–670.

Glanzer, M., Fischer, B., & Dorfman, D. (1984). Short-term storage in reading. *Journal of Verbal Learning and Verbal Behavior, 23,* 467–486.

Gorrell, P. G. (1987). *Studies of human syntactic processing: Ranked-parallel versus serial models.* Unpublished doctoral dissertation, University of Connecticut, Storrs.

Haier, R. J., Siegel, B. V., Nuechterlein, K. H., Hazlett, E., Wu, J. C., Paek, J., Browning, H. L., & Buchsbaum, M. S. (1988). Cortical glucose metabolic rate correlates of abstract reasoning and attention studied with positron emission tomography. *Intelligence, 12,* 199–217.

Hirst, W., Spelke, E. S., Reaves, C. C., Caharack, G., & Neisser, R. (1980). Dividing attention without alternation or automaticity. *Journal of Experimental Psychology: General, 109,* 98–117.

Hitch, G. J., & Baddeley, A. D. (1976). Verbal reasoning and working memory. *Quarterly Journal of Experimental Psychology, 28,* 603–621.

Hunt, E. B. (1978). Mechanics of verbal ability. *Psychological Review, 85,* 199–230.

Hunt, E. B., Lunneborg, C., & Lewis, J. (1975). What does it mean to be high verbal? *Cognitive Psychology, 2,* 194–227.

Just, M. A., & Carpenter, P. A. (1980). A theory of reading: From eye fixations to comprehension. *Psychological Review, 87,* 329–354.

Just, M. A., & Carpenter, P. A. (1987). *The psychology of reading and language comprehension.* Newton, MA: Allyn & Bacon.

Just, M. A., Carpenter, P. A., & Woolley, J. D. (1982). Paradigms and processes in reading comprehension. *Journal of Experimental Psychology: General, 111,* 228–238.

Kahneman, D. (1973). *Attention and effort.* Englewood Cliffs, NJ: Prentice-Hall.

Keenan, J. M., Baillet, S. D., & Brown, P. (1984). The effects of causal cohesion on comprehension and memory. *Journal of Verbal Learning and Verbal Behavior, 23,* 115–126.

Kemper, S. (1986). Imitation of complex syntactic constructions by elderly adults. *Applied Psycholinguistics, 7,* 277–287.

Kemper, S. (1988). Geriatric psycholinguistics: Syntactic limitations of oral and written language. In L. Light & D. Burke (Eds.), *Language, memory, and aging* (pp. 58–76). New York: Cambridge University Press.

King, J., & Just, M. A. (1991). Individual differences in syntactic processing: The role of working memory. *Journal of Memory and Language, 30,* 580–602.

Klapp, S. T., Marshburn, E. A., & Lester, P. T. (1983). Short-term memory does not involve the "working memory" of information processing: The demise of a common assumption. *Journal of Experimental Psychology: General, 112,* 240–264.

Kurtzman, H. (1985). *Studies in syntactic ambiguity resolution.* Doctoral dissertation, MIT, Cambridge, MA. Distributed by Indiana University Linguistics Club, Bloomington.

Kynette, D., & Kemper, S. (1986). Aging and the loss of grammatical forms: A cross-sectional study of language performance. *Language and Communication, 6,* 65–72.

Larkin, W., & Burns, D. (1977). Sentence comprehension and memory for embedded structure. *Memory & Cognition, 5,* 17–22.

Lesgold, A. M., Roth, S. F., & Curtis, M. E. (1979). Foregrounding effects in discourse comprehension. *Journal of Verbal Learning and Verbal Behavior, 18,* 291–308.

Lyon, D. (1977). Individual differences in immediate serial recall: A matter of mnemonics? *Cognitive Psychology, 9,* 403–411.

MacDonald, M. C., Just, M. A., & Carpenter, P. A. (1992). Working memory constraints on the processing of syntactic ambiguity. *Cognitive Psychology, 24,* 56–98.

Marcus, M. P. (1980). *A theory of syntactic recognition for natural language.* Cambridge, MA: MIT Press.

Masson, M. E. J., & Miller, J. A. (1983). Working memory and individual differences in comprehension and memory of text. *Journal of Educational Psychology, 75,* 314–318.

McClelland, J. L. (1979). On the time relations of mental processes: An examination of systems of processes in cascade. *Psychological Review, 86,* 287–330.

McClelland, J. L., & Rumelhart, D. E. (1988). *Explorations in parallel distributed processing: A handbook of models, programs, and exercises.* Cambridge, MA: MIT Press.

Navon, D. (1984). Resources—A theoretical soup stone? *Psychological Review, 91,* 216–234.

Navon, D., & Gopher, D. (1979). On the economy of the human processing system. *Psychological Review, 86*, 214–255.

Norman, D. A., & Bobrow, D. G. (1975). On data-limited and resource-limited processes. *Cognitive Psychology, 7*, 44–64.

Perfetti, C. A., & Goldman, S. R. (1976). Discourse memory and reading comprehension skill. *Journal of Verbal Learning and Verbal Behavior, 14*, 33–42.

Sanford, A. J., & Garrod, S. C. (1981). *Understanding written language: Explorations in comprehension beyond the sentence.* New York: Wiley.

Schneider, W., & Shiffrin, R. M. (1977). Controlled and automatic human information processing: I. Detection, search, and attention. *Psychological Review, 84*, 1–66.

Shallice, T. (1982). Specific impairments of planning. *Philosophical Transactions of the Royal Society of London B, 298*, 199–209.

Shallice, T. (1988). *From neuropsychology to mental structure.* Cambridge, England: Cambridge University Press.

Sharkey, N. E., & Mitchell, D. C. (1985). Word recognition in a functional context: The use of scripts in reading. *Journal of Memory and Language, 24*, 253–270.

Sheldon, A. (1974). The role of parallel function in the acquisition of relative clauses in English. *Journal of Verbal Learning and Verbal Behavior, 13*, 272–281.

St. John, M. F., & McClelland, J. L. (1990). Learning and applying contextual constraints in sentence comprehension. *Artificial Intelligence, 46*, 217–257.

Thibadeau, R., Just, M. A., & Carpenter, P. A. (1982). A model of the time course and content of reading. *Cognitive Science, 6*, 157–203.

Turner, M. L., & Engle, R. W. (1989). Is working memory capacity task dependent? *Journal of Memory and Language, 28*, 127–154.

vanDijk, T. A., & Kintsch, W. (1983). *Strategies of discourse comprehension.* San Diego, CA: Academic Press.

Waltz, D. L., & Pollack, J. B. (1985). Massively parallel parsing: A strongly interactive model of natural language interpretation. *Cognitive Science, 9*, 51–74.

Wickens, C. D. (1984). Processing resources in attention. In R. Parasuraman & D. R. Davies (Eds.), *Varieties of attention* (pp. 63–102). San Diego, CA: Academic Press.

Winograd, T. (1983). *Language as a cognitive process.* Reading, MA: Addison-Wesley.

B.   *Neural Network Models*

Neural Networks

Chapter 6

How Neural Networks Learn from Experience

Geoffrey E. Hinton

The brain is a remarkable computer. It interprets imprecise information from the senses at an incredibly rapid rate. It discerns a whisper in a noisy room, a face in a dimly lit alley and a hidden agenda in a political statement. Most impressive of all, the brain learns—without any explicit instructions—to create the internal representations that make these skills possible.

Much is still unknown about how the brain trains itself to process information, so theories abound. To test these hypotheses, my colleagues and I have attempted to mimic the brain's learning processes by creating networks of artificial neurons. We construct these neural networks by first trying to deduce the essential features of neurons and their interconnections. We then typically program a computer to simulate these features.

Because our knowledge of neurons is incomplete and our computing power is limited, our models are necessarily gross idealizations of real networks of neurons. Naturally, we enthusiastically debate what features are most essential in simulating neurons. By testing these features in artificial neural networks, we have been successful at ruling out all kinds of theories about how the brain processes information. The models are also beginning to reveal how the brain may accomplish its remarkable feats of learning.

In the human brain, a typical neuron collects signals from others through a host of fine structures called dendrites. The neuron sends out spikes of electrical activity through a long, thin strand known as an axon, which splits into thousands of branches. At the end of each branch, a structure called a synapse converts the activity from the axon into electrical effects that inhibit or excite activity in the connected neurons. When a neuron receives excitatory input that is sufficiently large compared with its inhibitory input, it sends a spike of electrical activity down its axon. Learning occurs by changing the effectiveness of the synapses so that the influence of one neuron on another changes.

Artificial neural networks are typically composed of interconnected "units," which serve as model neurons. The function of the synapse is modeled by a modifiable weight, which is associated with each connection. Most artificial networks do not reflect the detailed geometry of the dendrites and axons, and they express the electrical output of a neuron as a single number that represents the rate of firing—its activity.

Each unit converts the pattern of incoming activities that it receives into a single outgoing activity that it broadcasts to other units. It performs this conversion in two stages. First, it multiplies each incoming activity by the weight on the connection and adds together all these weighted inputs to get a quantity called the total input. Second, a unit uses an input-output function that transforms the total input into the outgoing activity.

The behavior of an artificial neural network depends on both the weights and the input-output function that is specified for the units. This function typically falls into one of three categories: linear, threshold or sigmoid. For linear units, the output activity is proportional to the total weighted input. For threshold units, the output is set at one of two levels, depending on whether the total input is greater than or less than some threshold value. For sigmoid units, the output varies continuously but not linearly as the input changes. Sigmoid units bear a greater resemblance to real neurons than do linear or threshold units, but all three must be considered rough approximations.

To make a neural network that performs some specific task, we must choose how the units are connected to one another, and we must set the weights on the connections appropriately. The connections determine whether it is possible for one unit to influence another. The weights specify the strength of the influence.

The most common type of artificial neural network consists of three groups, or layers, of units: a layer of input units is connected to a layer of "hidden"

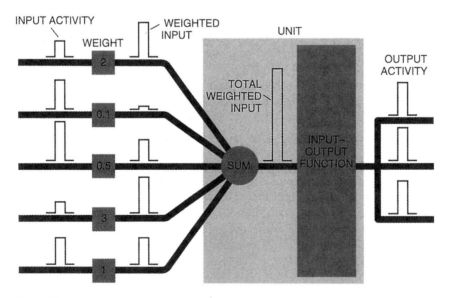

Figure 6.1
Idealization of a neuron processes activities, or signals. Each input activity is multiplied by a number called the weight. The "unit" adds together the weighted inputs. It then computes the output activity using an input-output function.

units, which is connected to a layer of output units. The activity of the input units represents the raw information that is fed into the network. The activity of each hidden unit is determined by the activities of the input units and the weights on the connections between the input and hidden units. Similarly, the behavior of the output units depends on the activity of the hidden units and the weights between the hidden and output units.

This simple type of network is interesting because the hidden units are free to construct their own representations of the input. The weights between the input and hidden units determine when each hidden unit is active, and so by modifying these weights, a hidden unit can choose what it represents.

We can teach a three-layer network to perform a particular task by using the following procedure. First, we present the network with training examples, which consist of a pattern of activities for the input units together with the desired pattern of activities for the output units. We then determine how closely the actual output of the network matches the desired output. Next we change the weight of each connection so that the network produces a better approximation of the desired output.

For example, suppose we want a network to recognize handwritten digits. We might use an array of, say, 256 sensors, each recording the presence or absence of ink in a small area of a single digit. The network would therefore need 256 input units (one for each sensor), 10 output units (one for each kind of digit) and a number of hidden units. For each kind of digit recorded by the sensors, the network should produce high activity in the appropriate output unit and low activity in the other output units.

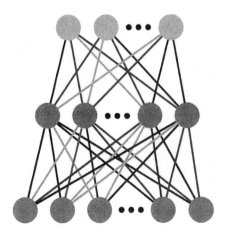

Figure 6.2
Common neural network consists of three layers of units that are fully connected. Activity passes from the input units to the hidden units and finally to the output units.

To train the network, we present an image of a digit and compare the actual activity of the 10 output units with the desired activity. We then calculate the error, which is defined as the square of the difference between the actual and the desired activities. Next we change the weight of each connection so as to reduce the error. We repeat this training process for many different images of each kind of digit until the network classifies every image correctly.

To implement this procedure, we need to change each weight by an amount that is proportional to the rate at which the error changes as the weight is changed. This quantity—called the error derivative for the weight, or simply the EW—is tricky to compute efficiently. One way to calculate the EW is to perturb a weight slightly and observe how the error changes. But that method is inefficient because it requires a separate perturbation for each of the many weights.

Around 1974, Paul J. Werbos invented a much more efficient procedure for calculating the EW while he was working toward a doctorate at Harvard University. The procedure, now known as the back-propagation algorithm, has become one of the more important tools for training neural networks.

The back-propagation algorithm is easiest to understand if all the units in the network are linear. The algorithm computes each EW by first computing the EA, the rate at which the error changes as the activity level of a unit is changed. For output units, the EA is simply the difference between the actual and the desired output. To compute the EA for a hidden unit in the layer just before the output layer, we first identify all the weights between that hidden unit and the output units to which it is connected. We then multiply those weights by the EAs of those output units and add the products. This sum equals the EA for the chosen hidden unit. After calculating all the EAs in the hidden layer just before the output layer, we can compute in like fashion the EAs for other layers, moving from layer to layer in a direction opposite to the way activities propagate through the network. This is what gives back propagation its name. Once the EA has been computed for a unit, it is straightforward to compute the EW for each incoming connection of the unit. The EW is the product of the EA and the activity through the incoming connection.

For nonlinear units, the back-propagation algorithm includes an extra step. Before back-propagating, the EA must be converted into the EI, the rate at which the error changes as the total input received by a unit is changed. (The details of this calculation are given in box 6.2.)

The back-propagation algorithm was largely ignored for years after its invention, probably because its usefulness was not fully appreciated. In the early 1980s, David E. Rumelhart, then at the University of California at San Diego, and David B. Parker, then at Stanford University, independently rediscovered the algorithm. In 1986, Rumelhart, Ronald J. Williams, also at the University of California at San Diego, and I popularized the algorithm by demonstrating that

Box 6.1
How a Neural Network Represents Handwritten Digits

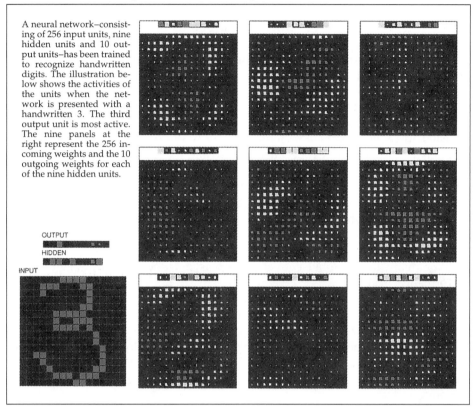

A neural network–consisting of 256 input units, nine hidden units and 10 output units–has been trained to recognize handwritten digits. The illustration below shows the activities of the units when the network is presented with a handwritten 3. The third output unit is most active. The nine panels at the right represent the 256 incoming weights and the 10 outgoing weights for each of the nine hidden units.

OUTPUT

HIDDEN

INPUT

it could teach the hidden units to produce interesting representations of complex input patterns.

The back-propagation algorithm has proved surprisingly good at training networks with multiple layers to perform a wide variety of tasks. It is most useful in situations in which the relation between input and output is nonlinear and training data are abundant. By applying the algorithm, researchers have produced neural networks that recognize handwritten digits, predict currency exchange rates and maximize the yields of chemical processes. They have even used the algorithm to train networks that identify precancerous cells in Pap smears and that adjust the mirror of a telescope so as to cancel out atmospheric distortions.

Within the field of neuroscience, Richard Andersen of the Massachusetts Institute of Technology and David Zipser of the University of California at San Diego showed that the back-propagation algorithm is a useful tool for explaining the function of some neurons in the brain's cortex. They trained a neural network to respond to visual stimuli using back propagation. They then found that the responses of the hidden units were remarkably similar to those of real neurons responsible for converting visual information from the retina into a form suitable for deeper visual areas of the brain.

Yet back propagation has had a rather mixed reception as a theory of how biological neurons learn. On the one hand, the back-propagation algorithm has made a valuable contribution at an abstract level. The algorithm is quite good at creating sensible representations in the hidden units. As a result, researchers gained confidence in learning procedures in which weights are gradually adjusted to reduce errors. Previously, many workers had assumed that such methods would be hopeless because they would inevitably lead to locally optimal but globally terrible solutions. For example, a digit-recognition network might consistently home in on a set of weights that makes the network confuse ones and sevens even though an ideal set of weights exists that would allow the network to discriminate between the digits. This fear supported a widespread belief that a learning procedure was interesting only if it were guaranteed to converge eventually on the globally optimal solution. Back propagation showed that for many tasks global convergence was not necessary to achieve good performance.

On the other hand, back propagation seems biologically implausible. The most obvious difficulty is that information must travel through the same connections in the reverse direction, from one layer to the previous layer. Clearly, this does not happen in real neurons. But this objection is actually rather superficial. The brain has many pathways from later layers back to earlier ones, and it could use these pathways in many ways to convey the information required for learning.

A more important problem is the speed of the back-propagation algorithm. Here the central issue is how the time required to learn increases as the network gets larger. The time taken to calculate the error derivatives for the weights on a given training example is proportional to the size of the network because the amount of computation is proportional to the number of weights. But bigger networks typically require more training examples, and they must update the weights more times. Hence, the learning time grows much faster than does the size of the network.

The most serious objection to back propagation as a model of real learning is that is requires a teacher to supply the desired output for each training example. In contrast, people learn most things without the help of a teacher. Nobody presents us with a detailed description of the internal representations of the world that we must learn to extract from our sensory input. We learn to understand sentences or visual scenes without any direct instructions.

How can a network learn appropriate internal representations if it starts with no knowledge and no teacher? If a network is presented with a large set of

Box 6.2
The Back-Propagation Algorithm

To train a neural network to perform some task, we must adjust the weights of each unit in such a way that the error between the desired output and the actual output is reduced. This process requires that the neural network compute the error derivative of the weights (EW). In other words, it must calculate how the error changes as each weight is increased or decreased slightly. The back-propagation algorithm is the most widely used method for determining the EW.

To implement the back-propagation algorithm, we must first describe a neural network in mathematical terms. Assume that unit j is a typical unit in the output layer and unit i is a typical unit in the previous layer. A unit in the output layer determines its activity by following a two-step procedure. First, it computes the total weighted input x_j, using the formula

$$x_j = \sum_i y_i w_{ij},$$

where y_i is the activity level of the ith unit in the previous layer and w_{ij} is the weight of the connection between the ith and jth unit.

Next, the unit calculates the activity y_j using some function of the total weighted input. Typically, we use the sigmoid function:

$$y_j = \frac{1}{1 + e_j^{-x}}.$$

Once the activities of all the output units have been determined, the network computes the error E, which is defined by the expression

$$E = \frac{1}{2} \sum_j (y_j - d_j)^2,$$

where y_j is the activity level of the jth unit in the top layer and d_j is the desired output of the jth unit.

The back-propagation algorithm consists of four steps:

1. Compute how fast the error changes as the activity of an output unit is changed. This error derivative $\partial E / \partial y$ is the difference between the actual and the desired activity.

$$\frac{\partial E}{\partial y_j} = y_j - d_j$$

2. Compute how fast the error changes as the total input received by an output unit is changed. This quantity $\partial E / \partial x$ is the answer from step 1 multiplied by the rate at which the output of a unit changes as its total input is changed.

$$\frac{\partial E}{\partial x_j} = \frac{\partial E}{\partial y_j} \frac{dy_j}{dx_j} = y_j - d_j y_j (1 - y_j)$$

3. Compute how fast the error changes as a weight on the connection into an output unit is changed. This quantity $\partial E / \partial w$ is the answer from step 2 multiplied by the activity level of the unit from which the connection emanates.

$$\frac{\partial E}{\partial w_{ij}} = \frac{\partial E}{\partial x_j} \frac{\partial x_j}{\partial w_{ij}} = \frac{\partial E}{\partial x_j} y_i$$

Box 6.2 (continued)

4. Compute how fast the error changes as the activity of a unit in the previous layer is changed. This crucial step allows back propagation to be applied to multilayer networks. When the activity of a unit in the previous layer changes, it affects the activities of all the output units to which it is connected. So to compute the overall effect on the error, we add together all these separate effects on output units. But each effect is simple to calculate. It is the answer in step 2 multiplied by the weight on the connection to that output unit.

$$\frac{\partial E}{\partial y_i} = \sum_j \frac{\partial E}{\partial x_j} \frac{\partial x_j}{\partial y_i} = \sum_j \frac{\partial E}{\partial x_j} w_{ij}$$

By using steps 2 and 4, we can convert the $\partial E/\partial y$ of one layer of units into $\partial E/\partial y$ for the previous layer. This procedure can be repeated to get the $\partial E/\partial y$ for as many previous layers as desired. Once we know the $\partial E/\partial y$ of a unit, we can use steps 2 and 3 to compute the $\partial E/\partial w$ on its incoming connections.

patterns but is given no information about what to do with them, it apparently does not have a well-defined problem to solve. Nevertheless, researchers have developed several general-purpose, unsupervised procedures that can adjust the weights in the network appropriately.

All these procedures share two characteristics: they appeal, implicitly or explicitly, to some notion of the quality of a representation, and they work by changing the weights to improve the quality of the representation extracted by the hidden units.

In general, a good representation is one that can be described very economically but nonetheless contains enough information to allow a close approximation of the raw input to be reconstructed. For example, consider an image consisting of several ellipses. Suppose a device translates the image into an array of a million tiny squares, each of which is either light or dark. The image could be represented simply by the positions of the dark squares. But other, more efficient representations are also possible. Ellipses differ in only five ways: orientation, vertical position, horizontal position, length and width. The image can therefore be described using only five parameters per ellipse.

Although describing an ellipse by five parameters requires more bits than describing a single dark square by two coordinates, we get an overall savings because far fewer parameters than coordinates are needed. Furthermore, we do not lose any information by describing the ellipses in terms of their parameters: given the parameters of the ellipse, we could reconstruct the original image if we so desired.

Almost all the unsupervised learning procedures can be viewed as methods of minimizing the sum of two terms, a code cost and a reconstruction cost. The

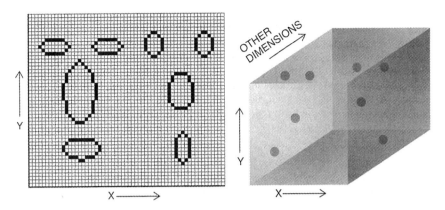

Figure 6.3
Two faces composed of eight ellipses can be represented as many points in two dimensions. Alternatively, because the ellipses differ in only five ways—orientation, vertical position, horizontal position, length and width—the two faces can be represented as eight points in a five-dimensional space.

code cost is the number of bits required to describe the activities of the hidden units. The reconstruction cost is the number of bits required to describe the misfit between the raw input and the best approximation to it that could be reconstructed from the activities of the hidden units. The reconstruction cost is proportional to the squared difference between the raw input and its reconstruction.

Two simple methods for discovering economical codes allow fairly accurate reconstruction of the input: principal-components learning and competitive learning. In both approaches, we first decide how economical the code should be and then modify the weights in the network to minimize the reconstruction error.

A principal-components learning strategy is based on the idea that if the activities of pairs of input units are correlated in some way, it is a waste of bits to describe each input activity separately. A more efficient approach is to extract and describe the principal components—that is, the components of variation shared by many input units. If we wish to discover, say, 10 of the principal components, then we need only a single layer of 10 hidden units.

Because such networks represent the input using only a small number of components, the code cost is low. And because the input can be reconstructed quite well from the principal components, the reconstruction cost is small.

One way to train this type of network is to force it to reconstruct an approximation to the input on a set of output units. Then back propagation can be used to minimize the difference between the actual output and the desired output. This process resembles supervised learning, but because the desired output is exactly the same as the input, no teacher is required.

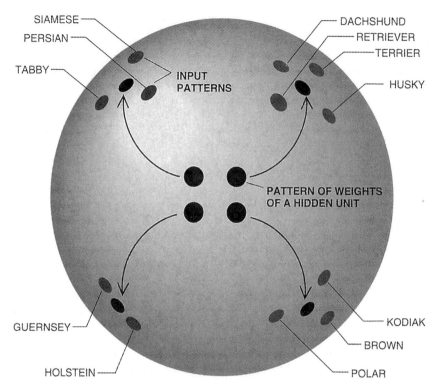

Figure 6.4
Competitive learning can be envisioned as a process in which each input pattern attracts the weight pattern of the closest hidden unit. Each input pattern represents a set of distinguishing features. The weight patterns of hidden units are adjusted so that they migrate slowly toward the closest set of input patterns. In this way, each hidden unit learns to represent a cluster of similar input patterns.

Many researchers, including Ralph Linsker of the IBM Thomas J. Watson Research Center and Erkki Oja of Lappeenranta University of Technology in Finland, have discovered alternative algorithms for learning principal components. These algorithms are more biologically plausible because they do not require output units or back propagation. Instead they use the correlation between the activity of a hidden unit and the activity of an input unit to determine the change in the weight.

When a neural network uses principal-components learning, a small number of hidden units cooperate in representing the input pattern. In contrast, in competitive learning, a large number of hidden units compete so that a single hidden unit is used to represent any particular input pattern. The selected hidden unit is the one whose incoming weights are most similar to the input pattern.

Now suppose we had to reconstruct the input pattern solely from our knowledge of which hidden unit was chosen. Our best bet would be to copy the pattern of incoming weights of the chosen hidden unit. To minimize the reconstruction error, we should move the pattern of weights of the winning hidden unit even closer to the input pattern. This is what competitive learning does. If the network is presented with training data that can be grouped into clusters of similar input patterns, each hidden unit learns to represent a different cluster, and its incoming weights converge on the center of the cluster.

Like the principal-components algorithm, competitive learning minimizes the reconstruction cost while keeping the code cost low. We can afford to use many hidden units because even with a million units it takes only 20 bits to say which one won.

In the early 1980s Teuvo Kohonen of Helsinki University introduced an important modification of the competitive learning algorithm. Kohonen showed how to make physically adjacent hidden units learn to represent similar input patterns. Kohonen's algorithm adapts not only the weights of the winning hidden unit but also the weights of the winner's neighbors. The algorithm's ability to map similar input patterns to nearby hidden units suggests that a procedure of this type may be what the brain uses to create the topographic maps found in the visual cortex.

Unsupervised learning algorithms can be classified according to the type of representation they create. In principal-components methods, the hidden units cooperate, and the representation of each input pattern is distributed across all of them. In competitive methods, the hidden units compete, and the representation of the input pattern is localized in the single hidden unit that is selected. Until recently, most work on unsupervised learning focused on one or another of these two techniques, probably because they lead to simple rules for changing the weights. But the most interesting and powerful algorithms probably lie somewhere between the extremes of purely distributed and purely localized representations.

Horace B. Barlow of the University of Cambridge has proposed a model in which each hidden unit is rarely active and the representation of each input pattern is distributed across a small number of selected hidden units. He and his co-workers have shown that this type of code can be learned by forcing hidden units to be uncorrelated while also ensuring that the hidden code allows good reconstruction of the input.

Unfortunately, most current methods of minimizing the code cost tend to eliminate all the redundancy among the activities of the hidden units. As a result, the network is very sensitive to the malfunction of a single hidden unit. This feature is uncharacteristic of the brain, which is generally not affected greatly by the loss of a few neurons.

The brain seems to use what are known as population codes, in which information is represented by a whole population of active neurons. That point was

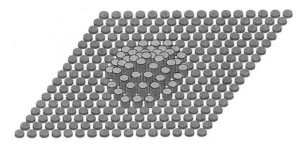

Figure 6.5
Population coding represents a multiparameter object as a bump of activity spread over many hidden units. Each disk represents an inactive hidden unit. Each cylinder indicates an active unit, and its height depicts the level of activity.

beautifully demonstrated in the experiments of David L. Sparks and his co-workers at the University of Alabama. While investigating how the brain of a monkey instructs its eyes where to move, they found that the required movement is encoded by the activities of a whole population of cells, each of which represents a somewhat different movement. The eye movement that is actually made corresponds to the average of all the movements encoded by the active cells. If some brain cells are anesthetized, the eye moves to the point associated with the average of the remaining active cells. Population codes may be used to encode not only eye movements but also faces, as shown by Malcolm P. Young and Shigeru Yamane at the RIKEN Institute in Japan in recent experiments on the inferior temporal cortex of monkeys.

For both eye movements and faces, the brain must represent entities that vary along many different dimensions. In the case of an eye movement, there are just two dimensions, but for something like a face, there are dimensions such as happiness, hairiness or familiarity, as well as spatial parameters such as position, size and orientation. If we associate with each face-sensitive cell the parameters of the face that make it most active, we can average these parameters over a population of active cells to discover the parameters of the face being represented by that population code. In abstract terms, each face cell represents a particular point in a multidimensional space of possible faces, and any face can then be represented by activating all the cells that encode very similar faces, so that a bump of activity appears in the multidimensional space of possible faces.

Population coding is attractive because it works even if some of the neurons are damaged. It can do so because the loss of a random subset of neurons has little effect on the population average. The same reasoning applies if some neurons are overlooked when the system is in a hurry. Neurons communicate by sending discrete spikes called action potentials, and in a very short time interval, many of the "active" neurons may not have time to send a spike. Nevertheless, even in such a short interval, a population code in one part of the brain can still give rise to an approximately correct population code in another part of the brain.

At first sight, the redundancy in population codes seems incompatible with the idea of constructing internal representations that minimize the code cost. Fortunately, we can overcome this difficulty by using a less direct measure of code cost. If the activity that encodes a particular entity is a smooth bump in which activity falls off in a standard way as we move away from the center, we can describe the bump of activity completely merely by specifying its center. So a fairer measure of code cost is the cost of describing the center of the bump of activity plus the cost of describing how the actual activities of the units depart from the desired smooth bump of activity.

Using this measure of the code cost, we find that population codes are a convenient way of extracting a hierarchy of progressively more efficient encodings of the sensory input. This point is best illustrated by a simple example. Consider a neural network that is presented with an image of a face. Suppose the network already contains one set of units dedicated to representing noses, another set for mouths and another set for eyes. When it is shown a particular face, there will be one bump of activity in the nose units, one in the mouth units and two in the eye units. The location of each of these activity bumps represents the spatial parameters of the feature encoded by the bump. Describing the four activity bumps is cheaper than describing the raw image, but it would obviously be cheaper still to describe a single bump of activity in a set of face units, assuming of course that the nose, mouth and eyes are in the correct spatial relations to form a face.

This raises an interesting issue: How can the network check that the parts are correctly related to one another to make a face? Some time ago Dana H. Ballard of the University of Rochester introduced a clever technique for solving this type of problem that works nicely with population codes.

If we know the position, size and orientation of a nose, we can predict the position, size and orientation of the face to which it belongs because the spatial relation between noses and faces is roughly fixed. We therefore set the weights in the neural network so that a bump of activity in the nose units tries to cause an appropriately related bump of activity in the face units. But we also set the thresholds of the face units so that the nose units alone are insufficient to activate the face units. If, however, the bump of activity in the mouth units also tries to cause a bump in the same place in the face units, then the thresholds can be overcome. In effect, we have checked that the nose and mouth are correctly related to each other by checking that they both predict the same spatial parameters for the whole face.

This method of checking spatial relations is intriguing because it makes use of the kind of redundancy between different parts of an image that un-

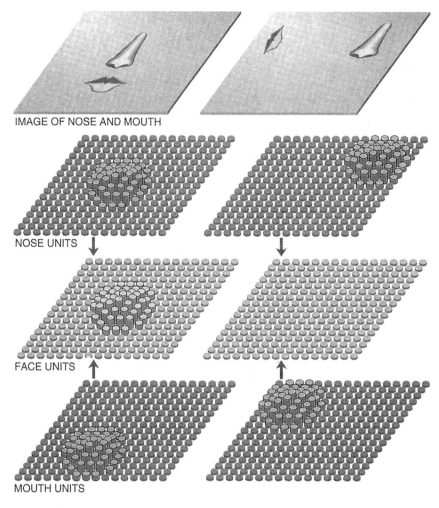

Figure 6.6
Bumps of activity in sets of hidden units represent the image of a nose and a mouth. The population codes will cause a bump in the face units if the nose and mouth have the correct spatial relation (left). If not, the active nose units will try to create a bump in the face units at one location while the active mouth units will do the same at a different location. As a result, the input activity to the face units does not exceed a threshold value, and no bump is formed in the face units (right).

supervised learning should be good at finding. It therefore seems natural to try to use unsupervised learning to discover hierarchical population codes for extracting complex shapes. In 1986, Eric Saund of M.I.T. demonstrated one method of learning simple population codes for shapes. It seems likely that with a clear definition of the code cost, an unsupervised network will be able to discover more complex hierarchies by trying to minimize the cost of coding the image. Richard Zemel and I at the University of Toronto are now investigating this possibility.

By using unsupervised learning to extract a hierarchy of successively more economical representations, it should be possible to improve greatly the speed of learning in large multilayer networks. Each layer of the network adapts its incoming weights to make its representation better than the representation in the previous layer, so weights in one layer can be learned without reference to weights in subsequent layers. This strategy eliminates many of the interactions between weights that make back-propagation learning very slow in deep multi-layer networks.

All the learning procedures discussed thus far are implemented in neural networks in which activity flows only in the forward direction from input to output even though error derivatives may flow in the backward direction. Another important possibility to consider is networks in which activity flows around closed loops. Such recurrent networks may settle down to stable states, or they may exhibit complex temporal dynamics that can be used to produce sequential behavior. If they settle to stable states, error derivatives can be computed using methods much simpler than back propagation.

Although investigators have devised some powerful learning algorithms that are of great practical value, we still do not know which representations and learning procedures are actually used by the brain. But sooner or later, computational studies of learning in artificial neural networks will converge on the methods discovered by evolution. When that happens, a lot of diverse empirical data about the brain will suddenly make sense, and many new applications of artificial neural networks will become feasible.

Hopfield Networks

Chapter 7

The Hopfield Model

John Hertz, Anders Krogh, and Richard G. Palmer

1 The Associative Memory Problem

Associative memory is the "fruit fly" or "Bohr atom" problem of this field. It illustrates in about the simplest possible manner the way that collective computation can work. The basic problem is this:

> Store a set of p patterns ξ_i^μ in such a way that when presented with a new pattern ζ_i, the network responds by producing whichever one of the stored patterns most closely resembles ζ_i.

The patterns are labelled by $\mu = 1, 2, \ldots, p$, while the units in the network are labelled by $i = 1, 2, \ldots, N$. Both the stored patterns ξ_i^μ and the test patterns ζ_i can be taken to be either 0 or 1 on each site i, though we will adopt a different convention shortly.

We could of course do this serially in a conventional computer simply by storing a list of the patterns ξ_i^μ, writing a program which computed the Hamming distance[1]

$$\sum_i [\xi_i^\mu (1 - \zeta_i) + (1 - \xi_i^\mu)\zeta_i] \tag{1}$$

between the test pattern ζ_i and each of the stored patterns, finding which of them was smallest, and printing the corresponding stored pattern out.

Here we want to see how to get a McCulloch-Pitts network to do it. That is, if we *start* in the configuration $n_i = \zeta_i$, we want to know what (if any) set of w_{ij}'s will make the network go to the state with $n_i = \xi_i^{\mu_0}$, where it is pattern number μ_0 that is the smallest distance (1) from ζ_i. Thus we want the memory to be **content-addressable** and insensitive to small errors in the input pattern.

A content-addressable memory can be quite powerful. Suppose, for example, we store coded information about many famous scientists in a network. Then the starting pattern "evolution" should be sufficient to recall everything about Darwin, and "$E = mc^3$" should recall Einstein, despite the error in the input pattern. Note that *some* pattern will always be retrieved for any clue (unless we invent a "don't know" pattern); the network will never retrieve a linear combination of, say, Darwin and Wallace in response to "evolution" but will pick the

Figure 7.1
Example of how an associative memory can reconstruct images. These are binary images with 130×180 pixels. The images on the right were recalled by the memory after presentation of the corrupted images shown on the left. The middle column shows some intermediate states. A sparsely connected Hopfield network with seven stored images was used.

best match according to what has been stored. This depends on the nonlinearity of the network, and obviously has advantages for many practical applications.

Other common examples of applications for an associative memory are recognition and reconstruction of images (see Fig. 7.1), and retrieval of bibliographic information from partial references (such as from an incomplete title of a paper).

Figure 7.2 shows schematically the function of the dynamic associative (or content-addressable) memories that we construct in this chapter. The space of all possible states of the network—the **configuration** space—is represented by the region drawn. Within that space are stored patterns called **attractors**. The dynamics of the system carries starting points into one of the attractors, as shown by the trajectories sketched. The whole configuration space is thus divided up into **basins of attraction** of the different attractors. This picture is very idealized, and in particular the space should really be a discrete set of

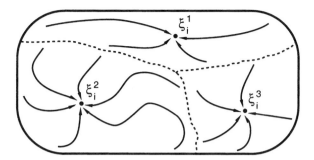

Figure 7.2
Schematic configuration space of a model with three attractors.

points (on a hypercube), not a continuous region. But it is nevertheless a very useful image to keep in mind.

In the next section we treat the basic Hopfield [1982] model of associative memory. In Section 3 we turn to statistical mechanics, studying some magnetic systems that are analogous to our networks. Then in Section 4 we define a stochastic version of the original model, and analyze it using statistical mechanics methods. Finally, Section 5 presents a heuristic derivation of the famous $0.138N$ capacity of the Hopfield model. Various embellishments and generalizations of the basic model are discussed in the next chapter.

2 The Model

For mathematical convenience we now transform to a formulation where the activation values of the units are $+1$ (firing) and -1 (not firing) instead of 1 and 0. We denote[2] them by S_i rather than n_i. Conversion to and from the $n_i = 0$ or 1 notation is easy via $S_i = 2n_i - 1$. The dynamics of the network reads

$$S_i := \text{sgn}\left(\sum_j w_{ij} S_j - \theta_i \right) \tag{2}$$

where we take the sign function $\text{sgn}(x)$ (illustrated in Fig. 7.3) to be

$$\text{sgn}(x) = \begin{cases} 1 & \text{if } x \geq 0; \\ -1 & \text{if } x < 0; \end{cases} \tag{3}$$

and the threshold θ_i is related to the μ_i in (1.1) by $\theta_i = 2\mu_i - \sum_j w_{ij}$. In the rest of this chapter we drop these threshold terms, taking $\theta_i = 0$, because they are not useful with the random patterns that we will consider. Thus we use

$$S_i := \text{sgn}\left(\sum_j w_{ij} S_j \right). \tag{4}$$

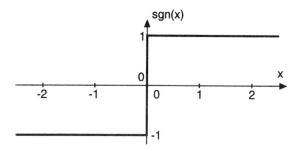

Figure 7.3
The function sgn (x).

There are at least two ways in which we might carry out the updating specified by (4). We could do it *synchronously*, updating all units simultaneously at each time step. Or we could do it *asynchronously*, updating them one at a time. Both kinds of models are interesting, but the asynchronous choice is more natural for both brains and artificial networks. The synchronous choice requires a central clock or pacemaker, and is potentially sensitive to timing errors. In the asynchronous case, which we adopt henceforth, we can proceed in either of two ways:

· At each time step, select at random a unit i to be updated, and apply the rule (4).
· Let each unit independently choose to update itself according to (4), with some constant probability per unit time.

These choices are equivalent (except for the distribution of update intervals) because the second gives a random sequence; there is vanishingly small probability of two units choosing to update at exactly the same moment. The first choice is appropriate for simulation, with central control, while the second is appropriate for autonomous hardware units.

We also have to specify for how long (for how many updatings) we will allow the network to evolve before demanding that its units' values give the desired stored pattern. One possibility in the case of *synchronous* updating is to require that the network go to the correct memorized pattern right away on the first iteration. In the present discussion (using asynchronous updating) we demand only that the network settle eventually into a stable configuration— one for which no S_i changes any more.

Rather than study a specific problem such as memorizing a particular set of pictures, we examine the more generic problem of a *random* set of patterns drawn from a distribution. For convenience, we will usually take the patterns to be made up of independent bits ξ_i which can each take on the values $+1$ and -1 with equal probability.

Our procedure for testing whether a proposed form of w_{ij} is acceptable is first to see whether the patterns to be memorized are themselves stable, and then to check whether small deviations from these patterns are corrected as the network evolves.

One Pattern
To motivate our choice for the connection weights, we consider first the simple case where there is just one pattern ξ_i that we want to memorize. The condition for this pattern to be stable is just

$$\text{sgn}\left(\sum_j w_{ij}\xi_j \right) = \xi_i \quad \text{(for all } i) \tag{5}$$

because then the rule (4) produces no changes. It is easy to see that this is true if we take

$$w_{ij} \propto \xi_i\xi_j \tag{6}$$

since $\xi_j^2 = 1$. For later convenience we take the constant of proportionality to be $1/N$, where N is the number of units in the network, giving

$$w_{ij} = \frac{1}{N}\xi_i\xi_j. \tag{7}$$

Furthermore, it is also obvious that even if a number (fewer than half) of the bits of the starting pattern S_i are wrong (i.e., not equal to ξ_i), they will be overwhelmed in the sum for the net input

$$h_i = \sum_j w_{ij}S_j \tag{8}$$

by the majority that are right, and $\text{sgn}(h_i)$ will still give ξ_i. An initial configuration near (in Hamming distance) to ξ_i will therefore quickly relax to ξ_i. This means that the network will correct errors as desired, and we can say that the pattern ξ_i is an **attractor**.

Actually there are two attractors in this simple case; the other one is at $-\xi_i$. This is called a **reversed state**. All starting configurations with *more* than half the bits different from the original pattern will end up in the reversed state. The configuration space is symmetrically divided into two basins of attraction, as shown in Fig. 7.4.

Many Patterns
This is fine for one pattern, but how do we get the system to recall the most similar of many patterns? The simplest answer is just to make w_{ij} a superposition of terms like (7), one for each pattern:

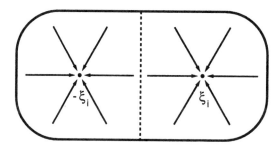

Figure 7.4
Schematic configuration space for the one pattern case, including the reversed state.

$$w_{ij} = \frac{1}{N} \sum_{\mu=1}^{p} \xi_i^{\mu} \xi_j^{\mu}. \tag{9}$$

Here p is the total number of stored patterns labelled by μ.

This is usually called the "Hebb rule" or the "generalized Hebb rule" because of the similarity between (9) and a hypothesis made by Hebb [1949] about the way in which synaptic strengths in the brain change in response to experience: Hebb suggested changes proportional to the correlation between the firing of the pre- and post-synaptic neurons. If we apply our set of patterns ξ_i^{μ} to the network during a **training phase**, and adjust the w_{ij} strengths according to such pre/post correlations, we arrive directly at (9). Technically, however, (9) goes beyond Hebb's original hypothesis because it changes the weights positively when neither of the units is firing ($\xi_i^{\mu} = \xi_j^{\mu} = -1$). This is probably not physiologically reasonable. Equation (9) can even cause a particular connection to change from excitatory to inhibitory or vice versa as more patterns are added, which is never believed to occur at real synapses. It is possible to modify the equation in various ways to remedy these defects [Toulouse et al., 1986], but here we use the simple form (9) unchanged.

An associative memory model using the Hebb rule (9) for all possible pairs ij, with binary units and asynchronous updating, is usually called a **Hopfield model**. The term is also applied to various generalizations discussed in the next chapter. Although most of the ingredients of the model were known earlier, Hopfield's influential paper [Hopfield, 1982] brought them together, introduced an energy function, and emphasized the idea of stored memories as dynamical attractors. Earlier related models, often also using the Hebb rule, are reviewed by Cowan and Sharp [1988a,b]. Particularly important is the Little model [Little and Shaw, 1975, 1978], which is based however on *synchronous* updating.

Let us examine the stability of a particular pattern ξ_i^{ν}. The stability condition (5) generalizes to

$$\text{sgn}(h_i^{\nu}) = \xi_i^{\nu} \quad (\text{for all } i) \tag{10}$$

where the net input h_i^v to unit i in pattern v is

$$h_i^v \equiv \sum_j w_{ij} \xi_j^v = \frac{1}{N} \sum_j \sum_\mu \xi_i^\mu \xi_j^\mu \xi_j^v. \tag{11}$$

We now separate the sum on μ into the special term $\mu = v$ and all the rest:

$$h_i^v = \xi_i^v + \frac{1}{N} \sum_j \sum_{\mu \neq v} \xi_i^\mu \xi_j^\mu \xi_j^v. \tag{12}$$

If the second term were zero, we could immediately conclude that pattern number v was stable according to (10). This is still true if the second term is small enough: *if its magnitude is smaller than 1 it cannot change the sign of h_i^v, and* (10) *will still be satisfied.*

It turns out that the second term, which we call the **crosstalk term**, *is* less than 1 in many cases of interest if p (the number of patterns) is small enough. We will discuss the details shortly; let us assume for now that the crosstalk term is small enough for all i and v. Then the stored patterns are all stable—if we start the system from one of them it will stay there. Furthermore, a small fraction of bits different from a stored pattern will be corrected in the same way as in the single-pattern case; they are overwhelmed in the sum $\sum_j w_{ij} S_j$ by the vast majority of correct bits. A configuration near (in Hamming distance) to ξ_i^v thus relaxes to ξ_i^v. This shows that the chosen patterns are truly attractors of the system, as already anticipated in Fig. 7.2. The system works as expected as a content-addressable memory.

Storage Capacity
Consider the quantity

$$C_i^v \equiv -\xi_i^v \frac{1}{N} \sum_j \sum_{\mu \neq v} \xi_i^\mu \xi_j^\mu \xi_j^v. \tag{13}$$

This is just $-\xi_i^v$ times the crosstalk term in (12). If C_i^v is negative the crosstalk term has the same sign as the desired ξ_i^v term, and thus does no harm. But if C_i^v is positive and larger than 1, it changes the sign of h_i^v and makes bit (or unit) i of pattern v unstable; if we start the system in the desired memory state ξ_i^v, it will *not* stay there.

The C_i^v's just depend on the patterns ξ_j^μ that we attempt to store. For now we consider purely *random* patterns, with equal probability for $\xi_j^\mu = +1$ and for $\xi_j^\mu = -1$, independently for each j and μ. Then we can estimate the probability P_{error} that any chosen bit is unstable:

$$P_{\text{error}} = \text{Prob}(C_i^v > 1). \tag{14}$$

Clearly P_{error} increases as we increase the number p of patterns that we try to store. Choosing a criterion for acceptable performance (e.g., $P_{\text{error}} < 0.01$) lets us find the storage **capacity** p_{max} of the network: the maximum number of patterns that can be stored without unacceptable errors. As we will see, there are actually several different expressions for p_{max}, depending on the type of criterion we use for P_{error}.

Let us first calculate P_{error}. It depends on the number of units N and the number of patterns p. We assume that both N and p are large compared to 1, because this is typically the case and because it makes the mathematics easier. Now C_i^ν is $1/N$ times the sum of about Np independent random numbers,[3] each of which is $+1$ or -1. From the theory of random coin tosses [Feller, 1968] it has therefore a **binomial distribution** with mean zero and variance $\sigma^2 = p/N$. But since Np is assumed large this can be approximated by a Gaussian distribution with the same mean and variance, as shown in Fig. 7.5.

The probability P_{error} that C_i^ν exceeds 1 is just the shaded area in Fig. 7.5. Thus

$$P_{error} = \frac{1}{\sqrt{2\pi}\sigma} \int_1^\infty e^{-x^2/2\sigma^2}\, dx$$

$$= \frac{1}{2}[1 - \mathrm{erf}(1/\sqrt{2\sigma^2})] = \frac{1}{2}[1 - \mathrm{erf}(\sqrt{N/2p})] \tag{15}$$

where the **error function** $\mathrm{erf}(x)$ is defined by

$$\mathrm{erf}(x) \equiv \frac{2}{\sqrt{\pi}} \int_0^x \exp(-u^2)\,du. \tag{16}$$

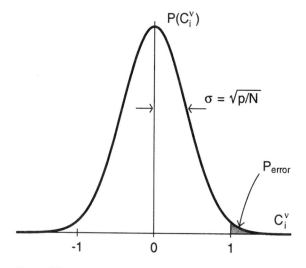

Figure 7.5
The distribution values for the crosstalk C_i^ν given by (13). For p random patterns and N units this is a Gaussian with variance $\sigma^2 = p/N$. The shaded area is P_{error}, the probability of error per bit.

Table 7.1 shows the values of p/N required to obtain various values of P_{error}. Thus if we choose the criterion $P_{error} < 0.01$ for example, we arrive at $p_{max} = 0.15N$.

This calculation only tells us about the *initial* stability of the patterns. If we choose $p < 0.185N$ for example, it tells us that no more than 1% of the pattern bits will be unstable initially. But if we start the system in a particular pattern ξ_i^ν and about 1% of the bits flip, what happens next? It may be that the first few flips will cause more bits to flip. In the worst case there could be an avalanche phenomenon in which more and more bits flip until the final state bears little or no resemblance to the original pattern. So our estimates for p_{max} are upper bounds; smaller values may be required to keep the final attractors close to the desired patterns. An avalanche occurs if $p > 0.138N$, making the whole memory useless. Thus $p_{max} = 0.138N$ if we are willing to accept the errors that occur up to that point. At $p = 0.138N$ table 7.1 shows that only 0.37% of the bits will be unstable initially, though it turns out that about 1.6% of them flip before a stable attractor is reached.

An alternative definition of the capacity insists that most of the memories be recalled *perfectly*. Since each pattern contains N bits, we need $P_{error} < 0.01/N$ to get all N bits right with 99% probability.[4] This clearly implies $p/N \to 0$ as $N \to \infty$, so we can use the asymptotic expansion of the error function

$$1 - \text{erf}(x) \to e^{-x^2}/\sqrt{\pi}x \quad (\text{as } x \to \infty) \tag{17}$$

to obtain

$$\log(P_{error}) \approx -\log 2 - N/2p - \tfrac{1}{2}\log \pi - \tfrac{1}{2}\log(N/2p). \tag{18}$$

This turns the condition $P_{error} < 0.01/N$ into

$$-\log 2 - N/2p - \tfrac{1}{2}\log \pi - \tfrac{1}{2}\log(N/2p) < \log 0.01 - \log N \tag{19}$$

or, taking only the leading terms for large N,

$$N/2p > \log N \tag{20}$$

giving the capacity $p_{max} = N/2\log N$ for this case.

Table 7.1
Capacities

P_{error}	p_{max}/N
0.001	0.105
0.0036	0.138
0.01	0.185
0.05	0.37
0.1	0.61

Even more stringently, we could ask that *all* the patterns be recalled perfectly. This requires us to get Np bits right with, say, 99% probability, and so needs $P_{\text{error}} < 0.01/pN$. It is easy to see that this changes (20) to

$$N/2p > \log(Np) \tag{21}$$

which gives $p_{\text{max}} = N/4\log N$ because $\log(Np) \sim \log N^2 = 2\log N$ in leading order.

Note that we have assumed in the perfect recall cases that the C_i^ν's are independent of one another. Closer examination shows that this is justified. More detailed derivations of the $N/\log N$ results are available in Weisbuch and Fogelman-Soulié [1985] and McEliece et al. [1987].

In summary, the capacity p_{max} is proportional to N (but never higher than $0.138N$) if we are willing to accept a small percentage of errors in each pattern, but is proportional to $N/\log N$ if we insist that most or all patterns be recalled perfectly.

Realistic patterns will *not* in general be random, though some precoding can make them more so. The Hopfield model is usually studied with random patterns for mathematical convenience, though the effect of correlated patterns has also been examined. At the other extreme, if the different patterns are strictly *orthogonal*, i.e.,

$$\sum_j \xi_j^\mu \xi_j^\nu = 0 \quad \text{for all } \mu \neq \nu \tag{22}$$

then there is no crosstalk at all; $C_i^\nu = 0$ for all i and ν.

In this orthogonal case the memory capacity p_{max} is apparently N patterns, because at most N mutually orthogonal bit strings of length N can be constructed. But the *useful* capacity is somewhat smaller. Trying to embed N orthogonal patterns with the Hebb rule actually makes *all* states stable; the system stays wherever it starts, and is useless as a memory. This occurs because the orthogonality conditions (22) lead necessarily to[5]

$$w_{ij} = \begin{cases} 1 & \text{if } i = j; \\ 0 & \text{otherwise.} \end{cases} \tag{23}$$

so each unit is connected only to itself. To define a useful measure of capacity for such a case it is clearly necessary to insist on a finite basin of attraction around each desired pattern. This leads to a useful capacity slightly less than N.

The Energy Function
One of the most important contributions of the Hopfield [1982] paper was to introduce the idea of an *energy function* into neural network theory. For the networks we are considering, the energy function H is

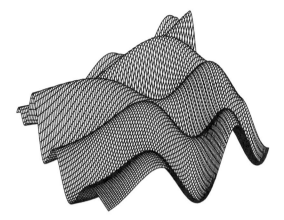

Figure 7.6
It is often useful (but sometimes dangerous) to think of the energy as something like this landscape. The z-axis is the energy and the 2^N corners of the hypercube (the possible states of the system) are formally represented by the x–y plane.

$$H = -\frac{1}{2} \sum_{ij} w_{ij} S_i S_j. \tag{24}$$

The double sum is over all i and all j. The $i = j$ terms are of no consequence because $S_i^2 = 1$; they just contribute a constant to H, and in any case we could choose $w_{ii} = 0$. The energy function is a function of the configuration $\{S_i\}$ of the system, where $\{S_i\}$ means the set of all the S_i's. We can thus imagine an **energy landscape** "above" the configuration space of Fig. 7.2. Typically this surface is quite hilly. Figure 7.6 illustrates the idea.

The central property of an energy function is that *it always decreases (or remains constant) as the system evolves according to its dynamical rule.* We will show this in a moment for (24). Thus the attractors (memorized patterns) in Fig. 7.2 are at local minima of the energy surface. The dynamics can be thought of as similar to the motion of a particle on the energy surface under the influence of gravity (pulling it down) and friction (so that it does not overshoot). From any starting point the particle (representing the whole state $\{S_i\}$ of the system) slides downhill until it comes to rest at one of these local minima—at one of the attractors. The basins of attraction correspond to the valleys or catchment areas around each minimum. Starting the system in a particular valley leads to the lowest point of that valley.

The term **energy function** comes from a physical analogy to magnetic systems that we will discuss in the next section. But the concept is of much wider applicability; in many fields there is a state function that always decreases during dynamical evolution, or that must be minimized to find a stable or optimum state. In some fields the convention is reversed; the function increases or must be maximized. The most general name, from the theory of dynamical systems, is **Lyapunov function** [Cohen and Grossberg, 1983]. Other terms are **Hamiltonian** in statistical mechanics, **cost function** or **objective function** in optimization theory, and **fitness function** in evolutionary biology.

For neural networks in general an energy function exists if the connection strengths are *symmetric*, i.e., $w_{ij} = w_{ji}$. In real networks of neurons this is an unreasonable assumption, but it is useful to study the symmetric case because of the extra insight that the existence of an energy function affords us. The Hebb prescription (9) which we are now studying automatically yields symmetric w_{ij}'s. Gérard Toulouse has called Hopfield's use of symmetric connections a "clever step backwards from biological realism." The cleverness arises from the existence of an energy function.

For symmetric connections we can write (24) in the alternative from

$$H = C - \sum_{(ij)} w_{ij} S_i S_j \tag{25}$$

where (ij) means all the distinct pairs ij, counting for example 12 as the same pair as 21. We exclude the ii terms from (ij); they give the constant C.

It now is easy to show that the dynamical rule (4) can only decrease the energy. Let S_i' be the new value of S_i given by (4) for some particular unit i:

$$S_i' = \text{sgn}\left(\sum_j w_{ij} S_j \right). \tag{26}$$

Obviously if $S_i' = S_i$ the energy is unchanged. In the other case $S_i' = -S_i$ so, picking out the terms that involve S_i,

$$
\begin{aligned}
H' - H &= -\sum_{j \neq i} w_{ij} S_i' S_j + \sum_{j \neq i} w_{ij} S_i S_j \\
&= 2S_i \sum_{j \neq i} w_{ij} S_j \\
&= 2S_i \sum_j w_{ij} S_j - 2w_{ii}.
\end{aligned}
\tag{27}
$$

Now the first term is negative from (26), and the second term is negative because the Hebb rule (9) gives $w_{ii} = p/N$ for all i. Thus the energy decreases every time an S_i changes, as claimed.

The **self-coupling terms** w_{ii} may actually be omitted altogether, both from the Hebb rule (where we can simply define $w_{ii} = 0$) and from the energy function. It is straightforward to check that they make no appreciable difference to the stability of the ξ_i^ν patterns in the large N limit. But they *do* affect the dynamics and the number of spurious states, and it turns out to be *better* to omit them [Kanter and Sompolinsky, 1987]. We can see why simply by separating the self-coupling term out of the dynamical rule (4):

$$S_i := \text{sgn}\left(w_{ii}S_i + \sum_{j \neq i} w_{ij}S_j \right). \tag{28}$$

If w_{ii} were larger than $\sum_{j \neq i} w_{ij}S_j$ in some state, then $S_i = +1$ and $S_i = -1$ could *both* be stable.[6] This can produce additional stable **spurious states** in the neighborhood of a desired attractor, reducing the size of the basin of attraction. If $w_{ii} = 0$, then this problem does not arise; for a given configuration of the other spins, S_i will always pick one of its states over the other.

Starting from an Energy Function
The idea of the energy function as something to be minimized in the stable states gives us an alternate way to derive the Hebb prescription (9). Let us start again with the single-pattern case. We want the energy to be minimized when the overlap between the network configuration and the stored pattern ξ_i is largest. So we choose

$$H = -\frac{1}{2N}\left(\sum_i S_i \xi_i \right)^2 \tag{29}$$

where the factor $1/2N$ is the product of inspired hindsight. For the many-pattern case, we can try to make each of the ξ_i^μ into local minima of H just by summing (29) over all the patterns:

$$H = -\frac{1}{2N}\sum_{\mu=1}^{p}\left(\sum_i S_i \xi_i^\mu \right)^2. \tag{30}$$

Multiplying this out gives

$$H = -\frac{1}{2N}\sum_{\mu=1}^{p}\left(\sum_i S_i \xi_i^\mu \right)\left(\sum_j S_j \xi_j^\mu \right) = -\frac{1}{2}\sum_{ij}\left(\frac{1}{N}\sum_{\mu=1}^{p} \xi_i^\mu \xi_j^\mu \right)S_i S_j \tag{31}$$

which is exactly the same as our original energy function (24) if w_{ij} is given by the Hebb rule (9).

This approach to finding appropriate w_{ij}'s is generally useful. If we can write down an energy function whose minimum satisfies a problem of interest, then we can multiply it out and identify the appropriate connection strength w_{ij} from the coefficient of $S_i S_j$. Of course we may find other terms, not of the $S_i S_j$ form. Constants are no problem, and terms linear in a single S_i can be represented by thresholds or by a connection to a clamped S_0 unit. But terms like $S_i S_j S_k$ take us outside the present framework of pairwise connections.

Spurious States

We have shown that the Hebb prescription (9) gives us (for small enough p) a dynamical system that has attractors—local minima of the energy function— at the desired points ξ_i^μ. These are sometimes called the **retrieval states**. But we have *not* shown that these are the only attractors. And indeed there are others.

First of all, the reversed states $-\xi_i^\mu$ are minima and have the same energy as the original patterns. The dynamics and the energy function both have a perfect symmetry, $S_i \leftrightarrow -S_i$ for all i. This is not too troublesome for the retrieved patterns; we could agree to reverse all the remaining bits when a particular "sign bit" is -1 for example.

Second, there are stable **mixture states** ξ_i^{mix}, which are not equal to any single pattern, but instead correspond to linear combinations of an odd number of patterns [Amit et al., 1985a]. The simplest of these are symmetric combinations of three stored patterns:

$$\xi_i^{\mathrm{mix}} = \mathrm{sgn}(\pm \xi_i^{\mu_1} \pm \xi_i^{\mu_2} \pm \xi_i^{\mu_3}). \tag{32}$$

All eight sign combinations are possible, but we consider for definiteness the case where all the signs are chosen as $+$'s. The other cases are similar. Observe that on average ξ_i^{mix} has the same sign as $\xi_i^{\mu_1}$ three times out of four; only if $\xi_i^{\mu_2}$ and $\xi_i^{\mu_3}$ both have the opposite sign can the overall sign be reversed. So ξ_i^{mix} is Hamming distance $N/4$ from $\xi_i^{\mu_1}$, and of course from $\xi_i^{\mu_2}$ and $\xi_i^{\mu_3}$ too; the mixture states lie at points equidistant from their components. This also implies that $\sum_i \xi_i^{\mu_1} \xi_i^{\mathrm{mix}} = N/2$ on average. Now to check the stability of (32), still with all $+$ signs, we can repeat the calculation of (11) and (12), but this time pick out the three special μ's:

$$h_i^{\mathrm{mix}} = \frac{1}{N} \sum_{j\mu} \xi_i^\mu \xi_j^\mu \xi_j^{\mathrm{mix}} = \frac{1}{2}\xi_i^{\mu_1} + \frac{1}{2}\xi_i^{\mu_2} + \frac{1}{2}\xi_i^{\mu_3} + \text{cross-terms}. \tag{33}$$

Thus the stability condition (10) is indeed satisfied for the mixture state (32). Similarly $5, 7, \ldots$ patterns may be combined. The system does not choose an *even* number of patterns because they can add up to zero on some sites, whereas the units have to be ± 1.

Third, for large p there are local minima that are not correlated with any finite number of the original patterns ξ_i^μ [Amit et al., 1985b]. These are sometimes called **spin glass states** because of a close correspondence to spin glass models in statistical mechanics.

So the memory does not work perfectly; there are all these additional minima in addition to the ones we want. The second and third classes are generally called **spurious minima**. Of course we only fall into one of them if we start close to it, and they tend to have rather small basins of attraction compared to the retrieval states. There are also various tricks, including finite temperature and biased patterns, that can reduce or remove the spurious minima.

Notes

1. The Hamming distance between two binary numbers means the number of bits that are different in the two numbers.
2. We reserve the symbol S_i for ± 1 units throughout.
3. There are actually $N(p-1)$ terms if we include the $i = j$ terms, or $(N-1)(p-1)$ terms if we don't, but these are both approximately Np for large N and p.
4. Strictly speaking we should write $(1 - P_{\text{error}})^N > 0.99$ here, but $P_{\text{error}} < 0.01/N$ is a good approximation from the binomial expansion.
5. Consider the matrix X with components $X_{\mu i} = \xi_i^\mu$. Equation (22) implies $XX^T = N1$, where 1 is the unit matrix, while the Hebb rule (9) may be written $w = (1/N)X^TX$. Using $(AB)^T = B^TA^T$ leads immediately to $w = 1$.
6. We assume that w_{ii} is positive or zero. The energy is no longer a Lyapunov function if negative self-couplings are allowed.

References

Amit, D. J., & Gutfreund, H. (1985). Spin-glass models of neural networks. *Physical Review A, 32*, 1007–1018.

Cohen, M. A., & Grossberg, S. (1983). Absolute stability of global pattern-formation and parallel memory storage by competitive neural networks. *IEEE Transactions on Systems, Man, and Cybernetics, 13*, 815–826.

Cowan, J. D., & Sharp, D. H. (1988). Neural nets. *Quarterly Reviews of Biophysics, 21*, 365–427.

Feller, W. (1968). On probabilities of large deviations. *Proceedings of the National Academy of Sciences, 61*, 1224–1227.

Hebb, D. O. (1949). *The organization of behavior: A neuropsychological theory*. NY: Wiley.

Hopfield, J. J. (1982). Neural networks and physical systems with emergent collective computational abilities. *Proceedings of the National Academy of Sciences-Biological Sciences, 79*, 2554–2558.

Kanter, I., & Sompolinsky, H. (1987). Associative recall of memory without errors. *Physical Review A, 35*, 380–392.

Little, W. A., & Shaw, G. L. (1978). Analytic study of memory storage capacity of a neural network. *Mathematical Biosciences, 39*, 281–290.

McEliece, R. J., Posner, E. C., Rodemich, E. R., & Venkate, S. H. (1987). The capacity of the Hopfield associative memory. *IEEE Transactions on Information Theory, 33*, 461–482.

Weisbush, G., & Fogelman-Soulie, F. (1985). Scaling laws for the attractors of Hopfield networks. *Journal de Physique Letters, 46*, L623–L630.

Back Propagation

Chapter 8

Learning Representations by Back-Propagating Errors

David E. Rumelhart, Geoffrey E. Hinton, and
Ronald J. Williams

There have been many attempts to design self-organizing neural networks. The aim is to find a powerful synaptic modification rule that will allow an arbitrarily connected neural network to develop an internal structure that is appropriate for a particular task domain. The task is specified by giving the desired state vector of the output units for each state vector of the input units. If the input units are directly connected to the output units it is relatively easy to find learning rules that iteratively adjust the relative strengths of the connections so as to progressively reduce the difference between the actual and desired output vectors.[1] Learning becomes more interesting but more difficult when we introduce hidden units whose actual or desired states are not specified by the task. (In perceptrons, there are "feature analysers" between the input and output that are not true hidden units because their input connections are fixed by hand, so their states are completely determined by the input vector: they do not learn representations.) The learning procedure must decide under what circumstances the hidden units should be active in order to help achieve the desired input–output behaviour. This amounts to deciding what these units should represent. We demonstrate that a general purpose and relatively simple procedure is powerful enough to construct appropriate internal representations.

The simplest form of the learning procedure is for layered networks which have a layer of input units at the bottom; any number of intermediate layers; and a layer of output units at the top. Connections within a layer or from higher to lower layers are forbidden, but connections can skip intermediate layers. An input vector is presented to the network by setting the states of the input units. Then the states of the units in each layer are determined by applying equations (1) and (2) to the connections coming from lower layers. All units within a layer have their states set in parallel, but different layers have their states set sequentially, starting at the bottom and working upwards until the states of the output units are determined.

The total input, x_j, to unit j is a linear function of the outputs, y_i, of the units that are connected to j and of the weights, w_{ji}, on these connections

$$x_j = \sum_i y_i w_{ji} \tag{1}$$

Units can be given biases by introducing an extra input to each unit which always has a value of 1. The weight on this extra input is called the bias and is equivalent to a threshold of the opposite sign. It can be treated just like the other weights.

A unit has a real-valued output, y_i, which is a non-linear function of its total input

$$y_j = \frac{1}{1 + e^{-x_j}} \tag{2}$$

It is not necessary to use exactly the functions given in equations (1) and (2). Any input–output function which has a bounded derivative will do. However, the use of a linear function for combining the inputs to a unit before applying the nonlinearity greatly simplifies the learning procedure.

The aim is to find a set of weights that ensure that for each input vector the output vector produced by the network is the same as (or sufficiently close to) the desired output vector. If there is a fixed, finite set of input–output cases, the total error in the performance of the network with a particular set of weights can be computed by comparing the actual and desired output vectors for every case. The total error, E, is defined as

$$E = \frac{1}{2} \sum_c \sum_j (y_{j,c} - d_{j,c})^2 \tag{3}$$

where c is an index over cases (input–output pairs), j is an index over output units, y is the actual state of an output unit and d is its desired state. To minimize E by gradient descent it is necessary to compute the partial derivative of E with respect to each weight in the network. This is simply the sum of the partial derivatives for each of the input–output cases. For a given case, the partial derivatives of the error with respect to each weight are computed in two passes. We have already described the forward pass in which the units in each layer have their states determined by the input they receive from units in lower layers using equations (1) and (2). The backward pass which propagates derivatives from the top layer back to the bottom one is more complicated.

The backward pass starts by computing $\partial E / \partial y$ for each of the output units. Differentiating equation (3) for a particular case, c, and suppressing the index c gives

$$\partial E / \partial y_j = y_j - d_j \tag{4}$$

We can then apply the chain rule to compute $\partial E / \partial x_j$

$$\partial E / \partial x_j = \partial E / \partial y_j \cdot dy_j / dx_j$$

Differentiating equation (2) to get the value of dy_j/dx_j and substituting gives

$$\partial E/\partial x_j = \partial E/\partial y_j \cdot y_j(1 - y_j) \tag{5}$$

This means that we know how a change in the total input x to an output unit will affect the error. But this total input is just a linear function of the states of the lower level units and it is also a linear function of the weights on the connections, so it is easy to compute how the error will be affected by changing these states and weights. For a weight w_{ji}, from i to j the derivative is

$$\partial E/\partial w_{ji} = \partial E/\partial x_j \cdot \partial x_j/\partial w_{ji}$$
$$= \partial E/\partial x_j \cdot y_i \tag{6}$$

and for the output of the ith unit the contribution to $\partial E/\partial y_i$ resulting from the effect of i on j is simply

$$\partial E/\partial x_j \cdot \partial x_j/\partial y_i = \partial E/\partial x_j \cdot w_{ji}$$

so taking into account all the connections emanating from unit i we have

$$\partial E/\partial y_i = \sum_j \partial E/\partial x_j \cdot w_{ji} \tag{7}$$

We have now seen how to compute $\partial E/\partial y$ for any unit in the penultimate layer when given $\partial E/\partial y$ for all units in the last layer. We can therefore repeat this procedure to compute this term for successively earlier layers, computing $\partial E/\partial w$ for the weights as we go.

One way of using $\partial E/\partial w$ is to change the weights after every input–output case. This has the advantage that no separate memory is required for the derivatives. An alternative scheme, which we used in the research reported here, is to accumulate $\partial E/\partial w$ over all the input–output cases before changing the weights. The simplest version of gradient descent is to change each weight by an amount proportional to the accumulated $\partial E/\partial w$

$$\Delta w = -\varepsilon \partial E/\partial w \tag{8}$$

This method does not converge as rapidly as methods which make use of the second derivatives, but it is much simpler and can easily be implemented by local computations in parallel hardware. It can be significantly improved, without sacrificing the simplicity and locality, by using an acceleration method in which the current gradient is used to modify the velocity of the point in weight space instead of its position

$$\Delta w(t) = -\varepsilon \partial E/\partial w(t) + \alpha \Delta w(t - 1) \tag{9}$$

where t is incremented by 1 for each sweep through the whole set of input–output cases, and α is an exponential decay factor between 0 and 1 that deter-

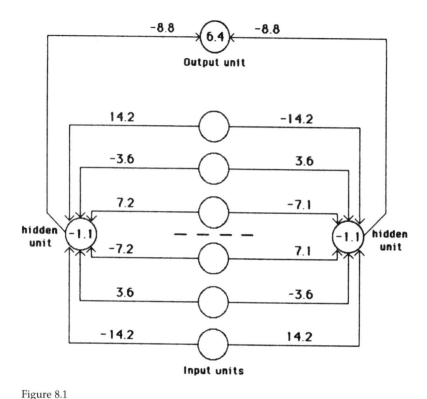

Figure 8.1
A network that has learned to detect mirror symmetry in the input vector. The numbers on the arcs are weights and the numbers inside the nodes are biases. The learning required 1,425 sweeps through the set of 64 possible input vectors, with the weights being adjusted on the basis of the accumulated gradient after each sweep. The values of the parameters in equation (9) were $\varepsilon = 0.1$ and $\alpha = 0.9$. The initial weights were ramdom and were uniformly distributed between −0.3 and 0.3. The key properly of this solution is that for a given hidden unit, weights that symmetric about the middle of the input vector are equal in magnitude and opposite in sign. So if a symmetrical pattern is presented, both hidden units will receive a net input units, and, because the hidden units have a negative bias, both will be off. In this case the output unit, having a positive bias, will be on. Note that the weights on each side of the midpoint are in the ratio 1:2:4. This ensures that each of the eight patterns that can occur above the midpoint sends a unique activation sum to each hidden unit, so the only pattern below the midpoint that can exactly balance this sum is the summetrical one. For all non-symmetrical patterns, both hidden units will receive non-zero activations from the input units. The two hidden units have indentical patterns of weights but with opposite signs, so for every non-symmetric pattern one hidden unit will come on and suppress the output unit.

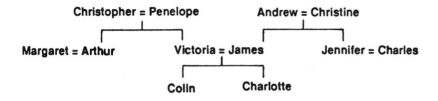

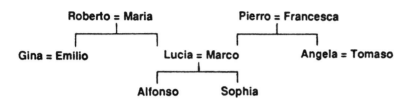

Figure 8.2
Two isomorphic family trees. The information can be expressed as a set of triples of the form ⟨person 1⟩ ⟨relationship⟩ ⟨person 2⟩, where the possible relationships are {father, mother, husband, wife, son, daughter, uncle, aunt, brother, sister, nephew, niece}. A layered net can be said to 'know' these triples if it can produce the third term of each triple when given the first two. The first two terms are encoded by activating two of the input units, and the network must then complete the proposition by activating the output unit that represents the third term.

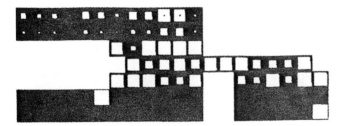

Figure 8.3
Activity levels in a five-layer network after it has learned. The bottom layer 24 input units on the left for representing ⟨person 1⟩ and 12 input units on the right for representing the relationship. The white squares insidethese two groups show the activity levels of the units. There is one active unit in the first group representing Colin and one in the second group representing the relationship 'has-aunt'. Each of the two input groups is totally connected to its own group of 6 units in the second layer. These groups learn to encode people and relationships as distributed patterns and activity. The second layer is totally connected to the central layer of 12 units, and these are connected to the penultimate layer of 6 units. The activity in the penultimate layer must activate the correct output units, each of which stands for a particular ⟨person 2⟩. In this case, there are two correct answers (marked by black dots) because Colin has two aunts. Both the input units and the output units laid out spatially with the English people in one row and the isomorphic Italians immediately below.

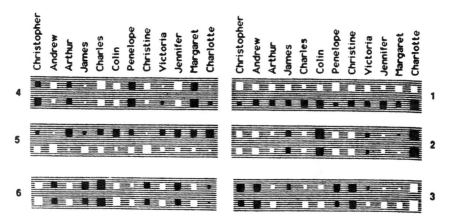

Figure 8.4

The weights from the 24 input units that represent people to the 6 units in the second layer that learn distributed representions of people. White rectangles, excitatory weights; black rectangles, inhibitory weights; area of the rectangle encodes the magnitude of the weight. The weights from the 12 English people are in the top row of each unit. Unit 1 is primarily concerned with the distinction between English and Italian and most of the other units ignore this distinction. This means that the represention of an English person is very similar to the representation of their Italian equivalent. The network is making use of the isomorphism between the two family trees to allow it to share structure and it will therefore tend to generalize sensibly from one tree to the other. Unit 2 encodes which generation a person belongs to, and unit 6 encodes which branch of the family they come from. The features captured by the hidden units are not at all explicit in the input and output encodings, since these use a separate unit for each person. Because the hidden features capture the underlying structure of the task domain, the network generalizes correctly to the four triples on which it was not trained. We trained the network for 1500 sweeps, using $\varepsilon = 0.005$ and $\alpha = 0.5$ for the first 20 sweeps and $\varepsilon = 0.01$ and $\alpha = 0.9$ for the remaining sweeps. To make it easier to interpret the weights we introduced 'weight-decay' by decrementing every weight by 0.2% after each weight change. After prolonged learning, the decay was balanced by $\partial E / \partial w$, so the final magnitude of each weight indicates its usefulness in reducing the error. To prevent the network needing large weights to drive the outputs to 1 or 0, the error was considered to be zero if output units that should be on had activities above 0.8 and output units that should be off had activities below 0.2.

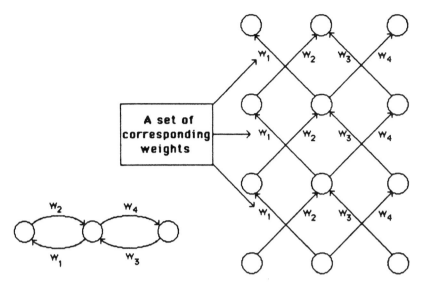

Figure 8.5
A synchronous iterative net that is run for three iterations and the equivalent layered net. Each time-step in the recurrent net corresponds to a layer in the layered net. The learning procedure for layered nets can be mapped into a learning procedure for iterative nets. Two complications arise in performing this mapping: first, in a layered net the output levels of the units in the intermediate layers during the forward pass are required for performing the backward pass (see equations (5) and (6)). So in an iterative net it is necessary to store the history of output states of each unit. Second, for a layered net to be equivalent to an iterative net, corresponding weights between different layers must have the same value. To preserve this property, we average $\partial E/\partial w$ for all the weights in each set of corresponding weights and then change each weight in the set by an amount proportional to this average gradient. With these two provisos, the learning procedure can be applied directly to iterative nets. These nets can then either learn to perform iterative searches or learn sequential structures[3].

mines the relative contribution of the current gradient and earlier gradients to the weight change.

To break symmetry we start with small random weights. Variants on the learning procedure have been discovered independently by David Parker (personal communication) and by Yann Le Cun.[2]

One simple task that cannot be done by just connecting the input units to the output units is the detection of symmetry. To detect whether the binary activity levels of a one-dimensional array of input units are symmetrical about the centre point, it is essential to use an intermediate layer because the activity in an individual input unit, considered alone, provides no evidence about the symmetry or non-symmetry of the whole input vector, so simply adding up the evidence from the individual input units is insufficient. (A more formal proof that intermediate units are required is given in ref. 2.) The learning procedure discovered an elegant solution using just two intermediate units, as shown in Fig. 8.1.

Another interesting task is to store the information in the two family trees (Fig. 8.2). Figure 8.3 shows the network we used, and Fig. 8.4 shows the 'receptive fields' of some of the hidden units after the network was trained on 100 of the 104 possible triples.

So far, we have only dealt with layered, feed-forward networks. The equivalence between layered networks and recurrent networks that are run iteratively is shown in Fig. 8.5.

The most obvious drawback of the learning procedure is that the error-surface may contain local minima so that gradient descent is not guaranteed to find a global minimum. However, experience with many tasks shows that the network very rarely gets stuck in poor local minima that are significantly worse than the global minimum. We have only encountered this undesirable behaviour in networks that have just enough connections to perform the task. Adding a few more connections creates extra dimensions in weight-space and these dimensions provide paths around the barriers that create poor local minima in the lower dimensional subspaces.

The learning procedure, in its current form, is not a plausible model of learning in brains. However, applying the procedure to various tasks shows that interesting internal representations can be constructed by gradient descent in weight-space, and this suggests that it is worth looking for more biologically plausible ways of doing gradient descent in neural networks.

Notes

1. Minsky, M. L. & Papert, S. *Perceptrons* (MIT, Cambridge, 1969).
2. Le Cun, Y. *Proc. Cognitiva* **85**, 599–604 (1985).
3. Rumelhart, D. E., Hinton, G. E. & Williams, R. J. in *Parallel Distributed Processing: Explorations in the Microstructure of Cognition*. Vol. 1: *Foundations* (eds Rumelhart, D. E. & McClelland, J. L.) 318–362 (MIT, Cambridge, 1986).

Supervised Learning

Chapter 9

Forward Models: Supervised Learning with a Distal Teacher

Michael I. Jordan and David E. Rumelhart

Recent work on learning algorithms for connectionist networks has seen a progressive weakening of the assumptions made about the relationship between the learner and the environment. Classical supervised learning algorithms such as the perceptron (Rosenblatt, 1962) and the LMS algorithm (Widrow & Hoff, 1960) made two strong assumptions: (1) The output units are the only adaptive units in the network, and (2) there is a "teacher" that provides desired states for all of the output units. Early in the development of such algorithms it was recognized that more powerful supervised learning algorithms could be realized by weakening the first assumption and incorporating internal units that adaptively recode the input representation provided by the environment (Rosenblatt, 1962). The subsequent development of algorithms such as Boltzmann learning (Hinton & Sejnowski, 1986) and backpropagation (LeCun, 1985; Parker, 1985; Rumelhart, Hinton, & Williams, 1986; Werbos, 1974) have provided the means for training networks with adaptive nonlinear internal units. The second assumption has also been weakened—learning algorithms that require no explicit teacher have been developed (Becker & Hinton, 1989; Grossberg, 1987; Kohonen, 1982; Linsker, 1988; Rumelhart & Zipser, 1986). Such "unsupervised" learning algorithms generally perform some sort of clustering or feature extraction on the input data and are based on assumptions about the statistical or topological properties of the input ensemble.

In this chapter we examine in some detail the notion of the "teacher" in the supervised learning paradigm. We argue that the teacher is less of a liability than has commonly been assumed and that the assumption that the environment provides desired states for the output of the network can be weakened significantly without abandoning the supervised learning paradigm altogether. Indeed, we feel that an appropriate interpretation of the role of the teacher is crucial in appreciating the range of problems to which the paradigm can be applied.

The issue that we wish to address is best illustrated by way of an example. Consider a skill-learning task such as that faced by a basketball player learning to shoot baskets. The problem for the learner is to find the appropriate muscle

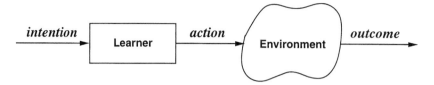

Figure 9.1
The distal supervised learning problem. Target values are available for the distal variables (the "outcomes") but not for the proximal variables (the "actions").

commands to propel the ball toward the goal. Different commands are appropriate for different locations of the goal in the visual scene; thus, a mapping from visual scenes to muscle commands is required. What learning algorithm might underly the acquisition of such a mapping? Clearly, clustering or feature extraction on the visual input is not sufficient. Moreover, it is difficult to see how to apply classical supervised algorithms to this problem, because there is no teacher to provide muscle commands as targets to the learner. The only target information provided to the learner is in terms of the outcome of the movement; that is, the sights and sounds of a ball passing through the goal.

The general scenario suggested by the example is shown in Figure 9.1. *Intentions* are provided as inputs to the learning system. The learner transforms intentions into *actions*, which are transformed by the environment into *outcomes*. Actions are *proximal* variables; that is, variables that the learner controls directly, while outcomes are *distal* variables, variables that the learner controls indirectly through the intermediary of the proximal variables. During the learning process, target values are assumed to be available for the distal variables but not for the proximal variables. Therefore, from a point of view outside the learning system, a "distal supervised learning task" is a mapping from intentions to desired outcomes. From the point of view of the learner, however, the problem is to find a mapping from intentions to actions that can be composed with the environment to yield desired distal outcomes. The learner must discover how to vary the components of the proximal action vector so as to minimize the components of the distal error.

The distal supervised learning problem also has a temporal component. In many environments the effects of actions are not punctate and instantaneous, but rather linger on and mix with the effects of other actions. Thus the outcome at any point in time is influenced by any of a number of previous actions. Even if there exists a set of variables that have a static relationship to desired outcomes, the learner often does not have direct control over those variables. Consider again the example of the basketball player. Although the flight of the ball depends only on the velocity of the arm at the moment of release—a static relationship—it is unlikely that the motor control system is able to control release velocity directly. Rather, the system outputs forces or torques, and these variables do not have a static relationship to the distal outcome.

In the remainder of the chapter we describe a general approach to solving the distal supervised learning problem. The approach is based on the idea that supervised learning in its most general form is a two-phase procedure. In the first phase the learner forms a predictive internal model (a forward model) of the transformation from actions to distal outcomes. Because such transformations are often not known a priori, the internal model must generally be learned by exploring the outcomes associated with particular choices of actions. This auxiliary learning problem is itself a supervised learning problem, based on the error between internal, predicted outcomes and actual outcomes. Once the internal model has been at least partially learned, it can be used in an indirect manner to solve for the mapping from intentions to actions.

The idea of using an internal model to augment the capabilities of supervised learning algorithms has also been proposed by Werbos (1987), although his perspective differs in certain respects from our own. There have been a number of further developments of the idea (Kawato, 1990; Miyata, 1988; Munro, 1987; Nguyen & Widrow, 1989; Robinson & Fallside, 1989; Schmidhuber, 1990), based either on the work of Werbos or our own unpublished work (Jordan, 1983; Rumelhart, 1986). There are also close ties between our approach and techniques in optimal control theory (Kirk, 1970) and adaptive control theory (Goodwin & Sin, 1984; Narendra & Parthasarathy, 1990). We discuss several of these relationships in the remainder of the paper, although we do not attempt to be comprehensive.

Distal Supervised Learning and Forward Models

This section and the following section present a general approach to solving distal supervised learning problems. We begin by describing our assumptions about the environment and the learner.

We assume that the environment can be characterized by a next-state function f and an output function g. At time step $n - 1$ the learner produces an *action* $\mathbf{u}[n - 1]$. In conjunction with the state of the environment $\mathbf{x}[n - 1]$ the action determines the next state $\mathbf{x}[n]$:

$$\mathbf{x}[n] = f(\mathbf{x}[n - 1], \mathbf{u}[n - 1]). \tag{1}$$

Corresponding to each state $\mathbf{x}[n]$ there is also a *sensation* $\mathbf{y}[n]$:

$$\mathbf{y}[n] = g(\mathbf{x}[n]). \tag{2}$$

(Note that sensations are output vectors in the current formalism—"outcomes" in the language of the introductory section). The next-state function and the output function together determine a state-dependent mapping from actions to sensations.

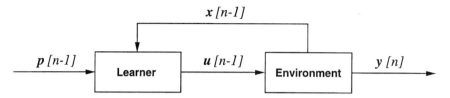

Figure 9.2
The composite performance system consisting of a learner and the environment. This system is a mapping from inputs $\mathbf{p}[n-1]$ to sensations $\mathbf{y}[n]$. The training data $\{\mathbf{p}_i[n-1], \mathbf{y}_i^*[n]\}$ specify desired input/output behavior across the composite system. Note that there is an implicit loop within the environment such that the output at time n depends on the state at time $n-1$ (cf. Equation 1).

In the current paper we assume that the learner has access to the state of the environment; we do not address issues relating to state representation and state estimation. State representations might involve delayed values of previous actions and sensations (Ljung & Söderström, 1986), or they might involve internal state variables that are induced as part of the learning procedure (Mozer & Bachrach, 1990). Given the state $\mathbf{x}[n-1]$ and given the *input* $\mathbf{p}[n-1]$, the learner produces an action $\mathbf{u}[n-1]$:

$$\mathbf{u}[n-1] = h(\mathbf{x}[n-1], \mathbf{p}[n-1]).^{[1]} \tag{3}$$

The goal of the learning procedure is to make appropriate adjustments to the input-to-action mapping h based on data obtained from interacting with the environment.

A *distal supervised learning problem* is a set of training pairs $\{\mathbf{p}_i[n-1], \mathbf{y}_i^*[n]\}$, where $\mathbf{p}_i[n-1]$ are the input vectors and $\mathbf{y}_i^*[n]$ are the corresponding desired sensations. For example, in the basketball problem, the input might be a high-level intention of shooting a basket, and a desired sensation would be the corresponding visual representation of a successful outcome. Note that the distal supervised learning problem makes no mention of the actions that the learner must acquire; only inputs and desired sensations are specified. From a point of view outside the learning system, the training data specify desired input/output behavior across the *composite performance system* consisting of the learner and the environment (see Figure 9.2). From the point of view of the learner, however, the problem is to find a mapping from inputs $\mathbf{p}[n-1]$ to actions $\mathbf{u}[n-1]$ such that the resulting distal sensations $\mathbf{y}[n]$ are the target values $\mathbf{y}^*[n]$. That is, the learner must find a mapping from inputs to actions that can be placed in series with the environment so as to yield the desired pairing of inputs and sensations. Note that there may be more than one action that yields a given desired sensation from any given state; that is, the distal supervised learning problem may be underdetermined. Thus, in the basketball example, there may be a variety of patterns of motor commands that yield the same desired sensation of seeing the ball pass through the goal.

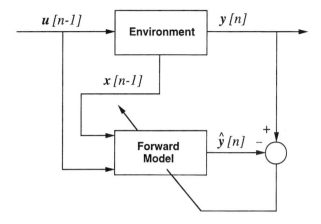

Figure 9.3
Learning the forward model using the prediction error $\mathbf{y}[n] - \hat{\mathbf{y}}[n]$.

Forward Models

The learner is assumed to be able to observe states, actions, and sensations and can therefore model the mapping between actions and sensations. A *forward model* is an internal model that produces a predicted sensation $\hat{\mathbf{y}}[n]$ based on the state $\mathbf{x}[n-1]$ and the action $\mathbf{u}[n-1]$. That is, a forward model predicts the consequences of a given action in the context of a given state vector. As shown in Figure 9.3, the forward model can be learned by comparing predicted sensations to actual sensations and using the resulting *prediction error* to adjust the parameters of the model. Learning the forward model is a classical supervised learning problem in which the teacher provides target values directly in the output coordinate system of the learner.[2]

Distal Supervised Learning

We now describe a general approach to solving the distal supervised learning problem. Consider the system shown in Figure 9.4, in which the learner is placed in series with a forward model of the environment. This *composite learning system* is a state-dependent mapping from inputs to predicted sensations. Suppose that the forward model has been trained previously and is a perfect model of the environment; that is, the predicted sensation equals the actual sensation for all actions and all states. We now treat the composite learning system as a single supervised learning system and train it to map from inputs to desired sensations according to the data in the training set. That is, the desired sensations $\mathbf{y}_i^*$ are treated as targets for the composite system. Any supervised learning algorithm can be used for this training process; however, the algorithm must be constrained so that it does not alter the forward model while the composite system is being trained. By fixing the forward model, we require the system to find an optimal composite mapping by varying only the mapping from inputs to actions. If the forward model is perfect, and if the learning algorithm finds the globally optimal solution, then the resulting (state-dependent) input-to-action mapping must also be perfect in the sense that it yields the desired composite input/output behavior when placed in series with the environment.

Consider now the case of an imperfect forward model. Clearly an imperfect forward model will yield an imperfect input-to-action map if the composite system is trained in the obvious way, using the difference between the desired sensation and the predicted sensation as the error term. This difference, the *predicted performance error* $(\mathbf{y}^* - \hat{\mathbf{y}})$, is readily available at the output of the composite system, but it is an unreliable guide to the true performance of the learner. Suppose instead that we ignore the output of the composite system and substitute the *performance error* $(\mathbf{y}^* - \mathbf{y})$ as the error term for training the composite system (see Figure 9.5). If the performance error goes to zero, the system has found a correct input-to-action map, regardless of the inaccuracy of the forward model. The inaccuracy in the forward model manifests itself as a bias during the learning process, but need not prevent the performance error from

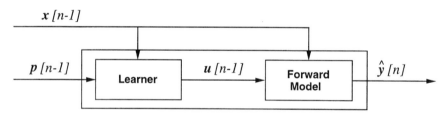

Figure 9.4
The composite learning system. This composite system maps from inputs $\mathbf{p}[n-1]$ to predicted sensations $\hat{\mathbf{y}}[n]$ in the context of a given state vector.

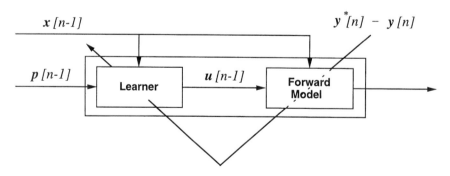

Figure 9.5
The composite system is trained using the performance error. The forward model is held fiexed while the composite system is being trained.

going to zero. Consider, for example, algorithms based on steepest descent. If the forward model is not too inaccurate the system can still move downhill and thereby reach the solution region, even though the movement is not in the direction of steepest descent.

To summarize, we propose to solve the distal supervised learning problem by training a composite learning system consisting of the learner and a forward model of the environment. This procedure solves implicitly for an input-to-action map by training the composite system to map from inputs to distal targets. The training of the forward model must precede the training of the composite system, but the forward model need not be perfect, nor need it be pre-trained throughout all of state space. The ability of the system to utilize an inaccurate forward model is important; it implies that it may be possible to interleave the training of the forward model and the composite system.

In the remainder of the chapter, we discuss the issues of interleaved training, inaccuracy in the forward model, and the choice of the error term in more detail. We first turn to an interesting special case of the general distal supervised learning problem—that of learning an inverse model of the environment.

Inverse Models

An *inverse model* is an internal model that produces an action $\mathbf{u}[n-1]$ as a function of the current state $\mathbf{x}[n-1]$ and the desired sensation $\mathbf{y}^*[n]$. Inverse models are defined by the condition that they yield the identity mapping when placed in series with the environment.

Inverse models are important in a variety of domains. For example, if the environment is viewed as a communications channel over which a message is to be transmitted, then it may be desirable to undo the distorting effects of the environment by placing it in series with an inverse model (Carlson, 1986). A second example, shown in Figure 9.6, arises in control system design. A controller receives the desired sensation $\mathbf{y}^*[n]$ as input and must find actions that cause actual sensations to be as close as possible to desired sensations; that is, the controller must invert the transformation from actions to sensations.[3] One approach to achieving this objective is to utilize an explicit inverse model of the environment as a controller.

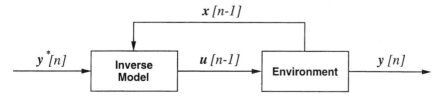

Figure 9.6
An inverse model as a controller.

Whereas forward models are uniquely determined by the environment, inverse models are generally not. If the environment is characterized by a many-to-one mapping from actions to sensations then there are generally an infinite number of possible inverse models. It is also worth noting that inverses do not always exist—it is not always possible to achieve a particular desired sensation from any given state. As we shall discuss, these issues of existence and uniqueness have important implications for the problem of learning an inverse model.

There are two general approaches to learning inverse models using supervised learning algorithms: the distal learning approach presented above and an alternative approach that we refer to as "direct inverse modeling" (cf. Jordan & Rosenbaum, 1989). We begin by describing the latter approach.

Direct Inverse Modeling

Direct inverse modeling treats the problem of learning an inverse model as a classical supervised learning problem (Widrow & Stearns, 1985). As shown in Figure 9.7, the idea is to observe the input/output behavior of the environment and to train an inverse model directly by reversing the roles of the inputs and outputs. Data are provided to the algorithm by sampling in action space and observing the results in sensation space.

Although direct inverse modeling has been shown to be a viable technique in a number of domains (Atkeson & Reinkensmeyer, 1988; Kuperstein, 1988; Miller, 1987), it has two drawbacks that limit its usefulness. First, if the environment is characterized by a many-to-one mapping from actions to sensations, then the direct inverse modeling technique may be unable to find an inverse.

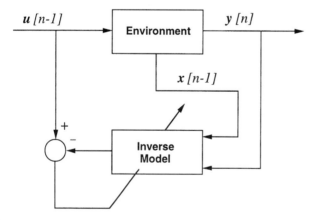

Figure 9.7
The direct inverse modeling approach to learning as inverse model.

The difficulty is that nonlinear many-to-one mappings can yield nonconvex inverse images, which are problematic for direct inverse modeling.[4] Consider the situation shown in Figure 9.8. The nonconvex region on the left is the inverse image of a point in sensation space. Suppose that the points labelled by X's are sampled during the learning process. Three of these points correspond to the same sensation; thus, the training data as seen by the direct inverse modeling procedure are one-to-many—one input is paired with many targets. Supervised learning algorithms resolve one-to-many inconsistencies by averaging across the multiple targets (the form of the averaging depends on the particular cost function that is used). As is shown in the figure, however, the average of points lying in a nonconvex set does not necessarily lie in the set. Thus the globally optimal (minimum-cost) solution found by the direct inverse modeling approach is not necessarily a correct inverse model. (We present an example of such behavior in a following section).

The second drawback with direct inverse modeling is that it is not "goal-directed." The algorithm samples in action space without regard to particular targets or errors in sensation space. That is, there is no direct way to find an action that corresponds to a particular desired sensation. To obtain particular solutions the learner must sample over a sufficiently wide range of actions and rely on interpolation.

Finally, it is also important to emphasize that direct inverse modeling is restricted to the learning of inverse models—it is *not* applicable to the general distal supervised learning problem.

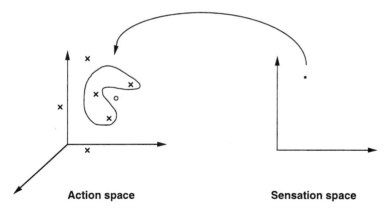

Action space   **Sensation space**

Figure 9.8
The convexity problem. The region on the left is the inverse image of the point on the right. The arrow represents the direction in which the mapping is learned by direct inverse modeling. The three points lying inside the inverse image are averaged by the learning procedure, yielding the vector represented by the small circle. The point is not a solution, because the inverse image is not convex.

The Distal Learning Approach to Learning an Inverse Model
The methods described earlier in this section are directly applicable to the problem of learning an inverse model. The problem of learning an inverse model can be treated as a special case of the distal supervised learning problem in which the input vector and the desired sensation are the same (that is, $\mathbf{p}[n-1]$ is equal to $\mathbf{y}^*[n]$ in Equation 3). Thus, an inverse model is learned by placing the learner and the forward model in series and learning an identity mapping across the composite system.[5]

A fundamental difference between the distal learning approach and direct inverse modeling approach is that rather than averaging over regions in action space, the distal learning approach finds particular solutions in action space. The globally optimal solution for distal learning is a set of vectors $\{\mathbf{u}_i\}$ such that the performance errors $\{\mathbf{y}_i^* - \mathbf{y}_i\}$ are zero. This is true irrespective of the shapes of the inverse images of the targets $\mathbf{y}_i^*$. Vectors lying outside of an inverse image, such as the average vector shown in Figure 9.8, do not yield zero performance error and are therefore not globally optimal. Thus nonconvex inverse images do not present the same fundamental difficulties for the distal learning framework as they do for direct inverse modeling.

It is also true that the distal learning approach is fundamentally goal-directed. The system works to minimize the performance error; thus, it works directly to find solutions that correspond to the particular goals at hand.

In cases in which the forward mapping is many-to-one, the distal learning procedure finds a particular inverse model. Without additional information about the particular structure of the input-to-action mapping, there is no way of predicting which of the possibly infinite set of inverse models the procedure will find. As is discussed below, however, the procedure can also be constrained to find particular inverse models with certain desired properties.

Distal Learning and Backpropagation

In this section we describe an implementation of the distal learning approach that utilizes the machinery of the backpropagation algorithm. It is important to emphasize at the outset, however, that backpropagation is not the only algorithm that can be used to implement the distal learning approach. Any supervised learning algorithm can be used as long as it is capable of learning a mapping across a composite network that includes a previously trained subnetwork; in particular, Boltzmann learning is applicable (Jordan, 1983).

We begin by introducing a useful shorthand for describing backpropagation in layered networks. A layered network can be described as a parameterized mapping from an input vector $\mathbf{x}$ to an output vector $\mathbf{y}$:

$$\mathbf{y} = \phi(\mathbf{x}, \mathbf{w}), \tag{4}$$

where $\mathbf{w}$ is a vector of parameters (weights). In the classical paradigm, the procedure for changing the weights is based on the discrepancy between a target vector $\mathbf{y}^*$ and the actual output vector $\mathbf{y}$. The magnitude of this discrepancy is measured by a cost functional of the form:

$$J = \frac{1}{2}(\mathbf{y}^* - \mathbf{y})^T(\mathbf{y}^* - \mathbf{y}). \tag{5}$$

(J is the sum of squared error at the output units of the network). It is generally desired to minimize this cost.

Backpropagation is an algorithm for computing gradients of the cost functional. The details of the algorithm can be found elsewhere (e.g., Rumelhart, et al., 1986); our intention here is to develop a simple notation that hides the details. This is achieved formally by using the chain rule to differentiate J with respect to the weight vector $\mathbf{w}$:

$$\nabla_{\mathbf{w}} J = -\frac{\partial \mathbf{y}}{\partial \mathbf{w}}^T (\mathbf{y}^* - \mathbf{y}). \tag{6}$$

This equation shows that any algorithm that computes the gradient of J effectively multiplies the error vector $\mathbf{y}^* - \mathbf{y}$ by the transpose Jacobian matrix $(\partial \mathbf{y}/\partial \mathbf{w})^T$.[6] Although the backpropagation algorithm never forms this matrix explicitly (backpropagation is essentially a factorization of the matrix; Jordan, 1988), Equation 6 nonetheless describes the results of the computation performed by backpropagation.[7]

Backpropagation also computes the gradient of the cost functional with respect to the activations of the units in the network. In particular, the cost functional J can be differentiated with respect to the activations of the input units to yield:

$$\nabla_{\mathbf{x}} J = -\frac{\partial \mathbf{y}}{\partial \mathbf{x}}^T (\mathbf{y}^* - \mathbf{y}). \tag{7}$$

We refer to Equation 6 as "backpropagation-to-weights" and Equation 7 as "backpropagation-to-activation." Both computations are carried out in one pass of the algorithm; indeed, backpropagation-to-activation is needed as an intermediate step in the backpropagation-to-weights computation.

In the remainder of this section we formulate a category of learning problems that requires that the learner have prior knowledge of an adequate set of state variables for describing the environment. (See Jordan and Rumelhart (1992) for a more general formulation that does not require this assumption). For simplicity it is assumed that the task is to learn an inverse model (that is, the inputs and the distal targets are assumed to be identical).

An Implementation of Distal Learning
In this section we consider the problem of optimizing the following cost functional, which measures the average magnitude of the performance error:

$$J = \frac{1}{2} E\{(\mathbf{y}^* - \mathbf{y})^T (\mathbf{y}^* - \mathbf{y})\}, \tag{8}$$

where E denotes expected value, where $\mathbf{y}$ is an unknown function of the state $\mathbf{x}$ and the action $\mathbf{u}$. The action $\mathbf{u}$ is the output of a parameterized inverse model of the form:

$$\mathbf{u} = h(\mathbf{x}, \mathbf{y}^*, \mathbf{w}),$$

where $\mathbf{w}$ is a weight vector.

Rather than optimizing J directly, by collecting statistics over the ensemble of states and actions, we utilize an online learning rule (cf. Widrow & Stearns, 1985) that makes incremental changes to the weights based on the instantaneous value of the cost functional:

$$J_n = \frac{1}{2} (\mathbf{y}^*[n] - \mathbf{y}[n])^T (\mathbf{y}^*[n] - \mathbf{y}[n]). \tag{9}$$

An online learning algorithm changes the weights at each time step based on the stochastic gradient of J; that is, the gradient of J_n:

$$\mathbf{w}[n+1] = \mathbf{w}[n] - \eta \nabla_{\mathbf{w}} J_n,$$

where η is a step size. To compute this gradient the chain rule is applied to Equation 9:

$$\nabla_{\mathbf{w}} J_n = -\frac{\partial \mathbf{u}^T}{\partial \mathbf{w}} \frac{\partial \mathbf{y}^T}{\partial \mathbf{u}} (\mathbf{y}^*[n] - \mathbf{y}[n]), \tag{10}$$

where the Jacobian matrices $(\partial \mathbf{y}/\partial \mathbf{u})$ and $(\partial \mathbf{u}/\partial \mathbf{w})$ are evaluated at time $n - 1$. The first and the third factors in this expression are easily computed: The first factor describes the propagation of derivatives from the output units of the inverse model (the "action units") to the weights of the inverse model, and the third factor is the distal error. The origin of the second factor is problematic, however, because the dependence of $\mathbf{y}$ on $\mathbf{u}$ is assumed to be unknown a priori. Our approach to obtaining an estimate of this factor has two parts: First, the system acquires a parameterized forward model over an appropriate subdomain of the state space. This model is of the form:

$$\hat{\mathbf{y}} = \hat{f}(\mathbf{x}, \mathbf{u}, \mathbf{v}), \tag{11}$$

where $\mathbf{v}$ is a vector of weights and $\hat{\mathbf{y}}$ is the predicted sensation. Second, the distal error is propagated backward through the forward model; this effectively multiplies the distal error by an estimate of the transpose Jacobian matrix $(\partial \mathbf{y}/\partial \mathbf{u})$.

Putting these pieces together, the algorithm for learning the inverse model is based on the following estimated stochastic gradient:

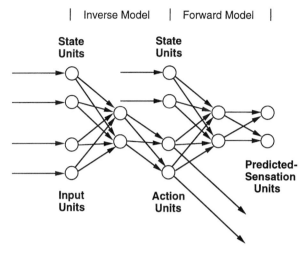

| Inverse Model | Forward Model |

Figure 9.9
A feedforward network that includes forward model. The action units are the output units of the system.

Table 9.1
The error signals and their sources

	Name	Source
$\mathbf{y}^* - \mathbf{y}$	performance error	environment, environment
$\mathbf{y} - \hat{\mathbf{y}}$	prediction error	environment, model
$\mathbf{y}^* - \hat{\mathbf{y}}$	predicted performance error	environment, model

$$\hat{\nabla}_{\mathbf{w}} J_n = -\frac{\partial \mathbf{u}}{\partial \mathbf{w}}^T \frac{\partial \hat{\mathbf{y}}}{\partial \mathbf{u}}^T (\mathbf{y}^*[n] - \mathbf{y}[n]). \qquad (12)$$

This expression describes the propagation of the distal error $(\mathbf{y}^*[n] - \mathbf{y}[n])$ backward through the forward model and down into the inverse model where the weights are changed.[8] The network architecture in which these computations take place is shown in Figure 9.9. This network is a straightforward realization of the block diagram in Figure 9.5. It is composed of an inverse model, which links the state units and the input units to the action units, and a forward model, which links the state units and the action units to the predicted-sensation units.

Learning the Forward Model
The learning of the forward model can itself be formulated as an optimization problem, based on the following cost functional:

$$L = \frac{1}{2}E\{(\mathbf{y} - \hat{\mathbf{y}})^T(\mathbf{y} - \hat{\mathbf{y}})\},$$

where $\hat{\mathbf{y}}$ is of the form given in Equation 11. Although the choice of procedure for finding a set of weights $\mathbf{v}$ to minimize this cost is entirely independent of the choice of procedure for optimizing J in Equation 8, it is convenient to base the learning of the forward model on a stochastic gradient as before:

$$\nabla_{\mathbf{v}}L_n = -\frac{\partial\hat{\mathbf{y}}^T}{\partial\mathbf{v}}(\mathbf{y}[n] - \hat{\mathbf{y}}[n]), \tag{13}$$

where the Jacobian matrix $(\partial\hat{\mathbf{y}}/\partial\mathbf{v})$ is evaluated at time $n-1$. This gradient can be computed by the propagation of derivatives within the forward model and therefore requires no additional hardware beyond that already required for learning the inverse model.

The Error Signals
It is important to clarify the meanings of the error signals used in Equations 12 and 13. As shown in Table 9.1, there are three error signals that can be formed from the variables $\mathbf{y}, \hat{\mathbf{y}}$, and $\mathbf{y}^*$—the *prediction error* $\mathbf{y} - \hat{\mathbf{y}}$, the *performance error* $\mathbf{y}^* - \mathbf{y}$, and the *predicted performance error* $\mathbf{y}^* - \hat{\mathbf{y}}$. All three of these error signals are available to the learner because each of the signals $\mathbf{y}^*, \mathbf{y}$ and $\hat{\mathbf{y}}$ are available individually—the target $\mathbf{y}^*$ and the actual sensation $\mathbf{y}$ are provided by the environment, whereas the predicted sensation $\hat{\mathbf{y}}$ is available internally.

For learning the forward model, the prediction error is clearly the appropriate error signal. The learning of the inverse model, however, can be based on either the performance error or the predicted performance error. Using the performance error (see Equation 12) has the advantage that the system can learn an exact inverse model even though the forward model is only approximate. There are two reasons for this: first, Equation 12 preserves the minima of the cost functional in Equation 9—they are zeros of the estimated gradient. That is, an inaccurate Jacobian matrix cannot remove zeros of the estimated gradient (points at which $\mathbf{y}^* - \mathbf{y}$ is zero), although it can introduce additional zeros (spurious local minima). Second, if the estimated gradients obtained with the approximate forward model have positive inner product with the stochastic gradient in Equation 10, then the expected step of the algorithm is downhill in the cost. Thus the algorithm can in principle find an exact inverse model even though the forward model is only approximate.

There may also be advantages to using the predicted performance error. In particular, it may be easier in some situations to obtain learning trials using the internal model rather than the external environment (Rumelhart, Smolensky, McClelland, & Hinton, 1986; Sutton, 1990). Such internal trials can be thought of as a form of "mental practice" (in the case of backpropagation-to-weights) or "planning" (in the case of backpropagation-to-activation). These procedures lead to improved performance if the forward model is sufficiently accurate. (Exact solutions cannot be found with such procedures, however, unless the forward model is exact).

Modularity
In many cases the unknown mapping from actions to sensations can be decomposed into a series of simpler mappings, each of which can be modeled independently. For example, it may often be preferable to model the next-state function and the output function separately rather than modeling them as a single composite function. In such cases, the Jacobian matrix $(\partial \hat{\mathbf{y}} / \partial \mathbf{u})$ can be factored using the chain rule to yield the following estimated stochastic gradient:

$$\hat{\nabla}_{\mathbf{w}} J_n = -\frac{\partial \mathbf{u}}{\partial \mathbf{w}}^T \frac{\partial \hat{\mathbf{x}}}{\partial \mathbf{u}}^T \frac{\partial \hat{\mathbf{y}}}{\partial \mathbf{x}}^T (\mathbf{y}^*[n] - \mathbf{y}[n]). \tag{14}$$

The estimated Jacobian matrices in this expression are obtained by propagating derivatives backward through the corresponding forward models, each of which are learned separately.

In the following two sections, we pursue the presentation of the distal learning approach in the context of two problem domains. The first section describes learning in a static environment, whereas the second section describes learning in a dynamic environment. In both sections, we utilize the local optimization formulation of distal learning.

Static Environments

An environment is said to be *static* if the effect of any given action is independent of the history of previous actions. In static environments the mapping from actions to sensations can be characterized without reference to a set of state variables. Such environments provide a simplified domain in which to study the learning of inverse mappings. In this section, we present an illustrative static environment and focus on two issues: (1) the effects of nonconvex inverse images in the transformation from sensations to actions and (2) the problem of goal-directed learning.

The problem that we consider is that of learning the forward and inverse kinematics of a three-joint planar arm. As shown in Figure 9.10 and Figure 9.11 the configuration of the arm is characterized by the three joint angles q_1, q_2, and q_3, and the corresponding pair of Cartesian variables x_1 and x_2. The function that relates these variables is the *forward kinematic* function $\mathbf{x} = g(\mathbf{q})$. It is obtained in closed form using elementary trigonometry:

$$\begin{bmatrix} x_1 \\ x_2 \end{bmatrix} = \begin{bmatrix} l_1 \cos(q_1) + l_2 \cos(q_1 + q_2) + l_3 \cos(q_1 + q_2 + q_3) \\ l_1 \sin(q_1) + l_2 \sin(q_1 + q_2) + l_3 \sin(q_1 + q_2 + q_3) \end{bmatrix}, \tag{15}$$

where l_1, l_2, and l_3 are the link lengths.

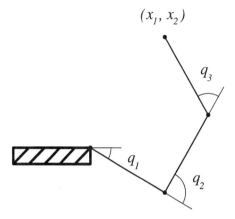

Figure 9.10
A three-point planar arm.

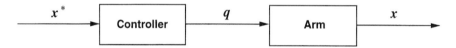

Figure 9.11
The forward and inverse mappings associated with the arm kinematics.

The forward kinematic function $g(\mathbf{q})$ is a many-to-one mapping—for every Cartesian position that is inside the boundary of the workspace, there are an infinite number of joint angle configurations to achieve that position. This implies that the *inverse kinematic* relation $g^{-1}(\mathbf{x})$ is not a function; rather, there are an infinite number of inverse kinematic functions corresponding to particular choices of points $\mathbf{q}$ in the inverse images of each of the Cartesian positions. The problem of learning an inverse kinematic controller for the arm is that of finding a particular inverse among the many possible inverse mappings.

Simulations

In the simulations reported below, the joint-angle configurations of the arm were represented using the vector $\left[\cos\left(q_1 - \frac{\pi}{2}\right), \cos(q_2), \cos(q_3)\right]^T$, rather than the vector of joint angles. This effectively restricts the motion of the joints to the intervals $\left[-\frac{\pi}{2}, \frac{\pi}{2}\right]$, $[0, \pi]$, and $[0, \pi]$, respectively, assuming that each component of the joint-angle configuration vector is allowed to range over the interval $[-1, 1]$. The Cartesian variables x_1 and x_2 were represented as real numbers ranging over $[-1, 1]$. In all of the simulations, these variables were represented directly as real-valued activations of units in the network. Thus, three units were used to represent joint-angle configurations and two units were used to represent Cartesian positions. Further details on the simulations are provided in Appendix A.

The Nonconvexity Problem

One approach to learning an inverse mapping is to provide training pairs to the learner by observing the input/output behavior of the environment and reversing the role of the inputs and outputs. This approach, which we referred to earlier as "direct inverse modeling," has been proposed in the domain of inverse kinematics by Kuperstein (1988). Kuperstein's idea is to randomly sample points $\mathbf{q}'$ in joint space and to use the real arm to evaluate the forward kinematic function $\mathbf{x} = g(\mathbf{q}')$, thereby obtaining training pairs $(\mathbf{x}, \mathbf{q}')$ for learning the controller. The controller is learned by optimization of the following cost functional:

$$J = \frac{1}{2} E\{(\mathbf{q}' - \mathbf{q})^T (\mathbf{q}' - \mathbf{q})\} \tag{16}$$

where $\mathbf{q} = h(\mathbf{x}^*)$ is the output of the controller.

As we discussed earlier, a difficulty with the direct inverse modeling approach is that the optimization of the cost functional in Equation 16 does not necessarily yield an inverse kinematic function. The problem arises because of the many-to-one nature of the forward kinematic function (cf. Figure 9.8). In particular, if two or more of the randomly sampled points $\mathbf{q}'$ happen to map to the same endpoint, then the training data that is provided to the controller is one-to-many. The particular manner in which the inconsistency is resolved depends on the form of the cost functional—use of the sum-of-squared error given in Equation 16 yields an arithmetic average over points that map to the same endpoint. An average in joint space, however, does not necessarily yield a correct result in Cartesian space, because the inverse images of nonlinear transformations are not necessarily convex. This implies that the output of the controller may be in error even though the system has converged to the minimum of the cost functional.

In Figure 9.12 we demonstrate that the inverse kinematics of the three-joint arm is not convex. To see if this nonconvexity has the expected effect on the direct inverse modeling procedure, we conducted a simulation in which a feedforward network with one hidden layer was used to learn the inverse kinematics of the three-joint arm. The simulation provided target vectors to the network by sampling randomly from a uniform distribution in joint space. Input vectors were obtained by mapping the target vectors into Cartesian space according to Equation 15. The initial value of the root-mean-square (RMS) joint-

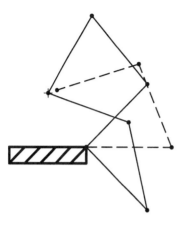

Figure 9.12
The nonconvexity of inverse kinematics. The dotted configuration is an average in joint space of the two solid configurations.

space error was 1.41, filtered over the first 500 trials. After 50,000 learning trials the filtered error reached asymptote at a value of 0.43. A vector field was then plotted by providing desired Cartesian vectors as inputs to the network, obtaining the joint-angle outputs, and mapping these outputs into Cartesian space using Equation 15. The resulting vector field is shown in Figure 9.13. As can be seen, there is substantial error at many positions of the workspace, even though the learning algorithm has converged. If training is continued, the loci of the errors continue to shift, but the RMS error remains approximately constant. Although this error is partially due to the finite learning rate and the random sampling procedure ("misadjustment," see Widrow & Stearns, 1985), the error remains above 0.4 even when the learning rate is taken to zero. Thus, misadjustment cannot account for the error, which must be due to the nonconvexity of the inverse kinematic relation. Note, for example, that the error observed in Figure 9.12 is reproduced in the lower left portion of Figure 9.13.

In Figure 9.14, we demonstrate that the distal learning approach can find a particular inverse kinematic mapping. We performed a simulation that was initialized with the incorrect controller obtained from direct inverse modeling. The simulation utilized a forward model that had been trained previously (the forward model was trained during the direct inverse modeling trials). A grid of 285 evenly spaced positions in Cartesian space was used to provide targets during the second phase of the distal learning procedure.[9] On each trial the error in Cartesian space was passed backward through the forward model and used to change the weights of the controller. After 28,500 such learning trials (100 passes through the grid of targets), the resulting vector field was plotted. As shown in the figure, the vector error decreases toward zero throughout the

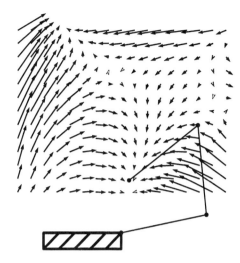

Figure 9.13
Near-asymptotic performance of direct inverse modeling. Each vector represents the error at a particular position in the workspace.

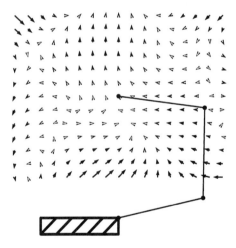

Figure 9.14
Near-asymptotic performance of distal learning.

workspace; thus, the controller is converging toward a particular inverse kinematic function.

Additional Constraints

A further virtue of the distal learning approach is the ease with which it is possible to incorporate additional constraints in the learning procedure and thereby bias the choice of a particular inverse function. For example, a minimum-norm constraint can be realized by adding a penalty term of the form $-\lambda \mathbf{x}$ to the propagated errors at the output of the controller. Temporal smoothness constraints can be realized by incorporating additional error terms of the form $\lambda(\mathbf{x}[n] - \mathbf{x}[n-1])$. Such constraints can be defined at other sites in the network as well, including the output units or hidden units of the forward model. It is also possible to provide additional contextual inputs to the controller and thereby learn multiple, contextually-appropriate inverse functions. These aspects of the distal learning approach are discussed in more detail in Jordan (1990, 1992).

Goal-Directed Learning

Direct inverse modeling does not learn in a goal-directed manner. To learn a specific Cartesian target, the procedure must sample over a sufficiently large region of joint space and rely on interpolation. Heuristics may be available to restrict the search to certain regions of joint space, but such heuristics are

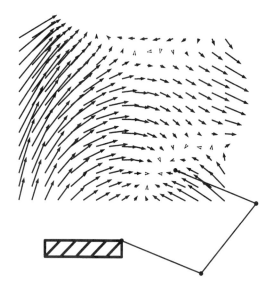

Figure 9.15
Goal-directed learning. A Cartesian target in the lower right portion of the figure was presented for ten successive trials. The error vectors are close to zero in the vicinity of the target.

essentially prior knowledge about the nature of the inverse mapping and can equally well be incorporated into the distal learning procedure.

Distal learning is fundamentally goal-directed. It is based on the performance error for a specific Cartesian target and is capable of finding an exact solution for a particular target in a small number of trials. This is demonstrated by the simulation shown in Figure 9.15. Starting from the controller shown in Figure 9.13, a particular Cartesian target was presented for ten successive trials. As shown in Figure 9.15, the network reorganizes itself so that the error is small in the vicinity of the target. After ten additional trials, the error at the target is zero within the floating-point resolution of the simulation.

Approximate Forward Models
We conducted an additional simulation to study the effects of inaccuracy in the forward model. The simulation varied the number of trials allocated to the learning of the forward model from 50 to 5000. The controller was trained to an RMS criterion of 0.001 at the three target positions $(-0.25, 0.25)$, $(0.25, 0.25)$, and $(0.0, 0.65)$. As shown in Figure 9.16, the results demonstrate that an accurate controller can be found with an inaccurate forward model. Fewer trials are needed to learn the target positions to criterion with the most accurate forward model; however, the dropoff in learning rate with less accurate forward models is relatively slight. Reasonably rapid learning is obtained even when the forward model is trained for only 50 trials, even though the average RMS error

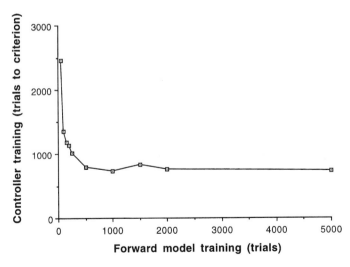

Figure 9.16
Number of trials required to train the controller to an RMS criterion of 0.001 as a function of the number of trials allocated to training the forward model. Each point is an average over three runs.

in the forward model is 0.34 m after 50 trials, compared to 0.11 m after 5000 trials.

Further Comparisons with Direct Inverse Modeling
In problems with many output variables, it is often unrealistic to acquire an inverse model over the entire workspace. In such cases the goal-directed nature of distal learning is particularly important because it allows the system to obtain inverse images for a restricted set of locations. However, the forward model must also be learned over a restricted region of action space, and there is no general a priori method for determining the appropriate region of the space in which to sample. That is, although distal learning is goal-directed in its acquisition of the inverse model, it is not inherently goal-directed in its acquisition of the forward model.

Because neither direct inverse modeling nor distal learning is entirely goal-directed, in any given problem it is important to consider whether it is more reasonable to acquire the inverse model or the forward model in a non-goal-directed manner. This issue is problem-dependent, depending on the nature of the function being learned, the nature of the class of functions that can be represented by the learner, and the nature of the learning algorithm. It is worth noting, however, that there is an inherent tradeoff in complexity between the inverse model and the forward model, due to the fact that their composition is the identity mapping. This tradeoff suggests a complementarity between the classes of problems for which direct inverse modeling and distal learning are appropriate. We believe that distal learning is more generally useful, however, because an inaccurate forward model is generally acceptable whereas an inaccurate inverse model is not. In many cases, it may be preferable to learn an inaccurate forward model that is specifically inverted at a desired set of locations rather than learning an inaccurate inverse model directly and relying on interpolation.

Dynamic Environments

To illustrate the application of distal learning to problems with environmental states, we consider the problem of learning to control a two-joint robot arm. Controlling a dynamic robot arm involves finding the appropriate torques to cause the arm to follow desired trajectories. The problem is difficult because of the nonlinear couplings between the motions of the two links and because of the fictitious torques due to the rotating coordinate systems.

The arm that we consider is the two-link version of the arm shown previously in Figure 10. Its configuration at each point in time is described by the joint angles $q_1(t)$ and $q_2(t)$, and by the Cartesian variables $x_1(t)$ and $x_2(t)$. The kinematic function $\mathbf{x}(t) = g(\mathbf{q(t)})$ that relates joint angles to Cartesian variables can be obtained by letting l_3 equal zero in Equation 15:

$$\begin{bmatrix} x_1(t) \\ x_2(t) \end{bmatrix} = \begin{bmatrix} l_1 \cos(q_1(t)) + l_2 \cos(q_1(t) + q_2(t)) \\ l_1 \sin(q_1(t)) + l_2 \sin(q_1(t) + q_2(t)) \end{bmatrix},$$

where l_1 and l_2 are the link lengths. The state space for the arm is the four-dimensional space of positions and velocities of the links.

The essence of robot arm dynamics is a mapping between the torques applied at the joints and the resulting angular accelerations of the links. This mapping is dependent on the state variables of angle and angular velocity. Let $\mathbf{q}$, $\dot{\mathbf{q}}$, and $\ddot{\mathbf{q}}$ represent the vector of joint angles, angular velocities, and angular accelerations, respectively, and let $\boldsymbol{\tau}$ represent the torques. In the terminology of earlier sections, $\mathbf{q}$ and $\dot{\mathbf{q}}$ together constitute the "state" and $\boldsymbol{\tau}$ is the "action." For convenience, we take $\ddot{\mathbf{q}}$ to represent the "next-state" (see the discussion below). To obtain an analog of the next-state function in Equation 1, the following differential equation can be derived for the angular motion of the links, using standard Newtonian or Lagrangian dynamical formulations (Craig, 1986):

$$M(\mathbf{q})\ddot{\mathbf{q}} + C(\mathbf{q}, \dot{\mathbf{q}})\dot{\mathbf{q}} + G(\mathbf{q}) = \boldsymbol{\tau}, \tag{17}$$

where $M(\mathbf{q})$ is an inertia matrix, $C(\mathbf{q}, \dot{\mathbf{q}})$ is a matrix of Coriolis and centripetal terms, and $G(\mathbf{q})$ is the vector of torque due to gravity. Our interest is not in the physics behind these equations per se, but in the functional relationships that they define. In particular, to obtain a "next-state function," we rewrite Equation 17 by solving for the accelerations to yield:

$$\ddot{\mathbf{q}} = M^{-1}(\mathbf{q})[\boldsymbol{\tau} - C(\mathbf{q}, \dot{\mathbf{q}})\dot{\mathbf{q}} - G(\mathbf{q})], \tag{18}$$

where the existence of $M^{-1}(\mathbf{q})$ is always assured (Craig, 1986). Equation 18 expresses the state-dependent relationship between torques and accelerations at each moment in time: Given the state variables $\mathbf{q}(t)$ and $\dot{\mathbf{q}}(t)$, and given the torque $\boldsymbol{\tau}(t)$, the acceleration $\ddot{\mathbf{q}}(t)$ can be computed by substitution in Equation 18. We refer to this computation as the *forward dynamics* of the arm.

An inverse mapping between torques and accelerations can be obtained by interpreting Equation 17 in the proper manner. Given the state variables $\mathbf{q}(t)$ and $\dot{\mathbf{q}}(t)$, and given the acceleration $\ddot{\mathbf{q}}(t)$, substitution in Equation 17 yields the corresponding torques. This (algebraic) computation is refered to as *inverse dynamics*. It should be clear that inverse dynamics and forward dynamics are complementary computations: Substitution of $\boldsymbol{\tau}$ from Equation 17 into Equation 18 yields the requisite identity mapping.

These relationships between torques, accelerations, and states are summarized in Figure 9.17. It is useful to compare this figure with the kinematic example shown in Figure 9.11. In both the kinematic case and the dynamic case, the forward and inverse mappings that must be learned are fixed functions of the instantaneous values of the relevant variables. In the dynamic case, this is due to the fact that the structural terms of the dynamical equations (the terms M, C, and G) are explicit functions of state rather than time. The dynamic case can be thought of as a generalization of the kinematic case in which additional

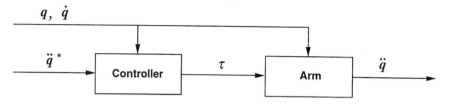

Figure 9.17
The forward and inverse mappings associated with the arm dynamics.

contextual (state) variables are needed to index the mappings that must be learned.[10]

Figure 9.17 is an instantiation of Figure 9.6, with the acceleration playing the role of the "next-state." In general, for systems described by differential equations, it is convenient to define the notion of "next-state" in terms of the time derivative of one or more of the state variables (e.g., accelerations in the case of arm dynamics). This definition is entirely consistent with the development in preceding sections; indeed, if the differential equations in Equation 17 are simulated in discrete time on a computer, then the numerical algorithm must compute the accelerations defined by Equation 18 to convert the positions and velocities at the current time step into the positions and velocities at the next time step.[11]

Learning a Dynamic Forward Model
A forward model of arm dynamics is a network that learns a prediction $\hat{\ddot{\mathbf{q}}}$ of the acceleration $\ddot{\mathbf{q}}$, given the position $\mathbf{q}$, the velocity $\dot{\mathbf{q}}$, and the torque τ. The appropriate teaching signal for such a network is the actual acceleration $\ddot{\mathbf{q}}$, yielding the following cost functional:

$$L = \frac{1}{2} E\{(\ddot{\mathbf{q}} - \hat{\ddot{\mathbf{q}}})^T (\ddot{\mathbf{q}} - \hat{\ddot{\mathbf{q}}})\}. \tag{19}$$

The prediction $\hat{\ddot{\mathbf{q}}}$ is a function of the position, the velocity, the torque and the weights:

$$\hat{\ddot{\mathbf{q}}} = \hat{f}(\mathbf{q}, \dot{\mathbf{q}}, \tau, \mathbf{w}).$$

For an appropriate ensemble of control trajectories, this cost functional is minimized when a set of weights is found such that $\hat{f}(\cdot, \mathbf{w})$ best approximates the forward dynamical function given by Equation 18.

An important difference between kinematic problems and dynamic problems is that it is generally infeasible to produce arbitrary random control signals in dynamical environments, because of considerations of stability. For example, if $\tau(t)$ in Equation 17 is allowed to be a stationary white-noise stochastic process, then the variance of $\mathbf{q}(t)$ approaches infinity (much like a random walk). This yields data that is of little use for learning a model. We have used two closely related approaches to overcome this problem. The first approach is to produce random *equilibrium* positions for the arm rather than random torques. That is, we define a new control signal $\mathbf{u}(t)$ such that the augmented arm dynamics are given by:

$$M(\mathbf{q})\ddot{\mathbf{q}} + C(\mathbf{q}, \dot{\mathbf{q}})\dot{\mathbf{q}} + G(\mathbf{q}) = k_v(\dot{\mathbf{q}} - \dot{\mathbf{u}}) + k_p(\mathbf{q} - \mathbf{u}), \tag{20}$$

for fixed constants k_p and k_v. The random control signal $\mathbf{u}$ in this equation acts as a "virtual" equilibrium position for the arm (Hogan, 1985) and the augmented dynamics can be used to generate training data for learning the forward model. The second approach also utilizes Equation 20 and differs from the first approach only in the choice of the control signal $\mathbf{u}(t)$. Rather than using random controls, the target trajectories themselves are used as controls (that is, the trajectories utilized in the second phase of learning are also used to train the forward model). This approach is equivalent to using a simple fixed-gain proportional-derivative (PD) feedback controller to stabilize the system along a set of reference trajectories and thereby generate training data.[12] Such use of an auxiliary feedback controller is similar to its use in the feedback-error learning (Kawato, et al., 1987) and direct inverse modeling (Atkeson & Reinkensmeyer, 1988; Miller, 1987) approaches. As is discussed below, the second approach has the advantage that it does not require the forward model to be learned in a separate phase.

Composite Control System
The composite system for controlling the arm is shown in Figure 18. The control signal in this diagram is the torque τ, which is the sum of two components:

$$\tau = \tau_{ff} + \tau_{fb},$$

where τ_{ff} is a feedforward torque and τ_{fb} is the (optional) feedback torque produced by the auxiliary feedback controller. The feedforward controller is the learning controller that converges toward a model of the inverse dynamics of the arm. In the early phases of learning, the feedforward controller produces small random torques, thus the major source of control is provided by the error-correcting feedback controller.[13] When the feedforward controller is first learned it produces torques that allow the system to follow desired trajectories with smaller error, thus the role of the feedback controller is diminished. Indeed, in the limit where the feedforward controller converges to a perfect inverse model, the feedforward torque causes the system to follow a desired trajectory without error and the feedback controller is therefore silent (assuming no disturbances). Thus the system shifts automatically from feedback-dominated control to feedforward-dominated control over the course of learning (see also Atkeson & Reinkensmeyer, 1988; Kawato, et al., 1987; Miller, 1988).

There are two error signals utilized in learning inverse dynamics: The prediction error $\ddot{\mathbf{q}} - \hat{\ddot{\mathbf{q}}}$ and the performance error $\ddot{\mathbf{q}}^* - \ddot{\mathbf{q}}$.[14] The prediction error is

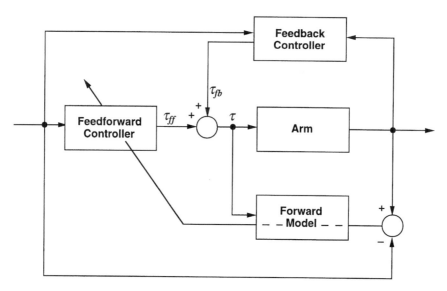

Figure 9.18
The composite control system.

used to train the forward model as discussed in the previous section. Once the forward model is at least partially learned, the performance error can be used in training the inverse model. The error is propagated backward through the forward model and down into the feedforward controller where the weights are changed.

The longer version of the paper (Jordan & Rumelhart, 1992) presents simulations for the dynamic arm, including cases in which an auxiliary feedback controller is present as well as cases in which such a controller is absent. Simulations are also presented which explore the problem of learning the forward model and the controller simultaneously.

Discussion

In this paper we have argued that the supervised learning paradigm is broader than is commonly assumed. The distal supervised learning framework extends supervised learning to problems in which desired values are available only for the distal consequences of a learner's actions and not for the actions themselves. This is a significant weakening of the classical notion of the "teacher" in the supervised learning paradigm. In this section we provide further discussion of the class of problems that can be treated within the distal supervised learning framework. We discuss possible sources of training data and we contrast distal supervised learning with reinforcement learning.

How is Training Data Obtained?

To provide support for our argument that distal supervised learning is more realistic than classical supervised learning, it is necessary to consider possible sources of training data for distal supervised learning. We discuss two such sources, which we refer to as *imitation* and *envisioning*.

One of the most common ways for humans to acquire skills is through imitation. Skills such as dance or athletics are often learned by observing another person performing the skill and attempting to replicate their behavior. Although in some cases a teacher may be available to suggest particular patterns of limb motion, such direct instruction does not appear to be a necessary component of skill acquisition. A case in point is speech acquisition—children acquire speech by hearing speech sounds, not by receiving instruction on how to move their articulators.

Our conception of a distal supervised learning problem involves a set of (intention, desired outcome) training pairs. Learning by imitation clearly makes desired outcomes available to the learner. With regard to intentions, there are three possibilities. First, the learner may know or be able to infer the intentions of the person serving as a model. Alternatively, an idiosyncratic internal encoding of intentions is viable as long as the encoding is consistent. For example, a child acquiring speech may have an intention to drink, may observe another person obtaining water by uttering the form "water," and may utilize the acoustic representation of "water" as a distal target for learning the articulatory movements for expressing a desire to drink, even though the other person uses the water to douse a fire. Finally, when the learner is acquiring an inverse model, as in the simulations reported in this paper, the intention is obviously available because it is the same as desired outcome.

Our conception of the distal supervised learning problem as a set of training pairs is of course an abstraction that must be elaborated when dealing with complex tasks. In a complex task such as dance, it is presumably not easy to determine the choice of sensory data to be used as distal targets for the learning procedure. Indeed, the learner may alter the choice of targets once he or she has achieved a modicum of skill. The learner may also need to decompose the task into simpler tasks and to set intermediate goals. We suspect that the role of external "teachers" is to help with these representational issues rather than to provide proximal targets directly to the learner.

Another source of data for the distal supervised learning paradigm is a process that we refer to as "envisioning." Envisioning is a general process of converting abstract goals into their corresponding sensory realization, without regard to the actions needed to achieve the goals. Envisioning involves deciding what it would "look like" or "feel like" to perform some task. This process presumably involves general deductive and inductive reasoning abilities as well as experience with similar tasks. The point that we want to emphasize is that envisioning need not refer to the actions that are needed to actually carry out a task; that is the problem solved by the distal learning procedure.

Comparisons with Reinforcement Learning

An alternative approach to solving the class of problems that we have discussed in this paper is to use reinforcement learning algorithms (Barto, 1989; Sutton, 1984). Reinforcement learning algorithms are based on the assumption that the environment provides an *evaluation* of the actions produced by the learner. Because the evaluation can be an arbitrary function, the approach is in principle applicable to the general problem of learning on the basis of distal signals.

Reinforcement learning algorithms work by updating the probabilities of emitting particular actions. The updating procedure is based on the evaluations received from the environment. If the evaluation of an action is favorable then the probability associated with that action is increased and the probabilities associated with all other actions are decreased. Conversely, if the evaluation is unfavorable, then the probability of the given action is decreased and the probabilities associated with all other actions are increased. These characteristic features of reinforcement learning algorithms differ in important ways from the corresponding features of supervised learning algorithms. Supervised learning algorithms are based on the existence of a signed error vector rather than an evaluation. The signed error vector is generally, although not always, obtained by comparing the actual output vector to a target vector. If the signed error vector is small, corresponding to a favorable evaluation, the algorithm initiates no changes. If the signed error vector is large, corresponding to an unfavorable evaluation, the algorithm corrects the current action in favor of a particular alternative action. Supervised learning algorithms do not simply increase the probabilities of all alternative actions; rather, they choose particular alternatives based on the directionality of the signed error vector.[15]

It is important to distinguish between learning *paradigms* and learning *algorithms*. Because the same learning algorithm can often be utilized in a variety of learning paradigms, a failure to distinguish between paradigms and algorithms can lead to misunderstanding. This is particularly true of reinforcement learning tasks and supervised learning tasks because of the close relationships between evaluative signals and signed error vectors. A signed error vector can always be converted into an evaluative signal (any bounded monotonic function of the norm of the signed error vector suffices); thus, reinforcement learning algorithms can always be used for supervised learning problems. Conversely, an evaluative signal can always be converted into a signed error vector (using the machinery that we have discussed; see also Munro, 1987); thus, supervised learning algorithms can always be used for reinforcement learning problems. The definition of a learning paradigm, however, has more to do with the manner in which a problem is naturally posed than with the algorithm used to solve the problem. In the case of the basketball player, for example, assuming that the environment provides directional information such as "too far to the left," "too long," or "too short," is very different from assuming that the environment provides evaluative information of the form "good," "better," or "best." Furthermore, learning algorithms differ in algorithmic complexity when applied across paradigms: Using a reinforcement learning algorithm to solve a supervised learning problem is likely to be inefficient because such algorithms do not take advantage of directional information. Conversely, using supervised learning algorithms to solve reinforcement learning problems is likely to be inefficient because of the extra machinery that is required to induce a signed error vector.

In summary, although it has been suggested that the difference between reinforcement learning and supervised learning is the latter's reliance on a "teacher," we feel that this argument is mistaken. The distinction between the supervised learning paradigm and the reinforcement learning paradigm lies in the interpretation of environmental feedback as an error signal or as an evaluative signal, not the coordinate system in which such signals are provided. Many problems involving distal credit assignment may be better conceived of as supervised learning problems rather than reinforcement learning problems if the distal feedback signal can be interpreted as a performance error.

Conclusions

There are a number of difficulties with the classical distinctions between "unsupervised," "reinforcement," and "supervised" learning. Supervised learning is generally said to be dependent on a "teacher" to provide target values for the output units of a network. This is viewed as a limitation because in many domains there is no such teacher. Nevertheless, the environment often does provide sensory information about the consequences of an action which can be employed in making internal modifications just as if a teacher had provided the information to the learner directly. The idea is that the learner first acquires an internal model that allows prediction of the consequences of actions. The internal model can be used as a mechanism for transforming distal sensory information about the consequences of actions into proximal information for making internal modifications. This two-phase procedure extends the scope of the supervised learning paradigm to include a broad range of problems in which actions are transformed by an unknown dynamical process before being compared to desired outcomes.

We first illustrated this approach in the case of learning an inverse model of a simple "static" environment. We showed that our method of utilizing a forward model of the environment has a number of important advantages over the alternative method of building the inverse model directly. These advantages are especially apparent in cases where there is no unique inverse model.

We also showed that this idea can be extended usefully to the case of a dynamic environment. In this case, we simply elaborate both the forward model and the learner (i.e., controller) so they take into account the current state of the environment.

We also suggested that comparative work in the study of learning can be facilitated by making a distinction between learning algorithms and learning paradigms. A variety of learning algorithms can often be applied to a particular instance of a learning paradigm; thus, it is important to characterize not only the paradigmatic aspects of any given learning problem, such as the nature of the interaction between the learner and the environment and the nature of the quantities to be optimized, but also the tradeoffs in algorithmic complexity that arise when different classes of learning algorithms are applied to the problem. Further research is needed to delineate the natural classes at the levels of paradigms and algorithms and to clarify the relationships between levels. We believe that such research will begin to provide a theoretical basis for making distinctions between candidate hypotheses in the empirical study of human learning.

Notes

This paper is an abridged version of Jordan and Rumelhart (1992). We wish to thank Michael Mozer, Andrew Barto, Robert Jacobs, Eric Loeb, and James McClelland for helpful comments on the manuscript. This project was supported in part by BRSG 2 S07 RR07047-23 awarded by the Biomedical Research Support Grant Program, Division of Research Resources, National Institutes of Health, by a grant from ATR Auditory and Visual Perception Research Laboratories, by a grant from Siemens Corporation, by a grant from the Human Frontier Science Program, and by grant N00014-90-J-1942 awarded by the Office of Naval Research.

1. The choice of time indices in Equations 1, 2, and 3 is based on our focus on the output at time n. In our framework a learning algorithm alters $\mathbf{y}[n]$ based on previous values of the states, inputs, and actions.
2. In the engineering literature, this learning process is referred to as "system identification" (Ljung & Söderström, 1986).
3. Control system design normally involves a number of additional constraints involving stability and robustness; thus, the goal is generally to invert the environment as nearly as possible subject to these additional constraints.
4. A set is *convex* if for every pair of points in the set all points on the line between the points also lie in the set.
5. An interesting analogy can be drawn between the distal learning approach and indirect techniques for solving systems of linear equations. In numerical linear algebra, rather than solving explicitly for a generalized inverse of the coefficient matrix, solutions are generally found indirectly (e.g., by applying Gaussian elimination to both sides of the equation $GA = I$, where I is the identity matrix).
6. The Jacobian matrix of a vector function is simply its first derivative—it is a matrix of first partial derivatives. That is, the entries of the matrix $(\partial \mathbf{y}/\partial \mathbf{w})$ are the partial derivatives of the each of the output activations with respect to each of the weights in the network.
7. To gain some insight into why a transpose matrix arises in backpropagation, consider a single-layer linear network described by $\mathbf{y} = W\mathbf{x}$, where W is the weight matrix. The rows of W are the incoming weight vectors for the output units of the network, and the columns of W are the

outgoing weight vectors for the input units of the network. Passing a vector forward in the network involves taking the inner product of the vector with each of the incoming weight vectors. This operation corresponds to multiplication by W. Passing a vector backward in the network corresponds to taking the inner product of the vector with each of the outgoing weight vectors. This operation corresponds to multiplication by W^T, because the rows of W^T are the columns of W.

8. Note that the error term $(\mathbf{y}^*[n] - \mathbf{y}[n])$ is not a function of the output of the forward model; nonetheless, activation must flow forward in the model because the estimated Jacobian matrix $(\partial \hat{\mathbf{y}}/\partial \mathbf{u})$ varies as a function of the activations of the hidden units and the output units of the model.

9. The use of a grid is not necessary; the procedure also works if Cartesian positions are sampled randomly on each trial.

10. This perspective is essentially that underlying the local optimization formulation of distal learning.

11. Because of the amplification of noise in differentiated signals, however, most realistic implementations of forward dynamical models would utilize positions and velocities rather than accelerations. In such cases the numerical integration of Equation 18 would be incorporated as part of the forward model.

12. A PD controller is a device whose output is a weighted sum of position errors and velocity errors. The position errors and the velocity errors are multiplied by fixed numbers (gains) before being summed.

13. As is discussed below, this statement is not entirely accurate. The learning algorithm itself provides a form of error-correcting feedback control.

14. As noted above, it is also possible to include the numerical integration of $\hat{\ddot{\mathbf{q}}}$ as part of the forward model and learn a mapping whose output is the predicted next-state $(\hat{\mathbf{q}}[n], \hat{\dot{\mathbf{q}}}[n])$. This approach may be preferred for systems in which differentiation of noisy signals is a concern.

15. As pointed out by Barto, Sutton & Anderson (1983), this distinction between reinforcement learning and supervised learning is significant only if the learner has a repertoire of more than two actions.

References

Atkeson, C. G., & Reinkensmeyer, D. J. (1988). Using associative content-addressable memories to control robots. *IEEE Conference on Decision and Control.* San Francisco, CA.

Barto, A. G. (1989). From chemotaxis to cooperativity: Abstract exercises in neuronal learning strategies. In R. M. Durbin, R. C. Maill, & G. J. Mitchison (Eds.), *The computing neurone.* Reading, MA: Addison-Wesley Publishers.

Barto, A. G., Sutton, R. S., & Anderson, C. W. (1983). Neuronlike adaptive elements that can solve difficult learning control problems. *IEEE Transactions on Systems, Man, and Cybernetics,* SMC-13, 834–846.

Becker, S. & Hinton, G. E. (1989). *Spatial coherence as an internal teacher for a neural network.* (Tech. Rep. CRG-TR-89-7). Toronto: University of Toronto.

Carlson, A. B. (1986). *Communication Systems.* New York: McGraw-Hill.

Craig, J. J. (1986). *Introduction to Robotics.* Reading, MA: Addison-Wesley Publishers.

Goodwin, G. C. & Sin, K. S. (1984). *Adaptive filtering prediction and control.* Englewood Cliffs, NJ: Prentice-Hall.

Grossberg, S. (1987). Competitive learning: From interactive activation to adaptive resonance. *Cognitive Science,* 11, 23–63.

Hinton, G. E. & Sejnowski, T. J. (1986). Learning and relearning in Boltzmann machines. In D. E. Rumelhart & J. L. McClelland (Eds.), *Parallel distributed processing: Volume 1,* 282–317. Cambridge, MA: MIT Press.

Hogan, N. (1984). An organising principle for a class of voluntary movements. *Journal of Neuroscience, 4*, 2745–2754.

Jordan, M. I. (1983). *Mental practice*. Unpublished dissertation proposal, Center for Human Information Processing, University of California, San Diego.

Jordan, M. I., & Rosenbaum, D. A. (1989). Action. In M. I. Posner (Ed.), *Foundations of Cognitive Science*. Cambridge, MA: MIT Press.

Jordan, M. I. (1990). Motor learning and the degrees of freedom problem. In M. Jeannerod (Ed.), *Attention and Performance, XIII*. Hillsdale, NJ: Erlbaum.

Jordan, M. I. (1992). Constrained supervised learning. *Journal of Mathematical Psychology, 36*, 396–425.

Jordan, M. I., & Rumelhart, D. E. (1992). Forward models: Supervised learning with a distal teacher. *Cognitive Science, 16*, 307–354.

Kawato, M. (1990). Computational schemes and neural network models for formation and control of multijoint arm trajectory. In W. T. Miller, III, R. S. Sutton, & P. J. Werbos (Eds.), *Neural Networks for Control*. Cambridge: MIT Press.

Kawato, M., Furukawa, K., & Suzuki, R. (1987). A hierarchical neural-network model for control and learning of voluntary movement. *Biological Cybernetics, 57*, 169–185.

Kirk, D. E. (1970). *Optimal control theory*. Englewood Cliffs, NJ: Prentice-Hall.

Kohonen, T. (1982). Self-organized formation of topologically correct feature maps. *Biological Cybernetics, 43*, 56–69.

Kuperstein, M. (1988). Neural model of adaptive hand-eye coordination for single postures. *Science, 239*, 1308–1311.

LeCun, Y. (1985). A learning scheme for asymmetric threshold networks. *Proceedings of Cognitiva 85*. Paris, France.

Linsker, R. (1988). Self-organization in a perceptual network. *Computer, 21*, 105–117.

Ljung, L. & Söderström, T. (1986). *Theory and practice of recursive identification*. Cambridge: MIT Press.

Miller, W. T. (1987). Sensor-based control of robotic manipulators using a general learning algorithm. *IEEE Journal of Robotics and Automation, 3*, 157–165.

Mozer, M. C. & Bachrach, J. (1990). *Discovering the structure of a reactive environment by exploration*. In D. Touretzky (Ed.), *Advances in Neural Information Processing Systems 2*. San Mateo, CA: Morgan Kaufmann.

Munro, P. (1987). A dual back-propagation scheme for scalar reward learning. *Proceedings of the Ninth Annual Conference of the Cognitive Science Society*. Hillsdale, NJ: Erlbaum.

Narendra, K. S. & Parthasarathy, K. (1990). Identification and control of dynamical systems using neural networks. *IEEE Transactions on Neural Networks, 1*, 4–27.

Nguyen, D. & Widrow, B. (1989). The truck backer-upper: An example of self-learning in neural networks. In: *Proceedings of the International Joint Conference on Neural Networks, 2*, 357–363. Piscataway, NJ: IEEE Press.

Parker, D. (1985). *Learning-logic*. (Tech. Rep. TR-47). Cambridge, MA: MIT Sloan School of Management.

Robinson, A. J. & Fallside, F. (1989). Dynamic reinforcement driven error propagation networks with application to game playing. *Proceedings of Neural Information Systems*. American Institute of Physics.

Rosenblatt, F. (1962). *Principles of neurodynamics*. New York: Spartan.

Rumelhart, D. E. (1986). Learning sensorimotor programs in parallel distributed processing systems. *US–Japan Joint Seminar on Competition and Cooperation in Neural Nets, II*. Unpublished presentation.

Rumelhart, D. E., Hinton, G. E., Williams, R. J. (1986). Learning internal representations by error propagation. In D. E. Rumelhart & J. L. McClelland (Eds.), *Parallel distributed processing*: *Volume 1*, 318–363. Cambridge, MA: MIT Press.

Rumelhart, D. E., Smolensky, P., McClelland, J. L. & Hinton, G. E. (1986). Schemata and sequential thought processes in PDP models. In D. E. Rumelhart & J. L. McClelland (Eds.), *Parallel distributed processing*: Volume 2, 7–57. Cambridge, MA: MIT Press.

Rumelhart, D. E. & Zipser, D. (1986). Feature discovery by competitive learning. In D. E. Rumelhart & J. L. McClelland (Eds.), *Parallel distributed processing*: Volume 1, 151–193. Cambridge, MA: MIT Press.

Schmidhuber, J. H. (1990). An on-line algorithm for dynamic reinforcement learning and planning in reactive environments. In: *Proceedings of the International Joint Conference on Neural Networks*, 2, 253–258. Piscataway, NJ: IEEE Press.

Sutton, R. S. (1984). *Temporal credit assignment in reinforcement learning*. (COINS Tech. Rep. 84-02). Amherst, MA: University of Massachusetts, Computer and Information Sciences.

Sutton, R. S. (1990). Integrated architectures for learning, planning, and reacting based on approximating dynamic programming. *Proceedings of the Seventh International Conference on Machine Learning*.

Werbos, P. (1974). *Beyond regression: New tools for prediction and analysis in the behavioral sciences*. Unpublished doctoral dissertation, Harvard University.

Werbos, P. (1987). Building and understanding adaptive systems: A statistical/numerical approach to factory automation and brain research. *IEEE Transactions on Systems, Man, and Cybernetics*, 17, 7–20.

Widrow, B. & Hoff, M. E. (1960). Adaptive switching circuits. *Institute of Radio Engineers, Western Electronic Show and Convention, Convention Record, Part 4*, 96–104.

Widrow, B., & Stearns, S. D. (1985). *Adaptive signal processing*. Englewood Cliffs, NJ: Prentice-Hall.

Appendix A

The networks used in all of the simulations were standard feedforward connectionist networks (see Rumelhart, Hinton, & Williams, 1986).

Activation functions—The input units and the output units of all networks were linear and the hidden units were logistic with asymptotes of -1 and 1.

Input and target values—In the kinematic arm simulations, the joint angles were represented using the vector $\left[\cos\left(q_1 - \frac{\pi}{2}\right), \cos(q_2), \cos(q_3)\right]^T$. The Cartesian targets were scaled to lie between -1 and 1 and fed directly into the network.

Initial weights—Initial weights were chosen randomly from a uniform distribution on the interval $[-0.5, 0.5]$.

Hidden units—A single layer of 50 hidden units was used in all networks. No attempt was made to optimize the number of the hidden units or their connectivity.

Parameter values—A learning rate of 0.1 was used in all of the kinematic arm simulations. The momentum was set to 0.5.

Recurrent Networks

Chapter 10

Finding Structure in Time

Jeffrey L. Elman

Introduction

Time is clearly important in cognition. It is inextricably bound up with many behaviors (such as language) which express themselves as temporal sequences. Indeed, it is difficult to know how one might deal with such basic problems as goal-directed behavior, planning, or causation without some way of representing time.

The question of how to represent time might seem to arise as a special problem unique to parallel-processing models, if only because the parallel nature of computation appears to be at odds with the serial nature of temporal events. However, even within traditional (serial) frameworks, the representation of serial order and the interaction of a serial input or output with higher levels of representation presents challenges. For example, in models of motor activity, an important issue is whether the action plan is a literal specification of the output sequence, or whether the plan represents serial order in a more abstract manner (e.g., Fowler, 1977, 1980; Jordan & Rosenbaum, 1988; Kelso, Saltzman, & Tuller, 1986; Lashley, 1951; MacNeilage, 1970; Saltzman & Kelso, 1987). Linguistic theoreticians have perhaps tended to be less concerned with the representation and processing of the temporal aspects to utterances (assuming, for instance, that all the information in an utterance is somehow made available simultaneously in a syntactic tree); but the research in natural language parsing suggests that the problem is not trivially solved (e.g., Frazier & Fodor, 1978; Marcus, 1980). Thus, what is one of the most elementary facts about much of human activity—that it has temporal extend—is sometimes ignored and is often problematic.

In parallel distributed processing models, the processing of sequential inputs has been accomplished in several ways. The most common solution is to attempt to "parallelize time" by giving it a spatial representation. However, there are problems with this approach, and it is ultimately not a good solution. A better approach would be to represent time implicitly rather than explicitly. That is, we represent time by the effect it has on processing and not as an additional dimension of the input.

This article describes the results of pursuing this approach, with particular emphasis on problems that are relevant to natural language processing. The approach taken is rather simple, but the results are sometimes complex and unexpected. Indeed, it seems that the solution to the problem of time may interact with other problems for connectionist architectures, including the problem of symbolic representation and how connectionist representations encode structure. The current approach supports the notion outlined by Van Gelder (1990) (see also, Elman, 1989; Smolensky, 1987, 1988), that connectionist representations may have a functional compositionality without being syntactically compositional.

The first section briefly describes some of the problems that arise when time is represented externally as a spatial dimension. The second section describes the approach used in this work. The major portion of this article presents the results of applying this new architecture to a diverse set of problems. These problems range in complexity from a temporal version of the Exclusive-OR function to the discovery of syntactic/semantic categories in natural language data.

The Problem with Time

One obvious way of dealing with patterns that have a temporal extent is to represent time explicitly by associating the serial order of the pattern with the dimensionality of the pattern vector. The first temporal event is represented by the first element in the pattern vector, the second temporal event is represented by the second position in the pattern vector, and so on. The entire pattern vector is processed in parallel by the model. This approach has been used in a variety of models (e.g., Cottrell, Munro, & Zipser, 1987; Elman & Zipser, 1988; Hanson & Kegl, 1987).

There are several drawbacks to this approach, which basically uses a spatial metaphor for time. First, it requires that there be some interface with the world, which buffers the input, so that it can be presented all at once. It is not clear that biological systems make use of such shift registers. There are also logical problems: How should a system know when a buffer's contents should be examined?

Second, the shift register imposes a rigid limit on the duration of patterns (since the input layer must provide for the longest possible pattern), and furthermore, suggests that all input vectors be the same length. These problems are particularly troublesome in domains such as language, where one would like comparable representations for patterns that are of variable length. This is as true of the basic units of speech (phonetic segments) as it is of sentences.

Finally, and most seriously, such an approach does not easily distinguish relative temporal position from absolute temporal position. For example, consider the following two vectors.

[0 1 1 1 0 0 0 0 0]

[0 0 0 1 1 1 0 0 0]

These two vectors appear to be instances of the same basic pattern, but displaced in space (or time, if these are given a temporal interpretation). However, as the geometric interpretation of these vectors makes clear, the two patterns are in fact quite dissimilar and spatially distant.[1] PDP models can, of course, be trained to treat these two patterns as similar. But the similarity is a consequence of an external teacher and not of the similarity structure of the patterns themselves, and the desired similarity does not generalize to novel patterns. This shortcoming is serious if one is interested in patterns in which the relative temporal structure is preserved in the face of absolute temporal displacements.

What one would like is a representation of time that is richer and does not have these problems. In what follows here, a simple architecture is described, which has a number of desirable temporal properties, and has yielded interesting results.

Networks with Memory

The spatial representation of time described above treats time as an explicit part of the input. There is another, very different possibility: Allow time to be represented by the effect it has on processing. This means giving the processing system dynamic properties that are responsive to temporal sequences. In short, the network must be given memory.

There are many ways in which this can be accomplished, and a number of interesting proposals have appeared in the literature (e.g., Jordan, 1986; Pineda, 1988; Stornetta, Hogg, & Huberman, 1987; Tank & Hopfield, 1987; Waibel, Hanazawa, Hinton, Shikano, & Lang, 1987; Watrous & Shastri, 1987; Williams & Zipser, 1988). One of the most promising was suggested by Jordan (1986). Jordan described a network (shown in Figure 10.1) containing recurrent connections that were used to associate a static pattern (a "Plan") with a serially ordered output pattern (a sequence of "Actions"). The recurrent connections allow the network's hidden units to see its own previous output, so that the subsequent behavior can be shaped by previous responses. These recurrent connections are what give the network memory.

This approach can be modified in the following way. Suppose a network (shown in Figure 10.2) is augmented at the input level by additional units; call these *Context Units*. These units are also "hidden" in the sense that they interact exclusively with other nodes internal to the network, and not the outside world.

Imagine that there is a sequential input to be processed, and some clock which regulates presentation of the input to the network. Processing would then consist of the following sequence of events. At time *t*, the input units receive the first input in the sequence. Each unit might be a single scalar value

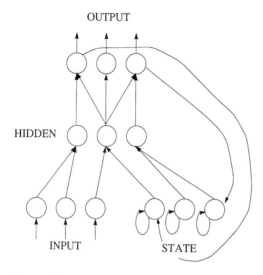

HIDDEN

INPUT   STATE

Figure 10.1
Architecture used by Jordan (1986). Connections from output to state units are one-for-one, with a fixed weight of 1.0. Not all connections are shown.

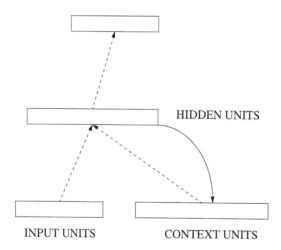

OUTPUT UNITS

HIDDEN UNITS

INPUT UNITS   CONTEXT UNITS

Figure 10.2
A simple recurrent network in which activations are copied from hidden layer to context layer on a one-for-one basis, with fixed weight of 1.0. Dotted lines represent trainable connections.

or a vector, depending upon the nature of the problem. The context units are initially set to 0.5.[2] Both the input units and context units activate the hidden units; the hidden units then feed forward to activate the output units. The hidden units also feed back to activate the context units. This constitutes the forward activation. Depending upon the task, there may or may not be a learning phase in this time cycle. If so, the output is compared with a teacher input, and back propagation of error (Rumelhart, Hinton, & Williams, 1986) is used to adjust connection strengths incrementally. Recurrent connections are fixed at 1.0 and are not subject to adjustment.[3] At the next time step, $t + 1$, the above sequence is repeated. This time the context units contain values which are exactly the hidden unit values at time t. These context units thus provide the network with memory.

Internal Representation of Time

In feed forward networks employing hidden units and a learning algorithm, the hidden units develop internal representations for the input patterns that recode those patterns in a way which enables the network to produce the correct output for a given input. In the present architecture, the context units remember the previous internal state. Thus, the hidden units have the task of mapping both an external input, and also the previous internal state of some desired output. Because the patterns on the hidden units are saved as context, the hidden units must accomplish this mapping and at the same time develop representations which are useful encodings of the temporal properties of the sequential input. Thus, the internal representations that develop are sensitive to temporal context; the effect of time is implicit in these internal states. Note, however, that these representations of temporal context need not be literal. They represent a memory which is highly task- and stimulus-dependent.

Consider now the results of applying this architecture to a number of problems that involve processing of inputs which are naturally presented in sequence.

Exclusive-Or

The Exclusive-Or (XOR) function has been of interest because it cannot be learned by a simple two-layer network. Instead, it requires at least three layers. The XOR is usually presented as a problem involving 2-bit input vectors $(00, 11, 01, 10)$ yielding 1-bit output vectors $(0, 0, 1, 1$, respectively).

This problem can be translated into a temporal domain in several ways. One version involves constructing a sequence of 1-bit inputs by presenting the 2-bit inputs one bit at a time (i.e., in 2 time steps), followed by the 1-bit output; then continuing with another input/output pair chosen at random. A sample input might be:

1 0 1 0 0 0 0 1 1 1 1 0 1 0 1 ...

Here, the first and second bits are XOR-ed to produce the third; the fourth and fifth are XOR-ed to give the sixth; and so on. The inputs are concatenated and presented as an unbroken sequence.

In the current version of the XOR problem, the input consisted of a sequence of 3,000 bits constructed in this manner. This input stream was presented to the network shown in Figure 10.2 (with 1 input unit, 2 hidden units, 1 output unit, and 2 context units), one bit at a time. The task of the network was, at each point in time, to predict the next bit in the sequence. That is, given the input sequence shown, where one bit at a time is presented, the correct output at corresponding points in time is shown below.

>   **input:**   1 0 1 0 0 0 0 1 1 1 1 0 1 0 1...
>
>   **output:**   0 1 0 0 0 0 1 1 1 1 0 1 0 1 ?...

Recall that the actual input to the hidden layer consists of the input shown above, as well as a copy of the hidden unit activations from the previous cycle. The prediction is thus based not just on input from the world, but also on the network's previous state (which is continuously passed back to itself on each cycle).

Notice that, given the temporal structure of this sequence, it is only sometimes possible to predict the next item correctly. When the network has received the first bit—**1** in the example above—there is a 50% chance that the next bit will be a **1** (or a **0**). When the network receives the second bit (**0**), however, it should then be possible to predict that the third will be the XOR, **1**. When the fourth bit is presented, the fifth is not predictable. But from the fifth bit, the sixth can be predicted, and so on.

In fact, after 600 passes through a 3,000-bit sequence constructed in this way, the network's ability to predict the sequential input closely follows the above schedule. This can be seen by looking at the sum squared error in the output prediction at successive points in the input. The error signal provides a useful guide as to when the network recognized a temporal sequence, because at such moments its outputs exhibit low error. Figure 10.3 contains a plot of the sum squared error over 12 time steps (averaged over 1,200 cycles). The error drops at those points in the sequence where a correct prediction is possible; at other points, the error is high. This is an indication that the network has learned something about the temporal structure of the input, and is able to use previous context and current input to make predictions about future input. The network, in fact, attempts to use the XOR rule at all points in time; this fact is obscured by the averaging of error, which is done for Figure 10.3. If one looks at the output activations, it is apparent from the nature of the errors that the network predicts successive inputs to be the XOR of the previous two. This is guaranteed to be successful every third bit, and will sometimes, fortuitously, also result in correct predictions at other times.

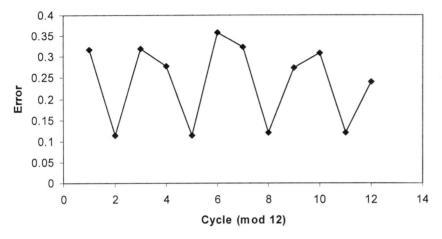

Figure 10.3
Graph of root mean aquared error over 12 consecutive inputs in sequential XOR task. Data points are averaged over 1200 trials.

It is interesting that the solution to the temporal version of XOR is somewhat different than the static version of the same problem. In a network with two hidden units, one unit is highly activated when the input sequence is a series of identical elements (all 1 s of 0 s), whereas the other unit is highly activated when the input elements alternate. Another way of viewing this is that the network develops units which are sensitive to high- and low-frequency inputs. This is a different solution than is found with feed-forward networks and simultaneously presented inputs. This suggests that problems may change their nature when cast in a temporal form. It is not clear that the solution will be easier or more difficult in this form, but it is an important lesson to realize that the solution may be different.

In this simulation, the prediction task has been used in a way that is somewhat analogous to auto-association. Auto-association is a useful technique for discovering the intrinsic structure possessed by a set of patterns. This occurs because the network must transform the patterns into more compact representations; it generally does so by exploiting redundancies in the patterns. Finding these redundancies can be of interest because of what they reveal about the similarity structure of the data set (cf. Cottrell et al. 1987; Elman & Zipser, 1988).

In this simulation, the goal is to find the temporal structure of the XOR sequence. Simple auto-association would not work, since the task of simply reproducing the input at all points in time is trivially solvable and does not require sensitivity to sequential patterns. The prediction task is useful because its solution requires that the network be sensitive to temporal structure.

Table 10.1
Vector definitions of alphabet

	Consonant	Vowel	Interrupted	High	Back	Voiced	
b	[1	0	1	0	0	1	]
d	[1	0	1	1	0	1	]
g	[1	0	1	0	1	1	]
a	[0	1	0	0	1	1	]
l	[0	1	0	1	0	1	]
u	[0	1	0	1	1	1	]

Structure in Letter Sequences

One question which might be asked is whether the memory capacity of the network architecture employed here is sufficient to detect more complex sequential patterns than the XOR. The XOR pattern is simple in several respects. It involves single-bit inputs, requires a memory which extends only one bit back in time, and has only four different input patterns. More challenging inputs would require multi-bit inputs of greater temporal extent, and a larger inventory of possible sequences. Variability in the duration of a pattern might also complicate the problem.

An input sequence was devised which was intended to provide just these sorts of complications. The sequence was composed of six different 6-bit binary vectors. Although the vectors were not derived from real speech, one might think of them as representing speech sounds, with the six dimensions of the vector corresponding to articulatory features. Table 10.1 shows the vector for each of the six letters.

The sequence was formed in two steps. First, the three consonants (b, d, g) were combined in random order to obtain a 1,000-letter sequence. Then, each consonant was replaced using the rules

$$b \rightarrow ba$$

$$d \rightarrow dii$$

$$g \rightarrow guuu$$

Thus, an initial sequence of the form **dbgbddg** ... gave rise to the final sequence **diibaguuubadiidiiguuu** ... (each letter being represented by one of the above 6-bit vectors). The sequence was semi-random; consonants occurred randomly, but following a given consonant, the identity and number of following vowels was regular.

The basic network used in the XOR simulation was expanded to provide for the 6-bit input vectors; there were 6 input units, 20 hidden units, 6 output units, and 20 context units.

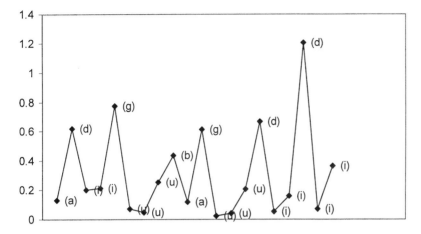

Figure 10.4
Graph of root mean squared error in letter prediction task, indicate the correct output prediction at each point in time. Error is computed over the entire output vector.

The training regimen involved presenting each 6-bit input vector, one at a time, in sequence. The task for the network was to predict the next input. (The sequence wrapped around, that the first pattern was presented after the last.) The network was trained on 200 passes through the sequence. It was then tested on another sequence that obeyed the same regularities, but created from a different initial randomization.

The error signal for part of this testing phase is shown in Figure 10.4. Target outputs are shown in parenthesis, and the graph plots the corresponding error for each prediction. It is obvious that the error oscillates markedly; at some points in time, the prediction is correct (and error is low), while at other points in time, the ability to predict correctly is quite poor. More precisely, error tends to be high when predicting consonants, and low when predicting vowels.

Given the nature of the sequence, this behavior is sensible. The consonants were ordered randomly, but the vowels were not. Once the network has received a consonant as input, it can predict the identity of the following vowel. Indeed, it can do more; it knows how many tokens of the vowel to expect. At the end of the vowel sequence it has no way to predict the next consonant; at these points in time, the error is high.

This global error pattern does not tell the whole story, however. Remember that the input patterns (which are also the patterns the network is trying to predict) are bit vectors. The error shown in Figure 10.4 is the sum squared error over all 6 bits. Examine the error on a bit-by-bit basis; a graph of the error for bits [1] and [4] (over 20 time steps) is shown in Figure 10.5. There is a striking difference in the error patterns. Error on predicting the first bit is consistently

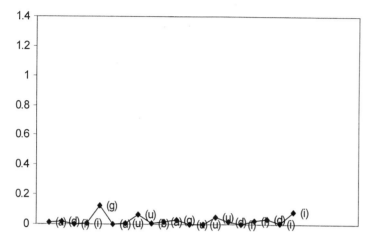

Figure 10.5 (a)
Graph of root mean squared error in letter prediction task. Error is computed on bit 1, representing the feature CONSONANTAL.

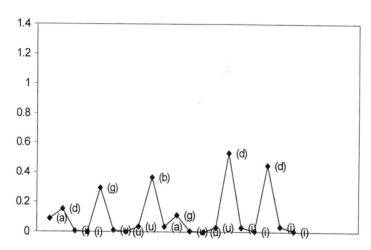

Figure 10.5 (b)
Graph of root mean squared error in letter prediction task. Error is computed on bit 4, representing the feature HIGH.

lower than error for the fourth bit, and at all points in time. Why should this be so?

The first bit corresponds to the features **Consonant**; the fourth bit corresponds to the feature **High**. It happens that while all consonants have the same value for the feature **Consonant**, they differ for **High**. The network has learned which vowels follow which consonants; this is why error on vowels is low. It has also learned how many vowels follow each consonant. An interesting corollary is that the network also knows how soon to expect the next consonant. The network cannot know *which* consonant, but it can predict correctly that a consonant follows. This is why the bit patterns for **Consonant** show low error, and the bit patterns for **High** show high error. (It is this behavior which requires the use of context units; a simple feed-forward network could learn the transitional probabilities from one input to the next, but could not learn patterns that span more than two inputs.)

This simulation demonstrates an interesting point. This input sequence was in some ways more complex than the XOR input. The serial patterns are longer in duration; they are of variable length so that a prediction depends upon a variable amount of temporal context; and each input consists of a 6-bit rather than a 1-bit vector. One might have reasonably thought that the more extended sequential dependencies of these patterns would exceed the temporal processing capacity of the network. But almost the opposite is true. The fact that there are subregularities (at the level of individual bit patterns) enables the network to make partial predictions, even in cases where the complete prediction is not possible. All of this is dependent upon the fact that the input is structured, of course. The lesson seems to be that more extended sequential dependencies may not necessarily be more difficult to learn. If the dependencies are structured, that structure may make learning easier and not harder.

Discovering the Notion "Word"

It is taken for granted that learning a language involves (among many other things) learning the sounds of that language, as well as the morphemes and words. Many theories of acquisition depend crucially upon such primitive types as word, or morpheme, or more abstract categories as noun, verb, or phrase (e.g., Berwick & Weinberg, 1984; Pinker, 1984). Rarely is it asked how a language learner knows when to begin or why these entities exist. These notions are often assumed to be innate.

Yet, in fact, there is considerable debate among linguists and psycholinguists about what representations are used in language. Although it is commonplace to speak of basic units such as "phoneme," "morpheme," and "word," these constructs have no clear and uncontroversial definition. Moreover, the commitment to such distinct levels of representation leaves a troubling residue of entities that appear to lie between the levels. For instance, in many languages, there are sound/meaning correspondences which lie between the phoneme and the morpheme (i.e., sound symbolism). Even the concept "word" is not as straightforward as one might think (cf. Greenberg, 1963; Lehman, 1962). In English, for instance, there is no consistently definable distinction among words (e.g., "apple"), compounds ("apple pie") and phrases ("Library of Congress" or "man in the street"). Furthermore, languages differ dramatically in what they treat as words. In polysynthetic languages (e.g., Eskimo), what would be called words more nearly resemble what the English speaker would call phrases or entire sentences.

Thus, the most fundamental concepts of linguistic analysis have a fluidity, which at the very least, suggests an important role for learning; and the exact form of the those concepts remains an open and important question.

In PDP networks, representational form and representational content often can be learned simultaneously. Moreover, the representations which result have many of the flexible and graded characteristics noted above. Therefore, one can ask whether the notion "word" (or something which maps on to this concept) could emerge as a consequence of learning the sequential structure of letter sequences that form words and sentences (but in which word boundaries are not marked).

Imagine then, another version of the previous task, in which the latter sequences form real words, and the words form sentences. The input will consist of the individual letters (imagine these as analogous to speech sounds, while recognizing that the orthographic input is vastly simpler than acoustic input would be). The letters will be presented in sequence, one at a time, with no breaks between the letters in a word, and no breaks between the words of different sentences.

Such a sequence was created using a sentence-generating program and a lexicon of 15 words.[4] The program generated 200 sentences of varying length, from four to nine words. The sentences were concatenated, forming a stream of 1,270 words. Next, the words were broken into their letter parts, yielding 4,963 letters. Finally, each letter in each word was converted into a 5-bit random vector.

The result was a stream of 4,963 separate 5-bit vectors, one for each letter. These vectors were the input and were presented one at a time. The task at each point in time was to predict the next letter. A fragment of the input and desired output is shown in Table 10.2.

A network with 5 input units, 20 hidden units, 5 output units, and 20 context units was trained on 10 complete presentations of the sequence. The error was relatively high at this point; the sequence was sufficiently random that it would be difficult to obtain very low error without memorizing the entire sequence (which would have required far more than 10 presentations).

Nonetheless, a graph of error over time reveals an interesting pattern. A portion of the error is plotted in Figure 10.6; each data point is marked with the

Table 10.2
Fragment of training sequence for letters-in-words simulation

Input		Output	
01101	(*m*)	00001	(*a*)
00001	(*a*)	01110	(*n*)
01110	(*n*)	11001	(*y*)
11001	(*y*)	11001	(*y*)
11001	(*y*)	00101	(*e*)
00101	(*e*)	00001	(*a*)
00001	(*a*)	10010	(*r*)
10010	(*r*)	10011	(*s*)
10011	(*s*)	00001	(*a*)
00001	(*a*)	00111	(*g*)
00111	(*g*)	01111	(*o*)
01111	(*o*)	00001	(*a*)
00001	(*a*)	00010	(*b*)
00010	(*b*)	01111	(*o*)
01111	(*o*)	11001	(*y*)
11001	(*y*)	00001	(*a*)
00001	(*a*)	01110	(*n*)
01110	(*n*)	00100	(*d*)
00100	(*d*)	00111	(*g*)
00111	(*g*)	01001	(*l*)
01001	(*l*)	10010	(*r*)
10010	(*r*)	01100	(*l*)
01100	(*l*)	01100	(*l*)
11001	(*l*)		

letter that should be predicted at that point in time. Notice that at the onset of each new word, the error is high. As more of the word is received the error declines, since the sequence is increasingly predictable.

The error provides a good clue as to what the recurring sequences in the input are, and these correlate highly with words. The information is not categorical, however. The error reflects statistics of co-occurrence, and these are graded. Thus, while it is possible to determine, more or less, what sequences constitute words (those sequences bounded by high error), the criteria for boundaries are relative. This leads to ambiguities, as in the case of the *y* in *they* (see Figure 10.6); it could also lead to the misidentification of common sequences that incorporate more than one word, but which co-occur frequently enough to be treated as a quasi-unit. This is the sort of behavior observed in children, who at early stages of language acquisition may treat idioms and other formulaic phrases as fixed lexical items (MacWhinney, 1978).

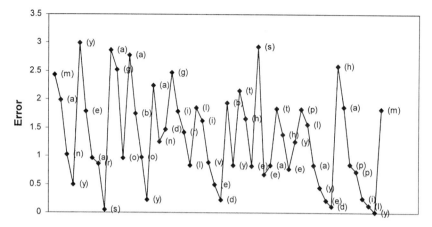

Figure 10.6
Graph of root mean squared error in letter-in-word prediction task.

This simulation should not be taken as a model of word acquisition. While listeners are clearly able to make predictions based upon partial input (Grosjean, 1980; Marslen-Wilson & Tyler, 1980; Salasoo & Pisoni, 1985), prediction is not the major goal of the language learner. Furthermore, the co-occurrence of sounds is only part of what identifies a word as such. The environment in which those sounds are uttered, and the linguistic context, are equally critical in establishing the coherence of the sound sequence and associating it with meaning. This simulation focuses only on a limited part of the information available to the language learner. The simulation makes the simple point that there is information in the signal that could serve as a cue to the boundaries of linguistic units which must be learned, and it demonstrates the ability of simple recurrent networks to extract this information.

Discovering Lexical Classes from Word Order

Consider now another problem which arises in the context of word sequences. The order of words in sentences reflects a number of constraints. In languages such as English (so-called "fixed word-order" languages), the order is tightly constrained. In many other languages (the "free word-order" languages), there are more options as to word order (but even here the order is not free in the sense of random). Syntactic structure, selective restrictions, subcategorization, and discourse considerations are among the many factors which join together to fix the order in which words occur. Thus, the sequential order of words in sentences is neither simple, nor is it determined by a single cause. In addition, it has been argued that generalizations about word order cannot be accounted for solely in terms of linear order (Chomsky 1957, 1965). Rather, there is an abstract

Table 10.3
Categories of Lexical Items Used in Sentence Simulation

Category	Examples
NOUN-HUM	man, woman
NOUN-ANIM	cat, mouse
NOUN-INANIM	book, rock
NOUN-AGRESS	dragon, monster
NOUN-FRAG	glass, plate
NOUN-FOOD	cookie, break
VERB-INTRAN	think, sleep
VERB-TRAN	see, chose
VERB-AGPAT	move, break
VERB-PERCEPT	smell, see
VERB-DESTROY	break, smash
VERB-EAT	eat

structure which underlies the surface strings and it is this structure which provides a more insightful basis for understanding the constraints on word order.

While it is undoubtedly true that the surface order of words does not provide the most insightful basis for generalizations about word order, it is also true that from the point of view of the listener, the surface order is the only visible (or audible) part. Whatever the abstract underlying structure is, it must be cued by the surface forms, and therefore, that structure is implicit in them.

In the previous simulation, it was demonstrated that a network was able to learn the temporal structure of letter sequences. The order of letters in that simulation, however, can be given with a small set of relatively simple rules.[5] The rules for determining word order in English, on the other hand, will be complex and numerous. Traditional accounts of word order generally invoke symbolic processing systems to express abstract structural relationships. One might, therefore, easily believe that there is a qualitative difference in the nature of the computation needed for the last simulation, which is required to predict the word order of English sentences. Knowledge of word order might require symbolic representations that are beyond the capacity of (apparently) non-symbolic PDP systems. Furthermore, while it is true, as pointed out above, that the surface strings may be cues to abstract structure, considerable innate knowledge may be required in order to reconstruct the abstract structure from the surface strings. It is, therefore, an interesting question to ask whether a network can learn any aspects of that underlying abstract structure.

Simple Sentences
As a first step, a somewhat modest experiment was undertaken. A sentence generator program was used to construct a set of short (two- and three-word) utterances. Thirteen classes of nouns and verbs were chosen; these are listed in Table 10.3. Examples of each category are given; it will be noticed that instances

Table 10.4
Templates for Sentence Generator

WORD 1	WORD 2	WORD 3
NOUN-HUM	VERB-EAT	NOUN-FOOD
NOUN-HUM	VERB-PERCEPT	NOUN-INANIM
NOUN-HUM	VERB-DESTROY	NOUN-FRAG
NOUN-HUM	VERB-INTRAN	
NOUN-HUM	VERB-TRAN	NOUN-HUM
NOUN-HUM	VERB-AGPAT	NOUN-INANIM
NOUN-HUM	VERB-AGPAT	
NOUN-ANIM	VERB-EAT	NOUN-FOOD
NOUN-ANIM	VERB-TRAN	NOUN-ANIM
NOUN-ANIM	VERB-AGPAT	NOUN-INANIM
NOUN-ANIM	VERB-AGPAT	
NOUN-INANIM	VERB-AGPAT	
NOUN-AGRESS	VERB-DESTROY	NOUN-FRAG
NOUN-AGRESS	VERB-EAT	NOUN-HUM
NOUN-AGRESS	VERB-EAT	NOUN-ANIM
NOUN-AGRESS	VERB-EAT	NOUN-FOOD

of some categories (e.g., VERB-DESTROY) may be included in others (e.g., VERB-TRAN). There were 29 different lexical items.

The generator program used these categories and the 15 sentence templates given in Table 10.4 to create 10,000 random two- and three-word sentence frames. Each sentence frame was then filled in by randomly selecting one of the possible words appropriate to each category. Each word was replaced by a randomly assigned 31-bit vector in which each word was represented by a different bit. Whenever the word was present, that bit was flipped on. Two extra bits were reserved for later simulations. This encoding scheme guaranteed that each vector was orthogonal to every other vector and reflected nothing about the form class or meaning of the words. Finally, the 27,534 word vectors in the 10,000 sentences were concatenated, so that an input stream of 27,534 31-bit vectors was created. Each word vector was distinct, but there were no breaks between successive sentences. A fragment of the input stream is shown in Column 1 of Table 10.5, with the English gloss for each vector in parentheses. The desired output is given in Column 2.

For this simulation a network similar to that in the first simulation was used, except that the input layer and output layers contained 31 nodes each, and the hidden and context layers contained 150 nodes each.

The task given to the network was to learn to predict the order of successive words. The training strategy was as follows. The sequence of 27,354 31-bit vectors formed an input sequence. Each word in the sequence was input, one at a time, in order. The task on each input cycle was to predict the 31-bit vector corresponding to the next word in the sequence. At the end of the 27,534 word

Table 10.5
Fragment of Training Sequences for Sentence Simulation

Input	Output
0000000000000000000000000000010 (woman)	0000000000000000000000000010000 (smash)
0000000000000000000000000010000 (smash)	0000000000000000000001000000000 (plate)
0000000000000000000001000000000 (plate)	0000010000000000000000000000000 (cat)
0000010000000000000000000000000 (cat)	0000000000000000000100000000000 (move)
0000000000000000000100000000000 (move)	0000000000000000100000000000000 (man)
0000000000000000100000000000000 (man)	0001000000000000000000000000000 (break)
0001000000000000000000000000000 (break)	0000100000000000000000000000000 (car)
0000100000000000000000000000000 (car)	0100000000000000000000000000000 (boy)
0100000000000000000000000000000 (boy)	0000000000000000000100000000000 (move)
0000000000000000000100000000000 (move)	0000000000001000000000000000000 (girl)
0000000000001000000000000000000 (girl)	0000000001000000000000000000000 (eat)
0000000001000000000000000000000 (eat)	0010000000000000000000000000000 (bread)
0010000000000000000000000000000 (bread)	0000000010000000000000000000000 (dog)
0000000010000000000000000000000 (dog)	0000000000000000000100000000000 (move)
0000000000000000000100000000000 (move)	0000000000000000001000000000000 (mouse)
0000000000000000001000000000000 (mouse)	0000000000000000001000000000000 (mouse)
0000000000000000001000000000000 (mouse)	0000000000000000000100000000000 (move)
0000000000000000000100000000000 (move)	1000000000000000000000000000000 (book)
1000000000000000000000000000000 (book)	0000000000000001000000000000000 (lion)

sequence, the process began again, without a break, starting with the first word. The training continued in this manner until the network had experienced six complete passes through the sequence.

Measuring the performance of the network in this simulation is not straight-forward. RMS error after training dropped to 0.88. When output vectors are as sparse as those used in this simulation (only 1 out of 31 bits turned on), the network quickly learns to turn off all the output units, which drops error from the initial random value of ~15.5 to 1.0. In this light, a final error of 0.88 does not seem impressive.

Recall that the prediction task is nondeterministic. Successors cannot be predicted with absolute certainty; there is a built-in error which is inevitable. Nevertheless, although the prediction cannot be error-free, it is also true that word order is not random. For any given sequence of words there are a limited number of possible successors. Under these circumstances, the network should learn the expected frequency of occurrence of each of the possible successor words; it should then activate the output nodes proportional to these expected frequencies.

This suggests that rather than testing network performance with the RMS error calculated on the actual successors, the output should be compared with the expected frequencies of occurrence of possible successors. These expected latter values can be determined empirically from the training corpus. Every word in a sentence is compared against all other sentences that are, up to that point, identical. These constitute the comparison set. The probability of occurrence for all possible successors is then determined from this set. This yields a vector for each word in the training set. The vector is of the same dimensionality as the output vector, but rather than representing a distinct word (by turning on a single bit), it represents the likelihood of each possible word occurring next (where each bit position is a fractional number equal to the probability). For testing purposes, this likelihood vector can be used in place of the actual teacher and a RMS error computed based on the comparison with the network output. (Note that it is appropriate to use these likelihood vectors only for the testing phase. Training must be done on actual successors, because the point is to force the network to learn the probabilities.)

When performance is evaluated in this manner, RMS error on the training set is 0.053 (SD = 0.100). One remaining minor problem with this error measure is that although the elements in the likelihood vectors must sum to 1.0 (since they represent probabilities), the activations of the network need not sum to 1.0. It is conceivable that the network output learns the relative frequency of occurrence of successor words more readily than it approximates exact probabilities. In this case the shape of the two vectors might be similar, but their length different. An alternative measure which normalizes for length differences and captures the degree to which the shape of the vectors is similar is the cosine of the angle between them. Two vectors might be parallel (cosine of 1.0) but still yield an RMS error, and in this case it might be felt that the network has extracted the crucial information. The mean cosine of the angle between network output on training items and likelihood vectors is 0.916 (SD = 0.123). By either measure, RMS or cosine, the network seems to have learned to approximate the likelihood ratios of potential successors.

How has this been accomplished? The input representations give no information (such as form class) that could be used for prediction. The word vectors are orthogonal to each other. Whatever generalizations are true of classes of words must be learned from the co-occurrence statistics, and the composition of those classes must itself be learned.

If indeed the network has extracted such generalizations, as opposed simply to memorizing the sequence, one might expect to see these patterns emerge in the internal representations which the network develops in the course of learning the task. These internal representations are captured by the pattern of hidden unit activations which are evoked in response to each word and its context. (Recall that hidden units are activated by both input units and context units. There are no representations of words in isolation.)

The nature of these internal representations was studied in the following way. After the learning phase of six complete passes through the corpus, the connection strengths in the network were frozen. The input stream was passed through the network one final time, with no learning taking place. During this testing, the network produced predictions of future inputs on the output layer. These were ignored. Instead, the hidden unit activations for each word + context input were saved, resulting in 27,354 150-bit vectors. Each word occurs many times, in different contexts. As a first approximation of a word's proto-typical or composite representation, all hidden unit activation patterns produced by a given word (in all its contexts) were averaged to yield a single 150-bit vector for each of the 29 unique words in the input stream.[6] (In the next section it will be shown how it is possible to study the internal representations of words in context.) These internal representations were then subject to a hierarchical clustering analysis. Figure 10.7 shows the resulting tree; this tree reflects the similarity structure of the internal representations these lexical items. Lexical items which have similar properties are grouped together lower in the tree, and clusters of similar words which resemble other clusters are connected higher in the tree.

The network has discovered that there are several major categories of words. One large category corresponds to *verbs*; another category corresponds to *nouns*. The verb category is broken down into groups that *require a direct object*, or are *intransitive*, or where a *direct object is optional*. The noun category is broken into two major groups: *inanimates*, and *animates*. Animates are divided into *human* and *nonhuman*; the nonhuman are divided into *large animals* and *small animals*. Inanimates are broken into *breakable*, *edibles*, and nouns which appeared as subjects of agentless active verbs.

The network has developed internal representations for the input vectors which reflect facts about the possible sequential ordering of the inputs. The network is not able to predict the precise order of words, but it recognizes that (in this corpus) there is a class of inputs (namely, verbs) that typically follow other inputs (namely, nouns). This knowledge of class behavior is quite detailed; from the fact that there is a class of items which always precedes "chase," "break," "smash," it infers that the large animals form a class.

Several points should be emphasized. First, the category structure appears to be hierarchical. Thus, "dragons" are large animals, but also members of the class of [−human, +animate] nouns. The hierarchical interpretation is achieved through the way in which the spatial relations (of the representations) are organized. Representations that are near one another in the representational space form classes, while higher level categories correspond to larger and more general regions of this space.

Second, it is also true that the hierarchy is "soft" and implicit. While some categories may be qualitatively distinct (i.e., very far from each other in space), there may also be other categories that share properties and have less distinct boundaries. Category membership in some cases may be marginal of unambiguous.

Finally, the content of the categories is not known to the network. The network has no information available which would "ground" the structural infor-

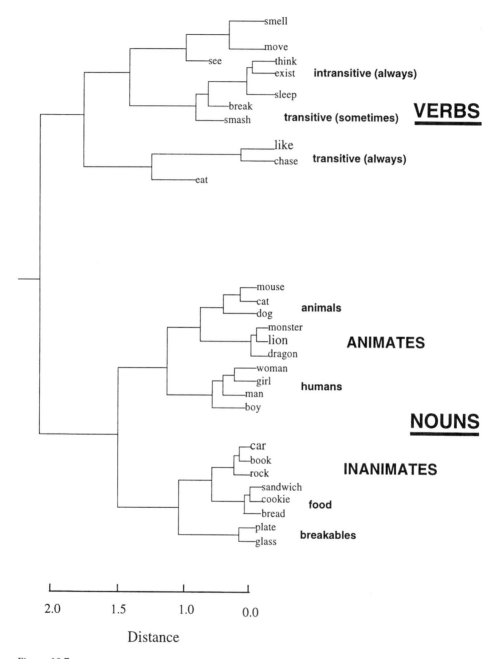

Figure 10.7
Hierarchical cluster diagram of hidden unit activation vectors in simple sentence prediction task.
Labels indicate the inputs which produced the hidden unit vectors; inputs were presented in context, and the hidden unit vectors averaged across multiple contexts.

mation in the real world. In this respect, the network has much less information to work with than is available to real language learners.[7] In a more realistic model of acquisition, one might imagine that the utterance provides one source of information about the nature of lexical categories; the world itself provides another source. One might model this by embedding the "linguistic" task in an environment; the network would have the dual task of extracting structural information contained in the utterance, and structural information about the environment. Lexical meaning would grow out of the associations of these two types of input.

In this simulation, an important component of meaning is context. The representation of a word is closely tied up with the sequence in which it is embedded. Indeed, it is incorrect to speak of the hidden unit patterns as word representations in the conventional sense, since these patterns also reflect the prior context. This view of word meaning (that is, its dependence upon context) can be demonstrated in the following way.

Freeze the connections in the network that has just been trained, so that no further learning occurs. Imagine a novel word, *zog*, which the network has never seen before, and assign to this word a bit pattern which is different from those it was trained on. This word will be used in place of the word *man;* everywhere that *man* could occur, *zog* will occur instead. A new sequence of 10,000 sentences is created, and presented once to the trained network. The hidden unit activations are saved, and subjected to a hierarchical clustering analysis of the same sort used with the training data.

The resulting tree is shown in Figure 10.8. The internal representation for the word *zog* bears the same relationship to the other words as did the word *man* in the original training set. This new word has been assigned an internal representation that is consistent with what the network has already learned (no learning occurs in this simulation) and the new word's behavior. Another way of looking at this is in certain contexts, the network expects *man*, or something very much like it. In just such a way, one can imagine real language learners making use of the cues provided by word order to make intelligent guesses about the meaning of novel words.

Although this simulation was not designed to provide a model of context effects in word recognition, its behavior is consistent with findings that have been described in the experimental literature. A number of investigators have studied the effects of sentential context on word recognition. Although some researchers have claimed that lexical access is insensitive to context (Swinney, 1979), there are other results which suggest that when context is sufficiently strong, it does indeed selectively facilitate access to related words (Tabossi, Colombo, & Job, 1987). Furthermore, individual items are typically not very predictable but classes of words are (Schwanenflugel & Shoben, 1985; Tabossi, 1988). This is precisely the pattern found here, in which the error in predicting the actual next word in a given context remains high, but the network is able to predict the approximate likelihood of occurrence of classes of words.

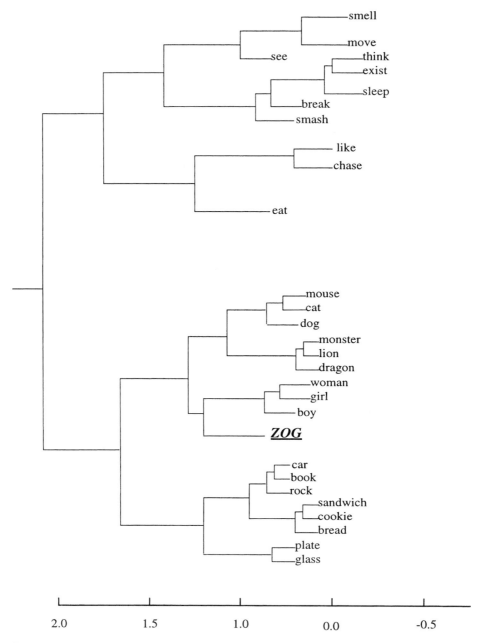

Figure 10.8
Hierarchical clustering diagram of hidden unit activation vectors in simple sentence prediction task, with the addition of the novel input ZOG.

Types, Tokens, and Structured Representations

There has been considerable discussion about the ways in which PDP networks differ from traditional computational models. One apparent difference is that traditional models involve symbolic representations, whereas PDP nets seem, to many people, to be non- or perhaps subsymbolic (Fodor & Pylyshyn, 1988; Smolensky, 1987, 1988). This is a difficult and complex issue, in part because the definition of symbol is problematic. Symbols do many things, and it might be more useful to contrast PDP versus traditional models with regard to the various functions that symbols can serve.

Both traditional and PDP networks involve representations which are symbolic in the specific sense that the representations refer to other things. In traditional systems, the symbols have names such as A, or x, or β. In PDP nets, the internal representations are generally activation patterns across a set of hidden units. Although both kinds of representations do the task of referring, there are important differences. Classical symbols typically refer to classes or categories, but in PDP nets the representations may be highly context-dependent. This does not mean that the representations do not capture information about category or class (this should be clear from the previous simulation); it does mean that there is also room in the representation scheme to pick out individuals.

This property of PDP representations might seem to be a serious drawback to some. In the extreme, it suggests that there could be separate representations for the entity *John* in every different context in which that entity can occur, leading to an infinite number of *John$_i$*. But rather than being a drawback, I suggest this aspect of PDP networks significantly extends their representational power. The use of distributed representations, together with the use of context in representing words (which is a consequence of simple recurrent networks) provides one solution to a thorny problem—the question of how to represent type/token differences—and sheds insight on the ways in which distributed representations can represent structure.

In order to justify this claim, let me begin by commenting on the representational richness provided by the distributed representations developed across the hidden units. In localist schemes, each node stands for a separate concept. Acquiring new concepts usually requires adding new nodes. In contrast, the hidden unit patterns in the simulations reported here have tended to develop distributed representations. In this scheme, concepts are expressed as activation patterns over a fixed number of nodes. A given node participates in representing multiple concepts. It is the activation pattern in its entirety that is meaningful. The activation of an individual node may be uninterpretable in isolation (i.e., it may not even refer to a feature or micro-feature).

Distributed representations have a number of advantages over localist representations (although the latter are not without their own benefits).[8] If the units are analog (i.e., capable of assuming activation states in a continuous range between some minimum and maximum values), then, in principle, there is no limit to the number of concepts which can be represented with a finite set of units. In the simulations here, the hidden unit patterns do double duty. They are required not only to represent inputs, but to develop representations which will serve as useful encodings of temporal context that can be used when processing subsequent inputs. Thus, in theory, analog hidden units would also be capable of providing infinite memory.

Of course, there are many reasons why in practice the memory is bounded, and why the number of concepts that can be stored is finite. There is limited numeric precision in the machines on which these simulations are run; the activation function is repetitively applied to the memory and results in exponential decay; and the training regimen may not be optimal for exploiting the full capacity of the networks. For instance, many of the simulations reported here involve the prediction task. This task incorporates feedback on every training cycle. In other pilot work, it was found that there was poorer performance in tasks in which there was a delay in injecting error into the network. Still, the representational capacity of these simple recurrent networks remains an open question (but, see Servan-Schreiber, Cleeremans, & McClelland, 1988).

Having made these preliminary observations, the question of the context-sensitivity of the representations developed in the simulations reported here will be addressed. Consider the sentence-processing simulation. It was found that after learning to predict words in sentence sequences, the network developed representations that reflected aspects of the words' meaning as well as their grammatical category. This was apparent in the similarity structure of the internal representation of each word; this structure was presented graphically as a tree in Figure 10.7.

In what sense are the representations, which have been clustered in Figure 10.7, context sensitive? In fact, they are not; recall that these representations are composites of the hidden unit activation patterns in response to each word averaged across many different contexts. So the hidden unit activation pattern used to represent *boy*, for instance, was really the mean vector of activation patterns in response to *boy* as it occurs in many different contexts.

The reason for using the mean vector in the previous analysis was in large part practical. It is difficult to do a hierarchical clustering of 27,454 patterns, and even more difficult to display the resulting tree graphically. However, one might want to know whether the patterns displayed in the tree in Figure 10.7 are in any way artifactual. Thus, a second analysis was carried out, in which all 27,454 patterns were clustered. The tree cannot be displayed here, but the numerical results indicate that the tree would be identical to the tree shown in Figure 10.7; except that instead of ending with the terminals that stand for the different lexical items, the branches would continue with further arborization containing the specific instances of each lexical item in its context. No instance of any lexical item appears inappropriately in a branch belonging to another.

It would be correct to think of the tree in Figure 10.7 as showing that the network has discovered that there are 29 *types* (among the sequence of 27,454 inputs). These types are the different lexical items shown in that figure. A finer grained analysis reveals that the network also distinguishes between the specific occurrences of each lexical item, that is, the *tokens*. The internal representations of the various tokens of a lexical type are very similar. Hence, they are all gathered under a single branch in the tree. However, the internal representations also make subtle distinctions between (for example), *boy* in one context and *boy* in another. Indeed, as similar as the representations of the various tokens are, no two tokens of a type are exactly identical.

Even more interesting is that there is a substructure of the representations of the various types of a token. This can be seen by looking at Figure 10.9, which shows the subtrees corresponding to the tokens of *boy* and *girl*. (Think of these as expansions of the terminal leaves for *boy* and *girl* in Figure 10.8.) The individual tokens are distinguished by labels which indicate their original context.

One thing that is apparent is that subtrees of both types (*boy* and *girl*) are similar to one another. On closer scrutiny, it is seen that there is some organization here; (with some exceptions) tokens of *boy* that occur in sentence-initial position are clustered together, and tokens of *boy* in sentence-final position are clustered together. Furthermore, this same pattern occurs among the patterns representing *girl*. Sentence-final words are clustered together on the basis of similarities in the preceding words. The basis for clustering of sentence-initial inputs is simply that they are all preceded by what is effectively noise (prior sentences). This is because there are no useful expectations about the sentence-initial noun (other than that it will be a noun) based upon the prior sentences. On the other hand, one can imagine that if there were some discourse structure relating sentences to each other, then there might be useful information from one sentence which would affect the representation of sentence-initial words. For example, such information might disambiguate (i.e., give referential content to) sentence-initial pronouns.

Once again, it is useful to try to understand these results in geometric terms. The hidden unit activation patterns pick out points in a high (but fixed) dimensional space. This is the space available to the network for its internal representations. The network structures that space in such a way that important relations between entities are translated into spatial relationships. Entities which are nouns are located in one region of space and verbs in another. In a similar manner, different types (here, lexical items) are distinguished from one another by occupying different regions of space; but also, tokens of a same type are differentiated. The differentiation is nonrandom, and the way in which tokens of one type are elaborated is similar to elaboration of another type. That is, $John_1$ bears the same spatial relationtionship to $John_2$ as $Mary_1$ bears to $Mary_2$.

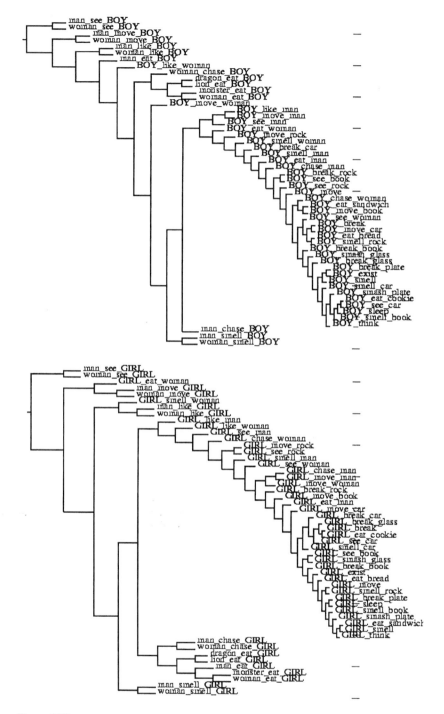

Figure 10.9
Hierarchical cluster diagram of hidden unit activation vectors in response to some occurrences of the inputs BOY and GIRL. Upper-case labels indicate the actual input; lower-case labels indicate the context for each input.

This use of context is appealing, because it provides the basis both for establishing generalizations about classes of items and also allows for the tagging of individual items by their context. The result is that types can be identified at the same time as tokens. In symbolic systems, type/token distinctions are often made by indexing or binding operations; the networks here provide an alternative account of how such distinctions can be made without indexing or binding.

Conclusions

There are many human behaviors which unfold over time. It would be folly to try to understand those behaviors without taking into account their temporal nature. The current set of simulations explores the consequences of attempting to develop representations of time that are distributed, task-dependent, and in which time is represented implicitly in the network dynamics.

The approach described here employs a simple architecture, but is surprisingly powerful. There are several points worth highlighting.

• *Some problems change their nature when expressed as temporal events*. In the first simulation, a sequential version of the XOR was learned. The solution to this problem involved detection of state changes, and the development of frequency-sensitive hidden units. Casting the XOR problem in temporal terms led to a different solution than is typically obtained in feed-forward (simultaneous input) networks.

• *The time-varying error signal can be used as a clue to temporal structure*. Temporal sequences are not always uniformly structured, nor uniformly predictable. Even when the network has successfully learned about the structure of a temporal sequence, the error may vary. The error signal is a good metric of where structure exists; it thus provides a potentially very useful form of feedback to the system.

• *Increasing the sequential dependencies in a task does not necessarily result in worse performance*. In the second simulation, the task was complicated by increasing the dimensionality of the input vector, by extending the duration of the sequence, and by making the duration of the sequence variable. Performance remained good, because these complications were accompanied by redundancy, which provided additional cues for the task. The network was also able to discover which parts of the complex input were predictable, making it possible to maximize performance in the face of partial unpredictability.

• *The representation of time—and memory—is highly task-dependent*. The networks here depend upon internal representations which have available, as part of their input, their own previous state. In this way the internal representations intermix the demands of the task with the demands imposed by carrying out that task over time. There is no separate "representation of time." There is simply the representation of input patterns in the context of a given output function; it just happens that those input patterns are sequential. That representation, and thus the representation of time, varies from task to task. This presents a somewhat novel view of memory. In this account, memory is neither passive nor a separate subsystem. One cannot properly speak of a memory for sequences; that memory is inextricably bound up with the rest of the processing mechanism.

• *The representations need not be "flat," atomistic, or unstructured.* The sentence task demonstrated that sequential inputs may give rise to internal representations which are hierarchical in nature. The hierarchy is implicit in the similarity structure of the hidden unit activations and does not require an a priori architectural commitment to the depth or form of the hierarchy. Importantly, distributed representations make available a space which can be richly structured. Categorical relationships as well as type/ token distinctions are readily apparent. Every item may have its own representation, but because the representations are structured, relations between representations are preserved.

The results described here are preliminary in nature. They are highly suggestive, and often raise more questions than they answer. These networks are properly thought of as dynamical systems, and one would like to know more about their properties as such. For instance, the analyses reported here made frequent use of hierarchical clustering techniques in order to examine the similarity structure of the internal representations. These representations are snapshots of the internal states during the course of processing a sequential input. Hierarchical clustering of these snapshots gives useful information about the ways in which the internal states of the network at different points in time are similar or dissimilar. But the temporal relationship between states is lost. One would like to know what the trajectories between states (i.e., the vector field) look like. What sort of attractors develop in these systems? It is a problem, of course, that the networks studied here are high-dimensional systems, and consequently difficult to study using traditional techniques. One promising approach, which is currently being studied, is to carry out a principal components analysis of the hidden unit activation pattern time series, and then to construct phase state portraits of the most significant principal components (Elman, 1989).

Another question of interest is the memory capacity of such networks. The results reported here suggest that these networks have considerable representational power; but more systematic analysis using better defined tasks is clearly desirable. Experiments are currently underway using sequences generated by finite state automata of various types; these devices are relatively well understood, and their memory requirements may be precisely controlled (Servan-Schreiber et al., 1988).

One of the things which feedforward PDP models have shown is that simple networks are capable of discovering useful and interesting internal representations of many static tasks. Or put the other way around: Rich representations are implicit in many tasks. However, many of the most interesting human behaviors have a serial component. What is exciting about the present results is that they suggest that the inductive power of the PDP approach can be used to discover structure and representations in tasks which unfold over time.

Notes

I would like to thank Jay McClelland, Mike Jordan, Mary Hare, Dave Rumelhart, Mike Mozer, Steve Poteet, David Zipser, and Mark Dolson for many stimulating discussions. I thank McClelland, Jordan, and two anonymous reviewers for helpful critical comments on an earlier draft of this article.

This work was supported by contract N000114-85-K-0076 from the Office of Naval Research and contract DAAB-07-87-C-H027 from Army Avionics, Ft. Monmouth.

1. The reader may more easily be convinced of this by comparing the locations of the vectors **[1 0 0]**, **[0 1 0]**, and **[0 0 1]** in 3-space. Although these patterns might be considered "temporally displaced" versions of the same basic pattern, the vectors are very different.
2. The activation function used here bounds values between 0.0 and 1.0.
3. A little more detail is in order about the connections between the context units and hidden units. In the networks used here, there were one-for-one connections between each hidden unit and each context unit. This implies that there are an equal number of context and hidden units. The upward connections between the context units and the hidden units were fully distributed, such that each context unit activates all the hidden units.
4. The program used was a simplified version of the program described in greater detail in the next simulation.
5. In the worst case, each word constitutes a rule. Hopefully, networks will learn that recurring orthographic regularities provide additional and more general constraints (cf. Sejnowski & Rosenberg, 1987).
6. Tony Plate (personal communication) has pointed out that this technique is dangerous, inasmuch as it may introduce a statistical artifact. The hidden unit activation patterns are highly dependent upon preceding inputs. Because the preceding inputs are not uniformly distributed (they follow precisely the co-occurrence conditions which are appropriate for the different categories), this means that the mean hidden unit pattern across all contexts of a specific item will closely resemble the mean hidden unit pattern for other items in the same category. This could occur even without learning, and is a consequence of the averaging of vectors which occurs prior to cluster analysis. Thus the results of the averaging technique should be verified by clustering individual tokens; tokens should always be closer to other members of the same type than to tokens of other types.
7. Jay McClelland has suggested a humorous—but entirely accurate—metaphor for this task: It is like trying to learn a language by listening to the radio.
8. These advantages are discussed at length in Hinton, McClelland, and Rumelhart (1986).

References

Berwick, R. C., & Weinberg, A. S. (1984). *The grammatical basis of linguistic performance*. Cambridge, MA: MIT Press.

Chomsky, N. (1957). *Syntactic structures*. The Hague: Moutin.

Chomsky, N. (1965). *Aspects of the theory of syntax*. Cambridge, MA: MIT Press.

Cottrell, G. W., Munro, P. W., & Zipser, D. (1987). Image compression by back propagation: A demonstration of extensional programming. In N. E. Sharkey (Ed.), *Advances in cognitive science* (Vol. 2). Chichester, England: Ellis Horwood.

Elman, J. L. (1989). *Structured representations and connectionist models*. (CRL Tech. Rep. No. 8901). San Diego: University of California, Center for Research in Language.

Elman, J. L., & Zipser, D. (1988). Discovering the hidden structure of speech. *Journal of the Acoustical Society of America, 83*, 1615–1626.

Fodor, J., & Pylyshyn, Z. (1988). Connectionism and cognitive architecture: A critical analysis. In S. Pinker & J. Mehler (Eds.), *Connections and symbols* (pp. 3–71). Cambridge, MA: MIT Press.

Fowler, C. (1977). *Timing control in speech production*. Bloomington, IN: Indiana University Linguistics Club.

Fowler, C. (1980). Coarticulation and theories of extrinsic timing control. *Journal of Phonetics, 8*, 113–133.

Frazier, L., & Fodor, J. D. (1978). The sausage machine: A new two-stage parsing model. *Cognition, 6*, 291–325.

Greenberg, J. H. (1963). *Universals of language*. Cambridge, MA: MIT Press.

Grosjean, F. (1980). Spoken word recognition processes and the gating paradigm. *Perception & Psychophysics, 28*, 267–283.

Hanson, S. J., & Kegl, J. (1987). Parsnip: A connectionist network that learns natural language grammar from exposure to natural language sentences. *Ninth Annual Conference of the Cognitive Science Society*, Seattle, Washington. Hillsdale, NJ: Erlbaum.

Hinton, G. E., McClelland, J. L., & Rumelhart, D. E. (1986). Distributed representations. In D. E. Rumelhart & J. L. McClelland (Eds.), *Parallel distributed processing: Explorations in the microstructure of cognition* (Vol. 1, pp. 77–109). Cambridge, MA: MIT Press.

Jordan, M. I. (1986). Serial order: A parallel distributed processing approach (Tech. Rep. No. 8604). San Diego: University of California, Institute for Cognitive Science.

Jordan, M. I., & Rosenbaum, D. A. (1988). *Action* (Tech. Rep. No. 88-26). Amherst: University of Massachusetts, Department of Computer Science.

Kelso, J. A. S., Saltzman, E., & Tuller, B. (1986). The dynamical theory of speech production: Data and theory. *Journal of Phonetics, 14*, 29–60.

Lashley, K. S. (1951). The problem of serial order in behavior. In L. A. Jeffress (Ed.), *Cerebral mechanisms in behavior*. New York: Wiley.

Lehman, W. P. (1962). *Historical linguistics: An introduction*. New York: Holt, Rinehart, and Winston.

MacNeilage, P. F. (1970). Motor control of serial ordering of speech. *Psychological Review, 77*, 182–196.

MacWhinney, B. (1978). The acquisition of morphophonology. *Monographs of the Society for Research in Child Development, 43*, (Serial No. 1).

Marcus, M. (1980). *A theory of syntactic recognition for natural language*. Cambridge, MA: MIT Press.

Marslen-Wilson, W., & Tyler, L. K. (1980). The temporal structure of spoken language understanding. *Cognition, 8*, 1–71.

Pineda, F. J. (1988). Generalization of back propagation to recurrent and higher order neural networks. In D. Z. Anderson (Ed.), *Neural information processing systems*. New York: American Institute of Physics.

Pinker, S. (1984). *Language learnability and language development*. Cambridge, MA: Harvard University Press.

Rumelhart, D. E., Hinton, G. E., & Williams, R. J. (1986). Learning internal representations by error propagation. In D. E. Rumelhart & J. L. McClelland (Eds.), *Parallel distributed processing: Explorations in the microstructure of cognition* (Vol. 1, pp. 318–362). Cambridge, MA: MIT Press.

Salasoo, A., & Pisoni, D. B. (1985). Interaction of knowledge sources in spoken word identification. *Journal of Memory and Language, 24*, 210–231.

Saltzman, E., & Kelso, J. A. S. (1987). Skilled actions: A task dynamic approach. *Psychological Review, 94*, 84–106.

Schwanenflugel, P. J., & Shoben, E. J. (1985). The influence of sentence constraint on the scope of facilitation for upcoming words. *Journal of Memory and Language, 24*, 232–252.

Sejnowski, T. J., & Rosenberg, C. R. (1987). Parallel networks that learn to pronounce English text. *Complex Systems, 1*, 145–168.

Servan-Schreiber, D., Cleeremans, A., & McClelland, J. L. (1988). *Encoding sequential structure in simple recurrent networks* (CMU Tech. Rep. No. CMU-CS-88-183). Pittsburgh, PA: Carnegie-Mellon University, Computer Science Department.

Smolensky, P. (1987). *On variable binding and the representation of symbolic structures in connectionist systems* (Tech. Rep. No. CU-CS-355-87). Boulder, CO: University of Colorado, Department of Computer Science.

Smolensky, P. (1988). On the proper treatment of connectionism. *The Behavioral and Brain Sciences, 11*.

Stornetta, W. S., Hogg, T., & Huberman, B. A. (1987). A dynamical approach to temporal pattern processing. *Proceedings of the IEEE Conference on Neural Information Processing Systems.* Denver, CO.

Swinney, D. (1979). Lexical access during sentence comprehension: (Re)consideration of context effects. *Journal of Verbal Learning and Verbal Behavior, 6*, 645–659.

Tabossi, P. (1988). Effects of context on the immediate interpretation of unambiguous nouns. *Journal of Experimental Psychology: Learning, Memory, and Cognition, 14*, 153–162.

Tabossi, P., Colombo, L., & Job, R. (1987). Accessing lexical ambiguity: Effects of context and dominance. *Psychological Research, 49*, 161–167.

Tank, D. W., & Hopfield, J. J. (1987, June). Neural computation by concentrating information in time. *Proceedings of the IEEE International Conference on Neural Networks.* San Diego, CA.

Van Gelder, T. J. (1990). Compositionality: Variations on a classical theme. *Cognitive Science, 14*, 355–384.

Waibel, A., Hanazawa, T., Hinton, G., Shikano, K., & Lang, K. (1987). *Phoneme recognition using time-delay neural networks* (ATR Tech. Rep. TR-1-0006). Japan: ATR Interpreting Telephony Research Laboratories.

Watrous, R. L., & Shastri, L. (1987). Learning phonetic features using connectionist networks: An experiment in speech recognition. *Proceedings of the IEEE International Conference on Neural Networks.* San Diego, CA.

Williams, R. J., & Zipser, D. (1988). *A learning algorithm for continually running fully recurrent neural networks* (Tech. Rep. No. 8805). San Diego: University of California, Institute for Cognitive Science.

Adaptive Resonance Theory

Chapter 11

A Self-Organizing Neural Network for Supervised Learning, Recognition, and Prediction

Gail A. Carpenter and Stephen Grossberg

As we humans move through our world, we can attend to both familiar and novel objects. Part of what makes us human is our ability to rapidly recognize, test hypotheses about, and name novel objects without disrupting our memories of familiar objects. This article describes a way of achieving these human characteristics in a self-organizing neural network called fuzzy ARTMAP. This architecture is capable of fast but stable on-line recognition learning, hypothesis testing, and adaptive naming in response to an arbitrary stream of analog or binary input patterns.

The fuzzy ARTMAP neural network combines a unique set of computational abilities that are needed to function autonomously in a changing world (see Table 11.1) and that alternative models have not yet achieved. In particular, fuzzy ARTMAP can autonomously learn, recognize, and make predictions about rare events, large nonstationary databases, morphologically variable types of events, and many-to-one and one-to-many relationships.

Fast Learning of Rare Events

An autonomous agent must be able to learn about rare events with important consequences, even if such events are similar to many other events that have different consequences (Fig. 11.1). For example, a rare medical case may be the harbinger of a new epidemic. A faint astronomical signal may signify important consequences for theories of the universe. A slightly different chemical assay may predict the biological effects of a new drug. Many traditional learning schemes use a form of slow learning that tends to average similar event occurrences. In contrast, fuzzy ARTMAP systems can rapidly learn rare events whose predictions differ from those of similar events.

Stable Memory of Nonstationary Data
Rare events typically occur in a nonstationary environment, such as a large database, in which event statistics may change rapidly and unexpectedly. Individual events may also occur with variable frequencies and durations, and

Table 11.1
Autonomous learning and control in a nonstationary world

A fuzzy ARTMAP system can reconcile conflicting properties and autonomously learn about:

Rare events
  • requires fast learning

Large nonstationary databases
  • requires stable learning

Morphologically variable events
  • requires multiple scales of generalization (fine/coarse)

One-to-many and many-to-one relationships
  • requires categorization, naming, and expert knowledge

To realize these properties, ARTMAP systems:

Pay attention
  • ignore masses of irrelevant data

Test hypotheses
  • discover predictive constraints hidden in data streams

Choose best answers
  • quickly select globally optimal solution at any stage of learning

Calibrate confidence
  • measure on-line how well a hypothesis matches the data

Discover rules
  • identify transparent if-then relations at each learning stage

Scale
  • preserve all desirable properties in arbitrarily large problems

---

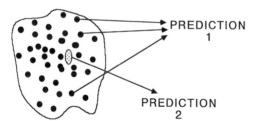

Figure 11.1
Fuzzy ARTMAP can make a different prediction for a rare event than for all the similar events that surround it.

arbitrarily large numbers of events may need to be processed. Each of these factors tends to destabilize the learning process within traditional algorithms. New learning in such algorithms tends to unselectively wash away the memory traces of old, but still useful, knowledge. Learning a new face, for instance, could erase the memory of a parent's face, or learning a new type of expertise could erase the memory of previous expert knowledge.

Adaptive Fitting of Morphological Variability
Many environments contain information that may be either coarsely or precisely defined. In other words, the morphological variability of the data may change through time. For example, it may be necessary merely to recognize that an object is an airplane, or that it is a particular type of airplane that is flown for a particular purpose by a particular country. Under autonomous learning conditions, no teacher is typically available to instruct a system about how coarse the definition of particular types of data should be. Multiple scales of generalization, from fine to coarse, need to be available on an as-needed basis. Fuzzy ARTMAP is able to automatically adjust its scale of generalization to match the morphological variability of the data. It embodies a Minimax Learning Rule that conjointly minimizes predictive error and maximizes generalization using only information that is locally available under incremental learning conditions in a nonstationary environment.

Learning Many-to-One and One-to-Many Maps
Autonomous agents must also be able to learn many-to-one and one-to-many relationships. Many-to-one learning takes two forms: categorization and naming (Fig. 11.2). For instance, during categorization of printed letter fonts, many similar samples of the same printed letter may establish a single recognition category, or compressed representation. Different printed letter fonts or written samples of the letter may establish additional categories. Each of these categories carries out a many-to-one map of its exemplars. During naming, all of the categories that represent the same letter may be associatively mapped into the letter name or prediction. There need be no relationship whatsoever between the visual features that define a printed letter A and a written letter A, yet both categories may need to be assigned the same name for cultural, not visual, reasons.

One-to-many learning is used to build up expert knowledge about an object or event (Fig. 11.3). A single visual image of a particular animal, for example, may lead to learning that predicts: animal, dog, beagle, and my dog Rover. Likewise, a computerized record of a patient's medical check-up may lead to a series of predictions about the patient's health; or a chemical assay of a sample of coal or petroleum may lead to many predictions about its uses as an energy source or material.

MANY-TO-ONE MAP

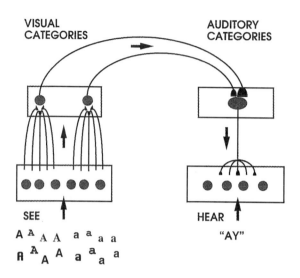

Figure 11.2
Many-to-one learning combines categorization of many exemplars into one category, and labeling of many categories with the same name.

In many learning algorithms, the attempt to learn more than one prediction about an event leads to unselective forgetting of previously learned predictions, for the same reason that these algorithms become unstable in response to non-stationary data.

Error-Based Learning and Alternatives

Error-based learning systems, including the back propagation algorithm, find it difficult, if not impossible, to achieve any of these computational goals [1–3]. Back propagation compares its actual prediction with a correct prediction and uses the error to change adaptive weights in a direction that is error-reducing. Fast learning would zero the error on each learning trial, and therefore cause massive forgetting. Statistical changes in the environment drag the adaptive weights away from their estimates of the previous environment. Longer event durations zero the error further, also destabilizing previous memories for the same reason that fast learning does. The selection of a fixed number of hidden units tends to fix a uniform level of generalization. Error-based learning also tends to force forgetting of previous predictions under one-to-many learning

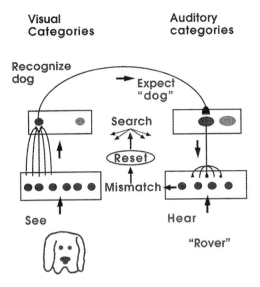

ONE-TO-MANY MAP

Expert Knowledge

Figure 11.3
One-to-many learning enables one input vector to be associated with many output vectors. If the system predicts an output that is desconfirmed at a given stage of learning, the predictive error drives a memory search for a new category to associate with the new prediction, without degrading its previous knowledge about the input vector.

conditions, because the present correct prediction treats all previously learned predictions as errors. Ratcliff has noted, moreover, that back propagation fails to simulate human cognitive data about learning and forgetting [4].

Fuzzy ARTMAP exhibits the properties outlined so far in this article because it implements a qualitatively different set of heuristics than error-based learning systems. These heuristics are embodied in the following types of processes:

Pay attention A fuzzy ARTMAP system can learn top-down expectations (also called primes, or queries) that enable the system to ignore masses of irrelevant data. A large mismatch between a bottom-up input vector and a top-down expectation can drive an adaptive memory search that carries out hypothesis testing and match-based learning.

Carry out hypothesis testing and match-based learning A fuzzy ARTMAP system actively searches for recognition categories, or hypotheses, whose top-down expectations provide an acceptable match to bottom-up data. The top-down expectation focuses attention upon and binds that cluster of input features that it deems to be relevant. If no available category or hypothesis provides a good enough match, then selection and learning of a new category and top-down expectation is automatically initiated. When the search discovers a category that provides an acceptable match, the system locks into an attentive resonance in which the input pattern refines the adaptive weights of the category based on any new information that it contains.

Thus, the fuzzy ARTMAP system carries out match-based learning, rather than error-based learning. A category modifies its previous learning only if its top-down expectation matches the input vector well enough to risk changing its defining characteristics. Otherwise, hypothesis testing selects a new category on which to base learning of a novel event.

Choose the globally best answer In many learning algorithms, local minima or less-than-optimal solutions are selected to represent the data as learning proceeds. In fuzzy ARTMAP, at any stage of learning, an input exemplar first selects the category whose top-down expectation provides the globally best match. A top-down expectation thus acts as a prototype for the class of all the input exemplars that its category represents. Before learning self-stabilizes, familiar events gain direct access to the "globally best" category without any search, even if they are interspersed with unfamiliar events that drive hypothesis testing for better matching categories. After learning self-stabilizes, every input directly selects the globally best category without any search.

Calibrate confidence A confidence measure called *vigilance* calibrates how well an exemplar matches the prototype that it selects. In other words, vigilance measures how well the chosen hypothesis matches the data. If vigilance is low, even poor matches are accepted. Many different exemplars can then be incorporated into one category, so compression and generalization by that category are high. If vigilance is high, then even good matches may be rejected, and hypothesis testing may be initiated to select a new category. In this case, few exemplars activate the same category, so compression and generalization are low. A high level of vigilance can select a unique category for a rare event that predicts an outcome different from that of any of the similar exemplars that surround it.

The Minimax Learning Rule is realized by adjusting the vigilance parameter in response to a predictive error. Vigilance is increased just enough to initiate hypothesis testing to discover a better category, or hypothesis, with which to match the data. In this way, a minimum amount of generalization is sacrificed to correct the error. This process is called match tracking because vigilance tracks the degree of match between exemplar and prototype in response to a predictive error.

Perform rule extraction At any stage of learning, a user can translate the state of a fuzzy ARTMAP system into an algorithmic set of rules. From this perspective, fuzzy ARTMAP can be interpreted as a type of self-organizing expert system. These rules evolve as the system is exposed to

Table 11.2
ARTMAP benchmark studies

Medical database—mortality following coronary bypass grafting (CABG) surgery
Fuzzy ARTMAP significantly outperforms:
- Logistic regression
- Additive model
- Bayesian assignment
- Cluster analysis
- Classification and regression trees
- Expert panel-derived sickness scores
- Principal component analysis

Mushroom database
- Decision trees (90–95% correct)
- ARTMAP (100% correct)
  Training set an order of magnitude smaller

Letter recognition database
- Genetic algorithm (82% correct)
- Fuzzy ARTMAP (96% correct)

Circle-in-the-square task
- Back propagation (90% correct)
- Fuzzy ARTMAP (99.5% correct)

Two-spiral task
- * Back propagation (10,000–20,000 training epochs)
- Fuzzy ARTMAP (1–5 training epochs)

---

new inputs. This feature is particularly important in applications such as medical diagnosis from a large database of patient records. Some medical and other benchmark studies that compare the performance of fuzzy ARTMAP with alternative recognition and prediction models are summarized in Table 11.2. One of the benchmarks is discussed below, and others are described in two references [5–6].

Properties scale One of the most serious deficiencies of many artificial intelligence algorithms is that their desirable properties tend to break down as small-scale problems are generalized to large-scale problems. In contrast, all of the desirable properties of fuzzy ARTMAP scale to arbitrarily large problems. However, fuzzy ARTMAP is meant to solve a particular type of problem—it is not intended to solve all problems of learning or intelligence. The categorization and prediction problems that ARTMAP does handle well are core problems in many intelligent systems, and have been technology bottlenecks for many alternative approaches.

A summary is now given of Adaptive Resonance Theory, or ART, networks for unsupervised learning and categorization. Then a connection between certain ART systems and fuzzy logic is noted. Fuzzy ART networks for unsupervised learning and categorization are next described. Finally, fuzzy ART

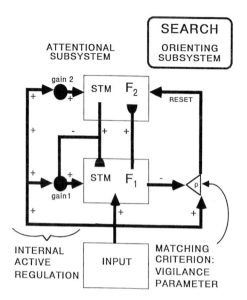

Figure 11.4
Typical ART 1 neural network.

modules are combined into a fuzzy ARTMAP system that is capable of super-vised learning, recognition, and prediction. A benchmark comparison of fuzzy ARTMAP with genetic algorithms is then summarized.

A Review of Unsupervised ART Systems

The Adaptive Resonance Theory, or ART, was introduced as a theory of human cognitive information processing [7–8]. The theory has since led to an evolving series of real-time neural network models for unsupervised category learning and pattern recognition. These models are capable of learning stable recognition categories in response to arbitrary input sequences with either fast or slow learning. Model families include ART 1 [9], which can learn to categorize binary input patterns presented in an arbitrary order; ART 2 [10], which can learn to categorize either analog or binary input patterns presented in an arbitrary order; and ART 3 as in [11], which can carry out parallel searches by testing hypotheses about distributed recognition codes in a multilevel network hierar-chy. Variations of these models adapted to the demands of individual applica-tions have been developed by a number of authors.

An example from the family of ART 1 models and a typical ART search cycle are illustrated in Figs. 11.4 and 11.5, respectively. Level F_1 in Fig. 11.4 contains a network of nodes, each of which represents a particular combination of sensory

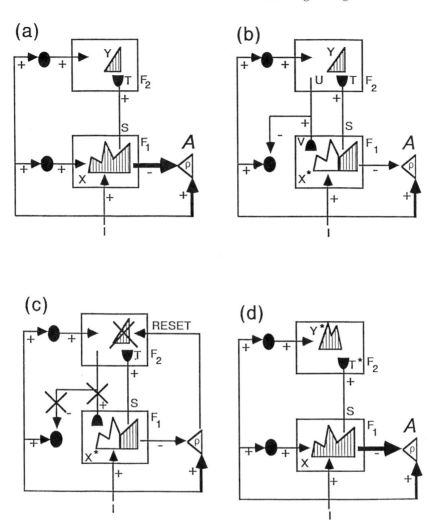

Figure 11.5

ART search for an F_2 code: (a) The input pattern **I** generates the specific STM activity pattern **X** at F_1 as it nonspecifically activates the orienting subsystem A. Pattern **X** both inhibits A and generates the output signal pattern **S**. Signal pattern **S** is transformed into the input pattern **T**, which activates the STM pattern **Y** across F_2. (b) Pattern **Y** generates the top-down signal pattern **U** which is transformed into the prototype pattern **V**. If **V** mismatches **I** at F_1, then a new STM activity pattern **X***is generated at F_1. The reduction in total STM activity that occurs when **X** is transformed into **X*** causes a decrease in the total inhibition from F_1 to A. (c) If the matching criterion fails to be met, A releases a nonspecific arousal wave to F_2, which resets the STM pattern at F_2. (d) After **Y** is inhibited, its top-down prototype signal is eliminated, and **X** can be reinstated at F_1. Enduring traces of the prior reset lead **X** to activate a different STM pattern **Y***at F_2. If the top-down prototype due to **Y*** also mismatches **I** at F_1, then the search for an appropriate F_2 code continues.

features. Level F_2 contains a network of nodes that represent recognition codes that are selectively activated by patterns of activation across F_1. The activities of nodes in F_1 and F_2 are also called short term memory (STM) traces. STM is the type of memory that can be rapidly reset without leaving an enduring trace. For instance, it is easy to reset a person's STM of a list of numbers by distracting the person with an unexpected event. STM is distinct from LTM, or long term memory, which is the type of memory that we usually ascribe to learning. For example, we do not forget our parent's names when we are distracted by an unexpected event.

As shown in Fig. 11.5a, an input vector I registers itself as a pattern X of activity across level F_1. The F_1 output vector S is then transmitted through the multiple converging and diverging adaptive filter pathways emanating from F_1. This transmission event multiplies vector S by a matrix of adaptive weights, or LTM traces, to generate a net input vector T to level F_2. The internal competitive dynamics of F_2 contrast-enhance vector T. A compressed activity vector Y is thereby generated across F_2. In ART 1, the competition is tuned so that the F_2 node that receives the maximal $F_1 \rightarrow F_2$ input is selected. Only one component of Y is nonzero after this choice takes place. Activation of such a winner-take-all node defines the category, or symbol, of I. Such a category represents all inputs, I, that maximally activate the corresponding node. So far, these are the rules of a self-organizing feature map, also called competitive learning or learned vector quantization. Such models were developed by Grossberg [12–16] and von der Malsburg [17–18]. Cohen and Grossberg [19–20], Grossberg and Kuperstein [21], and Kohonen [22] have applied them extensively to problems in speech recognition and adaptive sensory-motor control, among others.

Activation of an F_2 node may be interpreted as "making a hypothesis" about input I. When Y is activated, it generates an output vector U that is sent top-down through the second adaptive filter. After multiplication by the adaptive weight matrix of the top-down filter, a net vector V is input to F_1 (Fig. 11.5b). Vector V plays the role of a learned top-down expectation. Activation of V by Y may be interpreted as "testing the hypothesis" Y, or "reading out the category prototype" V. The ART 1 network is designed to match the "expected prototype" V of the category against the active input pattern, or exemplar, I. Nodes that are activated by I are suppressed if they do not correspond to large LTM traces in the prototype pattern V. Thus F_1 features not "expected" by V are suppressed. Expressed in a different way, the matching process may change the F_1 activity pattern X by suppressing activation of all the feature detectors in I that are not "confirmed" by hypothesis Y. The resultant pattern X^* encodes the cluster of features in I that the network deems relevant to the hypothesis Y, based upon its past experience. Pattern X^* encodes the pattern of features to which the network "pays attention."

If V is close enough to the input I, then a state of resonance develops as the attentional focus takes hold. Pattern X^* of attended features reactivates hypothesis $\mathbf{Y}$ which, in turn, reactivates $\mathbf{X}^*$. The network locks into a resonant state through the mutual positive feedback that dynamically links $\mathbf{X}^*$ with $\mathbf{Y}$. The resonant state persists long enough for learning to occur; hence the term Adaptive Resonance Theory. ART systems learn prototypes, rather than exemplars, because the attended feature vector $\mathbf{X}^*$, rather than $\mathbf{I}$ itself, is learned.

This attentive matching process is realized by combining three different types of inputs at level F_1: bottom-up inputs, top-down expectations, and attentional gain control signals (Fig. 11.4). The attentional gain control channel sends the same signal to all F_1 nodes; it is a "nonspecific," or modulatory channel. Attentive matching obeys the 2/3 Rule: an F_1 node can be fully activated only if two of the three input sources that converge upon it send positive signals at a given time [9]. The 2/3 Rule shows how an ART system can be "primed" to expect a subsequent event. A top-down expectation activates to subthreshold levels the F_1 nodes in its prototype. None of the nodes are activated well enough to generate output signals in the absence of their "second third" of the 2/3 Rule. They are nonetheless "primed," or ready, to fire rapidly and vigorously if a bottom-up input does match their prototype well enough. Thus ART systems are "intentional" or "goal-oriented" systems in the sense that their expectations can be primed to selectively seek out data in which they are interested.

The 2/3 Rule also allows an ART system to react to inputs in the absence of prior priming, because a bottom-up input directly activates its target F_1 features and indirectly activates them via the nonspecific gain control channel to satisfy the 2/3 Rule (Fig. 11.5a). After the input instates itself at F_1, which leads to selection of hypothesis $\mathbf{Y}$ and top-down expectation $\mathbf{V}$, the 2/3 Rule ensures that only those F_1 nodes that are confirmed by the expectation can remain active in STM.

The criterion of an acceptable 2/3 Rule match is defined by a dimensionless parameter called vigilance. Vigilance weighs how close exemplar $\mathbf{I}$ must be to the top-down prototype $\mathbf{V}$ in order for resonance to occur. Because vigilance can vary across learning trials, recognition categories capable of encoding widely differing degrees of generalization, or morphological variability, can be learned by a single ART system. Low vigilance leads to broad generalization and abstract prototypes. High vigilance leads to narrow generalization and to prototypes that represent fewer input exemplars. Within the limit of very high vigilance, prototype learning reduces to exemplar learning. Thus, a single ART system may be used, say, to recognize abstract categories of faces and dogs, as well as individual faces and dogs. Exemplars can be coded by specialized "grandmother cells" at the same time that abstract prototypes are coded by general categories of the same network. The particular combination of prototypes that is learned depends upon the predictive success of the learned categories in a particular task environment.

If the top-down expectation $\mathbf{V}$ and the bottom-up input $\mathbf{I}$ are too novel, or unexpected, to satisfy the vigilance criterion, then a bout of hypothesis testing—a memory search—is triggered. Searching leads to the selection of a better recognition code, symbol, category, or hypothesis to represent I at level F_2. An orienting subsystem mediates the search process (Fig. 11.4). The orienting subsystem interacts with the attentional subsystem to enable the attentional subsystem to learn new F_2 representations with which to remember novel events without risking unselective forgetting of its previous knowledge (Figs. 11.5c and 11.5d).

The search process prevents associations from forming between Y and X^* if X^* is too different from I to satisfy the vigilance criterion. The search process resets Y before such an association can form, as shown in Fig. 11.5c. A familiar category may be selected by the search if its prototype is similar enough to I to satisfy the vigilance criterion. The prototype may then be refined in light of new information carried by I. If I is too different from any of the previously learned prototypes, then an uncommitted F_2 node is selected and learning of a new category is initiated. A network parameter controls how far the search proceeds before an uncommitted node is chosen.

As inputs that correspond to a particular category are practiced over learning trials, the search process converges upon a stable learned recognition category in F_2. This process corresponds to making the inputs "familiar" to the network. After familiarization takes place, all inputs coded by that category access it directly in a single pass, and searching is automatically disengaged. The selected category's prototype provides the globally best match to the input pattern. While stable learning proceeds online, familiar inputs directly activate their categories and novel inputs continue to trigger adaptive searches for better categories, until the network's memory capacity is reached.

Uses for ART Systems

ART systems have been used to explain and predict a variety of cognitive and brain data that have as yet received no other theoretical explanation [23–26]. A formal lesion of the orienting subsystem, for example, creates a memory disturbance that mimics properties of medial temporal amnesia [27–28]. These and related data correspondences to orienting properties have led to a neurobiological interpretation of the orienting subsystem in terms of the hippocampal formation of the brain. In visual object-recognition applications, the interactions within the F_1 and F_2 levels of the attentional subsystem are interpreted in terms of data concerning the prestriate visual cortex and the inferotemporal cortex [29], with the attentional gain control pathway interpreted in terms of the pulvinar region of the brain.

From a computer science perspective, ART systems have an interpretation that is no less interesting. The read-out of top-down expectation V may be interpreted as a type of hypothesis-driven query. The matching process at F_1 and the hypothesis testing process at F_2 may be interpreted as query-driven symbolic substitutions. From this perspective, ART systems provide examples of new types of self-organizing production systems [30]. This interpretation of ART networks as production systems indicates how they contribute to artificial intelligence, a major goal of which is to understand the cognitive operations of human thinking in terms of production systems. The ability of ART production systems to explain many cognitive and neurobiological data that cannot be explained by classical production systems illustrates how ART systems have brought us closer to realizing this goal of artificial intelligence.

ARTMAP Systems

By incorporating predictive feedback into their control of the hypothesis testing cycle, the ARTMAP systems that are described below embody self-organizing production systems that are also goal-oriented. The fact that fuzzy logic may also be usefully incorporated into ART systems blurs the traditional boundaries between artificial intelligence and neural networks even further.

ARTMAP systems are capable of compressing different sorts of information into many distinct recognition categories that may all be used to make the same prediction, as shown in Fig. 11.2. The expertise of such an ARTMAP system can be inferred by a direct study of the rules it uses to arrive at predictions. This may be done at any stage of the learning process.

Suppose, for example, that the input vectors in Fig. 11.2 are of biochemicals instead of letter fonts, and that the outputs are indices of desired drug effects on behavior rather than letter names. There may be multiple ways in which different biochemicals can achieve the same clinical effect on behavior. At any point in the learning process, the operator of an ARTMAP system can test how many recognition categories have been detected that give rise to the desired clinical effect. The operator simply needs to check which LTM traces are large in the pathways from learned recognition categories to the desired output node. Within each recognition category, the prototype, or vector of large LTM traces, characterizes a particular rule or bundle of biochemical features that predicts the desired clinical effect. The "if-then" nature of the rule derives from the associative nature of ARTMAP predictions: "if the biochemical has features close enough to a particular prototype, then it predicts the desired outcome." A list of all the prototype vectors provides a transparent set of rules whereby one can predict the desired outcome.

Many such rules may coexist without mutual interference due to the competitive interactions whereby each hypothesis **Y** in Fig. 11.5 is compressed. Associative networks such as back propagation often mix multiple rules with the same LTM traces because they do not have the competitive dynamics to separate them.

This particular type of rule-based system may also exhibit aspects of "creativity." ARTMAP systems, albeit "supervised," do not use the correct answers

ART 1 (BINARY)	FUZZY ART (ANALOG)

CATEGORY CHOICE

$$T_j = \frac{|\mathbf{I} \cap \mathbf{w}_j|}{\alpha + |\mathbf{w}_j|} \qquad\qquad T_j = \frac{|\mathbf{I} \wedge \mathbf{w}_j|}{\alpha + |\mathbf{w}_j|}$$

MATCH CRITERION

$$\frac{|\mathbf{I} \cap \mathbf{w}|}{|\mathbf{I}|} \geq \rho \qquad\qquad \frac{|\mathbf{I} \wedge \mathbf{w}|}{|\mathbf{I}|} \geq \rho$$

FAST LEARNING

$$\mathbf{w}_j^{(new)} = \mathbf{I} \cap \mathbf{w}_j^{(old)} \qquad \mathbf{w}_j^{(new)} = \mathbf{I} \wedge \mathbf{w}_j^{(old)}$$

$$\cap = \begin{array}{c}\text{logical AND}\\\text{intersection}\end{array} \qquad \wedge = \begin{array}{c}\text{fuzzy AND}\\\text{minimum}\end{array}$$

Figure 11.6
Comparison of ART 1 and Fuzzy ART.

to directly force changes in LTM traces, as do supervised systems such as back propagation. ARTMAP systems use the fact that its answers are wrong, along with its present state of knowledge, to test new hypotheses until it discovers, on its own, new representations that are capable of predicting the correct answers.

ART Systems and Fuzzy Logic

Fuzzy ART is a form of ART 1 that incorporates fuzzy logic operations [31]. Although ART 1 can learn to classify only binary input patterns, fuzzy ART can learn to classify both analog and binary input patterns. In addition, fuzzy ART reduces to ART 1 in response to binary input patterns. Learning both analog and binary input patterns is achieved by replacing appearances of the intersection operator in ART 1 by the MIN operator of fuzzy set theory (Fig. 11.6). The MIN operator ($\wedge$) reduces to the intersection operator ($\cap$) in the binary case. Of particular interest is the fact that, as parameter α approaches zero, function Tj, which controls category choice through the bottom-up filter (Fig. 11.5), reduces to the operation of fuzzy subsethood [32]. T_j then measures the degree to which the adaptive weight vector $\mathbf{w}_j$ is a fuzzy subset of input vector $\mathbf{I}$.

In fuzzy ART, input vectors are normalized at a preprocessing stage (Fig. 11.7). This normalization procedure, called complement coding, leads to a symmetric theory in which the MIN operator ($\wedge$) and the MAX operator ($\vee$) of fuzzy set theory play complementary roles [33]. The categories formed by fuzzy ART are then hyper-rectangles. Fig. 11.8 illustrates how MIN and MAX define these rectangles in the 2-dimensional case. The MIN and MAX values define the acceptable range of feature variation in each dimension. Complement coding uses on-cells (with activity $\mathbf{a}$ in Fig. 11.7) and off-cells (with activity $\mathbf{a}^c$) to rep-

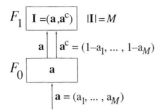

F_1 $\boxed{\mathbf{I} = (\mathbf{a}, \mathbf{a}^c)}$ $|\mathbf{I}| = M$

$\mathbf{a}$ $\mathbf{a}^c = (1 - a_1, \ldots, 1 - a_M)$

F_0 $\boxed{\mathbf{a}}$

$\mathbf{a} = (a_1, \ldots, a_M)$

Figure 11.7
Complement coding uses on-cell and off-cell pairs to normalize input vectors.

$\wedge$ Fuzzy AND (conjunction)

$\vee$ Fuzzy OR (disjunction)

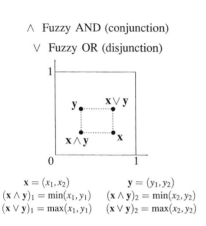

$\mathbf{x} = (x_1, x_2)$ $\mathbf{y} = (y_1, y_2)$
$(\mathbf{x} \wedge \mathbf{y})_1 = \min(x_1, y_1)$ $(\mathbf{x} \wedge \mathbf{y})_2 = \min(x_2, y_2)$
$(\mathbf{x} \vee \mathbf{y})_1 = \max(x_1, y_1)$ $(\mathbf{x} \vee \mathbf{y})_2 = \max(x_2, y_2)$

Figure 11.8
Fuzzy AND and OR operations generate category hyper-rectangles.

resent the input pattern, and preserves individual feature amplitudes while normalizing the total on-cell/off-cell vector.

The on-cell portion of a prototype encodes features that are critically present in category exemplars, while the off-cell portion encodes features that are critically absent. Each category is then defined by an interval of expected values for each input feature. For instance, we learn by example that men usually have hair on their heads. Fuzzy ART would encode this feature as a wide interval ([A, 1]) of expectations of "hair on head" for the category "man". Similarly, since men sometimes wear hats, the feature "hat on head" would be encoded by a wide interval ([0, B]) of expectations. On the other hand, a dog almost always has hair on its head but almost never wears a hat. These features for the category "dog" would thus be encoded by two narrow intervals ([C, 1]) for hair and [0, D] for hat) corresponding to narrower ranges of expectations for these two features.

Learning in fuzzy ART is stable because all adaptive weights can only decrease in time. Decreasing weights correspond to increasing sizes of category "boxes". Smaller vigilance values lead to larger category boxes, and learning stops when the input space is covered by boxes. The use of complement coding works with the property of increasing box size to prevent a proliferation of categories. With fast learning, constant vigilance, and a finite input set of arbitrary size and composition, learning stabilizes after just one presentation of each input pattern. A fast-commit, slow-recode option combines fast learning with a forgetting rule that buffers system memory against noise. Using this option, rare events can be rapidly learned, yet previously learned memories are not rapidly erased in response to statistically unreliable input fluctuations. See the appendix entitled "Fuzzy ART Algorithm" for an explanation of defining equations of fuzzy ART.

When the supervised learning of fuzzy ARTMAP controls category formation, a predictive error can force the creation of new categories that could not otherwise be learned due to monotone increases in category size through time in the unsupervised case. Supervision permits the creation of complex categorical structures without a loss of stability.

Fuzzy ARTMAP

Each fuzzy ARTMAP system includes a pair of fuzzy ART modules (ART_a and ART_b), as shown in Fig. 11.9. During supervised learning, ART_a receives a

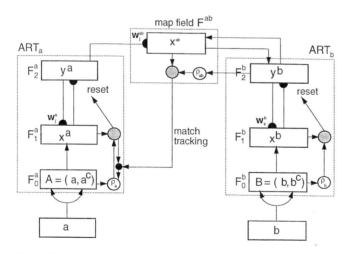

Figure 11.9

Fuzzy ARTMAP architecture. The ART_a complement coding preprocessor transforms the M_a-vector a into the $2M_a$-vector $\mathbf{A} = (\mathbf{a}.\mathbf{a}^c)$ at the ART_a field F_0^a. $\mathbf{A}$ is the input vector to the ART_a field F_1^a. Similarly, the input to F_1^b is the $2M_b$-vector $(\mathbf{b}.\mathbf{b}^c)$. When a prediction by ART_a is disconfirmed at ART_b, inhibition of map field activation induces the match tracking process. Match tracking raises the ART_a vigilance ρ_a to just above the F_1^a to F_0^a match ratio $|\mathbf{x}^a|/|\mathbf{A}|$. This triggers an ART_a search which leads to activation of either an ART_a category that correctly predicts $\mathbf{b}$ or to a previously uncommited ART_a category node.

stream $\{\mathbf{a}^{(p)}\}$ of input patterns and ART_b receives a stream $\{\mathbf{b}^{(p)}\}$ of input patterns, where $\mathbf{b}^{(p)}$ is the correct prediction given $\mathbf{a}^{(p)}$. These modules are linked by an associative learning network and an internal controller that ensures autonomous system operation in real time.

The controller is designed to create the minimal number of ART_a recognition categories, or "hidden units," needed to meet accuracy criteria. As noted above, this is accomplished by realizing a Minimax Learning Rule that conjointly minimizes predictive error and maximizes predictive generalization. This scheme automatically links predictive success to category size on a trial-by-trial basis using only local operations. It works by increasing the vigilance parameter ρ_a of ART_a by the minimal amount needed to correct a predictive error at ART_b (Fig. 11.10).

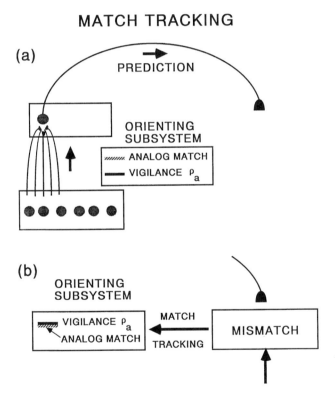

Figure 11.10
Match tracking: (a) A prediction is made by ART_a when the vigilance ρ_a is less than the analog match value. (b) A predictive error at ART_b increases the vigilance value of ART_a until it just exceeds the analog match value, and there-by triggers hypothesis testing that searches for a more predictive bundle of features to which to attend.

Parameter ρ_a calibrates the minimum confidence that ART_a must have in a recognition category (hypothesis) that is activated by an input $\mathbf{a}^{(p)}$, in order for ART_a to accept that category instead of searching for a better one through an automatically controlled process of hypothesis testing. As in ART 1, lower values of ρ_a enable larger categories to form. These lower ρ_a values lead to broader generalization and higher code compression. A predictive failure at ART_b increases the minimal confidence ρ_a by the least amount needed to trigger hypothesis testing at ART_a, using a mechanism called match tracking [5]. *Match tracking* sacrifices the minimum amount of generalization necessary to correct the predictive error.

Match tracking presents the idea that the system must have accepted hypotheses with too little confidence to satisfy the demands of a particular environment; it increases the criterion confidence just enough to trigger hypothesis testing. Hypothesis testing leads to the selection of a new ART_a category, which focuses attention on a new cluster of $\mathbf{a}^{(p)}$ input features that is better able to predict $\mathbf{b}^{(p)}$. Due to the combination of match tracking and fast learning, a single ARTMAP system can learn a different prediction for a rare event than for a cloud of similar frequent events in which it is embedded. The equations for fuzzy ART and fuzzy ARTMAP are given in the appendix in algorithmic form.

A Fuzzy ARTMAP Benchmark

Fuzzy ARTMAP has been benchmarked against a variety of machine learning, neural network, and genetic algorithms with considerable success (Table 11.2). One study used a benchmark machine learning task that Frey and Slate developed and described as a "difficult categorization problem" [34]. The task requires a system to identify an input exemplar as one of 26 capital letters, A through Z. The database was derived from 20,000 unique black-and-white pixel images. The task is difficult because of the wide variety of letter types represented: The twenty "fonts represent five different stroke styles (simplex, duplex, complex, and Gothic) and six different letter styles (block, script, italic, English, Italian, and German)." In addition, each image was randomly distorted, leaving many of the characters misshapen. Sixteen numerical feature attributes were then obtained from each character image, and each attribute value was scaled to a range of 0 to 15. The resulting Letter Image Recognition file is archived in the UCI Repository of Machine Learning Databases and Domain Theories, maintained by David Aha and Patrick Murphy (ml_repository@ics.uci.edu on Internet).

Frey and Slate used this database to test performance of a family of classifiers based on Holland's genetic algorithms [35]. The training set consisted of 16,000 exemplars, with the remaining 4000 exemplars used for testing. Genetic algorithm classifiers having different input representations, weight-update and rule-creation schemes, and system parameters were systematically compared.

Training was carried out for five epochs, plus a sixth "verification" pass during which no new rules were created but a large number of unsatisfactory rules were discarded. In Frey and Slate's comparative study, these systems had correct prediction rates that ranged from 24.5 percent to 80.8 percent on the 4000-item test set. The best performance was obtained using an integer input representation, a reward-sharing weight update, an exemplar method of rule creation, and a parameter setting that allowed an unused or erroneous rule to stay in the system for a long time before being discarded. After training in the best case, 1302 rules and 8 attributes per rule were created, as were over 35,000 more rules that were discarded during verification. (For purposes of comparison, a rule is somewhat analogous to an ART_a category in ARTMAP, and the number of attributes per rule is analogous to the size $|\mathbf{w}_j^a|$ of an ART_a category weight vector.)

Building on the results of their comparative study, Frey and Slate investigated two types of alternative algorithms: an accuracy-utility bidding system that had slightly improved performance (81.6 percent) in the best case, and an exemplar/hybrid rule creation scheme that further improved performance to a maximum of 82.7 percent but required the creation of over 100,000 rules prior to the verification step.

Fuzzy ARTMAP had an error rate on the letter-recognition task that was consistently less than one third that of the three best Frey-Slate genetic algorithm classifiers described above. In particular, after one to five epochs, individual fuzzy ARTMAP systems had a robust prediction rate of 90 to 94 percent on the 4000-item test set. A voting strategy consistently improved this performance. The voting strategy is based on the observation that ARTMAP fast learning typically leads to different adaptive weights and recognition categories for different orderings of a given training set, even when overall predictive accuracy of all simulations is similar.

The different category structures cause the set of test items where errors occur to vary from one simulation to the next. The voting strategy uses an ARTMAP system that is trained several times on input sets with different orderings. The final prediction for a given test set item is the one made by the largest number of simulations. Because the set of items making erroneous predictions varies from one simulation to the next, voting cancels many of the errors.

Such a voting strategy can also be used to assign confidence estimates to competing predictions given small, noisy, or incomplete training sets. Voting consistently eliminated 25 to 43 percent of the errors, giving a robust prediction rate of 92 to 96 percent. Fuzzy ARTMAP simulations each created fewer than 1070 ART_a categories, compared to the 1040 to 1302 final rules of the three genetic classifiers with the best performance rates. Most fuzzy ARTMAP learning occurred on the first epoch, with test set performance on systems trained for one epoch typically over 97 percent compared to systems exposed to inputs for five epochs.

Conclusion

Fuzzy ARTMAP is one of a rapidly growing family of attentive self-organizing learning, hypothesis testing, and prediction systems that have evolved from the biological theory of cognitive information processing of which ART forms an important part [16, 23–26]. Unsupervised ART modules have found their way into such diverse applications as the control of mobile robots, learning and searching of airplane part inventories, medical diagnosis, 3-D visual object recognition, music recognition, seismic recognition, sonar recognition, and laser radar recognition [36–40].

All of these applications exploit the ability of ART systems to rapidly learn to classify large databases in a stable fashion, to calibrate their confidence in a classification, and to focus attention upon those groups of features that they deem to be important based upon their past experience. We anticipate that the growing family of supervised ARTMAP systems will find an even broader range of applications due to their ability to adapt the number, shape, and scale of their category boundaries to meet the online demands of large nonstationary databases.

The algorithmic equations that define fuzzy ART and fuzzy ARTMAP are summarized in the appendix that follows.

Appendix: Fuzzy ART Algorithms

ART Field Activity Vectors   Each ART system includes a field F_0 of nodes that represent a current input vector; a field F_1 that receives both bottom-up input from F_0 and top-down input from a field F_2 that represents the active code, or category. The F_0 activity vector is denoted $\mathbf{I} = (I_1, \ldots, I_M)$, with each component I_i in the interval $[0, 1], i = 1, \ldots, M$. The F_1 activity vector is denoted $\mathbf{x} = (x_1, \ldots, x_M)$ and the F_2 activity vector is denoted $\mathbf{y} = (y_1, \ldots, y_N)$. The number of nodes in each field is arbitrary.

Weight Vector   Associated with each F_2 category node $j(j = 1, \ldots, N)$ is a vector $\mathbf{w}_j \equiv (w_{j1}, \ldots, w_{jM})$ of adaptive weights, or LTM traces. Initially,

$$w_{j1}(0) = \cdots = w_{jM}(0) = 1; \tag{1}$$

Each category is then said to be uncommitted. After a category is selected for coding, it becomes committed. As shown below, each LTM trace w_{ji} is monotone nonincreasing through time and hence converges to a limit. The fuzzy ART weight vector $\mathbf{w}_j$ subsumes both the bottom-up and top-down weight vectors of ART 1.

Parameters   Fuzzy ART dynamics are determined by a choice parameter $\alpha > 0$; a learning rate parameter $\beta \in [0, 1]$; and a vigilance parameter $\rho \in [0, 1]$.

Category Choice   For each input $\mathbf{I}$ and F_2 node j, the choice function T_j is defined by:

$$T_j(\mathbf{I}) = \frac{|\mathbf{I} \wedge \mathbf{w}_j|}{\alpha + |\mathbf{w}_j|}, \tag{2}$$

where the fuzzy AND [33] operator $\wedge$ is defined by:

$$(\mathbf{p} \wedge \mathbf{q})_i \equiv \min(p_i, q_i) \tag{3}$$

and where the norm $| \cdot |$ is defined by:

$$|\mathbf{p}| \equiv \sum_{i=1}^{M} |p_i|. \tag{4}$$

for any M-dimensional vectors $\mathbf{p}$ and $\mathbf{q}$. For notational simplicity, $T_j(\mathbf{I})$ in (2) is often written as T_j when the input $\mathbf{I}$ is fixed.

The system is said to make a category choice when at most one F_2 node can become active at a given time. The category choice is indexed by J, where

$$T_J = \max\{T_j : j = 1 \ldots N\}. \tag{5}$$

If more than one T_J is maximal, the category j with the smallest index is chosen. In particular, nodes become committed in order $j = 1, 2, 3, \ldots$. When the Jth category is chosen, $y_J = 1$; and $y_j = 0$ for $j \neq J$. In a choice system, the F_1 activity vector x obeys the equation

$$x = \begin{cases} \mathbf{I} & \text{if } F_2 \text{ is inactive} \\ \mathbf{I} \wedge \mathbf{w}_J & \text{if the } J^{th}F_2 \text{ node is chosen.} \end{cases} \tag{6}$$

Resonance or Reset   Resonance occurs if the match function $|\mathbf{I} \wedge \mathbf{w}_J|/|\mathbf{I}|$ of the chosen category meets the vigilance criterion:

$$\frac{|\mathbf{I} \wedge \mathbf{w}_J|}{|\mathbf{I}|} \geq \rho; \tag{7}$$

that is, by (6), when the Jth category is chosen, resonance occurs if

$$|x| = |\mathbf{I} \wedge \mathbf{w}_J| \geq \rho |\mathbf{I}|. \tag{8}$$

Learning then ensues, as defined later in this sidebar. Mismatch reset occurs if

$$\frac{|\mathbf{I} \wedge \mathbf{w}_J|}{|\mathbf{I}|} < \rho; \tag{9}$$

that is, if:

$$|x| = |\mathbf{I} \wedge \mathbf{w}_J| < \rho |\mathbf{I}|. \tag{10}$$

Then the value of the choice function T_J is set to 0 for the duration of the input presentation to prevent the persistent selection of the same category during search. A new index J is then chosen, by (5). The search process continues until the chosen J satisfies (7).

Learning   Once search ends, the weight vector $\mathbf{w}_J$ is updated according to the equation

$$\mathbf{w}_J^{(\text{new})} = \beta(\mathbf{I} \wedge \mathbf{w}_J^{(\text{old})}) + (1 - \beta)\mathbf{w}_J^{(\text{old})}. \tag{11}$$

Fast learning corresponds to setting $\beta = 1$. The learning law used in the EACH system of Salzberg is equivalent to equation (11) in the fast-learn limit with the complement coding option described below [41].

Fast-Commit Slow-Recode Option   For efficient coding of noisy input sets, it is useful to set $\beta = 1$ when J is an uncommitted node, and then to take $\beta < 1$ after the category is committed. Then $\mathbf{w}_j^{(\text{new})} = \mathbf{I}$, and the first time category J becomes active. Moore introduced the learning law (11), with fast commitment and slow recoding, to investigate a variety of generalized ART 1 models [42]. Some of these models are similar to fuzzy ART, but none includes the complement coding option. Moore described a category proliferation problem that can occur in some analog ART systems when a large number of inputs erode the norm of weight vectors. Complement coding solves this problem.

Input Normalization/Complement Coding Option   Proliferation of categories is avoided in fuzzy ART if inputs are normalized. Complement coding is a normalization rule that preserves amplitude information. Complement coding represents both the on-response and the off-response to an input vector $\mathbf{a}$ (Fig. 11.7). To define this operation in its simplest form, let $\mathbf{a}$ itself represent the on-response. The complement of $\mathbf{a}$, denoted by $\mathbf{a}^c$, represents the off-response, where

$$a_i^c \equiv 1 - a_i. \tag{12}$$

The complement-coded input $\mathbf{I}$ to the field F1 is the 2M-dimensional vector:

$$\mathbf{I} = (\mathbf{a}, \mathbf{a}^c) \equiv (a_1, \ldots, a_M, a_1^c, \ldots, a_M^c). \tag{13}$$

Note that

$$|\mathbf{I}| = |(\mathbf{a}, \mathbf{a}^c)|$$

$$= \sum_{i=1}^{M} a_i + \left(M - \sum_{i=1}^{M} a_i \right)$$

$$= M, \tag{14}$$

so inputs preprocessed into complement coding form are automatically normalized. Where complement coding is used, the initial condition (1) is replaced by

$$w_{j1}(0) = \cdots = w_{j,2M}(0) = 1. \tag{15}$$

Fuzzy ARTMAP Algorithm
The fuzzy ARTMAP system incorporates two fuzzy ART, modules ART_a and ART_b, that are linked together via an inter-ART module F^{ab} called a map field. The map field is used to form predictive associations between categories and to realize the match tracking rule whereby the vigilance parameter of ART_a increases in response to a predictive mismatch at ART_b. The interactions mediated by the map field F^{ab} may be operationally characterized as follows.

ART_a and ART_b   Inputs to ART_a and ART_b are in the complement code form: for ART_a, $\mathbf{I} = \mathbf{A} = (\mathbf{a}, \mathbf{a}^c)$; for ART_b, $\mathbf{I} = \mathbf{B} = (\mathbf{b}, \mathbf{b}^c)$ (Fig. 11.9). Variables in ART_a or ART_b are designated by subscripts or superscripts "*a*" or "*b*". For ART_a, let $\mathbf{x}^a \equiv (x_1^a \ldots x_{2Ma}^a)$ denote the F_1^a output vector; let $\mathbf{y}^a \equiv (y_1^a \ldots y_{Na}^a)$ denote the F_1^a output vector; and let $\mathbf{w}_j^a \equiv (w_{j1}^a, w_{j2}^a, \ldots, w_{j,2Ma})$ denote the jth ART_a weight vector. For ART_b, let $\mathbf{x}^b \equiv (x_1^b \ldots x_{2M_b}^b)$ denote the F_1^b output vector; let $\mathbf{y}^b \equiv (y_1^b \ldots y_{Nb}^b)$ denote the F_2^b output vector; and let $\mathbf{w}_k^b \equiv (w_{k1}^b, w_{k2}^b, \ldots, w_{k,2M_b}^b)$ denote the kth ART_b weight vector. For the map field, let $\mathbf{x}^{ab} \equiv (x_1^{ab}, \ldots, x_{N_b}^{ab})$ denote the F^{ab} output vector, and let $\mathbf{w}_j^{ab} \equiv (w_{j1}^{ab}, \ldots, w_{jN_b}^{ab})$ denote the weight vector from the jth F_2^a node to F^{ab}. Vectors $\mathbf{x}^a$, $\mathbf{y}^a$, $\mathbf{x}^b$, $\mathbf{y}^b$, and $\mathbf{x}^{ab}$ are set to $\mathbf{0}$ between input presentations.

Map Field Activation   The map field F^{ab} is activated whenever one of the ART_a or ART_b categories is active. If node J of F_2^a is chosen, then its weights $\mathbf{w}_J^{ab}$ activate F^{ab}. If node K in F_2^b is active, then the node K in F^{ab} is activated by 1-to-1 pathways between F_2^b and F^{ab}. If both ART_a and ART_b are active, then F^{ab} becomes active only if ART_a predicts the same category as ART_b via the weights $\mathbf{w}_J^{ab}$. The F^{ab} output vector $\mathbf{x}^{ab}$ obeys

$$
\mathbf{x}^{ab} = \begin{cases} \mathbf{y}^b \wedge \mathbf{w}_J^{ab} & \text{if the Jth } F_2^a \text{ node is active and } F_2^b \text{ is active} \\ \mathbf{w}_J^{ab} & \text{if the Jth } F_2^a \text{ node is active and } F_2^b \text{ is inactive} \\ \mathbf{y}^b & \text{if } F_2^a \text{ is inactive and } F_2^b \text{ is active} \\ \mathbf{0} & \text{if } F_2^a \text{ is inactive and } F_2^b \text{ is inactive} \end{cases} \tag{16}
$$

By (16), $\mathbf{x}^{ab} = 0$ if the prediction $\mathbf{w}_J^{ab}$ is disconfirmed by $\mathbf{y}^b$. Such a mismatch event triggers an ART_a search for a better category.

Match Tracking   At the start of each input presentation the ART_a vigilance parameter ρ_a equals a baseline vigilance $\overline{\rho_a}$. The map field vigilance parameter is ρ_{ab}. If

$$
|\mathbf{x}^{ab}| < \rho_{ab}|\mathbf{y}^b|, \tag{17}
$$

then ρ_a is increased until it is slightly larger than $|\mathbf{A} \wedge \mathbf{w}_J^a||\mathbf{A}|^{-1}$, where ^{A} is the input to F_1^a, in complement coding form. Then,

$$
|\mathbf{x}^a| = |\mathbf{A} \wedge \mathbf{w}_j^a| < \rho_a|\mathbf{A}|, \tag{18}
$$

where J is the index of the active F_2^a node, as in (10). When this occurs, ART_a search leads either to activation of another F_2^a node J with

$$|\mathbf{x}^a| = |\mathbf{A} \wedge \mathbf{w}_J^a| \geq \rho_a |\mathbf{A}| \tag{19}$$

and

$$|\mathbf{x}^{ab}| = |\mathbf{y}^b \wedge \mathbf{w}_J^{ab}| \geq \rho_{ab} |\mathbf{y}^b|; \tag{20}$$

or, if no such node exists, to the shut-down of F_2^a for the remainder of the input presentation.

Map Field Learning   Learning rules determine how the map field weights w_{jk}^{ab} change through time, as follows: Weights w_{jk}^{ab} in $F_2^a \rightarrow F^{ab}$ paths initially satisfy

$$w_{jk}^{ab}(0) = 1. \tag{21}$$

During resonance with the ART_a category J active, $\mathbf{w}_J^{ab}$ approaches the map field vector $\mathbf{x}^{ab}$. With fast learning, once J learns to predict the ART_b category K, that association is permanent; that is, $w_{JK}^{ab} = 1$ for all time.

Acknowledgements

The authors wish to thank Kelly Dumont and Diana Meyers for their valuable assistance in the preparation of the manuscript.

References

[1] D. B. Parker, "Leaning-Logic," Invention Report, 581-64, File 1, Office of Technology Licensing, Stanford University, Stanford, Calif., October, 1982.

[2] D. E. Rumelhart, G. Hinton, and R. Williams, "Learning Internal Representations by Error Propagation," Parallel Distributed Processing, D. E. Rumelhart and J. L. McClelland (Eds.), Cambridge, Mass, MIT Press, 1986.

[3] P. Werbos, "Beyond Regression: New Tools for Prediction and Analysis in the Behavioral Sciences," Ph.D. Thesis, Harvard University, Cambridge, Mass, 1974.

[4] R. Ratcliff, "Connectionist Models of Recognition Memory: Constraints Imposed by Learning and Forgetting Functions," *Psychological Review*, 97, pp. 285–308, 1990.

[5] G. A. Carpenter, S. Grossberg, and J. H. Reynolds, "ARTMAP: Supervised Real-time Learning and Classification of Nonstationary Data by a Self-organizing Neural Network," Neural Networks, 4, pp. 565–88, 1991.

[6] G. A. Carpenter, S. Grossberg, N. Markuzon, J. H. Reynolds, and D. B. Rosen, "Fuzzy ART-MAP: A Neural Network Architecture for Incremental Supervised Learning of Analog Multidimensional Maps," *IEEE Trans. on Neural Networks*, 3, 1992.

[7] S. Grossberg, "Adaptive Pattern Classification and Universal Recoding, II: Feedback, Expectation, Olfaction, and Illusions," *Biological Cybernetics*, 23, pp. 187–202, 1976.

[8] S. Grossberg, "How Does a Brain Build a Cognitive Code?" *Psychological Review*, 1, pp. 1–51, 1980.

[9] G. A. Carpenter and S. Grossberg, "A Massively Parallel Architecture for a Self-organizing Neural Pattern Recognition Machine," *Computer Vision, Graphics, and Image Processing*, 37, pp. 54–115, 1987.

[10] G. A. Carpenter and S. Grossberg, "ART 2: Stable Self-organization of Pattern Recognition Codes for Analog Input Patterns," *Applied Optics*, 26, pp. 4919–30, 1987.

[11] G. A. Carpenter and S. Grossberg, "ART 3: Hierarchical Search Using Chemical Transmitters in Self-organizing Pattern Recognition Architectures," *Neural Networks*, 3, pp. 129–152, 1990.

[12] S. Grossberg, "Neural Expectation: Cerebellar and Retinal Analogs of Cells Fired by Learnable or Unlearned Pattern Classes," *Kybernetik*, 10, pp. 49–57, 1972.

[13] S. Grossberg, "On the Development of Feature Detectors in the Visual Cortex with Applications to Learning and Reaction-diffusion Systems," *Biological Cybernetics*, 21, pp. 145–59, 1976.

[14] S. Grossberg, "Adaptive Pattern Classification and Universal Recoding, I: Parallel Development and Coding of Neural Feature Detectors," *Biological Cybernetics*, 23, pp. 121–34, 1976.

[15] S. Grossberg, "A Theory of Human Memory: Self-organization and Performance of Sensory-motor Codes, Maps, and Plans. Progress in Theoretical Biology, Vol. 5., R. Rosen and F. Snell (Eds.), New York, Academic Press, 1978. (Reprinted in S. Grossberg, Studies of Mind and Brain: Neural Principles of Learning, Perception, Development, Cognition, and Motor Control, Reidel Press, 1982).

[16] S. Grossberg, Studies of Mind and Brain: Neural Principles of Learning, Perception, Development, Cognition, and Motor Control, (Reidel Press, 1982).

[17] C. von der Malsburg, "Self-organization of Orientation Sensitive Cells in the Striate Cortex," *Kybernetik*, 14, pp. 85–100, 1973.

[18] D. J. Willshaw and C. von der Malsburg, "How Patterned Neural Connections Can Be Set Up by Self-organization," *Proceedings of the Royal Society of London (B)*, 194, pp. 431–45, 1976.

[19] M. Cohen and S. Grossberg, "Neural Dynamics of Speech and Language Coding: Developmental Programs, Perceptual Grouping, and Competition for Short Term Memory," *Human Neurobiology*, 5, pp. 1–22, 1986.

[20] M. Cohen and S. Grossberg, "Masking Fields: A Massively Parallel Architecture for Learning, Recognizing, and Predicting Multiple Groupings of Patterned Data," *Applied Optics*, 26, pp. 1866–1891, 1987.

[21] S. Grossberg and M. Kuperstein, Neural dynamics of adaptive sensory-motor control: Ballistic eye movements, (Amsterdam, Elsevier/North Holland, 1986). Also in Expanded Edition, pub. by Pergamon Press, 1989).

[22] T. Kohonen, Self-organization and Associative Memory, Springer-Verlag, 1988.

[23] G. A. Carpenter and S. Grossberg (Eds.), Pattern Recognition by Self-organizing Neural Networks, (MIT Press, 1991).

[24] S. Grossberg (Ed.), The Adaptive Brain, I: Cognition, Learning, Reinforcement, and Rhythm, Elsevier/North-Holland, 1987.

[25] S. Grossberg (Ed.), The Adaptive Brain, II: Vision, Speech, Language, and Motor Control, Elsevier/North-Holland, 1987.

[26] S. Grossberg (Ed.), Neural Networks and Natural Intelligence, MIT Press, 1988).

[27] G. Carpenter and S. Grossberg, "Neural Dynamics of Category Learning and Recognition: Attention, Memory Consolidation, and Amnesia" In S. Grossberg (Ed.), The Adaptive Brain, I: Cognition, Learning, Reinforcement, and Rhythm, pp. 238–86, Elsevier/North Holland, 1987.

[28] S. Grossberg and J. W. L. Merrill, "A Neural Network Model of Adaptively Timed Reinforcement Learning and Hippocampal Dynamics," *Cognitive Brain Research*, 1992.

[29] R. Desimone, "Neural Circuits for Visual Attention in the Primate Brain," Neural networks for vision and image processing, G. A. Carpenter and S. Grossberg (Eds.), pp. 343–364, (Cambridge, Mass: MIT Press, 1992).

[30] J. E. Laird, A. Newell, and P. S. Rosenbloom, "SOAR: An Architecture for General Intelligence," *Artificial Intelligence*, 33, pp. 1–64, 1987.

[31] G. A. Carpenter, S. Grossberg, and D. B. Rosen, "Fuzzy ART: Fast Stable Learning and Categorization of Analog Patterns by an Adaptive Resonance System," *Neural Networks*, 4, pp. 759–71, 1991.

[32] B. Kosko, "Fuzzy Entropy and Conditioning," *Information Sciences*, 40, pp. 165–174, 1986.

[33] L. Zadeh, "Fuzzy Sets," *Information Control*, 8, pp. 338–353, 1965.

[34] P. W. Frey and D. J. Slate, "Letter Recognition Using Holland-style Adaptive Classifiers," *Machine Learning*, 6, pp. 161–82, 1991.

[35] J. H. Holland, "Adaptive Algorithms for Discovering and Using General Patterns in Growing Knowledge Bases," *International Journal of Policy Analysis and Information Systems*, 4, pp. 217–40, 1980.

[36] A. J. Baloch and A. M. Waxman, "Visual Learning, Adaptive Expectations, and Learning Behavioral Conditioning of the Mobil Robot MAVIN," *Neural Networks*, 4, pp. 271–302, 1991.

[37] T. Caudell, S. Smith, C. Johnson, D. Wunsch, and R. Escobedo, "An Industrial Application of Neural Networks to Reusable Design," Adaptive neural systems, Technical Report BCS-CS-ACS-91-001, pp. 185–90, The Boeing Company, Seattle, Wash., 1991).

[38] R. O. Gjerdingen, "Categorization of Musical Patterns by Self-organizing Neuronlike Networks," *Music Perception*, 7, pp. 339–70, 1990.

[39] P. Goodman, V. Kaburlasos, D. Egbert, G. Carpenter, S. Grossberg, J. Reynolds, K. Hammermeister, G. Marshall, and F. Grover, "Fuzzy ARTMAP Neural Network Prediction of Heart Surgery Mortality," Proceedings of the Wang Institute Research Conference: Neural Networks for Learning, Recognition, and Control, p. 48 (Boston, Mass: Boston University, 1992).

[40] M. Seibert and A. M. Waxman, "Learning and Recognizing 3D Objects from Multiple Views in a Neural System," Neural Networks for Perception, H. Wechler (Ed.) Vol. 1, pp. 426–444, (New York: Academic Press, 1992).

[41] S. L. Salzberg, Learning with Nested Generalized Exemplars (Boston: Kluwer Academic Publishers, 1990).

[42] B. Moore, "ART 1 and Pattern Clustering," *Proceedings of the 1988 Connectionist Models Summer School*, D. Touretzky, G. Hinton, and T. Sejnowski, Eds., pp. 174–85, Morgan Kaumann, 1989.

Optimality Theory

Chapter 12

Optimality: From Neural Networks to Universal Grammar

Alan Prince and Paul Smolensky

It is evident that the sciences of the brain and those of the mind are separated by many gulfs, not the least of which lies between the formal methods appropriate for continuous dynamical systems and those for discrete symbol structures. Yet recent research provides evidence that integration of these sciences may holds significant rewards. Research on neural computation has identified optimization as an organizing principle of some generality, and current work is showing that optimization principles can be successfully adapted to a central domain within the theory of mind: the theory of grammar. In this article, we explore how a reconceptualization of linguistic theory through optimization principles provides a variety of insights into the structure of the language faculty, and we consider the relations between optimality in grammar and optimization in neural networks.

Some of the contributions of the optimization perspective on grammar are surprising. The distinction between linguistic knowledge in the abstract and the use of this knowledge in language processing has often been challenged by researchers adopting neural network approaches to language; yet we show here how an optimization architecture in fact strengthens and rationalizes this distinction. In turn, this leads to new formal methods by which grammar learners can cope with the demands of their difficult task, and new explanations for the gap in complexity between the language children produce and the language they can comprehend. Optimization also provides a fresh perspective on the nature of linguistic constraints, on what it is that grammars of different human languages share, and on how grammars may differ. And this turns out to provide considerable analytical leverage on central aspects of the long-standing problems in language acquisition.

Optimality Theory

Linguistic research seeks to characterize the range of structures available to human language and the relationships that may obtain between them, particularly as they figure in a competent speaker's internalized "grammar" or implicit knowledge of language. Languages appear to vary widely, but the same structural themes repeat themselves over and over again, in ways that are sometimes obvious and sometimes clear only upon detailed analysis. The challenge, then, is to discover an architecture for grammars that both allows variation and limits its range to what is actually possible in human language.

A primary observation is that grammars contain constraints on the well-formedness of linguistic structures, and these constraints are heavily in conflict, even within a single language. A few simple examples should bring out the flavor of this conflict. English operates under constraints entailing that its basic word order is subject-verb-object; yet in a sentence like *what did John see?* it is the object that stands first. This evidences the greater force of a constraint requiring question-words like *what* to appear sentence-initially. Yet even this constraint is not absolute: One must say *who saw what?* with the object question-word appearing in its canonical position; the potential alternative, *who what saw?*, with all question-words clumped at the front, which is indeed grammatical in some languages, runs afoul of another principle of clause structure that is, in English, yet stronger than the requirement of initial placement of question-words. Thus, *who saw what?* is the grammatical structure, satisfying the constraints of the grammar not perfectly, but optimally: No alternative does better, given the relative strength of the constraints in the grammar of English.

Similar conflicts abound at all levels of linguistic structure. In forming the past tense of "slip," spelled "slipped" but pronounced *slipt*, a general phonological constraint on voicing in final consonant sequences favors the pronunciation *pt* over *pd*, conflicting with the requirement that the past-tense marker be given its basic form *-d*; and the phonological constraint prevails (1). In an English sentence like *it rains*, a constraint requiring all words to contribute to meaning (unlike the element *it* in this usage) conflicts with a structural constraint requiring all sentences to have subjects; and the latter controls the outcome. Such examples indicate that a central element in the architecture of grammar is a formal means for managing the pervasive conflict between grammatical constraints.

The key observation is this: In a variety of clear cases where there is a strength asymmetry between two conflicting constraints, no amount of success on the weaker constraint can compensate for failure on the stronger one. Put another way: Any degree of failure on the weaker constraint is tolerated, so long as it contributes to success on the stronger constraint. Extending this observation leads to the hypothesis that a grammar consists entirely of constraints arranged in a strict domination hierarchy, in which each constraint is strictly more important than—takes absolute priority over—all the constraints lower-ranked in the hierarchy. With this type of constraint interaction, it is only the ranking of constraints in the hierarchy that matters for the determination of optimality; no particular numerical strengths, for example, are necessary. Strict domination thus limits drastically the range of possible strength-interactions between constraints to those representable with the algebra of total order.

Strict domination hierarchies composed of very simple well-formedness constraints can lead to surprisingly complex grammatical consequences. Furthermore, different rankings of the same set of constraints can give rise to strikingly different linguistic patterns. These properties show that strict domination, though a narrow mechanism, answers to the basic requirements on the theory of human language, which must allow grammars to be built from simple parts whose combination leads to specific kinds of complexity and diversity. Optimality theory, originally presented in 1991 (2), offers a particularly strong version of a strict-domination-based approach to grammatical optimization. Optimality theory hypothesizes that the set of well-formedness constraints is universal: not just universally available to be chosen from, but literally present in every language. A grammar for a particular language results from imposing a strict-domination ranking on the entire universal constraint set. Also universal is the function that determines, for each input to the grammar, the set of candidate output structures that compete for optimality; every language considers exactly the same set of options for realizing an input. The observed force of a given constraint can vary from absolute (never violated) to nil (always violated), with many stops and steps along the way, depending on its position in the strict domination hierarchy for a given language, and depending on the membership in the output candidate set for a given input.

Optimality theory thus provides a direct answer to the classic questions of linguistic theory: What do the grammars of different languages have in common, and how may they differ? What they share are the universal constraints and the definition of which forms compete; they differ in how the constraints are ranked, and, therefore, in which constraints take priority when conflicts arise among them. For example, the two constraints in conflict in English *it rains* are ranked differently in Italian: The constraint against meaningless words outranks that against subjectless sentences, and the resulting grammatical sentence is simply *piove* (literally, "rains").

Optimality theory connects a number of lines of research that have occupied linguists in the last several decades: the articulation of universal formal principles of grammars; the generalization of well-formedness constraints across the outputs of formally disparate mechanisms; the descriptive use of informal notions of linguistic optimization; and output-oriented analysis (3). Such a unification is made possible by the basic notion that grammaticality means optimally satisfying the conflicting demands of violable constraints.

Markedness and Faithfulness Constraints

Within the universal constraint set, several subclasses have been distinguished. One class of universal constraints in optimality theory formalizes the notion of structural complexity, or markedness (4). Grossly speaking, an element of linguistic structure is said to be marked if it is more complex than an alternative along some dimension; the relevant dimensions may sometimes correlate with comprehension, production, memory, or related physical and cognitive functions. The word-final consonant cluster *pd* is more marked than *pt*; sentences lacking subjects are more marked than those with subjects. Marked elements tend to be absent altogether in certain languages, restricted in their use in other languages, later-acquired by children, and in other ways avoided. This cluster of properties diagnostic of marked elements is given a uniform explanation in optimality theory, which follows from their formal characterization: Marked structures are those that violate structural constraints. We will call the set of all such constraints STRUCTURE.

Phonological STRUCTURE constraints often induce context-dependent alteration of pronunciations. For example, the markedness of *pd* relative to *pt* is responsible for the alteration of the past-tense suffix *d* to *t* in "slipped"; this is a context in which the more marked cluster is avoided. A more dramatic alteration is common in French, driven by syllabic markedness constraints. [Our presentation simplifies somewhat for ease of exposition (5).] One such constraint, NoCODA, is violated by any syllable ending with a consonant—a closed syllable; the syllable-closing consonant is called a coda. Closed syllables are marked relative to syllables ending with a vowel. Another constraint, ONSET, is violated by syllables that begin with a vowel.

In French, the masculine form of the word for "small," written "petit," is pronounced with or without the final *t*, depending on the context. Spelling, though often merely conventional, in this case accurately represents the abstract sound-sequence that a speaker internalizes when the word is learned; we write this sequence /petit/. When the following word is vowel-initial, the final *t* is pronounced, beginning a syllable—*pe.ti.t oeuf* "little egg." Elsewhere—when the following word begins with a consonant, or when there is no following word—/petit/ is pronounced *pe.ti*, with loss of the final lexical *t*—*pe.ti. chien* "little dog." (Adjacent syllables are separated by a period in the examples.) The phonological grammar of French determines how "small" is pronounced in a given context, that is, which grammatical "output" (pronunciation) corresponds to an "input" /petit.../. The final *t* is not pronounced when so doing would violate NoCODA; the constraint ONSET determines that when the *t* precedes a vowel, it begins a syllable and is pronounced.

A second class of universal constraints in optimality theory; FAITHFULNESS constraints, is a direct consequence of the optimization perspective (6). An optimal (grammatical) representation is one that optimally satisfies the constraint ranking among those representations containing a given input. The existence of many different optimal representations is due to the existence of many different inputs. The FAITHFULNESS constraints tie the success of an output candidate to the shape of the corresponding input; each FAITHFULNESS constraint asserts that an input and its output should be identical in a certain respect. For example, the constraint called PARSE asserts that every segment of the input must appear in the output; it penalizes deletion of material in the input-output mapping. [The French input-output pair (/petit/, *pe.ti*) shows a violation of Parse.] Another constraint, known as Fill, penalizes insertion of new material that is not present in the input. Other constraints demand featural identity—one of these is violated when the English past-tense suffix *d* is pronounced *t*. As with all constraints in the universal set, these constraints are violable, and much grammar turns on resolving the tension between Structure constraints, which favor simple structures, and the Faithfulness constraints, which favor exact replication of the input, even at the cost of structural complexity.

As a general illustration of this relation, consider the confrontation between Parse and NoCoda, which must play out in every language. These constraints are in conflict, because one way to avoid a closed syllable (thereby satisfying NoCoda) is to delete any consonant that would appear in syllable-final position (thereby violating Parse, which forbids deletion). Consider first a grammar in which NoCoda dominates Parse, which we will write as NoCoda ≫ Parse. Syllabification is grammatically predictable, and therefore need not be present in the input. Suppose a hypothetical unsyllabified input word /batak/ is submitted to this grammar for syllabification and pronunciation. A large range of syllabified candidate outputs (pronunciations) is to be evaluated, among which we find the faithful *ba.tak*, and the progressively less faithful *ba.ta, bat, ba, b* and Ø [silence], as well as *a.tak, tak, ak*, and many, many others. Observe that a very wide range of candidate output options is considered; it is the universal constraint set, ranked, which handles the bulk of the selection task.

Which of these candidates is optimal, by the hierarchy NoCoda ≫ Parse? The faithful form *ba.tak*, which ends on a closed syllable, is ruled out by top-ranked NoCoda, because there are other competing output candidates that satisfy the constraint, lacking closed syllables. Among these, *ba.ta* is the most harmonic, because it involves the least violation of Parse—a single deletion. It is therefore the optimal output for the given input: The grammar certifies the input-output pair (/batak/, *ba.ta*) as well-formed; the final lexical *k* is unpronounced. The optimality computation just sketched can be represented conveniently in a constraint tableau as shown in Fig. 12.1A. (For the sake of expositional simplicity, we are ignoring candidate outputs like *ba.ta.ki*, in which new material—the vowel *i*—appears at the end, resulting in a form that also avoids closed syllables successfully. Dealing with such forms involves ranking the anti-insertion constraint Fill with respect to Parse; when Fill ≫ Parse, deletion rather than insertion is optimal.) We conclude that in a language where NoCoda ≫ Parse, all syllables must be open; for any output candidate with a closed syllable, there is always a better competitor that lacks it.

Consider now a grammar in which, contrariwise, we have Parse ≫ NoCoda (Fig. 12.1B). Given the input /batak/, we have exactly the same set of output candidates to consider, because the candidate set is determined by universal

A

/batak/		NoCoda	Parse
a	*ba.tak*	*!	
b ☞	*ba.ta*		*
c	*bat*	*!	* *
d	*ba*		* *! *

B

/batak/		Parse	NoCoda
a ☞	*ba.tak*		*
b	*ba.ta*	*!	
c	*bat*	*! *	*
d	*ba*	*! * *	

Figure 12.1

A constraint tableau in optimality theory. The table in (A) displays the optimality computation in graphic form. The input is listed at the head of the first column, and (selected) output candidates occupy the cells below it. The constraints in the hierarchy are listed in domination order left-to-right across the first row. Other rows show the evaluation of a candidate with respect to the constraint hierarchy. The hand points to the optimal candidate. An asterisk indicates a constraint violation; the number of asterisks in a cell corresponds to the number of times the constraint is violated; for example, there are three asterisks in the Parse cell of row (d) because the input-output pair (/batak/, *ba*) involves three instances on nonparsing or deletion of segments. The exclamation point marks a fatal violation—one that ensures suboptimal status. Cells after the fatal violation are shaded, indicating that success or failure on the constraint heading that column is irrelevant to the optimality status of the candidate, which has already been determined by a higher-ranked constraint. In this example, which recapitulates the discussion of the mini-grammar NoCoda ≫ Parse in the text, the interaction of just two constraints is depicted, and only a small sampling of the candidate set is shown. Given this ranking, the word /batak/ would be pronounced *bata*, as in the optimal candidate (b). Tableau B shows the effect of reranking; in a different language, in which Parse ≫ NoCoda, candidate (a) would be optimal; /batak/ would therefore be pronounced *batak*.

principles. But now the one violation of Parse in *ba.ta* is fatal; instead, its competitor *ba.tak*, which has no losses, will be optimal. (In the full analysis, we set Fill ≫ NoCoda as well, eliminating insertion as an option.) The dominance of the relevant Faithfulness constraints ensures that the input will be faithfully reproduced, even at the cost of violating the Structure constraint NoCoda. This language is therefore one like English in which syllables will have codas, if warranted by the input.

Domination is clearly "strict" in these examples: No matter how many consonant clusters appear in an input, and no matter how many consonants appear in any cluster, the first grammar will demand that they all be simplified by deletion (violating Parse as much as is required to eliminate the occasion for syllable codas), and the second grammar will demand that they all be syllabified (violating NoCoda as much as is necessary). No amount of failure on the violated constraints is rejected as excessive, as long as failure serves the cause of obtaining success on the dominating constraint.

Constraint interaction becomes far more intricate when crucial ranking goes to a depth of three or more; it is not unusual for optimal forms to contain violations of many constraints. Optimality-theoretic research in syllable structure expands both the set of relevant Structure constraints and the set of Faithfulness constraints that ban relevant disparities between input and output. The set of all possible rankings provides a restrictive typology of syllable structure patterns that closely matches the basic empirical findings in the area, and even refines prior classifications. Many other areas of phonology and syntax have been subject to detailed investigation under optimality theory (7). Here as elsewhere in cognitive science, progress has been accompanied by disputes at various levels, some technical, others concerning fundamental matters. The results obtained to date, however, provide considerable evidence that optimization ideas in general and optimality theory in particular can lead to significant advances in resolving the central problems of linguistic theory.

Optimality Theory and Neural Network Theory

The principal empirical questions addressed by optimality theory, as by other theories of universal grammar, concern the characterization of linguistic forms in and across languages. A quite different question is, can we explicate at least some of the properties of optimality theory itself on the basis of more fundamental cognitive principles? A significant first step toward such an explanation, we will argue, derives from the theory of computation in neural networks.

Linguistic research employing optimality theory does not, of course, involve explicit neural network modeling of language. The relation we seek to identify between optimality theory and neural computation must be of the type that holds between higher level and lower level systems of analysis in the physical sciences. For example, statistical mechanics explains significant parts of thermodynamics from the hypothesis that matter is composed of molecules, but the concepts of thermodynamic theory, like "temperature" and "entropy," involve no reference whatever to molecules. Like thermodynamics, optimality theory is a self-contained higher-level theory; like statistical mechanics, we claim, neural computation ought to explain fundamental principles of the higher level theory by deriving them as large-scale consequences of interactions at a much lower level. Just as probabilistic systems of point particles in statistical mechanics give rise to nonprobabilistic equations governing bulk continuous media in thermodynamics, so too should the numerical, continuous optimization in neural networks give rise to a qualitatively different formal system at a higher level of analysis: the nonnumerical optimization over discrete symbolic representations —the markedness calculus—of optimality theory.

To make contact with the abstract level at which mental organization like that of grammar resides, the relevant concepts of neural computation must capture rather high-level properties (8). Because of the complexity and nonlinearity of general neural network models, such concepts are in short supply; one of the few available is the method of Lyapunov functions. Such a function assigns a number to each possible global state of the dynamical system in such a way that as the system changes state over time, the value of the function continually increases. Lyapunov functions have been identified for a variety of model neural networks, and given various names, the term "energy function" being the most popular (9). We will use the term "harmony function" because the work we discuss follows most directly along the path initiated in harmony theory (10).

In the particular class of model neural networks admitting a harmony function, the input to a network computation consists of an activation pattern held fixed over part of the network. Activation then flows through the net to construct a pattern of activity that maximizes—optimizes—harmony, among all those patterns of activity that include the fixed input pattern. The harmony of a pattern of activation is a measure of its degree of conformity to the constraints implicit in the network's "synapses" or connections. As illustrated in Fig. 12.2, A to C, an inhibitory connection between two model "neurons" or "units," modeled as a negative weight, embodies a constraint that when one of the units is active, the other should be inactive; this is the activation configuration that maximizes harmony at that connection. An excitatory connection, modeled as a positive weight, embodies the constraint that when one of the units is active, the other should be active as well. In a complex, densely interconnected network of units, such constraints typically conflict; and connections with greater numerical magnitude embody constraints of greater importance to the outcome. A complete pattern of activation that maximizes harmony is one that optimally balances the typically conflicting demands of all the constraints in the network.

An activity pattern can be understood as a representation of the information that it constitutes; the harmony of any activity pattern measures the well-formedness of that representation with respect to the constraint-system embodied in the connection weights. For a fixed input, a harmony-maximizing network produces the output it does because that is the most well-formed representation containing the input. The knowledge contained in the network is the set of constraints embodied in its synaptic connections, or equivalently, the harmony function these constraints define. This knowledge can be used in different ways during processing, by fixing input activity in different parts of the network and then letting activation flow to maximize harmony (Fig. 12.2D).

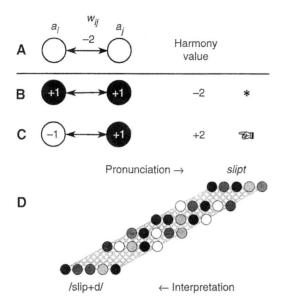

Figure 12.2

Harmony maximization in a neural network. The basic harmony function for a neural network is simply $H = \sum_{ij} a_i w_{ij} a_j$, where a_i is the activation of unit (abstract neuron) i and w_{ij} is the strength or weight of the connection to unit i from unit j. In (A), units i and j are connected with a weight of -2; this inhibitory connection constitutes a constraint that if one of these units is active, the other should be inactive. The microactivity pattern shown in (B) violates this constraint (marked with an asterisk): Both units have activity $+1$, and the constraint violation is registered in the negative harmony $a_i w_{ij} a_j = (+1)(-2)(+1) = -2$. The activity pattern in (C) satisfies the constraints, with harmony $+2$. Of these two micropatterns, the second maximizes harmony, as indicated by the hand. In a network containing many units, the harmony of a complete activity pattern is just the sum of all the micro-harmonies computed from each pair of connected units. In (D), a hypothetical network is depicted for relating English phonological inputs and outputs. The topmost units contain a pattern for the pronunciation *slipt* "slipped"; the units at the bottom host a pattern for the corresponding interpretation /slip+d/. In between, units support a pattern of activity representing the full linguistic structure, including syllables, stress feet, and so on. The connections in the network encode the constraints of English phonology. When the pattern for /slip+d/ is imposed on the lowest units, activation flows to maximize harmony, giving rise to the pattern for *slipt* on the uppermost units; this is production-directed processing. In comprehension, the pattern for *slipt* is imposed on the uppermost units, and harmony maximization fills in the rest of the total pattern, including the interpretation /slip+d/.

Because the harmony function for a neural network performs the same well-formedness-defining function as the symbol-sensitive mechanisms of grammar, it is natural to investigate harmony maximization as a means of defining linguistic grammars. In carrying out this program, two major problems arise: finding a suitable notion of optimization over linguistic structures; and finding a relation between this abstract measure and the numerical properties of neural computation. The second problem might seem sufficiently intractable to undermine the enterprise, no matter how the first is executed. Linguistic explanations depend crucially on representations that are complex hierarchical structures: Sentences are built of phrases nested one inside the other; words are constructed from features of sounds, grouped to form phonetic segments, themselves grouped to form syllables and still large units of prosodic structure. At first glance, the assumption that mental representations have such structure does not seem compatible with neural network models in which representations are patterns of activation—vectors, mere strings of numbers. But a family of interrelated techniques developed over the past decade show that patterns of activation can possess a precise mathematical analog of the structure of linguistic representations (11); the basic idea is illustrated in Fig. 12.3.

In this setting, the harmony of a linguistic structure is just the harmony of the pattern of activity realizing that structure. The connections in the network define which linguistic structures have maximal harmony—which are grammatical. This directly suggests the notion of a "harmonic grammar," a set of soft or violable constraints on combinations of linguistic elements, in which each constraint would have a numerical strength (12). This strength is the quantity by which the harmony of a linguistic representation is diminished when the constraint is violated; through an activation-passing computation implementing the harmony function, the strengths determine which constraints are respected, and to what degree, whenever there is conflict; a grammatical structure is then one that best satisfies the total set of constraints defining the grammar, that is, has maximal harmony.

This conception is straightforward, but obviously incomplete, for it is far from true that every weighting of the set of linguistic constraints produces a possible human language. To delimit the optimizing function narrowly enough, the strength relation between constraints must be severely regimented. And this is exactly what strict domination provides: In optimality theory, no amount of success on weaker constraints can compensate for failure on a stronger one. This corresponds to the numerical strength of a constraint being much greater than the strengths of those constraints ranked lower than it in the hierarchy; so much so that the combined force of all the lower-ranked constraints can never exceed the force of the higher-ranked constraint. But as we have seen, strict domination means constraint interaction in grammar is highly restricted: Only the relative ranking of constraints, and not particular numerical strengths, can be grammatically relevant. The grammatical consequence is that, in many cases

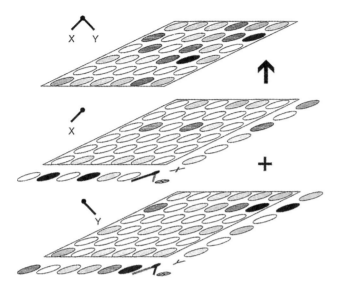

Figure 12.3
Realizing structured representations as patterns of activity in neural networks. The top plane shows a pattern of activity **p** realizing the structure $\overset{\wedge}{X\ Y}$ (for example, a sentence in which X is the noun-phrase subject *big dogs* and Y a verb-phrase predicate *bite*); gray levels schematically indicate the activity levels of units in a neural network (circles). This pattern is produced by superimposing a pattern **x** realizing X in the left position (middle plane) on another pattern **y** realizing Y in the right position (bottom plane). Within the middle plane, the pattern **x** is a pattern **X** for X (right edge) times a pattern **p′** for "left position" (bottom edge). The product operation here is the tensor product: In **x**, the activity level of the unit in row i and column j is just the activation of unit i in **X** times the activation of unit j in **p′**; and analogously for pattern **y**. Algebraically:

$$\mathbf{p} = \mathbf{x} + \mathbf{y}; \quad \mathbf{x} = \mathbf{p}' \otimes \mathbf{X}; \quad \mathbf{y} = \mathbf{p}' \otimes \mathbf{Y}; \quad (\mathbf{x})_{ij} = (\mathbf{p}')_i (\mathbf{X})_j; \quad (\mathbf{y})_{ij} = (\mathbf{p}')_i (\mathbf{Y})_j$$

Because tensor products may be nested one inside the other, patterns may realize structures embedded in other structures. Through simple neural network operations, massively parallel structure manipulation may be performed on such patterns.

studied to date, the set of all rankings delimits a narrow typology of possible linguistic patterns and relations.

That strict domination governs grammatical constraint interaction is not currently explained by principles of neural computation; nor do these principles explain the universality of constraints that is central to optimality theory and related approaches. These are stimulating challenges for fully integrating optimality theory with a neural foundation. But the hypothesis that grammar is realized in a harmony-maximizing neural network rationalizes a significant set of crucial characteristics of optimality theory: Grammaticality is optimality; competition for optimality is restricted to representations containing the input; complexity arises through the interaction of simple constraints, rather than within the constraints themselves; constraints are violable and gradiently satis-fiable; constraints are highly conflicting; conflict is adjudicated via a notion of relative strength; a grammar is a set of relative strengths; learning a grammar is adjusting these strengths. OT's markedness calculus is exactly neural network optimization, specialized to the case of strict domination.

If the hypothesis that grammar is realized in a harmony-maximizing neural network is correct, we would expect that it would lead to new developments in optimality theory. We now turn to recent work.

Linguistic Knowledge and Its Use

Just as a numerically valued harmony function orders the activity patterns in a model neural network from highest to lowest harmony, the ranking of con-straints of an optimality theoretic grammar orders linguistic structures from most to least harmonic: from those that best to those that least satisfy the con-straint hierarchy. It is the constraint ranking and the ordering of structures it provides that is OT's characterization of knowledge of grammar.

Using this knowledge involves finding the structures that maximize har-mony, and this can be done in several ways (13), directly following the lead of the corresponding neural network approach of Fig. 12.3. Use of grammatical knowledge for comprehending language involves taking the pronunciation of, say, a sentence, and finding the maximal-harmony linguistic structure with that pronunciation. This structure groups the given words into nested phrases, and fills in implied connections between words, such as the possible interpretive link between *John* and *him* in *John hopes George admires him* (him = John), and the necessary anti-link in *John admires him* (him John). The maximum-harmony structure projected from the pronounced sentence by the grammar plays an important role in determining its meaning.

Producing a sentence is a different use of the very same grammatical knowl-edge. Now the competition is among structures that differ in pronunciation, but share a given interpretation. The ordering of structures from most to least har-monic constitutes grammatical knowledge that is separate from its use, via optimization, in comprehension and production; this is depicted schematically in Fig. 12.4.

This view leads to a new perspective on a classic problem in child language. It is well known that, broadly speaking, young children's linguistic abilities in comprehension greatly exceed their abilities in production. Observe that this is a richer problem than many perception-action disparities—for example, we can recognize a violin without being able to play one—because real language com-prehension requires sophisticated grammatical knowledge. In many cases, both the comprehension and production abilities can be captured by grammars, the "comprehension grammar" being closer to the adults' than is the "production grammar." Yet a grammar is usually seen as a characterization of linguistic

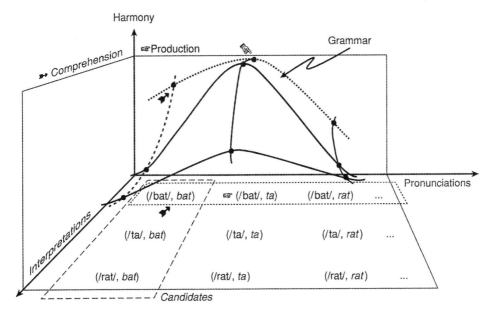

Figure 12.4
Knowledge of versus use of grammar in optimality theory. The pair (/bat/, *ta*) represents a structure in which the lexical item /bat/ is simplified and pronounced *ta*. The horizontal plane contains all such structures, and the vertical axis shows the relative harmony of each structure, and ordinal rather than a numerical scale. This harmony surface schematically depicts a young child's knowledge of grammar; STRUCTURE dominates FAITHFULNESS. This knowledge can be used by optimization in two ways. In the production of "bat," the row of structures containing /bat/ compete (dotted box); the maximum-harmony structure best-satisfies top-ranked STRUCTURE with the simplified pronunciation *ta* (peak of the dotted curve): this is marked ☞. In comprehension, the pronunciation *bat* is given, and competition is between the column of structures containing *bat* (dashed box). Because these are all pronounced *bat*, they tie with respect to STRUCTURE, so lower-ranked FAITHFULNESS determines the maximum-harmony structure to be (/bat/, *bat*), marked with ➻ (peak of the dashed curve). Correct comprehension results from the same grammar that gives incorrect—simplified—production.

competence independent of the cognitive factors involved in language use—so how can a child have two grammars, one for each type of use?

Optimality theory provides a conceptual resolution of this dilemma (14). The child has only one grammar (constraint ranking) at a given time, a grammar that is evolving toward the adult grammar by reranking of constraints. Early child grammars have an interesting property: When used for production, only the simplest linguistic structures are produced. But when used for comprehension, the same grammar allows the child to cope rather well with structures much more complex than those they can produce.

The reason is essentially this. In early child grammars, STRUCTURE constraints outrank FAITHFULNESS constraints. In production, the input is an interpretation, and what competes are different pronunciations of the given interpretation. The winner is a structure that sacrifices faithfulness to the input in order to satisfy STRUCTURE: This is a structure simpler than the corresponding adult pronunciation. (In the example of Fig. 12.4, the word /bat/ is simplified to *ta*.) But during comprehension, the competition is defined differently: It is between structures that all share the given adult pronunciation, which is fixed and immutable, under the comprehension regime, as the input to the grammar. These competitors are all heavy violators of STRUCTURE, but they tie in this respect; so the STRUCTURE constraints do not decide among them. The winner must then be decided by lower-ranked FAITHFULNESS constraints. (Thus in Fig. 12.4, the adult pronunciation *bat* is correctly comprehended as the word /bat/ even though the child's own pronunciation of /bat/ is *ta*.) Thus, production is quite "unfaithful" to adult language because FAITHFULNESS constraints are out-voted by the dominant STRUCTURE constraints. But comprehension is more "faithful" to adult language because the crucial unfaithful candidates are simply out of the competition; they do not have the given (adult) pronunciation, which is held fixed in the comprehension regime as the input to the grammar. That two such different outcomes can arise from one and the same constraint ranking is a typical effect of optimization in optimality theory: Constraints that are decisive in some competitions (STRUCTURE during production) fail to decide in other competitions (comprehension), depending on the character of the candidate set being evaluated, which allows lower-ranked constraints (FAITHFULNESS) to then determine the optimal structure.

This result resolves several related difficulties of two previous conceptions of child language. In the first, a grammar is a set of rules for sequentially transforming structures, ultimately producing the correct pronunciation of a given expression. This conception fails to adequately separate knowledge and use of grammar, so that a set of rules producing correct pronunciations is incapable of operating in the reverse direction, comprehension, transforming a pronunciation into an interpretation. (Even if the rule system could be inverted, children's "unfaithful production" and relatively "faithful comprehension" are simply not inverses of one another—the challenge is to provide a principled account for this divergence with a single grammar.) Furthermore, child grammars in this conception are typically considerably more complex than adult grammars, because many more transformations must be made in order to produce the "unfaithful" distortions characteristic of child productions.

In the second nonoptimization-based conception, a grammar is a set of inviolable constraints: A structure that violates any one of the constraints is ipso facto ungrammatical. Languages differ in the values of certain "parameters" that modify the content or applicability of constraints. Thus the gap between child linguistic production and comprehension must be seen as resulting from two different sets of parameters, one for each type of use. Again, this fails to separate knowledge from use of grammar, and fails to provide any principled link between production and comprehension. By contrast, conceiving of grammar as optimization provides a natural distinction between use and knowledge of language, in such a way that a single grammar naturally provides relatively "faithful" comprehension at the same time as relatively "unfaithful" production.

The optimization perspective also offers a principled approach to a vexing fundamental problem in grammar learning. The constraints of a grammar refer to many "hidden" properties of linguistic structures, properties that are not directly observable in the data available for learning a language. For example, the way that words are grouped into nested syntactic phrases, or sounds grouped into prosodic constituents, is largely unobservable (or only ambiguously and inconsistently reflected in observables), and yet can differ from language to language. Learning a grammar requires access to this hidden linguistic structure, so that the grammar may be adjusted to conform to the configurations of hidden structure characteristic of the language being learned. But the hidden structure itself must be inferred from prior knowledge of the grammar: It cannot be directly observed.

Within optimality theory, these coupled problems can be solved by successive approximation, as in related optimization problems outside grammar. The learner starts with an initial grammar (indeed, the early child grammar mentioned above). This grammar is used in the "comprehension direction" to impute hidden structure to the pronounced data of the target language. This hidden structure will initially be in error, because the grammar is not yet correct, but this structure can nonetheless be used to adjust the grammar so that, in the production direction, it outputs the inferred structures. With this revised grammar, the process continues with new learning data. As the grammar gets closer to the correct one, the hidden structure it assigns to learning data gets closer to the correct structure. While there are as yet no mathematical results demonstrating the success of this incremental learning method under general conditions, it has proved quite effective in related optimization problems such as speech recognition (15), and quite successful in preliminary computer simulation studies of optimality theory grammar learning (16).

The central subproblem of this incremental learning strategy is this: Given learning data including hidden structure (inferred on the basis of the current grammar), how can the grammar be improved? Here OT's optimization characterization of universal grammar provides considerable power. The grammars of human languages differ, according to the core hypothesis of optimality theory, only in the way they rank the universal constraints. Thus improving a grammar requires only reranking the constraints. Given a grammatical structure from the language to be learned, there is a straightforward way to minimally rerank constraints to make that structure optimal, hence grammatical, in the revised grammar. And this procedure can be proved to efficiently converge on a correct grammar, when one exists. "Efficient" here means that, even though there are $n!$ different constraint rankings of n universal constraints, no more than $n(n-1)$ informative learning examples are needed to converge on the correct ranking (17). Corresponding results are not available within alternative general theories of how human grammars may differ; this is an indication of the learnability advantage arising from the highly structured nature of OT's optimization characterization of universal grammar.

Will the connection between optimization in grammatical theory and optimization in neural networks lead to further progress at either level of cognitive theory? Will other theoretical connections between the sciences of the brain and of the mind prove fruitful? Of course, only time will tell. But we believe there is already in place a significant body of evidence that even a single high-level property of neural computation, properly treated, can yield a surprisingly rich set of new insights into even the most well-studied and abstract of symbol-processing cognitive sciences, the theory of grammar (18).

References and Notes

1. Basic work on this phenomenon in neural network models, and critiques, include D. E. Rumelhart and J. L. McClelland, in *Parallel Distributed Processing: Explorations in the Microstructure of Cognition, Volume 2: Psychological and Biological Models*, J. L. McClelland, D. E. Rumelhart, PDP Research Group, Eds. (MIT Press/Bradford Books, Cambridge, MA, 1986), pp. 216–271; S. Pinker and J. Mehler, Eds., *Connections and Symbols* (MIT Press. Cambridge, MA, 1988).

2. A. Prince and P. Smolensky, *Notes on Connectionism and Harmony Theory in Linguistics*. (Technical Report, Department of Computer Science, University of Colorado, Boulder, CO, 1991); *Optimality Theory: Constraint Interaction in Generative Grammar* (Technical Report, Rutgers Center for Cognitive Science, Rutgers University, New Brunswick, NJ and Department of Computer Science, University of Colorado, Boulder, CO, 1993; also Linguistic Inquiry Monograph Series, MIT Press, Cambridge, MA, to appear); J. McCarthy and A. Prince. *Prosodic Morphology I* (Technical Report RuCCS-TR-3, Rutgers Center for Cognitive Science, Rutgers University, New Brunswick, NJ, 1993); also Linguistic Inquiry Monograph Series, MIT Press, Cambridge, MA, to appear); J. McCarthy and A. Prince, in *Yearbook of Morphology 1993*, G. Booij and J. van Marle, Eds. (Kluwer, Boston, 1993), pp. 79–153. These are a few of the basic references for optimality theory, addressing primarily phonology. The following basic works address syntax, including the topics mentioned in the text: J. Grimshaw, *Linguist. Inq.*, in press; V. Samek-Lodovici, thesis. Rutgers University, New Brunswick, NJ (1996), G. Legendre, P. Smolensky, C. Wilson, in *Is the Best Good Enough? Proceedings of the Workshop on Optimality in Syntax*, P. Barbosa, D. Fox, P. Hagstrom, M. McGinnis, D. Pesetsky, Eds. (MIT Press and MIT Working Papers in Linguistics, Cambridge, MA, in press). These and many other optimality theory papers may be accessed electronically [see (7)].

3. Selected basic sources: Formal universalism: N. Chomsky, *Aspects of the Theory of Syntax* (MIT Press, Cambridge, MA, 1965); ——— and M. Halle, *The Sound Pattern of English* (Harper and Row, New York, 1968). Substantive process and product universalism: D. Stampe, *A Dissertation on Natural Phonology* (Garland, New York, 1979); D. Perlmutter, Ed., *Studies in Relational Grammar 1* (Univ. of Chicago Press, Chicago, 1983). Constraints across rules: C. Kisseberth, *Linguist. Inq.* 1, 291 (1970); N. Chomsky, *Lectures on Government and Binding* (Foris, Dordrecht, Netherlands, 1981), Markedness and informal optimization: J. Goldsmith, Ed., *The Last Phonological Rule* (Univ. of Chicago Press, Chicago, 1993); D. Archangeli and D. Pulleyblank, *Grounded Pho-*

nology (MIT Press, Cambridge, MA, 1994); L. Burzio, *Principles of English Stress* (Cambridge Univ. Press, New York, 1994); N. Chomsky, *The Minimalist Program* (MIT Press, Cambridge, MA, 1995). Output orientation: D. Perlmutter. *Deep and Surface Structure Constraints in Syntax* (Holt, Reinhart, and Winston, New York, 1971); J. Bybee and D. Slobin, *Language* 58, 265 (1982); J. McCarthy and A. Prince, *Prosodic Morphology 1986* (Technical Report RuCCS-TR-32. Rutgers Center for Cognitive Science, Rutgers University, New Brunswick, NJ, 1986/1996).

4. R. Jakobson, *Selected Writings I* (Mouton, The Hague, 1962); N. Trubetzkoy, *Grundzüge der Phonologie* (1939; translation: *Principles of Phonology*, Univ. of California Press, Berkeley, CA, 1969); N. Chomsky and M. Halle, *The Sound Pattern of English* (Harper and Row, New York, 1968), chapter 9.

5. For details, see B. Tranel, *French Liaison and Elision Revisited: A Unified Account Within Optimality Theory* (ROA-15, http://ruccs.rutgers.edu/roa.html, 1994).

6. For significant extensions of FAITHFULNESS within optimality theory, see J. McCarthy and A. Prince, in *The Prosody-Morphology Interface*, R. Kager, W. Zonneveld, H. van der Huist, Eds. (Blackwell, Oxford, UK, in press); L. Benua, in *Papers in Optimality Theory*. J. Beckman, L. Walsh Dickey, S. Urbanczyk, Eds. (Linguistics Department, Univ. of Massachusetts, Amherst, MA, 1995), pp. 77–136.

7. Examples include segmental repertories, stress patterns, vowel harmony, tonology, reduplicative and templatic morphology, syntax-phonology and morphology-phonology relations, case and voice patterns, principles of question formation, interaction of syntactic movement and clause patterns, structure of verbal complexes, order and repertory of clitic elements, the interaction between focus and the placement and retention of pronominal elements, the interpretation of anaphoric relations, the nature of constraints like the obligatory contour principle, and the compatibility of related grammatical processes. Readers interested in pursuing any of these topics may consult the Rutgers Optimality Archive at http://ruccs.rutgers.edu/roa.html, which includes many papers and an extensive bibliography.

8. P. Smolensky, *Behav. Brain Sci.* 11, 1 (1988); S. Pinker and A. Prince, *Cognition* 28, 73 (1988); M. McCloskey, *Psychol. Sci.* 2, 387 (1991); A. Prince, *in Defense of the Number i: Anatomy of a Linear Dynamical Model of Linguistic Generalizations* (Technical Report RuCCS-TR-1, Rutgers Center for Cognitive Science, Rutgers University, New Brunswick NJ, 1993).

9. J. J. Hopfield, *Proc. Natl. Acad. Sci. U.S.A.* 79, 2554 (1982); M. A Cohen and S. Grossberg. *IEEE Trans. Syst. Man Cybernet.* 13, 815 (1983); P. Smolensky, *Proc. Natl. Conf. Artif, Intell. AAAI-83*, 378 (1983); G. E. Hinton and T. J. Sejnowski, *Proceedings of the IEEE Computer Society Conference on Computer Vision and Pattern Recognition* (1983), p. 448; J. J. Hopfield, *Proc. Natl. Acad. Sci. U.S.A.* 81, 3088 (1984); R. M. Golden, *Biol. Cybernet.* 59, 109 (1988). For recent review articles, see M. W. Hirsch, in *Mathematical Perspectives on Neural Networks*, P. Smolensky, M. C. Mozer, D. E. Rumelhart, Eds. (LEA Mahwah, NJ, 1996), pp. 271–323; P. Smolensky, in ibid., pp. 245–270.

10. P. Smolensky, in *Parallel Distributed Processing: Explorations in the Microstructure of Cognition. Volume 1: Foundations.* D. E. Rumelhart, J. L. McClelland PDP Research Group. Eds. (MIT Press/ Bradford Books, Cambridge, MA, 1986), pp. 194–281.

11. R. Pike, *Psychol. Rev.* 9, 281 (1984); C. P. Dolan, thesis. University of California, Los Angeles (1989); —— and P. Smolensky, *Connection Sci.* 1, 53 (1989); P. Smolensky, *Artif, Intell.* 46, 159 (1990); T. Plate, thesis, University to Toronto (1994).

12. G. Legendre, Y. Miyata, P. Smolensky, *Proc. Annu. Conf. Cognit. Sci. Soc.* 12, 388 (1990); *ibid.*, p. 884.

13. B. Tesar and P. Smolensky, *Linguist. Inq.*, in press: *Learnability in Optimality Theory* (Technical Report. Cognitive Science Department, Johns Hopkins University, Baltimore, MD, 1996).

14. P. Smolensky, *Linguist. Inq.* 27, 720 (1996).

15. L. E. Baum and T. Petrie, *Ann. Math. Stat.* 37, 1559 (1966); L. R. Bahl, F. Jelinek, R. L. Mercer, *IEEE Trans. Pattern Anal. Mach. Intell.* PAMI-5 (1983), pp. 179–190. For recent review articles, see A. Nadas and R. L. Mercer, in *Mathematical Perspectives on Neural Networks*, P. Smolensky, M. C.

Mozer, D. E. Rumelhart, Eds. (LEA, Mahwah, NJ, 1996), pp. 603–650; P. Smolensky, in *ibid.*, pp. 453–494.

16. B. Tesar, *Lingua*, in press.
17. References in (13) and B. Tesar and P. Smolensky. *The Learnability of Optimality Theory: An Algorithm and Some Basic Complexity Results* (Technical Report, Department of Computer Science, University of Colorado, Boulder, CO, 1993).
18. As indicated in the cited publications, much of the work discussed here was carried out jointly with our collaborators G. Legendre, J. McCarthy, and B. Tesar: we are grateful to them and to our colleagues L. Burzio, R. Frank, J. Grimshaw, and C. Wilson for stimulating conversations and invaluable contributions. For support of the work presented here, we acknowledge a Guggenheim Fellowship, the Johns Hopkins Center for Language and Speech Processing, and NSF grants BS-9209265 and IRI-9213894.

Part II
Case Studies in Cognitive Modeling

Perceptual Recognition

Chapter 13

Dynamic Binding in a Neural Network for Shape Recognition

John E. Hummel and Irving Biederman

A brief glance at Figure 13.1 is sufficient to determine that it depicts three views of the same object. The perceived equivalence of the object across its views evidences the fundamental capacity of human visual recognition: Object recognition is invariant with viewpoint. That is, the perceived shape of an object does not vary with position in the visual field, size, or, in general, orientation in depth. The object in Figure 13.1 is unfamiliar, so the ability to activate a viewpoint invariant representation of its shape cannot depend on prior experience with it. This capacity for viewpoint invariance independent of object familiarity is so fundamental to visual shape classification that modeling visual recognition is largely a problem of accounting for it.[1]

This chapter presents a neural network model of viewpoint invariant visual recognition. In contrast with previous models based primarily on template or feature list matching, we argue that human recognition performance reflects the activation of a viewpoint invariant structural description specifying both the visual attributes of an object (e.g., edges, vertices, or parts) and the relations among them. For example, the simple object in Figure 13.1 might be represented as a vertical cone on top of a horizontal brick. Such a representation must bind (i.e., conjoin) the shape attribute *cone shaped* with the relational attribute *on top of* and the attribute *brick shaped* with the attribute *below*; otherwise, it would not specify which volume was on top of which. It is also necessary to use the same representation for *cone shaped* whether the cone is on top of a brick, below a cylinder, or by itself in the image otherwise the representation would not specify that it was the same shape each time. Traditional connectionist/neural net architectures cannot represent structural descriptions because they bind attributes by positing separate units for each conjunction (cf. Fodor & Pylyshyn, 1988). The units used to represent *cone shaped* would differ depending on whether the cone was on top of a brick, below a cylinder, or instantiated in some other relation. Representing structural descriptions in a connectionist architecture requires a mechanism for binding attributes dynamically; that is, the binding of attributes must be temporary so that the same units can be used in multiple conjunctions. A primary theoretical goal of this chapter is to describe how this dynamic binding can be achieved.

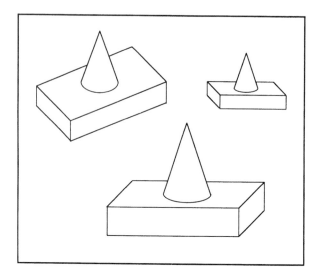

Figure 13.1
This object is readily detectable as constant across the three views despite its being unfamiliar.

Structural Description

A *structural description* (Winston, 1975) explicitly represents objects as configurations of attributes (typically parts) in specified relations to one another. For example, a structural description of the object in Figure 13.1 might consist of *vertical cone on top of horizontal brick*. Structural description models avoid the pitfalls of the implicit relations continuum: They are sensitive to attribute structures, but because they represent the relations among those attributes, they are not prone to illusory recognition. These models can also provide a natural account of the fundamental characteristics of human recognition. Provided the elements of the structural description are invariant with viewpoint, recognition on the basis of that description will also be invariant with viewpoint. Provided the description can be activated bottom up on the basis of information in the 2-D image, the luxury of viewpoint invariance will be enjoyed for unfamiliar objects as well as familiar ones.

Proposing that object recognition operates on the basis of viewpoint-invariant structural descriptions allows us to understand phenomena that extant template and feature theories cannot handle. However, it is necessary to address how the visual system could possibly derive a structural description in the first place. This article presents an explicit theory, implemented as a connectionist network, of the processes and representations implicated in the derivation of viewpoint-invariant structural descriptions for object recognition. The point of departure for this effort is Biederman's (1987) theory of recognition by components (RBC). RBC states that objects are recognized as configurations of simple, primitive volumes called *geons* in specified relations with one another. Geons are recognized from 2-D viewpoint-invariant[2] properties of image contours such as whether a contour is straight or curved, whether a pair of contours is parallel or nonparallel, and what type of vertex is produced where contours coterminate. The geons derived from these 2-D contrasts are defined in terms of viewpoint-invariant 3-D contrasts such as whether the cross-section is straight (like that of a brick or a pyramid) or curved (like that of a cylinder or a cone) and whether the sides are parallel (like those of a brick) or nonparallel (like those of a wedge).

Whereas a template representation necessarily commits the theorist to a coordinate space, 2-D or 3-D, the structural description theory proposed here does not. This is important to note because structural descriptions have been criticized for assuming a metrically specified representation in a 3-D object-centered coordinate space. Failing to find evidence for 3-D invariant recognition for some unfamiliar objects, such as crumpled paper (Rock & DiVita, 1987), bent wires (Edelman & Weinshall, 1991; Rock & DiVita, 1987), and rectilinear arrangements of bricks (Tarr & Pinker, 1989), some researchers have rejected structural description theories in favor of representations based on multiple 2-D views. But the wholesale rejection of structural descriptions on the basis of such data is unwarranted. RBC (and the implementation proposed here) predict these results. Because a collection of similarly bent wires, for example, tend not to activate distinctive viewpoint-invariant structural descriptions that allow one wire to be distinguished from the other wires in the experiment, such objects should be difficult to recognize from an arbitrary viewpoint.

Connectionist Representation and Structural Description: The Binding Problem

Given a line drawing of an object, the goal of the current model is to activate a viewpoint-invariant structural description[3] of the object and then use that description as the basis for recognition. Structural descriptions are particularly challenging to represent in connectionist architectures because of the binding problem. *Binding* refers to the representation of attribute conjunctions (Feldman, 1982; Feldman & Ballard, 1982; Hinton, McClelland, & Rumelhart, 1986; Sejnowski, 1986; Smolensky, 1987; von der Malsburg, 1981). Recall that a structural description of the nonsense object in Figure 13.1 must specify that *vertical* and *on top of* are bound with *cone shaped*, whereas *horizontal* and *below* are bound with *brick shaped*. This problem is directly analogous to the problem encountered by the feature matching models: Given that some set of attributes is present in the system's input, how can it represent whether they are in the proper configuration to define a given object?

The predominant class of solutions to this problem is conjunctive coding (Hinton et al., 1986) and its relatives, such as tensor product coding (Smolensky, 1987), and the interunits of Feldman's (1982) dynamic connections network.

A conjunctive representation anticipates attribute conjunctions and allocates a separate unit or pattern for each. For example, a conjunctive representation for the previously mentioned shape attributes would posit one pattern for *vertical cone on top of* and completely separate patterns for *horizontal cone on top of*, *horizontal cone below*, and so forth. A fully *local* conjunctive representation (i.e., one in which each conjunction is coded by a single unit) can provide an unambiguous solution to the binding problem: On the basis of which units are active, it is possible to know exactly how the attributes are conjoined in the system's input. *Vertical cone on top of horizontal brick* and *vertical brick on top of horizontal cone* would activate nonoverlapping sets of units. However, local conjunctive representations suffer a number of shortcomings.

The most apparent difficulty with local conjunctive representations is the number of units they require: The size of such a representation grows exponentially with the number of attribute dimensions to be represented (e.g., 10 dimensions, each with 5 values would require 5^{10} units). As such, the number of units required to represent the universe of possible conjunctions can be prohibitive for complex representations. Moreover, the units have to be specified in advance, and most of them will go unused most of the time. However, from the perspective of representing structural descriptions, the most serious problem with local conjunctive representations is their insensitivity to attribute structures. Like a template, a local conjunctive unit responds to a specific conjunction of attributes in an all-or-none fashion, with different conjunctions activating different units. The similarity in shape between, say, a cone that is on top of something and a cone that is beneath something is lost in such a representation.

These difficulties with local conjunctive representations will not come as a surprise to many readers. In defense of conjunctive coding, one may reasonably protest that a fully local conjunctive representation represents the worst case, both in terms of the number of units required and in terms of the loss of attribute structures. Both these problems can be attenuated considerably by using coarse coding and other techniques for distributing the representation of an entity over several units (Feldman, 1982; Hinton et al., 1986; Smolensky, 1987). However, in the absence of a technique for representing attribute bindings, distributed representations are subject to cross talk (i.e., mutual interference among independent patterns), the likelihood of which increases with the extent of distribution. Specifically, when multiple entities are represented simultaneously, the likelihood that the units representing one entity will be confused with the units representing another grows with the proportion of the network used to represent each entity. von der Malsburg (1987) referred to this familiar manifestation of the binding problem as the *superposition catastrophe*. Thus, the costs of a conjunctive representation can be reduced by using a distributed representation, but without alternative provisions for binding the benefits are also reduced.

This tradeoff between unambiguous binding and distributed representation is the connectionist's version of the implicit relations continuum. In this case, however, the relations that are coded implicitly (i.e., in the responses of conjunctive units) are binding relations. Escaping this continuum requires a way to represent bindings dynamically. That is, we need a way to temporarily and explicitly bind independent units when the attributes for which they code occur in conjunction.

Recently, there has been considerable interest in the use of temporal synchrony as a potential solution to this problem. The basic idea, proposed as early as 1974 by Peter Milner (Milner, 1974), is that conjunctions of attributes can be represented by synchronizing the outputs of the units (or cells) representing those attributes. To represent that Attribute A is bound to Attribute B and Attribute C to Attribute D, the cells for A and B fire in synchrony, the cells for C and D fire in synchrony, and the AB set fires out of synchrony with the CD set. This suggestion has since been presented more formally by von der Malsburg (1981, 1987) and many others (Abeles, 1982; Atiya & Baldi, 1989; Baldi & Meir, 1990; Crick, 1984; Crick & Koch, 1990; Eckhorn et al., 1988; Eckhorn, Reitboeck, Arndt, & Dicke, 1990; Gray et al., 1989; Gray & Singer, 1989; Grossberg & Somers, 1991; Hummel & Biederman, 1990a; Shastri & Ajjanagadde, 1990; Strong & Whitehead, 1989; Wang, Buhmann, & von der Malsburg, 1991).

Dynamic binding has particularly important implications for the task of structural description because it makes it possible to bind the elements of a distributed representation. What is critical about the use of synchrony in this capacity is that it provides a degree of freedom whereby multiple independent cells can specify that the attributes to which they respond are currently bound. In principle, any variable could serve this purpose (e.g., Lange & Dyer, 1989, used signature activations), so the use of synchrony, per se, is not theoretically critical. Temporal synchrony simply seems a natural choice because it is easy to establish, easy to exploit, and neurologically plausible.

This article presents an original proposal for exploiting synchrony to bind shape and relation attributes into structural descriptions. Specialized connections in the model's first two layers parse images into geons by synchronizing the oscillatory outputs of cells representing local image features (edges and vertices): Cells oscillate in phase if they represent features of the same geon and out of phase if they represent features of separate geons. These phase relations are preserved throughout the network and bind cells representing the attributes of geons and the relations among them. The bound attributes and relations constitute a simple viewpoint-invariant structural description of an object. The model's highest layers use this description as a basis for object recognition.

The model described here is broad in scope, and we have made only modest attempts to optimize any of its individual components. Rather, the primary theoretical statement concerns the general nature of the representations and processes implicated in the activation of viewpoint-invariant structural

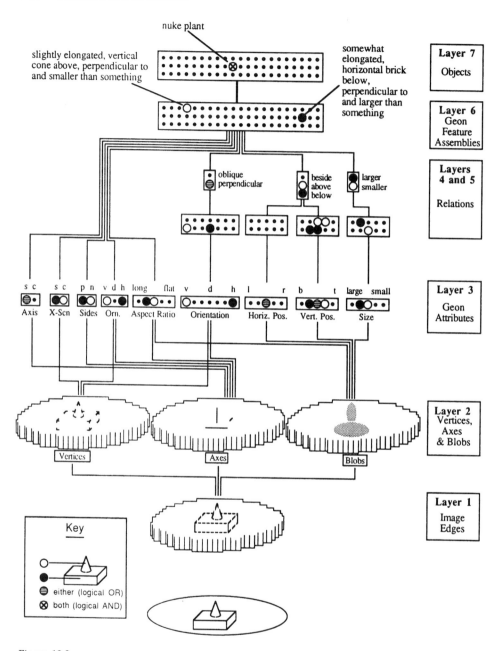

Figure 13.2

An overview of JIM's architecture indicating the representation activated at each layer by the image in the Key. (In Layers 3 and above, large circles indicate cells activated in response to the image, and dots indicate inactive cells. Cells in Layer 1 represent the edges (specifying discontinuties in surface descriptions for real-time object recognition. We have designed these representations and processes to have a transparent neural analogy, but we make no claims as to their strict neural realism.

A Neural Net Model of Shape Recognition

Overview

The model (JIM; John and Irv's model) is a seven-layer connectionist network that takes as input a representation of a line drawing of an object (specifying discontinuities in surface orientation and depth) and, as output, activates a unit representing the identity of the object. The model achieves viewpoint invariance in that the same output unit will respond to an object regardless of where its image appears in the visual field, the size of the image, and the orientation in depth from which the object is depicted. An overview of the model's architecture is shown in Figure 13.2. JIM's first layer (L1) is a mosaic of orientation-tuned cells with overlapping receptive fields. The second layer (L2) is a mosaic of cells that respond to vertices, 2-D axes of symmetry, and oriented, elongated blobs of activity. Cells in L1 and L2 group themselves into sets describing geons by synchronizing oscillations in their outputs.

Cells in L3 respond to attributes of complete geons, each cell representing a single value on a single dimension over which the geons can vary. For example, the shape of a geon's major axis (straight or curved) is represented in one bank of cells, and the geon's location is represented in another, thereby allowing the representation of the geon's axis to remain unchanged when the geon is moved in the visual field. The fourth and fifth layers (L4 and L5) determine the relations among the geons in an image. The L4–L5 module receives input from L3 cells representing the metric properties of geons (location in the visual field, size, and orientation). Once active, units representing relations are bound to the geons they describe by the same phase locking that binds image features together for geon recognition. The output of L3 and L5 together constitute a structural description of an object in terms of its geons and their relations. This representation is invariant with scale, translation, and orientation in depth.

orientation and depth) in an object's image. Layer 2 represents the vertices, axes, and blobs defined by conjunctions of edges in Layer 1. Layer 3 represents the geons in an image in terms of their defining dimentions: Axis shape (Axis), straight (s) or curved (c); Cross-section shape (X-son) straight or curved; whether the sides are parallel (p) or nonparallel (n); Coarse orientation (Orn.), vertical (v), diagonal (d), or horizontal (h); aspect ratio, elongated (long) to flattened (flat); Fine orientation (Orientation), vertical, two different diagonals, and four different horinzontals; Horizontals position (Horiz. Pos.) in the visual field, left (l) to right (r); Vertical position in the visual field, bottom (b) to top (t); and size, small (near 0% of the visual field) to large (near 100% of the visual field). Layers 4 and 5 represent the relative orientations, locations, and sizes of the geons in an image. Cells in Layer 6 respond to specific conjuntions of cells activated in Layers 3 and 5, cells in Layer 7 respond to complete objects, defined as conjunctions of cells in Layer 6.)

The model's first layer is
divided into 22 X 22 locations.

At each location there are
48 cells.

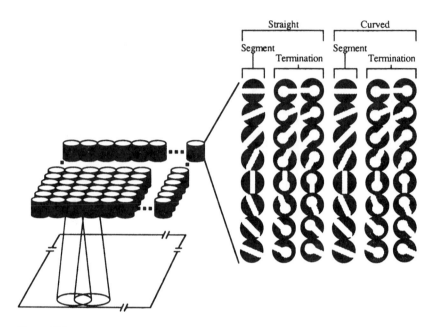

Figure 13.3
Detail of the model's first layer. (Image edges are represented in terms of their location in the visual field, orientation, curvature, and whether they terminate within the cell's receptive field or pass through it.)

The model's sixth layer (L6) takes its input from both the third and fifth layers. On a single time slice (ts), the input to L6 is a pattern of activation describing one geon and its relations to the other geons in the image (a *geon feature assembly*). Each cell in L6 responds to a particular geon feature assembly. The cells in L7 sum the outputs of the L6 cells over time, combining two or more assemblies into a representation of a complete object.

Layer 1: Representation of a Line Drawing
The model's input layer (L1) is a mosaic of orientation-tuned cells with over-lapping receptive fields (Figures 13.3 and 13.4). At each of 484 (22 × 22) locations,[4] there are 48 cells that respond to image edges in terms of their orientation, curvature (straight vs. curved), and whether the edge terminates within the cell's receptive field (termination cells) or passes through (segment cells). The receptive field of an L1 cell is thus defined over five dimensions: x, y, orientation, straight versus curved, and termination versus segment. The net input to L1 cell i (N_i) is calculated as the sum (over all image edges j) of prod-

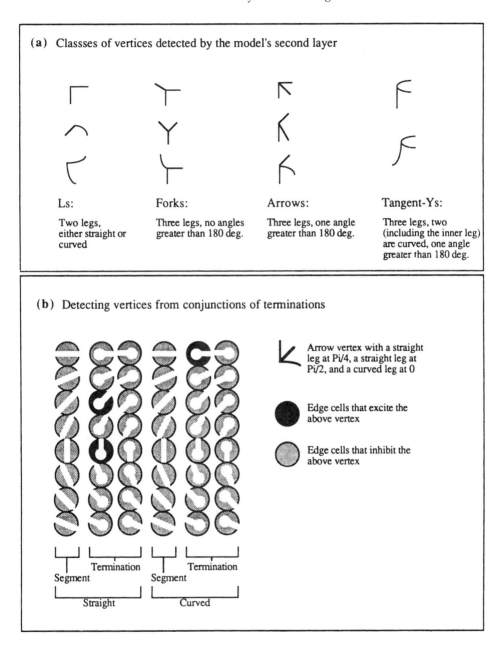

Figure 13.4

a: An illustration of the types of vertices detected in the model's second layer. b: An illustration of the mapping from the edge cells in a given location in Layer 1 to a vertex cell in the corresponding location of Layer 2. deg. = degree.

ucts (over all dimensions k):

$$N_i = \sum_j \prod_k (1 - |E_{jk} - C_{ik}|/W_k)^+, \tag{1}$$

where E_{jk} is the value of edge j on dimension k (e.g., the value 1.67 radians on the dimension orientation), C_{ik} is cell i's preferred value on dimension k (e.g., 1.85 radians), and W_k is a parameter specifying the width of a cell's tuning function in dimension k. The superscripted $+$ in Equation 1 indicates truncation below zero; L1 cells receive no negative inputs. The value of edge j on the dimensions x and y (location) is determined separately for each cell i as the point on j closest to C_{ix}, C_{iy}. Image segments are coded coarsely with respect to location: W_x and W_y are equal to the distance between adjacent clusters for segment cells (i.e., if and only if cells i and j are in adjacent clusters, then $|C_{ix} - C_{jx}| = W_x$). Within a cluster, segment cells are inhibited by termination cells of the same orientation. To reduce the calculations and data structures required by the computer simulation, edge orientation is coded discretely (i.e., one cell per cluster codes the orientation of a given image edge), and for terminations, location is also coded discretely (a given termination represented by activity in only one L1 cell). The activation of cell i (A_i) is computed as the Weber function of its net input:

$$A_i = N_i/(1 + N_i). \tag{2}$$

Layer 2: Vertices, Two-Dimensional Axes, and Blobs
The model's second layer (L2) is a mosaic of cells that respond to vertices, 2-D axes of parallel and nonparallel symmetry, and elongated, oriented blobs at all locations in the visual field.

Vertices   At each location in the visual field, there is one cell for every possible two- and three-pronged vertex. These include *L*s, arrows, forks, and tangent *Y*s (see Biederman, 1987; Malik, 1987) at all possible orientations (Figure 13.4a). In addition, there are cells that respond to oriented *lone terminations*, endpoints of edges that do not coterminate with other edges, such as the stem of a T vertex. Vertex cells at a given location receive input only from cells in the corresponding location of the first layer. They receive excitatory input from consistent L1 termination cells (i.e., cells representing terminations with the same orientation and curvature as any of the vertex's legs) and strong inhibition from segment cells and inconsistent termination cells (Figure 13.4b). Each L2 lone termination cell receives excitation from the corresponding L1 termination cell, strong inhibition from all other L1 terminations at the same location, and neither excitation nor inhibition from segment cells. The strong inhibition from L1 cells to inconsistent L2 cells ensures that (a) only one vertex cell will ever become active at a given location and (b) no vertex cells will become active in response to vertices with more than three prongs.

Axes and Blobs   The model also posits arrays of axis-sensitive cells and blob-sensitive cells in L2. The axis cells represent 2-D axes of parallelism (straight and curved) and non-parallel symmetry (straight and curved). However, the connections between these cells and the edge cells of L1 have not been implemented. Computing axes of symmetry is a difficult problem (cf. Brady, 1983; Brady & Asada, 1984; Mohan, 1989) the solution of which we are admittedly assuming. Currently, the model is given, as part of its input, a representation of the 2-D axes in an image. Similarly, cells sensitive to elongated, oriented regions of activity (blobs) are posited in the model's second layer but have not been implemented. Instead, blobs are computed directly by a simple region-filling algorithm.[5] These computations yield information about a geon's location, computed as the blob's central point, size, and elongation. Elongation is computed as the square of the blob's perimeter divided by its area (elongation is an inverse function of Ullman's, 1989, compactness measure).

Axis and blob cells are assumed to be sensitive to the phase relations established in L1 and therefore operate on parsed images (image parsing is described in the next section). Because this assumption restricts the computation of blobs and axes to operate on one geon at a time, it allows JIM to ignore axes of symmetry that would be formed between geons.

Image Parsing: Grouping Local Image Features Into Geons

Image parsing is a special case of the binding problem in which the task is to group features at different locations in the visual field. Fox example, given that many local features (edges, vertices, axes, and blobs) are active, how can the model know which belong together as attributes of the same geon (Figure 13.5)? As solving this problem is a prerequisite to correct geon identification, an image-parsing mechanism must yield groups that are useful for this purpose. The most commonly proposed constraint for grouping—location or proximity (Crick, 1984; Treisman & Gelade, 1980)—is insufficient in this respect. Even if there could be an a priori definition of a location (what criterion do we use to decide whether two visual entities are at the same location?), such a scheme would fail when appropriate grouping is inconsistent with proximity, as with Segments a and b in Figure 13.5. JIM parses images into geons by synchronizing cells in L1 and L2 in a pair-wise fashion according to three simple constraints on shape perception. The mechanism for synchronizing a pair of cells is described first, followed by a discussion of the constraints exploited for grouping.

Synchronizing a Single Pair of Cells   Each edge and vertex cell i is described by four continuous state variables, activation (A_i), output (O_i), output refractory (R_i), and refractory threshold (Θ_i), that vary from zero to one. A cell will generate an output if and only if it is active and its output refractory is below threshold:

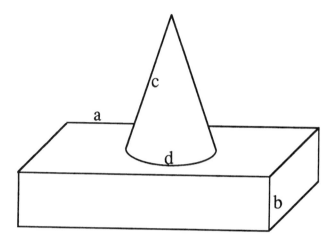

Figure 13.5
How does the brain determine that Segments a and b belong together as features of the brick, whereas c and d belong together as features of the cone? (Note that proximity alone is not a reliable cue: a is closer to both c and d than to b.)

$$\text{if and only if } A_i > 0 \quad \text{and} \quad R_i \leq \Theta_i,$$

$$\text{then } O_i = A_i, \text{ otherwise } O_i = 0. \tag{3}$$

When cell i is initially activated, R_i is set to 1.0 and Θ_i is set to a random value between 0 and 1. R_i decays linearly over time:

$$R_i(t) = R_i(t-1) - k, \quad k \ll 1.0, \tag{4}$$

where t refers to the current time slice. (A time slice is a discrete interval within which the state of the network is updated.) When its refractory reaches threshold $(R_i \leq \Theta_i)$, the cell fires $(O_i = A_i)$, resets its refractory $(R_i = 1.0)$, and re-randomizes its refractory threshold. An active cell in isolation will fire with a mean period of $0.5/k$ time slices[6] and an amplitude[7] of A_i.

Two cells can synchronize their outputs by exchanging an enabling signal over a *fast enabling link* (FEL). FELs are a class of fast, binary links completely independent of the standard connections that propagate excitation and inhibition: Two cells can share a FEL without sharing a standard connection and vice versa. FELs induce synchrony in the following manner: When cell j fires, it propagates not only an output along its connections but also an enabling signal along its FELs. An enabling signal is assumed to traverse a FEL within a small fraction of a time slice. When the enabling signal arrives at an active cell i, it causes i to fire immediately by pushing its refractory below threshold:

$$R_i(t_n) = R_i(t_o) - \Sigma_j FEL_{ij}E_j \tag{5}$$

where $R_i(t_o)$ is the refractory of cell i at the beginning of t, $R_i(t_n)$ is the refractory at some later period within t, FEL_{ij} is the value of the FEL (0 or 1) from j to i, and E_j (the enabling signal from cell j) is 1 if $O_j > 0$, and 0 otherwise. Note that the refractory state of a cell will go below threshold[8]—causing the cell to fire— whenever at least one cell with which it shares a FEL fires. When a cell fires because of an enabling signal, it behaves just as if it had fired on its own: It sends an output down its connections, an enabling signal down its FELs, sets its refractory to 1.0, and randomizes its refractory threshold.

An enabling signal induces firing on the same time slice in which it is generated; that is, its recipient will fire in synchrony with its sender. Furthermore, the synchrony is assumed to be transitive. If Cell A shares a FEL with Cell B and B shares one with C, then C will fire when A fires provided both B and C are active. It is important to note that enabling signals have no effect on, and do not pass through, inactive cells: if B is inactive, then A's firing will have no effect on either B or C. In the current model, the FELs are assumed to have functionally infinite propagation speed, allowing two cells to fire in synchrony regardless of the number of intervening FELs and active cells. Although this assumption is clearly incorrect, it is also much stronger than the computational task of image parsing requires. In the Discussion section, we explore the implications of the temporal parameters of cells and FELs.

The property of transitivity, the absence of propagation through inactive cells, and functionally infinite propagation speed allow us to define a *FEL chain*: Two cells, A and B, are said to lie on the same FEL chain if at least one path can be found from A to B by traversing FELs and active cells. All cells on the same FEL chain will necessarily fire in synchrony. Cells on separate FEL chains will not necessarily fire in synchrony, but they may fire in synchrony by accident (i.e., if their respective output refractories happen to go below threshold at the same time). The possibility of accidental synchrony has important implications for the use of synchrony to perform binding. These implications are addressed in the Discussion section. However, in this section, it is assumed that if two cells lie on different FEL chains, they will not fire in synchrony.

Layer 3: Geons

The model's first two layers represent the local features of an image and parse those features into temporal packages corresponding to geons. The third layer uses these grouped features to determine the attributes of the geons in the image. Each cell in L3 responds to a single geon attribute and will respond to any geon that possesses that attribute, regardless of the geon's other properties. For example, the cell that responds to geons with curved axes will respond to a large, curved brick in the upper left of the visual field, a small, curved cone in the lower right, and so forth. Because the geons' attributes are represented independently, an extraordinarily small number of units (58) is sufficient to represent the model's universe of geons and relations. The binding of attributes into geons is achieved by the temporal synchrony established in the first and second layers. It is at this level of the model that viewpoint invariance is achieved, and the first elements of a structural description are generated.

Representation of Geons   Cells in the model's third layer receive their inputs from the vertex, axis, and blob cells of L2. The details of the L2 to L3 mapping are described after the representation of L3 is described. Layer 3 consists of 51 cells that represent geons in terms of the following eight attributes (Figure 13.2):

Shape of the major axis   A geon's major axis is classified either as straight (as the axis of a cone) or curved (like a horn). This classification is *contrastive* in that degrees of curvature are not discriminated. One L3 cell codes for straight axes and one for curved.

Shape of the cross section   The shape of a geon's cross section is also classified as either straight (as the cross section of a brick or wedge) or curved (like a cylinder or cone). This attribute is contrastive, and the model does not discriminate different shapes within these categories: A geon with a triangular cross section would be classified as equivalent to a geon with a square or hexagonal cross section. One L3 cell codes for straight cross sections and one for curved.

Parallel versus nonparallel sides   Geons are classified according to whether they have parallel sides, such as cylinders and bricks, or nonparallel sides, like cones and wedges. This attribute is also contrastively coded in two cells: one for parallel and one for nonparallel.

Together, these three attributes constitute a distributed representation capable of specifying eight classes of geons: *Brick* (straight cross section, straight axis, and parallel sides), *Cylinder* (curved cross section, straight axis, and parallel sides), *Wedge* (straight cross section, straight axis, and nonparallel sides), *Cone* (curved cross section, straight axis, and nonparallel sides), and their curved-axis counterparts. Contrasts included in Biederman's (1987) RBC theory that are not discriminated by JIM include (a) whether a geon with nonparallel sides contracts to a point (as a cone) or is truncated (as a lamp shade), (b) whether the cross section of a geon with nonparallel sides both expands and contracts as it is propagated along the geon's axis (as the cross section of a football) or only expands (as the cross section of a cone), and (c) whether the cross section is symmetrical or asymmetrical.

Aspect ratio   A geon's aspect ratio is the ratio of the diameter of its cross section to the length of its major axis. The model codes five categories of aspect ratio: approximately 3 or more to 1 (3+:1), 2:1, 1:1, 1:2, and 1:3+. These categories are coded coarsely in one cell per category: Each aspect ratio cell responds to a range of aspect ratios surrounding its preferred value, and cells with adjacent preferred values respond to overlapping ranges.

Coarse orientation A geon's orientation is represented in two separate banks of cells in L3: a *coarse* bank, used directly for recognition (i.e., the outputs go to L6), and a *fine* bank, described later, used to determine the orientation of one geon relative to another (the outputs go to L4). The coarse bank consists of three cells, one each for horizontal, diagonal, and vertical orientations (Figure 13.2). The coarse orientation cells pass activation to L6 because the orientation classes for which they are selective are diagnostic for object classification, as with the difference between the vertical cylinder in a coffee mug and the horizontal cylinder in a klieg light. However, finer distinctions, such as left-pointing horizontal versus right-pointing horizontal, typically do not distinguish among basic level classes. A klieg light is a klieg light regardless of whether it is pointing left or right.

Fine orientation The coarse representation of orientation is not precise enough to serve as a basis for determining the relative orientation of two geons. For example, two geons could be perpendicular to one another and be categorized with the same orientation in the coarse representation (e.g., both legs of a T square lying on a horizontal surface would activate the coarse horizontal cell). The more precise fine representation is used to determine relative orientation. The fine cells code seven orientation classes (Figure 13.6): two diagonal orientations (left end up and right end up), four horizontal orientations (perpendicular to the line of sight, left end closer to viewer, right end closer, and end toward viewer), and one vertical orientation. Each orientation is represented by one cell.

Size A geon's size is coded coarsely in 10 cells according to the proportion of the visual field it occupies. The activation (A_i) of a size cell in response to a geon is given by

$$A_i = (1 - |C_i - G|/W_i)^+, \tag{7}$$

where C_i is the preferred size of cell i, W_i is the width of the cell's receptive field (0.1 for size cells), and G is the proportion of the visual field occupied by the geon. The preferred sizes of the L3 size cells start at 0.0 and advance in increments of 0.1 up to 0.9.

Location in the visual field A geon's location in the visual field is defined as the position of its centroid (the mean x- and y-coordinates for the set of all points inside the geon). The horizontal and vertical components of a geon's position are coded independently and coarsely in 10 cells each. The activation of a location cell is given by Equation 7, where C_i corresponds to the cell's preferred position. Location cells are ordered by positions starting at the left and bottom edges of the visual field and are incremented in equal intervals to the right and top edges, respectively. For example, the cell for $x = 1$ (far left) responds when a geon's centroid is close to the left edge of the visual field, $y = 1$ responds to centroids near

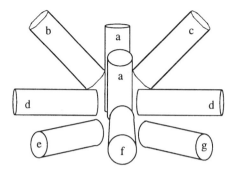

Fine Orientations	Coarse Orientations
a. Vertical	Vertical
b. Diagonal, left end up c. Diagonal, right end up	Diagonal

d. Horizontal
e. Horizontal, left end closer
    to viewer
f. Horizontal, end toward
    viewer
g. Horizontal, right end closer
    to viewer
	Horizontal

Figure 13.6
The fine orientation cells code seven geon orientations. (The coarse orientation cells code only three. Each fine orientation corresponds to exactly one coarse orientation.)

the bottom edge, and $x = 5$ responds to centroids just to the left of the vertical midline of the visual field.

Activating the Geon Attribute Cells   Cells in the model's third layer receive their inputs from the vertex, axis, and blob cells of L2, but the second and third layers of the model are not fully interconnected. Rather, L3 cells receive bottom-up excitation from consistent L2 cells only, and L3 cells representing inconsistent hypotheses (e.g., curved axis and straight axis) are mutually inhibitory. For example, L2 vertex cells send their outputs to the L3 cells for straight and curved cross section, but neither excite nor inhibit the L3 size cells. With the exception of cells for size, location, and aspect ratio, L3 cells compute their activations and outputs by Equation 2. The lateral inhibition among inconsistent L3 cells is implemented by normalizing the net inputs (N_i) to the L3 cells by the equation

$$N_i = N_i^k / (\Sigma_j N_j^k + N_i^k), \quad k > 1, \tag{8}$$

for all j such that cell j inhibits cell i.

Summary of Layers 1–3
The model's first three layers parse an image into its constituent geons and activate independent representations of each of the geon's attributes. For example, given the image in Figure 13.1, the model will parse the local features of the cone and the brick into separate groups, features within a group firing in synchrony. Each group then activates the cells in L3 that describe the geon they comprise. L3 cells are temporally yoked to their inputs: They fire only on time slices in which they receive inputs. When the L2 cells representing the cone fire, the L3 cells for straight axis, curved cross section, nonparallel sides, vertical, and the cells for its aspect ratio, size, and location become active and fire. Likewise, when the L2 cells representing the brick fire, the L3 cells for straight axis, straight cross section, parallel sides, horizontal, and the cells for its aspect ratio, size, and location will fire.

Layers 4 and 5: Relations Among Geons   Of the eight attributes represented in L3, five—axis shape, cross-section shape, parallelism of sides, coarse orientation, and aspect ratio—pass activation directly to the model's sixth layer (Figure 13.2). The remaining attributes—size, location, and fine orientation—pass activation to Layer 4, which, in conjunction with Layer 5, derives relative size, relative location, and relative orientation. The computational goals of Layers 4 and 5 are threefold. First, the relations among geons must be made explicit. For example, rather than representing that one geon is below another implicitly by representing each of their locations, the *below* relation is made explicit by activating a unit that corresponds uniquely to it. Second, the relations must be bound to the geons they describe. If one geon is below another in the visual field, the unit for below must be synchronized with the other units describing that geon. Finally, the relations must be invariant with geon identity and viewpoint so that, for example, the below unit will fire whenever one geon is below another, regardless of the shape of the geons, their locations in the visual field, orientation in depth, and size.

These goals are satisfied in two steps. In the first, L4 cells act as AND gates, responding when conjunctions of L3 cells fire on different (but nearby) time slices. In the second step, L5 cells OR together the outputs of multiple L4 cells, responding to the relations in a viewpoint-invariant manner. As illustrated in Figure 13.7, each L4 cell responds to a specific relation (e.g., below) in conjunction with a specific value on the dimension over which that relation is defined (e.g., $y = 1$). L4 cells respond to the following types of conjunctions: above–below conjoined with position in y, right–left with position in x, larger–smaller with size, and perpendicular–oblique with orientation. L5 contains only one cell for each relation: above, below, beside (which replaces the left–right distinction), larger, smaller, perpendicular, and oblique.

L4 cells receive both excitatory inputs and enabling signals from L3 (Figure 13.8). An L3 cell will excite an L4 cell if the L4 cell's value satisfies its relation with respect to the L3 cell. For example, the L3 $y = 3$ cell excites the L4 cell for

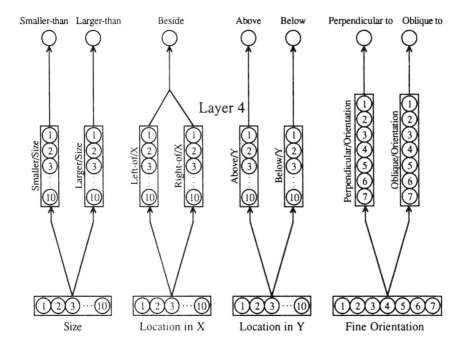

Figure 13.7
Detail of Layers 4 and 5. (Each Layer 4 cell responds to a specific relation [e.g., below] in conjunction with a specific value on the dimension over which that relation is defined [e.g., $Y = 1$]. Layer 5 contains only one cell for each relation.)

below$|y = 1$, because $y = 1$ is below $y = 3$ ($y = 1$ satisfies below with respect to $y = 3$). $y = 3$ also excites above$|y = 5$, above$|y = 6$, and so forth. Excitatory connections from L3 to L4 are unit strength, and there are no inhibitory connections. L4 cells sum their inputs over time by the equation

$$\Delta A_i = \gamma E_i(1 - A_i) - \delta A_i, \tag{9}$$

where A_i is the activation of L4 cell i, E_i is its excitatory input, and γ and δ are growth and decay parameters, respectively. L3 cells send enabling signals to L4 cells that respond to the same value; for example, $y = 1$ sends enabling signals to below$|y = 1$. L4 cells ensure proper geon-relation binding by firing only when they receive enabling signals. The invariant L5 relation cells sum the outputs of the corresponding L4 cells. For example, the L5 below cell receives excitation from below$|y = 1$, below$|y = 2$, and so on.

Computing BELOW

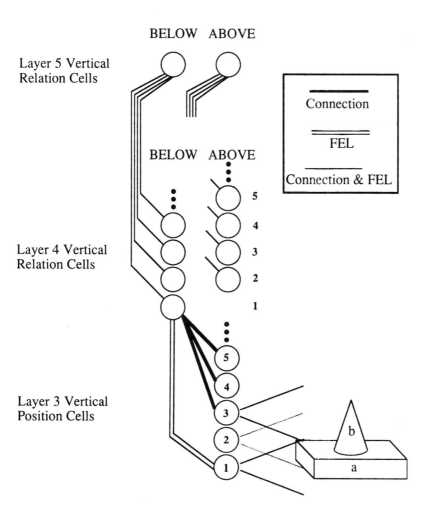

Figure 13.8
Operation of Layers 4 and 5 illustrated with the relation below. (FEL = fast enabling link.)

The relation *below* is used to illustrate how this architecture activates and binds invariant relations to geons, but the mechanism works in exactly the same way for all relations. Suppose, as shown in Figure 13.8, there is a geon near the bottom of the visual field (Geon A) and another nearer the middle (Geon B). $y = 1$ and $y = 2$ will fire in synchrony with the other L3 units describing Geon A, say, on time slices 1, 5, and 9. Similarly, $y = 2$ and $y = 3$ will fire in synchrony with the other properties of Geon B, say, on time slices 3, 7, and 11. Recall that below$|y = 1$ receives an excitatory input from $y = 3$. Therefore, when $y = 3$ fires (Time Slice 3), below$|y = 1$ will receive an excitatory input, and its activation will go above zero. On Time Slice 5, $y = 1$ will fire and send an enabling signal to below$|y = 1$, causing it to fire (i.e., in synchrony with $y = 1$ and, by transitivity, Geon A's other properties). Then below$|y = 1$ sends an excitatory signal to the L5 below cell, causing it to fire with geon A's other properties. In a directly analogous manner, *above* will come to fire in synchrony with the other properties of Geon B.

One problem with this architecture is a potential to "hallucinate" relations between a geon and itself. Such hallucinations can result if a geon's metric properties are coded coarsely, as they are in this model. For example, a given geon's vertical position in the visual field might be represented by simultaneous activity in both $y = 2$ and $y = 3$. Because $y = 2$ is below $y = 3$, the L4 below$|y = 2$ cell could become active and fire in response to the presence of that geon even if there are no others in the visual field. This problem is overcome by giving each L4 cell a blind spot for the L3 value directly flanking its preferred value. For example, below$|y = 2$ receives excitation from $y = 4$, $y = 5$, ... $y = 10$ but not from $y = 3$. The L4 blind spot prevents hallucinations, but it has the negative side effect that, for small enough differences in metric values, relations may be undetectable. For example, two very flat geons, one on top of the other, may activate the same L3 vertical position cells, only with slightly different ratios (say, one excites $y = 2$ strongly and $y = 3$ weakly; the other excites $y = 2$ weakly and $y = 3$ strongly). Because of the blind spot, the model would be insensitive to the above–below relation between such geons.

Layers 6 and 7: Geon Feature Assemblies and Objects
Together, Layers 3 and 5 produce a pattern of activation, termed a *geon feature assembly* (GFA), describing a geon in terms of its shape and general orientation as well as its location, size, and orientation relative to the other geons in the image. The collection of GFAs (over different time slices) produced in response to an object constitutes a simple structural description that is invariant with translation, scale, and orientation in depth. Furthermore, the model will produce the same description just as quickly in response to an object whether it is "viewing" that object for the first time or the twentieth. In this sense, the model's first five layers accomplish the primary theoretical goals of this effort. However, to assess the sufficiency of this representation for viewpoint-invariant

recognition, we have included two additional layers (6 and 7) that use the L3–L5 output to perform object classification.

The connections and FELs in JIM's first five layers are fixed, reflecting our assumption that the perceptual routines governing the activation of structural descriptions remain essentially unchanged past infancy. The acquisition of new objects is assumed to consist entirely in the recruitment of units (using modification of connections to existing cells) in Layers 6 and 7. There is an important and difficult question here as to exactly how and when new object classes are acquired. For example, when we see an object that is similar in shape to some familiar class of objects, how do we decide whether it is similar enough to belong to that class or whether it should become the first member of a new object class? ("I think it's a hot dog stand, but it could be some kind of device for sweeping the sidewalk.") Proper treatment of this question requires a theory of categorization, and the emphasis of this effort is on viewpoint invariance. Although it is possible that JIM's GFAs could serve as the representation in such a theory, a complete theory also requires processes to operate on its representations. Rather than attempt to propose such a theory, we have chosen instead to use a theoretically neutral procedure for providing the model with its vocabulary of objects. This simplified "familiarization" procedure is described shortly. First, let us consider how the model's last two layers activate a representation of a familiar object class given a structural description as input.

Given that almost any upright view of an object will produce the same GFA pattern in L3–L5 (within a small range of error), the task of classifying an object from its GFA pattern is straightforward. It is accomplished by allowing cells in L6 to be recruited by specific GFAs and cells in L7 to be recruited by conjunctions of L6 cells. If an object is in JIM's vocabulary, then each of its GFAs will activate a different cell in L6 (henceforth, GFA cells). The outputs of the GFA cells are summed over separate time slices to activate an L7 unit representing the class of the object.

The cells of L6 are fully interconnected to L5 and to the subset of L3 that passes activation to L6 (i.e., all L3 cells except those for size, position, and fine orientation). One L6 cell is a dummy cell, with unit strength excitatory connections from all L3–L5 cells. This cell is included to mimic the effect of GFA cells that are still free to be recruited in response to novel object classes. The remaining cells are selective for specific conjunctions of geon and relation attributes (for the current vocabulary, there are 20). For example, one GFA cell receives strong excitation from the L3 cells for curved cross section, straight axis, nonparallel sides, vertical, aspect ratio 1:1, and aspect ratio 1:2, and from the L5 cells for above, smaller than, and perpendicular to; the remaining connections to this cell are negligibly small. Thus, this GFA cell is selective for slightly elongated vertical cones that are above, smaller than, and perpendicular to other geons. Other GFA cells are selective for different patterns, and all GFA cells (including the dummy cell) are mutually inhibitory.

The most difficult problem confronting a GFA cell is that the pattern for which it is selective is likely to overlap considerably with the patterns selected by its competitors. For example, many objects contain geons with curved cross sections or geons that are below other geons, and so forth. Furthermore, some GFAs may be subsets of others: One GFA cell might respond to vertical cylinders below other geons, and another might respond to vertical cylinders below and beside other geons. To allow the GFA cells to discriminate such similar patterns, we adopted an excitatory input rule described by Marshall (1990), and others:

$$E_i = \Sigma_j O_j w_{ij} / (\alpha + \Sigma_j w_{ij}), \tag{10}$$

where E_i is the excitatory input to L6 cell i, O_j is the output of cell j (in L3 or L5), w_{ij} is the weight of the connection from j to i, and α is a constant. This equation normalizes a cell's excitatory input to a Weber function of the sum of its excitatory connections, making it possible for the cell to select for patterns that overlap with—or are even embedded within—the patterns selected by other cells. To illustrate, consider a simple network with two output cells (corresponding to L6 cells in JIM) and three input cells (corresponding to the L3–L5 cells), as shown in Figure 13.9. For simplicity, assume outputs and connection weights of 0 or 1, and let $\alpha = 1$. Output Cell 1 is selective for input Pattern ABC; that is, $w_{1A} = w_{1B} = w_{1C} = 1$, and Output Cell 2 is selective for Pattern AB. If ABC is presented to this network (i.e., $O_A = O_B = O_C = 1$), then, by Equation 10, E_1 will be 0.75, and E_2 will be 0.67. In response to ABC, Cell 1 receives a greater net input and therefore inhibits Cell 2. By contrast, if Pattern AB is presented to the network, E_1 will be 0.50, E_2 will be 0.67, and Cell 2 will inhibit Cell 1.

By allowing the GFA cells to select for overlapping and embedded patterns, this input rule allows JIM to discriminate objects with very similar structural descriptions: Each possible pattern of activation over L3 and L5 cells could potentially recruit a different GFA cell in L6. Given 21 inputs to L6, the number of GFA cells could in principle be as great as 2^{21} (or larger, if more than two degrees of activity were discriminated). However, because GFA cells are recruited only as the model adds objects to its vocabulary, the number of such cells that would realistically be required (even to represent the approximately 150,000 object models familiar to an adult [Biederman, 1988] is considerably smaller).

Simulations

JIM was implemented and run on an IBM PSII, Model 70. Simulations tested JIM's capacity for invariance with translation, scale changes, left–right image reflection, and rotations in depth and in the visual plane. These simulations were conducted in two phases, a familiarization phase and a test phase. During familiarization, the model was presented with one view of each of 10 simple

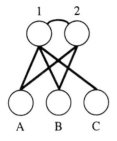

Excitatory Weights:

$w_{1A} = w_{1B} = w_{1C} = 1$

$w_{2A} = w_{2B} = 1, \ w_{2C} = 0$

Net Excitatory Input:

$$E_i = \sum_{j=A}^{C} O_j w_{ij} / (\alpha + \sum_{j=A}^{C} w_{ij}), \ \alpha = 1$$

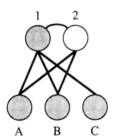

Input Pattern [ABC]:

$O_A = O_B = O_C = 1$

$E_1 = (3)/(1 + 3) = 0.75$

$E_2 = (2)/(1 + 2) = 0.67$

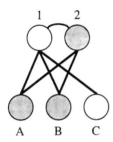

Input Pattern [AB]:

$O_A = O_B = 1, O_C = 0$

$E_1 = (2)/(1 + 3) = 0.50$

$E_2 = (2)/(1 + 2) = 0.67$

Figure 13.9
The Weber fraction excitatory input rule allows Output Cell 2 to select for Input Pattern AB and Output Cell 1 to select for Input Pattern ABC.

objects and allowed to modify the connection weights to L6 and L7 in response to the patterns of activity produced in L3 and L5. After familiarization, the connections were not allowed to change. During the test phase, JIM was presented with each object in 10 views: the original (baseline) view that was used for familiarization and 9 novel views. Its performance was evaluated by comparing its L7 responses to the test images with its baseline responses at that layer.

Familiarization: Creating the Object Vocabulary
Let us refer to the vector of bottom-up excitatory connection weights to a GFA cell as its *receptive field*. Before familiarization, all GFA cells (expect for the

dummy cell) were initialized: their receptive fields were set to vectors of zeros, and their output connections to all L7 object cells were set to −0.5.

JIM's vocabulary currently consists of 2 three-geon objects and 8 two-geon objects. The baseline view of each object is depicted in Figure 13.10. JIM was familiarized with one object at a time, each by the following procedure: The model was given the baseline image of an object as input and run for 20 time slices (ts). Each time the L1–L2 features of a geon fired, L3 and L5 produced a GFA as output. The GFA from the latest ts associated with each geon was selected as the familiarization GFA (denoted GFA*) for that geon. For example, the GFA*s for the telephone in Figure 13.10 were selected by presenting the baseline image to the model and running the model for 20 ts. Assume that the L2 features of the brick fired on ts 2, 7, 11, and 15, and those of the wedge fired on 4, 8, 13, and 18. The L3/L5 outputs for ts 15 would be selected as GFA* for the brick, and those for ts 18 as GFA* for the wedge.

Once an object's GFA*s were generated, the object was added to JIM's vocabulary by recruiting one L6 GFA cell for each GFA* and one L7 object cell for the object as a whole. For each GFA*, i, a GFA cell was recruited by computing the Euclidean distance[9] (D_{ij}) between i and the receptive fields of all previously recruited GFA cells, j. If, for all j, D_{ij} was greater than 0.5, a new GFA cell was recruited for GFA* i by setting the receptive field of an unrecruited GFA cell (i.e., one still in its initialized state) equal to GFA* i and setting the connection from that GFA cell to the associated object cell to 1.0. If a previously recruited cell, j, was found such that $D_{ij} \leq 0.5$, then the receptive field of that cell was set to the mean of itself and GFA* i, and its connection to the associated object cell was set to 1.0. This procedure recruited 20 GFA cells for the complete set of 22 GFA*s in the training set.

It is particularly important to note that this procedure establishes the model's vocabulary on the basis of only one view of each object. As such, exposure to many different views of each object cannot account for any viewpoint invariance demonstrated in the model's recognition performance. Also, this procedure is tantamount to showing the model a line drawing and instructing it that "this is an X." In an earlier version of the model (Hummel & Biederman, 1990b), the object vocabulary was developed by allowing the sixth and seventh layers to self-organize in response to GFA*s selected as described earlier. With a five-object training set, that procedure settled on a stable pattern of connectivity in L6 and L7, and the resulting connections produced recognition results very similar to those produced by the current version of the model. However, where the current familiarization procedure is capable of acquiring objects one at a time, the self-organizing system required all the objects to be presented at the same time. Where the current procedure establishes a pattern of connectivity in one exposure to an object, the self-organizing algorithm required 3,000 presentations of the training set to settle into a stable configuration. The self-organization was also highly sensitive to its parameters and to the ratio of the

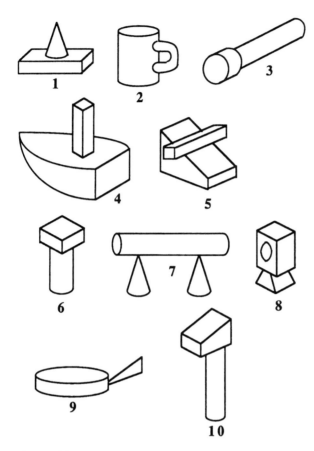

Figure 13.10
The baseline view of each object in JIM's vocabulary. (Objects 7 and 8 contain three geons, all others contain two. Objects 8 and 9 contain ambiguous geons: the central ellipse in Object 8 contains no axis information, and the "handle" on the "frying pan" [Object 9] contains no cross-section information. Objects 1 and 10 have the same geon and relation attributes in different combinations [see Figure 13.2].)

number of GFA*s to the number of L6 cells (e.g., it would not settle unless the number of L6 cells exactly equaled the number of GFA*s). We decided to use the current familiarization procedure instead because we want the model's behavior to reflect the performance of its 1st five layers rather than the idiosyncrasies of any particular learning algorithm.

Test Simulations: Conditions and Procedure

After familiarization, JIM's capacity for viewpoint-invariant recognition was evaluated by running two blocks of simulations. Each block consisted of 100 runs of the model, 10 objects presented in each of 10 conditions: Condition 1, Baseline, in which the original (familiarization) image was presented; Condition 2, Translation, in which the original image was moved to a new position in the visual field; Condition 3, Size, in which the original image was reduced to between 70% and 90% of its original size; Condition 4, Mirror Reversal of the original image; Condition 5, Depth rotation of 45° to 70° of the original object; Conditions 6 to 10, in which five images were created by rotating the original image in the visual plane (22.5°, 45°, 90°, 135°, and 180°). Blocks 1 and 2 differed only in the number, N, of ts for which the model was allowed to run on each image: In Block 1, $N = 20$, and in Block 2, $N = 40$.

Simulations were conducted by activating the set of L1 edge cells and L2 axis cells corresponding to the image of an object and allowing the model to run for N ts. Cells in all layers of the model updated their activations and outputs as described in the previous sections. On each of the n ts in which L1–L2 outputs were generated,[10] the activity of the target cell (the L7 cell corresponding to the correct identity of the object) was monitored. No data were collected on those $(N - n)$ ts in which no output was generated.

Four response metrics were calculated for each simulation because, alone, any one metric has the potential to yield a misleading characterization of performance. The metrics calculated were maximum activation of the target cell activated during the simulation (Max), mean activation of the target cell over the n ts in which data were collected, proportion (P) of all object cell mean activations attributable to the target cell, and the mean activation multiplied by proportion (MP). Max and mean provide raw measures of the target cell's response to an image. P and MP reflect the strength of the target cell's response relative to the responses of all other object cells.

As is evident in Figure 13.11, all the response metrics yielded the same qualitative picture of the model's performance, so most simulations are reported only in terms of max. For each block of simulations, JIM's performance in each condition (e.g., baseline, translation, and so forth) is reported in terms of the mean (over objects) of max, but the ordinate of each graph is labeled with the individual response metric (e.g., if the graph shows mean max's over objects in each condition, the ordinate will be labeled *max*). Error bars indicate the standard error of the mean. Because each metric is proportional to the strength and

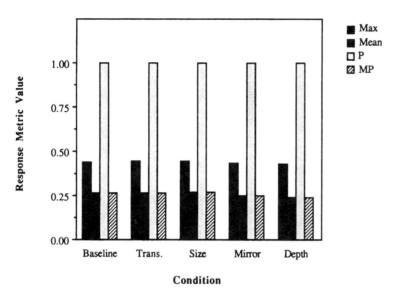

Figure 13.11
JIM's performance in the baseline, translation (Trans.) only, size, mirror-image reverse (Mirror), and depth rotated (Depth) conditions expressed in terms of the average-maximum (Max), mean proportion (P), and mean activation multiplied by proportion (MP) response metrics over objects in each condition. (These data were gathered in simulations lasting 20 time slices.)

correctness of the model's response to an image, high values of the response metrics are assumed to correspond to low reaction times and error rates in human subjects.

Test Simulations: Results
There is a stochastic component to the refractory thresholds of the cells in L1 and L2, so the output of the target cell in response to an image is subject to random variation. Specifically, the cell's output will reflect the number of times the features of each geon in the image fires, the number of ts between different geon's firing, and the order in which they fire. To derive an estimate of the amount of variation that can be expected for a given image of an object, the baseline view of Object 1 was run 20 times for 20 ts per simulation and 20 times for 40 ts per simulation. The means and standard deviations (unbiased estimate) of the four response metrics obtained in the 20-ts runs were max $= 0.499$ $(SD = 0.016)$, mean $= 0.304$ $(SD = 0.022)$, P $= 1.0$ $(SD = 0.0)$, and MP $= 0.304$ $(SD = 0.022)$. The values obtained in the 40-ts runs were max $= 0.605$ $(SD = 0.005)$, mean $= 0.436$ $(SD = 0.012)$, P $= 1.0$ $(SD = 0.0)$, and MP $= 0.436$ $(SD = 0.012)$. These figures are reported only to provide an estimate of the amount of random variation that can be expected in JIM's performance.

Translation, Size, Mirror Reversal, and Rotation in Depth   Recall that humans evidence no perceptual cost for image translations, scale changes, and mirror-image reversals (Biederman & Cooper, 1991, 1992), and only a very modest cost for rotations in depth, even with nonsense objects (Gerhardstein & Biederman, 1991). Similarly, JIM's performance reveals complete invariance with translation, size, and mirror-image reversals. Although every test condition entailed translating the original image (it is impossible to scale, rotate, or mirror reflect an image without affecting where its constituent edges fall in the visual field), JIM was tested on one image that underwent only a translation from the baseline image. JIM was also tested with one scaled image (reduced to between 70% and 90% of its original size), one left–right mirror-reflected image, and one depth-rotated image of each object. Limitations of the stimulus creation program made precise rotations in depth impossible (the stimulus creation program represents objects as 2-D line drawings rather than 3-D models). Therefore, each depth rotated image was created by rotating the object approximately 45° to 70° from its baseline orientation; these included rotations both about the object's vertical axis and about a horizontal axis perpendicular to the line of sight.

Figure 13.11 depicts JIM's performance in each of these conditions in terms of all four response metrics in Block 1 (simulations lasting 20 ts). By each response metric, performance in these conditions was indistinguishable from baseline performance. Figure 13.12 shows the max for these conditions in Block 2 (40 ts). These figures also reveal complete invariance in each condition, with the exception of a very modest cost for rotation in depth. This cost most likely reflects changes in the geons' aspect ratios resulting from the depth rotations. Note that mean P over objects was 1.0 for all conditions in Block 1, indicating that in each simulation only the target cell achieved a mean activation greater than zero. Although it is not shown, the mean P over objects was also 1.0 for all these conditions in Block 2.

Rotation in the Visual Plane   By contrast to rotations in depth, humans evidence a perceptual cost for recognizing images that have been rotated in the visual plane (Jolicoeur, 1985). Typically, subjects show a monotonic increase in response time and error rate, with the number of degrees rotated from upright to approximately 135°. Subjects respond faster at 180° (when the object is upside down) than they do at 135°, producing a W-shaped rotation function over 360° (Jolicoeur, 1985).

JIM's performance under rotations in the visual plane was tested with stimuli rotated 22.5°, 45°, 90°, 135°, and 180° from be baseline images. Figures 13.13 and 13.14 show max as a function of degrees of rotation for Blocks 1 and 2, respectively. Again, JIM's performance revealed a trend very similar to that of human subjects. In terms of JIM's operation, the cusp in the rotation function at 180° reflects two effects. First, for objects with a primarily vertical structure (i.e., the spatial relations among the geons include *above* and *below*, but not *beside*),

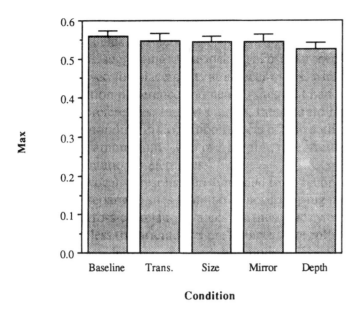

Figure 13.12
JIM's performance in the baseline, translation (Trans.) only, size, mirror-image reversed (Mirror), and depth rotated (Depth) conditions expressed in terms of the average maximum (Max) response metric over objects in each condition. (These data were gathered in simulations lasting 40 time slices.)

rotations between upright (0°) and 180° create spurious *beside* relations that are absent in the upright and 180° views. For example, rotate a lamp 45° in the visual plane and the lampshade, which is above the base in the upright view, will be above and beside the base. Continue to rotate the lamp until it is upside down and this spurious *beside* relation disappears. Second, a 180° rotation in the visual plane preserves the original coarse orientations of the object's component geons (*horizontal, diagonal,* or *vertical*) more than rotations greater or less than 180°.

Discussion of Test Simulations
The simulations reported earlier reveal a high degree of translation, scale, and mirror-reflection invariance in JIM's recognition of objects. Performance with objects rotated in depth and in the visual plane also resembles the performance of human subjects under similar circumstances. Comparison of results from Block 1 and Block 2 suggests that the length of time for which a simulation is run has little or no qualitative impact on the model's performance (mean and max were higher on average for the 40 ts simulations, but the relative values across conditions were unaffected). Similarly, comparison of the various

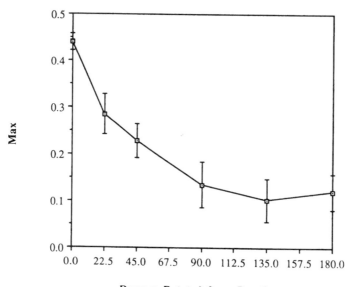

Degrees Rotated from Baseline

Figure 13.13
JIM's recognition performance as a function of degrees rotated in the visual plane from baseline (0.0°). (Performance is expressed in terms of the average maximum [Max] response metric over objects in each condition. These data were gathered in simulations lasting 20 time slices.)

response metrics suggests that the observed results are not dependent on the particular metric used. However, because the results are based on simulations with only 10 objects, it could be argued that they reflect the model's use of some sort of diagnostic feature for each object, rather than the objects' structural descriptions.

This diagnostic feature hypothesis is challenged by the results of two additional test conditions conducted with images of the objects in JIM's vocabulary. In the first condition, a scrambled image of each object was created by randomly rearranging blocks of the original image such that the edges' orientations were unchanged and the vertices remained intact. An example of a scrambled image is given in Figure 13.15. If JIM's performance reflects the use of a diagnostic list of 2-D features for each object, it would be expected to achieve at least moderate activation in the target cell corresponding to each scrambled image (although the axes of parallelism and symmetry are destroyed by the scrambling, the vertices are preserved), but if it is sensitive to the relations among these features, it would be expected to treat these images as unfamiliar. In the second condition, the intact baseline images were presented to the model, but the binding mechanism was disabled, forcing the separate geons to fire in synchrony. This condition demonstrated the effect of accidental synchrony on

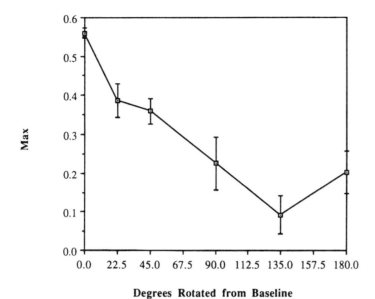

Degrees Rotated from Baseline

Figure 13.14
JIM's recognition performance as a function of degrees rotated in the visual plane from baseline (0.0°). (Performance is expressed in terms of the averagemaximum [Max] response metric over objects in each condition. These data were gathered in simulations lasting 40 time slices.)

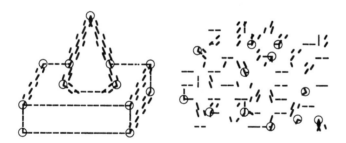

Figure 13.15
Left: The representation of the baseline image of Object 1 in JIM's first layer. (Line segments correspond to active cells in Layer 1, the location and orientation of a segment corresponding to the preferred location and orientation of the cell, respectively. Circles indicate locations in Layer 2 containing active vertex (or lone termination) cells. Right: The scrambled image version of the baseline image for Object 1. Verticles and edges orientations are preserved, but the positions of 2×2 blocks of the 22×22 cluster input layer are randomly rearranged.)

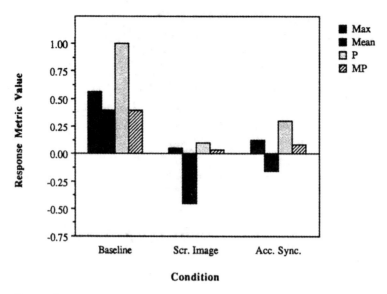

Figure 13.16
JIM's recognition performance in the baseline, scrambled image (Scr. Image), and forced accidental synchrony (Acc. Sync.) conditions. (Performance is expressed in terms of all response metrics [averaged over objects in each condition]. These data were gathered in simulations lasting 40 time slices. Max = maximum activation of the target cell activated during the simulations; P = mean activation multiplied by proportion.)

JIM's performance; if the model's capacity for image parsing is truly critical to its performance, recognition would be expected to fail in this condition as well. Simulations in both conditions lasted for 40 ts. JIM's performance on the scrambled image and forced accidental synchrony conditions is shown in Figure 13.16. In both conditions, performance was reduced to noise levels.

Discussion

JIM is capable of activating a representation of an object given a line drawing of that object as input. Moreover, that representation is invariant with translation, scale, and left–right mirror reversal even when the model has previously been exposed to only one view of the object. This section discusses the important aspects of JIM's design and explores their implications. Specifically, the implications of the independent attribute representation used in L3 and L5 are reviewed shortly. The model's use of dynamic binding plays a pivotal role in this capacity for independent attribute representations. The theoretical and empirical implications of using temporal synchrony for dynamic binding is discussed in some detail. Also addressed are additional findings for which JIM provides an account, some novel predictions for human recognition performance, and some limitations of the current architecture.

The Nature of Temporal Binding and Its Empirical Consequences

What Temporal Binding Is Not   The notion of temporal binding is only starting to become familiar to most psychologists, and its empirical consequences are not obvious. Specifically, binding through temporal synchrony as described here should not be confused with the grouping of stimulus elements that are presented in close temporal contiguity. Indeed, JIM produces temporal asynchrony for the different geons in an object even though they are presented simultaneously. The confusion between binding through synchrony and grouping features presented in close temporal contiguity is not hypothetical. A report by Keele, Cohen, Ivry, Liotti, and Yee (1988) is critical of temporal binding on the grounds that temporal contiguity in stimulus presentation did not predict feature binding.

Keele et al. (1988) conducted three experiments testing whether common location or common time of occurrence is a stronger cue to feature binding in rapidly presented images. In each experiment, illusory conjunctions were better predicted by common location in the visual field than by co-occurrence in time. Failing to find support for the primacy of stimulus contiguity in feature binding, these researchers rejected temporal binding theory. However, what their data show is that location is a more critical cue than temporal coincidence in determining how features should be conjoined. Such data do not and cannot falsify the hypothesis that synchronous activity is the manner in which a feature conjunction—even one established on the basis of common location—is represented. How a binding is represented and what cues are used to determine that binding are different issues entirely. Although it is possible to evaluate a given set of proposed binding cues with behavioral measures, we suggest that behavioral tests are inadequate in principle to falsify the temporal binding hypothesis. Rather, questions about the neural mechanism of binding, by definition, reside in the domain of neuroscience.

Limitations of the Current Implementation

The current implementation of JIM is limited in a number of respects. Some of these limitations derive from simplifying assumptions we have made to keep the implementation manageable, and others reflect fundamental questions that remain to be addressed. We shall focus the discussion primarily on the latter.

Several extensions suggest themselves for exploration. Among the first is the compatibility of the proposed constraints for parsing and recognition with natural images. In this implementation, we have assumed that recognition starts with a clean representation of the surface and depth discontinuities describing a line drawing of an object. Implicitly, we have also assumed that this representation could be achieved without top-down influences from geons or objects. However, forming a representation of orientation and depth discontinuities from natural images is clearly a nontrivial problem, and it may be the case that it cannot be solved without top-down mediation. These considerations motivate two lines of exploration. The first is the compatibility of our FELs with output from available edge-detection algorithms, and the second is the use of FELs and geons to interactively derive depth discontinuities from natural images. In particular, edge definition may be facilitated by constraints from geons (Biederman, 1987).

JIM's capacity for representing shape is most limited by its impoverished vocabulary of geons and relations. JIM is capable of discriminating eight geon types, whereas RBC posits 24. The most important relations omitted from JIM's current vocabulary are the connectedness relations, which describe how the various geons in an image are connected to one another. The simplest of these is the binary relation *connected* versus *not connected*. JIM does not discriminate two geons that are physically joined from two that are not. For example, its representation of a table would express only the relative angles, locations, and sizes of the various parts (such as the top and the legs), neglecting that the top is connected to each of the legs but that the legs do not touch one another. Other connectedness relations include whether two geons are joined end to end (like the cylinders of a flashlight) or end to side (like the join between a camera body and lens) and centeredness (whether one geon connects to another near the center of the latter's side or near an edge).

Expanding the current architecture to capture more relational and shape attributes will require additional structures. In particular, it is not clear that the current architecture in L4 and L5 could be applied directly to the problem of deriving connectedness relations. However, given that architectures capable of deriving them can be described, new attributes can be added to JIM's representation at a cost of one cell per attribute. None of the additional properties seem incompatible with the existing structure. Therefore, there is no reason to think that expanding the model to capture them will require violating any important assumptions underlying its current design.

Among JIM's most serious weaknesses is an inability to deal with multiple objects in an image. Expanding it to deal with multiple objects will almost certainly entail addressing questions of scale, visual attention, and additional problems in grouping such as figure–ground segmentation. Although we do not expect these extensions to be straightforward, we also do not expect that they will require abandoning the basic tenets underlying JIM's current design. If we regard JIM's current domain as a subset of the processing that occurs within the focus of attention, then its failure with multiple objects is not psychologically unrealistic. Biederman, Blickle, Teitelbaum, and Klatsky (1988) found that search time for a target object in a nonscene display (objects were arrayed in a circular arrangement, as the numbers on the face of a clock) was a linear function of the number of distractor objects in the display, suggesting that subjects were attending to one object at a time. This finding seems anomalous in the context of the finding that complete scenes can be recognized in the same time it takes to recognize a single object (Biederman, 1981). However, Mezzanotte (1981) demonstrated that scene recognition does not require that the individual objects in the scene be identifiable in isolation. Rather, as argued by Biederman (1988), familiar groups of interacting objects may be treated by the visual system as a single object, that is, as configurations of geons in particular relations.

Summary and Conclusions

We have described a neural net architecture that takes as input a retinotopically mapped representation of the surface and depth discontinuities in an object's image and activates a representation of the object that is invariant with translation and scale and largely invariant with viewpoint. JIM's behavior conforms well to empirical data on human object recognition performance. The fundamental principle underlying its design is that an object is represented as a structural description specifying its parts and the relations among them. This design principle frees JIM from trading off attribute structures for an implicit representation of the relations among those attributes. Also, it permits shape representation to be achieved with a remarkably small number of units. JIM's capacity for structural description derives from its solution to the dynamic binding problem. Dynamic binding is thus critical for shape representation, but it is subject to intrinsic capacity limitations. In the case of binding through synchrony, the limits derive from the temporal parameters of cells and the links among them. We speculate that observed limitations on visual attention in human subjects may reflect the limits of a natural dynamic binding mechanism.

Notes

This research was supported by National Science Foundation graduate and Air Force Office of Scientific Research (AFOSR) postdoctoral fellowships to John E. Hummel and by AFOSR research grants (88-0231 and 90-0274) to Irving Biederman. We are grateful to Dan Kersten, Randy Fletcher, Gordon Legge, and the reviewers for their helpful comments on an earlier draft of this chapter and to Peter C. Gerhardstein for his help on early simulations.

1. Though the perceived shape is invariant, we are of course aware of the differences in size, orientation, and position among the entities in Figure 13.1. Those attributes may be processed by a system subserving motor interaction rather than recognition (Biederman & Cooper, 1992).
2. The term *viewpoint invariant* as used here refers to the tendency of the image feature's classification to remain unchanged under changes in viewpoint. For instance, the degree of curvature associated with the image of the rim of a cup will change as the cup is rotated in depth relative to the viewer. However, the fact that edge is curved rather than straight will remain unchanged in all but a few accidental views of the cup.
3. Henceforth, it is assumed that the elements of the structural description are geons and their relations.

4. To reduce the computer resources required by the implementation, a square lattice (rather than a more realistic hexagonal lattice) was used in the simulations reported here. However, the use of a square lattice is not critical to the model's performance.

5. Regions containing geons are filled by an iterative algorithm that activates a point in the visual field if (a) there is an active edge cell at that location or (b) it is surrounded by active points in X or Y. This nonconnectionist algorithm fills regions occupied by geons. These regions are then assumed to correspond to the receptive fields of blob cells in the second layer. The properties of the receptive field (such as area, perimeter, and central point) are calculated directly from the region by counting active points.

6. The mean refractory threshold for a cell (Θ_i) will be 0.5. Assuming that $\Theta_i = 0.5$, it will take $0.5/k$ time slices for R_i to decay from 1.0 to Θ_i.

7. Real neurons spike with an approximately constant amplitude. A cell's firing can be thought of as a burst of spikes, with amplitude of firing proportional to the number of spikes in the burst.

8. $\Sigma_j FEL_{ij} \geq 1.0 \geq R_i(t_o)$. Therefore $[R_i(t_o) - \Sigma_j FEL_{ij}] = R_i(t_n) \leq 0 \leq \Theta_i$.

9. Recall that both the GFAs and the L6 receptive fields are 21-dimensional vectors. The Euclidean distance (D_{ij}) between two vectors, i and j, is calculated as the square root of the sum over vector elements of the squared differences of corresponding vector elements: $D_{ij} = (\Sigma_k (i_k - j_k)^2)^{0.5}$.

10. Because there is a stochastic component to the L1 and L2 cells' firing, a subset of the time slices will pass during any given run without any L1 or L2 cells firing (and, therefore, no other cells will fire). On these time slices, no data were gathered.

References

Abeles, M. (1982). *Local cortical circuits: Studies of brain function* (Vol. 6), New York: Springer.

Atiya, A., & Baldi, P. (1989). Oscillations and synchronizations in neural networks: An exploration of the labeling hypothesis. *International Journal of Neural Systems, 1,* 103–124.

Baldi, P., & Meir, R. (1990). Computing with arrays of coupled oscillators: An application to preattentive texture discrimination. *Neural Computation, 2,* 459–471.

Biederman, I. (1981). On the semantics of a glance at a scene. In M. Kubovy & J. R. Pomerantz (Eds.), *Perceptual organization* (pp. 213–263). Hillsdale, NJ: Erlbaum.

Biederman, I. (1987). Recognition-by-components: A theory of human image understanding. *Psychological Review, 94,* 115–147.

Biederman, I. (1988). Aspects and extensions of a theory of human image understanding. In Z. Pylyshyn (Ed.), *Computational processes in human vision* (pp. 370–428). Norwood, NJ: Ablex.

Biederman, I., Blickle, T., Teitelbaum, R., & Klatsky, G. (1988). Object search in nonscene displays. *Journal of Experimental Psychology: Learning, Memory, and Cognition, 14,* 456–467.

Biederman, I., & Cooper, E. E. (1991). Evidence for complete translational and reflectional invariance in visual object priming. *Perception, 20,* 585–593.

Biederman, I., & Cooper, E. E. (1992). Size invariance in human shape recognition. *Journal of Experimental Psychology: Human Perception and Performance, 18,* 121–133.

Brady, M. (1983). Criteria for representations of shape. In J. Beck, B. Hope, & A. Rosenfeld (Eds.), *Human and machine vision.* (pp. 39–84). San Diego, CA: Academic Press.

Brady, M., & Asada, H. (1984). Smoothed local symmetries and their implementation. *International Journal of Robotics Research, 3,* 36–61.

Crick, F. H. C. (1984). The function of the thalamic reticular spotlight: The searchlight hypothesis. *Proceedings of the National Academy of Sciences, 81,* 4586–4590.

Crick, F. H. C., & Koch, C. (1990). Towards a neurobiological theory of consciousness. *Seminars in Neuroscience, 2,* 263–275.

Eckhorn, R., Bauer, R., Jordan, W., Brish, M., Kruse, W., Munk, M., & Reitboeck, H. J. (1988). Coherent oscillations: A mechanism of feature linking in the visual cortex? Multiple electrode and correlation analysis in the cat. *Biological Cybernetics, 60,* 121–130.

Eckhorn, R., Reitboeck, H., Arndt, M., & Dicke, P. (1990). Feature linking via synchronization among distributed assemblies: Simulations of results from cat visual cortex. *Neural Computation, 2,* 293–307.

Edelman, S., & Weinshall, D. (1991). A self-organizing multiple-view representation of 3D objects. *Biological Cybernetics, 64,* 209–219.

Feldman, J. A. (1982). Dynamic connections in neural networks. *Biological Cybernetics, 46,* 27–39.

Feldman, J. A., & Ballard, D. H. (1982). Connectionist models and their properties. *Cognitive Science, 6,* 205–254.

Fodor, J. A., & Pylyshyn, Z. W. (1988). Connectionism and cognitive architecture: A critical analysis. *Cognition, 28,* 1–71.

Gerhardstein, P. C., & Biederman, I. (1991, May). *Priming depth-rotated object images: Evidence for 3D invariance.* Paper presented at the Meeting of the Association for Research in Vision and Ophthalmology, Sarasota, FL.

Gray, C. M., Konig, P., Engel, A. E., & Singer, W. (1989). Oscillatory responses in cat visual cortex exhibit inter-column synchronization which reflects global stimulus properties. *Nature, 338,* 334–337.

Gray, C. M., & Singer, W. (1989). Stimulus specific neuronal oscillations in orientation columns of cat visual cortex. *Proceedings of the National Academy of Sciences, 86,* 1698–1702.

Grossberg, S., & Somers, D. (1991). Synchronized oscillations during cooperative feature linking in a cortical model of visual perception. *Neural Networks, 4,* 453–466.

Hinton, G. E., McClelland, J. L., & Rumelhart, D. E. (1986). Distributed representations. In D. E. Rumelhart, J. L. McClelland, and the PDP Research Group, *Parallel distributed processing: Explorations in the microstructure of cognition. Volume I: Foundations* (pp. 77–109). Cambridge, MA: MIT Press/Bradford Books.

Hummel, J. E., & Biederman, I. (1990a). Dynamic binding: A basis for the representation of shape by neural networks. In M. P. Palmarini, *Proceedings of the 12th Annual Conference of the Cognitive Science Society* (pp. 614–621). Hillsdale, NJ: Erlbaum.

Hummel, J. E., & Biederman, I. (1990b, November). *Binding invariant shape descriptors for object recognition: A neural net implementation.* Paper presented at the 21st Annual Meeting of the Psychonomics Society, New Orleans, LA.

Jolicoeur, P. (1985). The time to name disoriented natural objects. *Memory & Cognition, 13,* 289–303.

Keele, S. W., Cohen, A., Ivry, R., Liotti, M., & Yee, P. (1988). Test of a temporal theory of attentional binding. *Journal of Experimental Psychology: Human Perception and Performance, 14,* 444–452.

Lange, T., & Dyer, M. (1989). *High-level inferencing in a connectionist neural network.* (Tech. Rep. No. UCLA-AI-89-12), Los Angeles: University of California, Computer Science Department.

Malik, J. (1987). Interpreting line drawings of curved objects. *International Journal of Computer Vision, 1,* 73–103.

Marshall, J. A. (1990). A self-organizing scale-sensitive neural network. *Proceedings of the International Joint Conference on Neural Networks, 3,* 649–654.

Mezzanotte, R. J. (1981). *Accessing visual schemata: Mechanisms invoking world knowledge in the identification of objects in scenes,* Unpublished doctoral dissertation, State University of New York at Buffalo, Department of Psychology.

Milner, P. M. (1974). A model for visual shape recognition. *Psychological Review, 81,* 521–535.

Mohan, R. (1989). *Perceptual organization for computer vision.* Unpublished doctoral dissertation, University of Southern California, Department of Computer Science.

Rock, I., & DiVita, J. (1987). A case of viewer-centered perception. *Cognitive Psychology, 19,* 280–293.

Sejnowski, T. J. (1986). Open questions about computation in cerebral cortex. In J. L. McClelland, & D. E. Rumelhart. (Eds.), *Parallel distributed processing: Explorations in the microstructure of cognition* (pp. 372–389). Cambridge, MA: MIT Press.

Shastri, L., & Ajjanagadde, V. (1990). *From simple associations to systematic reasoning: A connectionist representation of rules, variables and dynamic bindings* (Tech. Rep. No. MS-CIS-90-05). Philadelphia: University of Pennsylvania, Department of Computer and Information Sciences.

Smolensky, P. (1987). *On variable binding and the representation of symbolic structures in connectionist systems* (Internal Rep. No. CU-CS-355-87). Boulder, CO: University of Colorado, Department of Computer Science & Institute of Cognitive Science.

Strong, G. W., & Whitehead, B. A. (1989). A solution to the tag-assignment problem for neural networks. *Behavioral and Brain Sciences, 12,* 381–433.

Tarr, M. J., & Pinker, S. (1989). Mental rotation and orientation dependence in shape recognition. *Cognitive Psychology, 21,* 233–283.

Treisman, A., & Gelade, G. (1980). A feature integration theory of attention. *Cognitive Psychology, 12,* 97–136.

Ullman, S. (1989). Aligning pictorial descriptions: An approach to object recognition. *Cognition, 32,* 193–254.

von der Malsburg, C. (1981). *The correlation theory of brain function* (Internal Rep. No. 81-2). Gottingen, Germany: Max-Plank-Institute for Biophysical Chemistry, Department of Neurobiology.

von der Malsburg, C. (1987). Synaptic plasticity as a basis of brain organization. In J. P. Chaneaux & M. Konishi (Eds.), *The neural and molecular bases of learning* (pp. 411–432). New York: Wiley.

Wang, D., Buhmann, J., & von der Malsburg, C. (1991). Pattern segmentation in associative memory. *Neural Computation, 2,* 94–106.

Winston, P. (1975). Learning structural descriptions from examples. In P. Winston (Ed.), *The psychology of computer vision* (pp. 157–209). New York: McGraw-Hill.

Executive Processes

Chapter 14

Context, Cortex, and Dopamine: A Connectionist Approach to Behavior and Biology in Schizophrenia

Jonathan D. Cohen and David Servan-Schreiber

Schizophrenia is marked by a wide variety of behavioral deficits, including disturbances of attention, language processing, and problem solving. At the same time, findings of biological abnormalities in schizophrenia continue to accumulate, including disturbances in specific neurotransmitter systems (e.g., dopamine and norepinephrine) and anatomic structures (e.g., prefrontal cortex and hippocampus). For the most part, however, the behavior and biology of schizophrenia have remained separate fields of inquiry. Despite a modern consensus that information-processing deficits in schizophrenia are the result of underlying biological abnormalities, few efforts have been made to specify exactly how these phenomena relate to one another.

In this chapter we address this issue by drawing on a recent development within cognitive science: the parallel distributed processing, or *connectionist*, framework. This framework provides a means for building computer simulation models of performance in specific behavioral tasks. However, connectionist models differ from other computer simulation models of behavior in their use of information-processing mechanisms that incorporate important features of biological computation. Using this framework, it is possible to develop models that explore the effects of biologically relevant variables on behavior. In this article we explore the ability of such models to explain aspects of schizophrenic behavior in terms of specific underlying biological disturbances.

At the behavioral level, we focus on schizophrenic disturbances of selective attention and language. We describe a set of connectionist models that simulate both normal and schizophrenic patterns of performance in three experimental tasks: two that tap attentional performance (the Stroop task and the continuous performance test) and one that measures language-processing abilities (a lexical disambiguation task). The models make use of a common set of information-processing mechanisms and show how a number of seemingly disparate observations about schizophrenic behavior can all be related to a single functional deficit: a disturbance in the internal representation of context.

Furthermore, the models suggest that this functional deficit may be explained by a specific biological disturbance: a reduction in the effects of dopamine in prefrontal cortex. First, we show how a particular parameter of the models can be used to simulate the neuromodulatory effects of dopamine at the cellular level. We then describe the results of disturbing this parameter within a module corresponding to the function of prefrontal cortex in each of the three behavioral simulations. In each case, this disturbance leads to changes in performance that quantitatively match those observed for schizophrenics in the corresponding tasks. Taken together, these findings suggest that a number of the disturbances of selective attention and language found in schizophrenia may result from a common information-processing deficit (a disturbance in the internal representation of context) which, in turn, may be explained by a single biological abnormality (a reduction of dopaminergic activity in prefrontal cortex).

Before proceeding, it is important to acknowledge that the models we present in this article focus on a specific set of behavioral and biological phenomena associated with schizophrenia. Although we recognize that these represent only a subset of the many disturbances observed in schizophrenia, we suggest that they form a coherent subcomponent of this illness. Our hope is that a more precise account of this subcomponent will help delimit its role in schizophrenia and provide a framework for tackling other phenomena such as hallucinations and delusions.

We begin by reviewing data concerning cognitive and biological deficits in schizophrenia that are relevant to our argument. There are four components to this argument: (a) Schizophrenics' performance in a variety of cognitive tasks indicates a decreased ability to use context for choosing appropriate behavior; (b) frontal cortex is directly involved in, and necessary for the internal representation and maintenance of, context information; (c) schizophrenia is associated with abnormalities of frontal cortex; (d) the normal function of frontal cortex relies on the activity of the mesocortical dopamine system, which also appears to be disturbed in schizophrenia. Following our review of the empirical literature, we present a set of connectionist models that show how the behavioral phenomena can be causally related to specific biological mechanisms.

Background

Cognitive Deficits in Schizophrenia

Disturbances in the Internal Representation of Context   A large number of experiments have revealed schizophrenic deficits in information-processing tasks (for example, see Chapman, 1980). Although these encompass a variety of different processing domains—including selective attention, signal detection, memory, language processing, and problem solving—we believe that many of these may reflect a common underlying deficit: a degradation in the ability to construct and maintain an internal representation of context. By an *internal representation of context* we mean information held in mind in such a form that it can be used to mediate an appropriate behavioral response. This can be a set of task instructions, a specific prior stimulus, or the result of processing a sequence of prior stimuli (e.g., the interpretation resulting from processing a sequence of words in a sentence). By this definition, context information is relevant to but does not form part of the content of the actual response. This distinguishes context information from the kind of information traditionally thought to be stored in short-term memory. We usually think of short-term memory as storing recently presented information, the identity of which must later be retrieved—"declarative" representations in the sense used by Anderson (1983). In contrast, we think of internal representations of context as information stored in a form that allows it to mediate a response to the stimulus other than the simple reporting of its identity. Although it is possible, in principle, that the same representations (and mechanisms) could be involved in both cases, there is evidence that, in fact, the internal representation of context can be dissociated from short-term memory. For example, human infants younger than 6 months show evidence of knowing that an object is hidden behind a cover before they can use that information to reach for the object (Baillargeon, 1990). Similarly, schizophrenics show normal performance on a number of short-term memory tasks (e.g., Larsen & Fromholt, 1976; Oltmanns & Neale, 1975); however, in tasks that rely on the internal representation of context, they consistently show deficits. To illustrate this, we focus on three different tasks: a selective attention task, a signal detection task, and a lexical disambiguation task. In each case, we consider the role that the internal representation of context plays in the task and how schizophrenic deficits in both attention and language performance may be related to a degradation in this internal representation.

Attentional Tasks Since its definition as an illness, schizophrenia has been associated with deficits of selective attention (Bleuler, 1911; Kraeplin, 1950). Investigators who have focused on the phenomenology of schizophrenia have often reported that patients appear to be highly distractible and unable to screen out irrelevant stimuli from the environment (e.g., Garmezy, 1977; Lang & Buss, 1965; McGhie, 1970; McGhie & Chapman, 1961). A laboratory task that has been used extensively to study selective attention is the Stroop task (Stroop, 1935; for reviews, see Dyer, 1973, and MacLeod, 1991), and several experiments have been conducted using this task with schizophrenics.

THE STROOP TASK This task taps a fundamental aspect of selective attention: the ability to respond to one set of stimuli even when other, more compelling stimuli are available. The standard paradigm consists of two subtasks. In one, subjects name the color of the ink in which a word is printed. In the other, subjects read the word aloud while ignoring ink color. Three types of stimuli are used: conflict stimuli, in which the word and the ink color are different (e.g., the word RED in green ink); congruent stimuli, in which they are the same (e.g., the word RED in red ink); and control stimuli. The control stimuli for word

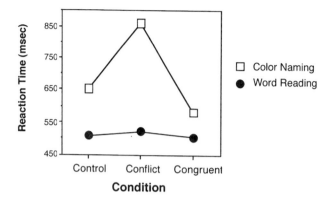

Figure 14.1
Perfomance in the standard Stroop task (after Dunbar & MacLeod, 1984). (Data are average reaction times to stimuli in each of the three conditions of the two tasks.)

reading are typically color words printed in black ink; for color naming they are usually a row of XXXXs printed in a particular color. The subjective experience of performing this task is that word reading is much easier, and there is no difficulty in ignoring the color of the ink. In contrast, it is much harder to ignore the word when the task is to name ink color.

These experiences are reflected in the time it takes for subjects to respond to stimuli of each type (see Figure 14.1). Three basic effects are observed: (a) Word reading is faster than color naming, (b) ink color has no effect on the speed of word reading, and (c) words have a large effect on color naming. For example, subjects are slower to respond to the color red when the word GREEN is written in red ink than when the word RED or a series of Xs appear in red ink. Thus, normal subjects have a harder time selectively attending to colors—and ignoring words—than the reverse. This is commonly referred to as the Stroop effect. If schizophrenics suffer from a deficit in selective attention, then they should show a larger Stroop effect; that is, they should be even worse than normal subjects in ignoring word information and should therefore show a greater interference effect.

Table 14.1 reports data from three empirical studies comparing normal and schizophrenic performance in the Stroop task.[1] Performance of control subjects conformed with the standard findings in this task: Subjects were faster at reading words than at naming colors, and words interfered with color naming. Schizophrenics also showed this pattern of results. However, in all three studies schizophrenics differed significantly from controls in two important ways: (a) Schizophrenics showed an overall slowing of responses, and (b) they showed a statistically disproportionate slowing of responses in the interference condition of the color-naming task. As we noted earlier, a deficit in selective

Table 14.1
Performance of normal and schizophrenic subjects in three studies using the Stroop task

Condition	Wapner & Krus (1960)	Abramczyk, Jordan, & Hegel (1983)	Wysocki & Sweet (1985)
Normal controls			
Word reading	0.39	0.43	0.44
Color naming	0.57	0.60	0.64
Color naming interference	0.98	1.00	1.13
Schizophrenics			
Word reading	0.57	0.50	0.52
Color naming	0.78	0.77	0.84
Color naming interference	1.51	1.40	1.49

Note. All of these studies used the original form of the Stroop task, in which subjects are given three cards, one with color words written in black ink (word reading), one with color patches or XXXs printed in different colors (color naming), and one with color words each written in a conflicting ink color (color naming interference). Data are presented as the average response time (in seconds) for stimuli of each type.

attention would predict this increase in interference. However, because an overall slowing of reaction time is also observed, the significance of this increase in interference must be questioned: This may simply reflect an unanticipated effect of general slowing of performance, rather than the effects of a specific attentional deficit (see Chapman & Chapman, 1978, for a discussion of differential vs. generalized deficits). This issue has not been resolved in the literature. Later we will show how a simulation model of this task can shed new light on this issue by helping to distinguish the effects of a general slowing from those of a specific attentional deficit.

Considerations of the Stroop effect typically focus on the role of selective attention. However, a reliable internal representation of context is also crucial to this task. In order to respond to the appropriate dimension of the stimulus, the subject must hold in mind the task instructions for that trial. These provide the necessary context for interpreting the stimulus and generating the correct response. In Stroop experiments, trials are typically blocked by task (e.g., all color naming, or all word reading) so that the proper context is consistent and regularly reinforced. This places only moderate demands on the maintenance of an internal representation of context. However, in other attentional tasks—such as certain variants of the continuous performance test—this is not the case.

THE CONTINUOUS PERFORMANCE TEST (CPT)   This task (Rosvold, Mirsky, Sarason, Bransome, & Beck, 1956) has been used extensively to study attentional deficits in schizophrenics. In the CPT, subjects are asked to detect a target event among a sequence of briefly presented stimuli and to avoid responding to distractor stimuli. The target event may be the appearance of a single stimulus (e.g., "Detect the letter X appearing in a sequence of letters"), or a stimulus appearing in a particular context (e.g., "Respond to X only when it follows A"). The percentages of correctly reported targets (hits) and erroneous responses to distractors (false alarms) are used to compute a measure of the subject's ability to discriminate target from nontarget events (d') independent of response criterion (cf. Green & Swets, 1966). Schizophrenics (and often their biological relatives) show lower hit rates and similar or higher false alarm rates compared to normal subjects and patient controls, indicating poorer signal detection ability (e.g., Cornblatt, Lenzenweger, & Erlenmeyer-Kimling, 1989; Erlenmeyer-Kimling & Cornblatt, 1978; Kornetsky, 1972; Nuechterlein, 1983, 1984; Rutschmann, Cornblatt, & Erlenmeyer-Kimling, 1977; Spohn, Lacoursiere, Thomson, & Coyne, 1977). The fact that schizophrenics show impaired signal detection performance, independent of response criterion, indicates that their poorer performance is not due simply to a lack of motivation (e.g., ignoring the task altogether) or to arbitrary responding (Swets & Sewall, 1963). It is interesting that their deficit is most apparent in versions of the task that make high processing demands: when stimuli are degraded or when information about the previous stimulus is necessary. For example, in one version—the "CPT-double" —a target event consists of the consecutive reoccurrence of any stimulus. As such, the previous stimulus provides the context necessary to decide whether or not the current one is a target; inability to use this context will impair performance. Schizophrenics perform especially poorly in this and similar versions of the task (Cornblatt et al., 1989; Nuechterlein, 1984). Note that here, in contrast to the Stroop task, elements of context change from trial to trial, so that there is additional demand placed on maintaining an internal representation of context.

OTHER MEASURES OF ATTENTION   In addition to the Stroop task and the CPT, there are a number of other information-processing paradigms in which schizophrenics exhibit performance deficits that have been related to selective attention, including the span of apprehension task (Neale, 1971), dichotic listening tasks (Spring, 1985; Wielgus & Harvey, 1988), and a variety of reaction time tasks (see Nuechterlein, 1977, for a review of the early literature, and Borst & Cohen, 1989, and R. Cohen, Borst, & Rist, 1989, for more recent work). Interpretations of schizophrenic performance in these tasks still frequently refer to Shakow's (1962) original formulation in terms of major and minor sets: Normal subjects are able to adopt a "major set" that takes account of all of the various factors involved in performing a task; schizophrenics are unable to do so, relying instead on a "minor set" that takes account of only a limited set of factors (e.g., the most recent events). Shakow (1962) argued that this is indicative of "the various difficulties created by context [sic].... It is as if, in the scanning process which takes place before the response to a stimulus is made, the schizophrenic is unable to select out the material relevant for optimal response" (p. 25). As yet, however, there is no generally accepted understanding of the specific information-processing mechanisms that are involved in maintaining an attentional set and that explain their relationship to schizophrenic disturbances in the processing of context.

Schizophrenic Language Deficits   Perhaps the clearest demonstration of deficits in the processing of context can be found in studies of schizophrenic language performance. The classic example of this comes from Chapman, Chapman, and Miller's (1964) study of schizophrenics' interpretation of lexical ambiguities. They found that schizophrenics tended to interpret the strong (dominant) meaning of a homonym used in a sentence even when context provided by the sentence mediated the weaker (subordinate) meaning. For example, given the sentence "The farmer needed a new *pen* for his cattle," schizophrenics interpreted the word *pen* to mean "writing implement" more frequently than did control subjects. They did not differ from control subjects in the number of unrelated meaning responses that were made (e.g., interpreting "pen" to mean "fire truck"), nor did they differ in the number of errors made when the strong meaning of the homonym was correct. These findings have been replicated in a number of studies (e.g., Benjamin & Watt, 1969; Blanley, 1974; J. D. Cohen, Targ, Kristoffersen, & Spiegel, 1988; Strauss, 1975).

Other studies of language performance also indicate that schizophrenics make poor use of context, including studies using cloze analysis (guessing the words deleted from a transcript of speech—e.g., Salzinger, Portnoy, & Feldman, 1964; Salzinger, Portnoy, Pisoni, & Feldman, 1970), speech reconstruction (ordering sentences that have been randomly rearranged—Rutter, 1979), and cohesion analysis (examining the types of references used in speech—e.g., Harvey, 1983; Rochester & Martin, 1979). (For reviews of this literature see Cozolino, 1983; Maher, 1972; Schwartz, 1982.) Whereas a disturbance in the internal representation of context may not account for all of the language and thought disturbances that have been observed in schizophrenics (e.g., idiosyncratic verbalizations, clang associations, or neologisms), it may be directly related to at least one aspect of the clinical presentation of this illness: the concreteness that is characteristic of schizophrenic thought processes. For example, the inability to evoke subtler, but contextually appropriate, meanings of common words may explain overly literal interpretation of proverbs and metaphors.

In language processing, as in attentional tasks, schizophrenics seem to suffer particularly from a restriction in the temporal range over which they are able to use context. Thus, for example, Salzinger et al. (1964, 1970) found that schizophrenics and normal subjects performed comparably well in "clozing" speech (i.e., guessing words deleted from a sample of normal speech) when contextual cues were local (e.g., when the missing word was surrounded by only two or three words). However, when remote cues were possible (e.g., when the missing word was surrounded by larger numbers of words), normal subjects improved in their ability to predict the word, whereas schizophrenics did not. This suggests that normal subjects were able to make use of the additional context provided by more remote cues but that schizophrenics could not. Conversely, Salzinger also showed that it is easier for normal subjects to cloze small segments of schizophrenic speech than larger ones. This implies that broader segments of schizophrenic discourse do not add contextual constraint, presumably because schizophrenics produce contextual references that span more limited segments of speech. On the basis of these data, Salzinger (1971) proposed an immediacy hypothesis which stated that "the behavior of schizophrenic patients is often controlled by stimuli which are immediate in their spatial and temporal environment than is that of normals" (p. 608).

Recently, we tested the idea that schizophrenics are restricted in the temporal range over which they can process linguistic context (J. D. Cohen et al., 1988). We designed a lexical ambiguity task, similar to the one used by Chapman et al. (1964), in which we could manipulate the temporal parameters involved.

Subjects were presented with sentences made up of two clauses; each clause appeared one at a time on a computer screen. One clause contained an ambiguous word in neutral context (e.g., "you need a PEN"), and the other clause provided disambiguating context (e.g., "in order to keep chickens" or "in order to sign a check"). Clauses were designed so that they could be presented in either order: context first or context last. The ambiguity in each sentence always appeared in capital letters so that it could be identified by the subject. Ambiguities were used that had previously been shown to have a strong (dominant) and a weak (subordinate) meaning, and a context clause was designed for each of the two meanings. Subjects were presented with the sentences and, following each, were asked to interpret the meaning of the ambiguity as it was used in the sentence.

Sentences were distributed across three conditions: (a) weak meaning correct, context last; (b) weak meaning correct, context first; and (c) strong meaning correct, context first. For example, a given subject would have seen the ambiguity PEN in one of the three following conditions and then chosen his or her response from the list of possible meanings:

(a)   without a PEN
               [*clear screen, pause*]
                              you can't keep chickens

                    —*or*—

(b)   you can't keep chickens
               [*clear screen, pause*]
                              without a PEN

                    —*or*—

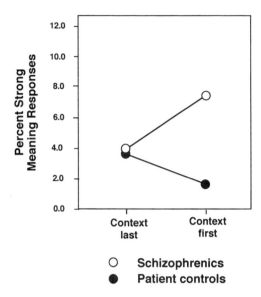

Figure 14.2
Medians for the rates of strong-meaning responses for schizophernics and patient controls when the weak meaning was correct. (Because of the low overall rate of weak-meaning responses when the strong meaning was correct, and of unrelated responses in all conditions, as well as the lack of any significant differences between groups in groups in these types of errors, these data are not shown.)

(c)   you can't sign a check
            [*clear screen, pause*]
                            without a PEN
            [*clear screen, pause*]

The meaning of the word in capital letters is:

a writing implement   [*dominant meaning*]
a fenced enclosure   [*subordinate meaning*]
a kind of truck   [*unrelated meaning*]

The results of this study (shown in Figure 14.2) corroborated both Chapman et al.'s (1964) original findings and the explanation of their findings in terms of a restriction in the temporal range over which schizophrenics are able to use context. As Chapman et al. found, schizophrenics made significantly more dominant meaning errors than did controls when the weak meaning was correct. However, this occurred only when the context came first, as in Condition (b). When context came last, schizophrenics correctly chose the weak meaning. This was the only type of error that reliably distinguished schizophrenics from controls. Thus, schizophrenics appear to have had difficulty using context but only when it was temporally remote (i.e., came first), and not when it was more recently available (i.e., came last). This effect is consistent with Salzinger's (1971) immediacy hypothesis. Moreover, it suggests that an impairment observed in language tasks may be similar in nature to the impairments observed in attentional tasks: a difficulty in maintaining and using the internal representation of context to control action.

Biological Disturbances in Schizophrenia

In parallel to research on schizophrenic information-processing deficits, there has been intensive research on biological abnormalities in this illness. Some of these involve systems that are believed to play a central role in the construction and maintenance of internal representations of context: prefrontal cortex and the mesocortical dopamine system.

Prefrontal Cortex and the Internal Representation of Context   Recent studies have begun to supply direct evidence that frontal areas are involved in maintaining internal representations of context for the control of action. For example, in neurophysiological studies, Fuster (1980, 1985a, 1985b), Goldman-Rakic (1987), and others (e.g., Barone & Joseph, 1989a, 1989b) have observed cells in prefrontal cortex that are specific to a particular stimulus and response and that remain active during a delay between these. These investigators have argued that neural patterns of activity are maintained in prefrontal cortex that encode the temporary information needed to guide a response. At the behavioral level, these authors and others (e.g., Damasio, 1979; Mishkin & Pribram, 1955; Passingham, 1985; Rosenkilde, 1979; Rosvold, Szwarcbart, Mirsky, & Mishkin, 1961; Stuss & Benson, 1984) have reported data suggesting that prefrontal cortex is needed to perform tasks involving delayed responses to ambiguous stimuli. Diamond and Goldman-Rakic (1989) have emphasized that prefrontal representations are required, in particular, to overcome reflexive or previously reinforced response tendencies in order to mediate a contextually relevant—but otherwise weaker—response (see also Diamond, 1985, 1990a, 1990c; Diamond & Doar, 1989). Diamond cites extensive data from lesion studies in adult monkeys and from developmental studies in human and monkey infants that use a variety of behavioral tasks (including object retrieval, visual paired comparisons, delayed response, and the A B̄ task). Results from these and many previous studies suggest that prefrontal cortex is directly involved in maintaining representations that inhibit reflexive or habitually reinforced behaviors to attain a goal.

For example, in the A B̄ task (pronounced "A not B"; Piaget, 1937/1954) subjects observe a desired object being hidden at one of two locations that are identical in appearance. Following a delay—during which fixation is drawn away from the hiding place—subjects are allowed to retrieve the object. The object is hidden at the same location until the subject has successfully retrieved it some number of times, after which the hiding place is switched. Normal adult monkeys and 5-year-old human children can successfully retrieve the object with delays between hiding and retrieval of 2 min or more. Monkeys with lesions of prefrontal cortex, as well as human infants younger than 6 months (in whom the frontal lobes are still in a rudimentary stage of development), can perform the task successfully only if there is no delay between the cue and test phases. With delays as short as 2 s, they show perseveration of previously reinforced responses: a return to the location at which the object was last retrieved (Diamond & Goldman-Rakic, 1989). This pattern of errors is specific to subjects lacking prefrontal cortex and is not found with lesions of the hippocampus or parietal lobes, where performance is either normal or at chance (Diamond, 1990b, 1990c).

Thus, it appears that prefrontal cortex is responsible for maintaining a representation (the location of the hidden object) required to inhibit a dominant response (return to the most recently rewarded location). Note, furthermore, that these findings help distinguish the internal representation of context from memory for specific associations between stimuli and responses. They indicate that these two functions are supported by different neural structures, with prefrontal cortex involved only in the former. It is precisely because lesions of prefrontal cortex affect internal representations of context and not associative memory that perseverations based on learned associations can occur. In contrast, lesions that involve other areas subserving such associations (e.g., hippocampus or parietal lobes) result in random, rather than perseverative, behavior (e.g., Diamond, 1990b).

The performance deficits observed for infants and frontally lesioned monkeys on delay tasks are similar to those observed for adult frontal lobe patients on the Wisconsin Card Sort Task (WCST; Grant & Berger, 1948). In this task, subjects are presented with a series of cards containing figures that vary in shape, color, and number. They are asked to sort the cards into piles according to a rule that the experimenter has in mind (e.g., "separate the cards by color"). However, subjects are not explicitly told the rule for sorting; rather, they are given feedback for each card as to whether or not they have sorted it properly. Normal subjects discover the rule quickly. Once they have demonstrated that they know it (i.e., by correctly sorting a certain number of cards in a row) the experimenter switches the rule, and the subject is required to discover the new rule. Patients with damage to the frontal lobes do poorly on this task (e.g., Milner, 1963; Nelson, 1976; Robinson, Heaton, Lehman, & Stilson, 1980). Although they are able to discover the first rule without too much difficulty, they are unable to switch to a new one: They continue to sort according to the old rule.

As in delay tasks, this behavior can be viewed as a failure to use contextual information—in this case, feedback from the experimenter—to overcome a response pattern that was correct on previous trials. Furthermore, there are additional indications from these tasks that a specific failure to use internal representations of context is involved, as distinct from a disturbance in declarative, or short-term, memory. In both the WCST and in delayed response tasks, subjects have been observed who show perseveratory behavior despite indications that they remember the relevant prior information. Thus, subjects in the WCST will sometimes comment that they know their perseveratory response is incorrect even as they carry it out (Goldberg, Weinberger, Berman, Pliskin, & Podd, 1987). Similarly, in the A B̄ task, subjects have been observed looking at the cued (new) location while reaching for the old (incorrect) one (Diamond & Goldman-Rakic, 1989). These kinds of observations support a dissociation between declarative, or short-term, memory on the one hand, and the internal representation of context needed to actually control the response, on the other. We assume that it is the latter—representation of response-specific contextual information—that is mediated by prefrontal cortex.

Note that in both the WCST and the A B̄ task, subjects with poor prefrontal function are not impaired in their ability to learn the basic elements of the task. Rather, they are impaired in their ability to use an internal representation of context to override the effects of prior experience in the task. This characterization of frontal lobe function fits well with clinical descriptions of the "disinhibition syndrome" that often accompanies frontal lobe pathology (e.g., Stuss & Benson, 1984). It is also consistent with difficulties that have been observed for frontal lobe patients in performing the Stroop task (Perret, 1974) and similar tasks in clinical use (e.g., the "go–no-go" paradigm) that require the subject to use task instructions to inhibit a dominant response tendency.

Finally, physiological measures have begun to provide converging evidence for the role of prefrontal cortex in supporting internal representations of context. Using measures of regional cerebral blood flow (rCBF), Weinberger and his collaborators (Berman, Illowsky, & Weinberger, 1988; Weinberger, Berman, & Chase, 1988; Weinberger, Berman, & Zec, 1986) have demonstrated that, in normal subjects, prefrontal metabolism correlates with WCST performance. Furthermore, this correlation is specific to prefrontal cortex (vs. other cortical areas). This finding corroborates the results of neuropsychological studies that link WCST performance with frontal lobe function (e.g., Nelson, 1976; Robinson et al., 1980). Weinberger's group also showed that not all cognitive tasks requiring effort and concentration are accompanied by such an increase in prefrontal activity. For example, during the Raven Progressive Matrices test—in which the task-relevant information is visually available at all times—metabolism increased in parietal and occipital areas but not in frontal areas.

Other tasks that rely on internal representations of context also appear to activate prefrontal cortex. R. M. Cohen and his colleagues (R. M. Cohen et al., 1987; R. M. Cohen, Semple, Gross, Holcomb, et al., 1988) used positron emission tomography (PET) to measure regional brain metabolism during performance of an auditory-discrimination version of the CPT. They found an increase in prefrontal metabolism in normal subjects, which correlated with performance on the task: Subjects who made more commission errors (false alarms) showed less of an increase in metabolism in prefrontal areas. Not all studies examining frontal lobe function during CPT performance have yielded positive results (e.g., Berman, Zec, & Weinberger, 1986). However, differing results may be attributable to differences in the actual tasks and conditions that were run. We will return to this issue in the General Discussion section.

In summary, evidence from attentional tasks (e.g., the CPT and the Stroop task), problem-solving tasks (e.g., the WCST and the A B̄ task), and from physiological imaging studies suggests that areas of the frontal cortex support the representation of information needed for response selection. A disturbance in this representation is most apparent when experimental tasks involve competing, prepotent responses. These dominant responses may have developed during the task itself (as in the WCST and the A B̄ task), or they may have existed prior to the experiment (e.g., the Stroop task). A disturbance in the prefrontal representation manifests as a bias toward prepotent, but task-inappropriate, response tendencies (e.g., interference in the Stroop task; perseveratory patterns in the WCST and the A B̄ task). The data reviewed earlier concerning schizophrenic performance deficits fit with this profile: an insensitivity to context and a dominant response tendency. It is not surprising to find, therefore, that frontal lobe deficits have been implicated in schizophrenia.

Frontal Deficits in Schizophrenia   The idea that the frontal lobes may be involved in schizophrenia is not new. Kraeplin (1950), who first defined this illness (as *dementia praecox*), wrote

> On various grounds it is easy to believe that the frontal cortex, which is especially well developed in man, stands in closer relation to his higher intellectual abilities, and that these are the faculties which in our patients invariably show profound loss. (p. 219)

Schizophrenics show typical frontal lobe deficits on neuropsychological tests (see Kolb & Whishaw, 1983, for a review), including the WCST (e.g., Malmo, 1974) and the Stroop task (e.g., Abramczyk et al., 1983; Wapner & Krus, 1960; Wysocki & Sweet, 1985). Several studies using imaging and electrophysiological techniques have also provided evidence suggesting frontal involvement in schizophrenia. Using rCBF, Ingvar and Franzen (1974; Franzen & Ingvar, 1975) reported abnormal perfusion of frontal areas in schizophrenics, and Buchsbaum et al. (1982) found abnormalities of glucose utilization localized to similar areas. Andreasen et al. (1986) reported evidence of frontal lobe atrophy in computerized tomographic (CT) images, and other data indicate that ventricular enlargement in schizophrenics (e.g., Andreasen et al., 1986; Weinberger et al., 1980) is associated with frontal lobe atrophy (Morihisa & McAnulty, 1985). Farkas et al. (1984) demonstrated a correlation between abnormal structure (CT) and perfusion (PET) of the frontal lobes, and Morihisa and McAnulty

(1985) showed a correlation between structural (CT) and electrophysiological abnormalities.

Not all studies using physiological imaging techniques have found metabolic abnormalities of the frontal lobes in schizophrenics (e.g., Gur et al., 1987). However, in recent studies investigators have begun to use these techniques to examine frontal activity under specific behavioral conditions. Weinberger et al. (1986) demonstrated abnormal perfusion of prefrontal cortex during performance of the WCST. Similarly, R. M. Cohen et al. (1987; R. M. Cohen, Semple, Gross, Nordahl, et al., 1988) showed that schizophrenics fail to show the normal pattern of increased perfusion of prefrontal cortex during performance of a version of the CPT. These studies suggest that anatomic and physiological deficits of frontal cortex may indeed be associated with some of the behavioral deficits that have been observed in schizophrenics.

Dopamine, Prefrontal Cortex, and Schizophrenia   The hypothesis that frontal lobe dysfunction is involved in schizophrenia fits well with the prevailing neurochemical and psychopharmacological data concerning this illness. Prefrontal cortex is a primary projection area for the mesocortical dopamine system, a disturbance of which has consistently been implicated in schizophrenia (e.g., Losonczy, Davidson, & Davis, 1987; Meltzer & Stahl, 1976; Nauta & Domesick, 1981). The dopamine hypothesis is one of the most enduring biological hypotheses concerning schizophrenia. Evidence for this hypothesis comes from a variety of sources. Perhaps the strongest argument is the chemical specificity of the neuroleptics, which are used to treat the symptoms of schizophrenia. In vitro studies have demonstrated that neuroleptics have a specific affinity for dopamine binding sites and that this affinity is correlated with their clinical potency (B. M. Cohen, 1981; Creese, Burt, & Snyder, 1976; Snyder, 1976). Furthermore, drugs that influence dopamine activity in the central nervous system—such as amphetamines and L-dopa—exacerbate symptoms in psychotic patients (Angrist, Peselow, Rubinstein, Wolkin, & Rotrosen, 1985; Davidson et al., 1987; Janowsky, Huey, Storms, & Judd, 1977; Lieberman et al., 1984) and may induce psychosis in nonpsychotic individuals (e.g., Janowsky & Rich, 1979; Snyder, 1972). Studies of the plasma (Bowers, Heninger, & Sternberg, 1980; Pickar et al., 1984) and cerebrospinal fluid (Sedvall, Fyro, Nyback, Wiesel, & Wode-Helgodt, 1974) of schizophrenics have revealed abnormal levels of dopamine metabolites. Finally, several postmortem studies have found evidence for an elevation in the number of dopamine receptors in schizophrenics compared to controls (e.g., Cross, Crow, & Owen, 1981; Seeman et al., 1984; Tyrone & Seeman, 1980), and this elevation has been found to correlate with the previous experience of hallucinations and delusions (Crow et al., 1984).

Whereas different investigators have argued that central dopamine activity is either reduced (e.g., Early, Posner, Reiman, & Raichle, 1989; Karoum, Karson, Bigelow, Lawson, & Wyatt, 1987) or increased (e.g., Creese et al., 1976; Snyder,

1972, 1976) in schizophrenia, one hypothesis is that both conditions may occur (either within or across individuals) and that each is associated with a different psychopathological profile. For example, both Crow (1980) and Mackay (1980) suggested that the symptoms of schizophrenia can be divided into two subtypes, one that reflects dopamine overactivity (positive symptoms—e.g., hallucinations and delusions) and another that reflects dopamine underactivity (negative symptoms—e.g., motivational difficulties, cognitive impairment, paucity in content of speech, flattening of affect, and deficits in social functioning). Several authors have argued that it is the negative symptoms of schizophrenia that are most often associated with frontal lobe deficits (e.g., Andreasen, Flaum, Swayze, Tyrrell, & Arndt, 1990; Andreasen et al., 1986, 1991; Goldman-Rakic, 1991; Levin, 1984). This is consistent with mounting evidence that mesocortical dopamine activity in prefrontal cortex is directly related to cognitive function and that a reduction of this activity can produce many of the cognitive deficits observed in schizophrenics. Thus, McCulloch, Savaki, McCulloch, Jehle, and Sokoloff (1982) showed that activation of mesocortical dopaminergic neurons increases metabolic activity in the prefrontal cortex of animals. Conversely, lesions of the same dopamine projections reduce metabolism in prefrontal cortex and impair cognitive functions usually associated with this brain region, such as the execution of search strategies or delayed-alternation tasks (Oades, 1981; Simon, Scatton, & Le Moal, 1980). For example, rhesus monkeys could not perform a delayed-alternation task following selective destruction of dopamine terminals in prefrontal cortex (Brozoski, Brown, Rosvold, & Goldman, 1979). This deficit was as severe as that following full surgical ablation of the same area of cortex. Moreover, performance recovered almost entirely with dopamine agonists such as L-dopa and apomorphine. Similar findings have been reported with respect to attentional impairments (e.g., Corwin, Kanter, Watson, Heilman, Valenstein, & Hashimoto, 1986) and, more recently, working memory deficits (Sawaguchi & Goldman-Rakic, 1991). Finally, studies of human patients suffering from Parkinson's disease—in which dopamine function is markedly impaired—provide similar evidence: Even when these patients do not display clinically significant cognitive deficits, they display impairments on the WCST similar to those observed in frontal lobe subjects (Bowen, Kamienny, Burns, & Yahr, 1975). This deficit is less pronounced in patients receiving the dopamine precursor L-dopa, which often has therapeutic efficacy in reestablishing dopaminergic tone.

In view of these findings, several authors have proposed that reduced dopaminergic tone in prefrontal cortex may be associated with frontal lobe abnormalities in schizophrenia and may be responsible for several of the cognitive deficits that have been observed. Levin (1984) reviewed a wide variety of behavioral data in support of this hypothesis (also see Goldman-Rakic, 1991; Levin, Yurgelun-Todd, & Craft, 1989). Recently, physiological data have also begun to accumulate. Weinberger, Berman, and Illowsky (1988) reported that levels of the dopamine metabolite homovanillic acid in the cerebrospinal fluid of schizophrenics show a strong correlation with prefrontal activity during WCST performance. In another study, Geraud, Arne-Bes, Guell, and Bes (1987) were able to reverse the metabolic hypofrontality observed in schizophrenics on PET by administration of a dopamine agonist. Thus, there is growing evidence that dopamine is closely related to the activity of prefrontal cortex and that a disturbance in this system may be involved in schizophrenic cognitive deficits. What is lacking, however, is a coherent account of these findings in terms of mechanisms that link biological processes with performance in behavioral tasks.

Summary

We have reviewed evidence suggesting (a) that schizophrenics suffer from an inability to construct and maintain internal representations of context for the control of action, (b) that prefrontal cortex plays a role in maintaining such representations, (c) that an intact mesocortical dopamine system is necessary for the normal function of prefrontal cortex, and (d) that disturbances of both prefrontal cortex and the mesocortical dopamine system appear to be involved in schizophrenia. However, despite a growing recognition that these findings are related, no theory has yet been proposed that answers the following question: How does a disturbance of dopamine activity in prefrontal cortex lead to the pattern of cognitive deficits observed in schizophrenia? In the section that follows, we describe simulation models developed within the connectionist framework that attempt to answer this question.

Connectionist Simulations

We have constructed a set of simulation models that show how the connectionist framework can be used to link the biological and behavioral processes just discussed. In this section, we present three such models, which simulate performance in three of the experimental tasks discussed previously: the Stroop task, the CPT, and the lexical disambiguation task. In each case, we show that a simulation of reduced dopamine effect in a component of the model identified with the function of prefrontal cortex results in performance deficits that are quantitatively similar to those observed for schizophrenics in the corresponding tasks. As background for understanding these models, we first provide a brief overview of the connectionist framework.

The Connectionist Framework

The principles of connectionism, or parallel distributed processing (McClelland & Rumelhart, 1986; Rumelhart & McClelland, 1986b), provide a framework for building computer models that can simulate cognitive phenomena. At the same time, these principles are meant to capture the salient details of the mechanisms underlying information processing in the brain. They can be roughly divided into those having to do with processing and those having to do with training.

Processing Each unit in a connectionist network (see Figure 14.3) is a simple summing device: It accumulates inputs from other units and adjusts its output in response to these inputs. Typically, units are grouped into modules, and modules are connected into pathways. Information is represented as the pattern of activation over the units in a module. The activation of each unit is a real-valued number varying continuously between a minimum and maximum value, which can be thought of as the unit's probability of firing. The responsivity of each unit is scaled by its *gain* parameter, which serves as a multiplier for the effects of excitatory and inhibitory inputs to the unit. Processing occurs by the propagation of signals (spread of activation) among units within and between modules. This occurs via the connections that exist between units. The connections between the units of different modules constitute processing pathways.

Training The ability of this type of system to perform a given task depends on its having an appropriate set of connection weights in the pathway that runs from the input modules to the output modules relevant to the task. The connections in a pathway are set by learning. Although a number of different connectionist learning techniques have been described, the generalized delta rule, or back propagation algorithm (Rumelhart, Hinton, & Williams, 1986), is in widest use. In brief, this involves the following series of operations: (a) present an input pattern to the network; (b) allow activation to spread to the output level; (c) compute the difference (error) for each output unit between its current activation and the one desired (i.e., the one specified by the target, or teaching pattern); (d) "back propagate" these error signals toward the input units. The back propagation algorithm provides a way for each unit in a pathway to compute the adjustment it must make to its connection weights so as to best reduce the error at the output level. A common criticism of this algorithm is that it is not biologically plausible. That is, it is difficult to imagine that real neural systems rely on the back propagation of error signals for learning. However, back propagation implements the general phenomenon of *gradient descent*—the gradual reduction of error by incremental adjustments in connection weights. Gradient descent has proven to be a powerful concept for describing many of the details concerning human learning behavior (e.g., J. D. Cohen, Dunbar, & McClelland, 1990). Thus, it may be that back propagation offers a reasonable approximation of the type of learning that occurs in neural systems, even if the actual algorithm is different.

It is important to recognize also that most connectionist models are not intended to be detailed circuit diagrams of actual neural networks. Rather, like statistical mechanical models in physics and chemistry, connectionist models

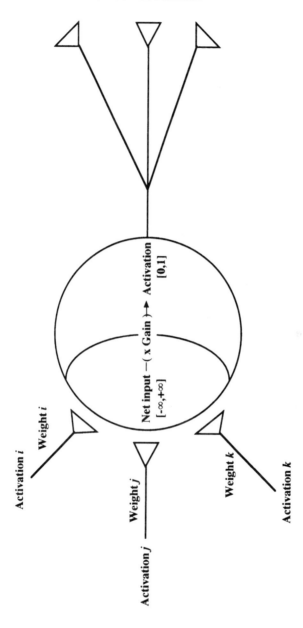

Figure 14.3
Schematic representation of a typical unit in a connectionist system.

are designed to capture those features of a lower level system (information-processing mechanisms in the brain) that are most relevant at a higher level of analysis (cognition and behavior). Thus, an important goal in constructing such models is to make it possible to examine the effects of biological variables on behavior without having to reproduce the entire brain.

We believe that developing biologically plausible models of information processing will (a) lead to more realistic models of cognitive phenomena and (b) make it possible to relate behavior directly to biological processes (for an in-depth discussion, see Rumelhart & McClelland, 1986c). Connectionist models have begun to show promise along these lines in their ability to explain a variety of phenomena at both the biological and behavioral levels. These include the computation of spatial orientation from retinal and eye-position information (Zipser & Andersen, 1988), the computation of object shape from shading information (Lehky & Sejnowski, 1988), the acquisition of regular and irregular verb forms in English (Rumelhart & McClelland, 1986a), text-to-speech translation and disturbances of this phenomenon in surface dyslexia (Patterson, Seidenberg, & McClelland, 1989; Seidenberg & McClelland, 1989), and access to word meaning from word form in deep dyslexia (Hinton & Shallice, 1991).

Using the connectionist framework, we developed simulation models of three tasks relevant to research on schizophrenia: the Stroop task, the continuous performance test, and the lexical disambiguation task described earlier. Each model was designed to simulate normal performance in one of these tasks. Although the models differ in the details necessary to capture differences between these tasks, all three rely on a common set of information-processing principles (as just described) and, in particular, share a common mechanism for representing and maintaining context. In each case, this mechanism relies on a specific module that we identify with the function of the prefrontal cortex. After establishing the ability of each model to capture normal performance of its particular task, we examined the effects that reducing the gain of units in the context module had on performance in order to explore the hypothesis that such a disturbance can account for schizophrenic deficits in that task. We begin our description of the models by showing how the physiological influence of dopamine can be simulated by changes in the gain parameter of individual units. We then describe simulations which show that a change in gain in the module used to represent context can account for differences between normal and schizophrenic performance in the Stroop, CPT, and lexical disambiguation tasks.

Simulation of the Physiological Effects of Dopamine
In contrast to other neurotransmitter systems, such as amino acids or peptides, the anatomy and physiology of dopamine systems are not suited to the trans-

mission of discrete sensory or motor messages. Rather, like other catecholamine systems, dopamine systems are in a position to modulate the state of information processing in entire brain areas over prolonged periods of time. Several anatomical and physiological observations support this contention. Dopamine neurons originate in discrete nuclei localized in the brain stem, and their fibers project radially to several functionally different areas of the central nervous system. The baseline firing rate of these neurons is low and stable, and the conduction velocity along their fibers is slow. These characteristics result in a steady state of transmitter release and relatively long-lasting postsynaptic effects that are conducive to modulatory influences. Most important, recent evidence suggests that, at least under certain circumstances, the effect of dopamine release is not to directly increase or reduce the firing frequency of target cells (e.g., Chiodo & Berger, 1986; Schneider, Levine, Hull, & Buchwald, 1984); rather, like norepinephrine, dopamine can modulate the response properties of postsynaptic cells such that both inhibitory and excitatory responses to other afferent inputs are potentiated. Some investigators have described this effect as an increase in the "signal-to-noise ratio" of the cells' behavior (Foote, Freedman, & Oliver, 1975) or an "enabling" of the cells' response (Bloom, Schulman, & Koob, 1989).

The modulatory effects of dopamine have been investigated mostly in the striatum, where they are similar to those observed for norepinephrine elsewhere. The results of investigations conducted directly in the prefrontal cortex are less clear. Some studies (Bunney & Aghajanian, 1976; Ferron, Thierry, Le Douarin, & Glowinski, 1984; Reader, Ferron, Descarries, & Jasper, 1979; Bunney & Sesack, 1987) report a potentiation of inhibitory responses but a reduction of excitatory responses. However, in these studies the amount of dopamine released also produced a direct decrease in the baseline firing rate of the cells. This direct decrease in baseline firing rate has also been observed in striatal cells, but only when large amounts of dopamine were released and not for smaller amounts (Chiodo & Berger, 1986). Thus, the reduction of excitatory responses in prefrontal cortex that has been reported may be related to the use of high concentrations of dopamine.[2] The effects of smaller concentrations— which do not affect baseline firing rate—have not been tested. More consistent with the idea of dopamine-induced *potentiation* are the results of two other studies, conducted in primate prefrontal cortex (Aou, Nishino, Inokuchi, & Mizuno, 1983; Sawaguchi & Matsumura, 1985), in which inhibitory as well as excitatory effects of dopamine iontophoresis were found.[3]

In our models, we assume that the effects of dopamine on cells in prefrontal cortex—at concentrations relevant to the behavioral tasks we are interested in—are similar to the effects that have been observed in striatal cells: a potentiation of cell responses. Two caveats are warranted by this assumption. First, although potentiation is compatible with existing data, as just noted, it has not been substantiated directly in physiological studies of prefrontal cortex. Second, the mechanism by which dopamine potentiates both excitatory and inhibitory inputs has not yet been elucidated. In particular, it is not clear whether this is a direct effect of dopamine on the target cell or whether potentiation arises from local interactions among inhibitory and excitatory cells. We will consider both of these issues further in the General Discussion section. In the simulations described in this section we have not concerned ourselves with the detailed mechanisms of how potentiating effects arise at the cellular level; we have focused instead on their functional significance by capturing the effects of potentiation with a single parameter.

In the models we simulate the action of dopamine by changing gain, which is a parameter of the function that relates a unit's input to its activation value. Thus, first we assume that the relationship between the input to a neuron and its firing rate can be simulated as a nonlinear function relating the net input of a unit in the model to its activation value. Physiological experiments suggest that in biological systems the shape of this function is sigmoid, with its steepest slope around the baseline firing rate (e.g., Burnod & Korn, 1989; Freeman, 1979). The same experiments also indicate that small increments in excitatory drive produce changes in firing frequency that are greater than those produced by equivalent increments in inhibitory input. These properties can be captured by the logistic function with a constant negative bias (see Figure 14.4, gain = 1.0):

$$\text{activation} = \frac{1}{1 + e^{-(\text{gain}*\text{net}) + \text{bias}}}.$$

The potentiating effects of dopamine can then be simulated by increasing the gain parameter of the logistic function. As Figure 14.4 illustrates, with a higher gain (gain = 2.0) the unit is more sensitive to afferent signals, whereas its baseline firing rate (net input = 0) remains the same. Elsewhere we have shown that such a change in gain can simulate a number of different catecholaminergic effects at both the biological and behavioral levels (e.g., the influence of catecholamines on the receptive field of individual units, the influence of amphetamines on stimulus detection in humans, and stimulus response generalization in both humans and rats; see Servan-Schreiber, 1990; Servan-Schreiber, Printz, & Cohen, 1990).

To simulate the effect of a neuromodulator, such as dopamine, we change gain equally for all units in the model that are assumed to be influenced by that neuromodulator. For example, the mesocortical dopamine system has extensive projections to prefrontal cortex. To model the action of dopamine in this brain area, we change the gain of all units in the module corresponding to this area. In the following models, decreased dopaminergic activity in prefrontal cortex was simulated by reducing the gain of units in the module used to represent and maintain context.

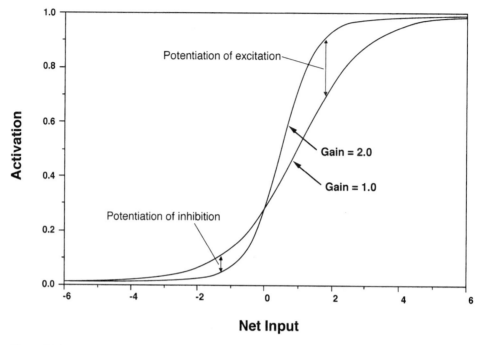

Figure 14.4
The influence of the gain parameter on the logistic activation function of an individual unit. (Note that with an increase in gain, the effect of the net input on the unit's activation is increased, whereas the reverse is true with a decrease in the gain. These effects simulate the consequences of dopamine release on target neurons in the central nervous system.)

A Connectionist Model of Selective Attention (the Stroop Effect)

Architecture and Processing Elsewhere we have described a connectionist model of selective attention that simulates human performance in the Stroop task (J. D. Cohen et al., 1990). In brief, this model consists of two processing pathways, one for color naming and one for word reading (see Figure 14.5). Simulations are conducted by activating input units corresponding to stimuli used in an actual experiment (e.g., the input unit representing the color red in the color naming pathway) and allowing activation to spread through the network. This leads to activation of the output unit corresponding to the appropriate response (e.g., "red"). Reaction time is considered to be linearly related to the number of cycles it takes for an output unit to accumulate a specified amount of activation.

Training The model is trained to produce the appropriate behavior by presenting it with the input patterns for each of the responses it is expected to make and using the back propagation learning algorithm to adjust the connec-

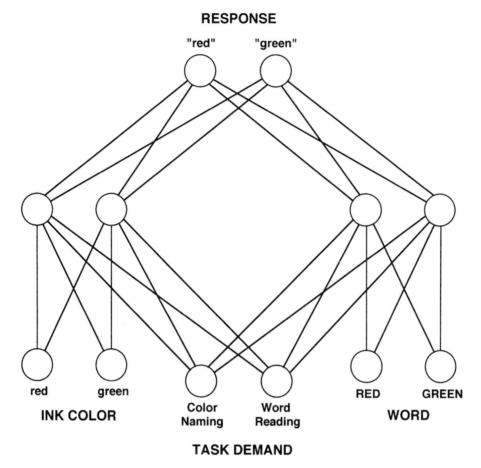

Figure 14.5
Network architecture. (Units at the bottom are input units, and units at the top are the output [response] units. From "On the Control of Automatic Processes: A Parallel Distributed Processing Account of the Stroop Effect" by J. D. Cohen, K. Dunbar, and J. L. McClelland, 1990, *Psychological Review 97*, 336. Copyright 1990 by the American Psychological Association.)

tion weights accordingly. During training, the model is given more experience with (i.e., a greater number of training trials on) the word-reading task than the color-naming task. This corresponds to the common assumption that human adults have had more experience generating a verbal response to written words than to colors they see. Because of this, the connection weights in the word-reading pathway become greater than those in the color-naming pathway. As a result, when the network is presented with conflicting inputs in the two pathways (e.g., the word RED and the color green), it responds preferentially to the word input. Of course, human subjects are able to overcome this tendency and respond to the color instead of the word when requested to do so. To capture this effect in the model, a set of units are included that represent the intended behavior (i.e., color naming vs. word reading). Thus, the specification of a particular task is represented by the appropriate pattern of activation over a set of "task demand" units. These are connected to the intermediate units in each of the two pathways and modulate their responsivity. For example, when the pattern corresponding to "color naming" is activated over the task demand units, activation spreading from these units has a sensitizing effect on processing units in the color pathway while it "desensitizes" units in the word pathway. This modulates the flow of information in the two pathways, favoring the color pathway. The result is that although the connection strengths in the color pathway are weaker, a signal presented to this pathway is able to overcome the otherwise dominant response mediated by the word pathway. In other words, the model is able to selectively attend to information in the task-relevant pathway. Note that spreading activation and attentional modulation are not different processes. Attentional modulation of both pathways is a consequence of activation spreading from the task demand units to the intermediate units in each pathway. Thus, both the "direct processing" of information as well as its attentional modulation rely on the same mechanisms of processing (see J. D. Cohen et al., 1990, for a more detailed discussion).

Simulation   This simple model is able to simulate a wide variety of empirical phenomena associated with the Stroop task. It captures all of the phenomena depicted in Figure 14.1 (asymmetry in speed of processing between word reading and color naming, the immunity of word reading to the effects of color, the susceptibility of color naming to interference and facilitation from words, and greater interference than facilitation effects). It also captures the influence of practice on interference and facilitation effects, the relative nature of these effects (i.e., their dependence on the nature of a competing process), stimulus onset asynchrony effects, and response set effects (see J. D. Cohen et al., 1990).

The model also clarifies the relationship between attention and the internal representation of context. Stimuli that vary in more than one dimension are inherently ambiguous (e.g., "Should I respond to the word or the color?"). Task instructions provide the context necessary to disambiguate the stimulus and choose the appropriate response. Furthermore, task instructions must be represented internally because, as we have said, the stimuli themselves do not indicate which task to perform. In the model, this internal representation was captured as a pattern of activation in the task demand module. This had a direct attentional effect: It was responsible for the model's selecting one pathway for the processing of information and not the other. Thus, the model suggests that attentional selection can be thought of as the mediating effects that the internal representation of context has on processing.

These ideas are directly relevant to schizophrenic deficits. If prefrontal cortex is responsible for maintaining the internal representation of context, and if schizophrenia involves a disturbance of frontal lobe function, then we should be able to simulate schizophrenic deficits in the Stroop task by disturbing processing in the task demand module. More specifically, if frontal lobe dysfunction in schizophrenia is due to a reduction in the activity of its dopaminergic supply, then we should be able to simulate this by reducing the gain of units in the task demand module.

Panel B of Figure 14.6 shows the results of this simulation, in which the gain of only the task demand units was reduced; all other units were unperturbed. This change in the context (i.e., task demand) module produces effects similar to those observed for schizophrenics: an increase in overall response time, with a disproportionate increase on color-naming conflict trials. It is important to emphasize here that this simulation was conducted without making any changes to the original Stroop model (J. D. Cohen et al., 1990) other than manipulating the gain of units in the task demand module, as motivated by our hypothesis.

It is interesting that the simulation shows that a lesion restricted to the mechanism for representing context can produce an *overall* degradation of performance in addition to the expected specific attentional deficit (i.e., increased interference). The overall slowing occurs because, according to this model, all processes rely on attention to some degree (see J. D. Cohen et al., 1990, for a detailed discussion). Disproportionate slowing occurs in the conflict condition because weaker, less automatic processes (e.g., color naming) rely more on selective attention (i.e., mediating context) than do stronger, more automatic ones (e.g., word reading), particularly when these are in competition.

The model also allows us to address a problem that frequently besets the interpretation of schizophrenic deficits. Recall the argument that, given an overall degradation of performance, it is difficult to know whether poor performance in a particular experimental condition is due to a specific deficit or to a more generalized one responsible for the overall degradation. This reflects a limitation in our ability to attribute cause when the information we have about a system is restricted to its behavior and we lack any knowledge about underlying mechanisms. However, the model provides us with a tool for specifying possible mechanisms and studying the behavior they produce. Earlier, we

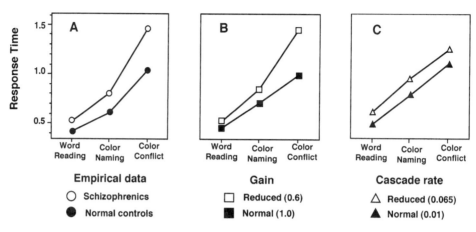

Figure 14.6
Stroop task performance for normal and schizophrenic subjects, and results from simulations manipulating the gain parameter (task demand units only) and cascade rate (all units) in the network. (Empirical data are the response times in [in seconds] for stimuli in each condition of the Stroop task, averaged over the three empirical studies reported in Table 14.1. Simulation data are the number of cycles required for processing stimuli of each type, averaged over 1,000 trials of each type and scaled by a constant [0.02] to facilitate comparison between these and the empirical data. The 5% confidence intervals for all simulation data are all less than 0.02.)

described a mechanism for a specific attentional deficit: a disturbance in the context module. We can compare this to a more generalized deficit—one that produces an overall slowing of response—by decreasing the rate at which information accumulates for units in the network. This is determined by a parameter called the *cascade rate*. We tested for the effects of a generalized deficit of this sort by reducing the cascade rate for all units in network. The reduction in cascade rate was selected by matching the degree of slowing in the word-reading condition of the simulation to the amount of slowing observed for schizophrenics relative to control subjects in the empirical data. The results of this manipulation are shown in Panel C of Figure 14.6. There is an overall slowing of response, but no disproportionate slowing in the interference condition. Thus, slowing the processing rate of units throughout the network is unable to account for schizophrenic performance in the interference condition of the task. We explored other deficits that produce an overall slowing of response (e.g., an increase in the response threshold) with similar results. In contrast, as we noted above, impairment of the context module produces both effects: Slowing occurs in all conditions but is most pronounced in the interference condition.

Chapman and Chapman (1978) pointed out the danger in assuming that degraded performance in a particular task condition necessarily reflects a deficit in processes related to that condition. If the condition is also the hardest one for normal subjects (as is the case for the interference condition of the color-naming task), then even a disproportionate degradation of performance in that condition could be caused by a generalized deficit (i.e., one that is not specific to any particular processing component). We have tried to show how a simulation model can help us deal with this problem. Our model demonstrates that a specific attentional deficit provides a better account for the data than a number of possible generalized deficits. Furthermore, the model provides a new interpretation of the data, reversing the typical view: It shows how a general degradation in performance can arise from a specific deficit, rather than the other way around. To our knowledge, this possibility has not been considered in the literature. Of course, our results do not preclude the possibility that some other model could account for the findings in terms of a different deficit—specific or generalized. However, by providing an explanation of the findings in terms of an explicit set of information-processing mechanisms, we have set a threshold for explanation that must be met by competing alternatives. Furthermore, we have shown how simulation models can be used to deal with the problem of differential deficits described by Chapman and Chapman. When tasks (or conditions) differ in difficulty, it is still possible to compare competing hypotheses by specifying the mechanisms believed to underlie the deficit and comparing their ability to account for the empirical data.

Finally, as discussed earlier, the model relates a disturbance in selective attention directly to the processing of context. Selective attention is viewed as the effects that context has on processing, and a failure to maintain an appropriate contextual representation (e.g., the task demand specification) leads directly to a failure in selective attention. In the Stroop task, this manifests as an increased susceptibility to interference in the color-naming task. This interference, in turn, reflects the increased influence of dominant response processes (e.g., word reading) that occurs with the weakening of attention. Schizophrenic performance has often been characterized as reflecting a dominant response tendency (e.g., Chapman et al., 1964; Maher, 1972), although no specific mechanism has previously been proposed for this. We will return to this issue later in our discussion of schizophrenic language performance.

Simulation of the Continuous Performance Test (CPT)
The Stroop model shows how contextual information and its attentional effects can be represented in a connectionist model and how a specific disturbance in this mechanism can explain important aspects of schizophrenic performance. One question we might ask is: How general are these findings? Here, we extend the principles described in the Stroop model to account for performance in the CPT.

As we discussed earlier, schizophrenics show consistent deficits in the CPT. This is particularly true for variants in which demand is placed on the active maintenance of internal representations of context. For example, in the CPT-

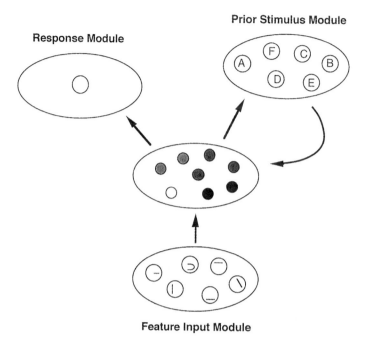

Figure 14.7
Network used to simulate the continuous performance test-double. (Note the bidirectional connections between units in the intermediate and prior stimulus modules.)

double, a target consists of any consecutive reoccurrence of a stimulus (e.g., a B immediately following a B). Thus, subjects must be able to use a representation of the previous stimulus as context for responding to the subsequent one. We have argued that such response-specific representations are maintained in prefrontal cortex and that this function of prefrontal cortex is impaired in schizophrenics. Indeed, schizophrenics perform poorly in the CPT-double and similar versions (Cornblatt et al., 1989; Nuechterlein, 1984). We suggest that, like deficits in the Stroop task, this impairment can be explained by a reduction of dopaminergic tone in prefrontal cortex resulting in an impairment of the internal representation of context. If this is so, then we should be able to simulate schizophrenic deficits in the CPT-double using the same manipulation used to produce deficits in the Stroop task: a reduction of gain in the module responsible for representing and, in this case, maintaining context. To test this, we constructed a network to perform the CPT-double.

The network consisted of four modules: an input module, an intermediate (associative) module, a module for representing the prior stimulus, and a response module (see Figure 14.7). The input module was used to represent the visual features of individual letters. Stimulus presentation was simulated by activating the input units corresponding to the features of the stimulus letter. This produced a unique pattern of activation for each letter. The network was trained to record the presentation of a given input pattern by activating the appropriate unit in the prior stimulus module. In addition, the network was trained to activate the unit in the response module whenever a stimulus letter appeared twice or more in a row. To do this, however, the network must be able to use the information stored in the prior stimulus module. To make this possible, a set of connections was added from the prior stimulus module back to the intermediate module. Intermediate units could thus receive "bottom up" information from the feature units (representing the current input) and "top down" information from the prior stimulus units. This allowed the network to compare the current and previous inputs and thereby learn to activate the response unit whenever these were the same—that is, whenever two consecutive letters were identical.

Note that the prior stimulus units in this model played the same role as the task demand units did in the Stroop model. The representation over the prior stimulus units in the CPT model provided the context for disambiguating the response to a particular pattern of input, just as the task demand units did in the Stroop model. The only important difference is that the context in the CPT model was determined by the previous input and therefore changed from trial to trial. We should emphasize, however, that the function of the prior stimulus module should not be thought of as a form of declarative, short-term memory. For the sake of clarity, we have labeled information in this module as individual letters. However, we imagine that in actuality this information is stored in a form that can be used to govern response selection but that may not be suitable for identification or reporting of the actual letter.

Following training, the network was able to perform the CPT-double task perfectly for a set of 10 different stimuli. To simulate the performance of normal subjects—who typically miss on 17% of trials and produce false alarms on 5% of trials (see Figure 14.8)—we added noise to processing. Noise in neural systems is usually attributed to afferent signals that are independent of the relevant stimulus. To simulate this distortion of input, we added a small amount of random, normally distributed noise to the net input of each unit on every processing cycle. The amount of noise was adjusted to match the performance of the network with that of human subjects. The results of this simulation also appear in Figure 14.8 (gain = 1.0). Then, to simulate schizophrenic performance, we disturbed processing in the prior stimulus module—which was responsible for representing and maintaining context—by decreasing the gain of these units to the same level used in the Stroop simulation (0.6). No other changes were made to the model. The percentage of misses increased to 44.9%, and false alarms increased slightly to 8.9%. These results closely match those from empirical studies of schizophrenic subjects (see Figure 14.8).

Although some authors have interpreted schizophrenic performance in the CPT in terms of a deficit in sensory processing, our model suggests an alterna-

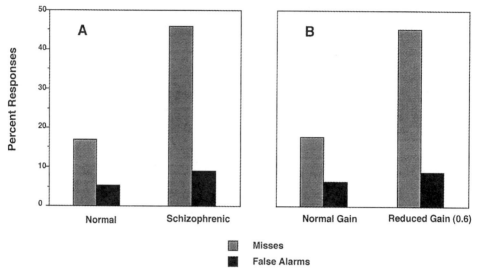

Figure 14.8
Percentage of misses and false alarms for (A) normal and schizophrenic subjects in the continuous performance test, and (B) the simulation run with normal and reduced gain on units in the prior stimulus module. (Empirical data are taken from Cornblatt, Lenzenweger, and Erlenmeyer-Kimling [1989]. That article reported d' and ln beta values; we obtained the values for misses and false alarms from B. Cornablat directly [personal communication, March 1990]. In addition, Corblatt et al. [1989] distinguised between "false alarms" [responses to stimuli similar to the target] and "random errors"; because both types of errors consist of responses to nontarget stimuli, we have combined these and considered them together as false alarms. Simulation data are based on 1,000 trials run in each condition. The 5% confidence intervals for the normal gain condition were ±2.3% for misses and ±1.7% for false alarms; for the reduced gain condition they were ±3.1% for misses and ±1.8% for false alarms.)

tive hypothesis: Performance deficits are due to a degradation in the internal representation required—as context—for processing the current stimulus. We hypothesize that this representation is maintained in prefrontal cortex and is directly influenced by changes in the dopaminergic supply to this area. This hypothesis is consistent with our account of Stroop performance and with disturbances of language processing, which we turn to next.

Simulation of Context-Dependent Lexical Disambiguation
In the two previous simulations, we focused on different aspects of schizophrenic performance deficits and the mechanisms involved. The Stroop simulation showed how a disturbance in the internal representation of context can lead to dominant response tendencies. In the CPT simulation, we introduced a mechanism for generating and maintaining previously generated representations of context, and showed how a disturbance in this mechanism could ac-

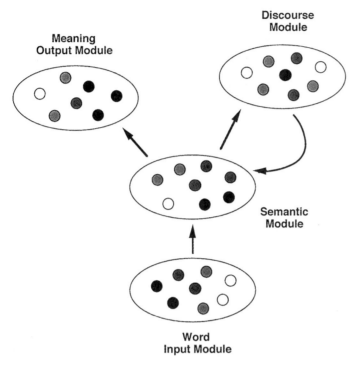

Figure 14.9
Schematic diagram of the language-processing model. (Patterns of activation over the units in the input module are assumed to represent the current sensory stimulus [e.g., the orthographic code for a written word], whereas the output module is assumed to represent the information necessary to generate an overt response [e.g., the phonological code needed to pronounce the meaning of the word]. Note that the connections between the semantic and discourse modules are bidirectional.)

count for experimental results. The lexical disambiguation task (described earlier) allows us to explore both of these factors (dominant response biases and maintenance of the internal representation of context) within a single paradigm. The results of our study using this task replicated the finding of others that schizophrenics show a tendency to respond to the dominant meaning of lexical ambiguities even when context confers the weaker, less frequent meaning. However, our results suggested that this tendency is significant only when context is temporally remote, implicating a deficit in the maintenance of context. Here, we show how this language-processing deficit can be simulated using the same principles that we used to account for schizophrenic performance in the Stroop task and the CPT.

Architecture and Processing   To simulate performance in the lexical disambiguation task, we constructed a network (see Figure 14.9) with the same basic architecture as the CPT model. In this case, the input module was used to represent lexical stimuli (e.g., the word PEN). The network was trained to associate patterns of activation in this module with patterns in two other modules: a response module and a discourse module. Patterns in the response module specified the meaning of the input word (e.g., "writing implement"), whereas the discourse module was used to represent the topic of the current sequence of inputs (e.g., the meaning of a sentence or phrase, as opposed to the meaning of individual words). The intermediate module functioned as a semantic module, encoding an internal representation for the meaning of the input that could be used to generate an appropriate response in the output module and a relevant discourse representation in the discourse module. Analogous to the CPT model, there were two-way connections between the semantic module and the discourse module. Thus, once a discourse representation had been activated (e.g., by a prior input pattern), it could be used to influence the processing of subsequent stimuli in the semantic module. This provided the mechanism by which context could be used to resolve lexical ambiguity.

Training   The model was trained to produce an output and discourse representation for 30 different input words, some of which were ambiguous. In the case of ambiguous words, the model was trained to produce the response and discourse patterns related to one meaning (e.g., PEN → "writing implement" and *writing*; we use uppercase letters to denote input words, quotation marks to denote output responses, and italics to denote discourse representations) more than the other (e.g., PEN → "fenced enclosure" and *farming*). This asymmetry of training was analogous to training in the Stroop model (words more than colors), with a comparable result: When presented with an ambiguous input word, the network preferentially activated the strong (more frequently trained) response and discourse representations. To permit access to the weaker meaning, the network was sometimes presented with an ambiguous word along with one of its associated discourse representations (e.g., PEN and *farming*)[4] and trained to generate the appropriate response (i.e., "fenced enclosure"). Finally, the network was trained on a set of context words, each of which was related to one meaning of an ambiguity; these words (e.g., CHICKEN) were trained to produce their own meaning as the response ("fowl") as well as a discourse representation that was identical to the corresponding meaning of the related ambiguity (*farming*).

The combined effect of these training procedures was that when an ambiguous word was presented and no representation was active over the discourse units, the output was a blend of the two meanings of the word, with elements of the more frequently trained (dominant) meaning being more active than the other (subordinate) meaning. However, when a discourse representation was active, the model successfully disambiguated the input and activated only the relevant meaning response.

Simulations   First, we tested the model's ability to simulate—in very simple form—the use of context in natural language processing. Most words in English have more than one meaning; therefore, language processing relies on context provided by prior stimuli to disambiguate current ones. In the model, this occurred by constructing a discourse representation in response to each lexical input, which could then be used as context for processing subsequent stimuli. We tested the model for this ability by first presenting it with a context word (e.g., CHICKEN), allowing activation to spread through the network, and then presenting the ambiguity (e.g., PEN) and observing the output. Note that, in this case, the model was not directly provided with a discourse representation. Rather, it had to construct this from the first input and then use it to disambiguate the second. Tested in this way with all context-word/ambiguous-word pairs (e.g., either CHICKEN or PAPER followed by PEN), the model was able to consistently generate the meaning response appropriate for the context.

To simulate performance in our lexical disambiguation experiment, the model was presented with pairs of context and ambiguous words (representing the clauses used in the experiment) in either order (context first or last). Following each pair, the network was probed with the ambiguous word, simulating the subjects' process of reminding themselves of the ambiguity and choosing its meaning. To simulate the variability observed for human performance in this task, a small amount of noise was added to the activation of every unit in the model at each time step of processing. The amount of noise was adjusted so that the simulation produced an overall error rate comparable to that observed for control subjects in the experiment. The model's response in each trial was considered to be the meaning representation that was most active over the output units after the probe was presented. To simulate schizophrenic performance, we introduced a disturbance identical to the one used in the Stroop and CPT models: a reduction in gain of units in the context (discourse) module to the same level used in the other models (0.6). No other changes were made to the model. The results of this simulation show a strong resemblance to the empirical data (see Figure 14.10). They demonstrate both significant effects: (a) In the reduced gain mode, the simulation made about as many more dominant response errors as did schizophrenic subjects; however, (b) as with human subjects, this occurred only when context came first—gain did not have a significant effect when context came last. Gain also had little effect on other aspects of performance (e.g., number of unrelated errors) and in other conditions of the task (e.g., when the dominant meaning was correct), which corresponds well to the empirical findings. Thus, the model appears to be specific in its behavior; that is, it demonstrated performance deficits only in those conditions in which schizophrenics showed similar deficits, and not in conditions in which schizophrenic performance was similar to that of normal subjects.

The model provides a clear view of the relationship between dominant response bias, internal representation of context, and a reduction of gain. When

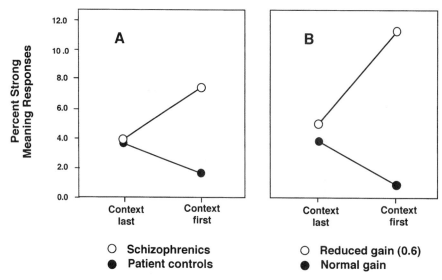

Figure 14.10
Percentage of strong-meaning responses when the weak meaning was correct for subjects in the empirical study and for the simulation (The rates of unrelated errors [not shown] and of weak-meaning responses when the strong meaning was correct were the same in the normal and reduced gain conditions of the simulation and were of the same magnitude as those observed for human subjects [about 1%–2%]. The 5% confidence intervals for the simulation data are ±1.1% for context last and ±0.6% for context first in the normal gain conditions, and ±1.3% for context last and ±2.0% for context first in the reduced gain condition.)

gain is reduced in the context module, the representation of context is degraded; as a consequence, it is more susceptible to the cumulative effects of noise. If a contextual representation is used quickly, this effect is less significant, and the representation is sufficient to overcome a dominant response bias. However, if time passes (as when context is presented first), the effects of noise accumulate, and the representation is no longer strong enough to reliably mediate the weaker of two competing responses. It is interesting that the cumulative effects of noise are offset by a priming effect when gain is normal in the discourse module. That is, when the internal representation of context is sufficiently robust, then its occurrence before the ambiguity allows it to prime the correct meaning, leading to better performance than when context follows the ambiguity. Note that a trend toward this effect is also observed in control subjects.

General Discussion

We began by reviewing behavioral data concerning deficits of selective attention and language processing in schizophrenia. We also reviewed data which indicate that prefrontal cortex and its dopaminergic supply are important for the construction and maintenance of internal representations of context and that disturbances in these systems are involved in schizophrenia. We then showed how the connectionist framework can be used to relate these findings to one another. We presented three models that (a) simulated quantitative aspects of performance in the Stroop task, the CPT, and a lexical disambiguation task; (b) elucidated the role of the internal representation of context—and its relationship to attention—in these various tasks; (c) related behavior in these tasks to biological processes; and (d) identified a specific disturbance in these processes that could account for schizophrenic patterns of performance.

The Role of Computational Modeling

A common objection to computer models of behavioral data is that such models have so many parameters that they can always be optimized to fit the data. For example, the number of units, the amount of training on different pathways, or the gain parameter could presumably be adjusted in each model to produce better fits. Such fits would not serve a useful purpose because they would be a reflection not of the correspondence between observed data and a mechanism of interest but only of the skill of the modeler.

In the simulations discussed here, the different parameters were indeed adjusted separately for each model. However, we did this only when attempting to fit the behavior of normal (or control) subjects. Once these parameters were determined, they were fixed; only the gain parameter was changed to simulate the behavior of schizophrenics. Furthermore, the gain parameter was reduced by exactly the same amount and in the same functional location in all three models. Thus, although it is true that the models were optimized to fit the normal data for each task, the fit to schizophrenic data was obtained by affecting only the variable (gain) motivated by our theory of schizophrenic deficits.

A related question is often asked: How do models contribute to an understanding of the data they simulate? After all, the data already exist, and the principles or ideas captured by a model can often be expressed more simply without the use of a computer program (indeed, one might contend that this must be so if the ideas are of any general value). McClelland (1988) provided an articulate reply to this question in describing the relevance of models to empirical investigations in psychology. He pointed out that models can (a) bring seemingly disparate empirical phenomena together under a single explanation, (b) provide new interpretations of existing findings, (c) reconcile contradictory evidence, and (d) lead to new predictions. Throughout the present discussion, we have tried to show how our models realize these different goals. For example, by showing that a disturbance in the internal representation of context can explain impairments of selective attention, language processing, and overall reaction time in schizophrenia, our models bring these seemingly disparate phenomena together under a single, unifying explanation. By revealing that an overall increase in reaction time could arise from a specific rather than a generalized information-processing deficit, they provide a reinterpretation of the data. They suggest a reconciliation of contradictory findings with respect to the CPT and prefrontal activation. And they lead to new predictions concerning normal and schizophrenic performance on behavioral tasks, as well as to predictions about dopamine effects on prefrontal metabolism. McClelland also emphasized the role that models play in formalizing theoretical concepts. By committing a set of ideas to a computer program and examining their ability to account for quantitative data, the ideas are put to a rigorous test of both their internal coherence and the resolution of their explanatory power.

Most important, however, is the role that modeling plays in the discovery process. At times the insights provided by a model may seem, in hindsight, to be obvious or not to have required the effort involved in constructing a computer simulation. On other occasions, one may be concerned with the possible circularity of a theory based on a model that has presumably been designed with the theory in mind. Usually, however, such perceptions fail to recognize that the insight and the emerging theory came from the process of developing the model itself. The three models described in this article were actually developed independently and for different purposes. The Stroop model was developed to account for normal performance in this task (J. D. Cohen et al., 1990); the CPT simulation was developed to explore gain as a model of catecholaminergic effects on behavior (Servan-Schreiber et al., 1990); and the language model was inspired by our work on the processing of ambiguous stimuli in recurrent networks (Cleeremans, Servan-Schreiber, & McClelland, 1989; Servan-Schreiber, Cleeremans, & McClelland, 1991). It was only when we compared the mechanisms at work in these different models that we realized how all relied on common principles of processing. This suggested a hypothesis about the relationship between biological and behavioral factors in schizophrenia. In this way, the models provided an important vehicle for the discovery—and not just the testing—of new ideas.

Conclusion

We have tried to show how the connectionist framework can be brought to bear on the relationship between some of the biological and cognitive disturbances characteristic of schizophrenia. The models we have presented suggest that a common information-processing deficit underlies impaired performance in selective attention and language-processing tasks and relate this deficit to decreased dopaminergic activity in prefrontal cortex. The models, and the simulations based on them, rely on many simplifying assumptions and provide, at best, a coarse approximation of the mechanisms underlying both normal and schizophrenic behavior. Although accounting for empirical data is a primary goal in the development of computer simulation models, McClelland (1988) argued that this may not be the only basis for their evaluation. Models are useful if they offer new interpretations of empirical phenomena, unify previously unrelated observations, reconcile conflicting findings, and predict new empirical facts. We have indicated how our models—simple as they are—may fulfill these different functions. In so doing, we hope that these models will help provide a more refined and integrated approach to the riddle of behavioral and biological disturbances in schizophrenia.

Notes

The order of authorship is alphabetical; both authors made equal contributions to the research and preparation of this article. Preliminary versions of this work were presented at the 142nd Annual Meeting of the American Psychiatric Association in May 1989 and at the Annual Meeting of the Cognitive Science Society in July 1990.

This work was supported by a National Institute of Mental Health (NIMH) Physician Scientist Award (MH00673) to Jonathan D. Cohen and an NIMH Individual Fellow Award (MH09696) to David Servan-Schreiber. Part of this work was also supported by a research grant from the Scottish Rite Schizophrenia Research Program, N.M.J., U.S.A., to Jonathan D. Cohen and a research fellowship from Western Psychiatric Institute and Clinic to David Servan-Schreiber.

We gratefully acknowledge the helpful suggestions made by David Galin, Steve Matthysse, James McClelland, Benoit Mulsant, and David Plaut during the development of our ideas and the preparation of this article. In addition, John Csernansky, Len Horowitz, Roy King, Tracy Kristoffersen, David Spiegel, Elisabeth Targ, and Sue Theimann participated in the design and implementation of the experimental study of schizophrenic language performance that we reported. We also thank our three reviewers for their careful consideration of our manuscript and their many useful suggestions.

1. To our knowledge, there are only five studies reported in the literature in which schizophrenics were tested using the standard Stroop task (Abramczyk, Jordan, & Hegel, 1983; Grand, Steingart, Freedman, & Buchwald, 1975; Mirsky et al., 1984; Wapner & Krus, 1960; Wysocki & Sweet, 1985). Only four of these report reaction times, and one involved only 4 subjects (Mirsky et al., 1984). The data for these 4 subjects, although statistically unreliable, conformed to the overall pattern of our predictions: Subjects showed disproportionate amounts of interference. It is interesting that this worsened when they were taken off of medication. The data for the three remaining studies reporting reaction times appear in Table 14.1.
2. For example, in Reader, Ferron, Descarries, and Jasper (1979) both the concentration of dopamine in the micropipette and the intensity of the iontophoretic current were almost one order of magnitude greater than the corresponding concentrations and current intensity used in the Chiodo and Berger (1986) study. Moreover, the effect of dopamine at these concentrations was to completely inhibit spontaneous firing in the target cells.
3. It is worth noting that different dopamine receptor subtypes predominate in the striatum and the prefrontal cortex. Whereas the potentiating effects of dopamine have been studied primarily within the striatum (where D2 receptors predominate), D1 receptors in this region have been shown to mediate potentiating effects (Hu & Wang, 1988).
4. Recall that the discourse module is connected to the semantic module with two-way connections, so that the discourse module can be used as either an input module or an output module, depending on whether the representation in this module is explicitly specified by the experimenter or is allowed to develop in response to activation it receives from the semantic module.

References

Abramczyk, R. R., Jordan, D. E., & Hegel, M. (1983). "Reverse" Stroop effect in the performance of schizophrenics. *Perceptual and Motor Skills, 56,* 99–106.

Anderson, J. R. (1983). *The architecture of cognition*. Cambridge, MA: Harvard University Press.

Andreasen, N. C., Flaum, M., Swayze, V. W., Tyrrell, G., & Arndt, S. (1990). Positive and negative symptoms in schizophrenia. *Archives of General Psychiatry, 47*, 615–621.

Andreasen, N. C., Nasrallah, H. A., Dunn, V., Olson, S. C., Grove, W. M., Ehrhardt, J. C., Coffman, J. A., & Crossett, J. H. W. (1986). Structural abnormalities in the frontal system of schizophrenia. *Archives of General Psychiatry, 43*, 136–144.

Angrist, B., Peselow, E., Rubinstein, M., Wolkin, A., & Rotrosen, J. (1985). Amphetamine response and relapse risk after depot neuroleptic discontinuation. *Psychopharmacology, 85*, 277–283.

Aou, S., Nishino, H., Inokuchi, A., & Mizuno, Y. (1983). Influence of catecholamines on reward-related neuronal activity in monkey orbitofrontal cortex. *Brain Research, 267*, 165–170.

Baillargeon, R. (1990, August). *Young infants' physical knowledge*. Paper presented at the 98th Annual Convention of the American Psychological Association, Boston, MA.

Barone, P., & Joseph, J. P. (1989a). Prefrontal cortex and spatial sequencing in macaque monkey. *Experimental Brain Research, 78*, 447–464.

Barone, P., & Joseph, J. P. (1989b). Role of the dorsolateral prefrontal cortex in organizing visually guided behavior. *Brain Behavior and Evolution, 33*, 132–135.

Benjamin, T. B., & Watt, N. F. (1969). Psychopathology and semantic interpretation of ambiguous words. *Journal of Abnormal Psychology, 74*, 706–714.

Berman, K. F., Illowsky, B. P., & Weinberger, D. R. (1988). Physiological dysfunction of dorsolateral prefrontal cortex in schizophrenia: Further evidence for regional and behavioral specificity. *Archives of General Psychiatry, 45*, 616–622.

Berman, K. F., Zec, R. F., & Weinberger, D. R. (1986). Physiological dysfunction of dorsolateral prefrontal cortex in schizophrenia: II. Role of neuroleptic treatment, attention and mental effort. *Archives of General Psychiatry, 43*, 126–135.

Blanley, P. H. (1974). Two studies on the language behavior of schizophrenics. *Journal of Abnormal Psychology, 83*, 23–31.

Bleuler, E. (1911). *Dementia praecox, or the group of schizophrenias*. New York: International Universities Press.

Bloom, F. E., Schulman, J. A., & Koob, G. F. (1989). Catecholamines and behavior. In U. Trendelenburg & N. Wiener (Eds.), *Handbook of experimental pharmacology* (Vol. 90, chap. 11, pp. 27–88). Berlin: Springer-Verlag.

Borst, U., & Cohen, R. (1989). Filling the preparatory interval with temporal information or visual noise: The crossover effect in schizophrenics and controls. *Psychological Medicine, 19*, 865–874.

Bowen, F. P., Kamienny, R. S., Burns, M. M., & Yahr, M. D. (1975). Parkinsonism: Effects of L-dopa treatment on concept formation. *Neurology, 25*, 701–704.

Bowers, M. B., Jr., Heninger, G. R., & Sternberg, D. (1980). Clinical processes and central dopaminergic activity in psychotic disorders. *Communications in Psychopharmacology, 4*, 177–188.

Brozoski, T. J., Brown, R. M., Rosvold, H. E., & Goldman, P. S. (1979). Cognitive deficit caused by regional depletion of dopamine in prefrontal cortex of Rhesus monkey. *Science, 205*, 929–931.

Bunney, B. S., & Aghajanian, G. K. (1976). Dopamine and norepinephrine innervated in the rat prefrontal cortex: Pharmacological differentiation using microiontophoretic techniques. *Life Sciences, 19*, 1783–1792.

Bunney, B. S., & Sesack, S. R. (1987). Electrophysiological identification and pharmacological characterization of dopamine sensitive neurons in the rat prefrontal cortex. In L. A. Chiodo & A. S. Freeman (Eds.), *Neurophysiology of dopaminergic systems—Current status and clinical perspectives* (pp. 129–140). Grosse Pointe, MI: Lakeshore.

Burnod, Y., & Korn, H. (1989). Consequences of stochastic release of neurotransmitters for network computation in the central nervous system. *Proceeding of the National Academy of Science (U.S.A.), 86*, 352–356.

Chapman, L. J. (1980). Recent advances in the study of schizophrenic cognition. *Schizophrenia Bulletin, 5*(4), 69–81.

Chapman, L. J., & Chapman, J. P. (1978). The measurement of differential deficit. *Journal of Psychiatric Research, 14,* 303–311.

Chapman, L. J., Chapman, J. P., & Miller, G. A. (1964). A theory of verbal behavior in schizophrenia. In B. A. Maher (Ed.), *Progress in experimental personality research* (Vol. 1, pp. 135–167). San Diego, CA: Academic Press.

Chiodo, L. A., & Berger, T. W. (1986). Interactions between dopamine and amino acid-induced excitation and inhibition in the striatum. *Brain Research, 375,* 198–203.

Cleeremans, A., Servan-Schreiber, D., & McClelland, J. L. (1989). Finite state automata and simple recurrent networks. *Neural Computation, 1,* 372–381.

Cohen, B. M. (1981). Dopamine receptors and antipsychotic drugs. *McLean Hospital Journal, 1*(2), 95–115.

Cohen, J. D., Dunbar, K., & McClelland, J. L. (1990). On the control of automatic processes: A parallel distributed processing model of the Stroop effect. *Psychological Review, 97,* 332–361.

Cohen, J. D., Targ, E., Kristoffersen, T., & Spiegel, D. (1988). *The fabric of thought disorder: Disturbances in the processing of context.* Unpublished manuscript.

Cohen, R., Borst, U., & Rist, F. (1989). *Cross-over and cross-modality effects in schizophrenia: Some old and some new data.* Unpublished manuscript.

Cohen, R. M., Semple, W. E., Gross, M., Holcomb, H. H., Dowling, M. S., & Nordahl, T. E. (1988). Functional localization of sustained attention: Comparison to sensory stimulation in the absence of instruction. *Neuropsychiatry, Neuropsychology, and Behavioral Neurology, 1,* 2–20.

Cohen, R. M., Semple, W. E., Gross, M., Nordahl, T. E., DeLisi, L. E., Holcomb, H. H., King, A. C., Morihisa, J. M., & Pickar, D. (1987). Dysfunction in a prefrontal substrate of sustained attention in schizophrenia. *Life Sciences, 40,* 2031–2039.

Cohen, R. M., Semple, W. E., Gross, M., Nordahl, T. E., Holcomb, H. H., Dowling, M. S., & Pickar, D. (1988). The effect of neuroleptics on dysfunction in a prefrontal substrate of sustained attention in schizophrenia. *Life Sciences, 43,* 1141–1150.

Cornblatt, B., Lenzenweger, M. F., & Erlenmeyer-Kimling, L. (1989). A continuous performance test, identical pairs version: II. Contrasting attentional profiles in schizophrenic and depressed patients. *Psychiatry Research, 29,* 65–85.

Corwin, J. V., Kanter, S., Watson, R. T., Heilman, K. M., Valenstein, E., & Hashimoto, A. (1986). Apomorphine has a therapeutic effect on neglect produced by unilateral dorsomedial prefrontal cortex lesions in rats. *Experimental Neurology, 94,* 683–698.

Cozolino, L. J. (1983). The oral and written productions of schizophrenic patients. In B. A. Maher (Ed.), *Progress in experimental personality research* (Vol. 12, pp. 101–152). San Diego, CA: Academic Press.

Creese, I., Burt, D. R., & Snyder, S. H. (1976). Dopamine receptor binding predicts clinical and pharmacological potencies of antischizophrenic drugs. *Science, 192,* 481–483.

Cross, A. J., Crow, T. J., & Owen, F. (1981). 3-H-flupenthixol binding in post-mortem brains of schizophrenics: Evidence for a selective increase in dopamine D2 receptors. *Psychopharmacology, 74,* 122–124.

Crow, T. J. (1980). Molecular pathology of schizophrenia: More than one disease process? *British Medical Journal, 137,* 383–386.

Crow, T. J., Cross, A. J., Johnson, J. A., Johnstone, E. C., Joseph, M. H., Owen, F., Owens, D. G. C., & Poulter, M. (1984). Catecholamines and schizophrenia: An assessment of the evidence. In A. R. Liss (Ed.), *Catecholamines: Neuropharmacology and central nervous system-therapeutic aspects* (pp. 11–20). New York: A. R. Liss.

Damasio, A. R. (1979). The frontal lobes. In K. M. Heilman & E. Valenstein (Eds.), *Clinical neuropsychology* (pp. 339–375). New York: Oxford University Press.

Davidson, M., Keefe, R. S. E., Mohs, R. C., Siever, L. J., Losonczy, M. F., Horvath, T. B., & Davis, K. L. (1987). L-dopa challenge and relapse in schizophrenia. *American Journal of Psychiatry, 144,* 934–938.

Diamond, A. (1985). Developmental of the ability to use recall to guide action, as indicated by infants' performance on A B̄. *Child Development, 56,* 868–883.

Diamond, A. (1990a). The development and neural bases of memory functions as indexed by the A B̄ and delayed response tasks in human infants and infant monkeys. In A. Diamond (Ed.), *The development and neural bases of higher cognitive functions* (pp. 267–317). New York: NY Academy of Science Press.

Diamond, A. (1990b). Rate of maturation of the hippocampus and the developmental progression of children's performance on the delayed non-matching to sample and visual paired comparison tasks. In A. Diamond (Ed.), *The development and neural bases of higher cognitive functions* (pp. 394–426). New York: NY Academy of Science Press.

Diamond, A. (1990c). Developmental time course in human infants and infant monkeys and the neural bases of inhibitory control in reaching. In A. Diamond (Ed.), *The development and neural bases of higher cognitive functions* (pp. 637–676). New York: NY Academy of Science Press.

Diamond, A., & Doar, B. (1989). The performance of human infants on a measure of frontal cortex function, the delayed response task. *Developmental Psychobiology, 22*(3), 271–294.

Diamond, A., & Goldman-Rakic, P. S. (1989). Comparison of human infants and rhesus monkeys on Piaget's A B̄ task: Evidence for dependence on dorsolateral prefrontal cortex. *Experimental Brain Research, 74,* 24–40.

Dunbar, K., & MacLeod, C. M. (1984). A horse race of a different color: Stroop interference patterns with transformed words. *Journal of Experimental Psychology: Human Perception and Performance, 10,* 622–639.

Dyer, F. N. (1973). The Stroop phenomenon and its use in the study of perceptual, cognitive, and response processes. *Memory and Cognition, 1,* 106–120.

Erlenmeyer-Kimling, L., & Cornblatt, B. (1978). Attentional measures in a study of children at high-risk for schizophrenia. *Journal of Psychiatric Research, 14,* 93–98.

Farkas, T., Wolf, A. P., Jaeger, J., Brodie, J. D., Christman, D. R., & Fowler, J. S. (1984). Regional brain glucose metabolism in chronic schizophrenia. *Archives of General Psychiatry, 41,* 293–300.

Ferron, A., Thierry, A. M., Le Douarin, C., & Glowinski, J. (1984). Inhibitory influence of the mesocortical dopaminergic system on spontaneous activity or excitatory response induced from the thalamic mediodorsal nucleus in the rat medial prefrontal cortex. *Brain Research, 302,* 257–265.

Foote, S. L., Freedman, R., & Oliver, A. P. (1975). Effects of putative neurotransmitters on neuronal activity in monkey auditory cortex. *Brain Research, 86,* 229–242.

Franzen, G., & Ingvar, D. H. (1975). Abnormal distribution of cerebral activity in chronic schizophrenia. *Journal of Psychiatric Research, 12,* 199–214.

Freeman, W. J. (1979). Nonlinear gain mediating cortical stimulus–response relations. *Biological Cybernetics, 33,* 243–247.

Fuster, J. M. (1980). *The prefrontal cortex.* New York: Raven Press.

Fuster, J. M. (1985a). The prefrontal cortex and temporal integration. In A. Peters & E. G. Jones (Eds.), *Cerebral cortex* (pp. 151–177). New York: Plenum Press.

Fuster, J. M. (1985b). The prefrontal cortex, mediator of cross-temporal contingencies. *Human Neurobiology, 4,* 169–179.

Garmezy, N. (1977). The psychology and psychopathology of attention. *Schizophrenia Bulletin, 3,* 360–369.

Geraud, G., Arne-Bes, M. C., Guell, A., & Bes, A. (1987). Reversibility of hemodynamic hypofrontality in schizophrenia. *Journal of Cerebral Blood Flow and Metabolism, 7,* 9–12.

Goldberg, T. E., Weinberger, D. R., Berman, K. F., Pliskin, N. H., & Podd, M. H. (1987). Further evidence of dementia of the prefrontal type in schizophrenia? *Archives of General Psychiatry, 44,* 1008–1014.

Goldman-Rakic, P. S. (1987). Circuitry of primate prefrontal cortex and regulation of behavior by representational memory. In F. Plum (Ed.), *Handbook of physiology—The nervous system, V* (pp. 373–417). Bethesda, MD: American Physiological Society.

Goldman-Rakic, P. S. (1991). Prefrontal cortical dysfunction in schizophrenia: The relevance of working memory. In B. Caroll (Ed.), *Psychopathology and the brain* (pp. 1–23). New York: Raven Press.

Grand, S., Steingart, I., Freedman, N., & Buchwald, C. (1975). Organization of language behavior and cognitive performance in chronic schizophrenia. *Journal of Abnormal Psychology, 84*, 621–628.

Grant, D. A., & Berger, E. A. (1948). A behavioral analysis of degree of reinforcement and ease of shifting to new responses in a Weigl type card sorting problem. *Journal of Experimental Psychology, 38*, 404–411.

Gur, R. E., Resnick, S. M., Gur, R. C., Alavi, A., Caroff, S., Kushner, M., & Reivich, M. (1987). Regional brain function in schizophrenia. II. Repeated evaluation with positron emission tomography. *Archives of General Psychiatry, 44*, 125–129.

Harvey, P. D. (1983). Speech competence in manic and schizophrenic psychoses: The association between clinically rated thought disorder and cohesion and reference performance. *Journal of Abnormal Psychology, 92*, 368–377.

Hinton, G. E., & Shallice, T. (1991). Lesioning an attractor network: Investigations of acquired dyslexia. *Psychological Review, 98*, 74–95.

Hoffman, R. E. (1987). Computer simulations of neural information processing and the schizophrenia–mania dichotomy. *Archives of General Psychiatry, 44*, 178–188.

Hu, X. T., & Wang, R. Y. (1988). Comparison of effects of D_1 and D_2 dopamine receptor agonists on neurons in the rat caudate putamen: An electrophysiological study. *The Journal of Neuroscience, 8*, 4340–4348.

Janowsky, D. S., Huey, L., Storms, L., & Judd, L. L. (1977). Methylphenidate hydrochloride effects on psychological tests in acute schizophrenic and nonpsychotic patients. *Archives of General Psychiatry, 34*, 189–194.

Janowsky, D. S., & Rich, C. (1979). Amphetamine psychosis and psychotic symptoms. *Psychopharmacology, 65*, 73–77.

Karoum, F., Karson, C. N., Bigelow, L. B., Lawson, W. B., & Wyatt, R. J. (1987). Preliminary evidence of reduced combined output of dopamine and its metabolites in chronic schizophrenia. *Archives of General Psychiatry, 44*, 604–607.

Kolb, B., & Whishaw, I. Q. (1983). Performance of schizophrenic patients on tests sensitive to left or right frontal, temporal, or parietal function in neurologic patients. *Journal of Mental and Nervous Disease, 171*, 435–443.

Kornetsky, C. (1972). The use of a simple test of attention as a measure of drug effects in schizophrenic patients. *Psychopharmacologia (Berlin), 8*, 99–106.

Kraeplin, E. (1950). *Dementia praecox and paraphrenia* (J. Zinkin, Trans.). New York: International Universities Press.

Lang, P. J., & Buss, A. H. (1965). Psychological deficit in schizophrenia: II. Interference and activation. *Journal of Abnormal Psychology, 70*, 77–106.

Larsen, S. F., & Fromholt, P. (1976). Mnemonic organization and free recall in schizophrenia. *Journal of Abnormal Psychology, 85*, 61–65.

Lehky, S. R., & Sejnowski, T. J. (1988). Network model of shape-from-shading: Neural function arises from both receptive and projective fields. *Nature, 333*, 452–454.

Levin, S. (1984). Frontal lobe dysfunctions in schizophrenia—II. Impairments of psychological and brain functions. *Journal of Psychiatry Research, 18*(1), 57–72.

Levin, S., Yurgelun-Todd, D., & Craft, S. (1989). Contributions of clinical neuropsychology to the study of schizophrenia. *Journal of Abnormal Psychology, 98*, 341–356.

Lieberman, J. A., Kane, J. M., Gadaleta, D., Brenner, R., Lesser, M. S., & Kinon, B. (1984). Methylphenidate challenge as a predictor of relapse in schizophrenia. *American Journal of Psychiatry,* *141,* 633–638.

Losonczy, M. F., Davidson, M., & Davis, K. L. (1987). The dopamine hypothesis of schizophrenia. In H. Y. Meltzer (Ed.), *Psychopharmacology: The third generation of progress* (pp. 715–726). New York: Raven Press.

Mackay, A. V. P. (1980). Positive and negative schizophrenic symptoms and the role of dopamine. *British Journal of Psychiatry, 137,* 379–386.

MacLeod, C. M. (1991). Half a century of research on the Stroop effect: An integrative review. *Psychological Bulletin, 109,* 163–203.

Maher, B. A. (1972). The language of schizophrenia: A review and interpretation. *British Journal of Psychiatry, 120,* 3–17.

Malmo, H. P. (1974). On frontal lobe functions: Psychiatric patient controls. *Cortex, 10,* 231–237.

McClelland, J. L. (1988). Connectionist models and psychological evidence. *Journal of Memory and Language, 27,* 107–123.

McClelland, J. L., & Rumelhart, D. E. (Eds.). (1986). *Parallel distributed processing explorations in the microstructure of cognition. Vol. 2: Psychological and biological models.* Cambridge, MA: MIT Press.

McCulloch, J., Savaki, H. E., McCulloch, M. C., Jehle, J., & Sokoloff, L. (1982). The distribution of alterations in energy metabolism in the rat brain produced by apomorphine. *Brain Research, 243,* 67–80.

McGhie, A. (1970). Attention and perception in schizophrenia. In B. A. Maher (Ed.), *Progress in experimental personality research* (Vol. 5, pp. 1–36). San Diego, CA: Academic Press.

McGhie, A., & Chapman, J. (1961). Disorders of attention and perception in early schizophrenia. *British Journal of Medical Psychology, 34,* 103–116.

Meltzer, H. Y., & Stahl, S. M. (1976). The dopamine hypothesis of schizophrenia: A review. *Schizophrenia Bulletin, 2,* 19–76.

Milner, B. (1963). Effects of different brain lesions on card sorting. *Archives of Neurology, 9,* 90–100.

Mirsky, A. F., DeLisi, L. E., Buchsbaum, M. S., Quinn, O. W., Schwerdt, P., Siever, L. J., Mann, L., Weingartner, H., Zec, R., Sostek, A., Alterman, I., Revere, V., Dawson, S. D., & Zahn, T. P. (1984). The Genain quadruplets: Psychological studies. *Psychiatry Research, 13,* 77–93.

Mishkin, M., & Pribram, K. H. (1955). Analysis of the effects of frontal lesions in monkey. I. Variations on delayed alternation. *Journal of Comparative and Physiological Psychology, 338,* 492–495.

Morihisa, J. M., & McAnulty, G. B. (1985). Structure and function: Brain electrical activity mapping and computed tomography in schizophrenia. *Biological Psychiatry, 20,* 3–19.

Nauta, J. H. W., & Domesick, V. B. (1981). Ramifications of the limbic system. In S. Matthysse (Ed.), *Psychiatry and the biology of the human brain: A symposium dedicated to Seymour S. Kety* (pp. 165–188). New York: Elsevier/North-Holland.

Neale, J. M. (1971). Perceptual span in schizophrenia. *Journal of Abnormal Psychology, 77,* 196–204.

Nelson, H. E. (1976). A modified card sorting test sensitive to frontal lobe defects. *Cortex, 12,* 313–324.

Nuechterlein, K. H. (1983). Signal detection in vigilance tasks and behavioral attributes among offspring of schizophrenic mothers and among hyperactive children. *Journal of Abnormal Psychology, 92,* 4–28.

Nuechterlein, K. H. (1984). Information processing and attentional functioning in the developmental course of schizophrenic disorders. *Schizophrenia Bulletin, 10,* 160–203.

Oades, R. D. (1981). Dopaminergic agonist and antagonistic drugs in the ventral tegmentum of rats inhibit and facilitate changes of food search behaviour. *Neuroscience Letters, 27,* 75–80.

Oltmanns, T. F., & Neale, J. M. (1975). Schizophrenic performance when distractors are present: Attentional deficit or differential task difficulty? *Journal of Abnormal Psychology, 84,* 205–209.

Passingham, R. E. (1985). Memory of monkeys (*Macaca mulatta*) with lesions in prefrontal cortex. *Behavioral Neuroscience, 99,* 3–21.

Patterson, K., Seidenberg, M. S., & McClelland, J. L. (1989). Connections and disconnections: Acquired dyslexia in a computational model of reading processes. In R. G. M. Morris (Ed.), *Parallel distributed processing: Implications for psychology and neurobiology:* Oxford: Clarendon Press.

Piaget, J. (1954). *The origins of intelligence in children.* New York: Basic Books. (Original work published 1937)

Pickar, D., Labarca, R., Linnoila, M., Roy, A., Hommer, D., Everett, D., & Paul, S. M. (1984). Neuroleptic-induced decrease in plasma homovanillic acid and antipsychotic activity in schizophrenic patients. *Science, 225,* 954–957.

Reader, T. A., Ferron, A., Descarries, L., & Jasper, H. H. (1979). Modulatory role for biogenic amines in the cerebral cortex: Microiontophoretic studies. *Brain Research, 160,* 217–229.

Robinson, A. L., Heaton, R. K., Lehman, R. A. W., & Stilson, D. W. (1980). The utility of the Wisconsin Card Sorting Test in detecting and localizing frontal lobe lesions. *Journal of Consulting and Clinical Psychology, 48,* 605–614.

Rochester, S. R., & Martin, J. R. (1979). *Crazy talk: A study in the discourse of schizophrenic speakers.* New York: Plenum Press.

Rosenkilde, K. E. (1979). Functional heterogeneity of the prefrontal cortex in the monkey: A review. *Behavioral Neural Biology, 25,* 301–345.

Rosvold, K. E., Mirsky, A. F., Sarason, I., Bransome, E. D., & Beck, L. H. (1956). A continuous performance test of brain damage. *Journal of Consulting Psychology, 20,* 343–350.

Rosvold, K. E., Szwarcbart, M. K., Mirsky, A. F., & Mishkin, M. (1961). The effect of frontal-lobe damage on delayed response performance in chimpanzees. *Journal of Comparative and Physiological Psychology, 54,* 368–374.

Rumelhart, D. E., Hinton, G. E., & Williams, R. J. (1986). Learning internal representations by backpropagating errors. *Nature, 323,* 533–536.

Rumelhart, D. E., & McClelland, J. L. (1986a). On learning the past tense of English verbs. In J. L. McClelland & D. E. Rumelhart (Eds.), *Parallel distributed processing: Explorations in the microstructure of cognition. Vol. 2: Psychological and biological models* (pp. 216–271). Cambridge, MA: MIT Press.

Rumelhart, D. E., & McClelland, J. L. (Eds.). (1986b). *Parallel distributed processing: Explorations in the microstructure of cognition. Vol. 1: Foundations.* Cambridge, MA: MIT Press.

Rumelhart, D. E., & McClelland, J. L. (1986c). PDP models and general issues in cognitive science. In D. E. Rumelhart & J. L. McClelland (Eds.), *Parallel distributed processing: Explorations in the microstructure of cognition. Vol. 1: Foundations* (pp. 110–146). Cambridge, MA: MIT Press.

Rutschmann, J., Cornblatt, B., & Erlenmeyer-Kimling, L. (1977). Sustained attention in children at risk for schizophrenia. *Archives of General Psychiatry, 34,* 571–575.

Salzinger, K. (1971). An hypothesis about schizophrenic behavior. *American Journal of Psychotherapy, 25,* 601–614.

Salzinger, K., Portnoy, S., & Feldman, R. S. (1964). Verbal behavior of schizophrenic and normal subjects. *Annals of the New York Academy of Sciences, 105,* 845–860.

Salzinger, K., Portnoy, S., Pisoni, D. B., & Feldman, R. S. (1970). The immediacy hypothesis and response-produced stimuli in schizophrenic speech. *Journal of Abnormal Psychology, 76,* 258–264.

Sawaguchi, T., & Goldman-Rakic, P. S. (1991). D1 dopamine receptors in prefrontal cortex: Involvement in working memory. *Science, 251,* 947–950.

Sawaguchi, T., & Matsumura, M. (1985). Laminar distributions of neurons sensitive to acetylcholine, noradrenaline and dopamine in the dorsolateral prefrontal cortex of the monkey. *Neuroscience Research, 2,* 255–273.

Schneider, J. S., Levine, M. S., Hull, C. D., & Buchwald, N. A. (1984). Effects of amphetamine on intracellular responses of caudate neurons in the cat. *Journal of Neuroscience, 4*, 930–938.

Schwartz, S. (1982). Is there a schizophrenic language? *Behavioral and Brain Sciences, 5*, 579–626.

Sedvall, G., Fyro, B., Nyback, H., Wiesel, F. A., & Wode-Helgodt, B. (1974). Mass fragmentometric determination of HVA in lumbar cerebrospinal fluid of schizophrenic patients during treatment with any psychotic drugs. *Journal of Psychiatric Research, 11*, 75–80.

Seeman, P., Ulpian, C., Bergeron, C., Riederer, P., Jellinger, K., Gbriel, E., Reynolds, G. P., & Tourtelotte, W. W. (1984). Bimodal distribution of dopamine receptor densities in brain of schizophrenics. *Science, 225*, 728–731.

Seidenberg, M. S., & McClelland, J. L. (1989). A distributed development model of word recognition and naming. *Psychological Review, 96*, 523–568.

Servan-Schreiber, D. (1990). *From physiology to behavior: Computational models of catecholamine modulation of information processing* (PhD thesis; Tech. Rep. CMU-CS-90-167). Pittsburgh, PA: Carnegie Mellon University, School of Computer Science.

Servan-Schreiber, D., Cleeremans, A., & McClelland, J. L. (1991). Graded state machines: The representation of temporal contingencies in simple recurrent networks. *Machine Learning*.

Servan-Schreiber, D., Printz, H. W., & Cohen, J. D. (1990). A network model of catecholamine effects: Gain, signal-to-noise ratio and behavior. *Science, 249*, 892–895.

Shakow, D. (1962). Segmental set: A theory of the formal psychological deficit in schizophrenia. *Archives of General Psychiatry, 6*, 1–17.

Simon, H., Scatton, B., & Le Moal, M. (1980). Dopaminergic A10 neurones are involved in cognitive functions. *Nature, 286*, 150–151.

Snyder, S. H. (1972). Catecholamines in the brain as mediators of amphetamine psychosis. *Archives of General Psychiatry, 27*, 169–179.

Snyder, S. H. (1976). The dopamine hypothesis of schizophrenia: Focus on the dopamine receptor. *American Journal of Psychiatry, 133*, 197–202.

Spohn, H. E., Lacoursiere, R. B., Thomson, K., & Coyne, L. (1977). Phenothiazine effects on psychological and psychophysiological dysfunction in chronic schizophrenics. *Archives of General Psychiatry, 34*, 633–644.

Spring, B. (1985). Distractibility as a marker of vulnerability to schizophrenia. *Psychopharmacology Bulletin, 21*, 509–512.

Strauss, M. E. (1975). Strong meaning-response bias in schizophrenia. *Journal of Abnormal Psychology, 84*, 293–298.

Stroop, J. R. (1935). Studies of interference in serial verbal reactions. *Journal of Experimental Psychology, 18*, 643–662.

Stuss, D. T., & Benson, D. F. (1984). Neuropsychological studies of the frontal lobes. *Psychological Bulletin, 95*, 3–28.

Swets, J. A., & Sewall, S. T. (1963). Invariance of signal detectability over stages of practice and levels of motivation. *Journal of Experimental Psychology, 66*, 120–126.

Tyrone, L., & Seeman, P. (1980). Elevation of brain neuroleptic/dopamine receptors in schizophrenia. *American Journal of Psychiatry, 137*, 191–197.

Wapner, S., & Krus, D. M. (1960). Effects of lysergic acid diethylamide, and differences between normals and schizophrenics on the Stroop color-word test. *Journal of Neuropsychiatry, 2*, 76–81.

Weinberger, D. R., Berman, K. F., & Chase, T. N. (1988). Mesocortical dopaminergic function and human cognition. *Annals of the New York Academy of Science, 537*, 330–338.

Weinberger, D. R., Berman, K. F., & Illowsky, B. P. (1988). Physiological dysfunction of dorsolateral prefrontal cortex in schizophrenia: A new cohort of evidence for a monoaminergic mechanism. *Archives of General Psychiatry, 45*, 606–615.

Weinberger, D. R., Berman, K. F., & Zec, R. F. (1986). Physiological dysfunction of dorsolateral prefrontal cortex in schizophrenia: I. Regional cerebral blood flow evidence. *Archives of General Psychiatry, 43*, 114–125.

Weinberger, D. R., Bigelow, L. B., Kleinman, J. E., Klein, S. T., Rosenblatt, J. E., & Wyatt, R. J. (1980). Cerebral ventricular enlargement in chronic schizophrenia. *Archives of General Psychiatry, 37,* 11–13.

Wielgus, M. S., & Harvey, P. D. (1988). Dichotic listening and recall in schizophrenia and mania. *Schizophrenia Bulletin, 14*(4), 689–700.

Wysocki, J. J., & Sweet, J. J. (1985). Identification of brain-damaged, schizophrenic, and normal medical patients using a brief neuropsychological screening battery. *International Journal of Clinical Neuropsychology, 7*(1), 40–49.

Zipser, D., & Andersen, R. A. (1988). A back-propagation programmed network that simulates response properties of a subset of posterior parietal neurons. *Nature, 331,* 679–684.

Attentional Neglect

Chapter 15

The End of the Line for a Brain-Damaged Model of Unilateral Neglect

Michael C. Mozer, Peter W. Halligan, and John C. Marshall

Introduction

Neglect

Unilateral neglect or *hemi-inattention* describes a collection of behavioral symptoms in which patients appear to ignore, forget, or turn away from contralesional space (Heilman, Watson, & Valenstein, 1993). Neglect after right-sided lesions is more frequent, long lasting, and severe than after equivalent lesions of the left hemisphere. The disorder can compromise visual, auditory, tactile, and olfactory modalities and may involve personal, peripersonal, extrapersonal, and "imaginal" space (Halligan & Marshall, 1993a). Unilateral neglect is far from a unitary phenomenon and has been shown to fractionate into a number of dissociable components in terms of sensory modality, spatial domain, laterality of response, motor output, and stimulus content (Barbieri & De Renzi, 1989). Furthermore, the lateralized behaviors observed cannot be explained in terms of concomitant sensorimotor deficits because neglect is manifested in free vision and under conditions of testing that do not necessarily require the use of motorically impaired limbs. Visual neglect has been repeatedly shown to double dissociate from hemiplegia, hemianopia, and hemianesthesia. Furthermore, the lesions that produce neglect are not restricted to primary sensory or motor cortex.

Unlike many brain-injured patients who rapidly learn to compensate for a visual field deficit or plegia of the upper limb, patients with unilateral neglect often continue to behave as if one half of space has ceased to exist in any meaningful form (Mesulam, 1985). As a result, patients with neglect commonly collide with objects on the left side of space, fail to eat from the left side of the plate, and may dress only one side of the body. When copying or drawing, patients tend to confine their drawings to the right side of the page; the drawings themselves often include adequate representations of the right side of the object with the left side either entirely omitted or grossly distorted.

A related condition, commonly found in association with recovery from florid neglect, is *extinction*. In extinction, a patient can report seeing or feeling an object on the side opposite the brain damage when one stimulus is presented, but fails to detect the same stimulus when a second stimulus is simultaneously presented to the unaffected side. Extinction is regarded by some researchers (e.g., Heilman, Watson, & Valenstein, 1993) as a milder form of neglect that is revealed in the course of partial recovery.

Line Bisection

Of all the clinical tests used to diagnose visual neglect, asking the patient to divide a horizontal line at its midpoint is by far the simplest and most widely employed (Bisiach et al., 1983; Bisiach et al., 1976; Halligan & Marshall, 1988; Schenkenberg, Bradford, & Ajax, 1980; Tegner & Levander, 1991). As a clinical test, line bisection can be traced back some hundred years to the practice of the first clinicians who documented spatial asymmetries of perception in patients with unilateral brain damage (Axenfeld, 1915; Poppelreuter, 1917).

Typically in a line bisection task, patients are shown a thin line centered on a sheet of paper, which is centered with respect to the midsaggital plane. They are instructed to mark the midpoint of the line with a rapid, ballistic movement. Patients with left-sided neglect behave as if they have failed to notice the full left extent of the line, generally transecting the line far to the right of center. Performance can be quantified by measuring the *transection displacement*, the deviation of the patient's mark from the true center. We follow the convention that a positive displacement is a shift to the right of center, indicating left neglect; a negative displacement is a shift to the left of center, indicating right neglect.

Halligan and Marshall have studied line bisection, extensively manipulating line length (Halligan & Marshall, 1988, 1989c; Marshall & Halligan, 1989, 1990a), orientation (Burnett-Stuart, Halligan, & Marshall, 1991; Halligan & Marshall, 1993b; Marshall & Halligan, 1990b), position (Halligan & Marshall, 1989b; Marshall & Halligan, 1990a), and the context in which the line is embedded (Halligan, Manning, & Marshall, 1991; Halligan & Marshall, 1989a, 1991a; Manning, Halligan, & Marshall, 1990). All of these variables have been shown to have reliable effects on the measured severity of neglect.

Computational Modeling of Neglect

We have replicated the pattern of results of neglect patients on the line bisection task in a computational model of two-dimensional object recognition and spatial attention (Mozer, 1991). The model, called MORSEL, was originally developed with two objectives in mind: (1) to build a computational mechanism that could analyze complex scenes consisting of multiple visual stimuli presented simultaneously, and (2) to account for a broad spectrum of psychological data, including perceptual errors that arise when several stimuli appear simultaneously in the visual field, facilitatory effects of context and redundant information, and attentional phenomena. The architecture and details of MORSEL arose from constraints imposed by these two objectives.

Mozer and Behrmann (1990) "lesioned" MORSEL in accordance with the damage that was hypothesized to occur in the brains of neglect patients. The lesioned model was then used to simulate some puzzling aspects of the performance of patients with neglect dyslexia—a reading disorder associated with neglect. For example, MORSEL could account for the data of Behrmann et al. (1990) indicating that patients, when shown a pair of words such as *cow* and *sun*, would generally report only the word on the right—a form of extinction. However, when the two words were related in that they could be combined to form a lexical item, e.g., *cow* and *boy*, extinction was less likely.

In the present work, we have used MORSEL, along with the lesion proposed in the earlier neglect modeling work, to simulate a set of findings on the line bisection task. The model, with no extensions or parameter adjustment, is successful in explaining a wide variety of effects. Interestingly, MORSEL makes an incorrect prediction for one minor aspect of the data, revealing a probable flaw in the model—most likely a technical, not conceptual, flaw. Nonetheless, the model makes interesting and testable predictions, and has the potential to be used as a diagnostic tool to better characterize the specific nature of a patient's deficit.

Description of MORSEL

At this point, readers might wish for a detailed description of the data that we model. We ask the reader's indulgence, however, and begin with an overview of MORSEL. Following this overview, we can then present the data side-by-side with simulation experiments. Readers who are not fully motivated now may wish first to skim the "Data and Simulation Accounts" section to get a sense for the results.

Input to MORSEL

MORSEL was designed primarily to model letter and word perception. In contrast to earlier models of word perception (e.g., McClelland & Rumelhart, 1981), MORSEL has the capability of processing several items simultaneously. MORSEL has a visual field or *retina* on which stimuli are presented. The retina is a 36×36 array of cells. In each cell is a set of five feature detectors. These detectors register, or *become active* in response to, the presence of certain features in their region of the retina. Four of the detectors register oriented lines and the fifth detector registers the termination of a line. Figure 15.1 shows a sample input to MORSEL representing the phrase BAD ARTIST. Each letter produces a 3×3 pattern of activity on the retina. (Note that we show only as many rows of the retina as are necessary in our figures.)

This primitive activity pattern is interpreted by a connectionist network called BLIRNET, which attempts to identify the letters and words appearing on the retina. Figure 15.2 shows a sketch of MORSEL, with the BLIRNET module mapping the retinal activity pattern to a representation of letters and words. We envision a potentially large collection of processing modules that analyze

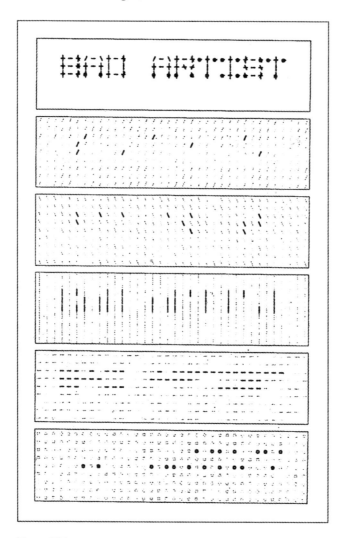

Figure 15.1

The top array shows the set of active feature detectors for a sample input, the phrase BAD ARTIST, presented on MORSEL's retina. The arrays below show activity by detector type. Each character in an array represents the activity of a single detector. The symbols −, /, |, and \ correspond to the 0°, 45°, 90°, 135° line detectors. A darkened symbol indicates that the detector is active.

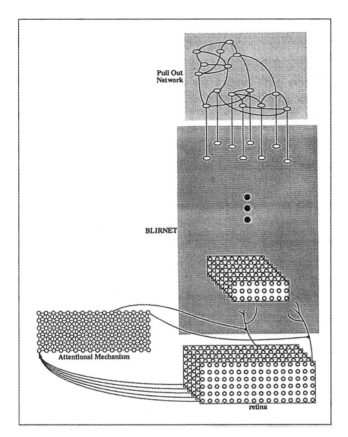

Figure 15.2
A sketch of MORSEL. The retinal representation is shown on the bottom right. Each circle corresponds to a detector or processing unit. The sheets of units correspond to a spatiotopic array of units all having the same feature type. The ovals at the top of the BLIRNET module are units that represent letters and words.

various properties of the retinal array. For the line bisection task, for example, a module is required that identifies the center of mass of the stimulus activity.

MORSEL has two means of performing attentional selection: a late-selection component called the *pull-out net* and an early-selection component called the *attentional mechanism* (AM). The pull-out net acts on the outputs of BLIRNET to select items that have a certain lexical status or semantic content. The AM acts on the input to BLIRNET to select certain spatial regions for processing. BLIRNET, and other processing modules that operate on the retinal representation, is limited in capacity, and hence requires the AM's direction to avoid processing too much information at once.

We omit details of BLIRNET and the pull-out net, as they are not relevant for the current simulations. The interested reader can consult Mozer (1991). The simulations of line bisection, however, are dependent on the behavior of the AM, and thus we describe this component in some depth.

The Attentional Mechanism

The AM receives advice about where to focus from various sources, resolves conflicting suggestions, and then constructs a "spotlight" centered on the selected region of the retina. The attentional spotlight serves to enhance the activation of input features within its bounds relative to those outside. This causes preferential treatment in BLIRNET and other processing modules. However, the AM does not act as an all-or-none filter. Information from unattended regions of the retina undergoes some degree of analysis by BLIRNET and other processing modules. This partial processing of unattended information distinguishes the AM from other early-selection filtering mechanisms that have been proposed (e.g., Koch & Ullman, 1985; LaBerge & Brown, 1989), although this is not relevant in the current work.

The AM receives input about where to focus from two sources. First, attention can be guided in a *bottom-up* manner by stimulus information so as to bias selection toward locations where stimuli are actually present. The connections in Figure 15.2 from the retina into the AM provide this input. Second, higher-levels of cognition can supply *top-down* control on the basis of task demands. For instance, if the task instructions are to report the left item in a multi-item display first, selection can be biased toward the left portion of the display initially; if the instructions are to read a page of text, a scanning mechanism can bias selection toward the top-left corner initially, and then advance left to right, top to bottom. (Butter, 1987 argues for a similar distinction between "reflex" and "voluntary" control of attention in humans.)

As shown in Figure 15.2, the AM is a set of units in one-to-one correspondence with the retinotopic feature maps serving as input to BLIRNET. Activity in an AM unit indicates that attention is focused on the corresponding retinal location and serves to *gate the flow of activity* from the retina into BLIRNET and other processing modules. Specifically, the activity level of a unit in a given location in the retinotopic array is transmitted to the processing modules with a probability that is monotonically related to the activity of the AM unit in the corresponding array location. However, the AM serves only to bias processing: it does not absolutely inhibit activations from unattended regions, but these activations are transmitted with a lower probability.

Each unit in the AM gets bottom-up input from the detectors in the corresponding location in all of the feature maps, as well as an unspecified top-down input. The dynamics of the AM generate a single, contiguous region of activity over the retinotopic array, with a bias toward locations indicated by bottom-up and top-down inputs. Details of the AM selection process are provided in Appendix 1. Figure 15.3 shows an example of the AM in operation. Two blobs of

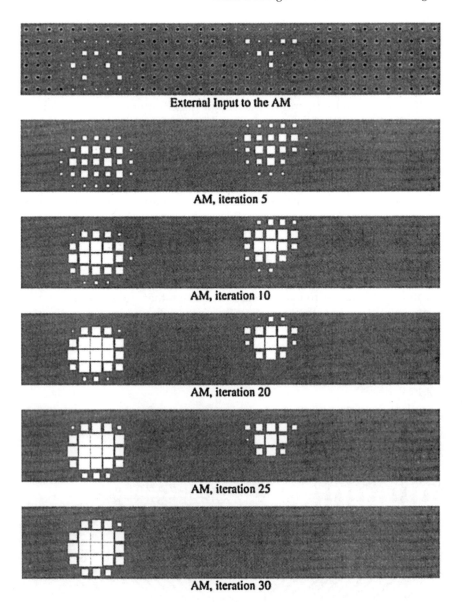

External Input to the AM

AM, iteration 5

AM, iteration 10

AM, iteration 20

AM, iteration 25

AM, iteration 30

Figure 15.3
An example of the AM selecting a single location. The top panel shows the external input to the AM. Arranged in a two-dimensional grid. The area of each white square is proportional to the magnitude of the external input to that location on the grid; the black dots indicate AM grid locations that receive no input. The lower five panels show activity in the AM as it settles over time. The area of each white square in these figures is proportional to the activity of the AM unit in the homologous position of the array. "Iteration" refers to the number of discrete time steps that have transpired.

activity are presented to the AM via its external inputs, and the AM settles on the left blob.[1]

Damaging MORSEL to Produce Neglect

To model data from neglect dyslexia, Mozer and Behrmann (1990) proposed a particular form of lesion to the model—damaging the bottom-up connections to the AM from the retinal feature arrays. The damage is graded monotonically, most severe at the left extreme of the retina and least severe at the right (assuming a right hemisphere lesion, as we will throughout this article). Figure 15.4 depicts the damaged connections into the AM. The graded damage is important; Mozer and Behrmann achieved what might be interpreted as object-based neglect via the graded damage. Complete destruction of the connections in the left field and fully intact connections in the right field would yield a qualitatively different sort of behavior. It is also important to contrast this proposal for lesioning the model with two alternatives. First, one might damage the visual recognition system (BLIRNET) itself. However, this would lead to blindness, and is inconsistent with the view of neglect as an attentional phenomenon and with the neuroanatomical lesion sites that give rise to neglect. Second, one might lesion the AM directly, either changing the activation dynamics or connectivity of the units such that damaged units integrated activity more slowly or had a weakened influence on the activity of other units. We conjecture that these types of lesions would yield a behavioral effect similar to the proposed lesion for the simulation studies reported in this article.

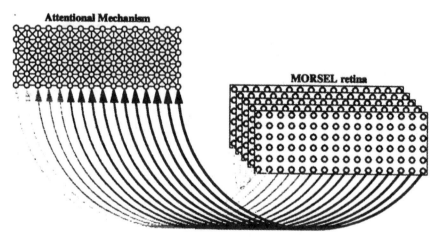

Figure 15.4
A sketch of the AM and some of its inputs from MORSEL's retina. Each detector on the retina connects to the homologous unit in the AM. In neglect, we propose that there is graded damage to these connections, causing retinal detectors to be less effective in activating the AM. The damage is depicted by the fainter connections toward the left side of the field.

The damage affects the probability that features present on the retina are detected by the AM. To the extent that features in a given location are not detected, the AM will fail to focus attention at that location. Note that this is not a "perceptual" deficit, in the sense that if somehow attention can be mustered, features will be analyzed normally by BLIRNET and other processing modules.

Mozer and Behrmann (1990) showed that this form of damage was compatible with early, peripheral effects observed in neglect dyslexia because the disruption directly affects a low-level representation. However, the damage was also compatible with late, higher-order effects in neglect dyslexia by virtue of the fact that the pull-out net is able to reconstruct elements of a string—via lexical and semantic knowledge—that are attenuated by the AM.

Modeling Line Bisection

Line bisection is a simple cognitive task; it does not require visual object recognition and does not invoke higher-order knowledge. For this reason, much of MORSEL, which deals with shape recognition and the top-down influence of semantic and lexical knowledge, is irrelevant. Only the early-selection attentional system—the AM—is pertinent. Thus, in terms of MORSEL, line bisection is an extremely pure and primitive cognitive task.

In brief, we model the line bisection task by presenting the line stimulus on the retina, allowing the AM to settle, and then supposing a motor process that places the transection point at the center of the attended region. We assume that the motor process thus veridically bisects the attended region; there is no motor neglect or motor bias.

Stimuli

Figure 15.5 shows the representation we constructed for a line stimulus appearing on MORSEL's retina. The line is made up of two rows of horizontal segments with terminators at the extremities.[2]

The number of features active in a given cell of MORSEL's retina determines the amount of input fed to the corresponding cell of the AM. Figure 15.6 shows the external input to the unlesioned AM for line stimuli of varying lengths, and Figure 15.7 shows the external input for line stimuli of various orientations.

To establish a correspondence between distances on the retina and physical distances in the world, we arbitrarily assume that each cell of the retina corresponds to an 8.47 mm $(= 1/3$ in) distance in the stimulus display. Consequently, the line lengths of 3 to 33 cells, depicted in Figure 15.6, correspond to stimulus lines of 25 to 279 mm.

Lesioning MORSEL

All parameters and details of MORSEL—including connection strengths, interconnectivity patterns, and time constants—were left unchanged from the ear-

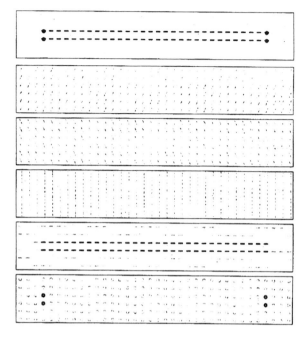

Figure 15.5
The Pattern of feature activity produced by a line or MORSEL's retina.

lier work of Mozer (1991) and Mozer and Behrmann (1990). However, MORSEL has several remaining degrees of freedom that relate to the nature of the attentional deficit, which presumably differs from patient to patient.

Specifically, four parameters determine a function relating the horizontal position of a feature on MORSEL's retina to the probability that the feature will be transmitted to the corresponding cell of the AM. This function is shown in Figure 15.8. It is a piecewise linear curve with a flat segment, followed by a segment with positive slope, followed by another flat segment. The left extreme of the curve represents the left edge of the retina, the right extreme of the curve represents the right edge of the retina. The probability that the AM will register a feature is low in the left field, and it is monotonically nondecreasing further to the right.

The curve is characterized by four parameters: (1) the probability of feature transmission on the right end of the retina (*saturation probability*), (2) the horizontal position on the retina where the probability reaches asymptote (*saturation position*), (3) the minimum transmission probability (*minimum probability*), and (4) the slope of the curve (*gradient*). Mozer and Behrmann (1990) used this same general type of curve, without the explicit parameterization, in their earlier neglect simulations. The basic notion of an attentional gradient is due

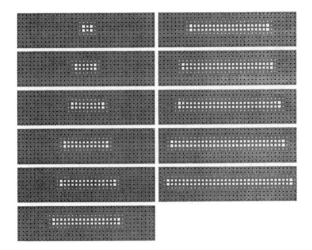

Figure 15.6
External input to the unlesioned AM for line stimuli of varying lengths. The size of a white square is proportional to the magnitude of the external input. The black dots indicate AM grid locations that receive no external input. Because both horinzontal and terminator detectors are active at the end-points of a line, external input is twice as large at the endpoint locations. Note that feature at given location on the retina provides input not just to the corresponding location on the AM but also provides a small amount of input to adjacent locations. This spillover results in the halo around the stimulus locations.

to Kinsbourne (1993). The parameterization of the curve allows a variety of transmission functions, including forms corresponding to normals (e.g., a minimum probability close to 1 and a gradient of 0), a homogeneous slope across the entire field (e.g., a shallow gradient and a saturation position at the far right edge), and a sharp discontinuity at the hemifield crossing (a very large gradient and a saturation position just to the right of fixation).

This curve representing damage is cleaner and sharper than one would expect from a biological system. Minimally, it should be curvilinear with no discontinuities in slope. However, minor changes to the form of the curve have little effect on the model's behavior, and the parameterization of curve is quite flexible in that it allows a wide variety of possible forms of damage.

It turns out that the behavior of the AM is robust over various transmission probability curves, except when extreme values of the parameters are selected. Interestingly, some sets of parameters do lead to odd and incorrect predictions. This does not invalidate MORSEL, but rather places constraints on the range of parameter values and their interrelationships that can occur in patients. This in itself is a useful contribution of the modeling effort. We say more about this issue below.

Rather than picking a single set of parameters somewhat arbitrarily, the simulations reported below explored a collection of parameter sets. Because

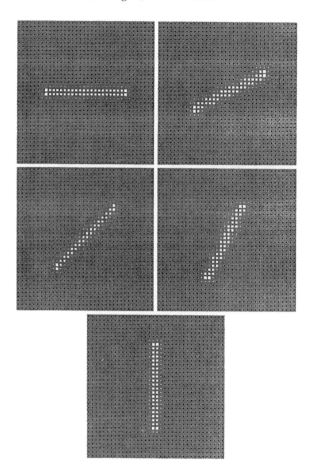

Figure 15.7
External input to the unlesioned AM for line stimuli of various orientations.

each patient presumably has a slightly different form of deficit, and because we are modeling mean performance across patients, it seems sensible to construct an ensemble of lesioned models, each with a slightly different transmission probability curve. Our ensemble was formed by considering saturation probabilities of .9 or 1.0, gradients of .01 or .02, saturation positions of 50%, 75%, or 100% from the left edge of the retina, and minimum probabilities of .2 or .4. The Cartesian product of these parameter values was formed, yielding 24 different transmission probability curves.

In most of our simulations, we modeled 10 replications of each of the 24 transmission probability curves, yielding a total of 240 simulated patients. The results reported below are means over these simulated patients. Except where

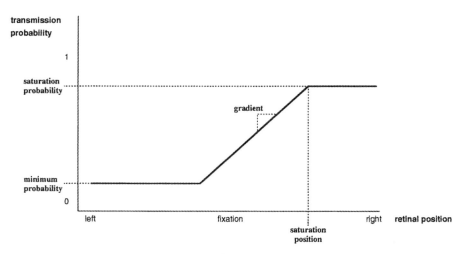

Figure 15.8
The transmission probability curve representing the damage to the attentional system is MORSEL. The function relates the position of a feature on MORSEL's retina to the probability that the feature will be detected by the corresponding cell of the AM. The function is for a left neglect patient: the probability that the AM will register a feature is low in the left field, and it is monotonically non-decreasing further to the right.

otherwise noted, we ran 10 trials per simulated patient per condition. This is the amount of data collected on real patients in the corresponding studies.

Methodology
When a stimulus is presented on MORSEL's retina, processing proceeds as follows. Activation is transmitted from the retina to the AM according to the transmission probability function. This triggers the AM to select a contiguous spatial region on the retina. The AM iterates toward a stable state over time. Examples of this in the normal and lesioned model are shown in Figures 15.9 and 15.10, respectively. The response of the unlesioned model is symmetric about the center of the line stimulus, whereas the response of the lesioned model is shifted toward the right side of the field. While Figure 15.10 shows the response on a single trial, of a version of the AM with a particular transmission probability function and a particular sampling of activation transmitted to the AM based on this function, it is quite typical, as will be evident from results presented in subsequent sections.[3]

Once the AM has settled, the center of mass of the blob of activity is computed using the formula:

$$p = \frac{\Sigma_x \Sigma_y x a_{xy}}{\Sigma_x \Sigma_y a_{xy}} \tag{1}$$

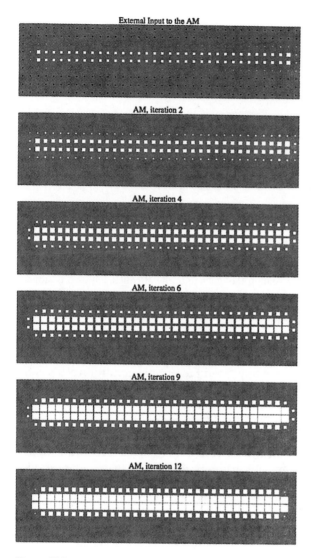

Figure 15.9
The unlesioned AM responding to a line stimulus. The top panel shows the external input to the AM. In this stimulation, the AM selects all locations containing features of the line, in addition to some neighboring locations, and its response is symmetric about the center of the line.

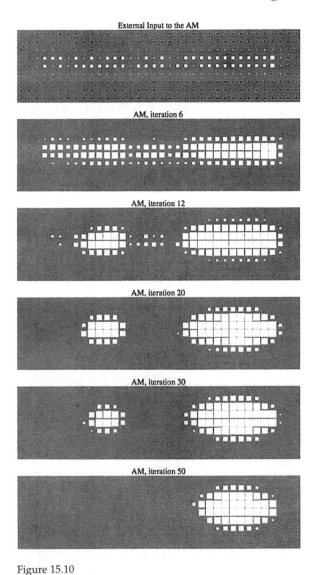

Figure 15.10
The lesioned version of the AM attending to a line stimulus. In contrast to Figure 15.9, the external input to the AM is degraded, particularly in the left region of the retina. Rather than processing the line as a single entity, the AM drops some portion of the line, resulting in a competition between the remaining portions of the line. The right portion wins out as its external input is stronger. The final state of the AM is not symmetric about the center of the stimulus line.

where a_{xy} is the activity of AM unit at location (x, y). If p_0 is the horizontal position of the true center of the line, then the transection displacement is $p - p_0$. This displacement can be scaled to units of millimeters, using the conversion factor described above.

There are several reasonable procedures for translating the AM pattern of activity into a transection response from the model. For instance, one could determine the leftmost and rightmost point of activity in the AM, call them p_l and p_r, and the transection point could be computed as the average, $p = (p_l + p_r)/2$. We experimented with several such alternative procedures. Fortunately, the results of simulations were quite robust to the readout procedure.

Data and Simulation Accounts

In this section, we describe the basic phenomena of line bisection, along with the model's explanation of the phenomena. A great deal of data has been collected on this task. We have attempted to sift through the data (including unpublished data) and characterize the consistent and robust phenomena, as well as curious but statistically reliable quirks.

1 Normal Performance
Studies of normal performance on line bisection have been carried out using college-aged subjects, elderly controls, and neurological patients without neglect (e.g., Bisiach et al., 1976; Bradshaw et al., 1985; Halligan & Marshall, 1989c; Heilman, Bowers, & Watson, 1984; Manning, Halligan, & Marshall, 1990). Some studies have shown overall mean leftward transection displacements, others have shown overall mean rightward displacements, while others have shown no overall bias. The mean displacements are quite small, less than 1–2% of the total line length in magnitude.

The variability across studies is not mysterious. It seems clear that individual subjects do show overall biases, roughly 3–4% of total line length. About half of the subjects transect to the left and half to the right. Consequently, with small sample sizes, one should expect small positive or negative means across subjects.

Two additional facts have emerged. First, the mean displacement for a given subject—either to the left or to the right—increases with the line length, although the effect is small because the displacements are small. Second, within-subject variability of transections is positively correlated with line length. For example, Manning, Halligan, & Marshall (1990) found a linear correlation between line length and standard deviation of responses to be .97; Halligan & Marshall (1988) found a correlation of .88.

Simulations   In the unlesioned version of MORSEL, the transmission probability curve is uniform across the visual field—there is no attentional bias or gradient.

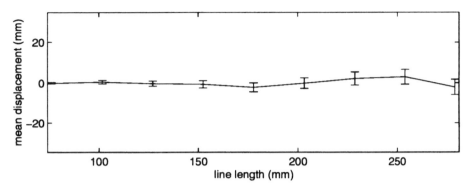

Figure 15.11
Simulation of unlesioned MORSEL on line bisection task as a function of line length. The bars indicate the standard error of the mean. Two hundred and forty simulated subjects were run, with 10 trials at each line length for each subject. The 10 trials were averaged, resulting in one data point at each line length for each subject.

To model normal performance, we must nonetheless specify the transmission probability. If the probability is 1.0 everywhere in the field, then the model will always select all features of the line (see Fig. 15.9) and will thus always bisect the line correctly. Some noise must be introduced into performance to model the variability among normals. One way to do this would be to assume noise in the motor response process, but it is also possible to introduce noise in perception by setting the transmission probability to, say, .9 uniformly across the field. (Mozer, 1991 also used a transmission probability of .9 to model normals.)

Figure 15.11 shows the mean transection displacement as a function of line length for the unlesioned model with uniform transmission probability of 0.9. The mean displacements are not reliably different from zero, regardless of the line length. However, there is a clearly monotonic relationship between the line length and the variability of the responses across simulated subjects: the standard deviation of transection displacements, which are linearly related to the error bars shown in the figure, get larger as the line length increases. This replicates the general pattern of normal human performance.

2 Effect of Line Length

In neglect patients, transection displacement is monotonically related to line length (Bisiach et al., 1983; Halligan & Marshall, 1988; Nichelli, Rinaldi, & Cubelli, 1989; Riddoch & Humphreys, 1983). Figure 15.12a shows a typical curve for a patient. For short lines of about 50 mm, the patient is fairly accurate, but as the line length increases, the transection point shifts farther to the right of center. Roughly, the displacement magnitude is proportional to the line length. The proportionality constant varies from one patient to another, but all show this general pattern.

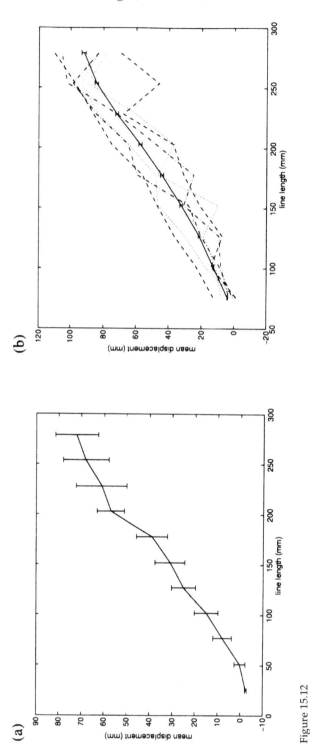

Figure 15.12

(a) Mean transection displacement as a function of line length for patient PP from Marshall and Halligan (1989). Each point is the average over 10 trials. The length of the vertical bar extending in each direction from the point is ±1 standard error of the mean. (b) Simulation of lesioned MORSEL on line bisection task as a function of line length. The dotted and dashed lines show typical curves from six simulated patients. The solid line with the error bars shows the mean across simulated patients.

Data from 43 patients with unilateral right hemisphere damage were reanalyzed to quantify this observation. Twenty-six of these patients were tested with lines varying from 18 to 180 mm in 18-mm increments; 16 were tested with lines of 25 to 279 mm in 25.4 mm increments. Ten trials were run for each line length. We examined the shape of the curves relating line length to transection displacement to determine the linearity of the relationship. Because subjects perform very well at the shortest lengths, and hence there is a floor effect, we removed lines of 50 mm and shorter from the analyses.

Of the 43 patients, 42 showed a strong linear relationship between line length and transection displacement. The mean percent of variance accounted for with a linear regression was 90.3%. With a quadratic term included in the regression, the percent variance accounted for rose only to 92.2%.

The one exception, patient MN, showed a significant quadratic component in his response function. The curve was negatively accelerated: in proportion to line length, MN showed less neglect for long lines than for short lines. MN was studied over 15 sessions to assess the reliability of his performance. Averaging MN's responses over the 15 sessions, a linear regression accounted for only 85.8% of the variance; a quadratic regression accounted for 97.6%.

Simulations   Varying-length lines were presented to the lesioned MORSEL. Figure 15.12b shows mean transection displacement as a function of line length averaged over the 240 simulated patients, as well as the data for six individual simulated patients who represent the sort of variability found in the data.

The mean curve is clearly linear. To examine the nature of the curve for individual simulated patients, we computed the proportion of variance accounted for by a linear regression and a quadratic regression (i.e., having both first- and second-order terms) for each simulated patient. Averaged over simulated patients, the linear fit accounted for 90.3% of the variance, and the quadratic fit 91.7%. This closely replicates the corresponding statistics from the human patients: 90.3% for the linear fit and 92.2% for the quadratic.

Over all simulated patients and line lengths, the mean transection displacement was 23% of the line length with a standard deviation of 12%. These figures match typical patient performance; for example, patient PP (Figure 15.12a) showed a mean displacement 22% of the line length and with a standard deviation of 13%.

Note that we omitted very short lines—having lengths of 25 or 51 mm—from Figure 15.12b and the regression analyses. This is because most of the simulated patients performed nearly perfectly at these lengths, resulting in a floor effect (Table 15.1) and corrupting the linearity of the relationship between line length and transection displacement. However, these very short lines were also omitted from the human performance statistics for the same reason; hence, the model and human data are comparable.

Table 15.1
Mean transection displacement for various line lengths—lesioned model

Line length (mm)	Mean displacement
25	0.1
51	1.1
76	3.9
102	12.7
127	21.4
152	32.4
178	44.2
203	57.4
229	71.6
254	84.3
279	92.0

3 Crossover of Displacements at Short Lengths

Typically, neglect patients transect to the right of the true midpoint. However, for very short line lengths—less than about 50 mm—some patients consistently bisect to the *left* of the midpoint (Halligan & Marshall, 1988; Marshall & Halligan, 1989). Thus, the left neglect observed for long lines becomes a sort of right neglect for the shortest lines. When this occurs, the transection displacements *cross over* the objective center of the lines. Linear extrapolation from the displacements for longer lines often predicts this counterintuitive phenomenon.

Account in Terms of the Model   Although this phenomenon is on the surface puzzling, we offer a simple explanation. The phenomenon might be viewed as emerging from a combination of two assumptions: (1) some normals consistently err to the left on line bisection; and (2) patients exhibit little or no neglect for short lines. The evidence for the first point was given earlier, and the leftward bias exhibited by some normals may be present even after brain damage. If this leftward bias is additive with large rightward shifts due to neglect, it will not be detected. However, if neglect plays no significant role for short lines, then the leftward bias might again dominate. Thus, rather than viewing the crossover phenomenon as fundamentally tied to neglect, one could sensibly attribute crossover to the *absence* of neglect for short lines.

Crossover in most human patients occurred only for line lengths of 25 and 51 mm. As Table 15.1 shows, the lesioned MORSEL produces little or no neglect at these line lengths, allowing even a slight leftward bias to push the responses to the left of the midpoint.

To quantify this argument, consider the combination of two independent influences on performance: left neglect which causes deviations to the right of the midpoint that are proportional to line length, and a fixed bias to deviate to the left of the midpoint for all line lengths. One can express this mathematically as

$$d = .5nl - b$$

where d is the observed transection displacement, l is the line length, n quantifies the severity of neglect ($0 =$ none, $1 =$ complete), and b is the fixed leftward bias. When the line length is sufficiently short, the contribution of the first term will be overwhelmed by the fixed leftward bias, and the displacement will end up negative, i.e., to the left of the midpoint.

Note that we make no assumptions concerning what system or systems produce the leftward bias. It is unrelated to brain damage, as normals exhibit these same biases. It could stem from perceptual, motor, or perhaps even spatial reasoning systems.

4 Response Variation as a Function of Line Length

At each line length, experimenters typically collect multiple responses from patients. The responses are averaged to factor out some sources of variability in performance. However, this variability is itself interesting. One can quantify the variability as the standard deviation of transection displacements over the trials for a given line length. This standard deviation tends to be proportional to line length. For example, patient AL was tested over six sessions and correlations between standard deviations and line length ranged from .55 to .89 (Halligan & Marshall, 1991b). Patients DF, MN, CC, BS, TB, EF, TR, and TM, reported in Halligan and Marshall (1993b), had correlations of .88, .94, .64, .96, .89, .92, .92, and .92, respectively. Patient PP's correlation was .93 (Marshall & Halligan, 1989; see Figure 15.12a). Patients PB (Halligan & Marshall, 1988), JH, and PS (Halligan & Marshall, 1989c) showed correlations of .84, .84, and .76, respectively.

Qualitatively, the distribution of responses is unimodal, with 5–25% of the transections being made to the left of center. The vast majority of these left-sided responses occurred at the shorter line lengths. In the case of the serial assessment of AL, the mean proportion of left-sided transections comprised 21% of the total responses. For the other neglect patients described above—DF, PP, MN, CC, BS, TB, EF, TR, TM, PB, JH, PS—the percentage of left-sided responses was as follows: 24, 18, 12, 0, 5, 5, 9, 8, 5, 17, 8, and 17.

Simulations We examined the distribution of transection displacements across simulated patients. The mean transection displacement for each patient and line length was computed over 10 trials. Then a histogram of displacements over the set of patients was constructed. Figure 15.13 shows this distribution for 229-mm lines using from data of 16 human patients (left) and 240 simulated patients (right). In both the human and simulation data, the distribution of responses is roughly unimodal.[4]

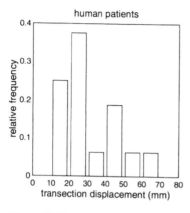
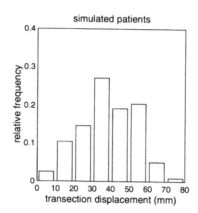

Figure 15.13
Distribution of mean transection displacements for 16 human patients (left) and 240 simulated patients (right) for 229-mm lines, averaged over 10 trials per patient.

The correlation coefficient between line length and standard deviation of transection displacements was computed for each simulated patient. Line lengths of 25 and 51 mm were included in these simulations because they were also used to compute the human patient correlations.

A mean correlation of .58 was obtained for the 240 simulated patients. This is perhaps lower than the correlations reported for humans (in the range .55–.95), but clearly nonzero and of the correct sign.[5]

5 Response Variation as a Function of Displacement
In the previous section, we characterized the variability of responses as a function of the length of lines. One can also consider the variability of responses as a function of mean displacement, for a given line length. Roughly, the standard deviation of transection displacements is proportional to the displacement: if a subject accurately bisects a line on average, then the variation from one attempt to the next will tend to be small; however, if the subject makes large rightward displacements, then the variability is generally larger. To quantify this effect, we reanalyzed the data of 20 patients transecting 180-mm lines, with 10 trials per patient. The correlation between mean displacement and standard deviation of the displacements was .51.

Simulations For a particular line length, we examined the relation between a simulated patient's mean transection displacement and the variability of the responses that constituted this mean. While the human patients showed a positive correlation, the simulated patients showed exactly the opposite pattern. For example, with 177-mm lines, the correlation was −.84, indicating that patients who produced larger displacements tended to show *less* variability in their responses. MORSEL thus fails to model this aspect of the data.

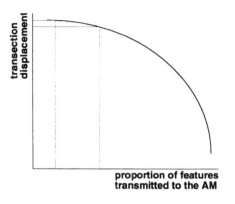
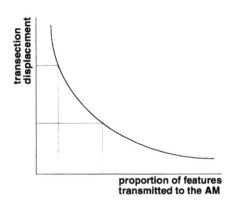

Figure 15.14
Two possible curves relating the expected transaction displacement as a function of the proportion of features on the left side of the retina that are successfully transmitted to the AM. The larger this proportion is, the less neglect should be expected.

While it would be extremely difficult to point to a specific component of MORSEL that is responsible for this failure, it is possible to describe a general characteristic that the model appears to possess, and how this characteristic is responsible for producing the observed simulation data.

Neglect in MORSEL corresponds to the failure of features registered on the retina to be detected by the AM, specifically features of the left side of the stimulus. The severity of neglect will be related to the degree to which the AM fails to detect the presence of these features. This is depicted schematically in the two graphs of Figure 15.14. Both graphs show the expected transection displacement as a function of the proportion of features on the left side of the retina that are successfully transmitted to the AM. When all features are transmitted, there will be no neglect, and the transection displacement will be zero; when the AM fails to detect features on the left side of the retina, transection displacements will be large. Thus, there should be a monotonic relationship between feature transmission probability and transection displacements. However, the relationship can be either negatively or positively accelerated, corresponding to the left and right curves in the figure, respectively.

For a particular lesion to MORSEL, the exact set and number of features transmitted to the AM on any trial will vary. This is because the operation of feature transmission is based on probability (see Fig. 15.8). Consequently, a particular lesion will produce a *range* of different values along the x-axis of the curves in Figure 15.14, as depicted by the two dotted vertical lines. This range in feature transmission rates will result in a range of transmission displacements, as depicted by the two dotted horizontal lines in Figure 15.8. One can clearly see in Figure 15.14 that with the curve on the left, larger transection displacements will occur with smaller variability, whereas with the curve on the right, larger transection displacements will occur with larger variability. The curve on the left corresponds to the behavior of the model; the curve on the right is what is required to fit the patient data.

While these curves are descriptive, translating them into a computation mechanism is not simple. The curve on the left emerges from the dynamics of the AM.[6] The difference between the curves—the sign of their second derivatives—is subtle indeed, and it will be a challenge to develop a revised version of the AM dynamics that achieves the desired behavior.

6 Effect of Stimulus Position

In the studies described above, stimulus lines were presented centered on a sheet of paper, which was also centered with respect to the midsaggital plane. One patient, PS, was studied not only in this condition, but also with a set of lines whose left endpoints all were anchored 1.5 mm from the left edge of the sheet of paper, and with another set whose right endpoints all were anchored 1.5 mm from the right edge of the sheet of paper (Marshall & Halligan, 1990a). Let us call these three conditions the *centered, left-aligned*, and *right-aligned* presentations. A variety of line lengths were tested, ranging from 12.5 mm to 279 mm in length. Note that the full extent of right-aligned lines 127 mm and shorter were entirely within right hemispace, and likewise for short left-aligned lines lying in the left hemispace.

Figure 15.15(a) shows PS's performance for centered, left-aligned, and right-aligned stimuli. In all three conditions, transection displacements are linearly related to line length. The average magnitude of neglect is no greater for left-aligned than for centered stimuli; right-aligned stimuli appear to produce less neglect. The slope of the linear relationship between line length and mean displacement can also be used as a measure of the severity of neglect; the larger the slope, the larger the displacement as a fraction of line length. The slopes for the three presentation conditions are shown in Table 15.2. All three of these slopes are quite large relative to slopes obtained for normals, which are in the neighborhood of .03. Although there appears to be somewhat less neglect for the right-aligned presentations by this measure, one cannot ascertain the statistical reliability of this conclusion from the one patient's data.[7]

If neglect occurs with respect to a reference frame that is centered on the sheet of paper or centered on the body midline, one would expect relatively severe neglect for left-aligned stimuli and relatively mild neglect for right-aligned stimuli. The support for this pattern of results is no strong. Instead, the data appears to provide evidence for neglect that occurs with respect to the reference frame of the stimulus itself.

Simulations   In the simulation experiments reported thus far, stimulus lines were centered on MORSEL's retina. Here, we add two conditions: lines whose endpoints are anchored either to the left or to the right side of the retina. Short

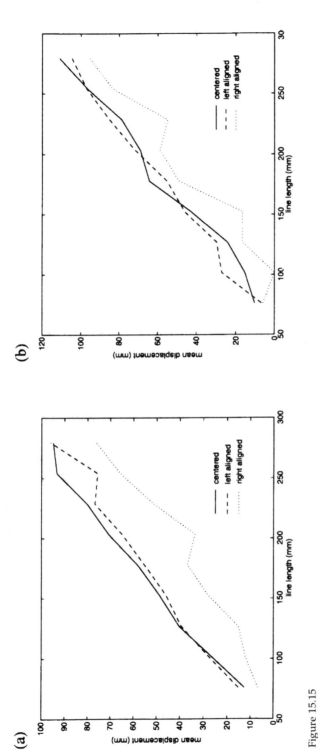

Figure 15.15

(a) Mean transection displacement as a function of line length for centered, left-aligned, and right-aligned presentations for patient PS, from Marshall and Halligan 1990. (b) Mean transection displacement as a function of line length for centered, left-aligned, and right-aligned stimulus presentations for one simulated patient. The transmission probability curve of this patient is characterized by a saturation probability of 9, a saturation position at the right edge of the retina, a gradient of .02, and a minimum transmission probability of 4. Other simulated patients with these parameters showed a similar pattern of results, indicating a systematic relationship between the parameters and the observed performance.

Table 15.2
Linear regression coefficient for different line placement conditions

	Left-aligned	Centered	Right-aligned
Patient PS	.369	.406	.299
Simulated patients	.479	.455	.449

lines thus lie entirely in one hemifield or the other, and the longer the line, the farther it extends into the opposite hemifield.

Figure 15.16 shows the transection displacement as a function of line length averaged over the 240 simulated patients, for centered, left-aligned, and right-aligned conditions. The centered-condition data are the same as those in Figure 15.12(b). The clear result is that the placement of the lines makes little difference in the pattern of neglect. Although the transmission probability varies as a function of absolute position of the stimulus, what appears to be critical to the AM's performance is the *relative* strength of the left and right extremes of a stimulus line. Thus, the AM produces object-centered neglect—neglect with respect to the left and right ends of the object—rather than retinotopic neglect—neglect with respect to the position on the retina. This behavior of the model is somewhat unintuitive because the deficit itself is retinotopic. Mozer and Behrmann (1990) similarly found that the retinal position of a stimulus word in the damaged MORSEL had a relatively minor influence on reading performance.

This simulation result is consistent with the data obtained from PS, the only human patient who has been studied in these conditions in two important respects as shown in Figure 15.15(a). First, there is severe neglect in all three conditions. Second, the slope of the functions in all three conditions are of the same order of magnitude, and are an order of magnitude larger than those obtained for normals. Because the simulation data represents a mean over 240 patients, whereas the human data are those of a single patient, a precise fit should not be expected. However, it is not difficult to find individual simulated patients whose data shows a remarkably similar pattern to that of PS; see Fig. 15.15(b).

7 Effect of Stimulus Orientation

In the studies described above, lines were presented horizontally on the page and horizontally with respect to the patient. Marshall and Halligan (1990b) and Burnett-Stuart, Halligan, & Marshall (1991) have explored performance as a function of stimulus orientation. Patients were presented with stimulus lines of a fixed length (180 mm) drawn at various orientations on the paper.

Figure 15.17(a) shows the mean transection displacement as a function of orientation for one patient for whom a large corpus of data was collected. Positive displacements are to the right of center, regardless of orientation. The

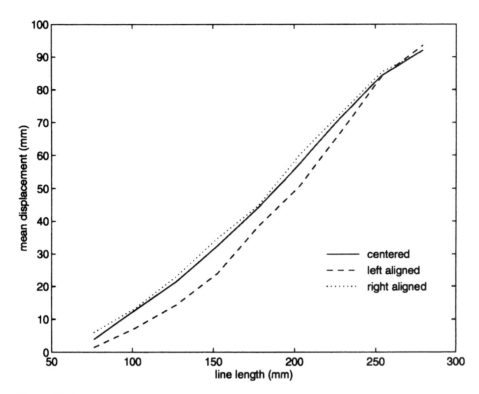

Figure 15.16
Mean transection displacement produced by simulations of lesioned MORSEL as a function of line length for centered, left-aligned, and right-aligned stimulus presentations.

angle 0° is horizontal; the angles 90° and −90° are vertical.[8] This particular patient shows relatively mild neglect; his transection displacements for horizontal lines are about one-third as large as are typically observed. Nonetheless, it is worth presenting this data because it clearly shows the pattern of results confirmed with statistical analyses: transection displacements are linearly related to the cosine of the orientation. That is, the severity of neglect is determined by the length of the projection of the line onto the horizontal axis (Burnett-Stuart et al., 1991).

Let us formalize this characterization of the results. The data obviously cannot be modeled by a straight line; it appears that a quadratic or cosine fit is necessary. Nonetheless, one can ask whether the data can be modeled by a piecewise linear function. That is, suppose we examine the data for orientations 0–90°. In the Burnett-Stuart et al. (1991) study of six patients, the fraction of the variance accounted for by a linear fit of these data is only 74.1%, whereas a cosine fit accounts for 88.8% of the variance.

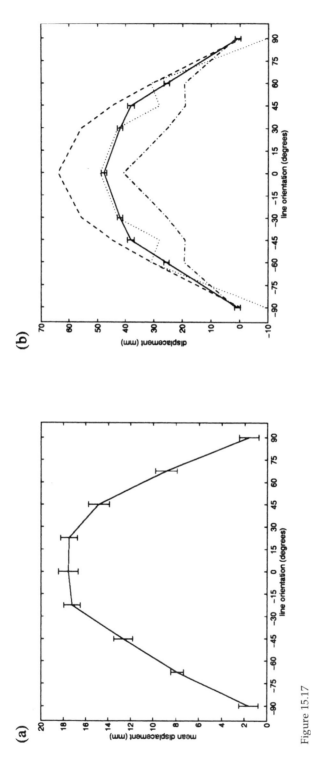

Figure 15.17

(a) Mean transection displacement as a fucntion of line orientation for patient MN, from Marshall and Halligan (1990b). Each point is the average over 60 trials. The vertical bars indicate ±1 standard error of the mean. (b) Simulation of lesioned MORSEL on line bisection task as a function of line orientation. The dotted and dashed lines show curves from three simulated patients. The solid line with the error bars shows the mean across simulated patients.

Table 15.3
Percent of variance accounted for in oriented line simulation

	Linear regression	Cosine regression
Human patients ($n = 6$)	74%	89%
Simulated patients ($n = 240$)	65%	72%

Interpreting the data is complicated somewhat by the fact that for some patients, neglect is not entirely a function of lateral extent, but also altitudinal extent (Butter et al., 1989; Rapcsak, Cimino, & Heilman, 1988). For these patients, one can conceptualize the axis of the attentional deficit as lying not along the horizontal, but rotated slightly clockwise (resulting in both left and upper-field neglect) or slightly counterclockwise (resulting in both left and lower field-neglect). Accordingly, for oriented lines, neglect is a function of the cosine of the angle, but there is a constant phase shift that reflects the fundamental axis of the deficit.[9]

Simulations   Stimuli used in this simulation experiment were fixed-length lines, corresponding to 180-mm lines viewed by human patients, at five orientations: 0°, 30°, 45°, 60°, and 90° (Fig. 15.7). Because of quantization effects on MORSEL's retina, it was tricky to generate the nonhorizontal and nonvertical lines. We matched the diagonal lines on the total number of input features and the average number of neighbors for each feature, which are the factors that seem to most affect the AM response.

Each of the 240 simulated patients was presented with 10 trials of each of the five different line orientations, and the mean transection displacement at each orientation was computed. Figure 15.17(b) shows the transection displacement as a function of line orientation. The dotted and dashed curves show typical responses of individual simulated patients, and the solid curve is the mean of the group, with error bars indicating the spread of the distribution.

Because the response of MORSEL for $-x°$ lines must necessarily mirror the response for $x°$ lines, the figure has been extended to include the orientations between −90° and 0°. Clearly, the mean displacement curve is bowed, non-monotonic in line orientation, and has the general shape of a cosine function.

For each simulated patient, we performed a linear and cosine regression to determine which type of curve best fits the individual's data for line orientations between 0° and 90°. The mean percent of variance accounted for in the two regression analyses is presented in Table 15.3. As it did for the human patients, the cosine regression yielded a reliably better fit for the simulated patients ($F(1,239) = 74$, $p < 0.001$). The explanation for this finding is simple: as we observed earlier, the critical factor in determining the severity of neglect in MORSEL is the difference in the transmission probability between the left and right ends of the stimuli. For oriented lines of a fixed length, this difference is monotonically related to the length of the projection of the stimulus line onto the horizontal axis, which in turn is proportional to the cosine of the line orientation.

One discrepancy between simulations and humans is that the simulated patients seem to show somewhat more variance in their responses than do the humans, which leads to slightly worse fits for both the linear and cosine regressions, as well as a weaker difference between the two. A partial explanation for this discrepancy may have to do with quantization effects on MORSEL's retina. In our preliminary simulation studies, we found that the responses of MORSEL were sensitive to small changes in the stimulus-induced activity pattern on the retina. A finer quantization of the retinal array should make the activity of any individual cell less critical and might reduce response variability. Another partial explanation for the discrepancy is the fact that the human experiments used 22.5° and 67.5° lines whereas the simulation used 30° and 60° lines. It was much simpler to construct 30° and 60° lines on MORSEL's retina due to quantization effects, but this created a uniform spacing of orientations, which may have masked differences between linear and cosine regressions.

We could model the performance of patients whose deficit was not strictly along the horizontal axis. This would be easy to do by rotating the attentional gradient on the map of the AM, corresponding to the sort of gradient that we suppose for these patients.

Discussion

MORSEL is an existing computational model whose architecture, dynamics, and parameters have been specified in earlier simulation studies. Even the form of the damage that occurs in unilateral neglect is dictated by earlier modeling work. Thus, MORSEL was not in any way designed to account for the line bisection data modeled here MORSEL makes strong predictions and the data were reexamined to determine whether the model and data were consistent.

We have shown that MORSEL can achieve a remarkable fit to the data. MORSEL can model the following phenomena: (1) no consistent across-subject bias is found in normals; (2) transection displacements are proportional to line length in neglect patients; (3) variability of displacements is proportional to line length, in both normals and patients; (4) position of the lines with respect to the body or the page on which they are drawn has little effect; and (5) for lines drawn at different orientations, displacements are proportional to the cosine of the orientation angle. MORSEL also fails to account for one observation: across patients, the variability of displacements for a particular line length is roughly proportional to mean displacement.

What have we learned from this modeling exercise? It has been valuable for a variety of reasons, on which we elaborate.

· In determining what data to model, we were forced to reexamine and reanalyze the patient data, combining results across multiple studies, separating robust and reliable patterns from quirks in individual patient performance. Prior to this effort, the main phenomena related to line bisection had never been distilled and summarized. We thus have a better understanding of the data.

· MORSEL is able to provide a comprehensive account of the varied corpus of data in a unified framework. We have pointed to essential properties of the model that are responsible for the observed effects. Phenomena that could be seen as puzzling without a theoretical framework—such as the finding that neglect is related to the total line length, despite the fact that the patient does not apprehend the entire line—have straightforward, mechanical explanations in terms of the model.

· MORSEL has been able to explain a large collection of new data with almost no additional assumptions or mechanisms. This increases our confidence in the correctness and importance of the model, and gives us further motivation to continue expanding the breadth and coverage of MORSEL.

· The one phenomenon that MORSEL mispredicts—the relation between the mean and variability of transection displacements—points to a possible problem with the model. We suspect that fixing this problem involves a fairly minor change to the dynamics of the AM, but it is difficult to determine at this point; making any change to the model requires verification that the change does not affect the model's behavior on any other data. However, we are confident that the change can be made without repercussion, as no other data previously modeled depends on the aspect of the AM that we have pointed to as the culprit of the misprediction. Indeed, whether or not the effort of fixing the model is warranted depends on whether we expect to run across data in the future that will require this correction. At this point, we suspect not.

· MORSEL provides an accurate portrayal of the average performance of groups of patients, yet it also possesses the flexibility—via the transmission probability curve that specifies the nature of the attentional deficit—to model individual differences. If we have confidence in the model's validity, we can use it prescriptively to *characterize the attentional deficit* of individual patients in terms of their transmission probability curves. We have done this in one case above to show that the stimulus-position effects observed for patient PS (left-aligned and centered stimuli producing comparable neglect, while right-aligned stimuli producing less) could be modeled by the selection of a particular transmission probability curve. We can do a similar sort of exploration in the model's parameter space to try to understand the behavior of the only patient of 43 studied who shows a significant quadratic component in his performance on varying-

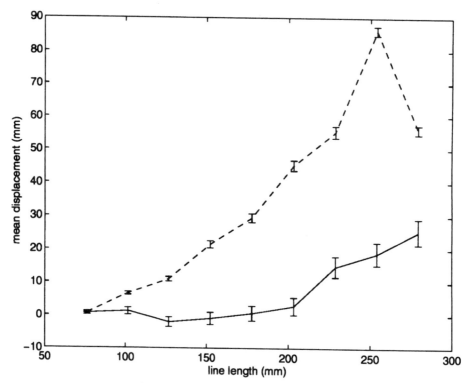

Figure 15.18

Simulation of lesioned MORSEL on line bisection task as a function of line length. The two lines show performance for two different transmission probability curves. The solid line—which corresponds to a saturation probability of .9, gradient of .01, saturation position on the right edge of the retina, and a minimum probability of .8—shows no neglect except for the longest lines. The dashed line—which corresponds to a saturation probability of 1.0, a gradient of .01, saturation position in the center of the retina, and a minimum probability of .8—shows proportionately less neglect for the longest line length than for the shorter line length. Neither of these patterns are observed in the human patient data, although a much less extreme version of the dashed line is occasionally found.

length lines. Thus, MORSEL could well be used as a diagnostic tool to characterize the specific nature of a patient's deficit.

A related and important application of MORSEL is in characterizing the sort of attentional deficits that are possible following brain damage. Exploring the model's parameter space, we have found that certain transmission probability curves yield patterns of data that are quite bizarre and have never been observed in patients, and thus are unlikely to occur in nature. Figure 15.18 shows two examples of this which result from shallow attentional gradients lying over just a small portion of the visual field. If we dichotomize the space of transmission probability curves into those that are and are not consistent with the human data, and if we have information about the site of a patient's lesion, we may gain insight into the underlying cortical organization and neural structures that give rise to certain types of deficits but not others.

· In the course of our modeling efforts, MORSEL has suggested experiments that should be run to help settle theoretical issues and to test additional predictions of the model. We are currently exploring the literature to determine if the relevant experiments have been conducted, and if not, we plan to conduct them in the future. The experiments will, for example, help disentangle perceptual and motor components of neglect, explore line thickness as a manipulation in bisection studies, explore the effects of brief, masked stimulus presentations, and collect more data on the effect of stimulus position and different frames of reference. For the masking studies, MORSEL makes the surprising prediction that under some conditions masking could alleviate neglect. In the last set of studies, MORSEL makes the strong prediction that, averaged over many patients, stimulus position should have little effect on performance, although there may be considerable individual differences. Assuming that these predictions are borne out, this may not be the end of the line for MORSEL after all!

Appendix 1: AM Dynamics

The task of the AM is to construct a "spotlight" of activity that highlights a single item appearing on MORSEL's retina. Defining an item to be a set of features in close proximity, the spotlight should form a *contiguous* region on the retina consistent with the bottom-up and top-down inputs to the AM.

In connectionism, the standard method of transforming this description of the target behavior of the AM into a network architecture is to view the AM's task as an *optimization* problem: To what activity value should each unit in the AM be set in order to best satisfy a number of possibly conflicting constraints? The two primary constraints here are that the AM should focus on locations suggested by the bottom-up and top-down inputs, and the AM should focus on a single item.

The first step in tackling such an optimization problem is to define a *Harmony* function (Smolensky, 1986) that computes the goodness of a given pattern of activity over the entire AM (the AM *state*). This goodness is a scalar quantity indicating how well the AM state satisfies the optimization problem. The maxima of the Harmony function correspond to desired states of the AM.

Given a Harmony function, H, one can ask how the activity of the AM unit at a retinal location (x, y), denoted a_{xy}, should be updated over time to increase Harmony and eventually reach states of maximal Harmony. The simplest rule, called *steepest ascent*, is to update a_{xy} in proportion to the derivative $\partial H / \partial a_{xy}$. If $\partial H / \partial a_{xy}$ is positive, then increasing a_{xy} will increase H; thus a_{xy} should be increased. If $\partial H / \partial a_{xy}$ is negative, then decreasing a_{xy} will increase H; thus a_{xy} should be decreased.

Returning to the problem faced by the AM, devising a Harmony function that computes whether the pattern of activity is contiguous is quite difficult. Instead of constructing a function that explicitly rewards contiguity, we have combined several heuristics that together generally achieve convex, contiguous patterns of activity.[10] The Harmony function used in the AM is:

$$H = \sum_{(x,y) \in \text{ALL}} ext_{xy} a_{xy} - \frac{\mu}{4} \sum_{(x,y) \in \text{ALL}} \sum_{(i,j) \in \text{NEIGH}_{xy}} (a_{ij} - a_{xy}^2) + \frac{\theta}{2} \sum_{(x,y) \in \text{ACTIVE}} (\gamma \bar{a} - a_{xy})^2,$$

where ALL is the set of all retinal locations, ext_{xy} is the net external (bottom-up and top-down) activity to the AM at location (x, y), NEIGH$_{xy}$ is the set of eight locations immediately adjacent to (x, y)—the *neighbors*, ACTIVE is the set of locations of all units with positive activity, $\bar{a}$ is the mean activity of all units with positive activity—

$$\bar{a} = \frac{1}{|\text{ACTIVE}|} \sum_{(x,y) \in \text{ACTIVE}} a_{xy},$$

and μ, θ, and γ are weighting parameters.

The first term encourages each unit to be consistent with the external bias. The second term encourages each unit to be as close as possible to its neighbors (so that if a unit is off and the neighbors are on, the unit will tend to turn on, and vice versa). The third term encourages units below the mean activity in the network to shut off, and units above the mean activity to turn on. The constant *gamma* serves as a discounting factor: with *gamma* less than 1, units need not be quite as active as the mean in order to be supported. Instead of using the average activity over *all* units, it is necessary to compute the average over the *active* units. Otherwise, the effect of the third term is to limit the total activity in the network, i.e., the number of units that can turn on at once. This is not suitable because we wish to allow large or small spotlights depending on the external input.

The update rule for a_{xy} is:

$$\Delta a_{xy} = \frac{\partial H}{\partial a_{xy}} = ext_{xy} + \mu \sum_{(i,j) \in \text{NEIGH}_{xy}} (a_{ij} - a_{xy}) - \theta(\gamma \bar{a} - a_{xy}).$$

Further, a_{xy} is prevented from going outside the range $[0, 1]$ by capping activity at these limits.[11]

To explain the activation function intuitively, consider the time course of activation. Initially, the activity of all AM units is reset to zero. Activation then feeds into each unit in proportion to its external bias (first term in the activation function). Units with active neighbors will grow the fastest because of neighborhood support (second term). As activity progresses, high-support neighborhoods will have activity above the mean; they will therefore be pushed even higher, while low-support neighborhoods will experience the opposite tendency (third term).

In all simulations, μ was fixed at $1/8$, θ at $1/2$, and γ at 0.11 times the total external input.

Acknowledgments

This research was supported by NSF Presidential Young Investigator award IRI-9058450 and grant 90–21 from the James S. McDonnell Foundation to MM, grants from the British Medical Research Council to PH and JM, and an Oxford McDonnell-Pew Centre Travel Grant. Our gracious thanks to Tim Shallice and Alphonso Caramazza for setting up the Trieste meeting that served as the catalyst for this work, and to Lesley Court for facilitating our communications across the Atlantic.

Notes

1. Mozer and Behrmann (1990) assumed a slight amount of blurring in the bottom-up input to the AM. Each retinal activation provided input not only to the corresponding location in the AM but also to the immediately adjacent locations, with a relative strength of 2%. This small amount of spread is unlikely to affect processing, but we have preserved it to maintain consistency with the original model.
2. The exact representation does not appear to be critical. We also experimented with lines having thicknesses of one and three cells, and the qualitative pattern of results was unchanged.
3. Examining the external input to the AM in Figure 15.10, one notices that the actual input strength varies from location to location, and some locations to the right of center actually have stronger input than some locations to the left of center. This is because the figure shows a particular sampling from retinal input based on the transmission probability function, rather than the *expected* input strength, which would increase monotonically from left to right.
4. This pattern is clearer for the simulation data, as there are 15 times as many patients composing the distribution. Note also that for the human data, patients were classified as normal if their displacements were less than 10 mm, causing the truncation of the distribution at the left end.
5. One parameter of the model that affects this correlation is the settling criterion—the total change in the AM activity pattern must drop below this criterion in order for a response to be

read out. In the simulations reported here, a criterion of .0001 was used. If this criterion is increased to .001, the correlation jumps to .75. This is because increasing the criterion terminates the settling process sooner, and the AM response tends to be more dependent on stimulus conditions (e.g., line length) earlier in the settling process. Of course, it is not valid to adjust parameter settings differently for each simulation, and if all other simulations were run again with a settling criterion of .001, other results would no doubt change. We mention this experiment only to indicate that the magnitude of the effect is sensitive to changes in minor parameter values, not to essential properties of the model.

6. It further does not give the whole story, because it says nothing about why shorter lines result in smaller displacements. We could simply relabel the y-axis "*relative* transection displacement" to deal with this issue, without influencing the discussion above.

7. Indeed, as a rough test, the slopes of the lines formed by consecutive pairs of data points in Figure 15.15(a) were compared for the centered and right-aligned conditions, yet no reliable difference was found ($F(1,7) < 1$).

8. Note that x° lines mirrored around the x-axis become $-x^\circ$ lines.

9. The cosine regression computed by Burnett-Stuart et al. (1991) includes a phase shift parameter to model the altitudinal component of neglect.

10. We should note that many other Harmony functions would suffice equally well, if not better, than the one presented here. Mozer & Behrmann (1990) experimented with several different functions, and the qualitative system behavior was unaffected by the details of the Harmony function.

11. To follow the objective function exactly, the third term should actually be zero if a_{xy} is currently inactive. However, including this term at all times prevents oscillation in the network and does not otherwise appear to affect the quality of the solution.

References

Axenfeld, D. (1915). Hemianopische Gesichtsfeldstroungen nach Schadelschussen. *Klin. Monatsble. Angerheilkd.*, *55*, 126–143.

Barbieri, C., & De Renzi, E. (1989). Patterns of neglect dissociation. *Behavioural Neurology*, *2*, 13–24.

Behrmann, M., Moscovitch, M., Black, S. E., & Mozer, M. C. (1990). Perceptual and conceptual mechanisms in neglect dyslexia: Two contrasting case studies. *Brain*, *113*, 1163–1183.

Bisiach, E., Bulgarelli, C., Sterzi, R., & Vallar, G. (1983). Line bisection and cognitive plasticity of unilateral neglect of space. *Brain and Cognition*, *2*, 32–38.

Bisiach, E., Capitani, E., Colombo, A., & Spinnler, H. (1976). Halving a horizontal segment: A study on hemisphere-damaged patients with focal cerebral lesions. *Archives Suisses de Neurologie, Neurochirgurie et de Psychiatrie*, *118*, 199–206.

Bradshaw, J. L., Nettleton, N. C., Nathan, G., & Wilson, L. E. (1985). Bisecting rods and lines: Effects of horizontal and vertical posture on left side underestimation by normal subjects. *Neuropsychologia*, *23*, 421–436.

Burnett-Stuart, G., Halligan, P. W., & Marshall, J. C. (1991). A Newtonian model of perceptual distortion in visuo-spatial neglect. *NeuroReport*, *2*, 255–257.

Butter, C. M. (1987). Varieties of attention and disturbances of attention: A neuropsychological analysis. In M. Jeannerod (Ed.), *Neurophysiological and neuropsychological aspects of spatial neglect* (pp. 1–24). Amsterdam: North Holland.

Butter, C. M., Evans, J., Kirsch, N., & Kewans, D. (1989). Altitudinal neglect following traumatic brain injury: A case report. *Cortex*, *25*, 135–146.

Halligan, P. W., Manning, L., & Marshall, J. C. (1991). Hemispheric activation versus spatio-motor cueing in visual neglect: A case study. *Neuropsychologia*, *29*, 165–175.

Halligan, P. W., & Marshall, J. C. (1988). How long is a piece of string? A study of line bisection in a case of visual neglect. *Cortex*, *24*, 321–328.

Halligan, P. W., & Marshall, J. C. (1989a). Laterality of motor response in visuo-spatial neglect: A case study. *Neuropsychologia, 27*, 1301–1307.

Halligan, P. W., & Marshall, J. C. (1989b). Perceptuo-cueing and perceptuo-motor compatibility in visuospatial neglect: A single case study. *Cognitive Neuropsychology, 6*, 423–435.

Halligan, P. W., & Marshall, J. C. (1989c). Line bisection in visuospatial neglect: Disproof of a conjecture. *Cortex, 25*, 517–522.

Halligan, P. W., & Marshall, J. C. (1991a). Left neglect for near but not far space in man. *Nature, 350*, 498–500.

Halligan, P. W., & Marshall, J. C. (1991b). Recovery and regression in visuo-spatial neglect: A case study of learning in line bisection. *Brain Injury, 5*, 23–31.

Halligan, P. W., & Marshall, J. C. (1993a). The history and clinical presentation of visual neglect. In I. H. Robertson & J. C. Marshall (Eds.), *Unilateral neglect: Clinical and experimental studies*. London: Erlbaum.

Halligan, P. W., & Marshall, J. C. (1993b). The bisection of horizontal and radial lines: A case study of normal controls and ten patients with left visuo-spatial neglect. *International Journal of Neuroscience, 70*, 149–169.

Heilman, K. M., Bowers, D., & Watson, R. T. (1984). Pseudoneglect in a patient with partial callosal disconnection. *Brain, 107*, 519–532.

Heilman, K. M., Watson, R. T., & Valenstein, E. (1993). Neglect and related disorders. In K. M. Heilman & E. Valenstein (Eds.), *Clinical neuropsychology* 2nd ed. (pp. 279–336). New York: Oxford University Press.

Kinsbourne, M. (1993). Orientational bias model of unilateral neglect: Evidence from attentional gradients within hemispace. In I. H. Robertson & J. C. Marshall (Eds.), *Unilateral neglect: Clinical and experimental studies*. Hove, UK: Erlbaum.

Koch, C., & Ullman, S. (1985). Shifts in selective visual attention: towards the underlying neural circuitry. *Human Neurobiology, 4*, 219–227.

LaBerge, D., & Brown, V. (1989). Theory of attentional operations in shape identification. *Psychological Review, 96*, 101–124.

Manning, L., Halligan, P. W., & Marshall, J. C. (1990). Individual variation in line bisection: A study of normal subjects with application to the interpretation of visual neglect. *Neuropsychologia, 28*, 647–655.

Marshall, J. C., & Halligan, P. W. (1989). When right goes left: An investigation of line bisection in a case of visual neglect. *Cortex, 25*, 503–515.

Marshall, J. C., & Halligan, P. W. (1990a). Line bisection in a case of visual neglect: Psychophysical studies with implications for theory. *Cognitive Neuropsychology, 7*, 107–130.

Marshall, J. C., & Halligan, P. W. (1990b). The psychophysics of visuo-spatial neglect: A new orientation. *Medical Science Research, 18*, 429–430.

McClelland, J. L., & Rumelhart, D. E. (1981). An interactive activation model of context effects in letter perception: Part I. An account of basic findings. *Psychological Review, 88*, 375–407.

Mesulam, M.-M. (1985). *Principles of behavioral neurology*. Philadelphia: F. A. Davis.

Mozer, M. C. (1991). *The perception of multiple objects: A connectionist approach*. Cambridge, MA: MIT Press/Bradford Books.

Mozer, M. C., & Behrmann, M. (1990). On the interaction of selective attention and lexical knowledge: A connectionist account of neglect dyslexia. *Cognitive Neuroscience, 2*, 96–123.

Nichelli, P., Rinaldi, M., & Cubelli, R. (1989). Selective spatial attention and length representation in normal subjects and in patients with unilateral spatial neglect. *Brain and Cognition, 9*, 57.

Poppelreuter, W. (1917). Die Storungan der Niederan und hoheren Seheistungen durch Nerletzung des Okzipitalhirns. In *Die Psychischen Schadigungen durch Kopfschuss in Kriege* (1914/1916). Vol. 1. Leipzig: Voss.

Rapcsak, S. Z., Cimino, C. R., & Heilman, K. M. (1988). Altitudinal neglect. *Neurology, 38*, 277–281.

Riddoch, M. J., & Humphreys, G. W. (1983). The effect of cueing on unilateral neglect. *Neuropsychologia, 21,* 589–599.

Schenkenberg, T., Bradford, D. C., & Ajax, E. T. (1980). Line bisection and unilateral visual neglect in patients with neurological impairment. *Neurology, 31,* 509–517.

Smolensky, P. (1986). Information processing in dynamical systems: Foundations of harmony theory. In D. E. Rumelhart & J. L. McClelland (Eds.), *Parallel distributed processing: Explorations in the microstructure of cognition.* Volume I: Foundations (pp. 194–281). Cambridge, MA: MIT Press/Bradford Books.

Tegner, R., & Levander, H. (1991). The influence of stimulus properties on visual neglect. *Journal of Neurology, Neurosurgery, and Psychiatry, 54,* 882–887.

List Memory

Chapter 16

An Integrated Theory of List Memory

John R. Anderson, Dan Bothell, Christian Lebiere, and Michael Matessa

From our vantage point on psychology it seems that more experiments have been run using the list memory paradigm than any other experimental paradigm (for recent reviews see Healy & McNamara, 1996; Raaijmakers & Shiffrin, 1992). This is a paradigm in which subjects are presented with a list of words and then are tested for their memory of the words. The test may involve an attempt to recall the words in the presented order (in which case it is called serial memory), an attempt to recall the words in any order (in which case it is called free recall), an attempt to recognize the words (in which case it is called recognition memory), or an attempt to do something involving the words but not requiring that the subject recall these words (like stem completion, in which case it is called implicit memory).

The list memory paradigm was the paradigm that Ebbinghaus used in the first experiments on human memory (although he used nonsense syllables). It continued to be used in a great many studies in the subsequent decades. Ebbinghaus and other early researchers usually used serial memory tests. With the rise of cognitive psychology, research on human memory grew in importance and the list memory paradigm seemed to rise with it. The free-recall paradigm was initially of great importance in showing the effects of organizational factors on memory. More recently, recognition memory has become important in discriminating among major theories of memory. The implicit memory research is almost exclusively a phenomenon of the past two decades, but has become one of the hottest areas of research in cognitive psychology. The serial memory version of this paradigm has not been forgotten and is currently prominent in the form of tests of immediate or working memory.

Most theoretical accounts one finds address phenomena in just one of these subdomains of list memory and have not tried to provide an integrated account that spans all of the sub-domains. Different subdomains involve different aspects of cognition—memory for serial order, free recall strategies, structure of lexical memory, etc. Therefore, it is natural that detailed accounts of specific subdomains should focus somewhat on different aspects of the cognitive system. Still the similarity of the learning experience (studying a list of words) creates the expectation that there should be some way of integrating these accounts. There are some theories that have striven for integrated accounts of list memory (e.g., Todam—Murdock, 1993; Lewandowsky & Murdock, 1989; SAM—Raaijmakers & Shiffrin, 1981; Gillund & Shiffrin, 1984; and now REM—Shiffrin & Steyvers, 1997). This paper will show that the ACT-R theory of cognition (Anderson, 1993; Anderson & Lebiere, 1998) also offers an integrated account. ACT-R is unique in that its basic assumptions were not fashioned to account for list memory but for cognition more generally.

In this chapter we will give a brief description of the ACT-R theory sufficient to understand its application to the list memory experiments. Then we will review the list memory experiments in the order of serial memory, recognition memory, free recall, and implicit memory.

The ACT-R Theory

ACT-R (Anderson, 1993; Anderson & Lebiere, 1998) is a theory which aspires to provide an integrated account of many aspects of human cognition. It assumes that a production system operates on a declarative memory. It is a successor to previous ACT production-system theories (Anderson, 1976, 1983) and continues the emphasis on activation-based processing as the mechanism for relating the production system to the declarative memory. Different traces in declarative memory have different levels of activation which determine their rates and probabilities of being processed by production rules. ACT-R is distinguished from the prior ACT theories in that the details of its design have been strongly guided by the rational analysis of Anderson (1990). As a consequence of the rational analysis, ACT-R is a production system tuned to perform adaptively given the statistical structure of the environment.

Declarative knowledge is represented in terms of *chunks* which are schema-like structures. Chunks are of different types and each type has an associated set of pointers encoding its contents. To emphasize that ACT-R applies to other domains besides list memory, we will describe an example of its representations from the domain of cognitive arithmetic. Figure 16.1 is a graphical display of a chunk of the type addition-fact, which encodes that $3 + 4 = 7$ with pointers to *three, four,* and *seven.* The B_i, W_j, and S_{ji} are quantities relevant to activation computation and they will be discussed in the next subsection.

According to ACT-R, procedural knowledge, such as mathematical problem-solving skills, is represented by *production rules* which coordinate the retrieval of declarative information like that in Fig. 16.1 for purposes of problem solving. For instance, suppose a child was at the point illustrated below in the solution of a multi-column addition problem:

$$531$$
$$\underline{+248}$$
$$9$$

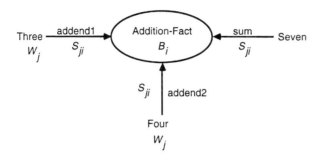

Figure 16.1
A chunk encoding the fact that $3 + 4 = 7$.

Focused on the tens column, the following production rule might apply from the simulation of multicolumn addition (Anderson, 1993):

> *Process-Column.*
>   IF the goal is to process a column containing digits d1
>   and d2 and d3 is the sum of d1 and d2
>   THEN set a subgoal to write out d3.

Each production consists of a condition and an action. In ACT-R each condition consists of a specification of the current goal (e.g., "the goal is to process a column containing digits d1 and d2") and some number of retrievals from declarative memory (e.g., "d3 is the sum of d1 and d2"). According to the ACT-R theory, an important component of the time to apply a production is the time to match the elements in the condition of a production. The time to match the goal is not a significant factor in the ACT-R theory because the goal is already in the focus of attention; but, ACT-R must retrieve chunks from declarative memory to match the rest of the condition and the time to match the condition is the sum of these retrieval times. The times to perform these retrievals will be important contributors to the latency for the production rule and the levels of activation of the chunks will determine these retrieval times. So, in this case, the time to apply this production will be determined by the level of activation of the chunk encoding $3 + 4 = 7$ in Fig. 16.1. The next subsection will explain how activation determines retrieval time. In addition to the retrieval time to match the condition, there are times associated with executing the action. This action latency is minimally 50 ms in the ACT-R theory but can be longer when significant motor actions are involved such as typing or speaking.

Much of the recent development of the ACT-R theory has focused on tasks like mathematical problem solving. However, the ACT theory originated as a theory focused on human memory (Anderson, 1976; Anderson & Bower, 1973). This chapter will propose that productions similar to those guiding problem solving in a mathematics domain are guiding recall in list memory paradigms.

So, one contribution of this paper will be to show that list-memory experiments can be viewed as problem-solving tasks.

Activation

Activation of declarative structures has always been an important concept in the ACT theories. Basically activation determines how available information will be.[1] The activation of a chunk is the sum of its base-level activation and the activations it receives from the elements currently in the focus of attention. Formally, the equation in ACT-R for the activation, A_i, of chunk i is

$$A_i = B_i + \sum_j W_j S_{ji}, \tag{1}$$

where B_i is the base-level activation of chunk i, W_j is the salience or source activation of element j in the focus of attention, and S_{ji} is the strength of association from element j to chunk i. For instance, in the context of retrieving the knowledge unit that $3 + 4 = 7$ in response to seeing 3 and 4 in a column, the W_j would be the source activations of the elements 3 and 4 in the column and the S_{ji} would be the strengths of association from these elements to the chunk encoding $3 + 4 = 7$.

Figure 16.1 illustrates these quantities in the network encoding of the chunk. It is assumed in ACT-R, in contrast to early versions of ACT (such as in Anderson, 1976) but as in ACT* (Anderson, 1983), that these activation levels are achieved rapidly and that time to "spread" activation is not a significant contributor to latency. However, unlike ACT* there is no multilink spread of activation. Rather, activation is simply a direct response to source elements like j. As such, the theory is much like the SAM theory (Raaijmakers & Shiffrin, 1981; Gillund & Shiffrin, 1984), except that activations in ACT-R are like logarithms of SAM familiarities since they add rather than multiply. It is important to keep conceptually separate the quantities A_i and W_j. The former are activations, which control retrieval from declarative memory, while the latter reflect the salience or attention given to the cues. The W_j are referred to as *source activations*.

According to Eq. (1), access to memory is going to vary with base-level activation (the B_i) and associative activation (determined by the W_j and the S_{ji}). The base-level activation of a chunk is a function of its history of use at times $t_1, \ldots, t_n$, where t_j measures how much time has passed since the jth use

$$B_i = \ln \left(\sum_{j=1}^{n} t_j^{-d} \right). \tag{2}[2]$$

As developed in Anderson and Schooler (1991), this equation produces both the Power Law of Forgetting (Rubin & Wenzel, 1996), where the strengths of individual experiences decay as power functions, and the Power Law of Learning

(Newell & Rosenbloom, 1981), where individual experiences accumulate strength as a power function of number of exposures. The decay effect is produced by the negative d exponent, while the practice effect is produced by the summation across experiences. Throughout this simulation we will use the ACT-R standard of setting the decay parameter d to 0.5. This has emerged as the value of d which gives good accounts of results across a wide range of domains.[3]

The associative activation in Eq. (1) is a product of the weights W_j and the strengths S_{ji}. The typical ACT-R assumption is that, if there are n sources of activation the W_j are all set to $1/n$. The associative strengths, S_{ji}, reflect the competition among the associations to the cue j. According to the ACT-R theory, $S_{ji} = S + \ln(P(i|j))$, where $P(i|j)$ is the probability that chunk i will be needed when j appears in the context. S is a constant.[4] Basically, this equation makes the strength of association between j and i a function of how likely i is in the presence of j. Built into this equation is the prediction of a fan effect (Anderson, 1974) in that the more things associated to j the less likely any of them will be, on average, in the presence of j. That is, if there are m elements associated to j their average probability will be $1/m$ and $S_{ji} = S - \ln(m)$. This is the simplification that will be used in all the simulations presented in the paper. Thus,

$$S_{ji} = S - \ln(m). \tag{3}$$

Anderson, Reder, and Lebiere (1996) introduced a new ACT-R assumption motivated by the many errors in algebra that seemed to be due to misretrieving arithmetic facts and algebraic transformations which were similar to the correct ones. Therefore, we extended the pattern-matching facility in ACT-R to allow partial matches between the conditions of productions and chunks in declarative memory. To favor more complete matches we added a mismatch penalty that reflected the degree of mismatch. The goodness of the match M_i of a chunk i to a condition in a production rule is

$$M_i = A_i - P, \tag{4}$$

where P is a mismatch penalty that depends on the similarity between the chunk and condition. In practice it becomes a parameter to be estimated. Thus, faced with the goal to retrieve the sum of $3 + 4$, the chunks $3 + 4 = 7$ and $3 + 1 = 4$ would have equal activation scores (both are associated to source elements 3 and 4), but $3 + 1 = 4$ would receive a mismatch penalty (because the addends 1 and 4 do not match). The chunk retrieved to match a production condition is the one with the largest match score. Normally, when a perfectly matching chunk competes with a partially matching chunk, the perfectly matching chunk will be retrieved because it has the largest match score. However, there is noise in the activation values and occasionally a partially matching chunk will be selected over a perfectly matching chunk because the activation noise gives it sufficiently more activation to overcome the mismatch penalty it suffers. When a partially matching chunk so beats out a perfectly matching chunk, there will be errors of commission in retrieval. Only when all chunks fail to reach an activation threshold does retrieval fail completely (errors of omission). Partially matching errors of commission are the cause of intrusions in recall while retrieval failures are the cause of recall blanks.

There now remains the issue of how to relate these match scores to dependent measures. With respect to latency, the time to retrieve a chunk i is related to its match score by the formula

$$\text{Time}_i = Fe^{-M_i}, \tag{5}$$

where F is a time scale factor. Equation (5) only describes the time to perform a retrieval in matching a production. To this we have to add the time for the production's action which is routinely estimated in ACT-R at 50 ms (in line with other production system models—Anderson, John, Just, Carpenter, Kieras, & Meyer, 1995) or more if a physical action is required (e.g., moving visual attention, speaking, and typing).

ACT-R retrieves the chunk i with the highest match score M_i, provided that match score is above a threshold of activation, τ. ACT-R assumes the match scores have noise added to them that is distributed according to a logistic distribution (which is like a normal distribution). Because of the noise there is only a probability of any match score being highest and only a probability of it being above threshold. The actual predictions reported in this paper are obtained by adding random noise to activation (assuming a logistic distribution) and doing Monte Carlo estimations to determine the most active chunk and whether it is above threshold. However, it is useful to have some closed formed descriptions of these probabilities. The probability of a chunk with expected value M_i being above the threshold τ is

$$\text{Prob}_i = \frac{1}{1 + e^{(M_i - \tau)/s}}, \tag{6}$$

where s is related to the variance in activation, σ^2, by the formula $\sigma^2 = \pi^2 s^2/3$.

Equation (6) misses one important contribution to memory error which is retrieval of the wrong chunk through partial matching. Because of the mismatch penalty (Eq. (4)), a partially matching chunk is usually less active than a perfectly matching chunk but sometimes the ordering can reverse because of random fluctuations in activation levels. The following equation describes the probability of retrieving chunk i as a function of its match score M_i:

$$\text{Probability of retrieving } i = \frac{e^{M_i/t}}{\sum_j e^{M_j/t}}, \tag{7}$$

where the summation is over all chunks and t is related to the variance in activations, σ^2, by the formula $\sigma^2 = \pi^2 t^2/6$ and is related to s in Eq. (6) by $t = \sqrt{2}s$. This is the same as the Boltzmann equation (Ackley, Hinton, & Sejnowsky, 1985; Hinton & Sejnowsky, 1986) in which context t is called temperature. Note that both Eqs. (6) and (7) are approximate descriptions of the system. Equation (6) ignores partial matching and Eq. (7) ignores the effect of the threshold.

This completes the description of the basic ACT-R theory. The key ideas are captured by each of the seven equations above:

> Equation (1): Chunk activation is the sum of a base-level activation and an associative activation.
> Equation (2): Base-level activation will show the influence of practice and time-based decay.
> Equation (3): Associative activation will depend on how many chunks are associated to a cue.
> Equation (4): The match score of a chunk to a production is a function of its level of activation and its degree of match.
> Equation (5): Latency in retrieving a chunk is an exponential function of its match score.
> Equation (6): Probability of retrieving a chunk is the probability that its noisy match score will be above a threshold.
> Equation (7): Probability of retrieving one chunk over others is the probability that its noisy match score will be the largest.

In subsequent sections we apply ACT-R models to simulate various experiments from the list memory paradigms. In all cases ACT-R predictions come from Monte Carlo runs of the computer simulation models. While the basic equations above characterize much of its behavior, there is always the potential for subtle interactions in the simulations which are not captured by the equations. Therefore, we have made all the simulations available on line and they can be reached by following the *Published ACT-R Models* link from the home page: http://act.psy.cmu.edu/. It is possible to change the parameters and run these simulations over the Web. The simulations are also capable of interacting with experimental software that can administer these experiments to subjects. These interactive simulations, which can be obtained by writing to the authors, are completeness proofs that the models specify all the processing involved in an experiment. One of the major goals in the ACT-R project is to achieve fully explicit theories of cognition that will yield the same computer traces that we see from human subjects interacting with the experimental software (Anderson, Lebiere, & Matessa, 1996). This reflects our dissatisfaction with theories (including past versions of ACT-R) that leave implicit aspects about how the theory relates to experimental data.

Serial Memory

The area of serial memory has had the longest history of research in psychology. It started with Ebbinghaus's interest in relatively permanent memory, evolved into an interest in transfer among lists, and most recently has been focused on theories of memory span. It has seen a fair amount of theory in the last third of this century (e.g., Baddeley, 1986; Burgess & Hitch, 1992; Conrad, 1964; Ebbinghaus, 1885; Estes, 1973; Lewandowsky & Murdock, 1989; Murdock, 1993; Shiffrin & Cook, 1978; Richman, Staszewski, & Simon, 1995; Wickelgren, 1965; Young, 1968). While we think the ACT-R theory is applicable to all types of serial recall paradigms, we will concentrate our presentation on the relatively immediate recall of relatively short lists, as this is where most of the recent interest has been. Much of the recent theory has been dominated by Baddeley's use of the phonological loop to account for memory span which assumes that the amount that can be maintained in a memory span is the number of words that can be rehearsed in approximately 2 s. Evidence for this proposal comes from research showing that people can maintain fewer words that take longer to articulate—because the words either have more syllables or have syllables that are longer to articulate. In one very influential study, Baddeley, Thompson, and Buchanan (1975) looked at the number of words (out of five) which could be repeated back as a function of syllable length. Over the range of syllables from one to five, they found that this was approximately equal to the number of words that could be said in 2 s.

We (Anderson & Matessa, 1997) published an application of the ACT-R theory to the memory span task.[5] The models reported there were mathematical approximations to the ACT-R theory while here we will report the results from actual running simulations. This allows us to more adequately deal with the effects of rehearsal strategy and partial matching. We could not always capture their effects in the Anderson and Matessa article with closed-form equations.

The ACT-R theory shares with Baddeley's theory an emphasis on time-based decay (based on base-level Eq. (2)). However, it also emphasizes important roles for associative interference (based on associative strength Eq. (3)) and for confusions among items in a list (based on partial matching Eq. (4)). In fact, there is good evidence for all of these factors as reviewed by Anderson and Matessa. Holding retention time constant, subjects perform worse when they must remember more items indicating associative interference. Confusions among items that are similar sounding (acoustic confusions) or are in similar positions (positional confusions) are a major fact of memory span performance. It is a challenge to be able to integrate these factors. In this section we will show that ACT-R is able to do this. Rather than reporting applications of ACT-R to past experiments as in Anderson and Matessa, we will show this with respect to some new data that we have gathered in our laboratory. These data were collected expressly to provide a powerful test of the predictions of the ACT-R theory about memory span.

An ACT-R Model of Serial Recall

One of the key issues in the history of research on serial memory concerns the nature of the representation of the serial list. Our assumption is that a list is organized as a set of groups and each group is represented as a set of items. Most critically, we assume that there is a chunk for each group encoding its position in the list and a chunk for each item encoding its position in the group. Positional coding, rather than associative chaining, has been advocated by a number of researchers (Burgess & Hitch, 1992; Conrad, 1965; Johnson, 1991; Shiffrin & Cook, 1978; Slamecka, 1967; Young, 1968). Figure 16.2 illustrates a possible representation for a list of nine digits grouped as 329 714 856. Each oval in Fig. 16.2 represents an ACT-R chunk. There is one chunk for each group and each element. A group chunk encodes the list the group is in, the size of the group, and its position in the list. Thus, the first group chunk encodes an item in position Group1 of Size3 in the list. This is indicated by pointers from *Group1*, *Size3*, and *List*. The elements are represented by chunks encoding the position of the element in the group, its group position in the list, the list it is in, and its content. Thus, for example, the first element 3 is encoded by a chunk with pointers to *1st. Group1*, *Three*, and *List*. Performance is going to depend critically on the retrieval of these chunks. Most critical is the link to the list

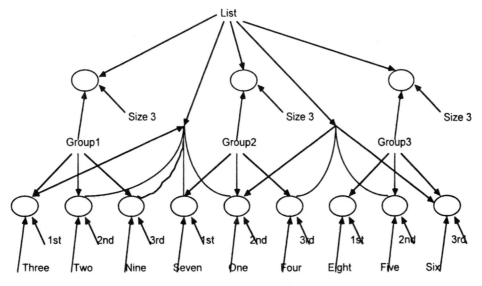

Figure 16.2
A network representation of the chunk structure encoding the 9-element list "329 714 856."

context. There are so many links to the *List* context in Fig. 16.2 that we have had
to merge them. However, in actual fact, *List* is the most unique index into each
chunk.[6] Terms like *1st*, *Group1*, and *Three*, will appear in thousands of contexts.
Thus, fan out of *List* becomes critical.

Retrieval of such chunks encoding list elements is orchestrated by a set of
productions of which the most critical is the following:

> *Get-Next.*
>   IF the goal is to retrieve the *n*th element of the *m*th group of the list
>   and *x* is the element at position *n* in group *m* in the list
> THEN set a subgoal to process *x*
>   and move the pointer to the $(n + 1)$th position.

This rule assumes that each element is indexed by its position. Each element
is then produced by the following production:

> *Type-Item.*
>   IF the goal is to process an item
>   and the item is associated with a key
> THEN type the key.

This production rule is specific to typing as the output mode since this is the
output modality in the experiment to be reported. Similar productions could
produce the response by means of written or verbal report.

In addition to retrieving the elements of a group, it is also necessary to
retrieve the groups themselves:

> *Retrieve-Group.*
>   IF the goal is to retrieve the *m*th group of the list
>   the best *x* is the group in position *m* of the list of size *s*
> THEN set as a goal to retrieve the *s* elements of the group starting in
>   position 1
>   and move the pointer to the $(m + 1)$th group.

The second line of this production retrieves the *m*th group and the size, *s*, of
the group (note in Fig. 16.2 the size is stored with each group). The group size is
important because it allows the system to know when to terminate recall of the
group.

Note that it is a feature of both Get-Next and Retrieve-Group that they recall
in the forward direction. This forward bias to serial recall played an important
role in Anderson and Matessa (1997) and will be a critical feature in the experiment reported here.

According to the ACT-R theory, the critical factor determining speed and
accuracy of retrieval will be the chunks that encode the group and item information. According to our activation Eq. (1) this activation will be a sum of base-
level activation and associative activation. The base-level activation will in turn

be determined by the amount of practice (through rehearsal) that these chunks received and how long ago those rehearsals were. As lists get longer the delays will tend to increase, thereby decreasing base-level activations (base-level Eq. (2)). The associative activation will come from the list element. As the list is longer, there will be greater interference because there will be more associations from the list element and less associative activation to any member of the list (associative strength Eq. (3)). Therefore, performance will go down with increased list length both because of increased delay affecting base-level activation and increased interference affecting associative activation.

While we will be presenting the results of Monte Carlo runs of our simulations, it is useful to have an equation which gives the approximate activation values that determine performance. Combining Eqs. (1)–(3) and using the approximation (Anderson, 1993) that

$$\sum_{j}^{n} t_j^{-d} \approx \frac{anT^{-d}}{1-d},$$

where T is total time; we get the equation

$$A_i = \ln\left(\frac{anT^{-d}}{1-d}\right) + W(S - \ln L),$$

where L is the list length. Collapsing constant factors and expanding, we get

$$\text{Activation} = B' + \ln n - d \ln T - W \ln L,$$

where B' reflects the constant factors, n is the number of presentations and rehearsals, T is time since presentation, L is the length of the list, d is the decay rate, and W is the attentional weighting of the list context. As noted earlier, we will set the decay parameter d to 0.5 throughout. The value of the W in this simulation is 1 since the list is the only useful source of activation. Thus, the effective equation for serial recall becomes

$$\text{Activation} = \ln n - 0.5 \ln T - \ln L \tag{8}$$

ignoring the constant factor B'. This equation is only approximate and we will be deriving our predictions from the running ACT-R simulation. This equation states that activation will increase logarithmically with number of rehearsals n and decrease logarithmically with delay T and list length L. The rehearsal and delay effects reflect base-level activation (Eq. (2)) while the list length effect reflects associative strength (Eq. (3)).

There is one additional important aspect to the ACT-R model of serial recall. We assume that the partial matching mechanism can result in positional confusions. Partial matching of the group slot will cause ACT-R to retrieve an element from a corresponding position in another group. Partial matching of the position slot will cause ACT-R to retrieve an element from another position in the current group. We assume that the degree of mismatch (P in partial-matching Eq. (4)) between elements is proportional to their distance apart. Thus, for instance, the mismatch between *First* and *Second*, *Second* and *Third*, or *Group1* and *Group2*, is *1D* while the degree of mismatch between *First* and *Third* or *Group2* and *Group4* is *2D*. *D* will be referred to as the scale factor for mismatches. This similarity-based confusion produces a majority of positional confusions between adjacent elements with only occasional confusions at greater distances. The existence of positional confusions within and between groups is well documented (e.g., Aaronson, 1968; Bjork & Healy, 1974; Lee & Estes, 1981; Nairne, 1992). We will not deal with acoustic confusions because the study to be reported involves digits which are not particularly confusable. Acoustic confusions are handled in Anderson and Matessa, again by the mechanism of partial matching.

Note that a positional element like "first" is just a cue for recall of an item just like "Montana" is a cue for answering the question, "Who is the governor of Montana?" Partial matching produces positional confusions in serial recall just as partial matching might result in confusion with the governor in Wyoming. In ACT-R the probability of such confusions is a function of the similarity of the cues (*first* versus *second*, or *Wyoming* versus *Montana*).

The ACT-R Simulation

We developed an ACT-R simulation of this task. Table 16.1 gives a trace of the simulation studying and recalling the nine-element list whose representation is given in Fig. 16.2. Part (a) illustrates the study process, part (b) illustrates the forward recall, and part (c) illustrates the backward recall. During study, ACT-R is interleaving study and rehearsal. The productions Attend-Start and Attend are responsible for encoding the digits as they appear on the screen. The first production, Attend-Start, encodes a digit at the beginning of a group, creating a chunk for both the group and the item. The second production, Attend, deals with the digits within a group.

The rehearsal strategy illustrated in Table 16.1a is one in which the system starts at the beginning of a list and keeps rehearsing until it comes to the end of the list. As the list keeps growing it takes longer to complete a rehearsal loop each time and usually it does not get to the end of the list in the last loop. Along with this linear rehearsal it interleaves rehearsal of the current item. Rehearse-Start initiates recall at the beginning of the list and Rehearse-Reset reinitiates recall at the beginning of the list when the current end of the list has been reached. The production Rehearse-Item is responsible for stepping through the items in serial order while Rehearse-Current is responsible for rehearsing the current item. These two productions compete and either is equally likely to fire next. This is a rehearsal strategy which is biased to rehearse the beginning of the list but has some probability of rehearsing all the members of the list.

Table 16.1
Study and recall of "329 714 856"

(a) Study		*(c) Backward recall*	
Cycle 0 Time 0.000: attend-start	Study 3	Cycle 13 Time 12.357: get-next	
Cycle 1 Time 0.200: rehearse-start		Cycle 14 Time 12.656: get-next	
Cycle 2 Time 0.334: rehearse-item	Rehearse 3	Cycle 15 Time 12.808: dispatch-three-items	
Cycle 3 Time 0.879: rehearse-reset		Cycle 16 Time 12.858: type-item	Recall 8
Cycle 4 Time 0.929: rehearse-item	Rehearse 3	Cycle 17 Time 13.359: type-item	Recall 7
Cycle 5 Time 1.462: rehearse-abort		Cycle 18 Time 13.866: type-item	Recall 4
Cycle 6 Time 1.512: attend	Study 2	Cycle 19 Time 14.369: get-next-start-skip	
Cycle 7 Time 1.712: rehearse-current	Rehearse 2	Cycle 20 Time 14.701: get-next	
Cycle 8 Time 2.246: rehearse-abort		Cycle 21 Time 14.986: get-next	
Cycle 9 Time 2.296: attend	Study 9	Cycle 22 Time 15.220: dispatch-three-items	
Cycle 10 Time 2.496: rehearse-current	Rehearse 9	Cycle 23 Time 15.270: skip-item	Skip
Cycle 11 Time 3.105: rehearse-abort		Cycle 24 Time 15.770: type-item	Recall 5
Cycle 12 Time 3.155: attend-start	Study 7	Cycle 25 Time 16.276: type-item	Recall 6
Cycle 13 Time 3.355: rehearse-item	Rehearse 2		
Cycle 14 Time 3.891: rehearse-item	Rehearse 9	*(c) Backward recall*	
Cycle 15 Time 4.518: rehearse-abort		Cycle 1 Time 9.000: start-group	
Cycle 16 Time 4.568: attend	Study 1	Cycle 2 Time 9.604: retrieve-group	
Cycle 17 Time 4.768: rehearse-next-group		Cycle 3 Time 9.920: retrieve-group	
Cycle 18 Time 4.942: rehearse-item	Rehearse 7	Cycle 4 Time 10.237: dispatch-three-group-backward	
Cycle 19 Time 5.573: rehearse-abort		Cycle 5 Time 10.287: get-next-start	
Cycle 20 Time 5.623: attend	Study 4	Cycle 6 Time 10.458: get-next-skip	
Cycle 21 Time 5.823: rehearse-item	Rehearse 1	Cycle 7 Time 10.620: get-next	
Cycle 22 Time 6.455: rehearse-abort		Cycle 8 Time 10.837: dispatch-three-items-backward	
Cycle 23 Time 6.505: attend-start	Study 8	Cycle 9 Time 10.887: type-item	Recall 6
Cycle 24 Time 6.705: rehearse-current	Rehearse 8	Cycle 10 Time 11.392: skip-item	Skip
Cycle 25 Time 7.212: rehearse-abort		Cycle 11 Time 11.896: type-item	Recall 8
Cycle 26 Time 7.262: attend	Study 5	Cycle 12 Time 12.401: start-group	
Cycle 27 Time 7.462: rehearse-current	Rehearse 5	Cycle 13 Time 12.942: retrieve-group	
Cycle 28 Time 8.019: rehearse-abort		Cycle 14 Time 13.165: dispatch-two-group-backward	
Cycle 29 Time 8.069: attend	Study 6	Cycle 15 Time 13.215: get-next-start	
Cycle 30 Time 8.269: rehearse-item	Rehearse 4	Cycle 16 Time 13.442: get-next	
Cycle 31 Time 8.872: rehearse-next-group		Cycle 17 Time 13.634: get-next	
Cycle 32 Time 9.052: rehearse-abort-last	Rehearse 6	Cycle 18 Time 13.755: dispatch-three-items-backward	
		Cycle 19 Time 13.805: type-item	Recall 4
(b) Forward recall		Cycle 20 Time 14.306: type-item	Recall 1
Cycle 1 Time 9.000: start-group		Cycle 21 Time 14.809: type-item	Recall 9
Cycle 2 Time 9.782: retrieve-group		Cycle 22 Time 15.315: start-group	
Cycle 3 Time 9.905: retrieve-group		Cycle 23 Time 15.842: dispatch-one-group-backward	
Cycle 4 Time 9.992: dispatch-three-groups		Cycle 24 Time 15.892: get-next-start	
Cycle 5 Time 10.042: get-next-start		Cycle 25 Time 15.988: get-next	
Cycle 6 Time 10.244: get-next		Cycle 26 Time 16.241: get-next-skip	
Cycle 7 Time 10.383: get-next		Cycle 27 Time 16.493: dispatch-three-items-backward	
Cycle 8 Time 10.644: dispatch-three-items		Cycle 28 Time 16.543: type-item	Skip
Cycle 9 Time 10.694: type-item	Recall 3	Cycle 29 Time 17.047: type-item	Recall 3
Cycle 10 Time 11.198: type-item	Recall 2	Cycle 30 Time 17.553: type-item	Recall 2
Cycle 11 Time 11.701: type-item	Recall 9		
Cycle 12 Time 12.208: get-next-start			

Rehearse-Abort stops rehearsal when a new item appears so that this new item can be encoded. Rehearse-Next-Group, which first appears on cycle 17, fires when one group has been rehearsed and switches rehearsal to the next group.

In forward recall (Table 16.1b), productions Retrieve-Group and Start-Group (a variant of Retrieve-Group for the first group) retrieve the group chunks. A production Dispatch-Three-Groups sets subgoals to retrieve the groups in the order encoded. For each group, the productions Get-Next and Get-Next-Start (a variant of Get-Next) retrieve the individual item chunks and Dispatch-Three-Items sets subgoals to type each in the order encoded. Then the production Type-Item types the individual digits. Note this scheme retrieves all the items in a group before typing any. This corresponds to the data we saw that indicated that our subjects tended to retrieve all the items in a group before typing any.

For backward recall, the rehearsal and encoding processes have identical structure since the subjects do not know how they will be tested. The structure of the recall (Table 16.1c) is the same except with respect to the productions that dispatch the subgoals. The production Dispatch-Three-Items-Backward is like Dispatch-Three-Items except that it sets the subgoals to type the items in opposite order. On the other hand, the productions for dispatching groups in backward order only subgoal one group at a time. In contrast the forward productions subgoaled all the groups. Therefore, when the group is completed in backward recall, the simulation must scan through all the groups in the list up to the to-be-recalled group. Thus, the structure for backward recall of the list in Fig. 16.2 is: recall group1, recall group2, recall group3, retrieve members of group3, recall group1, recall group2, retrieve members of group2, recall group1, and retrieve members of group1. This restarting is what produces recall latencies at the beginning of subsequent groups which are as long as the latency at the beginning of the first group. The backward protocol in Table 16.1 also illustrates failure to retrieve a couple of items. These are cases where the activation of the critical items randomly fell below threshold. It is also possible for the activation of the group chunk to randomly fall below threshold in which case the whole chunk will be skipped. The system is able to skip over the missing items and resume recall in place. It can use the visual structure of the recall display to know where to begin the next group.

In both the forward and backward recall it is the forward moving Retrieve-Group and GetItem productions that are responsible for retrieving the items. Forward or reverse recall is achieved by subgoaling the items to be recalled in either forward or reverse order by different Dispatch productions.

The protocol in Table 16.1 illustrates another feature of ACT-R's recall which results from the partial matching. In the forward recall (Table 16.1b) note that the 8 from the first position of the third group is introduced as the first member of the second group. In addition, the 7 which is the first member of the second group is recalled in the second position of the second group. Finally, because the 8 is "used up" nothing is recalled in the first position of the third group.[7] In the backward recall note that the 3 and the 2 of the first group (recalled last) are reversed. These kinds of positional confusions are typical of serial recall and are produced by partial matching of the positional information.

The exact timings of the item recalls and their probabilities of success depend on random fluctuations in the activation levels. We ran 620 trials per condition to correspond to the 620 observations that we got from our subjects. This yielded fairly stable predictions. These predictions depend on a number of parameters that we had to set for this simulation:

1. The activation noise level, s, which we set to 0.300 (corresponding to a variance of 0.296)—see probability Eq. (6).
2. The activation threshold, τ, which was set to -0.35—see probability Eq. (6).
3. The time scale parameter, F, for retrievals which we set to 220 ms—see latency Eq. (5).
4. The scale factor, D, for mismatches which was set to 2.5.

Then there were a number of productions which were given nondefault action times (the default is 50 ms). These times were just set to plausible ball-park values:

5. The time to encode an item which was 200 ms. This is the ballpark time that we have established from the simulations of visual attention (Anderson, Matessa, & Lebiere, 1997).
6. The response time to type an item which was set to 500 ms.
7. The time to rehearse an item which was set to 500 ms to reflect speech time.
8. The initiation time to start recall, for the Start-Group production, which was set to 500 ms.

The last four parameters are constant across all the simulations reported in this chapter, while the first four parameters, s, τ, F, and D were estimated to produce a good fit to this experiment. However, our search for these four parameters was informal and there is no guarantee that we found the ones which produce optimal fits. The D parameter, reflecting positional similarity, is unique to this experiment but the other three s, τ, and F are potentially estimated anew for each experiment. Table 16.2 at the end of the paper tracks all of the parameter estimates. At the end of the paper we will discuss the issue of variations in the s, τ, and F parameters across experiments.

Figures 16.3 and 16.4 show the resulting simulated recall behavior. The overall R^2 between the two sets of latencies is 0.946. The accuracy profiles do not match quite as well, producing an overall R^2 of 0.906. Nonetheless, the correspondences between the profiles are quite compelling. We think this indicates some of the power of ACT-R to account for a complex data pattern. We

Table 16.2
Parameter estimates of various experiments

	Serial recall	Burrows & Okada[a] (1975)	Raeburn[a] (1974)	Ratcliff, Clark, & Shiffrin (1990)	Murdock (1962)	Glenberg et al. (1980)	Roberts (1972)	Johnston, Dark, & Jacoby (1985)	Hayman & Tulving (1989)
s (noise)	0.3			0.55	0.7	0.6	0.85	0.65	0.3
τ (threshold)	−0.35			1.8	3.2	1.4	2.9	0.9	−.45
F (Latency scale)	0.22	4.15	2.29	2	2	2	2	1.3	0.5
D (Partial match serial position)	2.5		2.5						
P (Partial match list context)				1.5				1.5	1.5
Respond	0.5			0.5	0.5	0.5	0.5	0.5	0.5
Encoding	0.2		0.2	0.2	0.2	0.2	0.2	0.2	0.2
								0.5	
								0.7	
Rehearse	0.5	0.5	0.5	0.5	0.5	0.5	0.5	0.5	0.5
Intercept	0.5	0.5	0.6						
Time (R^2)	0.946	0.957	0.886	0.970	0.923	0.860	0.990	0.910	0.962
Accuracy (R^2)	0.906							0.921	
Base activation	0.24	2.19	1.1	2.5	0.35	−1.51	0.52	−1.47	−1.07
Associative activation	0.61	1.64	1.9	0.35	0.6	0.35	0.6	4.51	1.4
Average activation	0.85	3.83	3.0	2.85	0.95	−1.27	1.12	3.04	0.33

a. Since accuracy data are not modeled there was no need to estimate the s or τ parameters for these experiments. There was also no study process modeled in the Burrows and Okada experiment.

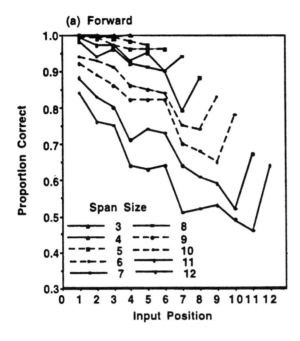

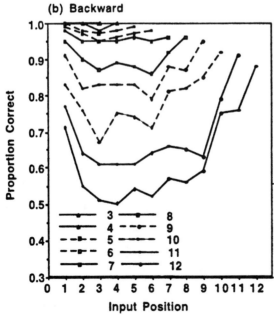

Figure 16.3
Results of simulation: Predicted probability of correct positional for items recalled in the forward direction (a) and for times recalled in the backward direction (b).

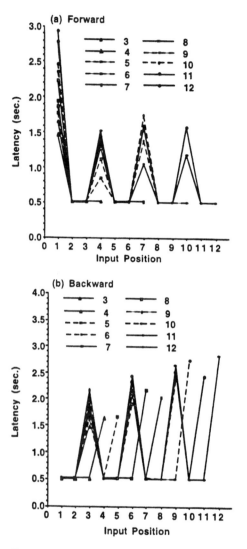

Figure 16.4
Results of simulation: Time to recall digits as a function of serial position and list length for (a) forward recall and (b) backward recall.

are predicting 300 numbers only estimating four parameters and without carefully optimizing our fit.

To summarize what lies behind the ACT-R account of the data: The latency data speak to a very systematic group-by-group recall procedure that subjects are using to pace their recall. This is incorporated into the basic production rules that execute the task. This is one of the things we get from the control structure provided by ACT-R's production system. Within this relatively fixed procedure there is considerable variation in latencies at group boundaries as a function of list length. Also, there is considerable variation in recall of items both as a function of list length and input position. ACT-R does not change the fundamental algorithm to predict these variations. These variations reflect the changes in activations of the elements being retrieved. These activations increase with rehearsal (base-level activation), decrease with time (base-level activation), and decrease with list length (associative activation). Also, there are fewer positional confusions (partial matching) at the end of lists. These are all basic processes in the ACT-R theory and they combine to form the behavioral profile that we see.

Both time-based decay and associative interference are required to account for the span limitations. The very different recall profiles for forward and backward recall reflect differences in the time at which the same items are recalled. This difference between items at identical input positions is produced by time-based decay. On the other hand, in the backward data we can look at recall of items which have the same delay between study and test but which vary in list length. For instance, the last item is always recalled first after the offset in its presentation. However, recall for this item systematically drops reflecting the contribution of associative interference from the other items. This difference between items with identical recall lag is evidence for associative interference.

In addition to associative activation and base-level decay, the rehearsal strategy assumed by ACT-R is critical. The tendency for the earlier items to receive greater rehearsal is one factor that is producing the primacy effect. The other factor is the lower positional confusions among items at the beginning of the list.

Recognition Memory

A different way of testing memory involves simply showing subjects the words in the list and asking them whether they recognize the items when they are mixed in with distractors (or foils) that they have not seen. Our model for this task is basically the one that Anderson and Bower (1972, 1974) developed 25 years ago where it is assumed that a memory trace is set up which encodes that an item occurred in a particular list. Thus, ACT-R records memory of the words in the list by means of chunks like the one illustrated in Fig. 16.5 which encodes that the word *imply* occurred in *List-3*. This is the same representation used in serial memory.[8] Recognition of a word is achieved by productions like

Figure 16.5
A chunk encoding that the word "imply" has occurred in List 3.

Recognize-a-Word.
   IF the goal is to judge whether the word occurred in a context
      and there is a trace of seeing the word in that context
THEN respond yes

This is a very straightforward model which views recognition memory as basically a simple process. The memory trace just consists of two items—the word and the list context. In recognizing a word, a subject has access to both sources of association (in contrast to free recall where the subject has only access to the list context). Thus, based on activation Eq. (1), the activation of a memory trace can be written

$$A = B + W_w S_w + W_L S_L$$

based on activation Eq. (1), where W_w is the weighting given to the word, S_w is the strength of association from the word to the trace, W_L is the weight of the list context, and S_L is the strength of association from the list context to the trace. While the word becomes an important additional source of activation the $W_w S_w$ term will remain constant across conditions. As in the case of the serial memory Eq. (8), we can expand the base level to show the effect of rehearsal time, decay, and list length

$$A = B' + \ln n - d \ln T - W_L \ln L,$$

where B' reflects constant effects including $W_w S_w$. Thus, just as in serial recall the critical variables remain the amount of rehearsal n, delay time T, and the list length L.

We can use the prior settings of the decay parameter, d, to 0.5 and assume an equal division of source activation between word and list context so that $W_L = 0.5$. Ignoring the constant, our equation becomes

$$\text{Activation} = \ln n - 0.5 \ln T - 0.5 \ln L. \tag{9}$$

This will be the critical activation equation for this section. This is identical to the serial memory equation [14] except that the list length is weighted by 0.5 reflecting the division of source activation (the Ws) between the list and the word. Again, this only gives an approximation to the results of the simulation and we will present data from simulation runs.

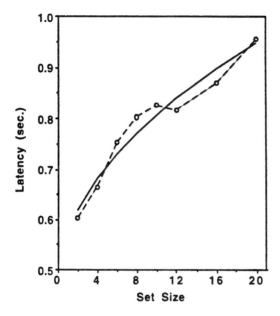

Figure 16.6
Observed (dashed lines) and predicted (solid lines) latencies for recognizing probes as a function of set size. From Burrows and Okada (1975).

An additional relevant factor in recognition memory involves partial matching to either the word or the list context. Partial matching to the word will produce false alarming for similar words. There are ample experiments that show effects of distractor similarity on recognition memory (e.g., Anisfeld & Knapp, 1968; Underwood & Freund, 1968). Similarly, subjects are likely to false alarm for a word if it occurred in a similar list (e.g., Anderson & Bower, 1974).

In this section we want to focus on three results which have proven important in the past 25 years of research and theory on recognition memory. These are latencies to recognize items, particularly in the Sternberg paradigm, and the relationship between list length and list strength, and the Tulving–Wiseman function. One subsection will be devoted to each topic.

The Sternberg Paradigm
The Sternberg paradigm is one in which subjects see a relatively small list of items and then are presented with a single item and have to judge whether that item is from the list. As the result was originally described and is still described in many textbooks, the claim is that there is a linear relationship between the number of items in the memory set and time to make this judgment. In fact the relationship is more typically curvilinear and extends out to lists as long as 20 items in length (Briggs, 1974). Figure 16.6 shows some data from Burrows

and Okada (1975) illustrating this relationship and a fit of our ACT-R model which we will describe below.

Since Burrows and Okada do not give us the details of presentation timing or practice, we simulated in ACT-R only the recognition judgment task and not the study. For this recognition judgment task we used a similar model as that which was used for our model of sentence recognition in studies of the fan effect (Anderson & Reder, 1999) which seems appropriate for time-pressured recognition judgments. Upon presentation of a probe the subject retrieves the most active item from the list:

> *Retrieve-a-Candidate.*
> IF the goal is to recognize whether a word is in the list
> and x is a word in the list
> THEN consider x as the retrieved word.

This is a variant of Recognize-a-Word given earlier and its latency is determined by the same activation quantity (given by recognition memory Eq. (9)). If the probe is a word in the list, that candidate word will be most active since it receives activation from the probe. Thus, it is only necessary to retrieve one candidate. The subject then checks whether the retrieved item matches the probe and responds "yes" if it does:

> *Match-Word.*
> IF the goal is to recognize whether a word is in the list
> and it matches the retrieved word
> THEN say yes.

In the case of a foil, some list member will be retrieved only to be rejected as mismatching the probe by Mismatch-Word:

> *Mismatch-Word.*
> IF the goal is to recognize whether a word is in the list
> and it does not match the retrieved word
> THEN say no.

For its success, this scheme relies on the fact that if the word was studied, the chunk encoding its occurrence in the list will be more active than chunks encoding the occurrence of other items. This will be the case because this chunk will receive activation from the probe word.

Since the model for the Burrows and Okada data is so simple we can develop a simple mathematical equivalent to display its predictions by adapting the recognition Eq. (9). Since we do not have the details to model the study process, the number of rehearsals, n, and delay, T, in that equation become irrelevant and the recognition equation becomes

$$\text{Activation} = 3.76 - 0.5 \ln L.$$

where L is the length of the list and 3.76 is the level of activation of an element in a list of length 1 in the ACT-R simulation. The 3.76 reflects the default activation that elements get in this ACT-R simulation. This activation value and the F parameter trade off such that there is only one degree of freedom in fitting the data. Thus, we left the activation value at its default and estimated F at 4.15. Then using retrieval time Eq. (4) our prediction for latency is

$$\text{Time} = I + Fe^{-A} = 0.5 + 4.15e^{-3.76}L^{0.5}$$
$$= 0.5 + 0.097L^{0.5},$$

where 0.5 is the fixed intercept I (reflecting encoding and response generation that will be used throughout this paper), F is the latency factor estimated at 4.15, and $0.097 = 4.15e^{-3.76}$.[9] The fit of this one-parameter model is basically identical to that of a logarithmic equation given by Burrows and Okada (which has two parameters) and is slightly worse than their bilinear model (which has four parameters). While this does involve the estimation of one parameter, it does make the parameter-free prediction that latency should increase as a function of the square root of list length. The data do correspond closely to this predicted form with an R^2 of 0.957 for the square root function as compared to 0.908 for a linear function.

   To have better tests for ACT-R, it would be useful to have data with better specification of the presentation timing and information about the effect of serial position on latency. Raeburn (1974) reports such an experiment in which items were presented at the rate of 1.5 s per item and tested at a delay of 1.2 s after the presentation of the last item. Figure 16.7 presents his data as a function of serial position of the targets plus the mean performance for foils.

   We developed a running ACT-R simulation of these data. In modeling these data, we want to carry over as much of the representations and processes as we can from our model in the previous section for serial memory given that the lists are of similar length and the timings are similar. We used the same productions for encoding and rehearsal and only changed the productions for making the recognition judgment. These recognition judgment productions are the same ones that we used for the Burrows and Okada simulation. As in the case of the Burrows and Okada data, we estimated the parameter, F, in fitting the data. This was estimated at 2.29 s. Also, only in this experiment did we have to estimate a nondefault intercept parameter—0.6 s rather than 0.5 s.

   The quality of the fit is quite good, with a mean error of prediction of 19 ms and an R^2 of 0.886 with just two parameters estimated. The data and the theory both reflect strong effects of target versus foil, set size, and serial position. It is worth reviewing what produces these effects in the ACT-R theory. The effect of target versus foil is due to the lower activation in the case of a foil for a trace retrieved by Retrieve-a-Candidate (because the probe does not provide source of activation to the retrieved trace). The effect of serial position reflects the

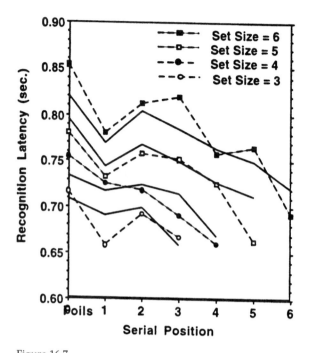

Figure 16.7
Data (in dashed lines) from Raeburn (1974): Time to recognize an item for lists of various lengths as a function of serial position. The predictions of the ACT-R theory are in solid lines.

effects of extra rehearsal of the beginning of the list and shorter recency of the end of the list. These are the same factors operating in the memory span except that time to recall in memory span is also affected by order of output in span tests. Finally, the effect of set size is due to the combined effects of decreased associative activation and increased decay of base-level activation since on average there will be longer delays between presentation and test.

Free Recall

Free recall is an experimental paradigm where the subject is allowed to recall the items of a list in any order. The removal of the constraint of recalling in serial order may seem to simplify the task from serial recall. However, in fact it complicates the task substantially because it frees the subject to choose among a wide variety of strategies for studying items and recalling them. Some subjects repeat groups of words over and over again, other subjects look for associative or categorical relationships among the words, and still other subjects make up stories involving these words. It has been shown that the more organizational structure a subject tries to impose on the material, the better memory they display (e.g., Mandler, 1967).

The generate-test model described in Anderson and Bower (1972) and realized in the FRAN simulation model (Anderson, 1972) was an attempt to extract the essence of these strategies. The basic assumptions of that model were:

1. The subject maintains a small set of about four items from the list which they rehearse and among which they try to find relationships. When a new item is encountered it enters this buffer and an old item is removed. This is basically the buffer model of Atkinson and Shiffrin (1968) with the added assumption that subjects search for semantic relationships among the items in the buffer.

2. At time of recall subjects try to generate candidate items, using among other things, the associative relationships that they have laid down.

3. Every time subjects generate a word they would then try to recognize it. Thus, the recognition process we discussed in the previous section was embedded as part of the recall process.

The SAM model of Raaijmakers and Shiffrin (1981) was another attempt to achieve an abstract characterization of this process. In that model traces were generated according to strength of association to the context and to the last retrieved item. There was a second stage in which an attempt was made to recover the word from the trace. The probability of this second stage was determined by overall activation rather than retrieval of contextual information as in the Anderson and Bower model.

In developing an ACT-R simulation of free-recall experiments we adopted a version that is simpler than either SAM or FRAN.[11] We assumed that subjects had a buffer of four elements for rehearsal and that, when a new element came in, the simulation randomly replaced a member of the buffer. This buffer was implemented by storing the four elements in four slots of the goal. After that the system randomly chose items to rehearse from the buffer as time allowed. At time of recall, the subject would first dump the members of the buffer, if it could,[12] and then recall items whose activation was above a threshold. Thus, if P_B is the probability the item is still in the buffer, the probability of recalling the item is approximately

$$\text{Probability of Recall} = P_B + (1 - P_B)P(\text{Activation} > \tau),$$

where τ is the threshold. The activation for an element would vary with the number of times it had been rehearsed, the length of time since those rehearsals, and the fan out of the list node (determined by list size). While we will present the results of actual simulations, it would be useful to have in hand an equation approximately giving the activation levels. In this case with a single source of activation (the LIST—the word is not presented), the operative equation is identical to the serial memory equation (8).

$$\text{Activation} = \ln n - 0.5 \ln T - \ln L, \tag{10}$$

where n is the number of encodings and rehearsals, T is the time since encoding, and L is the list length.

Serial Position Effects

One of the basic results about free recall is the serial-position curve which is a function giving probability of recall as a function of position of the item in the input sequence. Figure 16.8 shows some data gathered by Murdock (1962) looking at recall of lists that varied in length from 10 to 40 words, presented at 1 or 2 s for each word. These results show the classic recency effect (which is the high level of recall at the end of the list) and the primacy effect (which is the somewhat higher level of recall at the beginning of the list). The performance level is somewhat flat in intermediate positions with levels higher for shorter lists or for lists with more study time. Figure 16.8b shows the corresponding predictions of the ACT-R model. We preassigned the latency scale parameter F to have a value of 2.0 s for this experiment. The estimated parameters for this simulation were $\tau = 3.2$ and s (activation noise) $= 0.70$. The recency effect in ACT-R is produced by the probability that the item is still in the buffer plus the short delay in recall while the primacy effect is produced by the extra rehearsals given to the target item. The overall correspondence is quite good with an R^2 of 0.923 predicting 135 points.

Under this analysis the striking recency effect is due to both the decay of base-level activation and the tendency to rehearse and recall first the last few items of the list. In experiments where interfering activity is given after the list to wipe out the buffer, the advantage of the last few items disappear and they often show poorer recall, the so-called negative recency effect (Craik, 1970; Gardiner, Thompson, & Maskarinec, 1974). In experiments where an effort is made to eliminate rehearsal the primacy effect goes away and so does the negative recency effect when tested after a delay (Baddeley, 1986). In such studies, where subjects are prevented from forming a rehearsal buffer and forced just to process the item under study, one also sees a diminished positive recency effect. Performance tends to drop off continuously from the end of the list. These studies are perhaps the cleanest studies of free recall because they both eliminate the buffer and differential practice.

Reflections on the Model Fitting Enterprise

In a paper critical of model-fitting efforts, Roberts and Pashler (2000) complained that models are not applied across a range of experiments. We would submit this effort as one of a number exceptions to this assertion. While these are all list memory experiments they reflect a substantial variation in the testing procedures. There are a number of questions one can ask when a single theory

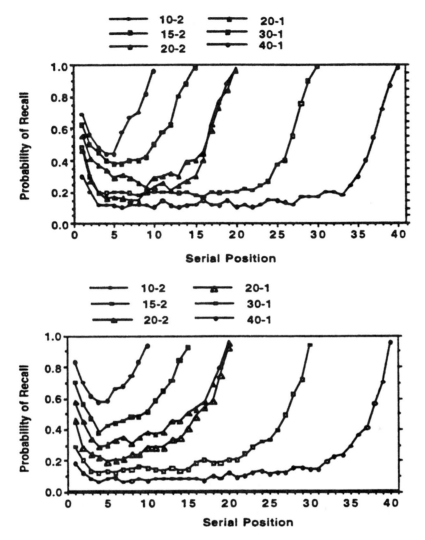

Figure 16.8
Probability of recall of lists of various lengths (10, 15, 20, 30, 40) and amount of study time (1 or 2 seconds) as a function of serial position. (a) Data from Murdock (1962). (b) Predictions of the ACT-R theory.

fits a range of experiments. Among these are whether the variations in parameter estimates across the experiments are reasonable and whether there are any hidden assumptions in the models. We will address these issues of parameter regularity and hidden assumptions.

Parameter Variation

Table 16.2 is a summary of the parameters used in fitting the models to the experiments and the proportion of variance accounted for. Except for the s, τ, and F, the parameters have been basically held constant across the experiments. The variations in s, the noise parameter, are rather small. One reason for variation in this parameter is that it will reflect heterogeneity in the population of subjects and variability in items and how subjects attend to them. The more variable they are the larger this parameter which controls variance in ACT-R activations. Better performance on some items will be modeled by higher ACT-R activations and worse performance by lower activations. Thus, the mixture of activations produced by s will tend to mirror the mixture of performances of subjects.

The other two parameters, τ and F, do appear to vary more dramatically from experiment to experiment. These two parameters map activation into performance. Probability of recall is a function of the distance between activation and the threshold τ. Latency is scaled by the parameter F. It turns out that the τ and F parameters are related to the mean activation level of memory chunks. The bottom line in Table 16.2 shows these activations at the point at which study is completed and before testing begins. In the experiments with multiple conditions these averages are calculated over the conditions. The activations are sums of base-level activations and associative activations when the goal is set to retrieve these items. These base-level and associative activations are also shown. It is apparent that these mean activations fluctuate from experiment to experiment. The exact activation levels in ACT-R are somewhat arbitrary. The activations reflect things like how many chunks are in the system and in any simulation the number is going to be much less than the true number.[13] It turns out that the τ and F parameters serve to map activation levels onto performance. This is particularly apparent in the case of the τ parameter where probability of recall is a function of the gap between τ and activation. Similarly, latency is a function of the gap between the logarithm of F and the activation level. Retrieval time will be proportional to the exponential of the difference between $\ln F$ and activation. If one adds a constant to all activation values one will get the same predictions if one adds that constant to τ and $\ln F$.

Figure 16.9 plots τ and $\ln F$ as a function of average activation level. We have separately plotted τ from the free-recall experiments (Murdock, Glenberg, Roberts—F does not vary across these experiments). While the relationship is not perfect there is an approximately linear relationship between τ and $\ln F$ and

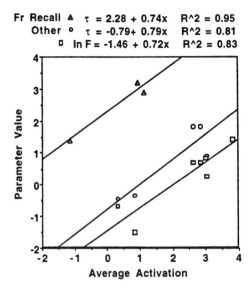

Figure 16.9
The relationship between average activation in an experiment and the threshold parameter τ and the logarithm of the latency factor.

average activation over the experiments. Thus, a major reason for the fluctuation in τ and F is to compensate for the arbitrary differences in mean activation levels from experiment to experiment. Activation is an interval scale in ACT-R where absolute differences are meaningful but there is no meaningful zero.

It might seem strange that the curve for the free recall τ is so far above other τ curve in Fig. 16.9. The reason for this is that in the free recall models a word can be recalled if, on any cycle, its noise brings it above threshold before recall terminated. Thus, there are many opportunities to recall a word in free recall while, in the recognition or serial memory paradigms, there is just one opportunity to recall the word. Because random noise was independent from cycle to cycle, this meant that chances were good for recall unless the threshold was very high. As discussed in Anderson and Lebiere (1998), the solution to this is to have the noise correlated from cycle to cycle in the simulation—something we did not pursue in the free-recall models.

While these studies reveal a general relationship between activation and the parameters, τ and F, there is no reason to believe the relationship should be perfect since there should be experiment and population differences in these parameters just as there should be in the s parameter. Differences in τ correspond to differences in levels of recall and bias. Some subjects in some experiments will show a greater recall and tendency to false alarm. This is captured by lower values of the τ parameter. Similarly, it is reasonable to assume that there will be population differences in retrieval speed (e.g., Salthouse, 1991). Moreover in some experiments subjects will have practiced more and so display higher activations. So all differences in activation levels are not arbitrary and so we should not always expect to see compensating changes in τ and F. Nonetheless, Fig. 16.9 suggests that variations in the average activation levels are a major reason our model fits for the large variation in the parameters, τ and F.

It is remarkable that the three functions in Fig. 16.9 are nearly parallel. Since τ and $\ln F$ both show approximately the same linear relationship to mean activation, they should show a simple relationship to one another. In fact, one can do a fairly good job in predicting F from τ for the nonfree recall experiments by the function

$$F = 0.348e^{\tau}. \tag{11}$$

This accounts for 93.9% of the variance in the F parameter across the nonfree-recall experiments where estimates of both τ and F where obtained.[14] So really in some cases, there is only one parameter being estimated per experiment, which can be conceived of as τ and the prediction is that retrieval time is about a third of a second when the activation is at the threshold τ. This equation also describes a situation where subjects can trade off increased accuracy for increased latency by lowering the threshold.

In conclusion, the parameter variation across experiments is exceedingly regular. The s parameter shows little variation and the F and τ parameters are related by the speed–accuracy equation above. We view this regularity as a major piece of evidence for the underlying ACT-R theory.

Assumptions in Modeling

In a couple of ways, the ACT-R models are exceedingly forthright in their assumptions. For instance, one can connect through the worldwide web, test these models, and examine their assumptions. In addition, it is the case that there are versions of these models which will interact with the same experiment-running software that could be used to run the experiments (and these can be obtained by writing to the authors). Thus, there are not any hidden assumptions about how the correspondence is made between the models and the empirical phenomena.

Each experiment simulation requires a number of assumptions (not part of the ACT-R theory) about how subjects approach these experiments. These assumptions are made in terms of the knowledge representations and production rules. We have tried to make explicit these key assumptions. They include things like a hierarchically grouped representation for serial lists, rehearsal assumptions, recognition confusions through partial matching of context, and use of a buffer of items in free recall. The predictions of the theory are dependent on the underlying architecture of ACT-R but also on these auxiliary modeling assumptions.

Interestingly, in almost no case are these auxiliary assumptions novel. They reflect ideas that have been in the field of list memory, often for decades. Indeed, most of these auxiliary assumptions are to be found in Anderson and Bower's (1973) chapter on verbal memory. The Anderson and Matessa serial memory model is basically the model presented there (which in turn reflected work like that of Johnson, 1970) augmented with ideas about positional encoding and Baddeley's ideas of time-based decay and rehearsal. The analysis of recognition and free recall is basically Anderson and Bower (1972) whose free recall component has strong influences from Atkinson and Shiffrin (1968). The implicit memory theory comes from the recent theories of Reder and of Bower which in turn show strong influence of the Anderson and Bower models.

This theory does contrast with the Anderson and Bower models in that it assumes no short-term store. One of the interesting aspects of this modeling enterprise is that it has produced models that seemlessly transition from what are considered short-term tasks like memory span and the Sternberg task to tasks that are considered long-term like recognition and free recall. In fact, these various tasks have long-term and short-term components. For instance, the 12 items that subjects had to remember in some of the conditions of our serial memory experiment or the 20 items required in Fig. 16.6 go beyond the traditional bounds of short-term memory. The recency function in free-recall is typically within the short-term span but is not in some of the experiments that have studied the IPI/RI ratio. ACT-R's ability to seemlessly transition among paradigms and to model effects of varying task parameters is produced by the retention function built into the base-level Eq. (2). This produces rapid initial decay and slower later decay. Thus, ACT-R provides evidence for the artificiality of the traditional separation between short-term memory and long-term memory.[15] While the elimination of the short-term store is a clear departure from Anderson and Bower, it is hardly a new idea in the field either.

One might ask what is contributed by the ACT-R theory? One could take the view that these results are predicted by theoretical ideas that predate ACT-R by at least two decades. However, this would ignore that the Anderson and Bower theory could only qualitatively integrate these various domains and only in relatively vague terms. The simulation models offered in this paper establish that all of these qualitative accounts can be woven into a consistent theory which predicts precisely the data obtained in actual experiments. They bring out a substantial systematicity in the underlying parameters across these experiments. They show that phenomena such as the Wiseman–Tulving functions are not inconsistent with the theory as had long been believed. They show that decay assumptions can produce the ratio-rule for the serial-position effect, which had not been suspected. Thus, the ACT-R theory serves the role claimed for it. That is, it integrates existing ideas in the field.

Notes

1. According to the ACT-R theory, the activation of a chunk reflects a preliminary estimate of how likely it is to match to a production at the current point in time. More precisely, activation estimates the log odds that the chunk will match to a production.
2. The summation in this equation could be viewed as describing a situation where each use resulted in additional synaptic efficacy but which then decayed away (e.g., a new receptor site which decays away with time). As n gets large we sometimes use approximations in ACT-R simulation. One might indeed imagine that the equation is also only an approximate characterization of change in synaptic efficacy in the case of large n.
3. This equation asserts that the critical variable is time but it is unlikely that this is truly clock time. It might be better read as number of intervening events or some other construct. However, our models will treat the critical variable as clock time because that is usually the variable directly manipulated in studies.
4. S is essentially a scale constant whose value is reflected in the setting of other parameters in ACT-R—in particular, F and τ—see Eqs. (5) and (6). It can be set in the simulation but if not set it will default to the log of the total number of chunks.
5. The theory was based on a slightly earlier version of the ACT-R theory than the one in this paper. The updated theory reported here also has a sufficiently efficient simulation that we are able to get predictions by Monte Carlo estimation.
6. The assumption here is that each list will have its own token. Perhaps to avoid ambiguity, we should have called this *List-7136*.
7. Each token of a digit in the list has a tag as to whether it has been recalled or not. A digit token will not recalled again if it is tagged as already recalled. This is implemented as a test in the production Get-Next.
8. In Fig. 16.5 we do not show encoding of position. As will be discussed, we will continue use of positional information for the short Sternberg lists but not for the longer lists.
9. While we estimated F at 4.15, it would have been mathematically equivalent to use the equation above and estimate .097 as our free parameter.
10. We have not estimated an optimal ACT-R but neither is the original Tulving and Wiseman function an optimal fit.
11. We do not deny the complexities. It is just that they are irrelevant to some of the principal effects in the literature that we will address here.
12. Items in the buffer still have to be retrieved to produce their name and there is a small probability that they will not be sufficiently active for this retrieval to succeed.
13. For instance, unless otherwise programmed into the simulation, the S in Associative Strength Eq. (3) defaults to the logarithm of the number of chunks in the system.
14. The free recall experiments provide very little constraints for the estimate of the F parameter and it was just arbitrarily set at 2 for all of these experiments.
15. This is not to say ACT-R denies the existence of transient sensory buffers. It is also the case that its current goal provides a transient abstract memory (which implemented our buffer for free recall).

References

Aaronson, D. (1968). Temporal course of perception in an immediate recall task. *Journal of Experimental Psychology, 76*, 129–140.

Ackley, D. H., Hinton, G. E., & Sejnowsky, T. J. (1985). A learning algorithm for Boltzmann machines. *Cognitive Science, 9*, 147–169.

Anderson, J. R. (1972). FRAN: A simulation model of free recall in G. H. Bower, (Ed.), *The psychology of learning and motivation, vol. 5.* New York: Academic Press.

Anderson, J. R. (1976). *Language, memory, and thought*. Hillsdale, NJ: Erlbaum.

Anderson, J. R. (1983). *The architecture of cognition*. Hillsdale, NJ: Erlbaum.

Anderson, J. R. (1990). *The adaptive character of thought*. Hillsdale, NJ: Erlbaum.

Anderson, J. R. (1993). *Rules of the mind*. Hillsdale, NJ: Erlbaum.

Anderson, J. R., & Bower, G. H. (1972). Recognition and retrieval processes in free recall. *Psychological Review*, 79, 97–123.

Anderson, J. R., & Bower, G. H. (1973). *Human associative memory*. Hillsdale, NJ: Erlbaum.

Anderson, J. R., & Bower, G. H. (1974). Interference in memory for multiple contexts. *Memory and Cognition*, 2, 509–514.

Anderson, J. R., John, B. E., Just, M. A., Carpenter, P. A., Kieras, D. E., & Meyer, D. E. (1995). Production system models of complex cognition. In Proceedings of the Seventeenth Annual Conference of the Cognitive Science Society (pp. 9–12). Hillsdale. NJ: Erlbaum Associates.

Anderson, J. R., & Lebiere, C. (1998). *Atomic components of thought*. Hillsdale, NJ: Erlbaum.

Anderson, J. R., Lebiere, C., & Matessa, M. (1996). *ACT-R: A working theory of human cognition*. Paper presented at the Psychonomics Society Conference.

Anderson, J. R., & Matessa, M. P. (1997). A production system theory of serial memory. *Psychological Review*, 104, 728–748.

Anderson, J. R., Matessa, M. P., & Lebiere, C. (1997). The ACT theory and the visual interface. *Human Computer Interaction*, 12, 439–462.

Anderson, J. R., & Reder, L. M. (1999). *The fan effect: New results and new theories. Journal of Experimental Psychology: General*, 128, 186–197.

Anisfeld, M., & Knapp, M. (1968). Association, synonymity, and directionality in false recognition. *Journal of Experimental Psychology*, 77, 171–179.

Atkinson, R. C., & Shiffrin, R. M. (1968). Human memory: A proposed system and its control processes. In K. Spence & J. Spence (Eds.), *The psychology of learning and motivation* (Vol. 2). New York: Academic Press.

Baddeley, A. D. (1986). *Working memory*. London: Oxford University Press.

Baddeley, A. D., Thompson, N., & Buchanan, M. (1975). Word length and the structure of short-term memory. *Journal of Verbal Learning and Verbal Behavior*, 14, 575–589.

Bjork, E. L., & Healy, A. F. (1974). Short-term order and item retention. *Journal of Verbal Learning and Verbal Behavior*, 13, 80–97.

Briggs, G. E. (1974). On the predictor variable for choice reaction time. *Memory & Cognition*, 2, 575–580.

Burgess, N., & Hitch, G. J. (1992). Toward a network model of the articulatory loop. *Journal of Memory and Language*, 31, 429–460.

Burrows, D., & Okada, R. (1975). Memory retrieval from long and short lists. *Science*, 188, 1031–1033.

Conrad, R. (1964). Acoustic confusions in immediate memory. *British Journal of Psychology*, 55, 75–84.

Conrad, R. (1965). Order error in immediate recall of sequences. *Journal of Verbal Learning and Verbal Behavior*, 4, 161–169.

Cowan, N. (1992). Verbal memory span and the timing of spoken recall. *Journal of Memory and Language*, 31, 668–684.

Craik, F. I. M. (1970). The fate of primary memory items in free recall. *Journal of Verbal Learning and Verbal Behavior*, 9, 143–148.

Ebbinghaus, H. (1885). *Memory: A contribution to experimental psychology* (translated by H. A. Ruger & C. E. Bussenues, 1913). New York: Teachers College, Columbia University.

Estes, W. K. (1973). Phonemic coding and rehearsal in short-term memory for letter strings. *Journal of Verbal Learning and Verbal Behavior*, 12, 360–372.

Gardiner, J. M., Thompson, C. P., & Maskarinec, A. S. (1974). Negative recency in initial free recall. *Journal of Experimental Psychology*, 103, 71–78.

Gillund, G., & Shiffrin, R. M. (1984). A retrieval model for both recognition and recall. *Psychological Review*, 91, 1–67.

Healy, A. F., & McNamara, D. S. (1996). Verbal learning and memory: Does the modal model still word? In J. T. Spence, J. M. Darley, & D. J. Foss (Eds.) *Annual Review of Psychology*, 47, 143–172.

Hinton, G. E., & Sejnowsky, T. J. (1986). Learning and relearning in Boltzmann machines. In Rumelhart, D. E., McClelland, J. L., and the PDP group. *Parallel distributed processing: Explorations in the microstructure of cognition. Volume 1: Foundations*. Cambridge, MA: MIT Press.

Johnson, N. F. (1970). The role of chunking and organization in the process of recall. In G. H. Bower (Ed.), *The Psychology of learning and motivation* (Vol. 4, pp. 171–247). New York: Academic Press.

Johnson, G. J. (1991). A distinctiveness model of serial learning. *Psychological Review*, 98, 204–217.

Lee, C. L., & Estes, W. K. (1981). Order and position in primary memory for letter strings. *Journal of Verbal Learning and Verbal Behavior*, 16, 395–418.

Lewandowsky, S., & Murdock, B. B., Jr. (1989). Memory for serial order. *Psychological Review*, 96, 25–57.

Mandler, G. (1967). Organization and memory. In K. W. Spence & J. T. Spence (Eds.), *The psychology of learning and motivation: Advances in research and theory* (Vol. 1, pp. 328–372). New York: Academic Press.

Murdock, B. B., Jr. (1962). The serial position effect in free recall. *Journal of Experimental Psychology*, 64, 482–488.

Murdock, B. B. (1993). TODAM2: A model for the storage and retrieval of item, associative, and serial-order information. *Psychological Review*, 100, 183–203.

Nairne, J. S. (1992). The loss of positional certainty in long-term memory. *Psychological Science*, 3, 199–202.

Raaijmakers, J. G. W., & Shiffrin, R. M. (1981). Search of associative memory. *Psychological Review*, 88, 93–134.

Raaijmakers, J. G. W., & Shiffrin, R. M. (1992). Models for recall and recognition. *Annual Review of Psychology*, 43, 205–234.

Raeburn, V. P. (1974). Priorities in item recognition. *Memory & Cognition*, 2, 663–669.

Richman, H. B., Stászewski, J. J., & Simon, H. A. (1995). Simulation of expert memory using EPAM IV. *Psychological Review*, 102, 305–330.

Roberts, S., & Pashler, H. (2000). How persuasive is a good fit? A comment on theory testing. *Psychological Review*, 107, 358–367.

Salthouse, T. A. (1991). *Theoretical perspectives on cognitive aging*. Hillsdale, NJ: Erlbaum.

Shiffrin, R. M., & Cook, J. R. (1978). A model for short-term item and order retention. *Journal of Verbal Learning and Verbal Behavior*, 17, 189–218.

Shiffrin, R. M., & Steyvers, M. (1997). A model for recognition memory: REM—Retrieving effectively from memory. *Psychonomic Bulletin & Review*, 4, 145–166.

Slamecka, N. (1967). Serial learning and order information. *Journal of Experimental Psychology*, 74, 62–66.

Underwood, B. J., & Freund, J. S. (1968). Effect of temporal separation of two tasks on proactive inhibition. *Journal of Experimental Psychology*, 78, 50–54.

Wickelgren, W. A. (1965a). Short-term memory for phonemically similar lists. *American Journal of Psychology*, 78, 567–574.

Wickelgren, W. A. (1965b). Short-term memory for repeated and non-repeated items. *Quarterly Journal of Experimental Psychology*, 17, 14–25.

Young, R. K. (1968). Serial learning. In T. R. Dixon & D. L. Horton (Eds.), *Verbal behavior and behavior theory* (pp. 122–148). Englewood Cliffs, NJ: Prentice-Hall.

Memory and Learning

Chapter 17

Why There Are Complementary Learning Systems in the Hippocampus and Neocortex: Insights from the Successes and Failures of Connectionist Models of Learning and Memory

James L. McClelland, Bruce L. McNaughton, and Randall C. O'Reilly

---

One of the most striking neuropsychological phenomena ever reported is the dramatic amnesia produced by bilateral lesions to the hippocampus and related temporal lobe structures (Scoville & Milner, 1957). A crucial aspect of this phenomenon is temporally graded retrograde amnesia. Considerable evidence now supports the conclusion that the influence of the hippocampal system on the ability to exploit information derived from past experience in a wide range of tasks is temporally circumscribed: Performance is impaired if the hippocampal system is damaged before or within a window of time after the initial experience; however, if the hippocampal system is left intact both during the experience and for a period of time thereafter, subsequent damage may have little or no impact on performance.

This change in dependence on the hippocampal system over time appears to be a slow, gradual process. This gradual change has often been called consolidation, but the term really only labels the phenomenon. In this article, we focus on consolidation and consider what produces it and why it occurs. We ask, Is the phenomenon a reflection of an arbitrary property of the nervous system, or does it reflect some crucial aspect of the mechanisms of learning and memory? Is the fact that consolidation can take quite a long time—up to 15 years or more in some cases—just an arbitrary parameter, or does it reflect an important design principle?

We begin with a brief overview of the neuropsychology of memory, emphasizing the temporally circumscribed role of the hippocampal system, and elaborate one possible account of the functional organization of memory that is broadly consistent with the neuropsychological evidence, as well as aspects of the underlying anatomy and physiology. We then describe results from connectionist modeling research that suggest reasons for this organization and for the phenomenon of gradual consolidation. From the insights gained through the consideration of these models, we develop illustrative simulation models of the phenomenon of temporally graded retrograde amnesia. These are not detailed neural models; rather, they illustrate, at an abstract level, what we take consolidation to be about. We discuss the implications of our view of the role of consolidation for findings related to age, species, and task differences in neocortical learning and for the form of representations used in the hippocampus, and we conclude with a comparison of our views and those of others who have theorized about the role of the hippocampal system in learning and memory. Although there are many points of compatibility, our approach differs from some others in treating gradual consolidation as reflecting a principled aspect of the design of the mammalian memory system.

Role of the Hippocampal System in Learning and Memory

The phrase *the hippocampal system* is widely used to refer to a system of interrelated brain regions found in a range of mammalian species that appear to play a special role in learning and memory. The exact boundaries of the hippocampal system are difficult to define, but it includes at least the hippocampus itself—the CA1–3 fields of Ammon's Horn and the dentate gyrus—the subicular complex, and the entorhinal cortex. It probably also encompasses adjacent structures including the perirhinal and parahippocampal cortices.

The literature on the effects of damage to the hippocampal system is quite vast. Here we summarize what we believe are the main points.

1. An extensive lesion of the hippocampal system can produce a profound deficit in new learning while leaving other cognitive functions and memory performance based on material acquired well before the lesion apparently normal. Dramatic evidence of this effect was first reported by Scoville and Milner (1957) in their description of the anterograde amnesia produced in patient HM as a result of bilateral removal of large portions of the hippocampal system and other temporal lobe structures. HM presented initially with a profound deficit in memory for events that occurred either after the lesion or during the weeks and months before it, but with intact intellectual function and information-processing skills and apparent sparing of his memory for more remote time periods.

2. The effects of lesions to the hippocampal system appear to be selective to certain forms of learning. In humans, the hippocampal system appears to be essential for the rapid formation of comprehensive associations among the various elements of specific events and experiences, in a form sufficient to sustain an explicit (Schacter, 1987) retrieval of the contents of the experience, so that they can be attested (explicitly recognized as memories), verbally described, or flexibly used to govern subsequent behavior. N. J. Cohen and Squire (1980) introduced the term *declarative memory* to encompass these forms of memory. Included in the category of declarative memories are *episodic memories*

(Tulving, 1983)—memories for the specific contents of individual episodes or events—as well as what are generally termed semantic memories, including knowledge of the meanings of words, factual information, and encyclopedic memories (see Squire, 1992, for a recent discussion). A paradigm example of this form of memory is paired-associates learning of arbitrary word pairs. Prior associations to the cue word are unhelpful in this task, which depends on recall of the word that previously occurred with the cue word in the list study context. Hippocampal system lesions produce profound impairments in learning arbitrary paired associates (Scoville & Milner, 1957). However, it should be noted that deficits are not apparently restricted to tasks that rely on memories that are explicitly accessed and used to govern task performance. For example, amnesics are also impaired in acquisition of arbitrary new factual information, whether or not the use of this information is accompanied by deliberate or conscious recollection of previous experience (Shimamura & Squire, 1987). Also, normal participants show sensitivity to novel associations after a single presentation in stem completion tasks, but profound amnesics do not (Schacter & Graf, 1986; Shimamura & Squire, 1989). Although recent evidence (Bowers & Schacter, 1993) suggests that normal participants who show sensitivity to novel associations are conscious of having accessed these associations on at least some trials, sensitivity to novel associations is dissociable in several ways from standard measures of explicit or declarative memory (Graf & Schacter, 1987; Schacter & Graf, 1989). Thus, at this point the extent to which deficits in amnesics are restricted to tasks that depend on conscious access to the contents of prior episodes or events is unclear. It does appear that, in humans, an intact hippocampal system is necessary for the formation of an association between arbitrarily paired words that is sufficiently strong after a single presentation to have an effect on subsequent performance, whether explicit memory is involved or not.

In the animal literature, the exact characterization of the forms of learning that depend on the hippocampal system remains a matter of intense investigation and debate. Sutherland and Rudy (1989) suggested that the hippocampal system is crucial for learning to make appropriate responses that depend not on individual cues but on specific combinations or conjunctions of cues, what they called *cue configurations*. The paradigmatic example of a task depending on cue configurations is the negative patterning task, in which animals receive reward for operant responses to a light and a tone but not the tone–light compound. Hippocampal system lesions lead to deficits in responding differently to the compound than to the individual cues (Rudy & Sutherland, 1989). N. J. Cohen and Eichenbaum (1993) have emphasized the importance of the hippocampal system for flexible access to memory traces, a characteristic that may be closely related to declarative memory in humans. A major alternative viewpoint is that of O'Keefe and Nadel (1978), who have suggested that the hippocampal system is especially relevant in the formation of memories involving places or locations in the environment, and there is a vast body of evidence that spatial learning is impaired after hippocampal lesions in rats. One view of spatial learning that is compatible with both the Sutherland and Rudy (1989) and the O'Keefe and Nadel (1978) theories is that place learning involves forming configural associations of locations and movements that would enable prediction of the spatial consequence of a given movement in a given spatial context (McNaughton, Leonard, & Chen, 1989). This can be seen as a special case of the Sutherland and Rudy (1989) theory, and it is possible that it may be the evolutionary forerunner of the more general processing capability. In any case, increasing evidence suggests that damage restricted to the hippocampus affects tasks that require the animal to learn responses specific to particular nonspatial combinations of cues, or to specific contexts, as well as tasks that depend on learning to navigate in a previously unfamiliar spatial environment (Jarrard, 1993; Rudy & Sutherland, 1994).[1] More extensive lesions of the hippocampal system lead to deficits in a broader range of tasks. In some cases, selective lesions to just the hippocampus produce little or no effect, although performance is severely disturbed by a complete lesion of the entire hippocampal system (for reviews, see Eichenbaum, Otto, & Cohen, 1994; Jarrard, 1993).

3. Some kinds of learning appear to be completely unaffected by hippocampal system lesions. Squire (1992) characterized these forms of memory as *nondeclarative* or *implicit* (Schacter, 1987), emphasizing that they influence behavior without depending on conscious or deliberate access to memory for the contents of the events that led to these influences. Another characterization emphasizes inflexibility of use of such memories; they appear to influence behavior maximally when there is a close match between the processing carried out during the learning event and the processing carried out when the later influence of the learning event is assessed (N. J. Cohen & Eichenbaum, 1993). This greater specificity appears to characterize implicit memory as it is observed in normals as well as amnesics (Schacter, 1987). Examples of forms of learning that are spared are gradually acquired skills that emerge over several sessions of practice, such as the skill of tracing a figure viewed in a mirror (B. Milner, 1966), reading mirror-reversed print (N. J. Cohen & Squire, 1980), or anticipating subsequent items in a sequence governed by a complex stochastic grammar (Cleeremans, 1993). Hippocampal patients also appear to be spared in their ability to learn the structure common to a set of items: They are as good as normals in judging whether particular test items come from the same prototype, or were generated by the same finite-state grammar, as the members of a previously studied list (Knowlton, Ramus, & Squire, 1992; Knowlton & Squire, 1993). Spared learning is also exhibited in repetition priming tasks. These are tasks that require participants to emit some response already within their capabilities, such as naming a word or picture (B. Milner, Corkin, & Teuber, 1968), reading aloud a pronounceable nonword (Haist, Musen, & Squire, 1991), or completing a word fragment with a lexically valid completion (Graf, Squire,

& Mandler, 1984). Repetition priming is exhibited when the participant is later required to process a previously presented item, and a single prior presentation is often sufficient. In many such tasks, hippocampal patients appear indistinguishable from normals in the extent to which they show facilitation from prior presentations, as long as care is taken to avoid the possibility that explicit recall is used to aid performance. Hippocampal patients exhibit spared priming of existing associations (i.e., an increase in the likelihood of producing *table* when giving a free associate to *chair* after prior presentation of *table* and *chair* together) but, as previously noted, do not show priming, as normals do, after a single prior presentation of an arbitrary, novel pair of words. Such priming effects can be obtained after multiple presentations of the novel arbitrary word pair (Squire, 1992). In animal studies, it is clear that some forms of classical or instrumental conditioning of responses to discrete salient cues are unaffected by hippocampal system damage (for reviews, see Barnes, 1988; O'Keefe & Nadel, 1978; Rudy & Sutherland, 1994). A fuller consideration of these forms of conditioning is presented in a later section.

4. Lesions to the hippocampal system and bilateral electroconvulsive treatment (ECT) appear to give rise to a temporally graded retrograde amnesia for material acquired in the period of time preceding the lesion. Recent electrophysiological studies (Barnes et al., 1994; Stewart & Reid, 1993) indicate that ECT has profound effects on hippocampal synapses. Although temporally graded retrograde amnesia has been the subject of controversy (Warrington & McCarthy, 1988; Warrington & Weiskrantz, 1978), we believe the evidence is substantial enough to be taken seriously, and it plays a major role in the theory developed here. Early indications that retrograde amnesia may be temporally graded, at least in certain forms of amnesia, came from the observations of Ribot (1882) and from the early report of patient HM by Scoville and Milner (1957). More recent quantitative studies of a wide range of hippocampal amnesics suggest several conclusions (Squire, 1992).

> 1. Hippocampal amnesics show a selective memory deficit for material acquired shortly before the date of their lesion. Memory for very remote material appears to be completely spared; in between, there is an apparent gradient.
> 2. The severity and temporal extent of the retrograde amnesia appear to vary with the extent of damage to the hippocampus and related structures.
> 3. In some severe cases, the retrograde gradient can extend over periods of 15 years or more.

Results from animal studies are generally consistent with the human data, although in the case of the animal work the retrograde gradient appears to cover a much briefer span of time. Studies in rats (Kim & Fanselow, 1992; Winocur, 1990) have produced retrograde gradients covering a period of days or weeks. Primate experiments (Zola-Morgan & Squire, 1990) have shown a severe impairment relative to controls for memory acquired 2 or 4 weeks before surgery but not for older memories.

A key observation is that there is a correspondence between the kinds of tasks that show retrograde amnesia and those that show anterograde amnesia. For example, Kim and Fanselow (1992) observed that the same rats who showed retrograde amnesia for the spatial context of a tone–shock association exhibited no retrograde amnesia for the simple tone–shock association itself. This same dissociation holds in anterograde amnesia.

A second crucial aspect of temporally graded retrograde amnesia is the fact that, after hippocampal lesions, performance on recent material can actually be worse than performance on somewhat older material. As Squire (1992) pointed out, this finding is crucial for the claim that some real consolidation takes place because it rules out the alternative interpretation that memories are initially stored in two forms whose effects are additive: a relatively transient, hippocampal-system-dependent form and a more persistent, hippocampal-system-independent form. On this account, there is no alteration of the form of memory over time; rather, there is merely decay. Nevertheless, because the decay of the hippocampal memory is more rapid, there would be a gradually diminishing difference between the two groups. Three animal studies now provide clear evidence against this simple dual-store interpretation (Kim & Fanselow, 1992; Winocur, 1990; Zola-Morgan & Squire, 1990); we show the data from these studies in Figure 17.1. In all three studies, performance of lesioned animals at test was better when there was a longer delay between study and test, supporting a real change in the form or location of memory. Also shown are data from human ECT patients (Squire & Cohen, 1979) taken from a measure called the *TV test* developed by Squire and Slater (1975). This test examined knowledge of single-season TV shows, for which memory depended primarily on exposure to the shows during the year in which they were aired. It is difficult to rule out the possibility that the depression in the years just before treatment affected initial storage. It also must be noted that the treatment may have affected more than just the hippocampal system. But no such difficulties apply to the findings from the animal studies, which are very clear in two of the cases: In both Winocur (1990) and Kim and Fanselow (1992), lesions occurring within 24 hr of the experience led to performance indistinguishable from chance, whereas lesions occurring at later points in time led to much better performance.

One Account of the Organization of Memory in the Brain

What follows is one account of the mechanisms of learning in the mammalian brain. The account is consistent with the data summarized earlier and with several important anatomical and physiological findings that we summarize later, and it has many points in common with the accounts offered in several

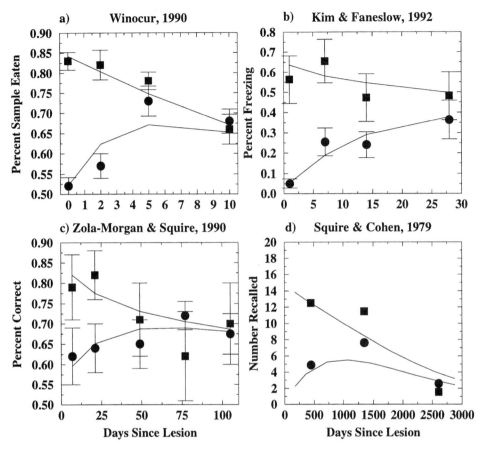

Figure 17.1

Panels a–c: Behavioral responses of animals receiving extensive hippocampal system lesions (circles) or control lesions (squares) as a function of the numbers of days elapsing between exposure to the relevant experiences and the occurrence of the lesion. Bars surrounding each data point indicate the standard error. Panel a shows the percentage choice of a specific food sample (out of two alternatives) by rats exposed to a conspecific that had eaten the food sample. Panel b shows fear (freezing) behavior shown by rats when returned to an environment in which they had experienced paired presentations of tones and footshock. Panel c shows choices of reinforced objects by monkeys exposed to 14 training trials with each of 20 object pairs. Panel d: Recall by depressed human participants of details of TV shows aired different numbers of years before the time of test after electroconvulsive treatment (circles) or just before treatment (squares). Here years have been translated into days to allow comparisons with the results from the animal studies. The curves shown in each panel are based on a simple model discussed in the text.

other synthetic treatments, beginning with Marr (1971). A comparison with these other treatments can be found in the General Discussion section.

Our account begins with the assumption that the brain exploits complementary learning systems. One system relies on adaptation of synaptic connections among the neurons directly responsible for information processing and behavior. The other relies on adaptation of synaptic connections within a special memory system that includes the hippocampus and related structures.

The Neocortical Processing System

Adaptation of synaptic connections undoubtedly occurs in a wide range of neural processing systems in the brain; however, for the cognitive forms of learning that are the principal focus of this article, we are concerned primarily with adaptive learning that is likely, in most cases, to occur in the neocortex. We suspect that the principles we propose for the neocortical system also apply to other adaptive processing systems in the brain such as those that are involved in some forms of skill learning, including the basal ganglia and the cerebellum. We comment in a later section on adaptive changes produced by animal conditioning paradigms in other systems such as the amygdala and various other subcortical brain structures.

We view the neocortex as a collection of partially overlapping processing systems; for simplicity of reference, however, we refer to these systems collectively as the *neocortical processing system*. We include in this system those neocortical structures that we take to share the role of providing the neural substrate for higher level control of behavior and cognitive processing, as well as other neocortical structures involved in sensory, perceptual, and output processes. Most but not all of the neocortex belongs to this system: The perirhinal and parahippocampal cortices are anatomically defined as neocortex, but they appear functionally to belong at least in part to the hippocampal memory system. It may be best to consider these as borderline areas in which the neocortical processing system and the hippocampal memory systems overlap. They certainly play a crucial role in mediating communication between the other parts of the hippocampal system and the neocortex.

We assume that performance of higher level behavioral and cognitive tasks depends on the elicitation of patterns of activation over the populations of neurons in various regions of the neocortical system by other patterns of activation over the same or different regions. For example, in an acquired skill (such as reading), the pattern produced by an input (such as a printed word) elicits a corresponding pattern representing an output (such as the motor program for pronouncing the word). In a free-association task, a pattern representing a stimulus word elicits another pattern representing the response word. When an arbitrary list associate in a paired-associates learning task is retrieved, the stimulus pattern must specify not only the stimulus word but also some information about the encoding context; however, the principle remains the same: Task performance occurs through the elicitation of one pattern of activation in response to another that serves as a cue. For this to work in tasks requiring the contextually appropriate retrieval of patterns of activation representing specific propositions, events, and so forth, the system must be structured in such a way that any aspect of the content of the target pattern, as well as patterns representing material associated with the target pattern, can serve as retrieval cues.

Patterns are elicited by the propagation of activation via synaptic connections among the neurons involved. The knowledge that underlies the processing capabilities of the neocortex is stored in these connections. Thus, the knowledge is assumed to be embedded in the very neural circuits that carry out the tasks that use the information.

We assume that every occasion of information processing in the neocortical system gives rise to adaptive adjustments to the connections among the neurons involved. The adjustments are widely distributed across all of the relevant connections but we assume they have relatively subtle effects; they tend to facilitate a repetition of the same act of processing or an essentially similar one at a later time or to facilitate reaching the same global state of activation (corresponding, for example, to an entire proposition or image) when given any fragment or associate of it as a cue.[2] We assume, however, that the changes that result from one or a few repetitions of an experience are not sufficient to support the reinstatement of a pattern representing a specific conjunction of arbitrary elements, such as the conjunction of an arbitrary pair of words in a paired-associates learning experiment or the conjunction of elements that together compose a specific episode or event.

Over the course of many repetitions of the same or substantially similar acts of information processing, the changes to the synaptic connections among neurons in the neocortical system will accumulate. When the changes arise from the repetition of the same specific content (e.g., the association between a particular word and its meaning), the accumulation of such changes will provide the basis for correct performance in tasks that depend on the specific content in question. When they reflect different examples of some sort of structured relationship between inputs and outputs (e.g., the structured relation that holds between the spellings of words and their sounds), they will provide the basis of an acquired cognitive skill.

The Hippocampal Memory System
The representation of an experience in the neocotical system consists of a widely distributed pattern of neural activity. As just noted, we assume that each experience gives rise to small adaptive changes but that these changes will generally not be sufficient to allow rapid learning of arbitrary associative conjunctions that we assume provide the substrate for explicit recall of the contents of specific episodes and for other hippocampal-system-dependent tasks. We

assume that performance in such tasks depends initially on substantial changes to the strengths of connections among neurons in the hippocampal system. Information is carried between the hippocampal system and the neocortical system via bidirectional pathways that translate patterns of activity in the neocortical system into corresponding patterns in the hippocampal system, and vice versa. We do not assume that the hippocampal system receives a direct copy of the pattern of activation distributed over the higher level regions of the neocortical system; instead, the neocortical representation is thought to be re-represented in a compressed format over a much smaller number of neurons in the hippocampal system. McNaughton (1989) has referred to this compressed pattern as a "summary sketch" of the current neocortical representation. Such compression can often occur without loss of essential information if there is redundancy in the neocortical representations. The familiar data compression schemes that are used for computer files exploit such redundancy, and very high levels of compression may be possible if the patterns being compressed are highly constrained or redundant. Artificial neural networks structurally similar to those suggested by Figure 17.2 are quite commonly used to perform pattern compression and decompression (Ackley, Hinton, & Sejnowski, 1985; Cottrell, Munro, & Zipser, 1987). Compression is carried out in these models by the connections leading from the input to a much smaller representation layer, and decompression occurs via connections leading back from the representation layer to the input layer. Intermediate layers can be interposed on either the input or the output side to increase the sophistication of the compression process, the decompression process, or both.

Within the hippocampus itself, we assume that the event or experience is represented by a sparse pattern of activity in which the individual neurons represent specific combinations or conjunctions of elements of the event that gave rise to the pattern of activation. We assume that once such a pattern of activity arises in the hippocampal memory system, it may potentially become a stable memory. Plastic changes to the synapses on fibers coming into the hippocampus tend to increase the likelihood that a subsequent fragment of the pattern will elicit the entire pattern, and plastic changes to synaptic connections among the neurons active in the pattern tend to make this pattern an attractor (i.e., a pattern toward which neighboring patterns or incomplete versions of the pattern will tend to converge). Several repetitions may be required for these changes to reach sufficient strength to subserve memory task performance. During recall, if a part of the pattern representing the episode arises again in the neocortical system, this will be translated into a part of the pattern corresponding to the previous event in the hippocampal memory system. If the input is sufficiently close to the stored pattern, and if the changes to the relevant synaptic efficacies were sufficiently large, this input would then lead the hippocampal memory system to tend to settle into the attractor, thereby filling in the missing aspects of the memory trace. The return pathways from the hippo-

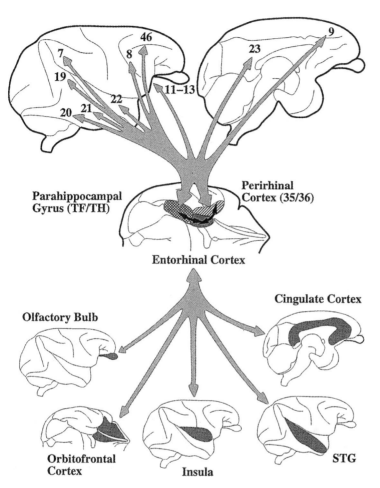

Figure 17.2
Schematic representation (from Squire, Shimamura, and Amaral, 1989) of the inputs and outputs of
the hippocampal system in the primate. The upper panel shows the frontal, temporal, and parietal
areas reciprocally connected with the parahippocampal gyrus and the perirhinal cortex, which in
turn connect reciprocally with the entorhinal cortex. The lower panel shows the areas that have
direct reciprocal connections with the entorhinal cortex.

campal system to the neocortex, together with preexisting intracortical connections, then reverse the translation carried out by the forward connections, thereby completing the neocortical reinstatement of the event pattern and enabling appropriate overt responses. Reinstatement in such a system is assumed to be a matter of degree, varying with the adequacy of the probe, the amount of initial learning, subsequent interference, and decay, and the sufficiency of a particular degree of pattern reinstatement for overt behavior will depend on the exact nature of the task and behavioral response required.

Reinstatement and Consolidation of Hippocampal Memories in the Neocortical System

As just described, reinstatement of patterns stored in the hippocampal memory system may occur in task-relevant situations, in which the memory trace is needed for task performance. We assume that reinstatement also occurs in off-line situations, including active rehearsal, reminiscence, and other inactive states including sleep (Marr, 1971). In such cases, we assume that reinstatement in the hippocampal memory system gives rise, via the return connections, to reinstatement in the neocortical processing system. This would have two important consequences. First, reinstatement of the stored event in an appropriate context would allow the stored information to be used for controlling behavioral responses. Second, reinstatement would provide the opportunity for an incremental adjustment of neocortical connections, thereby allowing memories initially dependent on the hippocampal system gradually to become independent of it. To the extent that the hippocampal memory system participates in this reinstatement process, it can be viewed not just as a memory store but as the teacher of the neocortical processing system.

In our view, the same consolidation process applies to the development of a neocortical substrate for performance in semantic, encyclopedic, and episodic memory tasks. As we define these terms here, semantic memory tasks are simply those that require the use of information about categories and concepts, encyclopedic tasks require the use of specific factual information, and episodic memory tasks are those that require the use of information contained in a specific previous event or episode in which the individual was an observer or participant. In our view, there is no special distinction between such tasks. Performance in all three depends initially on plastic changes within the hippocampal system, but the knowledge underlying the tasks can eventually be stored in the neocortical system via the gradual accumulation of small changes. Consider the specific episode or event in which one first encounters some particular fact, such as Neil Armstrong uttering the words "That's one small step for [a] man" when he first set foot on the moon. Such factual information would be encountered first in a particular context, in this case, perhaps, in the context of watching Armstrong live on TV as he set foot on the moon during a family reunion celebrating a grandfather's 70th birthday. If the event of Armstrong's landing is reinstated repeatedly, the accumulated changes to neocortical connections could eventually come to preserve the common aspects of the reinstated event. The result would allow the individual to perform correctly in the encyclopedic memory task of recalling what Armstrong said. If the previous reinstatements had specifically included information about the time and place of initial learning, then this information, too, would gradually become incorporated into the connection weights in the neocortical system and would sustain performance in an episodic memory task. If, however, the reinstatements occur in many different contexts, and if these reinstatements do not include other aspects of the original context of encoding, no reliable memory for any particular context would remain. Much the same process would also apply to the learning of semantic information, such as the fact that giraffes have long necks or the fact that a particular category label is the correct name to apply to a set of items derived from the same prototype. Knapp and Anderson (1984) and McClelland and Rumelhart (1985) have both presented connectionist models in which semantic memory and category learning can arise from the gradual accumulation of small changes resulting from individual events and experiences.

Summary

We can now summarize our account of the organization of the memory system by noting how it accounts for the main features of the pattern of deficits and spared performance found after a hippocampal system lesion. The deficit in the ability to learn new arbitrary associations involving conjunctions of cues from a few exposures would arise from the fact that these associations would have been stored in the (now destroyed) hippocampal system; the small changes that would occur in the neocortical system could contribute to repetition priming effects but would be insufficient to support normal rates of acquisition in semantic and episodic memory tasks and other tasks that depend on the acquisition of novel conjunctions of arbitrary material.

The spared acquisition of skills would arise from the gradual accumulation of small changes in the connections among the relevant neural populations in the neocortical system, as well as other relevant brain systems. The temporally extended and graded nature of retrograde amnesia would reflect the fact that information initially stored in the hippocampal memory system can become incorporated into the neocortical system only very gradually, as a result of the small size of the changes made on each reinstatement.

The ability of even very profound amnesics to acquire often-repeated material gradually (Glisky, Schacter, & Tulving, 1986a, 1986b; B. Milner et al., 1968) would likewise reflect this slow accumulation of changes in the neocortical system after the onset of amnesia. The fact that such learning is often restricted to the specific task contexts in which it was acquired follows from the assumption that the learning actually takes place directly within the connections among the neural populations that were activated during the acquisition process.

Our account of the organization of learning in the brain is intended as a provisional factual characterization. It embodies some unproven assumptions, and so it might be viewed as a theory of memory in some sense. We offer it, however, not as a theory in itself but as a starting place for theoretical discussion. Although it is neither fully explicit nor complete (some gaps, such as a consideration of spared conditioning of responses to individual salient cues, are discussed in later sections), the account appears to be broadly compatible with a large body of data, and it is consistent enough with many of the other accounts considered in the General Discussion section that we suggest it is useful to treat it as provisionally correct, at least in its essentials.

Key Questions About the Organization of Memory in the Brain

Supposing provisionally that our account is basically correct, we can now ask, why is it that the system is organized in this particular way? Two key functional questions arise:

1. Why is a hippocampal system necessary, if ultimately performance in all sorts of memory tasks depends on changes in connections within the neocortical system? Why are the changes not made directly in the neocortical system in the first place?
2. Why does incorporation of new material into the neocortical system take such a long time? Why are the changes to neocortical connections not made more rapidly, shortly after initial storage in the hippocampal system?

Successes and Failures of Connectionist Models of Learning and Memory

The answers we suggest to these questions arise from the study of learning in artificial neural network or connectionist models that adhere to many aspects of the account of the mammalian memory system provided earlier, but do not incorporate a special system for rapid acquisition of the contents of specific episodes and events. Such networks are similar to the neocortical processing system in that they may consist of several modules and pathways interconnecting the modules, but they are monolithic in the sense that knowledge is stored directly in the connections among the units of the system that carries out information processing, and there is no separate system for rapid learning of the contents of particular inputs.

Discovery of Shared Structure Through Interleaved Learning

The first and perhaps most crucial point is that, in such monolithic connectionist systems, there are tremendous ultimate benefits of what we call *interleaved learning*. By interleaved learning we mean learning in which a particular item is not learned all at once but is acquired very gradually, through a series of presentations interleaved with exposure to other examples from the domain. The adjustments made to connection weights on each exposure to an example are small; thus, the overall direction of connection adjustment is governed not by the particular characteristics of individual associations but by the shared structure common to the environment from which these individual associations are sampled.

Consider, in this context, some of the facts known about robins. It is known that a robin is a bird, it has wings, it has feathers, it can fly, it breathes, it must eat to stay alive, and so on. This knowledge is not totally arbitrary knowledge about robins but is, in fact, part of a system of knowledge about robins, herons, eagles, sparrows, and many other things. Indeed, much of the information accumulated about robins probably does not come from specific experience with robins but from other, related things. Some such knowledge comes from very closely related things of which people may have knowledge (e.g., other birds), whereas other knowledge may come from other things less closely related but still related enough in particular ways to support some knowledge sharing (e.g., other animals or even other living things). A key issue in the use of concepts is the fact that what counts as related is by no means obvious and is not, in general, predictable from surface properties. Birds are more related to, for example, reptiles and fish than they are to insects.

Connectionist models that use interleaved learning suggest how knowledge of relations among concepts may develop. Both Hinton (1989) and Rumelhart (1990; Rumelhart & Todd, 1993) developed simulations to illustrate how connectionist networks can learn representations appropriate for organized bodies of conceptual knowledge. We use the Rumelhart example here because it relates to the domain of knowledge about living things that we have already begun to consider as an example and because, as shown later, there are some empirical data about the development of children's knowledge that this model can help one understand. The specific example is highly simplified and abstract. It captures approximately the constraints that may be operative in the discovery of conceptual structure from an ensemble of sentences that convey simple propositional statements about living things, in that concepts are represented by arbitrary tokens (akin to words) rather than by percepts that directly provide some information about the concepts under consideration. The conceptual structure resides not in the direct appearance of the words that convey the concepts but in the relations that the concepts referred to by the words enter into with other concepts.

Human knowledge of the domain of living things appears to be organized hierarchically, with a principal grouping into plants and animals and then other, finer subgroupings within each of these broad classes (we refer not to objective biological information per se but to the cognitive representations that people have of this information). Previous symbolic approaches to knowledge

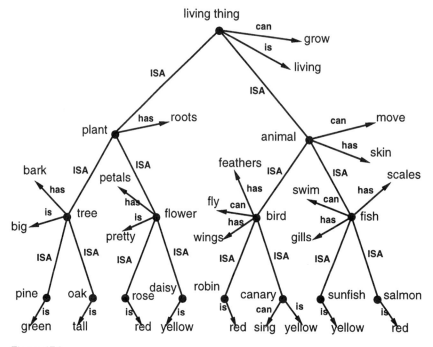

Figure 17.3
A semantic network of the type formerly used in models of the organization of knowledge in memory (from Rumelhart and Todd, 1993). All of the propositions used in training the network are based on the information actually encoded here. For example, the network indicates that living things can grow, that a tree is a plant, and that a plant is a living thing. Therefore, it follows that a tree can grow. All of these propositions are contained in the training set.

representation directly imported the hierarchical organization of knowledge into their structure, representing knowledge about concepts in a data structure known as a *semantic network* (Quillian, 1968; see Figure 17.3). Such networks are not to be confused with connectionist networks, because they represent and process information in fundamentally different ways. In the semantic network, concepts are organized hierarchically by means of links called *isa* links, as a short form of the statement *An X is a Y*. Given this organization, semantic networks can store knowledge of concepts in a succinct form, with information that is true of all of the concepts in an entire branch of the tree at the top of the branch. For example, the predicate *has feathers* can be stored at the *bird* node because it is true of all birds. This allows generalization to new instances. When a new type of thing is encountered, such as an egret, people need only to be told that it is a bird and to link the new node for *egret* to the node for *bird* by an *isa* link. Then their knowledge of egrets can inherit all that is known about birds.

Semantic networks of this type were very popular vehicles for representation for a period of time in the 1970s, but apparent experimental support (Collins & Quillian, 1969) for the hypothesis that people's knowledge of concepts is organized in this way was illusory (Rips, Shoben, & Smith, 1973). Computationally, semantic networks of this type become cumbersome to use when they contain a large amount of information (Fahlman, 1981). It becomes very difficult to determine when it is appropriate to consider a property to be essentially common to a category, even though there are exceptions, and when it is appropriate to consider a property sufficiently variable that it must be enumerated separately on the instances. The problem is compounded by the fact that most concepts are constituents of multiple intersecting hierarchies, in which case intractable inheritance conflicts can arise.

Connectionist models offer a very different way of accounting for the ability to generalize knowledge from one concept to another. According to this approach (Hinton, 1981; Touretzky & Geva, 1987), generalization depends on a process that assigns each concept an internal representation that captures its conceptual similarity to other concepts. This alternative approach appears to be more consistent with the psychological evidence (Rips et al., 1973), because the evidence favors the view that conceptual similarity judgments are made by comparing representations of concepts directly rather than searching for common parents in a hierarchically structured tree. This alternative also overcomes the vexing questions about how to handle partially regular traits and exceptions, because idiosyncratic as well as common properties can be captured in these representations.

The approach depends on exploiting the ability of a network to discover the relations among concepts through interleaved learning. The network is trained on a set of specific propositions about various concepts, and, in the course of training, it learns similar representations for similar concepts. By similar concepts, we mean concepts that enter into overlapping sets of propositions.

Rumelhart (1990) trained a network on propositions about a number of concepts: living things, plants, animals, trees, oaks, pines, flowers, roses, daisies, animals, birds, canaries, robins, fish, salmon, and sunfish. The training data were the set of true propositions either explicitly represented in or derivable from the semantic network shown in Figure 17.3. The connectionist network used to learn these propositions is shown in Figure 17.4. It consists of a number of nonlinear connectionist processing units organized into several modules, connected as illustrated in the figure. Arrows signify complete connectivity from all of the units in the module at the sending end of the arrows to all of the units at the receiving end. Input to the network is presented by activating the unit for a concept name in the concept input module on the upper left and the unit for a relation term in the relation input module on the lower left. The relations *isa, has, can,* and *is* are represented. The task of the network is to respond to each input by activating units in the appropriate module on the

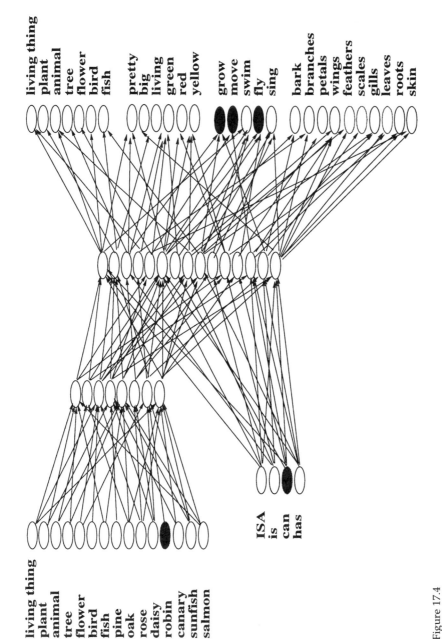

Figure 17.4
Depiction of the connectionist network used by Rumelhart (1990) to learn propositions about the concepts shown in Figure 17.3. The entire set of units used in the actual network is shown. Inputs are presented on the left, and activation propagates from left to right. In instances in which connections are indicated, every unit in the pool on the left (sending) side projects to every unit on the right (receiving) side. An input consists of a concept-relation pair; the input "robin can" is illustrated by a darkening of the active input units. The network is trained to turn on all of those output units that represent correct completions of the input pattern. In this case, the correct units to activate are "grow," "move," and "fly;" the units of these outputs are darkened as well. Subsequent analysis focuses on the concept representation units, the group of eight units to the right of the concept input units.

right corresponding to the correct completion or completions of the input. For example, in the case of the input *robin isa*, the network is trained to activate the output units for *living thing, animal, bird*, and *robin*. In the case of *robin can*, the network is trained to activate the output units for *grow, move*, and *fly*. The inputs and desired outputs for this latter case are indicated in the figure.

Before learning begins, the network is initialized with random weights. At first, when an input is presented, the output is random and bears no relation to the desired output. The goal is to adjust these connection weights, through exposure to propositions from the environment, so as to minimize the discrepancy between desired and obtained output over the entire ensemble of training patterns. This goal can be achieved by interleaved learning with a gradient descent learning procedure: During training, each pattern is presented many times, interleaved with presentations of the other patterns. After each pattern presentation, the error (i.e., the discrepancy between the desired output and the obtained output) is calculated. Each connection weight is then adjusted either up or down by an amount proportional to the extent that its adjustment will reduce the discrepancy between the correct response and the response actually produced by the network. The changes to the connection weights are scaled by a learning rate constant ε that is set to a small value so that only small changes are made on any given training trial. Thus, responses are learned slowly. Over time, some of the changes made to the connections are mutually cooperative, and some of the changes cancel each other out. The cooperative changes build up over time, with the end result that the set of connections evolves in a direction that reflects the aggregate influence of the entire ensemble of patterns.

To understand the results of the cooperative learning, we consider patterns of activation the network comes to produce on the eight units in the module to the right of the concept units in Figure 17.4. These units are called the *concept representation units*. The patterns of activation in this module can be considered to be the learned internal representations of each concept; the connections from the concept input units to the representation units can be viewed as capturing the mapping between input patterns and internal representations. The rest of the connections in the network can be seen as capturing the mapping from these internal representations, together with patterns on the relation units, to appropriate response patterns at the output layer.

In the course of learning, the network learns both how to assign useful representations and how to use these representations to generate appropriate responses. That is, it learns a set of input-to-representation weights that allow each concept to activate a useful internal representation, and it learns a set of weights in the rest of the network that allows these representations to produce the correct output, conditional on this representation and the relation input. Note that there is no direct specification of the representations that the network should assign; the representations—and the connection weights that produce them—arise as a result of the action of the learning procedure.

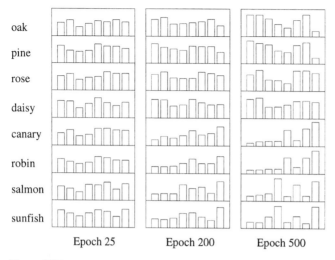

oak

pine

rose

daisy

canary

robin

salmon

sunfish

Epoch 25   Epoch 200   Epoch 500

Figure 17.5

Representations discovered in our replication of Rumelhart's (1990) learning experiment (with the network shown in Figure 17.4). Vertical bars indicate the activation of each of the eight concept representation units produced by activating the input unit for each of the eight specific concepts. The height of each vertical bar indicates the activation of the corresponding unit on a scale from 0 to 1. One can see that initially all of the concepts have fairly similar representations. After 200 epochs, there is a clear differentiation of the representations of the plants and animals, but the trees and flowers are still quite similar, as are the birds and the fish. After 500 epochs, the further differentiation of the plants into trees and flowers and of the animals into fish and birds is apparent.

We repeated Rumelhart's (1990) simulations, training the network for a total of 500 epochs (sweeps through the training set) using the gradient descent learning procedure.[3] The representations at different points in training are shown in Figure 17.5. These are simply the patterns of activation over the representation units that arise when the input unit corresponding to each of the eight specific concepts is activated. The arrangement and grouping of the representations, shown in Figure 17.6, reflect the similarity structure among these patterns, as determined by a hierarchical clustering analysis using Euclidian distance as the measure of similarity of two patterns. At an early point in learning (Epoch 25), the analysis reveals an essentially random similarity structure, illustrating that at first the representations do not reflect the structure of the domain (e.g., *oak* is grouped with *canary*, indicating that the representation of *oak* is more similar at this point to *canary* than it is to *pine*). At later points in training, however, the similarity structure begins to emerge. At Epoch 500, the complete hierarchical structure is apparent: The two trees (*oak* and *pine*) are more similar to each other than either is to any other concept, and the representations of the two flowers, the two birds, and the two fish are more similar to each other than either member of any of these pairs is to the representation of

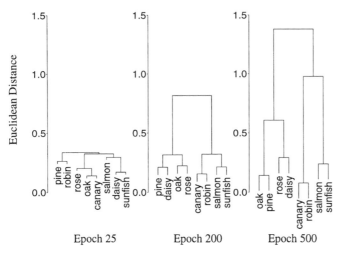

Figure 17.6
Similarity structure discovered in our replication of Rumelhart's (1990) learning experiment (with the representations shown in Figure 17.5). These analyses make the similarity relationships among the patterns shown in Figure 17.5 explicit. The clustering algorithm recursively links a pattern or previously formed group of patterns to another pattern or previously formed group. The process begins with the formation of a group consisting of the pair that is most similar. The elements combined are then replaced by the resulting group, and the process continues until everything has been joined into a single superordinate group. Similarity is measured by the Euclidean distance metric (sum of the squared differences between the activations of the corresponding elements in the two patterns). The height of the point where a subtree branches indicates the Euclidean distance of the elements joined at that branch point.

any other concept. Furthermore, the representations of the trees are more similar to the representations of the flowers than they are to the representations of any of the animals, and the representations of the birds are more similar to the representations of the fish than they are to the representations of any of the plants. Examination of the clustering of the representations at Epoch 200 shows that the network has, by this point, learned only the coarser distinction between plants and animals, because at this point the plants and animals are well differentiated but the differences within the plants and animals are very small and not yet completely systematic with respect to subtype. For example, *pine* is grouped with *daisy* rather than *oak*. Thus, it can be seen that the network exhibits a progressive differentiation of concepts, progressing from coarser to finer conceptual distinctions through the course of learning.

The similarity structure shown in Figure 17.6—for example, the fact that *oak* and *pine* are similar to each other but quite different from *canary* and *robin*— arises not because of intrinsic similarity among the inputs but because of similarity among the responses the network must learn to make when the various concepts are presented with the same relation term. The connections in the rest of the network exploit these similarities, so that what the network has learned about one concept tends to transfer to other concepts that use similar representations. We can illustrate this by examining what happens if, after training on the material already described, a new concept is added such as *sparrow*, and the network is taught only the correct response to the *sparrow isa* input, interleaving this example with the rest of the training corpus (Rumelhart, 1990, performed a very similar experiment). Through this further training, the network assigns a representation to *sparrow* that is similar to the representations for *robin* and *canary*. This allows correct performance, because such a representation is already associated with the correct output for the *isa* relation term. This representation is also already associated with the correct responses to be made when it is active in conjunction with the other relation terms. Therefore, the network will respond appropriately when the other relation terms are paired with *sparrow*, even though it has never been trained on these cases. In fact, the network correctly sets the activity of all those outputs on which *canary* and *sparrow* agree; when they disagree, it produces compromise activations reflecting the conflicting votes of the two known bird concepts.

Catastrophic Interference

The achievements of interleaved learning systems that we have just reviewed do not mean that such systems are appropriate for all forms of learning. Indeed, it appears that they are not at all appropriate for the rapid acquisition of arbitrary associations between inputs and responses, as is required, for example, in paired-associates learning experiments (e.g., Barnes & Underwood, 1959). When used in such tasks, connectionist systems like the one considered earlier exhibit a phenomenon McCloskey and Cohen (1989) termed *catastrophic interference*. Essentially the same point was also made independently by Ratcliff (1990).

To illustrate catastrophic interference, McCloskey and Cohen (1989) used a connectionist network slightly simpler than the one used by Rumelhart (1990). They were particularly interested in a paradigm called the *AB–AC* paradigm, which is commonly used to study the retroactive interference of one set of associations (*AC*) on recall of a set of associations previously acquired (*AB*). Here *AB* stands for a list of stimulus–response pairs of words (e.g., *locomotive–dishtowel*, *table–street*, and *carpet–idea*), and *AC* stands for a second such list involving the same stimulus words now paired with different responses (e.g., *locomotive–banana*, *table–basket*, and *carpet–pencil*). In such experiments, participants are repeatedly exposed to all of the items in a particular list. On each trial, they receive one *A* item, and the task is to produce the corresponding item on the list currently under study; the correct answer is given as feedback after each recall attempt. This is repeated for the *AB* list until performance reaches a strict criterion, and then the participant is switched to the *AC* list. At different

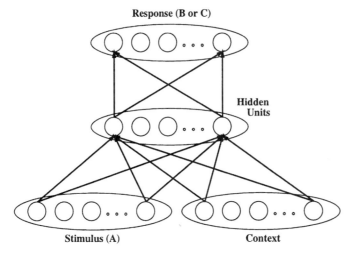

Figure 17.7
Our depiction of the network used by McCloskey and Cohen (1989) to demonstrate catastrophic interference in the back-propagation networks. All output units receive connections from all hidden units, and all hidden units receive inputs from both sets of input units.

points in the series of exposures to the *AC* list, the participant is asked to try to recall the *B* members of each pair, thereby providing an opportunity to examine the extent of interference of *AC* learning on recovery of the *AB* associations.

McCloskey and Cohen's (1989) network provided for a two-part input, as in Rumelhart's (1990) network (Figure 17.7). One subset of the input units was reserved for representing each *A* term, and a second subset was used to represent what is called the list context, essentially an arbitrary pattern indicating whether the items to be recalled are the *B* items or the *C* items. As in the experiment, they trained a network first on the *AB* list and then shifted to *AC* training, testing *AB* performance at different points along the way. The results are shown in Figure 17.8b and compared with typical human results in Figure 17.8a. The pattern McCloskey and Cohen termed catastrophic interference is evident in the network's performance. Whereas humans show a gradual loss of ability to retrieve the *AB* list and are still capable of operating more than 50% correct recall after the *AC* list performance has reached asymptote, the network shows virtually complete abolition of *AB* list performance before *AC* performance rises above 0% correct.

One possible response to this state of affairs might be to try to find ways of avoiding catastrophic interference in multilayer networks. In fact, several investigators have demonstrated ways of reducing the magnitude of interference in tasks like those studied by McCloskey and Cohen (1989; French, 1991, 1992; Hetherington & Seidenberg, 1989; Kortge, 1993; McRae & Hetherington,

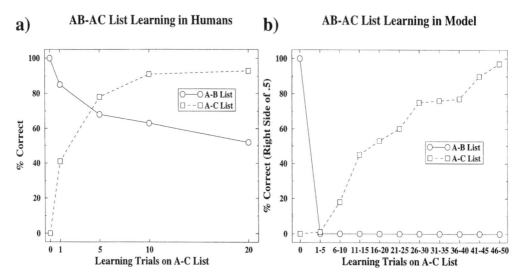

Figure 17.8
Panel a: Experimental data showing mild interference in humans in the AB–AC paradigm (Barnes & Underwood, 1959). Panel b: Simulation results demonstrating catastrophic interference (McCloskey & Cohen, 1989).

1993; Sloman & Rumelhart, 1992). Many of these proposals amount to finding ways of reducing overlap of the patterns that are to be associated with appropriate responses via connection weight adjustment. One might then be tempted to suggest that McCloskey and Cohen simply used the wrong kind of representation and that the problem could be eliminated by using sparser patterns of activation with less overlap. However, as French (1991) has noted, reducing overlap avoids catastrophic interference at the cost of a dramatic reduction in the exploitation of shared structure. In connectionist systems, what one learns about something is stored in the connection weights among the units activated in representing it. That knowledge can be shared or generalized to other related things only if the patterns that represent these other things overlap (Hinton, McClelland, & Rumelhart, 1986).

One could pursue the matter further, looking for ways of preserving as much of the ability to extract shared structure as possible while minimizing the problem of catastrophic interference. However, the existence of hippocampal amnesia, together with the sketch given earlier of the possible role of the hippocampal system in learning and memory, suggests instead that one might use the success of Rumelhart's (1990) simulation, together with the failure of McCloskey and Cohen's (1989), as the basis for understanding why there is a separate learning system in the hippocampus and why knowledge originally stored in this system is incorporated in the neocortex only gradually.

Incorporating New Material Into a Structured System of Knowledge Through
Interleaved Learning

To begin to address this issue, we consider the incorporation of new knowledge into a structured system. McCloskey and Cohen's (1989) simulation does not relate to structured knowledge, because the associations being learned are arbitrary paired associates arbitrarily grouped into lists. This issue can be explored, however, in the context of the semantic network simulation. We show later that attempts to acquire new knowledge all at once can lead to strong interference with aspects of what is already known. But we also show that this interference can be dramatically reduced if new information is added gradually, interleaved with ongoing exposure to other examples from the same domain of knowledge.

We illustrate these points by examining what happens if Rumelhart's (1990) network is taught some new facts that are inconsistent with the existing knowledge in the system: The facts in question are that penguins are birds, but they can swim and cannot fly. We consider two cases. The first one we call *focused learning*, in which the new knowledge is presented to the system repeatedly without interleaving it with continued exposure to the rest of the database about plants and animals. We compare this with *interleaved learning*, in which the new information about penguins is simply added to the training set so that it is interleaved with continued exposure to the full database. We use the same learning rate parameter in the two cases. It can be seen that, with focused learning, the network learns the material about penguins much more rapidly than in the case of interleaved learning (Figure 17.9a). In Figure 17.9, we use a measure called the absolute error, which reflects the mismatch between the network's output and the correct response. The absolute error is the sum, across all output units, of the absolute value of the difference between the correct activation and the obtained activation. The axis is inverted so that the upward direction represents better performance, and it is apparent that learning proceeds more rapidly in the focused case. However, as one teaches the network this new information, one can continue to test it on the knowledge it had previously acquired about other concepts. What is seen is a deleterious effect of the new learning on the network's performance with other concepts (Figure 17.9b). The measure is the average absolute error over all of the cases in which any concept (including a subordinate concept such as *robin* or *pine* or a superordinate concept such as *bird* or *animal*) is paired with the relation *can*. What happens is that, as the network learns that the penguin is a bird that can swim but not fly, it comes to treat all animals—and, to a lesser extent, all plants—as having these same characteristics. In the case of the fish, the effect is actually to improve performance slightly, because the penguin can do all of the same things the fish can do. In the case of the birds, of course, the effect is to worsen performance a great deal, specifically on the output units that differ between the birds and the penguin. The interference is not quite as catastrophic as in the

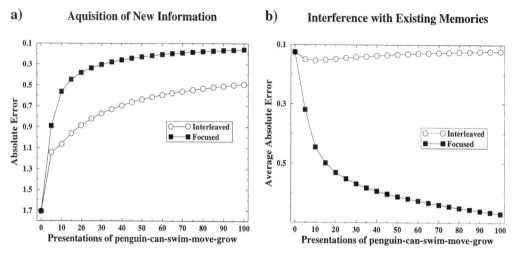

Figure 17.9
Effects of focused learning on the acquisition of new knowledge and on interference with existing
knowledge. Simulations were carried out with Rumelhart's (1990) network; the connection weights
resulting from the initial 500 epochs of training with the base corpus were used. This performance
measure, absolute error, is defined as the sum across output units of the absolute value of the difference between the correct response for each pattern and the actual response. The measure reaches
its optimal value of 0 when the output exactly matches the target. Better performance corresponds
to lower error, and the axis is inverted for better visual correspondence to standard memory performance curves. In the analysis of interference with other memories, the performance measure is
the average of the absolute error over all 15 of the cases in the initial training corpus involving the
"can" relation. The scales of each graph are different and are set to encompass the range of values
spanned in each case. The interference is much greater for some items than for others and falls
predominantly on those output units in which the correct answer for the preexisting memory differs
from the correct answer for the new information.

McCloskey–Cohen (1989) simulation, but it is far greater than what is seen with
interleaved learning.

With interleaved learning, incorporation of knowledge that penguins can
swim but not fly is very gradual, in two ways. First, the process is extended
simply because of the interleaving with continued exposure to the rest of the
corpus; second, the rate of progress per exposure, as shown in Figure 17.9, is
slowed down. However, this procedure has a great benefit: It results in very
little interference. Eventually, with enough practice, the network can in fact
learn to activate strongly the correct output for the input *penguin–can*, and it
learns to do so without ever producing more than a slight hint of interference
with what it already knows about other concepts. This is because the interleaved learning allows the network to carve out a place for the penguin,
adjusting its representation of other similar concepts and adjusting its connection weights to incorporate the penguin into its structured knowledge system.

We argue later that these effects are not just idiosyncratic characteristics of back-propagation networks but apply broadly to systems that learn by adjusting connection weights based on experience. Dramatic confirmation of catastrophic effects of focused learning in real brains—and of the benefits of interleaved learning—can be found in the recent work of M. M. Merzenich (personal communication, January 18, 1995). He found that highly repetitive sensory–motor tasks corresponding to focused learning lead to severe loss of differentiation of the relevant regions of sensory cortex: Practice produces a dramatic reduction in the diversity of responses of the neurons in these regions. This loss of differentiation was accompanied by a clinical syndrome called *focal dystonia*, which is a breakdown of sensory–motor coordination of the affected limb. This syndrome can be corrected in both monkeys and humans by physical therapy regimens that involve interleaved practice on a battery of different exercises.

The observation that interleaved learning allows new knowledge to be gradually incorporated into a structured system lies at the heart of our proposals concerning the role of the hippocampus in learning and memory. We see this gradual incorporation process as reflecting what goes on in the neocortex during consolidation. This view is quite close to the view of the consolidation process as it was envisioned by Squire, Cohen, and Nadel (1984):

> It would be simplistic to suggest that any simple biological change is responsible for consolidation lasting as long as several years, as indicated by the data from retrograde amnesia. Rather, this time period, during which the medial temporal region maintains its importance, is filled with external events (such as repetition and activities related to original learning) and internal processes (such as rehearsal and reconstruction). These influence the fate of as-yet unconsolidated information through remodeling the neural circuitry underlying the original representation. (p. 205)

Three Principles of Connectionist Learning

The simulations presented earlier suggest three principles of learning in connectionist systems.

> 1. The discovery of a set of connection weights that captures the structure of a domain and places specific facts within that structure occurs from a gradual, interleaved learning process.
> 2. Attempts to learn new information rapidly in a network that has previously learned a subset of some domain lead to catastrophic interference.
> 3. Incorporation of new material without interference can occur if new material is incorporated gradually, interleaved with ongoing exposure to examples of the domain embodying the content already learned.

Answers to the Key Questions

These principles allow us to formulate answers to the key questions about the organization of memory raised earlier.

> 1. Why is a hippocampal system necessary, if ultimately performance in all sorts of memory tasks depends on changes in connections within the neocortical system? Why are the changes not made directly in the neocortical system in the first place?

The principles indicate that the hippocampus is there to provide a medium for the initial storage of memories in a form that avoids interference with the knowledge already acquired in the neocortical system.

> 2. Why does incorporation of new material into the neocortical system take such a long time? Why are the changes to neocortical connections not made more rapidly, shortly after initial storage in the hippocampal system?

Incorporation takes a long time to allow new knowledge to be interleaved with ongoing exposure to exemplars of the existing knowledge structure, so that eventually the new knowledge may be incorporated into the structured system already contained in the neocortex. If the changes were made rapidly, they would interfere with the system of structured knowledge built up from prior experience with other related material.

Generality of the Relation Between Discovery of Shared Structure and Gradual, Interleaved Learning

Thus far, we have used a very specific example to consider discovery of shared structure through interleaved learning and catastrophic interference in focused learning. We selected this example to provide a concrete context in which to make these points and to illustrate as clearly as possible how much is at stake: Our claim is that experience can give rise to the gradual discovery of structure through interleaved learning but not through focused learning and that this gradual discovery process lies at the heart of cognitive, linguistic, and perceptual development.

In this section, we examine the issues more generally. We first consider what it means to discover the structure present in a set of inputs and experiences. Then we consider general reasons why the extraction of structure present in an ensemble of events or experiences requires slow learning. To conclude the section, we discuss the process of discovering structure in biologically realistic systems.

What Is Structure?

Throughout this article, we discuss the structure present in ensembles of events. What we mean by the term *structure* is any systematic relationship that exists within or between the events that, if discovered, could then serve as a basis for efficient representation of novel events or for appropriate responses to novel inputs. Marr (1970) noted that events almost never repeat themselves exactly, yet people do learn from past experience to respond appropriately to new experiences. If there is no structure—no systematicity in the relationship between inputs and appropriate responses—then, of course, there will be no basis for responding appropriately to novel inputs. But if a systematic relationship does exist between inputs and appropriate responses, and if the organism has discovered that relationship, then appropriate responding may be possible.

We can begin to make this point explicit by continuing within the domain of concepts about living things. In the Rumelhart (1990) model, the structure is the set of constraints that exist on the correct completions of propositions, given a concept and a relation term. For example, if something is a bird, then it has wings and it can fly. In a symbolic framework, such constraints are captured by storing propositions that apply to entire subtrees just once at the top of the subtree; similarity relations among concepts are captured by placing them in neighboring locations in the tree. In the connectionist framework, such constraints are captured in the connection weights, and the similarity relations among concepts are captured by using the weights to assign similar distributed representations. The patterns involving the concept *sparrow* conform, by and large, to the constraints embodied in the patterns involving the concepts for *robin* and *canary*; therefore, once *sparrow* is assigned a representation similar to the representations of *robin* and *canary*, appropriate representation and completion of propositions involving *sparrow* are possible.

In other domains, different kinds of structure can be found. For example, the English spelling system provides a notation that has a quasi-structured relation to the sound of English words. Once one has learned this structure from examples of existing words (including, for example, *save, wave, cave,* and *slave*), one can generalize correctly to novel forms (such as *mave*). As a third example of structure, consider redundancies present in visual patterns. Neighboring points tend to have similar depth, orientation, and reflectance properties; such sets of neighboring points define surfaces of objects. Similarly, if there is a discontinuity between two adjacent points in the pattern, the same discontinuity will tend to exist between other pairs of adjacent points close by; such sets of neighboring discontinuities define edges. The surfaces and edges constitute structure, and, given that the objects in images contain surfaces bordered by edges, it is efficient to represent images in terms of the properties and locations of the surfaces and edges. Such representations can be very efficient and can allow for completion of occluded portions of novel visual patterns.

Finally, an abstract but general example of structure is any correlation that may exist between particular pairs or larger sets of elements in a set of patterns. Such correlations, if discovered, could then be used to infer the value of one member of the set of elements from the values of the other members when a novel but incomplete pattern is presented. Furthermore, the presence of these correlations means that the patterns are partially redundant. This, in turn, means that one can represent patterns that exhibit these correlations by storing a single value for each correlated set of elements rather than the elements themselves, as is done in principal-components analysis.

Why Discovering Structure Depends on Slow Learning
Now that we have defined what we mean by structure, we are in a position to consider general reasons why the discovery of structure depends on gradual, interleaved learning. The reasons we consider are largely independent of specifics of the network organization, the training environment, or even the learning algorithm used. The first reason applies generally to procedures with the following characteristics:

> 1. The procedure is applied to a sequence of experiences, each representing a sample from an environment that can be thought of as a distribution or population of possible experiences.
> 2. The goal of learning is to derive a parameterized characterization of the environment that generated the sequence of samples rather than to store the samples themselves.
> 3. What is stored as a result of applying the procedure is not the examples, but only the parameterized characterization. As each new example is experienced, the parameterized characterization is adjusted, and that is the only residue of the example.
> 4. The adjustment process consists of a procedure that improves some measure of the adequacy of the parameterized characterization, as estimated from the data provided by the current training case.

We might call procedures with these characteristics stochastic, on-line, parameter updating procedures, but we call them simply *stochastic learning procedures* to emphasize their relation to the question of learning and memory. In such procedures, gradual learning is important if the parameterized characterization is to accurately capture the structure of the population of possible training examples.

Combining the Hippocampal and the Neocortical Learning Systems

We have shown how it is possible, using interleaved learning, to gradually discover the structure present in ensembles of events and experiences and to integrate new knowledge into the connection weights in a system without producing interference with what that system already knows. The problem is that acquiring new information in this way is very slow, and, if the cortical system works like the systems we have discussed, it would obviously be insufficient for meeting the demands of everyday life, in which information must often be acquired and retained on the basis of a single exposure. Our argument is that the hippocampus and related structures exist precisely to allow retention of the contents of specific episodes and events while avoiding interference with the structured knowledge held in the neocortex. As we have already reviewed, these structures are crucial for the rapid formation of memory traces for the contents of specific episodes and events.

Once a memory is stored in the hippocampal system, it can be reactivated and then reinstated in the neocortex. Such reinstatements will have two important consequences. First, reinstatement of the stored event in appropriate contexts would allow the reinstated pattern to be used for controlling behavioral responses (e.g., uttering the name of the person in front of one, when one has previously stored that name in association with the face). Second, reinstatement provides the opportunity for an incremental adjustment of neocortical connections, thereby allowing memories initially dependent on the hippocampal system to gradually become independent of it.

Experimental studies of consolidation generally use relatively arbitrary pairings of stimuli with other stimuli or responses, or both. For example, the experiment of Zola-Morgan and Squire (1990) discussed later required animals to learn totally arbitrary associations between food pellets and junk objects. It appears that consolidation of such arbitrary material occurs through the same process of gradual incorporation into the neocortical structures that is used for learning more structured material. As previously discussed, consolidation of arbitrary material allows efficient representation, and even experiences that have arbitrary elements generally share some structure with many other experiences that gradual consolidation will allow the system to exploit.

A key question arises as to the source of reinstatements of exemplars drawn from the existing knowledge structure, because their interleaving with new knowledge is crucial for the prevention of catastrophic interference. There are several (nonexclusive) possibilities, including direct reinstatement from the external environment and reactivation in the course of cognitive activity or reminiscence. In addition, spontaneous reactivation in the absence of external input may be possible. As discussed in an earlier section, multiple single-neuron recording in the hippocampus suggests such spontaneous reactivation during slow wave sleep (Wilson & McNaughton, 1994), and a similar process of reinstatement could apply to patterns arising from the structured knowledge in the neocortical system. Possibly, events reactivated in the hippocampus during slow wave sleep prime related neocortical patterns, so that these in turn become available for activation during REM sleep. This could permit both new and old information to be played back in closely interleaved fashion.

General Discussion

We have presented an account of the complementary roles of the hippocampal and neocortical systems in learning and memory, and we have studied the properties of computational models of learning and memory that provide a basis for understanding why the memory system may be organized in this way. We have illustrated through simple simulations how we see performance and consolidation arising from the joint contributions of the hippocampal system and the neocortical system.

We have treated the phenomenon of consolidation as a reflection of the gradual incorporation of new knowledge into representational systems located primarily in the neocortical regions of the brain. Our proposal has its roots in the work of Marr (1970, 1971) and Squire et al. (1984), but we have given it a clearer computational motivation than these earlier investigators, and we have pointed to computational mechanisms that indicate how the incorporation of new knowledge can gradually cause the structure itself to adapt. Nevertheless, our analysis is far from complete, and many details of the implementation and physiological realization of the complementary learning systems we have proposed remain obscure. Our analysis may address the two key questions we have posed in this article, but in so doing it raises many new ones. Answering these questions will depend on the emerging synthesis of computational, behavioral, and neurophysiological investigation.

Notes

James L. McClelland and Randall C. O'Reilly, Department of Psychology, Carnegie Mellon University, and the Center for the Neural Basis of Cognition; Bruce L. McNaughton, Departments of Psychology and Physiology and Arizona Research Laboratories, Division of Neural Systems, Memory and Aging, University of Arizona.

The work reported herein was supported by National Institute of Mental Health Grants MH00385, MH47566, and MH46823; by a collaborative grant from the Human Frontiers Program; by a Center Grant from the McDonnell-Pew Program in Cognitive Neuroscience; and by a fellowship from the Office of Naval Research.

We thank Carol Barnes, Sue Becker, Marlene Behrmann, Loren Frank, Mark Gluck, Robert French, Patrick Lynn, Mort Mishkin, Catherine Myers, David Plaut, William Skaggs, Craig Stark, Robert Sutherland, Larry Squire, and Matthew Wilson for useful discussions or comments on earlier versions of this article. Lynn Nadel's contributions to the initial formulation of some of these ideas and to several revisions of the article were extensive and are gratefully acknowledged.

The computational arguments developed here were sketched in a Society for Neurosciences abstract (McClelland, McNaughton, O'Reilly, & Nadel, 1992) and an invited review of several projects involving James L. McClelland that referred to the present article as a work in progress (McClelland, 1994). Preliminary versions of the simulations of retrograde amnesia in rats and monkeys were previously presented in a Psychonomic Society abstract (McClelland, McNaughton, & O'Reilly, 1993).

1. Jarrard (1993) treated the fact that Davidson, McKernan, and Jarrard (1993) found no effect of a lesion selective to the hippocampus per se in negative patterning as evidence against a role of the hippocampus in configural learning, but Rudy and Sutherland (1994) cited a total of six studies finding that selective hippocampal lesions lead to a deficit in negative patterning. Several of these studies used the ibotenate lesion of Jarrard (1989). Clearly, the debate is not yet settled. Further discussion of the relationship between spatial and configural approaches may be found in the General Discussion section.

2. In general, one expects adjustments of connection weights to produce a general facilitation of retrieval of the overall pattern through changes that occur among the neurons active in the

retrieved pattern itself, as well as a more specific facilitation of retrieval from the same cue as a result of changes that occur between the neurons representing the retrieved pattern and those representing the cue.

3. All of the simulation results reported here were fresh runs of the Rumelhart (1990) model that we carried out using the **bp** program of McClelland and Rumelhart (1988). We thank Rumelhart for supplying the pattern files used in his earlier simulations. Weights were initialized with values distributed uniformly between $-.5$ and $.5$ and were updated after every pattern presentation with no momentum. The learning rate parameter ε was set to 0.1. Targets for learning were .95 for units that should be "on" and .05 for units that should be "off."

References

Ackley, D. H., Hinton, G. E., & Sejnowski, T. J. (1985). A learning algorithm for Boltzmann machines. *Cognitive Science, 9,* 147–169.

Barnes, C. A. (1988). Spatial learning and memory processes: The search for their neurobiological mechanisms in the rat. *Trends in Neurosciences, 11,* 163–169.

Barnes, C. A., Jung, M. W., McNaughton, B. L., Korol, D. L., Andreasson, K., & Worley, P. F. (1994). LTP saturation and spatial learning disruption: Effects of task variables and saturation levels. *Journal of Neuroscience, 14,* 5793–5806.

Barnes, J. M., & Underwood, B. J. (1959). Fate of first-list associations in transfer theory. *Journal of Experimental Psychology, 58,* 97–105.

Bowers, J. S., & Schacter, D. L. (1993). Implicit memory and test awareness. *Journal of Experimental Psychology: Learning, Memory, and Cognition, 16,* 404–416.

Cleeremans, A. (1993). *Mechanisms of implicit learning: Connectionist models of sequence processing.* Cambridge, MA: MIT Press.

Cohen, N. J., & Eichenbaum, H. (1993). *Memory, amnesia, and the hippocampal system.* Cambridge, MA: MIT Press.

Cohen, N. J., & Squire, L. R. (1980). Preserved learning and retention of pattern analyzing skill in amnesia: Dissociation of knowing how and knowing that. *Science, 210,* 207–209.

Collins, A. M., & Quillian, M. R. (1969). Retrieval time from semantic memory. *Journal of Verbal Learning and Verbal Behavior, 8,* 240–247.

Cottrell, G. W., Munro, P., & Zipser, D. (1987). Learning internal representations from gray-scale images: An example of extensional programming. In *Proceedings of the 9th Annual Conference of the Cognitive Science Society* (pp. 462–473). Hillsdale, NJ: Erlbaum.

Davidson, T. L., McKernan, M. G., & Jarrard, L. E. (1993). Hippocampal lesions do not impair negative patterning: A challenge to configural association theory. *Behavioral Neuroscience, 107,* 227–234.

Eichenbaum, H., Otto, T., & Cohen, N. (1994). Two functional components of the hippocampal memory system. *Behavioral and Brain Sciences, 17,* 449–518.

Fahlman, S. E. (1981). Representing implicit knowledge. In G. E. Hinton & J. A. Anderson (Eds.), *Parallel models of associative memory* (pp. 145–159). Hillsdale, NJ: Erlbaum.

French, R. M. (1991). Using semi-distributed representations to overcome catastrophic forgetting in connectionist networks. In *Proceedings of the 13th Annual Cognitive Science Conference* (pp. 173–178). Hillsdale, NJ: Erlbaum.

French, R. M. (1992). Semi-distributed representations and catastrophic forgetting in connectionist networks. *Connection Science, 4,* 365–377.

Glisky, E. L., Schacter, D. L., & Tulving, E. (1986a). Computer learning by memory-impaired patients: Acquisition and retention of complex knowledge. *Neuropsychologia, 24,* 313–328.

Glisky, E. L., Schacter, D. L., & Tulving, E. (1986b). Learning and retention of computer-related vocabulary in memory-impaired patients: Method of vanishing cues. *Journal of Clinical and Experimental Neuropsychology, 8,* 292–312.

Graf, P., & Schacter, D. L. (1987). Selective effects of interference on implicit and explicit memory for new associations. *Journal of Experimental Psychology: Learning, Memory, and Cognition, 13,* 45–53.

Graf, P., Squire, L. R., & Mandler, G. (1984). The information that amnesic patients do not forget. *Journal of Experimental Psychology: Learning, Memory, and Cognition, 10,* 164–178.

Haist, F., Musen, G., & Squire, L. R. (1991). Intact priming of words and nonwords in amnesia. *Psychobiology, 19,* 275–285.

Hetherington, P. A., & Seidenberg, M. S. (1989). Is there 'catastrophic interference' in connectionist networks? In *Proceedings of the 11th Annual Conference of the Cognitive Science Society* (pp. 26–33). Hillsdale, NJ: Erlbaum.

Hinton, G. E. (1981). Implementing semantic networks in parallel hardware. In G. E. Hinton & J. A. Anderson (Eds.), *Parallel models of associative memory* (pp. 161–187). Hillsdale, NJ: Erlbaum.

Hinton, G. E. (1989). Learning distributed representations of concepts. In R. G. M. Morris (Ed.), *Parallel distributed processing: Implications for psychology and neurobiology* (pp. 46–61). Oxford, England: Clarendon Press.

Hinton, G. E., McClelland, J. L., & Rumelhart, D. E. (1986). Distributed representations. In D. E. Rumelhart & J. L. McClelland (Eds.), *Parallel distributed processing: Explorations in the microstructure of cognition* (Vol. 1, pp. 77–109). Cambridge, MA: MIT Press.

Jarrard, L. E. (1989). On the use of ibotenic acid to lesion selectively different components of the hippocampal formation. *Journal of Neuroscience Methods, 29,* 251–259.

Jarrard, L. E. (1993). On the role of the hippocampus in learning and memory in the rat. *Behavioral and Neural Biology, 60,* 9–26.

Kim, J. J., & Fanselow, M. S. (1992). Modality-specific retrograde amnesia of fear. *Science, 256,* 675–677.

Knapp, A., & Anderson, J. A. (1984). A signal averaging model for concept formation. *Journal of Experimental Psychology: Learning, Memory, and Cognition, 10,* 617–637.

Knowlton, B. J., Ramus, S. J., & Squire, L. R. (1992). Intact artificial grammar learning in amnesia: Dissociation of classification learning and explicit memory for specific instances. *Psychological Science, 3,* 172–179.

Knowlton, B. J., & Squire, L. R. (1993). The learning of categories: Parallel brain systems for item memory and category knowledge. *Science, 262,* 1747–1749.

Kohonen, T. (1984). *Self-organization and associative memory.* Berlin: Springer-Verlag.

Kortge, C. A. (1993). Episodic memory in connectionist networks. In *Proceedings of the Twelfth Annual Conference of the Cognitive Science Society* (pp. 764–771). Hillsdale, NJ: Erlbaum.

Marr, D. (1970). A theory for cerebral neocortex. *Proceedings of the Royal Society of London, Series B, 176,* 161–234.

Marr, D. (1971). Simple memory: A theory for archicortex. *Philosophical Transactions of the Royal Society of London, Series B, 262,* 23–81.

McClelland, J. L. (1994). The organization of memory: A parallel distributed processing perspective. *Revue Neurologique, 150,* 570–579.

McClelland, J. L., McNaughton, B. L., & O'Reilly, R. C. (1993). Why do we have a special learning system in the hippocampus? (Abstract 580). *Bulletin of the Psychonomic Society, 31,* 404.

McClelland, J. L., McNaughton, B. L., & O'Reilly, R. C., & Nadel, L. (1992). Complementary roles of hippocampus and neocortex in learning and memory. *Society for Neuroscience Abstracts, 18,* 1216.

McClelland, J. L., & Rumelhart, D. E. (1985). Distributed memory and the representation of general and specific information. *Journal of Experimental Psychology: General, 114,* 159–188.

McClelland, J. L., & Rumelhart, D. E. (1988). *Explorations in parallel distributed processing: A handbook of models, programs, and exercises.* Cambridge, MA: MIT Press.

McCloskey, M., & Cohen, N. J. (1989). Catastrophic interference in connectionist networks: The sequential learning problem. In G. H. Bower (Ed.), *The psychology of learning and motivation* (Vol. 24, pp. 109–165). New York: Academic Press.

McNaughton, B. L. (1989). The neurobiology of spatial computation and learning. In D. J. Stein (Ed.), *Lectures on complexity, Santa Fe Institute studies in the sciences of complexity* (pp. 389–437). Redwood, CA: Addison-Wesley.

McNaughton, B. L., Leonard, B., & Chen, L. (1989). Cortical-hippocampal interactions and cognitive mapping: A hypothesis based on reintegration of the parietal and inferotemporal pathways for visual processing. *Psychobiology, 17*, 230–235.

McRae, K., & Hetherington, P. A. (1993). Catastrophic interference is eliminated in pretrained networks. In *Proceedings of the Fifteenth Annual Conference of the Cognitive Science Society* (pp. 723–728). Hillsdale, NJ: Erlbaum.

Milner, B. (1966). Amnesia following operation on the temporal lobe. In C. W. M. Whitty & O. L. Zangwill (Eds.), *Amnesia* (pp. 109–133). London: Butterworth.

Milner, B., Corkin, S., & Teuber, H.-L. (1968). Further analysis of the hippocampal amnesia syndrome: 14-year follow-up study of H. M. *Neuropsychologia, 6*, 215–234.

O'Keefe, J., & Nadel, L. (1978). *The hippocampus as a cognitive map*. Oxford, England: Clarendon Press.

Quillian, M. R. (1968). Semantic memory. In M. Minsky (Ed.), *Semantic information processing*. Cambridge, MA: MIT Press.

Ribot, T. (1882). *Diseases of memory*. New York: Appleton-Century-Crofts.

Rips, L. J., Shoben, E. J., & Smith, E. E. (1973). Semantic distance and the verification of semantic relations. *Journal of Verbal Learning and Verbal Behavior, 12*, 1–20.

Rudy, J. W., & Sutherland, R. W. (1989). The hippocampal formation is necessary for rats to learn and remember configural discriminations. *Behavioral Brain Research, 34*, 97–109.

Rudy, J. W., & Sutherland, R. W. (1994). *Configural association theory and the hippocampal formation: An appraisal and reconfiguration*. Unpublished manuscript.

Rumelhart, D. E. (1990). Brain style computation: Learning and generalization. In S. F. Zornetzer, J. L. Davis, & C. Lau (Eds.), *An introduction to neural and electronic networks* (pp. 405–420). San Diego, CA: Academic Press.

Rumelhart, D. E., & Todd, P. M. (1993). Learning and connectionist representations. In D. E. Meyer & S. Kornblum (Eds.), *Attention and performance XIV: Synergies in experimental psychology, artificial intelligence and cognitive neuroscience* (pp. 3–30). Cambridge, MA: MIT Press.

Schacter, D. L. (1987). Implicit memory: History and current status. *Journal of Experimental Psychology: Learning, Memory, and Cognition, 13*, 501–518.

Schacter, D. L., & Graf, P. (1986). Preserved learning in amnesic patients: Perspectives from research on direct priming. *Journal of Clinical and Experimental Neuropsychology, 6*, 727–743.

Schacter, D. L., & Graf, P. (1989). Modality specificity of implicit memory for new associations. *Journal of Experimental Psychology: Learning, Memory, and Cognition, 15*, 3–21.

Scoville, W. B., & Milner, B. (1957). Loss of recent memory after bilateral hippocampal lesions. *Journal of Neurology, Neurosurgery, and Psychiatry, 20*, 11–21.

Shimamura, A. P., & Squire, L. R. (1987). A neuropsychological study of fact memory and source amnesia. *Journal of Experimental Psychology: Learning, Memory, and Cognition, 13*, 464–473.

Sloman, S. A., & Rumelhart, D. E. (1992). Reducing interference in distributed memories through episodic gating. In A. Healy, S. Kosslyn, & R. Shiffrin (Eds.), *Essays in honor of W. K. Estes* (Vol. 1, pp. 227–248). Hillsdale, NJ: Erlbaum.

Squire, L. R. (1992). Memory and the hippocampus: A synthesis from findings with rats, monkeys, and humans. *Psychological Review, 99*, 195–231.

Squire, L. R., & Cohen, N. (1979). Memory and amnesia: Resistance to disruption develops for years after learning. *Behavioral and Neural Biology, 25*, 115–125.

Squire, L. R., Cohen, N. J., & Nadel, L. (1984). The medial temporal region and memory consolidation: A new hypothesis. In H. Weingartner & E. Parker (Eds.), *Memory consolidation* (pp. 185–210). Hillsdale, NJ: Erlbaum.

Squire, L. R., & Slater, P. C. (1975). Forgetting in very long-term memory as assessed by an improved questionnaire technique. *Journal of Experimental Psychology: Human Learning and Memory, 104,* 50–54.

Stewart, C., & Reid, I. C. (1993). Electroconvulsive stimulation and synaptic plasticity in the rat. *Brain Research, 620,* 139–141.

Sutherland, R. W., & Rudy, J. W. (1989). Configural association theory: The role of the hippocampal formation in learning, memory and amnesia. *Psychobiology, 17,* 129–144.

Touretzky, D. S., & Geva, S. (1987). A distributed connectionist representation for concept structures. In *Proceedings of the 9th Annual Conference of the Cognitive Science Society* (pp. 155–164). Hillsdale, NJ: Erlbaum.

Tulving, E. (1983). *Elements of episodic memory.* New York: Oxford University Press.

Warrington, E. K., & McCarthy, R. A. (1988). The fractionation of retrograde amnesia. *Brain and Cognition, 7,* 184–200.

Warrington, E. K., & Weiskrantz, L. (1978). Further analysis of the prior learning effect in amnesic patients. *Neuropsychologia, 16,* 169–177.

Wilson, M. A., & McNaughton, B. L. (1994). Reactivation of hippocampal ensemble memories during sleep. *Science, 265,* 676–679.

Winocur, G. (1990). Anterograde and retrograde amnesia in rats with dorsal hippocampal or dorsomedial thalamic lesions. *Behavioral Brain Research, 38,* 145–154.

Zola-Morgan, S., & Squire, L. R. (1990). The primate hippocampal formation: Evidence for a time-limited role in memory storage. *Science, 250,* 288–290.

Category Learning

Chapter 18

ALCOVE: An Exemplar-Based Connectionist Model of Category Learning

John K. Kruschke

This chapter describes a connectionist model of category learning called ALCOVE (attention learning covering map). Any model of category learning must address the two issues of what representation underlies category knowledge and how that representation is used in learning. ALCOVE combines the exemplar-based representational assumptions of Nosofsky's (1986) generalized context model (GCM) with the error-driven learning assumptions of Gluck and Bower's (1988a, 1988b) network models. ALCOVE extends the GCM by adding a learning mechanism and extends the network models of Gluck and Bower by allowing continuous dimensions and including explicit dimensional attention learning. ALCOVE can be construed as a combination of exemplar models (e.g., Medin & Schaffer, 1978; Nosofsky, 1986) with network models (Gluck & Bower, 1988a, 1988b), as suggested by Estes (1988; Estes, Campbell, Hatsopoulos, & Hurwitz, 1989; Hurwitz, 1990). Dimensional attention learning allows ALCOVE to capture human performance where other network models fail (Gluck & Bower, 1988a), and error-driven learning in ALCOVE generates interactions between exemplars that allow it to succeed where other exemplar-based models fail (e.g., Estes et al., 1989; Gluck & Bower, 1988b).

ALCOVE is also closely related to standard back-propagation networks (Rumelhart, Hinton, & Williams, 1986). Although ALCOVE is a feed-forward network that learns by gradient descent on error, it is unlike standard back propagation in its architecture, its behavior, and its goals. Unlike the standard back-propagation network, which was motivated by generalizing neuronlike perceptrons, the architecture of ALCOVE was motivated by a molar-level psychological theory, Nosofsky's (1986) GCM. The psychologically constrained architecture results in behavior that captures the detailed course of human category learning in many situations where standard back propagation fares less well. Unlike many applications of standard back propagation, the goal of ALCOVE is not to discover new (hidden-layer) representations after lengthy training but rather to model the course of learning itself by determining which dimensions of the given representation are most relevant to the task and how strongly to associate exemplars with categories.

The purposes of this article are to introduce the ALCOVE model, demonstrate its application across a variety of category learning tasks, and compare it with other models to highlight its mechanisms. The organization of the article is as follows: First, the ALCOVE model is described in detail; then, its ability to differentially attend to relevant or irrelevant dimensions is demonstrated by applying it to the classic category learning task of Shepard, Hovland, and Jenkins (1961) and to the correlated-dimensions situation studied by Medin, Altom, Edelson, and Freko (1982). Next, the interaction of exemplars during learning is demonstrated by showing that ALCOVE learns Medin and Schwanenflugel's (1981) nonlinearly separable categories faster than the linearly separable ones. Afterward, the representation used in ALCOVE is contrasted with that used in standard back propagation, and it is shown that ALCOVE does not suffer the catastrophic retroactive interference seen in standard back propagation (McCloskey & Cohen, 1989; Ratcliff, 1990). Finally, I include a provocative demonstration of ALCOVE's ability to exhibit three-stage learning of rules and exceptions (cf. Rumelhart & McClelland, 1986) and speculate how ALCOVE might interact with a rule-hypothesizing system.

The Model

ALCOVE is a feed-forward connectionist network with three layers of nodes. Its basic computations are a direct implementation of Nosofsky's (1986) GCM. Like the GCM, ALCOVE assumes that stimuli can be represented as points in a multidimensional psychological space, as determined by multidimensional scaling (MDS) algorithms (e.g., Shepard, 1957, 1962a, 1962b). Each input node encodes a single psychological dimension, with the activation of the node indicating the value of the stimulus on that dimension. For example, if the first node corresponds to perceived size, and the perceived size of the given stimulus is some scale value v, then the activation of the first node is v. The activation of the ith input node is denoted a_i^{in}, and the complete stimulus is denoted by the column vector $a^{in} = (a_1^{in}, a_2^{in}, \ldots)^T$. Figure 18.1 shows the basic architecture of ALCOVE, illustrating the case of just two input dimensions (in general the model can have any number of input dimensions).

Each input node is gated by a dimensional attention strength, α_i. The attention strength on a dimension reflects the relevance of that dimension for the particular categorization task at hand. Before training begins, the model is initialized with equal attention strengths on all dimensions, and as training proceeds, the model learns to allocate more attention to relevant dimensions and less to irrelevant dimensions. Attention Learning is an important aspect of the model and gives ALCOVE the first two letters of its name. The function of the attention strengths will be described in more detail after the hidden nodes are described.

Each hidden node corresponds to a position in the multidimensional stimulus space. In the simplest version of ALCOVE, there is a hidden node placed at the

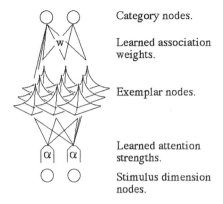

Category nodes.

Learned association
weights.

Exemplar nodes.

Learned attention
strengths.

Stimulus dimension
nodes.

Figure 18.1
The architecture of ALCOVE (attention learning covering map). (See The Model section.)

position of every training exemplar. For example, if the input dimensions are *perceived size* and *perceived brightness,* and one of the training stimuli has scale values of size = v and brightness = ξ, then there is a hidden node placed at the position (v, ξ). In a more complicated version, discussed at the end of the article, hidden nodes are scattered randomly across the space, forming a covering map of the input space. The covering map gives ALCOVE the last four letters of its name. Throughout the body of this article, however, the exemplar-based version is used.

For a given input stimulus, each hidden node is activated according to the psychological similarity of the stimulus to the exemplar at the position of the hidden node. The similarity function is the same as that used in the GCM, which in turn was motivated by Shepard's (1957, 1958, 1987) classic theories of similarity and generalization. Let the position of the jth hidden node be denoted as $(h_{j1}, h_{j2}, \ldots)$, and let the activation of the jth hidden node be denoted as a_j^{hid}. Then

$$a_j^{hid} = \exp\left[-c\left(\sum_i \alpha_i |h_{ji} - a_i^{in}|^r\right)^{q/r}\right],\tag{1}$$

where c is a positive constant called the *specificity* of the node, where the sum is taken over all input dimensions, and where r and q are constants determining the psychological-distance metric and similarity gradient, respectively. In the applications described in this article, separable psychological dimensions are assumed, so a city-block metric ($r = 1$) with exponential similarity gradient ($q = 1$) is used (Shepard, 1987). For integral dimensions, a Euclidean metric ($r = 2$) could be used (e.g., Nosofsky, 1987; Shepard, 1964).

The pyramids in the middle layer of Figure 18.1 show the activation profiles of hidden nodes, as determined by Equation 1 with $r = q = 1$. Because the acti-

Figure 18.2
Stretching the horizontal axis and shrinking the vertical axis causes exemplars of the two categories (denoted by dots and ×s) to have greater between-categories dissimilarity and greater within-category similarity. (The attention strengths in the network perform this sort of stretching and shrinking function. From "Attention, Similarity, and the Identification-Categorization Relationship" by R. M. Nosofsky, 1986, *Journal of Experimental Psychology: General*, 115, p. 42 © 1986 by the American Psychological Association. Adapted by permission.)

vation indicates the similarity of the input stimulus to the exemplar coded by the hidden node, the activation falls off exponentially with the distance between the hidden node and the input stimulus. The city-block metric implies that the iso-similarity contours are diamond shaped. The specificity constant, c, determines the overall width of the activation profile. Large specificities imply very rapid similarity decrease and hence a narrow activation profile, whereas small specificities correspond to wide profiles. Psychologically, the specificity of a hidden node indicates the overall cognitive discriminability or memorability of the corresponding exemplar. The region of stimulus space that significantly activates a hidden node will be loosely referred to as that node's *receptive field*.

Equation 1 indicates the role of the dimensional attention strengths, α_i. They act as multipliers on the corresponding dimension in computing the distance between the stimulus and the hidden node (cf. Carroll & Chang, 1970). A closely related type of attentional weighting was introduced by Medin and Schaffer (1978) in their context model and generalized into the form shown in Equation 1 by Nosofsky (1984, 1986).

The attention strengths stretch and shrink dimensions of the input space so that stimuli in different categories are better separated and stimuli within categories are better concentrated. Consider a simple case of four stimuli that form the corners of a square in input space, as indicated in Figure 18.2. If the two left stimuli are mapped to one category (indicated by dots), and the two right stimuli are mapped to another category (indicated by *x*s), then the separation of the categories can be increased by stretching the horizontal axis, and the proximity within categories can be increased by shrinking the vertical axis. Stretching a dimension can be achieved by increasing its attentional value; shrinking can be achieved by decreasing its attentional value. In ALCOVE, the dimensions most relevant to the category distinction learn larger attention strengths, and the less relevant dimensions learn smaller attention strengths.

Each hidden node is connected to output nodes that correspond to the possible response categories. The connection from the jth hidden node to the kth category node has a connection weight denoted w_{kj}. Because the hidden node is activated only by stimuli in a restricted region of input space near its corresponding exemplar, the connection weight is called the *association weight* between the exemplar and the category. The output (category) nodes are activated by the same linear rule used in the GCM and in the network models of Gluck and Bower (1988a, 1988b):

$$a_k^{out} = \sum_{\substack{hid \\ j}} w_{kj} a_j^{hid}. \tag{2}$$

In ALCOVE, unlike the GCM, the association weights are adjusted by an interactive, error-driven learning rule and can take on any real value, including negative values.

To compare model performance with human performance, the category activations must be mapped onto response probabilities. This is done in ALCOVE using the same choice rule as was used in the GCM and network models, which was motivated in those models by the classic works of Luce (1963) and Shepard (1957). Thus,

$$\Pr(K) = \exp(\phi a_K^{out}) \Big/ \sum_{\substack{out \\ k}} \exp(\phi a_k^{out}), \tag{3}$$

where ϕ is a real-valued mapping constant. In other words, the probability of classifying the given stimulus into category K is determined by the magnitude of category K's activation (exponentiated) relative to the sum of all category activations (exponentiated).

Here is a summary of how ALCOVE categorizes a given stimulus. Suppose, for example, that the model is applied to the situation illustrated in Figure 18.2. In this case, there are two psychological dimensions, hence two input nodes; four training exemplars, hence four hidden nodes; and two categories, hence two output nodes. When an exemplar is presented to ALCOVE, the input nodes are activated according to the component dimensional values of the stimulus. Each hidden node is then activated according to the similarity of the stimulus to the exemplar represented by the hidden node, using the attentionally weighted metric of Equation 1. Thus, hidden nodes near the input stimulus are strongly activated, and those farther away in psychological space are less strongly activated. Then the output (category) nodes are activated by summing across all the hidden (exemplar) nodes, weighted by the association weights between exemplars and categories, as in Equation 2. Finally, response probabilities are computed using Equation 3.

It was stated that the dimensional attention strengths, α_i, and the association weights between exemplars and categories, w_{kj}, are learned. The learning procedure is gradient descent on sum-squared error, as used in standard back propagation (Rumelhart et al., 1986) and in the network models of Gluck and Bower (1988a, 1988b). In the learning situations addressed by ALCOVE, each presentation of a training exemplar is followed by feedback indicating the correct response. The feedback is coded in ALCOVE as *teacher* values, t_k, given to each category node. For a given training exemplar and feedback, the error generated by the model is defined as

$$E = 1/2 \sum_{\substack{out \\ k}} (t_k - a_k^{out})^2, \tag{4a}$$

with the teacher values defined as

$$t_k = \begin{cases} \max(+1, a_k^{out}) \text{ if the stimulus} \\ \qquad \text{is in Category } K, \\ \min(-1, a_k^{out}) \text{ if the stimulus} \\ \qquad \text{is not in Category } K. \end{cases} \tag{4b}$$

These teacher values are defined so that activations "better than necessary" are not counted as errors. Thus, if a given stimulus should be classified as a member of the kth category, then the kth output node should have an activation of at least +1. If the activation is greater than 1, then the difference between the actual activation and +1 is not counted as error. Because these teacher values do not mind being outshone by their students, I call them "humble teachers." The motivation for using humble teacher values is that the feedback given to subjects is nominal, indicating only which category the stimulus belongs to and not the degree of membership. Hence, the teacher used in the model should only require some minimal level of category-node activation and should not require all exemplars ultimately to produce the same activations. Humble teachers are discussed further at the conclusion of the article.

On presentation of a training exemplar to ALCOVE, the association strengths and dimensional attention strengths are changed by a small amount so that the error decreases. Following Rumelhart et al. (1986), they are adjusted proportionally to the (negative of the) error gradient, which leads to the following learning rules (derived in the Appendix):

$$\Delta w_{kj}^{out} = \lambda_w (t_k - a_k^{out}) a_j^{hid}, \tag{5}$$

$$\Delta \alpha_i = -\lambda_\alpha \sum_{\substack{hid \\ j}} \left[\sum_{\substack{out \\ k}} (t_k - a_k^{out}) w_{kj} \right] a_j^{hid} c |h_{ji} - a_i^{in}|, \tag{6}$$

where the λs are constants of proportionality ($\lambda > 0$) called *learning rates*. The same learning rate, λ_w, applies to all the output weights. Likewise, there is only one learning rate, λ_α, for all the attentional strengths. The dimensional attention strengths are constrained to be nonnegative, as negative values have no psychologically meaningful interpretation. Thus, if Equation 6 were to drive an attention strength to a value less than zero, then the strength is set to zero.

Learning in ALCOVE proceeds as follows: For each presentation of a training exemplar, activation propagates to the category nodes as described previously. Then the teacher values are presented and compared with the actual category node activations. The association and attention strengths are then adjusted according to Equations 5 and 6. Several aspects of learning in ALCOVE deserve explicit mention.

First, learning is error driven. Both Equations 5 and 6 include the error term $(t_k - a_k^{out})$, so that changes are proportional to error. When there is no error, nothing changes. This is to be contrasted with learning rules that are based on accumulating constant increments on every trial, such as the array-exemplar model (Estes, 1986a, 1986b, 1988; Estes et al., 1989) and context model (Medin & Schaffer, 1978; Nosofsky, 1988b; Nosofsky, Kruschke, & McKinley, 1992). In such models, the system changes independently of its actual performance.

Second, because of the similarity-based activations of the hidden nodes, the training exemplars interact during learning. For example, consider two training exemplars that are similar to each other. Because of their similarity, when either one is presented, both corresponding hidden nodes are activated (one just partially); and because learning is proportional to the hidden node activations (see Equation 5), the association strengths from both exemplars are adjusted (as long as there is error present). This interactive property is also to be contrasted with models such as the array-exemplar model, in which learning affects isolated exemplars one at a time (see also Matheus, 1988). The interactive character of learning in ALCOVE is comparable to the competitive nature of learning noted by Gluck and Bower (1988a, 1988b) in their network models and gives ALCOVE the ability to account for the base-rate neglect phenomena they observed, as is described later.

There are other notable implications of interactive learning in ALCOVE. It implies that similar exemplars from the same category should enhance each other's learning. Thus, it suggests that prototypical exemplars should be learned faster than peripheral exemplars, if it can be assumed that prototypical exemplars tend to be centrally located near several other exemplars from the same category. That is desirable insofar as it is also observed in human data (e.g., Rosch, Simpson, & Miller, 1976). Interactive learning also suggests that the shape of the category boundary will have no direct influence on the difficulty of learning the category distinction; rather, difficulty should be based on the clustering of exemplars (subject to the additional complication of attentional learning). In particular, it suggests that it is not necessary for linearly separable categories to be easier to learn than nonlinearly separable categories. Human data again make this a desirable property (Medin & Schwanenflugel, 1981).

Figure 18.3
Attentional learning ALCOVE (attention learning covering map) cannot stretch or shrink diagonally. (Compare with Figure 18.2.)

A third property of learning in ALCOVE is that attention learning can only adjust the relative importance of the dimensions as given. ALCOVE cannot construct new dimensions to attend to. For example, consider the situation in Figure 18.3, in which the four training exemplars form the corners of a diamond in the psychological space. Ideally, one might like to stretch the space along the right diagonal to better separate the two categories and shrink along the left diagonal to make within-category exemplars more similar, but ALCOVE cannot do that. Fortunately, it appears that people cannot do that either, as is described later. This anisotropy in attentional learning implies that when modeling human data with ALCOVE, one must be certain that the input dimensions used in the model match the psychological dimensions used by the human subjects.

In all the applications described in this article, the psychological dimensions are separable, not integral (Garner, 1974), but the model does not necessarily depend on that. ALCOVE might accommodate psychologically integral dimensions by using a Euclidean distance metric ($r = 2$) in Equation 1 (Nosofsky, 1987; Shepard, 1964). There is evidence to suggest that people can, with effort, differentially attend to psychologically integral dimensions when given opportunity to do so (e.g., Nosofsky, 1987).

In summary, ALCOVE incorporates the exemplar-based representation of Nosofsky's (1987) GCM with error-driven learning as in Gluck and Bower's (1988a, 1988b) network models. ALCOVE extends the GCM in several ways: For learning association weights, it uses an error-driven, interactive rule, instead of a constant-increment rule, that allows association weights in ALCOVE to take on any positive or negative value. ALCOVE also provides a mechanism for attention-strength learning, whereas the GCM has none. ALCOVE extends Gluck and Bower's network models by allowing continuous input dimensions and by having explicit dimensional attention learning. In fitting ALCOVE to human data, there are four free parameters: (a) the fixed specificity c in Equation 1, (b) the probability-mapping constant ϕ in Equation 3, (c) the association weight-learning rate λ_w in Equation 5, and (d) the attention-learning rate λ_α in Equation 6.

Applications

Learning to Attend to Relevant Dimensions
In this section ALCOVE is applied to the category structures used in the classic research of Shepard, Hovland, and Jenkins (1961). There are three reasons for considering the work of Shepard et al.: First, the results of the study provide fundamental human data that any model of category learning should address, and in particular they have served as a benchmark for several recent models (e.g., Anderson, 1991; Gluck & Bower, 1988b; Nosofsky, 1984). Second, the structures described by Shepard et al. are well suited for demonstrating the capabilities of ALCOVE. Third, Shepard et al. argued explicitly that models of categorization based on reinforcement learning and graded generalization could not account for their data unless such models included some (unspecified) mechanism for selective attention. As ALCOVE does include such a mechanism, it faces a direct theoretical and empirical challenge.

The stimuli used by Shepard et al. (1961) varied on three binary dimensions. For example, figures could vary in shape (square vs. triangle), size (large vs. small), and color (filled vs. open). Each of the resulting eight training exemplars was assigned to one of two categories, such that both categories had four exemplars. It turns out that there are only six structurally distinct types of category assignments. Figure 18.4 shows the six types, with the eight exemplars indicated by the corners of a cube. The category assignment of an exemplar is indicated by either a filled or blank circle. For example, the top-left cube shows that for Category Type I, Exemplars 1 to 4 are assigned to the *blank* Category, and Exemplars 5 to 8 are assigned to the *filled* category. Any assignment of exemplars to categories, with four exemplars in each category, can be rotated or reflected into one of the structures shown in Figure 18.4.

A primary concern of Shepard et al. (1961) was to determine the relative difficulty of learning the six category types. Intuitively, Type I should be particularly easy to learn because only information about Dimension 1 is relevant to the categorization decision; variation on Dimensions 2 and 3 leads to no variation in category membership. However, Type II requires attention to both Dimensions 1 and 2 and therefore should be more difficult to learn. (Type II is the exclusive-or [XOR] problem in its two relevant dimensions.) Types III, IV, V, and VI require information about all three dimensions to make correct categorizations, but the dimensions are not equally informative in every type. For example, in Type V, six of eight exemplars can be correctly classified by considering only Dimension 1, with attention to Dimensions 2 and 3 needed only for the remaining two exemplars. On the other hand, Type VI requires equal attention to all the dimensions, because exemplars of each category are symmetrically distributed on the dimensions. (Type VI is the parity problem in three dimensions.) Thus, if it takes more cognitive effort or capacity to consider more dimensions, then Type I should be easiest to learn, followed by Types II, III, IV, V, and VI.

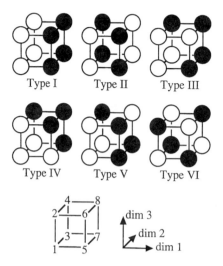

Figure 18.4
The six category types used by Shepard, Hovland, and Jenkins (1961). (The three binary stimulus dimensions [labeled by the trident at lower right] yield eight training examplars, numbered at the corners of the lower-left cube. Category assignments are indicated by the open or filled circles. From "Learning and Memorization of Classifications" by R. N. Shepard, C. L. Hovland, and H. M. Jenkins, 1961, *Psychological Monographs*, 75, 13, Whole No. 517, p. 4. In the public domain.)

Shepard et al. (1961) found empirically that the order of difficulty was I < II < (III, IV, V) < VI. That is, Type I was easiest, followed by Type II, followed by Types III, IV, and V (they were very close) and Type VI. Difficulty of learning was measured by the total number of errors made until the subject correctly classified each of the eight exemplars four times in a row. Other measures, such as number of errors in recall, and response time, showed the same ordering.

How does one explain, in a formal quantitative theory, the observed difficulty of the types? Perhaps the most direct approach is a stimulus generalization hypothesis: Category structures that assign highly similar stimuli to the same category and highly dissimilar stimuli to different categories should be relatively easy to learn, whereas structures in which similar stimuli are mapped to different categories and dissimilar stimuli are assigned to the same category should be relatively difficult to learn. Shepard et al. (1961) formalized that hypothesis by measuring interstimulus similarities (inferred from separately obtained identification-confusion data) and by computing the difficulty of category types by considering similarities of all pairs of exemplars from different categories. They considered several variants of the generalization hypothesis, all of which failed to predict the observed order of learning. They argued that "the most serious shortcoming of the generalization theory is that it does not provide for a process of abstraction (or selective attention)." (Shepard et al., 1961, p. 29). The idea was that by devoting attention to only relevant dimensions, confusability of stimuli that differed on those dimensions would be greatly reduced. In that way, Types I and II, especially, would be significantly easier to learn than predicted by a pure generalization theory.

The notion of selective attention was formalized by Nosofsky (1984, 1986) in his GCM. The GCM added attention factors to each dimension of the input space. By using optimal attention weights, which maximized the average percentage correct, or by using attention weights freely estimated to best fit the data, the GCM was able to correctly predict the relative difficulties of the six category types, but the GCM has no attention learning mechanism.

Shepard et al. (1961) considered a variety of learning theories, to see if any provided the necessary attention-learning mechanism. Their answer, in brief, was "no." *Cue conditioning* theories, in which associations between single cues (e.g., square) and categories are gradually reinforced, are unable to account for the ability to learn Types II, III, V, and VI, because no single cue is diagnostic of the category assignments. *Pattern conditioning* theories, in which associations between complete configurations of cues (e.g., large, white square) and categories are gradually reinforced, cannot account for the rapidity of learning Types I and II. They concluded:

> Thus, although a theory based upon the notions of conditioning and, perhaps, the adaptation of cues at first showed promise of accounting both for stimulus generalization and abstraction, further investigation indicated that it does not, in any of the forms yet proposed, yield a prediction of the difficulty of each of our six types of classifications. (Shepard et al., 1961, p. 32)

Gluck and Bower (1988a) combined cue and pattern conditioning into their "configural-cue model." The configural-cue model assumes that stimuli are represented by values on each single dimension, plus pairs of values on each pair of dimensions, plus triplets of values on each triplet of dimensions, and so on. Thus, for the stimuli from the Shepard et al. (1961) study, there are 6 one-value cues (two for each dimension), plus 12 two-value configural cues (four for each pair of dimensions), plus 8 three-value configural cues (the eight full stimuli themselves), yielding a total of 26 configural cues. Each configural cue is represented by an input node in a simple network, connected directly to category nodes. Presence of a configural cue is indicated by activating ($a = +1$) the corresponding input node, and absence is indicated by no activation. The model learns by gradient descent on sum-squared error. For the configural-cue model, Gluck and Bower made no explicit mapping from category-node activations to response probabilities, but in other network models they used the choice function of Equation 3 so that mapping is also assumed here. The configural-cue model has two parameters, the learning rate for the connection weights and the scaling constant ϕ in Equation 3. When applied to the six category types of Shepard et al., the result was that the configural-cue model failed to learn Type II fast enough (see Figure 12 of Gluck & Bower, 1988a), as measured either by cumulative errors during learning or by time until criterion error level is reached. Thus Shepard et al.'s conclusion persists: Some mechanism for selective attention seems to be needed.[1]

ALCOVE was applied to the six category types by using three input nodes (one for each stimulus dimension), eight hidden nodes (one for each training exemplar), and two output nodes (one for each category). It was assumed that the three physical dimensions of the stimuli had corresponding psychological dimensions. In the Shepard et al. experiments, the three physical dimensions were counterbalanced with respect to the abstract dimensions shown in Figure 18.4; therefore, the input encoding for the simulation gave each dimension equal scales (with alternative values on each dimension separated by one scale unit), and equal initial attentional strengths (set arbitrarily to $1/3$). The association weights were initialized at zero, reflecting the notion that before training there should be no associations between any exemplars and particular categories.

In the Shepard et al. (1961) study, the difficulty of any given type was computed by averaging across subjects, each of whom saw a different random sequence of training exemplars. In the simulation, sequence effects were eliminated by executing changes in association weights and attention strengths only after complete epochs of all eight training exemplars. (In the connectionist literature, epoch updating is also referred to as *batch* updating.)

Figure 18.5 (A and B) show learning curves generated by ALCOVE when there was no attention learning and when there was moderate attention learning, respectively. Each datum shows the probability of selecting the correct category, averaged across the eight exemplars within an epoch. For both graphs, the response mapping constant was set to $\phi = 2.0$, the specificity was fixed at $c = 6.5$, and the learning rate for association weights was $\lambda_w = 0.03$. In Figure 18.5A, there was no attention learning ($\lambda_\alpha = 0.0$), and it can be seen that Type II is learned much too slowly. In Figure 18.5B, the attention-learning rate was raised to $\lambda_\alpha = 0.0033$, and consequently Type II was learned second fastest, as observed in human data. Indeed, it can be seen in Figure 18.5B that the six types were learned in the same order as people, with Type I the fastest, followed by Type II, followed by Types III, IV, and V clustered together, followed by Type VI.

The dimensional attention strengths were redistributed as expected. For Category Type I, the attention strength on the relevant Dimension 1 increased, whereas attention to the two irrelevant Dimensions 2 and 3 dropped nearly to zero. For Type II, attention to the irrelevant Dimension 3 dropped to zero, whereas attention to the two relevant Dimensions 1 and 2 grew (equally for both dimensions). For Types III to VI, all three dimensions retained large

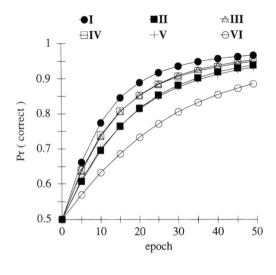

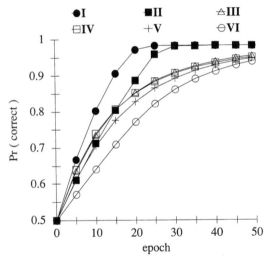

Figure 18.5
A: Results of applying ALCOVE (attention learning covering map) to the Shepard, Hovland, and Jenkins (1961) category types, with zero attention learning. Here Type II is learned as slowly as Type V (the Type V curve is mostly obscured by the Type II curve). B: Results of applying ALCOVE to the Shepard et al. category types, with moderate attention learning. Note that type II is now learned second fastest, as observed in human data. Pr = probability.

attention strengths. Type VI had all of its attention strengths grow, thereby better segregating all the exemplars. Such symmetrical growth of attention is functionally equivalent to increasing the specificities of all the hidden nodes (see Equation 1).

From a model-testing perspective, it is reassuring to note that the range of orderings illustrated in Figure 18.5 (A and B) are the only orderings that ALCOVE is capable of generating (when $r = q = 1$). When the attention-learning rate is set to higher values, the same ordering as in Figure 18.5B arises, but with Types I and II learned even faster. When the specificity is made larger (or smaller), the overall separation of the learning curves is lessened (or enlarged, respectively), but the same orderings persist. Adjusting the association-weight learning rate merely changes the overall number of epochs required to reach a certain probability correct.

ALCOVE accounts for the relative difficulty of Shepard et al.'s (1961) six category types by its ability to learn dimensional attention strengths. Such an attentional-learning mechanism is just the sort of thing Shepard et al. called for in their theoretical analyses. It is only fair to note, however, that Shepard et al. also concluded that in addition to abstracting the relevant dimensions, subjects formulated rules for specifying the categories. How ALCOVE might interact with a rule-generating system is discussed in a later section.

Learning to Attend to Correlated Dimensions
Medin et al. (1982) have noted that prototype and other "independent cue" models are not sensitive to correlations between cues. In several experiments, they pitted single-cue diagnosticity against correlated cues to see which would be the better determinant of human categorization performance. They used a simulated medical diagnosis paradigm in which subjects were shown hypothetical patterns of four symptoms. Each of the four symptoms could take on one of two values; for example, watery eyes versus sunken eyes. Subjects were trained on four exemplars of the fictitious disease Terrigitis (T) and four exemplars of the fictitious disease Midosis (M). In this situation the four symptoms are the four dimensions of the stimulus space, and the two diseases are the two alternative categories. The abstract structure of the categories is shown in Table 18.1. One important aspect of the structure is that the first two symptoms are individually diagnostic, in that p (Terrigitis | Symptom 1 = "1") = .75 and p (Terrigitis | Symptom 2 = "1") = .75, whereas the third and fourth symptoms are not individually diagnostic, each being associated with each disease 50% of the time. Another important aspect of the structure is that the third and fourth symptoms are perfectly correlated in the training set, so that their combination forms a perfect predictor of the disease category. Thus, symptoms three and four are either both 1 or both 0 for cases of Terrigitis, but they are different values for cases of Midosis.

Table 18.1
Patterns used by Medin, Altom, Edelson, and Freko (1982, experiment 4) and probabilities of classifying as Terrigitis after training

Exemplar	Symptoms	Observed	ALCOVE	Config cue
T1	1 1 1 1	.88	.82	.76
T2	0 1 1 1	.89	.78	.76
T3	1 1 0 0	.73	.82	.76
T4	1 0 0 0	.77	.78	.76
M1	1 0 1 0	.12	.22	.25
M2	0 0 1 0	.17	.18	.25
M3	0 1 0 1	.25	.22	.25
M4	0 0 0 1	.33	.18	.25
N1	0 0 0 0	.53	.59	.44
N2	0 0 1 1	.53	.59	.44
N3	0 1 0 0	.75	.64	.46
N4	1 0 1 1	.67	.64	.46
N5	1 1 1 0	.45	.41	.58
N6	1 1 0 1	.38	.41	.58
N7	0 1 1 0	.36	.36	.55
N8	1 0 0 1	.28	.36	.55

Note. Exemplar Labels T1–T4 refer to the four training exemplars for Terrigitis, and exemplar Labels M1–M4 refer to the four training exemplars for Midosis. Exemplar Labels N1–N8 refer to novel test patterns. Config cue = configural-cue model; ALCOVE = attention learning covering map. Data are from "Correlated Symptoms and Simulated Medical Classification" by D. L. Medin, M. W. Altom, S. M. Edelson, & D. Freko, 1982, *Journal of Experimental Psychology: Learning, Memory, and Cognition, 8,* p. 47. Copyright 1982 by the American Psychological Association. Adapted by permission.

If subjects learn to attend to the correlated third and fourth symptoms to make their diagnoses, then when tested with novel symptom patterns, they should choose Terrigitis whenever the third and fourth symptoms agree. On the other hand, if subjects learn to use the first and second symptoms, then they should choose Terrigitis more often when those symptom values are 1.

Subjects were trained on the first eight exemplars of Table 18.1 using a free-inspection procedure. Unlike training paradigms in which stimuli are shown sequentially with a definite frequency, Medin et al. (1982) allowed their subjects to freely inspect the eight exemplars during a 10-min period (each exemplar was written on a separate card). After the 10-min training period, subjects were shown each of the possible 16 symptom combinations and asked to diagnose them as either Terrigitis or Midosis. The results are reproduced in Table 18.1. Three important trends are evident in the data. First, subjects were fairly accurate in classifying the patterns on which they had been trained (Exemplars

T1–T4 and M1–M4), choosing the correct disease category 80% of the time. Second, subjects were sensitive to the diagnostic value of the first and second symptoms, in that Novel Patterns N3 and N4 were classified as Terrigitis more often than Patterns N1 and N2, and Patterns N5 and N6 were classified as Terrigitis more often than Patterns N7 and N8. Third, subjects were also apparently quite sensitive to the correlated features, because they classified Patterns N1 to N4, for which Symptoms 3 and 4 agree, as Terrigitis more than 50% of the time, and they classified patterns N5 to N8, for which Symptoms 3 and 4 differ, as Terrigitis less than 50% of the time.

The fourth column of Table 18.1 shows the results of applying ALCOVE. Eight hidden nodes were used, corresponding to the eight training exemplars. ALCOVE was trained for 50 sweeps, or epochs, on the eight patterns (T1 to T4 and M1 to M4). Association weights and attention strengths were updated after every complete sweep through the eight training patterns, because Medin et al. (1982) did not present subjects with a fixed sequence of stimuli. Best fitting parameter values were $\phi = 0.845$, $\lambda_w = 0.0260$, $c = 2.36$, and $\lambda_\alpha = 0.00965$, yielding a root-mean-squared deviation (RMSD) of 0.104 across the 16 patterns. (The number of epochs used was arbitrary and chosen only because it seemed like a reasonable number of exposures for a 10-min free-inspection period. The best fit for 25 epochs, for example, yielded an RMSD identical to three significant digits.)

All three of the main trends in the data are captured by ALCOVE. The trained exemplars were learned to 80% accuracy. The diagnosticities of the 1st two symptoms were picked up, because Patterns N3 and N4 were classified as Terrigitis with higher probability than Patterns N1 and N2, whereas Patterns N5 and N6 were classified as Terrigitis more often than Patterns N7 and N8. It is important to note that the correlated symptoms were detected, because Patterns N1 to N4 were classified as Terrigitis with more than 50% probability, and Patterns N5 to N8, with less than 50% probability.

ALCOVE accounts for the influence of correlated dimensions by increasing attention to those dimensions. When the attention-learning rate is very large, then the correlated Symptoms 3 and 4 get all the attention, and Symptoms 1 and 2 are ignored. On the contrary, when attentional learning is zero, then the diagnosticities of the first two dimensions dominate the results. The results reported in Table 18.1 are for an intermediate attentional-learning rate, for which Symptoms 3 and 4 get more attention than Symptoms 1 and 2, but some attention remains allocated to Symptoms 1 and 2.

The configural-cue model was also fitted to these data. For this situation, the configural-cue model requires 80 input nodes: 8 singlet nodes, 24 doublet nodes, 32 triplet nodes, and 16 quadruplet nodes. The model was trained for 50 epochs with epoch updating. The best-fitting parameter values were $\phi = 0.554$ and $\lambda_w = 0.0849$, yielding an RMSD of 0.217 across the 16 patterns, more than twice the RMSD of ALCOVE. As is clear from the results shown in Table 18.1, the configural-cue model is completely unable to detect the correlated symptoms, despite the presence of doublet nodes that are sensitive to pairwise combinations of dimensions. Contrary to human performance, the configural-cue model classifies Patterns N1 to N4 as Terrigitis with less than 50% probability and Patterns N5 to N8 with more than 50% probability. That qualitative reversal is a necessary prediction of the configural-cue model and cannot be rectified by another choice of parameter values.

Gluck, Bower, and Hee (1989) showed that if only single symptoms and pairwise symptom combinations were used, with no three-way or four-way symptom combinations, then correlated symptoms could be properly accentuated (for Experiment 3 from Medin et al., 1982). However, by not including the higher order combinations, the model was told a priori that pairwise combinations would be relevant, which begs the fundamental question at issue here: namely, how it is that the relevance is learned.

The simulation results shown in Table 18.1 are to be construed qualitatively, despite the fact that they are quantitative best fits. That is because the free-inspection training procedure used by Medin et al. (1982) might very well have produced subtle effects caused by subjects exposing themselves to some stimuli more frequently than to others, or studying different exemplars later in training than early on. The simulations, on the other hand, assumed equal frequency of exposure and constant relative frequencies throughout training. Moreover, there is a disparity in the number of parameters in the two models: ALCOVE has four, whereas the configural-cue model has two. Nevertheless, the qualitative evidence is clear: Because of attention learning, ALCOVE can account for sensitivity to correlated dimensions, whereas the configural-cue model cannot.

Interactive Exemplars in Linearly and Nonlinearly Separable Categories
The previous sections emphasized the role of attention learning. This section, instead, emphasizes the learning of association weights and illustrates how hidden nodes (exemplars) interact during learning because of their similarity-based activations. As suggested in the introduction, ALCOVE is only indirectly sensitive to the shape of category boundaries and is primarily affected by the clustering of exemplars and their distribution over stimulus dimensions. In particular, whether a category boundary is linear or nonlinear should have no direct influence, and it is possible that nonlinearly separable categories would be easier to learn than linearly separable ones.

A case in point comes from the work of Medin and Schwanenflugel (1981, Experiment 4). They compared two category structures, shown in Figure 18.6. One structure was linearly separable, whereas the other was not. The two structures were equalized, however, in terms of mean city-block distance between exemplars within categories and between exemplars from different categories. For example, the mean city-block separation of exemplars within categories for the linearly separable structure is $(2 + 2 + 2 + 2 + 2 + 2)/6 = 2$,

linearly   non-linearly
separable   separable

Figure 18.6

Category structures used by Medin and Schwanenflugel (1981, Experiment 4). (The linearly separable structure is a subset of Type IV in the Shepard, Hovland, and Jenkins, 1961, studies [cf. Figure 18.4], whereas the nonlinearly separable structure is the corresponding subset from Type III.)

and the mean within-category separation for the nonlinearly separable category is the same, $(1 + 2 + 3 + 1 + 2 + 3)/6 = 2$. The mean separation between categories is $1\frac{2}{3}$ for both structures.

When human subjects were trained on the two structures, it was found that the linearly separable structure was no easier to learn than the nonlinearly separable structure. This result contradicts predictions of prototype models, such as the single- and double-node models of Gluck and Bower (1988a, 1988b; see Nosofsky, 1991, for a derivation that they are a type of prototype model), but is consistent with models that are sensitive to relational information, such as Medin and Schaffer's (1978) context model, and Nosofsky's GCM. In another experiment run by Medin and Schwanenflugel (1981, Experiment 3), a significant advantage for nonlinearly separable categories was observed.

The configural-cue model is able to show an advantage for the nonlinearly separable category, if the scaling constant ϕ is not too large. Gluck (1991; Gluck et al., 1989) has shown that if the triplet nodes are removed from the configural-cue representation, leaving only the singlet and doublet nodes, the advantage for the nonlinearly separable categories remains. Unfortunately, such a move requires an a priori knowledge of which combinations of dimensions will be useful for the task.

When ALCOVE is applied to these structures, the nonlinearly separable structure is indeed learned faster than the linearly separable structure. This result is true for every combination of parameter values I have tested (a wide range). In particular, attentional learning is not needed to obtain this result. Therefore, it is the interaction of the exemplars, due to similarity and error-driven learning, that is responsible for this performance in ALCOVE. Whereas the mean city-block separations of exemplars were equalized for the two category structures, the mean similarities of exemplars were not equal. ALCOVE exploits that difference in the learning rule for association weights (Equations 1 and 5). The flavor of this explanation is no different from that given for the context model (Medin & Schwanenflugel, 1981). The point is not that ALCOVE necessarily fits these data better than other models with exemplar-similarity-based representations like Medin and Schaffer's (1978) context model but that error-driven learning in ALCOVE does not impair its ability to account for these fundamental data.

Summary

The importance of dimensional attention learning was demonstrated by applying ALCOVE to the six category types from Shepard et al. (1961) and to the Medin et al. (1982) categories involving correlated dimensions. The importance of interaction between exemplars, produced by similarity-based activations and error-driven association-weight learning, was demonstrated in accounting for the ability to learn nonlinearly separable categories faster than linearly separable categories. Subsequent sections address domains that use continuous dimensions to which the double-node and configural-cue models, as presently formulated, are not applicable.

ALCOVE Versus Standard Back Propagation

As stated in the introduction, ALCOVE differs from standard back propagation in its architecture, behavior, and goals. A *standard back-propagation network* (later referred to as *back-prop*) is a feed-forward network with linear-sigmoid nodes in its hidden layer and with hidden weights and output weights that learn by gradient descent on error. Linear-sigmoid nodes have activation determined by

$$a_j^{hid} = 1 \left/ \left[1 + \exp\left(- \sum_i^{in} w_{ji}^{hid} a_i^{in} \right) \right] \right. . \tag{7}$$

The linear-sigmoid function was motivated as a generalized, or smoothed, version of the linear-threshold function in neuronlike perceptrons (Rumelhart et al., 1986). In contrast, the activation functions of ALCOVE were motivated by molar-level psychological theory. The activation profiles of hidden nodes in ALCOVE and in backprop, as determined by Equations 1 and 7, are shown in Figure 18.7. Three important differences between the activation profiles are evident: First, the hidden node from ALCOVE has a limited receptive field, which means that the node is significantly activated only by inputs near its position. On the contrary, the hidden node from backprop is significantly activated by inputs from an entire half space of the input space. That difference in receptive field size has important consequences for how strongly hidden nodes interact during learning, as is demonstrated shortly. A second difference is that the level contours of the ALCOVE node are iso-distance contours (diamond shaped for a city-block metric), whereas the level contours of the backprop node are linear. (Examples of level contours are shown in Figure 18.7 by the lines that mark horizontal cross sections through the activation profiles.) This implies that backprop will be especially sensitive to linear boundaries between

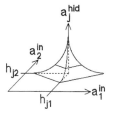 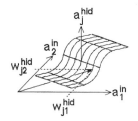

Figure 18.7
Activation profile of a hidden node in ALCOVE (attention learning covering map) is shown on the left (Equation 1, with $r = q = 1$). (Activation profile of a hidden node in standard back propagation is shown on the right [Equation 7].)

categories. A third difference between the structure of ALCOVE and backprop is that the linear level contours of the backprop node can be oriented in any direction in input space, whereas attention learning in ALCOVE can only stretch or shrink along the given input dimensions (recall the discussion accompanying Figure 18.3). Those three differences result in shortcomings of backprop that are now demonstrated with examples.

Insensitivity to Boundary Orientation
When backprop is applied to the six category types of Shepard et al. (1961; see Figure 18.4), Type IV is learned almost as fast as Type I and much too fast compared to human performance. (Backprop does not learn Type IV quite as quickly as Type I because it is also sensitive to the clustering of exemplars near the boundary; e.g., see Ahmad, 1988.) This result holds over a wide range of learning rates for the two layers of weights, with or without momentum (Rumelhart et al., 1986), for different ranges of initial weight values and over a wide range in the number of hidden nodes. Type IV is learned so quickly by back-prop because it can accentuate the diagonal axis through the prototypes of the two categories (Exemplars 1 and 8 in Figure 18.4), unlike ALCOVE. In other words, the linear level contours of the backprop nodes align with the linear boundary between the categories in Type IV, despite the diagonal orientation of that boundary. ALCOVE cannot direct attention to diagonal axes (see discussion accompanying Figure 18.3), so it does not learn Type IV so quickly.

Oversensitivity to Linearity of Boundary
When backprop is applied to the linearly or nonlinearly separable categories of Medin and Schwanenflugel (1981; see Figure 18.6), the result is that the linearly separable structure is learned much faster than the nonlinearly separable one, contrary to human (and ALCOVE's) performance (e.g., Gluck, 1991). The reason is that the linear level contours of backprop's hidden nodes can align with the linear boundary between categories.

Catastrophic Interference

McCloskey and Cohen (1989) and Ratcliff (1990) have shown that when a backprop network is initially trained on one set of associations, and subsequently trained on a different set of associations, memory for the first set is largely destroyed. Such catastrophic forgetting is not typical of normal humans and is a major shortcoming of backprop as a model of human learning and memory. As ALCOVE is also a feed-forward network that learns by gradient descent on error, it is important to test it for catastrophic forgetting.

A simple demonstration of catastrophic forgetting in back-prop is shown in Figure 18.8 (a–c). The task is to learn the four exemplars in two phases: First learn that $(0, -1) \rightarrow$ "box" and $(-1, 0) \rightarrow$ "circle", then in a second phase learn that $(0, +1) \rightarrow$ "box" and $(+1, 0) \rightarrow$ "circle". The two graphs in panels b and c show typical results of applying backprop and ALCOVE, respectively. Each graph shows probability of correct categorization as a function of training epoch. Phase 1 consisted of Training Epochs 1 to 10, and Phase 2 began after the 10th epoch. Two trends are clear in the backprop results: In Phase 1, generalization performance on the untrained exemplars shifts dramatically to worse than change, and in Phase 2 performance on the Phase 1 exemplars rapidly decays to worse than chance. On the contrary, ALCOVE shows virtually no interference between Phase 1 and Phase 2 exemplars (Figure 18.8c).

For the results in Figure 18.8b, the backprop network was made maximally comparable to ALCOVE. Thus, its input nodes were the same as in ALCOVE, and its output nodes were linear with weights initialized at zero, as in ALCOVE, with probability correct computed with Equation 3. There were 32 hidden nodes, with weights and thresholds initialized to random values between -2.5 and $+2.5$. Learning rates for output and hidden weights were both 0.06, with epoch updating. The same qualitative trends appear when using other parameter values and numbers of hidden nodes and for standard backprop using linear-sigmoid output nodes and output weights initialized to small random values. The results in Figure 18.8c were obtained by running ALCOVE with four hidden nodes centered on the four exemplars, using $\phi = 1.0$, $\lambda_w = .15$, $c = 2.0$, and $\lambda_\alpha = .06$, with epoch updating.

Backprop shows such severe interference because the receptive fields of its hidden nodes cover such a huge portion of input space. When training on Phase 1, the hidden nodes shift so that their linear level contours tend to align with the right diagonal in Figure 18.8a so that the two Phase 1 exemplars are accurately discriminated. In addition, nodes that happened to be initially placed in such an opportune orientation have their weights adjusted first and fastest. Unfortunately, those receptive fields cover the untrained Phase 2 exemplars in the same way, and the severe drop in generalization accuracy is the result. When subsequently trained on the Phase 2 exemplars, the same alignment of receptive fields occurs, but the category associations reverse, yielding the reversal of performance on the previously trained exemplars.

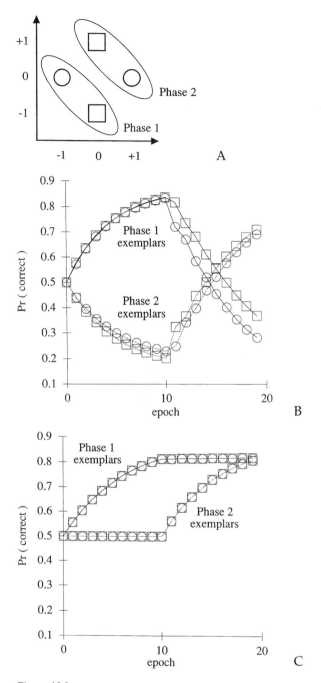

Figure 18.8
a: Category structure for demonstrating catastrophic forgetting in back propagation and resistance to forgetting in ALCOVE (attention learning covering map) b: Typical performance of back-propagation on the structure shown in Figure 18.8a. c: Performance of ALCOVE on the structure shown in Figure 18.8a. Pr = probability.

The receptive fields of hidden nodes in ALCOVE are much more localized, so that associations from exemplars to categories are not strongly affected by other exemplars, unless the exemplars are very similar. In general, the degree of interference generated in ALCOVE depends on two factors: the size of the receptive fields, as measured by the specificity parameter, c, and whether the exemplars from the two training phases have the same relevant or irrelevant dimensions.

The previous example was used because it was relatively easy to visualize the workings of the two models in terms of how receptive fields get distributed over the stimulus space. The relatively small interference in ALCOVE does not depend on using that particular configuration, however. Similar results also occur in a situation used by Ratcliff (1990) to demonstrate catastrophic forgetting in backprop. Ratcliff used the "4–4 encode" problem, in which a network with four input nodes and four output nodes must learn to reproduce isolated activity in each input node on the output nodes. That is, there are just four training patterns: $(+1, -1, -1, -1) \rightarrow (+1, -1, -1, -1), (-1, +1, -1, -1) \rightarrow (-1, +1, -1, -1)$, etc. (These patterns use values of -1 instead of 0 merely to maintain symmetry. Similar qualitative conclusions apply when 0 is used.) The models are initially trained on just the first three training pairs; then, in the second phase of training, they are shown only the fourth pattern pair.

For this demonstration, the backprop network had three hidden nodes, the same number as used by Ratcliff (1990). To maximize comparison with ALCOVE, the four output nodes were linear, and response probabilities were computed with Equation 3, using $\phi = 1.0$. Hidden and output weights had learning rates of 0.2. Hidden weights and biases were initialized randomly in the interval $(-2.5, +2.5)$. Similar qualitative trends obtain for other parameter values, numbers of hidden nodes, etc. (e.g., Ratcliff, 1990); 200 different randomly initialized runs were averaged.

ALCOVE used four hidden nodes, corresponding to the four training exemplars. Specificity of the hidden nodes was set to $c = 2.0$, with association-weight learning rate of 0.05 and attention-learning rate of 0.02. The response scaling constant was set as in the backprop model, $\phi = 1.0$. Similar qualitative trends obtain for other parameter values.

Both models were trained for 100 epochs on the 1st three pattern pairs, then 100 epochs on the fourth pattern pair. Response probabilities at the end of each phase are shown in Table 18.2. Backprop shows slightly more generalization error in Phase 1, classifying the untrained fourth pattern as one of the three trained patterns more than ALCOVE does. Backprop shows considerable retroactive interference from Phase 2 training: Correct response probabilities on the 1st three patterns drop from 70% to about 40%, and there is considerable bias for back-prop to choose the fourth output category even when presented with one of the 1st three input patterns. By contrast, ALCOVE shows no such severe interference. Correct response probabilities on the 1st three patterns

Table 18.2
Results of applying back propagation or ALCOVE to the 4–4 Encoder Problem

	Input	Back propagation	ALCOVE
End of Phase 1	+1 −1 −1 −1	.70 .10 .10 .10	.70 .10 .10 .10
	−1 +1 −1 −1	.10 .70 .10 .10	.10 .70 .10 .10
	−1 −1 +1 −1	.10 .10 .70 .10	.10 .10 .70 .10
	−1 −1 −1 +1[a]	.28 .31 .29 .12	.27 .27 .27 .19
End of Phase 2	+1 −1 −1 −1[a]	.40 .07 .08 .45	.69 .09 .09 .13
	−1 +1 −1 −1[a]	.08 .39 .07 .46	.09 .69 .09 .13
	−1 −1 +1 −1[a]	.08 .07 .40 .45	.09 .09 .69 .13
	−1 −1 −1 +1	.10 .10 .10 .70	.10 .10 .10 .70

Note. Data are the probabilities of choosing the corresponding output category. (For $\phi = 1.0$ and four output nodes, asymptotic correct performance in backprop is 0.71.) ALCOVE = attention learning covering map.
a. Input patterns were not trained during that phase.

decrease only slightly as a consequence of subsequent training on the fourth pattern. The exact amount of interference in ALCOVE is governed by the specificity and the attention-learning rate; the values used here were comparable to those that best fit human learning data in other studies.

In conclusion, the catastrophic forgetting that plagues back-prop is not found in ALCOVE because of its localized receptive fields. ALCOVE is able to show significant interference only when the subsequently trained patterns are highly similar to the initially trained patterns or when the second phase of training has different relevant or irrelevant dimensions than the first phase.

Localized Receptive Fields Versus Local Representations
Although the receptive fields of hidden nodes in ALCOVE are relatively localized, the hidden-layer representation is not strictly local, where *local* means that a single hidden node is activated by any one stimulus. In ALCOVE, an input can partially activate many hidden nodes whose receptive fields cover it, so that the representation of the input is indeed distributed over many hidden nodes. (This is a form of continuous coarse coding; see Hinton, McClelland, & Rumelhart, 1986.) However, the character of that distributed representation is quite different from that in backprop because of the difference in receptive fields (Figure 18.7). One might say that the representation in backprop is more distributed than the representation in ALCOVE and even that the representation in backprop is too distributed.

There are ways to bias the hidden nodes in backprop toward relatively localized representations, if the input patterns are restricted to a convex hypersurface in input space. For example, if the input patterns are normalized, they fall on a hypersphere in input space, in which case the linear level contours of the back-prop hidden nodes can "carve off" small pieces of the sphere. For concreteness, consider a two-dimensional input space, so that the normalized input patterns fall on a circle. A given linear-sigmoid hidden node "looks down" on this space and makes a linear cut through it, so that all input points to one side of the line produce node activations greater than .5, and all points to the other side of the line produce node activations less than .5. If the linear cut is made near the edge of the circle, then only a small piece of the available input space causes node activations above .5. In particular, Scalettar and Zee (1988) demonstrated that such localized representations are a natural consequence of learning noisy input patterns (with weight decay). Unfortunately, a system that learns a localized representation might also unlearn it, and so it is not clear if the approach taken by Scalettar and Zee could solve the problem of catastrophic forgetting in backprop.

Goals of Backprop Versus Goals of ALCOVE

I have tried to show that backprop and ALCOVE differ in their architecture and behavior. They are also different in their goals. A common goal of applications of backprop is to study the distributed representation discovered by the hidden nodes (e.g., Hanson & Burr, 1990; Lehky & Sejnowski, 1988; Rumelhart et al., 1986; Sejnowski & Rosenberg, 1987) but not to model the course of learning per se. The goals of ALCOVE are quite different. ALCOVE begins with a psychological representation derived from multidimensional scaling that is assumed to remain unchanged during learning. ALCOVE models the course of learning by adjusting attention strengths on the given dimensions and by adjusting association weights between exemplars and categories.

Learning Rules and Exceptions

So far the exemplar-similarity-based representation in ALCOVE has been compared with the featural- and configural-cue representations used in the network models of Gluck and Bower (1988a, 1988b) and with the "half-space receptor" representation in backprop. None of these representations directly addresses the fact that subjects in concept-learning tasks and many categorization tasks consciously generate another representation: rules (e.g., Bourne, 1970; Shepard et al., 1961). Ultimately, the relation of ALCOVE to rule generation must be determined. In this section I outline the beginnings of a theory of how ALCOVE might steer rule generation. The discussion is meant to be exploratory, suggestive, and perhaps provocative, but not conclusive.

One of the most widely known connectionist models of learning is the past-tense acquisition model of Rumelhart and McClelland (1986). That model learned to associate root forms of English verbs with their past-tense forms. The network consisted of input and output layers of nodes that represented *Wickel features*, which are triplets of phoneme features, one feature from each of three consecutive phonemes. The network had no hidden layer, and it learned the connection weights from the inputs to the outputs by using the perceptron convergence procedure, which can be considered to be a limiting case of backprop.

One of the main aspects of past-tense learning that Rumelhart and McClelland (1986) tried to model is the so-called three-stage or U-shaped learning of high-frequency irregular verbs. Children acquire these verbs, such as *go–went*, very early on, in Stage 1. Subsequently, they begin to acquire many regular verbs that form the past tense by adding *ed*. In this second stage, children apparently overgeneralize the rule and regularize the previously well-learned irregular verbs. For example, they might occasionally produce forms like *goed* or *wented*. Finally, in Stage 3, the high-frequency irregular verbs are relearned. Three-stage learning has traditionally been used as evidence that people generate rules. The second stage is explained by suggesting that children literally learn the rule and overapply it. Rumelhart and McClelland's (1986) model had no mechanism for explicit rule generation, so if it could account for three-stage learning, it would pose a challenge to the necessity of rule-based accounts.

The Rumelhart and McClelland (1986) model was indeed able to show three-stage learning of irregular verbs, but that was accomplished only by changing the composition of the training patterns during learning. The network was initially exposed to eight high-frequency irregular verbs and only two regulars. After 10 epochs of training, the network achieved fairly good performance on those verbs. Then the training set was changed to include 334 additional regular verbs and only 76 more irregulars, so the proportion of regulars suddenly jumped from 20% to 80%. As might be expected (especially considering the results on catastrophic forgetting discussed in the previous section), when flooded with regular verbs, the network rapidly learned the regulars but suffered a decrement in performance on the previously learned irregulars. With continued training on the full set of verbs, the network was able to relearn the irregulars. Thus, the transition from Stage 1 to Stage 2 was accomplished only with the help of a deus ex machina, in the form of a radically altered training set. Rumelhart and McClelland defended the approach by saying, "It is generally observed that the early, rather limited vocabulary of young children undergoes an explosive growth at some point in development (Brown, 1973). Thus, the actual transition in a child's vocabulary of verbs would appear quite abrupt on a time-scale of years so that our assumptions about abruptness of onset may not be too far off the mark" (Rumelhart & McClelland, 1986, p. 241). Several critics (e.g., Marcus et al., 1990; Pinker & Prince, 1988) were left unconvinced and argued that a cogent model would have the transition emerge from the learning mechanism, not exclusively from a discontinuity in the training corpus.

Connectionists are left with the challenge of how to model three-stage acquisition of high-frequency irregulars without changing the composition of

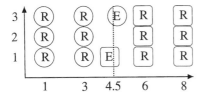

Figure 18.9
Category structure used for demonstration of three-stage learning of rules and exceptions. (The exemplars marked with an R follow the rule, which separates the two categories by the dotted line. Exemplars marked with an E are exceptions to the rule. The x values of the exceptions were 4.4 and 4.6.)

the training set during learning.[2] It is now shown that ALCOVE can exhibit three-stage learning of high-frequency exceptions to rules in a highly simplified abstract analogue of the verb-acquisition situation. For this demonstration, the input stimuli are distributed over two continuously varying dimensions as shown in Figure 18.9. Of the 14 training exemplars, the 12 marked with an R can be correctly classified by the simple rule, "If the value of the exemplar on Dimension 1 is greater than 4.5, then the exemplar is an instance of the box category; otherwise it is in the circle category." This type of rule is referred to as a *Type 1* rule by Shepard et al. (1961), because it segregates members of two categories on the basis of a single dimension. It is also called a *value-on-dimension* rule by Nosofsky, Clark, and Shin (1989), for obvious reasons. In Figure 18.9 there are two exceptions to the rule, marked with an E. The exceptions are presented with higher relative frequency than individual rule exemplars. The analogy to the verb situation is that most of the exemplars are regular, in that they can be classified by the rule, but a few exemplars are irregular exceptions to the rule. The circle and box categories are not supposed to correspond to regular and irregular verbs; rather, they are arbitrary output values (+1 and −1) used only to establish distinct types of mappings on the rule-based and exceptional cases.

ALCOVE was applied to the structure in Figure 18.9, using 14 hidden nodes and parameter values near the values used to fit the Medin et al. (1982) data: $\phi = 1.00$, $\lambda_\omega = 0.025$, $c = 3.50$, and $\lambda_\alpha = 0.010$. Epoch updating was used, with each rule exemplar occurring once per epoch and each exceptional case occurring four times per epoch, for a total of 20 patterns per epoch. (The same qualitative effects are produced with trial-by-trial updating, with superimposed trial-by-trial "sawteeth," what Plunkett and Marchman, 1991, called micro U-shaped learning.) The results are shown in Figure 18.10. The learning curve for the exceptions (filled circles) shows a distinct nonmonotonicity so that near Epochs 10 to 15 there is a reversal of learning on the exceptions. (ALCOVE is always performing gradient descent on total error, even when performance on the exceptions drops, because performance on the rule cases improves so

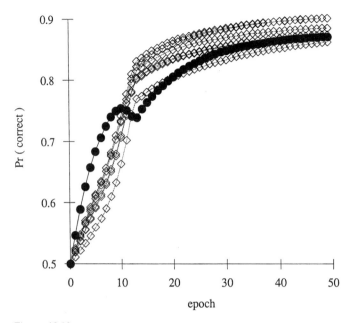

Figure 18.10
Results of applying ALCOVE (attention learning covering map) to the rules-and-exception structure of Figure 18.9 (Filled circles show probability of correct classification for exceptions, whereas open diamonds indicate probability of correct classification for the various rule cases. Pr = probability.)

rapidly.) The other important feature of the results is that the learning curves for exceptional and rule cases cross over, so that early in training the high-frequency exceptions are learned more accurately, but later in learning the rule cases are learned better. Thus, we have a clear case of three-stage, U-shaped learning.

It should be emphasized that in this demonstration, all parameter values were fixed throughout training, and the composition of the training set was also fixed throughout training. Moreover, there were no order-of-presentation effects because epoch updating was used.

The results shown here should not be construed as a claim that ALCOVE is appropriate for modeling language acquisition. On the contrary, linguistic stimuli, in their natural context, might not be adequately represented by a multidimensional similarity space as demanded by ALCOVE (but cf. Elman, 1989, 1990). Moreover, the results in Figure 18.10 should not be taken as a necessary prediction of ALCOVE, as some other combinations of parameter values do not show crossover or nonmonotonicities. Rather, the claim is that if such phenomena do occur in human learning, then ALCOVE might very well be able to model those effects.

How does three-stage learning happen in ALCOVE? In the initial epochs, the association weights between exemplars and categories are being established. The association weights from exceptions grow more quickly because the exceptions are presented more frequently. The attention strengths are not affected much in the early epochs because there is not much error propagated back to them by the weak association weights (see Equation 6). Thus, performance on the exceptions is initially better than on the rule cases entirely because of relative frequency.

The second stage begins as the association weights get big enough to back propagate error signals to the attention strengths. Then attention to the rule-irrelevant dimension rapidly decreases (in Figure 18.9, the vertical dimension shrinks). That has two effects: The rule cases rapidly increase their within-category similarity, thereby improving performance, and the two exceptional cases rapidly increase their between-categories similarity, thereby decreasing accuracy. In other words, once the system learns a little about which exemplars belong in which category, it temporarily ignores the dimension that best distinguishes the exceptions, to benefit the ruly majority.

Such an account of three-stage learning does not prohibit the simultaneous existence of a distinct rule generating system. On the contrary, I believe that a more complete model of human category learning should also include a rule system that would simultaneously try to summarize and generalize the performance of ALCOVE by hypothesizing and testing rules. ALCOVE could help steer the rule-generating system and act as a fallback when adequate rules are not yet found. In such a scenario, the rule-generating system is neither epiphenomenal nor redundant; one major benefit is that rules abstract and unitize category knowledge so it can be transferred to other tasks and stimulus domains.

Perhaps the primary question for such a rule-generating system is which rules should be hypothesized and tested first? The behavior of ALCOVE suggest that one should generate and test rules using the dimensions that are most relevant, where relevance is measured by the dimensional attention strength learned in ALCOVE. This approach is akin to ideas of Bourne et al. (1976), but the notion of driving the rule system with an attention-learning system is new, as far as I know. Details of such an interaction are yet to be worked out; I (Kruschke, 1990a, 1990b) described applications of the idea to the results of Medin, Wattenmaker, and Michalski (1987) and to the learning of exemplars within the six types of Shepard et al. (1961).

In this section I have made two main points: First, ALCOVE is a connectionist network that can show three-stage learning of rules and exceptions without changing the composition of the training set during learning. Second, such a demonstration does not necessarily challenge rule-based accounts; rather, I should like to see future work incorporate ALCOVE-like mechanisms with rule-based systems to capture a wider range of human learning.

Discussion

I have tried to demonstrate that ALCOVE has significant advantages over some other models of category learning. ALCOVE combines an exemplar-based representation with error-driven learning. The exemplar-based representation performs better than other models that also use error-driven learning but with different representations, such as the configural-cue model and backprop. Error-driven learning performs better than other models with exemplar-based representations but different learning rules, such as the array-exemplar model (Estes et al., 1989; Nosofsky et al., in press). In the remainder of the chapter I discuss variations, extensions, and limitations of ALCOVE.

Placement of Hidden Nodes
All the simulations reported here assumed that a hidden node was placed at the position of each training exemplar, and only at those positions, from the onset of training. That is a reasonable assumption in some circumstances; for example, when the subject previews all the training exemplars (without feedback) before training or when there are so few exemplars that the subject sees them all within a small number of trials. In general, however, the model cannot assume knowledge of the exemplars before it has been exposed to them. There are several ways to deal with that. One way is to recruit new exemplar nodes whenever a novel training exemplar is detected (Hurwitz, 1990). This requires some kind of novelty detection and decision device, which entails the introduction of new parameters, such as a threshold for novelty. An alternative method is to set some a priori bounds on the extent of the input space and randomly cover the space with hidden nodes (Kruschke, 1990a, 1990b). This also entails new parameters, such as the density of the nodes. A third possibility is to recruit a new node of every training trial, regardless of novelty. Careful comparison of these possibilities awaits future research, but I (Kruschke, 1990a, 1990b) reported some preliminary results that the covering map approach fit training data as well as the exemplar approach.

Humble Versus Strict Teacher
The simulations reported here assumed the use of a humble teacher (Equation 4b). This was not an ad hoc assumption, but was motivated by the fact that feedback in category-learning experiments is nominal and does not specify the magnitude of category membership. The humble teachers tell the output nodes that their activation values should reach at least a certain level to indicate minimal membership, but there is no upper limit placed on their activations.

There are situations where a strict teacher is appropriate. Perhaps the most important use of a strict teacher has been the modeling of overexpectation error in animal learning (e.g., Kamin, 1969; Kremer, 1978; Rescorla & Wagner, 1972). Overexpectation occurs when an animal is first trained to associate Conditioned

Stimulus (CS) 1 with an unconditioned stimulus (US), denoted $CS_1 \rightarrow US$, then trained on $CS_2 \rightarrow US$, and finally trained on the compound stimulus $(CS_1 + CS_2) \rightarrow US$. The result is that the final training on the compound stimulus actually reduces the individual association strengths from CS_1 and CS_2. A strict teacher with error-driven learning (the Rescorla-Wagner learning rule) can account for that, because at the beginning of training with the compound stimulus $(CS_1 + CS_2)$, the double-strength association overshoots the teacher and is counted as an overexpectation error, causing the individual associations to be reduced. In that situation, however, there is reason to believe that the feedback is encoded by the animal as having a certain magnitude, and not just nominally. For example, in many experiments the feedback was magnitude of electric shock or amount of food.

One difference between humble and strict teachers regards asymptotic performance. Strict teachers demand that all exemplars are equally good members of the category, in that they all activate the category nodes to the same degree. Humble teachers allow more typical exemplars to activate their category nodes more than peripheral exemplars, even after asymptotic training. That difference is robust when measured in terms of category node activations; however, when transformed into response probabilities by the choice rule (Equation 3), the difference is compressed by ceiling and floor effects and becomes very subtle. For the applications reported in this article, the difference in fits, using humble or strict teachers, is slight. Thus, although I believe the distinction between humble and strict teachers is conceptually well motivated, it remains for future research to decide conclusively which is best for modeling category learning.

Extensions of ALCOVE
Several reasonable extensions of ALCOVE that might allow it to fit a wider array of category learning phenomena, without violating the motivating principles of the model, are possible.

The choice rule in Equation 3 was used primarily because of historical precedents, but it is not a central feature of the model, and there might be better ways of mapping network behavior to human performance. For example, one might instead incorporate random noise into the activation values of the nodes and use a deterministic choice rule such as selecting the category with the largest activation (cf. McClelland, 1991). Also, the particular choice of teacher values in Equation 4b was arbitrary and motivated primarily by the precedent of Gluck and Bower (1988a, 1988b). It might be that a different choice of teacher values, for example, +1 for "in" and 0 (instead of −1) for "not in" would be more appropriate, especially in conjunction with different response rules.

Many researchers have suggested that training has local or regional attentional effects, rather than (or in addition to) global effects (e.g., Aha & Goldstone, 1990; Aha & McNulty, 1989; Medin & Edelson, 1988; Nosofsky, 1988a). ALCOVE is easily altered to incorporate local attention strengths by giving each hidden node j a full set of dimensional attention strengths α_{ji}. In this particular variation there are no new parameters added because there is still just one attention-learning rate. It remains to be seen if exemplar-specific attention strengths, or some combination of exemplar-specific and global attention strengths, can account for an even wider range of data.

A related approach to introducing local attentional effects is to adapt individual hidden node specificities. Specificity learning (by gradient descent on error) would adjust the receptive-field size of individual hidden nodes, so that nodes surrounded by exemplars assigned to the same category would enlarge their receptive fields to encompass those other exemplars, whereas nodes near exemplars assigned to other categories would reduce their receptive fields to exclude those other exemplars. One implication is that asymmetric similarities (Rosch, 1975; Tversky, 1977) would evolve: Peripheral or boundary exemplars would be more similar to central or typical exemplars than vice versa, because the receptive field of the central exemplar would cover the peripheral exemplar, but the receptive field of the peripheral exemplar would not cover the central exemplar.

Another possible extension retains global dimensional attention strengths but changes the dynamics of attention learning. In this article it was assumed that the attention strengths α_i were primitives in the formalization, in that attention strengths were not themselves a function of some other underlying variables. If, however, each attention strength α_i is some nonlinear function of an underlying variable β_i, then gradient descent with respect to β_i will lead to different changes in α_i than gradient descent with respect to α_i itself. For example, suppose we let $\alpha_i = 1/(1 + e_i^{-\beta})$. This has three potentially desirable features: First, it automatically keeps the attention strengths α_i nonnegative, so that it is not necessary to clip them at zero. Second, it automatically keeps the attention strengths bounded above, so that there is a built-in "capacity" limit (cf. Nosofsky, 1986). Third, and perhaps most important, the gradient-descent learning rule for β_i is the same as the learning rule for α_i (Equation 6) except for the inclusion of a new factor, $\partial \alpha_i / \partial \beta_i = \alpha_i(1 - \alpha_i)$. This implies that the attention strength will not change very rapidly if it is near one of its extreme values of $+1$ or 0. In particular, if the system has learned that one dimension is highly relevant (α_1, nearly 1) and a second dimension is irrelevant (α_2, nearly 0), then it will be reluctant to change those attention strengths. Such an extension might allow ALCOVE to model the ease shown by adults to learn intradimensional feedback reversals relative to interdimensional relevance shifts (Kendler & Kendler, 1962), which ALCOVE cannot capture in its present form (W. Maki, personal communication, October 1990).[3]

Limitations of ALCOVE
ALCOVE applies only to situations for which the stimuli can be appropriately represented as points in a multidimensional psychological similarity space.

Moreover, ALCOVE assumes that the basis dimensions remain unchanged during category learning, and it does not apply to situations in which subjects generate new dimensions of representation, or otherwise recode the stimuli, during learning. Predictions made by ALCOVE are therefore based on two sets of premises: One set regards the representational assumptions just stated. The other set regards the exemplar-similarity-based architecture and error-driven learning rules of the model. If ALCOVE should fail to capture data from a given situation, either or both of the sets of premises might be wrong.

Another, perhaps more severe, limitation of ALCOVE is that it does not have a mechanism for hypothesizing and testing rules, whereas people clearly do. As suggested in a previous section, ALCOVE might subserve a rule-generating system, steering its selection of candidate rules. Until such a combination of systems is created, Holland, Holyoak, Nisbett, and Thagard's (1986) assessment of the Rescorla-Wagner learning rule might also apply to ALCOVE: "The limits of [Rescorla and Wagner's] approach can be characterized quite simply—their equation is generally able to account for phenomena that primarily depend on strength revision but is generally unable to account for phenomena that depend on rule generation" (p. 167).

Notes

This article is based on a doctoral dissertation submitted to the University of California at Berkeley. The research was supported in part by Biomedical Research Support Grant RR 7031-25 from the National Institutes of Health.

I thank the members of my dissertation committee, Stuart Dreyfus, Jerry Feldman, Barbara Mellers, Rob Nosofsky, and Steve Palmer. I also thank Steve Palmer for his encouragement and helpfulness as my primary adviser. Rob Nosofsky gets special thanks for sharing with me (unpublished) data and many stimulating conversations and for commenting on earlier versions of this article. Roger Ratcliff and two anonymous reviewers of an earlier version of this article also provided very helpful comments.

1. Recognizing the need to address the dimensional attention issue in the configural-cue model, Gluck and Chow (1989) modified it by making the learning rates on different modules of configural cues self-adaptive. In the case of the Shepard, Hovland, and Jenkins (1961) category types, there were seven different modules of configural cues: a module for each of the three dimensions (each module containing 2 one-value cues), a module for each of the three distinct pairs of dimensions (each module containing 4 two-value configural cues), and a module for the combination of three dimensions (containing 8 three-value configural cues). The learning rates for the seven modules were separately self-modifying according to the heuristic described by Jacobs (1988), which says that if weights change consistently across patterns, then learning rates should increase. The modified configural-cue model was indeed able to capture the correct ordering of the six category types. Did the modified configural-cue model selectively attend to individual dimensions? That is a difficult question to answer. For example, in learning Type II, it seems likely (details were not provided in Gluck & Chow, 1989) that the modified configural-cue model increased its learning rates for the module that combined Dimensions 1 and 2, but decreased the learning rates of all other modules, in particular the modules that individually encode Dimensions 1 and 2. Thus, it increased attention to the combination of dimensions but decreased attention to the individual dimensions. Although this might or might not make sense psychologically, it is clear that further explication of the modified configural-cue model is needed. On the other

hand, ALCOVE makes dimensional attention strengths and explicit part of the model and, unlike the modified configural-cue model, allows continuous-valued input dimensions.

2. Plunkett and Marchman (1991) showed that a backprop network trained on an unchanging set exhibited micro U-shaped learning, meaning that performance on individual patterns and pattern types fluctuated from epoch to epoch, but gradually improved overall. Their simulations did not exhibit macro U-shaped learning, in which there is a decrease in accuracy on all irregulars over several consecutive epochs, accompanied by an increase in accuracy on regulars, but they argued that such macro U-shaped learning does not occur in children either. Marcus et al. (1990) reported that some aspects of macro U-shaped learning do occur, although they are indeed subtle.

3. Hurwitz (1990; "hidden pattern unit model Version 2") independently developed a closely related model that had hidden nodes with activation function determined by a multiplicative similarity rule (Medin & Schaffer, 1978). For direct comparison with ALCOVE's hidden nodes, Hurwitz's activation function can be formally reexpressed as follows:

$$a_j^{hid} = \prod_i (1/1 + e^{(\beta_i - k)})^{|h_{ji} - a_i^{in}|} = \exp\left[-\sum_i \underbrace{\ln(1 + e^{(\beta_i - k)})}_{\alpha_i} |h_{ji} - a_i^{in}| \right],$$

where k is a constant. Thus, Hurwitz's model can be construed as a version of ALCOVE with $r = q = 1$ in Equation 1 and with $\alpha_i = \ln(1 + e^{(\beta_i - k)})$. Hurwitz's model therefore keeps the attention strengths α_i nonnegative but unbounded above. Gradient descent with respect to β_i results in the right-hand side of Equation 6 except for the absence of the specificity c and the inclusion of a new factor, $\partial \alpha_i / \partial \beta_i = (1 - e^{-\alpha_i})$. That causes attention strengths near zero to be reluctant to change, but causes large attention strengths to change rapidly.

References

Aha, D. W., & Goldstone, R. (1990). Learning attribute relevance in context in instance-based learning algorithms. *Proceedings of the Twelfth Annual Conference of the Cognitive Science Society* (pp. 141–148). Hillsdale, NJ: Erlbaum.

Aha, D. W., & McNulty, D. M. (1989). Learning relative attribute weights for instance-based concept descriptions. *Proceedings of the Eleventh Annual Conference of the Cognitive Science Society* (pp. 530–537). Hillsdale, NJ: Erlbaum.

Ahmad, S. (1988). *A study of scaling and generalization in neural networks* (Tech. Rep. No. UIUCDCS-R-88-1454). Urbana-Champaign: University of Illinois at Urbana-Champaign, Computer Science Department.

Anderson, J. R. (1991). The adaptive nature of human categorization. *Psychological Review, 98,* 409–429.

Bourne, L. E. (1970). Knowing and using concepts. *Psychological Review, 77,* 546–556.

Bourne, L. E., Ekstrand, B. R., Lovallo, W. R., Kellogg, R. T., Hiew, C. C., & Yaroush, R. A. (1976). Frequency analysis of attribute identification. *Journal of Experimental Psychology: General, 105,* 294–312.

Brown, R. (1973). *A first language.* Cambridge, MA: Harvard University Press.

Carroll, J. D., & Chang, J. J. (1970). Analysis of individual differences in multidimensional scaling via an n-way generalization of "Eckart-Young" decomposition. *Psychometrika, 35,* 283–319.

Elman, J. L. (1989). *Representation and structure in connectionist models* (Tech. Rep. No. 8903). San Diego: University of California at San Diego, Center for Research in Language.

Elman, J. L. (1990). Finding structure in time. *Cognitive Science, 14,* 179–211.

Estes, W. K. (1986a). Array models for category learning. *Cognitive Psychology, 18,* 500–549.

Estes, W. K. (1986b). Memory storage and retrieval processes in category learning. *Journal of Experimental Psychology: General, 115,* 155–174.

Estes, W. K. (1988). Toward a framework for combining connectionist and symbol-processing models. *Journal of Memory and Language, 27,* 196–212.

Estes, W. K., Campbell, J. A., Hatsopoulos, N., & Hurwitz, J. B. (1989). Base-rate effects in category learning: A comparison of parallel network and memory storage–retrieval models. *Journal of Experimental Psychology: Learning, Memory, and Cognition, 15*, 556–576.

Garner, W. R. (1974). *The processing of information and structure*. Hillsdale, NJ: Erlbaum.

Gluck, M. A. (1991). Stimulus generalization and representation in adaptive network models of category learning. *Psychological Science, 2*, 50–55.

Gluck, M. A., & Bower, G. H. (1988a). Evaluating an adaptive network model of human learning. *Journal of Memory and Language, 27*, 166–195.

Gluck, M. A., & Bower, G. H. (1988b). From conditioning to category learning: An adaptive network model. *Journal of Experimental Psychology: General, 117*, 227–247.

Gluck, M. A., Bower, G. H., & Hee, M. R. (1989). A configural-cue network model of animal and human associative learning. *Proceedings of the Eleventh Annual Conference of the Cognitive Science Society*. Hillsdale, NJ: Erlbaum.

Gluck, M. A., & Chow, W. (1989). *Dynamic stimulus-specific learning rates and the representation of dimensionalized stimulus structures*. Unpublished manuscript.

Hanson, S. J., & Burr, D. J. (1990). What connectionist models learn: Learning and representation in connectionist networks. *Behavioral and Brain Sciences, 13*, 471–489.

Hinton, G. E., McClelland, J. L., & Rumelhart, D. E. (1986). Distributed representations. In D. E. Rumelhart & J. L. McClelland (Eds.), *Parallel distributed processing* (chapter 3). Cambridge, MA: MIT Press.

Holland, J. H., Holyoak, K. J., Nisbett, R. E., & Thagard, P. R. (1986). *Induction*. Cambridge, MA: MIT Press.

Hurwitz, J. B. (1990). *A hidden-pattern unit network model of category learning*. Unpublished doctoral dissertation, Harvard University.

Jacobs, R. A. (1988). Increased rates of convergence through learning rate adaptation. *Neural Networks, 1*, 295–307.

Kamin, L. J. (1969). Predictability, surprise, attention, and conditioning. In B. A. Campbell & R. M. Church (Eds.), *Punishment*. New York: Appleton-Century-Crofts.

Kendler, H. H., & Kendler, T. S. (1962). Vertical and horizontal processes in problem solving. *Psychological Review, 69*, 1–16.

Kremer, E. F. (1978). The Rescorla-Wagner model: Losses in associative strength in compound conditioned stimuli. *Journal of Experimental Psychology: Animal Behavior Processes, 4*, 22–36.

Kruschke, J. K. (1990a). *A connectionist model of category learning*. Doctoral dissertation, University of California at Berkeley. University Microfilms International.

Kruschke, J. K. (1990b). *ALCOVE: A connectionist model of category learning* (Cognitive Science Research Rep. No. 19). Bloomington: Indiana University.

Lehky, S. R., & Sejnowski, T. J. (1988). Network model of shape-from-shading: Neural function arises from both receptive and projective fields. *Nature, 333*, 452–454.

Luce, R. D. (1963). Detection and recognition. In R. D. Luce, R. R. Bush, & E. Galanter (Eds.), *Handbook of mathematical psychology* (pp. 103–189). New York: Wiley.

Marcus, G. F., Ullman, M., Pinker, S., Hollander, M., Rosen, T. J., & Xu, F. (1990). *Overregularization* (Occasional Paper No. 41). Cambridge, MA: MIT, Center for Cognitive Science.

Matheus, C. J. (1988). Exemplar versus prototype network models for concept representation (abstract). *Neural Networks, 1* (Suppl. 1), 199.

McClelland, J. L. (1991). Stochastic interactive processes and the effect of context on perception. *Cognitive Psychology, 23*, 1–44.

McCloskey, M., & Cohen, N. J. (1989). Catastrophic interference in connectionist networks: The sequential learning problem. In G. Bower (Ed.), *The psychology of learning and motivation* (Vol. 24, pp. 109–165). San Diego, CA: Academic Press.

Medin, D. L., Altom, M. W., Edelson, S. M., & Freko, D. (1982). Correlated symptoms and simulated medical classification. *Journal of Experimental Psychology: Learning, Memory, and Cognition, 8*, 37–50.

Medin, D. L., & Edelson, S. M. (1988). Problem structure and the use of base-rate information from experience. *Journal of Experimental Psychology: General, 117,* 68–85.

Medin, D. L., & Schaffer, M. M. (1978). Context theory of classification learning. *Psychological Review, 85,* 207–238.

Medin, D. L., & Schwanenflugel, P. J. (1981). Linear separability in classification learning. *Journal of Experimental Psychology: Human Learning and Memory, 7,* 355–368.

Medin, D. L., Wattenmaker, W. D., & Michalski, R. S. (1987). Constraints and preferences in inductive learning: An experimental study of human and machine performance. *Cognitive Science, 11,* 299–339.

Nosofsky, R. M. (1984). Choice, similarity, and the context theory of classification. *Journal of Experimental Psychology: Learning, Memory, and Cognition, 10,* 104–114.

Nosofsky, R. M. (1986). Attention, similarity, and the identification–categorization relationship. *Journal of Experimental Psychology: General, 115,* 39–57.

Nosofsky, R. M. (1987). Attention and learning processes in the identification and categorization of integral stimuli. *Journal of Experimental Psychology: Learning, Memory, and Cognition, 13,* 87–108.

Nosofsky, R. M. (1988a). On exemplar-based exemplar representations: Reply to Ennis (1988). *Journal of Experimental Psychology: General, 117,* 412–414.

Nosofsky, R. M. (1988b). Similarity, frequency, and category representations. *Journal of Experimental Psychology: Learning, Memory, and Cognition, 14,* 54–65.

Nosofsky, R. M. (1991). Exemplars, prototypes, and similarity rules. In A. Healy, S. Kosslyn, & R. Shiffrin (Eds.), *Essays in honor of W. K. Estes.* Hillsdale, NJ: Erlbaum.

Nosofsky, R. M., Clark, S. E., & Shin, H. J. (1989). Rules and exemplars in categorization, identification, and recognition. *Journal of Experimental Psychology: Learning, Memory, and Cognition, 15,* 282–304.

Nosofsky, R. M., Kruschke, J. K., & McKinley, S. (1992). Combining exemplar-based category representations and connectionist learning rules. *Journal of Experimental Psychology: Learning, Memory, and Cognition, 18,* 211–233.

Pinker, S., & Prince, A. (1988). On language and connectionism: Analysis of a parallel, distributed processing model of language acquisition. *Cognition, 28,* 73–193.

Plunkett, K., & Marchman, V. (1991). **U**-shaped learning and frequency effects in a multi-layered perceptron: Implications for child language acquisition. *Cognition, 38,* 43–102.

Ratcliff, R. (1990). Connectionist models of recognition memory: Constraints imposed by learning and forgetting functions. *Psychological Review, 2,* 285–308.

Rescorla, R. A., & Wagner, A. R. (1972). A theory of Pavlovian conditioning: Variations in the effectiveness of reinforcement and nonreinforcement. In A. H. Black & W. F. Prokasy (Eds.), *Classical conditioning: II. Current research and theory.* New York: Appleton-Century-Crofts.

Robinson, A. J., Niranjan, M., & Fallside, F. (1988). *Generalising the nodes of the error propagation network* (Tech. Rep. No. CUED/F-INFENG/TR.25). Cambridge, England: Cambridge University Engineering Department.

Rosch, E. (1975). Cognitive reference points. *Cognitive Psychology, 7,* 532–547.

Rosch, E., Simpson, C., & Miller, R. S. (1976). Structural bases of typicality effects. *Journal of Experimental Psychology: Human Perception and Performance, 2,* 491–502.

Rumelhart, D. E., Hinton, G. E., & Williams, R. J. (1986). Learning internal representations by back-propagating errors. In D. E. Rumelhart & J. L. McClelland (Eds.), *Parallel distributed processing* (Vol. 1, chapter 8). Cambridge, MA: MIT Press.

Rumelhart, D. E., & McClelland, J. L. (1986). On learning the past tenses of English verbs. In J. L. McClelland & D. E. Rumelhart (Eds.), *Parallel distributed processing* (Vol. 2, chapter 18). Cambridge, MA: MIT Press.

Scalettar, R., & Zee, A. (1988). Emergence of grandmother memory in feed forward networks: Learning with noise and forgetfulness. In D. Waltz & J. A. Feldman (Eds.), *Connectionist models and their implications: Reading from cognitive science* (pp. 309–327). Norwood, NJ: Ablex.

Sejnowski, T. J., & Rosenberg, C. R. (1987). Parallel networks that learn to pronounce English text. *Complex Systems, 1,* 145–168.

Shepard, R. N. (1957). Stimulus and response generalization: A stochastic model relating generalization to distance in psychological space. *Psychometrika, 22,* 325–345.

Shepard, R. N. (1958). Stimulus and response generalization: Deduction of the generalization gradient from a trace model. *Psychological Review, 65,* 242–256.

Shepard, R. N. (1962a). The analysis of proximities: Multidimensional scaling with an unknown distance function. I. *Psychometrika, 27,* 125–140.

Shepard, R. N. (1962b). The analysis of proximities: Multidimensional scaling with an unknown distance function. II. *Psychometrika, 27,* 219–246.

Shepard, R. N. (1964). Attention and the metric structure of the stimulus space. *Journal of Mathematical Psychology, 1,* 54–87.

Shepard, R. N. (1987). Toward a universal law of generalization for psychological science. *Science, 237,* 1317–1323.

Shepard, R. N., Hovland, C. L., & Jenkins, H. M. (1961). Learning and memorization of classifications. *Psychological Monographs, 75* (13, Whole No. 517).

Tversky, A. (1977). Features of similarity. *Psychological Review, 84,* 327–352.

Appendix: Derivation of Learning Rules

Here are derived the learning rules used in ALCOVE. Learning of any parameter in the model is done by gradient descent on a cost function such as sum-squared error. The purpose is to determine gradient-descent learning equations for the attention strengths, α_i, and the association weights, w_{kj}^{out}. All the derivations are simple insofar as they involve only the chain rule and algebra. On the other hand, they are complicated insofar as they involve several subscripts simultaneously, and care must be taken to keep them explicit and consistent. Subscripts denoting variables are in lowercase letters. Subscripts denoting constants are in uppercase letters. Vector notation is used throughout the derivations: Boldface variables denote vectors. For example, $\mathbf{a}^{out} = [\cdots a_k^{out} \cdots]^T$ is the column vector of output activation values for the current stimulus.

The General Case

I first compute derivatives using an unspecified cost function C and then treat the specific case of sum-squared error. Suppose that C is some function of the output of the network and perhaps of some other constants (such as teacher values for the output nodes). In general, any parameter x is adjusted by gradient descent on C, which means that the change in x is proportional to the negative of the derivative: $\Delta x = -\lambda_x \partial C / \partial x$, where λ_x is a (nonnegative) constant of proportionality, called the learning rate of parameter x.

I begin by rewriting Equation 1 in two parts, introducing the notation net_j^{hid}:

$$\text{net}_j^{hid} = \left(\sum_{\substack{in \\ i}} \alpha_i |h_{ji} - a_i^{in}|^r \right)^{1/r} \quad \text{and}$$

$$a_j^{hid} = \exp[-c(\text{net}_j^{hid})^q], \tag{A1}$$

where r and q are positive numbers. The special case of $r = 1$ (city-block metric) and $q = 1$ (exponential-similarity decay) are subsequently treated.

Because the output nodes are linear (Equation 2), the derivative of C with respect to the association weights between hidden and output nodes is

$$\frac{\partial C}{\partial w_{KJ}^{out}} = \frac{\partial C}{\partial a_K^{out}} \frac{\partial a_K^{out}}{\partial w_{KJ}^{out}} = \frac{\partial C}{\partial a_K^{out}} a_J^{hid}. \tag{A2}$$

The derivative $\partial C / \partial a_K^{out}$ must be computed directly from the definition of C, but it can presumably be evaluated locally in the Kth output node. Hence, the weight change resulting from gradient descent is locally computable.

In the applications reported in this article, there was never a need to alter the hidden node positions or specificities. Therefore, I do not compute the derivatives of the hidden node coordinates or specificities, although they certainly can be computed (e.g., Robinson, Niranjan, & Fallside, 1988). Now consider the attention strengths α_I. First note that

$$\frac{\partial C}{\partial \alpha_I} = \frac{\partial C}{\partial \mathbf{a}^{out}} \frac{\partial \mathbf{a}^{out}}{\partial \mathbf{a}^{hid}} \frac{\partial \mathbf{a}^{hid}}{\partial \alpha_I} = \left[\cdots \partial C / \partial a_{k^{out}} \cdots \right] \begin{bmatrix} \vdots \\ \cdots w_{kj}^{out} \cdots \\ \vdots \end{bmatrix} \begin{bmatrix} \vdots \\ \partial a_j^{hid} / \partial \alpha_I \\ \vdots \end{bmatrix}. \tag{A3a}$$

Computation of $\partial a_j^{hid} / \partial \alpha_I$ requires a bit more work:

$$\frac{\partial a_j^{hid}}{\partial \alpha_I} = \frac{\partial a_j^{hid}}{\partial \, net_j^{hid}} \frac{\partial \, net_j^{hid}}{\partial \alpha_I}$$

$$= -a_j^{hid} cq (net_j^{hid})^{(q-1)} \frac{1}{r} \left(\sum_{\substack{in \\ i}} \alpha_i |h_{ji} - a_i^{in}|^r \right)^{(1/r-1)} |h_{jI} - a_I^{in}|^r$$

$$= -a_j^{hid} c \frac{q}{r} (net_j^{hid})^{(q-r)} |h_{jI} - a_I^{in}|^r. \tag{A3b}$$

Substituting Equation A3b into Equation A3a yields

$$\frac{\partial C}{\partial \alpha_I} = \sum_{\substack{hid \\ j}} \left(\sum_{\substack{out \\ k}} \frac{\partial C}{\partial a_k^{out}} w_{kj}^{out} \right) a_j^{hid} c \frac{q}{r} (net_j^{hid})^{(q-r)} |h_{jI} - a_I^{in}|^r. \tag{A4}$$

The factors of Equation A4 are all available to input node I if one permits backwards connections from hidden nodes to input nodes that have connection weight equal to the fixed value 1. (Usually in back propagation the backward links are conceived as having the same value as adaptive forward links.) The mechanism for computing the derivatives is the same, in spirit, as that used in "standard" back propagation (Rumelhart, Hinton, & Williams, 1986): The partial derivatives computed at each layer are propagated backwards through the network to previous layers.

Equation A4 reveals some interesting behavior for the adaptation of the attentional parameter α_I. The equation contains the factor

$$F_j = a_j^{hid}(\text{net}_j^{hid})^{(q-r)}|h_{jI} - a_{Iin}|^r.$$

All the other factors of Equation A4 can be considered constants in the present context, so that the change in attention α_I is proportional to F_j. The question now is when is the change large, that is, when is F_j significantly nonzero? The precise answer depends on the values of q and r, but a qualitative generalization can be made about the form of F_j. The graph of F_j (not shown) is a "hyper dumbbell" shape that is centered on the input stimulus, with its axis of symmetry along the Ith dimension. Hence, the attentional parameter is only affected by hidden nodes within the hyper dumbbell region.

Sum-Squared Error
Now consider a specific case for the objective function C, the sum-squared error, as in Equation 4a. Note first that

$$\frac{\partial E}{\partial a_K^{out}} = -(t_K - a_K^{out}). \tag{A5}$$

This derivative (Equation A5) is continuous and well behaved, even with the humble-teacher values. Then Equation A5 can be substituted into each of Equations A2 and A4.

Special Case of $q = r = 1$
In the special case when $q = r$ (and in particular when $q = r = 1$), the learning equation for attention strengths simplifies considerably. In this special case, the term $\frac{q}{r}(\text{net}_j^{hid})^{(q-r)}$ in Equation A4 reduces to 1. The initial computation of a_j^{hid} also simplifies (cf. Equation A1). The learning rules reported in the text (Equations 5 and 6) are the result.

Procedural Learning

Chapter 19

How People Learn to Skip Steps

Stephen B. Blessing and John R. Anderson

As people solve the same type of problem again and again, not only do they get faster at doing that type of problem, but very often the process they use to solve the problems changes as well, often resulting in skipped steps (Koedinger & Anderson, 1990). This reorganization and skipping of steps allow people to solve problems more quickly, efficiently, and easily. One might expect this change in process to result in performance discontinuities in a person's acquisition of a skill because the person is undergoing what may be a radical reorganization of how that skill is performed. However, Newell and Rosenbloom (1981) showed that a variety of skills are acquired at a steady rate, one that follows a power function (an equation of the form $y = a + bx^c$, where a, b, and c are constants). In this article we examine the step-skipping phenomenon and its apparent relationship to the power law of learning.

Step skipping is often thought of as a compositional process, in which a person who used to take two or more steps to do a task now takes only one. Intuitively then, if a person does a problem in fewer steps in completing a task, he or she should take less time in performing that task. Research by Charness and Campbell (1988) showed that compositional processes account for about 70% of the speedup associated with acquiring a new skill, with the rest of the speedup accounted for by becoming faster at the operations themselves. Work done by Frensch and Geary (1993; Frensch, 1991) also indicated the importance of compositional processes, as distinct from a general speedup in performance, in learning a task. It is evident from this research that composition is an important component to acquiring a skill.

Given the importance of these compositional processes, a number of skill acquisition theories attempt to account for the change in process, including step skipping, that occurs when a person becomes expert in a particular domain. The adaptive control of thought—rational theory (ACT–R; Anderson, 1993) predicts that any new procedural skills arise by analogy to examples. Newell and Rosenbloom (1981; Rosenbloom & Newell, 1986) proposed that people acquire skill by a chunking process, in which responses are acquired in larger and larger chunks (patterns). Logan's (1988, 1990) instance theory states that skilled performance is generally characterized as the retrieval of a specific memory, and not the use of a procedure. As can be seen even from just these short descriptions, the proposed mechanisms in these theories differ greatly. These theories are discussed in more detail shortly, but first we want to introduce the phenomenon that we address in this article.

When asked to solve the equation $-x - A = B$ for x, some people who are facile in algebra will immediately write that $x = -B - A$. However, people who have just learned how to solve simple linear equations may not be able to go immediately from the initial problem statement to the solution. Rather, they may have to perform three steps, which may correspond to adding A to both sides, collecting $-A + A$ on the left, and multiplying through by -1 to solve successfully for x. At some point, people will probably learn to collapse into a single step the actions of removing the A from the left-hand side of the equation, changing the sign on the B, and adding $-A$ to the right-hand side. What happens during this transition, and how does it take place? Under what circumstances do people start skipping steps? In the experiments described in this chapter we examine this process. First, we discuss some of the learning mechanisms that have been proposed to account for step skipping.

Step-Skipping Explanations

There are a few theoretical approaches to step skipping that differ in their details but that involve the same problem-solving framework (Newell & Simon, 1972). As such, they make use of many of the ideas germane to that framework (e.g., operators and production rules, among others). An operator is a rule that can be applied to transform the current problem state into a different one. Operators are often conceived of as production rules, which are condition–action (IF–THEN) statements that act on the current problem state. A number of these explanations amount to the claim that step skipping involves replacing smaller grain operators by larger grain operators. Three such explanations are rule composition, chunking, and analogy. Another view, Logan's (1988, 1990) instance theory, differs from the previous three by stating that truly expert performance is not characterized by the application of operators but rather by retrieval of a specific example. We discuss each of these four explanations in turn.

Rule Composition

One view of how step skipping occurs is by collapsing operators that follow each other in a problem solution into a single operator (Anderson, 1983; Lewis, 1978). Such collapsing of adjacent operators is referred to as *rule composition*. These composed operators would then produce step-skipping behavior by not outputting the intermediate products that the single operators produced. For example, when first learning algebra and asked to solve the equation presented earlier, $-x - A = B$, the student would probably solve the problem in three steps (the application of three operators) by first adding a $+A$ to both sides, simplifying both sides to get $-x = B + A$, and finally multiplying through by -1 to get the final line, $x = -B - A$. Operator composition might compose the first two steps into a single operator that directly produced $-x = B + A$, and then compose this with the third step to create a single operator that produces the final result. Rule composition is an attractive idea because it provides a very concise account of how step skipping occurs.

Work by Lewis (1981), however, casts doubt on whether step skipping can merely be due to composition of adjacent steps. He investigated what he called *powerful operators*. These operators do the work of a series of others, as in the combination of the transposition and collection operators in algebra (shown previously). Their critical feature is that they can combine nonadjacent steps together, a condition that would not happen with standard rule composition. For example, a novice learning algebra would probably solve the equation $x + 2(x + 1) = 4$ by first multiplying both x and 1 by 2, and then adding x and $2x$ together for the next step. However, an expert would probably immediately write $3x = 2$, with the 2 and the x being multiplied and then added to the x before the 2 and the 1 are multiplied and subtracted from the 4. Thus, non-adjacent steps are being combined to produce the operator that writes out the $3x$. Lewis referred to this as the problem of going from a *two-pass* system (solving a problem in multiple steps) to a *one-pass* system (solving a problem in a single step).

Chunking

Newell's (1990) theory of cognition, *Soar*, has a single mechanism that attempts to provide a psychologically plausible account for all of skill acquisition. This mechanism, called *chunking*, operates when an impasse in the problem-solving process occurs. An impasse occurs when the Soar system reaches a state in which no operator applies or in which the knowledge to apply an operator does not exist. Once an impasse happens, Soar will set a subgoal to solve the impasse and then creates a new problem space in which to solve the subgoal. Once the subgoal has been solved, Soar creates a new operator, a chunk, using the results obtained after the impasse is resolved. The chunk is built by starting at the results of the impasse and backtracing (i.e., working backward) through the elements before the impasse that gave rise to these results. The operator that represents the chunk is then constructed by using these original elements that occurred before the impasse as the condition side of a production rule and the results after the impasse as the action side. These chunks could be thought of as a composite operator because the operators used to solve the subgoal would be represented by the resulting chunk. Under such a scheme, the learner builds larger and larger chunks. For example, a person may eventually create a single chunk (in the form of a production) that would produce $x = -B - A$ when presented with $-x - A = B$. It is important to note that within Soar, not only is the process by which a system solves a problem important, but the product is as well. Because of this, Soar avoids the problem of nonadjacent operators inherent in the rule composition view. In building the chunk, Soar backtraces from the results of solving an impasse to the conditions before the impasse.

Compiling Rules From Analogy
Within Anderson's (1993) ACT–R framework, cognitive skills are realized by production rules. Skilled performance is characterized by executing these production rules to do the task at hand. The only mechanism by which new production rules can enter the system is through analogy to an existing example in declarative memory. When given a task to do for which no production rules apply, ACT–R attempts to locate a previously acquired declarative example that exemplifies the application of the correct operator that is similar to the current goal. If a similar enough example is found, the analogy mechanism produces a production rule that will generate the correct action. In short, novices solve problems by referencing examples, whereas experts apply operators. Step skipping in which this analogy mechanism is used could be produced by forming analogies between examples that incorporated the application of multiple operators. A model of such a process, including a fuller account of the analogy mechanism, is presented after a discussion of the empirical results.

Retrieval of Examples
In Logan's (1988, 1990) theory, performance on a task is governed by a race between executing the appropriate operator and retrieving a specific example. When first starting to do a task, people will apply the necessary operators. Eventually a strong enough association will be made between a specific stimulus and its appropriate response, and so direct retrieval of the response can take place. In comparison to Anderson's (1993) theory, Logan's makes the opposite prediction—that novice performance is marked by application of operators, whereas skilled performance is done by retrieval of past examples. Step skipping in such a framework could perhaps occur once the task is done by direct memory retrieval. If one made the assumption that the retrieved memory trace of a problem solution could contain multiple steps of that problem solution, the problem solver could only produce the last step contained in the instance, thus eliminating intermediate steps. This would allow the problem solver to skip intermediate steps.

The two previous theories are not necessarily mutually exclusive, and evidence that supports both theories has been collected. In a study done by Anderson and Fincham (1994), some participants were given only examples of rule applications. Participants were able to extract the correct rules from the examples and were able to apply them to problems presented to them. Even in the absence of repeated examples, participants still exhibited power law learning, contrary to what the strong version of Logan's instance theory would predict. However, in unpublished follow-up studies, Anderson and Fincham (1994) found that learning was faster when examples were repeated. Carlson and Lundy (1992) also tested participants' ability to learn rules, varying the consistency of both the examples and the sequence of operation. They found separable benefits of both. That is, participants were able to learn faster either if the data were consistent (i.e., repeated examples) or if the order of operations was consistent.

The Current Experiments

The process by which people start skipping steps has not adequately been explored. Since the work done by Lewis (1978), few researchers have examined how people learn to skip steps in solving problems. One issue that arises when people begin to skip steps is whether they are actually mentally skipping steps or are only physically skipping steps. That is, people may just be going through each step in the problem mentally, and only performing some of the steps, as opposed to mentally going straight from the first step to the last step. We refer to this as *overtly* skipping steps versus *covertly* skipping steps. We discussed the above-indicated theories in terms of how they account for covert step skipping, but no experiments have been done to test their claims.

In the work presented in this article we examined the development of step skipping within a particular task, one similar to algebra. By a close examination of people performing our task, a better understanding of the skill acquisition process could be attained. Because the task was relatively easy, participants could reach expert status within a single experimental session. By comparing their knowledge and use of procedures at the beginning to that of the end, we established the two endpoints for which a process has to account. Furthermore, by examining the participants' actions between these two endpoints and from concurrent verbal protocols (Ericsson & Simon, 1990), we were able to investigate participants' use of examples, their step-skipping behavior, and their change from making each step explicit to skipping certain steps. From this analysis we were able to develop a process model of the observed behavior, part of which we have implemented as an ACT–R (Anderson, 1993) model.

Experiment 1

When and how do people start skipping steps when solving problems? Experiment 1 was designed to explore this question. By instructing participants in the rules of our task and letting them solve problems in it, but not forcing them to make all steps explicit, a situation was created in which we could study how problem solvers naturally learn to skip steps. Also, participants were instructed to think aloud while solving the problems. By studying these protocols, the relation between physically skipping steps and mentally skipping steps can be more closely examined. It could be the case that problem solvers who are

Table 19.1
How the symbols used in this task map onto algebraic symbols (experiments 1 and 2)

Algebraic symbol	Symbol in task
+	®
−	♥
*	#
/	©
Operands	Δ
	Γ
	Φ
	Ω
x	$\mathcal{P}$
=	↔

Table 19.2
Sample problem

Step	What participants saw	Algebraic mapping
Given step	♥Φ©Ω♥$\mathcal{P}$↔♥Δ	$-A \div B - x = -C$
Step 1	♥Φ©Ω♥$\mathcal{P}$® Φ↔♥Δ® Φ	$-A \div B - x + A = -C + A$
Step 2	©Ω♥$\mathcal{P}$↔♥Δ® Φ	$\div B - x = -C + A$
Step 3	©Ω♥$\mathcal{P}$#Ω↔♥Δ® Φ#Ω	$\div B - x^*B = -C + A^*B$
Step 4	♥$\mathcal{P}$↔♥Δ® Φ#Ω	$-x = -C + A^*B$
Step 5	$\mathcal{P}$↔®Δ♥ΦΦ#Ω	$x = +C - A^*B$

overtly skipping steps are still going through each step mentally, in which case no compositional processes are occurring.

As stated previously, the task we designed was an analog of algebra. The rules defining the task are given in Appendix A. In place of the standard four operators and Roman letters, we used Greek and various other symbols to mask the similarity to algebra. Table 19.1 lists the symbols we used and how they map onto the standard algebraic symbols. In most of our examples, we used the standard algebraic symbols so that the reader could use previous knowledge to decode parts of the task. Table 19.2 contains an example of one of the hardest problems, with all of the steps needed to solve the problem made explicit. The first step in solving this problem is to add ®Φ to both sides of the character string (the ↔ divides the string into left and right halves) in accordance with Rule 1. For the second step, the ... ♥Φ ... ®Φ is deleted from the left-hand side by application of Rule 5. For Steps 3 and 4, #Ω is added to both sides of the string (Rule 1 again), and then the ... ©Ω ... #Ω is deleted from the left-hand side (Rule 3). For the final step, Rule 8 is applied to eliminate the ♥

from in front of the $\mathcal{P}$. It should be noted that the rules are constructed such that this is the only order of steps possible in solving this problem.

Method

Participants   Twelve Carnegie Mellon University undergraduates were paid to participate in this experiment. We placed an ad on a local electronic bulletin board, which many undergraduates read, to solicit the participants.

Materials   We constructed an algebra analog for this experiment. Differences existed between this task and algebra, and so the mapping was not perfect. For example, the division–multiplication operator pair acted more like the addition–subtraction operator pair than in standard algebra. Also, this task had a more limited order of operations. There are rules of precedence (Rules 10 and 11 in Appendix A), but to keep the task simple, parentheses were not used as some of the allowable manipulations would look strange in algebra. Also, any operator was allowed in front of x, so it was possible to end up with an equation that looked like $^*x = A + B$. The order of operations was constrained so that at each step in any problem, only one rule was applicable. That is, at any intermediate step in solving a problem, only one operator can be used to achieve the next step in the problem. There was never a choice between operators.

In all, the task consisted of 11 rules that the participants used to manipulate the character strings to achieve the goal state, which was to "isolate" (i.e., solve for) the $\mathcal{P}$ symbol on the left-hand side of the equation. One rule (Rule 1 in Appendix A) resembled the algebraic rule that states the same thing can be added to both sides of an equation (e.g., one can add a $+A$ to both the left- and right-hand sides), four rules (Rules 2–5) dictated how operators and operands could be removed from one side of an equation (e.g., if $+A - A$ appeared on the left-hand side, it could be deleted from the equation), four rules (Rules 6–9) described how to remove a sign in front of the x symbol when one appeared, and two rules (Rules 10 and 11) provided information on precedence and the order of operations. The division removal rule (Rule 9, which applied when the equivalent of $/x$ appeared by itself on the left-hand side) depended on what the right-hand side of the equation contained. Because of this, the division removal rule had two incarnations: an easy one and a hard one.

These rules were presented to participants as screens of information, one rule per screen. The screens were similar to one another, with a schematic of how the rule applies, a short text description of the rule, and an example of an application of that rule. The task was implemented as a Hypercard 2.1 stack (Apple Computer, 1991) which was run on an accelerated Apple Macintosh IIci computer connected to a two-page monitor.[1]

Procedure   All participants were told to think aloud while solving the 200 problems they were given. (Because of a computer error, 1 participant received

Table 19.3
The four different types of problems (Experiment 1)

Step	Prototype equation[a]
Two step	$x \oplus A = \oplus B$
Three step	$\oplus x \oplus A = \oplus B$
Four step	$x \oplus A \oplus B = \oplus C$
Five step	$\oplus x \oplus A \oplus B = \oplus C$

a. The $\oplus$ represents any of the four operators. An operator can optionally appear as the first symbol on the right-hand side. $A, B,$ and C represent any of the four constants used. For Type 2 and Type 4 equations, the x can appear in any of the positions.

only 167 problems. This has been accounted for in the data, and the results do not suffer from this incident.) Before starting the task, each participant was instructed on what it meant to think aloud and was given two think-aloud warm-up tasks: one a mental addition problem and the other counting the windows in their childhood home. The rest of the experimental instructions was part of the Hypercard program. The participants had to go through all of the rule screens before starting to solve the problems. Once they started solving problems, participants could refer back to a particular rule screen by clicking on the appropriate button. Each participant received 50 problems of four different types, which are detailed in Table 19.3. The problems were randomly generated on-line within certain parameters to ensure that each rule was presented an equal number of times to each participant. The program kept track of the time between each symbol clicked and what symbol was clicked, so a complete record of the participants' responses to each problem was obtained.

Each problem was presented in a box near the top of the screen. The participant then used an on-screen keypad that contained all of the symbols used in the task to click out, with the mouse, a correct step that would follow from the problem or from one of the lines the participant had already clicked. A delete key was available to erase any character they had clicked. The participant's lines appeared in a box below the problem. Once the participant had clicked out a step, he or she clicked a special key to have the computer check the answer. If the step they had clicked out was a correct one, the computer would respond, "Good," and the participant could continue with the problem. If the line clicked out was the problem's solution, then the computer would respond, "Excellent," the box containing the participant's lines would clear, and a new problem would appear. If, however, the line was incorrect, the computer would respond, "Try again," the participant's line would be erased from the box below the problem and moved to a different location, and the participant would then have another chance to click out a correct line. If the second attempt was not correct, the computer would respond, "Here's the correct line," the next correct step (following from the last correct line) would appear, and a dialog box would

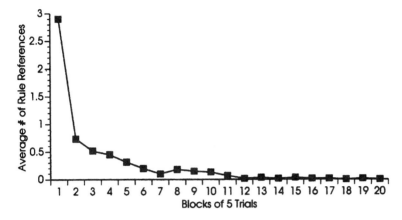

Figure 19.1
Mean number of rule references per problem by problem block (Experiment 1).

appear listing which rule the participant should have applied. The participant could also click on a button with a "?" to receive a hint. This feature was used very rarely, only 10 times in total by the 12 participants.

Results
Participants spent an average of 13.5 min going through the introduction and the rules of the task (15 screens in all). The average amount of time working on the 200 problems was 91 min, with the extremes being 61 min and 120 min. Each participant made references back to the rules 29.7 times on average. Figure 19.1 shows the average number of times participants referred back to the rules per problem for the first 100 problems (the number of referrals stays essentially at zero for the last 100 problems). Note that we have blocked trials together in this graph, and in the graphs to follow, to aid readability. Participants appeared to rapidly master the rule set.

Before examining the step-skipping behavior of the participants, and all of them did learn to skip at least some steps, it is worth looking at the overall time it took participants to work on the problems. Figure 19.2 graphs the total time participants spent on a problem of a particular type by block. For each problem type, a power curve of the form $y = a + bN^c$ (where a is the asymptote, b is the performance time on the first block, N is the block number, and c is the learning rate) has been fit to the data (Newell & Rosenbloom, 1981). As can be seen, the fit to the data was quite good. However, behind this quite regular quantitative finding, which was found in many different tasks, lie large differences in the qualitative aspects of how participants were solving the problems. As we see, different participants began skipping different steps at different times.

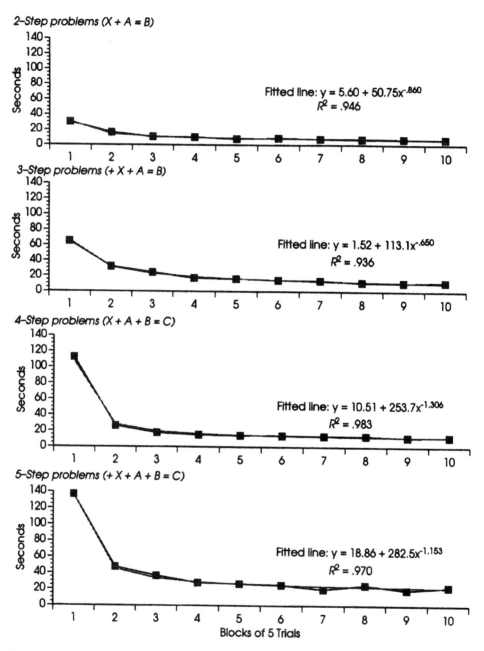

Figure 19.2
Overall time for solving problems by block for each problem type (Experiment 1).

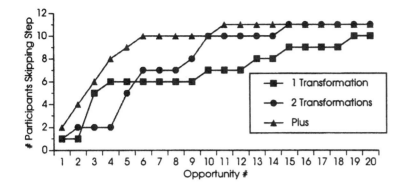

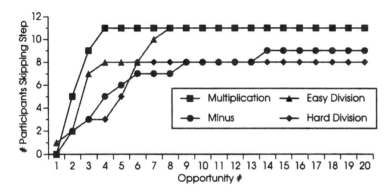

Figure 19.3
Step-skipping behavior of participants (Experiment 1).

Figure 19.3 depicts the overt step-skipping behavior of the participants. Each line represents a particular kind of step that a participant could skip and shows the number of participants that had consistently skipped that step as a function of the number of opportunities to skip the step. Referring to the example displayed in Table 19.2, skipping a one-transformation step would be skipping either Step 1 or Step 3. A participant would be credited with this if they clicked Step 2 or a later step on receiving the problem statement or Step 4 or 5 after clicking Step 2. Skipping two-transformation steps, possible only in four- and five-step problems, would occur when the participant received the problem statement and then clicked out Step 4 or Step 5. The other types of step skipping depicted in Figure 19.3 refer to the steps in which an operator was removed from in front of the x. From the example in Table 19.2, participants would have skipped the minus removal step if they did not click out Step 4. That is, participants were credited as having skipped the operator removal steps when they did not explicitly click out the step involving the operator and x by themselves on the left-hand side of the character string. Throughout the problem set, there were 300 opportunities to skip a one-transformation step (the two- and three-step problems each had one, and the four- and five-step problems each had two), 100 opportunities to skip two transformations at once (once on each four- and five-step problem), and 25 opportunities to skip all four rules dealing with removing each operator in front of the x. (Given the random nature of the problem generator, it would be expected that 9 of the 25 problems containing division removal would involve the hard version of that rule. In fact, each participant received an average of 8.1 problems involving the hard division removal rule.) Because of these differences in rule application opportunities, the graph in Figure 19.3 does not represent the order in which the participants began to skip the rules.

As noted, Figure 19.3 graphs consistent step skipping. Consistent skipping is defined not only as skipping the step on that opportunity but also on the next three opportunities in which that step could be skipped. In 72 of the 84 cases, once a participant started to skip a step they continued to skip that step. Thus, it was seldom the case that a participant would skip a step once, then on the next opportunity not skip that step. Of the 12 cases in which a participant would relapse into making a past-skipped step explicit, all were either the minus or the hard division operator elimination step. It should be stressed that this was a measure of overt step skipping, not covert step skipping. That is, this graph depicts only steps that participants were physically skipping. It could be the case that participants were still mentally going through each transformation, and so were not covertly skipping steps. However, by examining protocol data, to be discussed later, more light can be shed on this particular issue.

One of the curious features of the data is that we never saw a participant presented with a four- or five-step problem skip to Step 3 (see Table 19.2). That is, participants would first start skipping steps like Step 3. The additional complexity that occurred when an operator and operand were added to both sides, one of which would be taken away again on the next step, made this an unnatural step to skip. Participants only skipped to equations as simple as the original. It appears, for this task at least, there was somewhat of a natural progression in how steps were skipped, that of skipping the cancellation steps first (Steps 1 and 3), then the extra addition step (Step 2), and then the step that removed the operator in front of the x (Step 4).

The subjectively easier steps (in both our view and the view of the participants in postexperiment questioning) were generally skipped first. It is also the case that the more practiced rules were skipped first as well. The one-transformation step, for all participants, was always the first one skipped, usually followed by doing two transformations as one step. In all cases, once participants started skipping the one-transformation step for one operator–operand pair, they skipped it for all pairs. The typical order that the operator removal steps were skipped went (a) plus and multiplication (which were

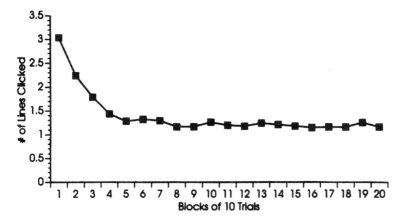

Figure 19.4
Mean number of lines clicked by problem block (Experiment 1).

essentially identical rules), (b) easy division, (c) minus, and then (d) hard division. Not all participants skipped all steps, as is evident from Figure 19.3. One participant only skipped the single-transformation steps. When asked why he made all the other steps explicit, he responded, "[I]f I tried to do two steps at once, it'll be just like four times the chance for error."

An interesting feature of the graph is that in almost all cases, the participants had to click out at least one instance of a step before it could be skipped. Only 1 participant never did a single transformation in two steps, only 1 participant never did two transformations on separate lines, 1 participant immediately skipped easy division, and 2 participants immediately skipped the plus-operator elimination step. For the rest, however, at least one occurrence had to be completed and, usually more, before that step was skipped.

The graph in Figure 19.4 shows the mean number of lines clicked out by the participants for each problem throughout the experiment. When this number is one, the participants are clicking out the answer as their first response after the problem is displayed, skipping all intermediate steps. At the start of the experiment, however, the participants were clicking out multiple lines per problem, and so this number is higher. Figure 19.5 graphs the mean seconds per character (i.e., total solution time divided by number of characters clicked), averaged over all participants, for each problem separated by the four different problem types. As can been seen, this measure steadily decreased throughout the experiment. Furthermore, as is evident from Figure 19.4, the number of characters that each participant clicked out per problem also decreased. This means that not only were participants getting faster at clicking out their answer, but they were also clicking out fewer lines (and therefore fewer symbols) per problem. All participants by the end of the experiment, except for the one, clicked out

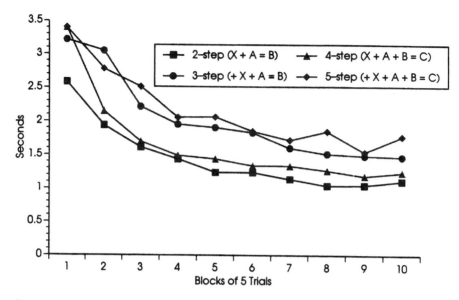

Figure 19.5
Mean seconds per character by block for each problem type (Experiment 1).

only the final line for most problems. Thus, hiding behind the regularity in Figure 19.2 are two more regularities depicted in Figures 19.4 and 19.5—a reduction in the number of physical actions and a reduction in the time per action.

As can be seen from Figure 19.5, the major difference in time per character occurs between problems with an even number of steps and problems with an odd number of steps. The difference between even and odd steps (two step = four step < three step = five step) was significant by a Duncan multiple range test ($p < .01$). The problems with an odd number of steps are the ones in which the participant had to remove a sign in front of the x. The importance of that fact becomes more apparent in Experiment 2.

All participants, except for the one, eventually got to the point where they would click out the final line (i.e., the solution) of a problem as their first line of input. The graph in Figure 19.6 examines the individual latencies between clicking the symbols for these solutions, which we termed *perfect solutions*, for the three-step problems. Because each participant started skipping steps at a different time, participants had a differing number of these perfect solutions. Each point on the graph represents at least 8 participants. The largest latency was before the first keypress (the x), in which the best fitting function was a power curve (see Table 19.4). The latencies between the other keypresses remained relatively constant throughout the problem set. An analysis of the

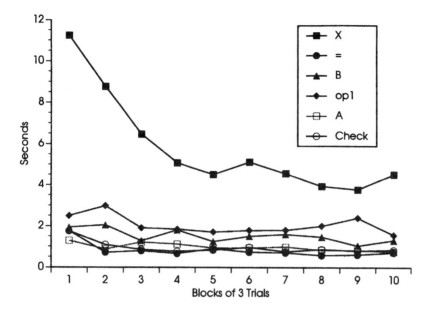

Figure 19.6
Latency by block between each character in "perfect" solutions of three-step problems (Experiment 1); op = operator.

other lines, the nonperfect solution lines, revealed a similar pattern. These results are suggestive that participants plan the whole line they are going to type next and then simply click out the sequence of symbols that constitute the line. The time to click out each line could therefore be divided into *planning* time and *execution* time. Planning time would be the time spent before the first keypress, and execution time would be the amount of time spent per character clicking out the rest of the line.

We fitted power functions, as in Figure 19.2, to the planning and execution time. Table 19.4 shows the best fitting power functions for each type of problem in the data set and with various constraints placed upon the parameters. As can be seen in Table 19.4, the fit was still good even when there were only six free parameters (where b varies for each type of problem and a and c are constrained to be the same across problem types). Performing F tests on the basis of the deviations and the number of free parameters did reveal that something is lost in planning time when going from 12 free parameters to 6 free parameters, $F(6, 28) = 8.44$, $MSE = 0.305$, $p < .05$. In contrast, nothing was lost by imposing the constraints on the execution time, $F(6, 28) = 1.07$, $MSE = 0.006$. Despite the slight loss of fit, it is impressive that the differences among conditions could be reduced to a 6-parameter model with little loss in prediction. In the 6-parameter model, the values of a and c are constant across number of steps skipped (and a

Table 19.4
Best fitting power functions ($y = a + bN^c$) for symbol in final line by problem type

Step	Planning		Execution	
	Latency	R^2	Latency	R^2
12 free parameters[a]				
Two step	$6.59N^{-0.545}$	.95	$1.14N^{-0.202}$	.89
Three step	$1.50 + 9.95N^{-0.628}$	.96	$0.81 + 0.74N^{-0.889}$	.94
Four step	$1.73 + 9.87N^{-1.151}$	.99	$0.33 + 0.99N^{-0.243}$	.76
Five step	$13.52N^{-0.375}$	.94	$1.58N^{-0.171}$	.74
9 free parameters[b]				
Two step	$0.77 + 5.95N^{-0.705}$	.94	$0.47 + 0.68N^{-0.425}$	.89
Three step	$2.04 + 9.49N^{-0.705}$	.96	$0.49 + 1.00N^{-0.425}$	.92
Four step	$10.92N^{-0.705}$	.98	$0.65 + 0.68N^{-0.425}$	.76
Five step	$4.09 + 9.78N^{-0.705}$	.89	$0.77 + 0.83N^{-0.425}$	.73
6 free parameters[c]				
Two step	$6.19N^{-0.477}$	.95	$1.13N^{-0.192}$	.89
Three step	$11.23N^{-0.477}$	.96	$1.40N^{-0.192}$	.89
Four step	$8.90N^{-0.477}$	.96	$1.36N^{-0.192}$	.76
Five step	$14.96N^{-0.477}$	.93	$1.63N^{-0.192}$	.74

Note. Parameters were constrained to be positive. If zero, it was not included in the equation.
a. No constraints.
b. c constrained to be the same fit value across problem type.
c. a and c constrained to be the same fit value (which for a was zero) across problem type.

estimates to be zero). Constraining a, the intercept term, implies that participants are converging to the same physical limit in producing these lines. Constraining c, the exponent, implies that participants have the same learning rate for each type of problem. The one parameter that separates the conditions is the multiplicative factor b. The variations in this parameter were quite large, particularly for the planning times. This parameter was large when more steps were being skipped, suggesting that participants may still have been going covertly through the steps and only overtly skipping them.

Discussion

An analysis of people learning this task sheds light on how people learn to skip steps, both overtly and, as to be discussed shortly, covertly. At the beginning, participants performed the task according to the given rules. When given a problem, they would either think over or refer back to the rules and pick the one rule that should be applied at that point. Some participants flipped back and forth between the screen with the problem and the relevant rule screen, making sure the rule was applicable in that situation. Soon, however, participants did not refer back to the rules. When they did refer to the rules, it appeared to the experimenter that they paid almost sole attention to the example at the bottom of the screen and not to the text description or the schematic.

The protocol data, as the following discussion shows, are useful at shedding further light on the processes the participants were going through as they learned the task. For example, as people went through the experiment, they also began to reorder the parts of a problem they considered first. This was evident from their protocols (see the first sequence in Appendix B). However, many of the protocols were simply verbalizations of what the participants were clicking. As such, a rigorous analysis of them would prove not useful. We present the protocols in the following text and in Appendix B as representative of the more substantive comments that the participants made. The participants at the beginning of the experiment, as per the given rules, would move the operator and operand pairs from the left-hand side to the right-hand side and would then consider the operator in front of the x, if one existed. By the end of the problems, participants were first considering the operator in front of the x, if one existed, and then performing the transposing operations. This represents a major strategy shift, but one that makes solving the problems in one step easier, as can be seen in Appendix B. When not skipping steps, it is obviously of no use to worry about any operator in front of the x until the very last step (Appendix B, Sequence 1, first problem). Even when participants began to skip all intermediate steps, they initially continued to consider the operator in front of x last (Appendix B, Sequence 2, first problem). However, later on, all 11 of the participants who consistently skipped all intermediate steps looked to see if an operator existed in front of the x (e.g., Sequence 1, second and third problems; Sequence 2, third problem—"I have to swap the ®s and ♥s," realizing there is a ♥ in front of the $\mathscr{P}$) before the end of the problem set.

Lastly, another difference between participants at the beginning of the experiment and those same participants at the end was the use of shortcuts. These shortcuts were also involved in making the problems easier to solve in one step. At the beginning of the experiment, of course, participants had no opportunity to make use of shortcuts because they were following the given rules. However, participants picked up a few shortcuts that aided in manipulating the character strings. Perhaps the most useful shortcut, and one that most participants acquired, helped in solving problems in which a minus sign was in front of the x. As an example, here is a problem with its worked-out solution:

$$-x + A = +B$$
$$-x + A - A = +B - A$$
$$-x = +B - A$$
$$x = -B + A.$$

If this was among the first of the problems presented to participants, they would transpose the $+A$ to the other side by using the inverse operator of plus, and when it came time to eliminate the minus sign from the x, the $-A$ would go back to what it was. Even when participants started doing these types of problems in one step, many would think of "double reversing" (4 participants said essentially that) the plus sign in front of the A. However, if this was near the end of the problem set, participants would see that there was a minus sign in front of the x, would know that the plus sign in front of the A would stay the same on the other side, and so would just carry it over (9 participants explicitly mentioned this property). The example in Appendix B, Sequence 2 is typical of how participants progressed through this task.

Once participants started doing problems, they soon began to skip steps. Many participants began skipping the single-transformation step after only two or three problems. Most of the time when participants began to skip steps, they would just click out a line, skipping a step in the process (Appendix B, Sequence 2, Problems 1 and 2 contain an example of this). Occasionally (three times), participants would explicitly say before clicking out the line "I think I'll skip a step here," and in the next line they would skip a step. Also, sometimes participants would have a line partially clicked out and would then delete the symbols they had, saying, "Oh, I can skip this step" (this was explicitly said twice), and would then click out a new line, skipping the step they had previously started to click. This directly raises the issue of overt versus covert step skipping. On the basis of the protocols, it appears that when participants started to skip steps, they were merely doing all the same operations in their head and were only overtly skipping steps. Later on it appears that participants were actually changing the rule base and therefore mentally skipping steps as well, as evidenced by participants planning to copy directly a $+$ over rather than going through a double reversal in their plan.

It would be interesting to graph the problems in which no step skipping occurred versus problems in which some of the intermediate steps were skipped versus problems in which all the intermediate steps were skipped, and then examine the best fitting power curve for each graph. In such a way, we could get a better handle on how these individual power curves conspired to produce the good fitting power curves seen in Figure 19.2. That is, it would be interesting to see if discontinuities exist between when people go from clicking out all of the steps to clicking out only some of them. Unfortunately, many of these graphs would have too few data points to properly fit a curve because participants began skipping some steps after only three or four exposures to the rule. The next experiment was designed such that people were explicitly told when to start step skipping so that such a comparison could be made. Also, in Experiment 2 we attempted to show that people can choose to initiate step skipping at any point in the experiment, even on the first trial. In contrast to some theoretical analyses, step skipping does not require first overtly performing the steps. When people start step skipping right away in this task it is highly plausible they are only overtly step skipping, having had no chance to rehearse skipping steps before beginning to solve problems. As these participants have never experienced the results of the step combinations, it is hard to imagine that they have rules yet to produce the results directly.

Experiment 2

In this experiment participants were told when they were allowed to start skipping steps. By exercising more control over participants' step-skipping behavior, a better analysis could be done of what transfers between making steps explicit and skipping steps. One group of participants was instructed to skip all intermediate steps immediately; whereas two other groups began the experiment clicking out all of the required steps. At different specified points in the experiment, these two groups were told when they had to begin skipping all intermediate steps. It was expected, on the basis of the participants in the first experiment, that participants in the first group, those who had to start overtly skipping steps immediately, would have a difficult time initially performing the task. By comparing across these three groups, inferences could be made as to whether the rule base that the participants used changed as the experiment progressed.

The task used for this experiment was almost identical to the one used in Experiment 1. However, this experiment contained no four- or five-step problems. A set of problems that took only one step, of the form $\oplus x = \oplus A \oplus B$, was added. These changes were made to ensure that all rules were used an equal number of times. One important feature of these materials is that, unlike Experiment 1, the final step contained the same number of symbols independent of number of steps skipped. This meant that when participants skipped steps, they were clicking out the same kind of line no matter how many steps were skipped.

Method

Participants   Thirty-six Carnegie Mellon University undergraduates participated in this experiment for course credit and pay. Data from 6 other participants were collected but not used in the analyses. Four of these participants used the hint facility on almost every problem, and 2 participants made more than three times the number of errors made by the other participants. These participants were evenly distributed through the three groups used in this experiment.

Materials   As stated in the introduction, the task used for this experiment was similar to the task used in Experiment 1. One-step problems were added, however, and the four- and five-step problems removed. Because there were no four- or five-step problems, the two rules that dealt with precedence (Rules 10 and 11 in Appendix A) were no longer needed, so this task made use of only nine rules. Finally, Rule 9 describing how to remove the division sign in front of x was also changed so that no matter what appeared on the right-hand side of the equation, the same procedure (switch the position of the two right-hand side operands) was applied.

Procedure   The procedure was similar to that of Experiment 1. These 36 participants, however, did not think aloud while solving the problems. The participants initially went through the nine rule screens and the screen of examples. Depending on which group the participant was placed in, the instructions differed. One group of participants was instructed that they must immediately skip all intermediate steps. That is, when given a problem, the first line they clicked out had to be the final line in the problem's solution. The other two groups were informed that to start with they must make each of the problem's steps explicit, and at some point during the experiment, they would be told when they had to start skipping steps. They were not told when that point would be within the problem set, but when that point arrived, a dialog box would appear on the screen saying that the participant must now skip all intermediate steps. For one of the two groups of participants, this dialog box appeared after they had completed 24 problems, and for the other group after 96 problems (halfway through the problem set). Twelve participants were in each of the three groups. Participants were allowed to take a break whenever they needed. Only 2 participants took a break, and no participant complained about the length of the experiment.

Results

Table 19.5 summarizes the amount of time participants spent on the experiment in each of the three groups. Time spent reading the instructions did not differ significantly among the three groups, $F(2, 33) = 0.87$, $MSE = 9.14$, $p > .1$. As to be expected, though, the time spent solving the problems did differ between the three groups, $F(2, 33) = 21.76$, $MSE = 66.48$, $p < .01$. Participants who could not start skipping steps until after 96 problems had to click out at least 288 lines; whereas participants in the other groups had to click out at least 192 (skip immediately) or 216 lines (skip-after-24 problems). Even though participants

Table 19.5
Mean time spent reading instructions and solving problems (experiment 2)

Step	Reading instructions[a] (min)	Solving problems (min)
Skip immediately	10.1	38.2
Skip after 24 problems	9.5	44.1
Skip after 96 problems	11.1	59.5

a. Thirteen screens.

who skipped steps immediately took a little longer per problem initially (see Figures 19.9 and 19.10), the number of lines required of the skip-after-96 group caused them to take longer in completing the experiment.

We also did an analysis of variance of how often participants entered incorrect lines. An error was when the participant clicked the checkmark button, but the current line was not a valid line. Participants in the three groups made statistically the same number of total errors, $F(2,33) = 1.39$, $MSE = 2.65$, $p > .1$. Even though participants in the skip-after-96 group had to click out more lines, we still expected participants who had to start skipping steps immediately to do worse, on the basis of our observations in Experiment 1. Figure 19.7 graphs the probability of a participant making an error on a line for each type of problem as a function of problem block, which was split into each of the three groups. Participants improved over the experiment, $F(7,231) = 25.61$, $MSE = 0.62$, $p < .001$. Not surprisingly, participants made more errors on the problems with more steps, $F(2,66) = 21.15$, $MSE = 1.07$, $p < .01$. The data were a bit erratic, but there was a significant interaction between problem block and group, $F(14,231) = 2.11$, $MSE = 0.62$, $p < .01$, which might be interpreted as participants making more errors when they first had to skip steps in the skip-immediate and skip-after-24 group. There was also a significant two-way interaction between problem block and number of steps, $F(14,462) = 3.16$, $MSE = 0.56$, $p < .001$, which could be interpreted as the participants improving less rapidly in the three-step condition. There were no other significant effects.

As in Figure 19.2 for Experiment 1, Figure 19.8 graphs the total time participants spent on a problem of a particular type by block. Only the curves for the two groups who had to do the intermediate steps before beginning to skip them are shown. Unlike Figure 19.2 for Experiment 1, there was a discontinuity for those participants who started skipping steps after problem 96 at the point where they were required to skip steps (marked by a vertical line in the graphs). The participants who skipped after 24 problems were in such a steep part of their learning curve that the discontinuity was less apparent, particularly with the trials blocked. In Experiment 1, the different times when participants started skipping steps masked such discontinuities. In fitting the curves shown in Figure 19.8, we made the assumption that once participants were required to skip steps, only the asymptote (the a parameter) would change, but not the multiplicative factor (the b parameter) or the learning rate (the c parameter). We also made the assumptions that the learning rate did not differ at all between the curves and that the different two-step and three-step problems had the same a and b parameters (these assumptions are similar to the most constrained model in Table 19.4). This resulted in a model with a total of six free parameters. When participants started to skip steps, then, they were essentially on the same learning curve, but the point to which they reached asymptote had been shifted down. This shift down corresponds to the decrease in the number of symbols that needed to be clicked out. The best fitting curves and their equations are also shown in Figure 19.8. This produced a better fit than not

1-Step problems (+ X = A + B)

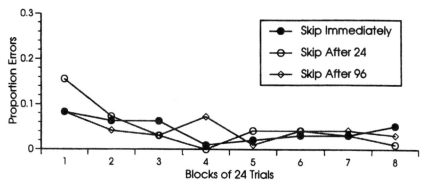

2-Step problems (X + A = B)

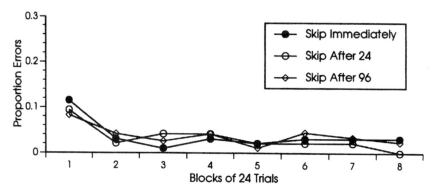

3-Step problems (+ X + A = B)

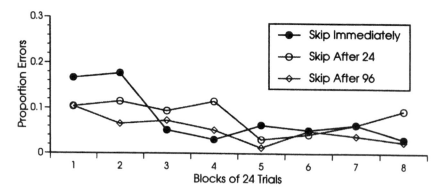

Figure 19.7
Probability of making an error by block for each problem type (Experiment 2).

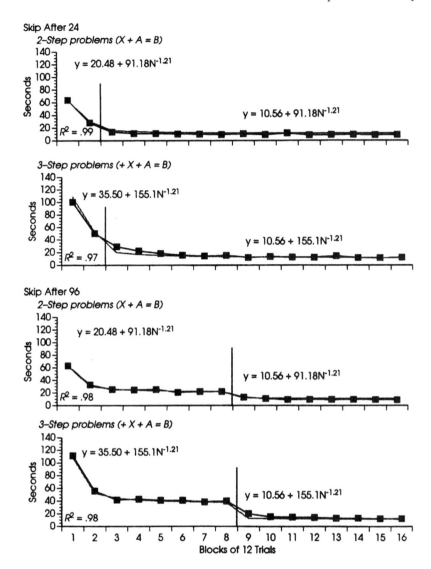

Figure 19.8
Overall time by block for each problem type (Experiment 2).

varying the a parameter at all over blocks, $F(1, 58) = 42.05$, $MSE = 235.80$, $p < .01$. Although this gave a fairly satisfactory global fit, as in Experiment 1, we looked at the timing of each symbol to get at the microstructure of the skill being learned.

On the basis of the observation from Experiment 1 that most of a participant's time was spent planning the first symbol, we split participants' time solving the problems of this experiment into two categories: planning time and execution time. A participant's planning time was the time spent before clicking out the first symbol of a line, and execution time was the rest of the time spent on that line. Figures 19.9 and 19.10 graph the execution and planning time, respectively, that participants spent on a per character basis on each type of problem, which was broken into the three groups.

Concerning participants' execution time, there was no difference between the three groups, $F(2, 33) = 0.09$, $MSE = 1.34$, $p > .1$. Participants did spend differing amounts of time executing the different problem types, $F(2, 66) = 40.18$, $MSE = 0.12$, $p < .01$, and got faster as they went through the experiment, $F(7, 231) = 75.97$, $MSE = 0.14$, $p < .01$. A multiple-comparison test showed that one- and two-step problems did not differ, but both differed from three-step problems. This could be interpreted as some planning time seeping into the execution time (or alternatively, it could amount to some concurrency of the two processes). There were also significant interactions between problem block and group, $F(14, 231) = 2.00$, $MSE = 0.14$, $p < .05$, and problem block, group, and number of steps $F(28, 462) = 2.36$, $MSE = 0.06$, $p < .001$. These interactions could be interpreted as participants taking longer when they have to skip steps, particularly for three-step problems at the beginning of the experiment. No other interactions were significant.

Looking at planning time, a significant difference was detected between the groups, $F(2, 33) = 4.22$, $MSE = 32.77$, $p < .05$. As in execution time, participants also differed in planning the different problem types, $F(2, 66) = 41.85$, $MSE = 4.88$, $p < .01$, and got faster at planning as they went through the experiment, $F(7, 231) = 41.52$, $MSE = 2.70$, $p < .01$. All interactions in planning time were highly significant: group by number of steps, $F(4, 66) = 14.42$, $MSE = 4.88$, $p < .001$, group by problem block, $F(14, 231) = 34.42$, $MSE = 2.70$, $p < .001$, number of steps by problem block, $F(14, 462) = 13.43$, $MSE = 1.67$, $p < .001$, and group by problem block by number of steps, $F(28, 462) = 18.46$, $MSE = 1.67$, $p < .001$. All of these can be interpreted as participants being slowed when they first have to skip steps, particularly in the three-step condition. This increase in planning time is evidence for covert execution of the steps that participants were now being asked to skip overtly. The participants who started skipping steps after 24 problems had longer latencies, in comparison to the group who skipped steps immediately, during the first block of trials in which they skipped steps, but in the next block of trials they were performing the same. Looking closer at the planning time for the three-step problems solved in

1–Step problems (+ X = A + B)

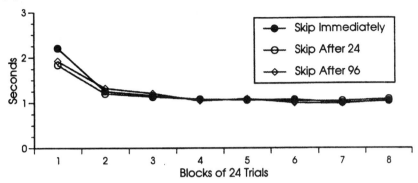

2–Step problems (X + A = B)

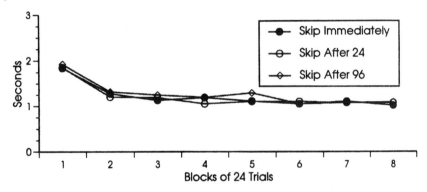

3–Step problems (+ X + A = B)

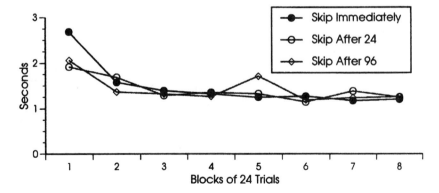

Figure 19.9
Execution time by block for each problem type (Experiment 2).

1–Step problems (+ X = A + B)

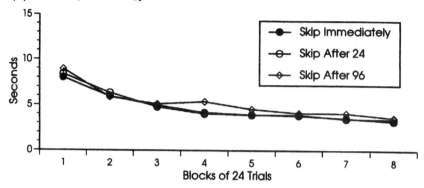

2–Step problems (X + A = B)

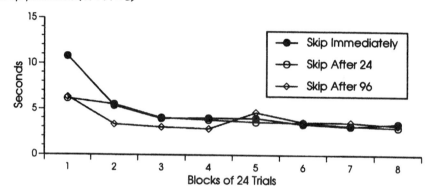

3–Step problems (+ X + A = B)

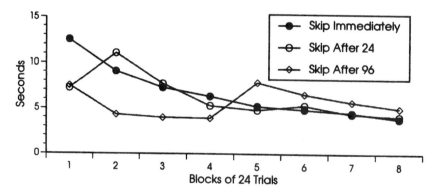

Figure 19.10
Planning time by block for each problem type (Experiment 2).

the last 96 problems, the times were significantly different from one another, $F(2, 33) = 3.52$, $MSE = 11.96$, $p < .05$. The line in Figure 19.10 representing the group of participants who did not skip steps until after Problem 96 is significantly different from the lines representing the other two groups by a Duncan multiple range test ($p < .05$), meaning that these participants never reached the performance level of the other two groups.

One of the striking results in Figure 19.10 is that, particularly for participants who skipped immediately, the differences in planning time among the one-, two-, and three-step problems disappeared over the course of the experiment. In the first block of 24 trials these participants were averaging 8.01, 10.78, and 12.52 s for the one-, two-, and three-step problems, respectively, whereas at the end of the experiment they averaged 3.23, 3.45, and 3.88 s, respectively.[2] It seems that, while participants were going through multiple transformations in planning these steps initially, or overtly skipping steps, they wound up planning all steps as single transformations, or covertly skipping steps. Protocols collected from 6 additional participants; 2 in each of the three groups, confirmed such a hypothesis. Like participants in Experiment 1, once they had to start overtly skipping steps, they went through each individual step mentally before clicking out the final line. After they had experience doing this, their protocols suggested, such as through the use of the shortcut mentioned previously, that they began to mentally skip steps as well.

We fit a simple mathematical model to the planning and execution times to more fully explain these findings. It assumes that planning of single steps and execution of steps speed up from the beginning of the experiment according to a power function. As in the final model fit in Table 19.4, we assumed separate parameters for a, b, and c for execution and planning, but these were constant across problem types (and as in Table 19.4, these constraints have the same implications). The model for execution and one-step planning is simply

$$a + bN^c, \tag{1}$$

where N is the number of blocks. However, the model is more complex in the case of planning multiple transformations. The model assumes that when participants are first asked to do a multistep problem in a single step, they mentally go through all of the steps. That is, at first they are only overtly skipping but are covertly still planning each line. However, each time that they do so there is a probability of forming a collapsed operator that will do it in a single step (and therefore covertly skipping as well). Thus, if a participant has been required to solve a two- or three-step problem in a single step M times, then the probability of still planning it in three steps is P^M and the probability of mentally planning it in one step is $1 - P^M$, where P is the probability of not collapsing a step. The latency for both planning and execution time is described by

$$a + (\text{no. of steps})^* P^M b N^c + (1 - P^M) b M^c, \tag{2}$$

Table 19.6
Best fitting parameters for planning and execution time (Experiment 2)

Time	Parameter		
	a	b	c
Execution	0.90	2.60	−0.337
planning	2.35	15.13	−0.495

Note. $P_2 = .963$ represents value for the two-step problem; $P_3 = .992$ represents value for the three-step problem.

where N is the total number of blocks, and M is the number of blocks in which the participant had to skip steps. The best fitting parameters, found by minimizing the sum-squared error, are displayed in Table 19.6. The overall R^2 for this model was .941. Figure 19.11 presents the planning predictions, which is to be compared with Figure 19.10. Note that the model predicts a longer planning time when required to start skipping steps, just as the participants actually did. We estimated two values of P for this model: .963 for two-step problems and .992 for three-step problems. This difference between the P values corresponds to the relatively less difficulty participants had in adapting to the skipping instructions for two-step problems. There are at least two possible factors to point to in understanding this difference. First, participants only have to compose two steps rather than three. Second, the two-step composition seems more natural in that it is very like algebraic movement rules and skips over an intermediate step.

General Discussion

Taken together, these two experiments provided a close examination of the step-skipping process, both overt step skipping and covert step skipping. The results of Experiment 1 supply a qualitative overview of how people begin to skip steps when left essentially on their own to learn how to solve problems. At first, the participants made all of the intermediate steps explicit. That is, they would apply the one necessary rule to the current line to arrive at the next line of the problem's solution. Only after participants applied each rule at least a couple of times did they begin overtly skipping that rule, and only later covertly skipping the rule. It was almost never the case that participants skipped a rule on the first opportunity they had to apply it. However, Experiment 2 indicated that overt skipping was a somewhat arbitrary choice on the participant's part, and they were capable of skipping right away. The experiment also indicated that their decision to skip brought a substantial reduction in total time due to the reduced execution time. Participants were still covertly planning each step, and it took longer for these covert planning steps to dis-

1-Step problems (+ X = A + B)

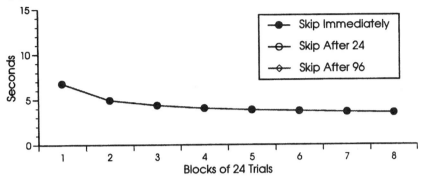

2-Step problems (X + A = B)

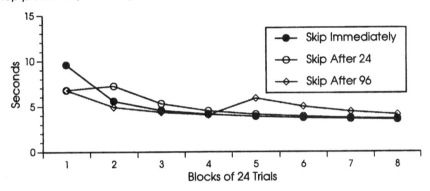

3-Step problems (+ X + A = B)

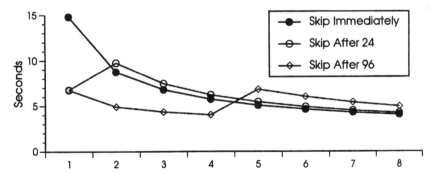

Figure 19.11
Predicted planning time by block for each problem type (Experiment 2).

appear. However, there was little evidence for multistep planning after the 192 trials.

The results of Experiment 1 demonstrate that even though participants showed an overall continuous improvement in performance (Figure 19.2), and the performance was consistent with the power law of learning, this masked large qualitative differences, such as step skipping (Figure 19.3). However, in Experiment 2, in which we controlled when participants were allowed to skip steps, discontinuities were observed (Figure 19.8). The separate parts of the discontinuities, though, were well fit by a power curve. Moreover, the clicking of individual symbols still followed a power law across the course of the experiments. Thus, it seems that the power law of learning is preserved at a more microscopic level.

It could be argued that discontinuities would not be observed when participants are not forced to skip steps, as in Experiment 1, because the two strategies (to skip or not to skip steps) are in competition with one another, as in a race model, and the faster of the two controls performance. When skipping steps becomes faster than not skipping steps, then that will be what the person does, without a discontinuity in performance.

Although other formalizations of how participants represent transformations are possible, we consider here and in the model to follow a production system framework. An important issue raised in these experiments was the grain size at which the participants represent these rules as productions. Participants could break up a rule into multiple productions for transforming individual characters, or they could have a single production rule that transformed a whole line mentally followed by a series of execution productions that clicked out each character. Evidence from these two experiments favors the latter possibility—that is, planning productions that apply at the line level. The longest latency for a line is before the first keystroke. This would be the time for the productions to fire that planned the line to be clicked. The time between all of the other keystrokes varied only a little as a function of condition. Once the production matches and fires, the next line is then ready to be clicked out, which would be handled by a set of execution productions that click out individual characters. While participants' planning time was greatly increased when they were instructed to skip steps, their execution times were almost unaffected.

An ACT–R Model

We developed an ACT–R model (Anderson, 1993) that captures the important qualitative aspects of people performing this task (in particular, the processes discussed in Experiment 1's *Discussion* section). Appendix C contains a more detailed account of the model, particularly of the analogy mechanism. An important distinction within the ACT–R architecture is between declarative knowledge, one's knowledge of facts (e.g., Washington, D.C. is the capital of the United States), and procedural knowledge, one's knowledge of how to perform actions (e.g., adding numbers together). One of the claims of the ACT–R theory is that all knowledge has declarative origins. That is, the only way new procedural knowledge, in the form of production rules, enters the system is by the process of analogizing to some previous declarative knowledge. This mechanism operates by forming an analogy from examples stored in declarative memory to the current goal.

The model of our task within ACT–R (Anderson, 1993), therefore, makes use of analogy to examples and creates production rules as a result of the analogy process (either the ones that do the original one-step transformations or the later ones that skip steps). This fits in nicely with the participants' behaviors because in the early stages of performing the task, they would refer to the rule screens and look specifically at the example at the bottom of the screen. Also, participants would try to recall what they did last time when faced with a similar configuration of symbols. Thus, participants were relying on examples to start out with, just as ACT–R predicts.

In formulating this model, and in keeping with the analyses previously presented, we made the assumption that each step in a problem's solution could be conceived of as the application of essentially two kinds of operators: those that planned the step and those that executed the step. Whereas there would be different operators for planning different lines, which would roughly correspond to the rules on the rule cards, the system would use the same set of execution operators for each step. That is, an operator would decide what string of symbols to output for the next step (i.e., what rule to apply), and a set of execution operators would produce that string. Our model concerned itself with the planning operators.

To begin the simulation, the model has some examples available to it, such as those found at the bottom of the rule screens as well as some other declarative knowledge about the operators and operands involved. To illustrate how ACT–R (Anderson, 1993) proceeds, suppose that for its current goal it has been encoded to solve the problem $x + A = B$. It has no productions that apply. However, one of the examples that it has, that the next line after $x * C = D$ is $x * C/C = D/C$, is similar to that of the current problem. It also has the knowledge that $/$ is the inverse operator of $*$ and that $-$ is the inverse operator of $+$. On the basis of that knowledge and the example given, the ACT–R analogy mechanism produces the following production (P):

IF the current goal is an equation of the form: (P1)
    x op1 CON1 $=$ CON2
    and op2 is the inverse of op1,
THEN the next step should be
        x op1 CON1 op2 CON1 $=$ CON2 op2 CON1.

Some of the mapping that the analogy mechanism does is relatively easy (e.g., the x in the first line goes with the x in the second line), but it does infer (by tracing through the working memory elements that contain $*$) that the $/$

appears because of the knowledge that $/$ is the inverse of $*$. After this production is constructed, it applies to the current goal to produce the result $x + A - A = B - A$. This result becomes the new goal.

Again, no productions apply to this new goal. However, the model has another example available to it, that the line that follows $x * C/C = D/C$ is $x = D/C$. Similar to last time, with this example and its other knowledge, the analogy mechanism creates this production

> IF the current goal is an equation of the form: (P2)
> x op1 CON1 op2 CON1 = CON2 op2 CON1
>   and op2 is the inverse of op1,
> THEN the next step should be
> x CON2 op2 CON1.

After firing, this production creates the final result, $x = B - A$. The model now has two productions that transform lines and a complete, worked-out solution of the form

$$x + A = B$$

$$x + A - A = B - A$$

$$x = B - A.$$

Once a production has been created to do a step, the person now has two bases for performing the task: either by reference to the production or by analogy to an example. This competition between production and example will be a function of the strength of the production and the activation of the example. The production will acquire strength with practice and gradually come to dominate the competition. This is consistent with the fact that in Experiment 1 participants did not stop referring to examples after their first opportunity. Presumably, this is because the resulting production was not yet strong enough and needed to be recreated by further analogy.

Let us now consider what may happen when the simulation is presented with a new, but similar, problem to solve (e.g., $x/B = D$). The simulation has one production that will apply, Production 1, but its strength will be low. It also has two declarative structures to which it can analogize: the original example and the declarative trace left from solving the first problem. The production's strength is low, and the activation from the example of the previous problem will be high, so the analogy mechanism will create a production that is identical to Production 1. This identity will be noted, and instead of creating a new production, the original production will gain strength. A similar process will occur to solve the next, final line of the problem.

The question now arises as to how the model will begin to overtly skip steps (as the participants did in the first experiment). Because it is quicker to solve problems by clicking out fewer lines, it is advantageous to skip steps, but the cost is an increased memory load because the person has to maintain a declarative structure representing the current line while retrieving and applying the next rule. Once participants, and the model, have gained a familiarity with the declarative structures that represent the task's problem space (or the experimenter dictates that intermediate steps must now be skipped), instead of clicking out intermediate steps, the intermediate steps can be maintained in working memory and the appropriate rules applied mentally (to decrease memory load) and some steps would be skipped. This corresponds to only overt step skipping. That is, the model, like the participants when they started to skip steps, still goes through the intermediate steps but does not click them out.

Once steps are overtly skipped, the solver will see on the screen a pair of lines with the step skipped and can store that pair in declarative memory to be used to form an analogy. In other words, once a solver or the model solves $x/B = D$ by mentally applying analogized productions similar to Production 1 and Production 2 and clicking out only $x = D * B$, a declarative structure will be formed linking $x/B = D$ with its solution, $x = D * B$. In that way, the system can analogize from a current problem to that new fact and produce the following production that skips a step:

> IF the current goal is an equation of the form: (P3)
> $x \ op1 \ CON1 = CON2$
>   and $op2$ is the inverse of $op1$,
> THEN the next step should be:
> $x = CON2 \ op2 \ CON1$.

Eventually, this production will accrue enough strength (by being generated repeatedly by the analogy mechanism) that it will be more powerful than the declarative examples. Once this happens, the model, by executing this production, will be covertly skipping steps.

In summary, all of the production rules start out by analogy to examples. The examples are either the line transformations on the rule screens or a line transformation it creates while solving the problem. Once ACT–R starts overtly skipping steps, it creates new examples of line transformations that contain skipped steps from which it can learn new rules that correspond to macro-operators. The new rules it learns gradually accrue strength and come to replace analogy to examples, which corresponds to covertly skipping steps. It is important to note that the rules created operate on whole lines and return whole lines as their answer. This corresponds to the result in both experiments that participants spent most of their time before clicking out the first symbol and then a relatively similar time clicking out the rest of the symbols of a line. That is, what the participants apparently did, and what the ACT–R model (Anderson, 1993) does, is to figure out what to do with the entire line and then click out the result.

Conclusions

One question of interest is if any person noticed the relationship between this task and algebra. This can be addressed best with respect to the 12 participants in Experiment 1 from whom protocols were obtained. Only 1 participant in Experiment 1 reported being aware of the similarity between this task and algebra. Another participant, after working on 60 problems in Experiment 1, began to make a mapping between the symbols in this task and algebraic symbols but did not complete the mapping. When questioned after the experiment, the participant reported thinking there was similarity but did not believe the mapping was going to provide any help in performing the task, so he abandoned it. Almost all participants in both experiments, when questioned after their participation, reported a similarity between this task and a logic type of task. From this finding, it appears that participants were not directly using their knowledge of algebra to perform the task.

This indirectly leads to the question of generality of these findings. What kinds of tasks lead to the sort of step skipping exhibited in the task used in these experiments? Step skipping is not possible, or simply is not done, in all tasks. Counting and simple addition represent two such tasks. A person counting cannot skip objects to be counted.[3] Children learning addition go directly from using some counting strategy to direct retrieval of the example (Siegler, 1986); they do not go from counting by ones to counting by twos to counting by fours. Retrieval of the answer can be conceived as a special kind of step skipping, but it is one that eliminates the algorithmic nature of the process. In our case, we argue that participants were not retrieving the final line but were still computing it (see below for more detail). Certainly, the kinds of tasks that support the type of step skipping discussed in this article are typically formal, procedurally oriented domains, such as algebra or physics. In such domains, steps are characterized by the application of a rule to the current state of the problem to reach the next meaningful state on the path to solution. Steps can be skipped by simply skipping the intermediate steps between the problem statement and its solution. This can be done by recognizing any sort of pattern that may be contained in the problem statements directly to reach the answer or some other intermediate step. However, it is the case that other less formal procedures support step skipping. For instance, students who are learning to draw human figures do so by drawing an oval for the head and then seven more for the other parts of the body. They then put hash marks on the ovals to serve as guides for such things as shoulders and hips. As the person becomes a more expert drawer, they begin to skip the steps of drawing certain ovals and the hash marks. This skipping of steps coincides with a more intuitive understanding of how to draw the human figure.

The ACT–R theory (Anderson, 1993) claims that any new procedural knowledge comes from declarative knowledge in the form of examples. The theory posits only a single mechanism to account for both the learning of the original rules and of the composed rules. Participants' behavior while performing this task is consistent with such a view (in how they referred to the examples and by their protocols), and an ACT–R simulation was created that modeled many of the important aspects of participant's performance. That is, both the participants and the model initially did each step in the solution procedure (when left on their own, as in Experiment 1) before skipping steps. In doing each individual step, the participants and model formed an analogy from an existing example to the current problem. When beginning to skip steps, they were most likely applying each separate operator mentally in order to skip a step. After noticing the relationship between these new pairs of lines, though, they formed by analogy a new, single operator that skips steps.

The other theories of skill acquisition also can be examined in light of these results. The rule composition view might seem to have the same problem with these data that Lewis (1981) raised. That is, people are composing together the planning steps, but these are not adjacent—for instance, the double reversals of the operators are separated at least by execution steps. However, the model we described proposed that people consciously reorganized their problem solving so that they went through a series of planning steps mentally before executing the results. Then the planning steps would be adjacent and composition could produce macrooperators. The remaining difficulty for the composition theory is that it does not deal with the original learning of the operators and the evidence for participant's reliance on examples.

Logan's (1988, 1990) instance theory as it is currently realized cannot adequately account for these data because at most only one or two examples were ever repeated for a participant, yet his or her performance still improved over the course of the experiment. Furthermore, once participants started to produce $x = B - A$ from $x + A = B$, they also would produce $x = C * D$ from $x/D = C$. That is, once they started to do single transformations in one step, they would do so for all operators. This generalization phenomenon poses a major problem to Logan's (1988, 1990) theory.

Modifications to instance theory could perhaps be made to explain the data in these experiments. For example, the generalization problem mentioned above could perhaps be solved by making the instances used by the problem solver smaller grained. That is, instead of using whole problems, or even whole lines, an instance could be only part of a line (an operator–operand pair perhaps). In that way, these instances could be pieced together by multiple retrievals to form a whole line. However, if that were the case, one would not expect to see the relatively large up-front planning time that was seen in these experiments. Rather, the expectation would be more consistent intercharacter times as the smaller grained instances were recalled. Another potential way to mend instance theory would be to allow instances to accept variables and thus allow nonexact retrieval matching to occur. This is perhaps a better solution, but it would seem to be basically introducing production rules into the theory, which would take away its distinct character. Moreover, in addressing the question of how such instances are variabilized, one comes against the same issues that ACT–R's (Anderson, 1993) analogy mechanism was designed to solve.

In these experiments, we have examined closely the power law of learning. At a gross level, as in Figure 19.2 from Experiment 1, our results were fit quite nicely by a power law. However, as we looked more deeply at people's performance at learning our task, we found discrete qualitative changes. Because these changes occurred at different points for different participants, the average result looked like a continuous power function. When we controlled the point of these qualitative changes (Experiment 2), we noticed discontinuities in the power law in terms of overall time. However, when we decomposed this overall time into its components, we found that these components still obeyed a power law. In summary, time to perform a complex task approximates a power law because its components do, and qualitative changes in these components are typically masked by averaging procedures.

Notes

The work presented in this article was supported by National Science Foundation Grant 91-08529 and Office of Naval Research Augmentation Award for Science and Engineering Research Training Grant N000149311010. We thank Richard Carlson, Jill Larkin, Marsha Lovett, and Herbert Simon for their comments on drafts of this article.
1. The maximum temporal resolution of Hypercard is $1/60$ of a second. The program that we used to collect data was written to minimize any inaccuracy due to this fact. Furthermore, the timing data of interest were sufficiently long enough that any inaccuracies due to poor temporal resolution should not matter.
2. The comparable means for the first block of data from the other two groups were 8.38, 6.18, and 7.49 for the participants who started skipping after Problem 24 and 8.93, 6.34, and 7.49 for the participants who started skipping after Problem 96. The comparable means for the last block of data from the other two groups were 3.46, 3.02, and 4.13 for the participants who started skipping after Problem 24 and 3.62, 3.25, and 5.02 for the participants who started skipping after Problem 96.
3. Subitizing (Chi & Klahr, 1975) could perhaps be construed as a case of skipping steps while counting, and indeed, people can be trained to enumerate recognized, repeated patterns (Lassaline & Logan, 1993). However, subitizing does not have the flavor of collapsing a sequence of different procedures into a single operation.

References

Anderson, J. R. (1983). *The architecture of cognition*. Cambridge, MA: Harvard University Press.

Anderson, J. R. (1993). *Rules of the mind*. Hillsdale, NJ: Erlbaum.

Anderson, J. R., & Fincham, J. M. (1994). Acquisition of procedural skills from examples. *Journal of Experimental Psychology: Learning, Memory, and Cognition, 20*, 1322–1340.

Carlson, R. A., & Lundy, D. H. (1992). Consistency and restructuring in learning cognitive procedural sequences. *Journal of Experimental Psychology: Learning, Memory, and Cognition, 18*, 127–141.

Charness, N., & Campbell, J. I. D. (1988). Acquiring skill at mental calculation in adulthood: A task decomposition. *Journal of Experimental Psychology: General, 117*, 115–129.

Chi, M. T. H., & Klahr, D. (1975). Span and rate of apprehension in children and adults. *Journal of Experimental Child Psychology, 19*, 434–439.

Ericsson, K. A., & Simon, H. A. (1990). *Protocol analysis: Verbal reports as data*. Cambridge, MA: MIT Press.

Frensch, P. A. (1991). Transfer of composed knowledge in a multistep serial task. *Journal of Experimental Psychology: Learning, Memory, and Cognition, 17*, 997–1016.

Frensch, P. A., & Geary, D. C. (1993). Effects of practice on component processes in complex mental addition. *Journal of Experimental Psychology: Learning, Memory, and Cognition, 19*, 433–456.

Hypercard 2.1 [Computer software]. (1991). Cupertino, CA: Apple Computer.

Koedinger, K. R., & Anderson, J. R. (1990). Abstract planning and perceptual chunks: Elements of expertise in geometry. *Cognitive Science, 14(4)*, 511–550.

Lassaline, M. E., & Logan, G. D. (1993). Memory-based automaticity in the discrimination of visual numerosity. *Journal of Experimental Psychology: Learning, Memory, and Cognition, 19*, 561–581.

Lewis, C. H. (1978). *Production system models of practice effects. Dissertation Abstracts International, 39*, 5105B. (University Microfilms No. 79-07, 120).

Lewis, C. H. (1981). Skill in algebra. In J. R. Anderson (Ed.), *Cognitive skills and their acquisition* (pp. 85–110). Hillsdale, NJ: Erlbaum.

Logan, G. D. (1988). Toward an instance theory of automatization. *Psychological Review, 95*, 492–527.

Logan, G. D. (1990). Repetition priming and automaticity: Common underlying mechanisms? *Cognitive Psychology, 22*, 1–35.

Newell, A. (1990). *Unified theories of cognition*. Cambridge, MA: Harvard University Press.

Newell, A., & Rosenbloom, P. S. (1981). Mechanisms of skill acquisition and the law of practice. In J. R. Anderson (Ed.), *Cognitive skills and their acquisition* (pp. 1–55). Hillsdale, NJ: Erlbaum.

Newell, A., & Simon, H. A. (1972). *Human problem solving*. Englewood Cliffs, NJ: Prentice Hall.

Rosenbloom, P. S., & Newell, A. (1986). The chunking of goal hierarchies: A generalized model of practice. In R. S. Michalski, J. G. Carbonell, & T. M. Mitchell (Eds.), *Machine learning: An artificial intelligence approach* (Vol. 2, pp. 123–140). Los Altos, CA: Morgan Kaufmann.

Siegler, R. S. (1986). Unities in strategy choices across domains. In M. Perlmutter (Ed.), *Minnesota Symposium on Child Development*. (Vol. 19, pp. 1–48). Hillsdale, NJ: Erlbaum.

Appendix A: Rules Used in Experiment 1

For Rules 2–5, participants were told that X represents any of the operand symbols, $\Delta, \Gamma, \Omega, \Phi$ (in the experiment they were called *object symbols*), and that the goal of each problem was to "isolate" the $\mathscr{P}$ on the left-hand side of the $\leftrightarrow$.

Rule 1

This rule allows you to take any connector symbol ($^{\copyright}, ^{\circledR}, \#, \heartsuit$) plus any object symbol ($\Delta, \Gamma, \Omega, \Phi$) and add them to both the left-hand side and the right-hand side of any character string. For example, if the current line was:

$$\mathscr{P}\#\Phi \leftrightarrow {}^{\circledR}\Delta$$

You could add $^{\copyright}\Phi$ to both sides to get:

$$\mathscr{P}\#\Phi^{\copyright}\Phi \leftrightarrow {}^{\circledR}\Delta^{\copyright}\Phi$$

Suppose the current line was ♥𝒫®Δ ↔ #Ω and you wanted to use Rule 1 with ♥Δ for the next line. That line would look like:

♥𝒫®Δ♥Δ ↔ #ΩσΔ

Rule 2
Schematically, Rule 2 states:

> The current line (on one side) contains: [...]#X[...]©X
> You may write: [...][...]

So, for Rule 2 to apply, the character string must contain the connector # and some object symbol together, and then the connector © and that same object symbol later on in the character string, but still on the same side.

To illustrate:

> The current string is: 𝒫#Δ©Δ ↔ ®Ω©Δ
> You may rewrite it as: 𝒫 ↔ ®Ω©Δ

Rule 3
Schematically, Rule 3 states:

> The current line (on one side) contains: [...]©X[...]#X
> You may write: [...][...]

For Rule 3 to apply, the character string must contain the connector © and some object symbol together, and then the connector # and that same object symbol later on in the character string, but still on the same side (either the right-hand side or the left-hand side).

As an example:

> The current string is: ®𝒫©Δ#Δ ↔ ♥Φ#Ω
> You may rewrite it as: ®𝒫 ↔ ♥Φ#Ω

Rule 4
Rule 4 states

> The current line (on one side) contains: [...]®X[...]♥X
> You may write: [...][...]

To apply Rule 4, the character string must contain the connector ® and some object symbol together, and then the connector ♥ and that same object symbol later on in the character string, but still on the same side (either the right-hand side or the left-hand side).

For example:

> The current string is: 𝒫®Δ♥Δ ↔ ♥ΦΔ
> You may rewrite it as: 𝒫 ↔ ♥Φ♥Δ

Rule 5
Rule 5 states:

> The current line (on one side) contains: $[\ldots]\heartsuit X[\ldots]^{\circledR}X$
> You may write: $[\ldots][\ldots]$

To apply Rule 5, the character string must contain the connector ♥ and some object symbol together, and then the connector ® and that same object symbol later on in the character string, but still on the same side (either the right-hand side or the left-hand side).

For example:

> The current string is: $\#\mathscr{P}\heartsuit\Phi^{\circledR} \leftrightarrow \#\Omega^{\circledR}\Phi$
> You may rewrite it as: $\#\mathscr{P} \leftrightarrow \#\Omega^{\circledR}\Phi$

Rule 6
Once you have used the preceding four rules to eliminate all but the $\mathscr{P}$ symbol and its connector from the left-hand side, these next four rules will allow you to get rid of that connector and thus correctly transform the character string.

When the left-hand side contains only $^{\circledR}\mathscr{P}$, in the next line you write you may eliminate the ® from the left-hand side, and leave the right-hand side exactly the same.

As an example:

> Current line: $^{\circledR}\mathscr{P} \leftrightarrow {}^{\circledcirc}\Omega^{\circledR}\Delta$
> Your next line: $\mathscr{P} \leftrightarrow {}^{\circledcirc}\Omega^{\circledR}\Delta$

Rule 7
Rule 7 is somewhat similar to Rule 6, in that when the left-hand side contains only $\#\mathscr{P}$, in the next line you write you may eliminate the # from the left-hand side and leave the right-hand side exactly the same.

As an example:

> Current line: $\#\mathscr{P} \leftrightarrow {}^{\circledR}\Phi\heartsuit\Gamma^{\circledcirc}\Omega$
> Your next line: $\mathscr{P} \leftrightarrow {}^{\circledR}\Phi\heartsuit\Gamma^{\circledcirc}\Omega$

Rule 8
When the left-hand side contains only $\heartsuit\mathscr{P}$, in the next line you write you may eliminate the ♥ from the left-hand side, but then change any occurrence of ® in the right-hand side to ♥, and any occurrence of ♥ to ®, leaving the other symbols alone.

To illustrate:

> Current line: $\heartsuit\mathscr{P} \leftrightarrow {}^{\circledR}\Omega\#\Gamma$
> Your next line: $\mathscr{P} \leftrightarrow \heartsuit\Omega\#\Gamma$

Rule 9

Rule 9 is somewhat more complicated. When the left-hand side contains only ©𝒫, in the next line you write you may eliminate the © from the left-hand side. If a © appears on the right-hand side, then you may rewrite the right-hand side, swapping the positions of the two symbols on either side of the ©. When the right-hand side does not contain a © connector symbol, you may simply rewrite the right-hand side, but putting a © first.

As examples of this rule:

Current line: ©𝒫 ↔ ♥Δ♥Φ©Ω
Your next line: 𝒫 ↔ ♥Δ♥Ω©Φ

But:

Current line: ©𝒫 ↔ ♥Δ♥Φ#Ω
Your next line: 𝒫 ↔ ©♥Δ♥Φ#Ω

These last two rules are very important and provide a standard method of attack for all problems.

Rule 10

Rule 10 states that you must eliminate all ♥ and ® connector symbols from the left-hand side before eliminating any # or © symbols.

Therefore, if the problem was #Δ®Φ♥𝒫 ↔ ♥Ω, you would have to eliminate the ®Φ before eliminating the #Δ.

Rule 11

Rule 11 states that you must eliminate the connector and object symbols from the left-hand side in a left-to-right fashion. However, Rule 10 has precedence over Rule 11. So if the current line was 𝒫#Γ®Φ©Ω ↔ ♥Φ, you would need to eliminate the ®Φ (because of Rule 10), then the #Γ before you eliminate the ©Ω.

Appendix B: Sample Protocols From Experiment 1

Problem	Protocol	Commentary
Sequence 1 (Participant 1)		
Problem 1		
®𝒫#Γ®Φ ↔ ®Ω	Let's see, ®, ®𝒫 is equivalent to ®Ω,	The participant first skips two
↓	®Ω then let's see, ® has precedence	transformations, not worrying
®𝒫 ↔ ®Ω♥Φ©Γ	so it's ♥Φ©Γ.	about what is in front of the 𝒫.
↓	(Computer: Good)	After that line is checked, he
𝒫 ↔ ®Ω♥Φ©Γ	Good. And, ummm, uh, let's see, so	then applies the rule that
	which gives me 𝒫 equivalent to,	removes the ® in front of the 𝒫.
	uhh, let's see, ®Ω, ♥Φ©Γ.	

Problem 2

®Φ♥Ω®𝒫 ↔♥Γ
↓
𝒫 ↔♥ΓΦ®Ω

Okay, ®𝒫, 𝒫 equivalent to ♥Γ, uh, uh oh, ♥Γ, just, I can worry about that later, ♥Γ, ♥Γ, ♥Φ®Ω.	The participant apparently looks to see what symbol is in front of the 𝒫.

Problem 3

®𝒫©Γ♥Δ ↔ Φ
↓
𝒫 ↔ Φ®Δ#Γ

Um, 𝒫, nothing interesting in front of it, goes to Φ, let's see, the ♥ gets precedence, so it's ®Δ#Γ.	The participant is considering the symbol in front of the 𝒫 first.

Sequence 2 (Participant 5)

Problem 1

♥𝒫®Ω ↔ Φ
↓
𝒫 ↔ Φ♥Ω

Okay. Okay. I have to eliminate the ®s with a ♥, and that ♥ will turn into a ®Ω, and then, that was supposed to have been, that was supposed to have been a ♥, okay. I'm not sure. . . .	First three-step problem done all in one line. The participant does all the steps in his head, first recalling the elimination rule, and then the rule concerning how to remove the ♥ in front of the 𝒫.

Problem 2

♥𝒫♥Φ ↔ Ω
↓
𝒫 ↔ Ω♥Φ

Okay. Get rid of the ♥s first with a ®, and then to get rid of the ♥s, you would change the ♥s to ®s. So I think I can do this on one line. This is that, and then I'll have to put, Φ, but it will just be ♥Φ.	Again, a similar three-step problem has been done on one line. He is faster and more sure of himself this time. Notice he mentioned the ®Φ changing to a ♥Φ.

Problem 3

♥𝒫®Γ ↔ ♥Δ
↓
𝒫 ↔ ®Δ®Γ

Okay. Umm, I have to swap the ®s and ♥s. So the original was that, goes to that, and this would stay as it is.	However, this time, he says, "this [the ®Γ] would stay as it is."

Problem 4

♥𝒫®Δ ↔ ®Φ
↓
𝒫 ↔ ♥Φ®Δ

Okay. Change that, to a ♥.	At the later problems, participants were very abbreviated in their protocols.

Note. In the first column the problem (as it was presented to the participant) is shown. Below that (as directed by the arrows) is what the participants clicked. The second column is the protocol that the participants produced while solving the problem. Participants developed their own names for the symbols (e.g., "squiggle" or "alpha" for the 𝒫), but in the protocol we substituted the actual symbol. The commentary in the third column explains the importance of the protocol.

Appendix C: The Adaptive Control of Thought—Rational (ACT–R) Model

This appendix elaborates on the ACT–R (Anderson, 1993) model, which was presented in the article. Because of space constraints, we focus on how the model composes, via the analogy mechanism, the production that covertly skips steps. A more detailed model can be found at the ACT–R World Wide Web site (http://sands.psy.cmu.edu/ACT/act/act-code.html).

We assumed a flat representation for the character strings. That is, the structure that contains the representation of a line is essentially just a list of the symbols placed in their correct slots. This assumption made it easier for the analogy mechanism, plus we had no real intuition as to what sort of hierarchical representation the participants actually used. In ACT–R (Anderson, 1993), our representation can be characterized by the following statement (*lhs* and *rhs* refer to the left-hand side and the right-hand side of the equation, respectively, as separated by the double arrow; *var* refers to variable; *op* refers to operator; and *con* refers to constant):

(WMEType equation lhs-var lhs-op1 lhs-con1 lhs-op2

lhs-con2 rhs-con1 rhs-op1 rhs-con2 achieved-by).

This creates a new working memory element (WME) type called *equation*, which has nine slots, one for each potential symbol, plus the achieved-by slot, which is a special slot used by the analogy mechanism telling the system the next step in a problem's solution. The only other important WME type is the one that defines the operators, which is defined by (WMEType operator reversed-by). Thus, these WMEs not only have the name of the operator but also the operator's inverse associated with them.

A problem can be expressed by the following WME:

(PROBLEM

    ISA equation
    LHS-VAR X
    LHS-OP1 $*$
    LHS-CON1 C
    RHS-CON1 D),

which is the problem $X * C = D$. Because the ACHIEVED-BY slot is not listed, it is assumed to be nil. For the purpose of this appendix, it is assumed that this problem is the current goal. Furthermore, the system has already solved the problem $X + A = B$ and has noted that the answer is $X = B - A$. These can be expressed by

$X + A = B$

(SOLVEDPROBLEM1

    ISA equation
    LHS-VAR X
    LHS-OP1 $+$
    LHS-CON1 A
    RHS-CON1 B
    ACHIEVED-BY SolvedProblem2)

and

$$X = B - A$$

> (SOLVEDPROBLEM2
>
> > ISA equation
> > LHS-VAR X
> > RHS-CON1 B
> > RHS-OP1 $-$
> > RHS-CON2 A).

The other two WMEs that are important for this illustration are the two that correspond to the operators used in the goal problem and SolvedProblem1:

> (+
>
> > ISA operator
> > REVERSED-BY $-$)

and

> (∗
>
> > ISA operator
> > REVERSED-BY /).

When the system solved the first problem $(X + A = B)$, it presumably either already had the productions needed to solve the problem or it had another example with which it analogized, which created two productions: one for going from $X + A = B$ to $X + A - A = B - A$, and another for going from $X + A - A = B - A$ to $X = B - A$. These productions will be in competition with the analogy mechanism. If the productions are weak, the system can analogize from the current problem $(X ∗ C = D)$ to SolvedProblem1. This will result in the following production, one that covertly skips steps:

> (p ANALOGIZED-PRODUCTION127
> > = Problem-Variable >
> > > ISA   equation
> > > LHS-VAR   = X-variable
> > > LHS-OP1   = ∗-variable
> > > LHS-CON1   = C-variable
> > > RHS-CON1   = D-variable
> > = ∗-variable >
> > > ISA   operator
> > > REVERSED-BY   = /-variable

```
==>
  = Equation-Operator-Subgoal >
       ISA                  equation
       LHS-VAR              = X-variable
       RHS-CON1            = D-variable
       RHS-OP2             = /-variable
       RHS-CON2            = C-variable
  !focus-on! = Equation-Operator-Subgoal)
```

The important thing to note about this production is that it found the mapping between the multiplication sign and the division sign to induce correctly how one goes from $X * C = D$ to $X = D/C$ (the three lines above the $\Rightarrow$ in the production). The analogy mechanism does this by finding the path from the $+$ in the previously solved problem to the WME that declares that the reverse operator of $+$ is $-$, where $-$ is also used in the previously found problem. The other symbols can be trivially mapped from their location in the problem statement to their location in the problem's solution. The !focus-on! command sets the newly created WME as the system's new goal.

Although the current simulation does not attempt to model the latencies recorded in either of the experiments, the ACT–R (Anderson, 1993) theory does specify how such predictions would be made. The latency of the analogy process is defined as the sum of the latencies of the WMEs retrieved in the process, which include the examples and the intermediate retrievals. The analogy process and the instantiation of the production occur sequentially. Therefore, the latency of the resulting instantiation is defined as the latency of the analogy process plus the matching latency. More information regarding how these latencies are computed, including the underlying equations, can be found in Anderson (1993).

Conceptual Learning

Chapter 20

Acquisition of Children's Addition Strategies: A Model of Impasse-Free, Knowledge-Level Learning

Randolph M. Jones and Kurt VanLehn

1 Introduction

This research focuses on modeling naturally occurring discovery processes in cognitive skill acquisition. In particular, it provides an explanation of the well-known SUM-to-MIN transition that children exhibit when they are learning to add (Ashcraft, 1982, 1987; Groen & Parkman, 1972; Groen & Resnick, 1977; Kaye, Post, Hall, & Dineen, 1986; Siegler & Jenkins, 1989; Svenson, 1975). On the surface, this transition appears to be a case of *symbol-level* or *speed-up* learning (Dietterich, 1986). The SUM and MIN strategies are both correct and complete addition algorithms, but the MIN strategy is much faster. However, closer inspection reveals that the transition involves changes to the *structure* of the solution, which cannot be explained by conventional symbol-level learning methods. In addition, children appear to invent the MIN strategy spontaneously, rather than in response to any failures or impasses in problem solving. Thus, a successful model of the SUM-to-MIN transition must make dramatic changes in the strategies, and it must be able to do so without the benefit of impasses to drive learning.

Earlier work attests to the complexity of modeling this structurally intricate strategy shift. Neches (1987) was able to model the transition using a machine learner based on compiler optimization techniques, but the model required implausibly large amounts of extremely detailed information about both ongoing processes and related past experiences. Moreover, it predicted that subjects would briefly display certain strategies on their way to the MIN strategy, but these strategies were not observed in subsequent empirical work (Siegler & Jenkins, 1989). Other intermediate strategies were observed instead.

The research problem is to find a learning method (or methods) that can make the SUM-to-MIN transition, use only plausible amounts of computation and memory, and explain the observed intermediate strategies. In this paper, we concentrate on explaining the results of a longitudinal study carried out by Siegler and Jenkins (1989). They found that children invent the MIN strategy and two intermediate strategies independently, without any instruction on the new strategies. More importantly, Siegler and Jenkins discovered that the invention of the MIN strategy does not appear to be driven by failures or impasses in solving problems. Finally, we argue that learning the MIN strategy requires a form of knowledge-level learning (Dietterich, 1986) that introduces new, more efficient behavior, rather than simply tuning or composing old knowledge.

2 The SUM-to-MIN Transition

When young children first learn to add two small numbers, they use the so-called SUM strategy. They create sets of objects to represent each addend, then count the objects in the union of the two sets. For example, suppose a child is asked, "What is 2 plus 3?" In order to solve this problem, the child says, "1, 2," while raising two fingers on the left hand; then "1, 2, 3," while raising three fingers on the right hand; then "1, 2, 3, 4, 5," while counting all the raised fingers. This is called the SUM strategy because its execution time is proportional to the sum of the two addends. Older children use a more efficient strategy, called the MIN strategy. In following this strategy, the child first announces the vale of the larger addend, then counts onward from it. For instance, in order to solve 2 + 3, the child would say, "3," then say, "4, 5," while raising two fingers on one hand. The execution time for the MIN strategy is proportional to the minimum of the two addends. Algorithms for the two strategies appear in Table 20.1.

Although the SUM strategy is taught in school, the MIN strategy appears to be invented by the children themselves. The best evidence for this comes from a longitudinal study by Siegler and Jenkins (1989). They interviewed eight children weekly for 11 weeks, each time asking them to solve about 15 orally presented addition problems. After each problem, they asked the children how they got their answers. They also told each child whether the answer was correct, and gave the child a gold star if it was. Finally, they analyzed videotapes of the session and classified the child's behavior on each problem according to the strategy that the child used. As far as Siegler and Jenkins could determine, the only instruction that the subjects received during this period was their school's normal instruction on the SUM strategy. Nonetheless, seven of the eight children eventually began to use the MIN strategy. Moreover, the children appear to have discovered this strategy during the video-taped sessions. The tapes make it clear that they received no help from the experimenter, so the MIN strategy appears to have been invented by the subjects themselves. In addition, Siegler and Jenkins found two transitional counting strategies that the subjects used while proceeding from SUM to MIN. These are the SHORTCUT SUM strategy, in which a subject raises and counts fingers from one to the final sum across both hands, and the FIRST strategy, which is similar to MIN, except that the order for adding two addends is not determined by their relative sizes.

A central issue for computational learning systems is deciding *when* to learn. A popular method is to learn when an *impasse* occurs, suggesting a hole in the

Table 20.1
A comparison of the SUM and MIN strategies

Initial SUM strategy	MIN strategy

1. Assign first addend
   to left hand;
	Assign larger addend
	   to left hand;

2. Assign second addend
   to right hand;
	Assign smaller addend
	   to right hand;

3. Let Counter be 0;	
4. Loop	
5. Raise finger on left hand;	
6. Let Counter be Counter + 1;	
7. Until Counter = left hand addend;	Let Counter be left hand addend;
8. Let Counter be 0;	
9. Loop	Loop
10. Raise finger on right hand;	Raise finger on right hand;
11. Let Counter be Counter + 1;	Let Counter be Counter + 1;

12. Until Counter =
   right hand addend;
	Until number of raised fingers =
	   right hand addend;

13. Let Counter be 0;	
14. Loop	
15. Mark raised finger;	
16. Let Counter be Counter + 1;	
17. Until number of marked fingers = number of raised fingers;	
18. Let Answer be Counter;	Let Answer be Counter;

system's knowledge base. The exact definition of "impasse" depends on the problem-solving architecture, but roughly speaking, an impasse occurs for a problem solver when it comes across a goal that cannot be achieved by any operator that is believed to be relevant to the task at hand. The essential idea of impasse-driven learning is to resolve the impasse somehow, then store the resulting experience in such a way that future impasses will be avoided or at least handled more efficiently. Many systems use impasse-driven learning, including LPARSIFAL (Berwick, 1985), OCCAM (Pazzani, Dyer & Flowers, 1986), SWALE (Schank, 1986), SOAR (Newell, 1990), SIERRA (VanLehn, 1990), and CASCADE (VanLehn & Jones, 1993; VanLehn, Jones & Chi, 1992). SOAR is perhaps the best-known impasse-driven learning system, but its definition of impasse is a bit idiosyncratic. It uses impasse-driven learning for *all* changes to memory. Because people automatically store a dense record of their on-going experiences (Tulving's episodic memory), a proper SOAR model must have impasses very frequently, perhaps several per second. Unlike SOAR, other models record their personal experiences with mechanisms that are separate from their impasse-driven learning mechanism. For them, an impasse corresponds to the subjective experience of getting stuck and knowing that you are stuck. In one detailed psychological study (VanLehn, 1991), this occurred about once every half hour. In this paper, we use "impasse" only for these higher level impasses.

Because of the importance of impasse-driven learning in current models of intelligence, Siegler and Jenkins looked specifically for signs of impasses in their study. In particular, they designed some of the problems to cause impasses by making one of the addends very large (e.g., $23 + 1$). They found that "The specific problems on which the children first used the MIN strategy were $2 + 5$, $4 + 1$, $3 + 1$, $1 + 24$, $5 + 2$, and $4 + 3$. These problems did not deviate from the characteristics of the overall set in any notable way" (p. 67). In fact, some of the children had earlier successfully solved exactly the same problem that they were working on when they discovered the MIN strategy. Although the large-addend problems did cause subjects who had already invented the MIN strategy to start using it more frequently, the problems did not cause those who had not invented the strategy to do so.

In addition, Siegler and Jenkins sought signs of impasses by examining solution times and errors in the vicinity of the discovery events. Solution times were longer than normal for the problems where the discovery occurred (a median of 17.8 seconds vs. overall median of 9.8 seconds) and for the problems immediately preceding the discovery trial (median 18 seconds). This might suggest some kind of impasse. However, the specific problems being worked on at those points were not particularly difficult. On the discovery trial, 71% of the problems involved addends that were both 5 or less and thus could each be stored on a single hand. This rate is almost identical to the rate of 72% for the set as a whole. Moreover, 88% of the problems encountered in the session prior to the discovery did not include a large addend. Using error rates as a measure of difficulty yielded a similar finding. Siegler and Jenkins report,

> Prior to discovering the min strategy, children had answered correctly 12 of the 16 problems that they had encountered within the session. This level of accuracy, 75%, was not substantially worse than the 85% correct answers that children generated across the entire practice set. Further, three of the four errors were generated by a single child; the other four children collectively made only one error on the 12 trials they encountered in the same session but before their discoveries. This, together with the fact that two other children used the min strategy for the first time on the first trial of a session, indicated that incorrect answers are not necessary to motivate discovery of a new strategy. However, the long solution times just prior to the discoveries do suggest a heightening of cognitive activity even without incorrect answers to motivate it. (p. 69)

The absence of impasses near the critical learning events presents a challenge for current theories of learning. However, Siegler and Jenkins suggest a reconciliation between their findings and the impasse-driven learning theories:

Two types of strategy changes can be distinguished: changes in which the main difference between the strategies is in the answers themselves, and changes in which the main differences are not in the answers that are generated but rather in the efficiency with which answers are generated and/or the aesthetic appeal of the procedures. The first type of strategy change may occur primarily as a result of encountering impasses, but the second may typically occur for other reasons. (p. 104)

Our analysis of the differences between the SUM and MIN strategies, together with Siegler and Jenkins' findings, provide some strict criteria that a model of the SUM-to-MIN transition should meet. First, the model should proceed from usage of the SUM strategy to the MIN strategy without any outside instruction (other than feedback on the correctness of the answers). It should invent the same transitional strategies that Siegler and Jenkins found in their subjects. It also must account for the ability to invent new strategies even when there are no impasses to drive learning. Finally, the model must incorporate a mechanism for knowledge-level learning, so that it can adapt its representation of the task domain. GIPS, the model we describe in the next section, meets these criteria.

3 The General Inductive Problem Solver

GIPS is a problem solver that uses *flexible means-ends analysis* as its performance mechanism (Jones, 1993; Langley & Allen, 1991). Its learning mechanism is based on Schlimmer's (1987; Schlimmer & Granger, 1986a, 1986b) STAGGER system, which uses a probabilistic induction technique to learn concept descriptions from examples. GIPS uses its induction algorithm to learn search-control knowledge for its operators, assigning credit and blame in a manner similar to SAGE (Langley, 1985) and LEX (Mitchell, Utgoff, & Banerji, 1983). However, GIPS also uses probabilistic induction to learn new preconditions on its operators, thus modifying the descriptions of the operators themselves. Inductive modification of preconditions (as opposed to inductive modification of search-control knowledge) appears to be a new machine-learning technique. Although it could be risky, in that it seems capable of destroying the correctness of the operator set, we show that when properly controlled, it can produce correctness-preserving speed increases that standard techniques have not been able to produce. From a cognitive-modeling perspective, both learning about search control and learning new operator representations play crucial roles in the SUM-to-MIN transition.

3.1 Representation of the Addition Domain
In this section, we describe GIPS' representation of the task domain. GIPS describes the world as a set of relations between objects. In the domain of

Table 20.2
A GIPS operator to increment the value of a counter

```
COUNT (?Hand, ?Initvalue, ?Finalvalue)
Preconditions:
  Hand (?Hand)
  Just-raised (?Hand)
  Counter-value (?Initvalue)
Add conditions:
  Counter-value (?Finalvalue)
Delete conditions:
  Counter-value (?Initvalue)
  Just-raised (?Hand)
Constraints:
  ?Finalvalue is ?Initvalue + 1
```

addition, these objects and relations include the numbers that are part of the problem, the state of the problem solver's "hands" while it is adding, and the value of a counter that the problem solver keeps "in its head." In addition, GIPS represents possible actions in the domain with operators that are similar in representation to those used by STRIPS (Fikes & Nilsson, 1971). Each includes a set of preconditions, add conditions, delete conditions, and possibly a set of constraints on the variable bindings.

As an example, consider the operator in Table 20.2, which increments the value of the counter. This operator has three variable parameters, ?Hand, ?Initvalue, and ?Final-VALUE (throughout this paper, an atom beginning with "?" represents a variable). The preconditions for the operator check the current value of the counter and make sure that the system has just raised a finger that needs to be counted. The constraint generates a final value for the counter by incrementing the initial value. GIPS' constraint mechanism allows constraints to propagate forwards or backwards, so this constraint can also compute the necessary initial value if it is given the final value as a goal. Finally, when the operator executes, it will delete the initial value of the counter and record the final value. In addition, it will delete the "just-raised" condition so that the finger will not be counted twice.

GIPS represents the addition domain with the 16 operators presented in Table 20.3. There are two particular operators, which we refer to as the ADDEND-REPRESENTED operators, that are involved in most of the strategy shifts. For future reference, the series of preconditions that the LEFT-ADDEND-REPRESENTED operator acquires in going from SUM to MIN appears in Table 20.4. For our study, we initialized GIPS' search-control and precondition knowledge for the 16 operators such that the system generates the SUM strategy on addition problems. We will discuss this initialization in more detail after presenting GIPS' performance algorithm and low-level knowledge representation.

Table 20.3
Operators for the addition domain

SELECT-HAND: Select an addend to be counted on each hand. The left hand is always counted first.

COUNT-OUT-LEFTHAND: Represent or count the left-hand addend.

COUNT-OUT-RIGHTHAND: Represent or count the right-hand addend.

START-COUNT: Keep track of the counter value while raising fingers.

START-RAISE: Begin raising fingers in order to represent an addend.

RAISE-FINGER: Raise a finger.

COUNT: Count the last raised finger by incrementing the counter value.

LEFT-ADDEND-REPRESENTED: Stop counting and raising fingers on the left hand.

RIGHT-ADDEND-REPRESENTED: Stop counting and raising fingers on the right hand.

CLOBBER-COUNTER: Set the counter value to zero.

COUNT-UP-BOTH-ADDENDS: Make sure both addends have been counted together.

START-MARK-COUNT: Keep a running count while marking raised fingers.

MARK-FINGER: Mark a finger that has already been raised.

MARK-COUNT: Count the last marked finger by incrementing the counter value.

END-MARK-COUNT: Stop marking fingers on a hand.

DETERMINE-ANSWER: Announce the answer.

Table 20.4
A series of preconditions for LEFT-ADDEND-REPRESENTED

SUM strategy (a):
  Raising (LeftHand)
  Assigned (LeftHand, ?Value)
  Counter-value (?Value)

SUM strategy (b):
  Raising (LeftHand)
  Assigned (LeftHand, ?Value)
  Counter-value (?Value)
  Raised-fingers (LeftHand,
    ?Value)

SHORTCUT SUM strategy (c):
  Raising (LeftHand)
  Assigned (LeftHand, ?Value)
  Raised-fingers (LeftHand,
    ?Value)

MIN strategy (d):
  Raising (LeftHand)
  Assigned (LeftHand, ?Value)

Table 20.5
Gips' algorithm for solving problems

```
TRANSFORM (CurState, Goals): Returns NewState
  If CurState satisfies Goals
    Then Return NewState as CurState
    Else Let OpSet be the ordered set of selected
                          operator instantiations;
        Let FailedOps be Nil;
        Loop for Operator in OpSet
            Let TempState be APPLY (CurState, Operator);
            If TempState is "Failed State"
               Then push Operator onto FailedOps and continue loop;
            Let TempState be TRANSFORM (TempState, Goals);
            If TempState is "Failed State"
               Then push Operator onto FailedOps and continue loop;
            Store (CurState, Goals) as a positive example for the
               selection concept of Operator;
            Store (CurState, Goals) as a negative example for the
               selection concept of each operator in FailedOps;
            Return NewState as Tempstate
        End loop;
        Return NewState as "Failed State";

APPLY (CurState, Op): Returns NewState
  Let P be PRECONDITIONS (Op);
  If CurState satisfies the execution concept of Op
    Then If the user says Op is executable
            Then Store CurState as a positive example for the
                   execution concept of Op;
                 Return NewState as EXECUTE (CurState, Op)
            Else Store CurState as a negative example for the
                   execution concept of Op;
  Let TempState be TRANSFORM (CurState, P);
  If TempState is "Failed State"
    Then Return NewState as "Failed State"
    Else Return NewState as APPLY (TempState, Op);
```

3.2 Performance Algorithm

As mentioned above, Gips' problem-solving algorithm (see Table 20.5) is a form of flexible means-ends analysis, borrowed from the Eureka system (Jones, 1993). As with standard means-ends analysis, the algorithm is based on trying to achieve a state change. The desired change is represented by a Transform, which is simply a pair consisting of the current state and some goals (an example appears in Table 20.6). In order to achieve this transformation, Gips selects an operator and attempts to apply it. If the operator's preconditions are met, Gips executes it and the current state changes. If some of the preconditions are not met, a new Transform is created with the preconditions as the new goals. When this Transform is achieved, Gips returns to the old Transform and

Table 20.6
An example of a TRANSFORM for the addition domain

Current State:	Goals:
On-Paper (First, Two)	Raising (LeftHand)
On-Paper (Second, Three)	Assigned (LeftHand, ?Value)
Assigned (LeftHand, Three)	Counter-Value (?Value)
Counter-Value (Zero)	
Raised-Fingers (LeftHand, Zero)	

attempts again to apply the operator. So far, this is simply a description of standard means-ends analysis.

The difference between standard and flexible means-ends analysis occurs in the selection of an operator to apply. Standard means-ends analysis requires that the actions of any selected operator directly address the goals of the TRANSFORM. In flexible means-ends analysis, operator selection is determined by a selection algorithm that can use any criteria to choose an operator. In order for the selection algorithm to be useful, it is usually under the direct control of the system's learning mechanism. In GIPS, operator selection is determined by *selection concepts*. Each operator is associated with an explicit concept that indicates when it should be selected. If the concept depends mostly on the current state of the TRANSFORM, then the operator will act like a forward-chaining inference rule and execute whenever the state is appropriate, regardless of the current goals. If the concept depends mostly on the goals of the TRANSFORM, then it will act like a backward-chaining inference rule. Typically, forward and backward operators intermingle during problem solving, yielding a psychologically plausible blend of goal-directed and opportunistic behavior.

In GIPS, each operator has a selection concept. The representation of a selection concept is similar to the representation of a TRANSFORM, consisting of a set of literals (predicates that may or may not be negated) describing the current state and goals. In addition, however, each literal in a selection concept has two numerical values associated with it: sufficiency and necessity. In order to evaluate the selection value of an operator, GIPS matches the literals against the current TRANSFORM. It determines the subset of literals that match (M) and fail to match (F), then calculates

$$\text{Selection Value} = \text{Odds}(C) \prod_{L \in M} S_L \prod_{L \in F} N_L,$$

where $\text{Odds}(C)$ is the prior odds that the concept's operator is worth selecting, S_L is the sufficiency of the literal, L, with respect to the concept, and N_L is the necessity of L with respect to the concept. A sufficiency score that is much greater than 1 indicates that a literal is very sufficient for the selection concept. That is, if S_L is a high value, then the selection value will be high if the literal, L, appears in the current TRANSFORM. In contrast, a literal is very necessary if the necessity value is much *less* than 1. In other words, if N_L is low, it means that the selection value will likely be low *unless L* appears in the current TRANSFORM.

The above formula is used by STAGGER, Schlimmer's (1987) concept formation system, to estimate the odds that a given object is an instance of a particular concept. However, a major difference between STAGGER and GIPS is the STAGGER worked exclusively with propositional knowledge representations. In contrast, the literals in GIPS' concepts are general predicates that can also contain variables. This means that the relations in a given TRANSFORM will generally only *partially* match the relations in a concept, and the TRANSFORM may in fact match the concept in more than one way. In these cases, GIPS finds a number of partial matches and calculates a selection value for each one. Each of these matches in turn represents a different instantiation of the operator attached to the selection concept. Thus, the selection procedure typically returns a number of different instantiations of a number of different operators. When all the operator instantiations have been found and their selection values have been calculated, GIPS throws out all the instantiations with a selection value less than 1. The remaining instantiations are ordered according to their selection values.

GIPS differs from standard means-ends systems in one more important way. In standard problem-solving systems, each operator has a set of *preconditions*, which are used in two ways. First, they determine when the operator can execute. Second, they dictate which subgoals should be set up via means-ends analysis when an operator is not yet executable. GIPS uses the preconditions to set up subgoals, but it does not use them to determine the executability of the operators. Rather, each operator has an associated *execution concept* that dictates when the system will try to execute it. GIPS' execution concepts are similar in form to selection concepts, except they contain literals describing the current state (but not the current goals).

As mentioned previously, GIPS' initial selection and execution concepts were set up to generate the SUM strategy for addition. The literals of each operator's selection concept were set to the preconditions and the goals that the operator could satisfy. The necessity and sufficiency of these literals were set so that they would be retrieved in either a backward-chaining or forward-chaining fashion, depending on the role of the operator in the domain. For example, pure backward-chaining operators had each of their goal literals set with high sufficiency. Forward-chaining operators had each of their current state literals set with high necessity. Finally, each operator had an initial set of preconditions, and the execution concept for each operator was initialized to the literals occurring in the preconditions, each with high necessity.

As an example, the initial preconditions for LEFT-ADDEND-REPRESENTED appear in Table 20.4(a), with its initial selection and execution concepts in Table 20.7. An examination of Table 20.7 shows that LEFT-ADDEND-REPRESENTED is likely to be selected when the current TRANSFORM's goals include `Raised (LeftHand)` or `Counted (LeftHand)` (high S value), *unless* these literals also appear in the TRANSFORM's current state (low S value). The operator is set

Table 20.7
The initial selection and execution concepts for LEFT-ADDEND-REPRESENTED

Selection					
CURRENT STATE	S	N	GOALS	S	N
Raising (LeftHand)	1.03	0.98			
Assigned (LeftHand, ?Value4)	1.03	0.98			
Counter-Value (?Value4)	1.03	0.98	Counter-Value (?Value4)	1.00	1.00
Raised (LeftHand)	0.01	1.01	Raised (LeftHand)	10.00	0.91
Counted (LeftHand)	0.71	1.01	Counted (LeftHand)	10.00	0.91
Execution					
CURRENT STATE	S	N			
Assigned (LeftHand, ?Value4)	2.71	0.05			
Raising (LeftHand)	2.71	0.05			
Counter-Value (?Value4)	2.71	0.05			

to execute only when all three of `Assigned (LeftHand, ?Value4)`, `Raising (LeftHand)`, and `Counter-Value (?Value4)` are matched by literals in the current TRANSFORM's state description (medium S value and low N value).

From our description of GIPS' general problem-solving algorithm, it is clear that there are exactly two types of choice that the system has to make while solving problems: the choice of which operator to apply next, and the choice of whether to execute an operator or subgoal on its preconditions. It is appealing to apply a uniform learning and decision mechanism in a system's performance algorithm, so GIPS uses its probabilistic concept-matching and learning mechanism for both of these decision points. Other problem solvers include additional types of decisions. For example, PRODIGY (Minton, 1988) makes an explicit decision for which subgoal to work on next, whereas that decision is implicit in GIPS' operator-selection decision. Our experiences indicate that a STAGGER-like algorithm can be used at any type of decision point, providing the same kinds of learning benefits to each. Thus, if we decided to have GIPS make an explicit choice about which subgoal to work on next, we would also use the concept-matching algorithm for that, enabling the system to learn and improve its behavior for choosing subgoals as well. In the following section, we discuss how execution and selection concepts change with experience. More importantly, we explain how changes in the execution concepts directly lead to representation changes in the operator preconditions.

3.3 Learning in GIPS

GIPS adjusts its selection concepts on the basis of its successes and failures while solving problems. When a TRANSFORM is finally solved, GIPS adjusts the sufficiency and necessity values of the successful operator so that the operator will be rated even higher the next time a similar TRANSFORM occurs. For each operator that initiated a failure path (i.e., it took the first step off a TRANSFORM's solution path), GIPS adjusts the values in its selection concept so that it will receive a lower value next time. Note that GIPS considers every TRANSFORM to be a "problem," so it can learn about any particular TRANSFORM even if it doesn't lie on the solution path to some global problem. In order to do this kind of learning, GIPS must store the current solution path and every operator that led off it. However, as soon as each individual TRANSFORM in a problem is finished, and the updating is completed, that portion of the solution path is discarded.

This method of assignment for credit and blame is similar to the method used by other problem-solving systems that include concept-learning mechanisms (Langley, 1985; Mitchell, Utgoff, & Banerji, 1983). These systems (and GIPS) can easily assign credit and blame, because they backtrack until they find a solution to the current problem. Then, each decision that leads off the final solution path is classified as a bad decision (a negative example), and each decision that lies on the final solution path is classified as a good decision (a positive example).

However, GIPS differs from these previous systems in the details of its concept-learning algorithm. GIPS computes the sufficiency and necessity scores for literals in a concept (S_L and N_L) with the following equations:

$$S_L = \frac{P(L \text{ matches } I \mid I \in C)}{P(L \text{ matches } I \mid I \notin C)},$$

$$N_L = \frac{P(L \text{ does not match } I \mid I \in C)}{P(L \text{ does not match } I \mid I \notin C)},$$

where $I \in C$ means that TRANSFORM instance, I, is a positive example of the concept, C, and "L matches I" means that literal, L, of the concept is matched by some literal in I. Thus, sufficiency and necessity for each literal are determined by four conditional probabilities.

GIPS learns by updating its estimates of these conditional probabilities. For each literal in a selection concept, GIPS records four values: t, the total number of examples (positive *and* negative) that the system has stored into this selection concept; p, the number of those that were positive examples; l, the total number of times this literal has been matched by any (positive or negative) example; and c, the number of times the literal has been matched in a positive example. In precise form, the conditional probabilities are estimated by

$$P(L \text{ matches } I \mid I \in C) = \frac{c}{p},$$

$$P(L \text{ matches } I \mid I \notin C) = \frac{l - c}{t - p},$$

$$P(L \text{ does not match } I \mid I \in C) = \frac{p - c}{p},$$

$$P(L \text{ does not match } I \mid I \notin C) = \frac{t + c - p - l}{t - p}.$$

As indicated in the algorithm in Table 20.5, GIPS learns by storing an instance (the literals describing the state and goals of the current TRANSFORM) as a positive or negative example of an operator's selection concept (depending on whether the operator led to a solution or a failed search path). Every time the system stores a TRANSFORM as a positive or negative example, it matches the literals in the TRANSFORM to the literals in the selection concept. If there are any literals in the new instance that do not already appear in the selection concept, they are added into the selection concept's representation. Finally, GIPS increments the appropriate counts for each literal: always incrementing t, incrementing p if the instance is a positive example, incrementing l if the literal is matched by a literal in the instance, and incrementing c if the instance is a positive example *and* the literal is matched. For the interested reader, Schlimmer (1987; Schlimmer & Granger, 1986a, 1986b) provides excellent, detailed descriptions of the learning algorithm and its behavior in classification tasks.

We have so far described how GIPS updates its selection concepts. These concepts determine when operators are selected to achieve a TRANSFORM, so they represent search-control knowledge. As we have mentioned, the system also must adapt its execution concepts. The conditional probabilities are updated identically to selection concepts. However, the assignment of credit and blame is a bit different.

Assignment of credit and blame for execution concepts can be computed in a manner similar to credit and blame for selection concepts. When GIPS thinks that a particular operator should execute, it blindly carries on and eventually generates an answer. However, it is possible that the answer will be wrong, indicating that the operator should not have executed (i.e., GIPS' execution concept for that operator is wrong). If GIPS is allowed to backtrack until it eventually generates the correct answer, it can precisely determine which situations should be stored as negative and positive instances of the execution concept, just as with selection concepts. We discovered that in some instances, when GIPS unfortunately generated multiple "bad" execution concepts, backtracking could take quite a while before the system would generate a correct answer and do the appropriate learning. We finessed this problem by giving the system immediate feedback on whether it would generate a correct answer when it attempted to execute operators.

Unfortunately, this does not tell the whole story on credit and blame assignment. In Siegler and Jenkins' study, they awarded each subject a gold star after the subject gave a correct answer, but they did not force the subjects to keep working on the problems until they could give a correct answer, as we do with GIPS. For a strict model of this experiment, we would give GIPS feedback after it generates a complete solution, and not force the system to backtrack. However, if GIPS is not allowed to backtrack, it must incorporate an incremental credit-assignment algorithm, such as the bucket-brigade algorithm (Holland, Holyoak, Nisbett, & Thagard, 1986). In our study, we were more concerned with the order of acquired strategies than the speed of acquisition, so we did not implement such an algorithm in the current version of GIPS. We are convinced that a more realistic credit-assignment algorithm would slow down learning, but would not disturb the order of strategy acquisition. However, future research with GIPS should certainly address this issue.

The final aspect of learning in GIPS involves changing the preconditions on operators. When GIPS successfully predicts that an operator should execute, but the probabilistic execution concept does not agree with the current preconditions of the operator, the system changes the preconditions appropriately. Operator preconditions in GIPS contain only the literals from the execution concept that GIPS has decided are very necessary. This symbolic representation is used to post subgoals when the system wants to apply an operator that it believes cannot yet be executed. Recall that a TRANSFORM includes literals representing the current goals, and these are matched against selection concepts for the operators. Thus, changing operator preconditions can lead directly to subsequent changes in the selection of operators while solving problems.

Logically, GIPS should include in its preconditions for an operator exactly the literals that are highly necessary (i.e., have very low values for N_L). In problem-solving terms, all the literals in the preconditions of an operator should be true (or matched) for the operator to be executable. Thus, it should add literals from the execution concept that have low N_L values to the preconditions, and it should drop literals that do not have low N_L values from the preconditions. However, in order to speed up GIPS' learning, we have adopted a heuristic approach for each of these cases.

First, consider the criterion for adding a new literal to the preconditions of an operator. Again, GIPS should ideally consider this action for any literal with a low value for N_L. An examination of the equation for N_L shows that it decreases as $P(L$ does not match $I \mid I \notin C)$ increases. Learning about necessity poses some difficulties, because GIPS can increase its estimate of $P(L$ does not match $I \mid I \notin C)$ only when it predicts that the operator associated with C should execute, but the user tells the system that it made an incorrect prediction (an error of commission). However, GIPS is generally conservative in attempting to execute operators, so this type of event is relatively rare. Thus, GIPS takes a long time to learn that any new literal is necessary for execution. To overcome this difficulty, we allow GIPS to use a different criterion for adding preconditions. Rather than looking for literals that are very necessary, it looks for literals that are somewhat sufficient (i.e., have relatively high values for S_L). Mathematically speaking, sufficiency is not a valid predictor of new preconditions, but it does have some heuristic value, because literals that are very necessary are also always somewhat sufficient (if not very sufficient). This heuristic can encourage GIPS to make errors of commission, and thus learn whether the new literal really is necessary to the execution concept.

Now let us consider the case of dropping a literal from the preconditions of an operator when its value for N_L becomes too big. Again looking at the equation for N_L, we see that N_L increases as $P(L$ does not match $I \mid I \in C)$ increases. This corresponds to the case where GIPS correctly predicts that the operator associated with C should execute, but L does not appear. Intuitively, this means that L is not necessary for the operator to execute, so we have some evidence that it should be removed from the preconditions. As far as the system is concerned, it is learning that there is no reason to subgoal on a literal if it is not actually a necessary precondition for the operator.

A "proper" implementation of the STAGGER algorithm for this case would increment the estimate for $P(L$ does not match $I \mid I \in C)$ slightly every time the operator successfully executes "early." Thus, it would slowly gather evidence that L is not necessary, and it would eventually delete L from the preconditions of the operator. The algorithm requires substantial evidence before it will do this, because it must learn that L really is unnecessary and that the system has not simply encountered a noisy instance. In order to speed up GIPS' learning of preconditions, we assume that the feedback on operator execution from the user is always correct (i.e., not noisy). This allows us to bias GIPS to increase $P(L$ does not match $I \mid I \in C)$ by a *large* value for this type of instance rather than just by a small increment. Thus, GIPS can drop a literal, L, from its preconditions for an operator the *first time* it successfully executes that operator without the presence of L, rather than waiting for a large number of confirming experiences.

4 Strategy Acquisition in the Addition Domain

This section presents GIPS' behavior through a series of different strategies for adding numbers. These strategy shifts arise from the learning algorithm incorporated into the system, and they correspond well with the shifts observed by Siegler and Jenkins. Siegler and Jenkins classified their subjects' behavior into eight strategies, of which four were based on counting (the others involved various kinds of recognition and guessing, which GIPS does not model). In this section, we describe each of the four counting strategies in the order in which they generally appear. However, it is important to note that children always intermingle their strategies, sometimes even on a trial-by-trial basis. We will discuss the issue of strategy variability in the following section.

4.1 The SUM Strategy

GIPS' initial strategy for addition is the SUM strategy. To better follow GIPS' behavior, we have provided a trace of the sum strategy for the problem $2 + 3$ in Table 20.8. In this trace, we have omitted calls to the `Transform` function, only listing when operators are selected to apply and when they actually execute. The first thing the system does is assign an addend to each hand. For example,

Table 20.8
Gips' initial Sum strategy for addition

Apply Select-hand
    (LeftHand, Two, RightHand, Three)
Execute Select-hand
    (LeftHand, Two, RightHand, Three)
Apply Determine-answer (?Answer)
  Apply Count-out-lefthand (?Value70)
    Apply Left-addend-represented
      (?Value70)
     Apply Start-raise (LeftHand)
     Execute Start-raise (LeftHand)
     Apply Start-count (LeftHand)
     Execute Start-count (LeftHand)
     Apply Raise-finger (LeftHand, 1)
     Execute Raise-finger (LeftHand, 1)
     Apply Count (1)
     Execute Count (1)
     Apply Raise-finger (LeftHand, 2)
     Execute Raise-finger (LeftHand, 2)
     Apply Count (2)
     Execute Count (2)
    Execute Left-addend-represented (2)
  Execute Count-out-Lefthand (2)
  Apply Clobber-counter
  Execute Clobber-counter
  Apply Count-out-righthand (?Value120)
    Apply Right-addend-represented
      (?Value120)
     Apply Start-raise (RightHand)
     Execute Start-raise (RightHand)
     Apply Start-count (RightHand)
     Execute Start-count (RightHand)
     Apply Raise-finger (RightHand, 1)
     Execute Raise-finger (RightHand, 1)
     Apply Count (1)
     Execute Count (1)
     Apply Raise-finger (RightHand, 2)
     Execute Raise-finger (RightHand, 2)
     Apply Count (2)
     Execute Count (2)
     Apply Raise-finger (RightHand, 3)
     Execute Raise-finger (RightHand, 3)
     Apply Count (3)
     Execute Count (3)
    Execute Right-addend-represented (3)
  Execute Count-out-righthand (3)

Apply Count-up-both-addends (?Answer)
  Apply Clobber-counter
  Execute Clobber-counter
  Apply Count-out-lefthand (?Value158)
    Apply End-mark-count
      (LeftHand, ?Value158)
     Apply Start-mark-count (LeftHand)
     Execute Start-mark-count (LeftHand)
     Apply Mark-finger (LeftHand, 1)
     Execute Mark-finger (LeftHand, 1)
     Apply Mark-count (1)
     Execute Mark-count (1)
     Apply Mark-finger (LeftHand, 2)
     Execute Mark-finger (LeftHand, 2)
     Apply Mark-count (2)
     Execute Mark-count (2)
    Execute End-mark-count (LeftHand, 2)
  Execute Count-out-lefthand (2)
  Apply Count-out-lefthand (?Value208)
    Apply End-mark-count
      (RightHand, ?Value208)
     Apply Start-mark-count (RightHand)
     Execute Start-mark-count (RightHand)
     Apply Mark-finger (RightHand, 1)
     Execute Mark-finger (RightHand, 1)
     Apply Mark-count (3)
     Execute Mark-count (3)
     Apply Mark-finger (RightHand, 2)
     Execute Mark-finger (RightHand, 2)
     Apply Mark-count (4)
     Execute Mark-count (4)
     Apply Mark-finger (RightHand, 3)
     Execute Mark-finger (RightHand, 3)
     Apply Mark-count (5)
     Execute Mark-count (5)
    Execute End-mark-count (RightHand, 5)
  Execute Count-out-righthand
    (RightHand, 5)
  Execute Count-up-both-addends (5)
Execute Determine-answer (5)

when adding 2 and 3, the system may assign the number 2 to the left hand and the number 3 to the right hand. However, in this strategy the order of the addends does not make a difference, so it could just as easily have switched them.

Next, the system begins its procedure of raising and counting a set of fingers on each hand. To accomplish this task, the ADDEND-REPRESENTED operators use a counter to determine when an addend is finished being represented on each hand (see Table 20.4(a)). For example, the preconditions of LEFT-ADDEND-REPRESENTED demand that the system be raising fingers on the left hand, and that the value of the counter be equal to the value of the left-hand addend. These preconditions are set up as subgoals, causing the selection of the START-RAISE and START-COUNT operators, which initialize the forward-chaining procedure of raising and counting fingers one at a time. These operators execute alternately until LEFT-ADDEND-REPRESENTED can execute, when the correct number of fingers have been counted on the left hand.

After the left hand has been counted, the CLOBBER-COUNTER operator immediately executes. This operator executes when all the fingers of a hand have been raised along with a running count. Its effects are to zero the value of the counter to prepare it for the next hand, and to mark the current hand as *uncounted*, because the counter's value has been changed. This entire procedure then repeats with the right hand.

After both hands have been counted, DETERMINE-ANSWER checks whether it can execute. It can only execute if both hands are marked as *counted*, but CLOBBER-COUNTER has caused this to be false. Therefore, the system again attempts to count up fingers on each hand, this time marking fingers that are already raised. For this procedure, no CLOBBER-COUNTER is necessary, because the number of raised fingers (rather than the value of the counter) is used to terminate the count for each hand. Finally, after each hand has been counted for the second time, GIPS announces the answer.

As the system repeatedly solves addition problems, it continuously updates the execution concepts for the two ADDEND-REPRESENTED operators. After a while, these two concepts encode several regularities that are always true when these operators execute. For example, there are always two addends in the problem description, and the number of "marked" fingers is always zero. Most importantly, however, the concepts encode the number of raised fingers as always equal to the counter value (which in turn is equal to the goal value for counting an addend). Literals representing this fact eventually get added into the preconditions for the ADDEND-REPRESENTED operators (see Table 20.4(b)). This action alone does not change the system's outward behavior, but it proves important for later strategies.

4.2 The SHORTCUT SUM Strategy

After the new preconditions have been added and a number of addition problems have been solved, the new literals in GIPS' execution concepts for LEFT-

Table 20.9
GIPS' SHORTCUT SUM strategy

Apply SELECT-HAND	
(LeftHand, Two, RightHand, Three)	Apply RIGHT-ADDEND-REPRESENTED
Execute SELECT-HAND	(?Value1022)
(LeftHand, Two, RightHand, Three)	Apply START-RAISE (RightHand)
Apply DETERMINE-ANSWER (?Answer)	Execute START-RAISE (RightHand)
Apply COUNT-OUT-LEFTHAND (?Value988)	Apply RAISE-FINGER (RightHand, 1)
Apply LEFT-ADDEND-REPRESENTED	Execute RAISE-FINGER (RightHand, 1)
(?Value988)	Apply COUNT (3)
Apply START-RAISE (LeftHand)	Execute COUNT (3)
Execute START-RAISE (LeftHand)	Apply RAISE-FINGER (RightHand, 2)
Apply RAISE-FINGER (LeftHand, 1)	Execute RAISE-FINGER (RightHand, 2)
Execute RAISE-FINGER (LeftHand, 1)	Apply COUNT (4)
Apply COUNT (1)	Execute COUNT (4)
Execute COUNT (1)	Apply RAISE-FINGER (RightHand, 3)
Apply RAISE-FINGER (LeftHand, 2)	Execute RAISE-FINGER (RightHand, 3)
Execute RAISE-FINGER (LeftHand, 2)	Apply COUNT (5)
Apply COUNT (2)	Execute COUNT (5)
Execute COUNT (2)	Execute RIGHT-ADDEND-REPRESENTED (3)
Execute LEFT-ADDEND-REPRESENTED (2)	Execute COUNT-OUT-RIGHTHAND (3)
Execute COUNT-OUT-LEFTHAND (2)	Apply COUNT-UP-BOTH-ADDENDS (?Answer)
Apply COUNT-OUT-RIGHTHAND	Execute COUNT-UP-BOTH-ADDENDS (5)
(?Value1022)	Execute DETERMINE-ANSWER (5)

ADDEND-REPRESENTED and RIGHT-ADDEND-REPRESENTED become so strong that GIPS decides that the operators should execute when the number of fingers raised on a hand is equal to the goal value even though the system has not yet incremented its count for the last finger. It turns out that the system can successfully solve the addition problem even if it executes this operator prematurely, so it deletes the condition that the current counter value must be equal to the goal value in the preconditions of the ADDEND-REPRESENTED operators (see Table 20.4(c)).

This change has a direct effect on GIPS' behavior (see Table 20.9). When attempting to apply LEFT-ADDEND-REPRESENTED, the value of the counter no longer appears in the preconditions, so it is not posted as a subgoal. This means that the START-COUNT operator is no longer selected. Thus, a running count is still kept while raising fingers, but the counter is not marked for use as the termination criterion. This means that CLOBBER-COUNTER will not execute, and that leads to two changes in strategy. First, the counter is not reset to zero after counting the left hand, and counting continues from the left hand's final value. Second, the hands are not marked as *uncounted*, so there is no need to count up the raised fingers again after the two hands have initially been counted. This behavior corresponds to the SHORTCUT SUM strategy, which was invented by all eight of Siegler and Jenkins' subjects.

This representation assumes that the student can determine without counting when the number of raised fingers on either hand is equal to the goal value. For example, in adding 2 + 3, just after saying, "five," and raising a third finger on the right hand, the subject must *see* that the number of fingers on the right hand is equal to 3, the number of fingers that they intended to raise. Before they began their study, Siegler and Jenkins tested their subjects' ability to recognize small numbers of objects without counting, and all the subjects could perform the skill adequately. Thus, we represent it in GIPS as a primitive skill, or a simple literal.

4.3 The SHORTCUT MIN Strategy

The next shift leads to an intermediate strategy between SHORTCUT SUM and MIN, which we call SHORTCUT MIN. Although Siegler and Jenkins do not classify SHORTCUT MIN as a distinct strategy from SHORTCUT SUM, they do note (p. 119) that some of their subjects begin to switch addends during SHORTCUT SUM so that they start counting with the larger addend on the left hand, rather than just picking whichever addend appears first in the problem. GIPS also accounts for this behavior.

An important feature of the SHORTCUT SUM strategy is that the problem solver's counter value is not equal to the number of fingers being raised on the right hand (i.e., the second hand). We hypothesize that this causes interference and subsequent failure. Such interference would not occur with the left hand, because the number of raised fingers in the SHORTCUT SUM strategy is always equal to the value of the counter for that hand. Unfortunately, interference is a phenomenon that GIPS does not yet model, so we were forced to simulate its effects. We assumed that interference between the value of the counter and the number of fingers raised on the right hand would cause a child to become confused and fail to solve the current problem. This behavior is confirmed by Siegler and Jenkins: "When children used the shortcut-sum approach, they were considerably more accurate on problems where the first addend was larger than on ones where the second addend was" (p. 71).

We simulated this process by causing GIPS to fail sometimes during the SHORTCUT SUM strategy when it decided to count the larger addend on its right hand. These failures caused the system to update its selection concept for the SELECT-HAND operator. Thus, GIPS learned to prefer assigning the larger of the two addends to its left hand (information on the relative sizes of the addends was explicitly included in the state representation). Note that the learning algorithm does not require a model of interference to make this strategy shift. It simply records the fact that failure is somewhat correlated with assigning a larger addend to the right hand.

4.4 The MIN Strategy

The final strategy shift occurs in a similar manner to the shift from SUM to SHORTCUT SUM. At this point, GIPS has attempted to execute the ADDEND-

Table 20.10
Gips' Min strategy

Apply Select-hand (LeftHand, Three, RightHand, Two)	Apply Start-raise (RightHand)
Execute Select-hand (LeftHand, Three, RightHand, Two)	Execute Start-raise (RightHand)
Apply Determine-answer (?Answer)	Apply Raise-finger (RightHand, 1)
Apply Count-out-lefthand	Execute Raise-finger (RightHand, 1)
(?Value1498)	Apply Count (4)
Apply Left-addend-represented	Execute Count (4)
(?Value1498)	Apply Raise-finger (RightHand, 2)
Apply Start-raise (LeftHand)	Execute Raise-finger (RightHand, 2)
Execute Start-raise (LeftHand)	Apply Count (5)
Execute Left-addend-represented (3)	Execute Count (5)
Execute Count-out-lefthand (3)	Execute Right-addend-represented (3)
Apply Count-out-righthand	Execute Count-out-righthand (3)
(?Value1516)	Apply Count-up-both-addends (?Answer)
Apply Right-addend-represented	Execute Count-up-both-addends (5)
(?Value1516)	Execute Determine-answer (5)

REPRESENTED operators at various times and has been given feedback each time as to whether it would be able to solve the current problem if it executed the operator at that time. Thus, it is slowly learning a "good" concept for when the ADDEND-REPRESENTED operators are executable. One of the things that proves to be true every time these operators execute is that the goal value for counting out a hand is equal to the addend assigned to that hand.

Eventually, the system attempts to execute the LEFT-ADDEND-REPRESENTED operator without having raised any fingers at all (see Table 20.10). When it succeeds in doing this, it deletes the precondition that the number of fingers raised on the hand be equal to the goal value (see Table 20.4(d)). The system has learned that it can simply start counting from the goal value for the left hand rather than starting from zero. Note that this behavior could not be generated directly from the initial SUM strategy, because it requires the counter to be used for counting the total sum, so it cannot aid in representing the right-hand addend. As with LEFT-ADDEND-REPRESENTED, GIPS also attempts to execute the RIGHT-ADDEND-REPRESENTED operator early, but this leads to failure. Thus, the system begins to exhibit the MIN strategy, in which the largest number (the left-hand number) is simply announced and used to continue counting the smaller number as in the SHORTCUT MIN strategy.

5 Summary and Analysis

Both the SUM strategy and the MIN strategy have three main subgoals: to represent the first addend, to represent the second addend, and to count the union of the representations. The SUM-to-MIN transition involves three independent modifications to the SUM strategy:

1. The process of representing the addends is run in parallel with counting up the union. In the SUM strategy, representing the two addends must be completed before counting up the union begins.
2. The order of addends is made conditional on their sizes so that the larger addend is represented by the easier process. That is, any interference that occurs with the second addend is more likely to occur if the addend is large. Clearly, this strategy change must take place after the first one, because there is no interference when representing an addend and counting the union take place separately.
3. The subgoal of representing one addend changes from explicitly constructing a set of objects to simply saying the addend.

The GIPS account for each of these transitions is as follows. The first transition is caused by a combination of correlational learning of preconditions and search-control learning. Initially, GIPS represents an addend on a hand by raising fingers and counting until the counter's value is equal to the addend value. In two steps, the system learns that recognizing the number of fingers raised on a hand is a better stopping criterion than the value of the counter. When the value of the counter disappears as a subgoal of representing an addend, it is still free to be used to count the union of objects.

6 Discussion

The GIPS analysis helps clarify several important, general issues about strategy change. Siegler and Jenkins observe that, "Not one child adopted a strategy that could be classified as indicating a lack of understanding of the goals of addition" (p. 107). In this respect, the subjects are similar to those of Gelman and Gallistel (1978), who found that very young children would invent correct strategies for counting a set of objects even when unusual constraints were placed on them to thwart their normal strategy. Gelman and Gallistel explain this remarkable competence by hypothesizing that children possess innate (or at least predetermined) principles of numerousity. Although linguists had earlier proposed the existence of innate constraints on language development, Gelman and Gallistel provided the first empirical evidence of innate constraints on non-linguistic development. This set off a heated debate in the developmental community. Siegler and Jenkins (p. 115) suggest that such constraints may exist on the development of addition strategies, but they do not give a specific list.

The initial knowledge given to GIPS does not involve any explicit principles of addition or counting. It is merely a set of operators and selection preferences that happen to generate the correct answers. It is able to avoid developing bad strategies because of the feedback it receives while solving problems. GIPS occasionally attempts to execute an operator in situations that would produce a wrong answer. If it were not told that the execution was wrong, it would develop wrong strategies. Thus, GIPS suggests one possible account for learning without the hypothesized innate constraints.

Siegler and Jenkins noticed that some children seemed consciously aware that they had invented a new strategy in that they could explain it on the first trial where they used it, and some even recognized that it was a "smart answer," in the words of one child. Other children denied using the MIN strategy even when the videotape showed that they had used it. For instance, one child said, "I never counted ... I knew it ... I just blobbed around." Siegler and Jenkins divided children into those who seemed conscious of the strategy and those who did not, and measured the frequency of their subsequent usage of the MIN strategy. The high awareness group used the MIN strategy on about 60% of the trials where they used any counting strategy. The low awareness group used the MIN strategy on less than 10% of the trials. This suggests that being aware of a newly discovered strategy facilitates its subsequent use.

This finding cannot be modeled by GIPS because GIPS has no way to distinguish a strategy that can be explained from one that is inaccessible to consciousness. However, the finding could probably be modeled by combining GIPS with a system that uses an analytical learning algorithm. The basic idea is simple. GIPS would discover a new strategy just as it does now, and a trace of the strategy's actions would remain in memory. This trace would be used as an example that is explained by the analytical system. (Siegler and Jenkins asked subjects after each problem to explain how they got their answer—a sort of mandatory reflection.) If enough of the trace can be recalled for the explanation to succeed, it annotates the steps in the trace and perhaps the operators whose executions produced the steps. These elaborations make it easier to retrieve the modified operators from memory, and they may help in assigning credit and blame, thus speeding the adjustment of the preconditions, selection, and execution concepts. These influences increase the usage of the new strategy on subsequent problems.

The GIPS analysis solves a number of puzzles raised by Siegler and Jenkins' study. These include the source of the various strategies that appear in the SUM-to-MIN transition and their order of appearance, as well as the ability to make significant strategy shifts without impasse-driven learning. GIPS also suggests a role for innate knowledge of the principles of addition in the ability to avoid inventing bad strategies, although this depends on the specific type of feedback given to the system. Thus, GIPS provides a plausible, computationally sufficient account of the discovery of the MIN strategy. However, Siegler and Jenkins produced a second set of findings on the gradual increase in usage of the newly discovered strategy. We have not yet tried to model these findings, but GIPS seems to provide an appropriate framework for doing so.

Finally, the Sum-to-Min transition does not appear to be explainable by conventional, symbol-level learning mechanisms. Rather, some of the important shifts require changes to the representation of the domain. Gips models these changes by altering preconditions on some of its operators. Adjusting operator preconditions is somewhat dangerous, because it can allow the system to corrupt a previously correct domain theory, but Gips demonstrates that such a mechanism can generate useful behavior shifts when controlled by feedback on its decisions.

Acknowledgments

This research benefited from discussions with Jeff Schlimmer and Bob Siegler. Comments from Clare Bates Congdon and the reviewers improved the technical quality of the paper. The research was supported in part by contract N00014-88-K-0080 from the Office of Naval Research, Cognitive Sciences Division, and a postdoctoral training grant from the Department of Health and Human Services.

References

Ashcraft, M. H. (1982). The development of mental arithmetic: A chronometric approach. *Developmental Review, 2*, 213–236.

Ashcraft, M. H. (1987). Children's knowledge of simple arithmetic: A developmental model and simulation. In C. J. Brainerd, R. Kail, and J. Bisanz (Eds.), *Formal methods in developmental psychology*. New York: Springer-Verlag.

Berwick, R. (1985). *The acquisition of syntactic knowledge*. Cambridge, MA: MIT Press.

Dietterich, T. G. (1986). Learning at the knowledge level. *Machine Learning, 1*, 287–316.

Fikes, R. E., and Nilsson, N. J. (1971). STRIPS: A new approach to the application of theorem proving to problem solving. *Artificial Intelligence, 2*, 189–208.

Gelman, R., and Gallistel, C. R. (1978). *The child's understanding of number*. Cambridge, MA: Harvard University Press.

Groen, G. J., and Parkman, J. M. (1972). A chronometric analysis of simple addition. *Psychological Review, 79*, 329–343.

Groen, G. J., and Resnick, L. B. (1977). Can preschool children invent addition algorithms? *Journal of Educational Psychology, 69*, 645–652.

Holland, J. H., Holyoak, K. J., Nisbett, R. E., and Thagard, P. R. (1986). *Induction: Processes of inference, learning, and discovery*. Cambridge, MA: MIT Press.

Jones, R. M. (1993). Problem solving via analogical retrieval and analogical search control. In A. L. Meyrowitz and S. Chipman (Eds.), *Foundations of knowledge acquisition: Machine learning*. Boston: Kluwer Academic.

Kaye, D. B., Post, T. A., Hall, V. C., and Dineen, J. T. (1986). The emergence of information retrieval strategies in numerical cognition: A development study. *Cognition and Instruction, 3*, 137–166.

Langley, P. (1985). Learning to search: From weak methods to domain-specific heuristics. *Cognitive Science, 9*, 217–260.

Langley, P., and Allen, J. A. (1991). The acquisition of human planning expertise. In L. A. Birnbaum and G. C. Collins (Eds.), *Machine Learning: Proceedings of the Eighth International Workshop* (pp. 80–84). Los Altos, CA: Morgan Kaufmann.

Minton, S. (1988). *Learning effective search control knowledge: An explanation-based approach*. Boston: Kluwer Academic.

Mitchell, T. M., Utgoff, P. E., and Banerji, R. (1983). Learning by experimentation: Acquiring and refining problem-solving heuristics. In R. S. Michalski, J. G. Carbonell, and T. M. Mitchell (Eds.), *Machine learning: An artificial intelligence approach*. Los Altos, CA: Morgan Kaufmann.

Newell, A. (1990). *Unified theories of cognition: The William James lectures*. Cambridge, MA: Harvard University Press.

Pazzani, M., Dyer, M., and Flowers, M. (1986). The role of prior causal theories in generalization. *Proceedings of the Fifth National Conference on Artificial Intelligence* (pp. 545–550). Los Altos, CA: Morgan Kaufmann.

Schank, R. (1986). *Explanation patterns: Understanding mechanically and creatively*. Hillsdale, NJ: Lawrence Erlbaum.

Schlimmer, J. C. (1987). Incremental adjustment of representations for learning. *Proceedings of the Fourth International Workshop on Machine Learning* (pp. 79–90). Los Altos, CA: Morgan Kaufmann.

Schlimmer, J. C., and Granger, R. H., Jr. (1986a). Beyond incremental processing: Tracking concept drift. *Proceedings of the Fifth National Conference on Artificial Intelligence* (pp. 502–507). Los Altos, CA: Morgan Kaufmann.

Schlimmer, J. C., and Granger, R. H., Jr. (1986b). Incremental learning from noisy data. *Machine Learning, 1*, 317–354.

Siegler, R. S., and Jenkins, E. (1989). *How children discover new strategies*. Hillsdale, NJ: Lawrence Erlbaum.

Svenson, O. (1975). Analysis of time required by children for simple additions. *Acta Psychologica, 39*, 289–302.

VanLehn, K. (1990). *Mind bugs: The origins of procedural misconceptions*. Cambridge, MA: MIT Press.

VanLehn, K. (1991). Rule acquisition events in the discovery of problem solving strategies. *Cognitive Science, 15*, 1–47.

VanLehn, K., and Jones, R. M. (1993). Integration of explanation-based learning of correctness and analogical search control. In S. Minton and P. Langley (Eds.), *Planning, scheduling and learning*. Los Altos, CA: Morgan Kaufmann.

VanLehn, K., Jones, R. M., and Chi, M. T. H. (1992). A model of the self-explanation effect. *Journal of the Learning Sciences, 2(1)*, 1–60.

Language Learning

Chapter 21

Learning from a Connectionist Model of the Acquisition of the English Past Tense

Kim Plunkett and Virginia A. Marchman

1 Introduction

In a recent journal article Marcus (1995) criticizes Plunkett and Marchman's (Plunkett and Marchman, 1993, henceforth PM) connectionist account of the acquisition of verb morphology for employing "misleading graphing practices" (p. 273), "including arbitrary, unexplained changes in how graphs were plotted" (p. 277) that exaggerate "the apparent very close similarity between the learning of the past tense by Adam and the ... model." Furthermore, Marcus suggests that the onset of overregularization errors in the model is "triggered ... by an externally imposed discontinuity" (p. 276). He argues that "children show a U-shaped sequence of development which does not depend on abrupt changes in input" (p. 278) and points out that "U-shaped development in the simulation occurs only after an abrupt change in training regimen." Finally, Marcus argues that the pattern of errors in the model do not conform to the pattern observed in young children: "Children overregularize vowel-change verbs more than no-change verbs; the simulation overregularizes vowel change verbs less often than no-change verbs" (p. 278) and "children, including Adam, overregularize more than they irregularize; the simulation overregularized less than it irregularized."

In this response, we briefly review the goals of the original model and reject Marcus' criticisms of our original comparisons between the model's profile of development and that observed in young children. We will demonstrate, following Plunkett and Marchman (1990), Plunkett and Marchman (1991), Plunkett and Marchman (1993), that externally imposed discontinuities in the training regime constitute neither necessary nor sufficient conditions for the onset of overregularizations in connectionist models of English past tense acquisition. Yet, this in no way undermines the claim made in PM and elsewhere that small vocabulary size allows young children to correctly produce both regular and irregular past tense forms, and that non-linearities in vocabulary growth are a contributing factor to the subsequent onset of overregularizations (Marchman and Bates, 1994). We also reject the claim that the errors produced by the PM model are substantively different from those of real children.

2 The Scope of the Model

The primary goal of the PM model was "to determine whether gradual *quantitative* and *structural* changes in the verb vocabulary can lead to *qualitative* shifts in the manner in which a network organizes the mapping relationship between verbs stems and their past tense forms" (p. 28). Following Rumelhart and McClelland (1986), Plunkett and Marchman (1991) and MacWhinney and Leinbach (1991), PM explored the extent to which the profile of mastery and pattern of children's past tense errors could be explained in terms of an hypothesized underlying process that systematizes relationships between phonological representations of verb stems and past tense forms. One key component was an incremental program of vocabulary growth in which new verbs are added to the training regimen at varying rates. Initially, the network was trained on a small vocabulary (10 regular and 10 irregular verbs), subsequently incremented by one verb every 5 training epochs. When 100 verbs had been introduced, the rate of the addition of new verbs was increased to one verb every training epoch. Token frequency depended on when the verbs were introduced to the training set. Thus, the incremental character of the training environment, a small initial vocabulary size, several verb types, variable token frequencies, assumptions about the phonological definitions of stem and past tense forms, and the learning architecture, constituted PM's identification of the factors that determine the profile of development and pattern of errors produced by children learning the English past tense.

Of course, several additional simplifying assumptions fell outside the overall goals of the model. The training vocabulary was an artificial language limited to triphonemic strings that conformed to the phonotactics of English. Second, the PM network cannot produce alternative forms for homophonic stems (Pinker and Prince, 1988) which are presumably differentiated by access to some representation of the verb's meaning—though see Cottrell and Plunkett (1994). Finally, PM utilizes phonological representations that do not interact with other components of the linguistic system. Insofar as these factors impinge upon the child's acquisition—and we don't pretend to have supplied an exhaustive listing—PM is bound to fall short of capturing all aspects of past tense acquisition. Nevertheless, this observation does not undermine PM's potential to contribute to our understanding of the extent to which children's performance can be explained with respect to a specific, tightly-constrained set of initial assumptions. We remain convinced that these assumptions were reasonable and valid, the model offered important insights into the factors determining language acquisition, and the field gained substantive and testable hypotheses for empirical studies in children.

3 Developmental Sequence

Much of the substance of the Marcus (1995) critique centres on PM's comparisons of the profile of overregularizations produced by the PM model and those produced by Adam (derived from data in Marcus et al., 1992). One major comparison involved Adam's rate of overregularization in tokens versus the model's rate as measured in types as a function of size of vocabulary. In Marcus (1995), Adam's overregularization rate is replotted as *types* against vocabulary size as measured in types. Not surprisingly, the rate at which Adam is estimated to overregularize increases. Marcus argues that the similarity between Adam and the model is reduced, and more substantively, that the claims of general similarity between PM and children are not justified. It may at first appear that types-versus-types is the appropriate basis for comparing model and child. However, apart from the fact that type overregularization rates were not available in the original monograph, further reflection confirms that our original strategy is the most appropriate given an understanding of the computational mechanisms underlying learning in these models.

Since Marcus does not provide a clear explanation of his procedure, we must assume type overregularization rate is determined by observing whether *any* overregularization errors occurred on an irregular verb, summing the number of verb types on which an error occurred and dividing by the total number of irregular past tense types produced on each session. For example, if the child produced 10 tokens each of two verb types and made 8 overregularization errors on one verb and 1 overregularization on the other, then type overregularization rate would be 100% (versus 45% measured in tokens). Since children can oscillate in their accuracy of production, type-based rates tend to inflate error profiles compared to calculations of tokens.

In contrast, the PM model will give a constant response to a given verb stem at a particular point in training. In connectionist models of this type, the weights are fixed during testing and activations are calculated in a non-probabilistic, deterministic fashion. The network cannot vary its response to different tokens of the same verb and will produce the same answer given all presentations of a single verb token. Of course, the model *could* have been given the opportunity to respond in a probabilistic fashion to different verb tokens. Yet, PM made no claims as to the source of this variability in children, and so we adopted the measure which was most appropriate given the context of the modelling endeavour. We chose to compare network performance with child performance at a more general level, refraining from drawing direct comparisons of absolute levels of overregularizations when they were clearly inappropriate—see PM (pp. 45–46).

Marcus goes on to note that "Adam continues overregularizing at vocabulary sizes of nearly 400" when "the PM model has long since stopped altogether" (p. 273). This difference is not reflective of key components of the model's behaviour, but is a consequence of simplifying assumptions regarding the training regime and vocabulary structure. Specifically, while Adam appears to be acquiring new irregular verbs throughout the period of development studied (see Figures 21 and 27 in Marcus et al., 1992, pp. 86 and 92), the PM model, in contrast, is introduced to its last irregular verb when vocabulary size reaches 269 (see PM, Table 2, p. 34). It is no surprise that errors stop shortly after the last irregular verb is introduced. Once the network has learned to accommodate these final irregulars, the predominant response characteristic is to add a suffix to all new remaining regular forms (see PM, Figure 4a, p. 48). Addition of further irregular verbs would have resulted in further overregularizations. Note also that the proportion of irregular verb types at the end of training is 8.4% for PM versus 25% for Adam (estimated from Marcus et al., 1992, Figure 27, p. 92). Adam has considerably more opportunities for error than the network.

Marcus criticizes PM for "truncating the x-axis range to only 320 verbs" (p. 273), prior to when Adam reaches the model's final vocabulary size of 500. However, it is at this point when Adam's overregularization rate also reduces temporarily to zero[1] (see Marcus et al., 1992, Figure 33, p. 108). Thus, PM truncated the comparison at the point at which overregularization errors are not observed in either the model or Adam.

The kind of detailed comparison of the profile of errors in the model and Adam suggested by Marcus (1995) is unwarranted and potentially misleading. Clearly, the training data used in the model are not the same as those available to Adam. The graphing practices and analyses performed in the original PM model reflect justifiable assumptions about the nature of the task the network is required to perform and conditions for comparison with children. Within the context of the goals established by PM, the mode of comparison offers a conservative and, we would argue, more appropriate assessment of the model's *general* capacity to capture the developmental sequence of overregularization errors observed in young children. The discrepancies that Marcus (1995) points out have no bearing on these issues.

4 Input

In PM, we plotted the simulation's overregularization rate *in types* and proportion of input vocabulary that is regular *in tokens* against vocabulary size (Figure 6, p. 61), with the goal of evaluating the role that vocabulary composition plays in the onset of overregularization errors. In the same figure, we also replotted the most comparable available data in Marcus et al. (1992), that is, Figure 28 which plots Adam's overregularization rate *in tokens* and proportion of input vocabulary that is regular *in types* against age. PM draws the following conclusion: "In general, then, the data for Adam as well as the simulations reported here do not demonstrate a relationship between changes in vocabulary composition and overgeneralization rate *after vocabulary size has achieved a particular level"* (original italics, p. 61).

Marcus (1995) again critiques this comparison, and replots Adam's over-regularization rate *in types* and proportion of input vocabulary that is regular *in tokens* against vocabulary size. Based on this re-analysis, Marcus (1995) shows that the proportion of parental input to Adam that is regular measured in tokens is considerably less than when this proportion is measured in types. This is to be expected since irregular verbs tend to have a high token frequency. The resulting low proportions of regular verbs in the parental input to Adam (<36%) appears to undermine PM's claim that "generalization is virtually absent when regulars contribute less than 50% of the items overall" (p. 55).

It is useful here to recall the theoretical assumptions of the model; namely, that children's overregularization errors can be explained in terms of their attempt to systematize the relationship between phonological representations of verbs stems *known to them* and phonological representations of the past tense forms *known to them*. Plunkett and Marchman (1991) argued for the importance of distinguishing between the *input* to the child and the *uptake* by the child. We assume that children do not learn simultaneously all the verbs they hear in the input, just those that are salient to them. Of course, a verb's saliency may change over developmental time, although we suppose that token frequency plays an important role throughout learning. Connectionist models use a filtered version of the verb's raw token frequency to guarantee that low frequency verbs will be processed by the network in finite time. In essence, the modeller specifies both the "uptake" and the "input" environment in the assessment of the degree to which absolute token frequencies influence the saliency of the training item. As a result, the incidence of low frequency forms in the "uptake" environment are inflated relative to the hypothesized "input" environment. In plotting Adam's parental input in token frequencies, Marcus fails to take account of the distinction between input and uptake that is crucial for assessing the impact of frequency in studies of children.

Even though the proportion of regulars in the input to Adam (measured in tokens) never exceeds 36%, throughout the period of development reported in Marcus et al. (1992), the number of different irregular verbs (i.e., types) that *Adam knows* is substantially less than the number of regular verbs that he knows (see Figure 27 in Marcus et al., 1992). These are precisely the conditions that PM predicts for generalization in the network and the eventual onset of overregularization errors: "Once the proportion of regular verbs exceeds 50%, the absolute number of regulars in the *training set* are allowed to act in consortium to produce generalization effects" (p. 55, italics added). Here, *training set* refers to the uptake training environment.

PM concluded, "We can identify two periods in the training of the network which are consistent with the hypothesis that vocabulary size plays a substantive role in the learning of inflectional verb morphology in young children. An early period of training results in a rapid transition in generalization characteristics ... no overregularization errors are observed ... In the second period (signalled by a flattening off in the rate of increase in proportion of regular verbs in the vocabulary), the generalization tendency is consolidated and the first overregularization errors are observed" (p. 63). The period of development reported by Marcus et al. (1992) and Marcus (1995) for Adam corresponds to this second period of development.

A stronger test of the PM model would be to show that overregularization errors can occur in children with small verb vocabularies where irregular verbs outnumber the regulars. Yet, Marcus et al. (1992) has already led us to reject this possibility by demonstrating the robustness of the developmental phenomenon that children pass through an initial period of error-free performance; that is, overregularizations do not occur when vocabularies are small. This pattern is also consistent with the non-linear relationship between vocabulary size and overgeneralizations observed in more than one thousand children using parental report (Marchman and Bates, 1994).

5 U-shaped Development

Marcus (1995) astutely notices that the onset of overregularizations in the PM network coincides with an increase in the rate of expansion of verb vocabulary after 100 verbs. If the implication of this observation is that this discontinuity is likely to be a *contributing* factor to the timing of the onset of overregularization errors, then we would agree. However, it is clear that Marcus would like us to believe that this "externally imposed" discontinuity is the primary cause of the onset of overregularization errors in these models. We disagree completely.

We should first remind readers that Plunkett and Marchman (1991) demonstrated that overregularization errors and U-shaped learning can be observed *in the absence of any discontinuities in vocabulary configuration*, that is, when vocabulary size is *held constant*. It is odd that Marcus would propose that discontinuity must play a strong causal role in the PM model. It is further puzzling that Marcus (1995), in his footnote 2, cites Kruschke's (Kruschke, 1990) erroneous claim that "Plunkett and Marchman (1991) does *not* exhibit U-shaped learning" (p. 61). While it is correct to claim that network performance monotonically improved *on average* throughout training, this improvement was achieved at the price of temporary local decrements in performance on specific verbs; that is, *micro U-shaped* learning. The claim that Plunkett and Marchman (1991) did not exhibit U-shaped learning is correct only if children's U-shaped behaviour results from *macro*, system-wide decrements in performance. Given that Plunkett and Marchman (1991) clearly predicted a micro U-shaped pattern and Marcus et al. (1992) confirmed this prediction, it is curious that Marcus (1995) reintroduces this misinterpretation.

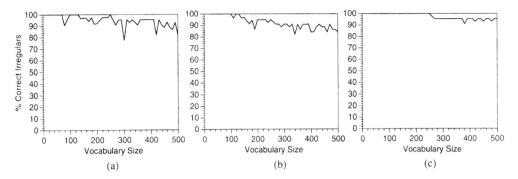

Figure 21.1
"1 – overregularization rate" (measured typewise) of verb past tense forms in three simulations where the epoch expansion schedule is held constant at one new verb every 5 epochs throughout training.

Of course, one goal of the PM model was to evaluate the impact of vocabulary *growth* on past tense acquisition. Plunkett and Marchman (1990) had already concluded that expansion rate discontinuities can impact the type and timing of overgeneralizations. However, we also concluded that this factor was neither a *necessary* nor a *sufficient* condition for the onset of errors. To drive the point home, we present data from 10 new simulations (identical to the PM model except for their random seeds) in which expansion rate discontinuities are either eliminated ($N = 5$) or shifted forward (i.e., introduced earlier in training, $N = 5$).

Fig. 21.1 plots the results (1 minus overregularization rate) for simulations in which verbs are added to the training set at a *constant* rate across training. Three (of five) individual simulations are presented here. Note that the point of onset of overgeneralizations varies considerably: Fig. 21.1(a) at vocabulary size of 80; Fig. 21.1(b) at 110 (the same point as PM); Fig. 21.1(c) at 260 verbs. Clearly, a discontinuity in expansion rate is not a *necessary* condition for the onset of overregularization errors ($M = 176$ across all five simulations).

Fig. 21.2 plots the results for three (of five) simulations in which the epoch expansion discontinuity is introduced early in training after 50 verbs (vs. 100 verbs). In Fig. 21.2(a) and (b), the onset of overregularizations occurs after 80 verbs; while in Fig. 21.2(c), the first error does not occur until 250! (overall $M = 152$). A comparison of the no-discontinuity versus the early-discontinuity results (paired on initial random seed) revealed no significant difference in point of error onset ($t(8) = -0.42$, $p = 0.68$), although it is likely that early discontinuities would consistently produce earlier errors in a larger sample of simulations. However, the onset of overregularization errors is *rarely coincidental* with the epoch increment discontinuity. Thus, as Plunkett and Marchman (1990) predicted and PM demonstrated (pp. 51–55), these data indicate that an epoch increment discontinuity is not a *sufficient* trigger for the onset of

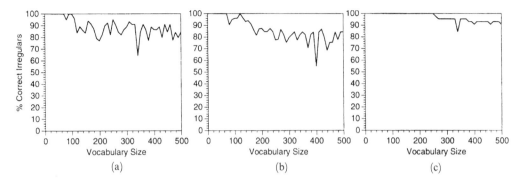

Figure 21.2
"1 – overregularization rate" (measured typewise) of verb past tense forms in three simulations where the epoch expansion schedule is switched from one new verb every 5 epochs to one new verb every epoch after vocabulary size reaches 50.

overregularization errors. Rather, the number of regular verbs needs to exceed a critical level before overregularizations occur (i.e., reaches a "critical mass").

It has been demonstrated repeatedly that discontinuities in the training environment to which connectionist networks are exposed do impact upon the profile of mastery and pattern of errors observed. It has also been demonstrated repeatedly that the presence of such discontinuities are neither a necessary nor a sufficient condition for errors to occur. These results predict that we should expect to find overregularization errors by children who exhibit non-linearities in the growth of their verb vocabularies as well as by children who do not exhibit such non-linearities. In PM, we chose to report on a simulation that underwent a particular schedule of vocabulary growth incorporating "non-linearities in rate of vocabulary growth that are sometimes observed in longitudinal studies of young children (Dromi, 1987)" (PM, pp. 33–34). This assumption of non-linear growth can be further justified by noting that data from the MacArthur Communicative Development Inventory (CDI: Toddler) (Fenson et al., 1993) suggest that the number of verbs in children's reported production vocabularies increases at a slow pace early in vocabulary growth, yet increases dramatically after vocabulary size exceeds about 100 items $(F(1,5) = 258.4, p < .001)$. Thus, while not the primary determinant of error onset in these networks, an acceleration in rate of vocabulary growth in children is nevertheless a compelling feature of acquisition that we chose to incorporate into our model.

6 Types of Errors

Evaluating errors on the 10 simulations reported above, we can confirm Marcus' observation that no-change verbs (M typewise = 8.1%) are more susceptible to overregularization than vowel change verbs (M typewise $= 5.8\%$) ($t(9) = 2.4$, $p < 0.04$). This can be traced to two factors. First, in PM's artificial language, no-change verbs all ended in an alveolar consonant, whereas vowel change verbs shared both a vowel and consonant with the other members of their family resemblance clusters. Thus, more phonological cues to class membership were available for vowel change verbs, an important determinant of accuracy of performance (Plunkett and Marchman, 1991). Interestingly, Bybee (1995) has recently pointed out that in English, "the set of verbs that undergo no change in the past tense ... all end in /t/ or /d/ and have lax vowels (with the exception of *beat* ...")" (p. 431). If this constraint were incorporated into PM, errors on no-change forms would be reduced.

Second, no-change overregularizations in children may be rare due to their phonological similarity to fully inflected regular forms (i.e., they already end in an alveolar consonant). That is, the language processor might be fooled into believing that a suffix has already been applied (Bybee and Slobin, 1982). This explanation is not appropriate to the PM model given that it does not code temporal information and that phonological information is not available in its 2-bit suffix representation. It is noteworthy that connectionist models that attempt to capture the full phonological coherence of no-change verbs and the phonological similarity of their endings to suffixed forms do not overregularize no-change more than vowel change verbs (MacWhinney and Leinbach, 1991; Rumelhart and McClelland, 1986).

The model reported in PM produced a total of 7 overregularization errors on vowel change verbs, only one of which was "stem + ed"; however, this does not reflect a general trend. Across the 10 new simulations, rates of "stem + ed" errors ($M = 2.4\%$) and "past + ed" errors ($M = 1.65\%$) on vowel change verbs are considerably higher than those observed in the original PM model (0.1% and 0.7%, respectively). However, we find no evidence to suggest that "past + ed" errors tend to be more prevalent overall ($t(9) = 0.982$, $p < 0.36$). On the contrary, the results suggest that further simulations would reveal a significant tendency in the opposite direction. Finally, contrary to Marcus' claim, overregularization rates ($M = 6.1\%$) were reliably higher than irregularization rates ($M = 4.3\%$) ($t(9) = 2.3$, $p < 0.05$). These data are consistent with Marcus' expectations about the rates of various types of errors.

At the same time, just as individual simulations vary considerably in the point of onset of errors, the precise patterns of errors and error types can differ across simulations. We consider this variability to be one of the strengths of this approach as it offers the opportunity to address issues associated with individual variation in language development. This variability also highlights the dangers of comparing the performance of any given simulation with the performance of specific children such as Adam. The connectionist approach predicts that the pattern of mastery of the English past tense will be highly sensitive to the specifics of each child's lexical history. Clearly, detailed comparisons between the performance of a *particular* simulation and a *particular* child, when the simulation is not designed to reflect that child's specific inventory of verbs, is likely to be misleading.

7 Concluding Remarks

What have we learned from this re-evaluation of the analyses conducted in the PM modelling endeavour? In our view, we have been reminded of the wealth of potential insights and empirically testable hypotheses that can derive from tightly constrained attempts to model significant characteristics of children's acquisition of the English past tense (see PM, pp. 58–59 for further discussion). However, it is also clear that those insights must be filtered by an understanding of the computational mechanisms underlying these types of models, as well as the simplifying assumptions that are built in by the modellers. Of course, a number of major issues remain to be addressed. All in all, however, we continue to be surprised just how much can be explained by appealing to such a small part of the complex apparatus that must be involved in children's acquisition of the English past tense.

Acknowledgments

Thanks to Patrick Juola and Donna Thal for comments on an earlier draft of the manuscript. The research was supported by grants to Kim Plunkett from the Economic and Social Sciences Research Council, UK and to Virginia Marchman from the National Institutes of Health–National Institute on Deafness and Other Communicative Disorders (5 R29 DC 02292).

Note

1. PM's Figure 3a (p. 46) incorrectly truncates the data for Adam at 4;7, missing the 4 remaining data points to 4;11 which show overregularization rates receding to zero. PM's Figure 6a plots all the data points for Adam up to 4;11. Although this omission may have caused some confusion, we fail to see that it has any bearing on the *arguments* presented in the original article.

References

Bybee, J. (1995). Regular morphology and the lexicon. *Language and Cognitive Processes, 10*(5), 425–455.

Bybee, J., & Slobin, D. I. (1982). Rules and schemas in the development and use of the English past tense. *Language, 58*, 265–289.

Cottrell, G. W., & Plunkett, K. (1994). Acquiring the mapping from meanings to sounds. *Connection Science, 6*(4), 379–412.

Dromi, E. (1987). *Early lexical development.* New York: Cambridge University Press.

Fenson, L., Dale, P., Reznick, S., Thal, D., Bates, E., Hartung, J., Pethick, S., & Reilly, J. (1993). *The MacArthur Communicative Development Inventories: User's guide and technical manual.* San Diego: Singular Publishing Group.

Kruschke, J. K. (1990). *ALCOVE: A connectionist model of category learning (Research Report 19).* Bloomington: Cognitive Science Program, Indiana University.

MacWhinney, B., & Leinbach, J. (1991). Implementations are not conceptualizations: Revising the verb learning model. *Cognition, 40,* 121–157.

Marchman, V., & Bates, E. (1994). Continuity in lexical and morphological development: A test of the critical mass hypothesis. *Journal of Child Language, 21*(2), 339–366.

Marcus, G. F. (1995). The acquisition of the English past tense in children and multilayered connectionist networks. *Cognition, 56,* 271–279.

Marcus, G. F., Ullman, M., Pinker, S., Hollander, M., Rosen, T. L., & Xu, F. (1992). Overregularization in language acquisition. *Monographs of the Society for Research in Child Development, 57,* Serial No. 228.

Pinker, S., & Prince, A. (1988). On language and connectionism: Analysis of a parallel distributed processing model of language acquisition. *Cognition, 28,* 73–193.

Plunkett, K., & Marchman, V. (1990). *From rote learning to system building* (Technical Report #9020). San Diego: University of California, Center for Research in Language.

Plunkett, K., & Marchman, V. (1991). U-Shaped learning and frequency effects in a multilayered perceptron: Implications for child language acquisition. *Cognition, 38,* 43–102.

Plunkett, K., & Marchman, V. (1993). From rote learning to system building: acquiring verb morphology in children and connectionist nets. *Cognition, 48,* 21–69.

Rumelhart, D. E., & McClelland, J. L. (1986). On learning the past tense of English verbs. In J. L. McClelland & D. E. Rumelhart (Eds.), *Parallel distributed processing: Explorations in the microstructure of cognition.* Cambridge, MA: MIT Press.

Learning Words

Chapter 22

Acquiring the Mapping from Meaning to Sounds

Garrison W. Cottrell and Kim Plunkett

1 Introduction

Most prior models of the acquisition of morphophonology in connectionist nets (MacWhinney & Leinbach, 1991; Plunkett & Marchman, 1991, 1993; Rumelhart & McClelland, 1986) have focused on the problem of learning the relationships between phonological representations of various paradigms of verbs. That is, they take the problem to be one of learning an *intra-level* mapping between phonological forms. Second, earlier models have used feedforward neural networks to model what is inherently a *temporal* process, that is, the generation of a phonological form. Our view is that the process of generation of phonological forms is inherently an *inter-level* process, one that involves a mapping from meanings to sounds. We assume that the generation process is a temporal process that proceeds in left-to-right fashion from the beginning to the end of the word. In this paper, we explore a particular model of this process, a connectionist network that generates one phoneme at a time from a fixed representation of the meaning of the word.

Our model is based on the work of Jordan (1986) and Elman (1990) (see Figure 22.1). We use a hidden-recurrent network to generate phonemes (represented as distinctive features) one at a time from a static input pattern (Jordan termed this the 'plan vector'). Jordan investigated, for simple cases, the types of plan vectors that made learning sequences easy. In our case, we use input vectors that make learning hard, because we view the mapping being learned as one from meanings to motor programs. Thus, the input vectors have a similarity structure that is unrelated to the output sequences. We use a second layer between this input and the recurrent hidden layer so that the network may learn the appropriate plan vector for the sequence. The problem we set for the network is to generate the appropriate sequence of phonemic forms corresponding to the different morphological paradigms for a verb.

We are not the first to attempt a model of this type (Gasser & Lee, 1990; Hare, 1990; Hare *et al.*, 1989; Jordan, 1986; Plaut & Shallice, 1993), however, we believe this is the first attempt to explore in a systematic fashion the effects of semantics on acquisition of surface forms. For example, Hare *et al.* (1989) used a network which used localist (one unit on) meaning vectors. Since localist

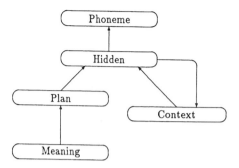

Figure 22.1
General network architecture. A meaning vector corresponding to the semantics of the present or past tense of the verb is held constant at the input layer while a sequence of phonemes is produced at the output layer. The context units permit the meaning vector to act as a plan for controlling the production of a sequence of phonemes in appropriate order. Phonemes are represented as vectors of distinctive features. Meanings are represented by two components: A lexical meaning plus the present vs. past tense. The plan layer has 50 units, the hidden and context 100, and the output layer 15 units. The input layer size varies with the representation used.

representations are inherently orthogonal, no similarity structure existed between different 'meanings.' In this paper, we use a representation of semantics as distortions of prototypes that imposes a *similarity structure* on the input to the network. Also, the target vocabulary has phonological regularities, resulting in a similarity structure in the output domain. These are associated at random. Thus the network is faced with a problem similar to that facing the child: there is a similarity structure in the input (presumably extracted from perceptual representations, and corresponding to objects and relations in the world) and there is a similarity structure in the targets (corresponding to the adult language forms), and there is a completely *arbitrary* relationship between the two.

Plaut and Shallice (1993), in a connectionist model of deep dyslexia, explored a similar problem, using a similar mapping structure (see below). However, where Plaut and Shallice were concerned with the effects of damage on a trained model, we are concerned with the learning trajectory, that is, the developmental aspects of the model. The Plaut and Shallice model used a small training set, which militated against a systematic evaluation of the role of semantic similarity in network performance. In contrast, we use a much larger training set which permits this evaluation. The size of our lexicon also allows us to analyze the effects of surface form similarity in a more systematic way. Finally, Plaut and Shallice did not explore inflectional variation in their model.

We use a familiar domain to instantiate the model; the acquisition of the past tense in English. Thus the model will take as input a vector representation of

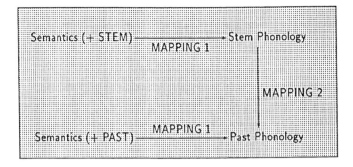

Figure 22.2
Two notions of "mapping." MAPPING 2 represents intra-level mappings between phonological representations of the stem and past tense forms of the verb. MAPPING 1 represents the inter-level mapping between the semantic representation of the verb and its various phonological forms. Under MAPPING 1 the relationship between the various phonological forms of the verb are expressed by the network in an indirect fashion.

the semantics of the verb, and produce as output the phonological representation. We assume this latter representation is a sequence of targets for a motor program.[1] In order for the model to produce different forms for the same verb, we include in our notion of semantics of the lexical item underlying semantic markers that distinguish surface phonological forms of present and past tense. This gives rise to a very different notion of the mapping from stems to past than the one that has been used previously (see Figure 22.2). The network of Rumelhart and McClelland (1986), for example, implemented an intra-level mapping between representations of the stem and past forms, corresponding to MAPPING 2 in Figure 22.2. Since we are implementing an inter-level mapping from meaning to form, corresponding to MAPPING 1 in Figure 22.2, MAPPING 2, which has been implemented directly by Rumelhart and McClelland, is implemented *indirectly* by our network. That is, it is a relationship between different network outputs, rather than a relationship between network inputs and outputs.

In learning to perform this task, the network must exploit phonological regularities that characterize the indirect relation between stems and their past tense forms. In particular, in the regular paradigm, the choice of the ending is conditioned by the identity of the final phoneme of the stem.[2] For example, if the verb ends in a dental, the epenthesized form of the past tense (/ed/, as in *flitted*) is required. Such phonological information is exploited by children and adults when prompted for the past tense form of a novel stem (Bybee & Slobin, 1982; Marchman, 1988), and must be captured by our network in some way. However, the phonological characteristics of the verb stem do not uniquely *determine* its past tense form. Although all verbs which have identical stem and past tense forms possess a dental final consonant (e.g., *hit* → *hit*), not all verbs that end in a dental consonant have identical stem and past tense forms (e.g. *flit* → *flitted*). Furthermore, connectionist models that learn purely intra-level phonological mappings cannot distinguish verb-stem homophones that take different past tense forms (Pinker & Prince, 1988). For example, to *brake* and to *break* take past tense forms *braked* and *broke* respectively. Since the inputs to a phonological–phonological network in these cases are identical, so will their outputs remain identical. Homophones are unproblematic, however, when the acquisition of verb morphology is conceived as proceeding from semantics to phonology, as they constitute a many-to-one mapping.

However, two new potential problems arise. First, as Pinker and Prince (1988) point out, the semantics of a verb is not a good predictor of the type of inflectional mapping that it must undergo. The three verbs *hit*, *strike* and *slap* are closely related semantically but they have different mapping types relating their stem and past tense forms (*hit* → *hit*, *strike* → *struck*, *slap* → *slapped*). The network must learn to *ignore* this semantic similarity in learning the mapping. Second, this same problem arises in general for the network, insofar as there is an arbitrary relationship between the meaning of the item and its phonological form. Similar inputs do *not* lead to similar outputs. In particular, highly similar inputs, modeling synonyms, provide a potential source of error in these networks.

The problem of similar inputs is perhaps uninteresting from the point of view of a neural network researcher: after all, one simply needs hidden units to separate inputs that are similar. Our interest in this problem stems from the observation that this is essentially the problem posed to the child seeking to acquire adult forms of words: the similarity structures at the input and target level have no relation to one another (except in the case of morphological variants of the same word).[3] This particular issue has not been studied, to our knowledge, in the connectionist literature, which tends to emphasize a different set of problems, such as how to learn parity more effectively. It is the cognitive modeling perspective that has led us to consider this kind of training set. We are thus less interested in whether the network achieves 100% effectiveness on the training set as we are in the stages the network passes through during learning. The former can depend a great deal on the particular learning method, parameters, and network topology. We suppose that the latter depends less on network learning than on the characteristics of the training set itself. That is, the data usually overwhelm the priors of the model. In neural network error-correction learning, it is often found that the network will attack the dimension in the data of highest variability first. Thus the network's stages of performance are driven by the data. In this work, we explore the effects of the distribution of environmental samples on the surface forms produced by the network over the learning phase. That is, we are interested in the *developmental predictions* of our model.

Our goals in this work are:

(1) To verify that the mapping from structured meanings to phonological forms can be learned by a recurrent network.
(2) To explore the effects of input and target similarity on the acquisition of the forms.
(3) To explore the ability of the network to learn the indirect mapping between the different surface forms of the same verbs.
(4) To analyze the errors of the network, compare these to children's errors, and to make predictions about these errors in the light of the semantic representations used.

We report on two sets of simulations that differ in the nature of the semantic representations used to encode verb meanings. In the first case, we simply map from localist semantics to surface form in order to test the recurrent network's ability to learn the mapping. In the second case, we introduce a similarity structure on the input semantics that is arbitrarily related to the phonological similarity structure of the target patterns. In each case, we provide an evaluation of the performance of the network on trained verbs and of the ability of the network to generalize to verb forms on which it has not been trained. In the second set of simulations, we provide a detailed analysis of the effects of output and input similarity on the mappings acquired.

Before passing on to the simulations, however, we first review some of the empirical issues relevant to this modeling effort, and secondly, make explicit the assumptions that we believe are important (and those that are not important) in developing this model.

2 Issues

2.1 How Does Semantics Influence the Acquisition of Adult Forms?

The problem we are most interested in here is how the structure of the meanings influences the acquisition of adult forms. We should be clear here that we are not, in the current study, looking at how semantics is acquired. Rather, we assume that all of the relevant conceptual distinctions are already available to the learner (but see the discussion later on assumptions). Given this, we are then interested in how a structured representation of meaning might influence the surface forms produced.

The study that comes closest to providing data on this subject is a cross-linguistic study of the acquisition of locative expressions (Johnston & Slobin, 1979). Johnston and Slobin (1979) compared the performance of children between the ages of 2;0 and 4;8 in producing locative expressions (*in, on, under, beside, between, back* and *front*), in English, Italian, Serbo-Croatian and Turkish. While the main intent of their study was to evaluate the order in which these

Table 22.1
Number of different vocabulary items (types) used for the seven concepts *in, on, under, behind, in front, beside* and *between* in four languages. Computed from Johnston and Slobin (1979, Table 2)

Turkish	Italian	English	Serbo-Croat
8	11	16	25

locative expressions were acquired in terms of their conceptual difficulty, one incidental result is relevant here. They found that the more ways that a language has to express a particular relationship, the later children learning that language mastered the forms, relative to children learning a language with fewer means for expressing the same concept. Children were scored for expressing a locative notion if they used it more often in appropriate circumstances than inappropriate ones. One of their main findings was that "children learning Turkish or Italian produced more different locative notions than those learning English or Serbo-Croatian." Compare this with the number of ways of expressing locative notions in the four languages (see Table 22.1).

In precisely the languages that had more ways to express locative notions, the children actually learned to produce *fewer* locative expressions when matched for age level. This is not so puzzling if we consider that in order to express essentially the same notions, Serbo-Croat children had to learn an average of 3.6 words compared to the Turkish children's 1.1 words. This means there are essentially 3.6 synonyms for each concept (*in, on, under,* etc.) in Serbo-Croat. Thus, the size of the vocabulary for each concept influences the pace of development. Here we see a direct influence of conceptual similarity on semantic differentiation and linguistic form. That is, synonyms are hard to learn.

2.2 What Is the Source of Children's Production Errors?
We suggest that there are three general ways in which the current model makes predictions for children's production errors. The first concerns the basic architecture of the model and how that impinges on our predictions about error sources. A second is how error-correction learning leads to variations in production. A third is how the target vocabulary leads to predictions about syllabic structure.

One remarkable fact about children's language production is that they fail to produce some sounds that they had no difficulty producing during the babbling stage (Jespersen, 1925; Jusczk, 1992). That is, they have a rather full phonemic inventory during babbling, but when word production starts, a very different picture emerges. They start with a very small phonemic inventory, and slowly add new sounds. One possible account for this gradual accumulation of phonemes is that they may have the targets for word production in advance, perhaps even in the form of the motor program for the phonemes, but are having trouble associating the motor program with the meaning of the word. To quote Jespersen (1925) (taken from Dale, 1972):

> It is strange that among an infant's sounds one can often detect sounds—for instance k, g, h and uvular r—which the child will find difficulty in producing afterwards when they occur in real words.... The explanation lies probably in the difference between doing a thing in play or without a plan—when it's immaterial which movement (sound) is made—and doing the same thing in fixed intention when this sound, and this sound only, is required....

That is, they are 'without a plan' for the word. This account naturally fits with the architecture of our model, which learns plans for the words, and assumes targets are available in advance. More specifically, on this view, the children lack a mapping from the plan specification to the sequence of phoneme motor programs.

One source for errors, then, will be in how hard this mapping is to learn. One can expect in advance, for example, that synonyms, which are essentially a one-to-many mapping for an architecture that maps from meaning to sound, will be difficult to learn. The model suggests a quite different account of the phenomenon of *over extension* to those typically suggested in the literature (Barrett, 1978; Clark, 1973; Plunkett & Sinha, 1992). Many children have been observed describing, for example, all four-legged things as 'doggie.' This is often accounted for in terms of the semantic features associated with a given label. Under-specification of the list of semantic features associated with a label results in that label being over-applied relative to the adult definition. As more features are acquired, more distinctions are made between the labels children apply to objects.

An alternative source of this type of error consists of the errors produced while learning the mapping between semantics and motor programs. Early in learning, the different features defining the children's early semantic representations are linked to different articulatory motor plans with varying connection strengths. For example, the feature FOUR-LEGGED associated with the semantic representations of CAT and DOG may be most strongly attached to the motor plan for producing the word 'doggie.' If other features that make up the semantic representation for CAT (e.g., MEOW) are not strongly attached to a different articulatory motor plan, then FOUR-LEGGED may win the competition for the phonological form used to express the particular meaning. Over-extensions then result from the inappropriate outcome of competition between the different motor plans that are connected to any given semantic representation. Over-extension is then viewed as arising from articulatory confusions as opposed to semantic confusions. Over-extensions are eliminated as bundles of semantic features redistribute their patterns of connectivity to articulatory plans.

The second source of error is error-correction learning. In a network, error-correction learning leads to the discovery of the primary dimensions of variation in the training set before the detections of the lower-level (fine-grained) distinctions. In this sense, the learning algorithm employed in the network performs an implicit principal components analysis. Thus, we expect the network to learn first the distinction between vowels and consonants since they are quite distant in the phonological representation used for the words in our simulations. Individual phonemes will be discovered gradually by the learning algorithm. However, due to the fact that different phonemes must be mapped by the same set of weights, discovery of some phonemes will lead to renewed errors in others. Thus, we will see W-shaped learning as has been observed in recent simulation experiments (Plunkett & Marchman, 1991).

Stemberger (1990) has proposed that children's speech errors can be viewed as resulting from the operation of an error-correction system that is attempting to adapt to a perfect target. Errors result from simply trying to reproduce these targets. His model differs from ours, however, in assuming that between the semantic and pragmatic levels and the ultimate motor programming level, there are distinct lexical, syntactic, syllabic and phonemic levels. Our proposal suggests a single program level (the recurrent network) between a meaning level and the motor programming level. That is, the meaning level specifies the program for the network in generating the sequence of phonetic features which taken together make up the phonemes of the word. These are then presumably passed on to an articulatory level as specifications for programs there. Although we state our case rather strongly here, clearly, more than one level may be required for particular inflectional forms such as reduplication (Corina, 1991; Gasser, 1994).

We discuss the third source of error, the target vocabulary itself, in the next section.

2.3 The Role of Phonological Form in Molding Children's Vocabularies

In a case study of language acquisition in two Danish children between the ages of 12 and 26 months, Plunkett (1993) describes how children consistently use non-standard (idiosyncratic non-adult) forms to refer to objects and actions in the world. In some cases, these idiosyncratic forms could be related to target words in the language. Plunkett suggests that the children are having difficulty segmenting adult speech into words, and are *overshooting* and *undershooting* the word boundaries. This explains at least some of his data. Other idiosyncratic expressions were unrelated to adult targets but were nevertheless used by the children in a meaningful and consistent fashion. Plunkett found an inverse relationship between the rate of use of these non-standard forms and adult forms in the child's vocabulary. Initially, the child's vocabulary was dominated by these non-standard forms, which then decreased as more adult forms were produced. This relation is depicted for the two children in Figure 22.3.

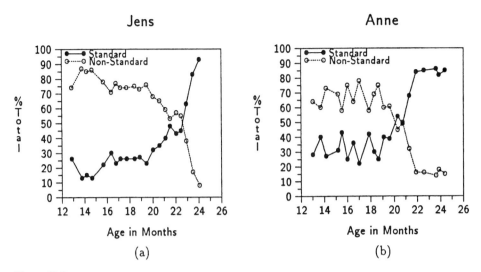

Figure 22.3
Vocabulary development in two Danish children. The number (types) of standard (adult-like) and non-standard (idiosyncratic) forms are plotted as a percentage of total vocabulary at different points in development during children's second year (Plunkett, 1993).

What influences the forms these pseudowords take? We have suggested earlier that one of the influences is semantics—similar inputs will initially lead to similar outputs. However, we also believe there are effects arising from the distribution of forms in the target language. Often error-correction learning algorithms find the average of the output first. This average will be weighted by the frequency of different forms. The network must then correct this over-shoot to produce the less frequent forms. In our simulations, there are three syllable structures taken by stems in the target language. We will see later that this leads to predictions about the order of acquisition of syllabic structures which go beyond this simple simulation.

3 Assumptions

The essential assumptions that the model incorporates are as follows:

(1) The child must associate meanings and forms.
(2) Each of the child's representation of meanings and phonological forms has its own intra-level similarity structure.
(3) The similarity structures that characterize meaning and phonology are uncorrelated. That is, similarity in meaning of two forms does not predict similarity at the phonological level of representation.
(4) The child learns this mapping in an associative network.

(5) Meaning includes features that correspond to morphological variants at the phonological level, such as tense.

We view the following assumptions as convenient and not essential to our conclusions:

(6) The child has available perfect versions of the input and target forms.
(7) The model uses back-propagation learning with a sum-squared error criterion.
(8) The model is learning an inflectional system that is analogous to the past tense system of English verbs.

The central concern of the model, therefore, is to evaluate the view that an important factor in determining the mapping from meaning to form is the influence of the similarity structures at the different levels of representation involved in the mapping. However, to avoid misunderstandings from the outset, we will discuss the last three assumptions that we have deemed inessential.

3.1 The Child Has Available Perfect Versions of the Input and Target Forms
That is, we assume the child has already divided the world up into categories and can distinguish them, and that the child has perceived the target forms correctly. Stemberger (1990) has argued that one can assume the child has perfect targets, and that most non-systematic errors can be explained in terms of a connectionist-style error-correction learning rule. Even though we make this assumption here for convenience, we would not want to assume in general that the process of perceptual and conceptual organization has advanced to this point before the child's attempts to communicate commence. For example, Plunkett (1993) has argued that segmentation of the adult input into lexical items is not perfect and is certainly a possible source of error in children's forms. In particular, he hypothesizes that different children may choose to segment the input into smaller or larger chunks, and that this is reflected in their production vocabulary. Likewise, Clark (1973) has argued that the child's semantic representations develop in concert with vocabulary growth. In this paper, we will identify another possible source of error that is in alignment with Stemberger's proposal, but we do not believe it is the only source of error.

A second potential problem that follows from this assumption is that the model has available to it, from the beginning, a past tense marker in its semantic representation. Marcus *et al.* (1992) have hypothesized that the recognition of the obligatory past tense marker plays a crucial role in over-regularization errors. While their position is controversial, we must agree that in our model the marker is available at an overly early stage. However, it will only play a role in terms of morphological variations being acquired along with stem forms. This will not affect the major issue we wish to address, namely, the issue of the effects of input and target similarity on acquisition. Again, we do not see this as an essential feature of our model, and could relax this assumption in future work. In fact, one could extend the model here to allow the inputs and targets to be learned even as the mapping is learned, and this would perhaps be more realistic. We prefer to deal with one issue at a time, however, and investigate the effects of learning the mapping without worrying for the moment about acquisition of semantics and phonology.

3.2 The Model Uses Back-propagation Learning with a Sum-squared Error Criterion

We are not wedded to back-propagation. It is simply a convenient method for training. Our choice of learning algorithm does have an effect on what is learned, however. In particular, under a rather loose set of criteria, any least squares estimator will learn the expected value of the output given the input (Duda & Hart, 1973). What this means is that initially, for very similar inputs, the network will produce averages of the target outputs. In our case, this will result in blends at the phonological level. Stemberger has observed semantic blends produced by children and adults, but for the most part, they are blends that start with segments from one word and then finish with segments from a related word, rather than blends on a phoneme-by-phoneme basis. However, there are systematic phonological errors that children make, and it is possible that some of these systematic errors have such blending as their source.

3.3 The Model Is Learning the Past Tense

This is perhaps the most simultaneously convenient and unfortunate assumption of our model: convenient because it is a familiar domain that we have worked with before, and is certainly familiar to many readers by now; unfortunate because it belies the generality of the model. This model might in theory be capable of representing the entire lexicon in the same network, although perhaps more plausibly with an appropriate mixture of experts architecture (Jacobs et al., 1991) (see Corina, 1991, and Gasser, 1994, for alternatives).

4 Methodology

All simulations utilize a simple recurrent network of the type developed by Elman (1990) (see Figure 22.1). In all simulations, the output phoneme consists of a 15-bit vector that reflects standard phonological contrasts. A noteworthy characteristic of this phonemic representation lies in its attempt to capture the sonority relationships between vowels and consonants [eliminated for space reasons. See original article for details.][4] The task of the network is to output a sequence of phonemes that correspond to the stem or past tense of the verb whose semantic representation is presented at the input. This task is a bit of a historical accident; indeed, we view the network as a model of how any morphophonological regularities may be acquired. That is, with sufficient variation in the input semantics, different noun and verb forms could presumably all be produced by the same network. Thus, this is a potential model of the morpho-phonological processes for the entire lexicon, not just one variation in verb morphology.

The distinction between stem and past tense forms is encoded by a 2-bit vector at the input level. The inventory of verbs (both stems and past tense forms) that the network is required to produce at the output is taken directly from previous simulations conducted by Plunkett and Marchman (1991), though note that a different phonological representation is used. In the current work, 504 stem/past tense pairings are used. Each stem consists of a consonant–vowel–consonant (CVC) string, a CCV string or a VCC string. Each string is phonologically well formed, even though it may not correspond to an actual English word. Verbs are assigned to one of four classes. Each class corresponds to a different type of transformation analogous to a distinct past tense form in English as in Plunkett and Marchman (1991). The first class follows the Regular rule in English. The three irregular classes are:

> (1) *Arbitrary verbs* have no systematic relationship between the stem and past tense form (*go → went*);
> (2) *Identity verbs* are unchanged between forms (*hit → hit*);
> (3) *Vowel Change verbs* undergo a change in vowel in CVC forms (*strike → struck*).

There were 2, 20 and 20 verbs in each of these classes, respectively, with frequencies of 5, 1 and 2 times that of the Regular verbs. Verbs are assigned randomly to each of the four classes, with the constraint that stems possess the appropriate characteristics of a given class.

Semantic representations of verbs are of two types. In the first set of simulations, each verb is represented in a localist manner in a 500-bit vector. An additional two units encode whether the network is to produce the stem of the verb or the appropriate past tense. In the second set of simulations, a similarity structure is imposed on the semantic representations by using distortions of several prototype vectors (Chauvin, 1988; Knapp & Anderson, 1984). Distortions may vary in their distance from the prototype. We use 50–70 prototype vectors (and thus as many categories), with an appropriate number of distortions to provide an input representation for every word. Note that each distortion corresponds to an individual word meaning, rather than as a 'noisy' example of a single word's meaning. Thus, similar inputs will have very different outputs.

The amount of distortion may vary. Thus, we can can essentially build a 'semantic network' of concepts, which corresponds to the structure of the semantic space that would be induced by a recursive clustering technique. In this paper, we explore an extremely simple semantic network structure. We do only one step of distortion of a prototype, corresponding to a very 'flat' semantic network. The amount of distortion around each prototype is held constant, but varies across prototypes to produce high, medium and low distortion clusters. The low distortion clusters we term the 'synonyms.'

Training proceeds by randomly selecting a plan vector (the verb's semantic representation) and a tense bit (stem or past tense). This composite vector is then presented at the input units over a number of time steps that correspond to the number of phonemes in the output form. All stems consist of three phonemes and thus involve three time steps. Past tense forms may involve 3, 4 or 5 phonemes. At each time step, the discrepancy between the actual output of the network and the target phoneme is used as the error signal to a back-propagation learning algorithm. We use a version of the TLEARN simulator developed by Jeff Elman at UCSD, modified to run on the Cray Y-MP. As part of the teaching signal, the verb plan is trained to produce an end-of-form signal (corresponding to the 'silence' phoneme). The 'context units' are reset to zero between forms. We used a learning rate of 0.1, and no momentum.

5 Analysis

The performance of the network is analyzed at regular intervals in training. In this paper, we present two types of analysis. First, we determine the hit rate for stems and past tense forms, both on the entire training set and on a class-by-class basis. The phoneme produced at any time step is determined by simply taking the closest legal phoneme to the output in terms of Euclidean distance. This is similar to the settling phase of an attractor network (cf. Plaut & Shallice, 1993). An output must match the target on all phonemes to be counted as a hit. In the error graphs, we report whether the output sequence is a hit or a miss. In the second set of experiments, we carry out further analysis of the outputs actually produced.

We analyze the generalization characteristics of the network by first training the network with 27 verb plans to produce only the stem form of the verb and with another 27 verb plans to produce only the past tense form of the verb. Each verb plan is then tested on the phonological form of the verb to which it has not been trained (e.g., 27 stem forms and 27 past tense forms). The output of the network on these novel inputs is used to evaluate the network's generalization properties.

Finally, in the second set of simulations, we provide a detailed analysis of the output of the network and relate the role of semantic similarity to the similarity of the phoneme sequences across different verbs, and the syllabic structure that the network extracts over the sequence of output phonemes.

6 Experiment One

This experiment tested the ability of the network to solve the problem using a 500-word vocabulary and orthogonal representations of the verb plan. We found that the network is equally fast at learning both stem and past tense forms and that learning undergoes a spurt in growth around the 20 epoch mark. In contrast, the test verbs differ with respect to their performance on stems and past tense forms. When a verb plan is trained to a past tense form, the network is quite accurate in predicting the correct stem ($\geq$90% after 70 epochs of training). On the other hand, generalization from stem to past tense never exceeds 55% over this training interval. Over several simulations starting with different random seeds, we find that performance on past to stem generalizations is always good, while stem to past varies. This result is to be expected given that the form of the past tense is a better predictor of the stem than the stem is of the past tense form (e.g., if the past tense of a verb is *talked*, then its stem form is unambiguous, but if the stem is *hit*, then in principle, its past tense form is underdetermined).

7 Experiment Two

This experiment reports the results of simulations using a 504-word vocabulary and semantically structured representations of the verb plan. This poses a much more difficult problem for the network, and a more interesting one from a psychological viewpoint. Since our main interest in this section is on the effects of input and output similarity on acquisition, we begin with an analysis of target similarity effects on the vocabulary profile, then turn to the effects of semantic structure. Finally, we analyze the performance of the network, with an emphasis on how well the indirect mapping from stem to past is learned. We thus perform four kinds of analyses on this network:

(1) We measure the changes in the stem output strings during learning from the point of view of the syllabic structure of the target language.
(2) We measure the changes in similarity of stem output strings during learning with respect to the semantic clusters.
(3) We measure the simple performance of the network in terms of hit rates and error rates.
(4) We measure the rate at which the indirect mapping from stem to past is learned irrespective of the correctness of the stem form.

7.1 Syllabic Structure Changes

The syllabic structure of the stem forms in the artificial language consist of CVC, CCV and VCC forms. In rough accord with their distribution in English, there are 368 CVCs, 63 VCCs and 46 CCVs.[5] In order to assess the vocabulary development of the network, we divide the stem output strings of the network into three classes:

(1) **Words:** strings that belong to the target vocabulary.
(2) **Pseudowords:** strings that are not in the target vocabulary but conform to the syllabic structure of the language—CVC, VCC or CCV.

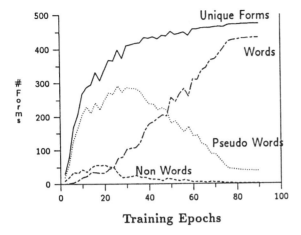

Figure 22.4
Vocabulary profiles of the network "language" (compiled from the training set stem outputs) over training. "Unique forms" is just the sum of the other three curves. See text for definitions of the classes.

(3) **Non-words:** strings that do not fit the above criteria—CCC, CVV, VCV, VVC and VVV.

A graph of the numbers of unique forms of each kind over learning, along with the total number of unique forms, is shown in Figure 22.4. Interestingly, before it has acquired many words in the language, the network has captured the syllabic structure, as evidenced by the high proportion of pseudowords in the set of unique forms. That is, there is a 'private' vocabulary burst before the burst in adult forms later. Over learning, there is an inverse relationship between these forms and the correct forms as the pseudowords migrate into the target vocabulary. This pair of curves is reminiscent of the set of curves found by Plunkett (1993). The total number of consistently produced non-(adult)-Danish forms was inversely related to the number of Danish words over the period studied. That is, the children had their own vocabulary early in development that was eventually replaced by target forms.

Note that in the simulation, the number of non-words actually *increases* just prior to the onset of the acquisition of adult forms (around 10–20 epochs). Why should this happen? Further analysis reveals a simple explanation for this effect. We assign each string of the network's stem outputs to one of the eight possible combinations of three segments of Cs and Vs regardless of whether the form is an adult form or not. Three of these classes characterize the target language's syllabic structure. A plot of the number of network outputs that belong to the three legal classes is given in Figure 22.5(a). Notice that the number in each class overshoots and undershoots the correct number several times during acquisition, but the largest swings are early in learning. In particular, no CCVs

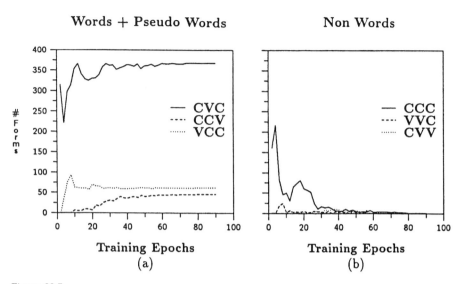

Figure 22.5
Syllabic structures of the network outputs on the training set over learning: (a) count of syllable structures that are correct for the language (irrespective of whether the outputs themselves match their targets); (b) number of incorrect forms.

are produced early on, and too few (and then too many) VCCs. That is, the network quickly starts to produce the most dominant form in the language (CVC), then must restructure to obtain the correct proportions. In order to extend to the target language syllabic structure, these strings have to mutate from CVC to CCV and VCC (and sometimes back again) during epochs 2–80. Suppose that the network only changes one segment at a time. Strings changing from CVC to CCV have to change the mid-vowel to a consonant and the coda consonant to a vowel. The possible intermediate forms are CCC and CVV. Similarly, between CVC to VCC, the possible intermediate forms are CCC and VVC. Indeed, a graph of the number of these forms produced by the network (Figure 22.5(b)) shows that they occur only during the onset of the cross-over from pseudowords to words. Also, the form that is on both paths, CCC, is the most common non-word produced.[6] The (logically possible) forms VVV and VCV never occur.

Thus, these simulations make the relatively unintuitive prediction that children may produce forms that are outside the target language yet which conform to the syllabic structure of the target language. This prediction is consistent with the finding (Plunkett, 1993) that children produce non-standard pseudowords during early language acquisition. A further prediction is that the predominant syllabic structure of these early pseudowords will concur with the dominant syllabic structure of the language. The migration of these syllabically

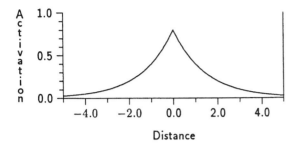

Figure 22.6
Pre-processing function for convolving distorted patterns.

legal, but nonstandard, forms to the correct target forms may result in a transitional period where illegal syllabic structures are generated. Those syllabic forms that are on more 'paths' between adult forms should be produced more often. Of course, not all illegal syllabic forms will be produced by the child, as they may be inarticulable (e.g. CCC). The current status of research on child phonology does not permit us to evaluate these predictions properly, though recent work in the area (Vihman *et al.*, 1985) tends to emphasize the constructive role of the child in the acquisition of its phonological system—a perspective consistent with current predictions.

7.2 Input Similarity Effects
The semantic structure consists of a number of semantic clusters, or groups. These are 100-element vectors formed in the following way. First, a prototype vector is formed by randomly choosing a certain number of bits to be 'on' in the prototype. Then, distortions of this prototype are generated by randomly shifting these bits in a uniform distribution with a specified range around its current position in the vector. A distortion level of 1 corresponds to selecting randomly (with probability $\frac{1}{3}$) the current position or one of the neighboring positions in the vector. Finally, the vectors are convolved with an exponentially decaying function shown in Figure 22.6, which enhances the similarity structure of the distortions within a prototype cluster. The whole three-stage process starting with the prototype pattern through the distorted pattern to the convolved distorted patterns is exemplified in Figure 22.7.

The structure of each semantic cluster is varied along two dimensions. First, the number of 1 s in the prototype is varied from 10 to 15. This is essentially varying the 'abstractness' of the categories (Plaut & Shallice, 1993). Second, the amount of distortion is varied between categories, so some categories are high distortion (level 6), medium (level 4) or small (level 1). We operationally define the level 1 distortion categories as the 'synonyms.'[7] In the following, we had 3 synonym classes, 45 medium distortion groups and 24 high distortion groups.

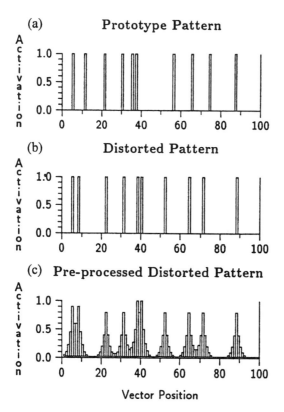

Figure 22.7
The creation of a meaning pattern: (a) a binary "prototype" vector is created; (b) the position of bits in the vector are jittered to create a distortion of the prototype; (c) the distorted pattern is convolved with the function in the previous figure to produce the final "meaning pattern." This process was based on the one used by Chauvin (1988).

This semantic structure has the advantage of avoiding the problem of defining exactly what the features represent, but has the disadvantage of being an exceptionally arbitrary and probably unrealistic structure. That is, it is unlikely that actual human categories have this structure; but for the moment, we are simply interested in what effects these variables have on our model. More realistic semantic structures, with hierarchies and non-uniform dispersion, are left for future work.

We hypothesized that the synonym groups would produce outputs that were more similar to one another than the non-synonym groups and the vocabulary as a whole. In order to test this hypothesis, we must have a quantitative measure of group similarity. If we use the absolute distance between the output vectors, this ignores the chance distribution of words (targets) to a group, which can result in more or less similar outputs. Instead, we consider the distance between output vectors *relative* to the distance between their targets:

$$\mathcal{RD}_{i,j} = \frac{dist_{i,j}^{O}}{dist_{i,j}^{T}}$$

where $dist_{i,j}$ is the sum of the distances between the corresponding phonemes of words i and j, using Euclidean distance between the vector representations, and the superscripts denote target and output. This is the distance between the output phonemes in a string *relative* to the distance they should be after learning. $\mathcal{RD}_{i,j}$ should tend to 1 as the network learns, since as the outputs approach their target values, the distances between them will approach the distances between the target values. If the network outputs the same string for words i and j, $\mathcal{RD}_{i,j}$ will be 0. If it produces the correct string for each, $\mathcal{RD}_{i,j}$ will be 1.

For each group of interest, we average this measure across all the pairs in the group, and subtract it from 1 to obtain a similarity measure:

$$\text{Similarly }(\mathcal{G}) = 1 - \frac{1}{N(N-1)} \sum_{\substack{i,j \in \mathcal{G} \\ i \neq j}} \mathcal{RD}_{i,j}$$

where i, j range over the members of $\mathcal{G}$, and $\mathcal{G}$ is of size N. If the network produces the same output for every member of $\mathcal{G}$, then Similarity $(\mathcal{G})$ will be 1. As the words' outputs approach their target values, Similarity $(\mathcal{G})$ will tend to 0.

We apply this similarity measure to the strings produced by the network for each of the 72 prototype classes. Figure 22.8(a) shows the average of this measure across the low-distortion (synonym) classes and the average across the high- and medium-distortion classes. Figure 22.8(b) shows the similarity measures $(\mathcal{G})$ when the similarity score of the *total* output of the network has been subtracted from each group score. The curves show that, in general, semantic classes produce surface forms that are more cohesive than the target forms of the network are as a whole. As it should, this effect disappears over training. This is the result of the network overcoming the false cue of input similarity.

As expected, the synonym classes have higher within-group similarity throughout training than non-synonym classes. It is noteworthy that during the period that the network begins acquiring the target vocabulary, i.e. from 20 to 40 epochs, the within-group similarity of the synonyms *increases* compared to the rest of the classes. That is, synonyms are forced to sound more alike than they did previously and more alike than the rest of the vocabulary at the beginning of acquisition. This is true on an absolute scale as well (where the relative similarity of the total vocabulary has not been subtracted off), as is shown in Figure 22.8(a). This figure also shows that even though there are many unique forms early on, as was shown in Figure 22.4, they are quite homogeneous. The explanation for the synonym effect in terms of network learn-

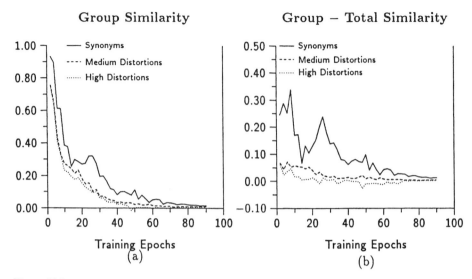

Figure 22.8

Input similarity effects: (a) Similarity ($\mathscr{S}$) plotted for the three semantic groups on the trained stem outputs (see text); (b) the same data, with the normalizing factor of Similarity (Total Vocabulary) subtracted off. This emphasizes the relative increase in "synonym" group similarity between 20 and 40 epochs.

ing is simply that patterns that are more easily learned (because they have less input similarity) are dominating the error gradient. The patterns may be characterized as *competing for representational resources* at the plan (first hidden) layer. The more similar inputs are pushed together at this layer while the network carves out representations for the more disparate meanings.

Examination of the network outputs over the training period reveals that many of the output strings for synonym classes during the second peak of similarity at 24 epochs are within 2 or 3 features of one another. An interesting question here is, what is the string the outputs of a synonym class are pushed towards? Is it a blend of all of the strings of the class, or does one string in the class 'capture' the output for that class? We tentatively find that when there is one lexical item that is more frequent than the others, it tends to capture the class. Interestingly, this is not the case if the more frequent item in a synonym class is an Arbitrary verb (*go/went*), probably due to the fact that the semantic representations of Arbitrary verbs map similar inputs to very different outputs (see Bartell *et al.* (1991) for a thorough discussion of this issue). In the case that synonym verbs are equally frequent, a blend of all of the outputs for the class is produced. This counterintuitive, and possibly simply wrong, prediction of our model in large part depends on the use of a mean-squared error criterion, which tends to produce the average of outputs for the same input. A different learning rule, such as contrastive Hebbian learning (Movellan, 1990) that learns distributions rather than expected values, could lead to a more satisfying result.

Taken in combination, these results suggest an unorthodox account of the source of the non-word forms found in Plunkett's subjects. These consistently used pseudowords are the result of two constraints or pressures on the child's language production:

(1) A pressure to produce forms that are in keeping with the syllabic structure of the language at the output level.

(2) A pressure to produce similar forms based on input similarity.

The child is thus producing the best approximation to a word in the language that is a blend of *all* of the words for that semantic class, with a tendency for this blend to be similar to the most frequent element of that class. A second counter-intuitive prediction of this work is that, during acquisition of the correct forms, the child will produce strings that may be inappropriate for the target language because they are *between* a common (over-acquired) form and a less common form.

9 Mapping Analysis

In this section, we analyze how well the network acquires the indirect mapping, described in Figure 22.2 as MAPPING 2. Although it may appear to the reader that we have already accomplished this in the previous section via a conventional 'hit-rate' analysis, we will soon see such hit-rate analyses on this kind of network can be misleading. Second, we will show that the indirect mapping can be learned independently of the ability of the network to produce the correct forms.

The approach taken here is to analyze the output of the network in terms of a hit rate for past tense forms *relative* to stem forms, irrespective of whether the *actual* stem is correct or not. This is to be contrasted with scoring the past output based on the *target* specified for the stem. For example, if the network produces /w^g/ when the stem is called for, we will score a regular hit if it produces /w^gd/ when the past is required. Since the past tense form is now evaluated relative to the network-generated stem form, we can classify the types of indirect MAPPING 2 relationships that the network has encoded.

Figure 22.9 shows a four-way classification of the network-defined indirect mapping—Regular (add a suffix), Vowel Change, Identity mapping and 'other' (essentially a garbage class). These graphs show each kind of mapping as a percentage of the total vocabulary. The proportion of Vowel Change and Identity mappings reflect the small number of such contingencies in the training set. The so-called 'other' mapping corresponds to no classifiable relation between the two forms in this case. We see that the Regular mapping constitutes a substantial proportion of the MAPPING 2 possibilities and is actually acquired much

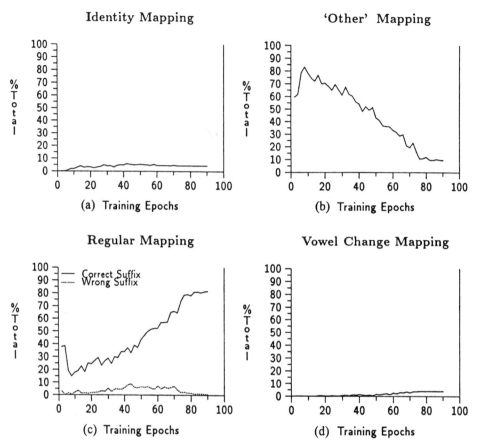

Figure 22.9

Percentage of total trained stems whose past forms is produced according to the different mapping types, measured based on the transformation of the (possibly incorrect) stem output of the network, and irrespective of the "correct" transformations for that lexical item. (a) Identity mapping; (b) "other" mapping ("other" is all transformations that could not be classified into one of the three rule-based classes); (c) Regular mapping; (d) Vowel Change mapping.

earlier than many of the vocabulary words! This again reflects the fact that the model has available a reliable morphological marker from the beginning of learning. The low fraction of incorrect suffixes suggests that the phonological constraints inherent in the Regular mapping are largely obeyed by the network.

Figure 22.10 shows the results of taking into account the correct mapping type for each lexical item, i.e. whether the MAPPING 2 relationship determined by the network is the same as that defined in the training set. Thus, for example, the Vowel Change graph shows the proportion of Vowel Change verbs in the training set that are indirectly mapped as a Vowel Change (again, irrespective of the correctness of the stem form). These graphs are thus analogous to the hit-rate graphs of the previous section. The most striking feature of these graphs is that they show a very different acquisition profile than the hit-rate graphs. Here, the Regulars are shown to have a head start, although the Identities soon overtake them. The Vowel Change mapping is much worse than expected. The reason for this is shown in the fourth graph, where we see that a large proportion of the Vowel Changes are actually treated as Identity verbs. Thus, the hit rates on the Vowel Change stems and pasts reported in the previous section are misleading because they display the hits on each form isolated from the behavior of the network on the alternate form. The current analysis reveals that the Vowel Change mapping is a very difficult one for this network. This would be expected by the low frequency of the transformation and the indirect way that the phonological conditioning must be induced.

Finally, this kind of analysis shows that, early in learning, there is more overregularization going on than could be gleaned from the other analyses. Figure 22.11 shows the percentage of each Vowel Change and Identities that are regularized.

10 Discussion

10.1 How Does Semantics Influence the Acquisition of Adult Forms?
The main variable we manipulated was similarity of meaning. The basic result from the simulations is that synonyms take longer to learn than words with highly differentiated meanings. This conforms to the results of Johnston and Slobin (1979), in that when meanings are similar, correct surface forms take longer to acquire. The explanation in terms of the model is that similar inputs tend to produce similar outputs. Thus, it takes longer to differentiate these forms at the output level. This explanation thus also makes a prediction that the forms produced by the child for synonyms will be more similar to one another than randomly chosen elements of the child's vocabulary.

We also found a 'squeeze' effect—when other words are being learned, surface forms of synonyms tend to become more similar. In their study, Johnston and Slobin (1979) evaluated children's competence with locative expressions at two time points, 4 months apart. They also found a decrement in performance

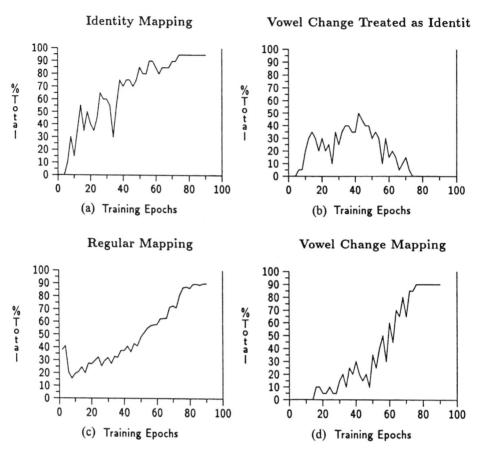

Figure 22.10
Proportion of mapping appropriate for each class. This is the same as in the previous figure, except that percentages are for each class as specified in the training set. (a) Shows the number of Identities actually treated as Identities. (b) Shows the proportion of Vowel Change verbs that were treated as Identities (no other interactions exist). The lower panels show the proportions of (c) Regulars and (d) Vowel Changes that were treated as such. Again, these proportions are calculated based on the transformation of the actual stem output, rather than the correct past.

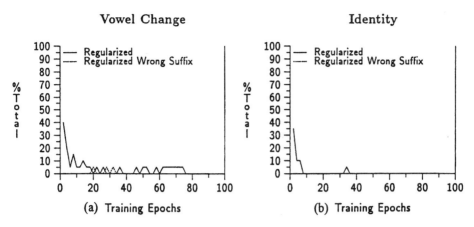

Figure 22.11
Over-regularizations in the MAPPING 2 of irregulars, when transformation of the actual stem form is used for scoring: (a) Vowel Change; (b) Identity.

at the later observation point for some children speaking a language with a highly differentiated vocabulary:

> The low Serbo-Croatian gain resulted in particular from the relatively large number of children who performed less well at Time II than at Time I (p. 536).

We speculate that this decrement in performance could be due to a squeeze effect. During error-correction learning, as the model differentiates the more disparate inputs, it does so at the cost of more similar inputs. We have characterized this as a competition for representational resources in the plan vector. In effect, synonyms become more like homonyms during the vocabulary burst. It is worth nothing that in earlier work (Cottrell & Plunkett, 1991), we found a much greater squeeze effect with a much smaller vocabulary (50 words). This may be more realistic in the case where semantics and surface forms are being learned simultaneously. Finally, in informal observation, we have noted that when these similar output forms were finally differentiated, they did so rapidly.

10.2 What Is the Source of Children's Production Errors?
The model predicts that a fundamental source of children's production errors arises from the need to connect meaning to form. Difficulties arise in assigning distinctive phonological forms to very similar underlying meanings. Thus, the model predicts that children will have difficulty in acquiring words for highly similar concepts. We have characterized this as due to a competition for representational resources. The network is learning a plan for producing this sequence

of phonemes. The network takes the easiest distinctions first, sacrificing the more difficult mappings until later. The model suggests that the most frequently practised word of a group of words with very similar meanings will be the one used for the whole group.

This is thus an alternative explanation for the source of over-extension errors to the standard account (Clark, 1973), where the errors are attributed to undifferentiated semantics. Clark hypothesizes that children will call all four-legged things 'doggie' simply because their semantic structures do not yet differentiate four-legged objects such as cows and dogs. In contrast, our model suggests that the dog mapping 'attracts' the cow mapping, since the inputs are similar. These explanations are not antithetical. As mentioned earlier, we do not take the assumption that the child has perfect versions of the input and target forms as an essential determinant of the behavior of the model. Rather, the model would respond on the basis of similarity of input representations even if the input forms were being learned at the same time as the mapping itself. Simply put, the model suggests that undifferentiated meanings may not be the only source of the error.

There will also be errors due to the architecture of the model. The obvious fact that the hardware for producing these words is shared between all words leads to the prediction that corrections to some forms will be detrimental to others. Thus, we see W-shaped learning curves on many forms. This kind of effect was predicted by Stemberger (1992) in his discussion of connectionist learning models, and has been demonstrated most effectively by Plunkett and Marchman (1991).

In the next section, we discuss a third source of errors attributable to the structure of the output domain.

10.3 How Do the Forms Themselves Mold the Child's Developing Vocabulary?

Plunkett (1993) has suggested that the idiosyncratic vocabularies of children arise because the children are having difficulties perceiving the boundaries between the words in the target language. The model presented here suggests an additional source of error. If one posits a single error-correcting system that is used for all words, then the words produced may reflect global regularities in the target domain, as our model demonstrated. Pseudowords that fit the syllabic structure of the adult vocabulary are acquired early, only later to be replaced by the correct forms as the system improves.

The kinds of forms produced reflect the frequencies of the forms in the target language. Our model showed a tendency to overshoot by overproducing the most frequent syllabic structure. The model then needed to recover from this by transforming the dominant syllabic structure into the less frequent ones. The restructuring involved producing forms that were not in the adult language, but were on trajectories between adult forms.

11 Conclusion

We have described a connectionist model of morphology acquisition in which input forms representing the meanings of words are mapped to sequences of outputs representing their phonological forms. The network is successful in producing appropriate forms, even though the input forms have a similarity structure that is independent of the similarity structure of the targets. Furthermore, the learning curves indicate a spurt-like acquisition profile. There is ample evidence for the spurt-like nature of vocabulary growth (McShane, 1979). It is unclear whether the acquisition of inflectional morphology in children shows a similar non-linear growth to that observed in the network.

We have also shown that the network is able to learn the relationship between different forms of the same verb, in spite of the fact that it is only exposed to these relations indirectly. In particular, we found that stem/past-tense pairs honored an appropriate form relationship, even when the stem's phonological form did not conform to the target signal. In effect, the model has acquired a generative capacity for inflecting verbs given that it knows one member of the paradigm. The model predicts that children are better at generalizing from past tense forms to stems than *vice versa*. Further analysis is needed to investigate what modifications must be made to the model in order to achieve better generalization in the structured input case. The results of Bartell *et al.* (1991) suggest that a layer of hidden units between the recurrent hidden layer and the output will aid generalization based on output similarity.

The analysis of the influence of input and target similarity on the acquisition of phonological form suggests some radical predictions. Children's non-adult forms may be a result of blending words from the same semantic category. Looked at another way, words are distorted by their neighbors in a semantic class. The effects of similarity at the phonological level suggest that children will initially overshoot and undershoot the correct proportion of syllabic structures for their language. During the correction phase, they will produce forms that do not belong to the syllabic structure of the language if these forms are between the most common form in the language and other forms. Finally, the model suggests that during the vocabulary burst, synonyms will be forced to be near-homonyms.

Acknowledgements

We thank Steen Ladegaard Knudsen for his assistance in programming, analysis and running of simulations, Scott Baden for his assistance in vectorizing our code for the Cray Y-MP, the Division of Engineering Block Grant for time on the Cray at the San Diego Supercomputer Center, and the members of the PDPNLP and GURU Research Groups at UCSD for helpful comments on earlier versions of this work.

Notes

1. To use these as specifications for a motor program, a forward model would need to be learned as outlined by Jordan and Rumelhart (1992).
2. See Plunkett and Marchman (1991) for details concerning the phonological conditioning of the suffix by the stem of the verb.
3. Of course, there is most likely some amelioration of this arbitrary relation as evidenced by the existence of sound symbolism. We ignore this here.
4. The phonological representation presented here was originally designed by Alan Prince and Kim Plunkett.
5. These numbers only add to 477 because 27 stems are left out of the training set for testing purposes.
6. We assume that the output of the model is actually a specification of a motor plan for that word. Presumably the articulators would prevent the production of CCCs.
7. These might better be called near-synonyms.

References

Barrett, M. D. (1978) Lexical development and overextension in child language. *Journal of Child Language, 5*, 205–219.

Bartell, B., Cottrell, G. W., & Elman, J. (1991) The role of input and target similarity in assimilation. *Proceedings of the 13th Annual Cognitive Science Society Conference*, Chicago, IL. Hillsdale, NJ: Lawrence Erlbaum Associates.

Bybee, J., & Slobin, D. I. (1982) Rules and schemas in the development and use of the English past tense. *Language, 58*, 265–289.

Chauvin, Y. (1988) *Symbol acquisition in humans and neural (PDP) networks.* PhD thesis, University of California, San Diego.

Clark, E. V. (1973) What's in a word? On the child's acquisition of semantics in his first language. In T. E. Moore (Ed.), *Cognitive development and the acquisition of language.* New York: Academic Press.

Corina, D. P. (1991) *Towards an understanding of the syllable: Evidence from linguistic, psychological, and connectionist investigations of syllable structure.* PhD thesis, University of California at San Diego, La Jolla, CA.

Cottrell, G. W., & Plunkett, K. (1991) Learning the past tense in a recurrent network: Acquiring the mapping from meanings to sounds. *Proceedings of the 13th Annual Cognitive Science Society Conference*, Chicago, IL. Hillsdale, NJ: Lawrence Erlbaum Associates.

Dale, P. S. (1972) *Language development: Structure and function.* New York: Dryden Press.

Duda, R. O., & Hart, P. E. (1973) *Pattern classification and scene analysis.* New York: Wiley.

Elman, J. L. (1990) Finding structure in time. *Cognitive Science, 14*, 179–211.

Gasser, M. (1994) Acquiring receptive morphology: A connectionist model. *Proceedings of the 32nd Annual Meeting of the Association for Computational Linguistics*, San Francisco, CA.

Gasser, M., & Lee, C. (1990) Networks that learn about phonological feature persistence. *Connection Science, 2*, 265–278.

Hare, M. (1990) The role of similarity in Hungarian vowel harmony: A connectionist account. *Connection Science, 2*, 123–150.

Hare, M., Corina, D., & Cottrell, G. W. (1989) A connectionist perspective on prosodic structure. *Proceedings of the 15th Annual meeting of the Berkeley Linguistics Society*, Berkeley, CA.

Jacobs, R., Jordan, M. I., Nowlan, S. J., & Hinton, G. E. (1991) Adaptive mixtures of local experts. *Neural Computation, 3*, 79–87.

Jespersen, O. (1925) *Language.* New York: Holt, Rinehart and Winston.

Johnston, J. R., & Slobin, D. I. (1970) The development of locative expressions in English, Italian, Serbo-Croatian and Turkish. *Journal of Child Language, 6*, 529–545.

Jordan, M. (1986) *Serial Order: A Parallel Distributed Processing Approach.* Technical Report #8604, Institute for Cognitive Science, University of California, San Diego.

Jordan, M. I., & Rumelhart, D. E. (1992) Forward models: Supervised learning with a distal teacher. *Cognitive Science, 16,* 307–354.

Jusczk, P. W. (1992) Developing phonological categories from the speech signal. In C. Ferguson, L. Menn & C. Stoel-Gammon (Eds), *Phonogical development.* Timonium, MD: York Press, pp. 17–64.

Knapp, A. G., & Anderson, J. A. (1984) Theory of categorization based on distributed memory storage. *Journal of Experimental Psychology: Learning, Memory and Cognition, 10,* 616–637.

McShane, J. (1979) The development of naming. *Linguistics, 17,* 879–905.

MacWhinney, B., & Leinbach, J. (1991) Implementations are not conceptualizations: Revising the verb learning model. *Cognition, 40,* 121–157.

Marchman, V. (1988) Rules and regularities in the acquisition of the English past tense. *Center for Research in Language Newsletter, 2.* University of California at San Diego, La Jolla, CA.

Marcus, G. F., Ullman, M., Pinker, S., Hollander, M., Rosen, T. J., & Xu, F. (1992) Overregularization in language acquisition. *Monographs of the Society for Research in Child Development, 57.*

Movellan, J. R. (1990) *Contrastive Hebbian Learning in Interative Networks.* Unpublished manuscript, Department of Psychology, Carnegie Mellon University.

Pinker, S., & Prince, A. (1988) On language and connectionism: Analysis of a parallel distributed processing model of language acquisition. *Cognition, 28,* 73–193.

Plaut, D. C., & Shallice, T. (1993) Deep dyslexia: A case study of connectionist neuropsychology. *Cognitive Neuropsychology, 10,* 377–500.

Plunkett, K. (1993) Lexical segmentation and vocabulary growth in early language acquisition. *Journal of Child Language, 20,* 43–60.

Plunkett, K., & Marchman, V. (1991) U-Shaped learning and frequency effects in a multi-layered perception: Implications for child language acquisition. *Cognition, 38,* 43–102.

Plunkett, K., & Marchman, V. (1993) From rote learning to system building: acquiring verb morphology in children and connectionist nets. *Cognition, 48,* 21–69.

Plunkett, K., & Sinha, C. G. (1992) Connectionism and developmental theory. *British Journal of Developmental Psychology, 10,* 209–254.

Rumelhart, D. E., & McClelland, J. L. (1986) On learning the past tense of English verbs. In J. L. McClelland, D. E. Rumelhart & PDP Research Group (Eds), *Parallel distributed processing: Explorations in the microstructure of cognition, #2: Psychological and biological models.* Cambridge, MA: MIT Press, pp. 216–271.

Stemberger, J. (1990) *The Acquisition of Morphology: Analysis of Symbolic Model of Language Acquisition.* Unpublished Manuscript, University of Minnesota.

Stemberger, J. (1992) A connectionist view of child phonology: Phonological processing without phonological processes. In C. Ferguson, L. Menn & C. Stoel-Gammon (Eds) *Phonological development.* Timonium, MD: York Press.

Vihman, M., Macken, M., Miller, R., Simmons, H., & Miller, J. (1985) Form babbling to speech: A re-assessment of the continuity issue. *Language, 61,* 397–443.

Reading Words

Chapter 23

Understanding Normal and Impaired Word Reading: Computational Principles in Quasi-Regular Domains

David C. Plaut, James L. McClelland, Mark S. Seidenberg, and Karalyn Patterson

Many aspects of language can be characterized as *quasi-regular*—the relationship between inputs and outputs is systematic but admits many exceptions. One such task is the mapping between the written and spoken forms of English words. Most words are *regular* (e.g., GAVE, MINT) in that their pronunciations adhere to standard spelling–sound correspondences. There are, however, many irregular or *exception* words (e.g., HAVE, PINT) whose pronunciations violate the standard correspondences. To make matters worse, some spelling patterns have a range of pronunciations with none clearly predominating (e.g., _OWN in DOWN, TOWN, BROWN, CROWN *vs.* KNOWN, SHOWN, GROWN, THROWN, or _OUGH in COUGH, ROUGH, BOUGH, THOUGH, THROUGH). Nonetheless, in the face of this complexity, skilled readers pronounce written words quickly and accurately and can also use their knowledge of spelling–sound correspondences to read pronounceable nonwords (e.g., MAVE, RINT).

An important debate within cognitive psychology is how best to characterize knowledge and processing in quasi-regular domains in order to account for human language performance. One view (e.g., Pinker, 1984, 1991) is that the systematic aspects of language are represented and processed in the form of an explicit set of rules. A rule-based approach has considerable intuitive appeal because much of human language behavior can be characterized at a broad scale in terms of rules. It also provides a straightforward account of how language knowledge can be applied productively to novel items (Fodor & Pylyshyn, 1988). However, as illustrated above, most domains are only partially systematic; accordingly, a separate mechanism is required to handle the exceptions. This distinction between a rule-based mechanism and an exception mechanism, each operating according to fundamentally different principles, forms the central tenet of so-called "dual-route" theories of language.

An alternative view comes out of research on connectionist or parallel distributed processing networks, in which computation takes the form of cooperative and competitive interactions among large numbers of simple, neuron-like processing units (McClelland, Rumelhart, & the PDP Research Group, 1986;

Rumelhart, McClelland, & the PDP Research Group, 1986). Such systems learn by adjusting weights on connections between units in a way that is sensitive to how the statistical structure of the environment influences the behavior of the network. As a result, there is no sharp dichotomy between the items that obey the rules and the items that do not. Rather, all items coexist within a single system whose representations and processing reflect the relative degree of *consistency* in the mappings for different items. The connectionist approach is particularly appropriate for capturing the rapid, on-line nature of language use as well as for specifying how such processes might be learned and implemented in the brain (although still at a somewhat abstract level; see Sejnowski, Koch, & Churchland, 1989, for discussion). Perhaps more fundamentally, connectionist modeling provides a rich set of general computational principles that can lead to new and useful ways of thinking about human performance in quasi-regular domains.

Much of the initial debate between these two views of the language system focused on the relatively constrained domain of English inflectional morphology, but very similar issues arise in the domain of oral reading, where there is a much richer empirical database with which to make contact. As in the domain of inflectional morphology, many researchers assume that accounting for the wealth of existing data on both normal and impaired word reading requires postulating multiple mechanisms. In particular, dual-route theorists (e.g., Besner & Smith, 1992; Coltheart, 1978, 1985; Coltheart, Curtis, Atkins, & Haller, 1993; Coltheart & Rastle, 1994; Marshall & Newcombe, 1973; Meyer, Schvaneveldt, & Ruddy, 1974; Morton & Patterson, 1980; Paap & Noel, 1991) have claimed that pronouncing exception words requires a lexical lookup mechanism that is separate from the sublexical spelling–sound correspondence rules that apply to regular words and nonwords (see also Humphreys & Evett, 1985, and the accompanying commentaries for discussion of the properties of dual-route theories). The separation of lexical and sublexical procedures is motivated primarily by evidence that they can be independently impaired, either by abnormal reading acquisition (developmental dyslexia) or by brain damage in a previously literate adult (acquired dyslexia). Thus *phonological* dyslexics, who can read words but not nonwords, appear to have a selective impairment of the sublexical procedure, whereas *surface* dyslexics, who can read nonwords but who "regularize" exception words (e.g., SEW ⇒ "sue"), appear to have a selective impairment of the lexical procedure.

Seidenberg and McClelland (1989), hereafter SM89, challenged the central claim of dual-route theories by developing a connectionist simulation that learned to map representations of the written forms of words (orthography) to representations of their spoken forms (phonology). The network successfully pronounces both regular and exception words and yet is not an implementation of two separate mechanisms (see Seidenberg & McClelland, 1992, for a demonstration of this last point). The simulation was put forward in support of a more general framework for lexical processing in which orthographic, phonological, and semantic information interact in gradually settling on the best representations for a given input (see Stone & Van Orden, 1989, 1994; Van Orden & Goldinger, 1994; Van Orden, Pennington, & Stone, 1990, for a similar perspective on word reading). A major strength of the approach is that it provides a natural account of the graded effects of spelling–sound consistency among words (Glushko, 1979; Jared, McRae, & Seidenberg, 1990) and how this consistency interacts with word frequency (Andrews, 1982; Seidenberg, 1985; Seidenberg, Waters, Barnes, & Tanenhaus, 1984; Taraban & McClelland, 1987; Waters & Seidenberg, 1985).[1] Furthermore, SM89 demonstrated that undertrained versions of the model exhibit some aspects of developmental surface dyslexia, and Patterson (1990; Patterson, Seidenberg, & McClelland, 1989) showed how damaging the normal model can reproduce some aspects of acquired surface dyslexia. The SM89 model also contributes to the broader enterprise of connectionist modeling of cognitive processes in which a common set of general computational principles are being applied successfully across a wide range of cognitive domains.

However, the SM89 work has a serious empirical limitation that undermines its role in establishing a viable connectionist alternative to dual-route theories of word reading in particular and in providing a satisfactory formulation of the nature of knowledge and processing in quasi-regular domains more generally. Specifically, the implemented model is significantly worse than skilled readers at pronouncing nonwords (Besner, Twilley, McCann, & Seergobin, 1990). This limitation has broad implications for the range of empirical phenomena that can be accounted for by the model (Coltheart et al., 1993). Poor nonword reading is exactly what would be predicted from the dual-route claim that no single system—connectionist or otherwise—can read both exception words and pronounceable nonwords adequately. Under this interpretation, the model had simply approximated a lexical lookup procedure: It could read both regular and exception words but had not separately mastered the sublexical rules necessary to read nonwords. An alternative interpretation, however, is that the empirical shortcomings of the SM89 simulation stem from specific aspects of its design and not from inherent limitations on the abilities of connectionist networks in quasi-regular domains. In particular, Seidenberg and McClelland (1990) suggested that the model's nonword reading might be improved—without adversely affecting its other properties—by using either a larger training corpus or different orthographic and phonological representations.

A second limitation of the SM89 work is that it did not provide a very extensive examination of underlying theoretical issues. The main emphasis was on demonstrating that a network that operated according to fairly general connectionist principles could account for a wide range of empirical findings on normal and developmentally impaired reading. Relatively little attention was paid in that article to articulating the general principles themselves or to evaluating their relative importance. Thus, much of the underlying theoretical foundation of the work remained implicit. Despite subsequent efforts at explicating these principles (Seidenberg, 1993), considerable confusion remains with regard to the role of connectionist modeling in contributing to a theory of word reading (or of any other cognitive process). Thus, some researchers (e.g., Forster, 1994; McCloskey, 1991) have claimed that the SM89 demonstration, while impressive in its own right, has not extended our understanding of word reading because the operation of the model itself—and of connectionist networks more generally—is too complex to understand. Consequently, "connectionist networks should not be viewed as theories of human cognitive functions, or as simulations of theories, or even as demonstrations of specific theoretical points" (McCloskey, 1991, p. 387; also see Massaro, 1988; Olsen & Caramazza, 1991). Although we reject the claim that connectionist modeling is atheoretical (see Seidenberg, 1993) and that there are no bases for analyzing and understanding networks (cf. Hanson & Burr, 1990), we agree that the theoretical principles and constructs for developing connectionist explanations of empirical phenomena are in need of further elaboration.

In this article, we develop a connectionist account of knowledge representation and cognitive processing in quasi-regular domains in the specific context of normal and impaired word reading. We draw on an analysis of the strengths and weaknesses of the SM89 work, with the dual aim of providing a more adequate account of the relevant empirical phenomena and of articulating in a more explicit and formal manner the theoretical principles that underlie the approach. We explore the use of alternative representations that make the regularities between written and spoken words more explicit. In the first simulation experiment, a network using the new representations learned to read both regular and exception words, including low-frequency exception words, and yet was still able to read pronounceable nonwords as well as skilled readers. The results open up the range of possible architectures that might plausibly underlie human word reading. A mathematical analysis of the effects of word frequency and spelling–sound consistency in a simpler but related system serves to clarify the close relationship of these factors in influencing naming latencies. These insights were verified in a second simulation. In a third simulation we developed an attractor network that reproduces the naming latency data directly in its time to settle on a response and thus obviates the need to use error as a proxy for reaction time. The implication of the semantic contribution to reading was considered in our fourth and final simulation in the context of accounting for the impaired reading behavior of acquired surface dyslexic patients with brain damage. Damage to the attractor network provides only a limited account of the relevant phenomena; a better account is provided by the performance of a network that learns to map orthography to phonology in the context of support from semantics. Our findings lead to a view of the reading system that incorporates a graded division of labor between semantic and phonological processes. Such a view is consistent with the more general SM89 framework and has some similarities with—but also important differences from—the standard dual-route account. In the General Discussion, we articulate these differences and clarify the implications of the current work for a broader range of empirical findings, including those raised by Coltheart et al. (1993) as challenges to the connectionist approach.

We begin with a brief critique of the SM89 model in which we try to distinguish its central computational properties from less central aspects of its design. An analysis of its representations led to the design of new representations that we used in a series of simulations analogous to the SM89 simulation.

The Seidenberg and McClelland Model

The General Framework

Seidenberg and McClelland's (1989) general framework for lexical processing is shown in Figure 23.1. Orthographic, phonological, and semantic information is represented in terms of distributed patterns of activity over separate groups of simple neuron-like processing units. Within each domain, similar words are represented by similar patterns of activity. Lexical tasks involve transformations among these representations—for example, oral reading requires the orthographic pattern for a word to generate the appropriate phonological pattern. Such transformations are accomplished via the cooperative and competitive interactions among units, including additional *hidden units* that mediate among

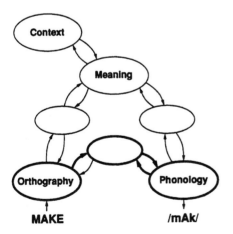

Figure 23.1
Seidenberg and McClelland's (1989) general framework for lexical processing. Each oval represents a group of units, and each arrow represent a group of connections. The implemented model is shown in bold.

the orthographic, phonological, and semantic units. Unit interactions are governed by weighted connections between them, which collectively encode the system's knowledge about how the different types of information are related. The specific values of the weights are derived by an automatic learning procedure on the basis of the system's exposure to written words, spoken words, and their meanings.

The SM89 framework is broadly consistent with a more general view of information processing that has been articulated by McClelland (1991, 1993) in the context of GRAIN networks. These networks embody the following general computational principles:

Graded: Propagation of activation is not all-or-none but rather builds up gradually over time.

Random: Unit activations are subject to intrinsic stochastic variability.

Adaptive: The system gradually improves its performance by adjusting weights on connections between units.

Interactive: Information flows in a bidirectional manner between groups of units, allowing their activity levels to constrain each other and to be mutually consistent.

Nonlinear: Unit outputs are smooth, nonlinear functions of their total inputs, significantly extending the computational power of the entire network beyond that of purely linear networks.

The acronym GRAIN is also intended to convey the notion that cognitive processes are expressed at a finer grain of analysis, in terms of interacting groups of neuronlike units, than is typical of most "box-and-arrow" information-processing models. Additional computational principles that are central to the SM89 framework but not captured by the acronym are the following:

Distributed Representations: Items in the domain are represented by patterns of activity over groups of units that participate in representing many other items.

Distributed Knowledge: Knowledge about the relationship between items is encoded across large numbers of connection weights that also encode many other mappings.

Much of the controversy surrounding the SM89 framework, and the associated implementation, stems from the fact that it breaks with traditional accounts of lexical processing (e.g., Coltheart, 1985; Morton & Patterson, 1980) in two fundamental ways. The first is in the representational status of words. Traditional accounts assume that words are represented in the structure of the reading system—in its *architecture*. Morton's (1969) "logogens" are well-known instances of this type of word representation. By contrast, within the SM89 framework the lexical status of a string of letters or phonemes is not reflected in the structure of the reading system. Rather, words are distinguished from non-words only by *functional* properties of the system—the way in which particular orthographic, phonological, and semantic patterns of activity interact (also see Van Orden et al., 1990).

The SM89 framework's second major break with tradition concerns the degree of uniformity in the mechanism(s) by which orthographic, phonological, and semantic representations interact. Traditional accounts assume that pronouncing exception words and pronouncing nonwords require separate lexical and sublexical mechanisms, respectively. By contrast, the SM89 framework employs far more homogeneous processes in oral reading. In particular, it eschews separate mechanisms for pronouncing nonwords and exception words. Rather, all of the system's knowledge of spelling–sound correspondences is brought to bear in pronouncing all types of letter strings. Conflicts among possible alternative pronunciations of a letter string are resolved not by structurally distinct mechanisms, but by cooperative and competitive interactions based on how the letter string relates to all known words and their pronunciations. Furthermore, the semantic representation of a word participates in oral reading in exactly the same manner as do its orthographic and phonological representations, although the framework leaves open the issue of how important these semantic influences are in skilled oral reading.

Regularity Versus Consistency   An issue that is intimately related to the tension between the SM89 framework and traditional dual-route theories concerns the distinction between regularity and consistency. Broadly speaking, a word is *regular* if its pronunciation can be generated "by rule," and it is *consistent* if its pronunciation agrees with those of similarly spelled words. Of course, to be useful these definitions must be operationalized in more specific terms. The most commonly proposed pronunciation rules are based on the most frequent grapheme–phoneme correspondences (GPCs) in the language, although such GPC rules must be augmented with considerable context-sensitivity to operate adequately (see Coltheart et al., 1993; Seidenberg, Plaut, Petersen, McClelland, & McRae, 1994, for discussion). Consistency, on the other hand, has typically been defined with respect to the orthographic body and the phonological rime (i.e., the vowel plus any following consonants). This choice can be partly justified on the grounds of empirical data. For example, Treiman, Mullennix, Bijeljac-Babic, and Richmond-Welty (1995) have recently demonstrated that, in naming data for all 1,329 monosyllabic words in English with a consonant-vowel-consonant (CVC) pronunciation, the consistency of the body (VC) accounts for significantly more variance in naming latency than the consistency of the onset plus vowel (CV). There are also pragmatic reasons for restricting consideration to body-level consistency—bodies constitute a manageable manipulation in the design of experimental lists. If experimenters had to consider consistency across orthographic neighborhoods at all possible levels, from individual graphemes up to the largest subword-sized chunks, their selection of stimulus words would be an even more agonizing process than it already is. Nonetheless, the general notion of consistency is broader than a specific instantiation in terms of body consistency, just as the general notion of regularity is broader than that defined by any particular set of spelling–sound correspondence rules.

On the basis of the frequent observation (e.g., Coltheart, 1978; Parkin, 1982; Waters & Seidenberg, 1985) that words with regular or typical spelling–sound correspondences (such as MINT) produce shorter naming latencies and lower error rates than words with exceptional correspondences (such as PINT), regularity was originally considered to be the critical variable. In 1979, however, Glushko argued that consistency provided a better account of empirical results. Although MINT may be a regular word according to GPC rules, its spelling–sound relationship is inconsistent with that of its orthographic neighbor, PINT. To the extent that the process of computing phonology from orthography is sensitive to the characteristics of the neighborhood, performance on a regular but inconsistent word like MINT may also be adversely affected. Glushko (1979) did indeed demonstrate longer naming latencies for regular inconsistent words than for regular words from consistent body neighborhoods, though this result was not always obtained in subsequent experiments (e.g., Stanhope & Parkin, 1987).

In 1990, Jared, McRae, and Seidenberg offered a more sophisticated hypothesis that captures aspects of results not handled by previous accounts referring solely to either regularity or consistency. According to Jared and colleagues, the magnitude of the consistency effect for a given word depends on the summed frequency of that word's *friends* (words with a similar spelling pattern and similar pronunciation) and of its *enemies* (words with a similar spelling pattern but a discrepant pronunciation). For example, an inconsistent word like MINT has a number of friends (e.g., LINT, TINT, PRINT) and just a single enemy, PINT. Against the strength of friends, the single enemy cannot exert a marked influence (especially when, as is true of PINT, the enemy is of relatively low frequency); its negative impact on the computation of the pronunciation of MINT will thus be small and perhaps undetectable. By contrast, an inconsistent word like GOWN, with many enemies (e.g., BLOWN, SHOWN, GROWN) as well as friends (e.g., DOWN, BROWN, TOWN), gives rise to a more substantial effect. Such words, with roughly balanced support from friends and enemies, have been termed *ambiguous* (with respect to the pronunciation of their body; Backman, Bruck, Hébert, & Seidenberg, 1984; Seidenberg et al., 1984).

The commonly observed effect of regularity also finds a natural explanation within Jared et al.'s (1990) account, because most regular words (as defined by GPC rules) have many friends and few (if any) enemies, whereas words with irregular spelling–sound correspondences (such as PINT or SEW) typically have many enemies and few (if any) friends. Given this correspondence, and following Glushko (1979) and Taraban and McClelland (1987), we will refer to words with many enemies and few if any friends as *exception* words, acknowledging that this definition excludes many words that would be considered exceptional according to GPC rules (e.g., many ambiguous words). Jared et al.'s hypothesis and supporting data also mesh well with other results demonstrating the inadequacy of a simple regular–irregular dichotomy, such as the "degrees of regularity" effect observed in acquired surface dyslexia (Shallice, Warrington, & McCarthy, 1983, also see Patterson & Behrmann, 1997, Plaut, Behrmann, Patterson, & McClelland, 1993, for more direct evidence of consistency effects in surface dyslexia).

It must be kept in mind, however, that a definition of consistency based solely on body neighborhoods, even if frequency-weighted, can provide only a partial account of the consistency effects that would be expected to operate over the full range of spelling–sound correspondences. Thus, for example, the word CHEF could not be considered inconsistent on a body-level analysis because all of the words in English with the body _EF (i.e., CLEF, REF) agree with its pronunciation. On a broader definition of consistency, however, CHEF is certainly inconsistent, because the overwhelmingly most common pronunciation of CH in English is the one appropriate to CHIEF, not CHEF. This broad view of consistency is also important when considering what might be called irregular consistent words—that is, words such as KIND, BOLD, and TOOK that have highly consistent body neighborhoods but that are nonetheless irregular according to GPC rules such as those of Coltheart et al. (1993). The processing of such items would be expected to be sensitive to the conflict between consistency at the body–rime level and inconsistency at the grapheme–phoneme level. In all of what follows, therefore, although we adopt the standard practice of using body-level manipulations for empirical tests, this should be interpreted as providing only an approximation of the true range of consistency effects.

Relationship to Other Approaches   A cursory inspection of Figure 23.1 might suggest that the SM89 framework is, in fact, a dual-route system: Orthography can influence phonology either directly or via semantics. To clarify this possible source of confusion, we must be more explicit about typical assumptions in dual-route theories concerning the structure and operation of the different procedures. As described earlier, the central distinction in such theories is between lexical and sublexical procedures. The sublexical procedure applies GPC rules to produce correct pronunciations for regular words, reasonable pronunciations for nonwords, and incorrect, "regularized" pronunciations for exception words. The lexical procedure produces correct pronunciations for all words and no response for nonwords. When the outputs of the two procedures conflict, as they do for exception words, some models (e.g., Paap & Noel, 1991) assume a "horse race," with the faster (typically lexical) procedure generating the actual response. Others (e.g., Monsell, Patterson, Graham, Hughes, & Milroy, 1992) suggest that output from the two procedures is pooled until a phonological representation sufficient to drive articulation is achieved (although the specific means by which this pooling occurs is rarely made explicit). The lexical procedure is often subdivided into a *direct* route that maps orthographic word representations directly onto phonological word representations, and an *indirect* route that maps via semantics. In these formulations, the "dual-route" model is in a sense a three-route model, although researchers typically assume that the indirect, semantic route would be too slow to influence skilled word pronunciation (Coltheart, 1985; Patterson & Morton, 1985).

By contrast, the nonsemantic portion of the SM89 framework does not operate by applying GPC rules, but by the simultaneous interaction of units. It is also capable of pronouncing all types of input, including exception words, although the time it takes to do so depends on the type of input. Furthermore, the semantic portion of the framework does not operate in terms of whole-word representations, but rather in terms of interacting units, each of which participates in the processing of many words. In addition, nonwords may engage semantics to some degree, although the extent to which this occurs is likely to be minimal (see the discussion of lexical decision in the General Discussion). Thus, the structure and operation of the SM89 framework is fundamentally different from existing dual-route theories.

The Implemented Model

The SM89 framework clearly represents a radical departure from widely held assumptions about lexical processing, but is it plausible as an account of human word reading? In the service of establishing the framework's plausibility, SM89 implemented a specific connectionist network that, they implicitly claimed, embodies the central theoretical tenets of the framework.

The network, highlighted in bold in Figure 23.1, contains three groups of units: 400 orthographic units, 200 hidden units, and 460 phonological units. The hidden units receive connections from all of the orthographic units and, in turn, send connections to all of the phonological units as well as back to all of the orthographic units. The network contains no semantic or context information.

Orthographic and phonological forms are represented as patterns of activity over the orthographic and phonological units, respectively. These patterns are defined in terms of context-sensitive triples of letters and phonemes (Wickelgren, 1969). It was computationally infeasible for SM89 to include a unit for each possible triple, so they used representations that require fewer units but preserve the relative similarities among patterns. In orthography, the letter triples to which each unit responds are defined by a table of 10 randomly selected letters (or a blank) in each of three positions. In the representation of a letter string, an orthographic unit is active if the string contains one of the letter triples than can be generated by sampling from each of the three positions of that unit's table. For example, GAVE would activate all orthographic units capable of generating _GA, GAV, AVE, or VE_.

Phonological representations are derived in an analogous fashion, except that a phonological unit's table entries at each position are not randomly selected phonemes, but rather all phonemes containing a particular phonemic feature (as defined by Rumelhart & McClelland, 1986). A further constraint is that the features for the first and third positions must come from the same phonetic dimension (e.g., place of articulation). Thus, each unit in phonology represents a particular ordered triple of phonemic features, termed a *Wickelfeature*. For example, the pronunciation /gAv/ would activate phonological units representing the Wickelfeatures [*back, vowel, front*], [*stop, long, fricative*], and many others (given that /g/ has *back* and *stop* among its features, /A/ has *vowel* and *long*, and /v/ has *front* and *fricative*). On average, a word activates 81 (20.3%) of the 400 orthographic units, and 54 (11.7%) of the 460 phonological units. We will return to an analysis of the properties of these representations after summarizing the SM89 simulation results.

The weights on connections between units were initialized to small random values. The network then was repeatedly presented with the orthography of each of 2,897 monosyllabic words and trained both to generate the phonology of the word and to regenerate its orthography (see Seidenberg & McClelland, 1989, for details). During each sweep through the training set, the probability that a word was presented to the network was proportional to a logarithmic function of its frequency (Kuçera & Francis, 1967). Processing a word involved setting the states of the orthographic units (as defined above), computing hidden unit states based on states of the orthographic units and the weights on connections from them, and then computing states of the phonological and orthographic units based on those of the hidden units. Back-propagation (Rumelhart, Hinton, & Williams, 1986a, 1986b) was used to calculate how to adjust the weights to reduce the differences between the correct phonological and orthographic representations of the word and those generated by the network. These weight changes were accumulated during each sweep through the training set; at the end, the changes were carried out and the process was repeated.

The network was considered to have named a word correctly when the generated phonological activity was closer to the representation of the correct pronunciation of the word than to that of any pronunciation which differed from the correct one by a single phoneme. For the example GAVE ⇒ /gAv/, the competing pronunciations are all those among /*Av/, /g*v/, or /gA*/, where /*/ is any phoneme. After 250 training sweeps through the corpus, amounting to about 150,000 word presentations, the network correctly named all but 77 words (97.3% correct), most of which were low-frequency exception words.

A considerable amount of empirical data on oral reading concerns the time it takes to name words of various types. A natural analogue in a model to naming

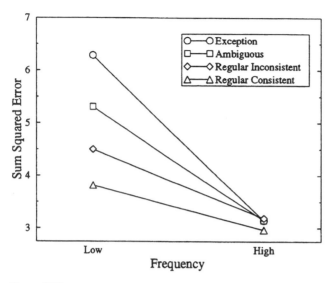

Figure 23.2
Mean phonological error scores produced by the Seidenburg and McClelland (1989) network for words with various degrees of spelling-sound consistency as a function of frequency.

latency in human readers would be the amount of computing time required to produce an output. SM89 could not use this measure because their network takes exactly the same amount of time—one update of each unit—to compute phonological output for any letter string. Instead, they approximated naming latency with a measure of the accuracy of the phonological activity produced by the network—the *phonological error score*. SM89 showed that the network's distribution of phonological error scores for various words reproduces the effects of frequency and consistency in naming latencies found in a wide variety of empirical studies that used the same words. Figure 23.2 presents particularly illustrative results in this regard, using high- and low-frequency words at four levels of consistency (listed in Appendix A and used in the current simulations):

> *Exception* words from Experiments 1 and 2 of Taraban and McClelland (1987): They have an average of 0.73 friends in the SM89 corpus (not counting the word itself) and 9.2 enemies.

> *Ambiguous* words generated by SM89 to be matched in Kuçera and Francis (1967) frequency with the exception words: They average 8.6 friends and 8.0 enemies.

> *Regular inconsistent* words, also from Taraban and McClelland (1987): These average 7.8 friends and only 2.1 enemies.

Regular consistent words that were the control items for the exception words in the Taraban and McClelland (1987) study: They have an average of 10.7 friends and 0.04 enemies (the foreign word COUP for the item GROUP, and one of the pronunciations of BASS for the item CLASS.

The relevant empirical effects in naming latency exhibited by the SM89 model are, specifically, as follows:

1. High-frequency words are named faster than low-frequency words (e.g., Forster & Chambers, 1973; Frederiksen & Kroll, 1976).
2. Consistent words are named faster than inconsistent words (Glushko, 1979), and latencies increase monotonically with increasing spelling–sound inconsistency (as approximated by the relative proportion of friends vs. enemies; Jared et al., 1990). Thus, regular inconsistent words like MOTH (cf. BOTH) are slower to be named than regular consistent words like MUST (Glushko, 1979), and exception words like PINT and SEW are the slowest to be named (Seidenberg et al., 1984). Performance on ambiguous words like GOWN (cf. GROWN) falls between that on regular inconsistent words and that on exception words, although this has been investigated directly only with respect to reading acquisition (Backman et al., 1984).
3. Frequency interacts with consistency (Seidenberg, 1985; Seidenberg et al., 1984; Waters & Seidenberg, 1985) such that the consistency effect is much greater among low-frequency words than among high-frequency words (where it may even be absent; see, e.g., Seidenberg, 1985), or equivalently, the frequency effect decreases with increasing consistency (perhaps being absent among regular words; see, e.g., Waters & Seidenberg, 1985).

In considering these empirical and simulation results, it is important to keep in mind that the use of a four-way classification of consistency is not in any way intended to imply the existence of four distinct subtypes of words; rather, it is intended to help illustrate the effects of what is actually an underlying continuum of consistency (Jared et al., 1990).[2]

The model also shows analogous effects of consistency in nonword naming latency. In particular, nonwords derived from regular consistent words (e.g., NUST from MUST) are faster to name than nonwords derived from exception words (e.g., MAVE from HAVE; Glushko, 1979; Taraban & McClelland, 1987). As mentioned in the Introduction, however, the model's nonword naming accuracy is much worse than that of skilled readers. Besner et al. (1990) reported that, on nonword lists from Glushko (1979) and McCann and Besner (1987), the model is only 59% and 51% correct, whereas skilled readers are 94% and 89% correct, respectively. Seidenberg and McClelland (1990) pointed out that the scoring criterion used for the network was more strict than that used for the human readers. We will return to the issue of scoring nonword reading performance; for the present purposes, it suffices to acknowledge that, even taking differences in scoring into account, the performance of the SM89 model on nonwords is inadequate.

The SM89 model replicates the effects of frequency and consistency in lexical decision (Waters & Seidenberg, 1985) when responses are based on *orthographic error scores*, which measure the degree to which the network succeeds at recreating the orthography of each input string. Again, however, the model is not as accurate at lexical decision under some conditions as are human readers (Besner et al., 1990; Fera & Besner, 1992).

Consistency also influences the ease with which word naming skills are acquired. Thus, less skilled readers—whether younger or developmentally dyslexic—show larger consistency effects than do more skilled readers (Backman et al., 1984; Vellutino, 1979). The model shows similar effects both early in the course of learning and when trained with limited resources (e.g., too few hidden units).

Finally, damaging the model by removing units or connections results in a pattern of errors that is somewhat similar to that of brain-injured patients with one form of surface dyslexia (Patterson, 1990; Patterson et al., 1989). Specifically, low-frequency exception words become particularly prone to being regularized (see Patterson, Coltheart, & Marshall, 1985). Overall, however, attempts to model surface dyslexia by "lesioning" the SM89 model have been less than satisfactory (see Behrmann & Bub, 1992; Coltheart et al., 1993, for criticism). We consider this and other types of developmental and acquired dyslexia in more detail after presenting new simulation results on normal skilled reading.

Evaluation of the Model

The SM89 implementation does, however, have serious limitations in accounting for some empirical data. Some of these limitations no doubt stem from the lack of unimplemented portions of the framework—most important, the involvement of semantic representations, but also perhaps visual and articulatory procedures. A full consideration of the range of relevant empirical findings will be better undertaken in the General Discussion in the context of the new simulation results. Consideration of the poor nonword reading performance of the SM89 network, however, cannot be postponed. This limitation is fundamental because nonword reading is unlikely to be improved by the addition of semantics. Furthermore, Coltheart et al. (1993) have argued that, primarily as a result of its poor processing of nonwords, the model is incapable of accounting for five of six central issues in normal and impaired word reading. More fundamental, by not reading nonwords adequately, the model fails to refute the claim of dual-route theorists that reading nonwords and reading exception words require separate mechanisms.

Seidenberg and McClelland (1990) argued that the model's poor nonword reading was not an inherent problem with the general framework, but rather was the result of two specific limitations in the implementation. The first is the limited size of the training corpus. The model was exposed to only about 3,000 words, whereas the skilled readers with whom it is compared know approximately 10 times that number. Given that the only knowledge that the model has available for reading nonwords is what it has derived from words, a limited training corpus is a serious handicap.

Coltheart et al. (1993) have argued that limitations of the SM89 training corpus cannot explain the model's poor nonword reading because a system that learns GPC rules using the same corpus performs much better. This argument is fallacious, however, because the effectiveness of a training corpus depends critically on other assumptions built into the training procedure. In fact, Coltheart and colleagues' procedure for learning GPC rules has built into it a considerable amount of knowledge that is specific to reading, concerning the possible relationships between graphemes and phonemes in various contexts. In contrast, SM89 applied a general learning procedure to representations that encode only ordered triples of letters and phonemic features but nothing of their correspondences. A demonstration that the SM89 training corpus is sufficient to support good nonword reading in the context of strong, domain-specific assumptions does not invalidate the claim that the corpus may be insufficient in the context of much weaker assumptions.

The second aspect of the SM89 simulation that contributed to its poor nonword reading was the use of Wickelfeatures to represent phonology. This representational scheme has known limitations, many of which are related to how well the scheme can be extended to more realistic vocabularies (see Lachter & Bever, 1988; Pinker & Prince, 1988, for detailed criticism). In the current context, Seidenberg and McClelland (1990) pointed out that the representations do not adequately capture phonemic structure. Specifically, the features of a phoneme are not bound with each other, but only with features of neighboring phonemes. As a result, the surrounding context can too easily introduce inappropriate features, producing many single-feature errors in nonword pronunciations (e.g., TIFE $\Rightarrow$ /tIv/).

Neither the specific training corpus nor the Wickelfeature representation are central to the SM89 general framework for lexical processing. If Seidenberg and McClelland (1990) are correct in suggesting that it is these aspects of the simulation that are responsible for its poor nonword reading, their more general framework remains viable. On the other hand, the actual performance of an implementation is the main source of evidence that SM89 put forward in support of their view of the reading system. As McCloskey (1991) has recently pointed out, it is notoriously difficult both to determine whether an implementation's failings are due to fundamental or incidental properties of its design, and to predict how changes to its design would affect its behavior. Thus, to support the SM89 connectionist framework as a viable alternative to rule-based, dual-route accounts, it is critical that we develop further simulations that account for the same range of findings as the original implementation and yet also pronounce nonwords as well as skilled readers do. In this article we present such simulations.

Orthographic and Phonological Representations

Wickelfeatures and the Dispersion Problem

For the purposes of supporting good nonword reading, the Wickelfeature phonological representation has a more fundamental drawback. The problem stems from the general issue of how to represent structured objects, such as words composed of ordered strings of letters and phonemes, in connectionist networks. Connectionist researchers would like their networks to have three properties (Hinton, 1990):

> 1. All the knowledge in a network should be in connection weights between units.
> 2. To support good generalization, the network's knowledge should capture the important regularities in the domain.
> 3. For processing to be fast, the major constituents of an item should be processed in parallel.

The problem is that these three properties are difficult to reconcile with each other.

Consider first the standard technique of using position-specific units, sometimes called a *slot-based* representation (e.g., McClelland & Rumelhart, 1981). The first letter goes in the first slot, the second letter in the second slot, and so forth. Similarly for the output, the first phoneme goes in the first slot, and so on. With enough slots, words up to any desired length can be represented.

This scheme satisfies Properties 1 and 3 above but at a cost to Property 2. That is, processing can be done in parallel across letters and phonemes using weighted connections, but at the cost of dispersing the regularities of how letters and phonemes are related. The reason is that there must be a separate copy of each letter (and phoneme) for each slot, and because the relevant knowledge is embedded in connections that are specific to these units, this knowledge must be replicated in the connections to and from each slot. To some extent this is useful in the domain of oral reading because the pronunciation of a letter may depend on whether it occurs at the beginning, middle, or end of a word. However, the slot-based approach carries this to an extreme, with unfortunate consequences. Consider the words LOG, GLAD, and SPLIT. The fact that the letter L corresponds to the phoneme /l/ in these words must be learned and stored three separate times in the system. There is no generalization of what is learned about letters in one position to the same letter in other positions. The problem can be alleviated to some degree by aligning the slots in various ways (e.g.,

Table 23.1
The Dispersion Problem

Slot-based representations

Left-justified					Vowel-centered					Context-sensitive triples ("Wickelgraphs")				
1	2	3	4	5	−3	−2	−1	0	1					
L	O	G				S	U	N		LOG:		_LO	LOG	OG_
G	L	A	D			S	W	A	M	GLAD:	_GL	GLA	LAD	AD_
S	P	L	I	T	S	P	L	I	T	SPLIT:	_SP	SPL	PLI	LIT	IT_

centered around the vowel; Daugherty & Seidenberg, 1992), but it is not eliminated completely (see Table 23.1). Adequate generalization still requires learning the regularities separately across several slots.

An alternative scheme is to apply the network to a single letter at a time, as in
Sejnowski and Rosenberg's (1987) NETtalk model.[3] Here, the same knowledge
is applied to pronouncing a letter regardless of where it occurs in a word, and
words of arbitrary length can be processed. Unfortunately, Properties 1 and 2
are now being traded off against Property 3. Processing becomes slow and sequential, which may be satisfactory in many domains but not in word reading.
Note that the common finding of small but significant effects of word length on
naming latency (e.g., Butler & Hains, 1979; Frederiksen & Kroll, 1976; Richardson, 1976) does not imply that the computation from orthography to phonology
operates sequentially over letters; a parallel implementation of this mapping
may also exhibit small length effects (as will be demonstrated in Simulation 3 of
this article).

The representations used by SM89 were an attempt to avoid the specific
limitations of the slot-based approach, but in the end they turn out to have a
version of the same problem. Elements such as letters and phonemes are represented, not in terms of their absolute spatial position or relative position
within the word, but in terms of the adjacent elements to the left and right. This
approach, which originated with Wickelgren (1969), makes the representation of each element context sensitive without being rigidly tied to position.
Unfortunately, however, the knowledge of spelling–sound correspondences is
still dispersed across a large number of different contexts, and adequate generalization still requires that the training effectively cover them all. Returning to
Table 23.1, one can see that although the words LOG, GLAD, and SPLIT share the
correspondence L ⇒ /l/, they have no triples of letters in common. A similar
property holds in phonology among triples of phonemes or phonemic features.
Thus, as in the slot-based approach, although the same correspondence is
present in these three cases, different units are activated. As a result, the
knowledge that is learned in one context—encoded as connection weights—
does not apply in other contexts, which thus hinders generalization.

Notice that the effect of dispersing regularities is much like the effect of limiting the size of the training corpus. The contribution that an element makes to the representation of the word is specific to the context in which it occurs. As a result, the knowledge learned from one item is beneficial only to other items which share that specific context. When representations disperse the regularities in the domain, the number of trained mappings that support a given pronunciation is effectively reduced. As a result, generalization to novel stimuli, as in the pronunciation of nonwords, is based on less knowledge and suffers accordingly. In a way, Seidenberg and McClelland's (1990) two suggestions for improving their model's nonword reading performance—enlarge the training corpus and improve the representations—amount to the same thing. Using improved representations that minimize the dispersion problem increases the effective size of the training corpus for a given pronunciation.

Condensing Spelling–Sound Regularities
The hypothesis guiding the current work was the idea that the dispersion problem prevented the SM89 network from exploiting the structure of the English spelling-to-sound system as fully as human readers do. We set out, therefore, to design representations that minimize this dispersion.

The limiting case of our approach would be to have a single set of letter units, one for each letter in the alphabet, and a single set of phoneme units, one for each phoneme. Such a scheme satisfies all three of Hinton's (1990) desired properties: All of the letters in a word map to all of its phonemes simultaneously via weighted connections (and presumably hidden units), and the spelling–sound regularities are condensed because the same units and connections are involved whenever a particular letter or phoneme is present. Unfortunately, this approach has a fatal flaw: It does not preserve the relative order of letters and phonemes. Thus, it cannot distinguish TOP from POT or SALT from SLAT.

It turns out, however, that a scheme involving only a small amount of replication is sufficient to provide a unique representation of virtually every uninflected monosyllabic word. By definition, a monosyllable contains only a single vowel, so only one set of vowel units is needed. A monosyllable may contain both an initial and a final consonant cluster, and almost every consonant can occur in either cluster, so separate sets of consonant units are required for each of these clusters. The remarkable thing is that this is nearly all that is necessary. The reason is that within an initial or final consonant cluster, there are strong phonotactic constraints that arise in large part from the structure of the articulatory system. At both ends of the syllable, each phoneme can occur only once, and the order of phonemes is strongly constrained. For example, if the phonemes /s/, /t/, and /r/ all occur in the onset cluster, they must be in that order, /str/. Given this, all that is required to specify a pronunciation is which

Table 23.2
Phonological and orthographic representations used in the simulations

Phonology[a]	
onset	s S C z Z j f v T D p b t d k g m n h l r w y
vowel	a e i o u @ ^ A E I O U W Y
coda	r l m n N b g d p s k s t s s z f v p k t S Z T D C j
Orthography	
onset	Y S P T K Q C B D G F V J Z L M N R W H CH GH GN PH PS RH SH TH TS WH
vowel	E I O U A Y AI AU AW AY EA EE EI EU EW EY IE OA OE OI OO OU OW OY UE UI UY
coda	H R L M N B D G C X F V J S Z P T K Q BB CH CK DD DG FF GG GH GN KS LL NG
	NN PH PP PS RR SH SL SS TCH TH TS TT ZZ U E ES ED

Note. The notation for vowels is slightly different from that used by Seidenberg and McClelland (1989). Also, the representations differ slightly from those used by Plaut and McClelland (1993; Seidenberg, Plaut, Petersen, McClelland, & McRae, 1994). In particular, /C/ and /j/ have been added for /tS/ and /dZ/, the ordering of phonemes is somewhat different, the mutually exclusive phoneme sets have been added, and the consonantal graphemes U, GU, and QU have been eliminated. These changes capture the relevant phonotactic constraints better and simplify the encoding procedure for converting letter strings into activity patterns over grapheme units.
a. /a/ in POT, /@/ in CAT, /e/ in BED, /i/ in HIT, /o/ in DOG, /u/ in GOOD, /A/ in MAKE, /E/ in KEEP, /I/ in BIKE, /O/ in HOPE, /U/ in BOOT, /W/ in NOW, /Y/ in BOY, /^/ in CUP, /N/ in RING, /S/ in SHE, /C/ in CHIN /Z/ in BEIGE, /T/ in THIN, /D/ in THIS. All other phonemes are represented in the conventional way (e.g., /b/ in BAT). The groupings indicate sets of mutually exclusive phonemes.

phonemes are present in each cluster—the phonotactic constraints uniquely determine the order in which these phonemes occur.

The necessary phonotactic constraints can be expressed simply by grouping phonemes into mutually exclusive sets and ordering these sets from left to right in accordance with the left-to-right ordering constraints within consonant clusters. Once this is done, reading out a pronunciation involves simply concatenating the phonemes that are active in sequence from left to right, including at most one phoneme per mutually exclusive set (see Table 23.2).

There are a few cases in which two phonemes can occur in either order within a consonant cluster (e.g., /p/ and /s/ in CLASP and LAPSE). To handle such cases, it is necessary to add units to disambiguate the order (e.g., /ps/). The convention is that if /s/ and /p/ are both active, they are taken in that order unless the /ps/ unit is active, in which case the order is reversed. To cover the pronunciations in the SM89 corpus, only three such units are required: /ps/, /ks/, and /ts/. Interestingly, these combinations are sometimes written with single letters (e.g., English x, German z) and are closely related to other stop-fricative combinations, such as /C/ (/tS/) and /j/ (/dZ/), that are typically considered to be single phonemes called *affricates*. If fact, /ts/ is often treated as an affricate and, across languages, is among the most common (see Maddieson, 1984), and postvocalic /ps/ and /ks/ behave similarly to affricates (Lass, 1984).

This representational scheme applies almost as well to orthography as it does to phonology because English is an alphabetic language (i.e., parts of the written form of a word correspond to parts of its spoken form). However, the spelling units that correspond to phonemes are not necessarily single letters. Rather, they are what Venezky (1970) termed *relational units*, sometimes called graphemes, that can consist of from one to four letters (e.g., L, TH, TCH, EIGH). Because the spelling–sound regularities of English are primarily grapheme–phoneme correspondences, the regularities in the system are captured most elegantly if the orthographic units represent the graphemes present in the string rather than simply the letters that make up the word.

Unfortunately, it is not always clear what graphemes are present in a word. Consider the word SHEPHERD. In this case, there is a P next to an H, so we might suppose that the word contains a PH grapheme, but in fact it does not; if it did it would be pronounced "she-ferd." It is apparent that the input is ambiguous in such cases. Because of this, there is no simple procedure for translating letter strings into the correct sequence of graphemes. It is, however, completely straightforward to translate a letter sequence into a pattern of activity representing all possible graphemes in the string. Thus, whenever a multiletter grapheme is present, its components are also activated. This procedure is also consistent with the treatment of /ps/, /ks/, and /ts/ in phonology.

To this point, the orthographic and phonological representations have been motivated purely by computational considerations: to condense spelling–sound regularities in order to improve generalization. Before turning to the simulations, however, it is important to be clear about the empirical assumptions that are implicit in the use of these representations. Certainly, a full account of reading behavior would have to include a specification of how the representations themselves develop prior to and during the course of reading acquisition. Such a demonstration is beyond the scope of the current work. In fact, unless we are to model everything from the eye to the mouth, we cannot avoid making assumptions about the reading system's inputs and outputs, even though, in actuality, these are learned, internal representations. The best we can do is ensure that these representations are at least broadly consistent with the relevant developmental and behavioral data.

The relevant assumptions about the phonological representations are that they are segmental (i.e., they are composed of phonemes) and that they are strongly constrained by phonotactics. We presume that this phonological structure is learned, for the most part, prior to reading acquisition, on the basis of speech comprehension and production. This is not to deny that phonological representations may become further refined over the course of reading acquisition, particularly under the influence of explicit phoneme-based instruction (see, e.g., Morais, Bertelson, Cary, & Alegria, 1986; Morais, Cary, Alegria, & Bertelson, 1979). For simplicity, however, our modeling work uses fully developed phonological representations from the outset of training.

Analogous assumptions apply with regard to the orthographic representations. We assume that they are based on letters and letter combinations and that the ordering of these obeys graphotactic constraints (although in English such constraints are generally weaker than those in phonology). Although these properties are not particularly controversial per se, orthographic representations must develop concurrently with reading acquisition. Thus, the use of fully articulated orthographic representations from the outset of reading acquisition is certainly suspect.

Again, a complete account of how orthographic representations develop from more primitive visual representations is beyond the scope of the current work. Here we provide only a general characterization of such an account. We suppose that children first learn visual representations for individual letters, perhaps much like those of other visual objects. In learning to read, they are exposed to words that consist of these familiar letters in various combinations. Explicit representations gradually develop for letter combinations that occur often or have unusual consequences (see Mozer, 1990). In the context of oral reading, many of these combinations are precisely those whose pronunciations are not predicted by their components (e.g., TH, PH), corresponding to Venezky's (1970) relational units. Of course, explicit representations may develop for other, regularly pronounced letter combinations. In the limit, the orthographic representation might contain all the letter combinations that occur in the language. Expanding our orthographic representation with multiletter units for all of these additional combinations would have little consequence because there would be little pressure for the network to learn anything about them, given that the correspondences of their components are already learned. In this way, the particular set of multiletter graphemes we use can be viewed as an efficient simplification of a more general orthographic representation that would be expected to develop through exposure to letter combinations in words.

To be clear, we do not claim that the orthographic and phonological representations we use are fully general. Some of their idiosyncrasies stem from the fact that their design took into account specific aspects of the SM89 corpus. Nonetheless, we do claim that the principles on which the representations were derived—in particular, the use of phonotactic and graphotactic constraints to condense spelling–sound regularities—are general.

Simulation 1: Feedforward Network

The first simulation was intended to test the hypothesis that the use of representations that condensed the regularities between orthography and phonology would improve the nonword reading performance of a network trained on the SM89 corpus of monosyllabic words. Specifically, the issue is whether a single mechanism, in the form of a connectionist network, can learn to read a reasonably large corpus of words, including many exception words, and yet also read

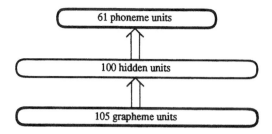

Figure 23.3
The architecture of the feedforward network. Ovals represent groups of units, and arrows represent complete connectivity from one group to another.

pronounceable nonwords as well as skilled readers. If such a network can be developed, it would undermine the claims of dual-route theorists that skilled word reading requires the separation of lexical and sublexical procedures for mapping print to sound.

Method

Network Architecture   The architecture of the network, shown in Figure 23.3, consisted of three layers of units. The input layer of the network contained 105 *grapheme* units, one for each grapheme in Table 23.2. Similarly, the output layer contained 61 *phoneme* units. Between these two layers was an intermediate layer of 100 *hidden* units. Each unit j had a real-valued activity level or state, s_j, that ranged between 0 and 1 and was a smooth, nonlinear (logistic) function, $\sigma(\cdot)$, of the unit's total input, x_j.

$$x_j = \sum_i s_i w_{ij} + b_j \tag{1}$$

and

$$s_j = \sigma(x_j) = \frac{1}{1 + \exp(-x_j)}, \tag{2}$$

where w_{ij} is the weight from unit i to unit j, b_j is the real-valued *bias* of unit j, and $\exp(\cdot)$ is the exponential function.

Each hidden unit received a connection from each grapheme unit and in turn sent a connection to each phoneme unit. In contrast to the Seidenberg and McClelland (1989) network, the grapheme units did not receive connections back from the hidden units. Thus, the network mapped only from orthography to phonology, not also from orthography to orthography (also see Phillips, Hay, & Smith, 1993). Weights on connections were initialized to small, random values, uniformly distributed between ±0.1. The bias terms for the hidden and phoneme units can be thought of as the weight on an additional connection from a unit whose state was always 1.0 (and so could be learned in the same way as other connection weights). Including biases, the network had a total of 17,061 connections.

Training Procedure   The training corpus consisted of the 2,897 monosyllabic words in the SM89 corpus, augmented by 101 monosyllabic words missing from that corpus but used as word stimuli in various empirical studies, for a total of 2,998 words.[4] Among these were 13 sets of homographs (e.g., READ ⇒ /rEd/ and READ ⇒ /red/)—for these, both pronunciations were included in the corpus. Most of the words were uninflected, although there were a few inflected forms that had been used in some empirical studies (e.g., ROLLED, DAYS). Although the orthographic and phonological representations are not intended to handle inflected monosyllables, they happen to be capable of representing those in the training corpus, and so these were left in. It should be kept in mind, however, that the network's exposure to inflected forms was extremely impoverished relative to that of skilled readers.

A letter string was presented to the network by clamping the states of the grapheme units representing graphemes contained in the string to 1, and the states of all other grapheme units to 0. In processing the input, hidden units computed their states based on those of the grapheme units and the weights on connections from them (according to Equations 1 and 2), and then phoneme units computed their states based on those of the hidden units. The resulting pattern of activity over the phoneme units represented the network's pronunciation of the input letter string.

After each word was processed by the network during training, backpropagation (Rumelhart et al., 1986a, 1986b) was used to calculate how to change the connection weights so as to reduce the discrepancy between the pattern of phoneme activity generated by the network and the correct pattern for the word (i.e., the derivative of the error with respect to each weight). A standard measure of this discrepancy, and the one used by SM89, is the summed squared error, E, between the generated and correct output (phoneme) states:

$$E = \sum_i (s_i - t_i)^2, \tag{3}$$

where s_i is the state of phoneme unit i and t_i is its correct (target) value. However, in the new representation of phonology, each unit can be interpreted as an independent hypothesis that a particular phoneme is present in the output pronunciation.[5] In this case, a more appropriate error measure is the *cross-entropy*, C, between the generated and correct activity patterns (see Hinton, 1989; Rumelhart, Durbin, Golden, & Chauvin, 1995), which is also termed the *asymmetric divergence* or the *Kullback–Leibler distance* (Kullback & Leibler, 1951):

$$C = -\sum_i t_i \log_2(s_i) + (1 - t_t) \log_2(1 - s_i). \tag{4}$$

Notice that the contribution to cross-entropy of a given unit i is simply $-\log_2(s_i)$ if its target is 1 and $-\log_2(1 - s_i)$ if its target is 0. From a practical point of view, cross-entropy has an advantage over summed squared error when it comes to correcting output units that are completely incorrect (i.e., on the opposite flat portion of the logistic function). This is a particular concern in tasks in which output units are off for most inputs—the network can eliminate almost all of its error on the task by turning all of the output units off regardless of the input, including those few that should be on for this input. The problem is that when a unit's state falls on a flat portion of the logistic function, very large weight changes are required to change its state substantially. As a unit's state diverges from its target, the change in cross-entropy increases much faster than the change in summed squared error (exponentially vs. linearly) so that cross-entropy is better able to generate sufficiently large weight changes.[6]

During training, we also gave weights a slight tendency to decay toward zero by augmenting the cross-entropy error function with a term proportional (with a constant of 0.0001 in the current simulation) to the sum of the squares of each weight, $\sum_{i<j} w_{ij}^2$. Although not critical, weight decay tends to aid generalization by constraining weights to grow only to the extent that they are needed to reduce the error on the task (Hinton, 1989).

In the SM89 simulation, the probability that a word was presented to the network for training during an epoch was a logarithmic function of its written frequency (Kučera & Francis, 1967). In the current simulation, we used the same compressed frequency values instead to scale the error derivatives calculated by back-propagation. This manipulation had essentially the same effect: More frequent words had a stronger impact than less frequent words on the knowledge learned by the system. In fact, using frequencies in this manner is exactly equivalent to updating the weights after each sweep through an expanded training corpus in which the number of times a word is presented is proportional to its (compressed) frequency. The new procedure was adopted for two reasons. First, by presenting the entire training corpus every epoch, learning rates on each connection could be adapted independently (Jacobs, 1988; but see Sutton, 1992, for a recently developed on-line version).[7] Second, by implementing frequencies with multiplication rather than sampling, we could use any range of frequencies; later, we will investigate the effects of using the actual Kučera and Francis (1967) frequencies in simulations. SM89 was constrained to use a logarithmic compression because less severe compressions would have meant that the lowest frequency words might never have been presented to their network.

The actual weight changes administered at the end of an epoch were a combination of the accumulated frequency-weighted error derivatives and a proportion of the previous weight changes:

$$\Delta w_{ij}^{[t]} = \varepsilon\varepsilon_{ij}\left(\frac{\partial C}{\partial w_{ij}} + \alpha\Delta w_{ij}^{[t-1]}\right), \tag{5}$$

where t is the epoch number, ε is the global learning rate (0.001 in the current simulation), ε_{ij} is the connection-specific learning rate, C is the cross-entropy error function with weight decay, and α is the contribution of past weight changes, sometimes termed *momentum* (0.9 after the first 10 epochs in the current simulation). We introduced momentum only after the first few initial epochs to avoid magnifying the effects of the initial weight gradients, which were very large because, for each word, any activity of all but a few phoneme units—those that should be active—produced a large amount of error (Plaut & Hinton, 1987).

Testing Procedure   The network, as described above, learned to take activity patterns over the grapheme units and produce corresponding activity patterns over the phoneme units. The behavior of human readers, however, is better described in terms of producing phoneme strings in response to letter strings. Accordingly, for a direct comparison of the network's behavior with that of human readers, we needed one procedure for encoding letter strings as activity patterns over the grapheme units and another procedure for decoding activity patterns over the phoneme units into phoneme strings.

The encoding procedure we used was the same one that generated the input to the network for each word in the training corpus. To convert a letter string into an activity pattern over the grapheme units, the string is parsed into onset consonant cluster, vowel, and final (coda) consonant cluster. This involved simply locating in the string the leftmost contiguous block composed of the letters A, E, I, O, U, or (non-initial) Y. This block of letters was encoded using vowel graphemes listed in Table 23.2—any grapheme contained in the vowel substring was activated; all others were left inactive. The substrings to the right and left of the vowel substring were encoded similarly using the onset and coda consonant graphemes, respectively. For example, the word SCHOOL activated the onset units S, C, H, and CH, the vowel units O and OO, and the coda unit L. Notice that in words like GUEST, QUEEN, and SUEDE, the U is parsed as a vowel although it functions as a consonant (cf. GUST, QUEUE, and SUE; Venezky, 1970). This is much like the issue with PH in SHEPHERD—such ambiguity was left for the network to cope with. The analogous encoding procedure for phonemes used to generate the training patterns for words was even simpler because monosyllabic pronunciations must contain exactly one vowel.

The decoding procedure for producing pronunciations from phoneme activities generated by the network was likewise straightforward. As shown in Table 23.2, phonemes are grouped into mutually exclusive sets, and these sets are ordered left to right (and top to bottom in the table). This grouping and ordering encode the phonotactic constraints that are necessary to disambiguate pronunciations. The response of the network was simply the ordered concatenation of all active phonemes (i.e., with state above 0.5) that were the most active in their set. There were only two exceptions to this rule. The first was that, because monosyllabic pronunciations must contain a vowel, the most active vowel was included in the network's response regardless of its activity level. The second exception relates to the affricate-like units /ps/, /ks/, and /ts/. As described earlier, if one of these units was active along with its components, the order of those components in the response was reversed.

The simplicity of these encoding and decoding procedures is a significant advantage of the current representations over those used by SM89. In the latter case, reconstructing a unique string of phonemes corresponding to a pattern of activity over triples of phonemic features is exceedingly difficult, and sometimes impossible (also see Mozer, 1991; Rumelhart & McClelland, 1986). In fact, SM89 did not confront this problem—rather, they simply selected the best among a set of alternative pronunciations on the basis of their error scores. In a sense, the SM89 model does not produce explicit pronunciations; it enables another procedure to select among alternatives. In contrast, the current decoding procedure does not require externally generated alternatives. Every possible pattern of activity over the phoneme units corresponds directly and unambiguously to a particular string of phonemes. Nonetheless, it should be kept in mind that the encoding and decoding procedures are external to the network and hence, constitute additional assumptions about the nature of the knowledge and processing involved in skilled reading, as discussed earlier.

Results

Word Reading   After 300 epochs of training, the network correctly pronounced all of the 2,972 nonhomographic words in the training corpus. For each of the 13 homographs, the network produced one of the correct pronunciations, although typically the competing phonemes for the alternatives were about equally active. For example, the network pronounced LEAD as /lEd/; the activation of the /E/ was 0.56, whereas the activation of /e/ was 0.44. These differences reflect the relative consistency of the alternatives with the pronunciations of other words.

Given the nature of the network, this level of performance on the training corpus is optimal. Because the network is deterministic, it always produces the same output for a given input. Thus, in fact, it is impossible for the network to learn to produce both pronunciations of any of the homographs. Note that this determinacy is not an intrinsic limitation of connectionist networks (see, e.g., Movellan & McClelland, 1993). It merely reflects the fact that the general principle of intrinsic variability was not included in the present simulation for practical reasons—to keep the computational demands of the simulation reasonable.

For the present purposes, the important finding is that the trained network reads both regular and exception words correctly. We were also interested in how well the network replicates the effects of frequency and consistency on naming latency. However, we will return to this issue after we consider the more pressing issue of the network's performance in reading nonwords.

Nonword Reading   We tested the network on three lists of nonwords from two empirical studies. The first two lists came from an experiment by Glushko (1979), in which he compared subjects' reading of 43 nonwords derived from regular words (e.g., HEAN from DEAN) with their reading of 43 nonwords derived from exception words (e.g., HEAF from DEAF). Although Glushko originally termed these *regular* nonwords and *exception* nonwords, respectively, they are more appropriately characterized in terms of whether their body neighborhood is consistent or not, and hence we will refer to them as *consistent* or *inconsistent* nonwords. The third nonword list came from a study by McCann and Besner (1987) in which they compared performance on a set of 80 pseudo-homophones (e.g., BRANE) with a set of 80 control nonwords (e.g., FRANE). We used only their control nonwords in the present investigation because we believe pseudohomophone effects are mediated by aspects of the reading system, such as semantics and the articulatory system, that were not implemented in our simulation (see the General Discussion).

As nonwords are, by definition, novel stimuli, exactly what constitutes the "correct" pronunciation of a nonword is a matter of considerable debate (see, e.g., Masterson, 1985; Seidenberg et al., 1994). The complexity of this issue will become apparent momentarily. For the purposes of an initial comparison, we considered the pronunciation of a nonword to be correct if it was regular, as defined by adhering to the GPC rules outlined by Venezky (1970).

Table 23.3 presents the correct performance of skilled readers reported by Glushko (1979) and by McCann and Besner (1987) on their nonword lists and the corresponding performance of the network. Table 23.4 lists the errors made by the network on these lists.

First consider Glushko's (1979) consistent nonwords. The network made only a single minor mistake on these items, just failing to introduce the transitional /y/ in MUNE. In fact, this inclusion varies across dialects of English (e.g.,

Table 23.3
Percentages of regular pronunciations of nonwords

| Reader | Glushko (1979) | | McCann and Besner (1987) |
	Consistent nonwords	Inconsistent nonwords	Control nonwords
Humans	93.8	78.3	88.6
Network	97.7	72.1	85.0

Table 23.4
Errors by the feedforward network in pronouncing nonwords

Glushko (1979)			McCann and Besner (1987)		
Nonword	Correct	Response	Nonword	Correct	Response
Consistent nonwords (1/43)			Control nonwords (12/80)		
MUNE	/myUn/	/m(y 0.43)Un/	*PHOYCE	/fYs/	/(f 0.42)Y(s 0.00)/
Inconsistent nonwords (12/43)			*TOLPH	/tolf/	/tOl(f 0.12)/
BILD	/bild/	/bIld	*ZUPE	/zUp/	/zyUp/
BOST	/bost/	/bOst/	SNOCKS	/snaks/	/snask(ks 0.31)/
COSE	/kOz/	/kOs/	*LOKES	/lOks/	/lOsk(ks 0.02)/
GROOK	/grUk/	/gruk/	*YOWND	/yWnd/	/(y 0.47)and/
LOME	/lOm/	/l∧m/	KOWT	/kWt/	/kOt/
MONE	/mOn/	/m∧n/	FAIJE	/fAj/	/fA(j 0.00)/
PILD	/pild/	/pIld/	*ZUTE	/zUt/	/zyUt/
PLOVE	/plOv/	/pl∧v/	*VEEZE	/vEz/	(v 0.40)Ez/
POOT	/pUt/	/put/	*PRAX	/pr@ks/	/pr@sk(ks 0.33)/
SOOD	/sUd/	/sud/	JINJE	/jinj/	/jIn(j 0.00)/
SOST	/sost/	/s∧st/			
WEAD	/wEd/	/wed/			

Note. /a/ in POT, /@/ in CAT, /e/ in BED, /i/ in HIT, /o/ in DOG, /u/ in GOOD, /A/ in MAKE, /E/ in KEEP, /I/ in BIKE, /O/ in HOPE, /U/ in BOOT, /W/ in NOW, /Y/ in BOY, /∧/ in CUP, /N/ in RING, /S/ in SHE, /C/ in CHIN, /Z/ in BEIGE, /T/ in THIN, /D/ in THIS. The activity levels of correct but missing phonemes are listed in parentheses. In these cases, the actual response is what falls outside the parentheses. Words marked with "*" remain errors after properties of the training corpus are considered (as explained in the text).

DUNE ⇒ /dUn/ vs. /dyUn/). In the training corpus, the four words ending in _UNE (DUNE, JUNE, PRUNE, TUNE) are all coded without the /y/. In any case, overall both the network and human readers have no difficulty on these relatively easy nonwords.

The situation is rather different for the inconsistent nonwords. Both the network and the human readers produced nonregular pronunciations for a significant subset of these items, with the network being slightly more prone to do so. However, a closer examination of the responses in these cases reveals why. Consider the nonword GROOK. The grapheme OO most frequently corresponds to /U/, as in BOOT, and so the correct (regular) pronunciation of GROOK is /grUk/. However, the body _OOK is almost always pronounced /u/, as in TOOK. The only exception to this among the 12 words ending in _OOK in the training corpus is SPOOK ⇒ /spUk/. This suggests that /gruk/ should be the correct pronunciation.

Actually, the issue of whether the network's pronunciation is correct or not is less relevant than the issue of whether the network behaves similarly to human readers. In fact, both the human readers and the network were sensitive to the context in which vowels occur, as is evidenced by their much greater tendency to produce irregular pronunciations for inconsistent nonwords compared with consistent nonwords. Glushko (1979) found that 80% of readers' irregular responses to inconsistent nonwords were consistent with some other pronunciation of the nonword's body in the Kuçera and Francis (1967) corpus, which left only 4.1% of all responses as actual errors. In the network, all of the irregular responses to inconsistent nonwords matched some other pronunciation in the training corpus for the same body, with half of these being the most frequent pronunciation of the body. None of the network's responses to inconsistent nonwords were actual errors. Overall, the network performed as well if not slightly better than skilled readers on the Glushko nonword lists.

Both the human readers and the network found McCann and Besner's (1987) control nonwords more difficult to pronounce, which is not surprising because the list contains a number of orthographically unusual nonwords (e.g., JINJE, VAWX). Overall, the network's performance was slightly worse than that of the human readers. However, many of the network's errors can be understood in terms of specific properties of the training corpus and network design. First, although there is no word in the training corpus with the body _OWT, medial ow is often pronounced /O/ (e.g., BOWL ⇒ /bOl/) and so KOWT ⇒ /kOt/ should be considered a reasonable response. Second, two of the errors were on inflected forms, SNOCKS and LOKES, and as previously acknowledged, the network had minimal experience with inflections and was not designed to apply to them. Finally, there are no instances in the training corpus of words containing the grapheme J in the coda, and so the network could not possible have learned to map it to /j/ in phonology. In a way, for a nonword like JINJE, the effective input to the network is JINE, to which the network's response /jIn/ is correct. This also applies to the nonword FAIJE. Excluding these and the inflected forms from the scoring, and considering KOWT ⇒ /kOt/ correct, the network performed correctly on 69/76 (90.8%) of the remaining control nonwords, which is slightly better than the human readers. Most of the remaining errors of the network involved correspondences that were infrequent or variable in the training corpus (e.g., PH ⇒ /f/, U ⇒ /yU/).

It must be acknowledged that the failure of the model on inflected forms and on those with J in the coda are real shortcomings that would have to be addressed in a completely adequate account of word reading. Our purpose in separating out these items in the above analysis simply acknowledges that the model's limitations are easily understood in terms of specific properties of the training corpus.

Is it a Dual-Route Model?   One possibility, consistent with dual-route theories, is that, over the course of learning the network partitioned itself into two subnetworks, one that reads regular words and another that reads exception

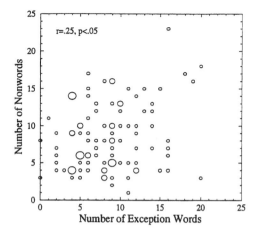

Figure 23.4
The numbers of exception words and nonwords ($n = 48$ for each) to which each hidden unit makes a significant contribution, as indicated by an increase in cross-entrophy error of at least 0.2 when the unit is removed from the network. Each circle represents one or more hidden units making significant contributions to the indicated numbers of exception words and nonwords.

words. If this were the case, some hidden units would contribute to exception words but not to nonwords, whereas others would contribute to nonwords but not to exception words. To test this possibility, we measured the contribution a hidden unit makes to pronouncing a letter string by the amount of increase in cross-entropy error when the unit is removed from the network. If the network had partitioned itself, there would be a negative correlation across hidden units between the number of exception words and the number of nonwords to which each hidden unit makes a substantial contribution (defined as greater than 0.2). In fact, for the Taraban and McClelland (1987) exception words and a set of orthographically matched nonwords (listed in Appendix A), there was a moderate positive correlation between the numbers of exception words and nonwords to which hidden units contributed, $r = .25$, $t(98) = 2.59$, $p = .011$ (see Figure 23.4). Thus, some units were more important for the overall task and some were less important, but the network had not partitioned itself into one system that learned the rules and another system that learned the exceptions.

Frequency and Consistency Effects   It is important to verify that in addition to producing good nonword reading, the new model replicates the basic effects of frequency and consistency in naming latency. Like the SM89 network, the current network takes the same amount of time to compute the pronunciation of any letter string. Hence, we must also resort to using an error score as an analogue of naming latency. In particular, we used the cross-entropy between the

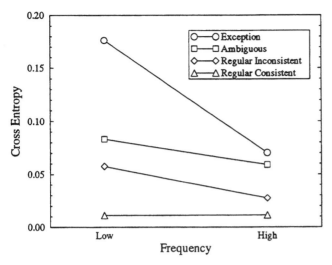

Figure 23.5
Mean cross-entrophy error produced by the feedforward network for words with various degrees of spelling-sound consistency as a function of frequency.

network's generated pronunciation of a word and its correct pronunciation, because this is the measure that the network was trained to minimize. Later we examine the effects of frequency and consistency directly in the settling time of an equivalently trained recurrent network when pronouncing various types of words.

Figure 23.5 shows the mean cross-entropy error of the network in pronouncing words of varying degrees of spelling–sound consistency as a function of frequency. Overall, high-frequency words produced less error than low-frequency words, $F(1, 184) = 17.1$, $p < .001$. However, frequency interacted significantly with consistency, $F(3, 184) = 5.65$, $p = .001$. Post hoc comparisons within each word type separately revealed that the effect of frequency reached significance at the .05 level only for exception words (although the effect for regular inconsistent words was significant at .053). The effect of frequency among all regular words (consistent and inconsistent) just failed to reach significance, $F(1, 94) = 3.14$, $p = .08$.

There was also a main effect of consistency in the error made by the network in pronouncing words, $F(3, 184) = 24.1$, $p < .001$. Furthermore, collapsed across frequency, all post hoc pairwise comparisons of word types were significant. Specifically, regular consistent words produced less error than regular inconsistent words, which in turn produced less error than ambiguous words, which in turn produced less error than exception words. Interestingly, the effect of consistency was significant when only high-frequency words are considered,

$F(3, 92) = 12.3$, $p < .001$. All pairwise comparisons were also significant except between exception words and ambiguous words. This contrasts with the performance of normal human readers, who typically show little or no effect of consistency among high-frequency words (e.g., Seidenberg, 1985; Seidenberg et al., 1984).

Summary

A feedforward connectionist network, which used orthographic and phonological representations that condense the regularities between these domains, was trained on an extended version of the SM89 corpus of monosyllabic words. After training, the network read regular and exception words flawlessly and yet also read pronounceable nonwords (Glushko, 1979; McCann & Besner, 1987) essentially as well as skilled readers. Minor discrepancies in performance could be ascribed to nonessential aspects of the simulation. Critically, the network did not segregate itself over the course of training into separate mechanisms for pronouncing exception words and nonwords. Thus, the performance of the network directly refutes the claims of dual-route theorists that skilled word reading requires the separation of lexical and sublexical procedures for mapping print to sound.

Furthermore, the error produced by the network on various types of words, as measured by the cross-entropy between the generated and correct pronunciations, replicates the standard findings of frequency, consistency, and their interaction in the naming latencies of human readers (Andrews, 1982; Seidenberg, 1985; Seidenberg et al., 1984; Taraban & McClelland, 1987; Waters & Seidenberg, 1985). A notable exception, however, is that, unlike human readers and the SM89 network, the current network exhibited a significant effect of consistency among high-frequency words.

Simulation 3: Interactivity, Componential Attractors, and Generalization

As outlined earlier, the current approach to lexical processing is based on a number of general principles of information processing, loosely expressed by the acronym GRAIN (for Graded, Random, Adaptive, Interactive, and Nonlinear). Together with the principles of distributed representations and knowledge, the approach constitutes a substantial departure from traditional assumptions about the nature of language knowledge and processing (e.g., Pinker, 1991). It must be noted, however, that the simulations presented so far involve only deterministic, feedforward networks and thus fail to incorporate two important principles: interactivity and randomness (intrinsic variability). In part, this simplification has been necessary for practical reasons: Interactive, stochastic simulations are far more demanding of computational resources. More important, including only some of the relevant principles in a given simulation enables more detailed analysis of the specific contribution that each makes to the overall behavior of the system. This has been illustrated most clearly in the current work with regard to the nature of the distributed representations used for orthography and phonology and the relative influences of frequency and consistency on network learning (adaptivity). Nonetheless, each such network constitutes only an approximation or abstraction of a more complete simulation that would incorporate all of the principles. The methodology of considering sets of principles separately relies on the assumption that there are no unforeseen, problematic interactions among the principles such that the findings with simplified simulations would not generalize to more comprehensive ones.

The current simulation investigates the implications of interactivity for the process of pronouncing written words and nonwords. Interactivity plays an important role in connectionist explanations of a number of cognitive phenomena (McClelland, 1987; McClelland & Elman, 1986; McClelland & Rumelhart, 1981) and constitutes a major point of contention with alternative theoretical formulations (Massaro, 1988, 1989). Processing in a network is interactive when units can mutually constrain each other in settling on the most consistent interpretation of the input. For this to be possible, the architecture of the network must be generalized to allow feedback or *recurrent* connections among units. For example, in the interactive activation model of letter and word perception (McClelland & Rumelhart, 1981; Rumelhart & McClelland, 1982), letter units and word units are bidirectionally connected so that the partial activation of a word unit can feed back to support the activation of letter units with which it is consistent.

A common way in which interactivity has been used in networks is in making particular patterns of activity into stable *attractors*. In an attractor network, units interact and update their states repeatedly in such a way that the initial pattern of activity generated by an input gradually settles to the nearest attractor pattern. A useful way of conceptualizing this process is in terms of a multidimensional *state space* in which the activity of each unit is plotted along a separate dimension. At any instant in time, the pattern of activity over all of the units corresponds to a single point in this space. As units change their states in response to a given input, this point moves in state space, eventually arriving at the point (attractor) corresponding to the network's interpretation. The set of initial patterns that settle to this same final pattern corresponds to a region around the attractor, called its *basin* of attraction. To solve a task, the network must learn connection weights that cause units to interact in such a way that the appropriate interpretation of each input is an attractor whose basin contains the initial pattern of activity for that input.

In the domain of word reading, attractors have played a critical role in connectionist accounts of the nature of normal and impaired reading via meaning

(Hinton & Sejnowski, 1986; Hinton & Shallice, 1991; Plaut & Shallice, 1993). According to these accounts, the meanings of words are represented in terms of patterns of activity over a large number of semantic features. These features can support structured, frame-like representations (e.g., Minsky, 1975) if units represent conjunctions of roles and properties of role fillers (Derthick, 1990; Hinton, 1981). Because only a small fraction of the possible combinations of features correspond to the meanings of actual words, it is natural for a network to learn to make these semantic patterns into attractors. Then, in deriving the meaning of a word from its orthography, the network need only generate an initial pattern of activity that falls somewhere within the appropriate semantic attractor basin; if so, the settling process will clean up this pattern into the exact meaning of the word.[8] If, however, the system is damaged, the initial activity for a word may fall within a neighboring attractor basin, typically corresponding to a semantically-related word. The damaged network will then settle to the exact meaning of that word, resulting in a semantic error (e.g., CAT read as "dog"). In fact, the occurrence of such errors is the hallmark symptom of a type of acquired reading disorder known as *deep dyslexia* (see Coltheart, Patterson, & Marshall, 1980, for more details on the full range of symptoms of deep dyslexia, and Plaut & Shallice, 1993, for connectionist simulations replicating these symptoms). In this way, attractors obviate the need for word-specific units in mediating between orthography and semantics (see Hinton, McClelland, & Rumelhart, 1986, for discussion).

When applied to the mapping from orthography to phonology, however, the use of interactivity to form attractors appears problematic. In particular, the correct pronunciation of a nonword typically does not correspond to the pronunciation of some word. If the network develops attractors for word pronunciations, one might expect that the input for a nonword would often be captured within the attractor basin for a similar word, resulting in many incorrect *lexicalizations*. More generally, attractors seem to be appropriate only for tasks, such as semantic categorization or object recognition, in which the correct response to a novel input is a familiar output. By contrast, in oral reading, the correct response to a novel input is typically a novel output. If it is true that attractors cannot support this latter sort of generalization, their applicability in reading specifically, and cognitive science more generally, would be fundamentally limited.

The current simulation demonstrates that these concerns are ill-founded and that, with appropriately structured representations, the principle of interactivity can operate effectively in the phonological pathway as well as in the semantic pathway (see Figure 23.1). The reason is that, in learning to map orthography to phonology, the network develops attractors that are *componential*—they have substructure that reflects common sublexical correspondences between orthography and phonology. This substructure applies not only to most words but also to nonwords, enabling them to be pronounced correctly. At the same time, the network develops attractors for exception words that are far less componential. Thus, rather than being a hindrance, attractors are a particularly effective style of computation for quasi-regular tasks such as word reading.

A further advantage of an attractor network over a feedforward network in modeling word reading is that the former provides a more direct analogue of naming latency. Thus far, we have followed SM89 in using an error measure in a feedforward network to account for naming latency data from skilled readers. SM89 offered two justifications for this approach. The first is based on the assumption that the accuracy of the phonological representation of a word would directly influence the execution speed of the corresponding articulatory motor program (see Lacouture, 1989, and Zorzi, Houghton, & Butterworth, 1995, for simulations embodying this assumption). This assumption is consistent with the view that the time required by the orthography-to-phonology computation itself does not vary systematically with word frequency or spelling–sound consistency. If this were the case, a feedforward network of the sort SM89 and we have used, which takes the same amount of time to process any input, would be a reasonable rendition of the nature of the phonological pathway in skilled readers.

An alternative justification for the use of error scores to model naming latencies, mentioned only briefly by SM89, is based on the view that the actual computation from orthography to phonology involves interactive processing such that the time to settle on an appropriate phonological representation does vary systematically with word type. The naming latencies exhibited by skilled readers are a function of this settling time, perhaps in conjunction with articulatory effects. Accordingly, a feedforward implementation of the mapping from orthography to phonology should be viewed as an abstraction of a recurrent implementation that would more accurately approximate the actual word reading system. Studying the feedforward implementation is still informative because many of its properties, including its sensitivity to frequency and consistency, depend on computational principles of operation that would also apply to a recurrent implementation—namely, adaptivity, distributed representations and knowledge, and nonlinearity. These principles merely manifest themselves differently: Influences that reduce error in a feedforward network serve to accelerate settling in a recurrent network. Thus, error in a feedforward network is a valid approximation of settling time in a recurrent network because they both arise from the same underlying causes; namely, additive frequency and consistency effects in the context of a nonlinear gradual ceiling effect. Nonetheless, even given these arguments, it is important to verify that a recurrent implementation that reads words and nonwords as accurately as skilled readers also reproduces the relevant empirical pattern of naming latencies directly in the time it takes to settle in pronouncing words.

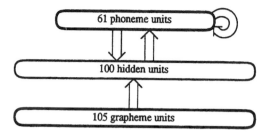

Figure 23.6
The architecture of the attractor network. Ovals represent groups of units, and arrows represent complete connectivity from one group to another.

Method

Network Architecture   The architecture of the attractor network is shown in Figure 23.6. The numbers of grapheme, hidden, and phoneme units were the same as in the feedforward networks, but the attractor network had some additional sets of connections. Each input unit was still connected to each hidden unit, which, in turn, was connected to each phoneme unit. In addition, each phoneme unit was connected to each other phoneme unit (including itself), and each phoneme unit sent a connection back to each hidden unit. The weights on the two connections between a pair of units (e.g., a hidden unit and a phoneme unit) were trained separately and did not have to have identical values. Including the biases of the hidden and phoneme units, the network had a total of 26,582 connections.

The states of units in the network change smoothly over time in response to influences from other units. In particular, the instantaneous change over time t of the input x_j to unit j is proportional to the difference between its current input and the summed contribution from other units:

$$\frac{dx_j}{dt} = \sum_i s_i w_{ij} + b_j - x_j. \tag{6}$$

The state s_j of unit j is $\sigma(x_j)$, the standard logistic function of its integrated input, which ranges between 0 and 1 (see Equation 2). For clarity, we will call the summed input from other units i (plus the bias) the *external* input to each unit, to distinguish it from the *integrated* input x, that governs the unit's state.

According to Equation 6, when a unit's integrated input is perfectly consistent with its external input (i.e., $x_j = \sum_i s_i w_{ij} + b_j$), the derivative is zero and the unit's integrated input, and hence its state, ceases to change. Notice that its activity at this point, $\sigma(\sum_i s_i w_{ij} + b_j)$, is the same as it would be if it were a standard unit that computes its state from the external input instantaneously (as in a feedforward network; see Equations 1 and 2). To illustrate this, and to provide some sense of the temporal dynamics of units in the network, Figure 23.7 shows the activity over time of a single unit, initialized to 0.5 and governed by Equation 6, in response to external input of various magnitudes. Notice that, over time, the unit state gradually approaches an asymptotic value equal to the logistic function applied to its external input.

For the purposes of simulation on a digital computer, it is convenient to approximate continuous units with finite difference equations in which time is discretized into *ticks* of some duration τ:

$$\Delta x_j = \tau \left(\sum_i s_i w_{ij} + b_j - x_j \right),$$

where $\Delta x_j = x_j^{[t]} - x_j^{[t-\tau]}$. Using explicit superscripts for discrete time, we can rewrite this as

$$x_j^{[t]} = \tau \left(\sum_i s_i^{[t-\tau]} w_{ij} + b_j \right) + (1 - \tau) x_j^{[t-\tau]}. \tag{7}$$

According to this equation, a unit's input at each time tick is a weighted average of its current input and that dictated by other units, where τ is the weighting proportion.[9] Notice that, in the limit (as $\tau \to 0$), this discrete computation becomes identical to the continuous one. Thus, adjustments to τ affect the accuracy with which the discrete system approximates the continuous one but do not alter the underlying computation being performed. This is of considerable practical importance, because the computational time required to simulate the system is inversely proportional to τ. A relatively larger τ can be used during the extensive training period (0.2 in the current simulation), when minimizing computation time is critical, whereas a much smaller τ can be used during testing (e.g., 0.01), when a very accurate approximation is desired. As long as τ remains sufficiently small for the approximations to be adequate, these manipulations do not fundamentally alter the behavior of the system.

Training Procedure   The training corpus for the network was the same as that used with the feedforward network trained on actual word frequencies. As in that simulation, the frequency value of each word was used to scale the weight changes induced by the word.

The network was trained with a version of back-propagation designed for recurrent networks, known as *back-propagation through time* (Rumelhart et al., 1986a, 1986b; Williams & Peng, 1990), and further adapted for continuous units (B. Pearlmutter, 1989). In understanding back-propagation through time, it may help to think of the computation in standard back-propagation in a three-layer feedforward network as occurring over time. In the forward pass, the states of input units are clamped at time $t = 0$. Hidden unit states are computed at $t = 1$ from these input unit states, and then output unit states are computed at $t = 2$ from the hidden unit states. In the backward pass, error is calculated for the output units based on their states ($t = 2$). Error for the hidden units and weight changes for the hidden-to-output connections are calculated based on the error of the output units ($t = 2$) and the states of hidden units ($t = 1$). Finally, the weight changes for the input-to-hidden connections are calculated based on the hidden unit error ($t = 1$) and the input unit states ($t = 0$). Thus, feedforward back-propagation can be interpreted as involving a pass forward in time to compute unit states, followed by a pass backward in time to compute unit error and weight changes.

Back-propagation through time has exactly the same form, except that, because a recurrent network can have arbitrary connectivity, each unit can receive contributions from any unit at any time, not just from those in earlier layers (for the forward pass) or later layers (for the backward pass). This means that each unit must store its state and error at each time tick so that these values are available to other units when needed. In addition, the states of noninput units affect those of other units immediately, so they need to be initialized to some neutral value (0.5 in the current simulation). In all other respects, back-propagation through time is computationally equivalent to feedforward back-propagation. In fact, back-propagation through time can be interpreted as "unfolding" a recurrent network into a much larger feedforward network with a layer for each time tick composed of a separate copy of all the units in the recurrent network (see Minsky & Papert, 1969; Rumelhart et al., 1986a, 1986b).

In order to apply back-propagation through time to continuous units, one must make the propagation of error in the backward pass continuous as well (B. Pearlmutter, 1989). If we use δ_j to designate the derivative of the error with respect to the input of unit j, then, in feedforward back-propagation

$$\delta_j = \frac{\partial C}{\partial s_j} \sigma'(x_j),$$

where C is the cross-entropy error function and $\sigma'(\cdot)$ is the derivative of the logistic function. In the discrete approximation to back-propagation through time with continuous units, this becomes

$$\delta_j^{[t]} = \tau \frac{\partial C}{\partial s_j^{[t+\tau]}} \sigma'(x_j^{[t+\tau]}) + (1 - \tau)\delta_j^{[t+\tau]}.$$

Thus, δ_j is a weighted average backward in time of its current value and the contribution from the current error of the unit. In this way, as in standard back-propagation, δ_j in the backward pass is analogous to x_j in the forward pass (cf. Equation 7).

Because output units can interact with other units over the course of processing a stimulus, they can indirectly affect the error for other output units. As a result, the error for an output unit becomes the sum of two terms: the error that is due to the discrepancy between its own state and its target and the error

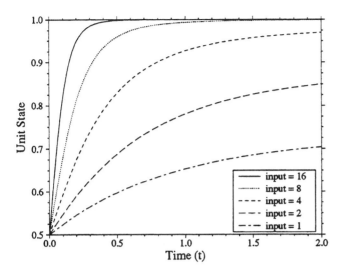

Figure 23.7
This state over time of a continuous unit when presented with fixed external input from other units of various magnitudes. The curves of state values for negative external input are the exact mirror images of these curves, approaching 0 instead of 1.

back-propagated to it from other units. The first term is often referred to as error that is *injected* into the network by the training environment, whereas the second term might be thought of as error that is *internal* to the network.

Given that the states of output units vary over time, they can have targets that specify what states they should be in at particular points in time. Thus, in back-propagation through time, error can be injected at any or all time ticks, not just at the last one as in feedforward backpropagation. Targets that vary over time define a trajectory that the output states will attempt to follow (see B. Pearlmutter, 1989, for a demonstration of this type of learning). If the targets remain constant over time, however, the output units will attempt to reach their targets as quickly as possible and remain there. In the current simulation, we used this technique to train the network to form stable attractors for the pronunciations of words in the training corpus.

It is possible for the states of units to change quickly if they receive a very large summed input from other units (see Figure 23.7). However, even for rather large summed input, units typically require some amount of time to approach an extreme value, and they may never reach it completely. As a result, it is practically impossible for units to achieve targets of 0 or 1 immediately after a stimulus has been presented. For this reason, in the current simulation, a less stringent training regime was adopted. Although the network was run for 2.0 units of time, error was injected only for the second unit of time;

units received no direct pressure to be correct for the first unit of time (although backpropagated internal error caused weight changes that encouraged units to move toward the appropriate states as early as possible). In addition, output units were trained to targets of 0.1 and 0.9 rather than 0 and 1, although no error was injected if a unit exceeded its target (e.g., reached a state of 0.95 for a target of 0.9). This training criterion can be achieved by units with only moderately large summed input (see the curve for input = 4 in Figure 23.7).

As with the feedforward network using actual frequencies, the attractor network was trained with a global learning rate $\varepsilon = 0.05$ (with adaptive connection-specific rates) and momentum $\alpha = 0.9$. Furthermore, as mentioned above, the network was trained using a discretization $\tau = 0.2$. Thus, units updated their states 10 times (2.0/0.2) in the forward pass, and they back-propagated error 10 times in the backward pass. As a result, the computational demands of the simulation were about 10 times that of one of the feedforward simulations. In an attempt to reduce the training time, we increased momentum to 0.98 after 200 epochs. To improve the accuracy of the network's approxima-tion to a continuous system near the end of training, we reduced τ from 0.2 to 0.05 at Epoch 1,800, and reduced it further to 0.01 at Epoch 1,850 for an addi-tional 50 epochs of training. During this final stage of training, each unit updated its state 200 times over the course of processing each input.

Testing Procedure   A fully adequate characterization of response generation in distributed connectionist networks would involve stochastic processing (see McClelland, 1991) and thus is beyond the scope of the present work. As an ap-proximation in a deterministic attractor network, we used a measure of the time it takes the network to compute a stable output in response to a given input. Specifically, the network responds when the average change in the states of the phoneme units falls below some criterion (0.00005 with $\tau = 0.01$ for the results below).[10] At this point, the network's naming latency is the amount of contin-uous time that has passed in processing the input, and its naming response is generated on the basis of the current phoneme states using the same procedure as for the feedforward networks.

Results

Word Reading   After 1,900 epochs of training, the network pronounced cor-rectly all but 25 of the 2,998 words in the training corpus (99.2% correct). About half of these errors were regularizations of low-frequency exception words (e.g., SIEVE ⇒ /sEv/, SUEDE ⇒ /swEd/, and TOW ⇒ /tW/). Most of the remaining errors would be classified as visual errors (e.g., FALL ⇒ /folt/, GORGE ⇒ /grOrj/, and HASP ⇒ /h@ps/), although four merely had consonants that failed to reach threshold (ACHE ⇒ /A/, BEIGE ⇒ /bA/, TZAR ⇒ /ar/, and WOUND ⇒ /Und/). All in all, the network came close to mastering the training corpus, although its performance was slightly worse than that of the equivalent feedforward network.

Even though the network settles to a representation of the phonemes of a word in parallel, the time it takes to do so increases with the length of the word. To demonstrate this, we entered the naming latencies of the network for the 2,973 words it pronounces correctly into a multiple linear regression, using as predictors (a) orthographic length (i.e., number of letters), (b) phonological length (i.e., number of phonemes), (c) logarithmic word frequency, and (d) a measure of spelling–sound consistency equal to the number of friends (including the word itself) divided by the total number of friends and enemies; thus, highly consistent words have values near 1 and exception words have values near 0. Collectively, the four factors accounted for 15.9% of the variance in the latency values, $F(4, 2,968) = 139.92$, $p < .001$. More important, all four factors accounted for significant unique variance after we factored out the other three (9.9%, 5.6%, 0.8%, and 0.1% for consistency, log-frequency, orthographic length, and phonological length, respectively, $p < .05$ for each). In particular, orthographic length was positively correlated with naming latency (semipartial $r = .089$) and accounted uniquely for 0.8% of its variance, $F(1, 2,968) = 40.0$, $p < .001$. To convert this correlation into an increase in reaction time (RT) per letter, we regressed the network's mean RTs for the Taraban and McClelland (1987) high-and low-frequency exception words and their regular consistent controls against the means for skilled readers reported by Taraban and McClelland; this resulted in a scaling of 188.5 ms per unit of simulation time (with an intercept of 257 ms). Given this scaling, the effect of orthographic length in the network is 4.56 ms/letter based on its semipartial correlation with RT (after factoring out the other predictors) and 7.67 ms/letter based on its direct correlation with RT ($r = .139$). Length effects of this magnitude are at the low end of the range found in empirical studies, although such effects can vary greatly with reading skill (Butler & Hains, 1979) and with the specific stimuli and testing conditions used (see Henderson, 1982).

Nonword Reading Table 23.5 lists the errors made by the network in pronouncing the lists of nonwords from Glushko (1979) and from McCann and Besner (1987). The network produced "regular" pronunciations to 40/43 (93.0%) of Glushko's consistent nonwords, 27/43 (62.8%) of the inconsistent nonwords, and 69/80 (86.3%) of McCann and Besner's control nonwords. If we accept as correct any pronunciation that is consistent with that of a word in the training corpus with the same body (and ignore inflected words and those with ʝ in the coda), the network pronounced correctly 42/43 (97.7%) of the inconsistent nonwords and 68/76 (89.5%) of the control nonwords. Although the performance of the network on the consistent nonwords was somewhat worse than that of the feedforward networks, it is about equal to the level of performance Glushko (1979) reported for subjects (93.8%; see Table 23.3). Thus, overall, the

Table 23.5
Errors by the attractor network in pronouncing nonwords

Glushko (1979)			McCann and Besner (1987)		
Nonword	Correct	Response	Nonword	Correct	Response
Consistent nonwords (3/43)			Control nonwords (11/80)		
*HODE	/hOd/	/hOdz/	*KAIZE	/kAz/	/skwAz/
*SWEAL	/swEl/	/swel/	*ZUPE	/zUp/	/zyUp/
*WOSH	/waS/	/wuS/	*JAUL	/jol/	/jOl/
Inconsistent nonwords (16/43)			*VOLE	/vOl/	/vOln/
BLEAD	/blEd/	/bled/	*YOWND	/yWnd/	/(y 0.04)Ond/
BOST	/bost/	/bOst/	KOWT	/kWt/	/kOt/
COSE	/kOz/	/kOs/	*VAWX	/voks/	/voNks/
COTH	/koT/	/kOT/	FAIJE	/fAj/	/fA(j 0.00)/
GROOK	/grUk/	/gruk/	*ZUTE	/zUt/	/zyUt/
LOME	/lOm/	/l∧m/	*YOME	/yOm/	/yam/
MONE	/mone/	/m∧n/	JINJE	/jinj/	/jIn(j 0.00)/
PLOVE	/plOv/	/plUv/			
POOT	/pUt/	/put/			
*POVE	/pOv/	/pav/			
SOOD	/sUd/	/sud/			
SOST	/sost/	/sOst/			
SULL	/s∧l/	/sul/			
WEAD	/wEd/	/wed/			
WONE	/wOn/	/w∧n/			
WUSH	/w∧S/	/wuS/			

Note. /a/ in POT, /@/ in CAT, /e/ in BED, /i/ in HIT, /o/ in DOG, /u/ in GOOD, /A/ in MAKE, /E/ in KEEP, /I/ in BIKE, /O/ in HOPE, /U/ in BOOT, /W/ in NOW, /Y/ in BOY, /∧/ in CUP, /N/ in RING, /S/ in SHE, /C/ in CHIN, /Z/ in BEIGE, /T/ in THIN, /D/ in THIS. The activity levels of correct but missing phonemes are listed in parentheses. In these cases, the actual response is what falls outside the parentheses. Words marked with "*" remain errors after properties of the training corpus are considered (as explained in the text).

ability of the attractor network to pronounce nonwords is comparable to that of skilled readers.

Frequency and Consistency Effects   Figure 23.8 shows the mean latencies of the network in pronouncing words of various degrees of spelling–sound consistency as a function of frequency. One of the low-frequency exception words from the Taraban and McClelland (1987) list was withheld from this analysis because it was pronounced incorrectly by the network (SPOOK ⇒ /spuk/). Among the remaining words, there were significant main effects of frequency, $F(3, 183) = 25.0$, $p < .001$, and consistency, $F(3, 183) = 8.21$, $p < .001$, and a significant interaction of frequency and consistency, $F(3, 183) = 3.49$, $p = .017$.

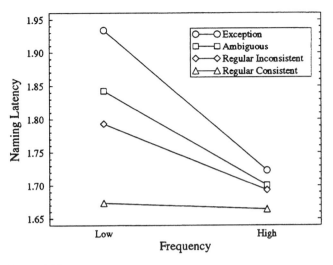

Figure 23.8
Naming latency of the attractor network trained on actual frequencies for words with various degrees of spelling-sound consistency as a function of frequency.

These effects also obtained in a comparison of only regular and exception words: frequency, $F(1, 91) = 10.2, p = .002$; consistency, $F(1, 91) = 22.0, p < .001$; frequency by consistency, $F(1, 91) = 9.31, p = .003$. Considering each level of consistency separately, the effect of frequency was significant for exception words, $F(1, 45) = 11.9, p = .001$, and for ambiguous words, $F(1, 46) = 19.8, p = .001$, and was marginally significant for regular inconsistent words, $F(1, 46) = 3.51, p = .067$. There was no effect of frequency among regular words ($F < 1$).

The naming latencies of the network showed a significant effect of consistency for low-frequency words, $F(3, 91) = 6.65, p < .001$, but not for high-frequency words, $F(3, 91) = 1.71, p = .170$. Among low-frequency words, regular consistent words were significantly different from each of the other three types (at $p < .05$), but regular inconsistent, ambiguous, and exception words were not significantly different from each other (although the comparison between regular inconsistent and exception words was significant at $p = .075$). Among high-frequency words, none of the pairwise comparisons was significant except between regular and exception words, $F(1, 46) = 4.87$, $p = .032$. Thus, overall, the naming latencies of the network replicate the standard effects of frequency and consistency found in empirical studies.

Network Analyses
The network's success at word reading demonstrates that, through training, it developed attractors for the pronunciations of words. How then is it capable of

reading nonwords with novel pronunciations? Why isn't the input for a non-word (e.g., MAVE) captured by the attractor for an orthographically similar word (e.g., GAVE, MOVE, MAKE)? We carried out a number of analyses of the network to gain a better understanding of its ability to read nonwords. Because nonword reading involves recombining knowledge derived from word pro-nunciation, we were primarily concerned with how separate parts of the input contribute to (a) the correctness of parts of the output and (b) the hidden rep-resentation for the input. As with naming latency, the item SPOOK was withheld from these analyses because it was mispronounced by the network.

Componential Attractors   In the first analysis we measured the extent to which each phonological cluster (onset, vowel, coda) depends on the input from each orthographic cluster. Specifically, for each word, we gradually reduced the activity of the active grapheme units in a particular orthographic cluster until, when the network was rerun, the phonemes in a particular phonological cluster were no longer correct.[11] This *boundary* activity level measures the importance of input from a particular orthographic cluster for the correctness of a particular phonological cluster; a value of 1 means that the graphemes in that cluster must be completely active; a value of 0 means that the phonemes are completely insensitive to the graphemes in that cluster. In state space, the boundary level corresponds to the radius of the word's attractor basin along a particular direction (assuming state space includes dimensions for the grapheme units).

This procedure was applied to the Taraban and McClelland (1987) regular consistent, regular inconsistent, and exception words, as well as to the corre-sponding set of ambiguous words. Words were excluded from the analysis if they lacked an orthographic onset or coda (e.g., ARE, DO). The resulting boundary values for each combination of orthographic and phonological clus-ters were subjected to an analysis of variance (ANOVA) with frequency and consistency as between-items factors and orthographic cluster and phonological cluster as within-item factors.

With regard to frequency, high-frequency words had lower boundary values than low-frequency words (0.188 vs. 0.201, respectively), $F(1, 162) = 6.48$, $p = .012$. However, frequency did not interact with consistency, $F(3, 162) = 2.10$, $p = .102$, nor did it interact with orthographic or phonological cluster, $F(2, 324) = 1.49$, $p = .227$, and $F(2, 324) = 2.46$, $p = .087$, respectively. Thus, we will consider high- and low-frequency words together in the remainder of the analysis.

There was a strong effect of consistency on the boundary values, $F(3, 162) = 14.5$, $p < .001$, and this effect interacted both with orthographic cluster, $F(6, 324) = 16.1$, $p < .001$, and with phonological cluster, $F(6, 324) = 20.3$, $p < .001$. Figure 23.9 presents the average boundary values of each ortho-graphic cluster as a function of phonological cluster, separately for words of each level of consistency. Thus, for each type of word, the set of bars for each phonological cluster indicates how sensitive that cluster is to input from each orthographic cluster. If we consider regular consistent words first, the figure shows that each phonological cluster depends almost entirely on the corresponding orthographic cluster and little, if at all, on the other clusters. For instance, the vowel and coda graphemes can be completely removed without affecting the network's pronunciation of the onset. There is a slight interdependence among the vowel and coda, consistent with the fact that word bodies capture important information in pronunciation (see, e.g., Treiman & Chafetz, 1987; Treiman et al., 1995). Nonetheless, neither the phonological vowel nor the coda cluster depends on the orthographic onset cluster. Thus, for a regular word like MUST, an alternative onset (e.g., N) can be substituted and pronounced without depending on or affecting the pronunciation of the body (producing the correct pronunciation of the nonword NUST).

Similarly, for regular inconsistent, ambiguous, and exception words, the correctness of the phonological onset and coda was relatively independent of noncorresponding parts of the orthographic input. The pronunciation of the vowel, by contrast, was increasingly dependent on the orthographic consonants as consistency decreased: $F(3, 166) = 47.7$, $p < .001$ for the main effect of consistency; $p < .05$ for all pairwise comparisons. In fact, most spelling–sound inconsistency in English involves unusual vowel pronunciations. Interestingly, for exception words, the vowel pronunciation was less sensitive to the orthographic vowel itself than it was to the surrounding (consonant) context: $F(1, 41) = 8.39$, $p = .006$ for orthographic onset versus vowel; $F(1, 41) = 6.97$, $p = .012$ for coda versus vowel. This makes sense, because the orthographic vowel in an exception word is a misleading indicator of the phonological vowel. Thus, in contrast to regular consistent words, words with ambiguous or exceptional vowel pronunciations depend on the entire orthographic input to be pronounced correctly.

These effects can be understood in terms of the nature of the attractors that develop when training on different types of words. The relative independence of the onset, vowel, and coda correspondences indicates that the attractor basins for regular words consist of three separate, orthogonal sub-basins (one for each cluster). When a word is presented, the network settles into the region in state space where these three sub-basins overlap, which corresponds to the word's pronunciation. However, each sub-basin can apply independently, so that "spurious" attractor basins exist where the sub-basins for parts of words overlap (see Figure 23.10). Each of these combinations corresponds to a pronounceable nonword that the network will pronounce correctly if presented with the appropriate orthographic input. This componentiality arises directly out of the degree to which the network's representations make explicit the structure of the task. By minimizing the extent to which information is replicated, the representations condense the regularities between orthography and phonology. Only small portions of the input and output are relevant to a particular regularity, which allows it to operate independently of other regularities.

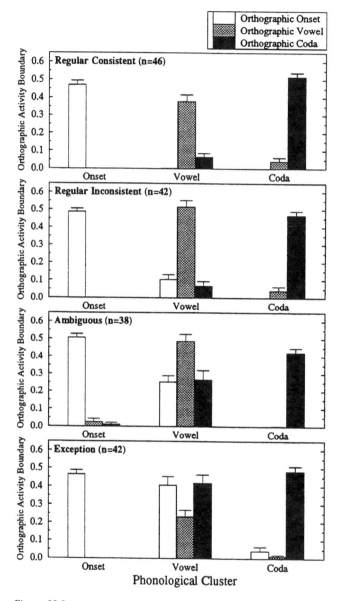

Figure 23.9
The degree of activity in each orthographic cluster required to activate each phonological cluster correctly, for words of various spelling-sound consistency. Words lacking either an onset or coda consonant cluster in orthography were excluded from the analysis.

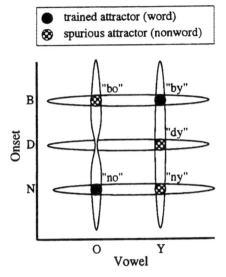

Figure 23.10
Depiction of how componential attractors for words can recombine to support pronunciations of nonwords. The attractor basins for words consist of orthogonal sub-basins for each of its clusters (only two are depicted here). Spurious attractors for nonwords exist where the sub-basins for parts of words overlap. To support the noncomponential aspects of attractors for exception words (e.g., DO), the sub-basins for vowels in the region of the relevant consonant clusters must be distorted somewhat (into dimensions in state space other than the ones depicted).

The attractor basins for exception words, by contrast, are far less componential than those for regular words (unfortunately, this cannot be depicted adequately in a two-dimensional diagram such as Figure 23.10). In this way, the network can pronounce exception words and yet still generalize well to nonwords. It is important to note, however, that the attractors for exception words are noncomponential only in their exceptional aspects—not in a monolithic way. In particular, whereas the consonant clusters in (most) exception words combine componentially, the correct vowel phoneme depends on the entire orthographic input. Thus, a word like PINT is in some sense three-quarters regular in that its consonant correspondences contribute to the pronunciations of regular words and nonwords just like those of other items. The traditional dual-route characterization of a lexical "lookup" procedure for exception words fails to do justice to this distinction.

Summary
Interactivity, and its use in implementing attractors, is an important computational principle in connectionist accounts of a wide range of cognitive phe-

nomena. Although the tendency of attractors to capture similar patterns might appear to make them inappropriate for tasks in which novel inputs require novel responses, such as pronouncing nonwords in oral reading, the current simulation showed that using appropriately structured representations led to the development of attractors with componential structure that supported effective generalization to nonwords. At the same time, the network also developed less componential attractors for exception words that violate the regularities in the task. In this way, attractors provide an effective means of capturing both the regularities and the exceptions in a quasi-regular task.

A further advantage of an attractor network in this domain is that its temporal dynamics in settling to a response provide a more direct analogue of readers' naming latencies than does error in a feedforward network. In fact, the time it took the network to settle to a stable pronunciation in response to words of varying frequency and consistency reproduced the standard pattern found in empirical studies.

General Discussion

The current work develops a connectionist approach to processing in quasi-regular domains as exemplified by English word reading. The approach derives from the general computational principles that processing is graded, random, adaptive, interactive, and nonlinear and that representations and knowledge are distributed (McClelland, 1991, 1993). When instantiated in the specific domain of oral reading, these principles lead to a view in which the reading system learns gradually to be sensitive to the statistical structure among ortho-graphic, phonological, and semantic representations and in which these representations simultaneously constrain each other in interpreting a given input.

In support of this view, we have presented a series of connectionist simulations of normal and impaired word reading. A consideration of the short-comings of a previous implementation (Seidenberg & McClelland, 1989) in reading nonwords led to the development of orthographic and phonological representations that better capture the relevant structure among the written and spoken forms of words. In Simulation 1, a feedforward network that used these representations learned to pronounce all of a large corpus of monosyllabic words, including the exception words, and yet also pronounced nonwords as well as skilled readers.

In Simulation 3, a recurrent network replicated the effects of frequency and consistency on naming latency directly in the time required to settle on a stable pronunciation. More critically, the attractors that the network developed for words over the course of training had componential structure that also supported good nonword reading.

Conclusions

At the end of their article, Coltheart et al. (1993) reached a conclusion that seemed to them "inescapable":

> Our ability to deal with linguistic stimuli we have not previously encountered ... can only be explained by postulating that we have learned systems of general linguistic rules, and our ability at the same time to deal correctly with exceptions to these rules ... can only be explained by postulating the existence of systems of word-specific lexical representations. (p. 606)

We have formulated a connectionist approach to knowledge and processing in quasi-regular domains, instantiated it in the specific domain of English word reading, and demonstrated that it can account for the basic abilities of skilled readers to handle correctly both regular and exception items while still generalizing well to novel items. Within the approach, the proficiency of humans in quasi-regular domains stems not from the existence of separate rule-based and item-specific mechanisms, but from the fact that the cognitive system adheres to certain general principles of computation in neural-like systems.

The more general lexical framework for word reading on which the current work is based contains a semantic pathway in addition to a phonological pathway. In contrast to the lexical and sublexical procedures in dual-route theories, which operate in fundamentally different ways, the two pathways in the current approach operate according to a common set of computational principles. As a result, the nature of processing in the two pathways is intimately related. In particular, a consideration of the pattern of impaired and preserved abilities in acquired surface dyslexia leads to a view in which there is a partial division of labor between the two pathways. The contribution of the phonological pathway is a graded function of frequency and consistency; items weak on both measures are processed particularly poorly. Overt accuracy on these items is not compromised, however, because the semantic pathway also contributes to the pronunciation of words (but not nonwords). The relative capabilities of the two pathways are open to individual differences, and these differences may become manifest in the pattern and severity of reading impairments following brain damage.

Needless to say, much remains to be done. The current simulations have specific limitations, such as the restriction to uninflected monosyllables and the lack of attention paid to the development of orthographic representations, which need to be remedied in future work. Furthermore, the nature of processing within the semantic pathway has been characterized in only the coarsest way. Finally, a wide range of related empirical issues, including phonological dyslexia, developmental dyslexia, lexical decision, and pseudohomophone and blocking effects, have been addressed in only very general terms. Nonetheless, the results reported here, along with those of others taking similar approaches, clearly suggest that the computational principles of connectionist modeling can lead to a deeper understanding of the central empirical phenomena in word reading in particular and in quasi-regular domains more generally.

Notes

David C. Plaut and James L. McClelland, Department of Psychology, Carnegie Mellon University, and the Center for the Neural Basis of Cognition; Mark S. Seidenberg, Neuroscience Program, University of Southern California; Karalyn Patterson, Medical Research Council Applied Psychology Unit, Cambridge, England.

This research was supported financially by National Institute of Mental Health Grants MH47566, MH01188, and MH00385, National Institute on Aging Grant Ag10109, National Science Foundation Grant ASC-9109215, and McDonnell-Pew Program in Cognitive Neuroscience Grant T89-01245-016.

We thank Marlene Behrmann, Derek Besner, Max Coltheart, Joe Devlin, Geoff Hinton, and Eamon Strain for helpful discussions and comments. We also acknowledge Derek Besner, Max Coltheart, and Michael McCloskey for directing attention to many of the issues addressed in this article.

1. The findings of these studies have often been cast as effects of *regularity* rather than *consistency*—we address this distinction in the next section.

2. This is particularly true with respect to the distinction between regular inconsistent words and ambiguous words, which differ only in the degree of balance between friends and enemies. In fact, a number of previous studies, including that of Taraban and McClelland (1987), failed to make this distinction. As a result, some of the Taraban and McClelland regular inconsistent words contain bodies that we categorize as ambiguous (e.g., DEAR, GROW). This has the unfortunate consequence that, occasionally, words with identical bodies are assigned into different consistency classes. However, in the current context, we are not concerned with individual items but solely with using the pattern of means across classes to illustrate overall consistency effects. In this regard, the word classes differ in the appropriate manner in their average relative numbers of friends and enemies. Thus, for continuity with earlier work, we will continue to use the Taraban and McClelland stimuli.

3. Bullinaria (1995) has recently developed a series of networks of this form that exhibit impressive performance in reading nonwords, although only very weak effects of word frequency. Coltheart et al. (1993) also took a sequential approach to solving the dispersion problem in that a correspondence learned from one position is applied to all positions unless a different correspondence is learned elsewhere.

4. The Plaut and McClelland (1993; Seidenberg et al., 1994) network was also trained on 103 isolated GPCs, as an approximation to the explicit instruction many children receive in learning to read. These correspondences were not included in the training of any of the networks reported in this article.

5. This is not precisely true because the procedure for determining the pronunciation based on phoneme unit activities, soon to be described, does not consider these units independently, and their states are not determined independently but are based on the same set of hidden unit states. Nonetheless, the approximation is sufficient to make cross-entropy a more appropriate error measure than summed squared error.

6. The derivative of cross-entropy with respect to an output unit's total input is simply the difference between the unit's state and its target:

$$\frac{\partial C}{\partial x_j} = \frac{\partial C}{\partial s_j}\frac{ds_j}{dx_j} = \left(\frac{1-t_j}{1-s_j} - \frac{t_j}{s_j}\right)s_j(1-s_j) = s_j - t_j.$$

7. The procedure for adjusting the connection-specific learning rates, called *delta-bar-delta* (Jacobs, 1988), works as follows. Each connection's learning rate is initialized to 1.0. At the end of each

epoch, the error derivative for that connection calculated by back-propagation is compared with its previous weight change. If they are both in the same direction (i.e., have the same sign), the connection's learning rate is incremented (by 0.1 in the current simulation); otherwise, it is decreased multiplicatively (by 0.9 in the current simulation).

8. This characterization of the derivation of word meanings is necessarily oversimplified. Words with multiple, distinct meanings would map to one of a number of separate semantic attractors. Shades of meaning across contexts could be expressed by semantic attractors that are *regions* in semantic space instead of single points. Notice that these two conditions can be seen as ends of a continuum involving various degrees of similarity and variability among the semantic patterns generated by a word across contexts (also see McClelland, St. John, & Taraban, 1989).

9. These temporal dynamics are somewhat different from those of the Plaut and McClelland (1993; Seidenberg et al., 1994) network. In that network, each unit's input was set instantaneously to the summed external input from other units; the unit's state was a weighted average of its current state and the one dictated by its instantaneous input.

10. This specific criterion was chosen because it gives rise to mean response times that are within the 2.0 units of time over which the network was trained; other criteria produce qualitatively equivalent results.

11. Final E was considered to be part of the orthographic vowel cluster.

References

Andrews, S. (1982). Phonological recoding: Is the regularity effect consistent? *Memory and Cognition, 10,* 565–575.

Backman, J., Bruck, M., Hébert, M., & Seidenberg, M. S. (1984). Acquisition and use of spelling–sound information in reading. *Journal of Experimental Child Psychology, 38,* 114–133.

Behrmann, M., & Bub, D. (1992). Surface dyslexia and dysgraphia: Dual routes, a single lexicon. *Cognitive Neuropsychology, 9,* 209–258.

Besner, D., & Smith, M. C. (1992). Models of visual word recognition: When obscuring the stimulus yields a clearer view. *Journal of Experimental Psychology: Learning, Memory, and Cognition, 18,* 468–482.

Besner, D., Twilley, L., McCann, R. S., & Seergobin, K. (1990). On the connection between connectionism and data: Are a few words necessary? *Psychological Review, 97,* 432–446.

Butler, B., & Hains, S. (1979). Individual differences in word recognition latency. *Memory and Cognition, 7,* 68–76.

Coltheart, M. (1978). Lexical access in simple reading tasks. In G. Underwood (Ed.), *Strategies of information processing* (pp. 151–216). New York: Academic Press.

Coltheart, M. (1985). Cognitive neuropsychology and the study of reading. In M. I. Posner & O. S. M. Marin (Eds.), *Attention and performance XI* (pp. 3–37). Hillsdale, NJ: Erlbaum.

Coltheart, M., Curtis, B., Atkins, P., & Haller, M. (1993). Models of reading aloud: Dual-route and parallel-distributed-processing approaches. *Psychological Review, 100,* 589–608.

Coltheart, M., Patterson, K., & Marshall, J. C. (Eds.). (1980). *Deep dyslexia.* London: Routledge & Kegan Paul.

Coltheart, M., & Rastle, K. (1994). Serial processing in reading aloud: Evidence for dual-route models of reading. *Journal of Experimental Psychology: Human Perception and Performance, 20,* 1197–1211.

Daugherty, K., & Seidenberg, M. S. (1992). Rules or connections? The past tense revisited. In *Proceedings of the 14th Annual Conference of the Cognitive Science Society* (pp. 259–264). Hillsdale, NJ: Erlbaum.

Derthick, M. (1990). Mundane reasoning by settling on a plausible model. *Artificial Intelligence, 46,* 107–157.

Fera, P., & Besner, D. (1992). The process of lexical decision: More words about a parallel distributed processing model. *Journal of Experimental Psychology: Learning, Memory, and Cognition, 18*, 749–764.

Fodor, J. A., & Pylyshyn, Z. W. (1988). Connectionism and cognitive architecture: A critical analysis. *Cognition, 28*, 3–71.

Forster, K. I. (1994). Computational modeling and elementary process analysis in visual word recognition. *Journal of Experimental Psychology: Human Perception and Performance, 20*, 1292–1310.

Forster, K. I., & Chambers, S. (1973). Lexical access and naming time. *Journal of Verbal Learning and Verbal Behaviour, 12*, 627–635.

Frederiksen, J. R., & Kroll, J. F. (1976). Spelling and sound: Approaches to the internal lexicon. *Journal of Experimental Psychology: Human Perception and Performance, 2*, 361–379.

Glushko, R. J. (1979). The organization and activation of orthographic knowledge in reading aloud. *Journal of Experimental Psychology: Human Perception and Performance, 5*, 674–691.

Hanson, S. J., & Burr, D. J. (1990). What connectionist models learn: Learning and representation in connectionist networks. *Behavioral and Brain Sciences, 13*, 471–518.

Henderson, L. (1982). *Orthography and word recognition in reading.* London: Academic Press.

Hinton, G. E. (1981). Implementing semantic networks in parallel hardware. In G. E. Hinton & J. A. Anderson (Eds.), *Parallel models of associative memory* (pp. 161–188). Hillsdale, NJ: Erlbaum.

Hinton, G. E. (1989). Connectionist learning procedures. *Artificial Intelligence, 40*, 185–234.

Hinton, G. E. (1990). Mapping part–whole hierarchies into connectionist networks. *Artificial Intelligence, 46*, 47–76.

Hinton, G. E., McClelland, J. L., & Rumelhart, D. E. (1986). Distributed representations. In D. E. Rumelhart, J. L. McClelland, & the PDP Research Group (Eds.), *Parallel distributed processing: Explorations in the microstructure of cognition: Vol. 1. Foundations* (pp. 77–109). Cambridge, MA: MIT Press.

Hinton, G. E., & Sejnowski, T. J. (1986). Learning and relearning in Boltzmann machines. In D. E. Rumelhart, J. L. McClelland, & the PDP Research Group (Eds.), *Parallel distributed processing: Explorations in the microstructure of cognition: Vol. 1. Foundations* (pp. 282–317). Cambridge, MA: MIT Press.

Hinton, G. E., & Shallice, T. (1991). Lesioning an attractor network: Investigations of acquired dyslexia. *Psychological Review, 98*, 74–95.

Humphreys, G. W., & Evett, L. J. (1985). Are there independent lexical and nonlexical routes in word processing? An evaluation of the dualroute theory of reading. *Behavioral and Brain Sciences, 8*, 689–740.

Jacobs, R. A. (1988). Increased rates of convergence through learning rate adaptation. *Neural Networks, 1*, 295–307.

Jared, D., McRae, K., & Seidenberg, M. S. (1990). The basis of consistency effects in word naming. *Journal of Memory and Language, 29*, 687–715.

Kučera, H., & Francis, W. N. (1967). *Computational analysis of present-day American English.* Providence, RI: Brown University Press.

Kullback, S., & Leibler, R. A. (1951). On information and sufficiency. *Annals of Mathematical Statistics, 22*, 79–86.

Lachter, J., & Bever, T. G. (1988). The relation between linguistic structure and theories of language learning: A constructive critique of some connectionist learning models. *Cognition, 28*, 195–247.

Lacouture, Y. (1989). From mean squared error to reaction time: A connectionist model of word recognition. In D. S. Touretzky, G. E. Hinton, & T. J. Sejnowski (Eds.), *Proceedings of the 1988 Connectionist Models Summer School* (pp. 371–378). San Mateo, CA: Morgan Kauffman.

Lass, R. (1984). *Phonology: An introduction to basic concepts.* Cambridge, England: Cambridge University Press.

Maddieson, I. (1984). *Patterns of sounds.* Cambridge, England: Cambridge University Press.

Marshall, J. C., & Newcombe, F. (1973). Patterns of paralexia: A psycholinguistic approach. *Journal of Psycholinguistic Research, 2*, 175–199.

Massaro, D. W. (1988). Some criticisms of connectionist models of human performance. *Journal of Memory and Language, 27*, 213–234.

Massaro, D. W. (1989). Testing between the TRACE model and the fuzzy logical model of speech perception. *Cognitive Psychology, 21*, 398–421.

Masterson, J. (1985). On how we read non-words: Data from different populations. In K. Patterson, M. Coltheart, & J. C. Marshall (Eds.), *Surface dyslexia* (pp. 289–299). Hillsdale, NJ: Erlbaum.

McCann, R. S., & Besner, D. (1987). Reading pseudohomophones: Implications for models of pronunciation and the locus of the word-frequency effects in word naming. *Journal of Experimental Psychology: Human Perception and Performance, 13*, 14–24.

McClelland, J. L. (1987). The case for interactionism in language processing. In M. Coltheart (Ed.), *Attention and performance XII: The psychology of reading* (pp. 3–36). Hillsdale, NJ: Erlbaum.

McClelland, J. L. (1991). Stochastic interactive processes and the effect of context on perception. *Cognitive Psychology, 23*, 1–44.

McClelland, J. L. (1993). The GRAIN model: A framework for modeling the dynamics of information processing. In D. E. Meyer, & S. Kornblum (Eds.), *Attention and performance XIV: Synergies in experimental psychology, artificial intelligence, and cognitive neuroscience* (pp. 655–688). Hillsdale, NJ: Erlbaum.

McClelland, J. L., & Elman, J. L. (1986). The TRACE model of speech perception. *Cognitive Psychology, 18*, 1–86.

McClelland, J. L., & Rumelhart, D. E. (1981). An interactive activation model of context effects in letter perception: Part 1. An account of basic findings. *Psychological Review, 88*, 375–407.

McClelland, J. L., Rumelhart, D. E., & the PDP Research Group (Eds.). (1986). *Parallel distributed processing: Explorations in the microstructure of cognition: Vol. 2. Psychological and biological models*. Cambridge, MA: MIT Press.

McClelland, J. L., St. John, M., & Taraban, R. (1989). Sentence comprehension: A parallel distributed processing approach. *Language and Cognitive Processes, 4*, 287–335.

McCloskey, M. (1991). Networks and theories: The place of connectionism in cognitive science. *Psychological Science, 2*, 387–395.

Meyer, D. E., Schvaneveldt, R. W., & Ruddy, M. G. (1974). Functions of graphemic and phonemic codes in visual word recognition. *Memory and Cognition, 2*, 309–321.

Minsky, M. (1975). A framework for representing knowledge. In P. H. Winston (Ed.), *The psychology of computer vision* (pp. 211–277). New York: McGraw-Hill.

Minsky, M., & Papert, S. (1969). *Perceptions: An introduction to computational geometry*. Cambridge, MA: MIT Press.

Monsell, S., Patterson, K., Graham, A., Hughes, C. H., & Milroy, R. (1992). Lexical and sublexical translation of spelling to sound: Strategic anticipation of lexical status. *Journal of Experimental Psychology: Learning, Memory, and Cognition, 18*, 452–467.

Morais, J., Bertelson, P., Cary, L., & Alegria, J. (1986). Literacy training and speech segmentation. *Cognition, 24*, 45–64.

Morais, J., Cary, L., Alegria, J., & Bertelson, P. (1979). Does awareness of speech as a sequence of phones arise spontaneously? *Cognition, 7*, 323–331.

Morton, J. (1969). The interaction of information in word recognition. *Psychological Review, 76*, 165–178.

Morton, J., & Patterson, K. (1980). A new attempt at an interpretation, Or, an attempt at a new interpretation. In M. Coltheart, K. Patterson, & J. C. Marshall (Eds.), *Deep dyslexia* (pp. 91–118). London: Routledge & Kegan Paul.

Movellan, J. R., & McClelland, J. L. (1993). Learning continuous probability distributions with symmetric diffusion networks. *Cognitive Science, 17*, 463–496.

Mozer, M. C. (1990). Discovering faithful "Wickelfeature" representations in a connectionist network. In *Proceedings of the 12th Annual Conference of the Cognitive Science Society* (pp. 356–363). Hillsdale, NJ: Erlbaum.

Mozer, M. C. (1991). *The perception of multiple objects: A connectionist approach*. Cambridge, MA: MIT Press.

Olsen, A., & Caramazza, A. (1991). The role of cognitive theory in neuropsychological research. In S. Corkin, J. Grafman, & F. Boller (Eds.), *Handbook of neuropsychology* (pp. 287–309). Amsterdam: Elsevier.

Paap, K. R., & Noel, R. W. (1991). Dual route models of print to sound: Still a good horse race. *Psychological Research, 53,* 13–24.

Parkin, A. J. (1982). Phonological recoding in lexical decision: Effects of spelling-to-sound regularity depend on how regularity is defined. *Memory and Cognition, 10,* 43–53.

Patterson, K. (1990). Alexia and neural nets. *Japanese Journal of Neuropsychology, 6,* 90–99.

Patterson, K., & Behrmann, M. (1997). Frequency and consistency effects in a pure surface dyslexia patient. *Journal of Experimental Psychology: Human Learning and Memory, 23,* 1217–1231.

Patterson, K., Coltheart, M., & Marshall, J. C. (Eds.). (1985). *Surface dyslexia*. Hillsdale, NJ: Erlbaum.

Patterson, K., & Morton, J. (1985). From orthography to phonology: An attempt at an old interpretation. In K. Patterson, M. Coltheart, & J. C. Marshall (Eds.), *Surface dyslexia* (pp. 335–359). Hillsdale, NJ: Erlbaum.

Patterson, K., Seidenberg, M. S., & McClelland, J. L. (1989). Connections and disconnections: Acquired dyslexia in a computational model of reading processes. In R. G. M. Morris (Ed.), *Parallel distributed processing: Implications for psychology and neuroscience* (pp. 131–181). London: Oxford University Press.

Pearlmutter, B. A. (1989). Learning state space trajectories in recurrent neural networks. *Neural Computation, 1,* 263–269.

Phillips, W. A., Hay, I. M., & Smith, L. S. (1993). *Lexicality and pronunciation in a simulated neural net* (Tech. Rep. CCCN-14). Stirling, Scotland: Centre for Cognitive and Computational Neuroscience, University of Stirling.

Pinker, S. (1984). *Language learnability and language development*. Cambridge, MA: Harvard University Press.

Pinker, S. (1991). Rules of language. *Science, 253,* 530–535.

Pinker, S., & Prince, A. (1988). On language and connectionism: Analysis of a parallel distributed processing model of language acquisition. *Cognition, 28,* 73–193.

Plaut, D. C., Behrmann, M., Patterson, K., & McClelland, J. L. (1993). Impaired oral reading in surface dyslexia: Detailed comparison of a patient and a connectionist network [Abstract 540]. *Psychonomic Society Bulletin, 31,* 400.

Plaut, D. C., & Hinton, G. E. (1987). Learning sets of filters using back propagation. *Computer Speech and Language, 2,* 35–61.

Plaut, D. C., & McClelland, J. L. (1993). Generalization with componential attractors: Word and nonword reading in an attractor network. In *Proceedings of the 15th Annual Conference of the Cognitive Science Society* (pp. 824–829). Hillsdale, NJ: Erlbaum.

Plaut, D. C., & Shallice, T. (1993). Deep dyslexia: A case study of connectionist neuropsychology. *Cognitive Neuropsychology, 10,* 377–500.

Richardson, J. T. E. (1976). The effects of stimulus attributes upon latency of word recognition. *British Journal of Psychology, 67,* 315–325.

Rumelhart, D. E., Durbin, R., Golden, R., & Chauvin, Y. (1995). Backpropagation: The basic theory. In D. E. Rumelhart & Y. Chauvin (Eds.), *Backpropagation: Theory and practice* (pp. 1–34). Cambridge, MA: MIT Press.

Rumelhart, D. E., Hinton, G. E., & Williams, R. J. (1986a). Learning internal representations by error propagation. In D. E. Rumelhart, J. L. McClelland, & the PDP Research Group (Eds.), *Parallel distributed processing: Explorations in the microstructure of cognition: Vol. 1. Foundations* (pp. 318–362). Cambridge, MA: MIT Press.

Rumelhart, D. E., Hinton, G. E., & Williams, R. J. (1986b). Learning representations by back-propagating errors. *Nature, 323,* 533–536.

Rumelhart, D. E., & McClelland, J. L. (1982). An interactive activation model of context effects in letter perception: Part 2. The contextual enhancement effect and some tests and extensions of the model. *Psychological Review, 89,* 60–94.

Rumelhart, D. E., & McClelland, J. L. (1986). On learning the past tenses of English verbs. In J. L. McClelland, D. E. Rumelhart, & the PDP Research Group (Eds.), *Parallel distributed processing: Explorations in the microstructure of cognition: Vol. 2. Psychological and biological models* (pp. 216–271). Cambridge, MA: MIT Press.

Rumelhart, D. E., McClelland, J. L., & the PDP Research Group (Eds.). (1986). *Parallel distributed processing: Explorations in the microstructure of cognition: Volume 1. Foundations.* Cambridge, MA: MIT Press.

Seidenberg, M. S. (1985). The time course of phonological code activation in two writing systems. *Cognition, 19,* 1–10.

Seidenberg, M. S. (1993). Connectionist models and cognitive theory. *Psychological Science, 4,* 228–235.

Seidenberg, M. S., & McClelland, J. L. (1989). A distributed, developmental model of word recognition and naming. *Psychological Review, 96,* 523–568.

Seidenberg, M. S., & McClelland, J. L. (1990). More words but still no lexicon: Reply to Besner et al. (1990). *Psychological Review, 97,* 477–452.

Seidenberg, M. S., & McClelland, J. L. (1992). *Connectionist models and explanatory theories in cognition* (Tech. Rep. PDP.CNS.92.4). Pittsburgh, PA: Carnegie Mellon University, Department of Psychology.

Seidenberg, M. S., Plaut, D. C., Petersen, A. S., McClelland, J. L., & McRae, K. (1994). Nonword pronunciation and models of word recognition. *Journal of Experimental Psychology: Human Perception and Performance, 20,* 1177–1196.

Seidenberg, M. S., Waters, G. S., Barnes, M. A., & Tanenhaus, M. K. (1984). When does irregular spelling or pronunciation influence word recognition? *Journal of Verbal Learning and Verbal Behaviour, 23,* 383–404.

Sejnowski, T. J., Koch, C., & Churchland, P. S. (1989). Computational neuroscience. *Science, 241,* 1299–1306.

Sejnowski, T. J., & Rosenberg, C. R. (1987). Parallel networks that learn to pronounce English text. *Complex Systems, 1,* 145–168.

Shallice, T., Warrington, E. K., & McCarthy, R. (1983). Reading without semantics. *Quarterly Journal of Experimental Psychology, 35A,* 111–138.

Stanhope, N., & Parkin, A. J. (1987). Further exploration of the consistency effect in word and nonword pronunciation. *Memory and Cognition, 15,* 169–179.

Stone, G. O., & Van Orden, G. C. (1989). Are words represented by nodes? *Memory and Cognition, 17,* 511–524.

Stone, G. O., & Van Orden, G. C. (1994). Building a resonance framework for word recognition using design and system principles. *Journal of Experimental Psychology: Human Perception and Performance, 20,* 1248–1268.

Sutton, R. S. (1992). Adapting bias by gradient descent: An incremental version of Delta-Bar-Delta. *Proceedings of the 10th National Conference on Artificial Intelligence* (pp. 171–176). Cambridge, MA: MIT Press.

Taraban, R., & McClelland, J. L. (1987). Conspiracy effects in word recognition. *Journal of Memory and Language, 26,* 608–631.

Treiman, R., & Chafetz, J. (1987). Are there onset- and rime-like units in printed words? In M. Coltheart (Ed.), *Attention and performance XII: The psychology of reading* (pp. 281–327). Hillsdale, NJ: Erlbaum.

Treiman, R., Mullennix, J., Bijeljac-Babic, R., & Richmond-Welty, E. D. (1995). The special role of rimes in the description, use, and acquisition of English orthography. *Journal of Experimental psychology: General, 124,* 107–136.

Van Orden, G. C., & Goldinger, S. D. (1994). Interdependence of form and function in cognitive systems explains perception of printed words. *Journal of Experimental Psychology: Human Perception and Performance, 20,* 1269.

Van Orden, G. C., Pennington, B. F., & Stone, G. O. (1990). Word identification in reading and the promise of subsymbolic psycholinguistics. *Psychological Review, 97,* 488–522.

Vellutino, F. (1979). *Dyslexia.* Cambridge, MA: MIT Press.

Venezky, R. L. (1970). *The structure of English orthography.* The Hague: Mouton.

Waters, G. S., & Seidenberg, M. S. (1985). Spelling–sound effects in reading: Time course and decision criteria. *Memory and Cognition, 13,* 557–572.

Wickelgren, W. A. (1969). Context-sensitive coding, associative memory, and serial order in (speech) behavior. *Psychological Review, 76,* 1–15.

Williams, R. J., & Peng, J. (1990). An efficient gradient-based algorithm for on-line training of recurrent network trajectories. *Neural Computation, 2,* 490–501.

Producing Language

Chapter 24

Language Production and Serial Order: A Functional Analysis and a Model

Gary S. Dell, Lisa K. Burger, and William R. Svec

More than 45 years ago, Lashley (1951) directed the attention of psychologists to the problem of serial order. Ordered behavior, he wrote, cannot simply be the product of associations between elementary responses. Instead, there must be a hierarchically organized plan or schema that is separate from the responses and yet determines their order. Although it took some time for Lashley's paper to be appreciated (Bruce, 1994), his insights are now acknowledged to be central to theory in memory (e.g., Murdock, 1974), psycholinguistics (e.g., Levelt, 1989; MacKay, 1987), and motor control (e.g., Rosenbaum, 1990).

This article examines the nature of order schemata in that behavior in which the serial-ordering problems are perhaps most acute, in language. We begin by reviewing evidence from serial-order errors in speech, particularly errors in which sounds or words are either *anticipated*, spoken ahead of their time, or *perseverated*, produced later than they should be. This evidence suggests that the past and future often impinge on the present while we are speaking and that the extent to which the language-production system is focused on the past or the future depends on a number of factors.

We then present an experimental study of one of these factors, the degree to which a spoken phrase is familiar. This study shows that, as a phrase gains familiarity, the pattern of order errors moves from one in which perseverations dominate to one in which anticipations are more common. This is termed the *anticipatory practice effect*. The ability of various serial-order theories to explain this effect is reviewed, and a simple quantitative model is developed from a class of existing activation-based theories (e.g., Dell, 1986; Estes, 1972; Houghton, 1990; MacKay, 1987). This model makes predictions about the relationship between speech rate, practice, overall error rate, and the extent to which errors are anticipatory or perseveratory. Most importantly, it states that the proportion of errors that are anticipatory should be predictable from the overall error rate, regardless of the combination of factors that led to that particular rate. This claim, called the *general anticipatory effect*, is tested in another experiment.

Ultimately, we argue that a theory of serial order in speech must satisfy a set of functional requirements: The system must activate the present, deactivate the past, and prepare to activate the future. Furthermore, the order schema that accomplishes these functions must be capable of doing so for both stored and novel sequences. We attempt to show that the general anticipatory effect follows from these functions, given certain assumptions. In short, we claim that when the language-production system is working well, it looks to the future and does not dwell on the past.

Serial-Order Errors in Speech

Everyday speech errors, or slips of the tongue, occur once or twice every 1,000 words on average for normal adults (Garnham, Shillcock, Brown, Mill, & Cutler, 1981; Hotopf, 1983). Young children appear to have a higher error rate (e.g., seven times the adult rate, for 2–3-year-olds; Wijnen, 1992), and aphasic patients may have error rates in their spontaneous speech that are hundreds of times greater than normal (e.g., Schwartz, Saffran, Bloch, & Dell, 1994).

Speech errors can be categorized along two dimensions: the size of the linguistic units involved and the nature of the disturbance. Linguistic units of all sizes can slip, from articulatory gestures to whole clauses (Fromkin, 1971; Mowrey & MacKay, 1990). The most commonly collected errors, at least in the languages that have been extensively studied, involve units that roughly correspond to phonemes, as in Errors 1–3 below, or to words (see Error 4) or morphemes (see Error 5). The nature of the disturbance refers to whether errors involve the intrusion of linguistic material from outside the utterance, called *noncontextual errors*, or from within the utterance, called *contextual* or *movement errors*. Anticipations and perseverations are contextual errors. Error 1 below can be categorized as the anticipation of the phoneme /f/. The /f/ was spoken too early and replaced the correct sound /p/.[1] In Error 2 the vowel sound /i/ is perseverated. When an anticipation and perseveration occur on corresponding units, the error is called an *exchange*; Error 3 is an exchange of phonemes, and Error 4 is an exchange of words.

1. cup of coffee → cuff of coffee (Fromkin, 1971)
2. beef noodle → beef needle (Fromkin, 1971)
3. left hemisphere → heft lemisphere (Fromkin, 1971)
4. fill the car up with gas → fill the gas up with car (Dell & Reich, 1981)
5. thinly sliced → slicely thinned (Stemberger, 1982)

To a considerable extent, error categorization is a theory-laden decision, both with respect to the size of the disrupted unit and the nature of the disruption. In our studies, we distinguish between errors that involve whole meaningful units (words, stem morphemes), which we call *word errors*, and those that involve smaller pieces of the speech stream, called *sound errors*. We further assume that many errors have contextual sources and specifically adopt the categories of anticipation, perseveration, and exchange to label these errors. These categories are widely accepted (e.g., Cutler, 1981; Fromkin, 1971; Garrett, 1975, 1980; MacKay, 1970, 1974; Shattuck-Hufnagel, 1979, 1983; Stemberger, 1985), although it is also acknowledged that it is not easy to tell whether an error is a word or sound error or if it is contextual or noncontextual and, if contextual, whether it is an anticipation, perseveration, or exchange.

Anticipations, perseverations, and exchanges are often informally explained by the need for several linguistic units to coexist in a buffer (e.g., Fromkin, 1971; MacKay, 1970; Reich, 1977). Buffers serve many functions in information-processing systems, two of which are particularly important for language. First, the nature of language, both its abstract linguistic structure and its articulatory manifestation in speech, dictates that the form of a particular unit may depend on nonadjacent units, and moreover, on units from both the past and future. Having the units co-occur in a buffer helps the system compute these dependencies.

Second, buffers allow the processing levels of a system to work separately (e.g., Reich, 1977). A buffer can store the products of an earlier level, thereby allowing later levels that use these products to work at their own rate. Language does appear to be produced by a multileveled system, each level being associated with its own representation of the utterance. These representations, seen as organized sets of symbols, serve as buffers. Much of the research on language production has been concerned with identifying the number and character of these representations (e.g., Garrett, 1975). Current theory (e.g., Bock & Levelt, 1994) distinguishes between *grammatical encoding, phonological encoding,* and storage in an *articulatory buffer*. Grammatical encoding builds a syntactic representation of the utterance. Words are chosen but not specified in terms of their sounds; these abstract word symbols are assigned to grammatical functions such as subject and object and are placed in slots in a syntactic frame that dictates their order. Phonological encoding comprises the assembly of the sounds of words and the generation of intonation. The articulatory buffer is capable of storing motor representations of syllable strings in advance of overt articulation (Sternberg, Monsell, Knoll, & Wright, 1978). Contextual speech errors occur during the manipulation of the grammatical and phonological representations. Specifically, sound errors are associated with the phonological representation, and most word errors are associated with the grammatical representation (Fromkin, 1971; Garrett, 1975; MacKay, 1982; Stemberger, 1985).

The association of speech errors with distinctly linguistic representational levels comes from a consideration of the variables that influence the errors. Here we offer a brief review, focusing on contextual speech error types. (See Berg, 1988; Dell, 1986; Fromkin, 1973, 1980; Garrett, 1975; MacKay, 1970; Shattuck-Hufnagel, 1979; Stemberger, 1985, for complete discussions.) A serial-order error can be characterized by a *target linguistic unit* and an *error unit*. In anticipations and perseverations, a single target is replaced by an error unit from within the utterance. In an exchange, each of the exchanging units is both a target and an error.[2]

Previous discussions of anticipations, perseverations, and exchanges hypothesize a close relationship among the types (Dell, 1986; MacKay, 1970; Shattuck-Hufnagel, 1979). An anticipatory error ("left hemisphere" → "heft ...") can evolve into an exchange ("heft lemisphere") because the replaced unit (e.g., /l/) seeks expression in the next available location in which it is allowed. Alternately, it can emerge as a simple anticipation ("heft hemisphere"), or the speaker can stop, thereby producing an incomplete anticipation ("heft ... I mean, left hemisphere"). Perseverations and exchanges are related in that both involve the production of a unit in a position later than the intended position. The three error types are further related in that they are influenced by the same variables. Anticipations, perseverations, and exchanges at the phonological level usually involve similar sounds from similar word and syllable positions, and the resulting errors are typically phonologically well formed (see, e.g., Errors 1–3, above). At the word level, the three error types usually involve target and error words of the same grammatical class (e.g., Error 4). Word and sound exchanges, however, differ somewhat from anticipations and perseverations in that the interacting units in an exchange are more constrained by similarity and tend to be closer together than those in anticipations and perseverations (Garrett, 1980).

Anticipations, Perseverations, and the "Good–Bad" Dimension

Serial-order errors that have a clear directionality—anticipations and perseverations—can be used to determine when behavior is focused on the past or the future. In particular, one can compare the extent to which errors are anticipatory versus perseveratory in certain situations or people. Such comparisons have been made with respect to four independent variables: the presence of aphasia, the speaker's age, the rate of speech, and the speaker's familiarity with the material uttered. These are discussed in turn.

Schwartz et al. (1994) noted that perseverations are a feature of many aphasic patients' speech and went on to show specifically that F.L., classified as a jargon-aphasic patient, made more perseverations than anticipations in his spontaneous speech. His anticipatory proportion (*AP*), which we define as the proportion of anticipation and perseveration errors that are anticipations, was .32. The same analysis performed on spontaneous speech errors from nonaphasic speakers, culled by Garnham et al. (1981) from a tape-recorded and transcribed source (the London–Lund corpus, Svartvik & Quirk, 1980), showed that nonaphasic speakers make more anticipations than perseverations; the *AP* was .75. The difference between the aphasic patient and the nonaphasic speakers' *AP* was highly reliable and, moreover, the error-pattern differences occurred for both sound and word errors.

Another variable that appears to influence the anticipatory proportion is age. Stemberger (1989) collected speech errors from adults and from two children with most of the observations coming at ages 2 and 3. He found that the adults' slips were predominately anticipatory $(AP = .60)$, while the children tended to perseverate more $(AP = .47)$, particularly when they were young (for age 2, $AP = .41$).

There is some evidence that the proportion of errors that are anticipatory decreases as speech rate increases. Dell (1990) had experimental participants say two- or three-word phrases within either a short or long deadline and found that anticipations and incomplete anticipations were unaffected by the deadline, but perseverations and exchanges were less likely at the long deadline. Hence, the anticipatory proportion increased as the available time for speaking increased.

Finally, Schwartz et al. (1994) investigated the effect of practice on saying difficult phrases, such as "chef's sooty shoe soles." Phrases were produced by normal adults in time with a metronome. There were eight practice blocks during which participants said each of the nine phrases in the study twice. Practice both reduced errors and had a large effect on the anticipatory proportion. For the first practice block, perseverations were more likely $(AP = .38)$, but by the eighth block, anticipations dominated $(AP = .70)$. This change in *AP* with practice is the anticipatory practice effect.

In summary, the anticipatory proportion is lower in the spontaneous speech of at least some aphasic patients and young children compared to normal adults and when speakers are producing unfamiliar compared to practiced phrases. There is also some evidence that a faster speech rate promotes a lower *AP*. According to Schwartz et al. (1994), the generalization from these data is that when the error rate is higher, errors tend to be more perseveratory. They distinguished between a "good" error pattern, in which errors were less likely and mostly anticipatory, and a "bad" error pattern characterized by more errors overall and by a high proportion of perseverations. Another feature of the good–bad dimension concerned the extent to which errors produced words over nonwords. The good pattern was associated with more slips with word outcomes.

Our goal is to examine the relation between the anticipatory proportion and other variables that affect overall error rate and to explain it by appealing to principles of serial ordering. But before we turn to these principles, we first replicate the anticipatory practice effect found by Schwartz et al. (1994). It is our view that practice is a particularly informative variable. In most theories of the production of verbal sequences, practice is assumed to increase the strength of the connections among units representing concepts, phrases, words, and sounds (e.g., Dell, Juliano, & Govindjee, 1993; Estes, 1972; Houghton, 1990; Jordan, 1986; MacKay, 1982, 1987; Rumelhart & Norman, 1982). Furthermore, variation in connection strength can be hypothesized to underlie the contrast between nonaphasic adults on the one hand and young children and aphasic patients on the other.

Experiment 1: Anticipatory Practice Effect

The goal of the first experiment is to replicate the anticipatory practice effect in a larger study than that of Schwartz et al. (1994). With a large data set, we can evaluate alternative accounts of the effect and see whether it generalizes across items.[3]

Method

Materials   The 16 phrases shown in Appendix A provided the materials that were practiced. Each phrase is a novel noun phrase consisting of four content words. Nine of these were also used by Schwartz et al. (1994). The onsets of each of the four content words in a phrase were chosen to make the phrases be tongue twisters. Specifically, each phrase made use of two similar word onsets (e.g., /s/ and /š/ in "chef's sooty shoe soles," or /b/ and /br/ in "Brad's burned bran buns"). The goal was to create phrases that are novel, meaningful, and short enough to be within memory span, but nonetheless are difficult to say at a normal speaking rate.

Participants   Forty-one students randomly sampled from the University of Illinois psychology participant pool received course credit for participation. All but one were native speakers of English, and the nonnative speaker's data were not examined, resulting in 40 participants.

Procedure   There were eight trial blocks, during each of which participants produced each of the 16 phrases twice. For the first trial block, a single trial went as follows: A prompt on a computer screen (Dell System 200, Dell Computer Corp., Houston, TX) informed the participant to press *y* on the keyboard, which displayed a phrase. The experimenter turned on an audiovisual metronome (Franz electric metronome [Model LM FB5], Franz Manufacturing Co., New Haven, CT) at a rate of 0.8 beats/s and repeated the phrase at this rate, aligning the stressed syllable of each word with a beat. The participant then repeated the phrase at the 0.8 rate. This is a very slow rate, and errors were extremely rare. The purpose of the participants' slow repetition was to verify their pronunciation of the phrase and to aid in memorization. The phrase then disappeared from the screen and was replaced by the prompt. The experimenter increased the metronome speed to 2.1 beats/s, which is a normal speech rate. When the participant pressed *y*, the phrase was redisplayed for 5 s for study. The phrase's disappearance after this interval was the signal for the participant to repeat the phrase from memory in time with the metronome. Participants were instructed to say the phrase twice with a four-beat pause between repetitions. This procedure was repeated for all 16 phrases to complete the first block. The second through eighth blocks were the same as the first with one exception. The participant did not repeat the phrase at the 0.8 rate; only the experimenter did. The phrases were presented in random order in each block.

Instructions consisted of running the participants through two trials on phrases that were not part of the experiment.

Error Coding   Tape recordings made of the experimental sessions (Marantz cassette recorder PMD201, Marantz Company, Inc., Chatsworth, CA) were transcribed by a trained assistant who was unaware of the research hypotheses. Transcriptions indicated phonemic content but not information about timing.

Error coding consisted of the following stages: (a) The transcriber identified utterances that contained at least one error; (b) transcriptions of these utterances were listed without information identifying what trial block they came from; error utterances that occurred several times in the experiment (e.g., "Bonnie's brown bread box" spoken as "Bronnie's brown bread box" occurred 18 times) were listed only once; and (c) a single coder (Gary S. Dell) identified and categorized the errors in each error utterance in the list. Hence, errors were categorized in ignorance of trial block, and identical error utterances were coded in the same way. The error categories were sound perseveration, sound anticipation, sound exchange, sound anticipation–perseveration, word perseveration, word anticipation, word exchange, word substitution, and other. The other category included noncontextual sound errors, affix errors, and word deletions. The sound anticipation–perseveration category was for sound errors that are ambiguous between anticipation and perseveration, specifically where the intruding sound occurs both before and after the target location and where these are equidistant (in words) from the location. (e.g., "chef's sooty *sue* soles" is sound anticipation–perseveration because there is an /s/-onset in both "sooty" and "soles").

Results and Discussion

There were 1,120 errors obtained making for an overall rate of 2.7 errors for every 100 words produced. Practice reduced errors considerably, from 5.9 errors/100 words in the first trial block to 1.5 errors/100 words in the eighth block. Table 24.1 gives the category totals for each block.

The relation between the log (number of errors) and log (trial block) was linear ($r = -.99$; see Figure 24.1) and is therefore consistent with other data showing performance to be a power function of practice (e.g., Anderson &

Table 24.1
Error totals, log–log slopes, anticipatory proportions (APs), and correlations for experiment 1

Category	Trial								Total	Slope	r
	1	2	3	4	5	6	7	8			
Sound	206	126	104	85	68	63	49	46	747	−.714	−.99
SA	56	38	37	22	25	23	23	20	244	−.487	−.95
SP	88	57	35	37	24	24	11	15	291	−.914	−.95
SE	26	9	11	11	10	10	10	6	93	−.462	−.80
SAP	36	22	21	15	9	6	5	5	119	−1.028	−.95
Word	87	72	53	35	38	20	19	29	353	−.726	−.92
WA	21	15	22	10	15	6	6	8	103	−.585	−.79
WP	47	30	18	6	11	6	5	8	131	−1.073	−.92
WE	16	22	7	16	7	5	8	6	87	−.566	−.73
WS	3	5	6	3	5	3	0	7	32		
Other	9	2	3	3	0	1	1	1	20		
Total	302	200	160	123	106	84	69	76	1,120	−.721	−.99
Anticipatory proportion	.36	.38	.53	.43	.53	.49	.64	.55			

Note. For categories with zero entries, no slope or correlation is computed. SA = sound anticipation; SP = sound perseveration; SE = sound exchange; SAP = sound anticipation–perseveration; WA = word anticipation; WP = word perseveration; WE = word exchange; WS = word substitution.

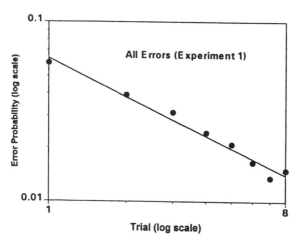

Figure 24.1
The effect of practice on overall error rate for Experiment 1.

Schooler, 1991; Logan, 1988; Newell & Rosenbloom, 1981). Our concern is less with the correctness of the power law, however, than with the fact that the obtained log/log slopes can be used to index learning and, particularly, that slope differences between error types indicate changes in the relative proportions of types with practice. These slopes and their corresponding correlations are given for the various error categories in Table 24.1.

The main result of the experiment was a clear anticipatory practice effect. The anticipatory proportion favored perseverations early in learning and favored anticipations after practice. AP was .37 pooled over the first two blocks and .59 over the last two blocks. This trend can be indexed by the difference in slopes for sound and word anticipations and perseverations. The slopes are nearly twice as great for perseverations. Furthermore, the slope differences were consistent across phrases. To show this, we computed log/log slopes for anticipations and perseverations for each phrase (combining word and sound errors). Because of the small number of errors in some phrases, particularly in the late practice blocks, some blocks had no errors in them for a particular phrase and error type, complicating the computation of logs. We dealt with this by randomly pooling each phrase with a zero entry for one or more blocks with another phrase with a zero entry somewhere doing this recursively until all phrases had nonzero entries for anticipations and perseverations for all eight blocks. This resulted in seven "superphrases." Each superphrase had a greater slope for perseverations than anticipations, with the mean of the differences being .513, $t(6) = 4.91, p < .002$.

In the following analyses, we show that this slope difference is robust in several respects. First, because of the potential ambiguities in coding utterances with multiple errors, we recomputed the slopes for anticipations and perseverations with all errors from multiple-error utterances removed. This reduced 769 anticipations and perseverations to 613 errors. The slopes, pooled over word and sound errors, was $-.477$ for anticipations and $-.923$ for perseverations, little changed from the original $-.510$ and $-.958$, respectively.

Next the slopes were recomputed with another subclass of errors removed, those sound anticipations and perseverations where the error unit occurred both before and after the target, but where one unit was closer to the target than the other and, hence, determined classification. Removing these cases resulted in 647 anticipations and perseverations, and the relevant slopes were $-.441$ and $-.927$, which are again very similar to the original slopes.

One feature of anticipations is that they tend to occur early in the phrase, whereas perseverations tend to occur later. For example, word perseverations cannot possibly occur on the first word and word anticipations cannot occur on the last. This raises the question of whether the anticipatory practice effect is a product of an interaction between serial position and learning or whether it is independent of any serial position effects. To examine this, we broke down word anticipations, word perseverations, sound anticipations, and sound perseverations by serial position and examined their slopes. The following error-type/position combinations had enough errors to compute slopes: sound-anticipation/1, word-anticipation/1, sound-perseveration/2, word-anticipation/2, sound-anticipation/3, word-perseveration/3, sound-perseveration/4, word-perseveration/4.[4] To eliminate zero entries, the eight trial blocks were reduced to four by combining the first with the second, the third with the fourth, and so on. The slopes from steepest to shallowest were −2.09 (sound-perseveration/2), −1.43 (word-perseveration/4), −1.26 (word-perseveration/3), −1.17 (sound-perseveration/4), −0.85 (word-anticipation/1), −0.81 (sound-anticipation/3), −0.52 (sound-anticipation/1), −0.44 (word-anticipation/2). The four perseveration slopes are steeper than the four anticipation slopes, and there is clearly no trend associated with serial position. Therefore the anticipatory practice effect is not a byproduct of differential learning across serial positions.

Finally, we consider the possibility that the anticipatory practice effect results from an increased tendency for participants to stop speaking after realizing that they have erred. With more practice, they may pause and correct themselves after making an initial anticipatory slip, for example, "sef's ... chef's sooty shoe soles," whereas with less practice, this error might have ended up as an exchange, "sef's shooty shoe soles." Because incomplete anticipations such as "sef's ... chef's sooty shoe soles" are counted as anticipations, an increased anticipatory proportion could conceivably result from an increased tendency to stop in the middle of exchanges. We therefore eliminated all errors from utterances in which speakers stopped before finishing. As expected, this eliminated more anticipations (84) than perseverations (36), but the difference in slopes for the remaining errors between anticipations (−.400) and perseverations (−.966) was actually a bit larger than originally. Clearly, the anticipatory practice effect is not due to an increasing relative proportion of incomplete anticipations.

In summary, the experiment found a strong anticipatory practice effect, one that is present on sound and word errors, generalizes across items and serial positions, and is robust over different conceptions of what constitutes an anticipation.

Before turning to the theoretical section of the article, there is one more empirical issue that needs to be briefly addressed. We have been assuming that practicing a phrase does something fairly specific to that phrase, for example, changes the connection weights among the linguistic units that represent the phrase. Alternately, the improvement with practice could be a general effect, such that practicing some phrases makes other phrases easy to say. Experiment 2 examined this issue by testing the production of a new group of phrases after eight practice blocks with the original group of phrases. If practice produces only specific effects, the error rate for the new group should be similar to that of the first block of the original group.

Experiment 2: Are Practice Effects Specific or General?

Method

The 16 phrases used in Experiment 1 were divided into two groups of 8. Using the same procedure as in Experiment 1, participants practiced one of the phrase groups for eight trial blocks and then on the ninth, or transfer, block recited the phrases for the other group. Twenty-two participants from the same population as Experiment 1 were tested, counter-balancing the assignment of phrase groups to Blocks 1–8 and the transfer block. Two participants were eliminated because of failure to keep time with the metronome, and one was eliminated because he was not a native speaker of English.

Results and Discussion

Audiotapes were transcribed by William R. Svec, and errors were coded as before by Gary S. Dell. As in Experiment 1, the error totals diminished with practice: 121, 64, 52, 34, 30, 29, 30, 29 for Blocks 1–8 respectively (log/log line, $r = -.97$, slope $= -.717$). On the transfer block, however, there were 98 errors, a total that is not significantly different from that of block 1 ($p > .10$). We conclude that practice effects are largely specific to the practiced phrases, although we cannot rule out the existence of a very small general effect. Because this experiment had fewer than one-quarter of the observations of Experiment 1, it lacked the power to test for the anticipatory practice effect. The expected pattern emerged, but the number of relevant errors is too small. The anticipatory proportion increased with practice ($AP = .53$ for Blocks 1 and 2, 77 errors; $AP = .61$ for Blocks 7 and 8, 23 errors) and, most importantly, went back down for the new items in the transfer block ($AP = .42$, 62 errors).

The results of Experiments 1 and 2 show that practice changes the error probability and error pattern associated with the practiced phrases. The next section considers these effects in the light of theories of serial order.

Serial Order and the Anticipatory Practice Effect

Why does practice create an error pattern that is more oriented to the future than the past? One can address this question in two ways, functionally and mechanistically. That is, one can ask why the system should work this way, given its purposes, and one can ask how it does so. We first provide a functional analysis of serial order and then consider the mechanisms involved in several activation-based theories that have been applied to language, asking how they achieve these functions. From these theories, we develop a formal model and show that it accounts for the anticipatory practice effect and makes the set of predictions that we termed the general anticipatory effect.

What Must a Serial-Order Mechanism Do?

The production of a sequence involves the ordered activation of representations of its elements. We use the designation *present* for the representational unit corresponding to the element that should currently be produced, *past* for the unit for the immediately preceding element, and *future* for the unit representing the element after the *present* element. The principal functions of a serial-order mechanism are as follows:

1. *Turn-On Function*. The system must activate the *present*. It must have some way of determining which unit is the present one and cause it to adopt an activated state.

2. *Turn-Off Function*. The system must deactivate the *past*. Most activation-based theories have assumed that an activated unit is associated with a large positive number and that this high level of activation does not decay immediately. Thus, when the present unit is not the initial one of a sequence, the system must counter the activation of previous units. The turn-off function serves this purpose.

In principle, any system that identifies and activates the *present* and deactivates the *past* is an effective serial-order mechanism. Practically speaking, though, a third function is required:

3. *Prime Function*. The system must prepare to activate the *future*. One factor that motivates the prime function can be called the *throw-away principle*: It is easier to throw away what you have than to find what you do not have. Applying this principle to serial order means that the turn-off function is easy: you can deactivate the past element because the system currently has access to it by virtue of its activated state. As we shall see, many models turn off the past through a *self-inhibition mechanism*: After each element has been fully activated, it throws itself away. The turn-on function, in contrast, is hard: the present element is something that you do not yet have. The prime function counters the throw-away principle by making the *present* something that you do, at least partially, have. It does this by initiating the process of activating units after the present one. As we shall see, the serial-order theories that have been applied to language implement the prime function by means of the activation of a *plan representation*, a unit or set of units that can influence fairly directly the activation of elements of the sequence. By virtue of the activation of the plan, each element is a step away from activation.

While some theories restrict priming to just activation of the plan, most assert that the activation of the plan causes anticipatory activation of units for upcoming elements. Actual activation of future elements is important for language because the appropriateness and form of the *present* often depends on what the *future* will be. Every language offers countless examples of these dependencies at the grammatical, phonological, and articulatory levels. For instance, in English whether you say *a* or *an* is governed by the form of the next word. Or, in German, the identity of the perfect auxiliary, *sein* (to be) or *haben* (have), depends on a verb that could be several words in the future.

Examples such as *a–an* are true future-oriented dependencies because one really must have a representation of the *future* to determine the *present*. You do not first decide whether to say *a* or *an* and then choose a next word that fits. The earlier depends on the later, rather than the reverse. Many dependencies in language, though, are past-oriented; a later item depends on an earlier one, for example, English subject–verb number agreement when constituents are in their normal order. *Mary is*, not *Mary are*. With past-oriented dependencies one can imagine two possible production mechanisms. One is a look-to-the-past mechanism. When deciding whether to say *is* or *are*, look back to what was already encoded for the subject of the sentence. The alternative is to program the *future* with the *present*. When *Mary* is the *present*, prepare the *future* verb that is to agree with it. To the extent that past-oriented dependencies are processed by this latter mechanism, they are much like future-oriented dependencies in that there is a need for co-activation of the *present* and *future*.

The tendency for a system to produce anticipations and perseverations should be related to the relative activation of the *past*, *present*, and *future*. To the extent that the turn-on and turn-off functions are working well, one would not expect perseverations. The balance between the turn-on and priming functions should affect the probability of anticipations. How effectively these functions are achieved and how this might vary with practice requires an analysis of the mechanisms behind them in serial-order models, to which we now turn.

Theories of Serial Order in Language

Hierarchies with Forward Lateral Inhibition   These models (e.g., Estes, 1972; Rumelhart & Norman, 1982) use a plan (or "chunk" or "control") unit that connects by excitatory links to all of the elementary units in the sequence. Hence, when the plan is activated, it tends to activate the elements. Plan units can themselves act as elements in higher-order plans creating the multileveled hierarchies that appear to be necessary to account for data on sequence generation (e.g., Gordon & Meyer, 1987; Rosenbaum, Kenny, & Derr, 1983) and language production (e.g., Bock & Loebell, 1990; Ferreira, 1993; Fowler, Treiman, & Gross, 1993; MacKay, 1973; Meyer, 1994). Furthermore, each elementary unit inhibits all other units after it with the result that, initially, only the first element has considerable activation. After the first element has reached a threshold level of activation, it is deemed to have been produced, and the unit undergoes self-inhibition: It turns itself off. As a consequence of the inactivity of the first unit, it no longer inhibits later units and, hence, the second unit gains activation and so on until the end of the sequence. The top part of Figure 24.2

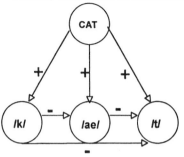

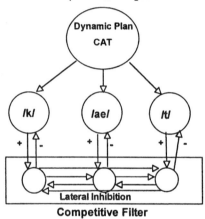

Figure 24.2

The mechanisms of forward-lateral-inhibition and competitive-queuing models illustrated with the sounds of the word *cat*. Excitatory connections are indicated by plus signs and inhibitory connections minus signs. Self-inhibition is not shown.

shows the connections involved in a forward-lateral-inhibition model representing the sounds of the word *cat*.

In forward-lateral-inhibition models, the prime function happens through the activation of the plan. Whether there is any anticipatory activation of the *future*, though, depends on the strength of the inhibitory connections and the exact nature of the activation function, but generally, the inhibition should dampen every unit except the *present*. The turn-off function is achieved by the self-inhibition of the *past*. Finally, the entire system effectively turns on the *present* because the prime function works with the turn-off function and the lateral inhibition so that the turn-off of the *past* automatically turns on the *present*.

Competitive-Queuing Model   Forward-lateral-inhibition models store a sequence by exciting its elements and using forward lateral inhibition among them to sort out the order. However, if the same response units are used for the same elements when they appear in different sequences, effective serial order is not always achieved because of interference among the sequences. For example, if response units for words are something like phonemes, words that are phonological anagrams, such as *cat, act,* and *tack,* cannot all be represented (see, e.g., Dell & O'Seaghdha, 1994; Houghton, 1990; and MacKay, 1987). A related problem concerns sequences with repeated elements such as the word *did.* How can the lateral inhibition between /I/ and /d/ sort out this sequence? The competitive-queuing model developed by Houghton (1990) provides a good alternative (see also Burgess & Hitch, 1992; Gupta & MacWhinney, 1997; and Hartley & Houghton, 1996). This model, based on interactive activation, learning, and serial-order principles pioneered by Grossberg (1978, 1982), has three layers of units: plan units, response units, and a *competitive filter.* Consider the sequence of phonemes in *cat,* as illustrated in the bottom of Figure 24.2. Plan units for *cat* connect to the response units /k/, /æ/, and /t/, such that there is, initially, a gradient of activation with /k/ being most activated, then /æ/, and then /t/. The gradient results from a time-varying signal in the plan that evolves from a state that can be interpreted as *beginning of cat* to one representing *end of cat* and from excitatory connection weights between plan and response units that are set by a supervised Hebbian learning algorithm. The activation levels of the response units are then copied into the competitive filter, which contains one unit for each response unit. However, the units in the competitive filter strongly inhibit one another with the result that only the most highly activated unit, the one for /k/, remains active. This constitutes the selection of the initial element. The competitive filter unit for /k/ then inhibits the response unit for /k/ in the middle layer, leading to a pattern in which /æ/ is most active, then /t/, and then /k/. The competitive filter is then reloaded and selects /æ/; /æ/ is then inhibited, leaving /t/ as the most active, and so on. Probably the most important difference between the competitive-queuing model and forward-lateral-inhibition models is that the competitive-queuing model separates the activation gradient in the middle layer from the competitive interactions that take place in the third layer. This enables the model to retain the anticipatory activation of future units (in the middle layer) while it is throwing all of the activation to the present unit (in the competitive filter layer). Moreover, anagrams and repeated elements are not a problem. The plans for *cat, act,* and *tack* can create different gradients among the response units /k/, /æ/, and /t/ because the gradients are determined by connections between the plans and the response units, not by lateral inhibition among the response units. The variation in each plan itself over time handles the repeated element problem (Houghton, 1990).

In sum, the competitive-queuing model effectively turns on the *present* by making it the most activated response unit, given the signal from the plan, and by inhibiting all non-*present* units in the competitive filter. It turns off the past by the architectural assumption of inhibition from each competitive filter unit to each response unit. Finally, it prepares the *future* by excitatory connections from plan units to response units.

Novel Serial Orders and Frame-Based Models   The models discussed thus far can store a sequence and reproduce it when called upon. So, a phrase such as *the big dog* can be produced if it was previously encountered and a suitable plan was stored. However, the language-production system must be able to order novel sequences during grammatical encoding and, to a lesser extent, during phonological encoding. We can assemble *a tiny aardvark* even though we have never heard or said it before because we know the categories of the words (determiner, adjective, noun) and we know how those categories should be ordered. Similarly, given the phonemes /ŋ/, /æ/, and /m/, English speakers know that there is only one way to order them, even if they have never encountered the string *mang* before.

Clearly, serial-order plans need to be extendable to novel sequences. Psycholinguistic models of production have addressed this need by including rule-governed *frames* as components to plans (Bock, 1982; Dell, 1986; Garrett, 1975; Levelt, 1989; MacKay, 1972; Shattuck-Hufnagel, 1979; Stemberger, 1991). A frame is a sequence (or hierarchy) of categorically specified slots. A syntactic frame would contain syntactic categories (e.g., Determiner–Adjective–Noun), and a phonological frame would have phonological categories (e.g., Onset–Nucleus–Coda). The serial order of a sequence is determined when elements are inserted into the slots. We should make clear that frames may be necessary, but are not sufficient for generating novel serial orders. The frame contains knowledge about how to order a novel set of elements; it does not uniquely determine the elements.

A good example of an activation-based model that includes frames is the node structure theory of MacKay (1982, 1987). The theory has been developed for both the order of words in sentences, the *phrasal system*, and for the order of sounds within words, the *phonological system*. Figure 24.3 illustrates the theory. Consider the sequence of words *the cat*. The relevant content nodes consist of nodes for the words *the* and *cat* and a phrasal node that we informally label *the cat* (for the complex concept of *cat–sing–def*). There are structural nodes for *Det* (for determiner) and *N* (for noun). The phrasal node has excitatory connections to *the, cat, Det,* and *N; Det* has positive connections to all determiners, including *the*; and *N* has positive connections to all nouns, including *cat*. An important feature of the model is that order is stored only in the structural nodes. Specifically, *Det* inhibits *N*, representing the rule that determiners come before nouns in noun phrases. These structural nodes and their connections constitute the

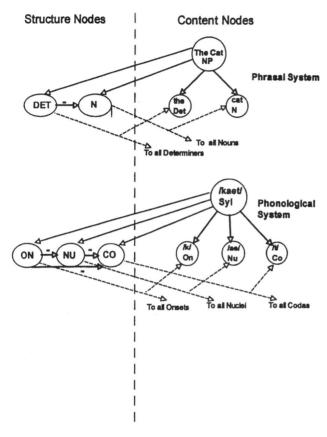

Figure 24.3
The phrasal and phonological systems in the node structure theory. Inhibitory connections are labeled by minus signs and excitatory connections are unlabeled. Content nodes are circles, and structure nodes are ovals. Self-inhibition is not shown. (NP = noun phrase; DET = determiner; N = noun; Syl = syllable; ON = onsets; NU = nuclei; CO = codas.).

frame. Note that the node structure theory is similar to the forward-lateral-inhibition models in that order is represented by lateral inhibition. However, the node structure theory differs by separating structure, where order is stored, from content, which derives its order from the structure.

More specifically, the node structure theory works like this: The production of *the cat* starts with the activation of *the cat*. Although many such phrasal nodes will already be stored in memory, one can assume that they can be created by the conjunction of existing features. The phrasal node then delivers some activation to *the, cat, Det*, and *N*. The structural nodes also receive input from a separate set of *timing nodes* (not shown in the figure), which control the rate of production. This results in a large buildup of activation in *Det* and *N*, and because *Det* inhibits *N*, only *Det* reaches a special "activation threshold," causing it to sustain its activation at a high level. *Det* then sends a large amount of activation to all determiners. The content node for *the* thus obtains activation both from *the cat* and from *Det*, sufficient for it to pass the activation threshold. This constitutes the filling of the *Det* slot with the word *the*. After a node has reached activation threshold and has had its activation level sustained for a period of time, it enters a period of self-inhibition. When *Det* becomes self-inhibited, the next structure node *N* then reaches threshold. The *N* sends activation to all nouns and so activation converges on *cat* causing it to reach threshold, effectively filling the *N*-slot with *cat*.

The ordering of the phonemes of a word such as *cat* uses the same kind of frame-based mechanism in the node structure theory. Here the content nodes might include the syllable *kæt*, and the phonemes /k/-*onset*, /æ/-*nucleus*, and /t/-*coda*, and the structural nodes would be *stressed syllable, onset, nucleus,* and *coda*. As in the phrasal system, order is represented by forward lateral inhibition between the structural nodes. By activating the syllable /kæt/, eventually the sequence /k/-onset, /æ/-nucleus, and /t/-coda would be produced.[5]

The node structure theory and other activation-based models with frames (e.g., Berg, 1988; Dell, 1986, 1988/1989; Eikmeyer & Schade, 1991; Gasser, 1988; Gupta & MacWhinney, 1997; Hartley & Houghton, 1996; Levelt, 1989; Meijer, 1994; Roelofs, 1992; Schade, 1992; Stemberger, 1985, 1990, 1991) have two advantages over the models without frames. First, as we explained before, they are consistent with our abilities to order novel sets of elements. Second, there is a fairly glaring empirical difficulty with the models without frames as theories of phonological encoding (Hartley & Houghton, 1996; MacKay, 1987). In the forward-lateral-inhibition and competitive-queuing models, the predicted pattern of misorderings of phonemes involves rearrangements of the phonemes within a word. So, /kæt/ would be predicted to slip to /tkæ/, /ækt/ or /ktæ/. Unfortunately, these kinds of errors never happen. Most commonly, phonological errors on a syllable like /kæt/ involve the substitution of sounds from nearby syllables, where the substituting sound emerges in the same syllabic position and where the resulting string of sounds is phonologically acceptable (Boomer & Laver, 1968; MacKay, 1970). For example "the cat is chasing ..." results in "the chat ..." or "the cass ..." as Error Examples 1–3 discussed previously. Categorically specified frames derived from the phonological patterns in the language, together with a mechanism that inserts sounds from particular categories into frame slots, provide for exactly the right kind of phonological errors (Dell, 1986; MacKay, 1982; Shattuck-Hufnagel, 1979; Stemberger, 1991).

Frame-based, spreading-activation approaches to serial order in language, such as the node structure theory, are numerous and diverse. Consequently, we will not review them all other than to note some dimensions of variation. The principal way that these theories vary concerns their assumptions about particular levels of processing. For example, the node structure theory has content nodes for phrases, words, morphemes, syllables, syllabic constituents, phonemes, and features. Other theories (e.g., Gupta & MacWhinney, 1997; Gupta, 1995; Roelofs, 1992) have fewer levels among content items. Theories also differ greatly in how the frames work. Schade (1992), for example, uses excitatory forward connections from frame element i to element $i + 1$ to store the order of categories, whereas the node structure theory uses forward lateral inhibition. Another dimension of difference concerns how many different frames are needed for particular processing levels. The theories of Dell (1986), Gupta (1995), and Hartley and Houghton (1996) used a single frame at the phonological level, one that was sufficiently flexible to handle all possible syllables. Others (e.g., Dell, 1988/1989; Stemberger, 1991) hypothesize the existence of several word-shape frames, one frame for each possible patterning of consonants and vowels in a word. Finally, frame-based models have differed on whether elements send activation to plans, as well as plans to elements. For example, Dell (1986), Harley (1993), Stemberger (1985), as well as the node structure theory, allow for two-way interaction between word plans and phonological elements. Roelofs (1995) does not.

In summary, frame-based approaches are both varied and complex. In fact, the added complexity of separate frames must be considered their main weakness, when compared to the models lacking frames. Individual models, of course, have strengths and weaknesses related to particular linguistic and psycholinguistic assumptions. For our purposes, though, frame-based, spreading-activation approaches share important general principles: The activation of the *present* is achieved by input from both a structural frame node and a higher level content node (e.g., in the node structure theory the phrasal node for word sequences or a word or syllable node for phoneme sequences). The *future* is prepared because input from the higher level content node is sent to all elements dominated by that node. Finally, the *past* is deactivated by a period of self-inhibition after a node has reached activation threshold.

PDP Recurrent Network Models   For the sake of completeness, we mention the parallel-distributed-processing (PDP) recurrent network models of serial order (e.g., Cleeremans & McClelland, 1991; Dell et al., 1993; Elman, 1990; Jordan, 1986). These models map between a plan representation and a sequence of outputs by means of a changing contextual representation that is derived from the network's previous state of activation and a set of hidden units that computes a nonlinear combination of the plan and the context. The connection strengths among the units are learned by back-propagation or related supervised algorithms. However, because the configuration of excitation and inhibition is determined by the particular sequences that are learned, rather than by architectural assumptions as in the previous models, it is not so easy to characterize. We can say, though, that if the learned sequences do not often exhibit immediate repetition of units (which is true for word or phoneme sequences), then the network should develop a general mechanism for turning off each *past* representation.

The PDP approaches have been used successfully to account for coarticulation (Jordan, 1986) and some facts about phonological speech errors (Dell et al., 1993). It is unclear, though, whether these models, insofar as they lack explicit frames, can account for the speech error patterns that have motivated the frame-based models (see Dell et al., 1993; Hartley & Houghton, 1996).

A General Model

All of the models discussed share four characteristics: (a) Learning involves the creation and strengthening of excitatory connections from plans to elements; (b) the abilities to activate the *present* and to prepare the *future* are achieved by these connections: Consequently, the activation of the *present* and the preparation of the *future* are linked; (c) the turn-off function is effective: That is, regardless of how activated the *past* is, it can be quickly brought down to an absolutely low level; and (d) the turn-off function does not require new learning.[6] These characteristics reflect what we earlier called the throw-away principle: Getting rid of what is already activated is easier than activating what is needed. People do not need to learn how to turn off the *past* the way they need to learn to activate the *present* and prepare the *future*.

These generalizations from the models allow us to account for the anticipatory practice effect. Compare Figure 24.4, which shows the hypothetical activations of the *past*, *present*, and *future* under good circumstances, that is, when a

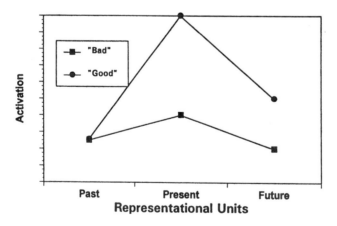

Figure 24.4
A mechanism for the anticipatory practice effect. The difference between good and bad circumstances occurs in the amount of activation of the *present* and *future*, not in the *past*.

sequence is well learned, and under bad circumstances, when it is not. The idea is that practice increases the activation of both the *present* and *future*, and does little to the *past*. Learning a sequence in all of the models involves the strengthening of connections between plans and their elements. This increases the potential to activate the *present* and the *future*. Practice does not, however, have much effect on the deactivation of the *past*, because this function is not achieved through the learning of the plan. Given that anticipations reflect the relative activation of the *present* and *future*, and perseverations, that of the *present* and *past*, the anticipatory proportion should increase with practice.

We now work out the empirical consequences of this account of the anticipatory practice effect. Rather than derive predictions from each model, though, we offer a new model that exhibits many of their common characteristics and is sufficiently simple in its size, activation function, and selection decisions to allow for formal derivations.

The model contains four nodes, one for the plan, and one each for *past*, *present*, and *future*. The plan connects to each element with a long-term positive weight, w, the value of which is a product of learning. These weights are temporarily altered during sequence production, the alteration depending on when the element in question is scheduled. The weight from plan to *past* becomes 0; the weight to the *present* remains at w; and the weight to the *future* becomes bw, where b is a positive fraction representing anticipatory activation. One can view these modifications as inputs to *past*, *present*, and *future* of 0, 1, and b, respectively, that combine multiplicatively with the inputs of w from the plan.

We adopt two perspectives on these short-term weight alterations. First, we view them as corresponding to various mechanisms in the particular serial-order models. In the forward-lateral-inhibition models and the node structure theory, the multiplicative input of 0 to the *past* is part of the self-inhibitory mechanism. In the competitive-queuing model, it is part of the competitive-filter-to-response-units inhibition. Parameter b corresponds to the joint effects of plan-to-element excitation and forward-lateral inhibition in the forward-lateral-inhibition models, to the extent of the activation gradient set up by plan-to-response-unit connection weights in the competitive-queuing model, and to the combination of priming from the higher level content node and upcoming frame nodes in the node structure theory.

Second, we have our own perspective on the weight modifications in the general model. For reasons mentioned before, we are persuaded that structural frames are needed for serial order in language. The order of a set of linguistic units must come, at least in part, from knowledge of how their categories are ordered. Let us therefore assume that *past*, *present*, and *future* are content nodes that belong to the categories X, Y, and Z, respectively. The frame consists of structural nodes for X, Y, and Z, specified for that order. We propose that the frame works by sending a signal of 0 to all members of the "past" category (here, X), a signal of 1.0 to all members of the "present" category (Y), and signal

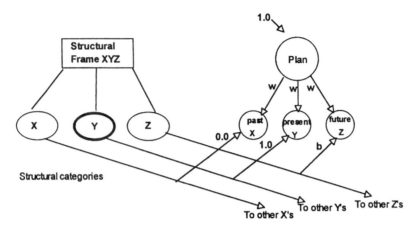

Figure 24.5
A general model of serial order in language. Content nodes (right) or *past, present,* and *future* receive inputs from the plan along connections of weight w and inputs from structural nodes (left). The figure indicates that structural node Y is the present category.

of b to all members of the "future" category (Z). These signals are multiplicative with other inputs to the content nodes resulting in net temporary weights of 0 to *past*, w to *present*, and bw to *future*. Notice that this perspective does not say how the order of categories within the frame itself is stored, but it is easy enough to build the competitive queuing, recurrent net, or the forward-lateral-inhibition mechanism (as MacKay does in the node structure theory) into the frame itself, so that the frame signals to the content nodes are ordered appropriately. We assume the existence of such a mechanism. Figure 24.5 illustrates the model, under the interpretation that the weight alterations derive from the frame.

The model uses assumptions about the initial activation of the nodes and a spreading activation rule to compute activations of each element. The relative activations of *past, present,* and *future* are then used to determine the probabilities of error. Specifically, an input of 1.0 is given to the plan element, and the past is assumed to have its activation initialized to some small positive value, c, reflecting its previous activation and the result of an effective turn-off mechanism. Activation spreads for n time steps according to a linear rule:

$$a(j, t) = a(j, t - 1)(1 - d) + \text{Input}(j, t). \tag{1}$$

Where $a(j, t)$ is the activation of node j at time step t, d is the decay rate, and $\text{Input}(j, t)$ is the net input to node j given by

$$\text{Input}(j, t) = \sum_i w(i, j) a(i, t - 1), \tag{2}$$

where $w(i, j)$ is the weight from node i to node j.

In computing the activation of the elements, we consider two kinds of input to the plan, a *pulsed* and a *clamped* input. The pulsed input assumes that, for each element in the sequence, the plan's activation is set to 1.0. However, the plan is subject to decay like any node and, hence, must get a new pulse for each element. The clamped input assumes that the plan's activation is held at 1.0 throughout the production of the sequence. Our consideration of these two cases arises because both kinds of input have been proposed in serial-order models (e.g., Dell, 1986, is pulsed; most others are explicitly or functionally clamped). As we will show, though, both kinds of input lead to the same principal predictions.

The absolute activation levels after n time steps for the *past, present*, and *future* after pulsed and clamped input to the plan are given by Equations 3–5 and Equations 6–8, respectively.

$$\text{(pulsed)} \ a(present) = nw(1-d)^{(n-1)} \tag{3}$$

$$\text{(pulsed)} \ a(past) = c(1-d)^{n} \tag{4}$$

$$\text{(pulsed)} \ a(future) = nwb(1-d)^{(n-1)} \tag{5}$$

$$\text{(clamped)} \ a(present) = w(1/d)[1-(1-d)^{n}] \tag{6}$$

$$\text{(clamped)} \ a(past) = c(1-d)^{n} \tag{7}$$

$$\text{(clamped)} \ a(future) = wb(1/d)[1-(1-d)^{n}] \tag{8}$$

What is important for determining order is the relative activation of the nodes. In this respect it is useful to define the perseverative tendency, P, as the ratio of $a(past)$ to $a(present)$ and the anticipatory tendency, A, as that of $a(future)$ to $a(present)$. These are given by Equations 9–11.

$$P = \frac{c(1-d)}{nw} \ \text{(pulsed)} \tag{9}$$

$$P = \frac{cd}{w[(1-d)^{-n}-1]} \ \text{(clamped)} \tag{10}$$

$$A = b \ \text{(both pulsed and clamped)} \tag{11}$$

We further assume that the element that is output after n time steps is determined by a stochastic decision rule (e.g., McClelland & Rumelhart, 1981) based on a transformation of the relative activation levels. The relative activation, R, of an element is the proportion of the total activation in the elements that that element has. These are given by Equations 12–14.

$$R(past) = \frac{P}{P+A+1} \tag{12}$$

$$R(present) = \frac{1}{P + A + 1} \tag{13}$$

$$R(future) = \frac{A}{P + A + 1} \tag{14}$$

The probability of selection of a particular element is then given by Equation 15.

$$\text{probability of selection for element } i = \frac{S(i)}{\sum_{j} S(j)}, \tag{15}$$

where $S(i) = e^{\mu R(i)}$, and μ is a parameter that determines how rapidly response strength grows with relative activation. The probability of a correct selection is therefore given by Equation 15 when i is the *present*. Anticipations and perseverations are analogous where i is the *future* and *past*, respectively.

Model Characteristics

Anticipatory Practice Effect   Practicing a sequence is assumed to increase w. The anticipatory practice effect then arises because the perseverative tendency, P, decreases as w increases (Equations 9 and 10), while the anticipatory tendency, A, (Equation 11) is independent of w. Consequently, the proportion of errors that are anticipatory increases as connection weights get larger. Figure 24.6

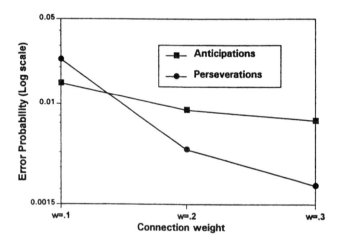

Figure 24.6
Anticipation and perseveration probabilities as a function of connection weight (w) in the general model when number of time steps (n) = 4, decay (d) = .5, residual activation rate (c) = .3, anticipatory activation rate (b) = .3, and response parameter (μ) = 10.

shows an example set of parameters. Increasing w makes both perseveratory and anticipatory errors less likely, but the effect on perseverations is much stronger, resulting in a higher anticipatory proportion for larger values of w. To put it less formally, the activation of the *present* and *future* are both linked to practice and so increase together. The activation of the *past* is not linked to practice and so its relative influence diminishes with practice.

The Effect of Speech Rate   The model makes two specific claims about speech rate, which is represented by n, the number of time steps passing during the retrieval of each element. The first of these is unsurprising: As n increases (as speech slows), errors become less likely. This claim is most definitely true empirically and gives the model a general basis for speed–accuracy trade-offs in production (e.g., Dell, 1986; MacKay, 1987). The second is more interesting: As n increases, the anticipatory proportion increases. This will be called the *anticipatory speech-rate effect*. The basis for the prediction can be seen by noting that n is similar to w in that P decreases as n increases, while A is independent of n. The actual relation between n and P differs in the clamped and pulsed cases and is not simple (see Equations 9 and 10). Nonetheless, any increase in time makes the perseveratory tendency smaller, while leaving the anticipatory tendency unaffected. Consequently, the anticipatory proportion increases as speech slows. Earlier, we suggested that there was some evidence for this relation from a deadline task (Dell, 1990), and one of the purposes of Experiment 3 will be to gather further data on this question.

The General Anticipatory Effect   One of the most striking characteristics of the model is that the anticipatory proportion can be predicted solely from overall error rate, provided that parameter b does not vary. That is, you do not need to know w, n, c, or d to predict the extent to which errors are anticipatory; you only need to know the overall error rate. This is illustrated in Figure 24.7, which shows the relation between the log (overall error probability) and the anticipatory proportion for various combinations of values of w, n, c, and d. Regardless of the combination, the predicted anticipatory proportion falls on the line. The actual place on the line is determined by P, which is a computed combination of w, n, c, and d.

The relation between overall correctness, regardless of parameter values, and anticipatory proportion was called the general anticipatory effect. It is, we believe, a far-reaching prediction from the model, because there are many variables that can affect overall error rate. Our claim is that any error-prone circumstance will be associated mostly with perseveratory errors, while relatively error-free cases will have relatively more anticipatory errors. Specifically, any variation in overall error rates that reflects the knowledge of individual sequences (w), time (n), activation decay (d), or residual activation in the *past* resulting from its turn-off (c), will be associated with a predictable anticipatory

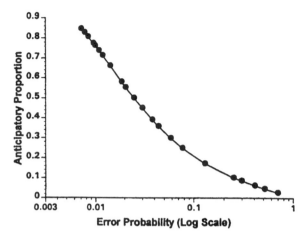

Figure 24.7
The general anticipatory effect in the model. The graphed points reflect a variety of values of connection weight (w) (.1–.3), number of time steps (n) (1–4), residual activation rate (c) (.2–.4), and decay (d) (.4–.6) with anticipatory activation rate (b) (.3) and response parameter (μ) (10) held constant.

proportion. This relation does not, however, hold for variation that can be attributed to parameter b, the signal sent from the frame to the *future* that mediates anticipatory activation. Varying b actually shifts the line relating error rate to anticipatory proportion that is defined by variation among the other four parameters, rather than leading to movement along the line. Given our conception of b as a feature of the structural frame, we see its magnitude as reflecting the grammatical or phonological structure of the intended utterance (e.g., the kind or size of phrases) or even the nature of the language itself (e.g., the location of the heads of phrases in the language). One should note, as well, that the general anticipatory effect also does not hold for variation in parameter μ, which governs the decision process.

Experiment 3 varies both practice and speech rate in an attempt to test the predictions about speech rate and the general anticipatory effect. We assume that practice effects w and speech rate affects n. It is predicted that increased practice and a slower speech rate will lead to fewer errors and to a greater anticipatory proportion. Most importantly, the anticipatory proportion should be predictable from overall error rate, regardless of the combination of practice and speech rate that led to that error rate. Specifically, the model expects an approximately linear relation between log (error rate) and anticipatory proportion, provided that the anticipatory proportion is not extreme (see Figure 24.7).

Experiment 3: General Anticipatory Effect

Method

Materials   The same 16 phrases were used. On the basis of a pilot experiment using a variety of speech rates, the phrases were placed in two groups of 8, such that each group of phrases was approximately equally error prone.

Participants   Forty-three students from the Illinois participant pool were tested. Two were eliminated because of failure to keep up with the metronome and one because of equipment failure, resulting in 40 official participants. Half of these produced the 8 phrases of Group 1 at a slow rate (1.73 beats/s) and the 8 phrases of Group 2 at a fast rate (2.83 beats/s). The other 20 students had the assignment of phrase groups to speech rates reversed.

Procedure   Each phrase was practiced for eight trial blocks, using much the same procedure as in Experiment 1. There were two differences. First, there was within-subject manipulation of speech rate. Each trial block involved practice at a fast rate for some phrases and a slow rate for others. Second, participants were asked to leave "at least two beats" between the two repetitions of each phrase. Experiment 1 had asked them to leave exactly four beats, which may have caused the speakers to covertly produce the digits "one, two, three, four," an undesirable source of phonological interference.

Results and Discussion

Tape recordings were transcribed by Lisa K. Burger, and errors were coded as before by Gary S. Dell. Table 24.2 shows the number of errors in each category as a function of speech rate and practice block. Both rate and practice had powerful effects on the overall error rate. The fast and slow rates were associated with 1,551 and 849 errors, respectively. Practice reduced errors from 14.3 per 100 words in the first block to 4.9 per 100 words for the eighth block for the fast rate. For the slow rate, these rates were 9.2 per 100 and 1.8 per 100, respectively. Figure 24.8 shows that the effect of practice was well captured by a linear log/log relation. Interestingly, the slope was marginally steeper for the slow rate than the fast rate, $t(15) = 1.94$, $p < .10$.

Given that the two independent variables had expected and strong effects on error rate, we now turn to aspects of the data that impact the model. First, the expectation of an anticipatory practice effect was examined. The number of anticipations and perseverations for each trial block was determined separately for each phrase (pooled across speech rate and word-versus-sound errors), and the data from phrases with zero entries were combined as before, with the result that there were nine "super-phrases." The average slope for the perseverations was significantly steeper than that for the anticipations, with the mean difference being .307, $t(8) = 3.00$, $p < .025$. This is a smaller difference than that

Table 24.2
Error totals, log–log slopes, anticipatory proportions (APs), and correlations for experiment 3

Category	Trial 1	2	3	4	5	6	7	8	Total	Slope	r
Slow rate											
Sound	154	110	80	69	68	50	36	35	602	−.710	−.97
SA	40	33	21	26	25	20	12	12	189	−.539	−.88
SP	70	42	33	25	25	15	11	15	236	−.834	−.96
SE	24	16	11	11	10	7	7	3	89	−.799	−.91
SAP	20	19	15	7	8	8	6	5	88	−.706	−.92
Word	64	45	25	19	17	16	13	9	208	−.903	−.98
WA	21	18	8	7	8	3	7	5	77	−.778	−.86
WP	22	17	13	7	8	11	3	4	85	−.842	−.86
WE	15	4	4	2	1	2	2	0	30		
WS	6	6	0	3	0	0	1	0	16		
Other	17	6	4	3	4	2	0	3	39		
Total	235	161	109	91	89	68	49	47	849	−.774	−.98
Anticipatory proportion	.40	.46	.39	.51	.50	.47	.56	.47			
Fast rate											
Sound	265	197	171	136	142	110	87	101	1209	−.507	−.97
SA	66	36	49	33	41	30	30	36	321	−.300	−.78
SP	108	85	76	53	47	48	29	40	486	−.574	−.94
SE	38	41	22	25	23	17	17	14	197	−.496	−.91
SAP	53	35	24	25	31	15	11	11	205	−.723	−.90
Word	81	39	43	28	18	19	26	21	275	−.659	−.91
WA	24	6	12	9	5	6	8	5	75	−.572	−.75
WP	33	25	19	9	9	10	16	11	132	−.572	−.81
WE	12	5	8	9	3	2	1	3	43	−.920	−.77
WS	12	3	4	1	1	1	1	2	25	−1.092	−.94
Other	20	16	5	7	8	4	4	3	67	−.880	−.91
Total	366	252	219	171	168	133	117	125	1551	−.549	−.99
Anticipatory proportion	.39	.28	.39	.40	.45	.38	.46	.45			

Note. For categories with zero entries, no slopes or correlations were computed. SA = sound anticipation; SP = sound perseveration; SE = sound exchange; SAP = sound anticipation–perseveration; WA = word anticipation; WP = word perseveration; WE = word exchange; WS = word substitution.

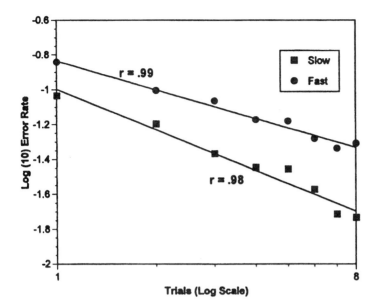

Figure 24.8
Overall error rate in Experiment 3 as a function of practice and speech rate.

found in Experiment 1 (.513), but it adequately replicates the anticipatory practice effect.

Next, we tested the prediction of an anticipatory speech-rate effect, that the anticipatory proportion will be greater with a slower speech rate. The *AP* was determined for each phrase for each rate, pooling across practice block and error categories. In support of the prediction, the *AP* was significantly greater for the slow rate (.45) than the fast rate (.39), $t(15) = 2.78$, $p < .025$.

The most important test of the model concerns the general anticipatory effect. Can the *AP* for each of the 16 conditions of the experiment, 2 (rates) × 8 (practice blocks), be predicted solely from overall error rate, that is, without regard for the combination of variables that led to that error rate? Figure 24.9 plots *AP* as a function of the log(10) of error rate per word and gives the resulting regression line. As predicted by the model, *AP* decreases linearly with the log of the overall error rate; slope $= -.193$, intercept $= .185$, $r = -.73$, $p < .001$. Each condition results in an *AP* that is close to the line, and deviations appear to be nonsystematic. Another way to illustrate the finding is to note that if the 8 points from the fast conditions and those from slow conditions are fit separately, the regression lines are very similar (fast conditions: slope $= -.154$, intercept $= .248$; slow conditions: slope $= -.193$, intercept $= .178$).

The data presented in Figure 24.9 support the general anticipatory effect with respect to two manipulations—practice and speech rate. These manipulations

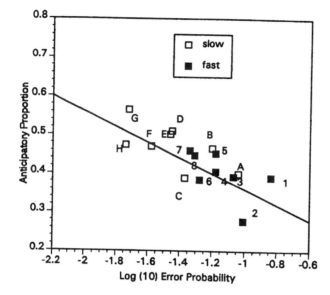

Figure 24.9
The general anticipatory effect illustrated for variation over speech rate and practice in Experiment 3. The numbers 1–8 and the letters A–H indicate practice Blocks 1–8 for the fast and the slow rates respectively.

are tied to specific parameters in the model, namely w and n, which work together to determine both how error-prone the system is and the extent to which errors are anticipatory.

Another factor affecting errors is individual speakers. There were large individual differences in error probability, particularly with the slow speaking rate, where error totals pooled over blocks ranged from 3 to 59 errors per speaker. This variation allows for another test of the general anticipatory effect. According to the model, if individuals differ in connection weights (w), residual activation in the *past* (c), decay rate (d), or a combination of any of these, and if this variation is large compared to individual variation in parameter b, the strength of the signal from the frame to the *future*, then the more error-prone speakers should have relatively more perseverations. The general anticipatory effect gives us this prediction without us having to know exactly which parameters are associated with individual differences—only that the differences are primarily associated with the cluster of parameters in Equations 9 and 10.

The prediction about individual differences was tested by examining each speaker's overall error rate and his or her *AP*. Because there was more individual variation in the slow speech-rate condition than in the fast one, error totals were kept separate for fast and slow rates for each speaker. Three of the resulting 80 speaker–condition cases were removed because they lacked antic-

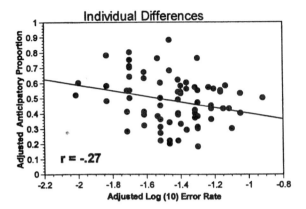

Figure 24.10
The general anticipatory effect illustrated for individual variation in Experiment 3. The error rates and anticipatory proportions (*APs*) are adjusted to remove the existing correlation between speech rate and *AP*. Each point represents a single participant for a particular speech rate.

ipations and perseverations, making for 77 data points. So that the points only reflect individual variation, each point was adjusted to remove the known correlation between *AP* and speech rate. If this covariation is not removed, the predicted relation between *AP* and error rate across speakers could emerge for the simple reason that faster rates have more errors and lower *APs*. The resulting scatter plot on the adjusted data is shown in Figure 24.10. In support of the general anticipatory effect, the more error-prone participants had lower *APs*, $r = -.27$, $p < .05$. The points scatter themselves around a regression line that is similar to the line derived by variation in practice and speech rate (slope $= -.188$, intercept $= .214$). The correlation, though, is much lower because each point is based on many fewer errors and, hence, noise is more dominant.

In summary, Experiment 3 replicated the anticipatory practice effect, found an anticipatory speech-rate effect, and most importantly, provided evidence for a general anticipatory effect. Variation in practice and speech rate, and individual differences, all led to the same relation between the log of overall error rate and the anticipatory proportion. These results provide good support for the principles behind the proposed serial-order model.

In the remainder of the article, we consider the scope of the general anticipatory effect, both with respect to other variables' influence on error rate and with respect to the universality of the functional relation found in Figure 24.9.

Is the General Anticipatory Effect General?

The relationship between overall error rate and the anticipatory proportion found in Experiment 3 should apply to other data sets as well. First, we consider whether the line presented in Figure 24.9 also fits the data from Experiments 1 and 2. Then we examine data sets from outside our experiments that used the same error categories that we did. Finally, we consider the potential for testing the general anticipatory effect in other domains, both linguistic and nonlinguistic.

Other Data Sets

Experiments 1 and 2   The line relating *AP* to log(overall error rate) derived from Experiment 3 should apply to the data from the earlier experiments. Experiment 3 found that variation due to practice, speech rate, and individual differences generates points along this line. According to the model, this is to be expected for any variation in the key parameters, the ones in Equations 9 and 10. Speech rate and practice are identified with parameters *n* and *w*, respectively. Individual differences are harder to identify with a single parameter. Nonetheless, the fact that individual *AP* was, to some extent, predictable from individual error rate suggests, within the context of the model, that some proportion of individual variation can be associated with the key parameters. Given these findings, the line in Figure 24.9 should fit the other experiments because the main differences among the experiments is their participants and speech rates. Importantly, the same phrases were used and the error-categorization scheme was the same. Any differences in overall error due to the particular speakers, speech rates, and interactions of these factors with practice, should still lead to a predictable *AP*.

Figure 24.11 takes the line derived from Experiment 3 and adds to it the relevant points for each practice block in Experiment 1. Experiment 2 is also included, but because of the many fewer errors in this experiment, Blocks 1–4 and Blocks 5–8 are pooled; the transfer block is kept separate. The points contributed by Experiments 1 and 2, by themselves, are associated with a line that is reliably different from zero ($r = -.65$, $p < .05$) and which is quite similar to the one from Experiment 3 (slope $= -.210$ compared to $-.193$; intercept $= .168$ compared to .185). At least within the confines of the materials and methods of these experiments, overall error rate, by itself, accounts for the bulk of the variation in *AP*, providing good support for the general anticipatory effect.

Natural Speech Samples   How far can we push the support for a general anticipatory effect? The strongest possible claim is that the particular line relating *AP* to error rate shown in Figures 24.9 and 24.11 applies to any speech sample from any persons or circumstances. Of course, the same definitions of error categories must be employed, and the sample should be based on a sufficient number of errors. There are two analyses of tape-recorded spontaneous speech samples that used the same error categories and coding that were used in the experiments, the London–Lund corpus of normal speech and the speech of the jargon-aphasic patient F.L., as analyzed by Schwartz et al. (1994). Because these data

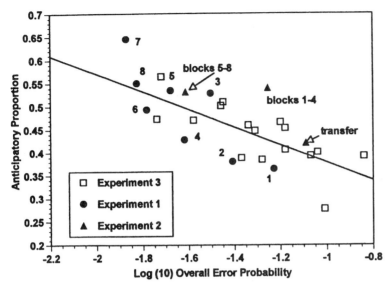

Figure 24.11
The general anticipatory effect for the conditions of Experiments 1–3. The numbers besides the filled circles label the practice blocks of Experiment 1. The regression line shown is based on the data from Experiment 3.

sets are complete samples, rather than just recordings of errors, they allow for the computation of overall error rate per word. Hence, it can be determined whether their observed *AP* is close to what would be predicted from the error rate. Figure 24.12 shows the line derived from Experiment 3 expanded to accommodate the range of the error rates from the London–Lund corpus (.0007 per word) and patient F.L. (.067 per word). The obtained *AP*s of .75 and .32, respectively, allow these points to be added to the figure.

Figure 24.12 also shows points from six other spontaneous speech samples. With one exception, these are based on large speech–error collections (not tape-recorded) and, hence, are not associated with any direct estimate of error rate, only with the relative proportions of error types. The collections of Shattuck-Hufnagel and Klatt (1979), Nooteboom (1969), Meringer (1908, as analyzed by Nooteboom, 1980), and Stemberger's (1989) adult corpus are all derived from nonaphasic adult speakers. Their error rates would be expected to be similar to that of the London–Lund corpus and, hence, these are graphed as if they have the same rate. Their *AP*s are, respectively, .75, .81, .70, and .60.[7] Stemberger's (1989) child corpus is derived from two children, ages 1–5, with the bulk of the observations coming at ages 2 and 3. Wijnen's (1992) analysis of recordings of two children, ages 2–3, found that the children's overall error rate (true speech errors as opposed to systematic errors) was around .005 per word, about seven

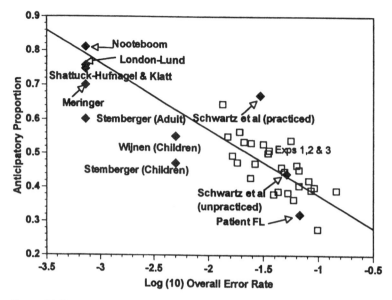

Figure 24.12
Extension of the general anticipatory effect to other error sets. Open squares represent points from Experiments 1–3 (see Figure 24.11). The labeled error collections are described in the text. The "practiced" and "unpracticed" conditions from Schwartz et al. (1994) correspond to Blocks 1–4 and 5–8, respectively. The regression line is based on the data from Experiment 3.

times greater than that of adults, and that the *AP* was .55. If we assume that the overall error rate for Stemberger's children is the same as that of Wijnen's, then the *AP* associated with them (.47) can also be placed on the figure.

The natural error corpora provide good support for the general anticipatory effect. The spontaneous speech of normal adults exhibits a low error rate and anticipatory proportions that are reasonably close to the predicted value. Patient F.L.'s high error rate is expected to be associated with a low *AP*, and it is. For children, their accuracy is somewhat less than that of adults, as is their *AP*. The two points associated with Stemberger (1989), however, are a little lower than predicted. Stemberger noted that he found a few more perseverations than other researchers, suggesting that error classification criteria may have differed among the corpora. All things considered, though, the *AP* of each corpus is well predicted by its overall error rate, using the same functional relation as was found in the experiments.

In general, we suggest the following conditions on tests of the function presented in Figure 24.12: (a) The error sample should be large enough for the overall error rate and *AP* to be accurately estimated; (b) errors need to be categorized as we have done; in particular, incomplete anticipations are counted as anticipations; (c) for experimental data, there must be a range in the materials; as a rule of thumb, at least 12 phrases might be needed to reduce the likelihood that any sound replacement asymmetries are confounded with anticipation versus perseveration locations; and (d) the speech sample should be English. With regard to this last condition, we note that two points on Figure 24.12, those associated with Nooteboom (1969) and Wijnen (1992), are based on Dutch, and one point, Meringer, is from German. Dutch and German, like English, are Germanic languages and are therefore relatively similar to English and each other. We also have data (not plotted on Figure 24.12) for a single French corpus based on Rossi and Peter-Defare's (1995) analysis. Here the *AP* is .65, which is within the range of that of corpora for Germanic languages. In general, though, languages differ greatly in their grammatical and phonological structures and, hence, would be expected to differ in the average value of *b*. Samples from a single language, if they are sufficiently large, should fall on a line, but each language or language group may have a different line.[8]

In summary, we feel we have sufficient evidence for the particular line shown in Figure 24.12 to predict that any speech sample adhering to the four conditions mentioned in the previous paragraph should produce a point on the line. Manipulation of either speaking conditions or speakers should result in an *AP* that is predictable from overall error rate.

Clinical Populations   Our analysis can be applied to clinical syndromes associated with speech-production errors, for example, aphasia, Alzheimer's dementia, and some forms of schizophrenia. Aphasic speech has long been characterized as both errorful and perseverative (e.g., Buckingham, Whitaker, & Whitaker, 1979; Sandson & Albert, 1984). The aphasic patient analyzed by Schwartz et al. (1994), F.L., makes about 100 times more errors than nonaphasic adults and makes more perseverations than anticipations. We predict that corresponding analyses with other patients will show that they have lower *AP*s than nonaphasic speakers and, in particular, that *AP* will be related to severity, as dictated by the line in Figure 24.12. There is indirect evidence that this prediction will be verified: Talo (1980) examined the spontaneous speech errors of aphasic patients and reported that anticipations were "rare" (p. 84). Helm-Estabrooks, Bayles, and Bryant (1994) found that perseverations made by aphasic patients in description and confrontation naming tasks were more likely in moderately impaired patients than in mildly impaired ones, where impairment was assessed by an aphasic diagnostic profile. Furthermore, Alzheimer's patients produced a number of perseverations intermediate between the aphasics and same-aged controls, providing additional evidence that perseveration is related to overall speech error rate. However, because anticipations were not recorded and, indeed, on confrontation naming tasks are not really possible, these data do not tell us whether the *AP* measure itself decreases as severity increases.

Schizophrenic speech has also been associated with perseveration (e.g., Andreasen, 1986; Chaika, 1982; Maher, 1983). In addition to perseverations of words and sounds that appear to be quite similar to those of nonaphasic and aphasic speakers, schizophrenic patients may also perseverate on topics (e.g., persistently speaking about towns in Iowa; Andreasen, 1986). Hence, it's hard to tell whether a deviation is a slip or was intended. To our knowledge, there is no quantitative analysis of schizophrenic speech that allows for *AP* to be computed and for this to be related to overall speech error rate. If such analyses could be performed on patient speech samples, our prediction is that the samples would exhibit the general anticipatory effect. However, because of the difficulty in determining the patients' intended utterances, it may be hard to get an estimate of overall error rate that can be compared to that of others.

What Is Causing the Variation in Error Rate and AP?
The general anticipatory effect allows for error variation due to any number of parameters to be associated with a predictable *AP*. For variation due to speech rate, there is a clear link to the time parameter, *n*. For the other factors that we have considered, in particular practice and differences among individuals due to age or the presence of brain damage, it is not so obvious which parameters are responsible. Here we argue that connection weight, *w*, is likely the most important parameter contributing to the effect.

Practice   We follow the serial-order models and attribute the effect of practice to increases in connection weights between the plan and its elements. Specifically, practice enhances the activation of the *present* and *future* at the expense of the *past*. So, as performance gets better, perseverations become relatively less common. There is a plausible alternative to this view. Perhaps practicing a phrase allows, instead, for more effective turn-off of the *past*. Such an explanation accords with theories of processing that emphasize the flexibility of inhibitory processes (e.g., see papers in Dagenbach & Carr, 1994).

The question of whether practice works on the turn-on and priming functions or on the turn-off of the *past* can be addressed with our experimental data. The model assumes that there is a competition between the *past, present,* and *future*. In reality, the competition includes linguistic units that are not a part of the sequence, and an intrusion of one of these creates a noncontextual error. Although these errors, represented by the "word substitution" and "other" categories, are relatively unlikely in the experiments, they occurred sufficiently often in the three experiments (*n* = 259) to determine how their probability changes with practice. If practice works by enhancing the *present* and the *future*, noncontextual errors would be expected to go away with practice at roughly the same rate as perseverations do. More specifically, if a node standing for a noncontextual error is introduced into the model and assigned an activation level, it is functionally like the *past* node, which was assigned a particular level of c. Consequently, if practice increases w, which causes the *present* and *future* to gain more activation, the probability of selecting the past or the noncontextual node becomes more reduced than that of selecting the future. The data should then show that the slope for noncontextual errors is more like that of perseverations than that of anticipations. If practice works, instead, by improving the turn-off of the *past*, a noncontextual node will be more like the *future* in that its activation will not change much relative to the *present*. Only the *past* will be greatly reduced. On this view, the slope for noncontextual errors will be more similar to anticipations than perseverations.

The number of anticipations, perseverations, and noncontextual errors as a function of practice block was determined, pooling across all experiments and word versus sound errors. The log–log slopes were $-.501$ for anticipations, $-.751$ for perseverations, and $-.756$ for noncontextual errors. A test of the null hypothesis that anticipations and noncontextual errors have the same slope can be rejected assuming that the alternative hypothesis is that the noncontextual errors are steeper, $t(6) = 2.02$, $p < .05$. It appears that practice eliminates noncontextual errors, as well as perseverations, more effectively than anticipations. This supports the claim that practice builds up the *present* and the *future*, which, in turn, is consistent with the assumption that practice affects w.

Developmental Effects   The finding that young children make more errors and have higher *AP*s than adults (Stemberger, 1989; Wijnen, 1992) is, in our view, explained most easily by proposing that w is lower in children. As was the case for practice, though, there are alternative accounts. For example, Berg and Schade (1990) attributed the finding of more perseverations with children to a difficulty in turning off the *past*. Their model (e.g., Berg, 1988; Schade, 1992) is an example of a frame-based activation model that uses self-inhibition to deactivate structure and content units after they have been fully activated. Less effective self-inhibition would correspond, in our model, to a higher value of c. Stemberger (1989) suggested that children may have a slower (smaller) decay of activation (our d) than adults. Each of these proposals, a decrease in w or d, or an increase in c, leads to more errors and a lower *AP* in the model. We favor the explanation for the difference between adults and children in terms of w because assigning the difference to w accords with the undeniable fact that children do, in fact, have less knowledge of phoneme and word sequences than adults do. Connection weight is supposed to represent this knowledge and, hence, the proposal that w is lower in children is motivated in a way that the alternatives are not. However, we acknowledge that the data on child speech errors are not sufficiently extensive to support one view over another.

The general anticipatory effect should apply to error increases associated with aging as well as those associated with children. To the extent that older adults make more speech errors, they should have a lower *AP*. This prediction applies whether the underlying deficit is in processing speed (e.g., Salthouse,

1985), information loss (Myerson, Hale, Wagstaff, Poon, & Smith, 1990), information transmission (Burke, MacKay, Worthley, & Wade, 1991), or inhibitory processes (Zacks & Hasher, 1994). Although it would not be easy to relate the particular theories of aging to particular parameters and processes in our model, one may be able to say that the theories as a group assign aging effects to the group of parameters associated with the general anticipatory effect, namely w, n, d, and c. These parameters regulate the model's ability to retrieve what it should be retrieving as a sequence is produced. To our knowledge, there are no extensive quantitative analyses of older adults' slips, and so the statement that the general anticipatory effect should apply to aging remains only a prediction.

Brain Damage   Accounts of the effect of brain damage on the language production system are numerous and varied (see e.g., Bates, Wulfeck, & Mac-Whinney, 1991; Caplan & Hildebrandt, 1988; Caramazza, 1984; Harley, 1993). The focus can be on either where the damage lies (that is, on what subsystem of the language processor is affected), or on what the deficit is. Our concern is with the latter issue. Given that most aphasic patients make excessive numbers of phonological and word slips, one can ask how these errors' greater prevalence can be best characterized in activation-based theories. Schwartz et al. (1994) and Harley and MacAndrew (1992) suggested that jargon aphasia could be the result of diminished connection strengths in a lexical network such as that proposed in the various frame-based activation models. In addition, aphasic errors have been attributed to a slower buildup of activation (e.g., Prather, Shapiro, Zurif, & Swinney, 1991, Haarmann & Kolk, 1991), diminished memory capacity (e.g., Haarmann, Just, & Carpenter, 1994) or loss of units in a highly distributed system (e.g., Farah, 1994). It turns out to be hard to discriminate among such proposals because functions such as processing speed, memory capacity, and so on can be viewed as basic parameters in some models or they can be derived from more elementary parameters in others. Similarly, loss of units in a network with distributed representations can act like reduced connection weights in a network with local representations. Consequently, any claims about the nature of the damage must be made in reference to a particular model.

There is one class of models of aphasic deficits that we believe our analysis makes unlikely. These are spreading activation models that propose that the aphasia is associated entirely with more activation noise in the system (e.g., Laine & Juhola, 1991). Although such models may successfully capture many features of the data, they may not be able to explain the apparent decrease in *AP* associated with aphasia. In our model, making the activation levels of the *past*, *present*, and *future* more noisy or making the decision process more noisy, while keeping all other aspects of the system the same, causes an increase in overall error rate without the lawful decrease in *AP*. If aphasic deficits are associated with a big drop in *AP*, as Schwartz et al. (1994) suggested, a model would have to concentrate the increased noise on the *past* more than on the *future* to actually flip an anticipation-dominant pattern to a perseveration-dominant one.

A related model of aphasia, that of Martin, Dell, Saffran, & Schwartz (1994; see also Martin & Saffran, 1992; Schwartz et al., 1994), attributes fluent aphasic production deficits to a relative increase in activation noise. It makes this happen by assuming that brain damage causes the activation levels in a lexical network to get so sufficiently small that intrinsic noise creates many errors. By itself, this proposal has the same problem as that of simply adding noise—reducing activation will not change an anticipatory pattern into a perseveratory one. However, in Martin et al.'s (1994) approach, activation can be made small in two ways: reducing connection weights or increasing decay rate. To the extent that low activation is caused by decreased weights, there should be a relative increase in perseverations. According to the various serial-order models presented here, reducing w should decrease AP. However, Martin et al.'s other mechanism, increased decay rate, does not naturally decrease AP. On the contrary, in our analysis, increasing d actually increases AP, particularly in the clamped case (see Equations 9 and 10). Thus, Martin et al. would predict that some patients, those with decreased connection strength, should exhibit a decreased AP in proportion to the severity of their deficit, while those with increased decay would have an AP that is higher than what would be expected from their error rate. In other words, patients of the former type, which they characterize as jargon-type patients, should fall on the line relating AP to error rate, while patients of the latter type, deep dysphasics, should be above the line.

Applications to Nonlinguistic Domains?
Thus far, the model has been applied to spoken language production. Our functional analysis, however, suggests that other behavioral systems should exhibit the kinds of phenomena that we have been studying. If the ordered behavior appears to have rules that allow for novel sequences, and particularly rules in which *present* elements depend on *future* ones, there is a need for structural frames and anticipatory priming. In short, to the extent that the behavior is languagelike, our model should apply. The model would not, for example, be expected to apply directly to simple behavioral perseveration, such as that shown by infants in search tasks (Piaget, 1954), because the relevant responses—looking for an object in one or another location—are not being generated as part of a system with languagelike dependencies. Moreover, there is no clear sense of what would constitute an anticipation. Nonetheless, the question of whether this kind of perseveration results from failure to represent the present or failure to eliminate the past is common to all discussions of perseveration and, hence, the model may provide a framework for formalization.

The closest domains to spoken language are writing and typing. However, because production in these domains is parasitic on the linguistic system down to the phonological level (Hotopf, 1983), successful tests of the model's predictions will not support a claim of generalization to nonlinguistic systems. The production of music may, instead, be a more fruitful domain. Music production is nonlinguistic, yet shares many features with language production (Palmer & van de Sande, 1993, 1995). Many performance errors can be classified as anticipatory or perseveratory, and it appears that there is lawful variation among error proportions. Palmer and Drake (1995) found that children at intermediate levels of piano skill had an *AP* of .74, while those with less skill had a significantly lower *AP* of .57. This finding is consistent with an anticipatory practice effect because the more advanced group had more years of piano training. However, because the more advanced group played more difficult pieces, it is difficult to interpret the results in the light of the model. In general, though, the model's predictions should be testable in nonlinguistic domains, such as music, in which complex behavioral sequences are produced.

Summary and Conclusions

Activation-based theories of serial order, when applied to language production, must satisfy four functional requirements: (a) the *present* must be activated (b) the *past* must be deactivated, (c) the *future* must be prepared, and (d) the system must be capable of assembling the order of novel sequences. We have reviewed activation-based theories and found that they tend to achieve the first three of these functions in similar ways. Each has a plan that is separated from the sequence elements, and the plan has excitatory connections to the elements, the strength of which is a product of learning. Furthermore, each has either a self-inhibitory turn-off mechanism or its functional equivalent, and this mechanism is part of the architecture of the system and, hence, does not have to be learned for each sequence. Finally, the activation of the *present* and the preparation of the *future* are achieved by plan-to-element connections with the result that the *present* and *future*'s activation are linked to the same parameters of the system. These features enable the models to explain the anticipatory practice effect.

   With regard to the fourth function, the ability to assemble novel sequences, only the frame-based theories of production appear to be sufficient. These theories propose that order is regulated, in part, by structures that represent patterns among categories of linguistic items, rather than items themselves. Such structures nicely account for the form of sound and word errors (Dell, 1986; Garrett, 1975; Hartley & Houghton, 1996; Levelt, 1989, 1992; MacKay, 1982, 1987; Roelofs, 1992; Shattuck-Hufnagel, 1979; Stemberger, 1990) and no model without frames has been shown to do so.[9] Moreover, experimental studies of language production have shown that structural frames have reality in the sense that they can be primed. Bock and Loebell (1990) found that syntactic structures persist across utterances in the absence of lexical, semantic, thematic, or prosodic overlap (see also, Bock, Loebell, & Morey, 1992; Bock,

1986). There are analogous effects for phonological structures (Meijer, 1994; Romani, 1992; Sevald, Dell, & Cole, 1995; Stemberger, 1990).

We offered a model that reflects the common characteristics of activation-based models with regard to the first three functional requirements and that incorporates structural frames. This model was able to account for the anticipatory practice effect and predicted the existence of an anticipatory speech-rate effect and a general anticipatory effect. Three experiments and analyses of error corpora from several populations provided support for the model. The centerpiece of this support, shown in Figures 8–13, was the finding that the anticipatory proportion can be predicted solely from overall error rate. Several factors that affect error rate—practice, speech rate, individual differences, age, or brain damage—appear to induce variation in anticipatory proportion along a single line. The findings are sufficiently compelling for us to hypothesize that any large sample of English speech should yield a point on the line and that corresponding analyses with other languages and even with complex nonlinguistic domains may discover similar relations between correctness and anticipatory proportion.

In sum, the data suggest that an error-prone language-production system is inherently perseveratory, while a relatively errorfree system tends to anticipate. Because of the functional requirements of serial order and the nature of language, the system should look to the future and not dwell on the past.

Notes

This research was supported by National Science Foundation Grant SBR 93-19368 and National Institutes of Health Grants DC-00191 and HD 21011 and grew out of a project involving Gary S. Dell, Myrna Schwartz, Eleanor Saffran, and Nadine Martin.

We are grateful for the advice of David Adams, Howard Berenbaum, Gary Bradshaw, Kay Bock, Cooper Cutting, Vic Ferreira, Zenzi Griffin, Susan Garnsey, Anita Govindjee, Prahlad Gupta, John Huitema, Gordon Logan, Gregory Murphy, Neal Pearlmutter, Brian Ross, Christine Sevald, and Ulrich Schade and for the contributions of Linda May, Julie Owles, and the Beckman Institute.

1. Many phoneme errors such as this one have an interpretation as phonological feature slips. If the voiceless labial stop acquires a continuent feature, the closest English sound is /f/.

2. We are not considering the categories of shift and contextual addition and deletion to be separate from serial-order errors involving replacement. Rather a perseveratory addition such as "black boxes" is simply viewed as a perseveration, with the target /b/ replaced by the error /bl/. Or the shift "back bloxes" is viewed as the exchange of /b/ and /bl/. This treatment of the error categories may not be justified generally (see, particularly, Garrett, 1975 and Stemberger, 1991), but for the purposes of elucidating anticipatory and perseveratory influences in speech it is a useful simplification.

3. In all of our experiments, we treat items as random effects and pool over participants. Because we have many fewer items than participants and item variance is larger than participant variance, this is the conservative approach.

4. Sound-perseveration/3 and sound-anticipation/2 had very few errors because of the patterning of onsets in the phrases—either ABBA or ABAB—and the rules about coding sound anticipation–perseverations. A contextual onset error in Position 2 was either sound-perseveration or sound anticipation–perseveration, while such an error in Position 3 was either sound-anticipation or sound anticipation–perseveration. Word-anticipation/3 had only eight errors.

5. To simplify the presentation, we are ignoring the node structure theory's use of rime constituents and phonological features.

6. This is not strictly true in the recurrent net PDP models. But it is largely so because learning a new linguistic sequence would make use of previous learning involving its elements. The connections responsible for turning off a unit after it has been produced would be mostly in place prior to the learning of a new sequence because linguistic units are almost never immediately repeated.

7. Because our experimental work, that of Schwartz et al. (1994), and that of Nooteboom (1969) classified incomplete anticipations along with anticipations, the incomplete anticipation categories of Shattuck-Hufnagel and Klatt (1979) and Stemberger (1989) have been included in their anticipation numbers. We do not claim that all incomplete anticipations are anticipations as opposed to exchanges. Our aim is simply to be consistent in classification.

8. The phonological errors in Spanish reported by Del Viso, Igoa, and Garcia-Albert (1991) appear to have more perseverations than anticipations, suggesting that Spanish may have a different line than the other languages studied.

9. For example, PDP recurrent network models, which lack separate frame structures (e.g., Dell et al., 1993), are not capable of explaining the existence of exchange errors and various frame-priming effects, although these models can produce a variety of structural and rulelike effects.

References

Anderson, J. R., & Schooler, L. J. (1991). Reflections of the environment in memory. *Psychological Science, 2*, 396–408.

Andreasen, N. (1986). Scale for the assessment of thought, language and communication (TLC). *Schizophrenia Bulletin, 12*, 473–482.

Bates, E., Wulfeck, B., & MacWhinney, B. (1991). Cross-linguistic research in aphasia: An overview. *Brain and Language, 41*, 123–148.

Berg, T. (1988). *Die Abbildung des Sprachproduktionprozess in einem Aktivationsflussmodell* [A spreading activation model of language production]. Tuebingen, Germany: Max Niemeyer.

Berg, T., & Schade, U. (1990). *Activation and inhibition in emergent processing systems.* Unpublished manuscript.

Bock, J. K. (1982). Towards a cognitive psychology of syntax: Information processing contributions to sentence formulation. *Psychological Review, 89*, 1–47.

Bock, J. K. (1986). Syntactic persistence in language production. *Cognitive Psychology, 18*, 355–387.

Bock, J. K., & Levelt, W. J. M. (1994). Language production: Grammatical encoding. In M. Gernsbacher (Ed.), *Handbook of psycholinguistics* (pp. 945–984). San Diego: Academic Press.

Bock, J. K., & Loebell, H. (1990). Framing sentences. *Cognition, 35*, 1–39.

Bock, J. K., Loebell, H., & Morey, R. (1992). From conceptual roles to structural relations: Bridging the syntactic cleft. *Psychological Review, 99*, 150–171.

Boomer, D. S., & Laver, J. D. M. (1968). Slips of the tongue. *British Journal of Disorders of Communication, 3*, 1–12.

Bruce, D. (1994). Lashley and the problem of serial order. *American Psychologist, 49*, 95–103.

Buckingham, H. W., Whitaker, H., & Whitaker, H. A. (1979). On linguistic perseveration. In H. Whitaker & H. A. Whitaker (Eds.), *Studies in Neurolinguistics* (Vol. 4, pp. 329–352). New York: Academic Press.

Burgess, N., & Hitch, G. J. (1992). Toward a network model of the articulatory loop. *Journal of Memory and Language, 31*, 429–460.

Burke, D. M., MacKay, D. G., Worthley, J. S., & Wade, E. (1991). On the tip of the tongue: What causes word finding failures in young and older adults? *Journal of Memory and Language, 30*, 542–579.

Caplan, D., & Hildebrandt, N. (1988). *Disorders of syntactic comprehension.* Cambridge, MA: MIT Press.

Caramazza, A. (1984). The logic of neuropsychological research and the problem of patient classification in aphasia. *Brain and Language, 21,* 9–20.

Chaika, E. (1982). A unified explanation for the diverse structural deviations reported for adult schizophrenics with disrupted speech. *Journal of Communication Disorders, 15,* 167–189.

Cleeremans, A., & McClelland, J. L. (1991). Learning the structure of event sequences. *Journal of Experimental Psychology: General, 120,* 235–253.

Cutler, A. (1981). The reliability of speech error data. *Linguistics, 19,* 561–582.

Dagenbach, D., & Carr, T. H. (1994). *Inhibitory processes in attention, memory, and language.* San Diego, CA: Academic Press.

Dell, G. S. (1986). A spreading activation theory of retrieval in language production. *Psychological Review, 93,* 283–321.

Dell, G. S. (1989). The retrieval of phonological forms in production: Tests of predictions from a connectionist model. In W. Marslen-Wilson (Ed.), *Lexical representation and process* (pp. 136–165). Cambridge, MA: MIT Press. (Reprinted from *Journal of Memory and Language,* Vol. 27, pp. 124–142, 1988).

Dell, G. S. (1990). Effects of frequency and vocabulary type on phonological speech errors. *Language and Cognitive Processes, 5,* 313–349.

Dell, G. S., Juliano, C., & Govindjee, A. (1993). Structure and content in language production: A theory of frame constraints in phonological speech errors. *Cognitive Science, 17,* 149–195.

Dell, G. S., & O'Seaghdha, P. G. (1994). Inhibition in interactive activation models of linguistic selection and sequencing. In D. Dagenbach & T. H. Carr (Eds.), *Inhibitory processes in attention, memory, and language* (pp. 409–453). San Diego, CA: Academic Press.

Dell, G. S., & Reich, P. A. (1981). Stages in sentence production: An analysis of speech error data. *Journal of Verbal Learning and Verbal Behavior, 20,* 611–629.

Del Viso, S., Igoa, J. M., & Garcia-Albert, J. E. (1991). On the autonomy of phonological encoding: Evidence from slips of the tongue in Spanish. *Journal of Psycholinguistic Research, 20,* 161–185.

Eikmeyer, H.-J., & Schade, U. (1991). Sequentialization in connectionist language-production models. *Cognitive Systems, 3,* 128–138.

Elman, J. L. (1990). Finding structure in time. *Cognitive Science, 14,* 213–252.

Estes, W. K. (1972). An associative basis for coding and organization in memory. In A. W. Melton & E. Martin (Eds.), *Coding processes in human memory* (pp. 161–190). Washington, DC: Winston.

Farah, M. J. (1994). Neuropsychological inference with an interactive brain: A critique of the "locality" assumption. *Behavioral and Brain Sciences, 17,* 43–104.

Ferreira, F. (1993). Creation of prosody during sentence production. *Psychological Review, 100,* 233–253.

Fowler, C. A., Treiman, R., & Gross, J. (1993). The structure of English syllables and polysyllables. *Journal of Memory and Language, 32,* 115–140.

Fromkin, V. A. (1971). The non-anomalous nature of anomalous utterances. *Language, 47,* 27–52.

Fromkin, V. A. (Ed.). (1973). *Speech errors as linguistic evidence* (pp. 11–45). The Hague, The Netherlands: Mouton.

Fromkin, V. A. (1980). *Errors in linguistic performance: Slips of the tongue, ear, pen, and hand.* New York: Academic Press.

Garnham, A., Shillcock, R. C., Brown, G. D. A., Mill, A. I. D., & Cutler, A. (1981). Slips of the tongue in the London–Lund corpus of spontaneous conversation. *Linguistics, 19,* 805–817.

Garrett, M. F. (1975). The analysis of sentence production. In G. H. Bower (Ed.), *The psychology of learning and motivation* (pp. 133–175). San Diego, CA: Academic Press.

Garrett, M. F. (1980). Levels of processing in sentence production. In B. Butterworth (Ed.), *Language production* (Vol. 1, pp. 177–210). London: Academic Press.

Gasser, M. E. (1988). A connectionist model of sentence generation in a first and second language (Tech. Rep. No. UCLA-AI-88-13). Los Angeles: University of California, Los Angeles, Computer Science Department.

Gordon, P. C., & Meyer, D. E. (1987). Control of serial order in rapidly spoken syllable sequences. *Journal of Memory and Language, 26,* 300–321.

Grossberg, S. (1978). A theory of human memory: Self-organization and performance of sensory-motor codes, maps, and plans. In R. Rosen & F. Snell (Eds.), *Progress in theoretical biology* (Vol. 5, pp. 233–374). New York: Academic Press.

Grossberg, S. (1982). *Studies of mind and brain: Neural principles of learning, perception, development, cognition, and motor control.* Boston: Reidel.

Gupta, P. (1995). *Word learning and immediate serial recall: Toward an integrated account.* Unpublished doctoral dissertation, Carnegie Mellon University, Pittsburgh, PA.

Gupta, P., & MacWhinney, B. (1997). Vocabulary acquisition and verbal short-term memory: Computational and neural bases. *Brain and Language, 59,* 267–333.

Haarmann, H. J., Just, M. A., & Carpenter, P. A. (1994). Computational modelling of normal and aphasic sentence comprehension. *Brain and Language, 47,* 389–391.

Haarmann, H. J., & Kolk, H. H. J. (1991). A computer model of the temporal course of agrammatic sentence understanding: The effects of variation in severity and sentence complexity. *Cognitive Science, 15,* 49–87.

Harley, T. A. (1993). Connectionist approaches to language disorders. *Aphasiology, 7,* 221–249.

Harley, T. A., & MacAndrew, S. B. G. (1992). Modelling paraphasias in normal and aphasic speech. In J. K. Kruschke (Ed.), *Proceedings of the 14th Annual Conference of the Cognitive Science Society* (pp. 378–383). Hillsdale, NJ: Erlbaum.

Hartley, T. A., & Houghton, G. (1996). A linguistically constrained model of short-term memory for nonwords. *Journal of Memory and Language, 35,* 1–31.

Helm-Estabrooks, N., Bayles, K., & Bryant, S. (1994). Four forms of perseveration in dementia and aphasia patients and normal elders. *Brain and Language, 47,* 457–460.

Hotopf, W. H. N. (1983). Lexical slips of the pen and tongue. In B. Butterworth (Ed.), *Language production* (Vol. 2, pp. 145–199). San Diego, CA: Academic Press.

Houghton, G. (1990). The problem of serial order: A neural network model of sequence learning and recall. In R. Dale, C. Mellish, & M. Zock (Eds.), *Current research in natural language generation* (pp. 287–319). London: Academic Press.

Jordan, M. I. (1986). Attractor dynamics and parallelism in a connectionist sequential machine. *Proceedings of the Eighth Annual Conference of the Cognitive Science Society* (pp. 531–546). Hillsdale, NJ: Erlbaum.

Laine, M., & Juhola, M. (1991). *Modelling aphasic naming disorders by computer simulation.* Paper presented at the Fourth Finnish Conference on Neurolinguistics, Turku, Finland.

Lashley, K. S. (1951). The problem of serial order in behavior. In L. A. Jeffress (Ed.), *Cerebral mechanisms in behavior* (pp. 112–136). New York: Wiley.

Levelt, W. J. M. (1989). *Speaking: From intention to articulation.* Cambridge, MA: MIT Press.

Levelt, W. J. M. (1992). Accessing words in speech production: Stages, processes, and representations. *Cognition, 42,* 1–22.

Logan, G. D. (1988). Toward an instance theory of automatization. *Psychological Review, 95,* 492–527.

MacKay, D. G. (1970). Spoonerisms: The structure of errors in the serial order of speech. *Neuropsychologia, 8,* 323–350.

MacKay, D. G. (1972). The structure of words and syllables: Evidence from errors in speech. *Cognitive Psychology, 3,* 210–227.

MacKay, D. G. (1973). Complexity in output systems: Evidence from behavioral hybrids. *American Journal of Psychology, 86,* 785–806.

MacKay, D. G. (1974). Aspects of the syntax of speech: Syllable structure and speech ratio. *Quarterly Journal of Experimental Psychology, 26,* 642–657.

MacKay, D. G. (1982). The problems of flexibility, fluency, and speed–accuracy trade-off in skilled behaviors. *Psychological Review, 89,* 483–506.

MacKay, D. G. (1987). *The organization of perception and action: A theory for language and other cognitive skills.* New York: Springer-Verlag.

Maher, B. A. (1983). A tentative theory of schizophrenic utterances. *Progress in Personality Research, 12*, 1–52.

Martin, N., Dell, G. S., Saffran, E. M., & Schwartz, M. F. (1994). Origins of paraphasias in deep dysphasia: Testing the consequences of a decay impairment to an interactive spreading activation model of lexical retrieval. *Brain and Language, 47*, 609–660.

Martin, N., & Saffran, E. M. (1992). A computational account of deep dysphasia: Evidence from a single case study. *Brain and Language, 43*, 240–274.

McClelland, J. L., & Rumelhart, D. E. (1981). An interactive activation model of context effects in letter perception: Part 1. An account of basic findings. *Psychological Review, 88*, 375–407.

Meijer, P. J. A. (1994). *Phonological encoding: The role of suprasegmental structures.* Unpublished doctoral dissertation, Nijmegen University, Nijmegen, The Netherlands.

Meringer, R. (1908). *Aus dem Leben der Sprache* [On the life of language]. Berlin, Germany: V. Behr's Verlag.

Meyer, A. S. (1994). Timing in sentence production. *Journal of Memory and Language, 33*, 471–492.

Mowrey, R. A., & MacKay, I. R. A. (1990). Phonological primitives: Electromyographic speech error evidence. *Journal of the Acoustical Society of America, 88*, 1299–1312.

Murdock, B. B., Jr. (1974). *Human memory: Theory and data.* Hillsdale, NJ: Erlbaum.

Myerson, J., Hale, S., Wagstaff, D., Poon, L. W., & Smith, G. A. (1990). The information-loss model: A mathematical theory of age-related cognitive slowing. *Psychological Review. 97*, 475–487.

Newell, A., & Rosenbloom, P. S. (1981). Mechanisms of skill acquisition and the law of practice. In J. R. Anderson (Ed.), *Cognitive skills and their acquisition* (pp. 1–55). Hillsdale, NJ: Erlbaum.

Nooteboom, S. G. (1969). The tongue slips into patterns. In A. G. Sciarone, A. J. van Essen, & A. A. Van Raad (Eds.), *Leyden studies in linguistics and phonetics* (pp. 114–132). The Hague, The Netherlands: Mouton.

Nooteboom, S. G. (1980). Speaking and unspeaking: Detection and correction of phonological and lexical errors in spontaneous speech. In V. A. Fromkin (Ed.), *Errors in linguistic performance* (pp. 87–95). New York: Academic Press.

Palmer, C., & Drake, C. (1995). *Musical skill acquisition: Better monitoring or planning?* Unpublished manuscript.

Palmer, C., & van de Sande, C. (1993). Units of knowledge in music performance. *Journal of Experimental Psychology: Learning, Memory, and Cognition, 19*, 457–470.

Palmer, C., & van de Sande, C. (1995). Range of planning in music performance. *Journal of Experimental Psychology: Human Perception and Performance, 21*, 947–962.

Piaget, J. (1954). *The construction of reality in the child.* New York: Basic.

Prather, P., Shapiro, L., Zurif, E., & Swinney, D. (1991). Real-time examination of lexical processing in aphasics. *Journal of Psycholinguistic Research, 20*, 271–281.

Reich, P. A. (1977). Evidence for a stratal boundary from slips of the tongue. *Forum Linguisticum, 2*, 211–217.

Roelofs, A. (1992). A spreading-activation theory of lemma retrieval in speaking. *Cognition, 42*, 107–142.

Roelofs, A. (1995). *A model of word-form encoding in speaking: Generating phonetic plans in context.* Unpublished manuscript.

Romani, C. A. (1992). *The representation of prosodic and syllabic structure in speech production.* Unpublished doctoral dissertation, Johns Hopkins University, Baltimore, MD.

Rosenbaum, D. A. (1990). *Human motor control.* San Diego, CA: Academic Press.

Rosenbaum, D. A., Kenny, S. B., & Derr, M. A. (1983). Hierarchical control of rapid movement sequences. *Journal of Experimental Psychology: Human Perception and Performance, 9*, 86–102.

Rossi, M., & Peter-Defare, E. (1995). Lapsus linguae: Word errors or phonological errors? *International Journal of Psycholinguistics, 11*, 5–38.

Rumelhart, D. E., & Norman, D. A. (1982). Simulating a skilled typist: A study of skilled cognitive motor performance. *Cognitive Science, 6*, 1–36.

Salthouse, T. A. (1985). *A theory of cognitive aging.* Amsterdam: North-Holland.

Sandson, J., & Albert, M. L. (1984). Varieties of perseveration. *Neuropsychologia, 22,* 715–732.

Schade, U. (1992). *Konnektionismus-Zur Modellierung der Sprachproduktion* [Connectionism: Modelling of language production]. Opladen, Germany: Westdeutscher Verlag.

Schwartz, M. F., Saffran, E. M., Bloch, D. E., & Dell, G. S. (1994). Disordered speech production in aphasic and normal speakers. *Brain and Language, 47,* 52–88.

Sevald, C. A., Dell, G. S., & Cole, J. (1995). Syllable structure in speech production: Are syllables chunks or schemas? *Journal of Memory and Language, 34,* 807–820.

Shattuck-Hufnagel, S. (1979). Speech errors as evidence for a serialorder mechanism in sentence production. In W. E. Cooper & E. C. T. Walker (Eds.), *Sentence processing: Psycholinguistic studies presented to Merrill Garrett* (pp. 295–342). Hillsdale, NJ: Erlbaum.

Shattuck-Hufnagel, S. (1983). Sublexical units and suprasegmental structure in speech production planning. In P. F. MacNeilage (Ed.), *The production of speech* (pp. 109–136). New York: Springer.

Shattuck-Hufnagel, S., & Klatt, D. (1979). The limited use of distinctive features and markedness in speech production: Evidence from speech error data. *Journal of Verbal Learning and Verbal Behavior, 18,* 41–55.

Stemberger, J. P. (1982). *The lexicon in a model of language production.* Unpublished doctoral dissertation, University of California, San Diego.

Stemberger, J. P. (1985). An interactive activation model of language production. In W. W. Ellis (Ed.), *Progress in the psychology of language* (Vol. 1, pp. 143–186). Hillsdale, NJ: Erlbaum.

Stemberger, J. P. (1989). Speech errors in early child language production. *Journal of Memory and Language, 28,* 164–188.

Stemberger, J. P. (1990). Wordshape errors in language production. *Cognition, 35,* 123–157.

Stemberger, J. P. (1991). Apparent anti-frequency effects in language production: The addition bias and phonological underspecification. *Journal of Memory and Language, 30,* 161–185.

Sternberg, S., Monsell, S., Knoll, R. L., & Wright, C. E. (1978). The latency and duration of rapid movement sequences: Comparisons of speech and typing. In G. E. Stelmach (Ed.), *Information processing in motor control and learning* (pp. 117–152). New York: Academic Press.

Svartvik, J., & Quirk, R. (1980). *A corpus of English conversation.* Lund, Sweden: CWK Gleerup.

Talo, E. S. (1980). Slips of the tongue in normal and pathological speech. In V. A. Fromkin (Ed.), *Errors in linguistic performance* (pp. 81–86). New York: Academic Press.

Wijnen, F. (1992). Incidental word and sound errors in young speakers. *Journal of Memory and Language, 31,* 734–755.

Zacks, R. T., & Hasher, H. (1994). Directed ignoring: Inhibitory regulation of working memory. In D. Dagenbach & T. H. Carr (Eds.), *Inhibitory processes in attention, memory, and language* (pp. 241–264). San Diego, CA: Academic Press.

Appendix A: Phrases Used in Experiments 1–3

Bonnie's brown bread box	Freida's fabulous freaky fabric
Brad's burned bran buns	Gloria's Greek green gloves
Brief beastly beach breezes	Pam's plain plaid pan
Chef's sooty shoe soles	Plastic potted pansy plants
Danny's dripping dish drain	Sappy shiny shop signs
Fine fresh free fish	Simple slender silver slippers
Five frantic fat frogs	Thirty-three throbbing thumbs
Floyd's fourth floor fort	Tike's tricky trike tire

Understanding Language

Chapter 25

Interference in Short-Term Memory: The Magical Number Two (or Three) in Sentence Processing

Richard L. Lewis

Introduction

An important goal in psycholinguistics in understanding the nature of short-term memory (or working memory) and its effects on comprehension. The classic short-term memory (STM) effect in sentence processing is severe difficulty on multiple center embedding (Miller, 1962; Miller & Chomsky, 1963). Over the past three decades, many theories of syntactic processing have been proposed to explain this effect, most attributing the problem to some kind of limited-capacity STM. However, these theories have developed (for the most part) independently of more traditional memory research, which has focused on uncovering general principles such as chunking (Miller, 1956; Simon, 1974) and interference (McGeoch & McDonald, 1931).

One principle of memory that has been neglected in theories of sentence processing is similarity-based interference. When to-be-remembered items are followed by stimuli that are similar along some dimensions, the original items are more quickly forgotten (Shulman, 1970; Waugh & Norman, 1965). This chapter attempts to gain some unification with traditional memory research by suggesting that an interesting range of core sentence processing phenomena can be explained as interference effects in a sharply limited syntactic working memory. This research follows the path Newell (1990) urged on psychology—attempting to explain a range of empirical phenomena with a small set of independently motivated architectural mechanisms and principles and their associated constants (Simon, 1974).

The chapter begins with a brief overview of theories of center embedding and their numeric bounds on processing. Next we shift to traditional accounts of short-term memory, focusing in particular on interference effects and the variety of codes used in short-term memory. The next few sections show how an interference theory of syntactic short-term memory can explain difficult and acceptable embeddings, some limitations on ambiguity resolution, length effects in garden path structures, and the general requirement for locality in syntactic structure. Finally, we speculate on some possible bases for the limitation of two or three, and discuss some empirical problems with the present model and its bound of two.

Center Embedding and Bounds on Processing

The difficulty in comprehending multiple center embedded object relative clauses in English (Miller & Chomsky, 1963) is one of the best known psycholinguistic phenomena.

(1)   The salmon that the man that the dog chased smoked fell.

Center embedding refers to what Miller and Chomsky (1963) called nesting of dependencies, which occurs when a constituent *X* is embedded in another constituent *Y*, with material in *Y* to both the left and right of *X*. *Self-embedding* is a special case of center embedding involving constituents of the same category. Self-embedding is the formal property that moves a grammar outside the scope of a finite device, but as Miller and Chomsky pointed out, center embedding in general increases memory load. The classic examples such as (1) exhibit double self-embedding (hence, center embedding) of both noun phrases (NPs) and sentences (Ss):

(2)   a.   [s The salmon that [s the man that [s the dog chased] smoked] fell.]
         b.   [NP The salmon that [NP the man that [NP the dog] chased] smoked.]

The difficulty of these constructions has been confirmed in a variety of experimental paradigms (Blauberg & Braine, 1974; Blumenthal, 1966; Hakes & Cairns, 1970; Marks, 1968; Miller & Isard, 1964; Wang, 1970). The basic result is that center embedding is always more difficult than right-branching, which can carry the same amount of content but exhibits no severe limits on depth of embedding. Although this fundamental contrast has been known for nearly 40 years now, it was not until Cowper (1976) and Gibson (1991) that the extent of the relevant cross-linguistic data began to be revealed.

Most theories that account for difficulty with center embeddings fall into three broad classes: linguistic metrics, architectures for parsing, and perceptual strategies [for a review, see Lewis (1995)]. *Metrics* define a measure over syntactic structure which predicts the perceived relative complexity of parsing different structures. The most sophisticated and empirically successful metric is Gibson's (1991). *Architectures* specify functional computational mechanisms for parsing, and characterize capacity limitations in terms of some fixed computational resource. PARSIFAL (Marcus, 1980) is one familiar example. The third and smallest class of theories, *perceptual strategies*, posits that difficulty arises from interactions among a set of perceptual mapping strategies that map surface strings to some underlying syntactic structure (Bever, 1970; Kac, 1981).

Table 25.1
Some posited processing bounds in sentence processing

Metric or architecture	Limited resource	Limit
Push-down automaton (Yngve, 1960)	Stack cells	$7 +/- 2$
Sausage Machine (Frazier & Fodor, 1978)	Lookahead word window	6
Open syntactic requirements (Gibson, 1991)		4
Register-vector finite state machine (Blank, 1989)	State for tracking clause level	3
FARSIFAL (Marcus, 1980)	Lookahead constituent buffer	3
Poker parser (Cowper, 1976)	Clausal processing track, hold cells	3
Connectionist net (Henderson, 1994)	Public stack; tree fragments	2; 4
Open sentence nodes (Kimball, 1973)		2
Open case relations (Stabler, 1994)		1 or 2
ACT (Anderson, Klein, & Lewis, 1977)	Control variables	1
Subroutine architecture (Miller & Isard, 1964)	Return address memory	1

Metrics and architectures require specific constant limits if they are to make absolute predictions of acceptability. Table 25.1 lists many of the theories of center embedding that have posited some specific bound. Despite the empirical successes represented in this table, only Yngve (1960) used an independently estimated constant [Miller's (1956) $7 +/- 2$]. The problem runs much deeper than just stipulating constants, however; there is often no psychological motivation for either the posited structure of short-term memory (stacks, lookahead buffers, etc.), or how the structure should be limited.

There have been attempts to unify linguistic processing with independently motivated psychological constructs. For example, Gathercole and Baddeley (1993) discussed the linguistic functions of the phonological loop, which has been used to account for a variety of immediate memory tasks (Baddeley, 1990; Simon & Zhang, 1985). Just and Carpenter (1992) proposed an activation-based, limited-capacity working memory that has been used to model individual differences in a range of cognitive tasks (Carpenter, Just, & Shell, 1990). Bever (1970) represented one of the earliest efforts to find a general cognitive and

Table 25.2
Kinds of immediate memory subject to interference

Conceptual/semantic	(Potter, 1976)
Kinesthetic	(Williams, Beaver, Spencer, & Rundell, 1969)
Odor	(Walk & Johns, 1984)
Sign language	(Poizner, Bellugi, & Tweney, 1981)
Tone	(Deutsch, 1970)
Verbal/phonological	(Schiffrin, 1973; Waugh & Norman, 1965)
Visual	(Logie, Zucco, & Baddeley, 1990)

perceptual basis for language processing. But in the domain of difficult and acceptable embeddings, none of these theories have come close to achieving the cross-linguistic coverage of the best syntactic metrics and architectures, in particular, those of Cowper (1976) and Gibson (1991).

Interference in a Multifaceted Working Memory

In this section, I will briefly attempt to establish two things. First, working memory uses a multiplicity of different codes, and exhibits interference effects when items are stored using similar codes. Second, the standard verbal STM tasks do not use the same codes that are functionally required by syntactic parsing. These two claims lead naturally to positing a portion of working memory that is coded specifically in terms of syntactic features, but which still exhibits interference effects.

Retroactive Interference and Within-Category Similarity Effects

Table 25.2 lists a set of content categories for which there is some evidence of interference effects in short-term memory, independent of decay. The table refers primarily to studies demonstrating *retroactive interference*, which occurs when a to-be-remembered stimulus is followed by a set of distractor items that the subject must attend to in some fashion.[1] The general finding is that distractor items that are similar in kind to the original stimulus cause forgetting, while dissimilar items are far less disruptive. For example, immediate memory for odor is disrupted by interpolated tasks involving odors, but is unaffected by a distracting verbal task such as counting backward (Walk & Johns, 1984).

   Most of this evidence is consistent with a model in which similarity has an effect only at a fairly gross level (visual vs. phonological, odor vs. verbal), and in which interference can be construed primarily as a matter of displacement (Waugh & Norman, 1965). However, there are *within-category* similarity effects which provide stronger support for the concept of similarity-based interference and demonstrate that the mechanisms of forgetting in working memory are probably more subtle and complex than displacement at a gross level.

The most familiar within-category effect is the phonological similarity effect. Ordered recall of phonologically similar lists of words, consonants, or nonsense trigrams is worse than recall of dissimilar lists (Baddeley, 1966; Conrad, 1963; Wickelgren, 1965). A similar effect was found with immediate memory for signs in American Sign Language, where the relevant measure of similarity was formational (Poizner, Bellugi, & Tweney, 1981). Similarity effects have also been demonstrated in visual memory tasks. For example, distractor gratings with similar orientations to the target stimuli produced more interference than those with dissimilar orientations (Magnussen, Greenslee, Asplund, & Dyrnes, 1991).

Traditional Verbal STM in Syntactic Processing
The suggestion that theories of center embedding have largely ignored traditional work on STM raises the important question: Does verbal short-term memory as studied in these classic experiments actually have anything to do with syntactic processing?

The answer may be: yes, but very little. The reason is fairly straightforward when one considers the functional requirements of parsing and remembering lists of unrelated stimuli. There is good evidence that traditional verbal memory tasks rely on phonological codes in working memory (Baddeley, 1990). Parsing, on the other hand, requires the temporary storage of partial syntactic structures. With the possible exception of linear precedence information, none of the functional models listed in Table 25.1 incorporate representations that resemble the content of phonological STM.

There is also empirical evidence for the independence of parsing from phonological STM. Early studies with center embedding clearly demonstrated conditions where phonological STM is intact, but parsing is impaired. For example, Larkin and Burns (1977) showed that subjects could repeat verbatim the words in a difficult center embedded sentence without being able to correctly parse the structure. Conversely, some brain-damaged subjects with severely impaired phonological short-term memories were still able to parse even complex constructions (e.g., Martin, 1993). Potter's (1982) RSVP (rapid serial visual presentation) experiments provided a condition where parsing is intact but phonological STM is impaired in normals.

The functional considerations, the evidence of a double dissociation between parsing and phonological STM, and the empirical success of purely syntactic theories suggest that most of the action in explaining difficult and acceptable embeddings is to be found in that part of working memory based on syntactic features, not phonological features.

An Interference Theory of Syntactic Working Memory

The STM theory presented here is part of a more comprehensive computational model of real-time sentence comprehension, NL-Soar (Lewis, 1993; Lewis &

Lehman, 1994). NL-Soar is built within Soar, a theory of the human cognitive architecture (Laird, Newell, & Rosenbloom 1987; Newell, 1990; Rosenbloom, Lehman, & Laird, 1993). In NL-Soar, Soar's working memory is used to store the partial products of incremental comprehension, including syntactic structure. The model of syntactic working memory described below grew out of an attempt to ensure that the most primitive cognitive processes in Soar operate efficiently (matching associations against working memory) (Lewis, 1993; Tambe, Newell, & Rosenbloom, 1990).

The part of NL-Soar's working memory that buffers partial constituents is called the H/D set, for Heads and Dependents. Assuming that the function of syntactic parsing is to build surface structure, X-bar positions (specificier of IP (spec-IP), complement of V' (comp-V'), adjunct of N' (adjoin-N'), etc.) (Chomsky, 1986) comprise one possible useful set of indices for partial structures. The Heads part of the H/D set indexes nodes by the structural positions they may head. The Dependents part of the H/D set indexes nodes by the structural relations they may fill. For example, (3a) gives the partial H/D set corresponding to the situation in (3b):

	Heads	comp-P':	[P' under]
(3) a.		comp-P':	[NP the basket]
	Dependents	comp-V':	[NP the basket]
		adjoin-N':	[PP under]

b.

Parsing is now a process of projecting X0 nodes (Pritchett, 1991), and matching potential heads with potential dependents. In (3), [P' under] and [NP the basket] may be joined by the structural relation comp-P', since [NP the basket] is indexed under comp-P' in the Dependents set, and [P' under] is indexed under comp-P' in the Heads set. Furthermore, [PP under] may potentially be adjoined to an N' as a postnominal modifier, so it is indexed under adjoin-N' in the Dependents set, and so on.

Once the PP *under the basket* has been formed, the H/D set contains the following:

(4)

Heads	comp-P′:	[P′ under [NP the basket]]
Dependents	adjoin-N′:	[PP under [NP the basket]]

When a node is assigned a structural position, it is removed from the Dependents set. However, because the H/D set provides all access to syntactic structure (i.e., it is not shunted off to another buffer for further processing), *under* must remain in the Heads set to support semantic interpretation.

In the example above, each relation indexes just one node, but in principle multiple constituents may be indexed by the same relation. Consider the case of a single object relative clause:

(5) a. The cat that the bird found jumped.

b. | Dependents | spec-IP: | [NP the cat], [NP the bird] |
|---|---|---|

In (5), both NPs must be momentarily indexed under spec-IP in the Dependents set, since both eventually occupy a subject position.

We can make this model an interference theory by simply placing a limit on the number of nodes that each relation may index. In this way, structures are similar and interfere with each other when they must be indexed by the same relations. How much should each relation index? If we assume a uniform limit across all relations in the H/D set, that limit must be at least two in order to achieve the minimal functionality required to parse natural language (Lewis, 1995). The reason is simple: To compose propositions (as in a relative or complement clause), two clauses must often be held simultaneously in working memory. Furthermore, clauses by their nature have similar structures and will often interfere with each other. We will return to a discussion of this memory bound later in the paper, but for now simply assume it to test its empirical adequacy.

Accounting for Some Limitations in Human Parsing

This section describes the model's explanation of a variety of cross-linguistic phenomena in parsing. The first few subsections deal with difficult and acceptable embeddings, presenting a subset of the 50+ constructions analyzed in Lewis (1995). The remaining subsections consider ambiguity resolution, garden path effects, and grammatical locality constraints.

Embedded Relative Clauses
Consider again the difficult center embedding:

(6) The boy that the man that the woman hired hated cried.

The Dependents set must index the three initial NPs under spec-IP, since all three NPs will eventually occupy subject position:

---

(7)   Dependents   spec-IP: [NP the boy], [NP the man],
                                [NP the woman]

Failure will occur at one of the final verbs (which verb depends on which NP is dropped from the H/D set). It is important to note that failure does not occur just because nodes are removed from the set. Just as in standard short-term memory tasks, interference is only a problem if the item that is interfered with must be accessed later.

The uniform limit of two nodes per relation in the H/D set theory does not entail a prohibition against all double center embedding. If that was the case, it would essentially be equivalent to Kimball's (1973) principle of two sentences, and fall prey to the same empirical problems. Consider the pseudocleft construction, which has something like a *wh*-clause in subject position:

(8)   a.   What the man saw was a dog.
      b.   [IP [NP [CP What the man saw]] was a dog.]

The initial *wh*-clause in pseudo-clefts is an indirect question (Baker, 1989; McCawley, 1988). The interaction of this structure with the H/D set leads to some interesting predictions. Because the initial *wh*-word does not occupy spec-IP, it should be possible to embed an additional relative clause within the indirect question without causing difficulty. This prediction turns out to be true (Gibson, 1991):

(9)   a.   What the woman that John married likes is smoked salmon.
           [s What [s the woman that [s John married] likes] is
           smoked salmon.]

---

		spec-IP:	[NP woman], [NP John]
b.	Dependents		
		spec-CP:	[NP what]

There are some triple-subject constructions that the model predicts should be difficult, yet seem easier to process than the classic (6):

(10)   a.   The reporter everyone I met trusts had predicted that Thieu would resign in the spring. (T. Bever, personal communication, August 4, 1995)
       b.   Isn't it true that example sentences that people that you know produce are more likely to be accepted? (De Roeck et al., 1982)

(11)   The claim that the man that John hired is incompetent upset me.
(Gibson, 1991)

Sentences like those in (10) are counterexamples to the claim that double center embedded relative clauses are always difficult in English. Example (11) also involves three subjects, but mixes a complement clause with a relative clause. Interestingly, the constructions in (10) and (11) fit the general prediction of the interference hypothesis that making the constituents more distinct or dissimilar is some way should help processing, as first noted by Bever (1970). The fact that they are nevertheless predicted to be difficult by the H/D set suggests that something may be missing in the way that the H/D set has formalized similarity.

Is the Problem Center Embedding or Gap-filling?
Difficulty can arise with center embedding independently of problems computing filler-gap relations, consistent with Miller and Chomsky's (1963) initial analysis. For example, Mazuka et al. (1989) found that double center embedding sentential complements and adjuncts in Japanese can cause difficulty, even though no filler-gap relations are involved:

(12)   Akira-ga Tosiko-ga Hazime-ga nakidasita toki okidasita no ni kizuita.
Akira NOM Tosiko NOM Hazime NOM started crying when got-up that noticed.
(Akira noticed that Toshiko got up when Hajime started crying.)

In (12), each of the NPs occupies subject position, requiring the H/D set to index three NPs on the spec-IP relation:

(13)	Dependents	spec-IP:	[NP Akira], [NP Tosiko], [NP Hazime]

Interestingly, the H/D set does predict that computing filler-gap relations can cause problems as well. Consider *tough-movement* constructions:

(14)   Fred$_i$ is tough [CP e$_i$ [c' for the man to please e$_i$]].

In (14), the matrix subject is related to the object of the embedded clause via movement through spec-CP. Embedding two relatives in such a construction is unacceptably difficult (Cowper, 1976):

(15)   Fred is easy for the woman who the man who hired me married to please.

Stacking three subject NPs cannot be the explanation of difficulty in (15), because at most two NPs must be buffered simultaneously under spec-IP (*woman* and *man*). Nevertheless, the H/D set cannot parse this construction because three CPs must be indexed simultaneously in the Heads set under spec-CP so that the traces can be properly generated:

---

(16) Heads   spec-CP: [CP for], [CP who], [CP who]

Is the Problem Stacking or Embedding?
The H/D set explanation for difficulty with center embedding places the blame on stacking (consecutive occurrences) of NPs, rather than center embedding per se. An interesting study by Hakuta (1981) was able to tease apart these two factors. Controlling for depth of embedding, he found that Japanese children had much less trouble with center embedded structures which were transformed so that the amount of stacking was reduced. Mazuka et al. (1989) also pointed out that difficult double center embeddings such as (12) become easy to process if one or two of the initial overt NPs are dropped. The H/D set predicts this because then only one or two NPs must be indexed under spec-IP.

Although the Hakuta (1981) study showed that stacking can be a source of difficulty in Japanese, it need not be. In fact, stacking NPs appears to be more acceptable in head-final languages such as Japanese. Remarkably, Japanese sentences that stack up to five initial NPs are acceptable for some speakers:

(17) John-wa Bill-ni Mary ga Sue-ni Bob-o syookai sita to it-ta.
John TOP Bill DAT Mary NOM Sue DAT Bob ACC introduced COMP say PERF.
(John said to Bill that Mary introduced Bob to Sue.)

Although such sentences are surely complex, they do not cause the failure associated with (6) or (12). The H/D set can handle structures such as (19) because no single structural relation must buffer more than two NPs[2]:

---

		spec IP:	[NP John], [NP Mary]
(18)	Dependents	comp-V':	[NP Bob]
		comp2-V':	[NP Bill], [NP Sue]

Limitations on Ambiguity Resolution
The H/D set has implications for ambiguity resolution as well. In particular, it makes the strong prediction that at most two nodes are available to assign the same structural relation at any given time. For example, consider the right branching structure in (19):

(19) a. Amparo saw the dog under the box on the table in the room next to the library.

---

b. Heads   adjoin-N':   [N' dog], [N' library]

At any given point, at most two noun phrases are available for postnominal modification, because only two NPs may be indexed under the adjoin-N' relation in the Heads set. [In fact, (19) can be successfully parsed by just keeping the most recent NP open for attachment.]

In this way, the H/D set naturally serves a function similar to *closure principles* (Church, 1980; Frazier & Rayner, 1982; Kimball, 1973), which keep a small set of syntactic nodes open for further attachment. The H/D set bears the closest resemblance to Church's (1980) closure principle, which posits that only the two most recent nodes of the same category may be kept open at any time. Church's principle and those derived from it have the best empirical coverage (Church, 1980; Gibson, 1991). The main differences between NL-Soar and Church's principle is that closure in NL-Soar derives from the structure of the parsing architecture, and the limit on open nodes is on the basis of similar structural relations, not categories.

Length Effects in Garden Path Structures
Consider the following easy and difficult structural ambiguities:

(20) John believed the professor was honest.

(21) The horse raced past the barn fell. (Bever, 1970)

One striking difference between many unproblematic ambiguities like (20) and the classic (21) is the distance between the ambiguity and the disambiguating material. In (21), the disambiguating information follows immediately on the heels of the ambiguity, while in the classic garden path, there is an intervening phrase (*past the barn*) between the ambiguous raced and the disambiguating *fell*. Such a difference leads naturally to the hypothesis that distance-to-disambiguation is a crucial factor.

However, the distance-to-disambiguation can be extended in structures like (21) without causing severe garden path effects (Pritchett, 1992):

(22) a. Ron believed the ugly little linguistics professor.
b. Ron believed the ugly little linguistics professor he had met the week before in Prague disliked him.

NL-Soar includes a limited repair mechanism for handling unproblematic ambiguities (Lewis, 1993). As long as the complement relation assigned by the relevant verb (in this case *believe*) is still accessible in working memory, then the structure can be repaired regardless of the length of the object noun phrase.

Nevertheless, Warner and Glass (1987) *did* manage to produce an apparently length-induced garden path effect, using exactly the same object/subject ambiguity:

(23)   The girls believe the man who believes the very strong ugly boys struck the dog killed the cats.

Surprisingly, NL-Soar accounts for such garden path effects. The intervening material is such that all the structural relations required for a successful repair cannot be held in the working memory. For the repair to be successful, the H/D set must support the following structure upon reading *struck*[3]:

(24) Heads	comp-V':	[v' believes], [v' believe],
		[v' struck]

This exceeds the capacity of two nodes per relation. Thus, the limited working memory produces a garden path effect because the relevant structural relations are not available to repair. The important factor is not simply the length of the intervening material, but the interaction of the structure of the intervening material with the structure to be repaired.[4]

Working Memory and Syntactic Locality

The H/D set suggests that some, but not all, extraction violations may be accounted for by interference effects in short-term memory. Consider the severe violation in (25):

(25)   *Who$_i$ does Phineas know a boy who hates the man who saw t$_i$?

The H/D set cannot maintain the structures in working memory necessary to establish the long distance relation between the object of *saw* and the initial *who*. The structure required to establish this relation involves three CPs (complement phrases):

(26)   [CP who does ... [CP who hates ... [CP who saw ...]]]

Binding the object trace with the wh-word antecedent requires accessing the antecedent in spec-CP (specifier of CP) and following three comp-C' (complement of C') links (among others) to reach the object position in the final embedded clause. This exceeds the two-valued capacity of the H/D set:

(27) Heads	spec-CP:	[CP who does]
	comp-C':	[c' who does], [c' who hates],
		[c' who saw]

In general, the H/D set will rule out extractions of the form

(28) $[\alpha \ldots X \ldots [\alpha \ldots [\alpha \ldots Y \ldots]]]$

which essentially corresponds to Ross's (1967) *wh*-island constraint when α is S. This is also enticingly close to subjacency (Chomsky, 1973), where the prohibition against crossing two bounding nodes corresponds to the limit of two in the H/D set. However, the H/D set clearly does not capture all the violations that subjacency captures, because α must be the same category in the H/D set, while subjacency predicts that violations occur when two bounding nodes are crossed, which may or may not be the same category (complex NP violations are an example, crossing S and NP bounding nodes.)

What the H/D set does predict is that eventually all long-distance dependencies will become unprocessable due to syntactic interference in short-term memory. Thus, there is clear motivation for some kind of locality constraint on grammatical representation. However, within the small range of processable extractions, there may still be other grammatical principles at work that rule out certain extractions.

The Bound of Two or Three in Other STM Phenomena

None of the posited processing bounds in sentence processing theories (Table 25.1) have had quite the magic of Miller's (1956) original $7 +/- 2$. The limitations were only motivated by one kind of data, and until Gibson (1991), even the coverage of that one kind of data was not compelling. I hope now to make good on an implicit promise in the title by showing that the constant two or three shows up often enough in other guises that it should at least raise an eyebrow.

We have already seen that a bound of two or three may be behind a variety of syntactic processing effects. But in addition to this, this constant seems to arise in immediate verbal memory tasks not involving phonological short-term memory. For example, when presentation of words is so rapid that subjects do not have time to encode them phonologically, average word span drops to 2.6 (Potter, 1982). Rapid presentation is not necessary to reduce memory span. Simon and Zhang (1985) found that the average span for Chinese homophones (all pronounced /gong/, so a purely phonological memory would not be very useful) was 2.7. Table 25.3 summarizes these and other phenomena.

Table 25.3 may represent nothing more than some coincidences. However, it is possible to give these data a plausible interference-based interpretation. For any, given task, subjects must adopt some means of coding stimuli in working memory. Furthermore, the subject must essentially come to the task prepared with this set of codes; there is not time in a single task to learn a new encoding scheme. For the vast majority of verbal short-term memory tasks, subjects adopt a phonological encoding, which provides a ready set of over-learned

Table 25.3
The magical number two (or three) in verbal short-term memory

Maximum subject NPs stacked in center-embedding (Lewis, 1993)	2 or 3
Phrases of a single category open for attachment (Church, 1980; Gibson, 1991; Gibson & Pearlmutter, 1994)	2 or 3
Bounding nodes crossed in Wh-movement for violation (Chomsky, 1973)	2
Average span for RSVP words (Potter, 1982)	2.6
Average span for unpronounceable Chinese radicals (Simon & Zhang, 1985)	3.0
Average span for Chinese homophones (Simon & Zhang, 1985)	2.7
Average reading span (Daneman & Carpenter, 1980)	3.15

features to discriminate the contents of memory. However, in tasks where a phonological code is not available or where phonological interference is too great, there may essentially be no means at hand to discriminate the to-be-remembered stimuli. This is the case with the tasks in Table 25.3, by design. In short, what we could be seeing in the data in Table 25.3 is the limited capacity of human memory to keep in mind only two or three similar chunks at the same time. It is of particular interest that the average reading span of subjects in the Daneman and Carpenter (1980) task falls into this range, because this leaves open the exciting possibility of unifying the interference theory presented here with the Just and Carpenter (1992) account of individual differences in working memory capacity.

Is Two Enough?

The predictions of the H/D set depend on the bound of two and adopting the full set of X-bar positions. Although the empirical coverage is promising [see Lewis (1995) for the full data set], there are still problems.

The most significant problem, noted earlier, is that there are constructions that require buffering three subjects, but that are nonetheless acceptable. As one additional example, Babyonyshev and Gibson (1997) point out that triple-embedded complement clauses in Japanese are acceptable, despite the fact that the first three NPs occupy spec-IP (and therefore should overload the H/D set):

(29)   Taroo-ga Akira-ga Hanako-ga nakidasita to itta to omotteiru.
Taroo Akira Hanako started-crying that said that knows.
(Taroo thinks that Akira said that Hanako started crying.)

This suggests that the bound should be three, and not two (as does some of the data in Table 25.3, if we take it seriously). Making this move, however, would require finding additional sources of difficulty in the standard double center embedding cases. The Gibson et al. metric does this because it assigns additional cost to the empty operator positions associated with the relative clauses. However, this may not be the correct generalization, for we are still left with the fact that the double center embedded (12) is very difficult, but contains no relative clauses. At present, neither theory can account for the contrast between (29) and (12). It appears that there may be additional cost associated with adjuncts in general, regardless of whether they involve relativization.

Conclusion

This chapter suggests that sentence processing theories can benefit from incorporating ideas from traditional work in short-term memory. NL-Soar demonstrates that it is possible to combine general principles of memory (in particular similarity-based interference) with linguistic analyses to produce a detailed model of syntactic working memory that is empirically powerful, and psychologically and functionally grounded.

NL-Soar's working memory captures two important theoretical convergences in recent accounts of syntactic short-term memory:

> • The source of memory load is open or unsatisfied syntactic relations (Abney & Johnson, 1991; Gibson, 1991; Stabler, 1994). This leads naturally to a focus on stacking, rather than embedding per se, as the source of difficulty (Gibson, 1991; Hakuta, 1981; Mazuka et al., 1989).
> • Increasing similarity makes things more difficult. This shows up clearly in the "broad but shallow" memory models of Reich (1969) and Stabler (1994), and the original self-embedding metric of Miller and Chomsky (1963).

Although the accumulated phenomena of short-term memory are vast, there is a great potential payoff for continued attempts to unify traditional STM phenomena with functional tasks such as language comprehension.

Notes

Preparation of this paper was supported by a grant from the James S. McDonnell Foundation to the Human Information Processing Group at Princeton University. Many thanks to Martin Chodorow, Terry Langendoen, Thad Polk, and an anonymous reviewer for helpful comments on the paper and research.

1. Although proactive interference (PI) may occur in short-term memory as well, PI as it has been studied may more properly be considered a phenomenon of long-term memory (Baddeley, 1990; Shulman, 1970).
2. The overt case marking does not in and of itself explain the contrast between Japanese and English stacked NPs. Note that the explicit case marking in (12)—with only three stacked NPs—does not seem to help.

3. In (23), *the man* and *the boys* are taken as complements of *believe* and *believes*, respectively. When *struck* arrives, it must be indexed under the Comp-V' relation so that it may take its complement. *Believes* must also still be available on the Comp-V' relation, because the complement of *believes* must change from the *boys* to *struck*. However, *believe* must also be on the Comp-V' relation, because the complement of *believe* must be changed from *the man* to *the man killed*.

4. Contrary to the theory presented here, Ferreira and Henderson (1991) presented evidence that the crucial factor is the length of the ambiguous region after the head of the object phrase, not the structural complexity. However, their material consisted of subject/object ambiguities that can cause difficulty even in short versions, in contrast to (21) above:

(33)   When the men hunt the birds typically scatter.

Thus, Ferreira and Henderson were investigating the factors that cause a mild but noticeable garden path effect to become a severe one, while the theory above is concerned with the structural factors that can cause a perfectly acceptable ambiguity to become a noticeable garden path. In short, both length and structure may play a role.

References

Abney, S. P., & Johnson, M. (1991). Memory requirements and local ambiguities of parsing strategies. *Journal of Psycholinguistic Research, 20,* 233–250.

Babyonyshev, M., and Gibson, E. (1997). The complexity of nested structures in Japanese. *Language: Journal of the Linguistic Society of America, 75,* 423–450.

Baddeley, A. D. (1966). Short-term memory for word sequences as a function of acoustic, semantic, and formal similarity. *Quarterly Journal of Experimental Psychology, 18,* 362–365.

Baddeley, A. D. (1990). *Human memory: Theory and practice.* Boston: Allyn and Bacon.

Baker, C. L. (1989). *English syntax.* Cambridge, MA: MIT Press.

Bever, T. G. (1970). The cognitive basis for linguistic structures. In J. R. Hayes (Ed.), *Cognition and the development of language.* New York: Wiley.

Blauberg, M. S., & Braine, M. D. S. (1974). Short-term memory limitations on decoding self-embedded sentences. *Journal of Experimental Psychology, 102,* 745–748.

Blumenthal, A. L. (1966). Observations with self-embedded sentences. *Psychonomic Science, 6,* 453–454.

Carpenter, P. A., Just, M. A., & Shell, P. (1990). What one intelligence test measures: A theoretical account of the processing in the Raven Progressive Matrices Test. *Psychological Review, 97,* 404–431.

Chomsky, N. (1973). Conditions on transformations. In S. R. Anderson & P. Kiparsky (Eds.), *A Festschrift for Morris Halle.* New York: Holt, Rinehart, and Winston.

Church, K. W. (1980). *On memory limitations in natural language processing* (Tech. Rep. MIT/LCL/TR-245). Cambridge, MA: Laboratory for Computer Science, Massachusetts Institute of Technology.

Conrad, R. (1963). Acoustic confusions and memory span for words. *Nature, 197,* 1029–1030.

Cowper, E. A. (1976). *Constraints on sentence complexity: A model for syntactic processing.* Unpublished doctoral dissertation, Brown University.

Daneman, M., & Carpenter, P. A. (1980). Individual differences in working memory and reading. *Journal of Verbal Learning and Verbal Behavior, 19,* 450–466.

De Roeck, A., Johnson, R., King, M., Rosner, M., Sampson, G., & Varile, N. (1982). A myth about center-embedding. *Lingua, 58,* 327–340.

Deutsch, D. (1970). Tones and numbers: Specificity of interference in immediate memory. *Science, 168,* 1604–1605.

Ferreira, F., & Henderson, J. M. (1991). Recovery from misanalyses of garden-path sentences. *Journal of Memory and Language, 30,* 725–745.

Frazier, L., & Fodor, J. D. (1978). The sausage machine: A new two-stage parsing model. *Cognition*, *6*, 291–325.

Gathercole, S. E., & Baddeley, A. D. (1993). *Working memory and language*. Hove, U.K.: Erlbaum.

Gibson, E. A. (1991). *A computational theory of human linguistic processing: Memory limitations and processing breakdown*. Doctoral dissertation, Carnegie Mellon. (Available Tech. Rep. CMU-CMT-91-125, from Center for Machine Translation, Carnegie Mellon University, Pittsburgh, PA 15213.)

Gibson, E. A., & Pearlmutter, N. (1994). A corpus-based analysis of psycholinguistic constraints on PP attachment. In C. Clifton, L. Frazier, & K. Rayner, (Eds.), *Perspectives in sentence processing*. Hillsdale, NJ: Erlbaum.

Hakes, D. T., & Cairns, H. S. (1970). Sentence comprehension and relative pronouns. *Perception & Psychophysics*, *8*, 5–8.

Hakuta, K. (1981). Grammatical description versus configurational arrangement in language acquisition: The case of relative clauses in Japanese. *Cognition*, *9*, 197–236.

Just, M. A., & Carpenter, P. A. (1992). A capacity theory of comprehension: Individual differences in working memory. *Psychological Review*, *99*, 122–149.

Kac, M. B. (1981). Center-embedding revisited. In *Proceedings of the Third Annual Conference of the Cognitive Science Society* (pp. 123–124). Hillsdale, NJ: Erlbaum.

Kimball, J. (1973). Seven principles of surface structure parsing in natural language. *Cognition*, *2*, 15–47.

Laird, J. E., Newell, A., & Rosenbloom, P. S. (1987). Soar: An architecture for general intelligence. *Artificial Intelligence*, *33*, 1–64.

Larkin, W., & Burns, D. (1977). Sentence comprehension and memory for embedded structure. *Memory & Cognition*, *5*, 17–22.

Lewis, R. L. (1993). *An architecturally-based theory of human sentence comprehension*. Doctoral dissertation, Carnegie Mellon University. (Available as Tech. Rep. CMU-CS-93-226 from Computer Science Dept., Carnegie Mellon University, 5000 Forbes Ave., Pittsburgh, PA 15213, or reports@cs.cmu.edu.)

Lewis, R. L. (1995). *A theory of grammatical but unacceptable embeddings*. Submitted manuscript, Cognitive Science Laboratory, Princeton University.

Lewis, R. L., & Lehman, J. F. (1994). *A theory of the computational architecture of sentence comprehension*. Submitted manuscript, Cognitive Science Laboratory, Princeton University.

Logie, R. H., Zucco, G. M., & Baddeley, A. D. (1990). Interference with visual short-term memory. *Acta Psychologica*, *75*, 55–74.

Magnussen, S., Greenlee, M. W., Asplund, R., & Dyrnes, S. (1991). Stimulus-specific mechanisms of visual short-term memory. *Vision Research*, *31*, 1213–1219.

Marcus, M. P. (1980). *A theory of syntactic recognition for natural language*. Cambridge, MA: MIT Press.

Marks, L. E. (1968). Scaling of grammaticalness of self-embedded English sentences. *Journal of Verbal Learning and Verbal Behavior*, *7*, 965–967.

Martin, R. C. (1993). Short-term memory and sentence processing: Evidence from neuropsychology. *Memory & Cognition*, *21*, 176–183.

Mazuka, R., Itoh, K., Kiritani, S., Niwa, S., Ikejiru, K., & Naitoh, K. (1989). Processing of Japanese garden path, center-embedded, and multiply left-embedded sentences. *Annual Bulletin of the Research Institute of Logopedics and Phoniatrics (Tokyo)*, *23*, 187–212.

McCawley, J. D. (1988). *The syntactic phenomena of English, volume 2*. Chicago: The University of Chicago Press.

McGeoch, J. A., & McDonald, W. T. (1931). Meaningful relation and retroactive inhibition. *American Journal of Psychology*, *43*, 579–588.

Miller, G. A. (1956). The magical number seven plus or minus two: Some limits on our capacity for processing information. *Psychological Review*, *63*, 81–97.

Miller, G. A. (1962). Some psychological studies of grammar. *American Psychologist*, *17*, 748–762.

Miller, G. A., & Chomsky, N. (1963). Finitary models of language users. In D. R. Luce, R. R. Bush & E. Galanter (Eds.), *Handbook of mathematical psychology* (vol. II). New York: John Wiley.

Miller, G. A., & Isard, S. (1964). Free recall of self-embedded English sentences. *Information and Control, 7,* 292–303.

Newell, A. (1990). *Unified theories of cognition.* Cambridge, MA: Harvard University Press.

Poizner, H., Bellugi, U., & Tweney, R. D. (1981). Processing of formational, semantic, and iconic information in American Sign Language. *Journal of Experimental Psychology: Human Perception and Performance, 7,* 1146–1159.

Potter, M. C. (1976). Short-term conceptual memory for pictures. *Journal of Experimental Psychology: Human Learning and Memory, 2,* 509–522.

Potter, M. C. (1982). *Very short-term memory: In one eye and out the other.* Paper presented at the 23rd Annual Meeting of the Psychonomic Society, Minneapolis.

Pritchett, B. L. (1991). Head position and parsing ambiguity. *Journal of Psycholinguistic Research, 20,* 251–270.

Pritchett, B. L. (1992). *Grammatical competence and parsing performance.* Chicago: University of Chicago Press.

Reich, P. (1969). The finiteness of natural language. *Language, 45,* 831–843.

Rosenbloom, P. S., Lehman, J. F., & Laird, J. E. (1993). Overview of Soar as a unified theory of cognition: Spring 1993. In Proceedings of the Fifteenth Annual Conference of the Cognitive Science Society (pp. 98–101). Hillsdale, NJ: Erlbaum.

Shiffrin, R. M. (1973). Information persistence in short-term memory. *Journal of Experimental Psychology, 100,* 39–49.

Shulman, H. G. (1970). Similarity effects in short-term memory. *Psychological Bulletin, 75,* 399–414.

Simon, H. A. (1974). How big is a chunk? *Science, 183,* 482–488.

Simon, H. A., & Zhang, G. (1985). STM capacity for Chinese words and idioms: Chunking and the acoustical loop hypotheses. *Memory & Cognition, 13,* 193–201.

Stabler, E. P. (1994). *The finite connectivity of linguistic structure.* Unpublished manuscript, University of California, Los Angeles.

Tambe, M., Newell, A., & Rosenbloom, P. S. (1990). The problem of expensive chunks and its solution by restricting expressiveness. *Machine Learning, 5,* 299–348.

Walk, H. A., & Johns, E. E. (1984). Interference and facilitation in short-term memory for odors. *Perception & Psychophysics, 36,* 508–514.

Wang, M. D. (1970). The role of syntactic complexity as a determiner of comprehensibility. *Journal of Verbal Learning and Verbal Behavior, 9,* 398–404.

Warner, J., & Glass, A. L. (1987). Context and distance-to-disambiguation effects in ambiguity resolution: Evidence from grammaticality judgments of garden path sentences. *Journal of Memory and Language, 26,* 714–738.

Waugh, N. C., & Norman, D. A. (1965). Primary memory. *Psychological Review, 72,* 89–104.

Wickelgren, W. A. (1965). Acoustic similarity and retroactive interference in short-term memory. *Journal of Verbal Learning and Verbal Behavior, 4,* 53–61.

Williams, H. L., Beaver, W. S., Spence, M. T., & Rundell, O. H. (1969). Digital and kinesthetic memory with interpolated information processing. *Journal of Experimental Psychology, 80,* 530–536.

Yngve, V. H. (1960). A model and an hypothesis for language structure. *Proceedings of the American Philosophical Society, 104,* 444–466.

Processing Similarity

Chapter 26

Similarity, Interactive Activation, and Mapping: An Overview

Robert L. Goldstone and Douglas L. Medin

---

1 Introduction

The act of comparison often seems to be an immediate, direct operation. Dogs and wolves appear similar simply because of the large perceptual overlap between their visual forms—they both have a head with a snout and ears, four legs, and a tail. In general, things seem similar if they share many properties. Abstract properties may also influence similarity; puppies and children seem similar because of their innocence, youth, and dependence on others. Once we find the appropriate set of property descriptions, so the argument goes, similarity assessment is a direct function of the objects' overlap/proximity on these descriptions. As such, the first step is to create representations of the to-be-compared objects in terms of their properties. Once the two property lists have been created, the similarity computation proceeds by comparing the two property lists for matching and mismatching features.

However, there is more to similarity than property listing and matching. Comparing scenes and objects with parts requires a more structured representation than a feature list, and requires a more sophisticated process than counting up matches and mismatches. Features are organized into objects; objects are organized into relations; and relations are organized into scenes. The parts of a scene are mapped onto the parts of the scene with which it is compared, and this process of finding corresponding parts has an important influence on the perceived similarity. The purposes of this chapter are to (a) demonstrate the process of mapping in human scene comparison, (b) present new experimental findings implicating mapping in similarity assessment, and (c) organize and interpret these results with an interactive activation model of mapping and similarity.

The organization of this chapter is as follows. First, we review the role of mapping and global consistency in both low-level visual perception and abstract analogy and then suggest that mapping and consistency also apply to similarity assessment. Next, we review current models of similarity and note that they have little to say about processes by which corresponding properties are aligned. We then describe some experiments on alignment processes associated with comparisons. We account for these results with an interactive activation model of alignment and contrast this model with a number of alternatives. Finally, we assess the role of mapping or alignment in comparisons more generally and offer some conclusions.

2 Mapping and Structure in Perceptual and Conceptual Comparisons

Similarity inhabits the broad middle ground between low-level visual perception and abstract analogy. The perception of similarity depends both on physical, concrete properties, and on knowledge-based, abstract properties. In both perceptual and conceptual comparisons, the act of mapping elements (finding the correspondences between scene parts) plays a fundamental role.

2.1 Perceptual Mapping Processes in Comparison

In perceiving objects in depth, people combine information obtained from their two eyes. The image locations from the left eye must be placed in correspondence with the image locations from the right eye. Marr and his colleagues (Marr, 1982; Marr & Poggio, 1979) have investigated algorithms that compute the depth of an object by: (a) selecting locations from the image in one eye, (b) identifying the same location in the other eye's image, and (c) measuring the disparity between the corresponding image points. The task of identifying corresponding locations is difficult because of the "false target problem"—the problem of finding the correct location-to-location correspondences given the large number of potential mappings between the dots in the two images. Thus, in Figure 26.1A, the image that falls on the left eye is integrated with the image

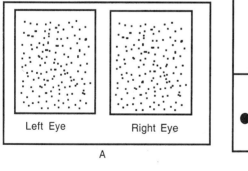

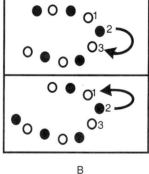

A   B

Figure 26.1
The importance of aligning scene parts in visual perception. In A, the dots that fall on the left eye must be fused with the dots that fall on the right eye in order to form an integrated and coherent perception. In B, the white dots belonging to the first frame of an apparent motion display must be placed into correspondence with the black dots belonging to the second frame. In the top display, Dot 2 is seen as moving to become Dot 3; in the bottom display, Dot 2 maps onto Dot 1.

that falls on the right eye by creating correspondences between the images' dots. These mappings are formed in random-dot stereograms by constraining correspondences such that (a) black dots can only match black dots (the similarity constraint), (b) one black dot matches no more than one black dot (the uniqueness constraint), and (c) the distance between matching dots usually varies gradually (the continuity constraint). While any dot in a scene can potentially match any number of dots in the other scene, one dot's correspondences are strongly constrained by the other correspondences that are established by other scene parts. This dependence of location mappings on other location mappings is a hallmark of "cooperative" algorithms.

Cooperative algorithms also are important in apparent motion phenomena. Single frame visual displays that are presented in fairly rapid succession can yield strong subjective impressions of motion (a fact the movie industry relies on). Reviews of this phenomena are found in Kolers (1972), Ramachandran and Antis (1986), and Ullman (1979). For subjective motion to occur, people must create correspondences between the separate image frames. In Figure 26.1B, two alternating displays of two frames each are depicted. The white circles are all displayed in one frame. The black circles appear in the second frame. (They are shaded black in the figure to show that they appear in the *second* frame.) The two frames are then alternated with each other on a computer screen once every quarter second. Subjectively, for the top apparent motion display, five dots are seen as rocking on a sideways horseshoe, with Dot 3 of the first frame corresponding to Dot 2 of the second frame. In the bottom display, the five dots subjectively move such that Dot 1 becomes Dot 2.

This small example suggests one method the mind uses to constrain motion perception—global optimization of correspondences. There is only one difference between the top and bottom display; in the top display the leftmost black dot is on the upper portion of the horseshoe, while in the bottom display the leftmost black dot is on the lower portion of the horseshoe. Although far removed from Dots 1, 2, and 3, the location of the leftmost black dot constrains the mappings of these dots. Mappings are created such that each white dot has a strong tendency to map onto one and only one black dot. Ullman (1979) and Marr (1982) argue that the subjectively perceived motion will be that motion which "maximizes the overall similarity between the frames" (Marr, 1982, p. 186). Interestingly, maximizing the overall similarity can proceed solely on the basis of local interactions between mappings.

In both the perception of depth and motion, there is evidence that mappings between scenes are constructed—mappings between the left and right visual images or mappings between frames that are separated in time. In both instances, the mappings that develop are partially constrained by local affinities and by global consistency. Mappings are sought out that: (a) place similar parts in correspondence (black dots tend to map onto other black dots), and (b) place parts in correspondence that are consistent with the other correspondences that have been established.

2.2 Analogical Mapping Processes in Comparison

Establishing mappings also plays a critical role in more conceptual processes. Analogies (Gentner & Clement, 1988) are understood by creating correspondences between elements from two domains. The comprehension of the atom / solar system analogy requires setting up correspondences between the atom's nucleus and the sun, between electrons and planets, etc.

Reminiscent of Marr's and Ullman's proposals, in Holyoak and Thagard's ACME system and Gentner's Structure Mapping Theory (SMT), comparison processes serve to: (a) place similar relations in correspondence, and (b) place relations in correspondence that are consistent with other relational correspondences. According to Gentner's systematicity principle (Gentner, 1983) and Holyoak and Thagard's "uniqueness" and "relational consistency" constraints (Holyoak & Thagard, 1989), elements are mapped onto each other so as to tend to yield coherent relational correspondences as opposed to isolated or inconsistent correspondences.

The current evidence suggests that analogies are created and evaluated by placing the elements (relations, and perhaps objects) of one domain into correspondence with the other domain. Furthermore, what correspondences are made depend on the other correspondences that have been established. In analogical reasoning, as in perceptual mapping, global consistency contrains the mappings that are created.

3 Models of Similarity and Mapping

Given that a global-consistency constraint on scene-to-scene mapping is found in both perceptual (apparent motion and stereoscopic vision) and conceptual (analogy) comparisons, it might well be expected that this constraint would also be found in people's judgments of similarity. One reason for thinking this is that the similarity of two objects or scenes depends on both perceptual and conceptual factors. Dogs and cats are similar both because they have roughly the same body shape (four legs, body, head) and because they are domesticated pets.

Given the above framework, it is surprising that the two predominant models of similarity in cognitive psychology, multidimensional scaling (MDS), and Tversky's (1977) Contrast model, provide no allowance for mappings that are constrained by other mappings (the global-consistency constraint). In fact, there is very little in either model to suggest that the process of mapping or aligning parts of scenes / objects is part of the process of computing similarity.

3.1 Multidimensional Scaling

The purpose of multidimensional scaling (MDS) is to discover the underlying dimensions that account for a given set of proximity data, and to provide an account for how the dimensional information is combined to yield a measure of similarity. The input to MDS routines may be similarity judgments, dissimilarity judgments, confusion probabilities, correlations, joint probabilities of occurrence, or any other measure of pairwise proximity. The output from an MDS routine will be a geometrical model of the data, with each object of the data set represented as a point in an N-dimensional space. The distance between two objects' points in the space is taken to be inversely related to the objects' similarity.

The MDS modeler observes the geometric space or a rotated version of the space, and subjectively determines labels for the dimensional axes. Richardson's (1938) fundamental insight, which is the basis of contemporary use of MDS, was to begin with subjects' judgments of pair-wise object (dis)similarity, and work backward to determine the dimensions and dimension values that subjects used in making their judgments.

A study by Smith, Shoben, and Rips (1974) illustrates a classic use of MDS. They obtained similarity ratings from subjects on many pairs of birds. Submitting these pair-wise similarity ratings to MDS analysis, they hypothesized underlying features that were used for representing the birds. Assigning subjective interpretations to the geometric model's axes, the experimenters postulated that birds were represented by such features as "ferocity" and "size."

3.2 Tversky's Contrast Model

A very influential model of similarity, the Contrast model, has been proposed by Amos Tversky and his associates (Gati & Tversky, 1984; Sattath & Tversky, 1987; Tversky, 1977). In the model, the similarity of two entities is taken to be a linear contrast of the features that the entities share, minus the features possessed by one entity that are not possessed by the other. The mathematical formulation

$$\text{SIM}(A, B) = \alpha \cdot F(\mathbf{A} \cap B) - \beta^* f(A - B) - \chi^* f(B - A)$$

is interpreted as: The similarity of A to B is a function of the features that A and B share, minus the features that A has that B does not have, minus again the features that B has that A does not have. The greek letters are simply weighting terms that depend on the subjects' task and the stimuli. Although not inherent to the Contrast model, the further assumption is often made that the function "f" satisfies feature additivity such that $f(x)$ for any set x is expressible as the *sum* of the measures of all the features that belong to x.

3.3 Assumptions Common to Both Models

There are many differences between the MDS model and the Contrast model. In fact, the Contrast model was in part formulated as an alternative to the metric MDS model's strong geometric assumptions regarding symmetry (Distance(A, B) = Distance(B, A)), the triangle inequality (Distance(A, B) + Distance(B, C) ≥ Distance(A, C)), and minimality (Distance(A, B) ≥

Distance(A, A) = $\varnothing$). However, the models share three assumptions with which we will take issue:

1. Entities are represented as a set of features (Contrast model) or dimension values (MDS). In the Contrast model, entities are represented by their set of features. Sets of features are compared for match and mismatch to determine the similarity of two entities. In the MDS models, entities are represented by their N-dimensional location; entities are defined by their values on each of the N dimensions.

2. Entity representations and feature weightings do not depend on the actual pair-wise comparison. This is very clear in MDS: once an MDS solution space has been derived, an entity's values are set. In some MDS schemes, the weights of the dimensions can vary (Carroll & Wish, 1974; Nosofsky, 1986) and in some schemes the context can change the MDS solution (Roth & Shoben, 1983). However, in all cases, once a context has been set up and all of the pairs have been presented, an entity's representation is fixed and the entity's features and feature weightings are defined. Primarily, both the Contrast model and MDS models work by setting up feature/dimension representations of all of the entities, and then comparing the entities (measuring distances or set overlap). The actual pair-wise comparison operation *uses* the previously established representations; it does not establish these representations.

3. The alignment process is straightforward and simple. If an object is simply represented by a list of features, then alignment is a trivial issue and global consistency provides no constraint on creating object-to-object correspondences. Features are placed in correspondence if they are identical (one scene's "red" feature is placed in correspondence with the "red" of the scene it is compared with). In the case of MDS, the dimensions provide the alignment, and values on these dimensions determine the degree or extent of matching. Although these assumptions may work for certain sets of stimuli, we shall soon see that often things are much more complicated.

The relatively unstructured representation of objects/scenes in MDS and the Contrast model stand in stark contrast to the richer first-order predicate logic and propositional representations invoked to explain analogical reasoning. The assumption that entities are represented by sets of features/dimension values makes no provision for hierarchical organization (features do not contain features as parts; features are nondecomposable primitives) or propositional organization (features do not take features as arguments).

We believe that issues of alignment are critical in visual similarity comparisons and that a major component of the comparison process involves setting up the correspondences between the objects/parts of the compared scenes. Furthermore, as with the perceptual and conceptual domains surveyed, we

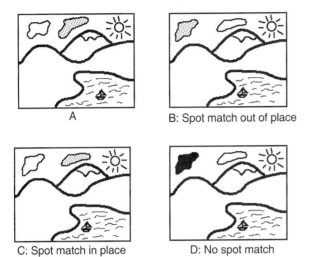

Figure 26.2
The influence of matches in place (MIPs) and matches out of place (MOPs) on similarity. If MIPs increase similarity more than MOPs, then Scene A will be more similar to scene C than Scene B. If MOPs increase similarity at all, then A will be more similar to B than D.

find that the alignment of objects is not independent of the other established correspondences—visual similarity is influenced by global consistency also. In opposition to the second assumption of comparison-independent representations, the weight that a particular feature has in a similarity calculation and the way it aligns cannot be determined before the actual similarity comparison process takes place. The process of placing scenes in correspondence changes the weights of matching and mismatching features. Finally, the model for alignment we present argues against the idea that determining correspondences is simple or can be ignored.

As a preview of the psychological experiments to come, consider Figure 26.2, which is based on a figure from Gati and Tversky (1984). Figure 26.2 is virtually identical to Gati and Tversky's stimuli except that a third mountain has been deleted and a cloud has been added. Previous research may have ignored issues of alignment by designing stimuli that lack many-to-one mappings or cross-mappings. Gati and Tversky compare scenes like Figure 26.2A to other scenes that have features such as clouds, houses, and mountains added or deleted. By collecting similarity ratings for several variations of the same scene, they can ascertain the importance of shared and distinctive features for similarity judgments.

However, it is not always easy to say what counts as a matching feature. For example, does the fact that both the right cloud of Figure 26.2A and the left cloud of Figure 26.2B are spotted count as a *matching feature* between these scenes? Does the feature "spots" increase the similarity of these scenes? It would seem that *how much* a *feature match increases similarity depends on whether it belongs to objects that correspond to each other or not.* If the right clouds of each scene were spotted, as they are in Figure 26.2A and 26.2C, then the shared spots would clearly increase similarity, but the spots would not increase similarity much if they belonged to the clouds of one scene and the sailboat of the other scene.

We will refer to feature matches between objects that are aligned with one another as *Matches in Place*, or MIPs. Feature matches between objects that are not aligned will be called *Matches out of Place*, or MOPs. We might presume that MIPs increase scene similarity more than MOPs—the fact that two scenes contain the feature "spotted" increases similarity more if the spots belongs to two clouds that correspond to each other than if the spots belong to non-corresponding objects. Thus, the similarity of Figures 26.2A and 26.2C is presumed to be higher than the similarity of Figures 26.2A and 26.2B. We might also presume that MOPs increase similarity more than no feature match at all —the fact that two noncorresponding objects are spotted results in a higher similarity than if the objects were not both spotted, all else being equal. Hypothetically, the similarity of Figures 26.2A and 26.2B is higher than the similarity of Figures 26.2A and 26.2D.

It is conceivable that a simple "feature list" representation of scenes could explain why feature matches only count if they belong to aligned objects. Instead of representing objects as containing "spotted" or "white" features, features could represent *conjunctions* of properties, such as "spotted cloud" or "right spotted cloud." If the clouds' features of Figure 26.2A are "left-spotted-cloud" and "right-spotted-cloud" while Figure 26.2B's features are "left-white-cloud" and "right-white-cloud" then the "feature list" representation could account for the inability of the scenes' matching spots to increase similarity. If these conjunctions were the encoded features, then Figure 26.2A and 26.2B have no cloud features in common at all.

Of course, it is reasonable to expect (and empirically supported, as we will see) that the matching spots increase the similarity of Figures 26.2A and 26.2B somewhat; the increase is just smaller than would be expected if the matching spots belonged to objects that were aligned. Keeping with the simple "feature list" representation of scenes, we could account for this pattern also, but only by positing both simple features such as "spotted" and conjunctive features such as "left white cloud." We need the simple features to account for the tendency of matching spots to increase similarity even when the spotted objects do not correspond to each other. We need the conjunctive features to account for the tendency for matching spots to increase similarity more if the spots belong to aligned objects than if they belong to nonaligned objects.

Problems with saving "feature list" representations by positing both simple and conjunctive features are that: (a) no account is given of how objects and object parts are aligned, (b) the number of features required grows exponentially with the complexity of the scenes, yielding a computationally intractable representation system, and (c) the account may not be able to handle, in detail, experimental evidence concerning how MOPs and MIPs influence similarity under various task manipulations. The first problem is that an unstructured similarity model, replete with simple and conjunctive features, still does not account for the intuition that objects and object parts are placed into correspondence during similarity comparisons. Scenes are still decomposed into a "flat" list of features with no hierarchical structure or account of how some features constrain others. The second problem is that, in order to account for all hypothetical similarity comparisons, $2^k - 1$ features are required for every object in a scene, where k is the number of object components. For example, if a scene has an object with four parts/features (a, b, c, and d), then 15 simple and conjunctive features (a, b, c, d, ab, ac, ad, bc, bd, cd, abc, abd, acd, bcd, $abcd$) are required just for this object to account for the scene's similarity to other related scenes. Fleshing out the third problem will be the central objective of the rest of this chapter. In the next section, we will review several experiments that investigate the influence of MIPs and MOPs on similarity ratings, indirect measures of similarity, and alignment judgments. Several of these experiments have been conducted in collaboration with Dedre Gentner. Throughout the review, the central point will be that the process of comparing scenes places scene parts in correspondence, and that this alignment process accounts for the influence of time, context, and feature distribution on scene comparison.

4 Experimental Support for Alignment in Comparison

4.1 Initial Investigation of Mapping and Similarity

The first experiment was designed to corroborate our intuitions about the influence of matches in and out of place on similarity. Briefly, two scenes were shown side by side on a computer screen. Each scene was composed of two butterflies. Each butterfly varied on four dimensions: head type, tail type, body shading, and wing shading. For each pair of scenes, subjects *assigned a similarity rating* (1–9, where 9 means "HIGHLY SIMILAR") and then *indicated which butterflies corresponded to each other* between the scenes. For each butterfly of one scene, subjects indicated the butterfly of the other scene that corresponded best to it, where subjects were left to define "correspond" themselves. The two scenes were constructed so that the number of matches in and out of place were varied.

Figure 26.3 shows two of the possible comparisons that were shown to subjects. In the top comparison, the only difference between the scene on the left and the scene on the right is related to the butterflies' body shadings. Butterfly C, while most likely corresponding to Butterfly A because they share three out of four features in common, possesses the body shading (wavy lines) of Butterfly

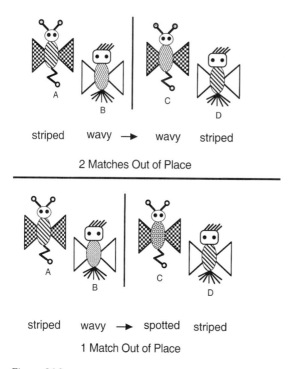

striped   wavy → wavy   striped

2 Matches Out of Place

striped   wavy → spotted   striped

1 Match Out of Place

Figure 26.3
Two possible displays from the initial experiment. In the top display, concentrating on the body shadings of the butterflies, there are 2 MOPs between the left scene and the right scene. In the bottom display, there is a single MOP along the body shading dimension.

B. Likewise, Butterfly D, though corresponding to B, has A's body shading. This is similar to the cross-mapping situation in analogy described earlier. Concentrating only on the body-shading dimension, there are two MOPs between the scenes—one between A and D, and the other between B and C.

The lower comparison of Figure 26.3 has one MOP along the body-shading dimension. Again, A corresponds to C, but has the same body shading as D. Butterflies B and C have different body shadings.

In all, there were six methods for changing a dimension from one butterfly scene to another. These methods resulted in the following numbers of MIPs and MOPs along a dimension: 2 MOPs, 1 MOP, 2 MIPs, 1 MIP, 1 MOP, and 1 MIP, and no matches at all.

On half of the trials, in going from the left scene to the right scene, we change the features of one dimension, in one of six ways. On the other half of the trials, we change two dimensions, each in one of six ways.

On one-third of the trials, the butterflies that correspond to each other are placed in the same relative positions in the two scenes. On one-third of the

Description	Similarity		Mapping Accuracy	
	True Mappings	False Mappings	One Dimension Changed	Two Dimensions Changed
Two matches in place	7.1	6.6	91%	—
One match in place, one match out of place	6.5	5.5	90%	83%
One match in place	6.4	6.0	90%	85%
No match	5.5	4.9	89%	83%
One match out of place	5.5	4.8	86%	76%
Two matches out of place	5.9	5.3	86%	62%

Figure 26.4
Results from initial experiment investigating the influence of MIPs and MOPs on similarity.

trials, the butterflies are given new unrelated positions. The particular features that were switched, the positions of the butterflies, and the particular values that the dimensions had were all randomized.

The results, as shown in the first column of Figure 26.4, reveal an influence of both matches in and out of place on similarity. First of all, similarity ratings for 0, 1, and 2 MIPs averaged 5.5, 6.4, and 6.1, respectively. MOPs have a much smaller effect; the ratings for 0, 1, and 2 MOPs averaged 5.5, 5.5, and 5.9, respectively. The fact that MIPs increase similarity more than MOPs can also be seen by looking at scene comparisons that have the same number of total matches. For example, the similarity rating in the first column for two MIPs is 7.1. This decreases to 5.9 in scenes where there are two MOPs. (In the first column, rating differences of 0.2 are significant at $p < .05$.) Further, the similarity rating for scenes with 1 MIP (6.4) is greater than the rating for scenes with 1 MOP (5.5).

We also find that if scenes share MOPs, feature matches that belong to butterflies that do not correspond to each other, then similarity is higher than if the scenes share no match along a dimension. In Figure 26.4, scenes with 2 MOPs are more similar than scenes with 1 MOP or no matches in common. However, there is no difference between scenes with 1 MOP and no matches at all. Interestingly, the phenomenon that (2 MOPs–1 MOP) > (1 MOP–0 MOPs) cannot be explained by an exponential relation between featural overlap and similarity (e.g., Nososky, 1986) because the finding holds even when the 0 and 1 MOPs displays are more similar overall than the 1 and 2 MOPs displays that are compared. Overall similarity is manipulated by varying the number of MIPs.

A question might arise: How does the experimenter know that a feature match is really in or out of place? A MOP would be a MIP if subjects gave the opposite mapping of butterflies than was expected. In Figure 26.3, the expected mapping was to place A and C in correspondence, and B and D. Perhaps the hypothesized influence of MOPs is due to trials in which the subject gives the unexpected mapping (A is aligned with D, B with C).

To address this objection, in the first column, we only include similarity ratings for trials where the subject and experimenter are in agreement as to which butterflies correspond to one another. These trials are called "true mapping" trials because the mappings that the subject gives are optimal in the sense of maximizing the number of matches that are MIPs as opposed to MOPs. In the top half of Figure 26.3, the mapping "A goes to C, B goes to D" results in six MIPs and two MOPs. The alternative mapping of "A goes to D, B goes to C" results in six MOPs and two MIPs. Thus, the first mapping is the "true mapping" and the second mapping is the "false mapping." According to the first column in Figure 26.4, MOPs increase similarity even when they are MOPs *for the subject*.

Additional support for the hypothesis that scene alignment influences similarity can be obtained by comparing the true mapping and the false mapping trials. If the subject makes the mapping that maximizes the number of matches in place (the true mapping), then similarity is greater than if subjects make a nonoptimal mapping. Both the true and false mappings result in the same number of total (MIPs + MOPs) scene matches; the true mapping results in a greater number of MIPs relative to MOPs. Thus, the difference between true and false mapping trials provides further evidence that MIPs increase similarity more than MOPs.

The relation between similarity and mapping can also be clarified by examining the percentages of true mapping trials for the different scene types. While the two rightmost columns of Figure 26.4 have the true mapping percentages, the rightmost column provides the most sensitive data; if only one dimension is changed, subjects do not make very many false mappings (and most of these are due to the different spatial locations of the butterflies in the scenes). If two dimensions are changed, we find that MOPs decrease mapping accuracy significantly (62% accuracy with 2 MOPs compared with 83% for 0 MOPs). There is also a much smaller, but significant influence of MIPs; the more MIPs there are, the greater the proportion of true mappings. The probability of finding the best correspondences between butterflies decreases as the number of MOPs increases and increases slightly as the number of MIPs increases.

A summary of the results from the first experiment reveals: (a) MIPs and MOPs both increase similarity, but MIPs increase similarity more, (b) if subject's give nonoptimal mappings, similarity is lower than if they give the optimal mapping, (c) MIPs simultaneously increase similarity ratings and mapping accuracy but MOPs increase similarity while decreasing mapping accuracy, and (d) the influence of a MOP depends on the other feature matches. The fourth conclusion is based on the significant difference in similarity between scenes with 2 MOPs and scenes with 1 MOP, but the lack of a difference between 1 MOP and no matches. The first two conclusions speak to our most central claim: the act of assessing similarity involves placing the parts of scenes in alignment with one another.

4.2 Other Experimental Findings

Although the following findings may seem rather loosely connected, the observations will later be integrated into a single account of mapping and similarity. The empirical results will be presented first, followed later by the model's explanations of the results.

4.2.1 MIPs and Feature Distribution

A robust effect found in our experiments is that the importance of a MIP on similarity depends on how other MIPs are distributed. First, similarity increases more if feature matches are concentrated in one pair of objects. Consider the two displays in Figure 26.5. In both cases, there are four MIPs between the scenes (only true mapping trials are included). In "concentrated" displays, such as the top display, the four MIPs are concentrated in one pair of butterflies. One pair of butterflies has four matching features, and the other pair of butterflies has no matching features. The average similarity rating for "concentrated" displays is significantly greater than the rating for "distributed" displays. In the lower "distributed" scene, two butterflies have three feature matches in common, and the other two butterflies have a single matching feature. Similarity decreases still further, to 4.6, when the MIPs are evenly split between the two pairs of butterflies. In short, a MIP increases similarity more if it is placed between objects that already share a large number of MIPs.

We get an analogous finding with dimensions. Namely, similarity is higher if feature matches are concentrated in a few dimensions rather than distributed across many dimensions. If four feature matches are concentrated in two dimensions (for example, wing shading and head), then similarity is higher than if the four feature matches are distributed across all four dimensions.

4.2.2 Nondiagnostic Features and Mapping Accuracy

Feature matches that cannot serve, by themselves, as cues for placing scene parts into correspondence still can increase mapping accuracy. Mapping accuracy can be measured as the

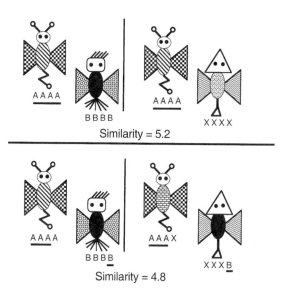

Figure 26.5
MIPs that are concentrated in a single pair of objects (top) increase similarity more than MIPs that are distributed over multiple pairs of objects (bottom).

percentage of time that subjects place butterflies in correspondence with each other in a manner that maximizes the number of MIPs. In the left scenes of Figure 26.6, three dimensions are nondiagnostic: wings, body, and tail. These dimensions are nondiagnostic because both butterflies have the same values on these three dimensions. In the top display, the butterflies in the right scene do not have any nondiagnostic features in common with the left butterflies. The ability of subjects to determine the optimal, or true mapping is poor; errors of mapping are made on 33% of trials.[1] A mapping error occurs if subjects respond that the top-left butterfly of the left scene corresponds to the bottom-right butterfly of the right scene.

Mapping performance greatly improves in the lower display, where the three nondiagnostic features of the left butterflies are also present in the right butterflies. Even though the nondiagnostic features provide no direct cue that the top-left butterflies correspond to each other (as do the bottom-right butterflies), the shared nondiagnostic features do increase responses on the basis of the HEAD dimension which *is* diagnostic for mapping. Subjects make their mappings on the basis of the butterfly heads more when other features between the scenes match than when they mismatch.

4.2.3 The Time Course of MIPs and MOPs   According to the feature integration theory developed by Anne Treisman and her associates (Treisman & Gelade, 1980), focused selective attention is required to bind object features to their

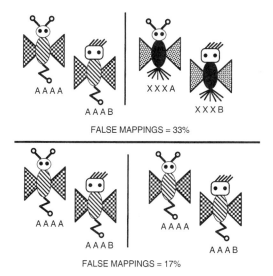

Figure 26.6
Nondiagnostic features, if shared by two scenes, can still increase mapping accuracy. In the top display, the nondiagnostic features of the left scene are not shared by the right scene's butterflies. In the bottom display, the left scene's nondiagnostic features are shared by the right scene's butterflies, thereby decreasing the number of mapping errors made.

objects/locations. If an object is displayed quickly, before attention can be directed to it, then the object's features will not be bound to the object. One result of unbound features is "illusory conjunctions"; features from different objects are combined together. The red color from one object, for example, may be perceptually conjoined with the circular shape of another object.

One might consider applying this logic to our paradigm. We might expect that MOPs would show most of their influence on similarity fairly early in processing, just as illusory conjunctions occur only before attention can bind features to objects. With time, as object-to-object correspondences become clear, only MIPs would show a large influence on similarity. The feature matches become *bound* to their correct correspondence with time. Until these correspondences are created, there would be little difference between a MIP and a MOP.

One of our "same/different" experiments supports this notion. Subjects saw two scenes and were required to report whether the scenes contained exactly the same butterflies. The error rate on "different" trials was used as a measure of similarity. Hypothetically, the more similar the two scenes are, the more likely a subject will be to incorrectly report that the scenes are the same. The butterflies in one of the scenes, the target scene, can be abstractly represented as AAAA and BBBB, signifying that the butterflies are composed of four features,

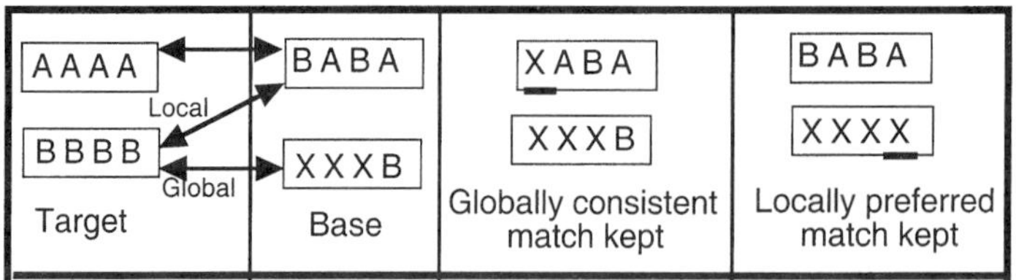

AAAA ↔ BABA Local / BBBB ↔ XXXB Global Target	Base	X A B A / X X X B Globally consistent match kept	B A B A / X X X X Locally preferred match kept
% confusions with Target, Slow Deadline	6%	6%	3%
% confusions with Target, Fast Deadline	27%	18%	21%

Figure 26.7
The temporal course of MIP and MOP influence. If subjects must respond within a very short time, then locally consistent matches increase similarity (as measured by % confusions) more than globally consistent matches. If subjects are given a longer deadline, then globally consistent matches increase similarity more than locally consistent matches.

and the features of one butterfly are completely different from the other butterfly's features. In the first panel of Figure 26.7 we compare the target scene to a base scene. If we require subjects to respond within 2.5 seconds, a slow deadline, subjects mistakenly think the scenes have the same butterflies 6% of the time. This error percentage increases to 27% if subjects are forced to respond within 1 second.

The important aspect of the target and base scenes is that both of the target butterflies have the most matching features with the top butterfly of the base scene. The top butterfly of the base scene, BABA, has two matches in common with both of the target scene's butterflies. Thus, if we ignore the fact that one object mapping can constrain another object mapping and just consider the locally preferred mappings, we would want to map both target butterflies onto the top butterfly of the base scene. However, if we maintain the global consistency of our mappings, then we would not permit this many-to-one mapping. The best globally consistent mapping is to map the top butterflies to each other, and the bottom butterflies to each other. MIPs are defined as feature matches between parts that are placed in "true" correspondence, and parts truly correspond if they belong to the set of consistent correspondences that results in the largest number of MIPs. As such, MIPs are matches between objects that are mapped in a globally consistent fashion; MOPs are matches between objects whose correspondence is not globally consistent.

In the next two scenes, we either take away one of the locally consistent matches leaving the global matches intact, or take away one of the globally consistent matches leaving the local matches intact. If we preserve the local match, then there are more confusion errors with the target display than if the global match is kept, *but only at the fast deadline.* At the slow deadline, keeping the global match increases similarity/errors more than keeping the local match. Locally consistent matches are more important than globally consistent matches for similarity *early* in processing (fast deadline). Later in processing, globally consistent matches are more important than locally consistent matches. It seems that it takes time to set up the influence that one object-to-object mapping has on another object-to-object mapping, and until this happens, error data show the influence of many-to-one mappings. At first, both butterflies of the target are mapped onto one butterfly of the other scene, but with time the influence of one mapping redirects the other mapping.

4.2.4 Sensitivity to Features of Aligned and Unaligned Objects   In addition to obtaining estimates of similarity and mapping judgments, a third source of data is the sensitivity with which subjects are able to report feature matches and mismatches. We have found that subjects are more sensitive in reporting feature matches and mismatches that occur between objects that are aligned than objects that are unaligned.

Subjects are presented scenes composed of two butterflies that are displayed on the screen for only five seconds. After the screen is erased, subjects first give a similarity rating for the two scenes. Then, two pointers appear on the screen, pointing to the previous locations of two butterflies. Subjects are told to respond as to whether the butterflies referred to by the pointers had matching values on a particular dimension (head, tail, body, or wings). Using the top display of Figure 26.3 as an illustration, the following four types of questions are asked, with the following results:

> *Aligned Matches:* Do A and C have the same WING SHADING? The correct answer (Yes) was given on 85% of trials.
> *Aligned Mismatches:* Do A and C have the same BODY SHADING? The correct answer (No) was given on 71% of trials.
> *Unaligned Matches:* Do A and D have the same BODY SHADING? The correct answer (Yes) was given on 52% of trials.
> *Unaligned Mismatches:* Do A and D have the same WING SHADING? The correct answer (No) was given on 80% of trials.

These data are based on displays where one scene is identical to another scene except along one dimension. The single changed dimension is changed by introducing one or two completely new butterfly features, or by *swapping* one or two butterfly features.

These data suggest both a response bias and a sensitivity change (for a discussion of these and other notions in signal detection theory, see Swets, Tanner, & Birdsall, 1961) due to the alignment of butterflies. The response bias is that if the butterflies correspond to one another, then subjects are more likely to respond "Yes, the features match" than if the butterflies are not aligned. The sensitivity change is reflected by the overall increase in accuracy in judgments for aligned butterflies over unaligned butterflies. A signal detection analysis indicates significantly greater sensitivity (d^1) for feature matches and mismatches that occur between butterflies that correspond to one another. Thus, it is not simply that people assume that all features that belong to corresponding objects match. Subjects are highly accurate at identifying *mismatching* features between corresponding objects, much more accurate than they are at reporting matching features for objects that do not correspond to one another. The act of placing objects into correspondence increases sensitivity to *all* of their feature correspondences, matching or mismatching. In order to know how likely a person will be to detect a matching or mismatching feature between two scenes' parts, it is necessary to know whether the parts correspond.

5 An Interactive Activation Model of Mapping and Similarity

5.1 A Brief Overview of SIAM

In attempting to provide a framework to organize the seemingly disconnected fragments of data reported, we have developed a model SIAM (Similarity as Interactive Activation and Mapping).[2] Originally inspired by McClelland and Rumelhart's (1981) interactive activation model of word perception, SIAM also bears many conceptual resemblances to Falkenhainer, Genter, and Forbus's (1990) SME, and many architectural and conceptual resemblances to Holyoak and Thagard's (1989) ACME system.

The primary unit of operation is the node. Nodes do only two things: (a) send activation to other nodes, and (b) receive activation from other nodes. As in ACME, nodes represent hypotheses that two entities correspond to one another in two scenes. In SIAM, there are two types of nodes: feature-to-feature nodes and object-to-object nodes.

Feature-to-feature nodes each represent a hypothesis that two features correspond to each other. There will be one node for every pair of features that belong to the same dimension; if each scene has O objects with F features each, there would be O^2F feature-to-feature nodes. As the activation of a feature-to-feature node increases, the two features referenced by the node will be placed in stronger correspondence. All node activations range from 0 to 1. In addition to activation, feature-to-feature nodes also have a "match value," a number between 0 and 1 that indicates how similar the two features' values on a dimension are. If two butterflies have the same type of head, then the node hypothesizing that these two heads correspond to each other would receive a match value of one. The match value decreases monotonically as the similarity of the butterflies' heads decreases. Match values in SIAM play a similar role to the semantic unit in ACME. Both structures serve to place parts that are primitively similar in correspondence. In addition, match values influence similarity directly; similarity is a function of the match values, weighted by the attention paid to them.

Each object-to-object node represents an hypothesis that two objects correspond to one another. There will be O^2 object-to-object nodes if there are O objects in each of two scenes. As the activation of an object-to-object node increases, the two objects are said to be placed in tighter correspondence with each other.

At a broad level, SIAM works by first creating correspondences between the features of scenes. At first, SIAM has "no idea" what objects belong together. Once features begin to be placed into correspondence, SIAM begins to place objects into correspondence that are consistent with the feature correspondences. Once objects begin to be placed in correspondence, activation is fed back down to the feature (mis)matches that are consistent with the object alignments. In this way, object matches influence activation of feature matches at the same time that feature matches influence the activation of object matches.

As in ACME and McClelland and Rumelhart's original work, activation spreads in SIAM by two principles: (a) nodes that are consistent send excitatory activation to each other, and (b) nodes that are inconsistent inhibit one another. Figure 26.8 illustrates the basic varieties of excitatory and inhibitory connections in SIAM. There are four ways in which the activation from one node influences the activation of another node:

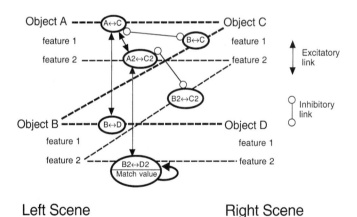

Left Scene   Right Scene

Figure 26.8
Sample connections present in SIAM. Correspondences that are consistent excite each other. Inconsistent correspondences inhibit each other. Nodes are represented by ovals. Excitatory and inhibitory links are represented by solid lines. Dashed lines represent the object or feature mapping indicated by the node.

1. Feature-to-feature nodes inhibit and excite other feature-to-feature nodes. Feature correspondences that result in two-to-one mappings are inconsistent; all other correspondences are consistent. The node that places Feature 2 of Object A in correspondence with Feature 2 of C (the A2 ↔ C2 node) is inconsistent with the node that places Feature 2 of C in correspondence with Feature 2 of B (the B2 ↔ C2 node). These nodes are inconsistent because they would place two features from one scene into correspondence with a single feature of the other scene. These nodes inhibit one another. The A2 ↔ C2 node is consistent with the B2 ↔ D2 node; consequently, these nodes will excite one another.

2. Object-to-object nodes inhibit and excite other object-to-object nodes. This is analogous to the previous type of connection. Object correspondences that are inconsistent inhibit one another. The node that places A and C in correspondence inhibits the node that places B and C in correspondence (A and B cannot both map onto C) and excites the node that places B and D in correspondence.

3. Feature-to-feature nodes excite, and are excited by, object-to-object nodes. Object-to-object nodes that are consistent with feature-to-feature nodes will be excited. The node that places A into correspondence with C is excited by the node that places Feature 2 of A into correspondence of Feature 2 of C. The excitation is bidirectional; a node placing two features in correspondence will be excited by the node that places the objects composed of the features into correspondence. In other words, the A ↔ C node sends activation back down to the A2 ↔ C2 node.

4. Match values excite feature-to-feature nodes. Features are placed in correspondence to the extent that their features match. If a match value is greater than .5 (a value of 1.0 signifies two identical features), then the activation of the node that places the features in correspondence will increase. Otherwise the feature-to-feature node activation decreases.

The net input to a node i is given by:

$$net_{i(t)} = \frac{\sum_{j=1}^{n}(A_{j(t)}W_{ij}) - MIN}{(MAX - MIN)}$$

Where n is the number of afferent links to node i (including excitatory links from match values to nodes), $A_{j(t)}$ is the activation of node j at time t, and W_{ij} is the weight of the link going from unit j to unit i. In the current modeling, all weights are set equal to 1.0 (for excitatory connections) or −1.0 (for inhibitory connections).[3] $Net_{i(t)}$ is the activation of node i normalized by the difference between the maximum (MAX) and minimum (MIN) activation values that i can possibly attain, given the number of inhibitory and excitatory afferents to i. $Net_{i(t)}$ is constrained to lie between 0 and 1. If i has 2 inhibitory and 1 excitatory afferents, then MIN $= -2$ (if both inhibitory inputs were completely activated, and the excitatory input was zero) and MAX $= 1$. The new activation of a node at time $t + 1$ is a synchronously updated function of the old activation at time t and the normalized input activation, $net_{i(t)}$, received by the node: if $net_{i(t)} > 0.5$ then

$$A(t + 1) = A(t) + (1 - A(t))^*(net_{i(t)} - 0.5)^*B, \text{ otherwise}$$
$$A(t + 1) = A(t) - A(t)^*(0.5 - net_{i(t)})^*B$$

where B is a parameter for the rate of activation adjustment.

Once a cycle of activation adjustment has passed, similarity is computed via:

$$\text{similarity} = \frac{\sum_{i=1}^{n}(\text{match value}_i^* A_i)}{\sum_{i=1}^{n} A_i}$$

As such, similarity is computed as a function of the match values for each feature-to-feature node, weighted by the activation of the node. Thus, the more active a feature-to-feature node is, the more the particular matching or mismatching value shared by the features will influence similarity. If the features have the same feature value, then similarity will increase more if the feature-to-feature node's activation is high. Likewise, similarity will decrease more if the features do not have the same value if they are also placed in strong correspondence. The activation of a feature-to-feature node can be interpreted as the attention paid to a matching/mismatching feature. The greater the activation of a feature-to-feature node, the more the feature match or mismatch will influence similarity. Similarity is normalized (by dividing by ΣA_i) such that the minimum similarity is 0.0 and the maximum similarity is 1.0. By normalizing similarity, the similarity of two-scene displays with different numbers of objects and features can be compared. It should not be assumed that similarity is algebraically computed by SIAM at the end of each cycle. Rather, this formula for similarity should be viewed as a shorthand way of characterizing the state of the network as a whole.

For the present modeling, the only parameter that is allowed to vary is the number of times SIAM cycles through the four methods of adjusting activations. Roughly speaking, the more cycles SIAM is allowed to complete, the more individual node activations will be influenced by global consistency. If SIAM runs for only a single cycle of activation adjustment, then MOPs and MIPs are almost equally weighted. If SIAM is allowed many cycles of activation adjustment, MIPs will become more influential than MOPs. Objects will begin to be placed into correspondence, and once objects are placed in correspondence, they will send activation down to the features that are compatible with their alignment. MIPs will generally be compatible with the most activated object-to-object correspondences, and thus will receive the most activation. The isolated body shading MOPs of Figure 26.3 will not receive much weight in the similarity calculation because they will not receive much activation from the node that hypothesizes that A corresponds to D. The A ↔ D node will not be highly activated because there are three inhibitory feature-to-feature nodes (head, tail, wings) and only one excitatory feature-to-feature node (body shading) activating it. In short, the influence of consistent feature-to-feature and object-to-object mappings becomes more pronounced as the number of iterations of activation adjustment increases. Aspects of the temporal course of human similarity assessments are modeled by varying the number of cycles SIAM executes.

SIAM is given two scene descriptions as an input. Each scene is organized into objects, and the objects are organized into features with feature values. A scene might be expressed as ((object 1 (head square) (tail zig-zag) (body-shading white) (wing-shading checkered)) (object 2 (head triangle) (tail zig-zag) (body-shading striped) (wing-shading spotted))). On the basis of the initial scene descriptions, SIAM constructs a network of feature-to-feature nodes and object-to-object nodes, and assigns initial match values (0 or 1) to feature-to-feature nodes. All node activations are initially set to 0.5. SIAM gives as output the similarity of the two scenes at every cycle of activation, the feature-to-feature correspondences (derived from the feature-to-feature node activations), the object-to-object correspondences, and the likelihood of performing a particular mapping (derived from the object-to-object activations).

5.2 Evaluation of SIAM

The results of fitting SIAM's output to subjects' data are shown in Figure 26.9. Data from three experiments are used: the original similarity rating study, the replication in which no mapping judgments are required, and the same/different response time experiment. Similarity, as measured by ratings and response time, is compared to predicted values from SIAM and three other models. SIAM is allowed to run from 1 to 20 cycles of activation adjustment. SIAM is fit to the subjects' data with only "number of cycles" fit as a free parameter. All other parameters are set to their default values. SIAM is fit to the average similarity assessments for each functionally different display, averaging over subjects and over the particular featural instantiation of the display type. For example, in the first experiment, similarity ratings are modeled for 21 different display types, each with a different combination of MIPs and MOPs. For the similarity rating data, SIAM at two cycles correlates best with subject data (Pearson's $r = .983$ if no mappings are required, $r = .968$ if subjects are required to place butterflies in correspondence with each other).[4] For the response time data, SIAM fits the data best when it is only allowed one cycle of activation adjustment ($r = .78$). The different settings of the "number of cycles" parameter are reasonable because the "same/different" judgments are made much more

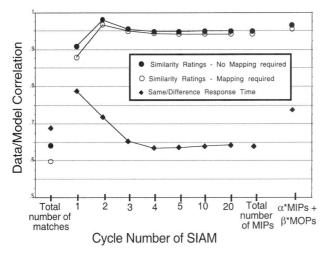

Figure 26.9

Data/Model correlations for SIAM (where SIAM is allowed to execute a variable number of cycles) and three other models (Far left: MIPs and MOPs are not distinguished; right: Only MIPs increase similarity; far right: MIPs and MOPs both influence similarity and are differentially weighted). SIAM at cycle 2 (for the rating data) and cycle 1 (for the response time date) correlates significantly better with the human data from three experiments than the other three models.

quickly than the similarity ratings are, and speed is modeled in SIAM by reducing the number of cycles.

The three models SIAM is compared against include models where MOPs and MIPs are treated the same and both influence similarity, where only MIPs influence similarity, and where MOPs and MIPs are differentially weighted and both influence similarity. All three models yield significantly inferior fits to the subject generated data for all three experimental tasks. The worst fit is provided by the model that claims that similarity is a function of the total number of matching features, irrespective of whether the match is a MIP or a MOP. This model can be considered the "no alignment is necessary" model because alignment is necessary to decide whether a match is in place or out of place. This model is not capable of explaining our basic experimental result that the importance of a match depends on whether it belongs to objects that correspond to one another. According to this model, all matches are treated equivalently. This model is tested by running a linear regression of "total number of MIPs and MOPs" on similarity assessments. The demise of this model supports our claim that object alignment is a necessary consideration when evaluating a feature's impact on similarity.

The second "straw-person" model characterizes similarity as only a function of MIPs; MOPs do not influence similarity at all. The ability of this model to fit the rating data is quite good, reaching correlations of $r = .95$ and $r = .94$ for the two sets of rating data. Its fit of the response time data is much worse, as might be expected given the more substantial influence of MOPs in this data set. SIAM's superior fit[5] supports the previous claim that pure "conjunctive feature" (combinations of simple features, such as "Red square") accounts of similarity are unable to explain the influence of MOPs on similarity. At the very least, we need both simple and conjunctive features.

The final model assumes that both MIPs and MOPs influence similarity, and that the two types of match receive different weights. Similarity is assumed to be a linear regression of "number of MIPs" and "number of MOPs," where the weights given to MIPs and MOPs are free parameters chosen to optimize the fit to the subject data. This model captures the intuition that MIPs and MOPs both increase similarity, and that MIPs increase similarity more than MOPs.

SIAM predicts the subjects' data from the three tasks with reliably greater accuracy than even this third, more sophisticated model. Therefore, SIAM's success at modeling the subject's data is not simply due to the fact that it weights both MIPs and MOPs, and weights MIPs more.

How does SIAM differ from a model that simply weights MIPs and MOPs differentially? Put another way, *why do we need the complex interactive activation that SIAM has?* For the particular data that were modeled, there are two contributory reasons:

1. SIAM correctly predicts that 2 MOPs increases similarity over 1 MOP, whereas the difference between 1 MOP and 0 MOP is not significant. If 2 MOPs are arranged as they were in the scene's shown subjects (see the top half of Figure 26.3), then the MOPs will mutually excite one another because they are consistent with each other. Even though the MOPs will not be consistent with the optimal mapping, they will activate nodes that will send excitatory activation to each other. Two MOPs will support each other if they are consistent with the same object-to-object mappings, and they will support each other more if they occur on the same dimension (because feature-to-feature modes facilitate other consistent feature-to-feature nodes). A single MOP will not receive much weight because there will be no other feature matches that support it. Therefore, the non-linear relation between number of MOPs and judged similarity is a natural outcome of the mutual support relations in the interactive activation process.

2. SIAM correctly predicts that concentrated feature matches increase similarity more than distributed feature matches. Experiments described earlier showed that if feature matches are concentrated on a single dimension or on a single object then similarity will be relatively high. In SIAM, the reason for this is (again) that concentrated matches will mutually excite each other. If there are four feature matches in common between two objects, then the objects will be placed in strong correspondence with one another. Therefore, the object-to-object node representing these objects will be highly activated. Once activated, the object-to-object node will send activation down to the features that compose

the objects. This "fed-back" activation results in a similarity assessment that strongly weights the four concentrated MIPs. Thus, the four feature matches influence similarity greatly because of the strong object correspondences they establish. Distributed MIPs will not activate any single object pair as strongly, and therefore, they will not receive as much "fed-back"activation.

There are also a number of advantages of SIAM over the other three models that have influenced its ability to account for other trends in the data.

1. SIAM provides an account for how we match objects. The best alternatives to SIAM are the model that has similarity as only a function of the number of MIPs, and the model that differentially weights MIPs and MOPs to arrive at a similarity assessment. *Both* of these models presume that there is a method for determining whether a match is a match in place or a match out of place. One model only includes MIPs, and the other model differentially weights MIPs. SIAM gives a process model for determining how objects and features are aligned and consequently gives a method for determining whether a given feature match is in or out of place. SIAM, in addition to computing similarity, also computes feature-to-feature and object-to-object alignments.

2. SIAM correctly makes time course predictions. SIAM predicts our results that a globally consistent feature match increases similarity more than a local match *late* in processing, whereas the locally consistent feature match increases similarity more than the global match *early* in processing. The more cycles SIAM executes, the more similarity is influenced by the requirement that object mappings be consistent. While two objects may strongly map onto one object at first, the nodes representing these incompatible mappings will strongly inhibit each other. If there is even a weak advantage to one of the mappings, then the other mapping will become increasingly weakened with time. SIAM also correctly predicts that MOPs increase early assessments of similarity more than late assessments, for the same reason. With time, object-to-object correspondences will begin to influence feature-to-feature correspondences, and with this influence, similarity will become selectively influenced by MIPs. The more cycles SIAM completes, the more any given node is activated so as to be consistent with all of the other nodes.

3. SIAM predicts that nondiagnostic features, if present in two scenes, increase subjects' accuracy in making the correct butterfly-to-butterfly mappings. Mapping accuracy in SIAM is modeled by comparing the magnitudes of object-to-object node activations. If the A-to-C node activation is 0.8 and the A-to-D activation is 0.4, then the probability of a subject mapping A to C is $0.8/(0.8 + 0.4) = 67\%$. The more features (diagnostic and nondiagnostic) that two objects share, the more strongly the objects will be placed in correspondence, and consequently, the more strongly all feature matches shared by the objects will be activated, including the diagnostic feature match. If the two scenes do not agree on the nondiagnostic features, no objects will be placed in strong correspondence, and no substantial level of activation will be fed back to

the diagnostic feature. In this way, SIAM correctly predicts that even features that provide no cue about what objects correspond to each other still can increase mapping accuracy.

4. SIAM predicts that sensitivity (in the signal detection sense of the word) is higher for feature matches and mismatches that occur in aligned objects than unaligned objects. If two objects are placed in strong correspondence, then all of the matching and mismatching features of those objects are made more important for similarity assessments. If we assume that sensitivity to (mis)matching features is a monotonically increasing function of the feature-to-feature node activation, then subjects will be more sensitive to aligned feature (mis)matches. Feature-to-feature node activations are used as indications of how much *attention* a particular correspondence receives; the more a feature-to-feature node is activated, the more the feature-to-feature value influences similarity. The more attention a feature-to-feature (mis)match receives, the greater the sensitivity will be for match/mismatch questions. McClelland and Elman's (1986) inter-active activation model of speech perception has received criticism for making a similar claim. Massaro (1989) argues that McClelland and Elman's TRACE model predicts non-constant phoneme sensitivities for different speech contexts (for a more recent version of TRACE that does not make this prediction see McClelland, 1991). No such sensitivity changes are empirically obtained in the spoken word stimuli that have been used. However, in the case of our butterfly scenes, we in fact *do* find sensitivity differences for feature matches depending on the alignments of objects. For our domain, the fact that an interactive activation model predicts context-dependent sensitivity changes is a point in favor of the model.

5.3 Comparisons and Future Directions

The empirical results presented here are problematic for traditional models of similarity that create independent representations of entities and compare these representations for matching and mismatching features (Contrast model), or for proximity on feature values (MDS). Even if entities are represented in terms of simple ("white") and conjunctive ("white spotted triangle") features, many of the more detailed results we obtained would not be predicted. In particular, no account would be given of: the nonlinear effect of MOPs (2 MOPs > 1 MOP = 0 MOPs), the difference between true and false mapping trials on similarity ratings, the relatively large impact of MOPs on similarity *early* in processing, the influence of nondiagnostic features on mapping accuracy, the increased similarity due to MIPs that are concentrated in few dimensions as opposed to distributed across many dimensions, and the influence of alignment on feature sensitivity.

In many ways, the closest neighbors to SIAM are models of analogy such as SME and ACME. Our empirical results were not compared with these models' predictions in a rigorous manner. SME and ACME were not principally designed to handle similarity data, and there are several issues that arise when they are applied to our results. In particular, if SME's assessment of a pair of scenes is limited to a single best GMAP (a single set of *consistent* correspondences between two structured representations), then SME does not predict that MOPs increase similarity. For a MOP to increase similarity, mutually exclusive correspondences must be integrated into a single estimate of similarity. SME would have to allow for multiple conflicting GMAPs to simultaneously increase similarity.

Likewise, MOPs do not increase similarity in ACME if similarity is measured as the numbers of "cycles to success, the number of cycles required for all of the correct individual mapping hypotheses to reach an activation level exceeding that of their nearest competitor." Instead, MOPs would decrease this measure of similarity because MOPs tend to activate globally inconsistent object-to-object alignments, and thus slow down convergence to the correct object-to-object mappings. ACME also incorporates a measure G, "a rough index of the overall fit of the emerging mapping to the constraints" imposed by the network. In some senses, G captures some notion of similarity: if the system is relatively "happy" in the correspondences it is setting up between scenes, G will tend to be high. G increases monotonically with the number of cycles of activation adjustment; as ACME settles into a solution, G necessarily increases. While G captures the notion that activations tend to strive for global consistency, it does not necessarily capture the notion of overall similarity. Human assessments of similarity do not always increase with time; in fact, with similarity measured as the number of errors on "different" trials, similarity virtually always decreases with longer display exposure or longer response deadlines. In SIAM, similarity is a function of activations and the feature match values. While a feature-to-feature activation may become increasingly influenced by object correspondences, if the features do not in fact have the same feature value then similarity will still be lowered by this mismatch. Massaro (1989) has argued that interactive activation models are nonoptimal because they distort environmental input more than is reasonable; the integrity of the information sources is compromised by other activations. In SIAM, the feature match values are not subject to modification by activations, and thus the information they provide is never lost by other activations. What changes is the weight given to the match values.

One of our central claims has been that scene representations are not completely determined prior to the comparison process. We have argued that the weight that a feature match or mismatch has depends on how the two scenes align with one another. However, there is a more fundamental way in which representations may not be precomputable. We have recently obtained results suggesting that the actual features that describe scenes may not be developed independently of the comparison. In Figure 26.10, when A is compared to B, more often than not, a subject will list as a shared feature the fact that both A

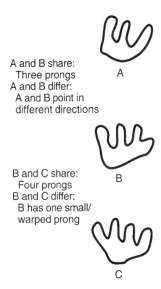

A and B share:
  Three prongs
A and B differ:
  A and B point in
  different directions

B and C share:
  Four prongs
B and C differ:
  B has one small/
  warped prong

Figure 26.10
Subjects are asked to compare B with A and C, listing similarities and differences. When B is compared to A, B is most often given the description "three prongs." When B is compared to C, B is most often given the description "four prongs."

and B have three prongs/fingers. However, a second group of subjects, asked to compare B and C, more than half of the time list as a shared feature the fact that both B and C have four prongs/fingers. Assuming these groups of subjects have the same initial tendency to see B as three vs. four pronged, we conclude that the featural description of B depends on what it is compared with. Given the implausibility of B having static, precomparison descriptions of both "three prongs" and "four prongs," we conclude that the prong description for B is at least partially created only once it has been paired with A or C. Not only are feature *saliences* influenced by the process of aligning scene parts, but the features themselves are determined by the comparison process as well. SIAM as currently conceived cannot handle this finding, but the finding is consistent with the general theory that entity representations are dynamically constructed on the basis of the actual comparison being made, and are not static or completely prewired.

6 Conclusions

The experiments and model presented here have pointed to three conclusions:

  1. The act of comparing things naturally involves aligning the parts of the things to be compared.

2. Similarity assessments are well captured by an interactive activation process between feature and object correspondences.

3. What counts as a feature match, and how much it will count, depends on the particular things being compared.

Comparison naturally involves alignment. Even when subjects are not instructed to do so, even when indirect measures of similarity are used, subjects in our experiments set up correspondences between the parts of things they compared. These correspondences influence the particular features that are attended, and the other correspondences that are created. Relative to feature matches between noncorresponding objects (MOPs), feature matches between corresponding objects (MIPs) increase similarity ratings, slow down subjects' responses to say scenes are different, increase the proportion of trials in which subjects call two different scenes the same, and influence categorization decisions. The actual correspondences set up by a subject influence the perceived similarity of two scenes.

Similarity assessments are well captured by an interactive activation process between feature and object correspondences. SIAM is able to capture empirical details not captured even by the model of similarity that makes a conceptual distinction between MIPs and MOPs and differentially weights the two types of matching features. SIAM gives good fits to data collected by subjects, and makes correct predictions with regard to the distribution of feature matches (concentrated MIPs increases similarity more than distributed MIPs), the time course of similarity (MOPs increase similarity more early in processing than later), and sensitivity to features (sensitivity is greater for feature (mis)matches belonging to aligned objects than unaligned objects). The most important insight of SIAM is that there is a relation of mutual dependency between hierarchical levels of a scene. Object correspondences depend on feature-to-feature similarities. The more features two objects have in common, the more strongly the objects will be placed in correspondence. Reciprocally, feature correspondences depend on object-to-object similarities. The greater the similarity between two objects, the more strongly the features of the objects will be placed in correspondence. How much a feature match counts toward similarity depends on whether it matches aligned objects. Feature and object alignments mutually influence each other, and together they determine the similarity of whole scenes. This picture of mutual dependency is in contrast to traditional models of similarity which have little to say concerning how feature matches and mismatches are determined.

What counts as a feature match, and how much it will count, depends on the particular things being compared. We have argued against models of comparison that develop independent representations of the things to be compared, and then evaluate these representations for overlap and proximity of values. Representations are not created independently—the weight that a feature has in a comparison cannot be determined until the feature is brought into alignment with its counterpart in the other scene. We cannot know a priori how much a given feature such as "triangle," if it matches, will influence similarity. The feature match may increase similarity a great deal, or not very much at all, depending on how the scene's parts are aligned more globally.

If we begin our analysis of the comparison process by assuming "A has these features, B has these features, and the features have saliences X, Y, and Z" then we may unwisely ignore the most interesting cognitive phenomena involved in comparing things. It may turn out that the cognitive processes most in need of explanation are not those processes responsible for integrating matching and mismatching features into a single estimate of similarity, but are those processes responsible for figuring out exactly what will *count* as matching and mismatching features and how much weight to give these features.

Notes

This research was supported by National Science Foundation, Grant BNS-88-12193, awarded to the second author.
1. One reason for such poor performance is that the butterflies that correspond to each other are not always placed in the same relative spatial locations as they are in Figure 26.6. If corresponding butterflies are given the same spatial locations, errors are made on only 18% of trials; this increases to 37% if the corresponding butterflies are given unrelated spatial locations, and to 41% if the spatial positions of butterflies are switched.
2. A simplified version of SIAM is presented. A slightly different activation function and network architecture is presented in Goldstone (1991).
3. Goldstone (1991) allows for different sources of information to have different weights. Separate weights are given for the influence of match values, features, and objects on feature-to-feature nodes, and for the influence of features and objects on object-to-object nodes. When the weight associated with the influence of objects on features is a free parameter, data fits are somewhat better than in the currently presented model. Individual weight terms are not required for each feature value/dimension because the experiments randomized these variables, and the modeled data collapse over different feature value/dimension configurations.
4. More cycles of activation adjustment would be required if B were set to a value less than one. In the version of SIAM discussed by Goldstone (1991), more cycles of activation adjustment are required for the best fitting model because node activations do not asymptote to zero (for MOPs) or one (for MIPs). Even after activations have asymptoted, there is still an influence of MOPs on similarity.
5. Although the differences in correlation are small, they are significant. When data/model correlations are near 1.00, very small differences are needed for statistical significance.

References

Beck, J. (1966). Effect of orientations and of shape similarity on perceptual grouping. *Perception and Psychophysics, 1,* 300–302.

Carroll, J. D., & Wish, M. (1974). Models and methods for three-way multidimensional scaling. In D. H. Krantz, R. C. Atkinson, R. D. Luce, & P. Suppes (Eds.), *Contemporary developments in mathematical psychology* (Vol. 2, pp. 57–105). San Francisco: Freeman.

Clement, C., & Gentner, D. (188). Systematicity as a selection constraint in analogical mapping. *Proceedings of the Tenth Annual Conference of the Cognitive Science Society* (pp. 421–419). Hillsadle, NJ: Erlbaum.

Falkenhainer, B., Forbus, K. D., & Gentner, D. (1990). The structure-mapping engine: Algorithm and examples. *Artificial Intelligence, 41,* 1–63.

Gati, I., & Tversky, A. (1984). Weighting common and distinctive features in perceptual and conceptual judgments. *Cognitive Psychology, 16,* 341–370.

Gentner, D. (1983). Structure-mapping: A theoretical framework for analogy. *Cognitive Science, 7,* 155–170.

Gentner, D., & Clement, C. (1988). Evidence for relational selectivity in the interpretation of analogy an metaphor. In G. H. Bower (Ed.), *The psychology of learning and motivation* (Vol. 22, pp. 307–358). New York: Academic Press.

Goldstone, R. L. (1991). *Similarity, interactive, activation, and mapping.* Unpublished doctoral dissertation, University of Michigan, Ann Arbor.

Hall, R. P. (1989). Computational approaches to analogical reasoning: A comparative analysis. *Artificial Intelligence, 39,* 39–120.

Holyoak, K. J., & Thagard, P. (1989). Analogical mapping by constrain satisfaction. *Cognitive Science, 13,* 295–355.

Keren, G., & Baggen, S. (1981). Recognition model of alphanumeric characters. *Perception and Psychophysics, 29,* 289–294.

Kolers, P. A. (1972). *Aspects of motion perception.* New York: Pergamon Press.

Markman, A. B., & Gentner, D. G. (1990). Analogical mapping during similarity judgments. *Proceedings of the Twelfth Annual Conference of the Cognitive Science Society* (pp. 38–44).

Marr, D. (1982). *Vision.* San Francisco: Freeman.

Marr, D., & Poggio, T. (1979). A computational theory of human stereo vision. *Proceedings of the Royal Society of London, 204,* 301–328.

Massaro, D. W. (1989). Testing between the TRACE model and the fuzzy logical model of speech perception. *Cognitive Psychology, 21,* 398–421.

McClelland, J. L. (1991). Stochastic interactive processes and the effect of context on perception. *Cognitive Psychology, 23,* 1–144.

McClelland, J. L., & Elman, J. L. (1986). The TRACE model of speech perception. *Cognitive Psychology, 18,* 1–86.

McClelland, J. L., & Rumelhart, D. E. (1981). An interactive activation model of context effects in letter perception: Part 1. An account of basic findings. *Psychological Review, 88,* 375–407.

Nosofsky, R. M. (1986). Attention, similarity, and the identification-categorization relationship. *Journal of Experimental Psychology: General, 115,* 39–57.

Ramachandran, V. S., & Antis, S. M. (1986). Perception of apparent motion. *Scientific American, 254,* 102–109.

Richardson. M. W. (1938). Multidimensional psychophysics. *Psychological Bulletin, 35,* 659–660.

Roth, E. M., & Shoben, E. J. (1983). The effect of context on the structure of categories. *Cognitive Psychology, 15,* 346–378.

Sattath, S., & Tversky, A. (1987). On the relation between common and distictive feature models. *Psychological Review, 94,* 16–22.

Smith, E. E., Shoben, E. J., & Rips, L. J. (1974). Structure and process in semantic memory: A featural model for semantic decisions. *Psychological Review, 81,* 214–241.

Swets, J. A., Tanner, W. P., & Birdsall, T. G. (1961). Decision processes in perception. *Psychological Review, 68,* 301–340.

Treisman, A., & Gelade, G. (1980). A feature-integration theory of attention. *Cognitive Psychology, 12,* 97–136.

Tversky, A. (1977). Features of similarity. *Psychological Review, 84,* 327–352.

Ullman, S. (1979). *The interpretation of visual motion.* Cambridge, MA: MIT Press.

Mapping Analogies

Chapter 27

Analogical Mapping by Constraint Satisfaction

Keith J. Holyoak and Paul Thagard

Introduction

At the core of analogical thinking lies the process of *mapping:* the construction of orderly correspondences between the elements of a source analog and those of a target. Identifying an appropriate mapping is crucial in allowing useful transfer of knowledge. In this chapter, a theory of analogical mapping based upon a small set of constraints is provided and a cooperative algorithm that allows the graceful integration of these constraints is described. The algorithm is implemented in a computer program that computes mappings between symbolic representations. The results of a number of applications of the computational model to a variety of analogies will be presented. The theory and implementation here are similar in many respects to those of Gentner and colleagues (Falkenhainer, Forbus, & Gentner, 1986; Gentner, 1983), but also differ in significant ways. Gentner has emphasized the importance of structural constraints in determining the correspondences between two analogs, but it is maintained here that semantic and pragmatic constraints must also be taken into account.

In order to formulate a theory of mapping, it is necessary to consider the relationship between mapping and other aspects of analogical thinking. The centrality of mapping is a point of general agreement among all theorists who have discussed the use of analogy, whether in problem solving (Carbonell, 1983, 1986; Gick, & Holyoak, 1980), in explanation (Gentner, 1983), in case-based reasoning (Hammond, 1986; Kolodner, Simpson, & Sycara, 1985) in theory formation (Darden, 1983; Thagard, 1988a), in the analysis of formal systems (Hesse, 1966; Polya, 1973), or in metaphor and other literary uses (Black, 1962; Gentner, 1982; Holyoak, 1982; Miller, 1979). There has been less agreement, however, on the relationship between mapping and other subprocesses of analogy, and on the related issue of whether a common set of principles governs mapping across different uses of analogies.

The view here is that analogy, and inference in general, must be understood pragmatically, taking into account the goals and purposes of the cognitive system (Holland, Holyoak, Nisbett, & Thagard, 1986; Holyoak, 1985). As many theorists have noted, it is useful to decompose analogy into four major components: (1) the retrieval or selection of a plausibly useful source analog, (2) mapping, (3) analogical inference or transfer, and (4) subsequent learning. In this article, the important issue of learning in the aftermath of analogy use will be set aside in order to focus on mapping and the components that immediately surround it: selection and transfer. These three subprocesses must collectively serve three crucial functions: picking out a plausibly useful source analog, identifying elements of the source that should determine transfer to the target, and effecting such transfer.

Is there, in fact, a general purpose mapping component that operates in fundamentally the same way for different varieties of analogy, and if so what role does it play in this overall task? This question can be addressed, indirectly, by examining the functions performed by the subprocesses of selection and transfer, and then considering what remains. Clearly, the selection component is crucial to the success of analogy. Spontaneous retrieval of a relevant source analog depends upon the presence of similar elements in the source and target (Gentner & Landers, 1985), including (in the case of problem analogs) similar constraints and goals (Brown, Kane, & Echols, 1986; Holyoak & Koh, 1987). In the absence of clear similarities, useful analogies are often missed (Gick & Holyoak, 1980); if misleading surface similarities are present, false analogies may be accessed and lead to negative transfer (Novick, 1988).

Once a possible source analog is retrieved spontaneously or provided by a teacher, further selection must be made of the aspects of the source relevant to the analogy. Analogies are virtually always used to serve some known purpose, and the purpose will guide selection. If, for example, one is simply asked to compare what is known about Nicaragua with what is known about Cuba, all elements of the two representations are relevant. But if one is asked to assess likely political trends in Nicaragua by analogy to Cuba, then only a subset of what is known about Cuba—roughly, facts which bear upon the development of its political system—need be mapped. For example, it is relevant to consider the degree to which Nicaragua's Daniel Ortega resembles Cuba's Fidel Castro. In contrast, suppose one is asked to predict the suitability of Nicaragua for sugar cane production, again by analogy to Cuba. The subset of knowledge about the source that is likely to be mapped will be very different—the similarity of Nicaragua to Cuba in terms of temperature and rainfall will loom much larger when the question concerns agriculture rather than politics. In examples such as these, the selection process can use pragmatic knowledge about the purpose of the analogy to identify not only a relevant source analog, but also *which aspects* of the source are important in the context. Much of the work of identifying aspects of the source that will determine transfer to the target can be done prior to mapping, based upon knowledge of the purpose of the analogy coupled with causal knowledge concerning the source.

Similarly, knowledge can be brought to bear on the transfer process *after* mapping has established correspondences between elements of the source and target. The mapping implicitly defines a set of inferences that could be made about the target, based upon correspondences with predicates and objects in the source domain. Thus if predicate P and object O in the source map onto P′ and O′ in the target, and the proposition P(O) holds in the source, then the proposition P′(O′) can be constructed as a candidate inference about the target. Whether a candidate inference will in fact be seriously considered as a plausible hypothesis about the target will depend upon such pragmatic factors as whether the inference is relevant to the analogist's goals in using the analogy and whether the inference is consistent with what is already known about the target domain.

Given what functions can reasonably be ascribed to the selection and transfer components of analogy, it appears that the central task of the mapping component is to take as inputs representations of a target analog and a plausibly relevant source, augmented if possible with information about the apparent pragmatic importance of elements of each analog, and to compute a set of correspondences between elements of the source and target that is likely to yield useful candidate inferences. Given that the analogist will often have imperfect knowledge of either or both analogs, a robust mapping process should be capable of operating even in the face of some uncertainty about what aspects of the two analogs are in fact most central for effective transfer.

A Constraint-Satisfaction Theory

The fundamental problem of analogical mapping is how to find appropriate correspondences between two analogs. If the analogs each have m predicates and n constants, and it is assumed that predicates map only to predicates and constants to constants, and that the mapping is one-to-one, then there are $m!n!$ possible mappings from which to select. Thus a typical analogy between analogs with 10 predicates and 5 constants each generates over 400 million possible mappings. Efficient selection of the best mapping requires that some constraints be placed upon what it might be. This problem is similar to that of stereoscopic vision (Marr & Poggio, 1976). Stereopsis requires that points in two visual images, one from each eye, be appropriately paired; however, there is no a priori basis for uniquely deciding which point should go with which. Similarly, given representations of two complex analogs, there is no a priori basis for establishing a determinate set of correspondences between elements in the two analogs. In order to account for stereopsis, Marr and Poggio proposed several qualitative constraints on the visual system. These constraints lead to the emergence of a unique set of point-to-point pairings, with each pairing consisting of points in each image arising from the same spatial position in the environment.

Numerous models of analogical mapping have been proposed by researchers in cognitive psychology and artificial intelligence, and a thorough review will not be attempted here (see Hall, 1989; Thagard, 1988b). Three classes of constraints tend to recur in theoretical treatments of analogy: structural,[1] semantic, and pragmatic. After discussing these constraints, a set of principles governing analogical mapping will be proposed.

Structural Consistency

Many theorists, particularly Gentner (1983), have stressed the importance of consistent structural correspondences as a criterion for an intuitively satisfying analogical mapping (Burstein, 1986; Falkenhainer et al., 1986; Gick & Holyoak, 1980; Hofstadter, 1984; Winston, 1980). Loosely speaking, a source analog can serve as a model for the target if objects in those two analogs can be placed into correspondence so that relations also correspond. A formal definition of structural consistency can be developed in terms of the concept of a *morphism*. Essentially the same characterization of structural consistency has been adopted in many different contexts, including formal model theory (Tarski, 1954), mathematical category theory (Maclane, 1971), and the theory of simulation (Ziegler, 1976). Within psychology, the concept of a morphism underlies the theory of measurement (Coombs, Dawes, & Tversky, 1970; Suppes & Zinnes, 1963), as well as theoretical treatments of mental representation (Halford, 1987; Halford & Wilson, 1980; Palmer, 1978), mental models (Holland et al., 1986), and analogy (Holyoak, 1984, 1985; Indurkhya, 1987; Palmer, 1989). In the case of analogy, let T be an ordered n-tuple representing a target analog consisting of a set of objects, O, and some number, n, of relations on O,

$$T = \langle O, R_1, R_2, \ldots R_n \rangle.$$

The representation of the source can similarly be defined as

$$S = \langle O', R_1', R_2', \ldots R_n' \rangle.$$

Let m be a mapping function that takes objects and relations in the target into objects and relations in the source,

$$m\colon o_i \to o_i'; R_i \to R_i'.$$

The mapping function m defines a valid isomorphism if, and only if, the mapping is one-to-one and for any objects and relations in T and S

$$o_i \, R_k \, o_j \text{ implies } m(o_i) \, m(R_k) \, m(o_j). \tag{1}$$

A valid analogy, A, is thus an ordered triple consisting of the relational systems T and S and a mapping function m with the above properties,

$$A = \langle T, S, m \rangle.$$

Figure 27.1 depicts the essence of a structurally valid analogy. Relations in the two analogs and the mapping function m are represented by directed lines.

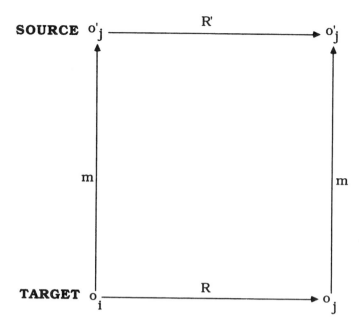

SOURCE o'_j ——————R'——————→ o'_j

m m

TARGET o_i ——————R——————→ o_j

Figure 27.1
Representing a structurally valid analogy as an isomorphism.

The consistency requirement expressed in (1) corresponds to the property of *commutativity of the diagram:* Following the arc representing the relation R_k between o_i and o_j in the target and then applying m produces the same result as first applying m to o_i to arrive at o'_i and then following the arc representing R'_i between o'_i and o'_j in the source.

Although (1) is stated for relations with two arguments, the basic principle can readily be generalized to *n*-place predicates (including $n = 1$, as an example below will illustrate). In more general terms, a proposition P in the target is in correspondence to a proposition P' in the source if, and only if, the predicate and arguments of P are mapped into the predicate and arguments of P' by a function m that leads to a structurally consistent analogy A. Note that the consistency requirement in (1) implies that it is not generally possible to decide whether any pair P and P' are in correspondence without considering the entire set of correspondences between propositions in T and S. This interdependence inherent in the constraint of structural consistency poses one of the major problems that must be solved by a computational model of mapping.

The strict formal definition of an isomorphism is clearly inappropriate as a characterization of the kinds of analogies of psychological interest, which virtually never have the structure of a valid isomorphism. Rather, some elements of the target may have no apparent corresponding element in the source (or vice versa); some correspondences may be many-to-one (a homomorphism) or one-to-many (violating the formal definition of a function); and the consistency requirement in (1) may occasionally be violated. None of these types of violations of the formal requirements for an isomorphism necessarily preclude the analogy being potentially useful to a human reasoner. Nonetheless, useful naturalistic analogies intuitively can be viewed as *approximations* to isomorphisms. In order to characterize mental representations that violate the strict definition of an isomorphism, Holland et al. (1986) extended the concept to homomorphisms with exceptions, or *quasi-homomorphisms*. Similarly, the theory to be proposed here treats the structural constraint of isomorphism as an ideal that can be satisfied to some imperfect degree, rather than as an absolute requirement for a successful mapping.

Semantic Similarity
The formal definition of an isomorphism makes no reference to the similarity of the objects and relations involved in the two analogs. Consider, for example, analogies between linear orderings (Halford, 1987). "John is taller than Bill, and Bill is taller than Sam" is analogous to "Mary is heavier than Susan, and Susan is heavier than Beth," with mappings between John and Mary, Bill and Susan, Sam and Beth, and the relations "taller than" and "heavier than." In this case both the objects and the relations being mapped are relatively similar. However, an equally valid analogy holds between the former analog and "communism is more radical than socialism, and socialism is more radical than capitalism," with mappings between John and communism, Bill and socialism, Sam and capitalism, and "taller than" and "more radical than." Even though similarity of relations and objects is sharply reduced in the latter analogy, the degree of structural consistency is the same in both cases.

Various theorists have suggested, and empirical evidence confirms, that object and predicate similarity influence the mapping process, with high semantic similarity leading to greater ease of mapping (Gentner & Toupin, 1986; Holyoak & Koh, 1987; Ross, 1987; Winston, 1980). The question therefore arises whether semantic similarity should be viewed as a distinct constraint on mapping, or whether it can somehow be assimilated to more basic constructs. Object similarity can potentially be reduced to predicate similarity: two objects are similar to the extent they serve as arguments of similar predicates. Predicate similarity may in turn be analyzed in terms of feature overlap (Tversky, 1977). One possibility, therefore, is to assimilate semantic similarity to structural consistency by imposing an added restriction on the latter constraint: corresponding relations must either be identical (Falkenhainer et al., 1986)[2] or share common features, such as a common superordinate (Burstein, 1986; Winston, 1980). A requirement of strict identity between corresponding relations does not seem satisfactory as a psychological model, since people can readily find mappings involving nonidentical relations (Burstein, 1986). (A number of relevant examples will be presented below.) Restrictions stated in terms of feature overlap (thus allowing mappings between similar rather than just identical relations) are much more plausible. However, the prerequisite requirement to provide a satisfactory analysis of natural language concepts in terms of semantic features remains a formidable challenge.

In addition to the sheer difficulty of reducing semantic similarity to structural consistency, there is empirical evidence that the two types of constraints have distinct consequences. Semantic similarity has a more pronounced effect on the retrieval of a source analog than on the mapping process (Gentner & Landers, 1985; Holyoak & Koh, 1987). In addition, although judgments of the aptness or soundness of analogies and metaphors are positively correlated with structural consistency, they are negatively correlated with similarity (Tourangeau & Sternberg, 1982). People's judgments thus reflect the intuition that although analogies based upon similar objects and relations are easy to map, they are less interesting or esthetically pleasing than "deeper" analogies between disparate situations. These separable effects of structural consistency and semantic similarity motivate treating the two kinds of constraints as distinct.

Pragmatic Centrality

Another major type of constraint on mapping that many theorists have proposed involves the pragmatic importance of the elements of the two analogs. Some treatments have emphasized the centrality of causal knowledge in determining the most appropriate mapping (Hesse, 1966; Winston, 1980); others have focused on the roles of high-level plans, goals, and functional knowledge (Anderson & Thompson, 1989; Burstein, 1986; Carbonell, 1983, 1986; Kedar-Cabelli, 1985). Although these models have important differences, they all share the view that the analogist uses explicit or implicit knowledge about the purpose the analogy is intended to serve to help direct the mapping process.

Although few would dispute that pragmatic knowledge influences the use of analogy, there remains disagreement as to the locus of its influence. Pragmatic considerations clearly weigh heavily in the initial selection of a plausibly useful source analog and in the subsequent transfer process. But do pragmatic considerations affect the mapping process itself? Gentner (1989, p. 215) proposes an architecture for analogy in which "plans and goals influence our thinking *before* and *after* the analogy engine" (i.e., the mapping mechanism) "but not during its operation." Gentner argues, very plausibly, that the goal of the analogist will typically have an impact on the representation of the target analog in working memory, which will in turn influence the retrieval of a source analog. Furthermore, the goal structure of a stored source problem may influence the mapping process indirectly by affecting the degree of structural consistency between the source and the target.

There are reasons to suspect, however, that pragmatic considerations—the analogist's judgments about which elements of the analog are most crucial to achieve a useful mapping—may also have a more direct influence on the mapping process. As noted earlier, the general form of analogical transfer is to find correspondences among elements of the source and of the target, and then construct candidate inferences about the target by essentially copying over propositions from the source after substituting the appropriate corresponding elements from the target domain. This form of transfer is very flexible, and allows analogies to be used in an exploratory fashion to derive unanticipated candidate inferences about the target (Gentner, 1989). The cost of this flexibility, however, is that the inference process is not goal directed; there is no guarantee that candidate inferences constructed in this fashion will be relevant to the analogist's purpose in using the analogy. In many uses of analogy, such as problem solving and explanation, the analogist has an implicit or explicit question in mind when trying to derive a mapping, and therefore intends to use the source analog to derive inferences that will provide specific information about the target. For example, Holyoak and Thagard (1989) suggest that in analogical problem solving, people may aim to generate a mapping sufficient to transfer useful subgoals.

When the analogist is trying to make a particular type of inference or to answer a specific question, a more goal-directed form of transfer is possible. In particular, if the target representation contains variables representing missing knowledge that the analogy is intended to provide, then the analogist may selectively favor possible correspondences that would allow these variables to be appropriately instantiated. For example, if a person is trying to answer the question, "What was the likely cause of the stock market crash of 1987?" by mapping the circumstances of that year to those involved in the crash of 1929, then it would be useful to favor correspondences that allow instantiation of the unknown cause of the crucial event in the target over correspondences that could not do so. Mappings guided by such questions will in effect generate goal-relevant candidate inferences directly, rather than depending upon the unconstrained generation and assessment of all possible inferences in the aftermath of mapping.

In addition to considerations of computational efficiency in guiding transfer, there is some suggestive empirical evidence indicating that pragmatic knowledge may influence the mapping process directly, rather than solely by affecting the representations over which the mapping is derived. Brown et al. (1986) found that young children who were directed to attend to the goal structure of problems were better able to transfer solutions to analogous problems than were children who were not so directed. These investigators found, however, that the latter children were nonetheless able to recall the critical goal elements when directly asked to do so. Their poor transfer performance thus seemed not to be due to simple failure to remember the goal elements (i.e., failure to include the goal elements in their representations of the source problems). Rather, the difficulty seemed related to selective attention, involving failure to view the goal elements as especially important during the mapping process. The theory to be proposed here assumes that the judged pragmatic importance of elements of analogs can directly constrain the mapping process, in addition to influencing earlier and later stages in the use of analogy.

Statement of Theory

The theory here assumes, as do many others, that analogical mapping can be viewed as a process of finding correspondences between elements of two structures. In propositional representations, the elements will include propositions, predicates, and objects. In other kinds of representations, such as pictorial ones, different types of elements may have to be mapped.

The major assertion of the theory is that mapping is governed by constraints of the three basic types discussed earlier: structural, semantic, and pragmatic. None of these constraints is absolute; rather, they provide "pressures" (in the sense of Hofstadter, 1984) that guide the emergence of a global mapping as a consequence of numerous local decisions about element correspondences.

Constraint 1   The structural constraint of *isomorphism* favors mappings that satisfy the consistency criterion in formula (1) and are one-to-one. Structural consistency requires that if a proposition in the target corresponds to a proposition in the source, then the constituent predicates and arguments of the paired propositions should also correspond. One-to-one mapping requires that each target element should correspond to only one element of the source, and that no two target elements should correspond to the same source element.

Constraint 2   **Semantic similarity** supports possible correspondences between elements to the degree that they have similar meanings.

Constraint 3   **Pragmatic centrality** favors correspondences that are pragmatically important to the analogist, either because a particular correspondence between two elements is presumed to hold, or because an element is judged to be sufficiently central that *some* mapping for it should be found.

The similarities and differences between the present theory and the structure-mapping theory developed by Gentner and colleagues (Falkenhainer et al., 1986; Gentner, 1983, 1989) can be characterized in terms of the above principles. The basic assumption that mapping involves finding structural correspondences is common to both approaches, as well as to virtually all other theoretical treatments. The isomorphism constraint here embodies the principles of structural consistency and one-to-one mapping employed by Falkenhainer et al.; however, in the present theory these principles are interpreted as pressures rather than as requirements. Isomorphism is also related to Gentner's *systematicity principle*, which states that mappings between higher-order relations (i.e., predicates such as "cause" and "implies" that take propositions as arguments) constrain mappings between first-order relations (i.e., predicates such as "kill" that take objects as arguments), which in turn constrain object mappings. Gentner's systematicity principle characterizes one important type of information that can be used to identify isomorphic structures.

The constraint of semantic similarity provides a stronger distinction between Gentner's theory and the one described here, which postulates semantic pressures interacting with the isomorphism constraint. By treating semantic similarity as a pressure distinct from isomorphism, the restriction that multiplace relations must be identical in order to be mapped is eliminated. As a consequence, this theory is able to provide a mechanism for mapping purely formal analogies that lack any identical or even similar relations. At the same time, the mapping process is guided by similarity information if it is available. Nonetheless, this difference between the two approaches should not be overstated. If identity of predicates is understood as a limiting case of semantic similarity, then the semantic similarity constraint here can be viewed as a weakening of Gentner's principle of finding correspondences between identical relations. The mapping model described by Burstein (1986) also allows mapped relations to be similar rather than identical. In the present theory, degree of similarity leads to preferences, rather than strict requirements, in identifying optimal correspondences.

The constraint of pragmatic centrality presented here departs most clearly from Gentner's theory, which maintains that people use only structural information in mapping. Gentner's approach emphasizes that attention to pragmatic considerations is restricted to stages of analogical reasoning occurring before and after the mapping process.

Further comparisons of the theory presented here with that of Gentner can be made at the level of the computational *implementations* of these theories. Below, the implementation of the theory in the program ACME will be contrasted with the implementation of Gentner's theoretical approach in the SME program (Falkenhainer, Forbus, & Gentner, 1989).

The mapping component is of course only one piece of an overall processing system for analogical reasoning. In addition to a natural-language interface, prior processes of analogical retrieval and selection are assumed that (a) propose a plausible source-target pair, and also may optionally provide (b) information about the degree of semantic similarity between pairs of source-target predicates, and (c) information about the pragmatic importance of elements of each analog. The present theory makes no assumptions about the nature of the processes that compute similarity and importance information. The similarity computation may be based upon decomposition of meanings into identities and differences (Hesse, 1966; Tversky, 1977); the importance computation may be based upon some form of causal or explanation-oriented analysis (Kedar-Cabelli, 1985), prior expectations, or instruction from a teacher. For the present purposes it will simply be assumed that the mapping component can receive a numerical index of the degree of semantic similarity between two predicates and of the pragmatic centrality of elements of the analogs. In general, this theory of mapping can be stated independently of any strong theory of similarity, memory retrieval, causal analysis, or of other subprocesses of analogical inference. The theory thus defines a mapping mechanism that can be potentially integrated within broader theories describing additional stages of analogical reasoning.

ACME: A Cooperative Algorithm for Mapping

The algorithm for evaluating mappings is suggested by Marr and Poggio's (1976) treatment of stereoscopic matching, which was based upon a *cooperative* algorithm, "... so-called because of the way in which local operations appear to cooperate in forming global order in a well-regulated manner" (Marr, 1982, p. 122). A cooperative algorithm is a procedure for parallel satisfaction of a set of interacting constraints. In the Marr and Poggio algorithm, a network of nodes is established, in which each node represents a possible pair of matched points, and excitatory and inhibitory connections between nodes represent constraints. The network is then allowed to run in order to find a globally optimal set of match hypotheses.

More generally, Marr (1982) argued that cooperative methods capture two principles that appear to govern fluent information processing: (1) the principle of *graceful degradation*, according to which degrading the input data should allow computation of a partial answer, and (2) the principle of *least commitment*, which requires avoiding doing something that may later have to be undone. Theorists working within the connectionist framework have argued that cooperative methods may be applicable to human memory retrieval and higher level reasoning (Rumelhart, Smolensky, McClelland, & Hinton, 1986). Several properties of an information-processing task can provide cues that a cooperative algorithm may be appropriate. A cooperative algorithm for parallel constraint satisfaction is preferable to any serial decision procedure when: (a) a global decision is composed of a number of constituent decisions, (b) each constituent decision should be based upon multiple constraints, (c) the outcome of the global decision could vary depending upon the order in which constraints are applied and constituent decisions are made, and (d) there is no principled justification for preferring any particular ordering of constraints or of constituent decisions. (For a philosophical discussion of the importance of parallel computation, see Thagard, 1986.)

Analogical mapping using constraints exhibits all of these features. Hofstadter (1984) pioneered the use of a cooperative process model for analogical mapping. In the Copycat model, a global mapping emerges from the parallel evaluation of evidence for interacting local hypotheses about element correspondences. Similarly, a cooperative algorithm for mapping analogies has been formulated and implemented here into a COMMON LISP program called ACME

(Analogical Constraint Mapping Engine). ACME constructs a network of units representing mapping hypotheses and relaxes into a state representing the best mapping.

Inputs to ACME
In order to apply the isomorphism constraint, a mapping model must have input representations rich enough to distinguish (a) among predicates such as *dog*, constants representing objects such as *Fido*, and identifiers representing propositions such as *dog (Fido)*, and (b) between predicates with different numbers of arguments. For example, *cow* can be represented as a one-place predicate taking one argument, as in *cow (Bossy)*, whereas *loves* is a two-place predicate taking two arguments, as in *loves (John, Mary)*. The algorithm described below, like the SME mapping program of Falkenhainer et al. (1986), takes as input structures consisting of sets of sentences in predicate calculus. No particular devotion to predicate calculus as a representation language (Thagard, 1984) is maintained here; it is used because of its simplicity and familiarity. Other more complex representation languages should be amenable to similar treatment.

Several more specific representational assumptions also deserve mention. Propositions may have hierarchical structure, with some predicates taking propositions as arguments. For example, *cause* is treated as a two-place predicate with propositions representing events or states as its arguments (Gentner, 1983). Functions of n arguments are treated as relations of $n + 1$ arguments holding among n objects and a value. Thus *height (John, 6 feet)* represents the fact that the height of John has the value six feet.

In order to represent queries that serve to focus attention on the pragmatically central aspects of a target analog, ACME allows some arguments to be variables marked with a question mark, as in "value?" Two kinds of queries are distinguished between here:

1. *Cross-structure* queries indicate that the answer to the query should come from seeing the relevant correspondences in the other analog. For example, if I tell you that Ortega is like Castro, and ask you what Ortega's political views are, then you could answer by transferring Castro's political views over to Ortega.

2. *Internal* queries indicate that the answer to a query is to be found within the structure that contains the query, with some element already present in the structure answering the query. In comparing the stock market crash of 1987 to the crash of 1929, you may expect to map a structure describing the 1929 crash to a structure describing the 1987 crash. In asking what caused the latter, you would expect to find some element of the 1987 structure that could provide the cause. This case differs from a cross-structure query in that you do not expect some element of the 1929

situation to answer your question for you directly. Rather, you hope that one result of mapping the 1987 and 1929 situations will be to fill in the relevant element in the 1987 structure using another component of that structure. ACME uses two question marks to indicate internal queries. For example, *cause (?proposition?, crash-of-'87)* represents the question, "What aspect of the situation was the cause of the crash of 1987?" As described below, internal queries are treated as variables that allow support to be passed to specific elements that might fill the role of the variable.

Each possible hypothesis about a possible pairing of an element from the source with a corresponding element of the target is assigned to a node or *unit*. Each unit has an *activation level*, ranging between some minimum and maximum values, which indicates the plausibility of the corresponding hypothesis, with higher activation indicating greater plausibility. Inferential dependencies between mapping hypotheses are represented by *weights* on *links* between units. Supporting evidence is given a positive weight, and disconfirmatory evidence is given a negative weight.

Setting Up a Mapping Network

The operation of the ACME program will now be described in greater detail. Figure 27.2 provides a schematic illustration of the kind of input that is provided to the program and of the kind of mapping network that the program builds. The input to the program consists of predicate-calculus representations of the source and target analogs, plus optional information about semantic similarity and pragmatic importance. It is assumed that a mapping may be computed either from a target analog to a source or vice versa. It is conjectured that the direction of mapping will vary depending upon the use of the analogy and the knowledge of the analogist. If the source is much more familiar than the target, then it may be best to try to map source elements to target elements. On the other hand, if the source is much more complicated than the target or if the target contains highly salient elements, then the analogist may attempt to map from the target to the source. In the example in Figure 27.2, the target is mapped to the source.

When given two structures as input, ACME automatically generates a network in accord with the constraints postulated by the theory. Each of the analogs in the simple abstract example depicted in Figure 27.2 includes four propositions, 2 one-place predicates, 2 two-place predicates, and 2 objects. The first step in building a mapping network is to construct *mapping units* corresponding to each possible hypothesis about pairings between elements. Two restrictions are used to limit the number of units formed. First, the *type* restriction limits possible correspondences to those between elements of the same basic type: propositions to propositions, *n*-place predicates to *n*-place predicates, and objects to objects.[3] Second, the *part-correspondence* restriction allows pairings only between

INPUT

TARGET	SOURCE	Semantic Weights For:	Pragmatic Information:
T1 A(a)	S1 M(m)	A=M C=O	IMPORTANT D
T2 B(b)	S2 N(n)		
T3 C(a,b)	S3 O(m,n)		
T4 D(b,a)	S4 P(n,m)		

PARTIAL RESULTING NETWORK

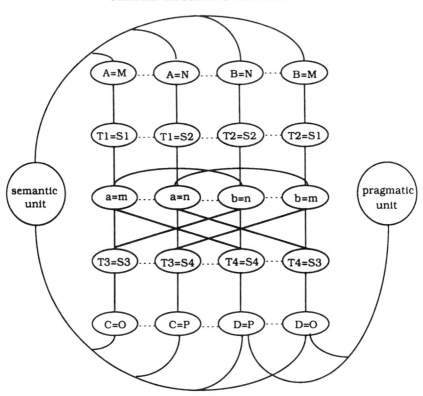

Figure 27.2
A schematic example of an ACME mapping network. Numbered capital letters represent proposition identifiers, unnumbered capital letters represent predicates, and lowercase letters represent objects. Solid lines represent excitatory connections, and dotted lines represent inhibitory connection. (See text for further explanation.)

propositions within corresponding major parts of the two analogs. The latter restriction only applies if the analogs are in fact divided into major parts. In the examples dealt with in this article, the part-correspondence restriction is only implemented for problem analogies. Problems can be divided into the basic parts of initial state, goal state, solution constraints, operators, and solution steps (Carbonell, 1983; Newell & Simon, 1972). ACME assumes that propositions describing initial states map to propositions describing initial states, propositions describing goals to propositions describing goals, and so on. Similarly, it would be possible to restrict mappings involving story structures to propositions within such corresponding major parts as the setting and resolution.

Neither of these restrictions on unit formation in the current implementation of ACME should be considered definitive. The type restriction can be viewed as a means of setting a low threshold of minimal similarity that is required in order to consider setting up a mapping unit linking two elements. The part-correspondence restriction can be viewed as a type of serial application of the isomorphism constraint on mapping, in which prior correspondences between high-level parts are used to constrain more detailed correspondences. Possible modifications of these restrictions will be discussed in the General Discussion.

The mapping units in Figure 27.2 thus represent all possible pairings of elements of the same basic type. For each two-place predicate in the target, for example, units are established for each possible pairing with a two-place source predicate (e.g., $C = O$ and $C = P$). The part-correspondence restriction is not illustrated in this simple example. Units corresponding to pairings between one-place predicates (e.g., $A = M$), pairings between objects (e.g., $a = m$), and pairings between propositions (e.g., $T1 = S1$) are also constructed.

As the units are established, links are formed between them to implement the constraint of structural consistency. All links are symmetrical, with the same weight regardless of direction. For example, excitatory links (represented by solid lines) are formed between $T1 = S1$ and $A = M$, $T1 = S1$ and $a = m$, and $A = M$ and $a = m$. All excitatory links have a default excitation weight given by parameter e. For predicates that take more than one argument, the argument mappings support each other, as in the link between $a = m$ and $b = n$ (which is suggested by both $T3 = S3$ and $T4 = S4$). Weights on links are additive, so that the weight between $a = m$ and $b = m$ will be double the value of e. Links are also created between predicate-mapping units and their corresponding argument-mapping units. Each potential correspondence between propositions thus generates an interconnected subnetwork of mutually consistent correspondences among elements of the propositions.[4] Figure 27.2 only shows a subset of the links that would be formed for this example. Figure 27.3 depicts the full set of excitatory links that would be created in the course of mapping two propositions with two-place predicates, T3 and S3.

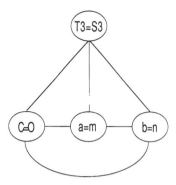

Figure 27.3
The subnetwork of excitatory and inhibitory connections among mapping units formed in the course of mapping propositions T3 and S3 (see Figure 27.2).

After all the units have been formed, inhibitory links (represented in Figure 27.2 by dashed lines) with weights equal to parameter *i* are formed to connect all units that represent alternative mappings for the same element. Thus the units $C = O$ and $C = P$ will be mutually inhibitory, as will $C = P$ and $D = P$. For clarity, Figure 27.2 depicts only a subset of all the links actually constructed, omitting, for example, the inhibitory links between $T2 = S1$ and $T1 = S1$.

In addition to the units representing mapping hypotheses, the network includes two special units. The *semantic unit* is used to convey information about the system's prior assessment of the degree of semantic similarity between each pair of meaningful concepts in the target and source, and the *pragmatic unit* similarly is used to convey information about the pragmatic importance of possible correspondences. The semantic-similarity constraint is enforced by placing excitatory links from the semantic unit to all units representing mappings between predicates. The weights on these links are made proportional to the degree of semantic similarity between the mapped concepts. Similarly, the pragmatic-centrality constraint is represented by weights on links connecting the pragmatic unit to relevant mapping units.

The list of semantic weights provides numerical values that reflect the degree of semantic similarity between target-source predicate pairs.[5] Semantic similarity values, which range from a minimum value *smin* (representing no similarity) to a maximum value *smax* (automatically given to identical predicates), are given to ACME by statements of the form:

(SIMILAR⟨concept-1⟩⟨concept-2⟩⟨degree⟩).

If no similarity degree is given, then ACME assumes the minimum value. Thus in Figure 27.2, semantic weights are only explicitly provided for the units $A = M$ and $C = O$, which represent units linking concepts with some degree of similarity that lie between the minimum value and identity.

Important elements are indicated by inputs of the form

(IMPORTANT⟨element⟩)

which sets up links with weights equal to parameter *p1* from the pragmatic unit to all units concerning the mapping of the element. Figure 27.2 shows D as an IMPORTANT element, so that there are excitatory links from the pragmatic unit to both of the units concerning how D could be mapped.

ACME also allows pragmatic support to be provided to a particular correspondence that the analogist may presume to hold. The input

(PRESUMED⟨hypothesis⟩)

sets up a mapping from the pragmatic unit directly to the unit representing that hypothesis, with a weight equal to parameter *p2*. Thus IMPORTANT provides support to the class of possible mappings for an important element, whereas PRESUMED provides support to a particular mapping hypothesis.

In addition to its use of pragmatic weights, ACME also represents pragmatic information related to questions for which an answer is sought by special query variables. Table 27.1 provides a summary of ACME's algorithm for forming a mapping network.

Running the Network
The manner in which the network is run to arrive at a solution is a straightforward application of constraint-satisfaction methods that have been investigated extensively in other applications (see Rumelhart et al., 1986). To initialize the network, the activation levels of the semantic and pragmatic units are fixed at 1, and the activations of all other units are set to some minimal value. On each cycle of activity, all units (except the semantic and pragmatic units) have their activation levels updated on the basis of the activation levels and weights associated with neighboring units and links. The updating procedure is based upon that suggested by Grossberg (1978). The activation level of unit j on cycle $t + 1$ is given by

$$a_j(t + 1) = a_j(t)(1 - d) + enet_j(max - a_j(t)) + inet_j(a_j(t) - min)$$

where d is a decay parameter, $enet_j$ is the net excitatory input, and $inet_j$ is the net inhibitory input (a negative number), with $min = -1$ and $max = 1$. The value of $enet_j$ is equal to $\Sigma_i w_{ij} o_i(t)$ for $w_{ij} > 0$, and the value of $inet_j$ is equal to the same quantity when $w_{ij} < 0$. The quantity $o_i(t)$ is the output on cycle t of a unit with activation a_i, with $o_i(t) = max(a_i(t), 0)$. On each cycle, updating is synchronous across all units (see Table 27.1). Activation values are constrained to range from *min* to *max*.[6]

The degree to which the activation levels of units satisfy the constraints imposed by the weights on links is approximated by a measure termed G, defined as

Table 27.1
Summary of the ACME algorithms for forming a mapping network and performing constraint satisfaction

---

Consider a mapping between structures T and S. Let $prop_{Ti}$ be the ith proposition of structure T, and let $pred_{Ti}$ be the predicate in the ith proposition of T, and let arg_{Tik} be the object or proposition corresponding to the kth argument of the ith proposition in T, with analogous definitions of $props_{Sj}$, $preds_{Sj}$, and $args_{Sjk}$.

I. Setting Up A Mapping Network

A. For each proposition $prop_{Ti}$ in T, consisting of ($pred_{Ti}$ (arg_{Ti1} arg_{Ti2} ... arg_{Tin})), for each proposition $props_{Sj}$ in S, consisting of ($preds_{Sj}$ ($args_{Sj1}$ $args_{Sj2}$ ... $args_{Sjm}$)), if $prop_{Ti}$ and $props_{Sj}$ are in the same part (e.g., goal) of their respective structure, and have the same number of arguments (i.e., n = m),

then: (1) construct the units $prop_{Ti}$ = $props_{Sj}$, $pred_{Ti}$ = $preds_{Sj}$, and each arg_{Tik} = $args_{Sjk}$;
(2) construct links between $prop_{Ti}$ = $props_{Sj}$ and $pred_{Ti}$ = $preds_{Sj}$;
(3) construct links between $prop_{Ti}$ = $props_{Sj}$ and each arg_{Tik} = $args_{Sjk}$;
(4) construct links between $pred_{Ti}$ = $preds_{Sj}$ and each arg_{Tik} = $args_{Sjk}$;
(5) construct links between each pair of arg_{Tik} = $args_{Sjk}$.
Note 1: These are excitatory links with equal weights set by a default excitation parameter e.
Note 2: A unit will not be formed if it would be redundant with a unit formed previously, but the weight on a link is incremented by e for each proposition that supports it.

B. Construct inhibitory links between any two units that represent incompatible mappings, with a negative weight set by a default inhibition parameter i.
Note 3: If a mapping unit connects an internal-query variable to some other element (i.e., ?query? = ⟨element⟩), then construct excitatory (rather than inhibitory) links to other units representing possible mapping to ⟨element⟩.

C. For each predicate-mapping unit $pred_{Ti}$ = $preds_{Sj}$, construct a link from the semantic unit based on the degree of semantic similarity between the two predicates, with a weight ranging from a minimum value *smin* if there is no similarity to a maximum value *smax* if the predicates are identical.

D. For each element (predicate, object, or proposition) listed as IMPORTANT, construct a link from the pragmatic unit to each unit concerning a mapping for that element, with a weight equal to a parameter *p1* for pragmatic centrality for IMPORTANT mappings.

E. For each unit listed as PRESUMED, construct a link from the pragmatic unit with a weight equal to a parameter *p2* for pragmatic centrality for PRESUMED mappings.

To summarize, A (1–5) and B implement the structural constraint of isomorphism, C implements the semantic similarity constraint, and D and E (along with Note 3) implement the pragmatic centrality constraint.

II. Running the Network

The algorithm for synchronously updating the units in the network is:
Clamp the activations of the semantic and pragmatic units at the maximum value. Set activations of all other units to an initial value (e.g., .01).
At each cycle,
1. For each unit u, calculate the new activation of u in accord with the equations in text, considering each unit u′ linked to u.
2. Set the activation of u to the new activation.

$$G(t) = \Sigma_i \Sigma_j w_{ij} o_i(t) o_j(t).$$

The value of G can be interpreted as a rough index of the overall fit of the emerging mapping to the constraints of isomorphism, similarity, and pragmatic centrality.[7]

Comparison with Other Simulation Models of Analogy
As noted earlier, many previous simulation models of analogical mapping have been proposed (see Hall, 1989; Thagard, 1988b). Other models have included structural, semantic, and pragmatic constraints on mapping, but no single model has integrated these constraints as ACME does. The most closely related previous simulation is the SME program (Falkenhainer et al., 1986). SME is designed as a "tool kit" for implementing different possible mapping rules; the comparison here is with SME operating with rules based upon Gentner's (1983, 1989) structure-mapping theory. ACME and SME have several important similarities; indeed, in many respects ACME can be characterized as an extension of SME, even though it operates differently. Both models provide content-independent accounts of the mapping process, and both derive a global "best" mapping from a set of constituent hypotheses about element correspondences (the mapping units of ACME and the "match hypotheses" of SME). Both programs operate on predicate-calculus representations of analogs, and both emphasize the role of proposition mappings in enforcing mappings between corresponding elements of the propositions.

In terms of the basic constraints, ACME's isomorphism constraint is a generalized version of the constraints of structural consistency and one-to-one mapping that are employed by SME. Two differences in ACME's treatment of structural constraints are notable. First, ACME treats isomorphism as a separate constraint from semantic similarity. Whereas SME requires multiplace relations to be identical in order to be mapped, ACME allows mappings between relations with no similarity beyond having the same number of arguments. ACME's more abstract version of the isomorphism constraint allows the program to compute mappings beyond the scope of SME. ACME can exploit its sensitivity to abstract isomorphism to *find* important similarities between predicates, rather than depending upon the similarities being precoded in the initial representations of the analogs. This creative aspect of analogy is not well captured by models of mapping that are more highly dependent upon pre-existing similarities or identities.

As we noted earlier, Gentner's systematicity principle, which is implemented in SME, describes one major type of information that can be used to identify isomorphisms: mappings of higher-order relations constrain mappings of first-order relations, which in turn constrain mappings of objects. ACME is also sensitive to systematicity, although such information is viewed symmetrically (e.g., not only do relation mappings constrain object mappings, but object mappings constrain relation mappings). The systematicity principle can be viewed as a special case of the general use of interrelated propositions to identify isomorphisms. In both ACME and SME, interrelated first-order relations also convey information about isomorphism, especially with multiplace relations. (The greater the number of arguments in a pair of mapped propositions, the greater the information provided about argument mappings.) Indeed, ACME (but not SME) can potentially find a unique mapping using no information except patterns of semantically unrelated monadic predicates (attributes), if these are in fact sufficient to create unique assignments of objects to sets of attributes. (An example of a mapping based solely upon attributes will be presented in the section on applications of ACME to formal isomorphisms.) Thus ACME's sensitivity to structure is by no means dependent upon higher-order relations.

A further difference between ACME and SME involves the "tightness" of structural constraints on mapping. SME begins the mapping process by identifying consistently mappable subsets of the analogs. Any violation of the strong restriction that mapped relations must be identical marks the limit of a consistently mappable subset. The program typically yields several such subsets, ranked in order of "goodness." In contrast, ACME treats the constraints of isomorphism, semantic similarity, and pragmatic centrality as pressures that operate in parallel to find a single mapping that best satisfies all of the converging and competing constraints to some (typically imperfect) degree. The program on any one run finds a single set of "best" mapping units (although relatively high activation levels on other units will convey information about possible alternative mappings). Whereas SME explicitly constructs global mappings and evaluates them, the global mappings selected by ACME are only implicitly determined by means of the links between mapping hypotheses.

More generally, ACME includes semantic and pragmatic constraints on the mapping component, as well as purely structural constraints. ACME prefers mappings between elements that are semantically similar, whereas SME excludes such information as relevant only to stages of analogy outside mapping. To implement the constraint of pragmatic centrality, ACME allows preferences for PRESUMED mappings and for mappings involving IMPORTANT elements. More subtly, it prefers mappings that have the potential to answer queries internal to a structure. Somewhat similarly, SME includes a preference for mappings that generate the greatest number of inferences; although not characterized as such by Falkenhainer et al. (1986), this preference might be construed as a pragmatic factor. However, the program does not consider whether the possible inferences are relevant to the goals of the analogist, as ACME does. In line with the emphasis on the pragmatic aspects of analogy, it is contended here that analogists will tend to prefer mappings that produce the inferences they are interested in, not inferences in general.

In its use of a connectionist architecture, ACME has important similarities to the Copycat program developed by Hofstadter (1984; Hofstadter & Mitchell, 1988), which also derives the globally best analogy from the outcomes of parallel competitions among interacting hypotheses about element correspondences. However, the constraints embodied in Copycat, like those used in SME, explicitly exclude pragmatic considerations.

ACME, SME, and Copycat are all much more complex than the mapping schemes implicitly included in simulation models that do not operate on cross-domain analogies (or, in the case of Copycat, on novel relational intradomain correspondences). If one is modeling only analogies within a highly structured domain, mapping can be virtually trivial (especially for small examples), since essentially the same predicates and arguments will exist in both domains. For example, in Anderson and Thompson's (1989) model of using analogies in programming LISP, each piece of LISP code is represented with an explicit form and function. Mapping consists merely of applying similar forms to code with similar functions. Work on case-based reasoning also tends to be restricted to intradomain analogies (e.g., Hammond, 1986; Kolodner & Simpson, 1988). If analogy is restricted to a single domain in which the same predicates and arguments turn up in both structures to be mapped, mapping becomes a very simple special case of the more complex processes used by ACME and SME for cross-domain analogies.

It should be noted that there are important ties between the theory's treatment of the basic constraints on mapping and ACME's use of an algorithm based upon parallel constraint satisfaction. In an abstract isomorphism, it is impossible to assess whether the mapping between any two propositions in the target and source is valid without considering the mappings of all other propositions, because the validity of any possible correspondence depends upon its relationship to the entire analogical structure. When the additional semantic and pragmatic constraints are included, the degree of interdependence between mapping hypotheses increases even further. Parallel constraint satisfaction is able to deal with this sort of extreme interdependence by allowing all local mapping decisions to emerge together in an incremental fashion.

Applications of ACME

Analogical reasoning can serve many different functions. Major contexts for analogy use include problem solving, when the solution to one problem suggests a solution to a similar one; argumentation, when similarities between two situations are used to contend that what is true in one situation is likely to be true in the other; and explanation, when a familiar topic is used to provide understanding of a less familiar one. In addition, analogical reasoning is also used to understand formal analogies of the sort found in mathematics, as well

Table 27.2
Summary of applications of ACME

Analogs	Number of units	Number of symmetric links
Lightbulb/radiation problems (4 versions) (Holyoak & Koh, 1987)	169–192	1373–1773
Fortress/radiation problems (Gick & Holyoak, 1980)	41	144
Cannibals and missionaries/farmer's dilemma problems (Gholson et al., 1988)	144	973
Contras inference	95	169
Politics inference (2 versions)	55–67	308–381
Water-flow/heat-flow explanation (2 versions) (Falkenhainer et al., 1986)	62–127	317–1010
Solar system/atom explanation (Falkenhainer et al., 1986)	93	733
Jealous animal stories (6 versions) (Gentner & Toupin, 1986)	125–214	1048–1783
Addition/union	162	1468
Attribute mapping	43	220
Midwife/Socrates (3 versions) (Kittay, 1987)	97–203	534–1702
Chemical analogies (8 different analogies) (Thagard et al., 1989)		

as metaphors, which can be employed to serve both explanatory and more aesthetic functions. Given the fundamental assumption that all uses of analogy involve the same basic mapping mechanism, it follows that a theory of analogical mapping should apply to a full range of examples.

Table 27.2 lists the principal analogies to which ACME has been applied, along with the number of units and links that were formed for each. All of these examples are discussed below, except for the chemical analogies presented in Thagard, Cohen, and Holyoak (1989). Because translation of analogies in natural language into predicate-calculus inputs is somewhat arbitrary, these applications do not constitute strict tests of the theory implemented in ACME. Nevertheless, they show that ACME is applicable to a wide variety of analogies and is consistent with experimental results that reveal when analogical mapping is difficult for people.

In order to demonstrate that ACME can account for performance on a wide variety of analogies using a consistent set of parameters, all parameters were held constant across the entire set of applications. Unless otherwise stated, all runs employed the Grossberg updating rule with $min = -1$, $max = 1$, and $d = .1$. Weight parameters were $e = .1$, $i = -.2$, $smin = 0$, $smax = .1$, $p1 = .1$, and $p2 = .3$. Mapping units were initialized at activation $= .01$. Intermediate similarity weights will be noted in those examples when they were used. The pragmatic centrality parameters were only used in a subset of the examples. The sensitivity of the program to variations in the parameter set will be described later.

Problem Analogies

Convergence Analogies   ACME has been applied to a number of problem analogies involving the use of a "convergence" solution, in which several weak forces are applied simultaneously to a centrally located object in order to achieve the effect of a single large force (Gick & Holyoak, 1980, 1983; Holyoak & Koh, 1987). In experimental work using these materials, the target analog has typically been a "radiation problem," in which a doctor must find a way to use a ray to destroy a stomach tumor without harming the surrounding tissue (Duncker, 1945), Holyoak and Koh (1987) compared the effectiveness of four alternative versions of a source analog based upon a "lightbulb problem," in which a broken filament in a lightbulb must be repaired. The four versions were defined by two types of variations. Surface similarity to the ray used in the target was varied by manipulating whether the force used in the lightbulb problem was a laser (highly similar to a ray) or an ultrasound beam (less similar). Similarity of problem constraints was also varied. The similar constraint in the source was the necessity to avoid breaking the fragile glass bulb surrounding the filament (analogous to avoiding injury to the tissue surrounding the tumor). The dissimilar constraint was that a force of sufficiently high intensity was not available. Table 27.3 presents predicate-calculus representations of the "laser/fragile-glass" version of the lightbulb problem and of the radiation problem. These, together with similar representations of the other lightbulb versions, were used as inputs to ACME. Each proposition in an analog is represented by a list consisting of a predicate, a list of arguments, and a name for the proposition. In the surface-similar versions, ACME was given a similarity weight of .08 for the mapping unit *ray-source = laser*. Pragmatic-centrality weights were not used in any of these examples of problem analogies, since all elements of the representations were selected to be important. In each run the possible mapping hypotheses were limited by the part-correspondence restriction (i.e., goal elements must map to goal elements, and so on).

Because of their complexity, a figure showing the full network created using the above input, with its 192 units and 1773 links, cannot be presented. However, Figure 27.4, reproduced directly from a screen dump of a graphics program running with ACME, shows the nodes connected to a typical unit, *ray-source = laser*. Thick lines indicate excitatory links and thin lines indicate inhibitory links; the weight of the link is specified by a number midway in the line. Beneath each node is a truncated number indicating the activation of the

Table 27.3

Predicate-calculus representations of lightbulb problem (laser, fragile-glass and insufficient-intensity versions) and radiation problems

---

Lightbulb problem (source)

    Start: (laser (obj_laser) f1)
               (bulb (obj_bulb) f2)
               (filament (obj_filament) f3)
               (surround (obj_bulb obj_filament) f4)
               (outside (obj_laser obj_bulb) f5)

  For good-constraint version, add:
               (can-produce (obj_laser obj_beams_high) fg6)
               (high-intensity (obj_beams_high_obj_filament) fg8)
               (can-destroy (obj_beams_high obj_bulb) fg9)
               (can-produce (obj_laser obj_beams_low) fg10)
               (low-intensity (obj_beams_low) fg11)
               (cannot-fuse (obj_beams_low obj_filament) fg12)
               (cannot-destroy (obj_beams_low obj_bulb) fg13)

  For poor-constraint version, add instead:
               (cannot-produce (obj_laser obj_beams_high) fp6)
               (high-intensity (obj_beams_high) fp7)
               (can-fuse (obj_beams_high obj_filament) fp8)
               (can-produce (obj_laser obj_beams_low) fp10)
               (low-intensity (obj_beams_low) fp11)
               (cannot-fuse (obj_beams_low obj_filament) fp12)
    Goals: (fuse (obj_laser obj_filament) f21)

  For good-constraint version, add:
               (not-destroyed (obj_bulb) fg22)

  For poor-constraint version, add instead:
               (can-produce (obj_laser obj_beams_high) fp22)

Radiation problem (target)

    Start: (ray-source (obj_ray) d1)
               (tissue (obj_tissue) d2)
               (tumor (obj_tumor) d3)
               (surround (obj_tissue obj_tumor) d4)
               (outside (obj_ray obj_tissue) d5)
               (can-produce (obj_ray obj_rays_high) d6)
               (high-intensity (obj_rays_high) d7)
               (can-destroy (obj_rays_high obj_tumor) d8)
               (can-destroy (obj_rays_high obj_tissue) d9)
               (can-produce (obj_ray obj_rays_low) d10)
               (low-intensity (obj_rays_low) d11)
               (cannot-destroy (obj_rays_low obj_tumor) d12)
               (cannot-destroy (obj_rays_low obj_tissue) d13)
    Goals: (destroy (obj_ray obj_tumor) d21)
               (not-destroyed (obj_tissue) d22)

Similarity: (similar ray-source laser .08)

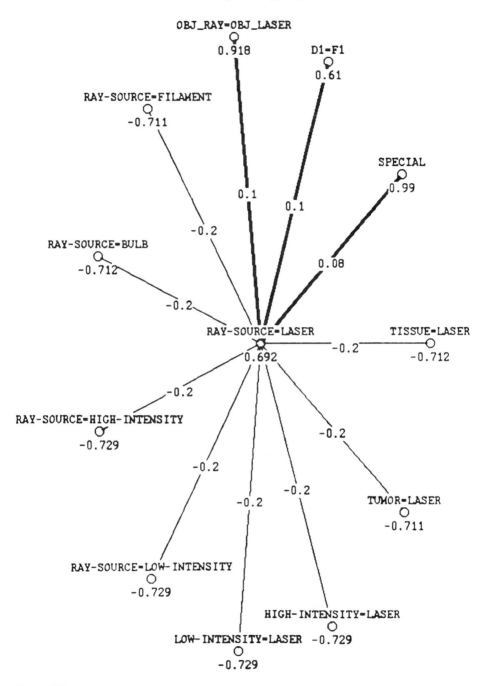

Figure 27.4
Output of a graphics program running with ACME, showing the subnetwork of excitatory and inhibitory connections to the unit *ray-source = laser*.

Table 27.4

Activation values of best mappings of radiation problem to lightbulb problem (laser/fragile-glass version)*

Network has settled by cycle 31.

Test: TEST0   Total times: 32

Thu May 5 15:17:40 EDT 1988

Laser analogy: basic, good constraint.

Units not yet reached asymptote: 0

Goodness of network: 4.84

Calculating the best mappings after 32 cycles.

Best mapping of RAY-SOURCE is LASER. 0.69

Best mapping of TISSUE is BULB. 0.59

Best mapping of TUMOR is FILAMENT. 0.59

Best mapping of SURROUND is SURROUND. 0.77

Best mapping of OUTSIDE is OUTSIDE. 0.77

Best mapping of CAN-PRODUCE is CAN-PRODUCE. 0.88

Best mapping of HIGH-INTENSITY is HIGH-INTENSITY. 0.71

Best mapping of CAN-DESTROY is CAN-DESTROY. 0.58

   Mapping with CAN-FUSE is also possible: 0.39

Best mapping of LOW-INTENSITY is LOW-INTENSITY. 0.71

Best mapping of CANNOT-DESTROY is CANNOT-DESTROY. 0.58

   Mapping with CANNOT-FUSE is also possible: 0.39

Best mapping of DESTROY is FUSE. 0.71

Best mapping of NOT-DESTROYED is NOT-DESTROYED. 0.71

Best mapping of OBJ_RAYS_LOW is OBJ_BEAMS_LOW. 0.88

Best mapping of OBJ_RAYS_HIGH is OBJ_BEAMS_HIGH. 0.88

Best mapping of OBJ_TUMOR is OBJ_FILAMENT. 0.90

Best mapping of OBJ_TISSUE is OBJ_BULB. 0.91

Best mapping of OBJ_RAY_ is OBJ_LASER. 0.92

---

* Values are activations of units after settling. This table and all other tables of mapping results are taken directly from ACME outputs, except that all numbers have been rounded to 2 decimal places.

named unit. The network can be browsed to show the connectivity of another node simply by clicking on that node.

   Table 27.4 presents the output of ACME after mapping the radiation problem with the laser/fragile-glass version of the lightbulb problem. This and all other tables of outputs to be presented gives the optimal mappings obtained after the network has settled at an asymptote, defined as the first cycle at which no unit has its activation adjusted by more than .001. For this example, the network settles after 31 cycles. The asymptotic value of G is also printed, along with the best mapping for each object, each predicate, and each proposition used as the argument of a higher-order relation. (No propositions appear as arguments in this example.) The program defines the "best" mapping of an element as the corresponding mapping unit with highest activation level, regardless of absolute magnitude; however, it is natural to interpret cases in which the most active unit is very weak (e.g., activation less than .20) as target elements that have no good map in the source. (There are no such unmapped elements in this example.)

ACME also displays any additional possible mappings for each element, defined as units other than the best, which have activations greater than a threshold set at .20. In most cases each element has a single clear best mapping, but the occasional secondary mappings are also of interest. For example, the predicate *can-destroy* in the radiation problem has *can-destroy* in the target problem as its best map (activation = .58), but has a secondary mapping to *can-fuse* (activation = .39). The reason for this dual mapping is apparent at the level of propositions (see Table 27.3). The high-strength ray can destroy the tissue just as the high-strength laser can destroy the bulb (i.e., $d9 = fg9$), but at the same time the high-strength ray can destroy the tumor just as the high-strength laser can fuse the filament ($d8 = fg8$). ACME finds the intuitively correct best mapping for both source propositions ($d9 = fg9$ has activation = .69, and $d8 = fg8$ has activation .68). However, at the level of predicate mappings, *can-destroy = can-destroy* is preferred to *can-destroy = can-fuse* because of the greater semantic similarity of the concepts in the former mapping.

This analogy demonstrates that ACME can successfully map relations without requiring that they be coded as identical or even similar (e.g., *destroy = fuse*, activation = .71). One could argue, of course, that these relations overlap at the level of their underlying semantic structures, as both are causatives. However, this is a very abstract similarity; intuitively, the differences between the two predicates (e.g., one involves destruction and the other construction) are at least as salient as their similarities. The operation of ACME suggests how the overall structure of an analog can force dissimilar predicates into correspondence. The mapping thus leads to (rather than results from) discovery of underlying similarities. Once two predicates have been mapped, their similarities are highlighted while their differences are forced into the background.

The output provided in Table 27.4 does not reflect the history of activation of units as the network settles. Such information can be displayed, however, by using a graphics program that runs simultaneously with ACME and graphs the activation values of selected units. Figure 5 depicts activation histories of all the units concerning the mappings of ray-source, tissue, and tumor. In each graph, the x-axis is for time over 60 cycles of updating, and the y-axis shows activations ranging between 1 and -1, with the horizontal line indicating activation of 0. For example, the unit *ray-source = laser* rises steadily and then asymptotes, while the other units concerning the mapping of ray-source asymptote at negative activation values. This graph illustrates the characteristic stability of the asymptotic activation levels of individual units.

Table 27.5
Ease of mapping four versions of lightbulb/radiation problem analogy

	Laser/ fragile-glass	Ultrasound/ fragile-glass	Laser/ insufficient- intensity	Ultrasound/ insufficient- intensity
Cycles to success	3	3	5	5
Percent convergence solutions prior to hint*	69	38	33	13
Percent convergence solutions with hint*	75	81	60	47

* Data from Holyoak and Koh (1987)

Table 27.5 presents results of running ACME on four versions of the convergence problem. The top row of the table presents the number of "cycles to success" for each version, defined as the number of cycles required for each correct mapping unit (for objects, predicates, and propositions used as arguments) to exceed the activation of its nearest competitor. It has generally been found that cycles to success provides a useful measure of relative difficulty of analogical mappings. Holyoak and Koh (1987) measured the percent of undergraduates who produced the convergence solution to the radiation problem after reading one of the four versions of the lightbulb problem, both before a hint to use the source was given, and in total, after a hint was provided. For comparison with ACME's mapping results, these data are provided at the bottom of Table 27.5. Since ACME is modeling mapping only, not retrieval, the more relevant comparison is with the number of solutions after a hint was given. ACME is able to find the correct set of mappings in all four cases. Cycles to success does not differ as a function of surface similarity. All versions of the analogy have such extensive structural correspondences that the extra weight from the semantic unit to the mapping unit corresponding to the more similar predicate pair, *ray-source = laser*, has no measurable impact upon mapping difficulty. As the data from the Holyoak and Koh (1987) study indicate, people are also able to derive the mapping equally well in the laser and ultrasound conditions once a hint is provided.

Cycles to success does increase slightly for the two poor-constraint versions. Most seriously, proposition d22 in the radiation problem, which expresses the major constraint of not destroying the healthy tissue, has no map at all in the poor-constraint versions of the lightbulb problems. This breakdown of the analogy is likely to be a major part of the reason transfer was impaired for human subjects in the poor-constraint conditions of the Holyoak and Koh (1987) experiment.

ACME has also been applied to another convergence analogy, in which the target is the radiation problem and the source is the "fortress problem" used by

Gick and Holyoak (1980). In the latter problem a general divides his army into small groups and has them converge simultaneously on a fortress to capture it. ACME is also able to find the appropriate mapping for this additional convergence analogy.

Homomorphs of Missionaries-and-Cannibals   ACME's performance on the convergence analogies indicates that it can find useful mappings in the absence of a strict isomorphism. Humans can sometimes show problem-solving transfer between homomorphs that require more extensive one-to-many or many-to-one mappings. Once such example has been provided by Gholson, Eymard, Long, Morgan, and Leeming (1988). In the "missionaries-and-cannibals" problem, it is necessary to get a number of missionaries and cannibals across a river in a boat without leaving any missionaries outnumbered, and hence eaten, by cannibals. The homomorphic "farmer's dilemma" problem requires a farmer to take a fox, a goose, and some corn across a mountain in his wagon without having the fox eat the goose or the goose eat the corn. These problems are not isomorphic since multiple missionaries and multiple cannibals map equally well to a single corn and a single fox, respectively. Gholson et al. (1988) found that third- and fourth-grade children who had learned a solution to the farmer's dilemma problem were facilitated in subsequently solving a simple version of the missionaries-and-cannibals problem (with three missionaries and two cannibals). However, no transfer was obtained in the reverse direction, from missionaries-and-cannibals to farmer's dilemma. A similar transfer asymmetry was obtained with adult subjects by Reed, Ernst, and Banerji (1974), using other missionaries-and-cannibals homomorphs.

Table 27.6 shows predicate-calculus representations of the two problems in the form in which they were given to ACME. These representations are simplified in that the constraints on which objects can be left together are not explicitly included; however, the representations contain the basic information required to indicate that each missionary and each cannibal have the same properties, so that the optimal mapping should be a homomorphism. Given that ACME forms inhibitory links in order to encourage one-to-one mappings, it is not obvious that the program could find many-to-one or one-to-many mappings. However, as the outputs presented in Table 27.7 demonstrate, ACME in fact sorts out the relations among the elements of the two problems very well, both when mapping from missionaries-and-cannibals to farmer's dilemma (many-to-one mappings, Table 27.7A) and from farmer's dilemma to missionaries-and-cannibals (one-to-many mappings, Table 27.7B). Thus in the former direction each missionary maps equally well to the corn, and each cannibal maps equally well to the fox. The goose is a weaker secondary map for both the missionaries and the cannibals; at the level of predicates, however, the only successful mapping units are *missionary = corn* and *cannibal = fox*. ACME is able to find many-to-one mappings at the level of objects because the positive

Table 27.6
Predicate-calculus representations of missionaries-and-cannibals and farmer's dilemma problems

Missionaries-and-Cannibals

Start: (missionary (obj_missionary1) m1)
         (missionary (obj_missionary2) m2)
         (missionary (obj_missionary3) m3)
         (cannibal (obj_cannibal1) m4)
         (cannibal (obj_cannibal2) m5)
         (boat (obj_boat) m6)
         (carries (obj_boat vbl_rower vbl_passenger) m7)
         (eat (obj_cannibal1 obj_missionary1) m8)
         (eat (obj_cannibal1 obj_missionary2) m9)
         (eat (obj_cannibal1 obj_missionary3) m10)
         (eat (obj_cannibal2 obj_missionary1) m11)
         (eat (obj_cannibal2 obj_missionary2) m12)
         (eat (obj_cannibal2 obj_missionary3) m13)

Goals: (cross_river (obj_missionary1) m14)
         (cross_river (obj_missionary2) m15)
         (cross_river (obj_missionary3) m16)
         (cross_river (obj_cannibal1) m17)
         (cross_river (obj_cannibal2) m18)
         (not_eaten (obj_missionary1) m19)
         (not_eaten (obj_missionary2) m20)
         (not_eaten (obj_missionary3) m21)

Farmer's Dilemma:

Start: (farmer (obj_farmer) f1)
         (fox (obj_fox) f2)
         (goose (obj_goose) f3)
         (corn (obj_corn) f4)
         (wagon (obj_wagon) f5)
         (carries (obj_wagon obj_farmer vbl_thing) f6)
         (eat (obj_fox obj_goose) f7)
         (eat (obj_goose obj_corn) f8)

Goals: (cross_mountain (obj_farmer) f9)
         (cross_mountain (obj_fox) f10)
         (cross_mountain (obj_goose) f11)
         (cross_mountain (obj_corn) f12)
         (not_eaten (obj_goose) f13)
         (not_eaten (obj_corn) f14)

Table 27.7
Results of mapping Missionaries-and-Cannibals to Farmer's Dilemma and Vice Versa

A. Missionaries-and-Cannibals to Farmer's Dilemma:

Network has settled by cycle 41.

Test: TEST22   Total times: 42

Mon May 2 17:09:08 EDT 1988

Mapping cannibals & missionaries (3) to farmer's dilemma.

Units not yet reached asymptote: 0

Goodness of network: 2.26

Calculating the best mappings after 42 cycles.

Best mapping of OBJ_MISSIONARY1 is OBJ_CORN. 0.37
   Mapping with OBJ_GOOSE is also possible: 0.26

Best mapping of OBJ_MISSIONARY2 is OBJ_CORN. 0.37
   Mapping with OBJ_GOOSE is also possible: 0.26

Best mapping of OBJ_MISSIONARY3 is OBJ_CORN. 0.37
   Mapping with OBJ_GOOSE is also possible: 0.26

Best mapping of OBJ_CANNIBAL1 is OBJ_FOX. 0.52
   Mapping with OBJ_GOOSE is also possible: 0.21

Best mapping of OBJ_CANNIBAL2 is OBJ_FOX. 0.52
   Mapping with OBJ_GOOSE is also possible: 0.21

Best mapping of OBJ_BOAT is OBJ_WAGON. 0.80

Best mapping of VBL_PASSENGER is VBL_THING. 0.75

Best mapping of VBL_ROWER is OBJ_FARMER. 0.75

Best mapping of NOT_EATEN is NOT_EATEN. 0.78

Best mapping of CROSS_RIVER is CROSS_MOUNTAIN. 0.82

Best mapping of EAT is EAT. 0.90

Best mapping of CARRIES is CARRIES. 0.79

Best mapping of BOAT is WAGON. 0.57

Best mapping of CANNIBAL is FOX. 0.60

Best mapping of MISSIONARY is CORN. 0.61

B. Farmer's Dilemma to Missionaries-and-Cannibals:

Network has settled by cycle 41.

Test: TEST23   Total times: 42

Mon May 2 17:11:11 EDT 1988

Mapping farmer's dilemma to cannibals & missionaries (3).

Units not yet reached asymptote: 0

Goodness of network: 2.26

Calculating the best mappings after 42 cycles.

Best mapping of FARMER is BOAT. −0.52

Best mapping of FOX is CANNIBAL. 0.60

Best mapping of GOOSE is MISSIONARY. −0.14

Best mapping of CORN is MISSIONARY. 0.60

Table 27.7 (continued)

Best mapping of WAGON is BOAT. 0.57

Best mapping of CARRIES is CARRIES. 0.79

Best mapping of EAT is EAT. 0.90

Best mapping of CROSS_MOUNTAIN is CROSS_RIVER. 0.82

Best mapping of NOT_EATEN is NOT_EATEN. 0.78

Best mapping of VBL_THING is VBL_PASSENGER. 0.75

Best mapping of OBJ_WAGON is OBJ_BOAT. 0.80

Best mapping of OBJ_CORN is OBJ_MISSIONARY3. 0.37

   Mapping with OBJ_MISSIONARY2 is also possible: 0.37

   Mapping with OBJ_MISSIONARY1 is also possible: 0.37

Best mapping of OBJ_GOOSE is OBJ_MISSIONARY3. 0.26

   Mapping with OBJ_CANNIBAL2 is also possible: 0.20

   Mapping with OBJ_CANNIBAL1 is also possible: 0.20

   Mapping with OBJ_MISSIONARY2 is also possible: 0.26

   Mapping with OBJ_MISSIONARY1 is also possible: 0.26

Best mapping of OBJ_FOX is OBJ_CANNIBAL2. 0.52

   Mapping with OBJ_CANNIBAL1 is also possible: 0.52

Best mapping of OBJ_FARMER is VBL_ROWER. 0.75

---

evidence favoring each of several object–object mappings (e.g., each cannibal to the fox) provides total excitation that exceeds the inhibition generated by inhibitory links between the competing units. In ACME, the structural constraint of one-to-one mapping, like that of structural consistency, is treated as a pressure rather than a requirement.

The mappings found by ACME may also help account for the asymmetry in transfer between the two problems observed by Gholson et al. (1988). Although subjects may map the problems in either direction, they of course only know the solution to one of them at the time of transfer. For simplicity, let us assume subjects were mapping from target to source, so that the mapping from missionaries-and-cannibals to farmer's dilemma (Table 27.7A) represents the basis for transfering knowledge about the farmer's dilemma to the various characters of missionaries-and-cannibals. It is clear from examining the solutions required for the two problems that there are no useful correspondences at the level of moves. However, subjects may have been able to use their experience with the source to help construct appropriate tests for legal moves. The basis for the analogy is that in each problem, to avoid illegal moves it is necessary to check, during the process of move selection, that objects are neither threats to, nor threatened by, other objects. If the source problem is the farmer's dilemma, then the mapping in Table 27.7A gives relatively clear guidance about the test required for each object in the missionaries-and-cannibals problem:

each cannibal should be viewed as a potential threat (like the fox), and each missionary should be viewed as potentially threatened (like the corn). This is the direction in which Gholson et al.'s subjects were able to transfer successfully.

In contrast, subjects who receive the missionaries-and-cannibals problem as the source will have less adequate guidance in dealing with the farmer's dilemma characters. As Table 27.7B indicates, the fox maps to each of the cannibals, and the corn maps to each of the missionaries; the predicate mappings *fox = cannibal* and *corn = missionary* emerge unambiguously. These mappings will correctly lead subjects to decide to view the fox as a threat and the corn as threatened. Note, however, that the mapping provides no clear guidance about how to treat the goose. The goose maps weakly to each of the missionaries and cannibals; the predicate *goose* has no good map at all. Intuitively, the goose in the farmer's dilemma problem is sometimes threatened and sometimes a threat; the missionaries-and-cannibals problem provides no clear information about how to deal with such ambiguity. Accordingly, transfer in this direction will be greatly impaired, as Gholson et al. observed.

Pragmatics in Analogical Arguments
In analogical arguments, one implies that what is true of one situation is also true of another situation. Such arguments have a long history in philosophy, being used, for example, to argue for the existence of other minds and the existence of God. (I know that I have a mind because of my experiences, and I infer that you also have a mind because you are similar to me in many other respects. Less metaphysically, I may infer that since my favorite candidate for the United States presidency is like former president John F. Kennedy, my candidate too will win the election.)

Analogical arguments may rely upon an unbiased assessment of similarities, but often people are motivated to reach particular conclusions. It is conjectured here that such motivations may bias people's judgments of similarity, just as Kunda (1987) has shown that generalization can be biased by personal motivation. Motivated analogical arguments would provide striking examples of the pragmatic nature of analogy, since judgments about what corresponds to what will be biased by the conclusion the analogy is intended to produce.

To illustrate the possible role of biases in analogical argumentation, ACME was used to simulate a very simple example of a motivated use of analogy, involving the issue of assessing the nature of the Contras' attempt to overthrow the government of Nicaragua in 1987. Table 27.8 shows the input representations provided to the program. The "Contras" structure contains only the minimal information that the Contras aim to overthrow the government of Nicaragua, leaving open the question of whether the U.S. should support them, and whether they should be viewed as terrorists or freedom fighters. The unknown but desired information about the Contras is signalled by variables representing cross-structure queries, such as *support?*. The "Others" analog

Table 27.8
Predicate-calculus representations for contras example

Contras

  (country (Nicaragua) c1)

  (govern (Sandinistas Nicaragua) c2)

  (aim-to-overthrow (Contras Sandinistas) c3)

  (terrorists? (Contras Contra-terror?) c4)

  (freedom-fighters? (Contras Contra-freedom?) c5)

  (should-support? (US Contras support?) c6)

Others

  (country (Hungary) h1)

  (govern (communists Hungary) h2)

  (aim-to-overthrow (Hungarians communists) h3)

  (freedom-fighters? (Hungarians freedom-fighters-yes) h5)

  (terrorists? (Hungarians terrorists-no) h4)

  (should-support? (US Hungarians support-yes) h6)

  (country (Israel) i1)

  (govern (Israelis Israel) i2)

  (aim-to-overthrow (PLO Israelis) i3)

  (terrorists? (PLO terrorists-yes) i4)

  (freedom-fighters? (PLO freedom-fighters-no) i5)

  (should-support? (US PLO support-no) i6)

Presumed: support? = support-yes

---

contains substructures corresponding to Hungarians wanting to overthrow their communist government, who are categorized as freedom fighters, and to the PLO wanting to overthrow the Israeli government, who are categorized as terrorists. The Contras structure has the same degree of structural and semantic similarity to each of the Hungarian and Israeli substructures, and maps to them equally well if no additional information is provided.

Suppose, however, that the analogist is motivated to support the Contras. This person will want *support?* to correspond to *support-yes*. To represent this type of bias in the mapping process, ACME's input in Table 27.8 includes the information that this is a PRESUMED mapping. Results of running ACME are shown in Table 27.9. The result of ACME's bias toward *support? = support-yes* is not only that the network indeed settles upon the mapping *support? = support-yes*, but that the Contras map to Hungarians rather than to PLO, so that *Contra-terror?* maps to *terrorists-no* and *Contra-freedom?* maps to *freedom-fighters-yes*. A very different result is produced if ACME is told that it is desirable to reach the conclusion that the Contras should not be supported: the Contras then map to the PLO and take on their characteristics. Thus a single entering bias can potentially alter the entire mapping that will be found.

Table 27.9
Output for contras example

Network has settled by cycle 103.
Test: TEST7   Total times: 104
Mon May 2 14:46:02 EDT 1988
Support the contras?
Units not yet reached asymptote: 0
Goodness of network: 2.53
Calculating the best mappings after 104 cycles.
Best mapping of NICARAGUA is HUNGARY. 0.75
Best mapping of SANDINISTAS is COMMUNISTS. 0.73
Best mapping of CONTRAS is HUNGARIANS. 0.75
Mapping with PLO is also possible: 0.42
Best mapping of CONTRA-TERROR? is TERRORISTS-NO. 0.68
Best mapping of CONTRA-FREEDOM? is FREEDOM-FIGHTERS-YES. 0.68
Best mapping of SUPPORT? is SUPPORT-YES. 0.77
Best mapping of US is US. 0.81
Best mapping of SHOULD-SUPPORT? is SHOULD-SUPPORT?. 0.84
Best mapping of FREEDOM-FIGHTERS? is FREEDOM-FIGHTERS? 0.77
Best mapping of TERRORISTS? is TERRORISTS?. 0.77
Best mapping of AIM-TO-OVERTHROW is AIM-TO-OVERTHROW. 0.78
Best mapping of GOVERN is GOVERN. 0.76
Best mapping of COUNTRY is COUNTRY. 0.69

Also modeled was a similar case of motivated analogy using three possible analogs. Suppose you are inferring some of the policies of your favorite political candidate. Then you will be motivated to infer that the candidate has properties that will make election possible. If you believe that a moderate will have the best chance of being elected, then you will be prone to view your candidate as most similar to another moderate; accordingly, you will infer that your candidate is more analogous to a known moderate politician than to a conservative or liberal. ACME models this behavior when it maps a target politician to an "Others" analog consisting of a liberal, a moderate, and a conservative. If the target is about equally similar to the three alternatives in structure and in semantic properties, then treating the mapping of "politics-value" to "moderate" as PRESUMED is sufficient to cause the target to map to the moderate candidate and take on that politician's characteristics.

Note, however, that such pragmatic biases can only *select* among mappings that are reasonably close in terms of the structural and semantic constraints. Pragmatic biases will not suffice, for example, to view an arch conservative as a moderate simply because moderates are believed to be electable. In a second version of the "politics" simulation, the target politician is represented as having the same properties as the known conservative, and then the program was run with a pragmatic weight indicating that the target was a moderate, as in the version described above. In early cycles, the target mapped most strongly to the moderate politician, but eventually the structural and semantic pressures dominated. At asymptote, ACME mapped the target politician to the conservative despite its pragmatic bias. Thus although pragmatic considerations can guide the mapping process, they cannot overwhelm other information.

Pragmatics in Explanatory Analogies

ACME has been applied to the explanatory analogies discussed by Gentner (1983, 1989) and Falkenhainer et al. (1986): the analogy between the flow of water caused by differential pressure and the flow of heat caused by differential temperature; and the analogy between the motion of planets around the sun and of electrons around an atomic nucleus. These examples allow a close comparison of the ACME and SME programs, since Falkenhainer et al. (1986) describe the representations used as input to SME in sufficient detail so that essentially the same information could be provided about each analog to ACME.

Table 27.10 presents predicate-calculus representations of the water-flow/heat-flow analogy that were used as inputs to ACME. Two versions were used. The basic version is based directly upon an example used as a test of SME by Falkenhainer et al. (1986). This version is of interest because it represents an analogy in which considerably more information is known about the source (water flow) than about the target (heat flow), as is often the case when a novel situation is explained in terms of a more familiar one. Despite surface representational differences, our predicate-calculus representations encode essentially the same information as that which Falkenhainer et al. provided to the SME program. The major exception is that ACME received an explicit representation of the pragmatic purpose of using the analogy. The internal query *?proposition?* in proposition h11 of the heat analog represents the unknown cause of heat flow.

Table 27.11A presents the activation levels of selected mapping hypotheses after the network settles in 80 cycles. Falkenhainer et al. constructed the example to include three impediments to a successful map from water flow to heat flow. ACME, like SME, is able to handle all three difficulties. First, the attribute *clear* in the water-flow analog has no acceptable map in the heat-flow analog, as is evident from the fact that no mapping unit for *clear* has an activation above 0. Second, the information that both water and coffee are liquids and have a flat top tends to encourage water to map to coffee rather than to heat. Despite this misleading similarity information, the structural information encoded in the network enables ACME, by cycle 3, to provide higher activation to the unit representing the hypothesis that water maps to heat. As the values in Table

Table 27.10
Predicate-calculus representation of water-flow and heat-flow analogs, and extended versions

---

Water-flow (source)

    (liquid (obj_water) w1)

    (flat-top (obj_water) w2)

    (clear (obj_beaker) w3)

    (diameter (obj_beaker obj_val1) w4)

    (diameter (obj_vial obj_val2) w5)

    (greater (obj_val1 obj_val2) w6)

    (pressure (obj_beaker obj_val3) w7)

    (pressure (obj_vial obj_val4) w8)

    (greater (obj_val3 obj_val4) w9)

    ; flow: from x to y of w via z

    (flow (obj_beaker obj_vial obj_water obj_pipe) w10)

    ; pressure difference causes flow:

    (cause (w9 w10) w11)

  Extended version adds:

    (volume (obj_beaker obj_val5) w11)

    (volume (obj_vial obj_val6) w12)

    (greater (obj_val5 obj_val6) w13)

    ; diameter difference causes volume difference

    (cause (w6 w13) w14)

Heat-flow (target)

    (liquid (obj_coffee) h1)

    (flat-top (obj_coffee) h2)

    (temperature (obj_coffee obj_val13) h7)

    (temperature (obj_ice_cube obj_val14) h8)

    (greater (obj_val13 obj_val14) h9)

    (flow (obj_coffee obj_ice_cube obj_heat obj_bar) h10)

    ; what causes heat flow?

    (cause (?proposition? h10) h11)

  Extended version adds:

    (volume (obj_coffee obj_val15) h11)

    (volume (obj_ice_cube obj_val16) h12)

    (greater (obj_val15 obj_val16) h13)

Table 27.11
Output for heat-flow example

A. Basic version:

Network has settled by cycle 80.

Test: TEST2   Total times: 81

Thu Dec 8 09:41:16 EST 1988

Analogy between water flow and heat flow

Units not yet reached asymptote: 0

Goodness of network: 2.84

Calculating the best mappings after 81 cycles.

Best mapping of LIQUID is LIQUID. 0.53

Best mapping of FLAT-TOP is FLAT-TOP. 0.53

Best mapping of CLEAR is LIQUID. −0.02 tied with FLAT-TOP.

Best mapping of DIAMETER is TEMPERATURE. 0.04

Best mapping of GREATER is GREATER. 0.76

Best mapping of PRESSURE is TEMPERATURE. 0.78

Best mapping of FLOW is FLOW. 0.82

Best mapping of CAUSE is CAUSE. 0.76

Best mapping of W9 is H9. 0.78

   Mapping with ?PROPOSITION? is also possible: 0.78

Best mapping of W10 is H10. 0.85

Best mapping of OBJ_PIPE is OBJ_BAR. 0.79

Best mapping of OBJ_VAL4 is OBJ_VAL14. 0.79

Best mapping of OBJ_VAL3 is OBJ_VAL13. 0.79

Best mapping of OBJ_VIAL is OBJ_ICE_CUBE. 0.85

Best mapping of OBJ_VAL2 is OBJ_VAL14. 0.02

Best mapping of OBJ_VAL1 is OBJ_VAL13. 0.02

Best mapping of OBJ_BEAKER is OBJ_COFFEE. 0.86

Best mapping of OBJ_WATER is OBJ_HEAT. 0.79

B. Extended version:

Network has settled by cycle 92.

Test: TEST6   Total times: 93

Thu Dec 8 10:02:42 EDT 1988

Extended map from water to heat.

Units not yet reached asymptote: 0

Goodness of network: 4.08

Calculating the best mappings after 93 cycles.

Best mapping of LIQUID is LIQUID. 0.52

Best mapping of FLAT-TOP is FLAT-TOP. 0.52

Best mapping of CLEAR is LIQUID. −0.004 tied with FLAT-TOP.

Best mapping of DIAMETER is TEMPERATURE. 0.10

Best mapping of GREATER is GREATER. 0.84

Best mapping of PRESSURE is TEMPERATURE. 0.74

Table 27.11 (continued)

Best mapping of FLOW is FLOW. 0.83

Best mapping of CAUSE is CAUSE. 0.76

Best mapping of VOLUME is VOLUME. 0.84

Best mapping of W6 is H9. −0.14

Best mapping of W14 is H14. 0.70

Best mapping of OBJ_VAL6 is OBJ_VAL16. 0.81

Best mapping of OBJ_VAL5 is OBJ_VAL15. 0.81

Best mapping of W9 is H9. 0.78

   Mapping with ?PROPOSITION? is also possible: 0.78

Best mapping of W10 is H10. 0.85

Best mapping of OBJ_PIPE is OBJ_BAR. 0.80

Best mapping of OBJ_VAL4 is OBJ_VAL14. 0.75

Best mapping of OBJ_VAL3 is OBJ_VAL13. 0.75

Best mapping of OBJ_VIAL is OBJ_ICE_CUBE. 0.89

Best mapping of OBJ_VAL2 is OBJ_VAL14. 0.09

Best mapping of OBJ_VAL1 is OBJ_VAL13. 0.09

Best mapping of OBJ_BEAKER is OBJ_COFFEE. 0.89

Best mapping of OBJ_WATER is OBJ_HEAT. 0.80

27.11 indicate, the mapping from water to heat emerges as a clear victor over the alternative possibility of mapping water to coffee.

The third and most serious impediment to a successful map is the irrelevant information concerning the diameters of the beaker and vial, encouraging the map of diameter to pressure in competition with the correct map of temperature to pressure. SME selects the correct map on the basis of Gentner's principle of systematicity, interpreted as a preference for mappings that yield the greatest number of possible inferences. In contrast, the preferability of the temperature-pressure map is viewed here as largely a pragmatic matter of the intended use of the analogy. If water flow is being used to explain heat flow, then aspects of water systems that affect its flow (pressure differences rather than diameter differences) should be favored in mapping.

In the representation of the heat-flow analogy in Table 27.10, the information-seeking purpose of the analogy is captured by the proposition (*cause* (*?proposition?* h10) h11) in the heat-flow representation, where "*?proposition?*" represents the unknown cause of heat flow. This internal-query variable signals that the purpose of the mapping is to identify an actual proposition in the heat situation that can fill the empty argument slot. Since *w9* concerning the greater temperature has this desired feature by virtue of its appearance in the proposition (*cause* (*w9 w10*) *w11*), whereas *w6* concerning the greater diameter does not, units for mapping the former are preferred to units for mapping the latter.

Because the mapping of *w9* to *h9* is therefore preferred to the mapping of *w6* to *h9*, the mapping of pressure to temperature is preferred to the mapping of diameter to temperature. (Note that because *?proposition?* is treated as a variable that supports rather than competes with specific values such as *h9* (see Table 27.1, Note 3), ACME reports both *?proposition?* and *h9* as the best maps for *w9*.)

Although SME and ACME both find the appropriate mappings in this example, some minor extensions serve to differentiate the performance of the two programs. For SME, it is crucial that the identical predicate "flow" be used in the water-flow and heat-flow situations, or else this correspondence would not be found. For ACME, this identity is not essential. The basic version of the analogy was also run with the predicates "water-flow" and "heat-flow," respectively, substituted for "flow" in the two analogs. The two distinct predicates were given a minimal similarity weight. Given that these predicates were the only four-place predicates in the analogs, and hence forced to map by the type restriction, this variation is not a serious challenge for ACME. The resulting asymptotic solution, which is reached after 78 cycles, is virtually identical to that shown in Table 27.11A; the mapping unit *water-flow = heat-flow* asymptotes at an activation of .80.

As noted above, SME prefers the mapping of pressure to temperature over the mapping of diameter to temperature for a different reason than ACME does. Whereas ACME bases its choice on the fact that only the former mapping is directly relevant to the purpose of the analogy, SME bases its choice upon the fact that only the former allows a causal inference to be constructed, because only temperature change is the cause of something in the water-flow situation. These two criteria can be separated by a small extension of the two analogs, as indicated in Table 27.10. In the extended version of the water-flow situation, it is assumed the analogist has noticed that the greater diameter of the beaker relative to the vial is the cause of the former having greater volume. It is further supposed that the analogist has observed in the heat-flow situation that the volume of the coffee exceeds that of the ice cube. If the internal query is not included in the latter representation, then the systematicity principle provides no basis for choosing between the two competing mappings involving temperature in this extended version. For if pressure maps to temperature, then it is possible to infer that temperature differences cause flow; whereas if diameter maps to temperature, it is possible to infer that temperature change is the cause of the observed differences between the volumes of the coffee and the ice cube. The latter inference is of course erroneous, but worse, it is irrelevant to the analogist's presumed goal of understanding heat flow. In contrast, as the output in Table 27.11B indicates, ACME's internal-query mechanism continues to produce a clear preference for mapping pressure to temperature in the extended version of the analogy.

ACME is also able to produce the appropriate mapping for the solar-system/ atom analogy that Falkenhainer et al. (1986) used to test SME. Since this anal-

Table 27.12
Precis of a "jealous animal" story as used in ACME simulation, in systematic and nonsystematic versions

---

The cat was jealous.
 (Nonsystematic version: The cat was strong.)

The cat was friends with a walrus.

The walrus played with a seagull.

The cat was angry.
 (Systematic version: Because the cat was jealous and the walrus played with the seagull, the cat was angry.)

The cat was reckless.
 (Systematic version: Because the cat was angry, it was reckless.)

The cat got in danger.
 (Systematic version: Because the cat was reckless, it got in danger.)

The seagull saved the cat.
 (Systematic version: Because the seagull saved the cat, the cat was friends with the seagull.)

---

ogy does not provide any additional complexities (the network settles with the correct solution after 40 cycles), the results will not be described further.

ACME has also been applied to analogies used by chemistry teachers to explain difficult concepts to students, but these results are reported elsewhere (Thagard et al., 1989).

Competing Constraints in Mapping Story Analogs

Additional evidence concerning ACME's ability to account for empirical evidence relating to the effect of systematicity on mapping is provided by a study performed by Gentner and Toupin (1986). This experiment investigated the effects both of systematicity and *transparency:* the degree to which similar objects serve similar functions in the analogy. Gentner and Toupin presented two groups of children, aged 4–6 years and 8–10 years, with a series of simple stories. After the child had acted out one version of a story with props, the experimenter asked him or her to act out the same story with different characters.

Table 27.12 presents a simplified version of one of these stories that served as the basis for a simulation by ACME, and Table 27.13 presents the actual predicate-calculus representation provided to the program. As indicated in Table 27.14, each source story was used across children in either a "systematic" or a "nonsystematic" form. The systematic version differed from the nonsystematic version in that it added additional information relevant to the causes of events in the story (e.g., the cat's jealousy caused its anger). Transparency was varied by manipulating the similarity of the animals in the various roles. In the example used in the simulation, the target analog involved a dog, seal, and penguin. In the S/S (similar objects/similar roles) condition, the source analog involved similar characters playing similar roles (cat, walrus, and seagull). In the D

Table 27.13
Predicate-calculus representation of a jealous animal story: Similar objects/similar roles (systematic and unsystematic versions)

(cat (obj_cat) b1)

(walrus (obj_walrus) b2)

(seagull (obj_seagull) b3)

(friends (obj_cat obj_walrus) b4)

(played (obj_walrus obj_seagull) b5)

(angry (obj_cat) b6)

(reckless (obj_cat) b7)

(endangered (obj_cat) b8)

(save (obj_seagull obj_cat) b9)

Systematic version adds:

(jealous (obj_cat) b10)

(befriend (obj_cat obj_seagull) b11)

(conjoin-event (b10 b5) b12)*

(cause (b12 b6) b13)

(cause (b6 b7) b14)

(cause (b7 b8) b15)

(cause (b9 b11) b16)

Unsystematic version adds instead:

(strong (obj_cat) b10)

* The interpretation of a conjoin-event is that two events are conjoined to make a third event. This device is needed so that cause can remain a two-place relation despite conjunctive causes.

Table 27.14
Mapping conditions for "jealous animal" stories

Test	Similar objects/ similar roles	Dissimilar objects	Similar objects/ dissimilar roles
dog	cat	camel	seagull
seal	walrus	lion	cat
penguin	seagull	giraffe	walrus

Table 27.15
Results of ACME runs for six versions of "jealous animal" stories

Version	Cycles to success
Systematic:	
S/S	3
D	4
S/D	38
Nonsystematic:	
S/S	3
D	4
S/D	no success

(dissimilar objects) condition, all the characters were quite different from those in the target (camel, lion, and giraffe). In the cross-mapped S/D (similar objects/dissimilar roles) condition, similar characters were used, but these played different roles than did the corresponding characters in the target (seagull, cat, and walrus).

Gentner and Toupin found that both systematicity and transparency affected the accuracy with which children enacted the target stories. The two effects interacted, in that performance was uniformly good, regardless of systematicity, in the S/S condition. As the transparency of the mapping decreased from the S/S to the D and the S/D conditions, performance declined, and the advantage of the systematic over the unsystematic version increased. The positive impact of systematicity was more pronounced for the older group of children.

In order to stimulate these results, predicate-calculus representations of the stories were used as inputs to ACME (see Table 27.13). If the similarity of the characters in the source and target was high, the similarity weight for the corresponding predicate-mapping unit was set at .06; if the similarity was low, the weight was set at .01. Units for pairings of identical predicates were given similarity weights of .1, the value of $smax$ in all the reported simulations. Table 27.15 presents the cycles to success (the first cycle at which the appropriate winning units emerged for all objects, predicates, and propositional arguments) in each of the six conditions. Values of cycles to success increased very slightly from the S/S to D conditions, and more dramatically to the cross-mapped S/D condition. Only in the latter condition did systematicity have an effect on cycles to success, as the network failed to settle on the correct mapping in the unsystematic S/D condition. In this most difficult condition, the network was unable to overcome the misleading impact of semantic similarity. Further exploration revealed that the correct solution can be obtained in the S/D condition if either the value of i is reduced from $-.2$ to $-.1$ or the value of min is raised from -1 to $-.3$; however, cycles to success remains higher in the unsystematic than the systematic S/D condition. Although ACME seems to show relatively fewer differences between the S/S and D conditions than did Gentner and Toupin's subjects, the program does capture the substantially greater difficulty of the cross-mapped S/D condition, and the role of systematicity in overcoming misleading semantic similarity.

As noted above, Gentner and Toupin found that the younger children benefited less from high systematicity than did the older children. The authors suggested that focus on systematicity increases with age. In terms of the present theory, it is possible that with age children learn to place greater weight on isomorphism, and less on the similarity constraint. It is also possible, however, that the younger children in the Gentner and Toupin (1986) study simply failed to grasp some of the causal structure provided in the systematic stories, and hence encoded the source stories imperfectly. Thus the lesser benefit they derived from the systematic versions need not imply insensitivity to the isomorphism constraint.

Finding Isomorphisms without Semantic or Pragmatic Information

A Formal Isomorphism   As pointed out in the comparison of ACME with SME, ACME is able to use structural information to map predicates that are not semantically identical or even similar. In fact, if two analogs are isomorphic, it should be possible to derive an appropriate mapping even in the complete absence of semantic or pragmatic information. Table 27.16 presents a formal analogy between addition of numbers and union of sets that was used to demonstrate this point. Both addition and union have the abstract mathematical properties of commutativity, associativity, and the existence of an identity element (0 for numbers, the empty set Φ for sets). ACME was given predicate-calculus representations of these two analogs, with no identical elements (note that number equality and set equality are given distinct symbols), and with all semantic weights set equal to the minimal value. This analogy is quite complex, as many propositions have the same predicate (*sum* or *union*), and many symbols representing intermediate results must be sorted out. Note that the representations given to the program did not explicitly group the components of each analog into three distinct equations. In the absence of any semantic or pragmatic information, only weights based upon isomorphism, coupled with the type restriction, provided information about the optimal mapping.

As the output in Table 27.17 indicates, ACME settles to a complete solution to this formal mapping problem after 59 cycles. The model is thus able to derive a unique mapping in the absence of any overlap between the elements of the source and target. ACME's ability to deal with such examples is crucially dependent upon its parallel constraint-satisfaction algorithm.

Isomorphism without Explicit Relational Predicates   The best mapping for the addition/union analogy, as for all the examples considered so far, involves a

Table 27.16
Formal isomorphism between addition of numbers and union of sets

Property	Addition	Union
Commutativity:	$N1 + N2 = N2 + N1$	$S1 \cup S2 \equiv S2 \cup S1$
Associativity:	$N3 + (N4 + N5) = (N3 + N4) + N5$	$S3 \cup [S4 \cup S5] \equiv [S3 \cup S4] \cup S5$
Identity:	$N6 + 0 = N6$	$S6 \cup \varnothing \equiv S6$

Predicate-calculus representations:

Numbers: (sum (num1 num2 num10) n1)
(sum (num2 num1 num11) n2)
(num_eq (num10 num11) n3)
(sum (num5 num6 num12) n3)
(sum (num4 num12 num13) n5)
(sum (num4 num5 num14) n6)
(sum (num14 num6 num15) n7)
(num_eq (num13 num15) n8)
(sum (num20 zero num20) n9)

Sets: (union (set1 set2 set10) s1)
(union (set2 set1 set11) s2)
(set_eq (set10 set11) s3)
(union (set5 set6 set12) s4)
(union (set4 set12 set13) s5)
(union (set4 set5 set14) s6)
(union (set14 set6 set15) s7)
(set_eq (set13 set15) s8)
(union (set20 empty-set set20) s9)

rich set of relational correspondences. It is important to understand, however, that the structural constraint of isomorphism is not strictly dependent upon explicit relational predicates in the analogs. In fact, ACME can identify isomorphisms between analogs that lack not only higher-order relations, but any relational predicates at all. To illustrate this point, Table 27.18A presents predicate-calculus versions of two completely arbitrary analogs, each involving three objects and three monadic predicates. Without any semantic or pragmatic information, ACME settles to a unique solution to this minimalist mapping problem after 71 cycles. The obtained mapping is given in Table 27.18B.

The basis for the mapping in this example is the fact that there is a unique set of element correspondences such that attributes asserted of each object in the source map consistently to attributes asserted of some object in the target. This information *could* be described in terms of relations; for example, an attribute of Bill ("smart") is *the same as* an attribute of Steve, just as an attribute of Rover

Table 27.17
Output after running addition/union analogy

Network has settled by cycle 59.

Test: TEST0   Total times: 60

Mon May 2 10:40:03 EDT 1988

Analogy between numbers and sets.

Units not yet reached asymptote: 0

Goodness of network: 3.31

Calculating the best mappings after 60 cycles.

Best mapping of NUM10 is SET10. 0.79

Best mapping of NUM2 is SET2. 0.82

Best mapping of NUM1 is SET1. 0.82

Best mapping of NUM11 is SET11. 0.79

Best mapping of NUM12 is SET12. 0.82

Best mapping of NUM6 is SET6. 0.82

Best mapping of NUM5 is SET5. 0.82

Best mapping of NUM13 is SET13. 0.79

Best mapping of NUM4 is SET4. 0.82

Best mapping of NUM14 is SET14. 0.82

Best mapping of NUM15 is SET15. 0.79

Best mapping of NUM20 is SET20. 0.66

Best mapping of ZERO is EMPTY-SET. 0.66

Best mapping of NUM_EQ is SET_EQ. 0.57

Best mapping of SUM is UNION. 0.83

("hungry") is *the same as* an attribute of Fido. The crucial point, however, is that such relational information is computed implicitly by the ACME algorithm, and need not be explicitly coded into the propositional input representations of the analogs.

One might well question whether ACME's ability to derive semantically empty isomorphisms based solely upon monadic predicates is overpowerful relative to human analogical reasoning. Accordingly, a small experiment was performed to find out whether people can find the mapping identified by ACME for this example. The five sentences corresponding to the five propositions in each analog (e.g., "Bill is smart") were listed in adjacent columns on a piece of paper. Sentences related to the same individual were listed consecutively; otherwise, the order was scrambled. Across subjects two different orders were used. The instructions simply stated, "Your task is to figure out what in the left set of sentences corresponds to what in the right set of sentences." Subjects were also told that the meaning of the words was irrelevant. The three individuals and three attributes of the analog on the left were listed on the bottom of the page; for each element, subjects were to write down what they

Table 27.18
Input and output for arbitrary attribute-mapping example

A. Input analogs:

Source   (smart (Bill) f1)
          (tall (Bill) f2)
          (smart (Steve) f3)
          (timid (Tom) f4)
          (tall (Tom) f5)

Target   (hungry (Rover) s1)
          (friendly (Rover) s2)
          (hungry (Fido) s3)
          (frisky (Blackie) s4)
          (friendly (Blackie) s5)

B. Output:

          Network has settled by cycle 71.
          Test: TEST3   Total times: 72
          Wed May 11 10:08:53 EDT 1988
          Abstract similarity.
          Units not yet reached asymptote: 0
          Goodness of network: 0.61
          Calculating the best mappings after 72 cycles.
          Best mapping of SMART is HUNGRY. 0.70
          Best mapping of TALL is FRIENDLY. 0.71
          Best mapping of TIMID is FRISKY. 0.54
          Best mapping of TOM is BLACKIE. 0.70
          Best mapping of STEVE is FIDO. 0.54
          Best mapping of BILL is ROVER. 0.71

believed to be the corresponding element of the analog on the right. Three minutes were allowed for completion of the task.

A group of 8 UCLA students in an undergraduate psychology class served as subjects. Five subjects produced the same set of six correspondences identified by ACME, 2 subjects produced four of the six, and 1 subject was unable to understand the task. These results indicate that finding the isomorphism for this example is within the capability of many college students.

Structure and Pragmatics in Metaphor
To explore the performance of ACME in metaphorical mapping, the program was given predicate-calculus representations of the knowledge underlying a metaphor that has been analyzed in detail by Kittay (1987). The metaphor is derived from a passage in Plato's *Theaetetus* in which Socrates declares himself

to be a "midwife of ideas," elaborating the metaphor at length. Table 27.19 contains predicate-calculus representations based upon Kittay's analysis of the source analog concerning the role of a midwife and of the target analog concerning the role of a philosopher-teacher. Roughly, Socrates claims that he is like a midwife in that he introduces the student to intellectual partners, just as a midwife often serves first as a matchmaker; Socrates helps the student evaluate the truth or falsity of his ideas much as a midwife helps a mother to deliver a child.

This metaphor was used to provide an illustration of the manner in which structural and pragmatic constraints interact in ACME. Table 27.19 presents predicate-calculus representations of two versions of the metaphor: an isomorphic version based directly upon Kittay's analysis, and a nonisomorphic version created by adding irrelevant and misleading information to the representation of the "Socrates" target analog. The best mappings obtained for each object and predicate in the target, produced by three runs of ACME, are reported in Table 27.20. The asymptotic activations of the best mappings are also presented. A mapping of "none" means that no mapping unit had an asymptotic activation greater than .20.

The run reported in the first column used the isomorphic version without any pragmatic weights. The network settles with a correct set of mappings after 34 cycles. Thus Socrates maps to the midwife, his student to the mother, the student's intellectual partner to the father, and the idea to the child. (Note that there is a homomorphic mapping of the predicates *thinks_about* and *tests_truth* to *in_labor_with*.) The propositions expressing causal relations in the two analogs are not essential here; deletion of them still allows a complete mapping to be discovered.

A very different set of mappings is reported in the middle column of Table 27.20 for the nonisomorphic version of the "Socrates" analog. This version provides additional knowledge about Socrates that would be expected to produce major interference with discovery of the metaphoric relation between the two analogs. The nonisomorphic version contains the information that Socrates drinks hemlock juice, which is of course irrelevant to the metaphor. Far worse, the representation encodes the information that Socrates himself was matched to his wife by a midwife; and that Socrates' wife had a child with the help of this midwife. Clearly, this nonisomorphic extension will cause the structural and semantic constraints on mapping to support a much more superficial set of correspondences between the two situations. And indeed, in this second run ACME finds only the barest fragments of the intended metaphoric mappings when the network settles after 105 cycles. Socrates' midwife now maps to the midwife in the source, and Socrates' wife and child map to the source mother and child. Socrates himself simply maps to the father. Most of the other crucial objects and predicates (other than *cause* and *helps*, which map to themselves) have no good mappings. The only major pieces of the intended analogy that

Table 27.19
Predicate-calculus representations of knowledge underlying the metaphor "Socrates is a midwife of ideas" (isomorphic and nonisomorphic versions)

Midwife (source)
  (midwife (obj_midwife) m1)
  (mother (obj_ m2)
  (father (obj_father) m3)
  (child (obj_child) m4)
  (matches (obj_midwife obj_mother obj_father) m5)
  (conceives (obj_mother obj_child) m6)
  (cause (m5 m6) m7)
  (in_labor_with (obj_mother obj_child) m8)
  (helps (obj_midwife obj_mother) m10)
  (give_birth_to (obj_mother obj_child) m11)
  (cause (m10 m11) m12)
Socrates (target)
  (philosopher (Socrates) s1)
  (student (obj_student) s2)
  (intellectual_partner (obj_partner) s3)
  (idea (obj_idea) s4)
  (introduce (Socrates obj_student obj_partner) s5)
  (formulates (obj_student obj_idea) s6)
  (cause (s5 s6) s7)
  (thinks_about (obj_student obj_idea) s8)
  (tests_truth (obj_student obj_idea) s9)
  (helps (Socrates obj_student) s10)
  (knows_truth_or_falsity (obj_student obj_idea) s11)
  (cause (s10 s11) s12)
Nonisomorphic version adds:
  (father (Socrates) s20)
  (poison (obj_hemlock) s21)
  (drink (Socrates obj_hemlock) s22)
  (midwife (obj_soc-midwife) s23)
  (mother (obj_soc-wife) s24)
  (matches (obj_soc-midwife obj_soc-wife Socrates) s25)
  (child (obj_soc-child) s26)
  (conceives (obj_soc-wife obj_soc-child) s27)
  (cause (s25 s27) s28)
  (in_labor_with (obj_soc-wife obj_soc-child) s29)
  (helps (obj_soc-midwife obj_soc-wife) s30)
  (give_birth_to (obj_soc-wife obj_soc-child) s31)
  (cause (s30 s31) s32)

Table 27.20
Best mappings, with asymptotic activation levels, for objects and predicates in three versions of the Socrates/Midwife metaphor

Cycles to settle	Versions					
	Isomorphic, nonpragmatic 34		Nonisomorphic, nonpragmatic 105		Nonisomorphic, pragmatic 83	
Objects:						
Socrates	obj_midwife	.87	obj_father	.80	obj_midwife	.86
obj_student	obj_mother	.69	obj_mother	.69	obj_mother	.69
obj_partner	obj_father	.81	none		obj_father	.80
obj_idea	obj_child	.90	obj_child	.69	obj_child	.70
*obj_soc-midwife	—		obj_midwife	.84	none	
*obj_soc-wife	—		obj_mother	.69	obj_mother	.69
*obj_soc-child	—		obj_child	.69	obj_child	.65
*obj_hemlock	—		none		none	
Predicates:						
philospher	midwife	.58	none		midwife	.81
student	mother	.59	none		none	
intellectual_partner	father	.57	none		father	.57
idea	child	.59	none		child	.58
introduces	matches	.77	none		matches	.67
formulates	conceives	.72	conceives	.27	conceives	.31
thinks_about	in_labor_with	.36	none		none	
tests_truth	in_labor_with	.36	none		none	
knows_truth_or_falsity	gives_birth_to	.72	gives_birth_to	.29	gives_birth_to	.31
helps	helps	.77	helps	.79	helps	.80
cause	cause	.84	cause	.84	cause	.84
*posion	—		none		none	
*drink	—		none		none	
*father	—		father	.70	none	
*midwife	—		midwife	.70	none	
*mother	—		mother	.69	mother	.69
*child	—		child	.69	none	
*matches	—		matches	.78	none	
*conceives	—		conceives	.48	conceives	.43
*in_labor_with	—		in_labor_with	.74	in_labor_with	.74
*gives_birth_to	—		gives_birth_to	.46	gives_birth_to	.43

* Elements with an asterisk appeared only in nonisomorphic version. Elements that map to "none" have no mapping unit with activation greater than .20.

survive are the mappings between the student and the mother and between the idea and the child.

Note, however, that the original statement of the metaphor, "Socrates is a midwife of ideas," provides some direct pragmatic guidance as to the intended mappings. Clearly, Socrates must map to the midwife, and the idea must map to *something*. This is precisely the kind of knowledge that ACME can represent using pragmatic weights. Accordingly, in a further run the mappings between propositions s1 and m1 and between the elements of those propositions (i.e., *s1 = m1*, *Socrates = obj_midwife*, and *philosopher = midwife*) were marked as PRESUMED; and proposition s4 and its elements (i.e., *s4*, *obj_idea*, and *idea*) were marked as IMPORTANT. The right column of Table 27.20 reports the results for the nonisomorphic version of the metaphor after these pragmatic weights were introduced. The pragmatic information was sufficient to allow almost complete recovery of the abstract metaphoric mappings. The network settled after 83 cycles. Socrates again maps to the midwife, and the partner to the father; almost all of the appropriate predicate mappings, such as those between *idea* and *child* and between *introduces* and *conceives*, are also recovered. Note that some of the more superficial mappings of objects, such as between Socrates' wife and the mother, also emerge. The behavior of the program across these versions of the metaphor thus dramatically illustrates both the power and the limitations of purely structural constraints, and the crucial role of pragmatic knowledge in finding abstract mappings in the face of misleading information.

Stability, Sensitivity, and Complexity Analyses
The discussion of ACME's applications is concluded by describing analyses that have been done to answer important questions about the stability, sensitivity, and computational complexity of the system. The chief stability question is whether networks settle into states in which units have stable activation values. Questions about sensitivity concern whether the performance of ACME depends upon specific parameter values or representations. Computational complexity concerns the danger of combinatorial explosion arising with large examples. These analyses show that ACME fares well on all these dimensions.

Localist connectionist networks such as the one used by ACME are sometimes unstable, undergoing oscillations in activation values of units. ACME is not subject to such instabilities for examples above, which in all of their versions have been run until stable activations have been reached by all units. In no case does ACME get a correct mapping and lose it by having an incorrect mapping catch up to, and surpass, the correct one. The stability of ACME is well typified by Figure 27.5, which illustrates how the activations of units proceed to stable levels. How quickly ACME settles depends upon the values of the parameters, but in no experiment has the time exceeded 220 cycles. The network typically settles in well under 100 cycles.

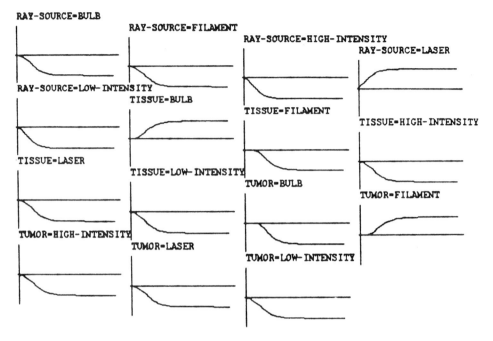

Figure 27.5
The activation history of several selected mapping units over 60 cycles of updating.

ACME has several important parameters, and the question naturally arises how sensitive ACME is to particular values for those parameters. The three most crucial ones are decay rate d, excitation e, and inhibition i. All of the runs reported above have used the same values: $d = .1$, $e = .1$, and $i = -.2$. Sensitivity experiments using the laser/radiation and basic water/heat-flow examples showed that ACME performs satisfactorily over a wide range of values for these parameters. Decay rates from .001 to .2 work equally well, with the higher values producing a faster rate of settling. Higher values for excitation also lead to faster settling; values ranging from .01 to .12 work for all examples. Excitation values higher than .12 are disruptive, however, because the gracefulness of the network depends upon reasonably small updatings of activation. If excitation is above .12, then after dozens of cycles the net input to a unit can exceed 1, producing instability manifested in long settling times. Inhibition values can range all the way to $-.9$ without causing problems, except that high inhibition can prevent ACME from overcoming an initially promising but incorrect mapping. Although it is not crucial to the functioning of the networks, it was found desirable to have inhibition higher than excitation, because that produces greater separation in the asymptotic values of best and second-best units. In order to have a large impact, the *p2* parameter for weights from the pragmatic unit for PRESUMED mappings works best at around .3; smaller values produce less differentiation while larger values do not produce significantly more differentiation.

How sensitive is ACME to representation changes? Although several of the examples examined involved isomorphic representations, such examples as the poor-constraint versions of the convergence problems, the missionaries-and-cannibals homomorphs, and the nonisomorphic version of the Socrates / midwife metaphor, show that ACME does not need to be spoon-fed isomorphic representations. The robustness of ACME in the face of representational changes was tested further by both complicating and simplifying existing examples. A bizarre analogy was created by combining the representations of the Contras and the Socrates analogs, and mapping it to a combination of the Hungarian and midwife analogs. ACME quickly partitioned the bizarre analogy into the appropriate sub-analogies. "Ablation" experiments were also performed on the good-constraint laser example, first by deleting every third proposition of the lightbulb problem and second, by deleting every second proposition of the tumor problem. ACME still found the appropriate mappings, except that in the first case, in which the predicate "filament" had been deleted, the tumor was left without any mapping unit with positive activation.

Finally, the computational complexity of ACME was analyzed. Mathematical analysis shows that the algorithm for constructing networks operates in time that is a polynomial (nonexponential) function of the number of elements in the input representations of the two structures that are mapped. Let $m1$ be the number of propositions in Structure 1, and $m2$ be the number of propositions in Structure 2. To simplify the algebra, let m be the higher of $m1$ and $m2$. Similarly, let n be the greater of the numbers of objects in the arguments of Structures 1 and 2. Since there can be only one predicate in a proposition, m also gives an upper limit on the number of predicates in a structure. Then

> the maximum possible number of units mapping propositions is m^*m;
> the maximum possible number of units mapping predicates is m^*m; and
> the maximum possible number of units mapping objects is n^*n.

So the maximum possible number of units altogether is

$$2m^2 + n^2.$$

Since there is at most only one link between any two units, if there are u units, then there can be at most $u(u-1)$ possible links, which is less than the number of units squared, or

$$4m^4 + 4m^2n^2 + n^4.$$

The semantic and pragmatic units add an additional maximum $2u$ links. Clearly, the number of links is not an exponential function of the number of elements in the input representations. In practice, the number of units and links are far lower than the calculated second- and fourth-power limits because of the various restrictions used in setting up the networks.

Unfortunately, no mathematical analysis can be given concerning how long it will take the network to settle as a function of number of units, since time of settling is a function of the degree to which the various constraints are satisfied as well as of the number of units. But the networks run so far do not take a long time to settle. Across the more than 20 examples, the greatest number of cycles to settling was 217 using the McClelland and Rumelhart updating rule and low excitation and inhibition values; the same example (the analogy between the radiation problem and the fortress problem) took only 62 cycles to settle with high excitation and decay values using the Grossberg updating rule. On a Sun 3/160 workstation, the runs typically take a few minutes, with most of that time spent in running the network to asymptote after the correct mapping units have already emerged as winners. For Falkenhainer et al.'s (1986) heat- and water-flow analogy, for example, ACME creates the network in less than 2 seconds of CPU time and settles in less than 25 seconds.

The algorithm for updating the network is fully parallel, and hence can theoretically operate in constant time if there is a processor corresponding to each link. A version of ACME in *LISP has been implemented on a 16384-processor CM2 Connection Machine, which takes advantage of the inherent parallelism of the updating algorithm. The largest example tested so far, which is considerably larger than any of the examples mentioned in Table 27.2, involves mapping representations of synopses of the plays *Hamlet* and *Macbeth* (cf. Winston, 1980). Each of these representations contains about 45 propositions, and the resulting network involves 730 units and 11801 links. The network settles after 402 cycles.

General Discussion

A new theory of anlogical mapping that integrates structural, semantic, and pragmatic constraints on how people map from one structure to another has been described here. The theory has been implemented in a connectionist computer program, ACME, which has been applied to a wide variety of analogies. The examples presented illustrate such capabilities as finding many-to-one and one-to-many mappings, mapping dissimilar relations, identifying purely structural isomorphisms without any semantic or pragmatic information, and using pragmatic knowledge to find useful mappings in the face of misleading structural and semantic resemblances. The program was able to provide qualitative simulations of a number of experimental findings concerning human analogical reasoning.

All of the examples considered here involved finding mappings between analogs at the same level of abstraction. It should be readily apparent, however, that ACME can also map structures that differ in level of abstraction, such as an instance and a schema. For example, rather than mapping a representation of the Contras onto a representation of the PLO, it would be possible to map the Contras onto a schema for "terrorists." Similarly, the same basic mapping process could map the radiation problem either onto the laser problem or onto a more abstract convergence schema (Gick & Holyoak, 1983). The present theory thus provides a unifying account of analogical mapping and mapping to schemas.

Although the constraint-satisfaction theory of analogical mapping appears powerful in its intended domain, many other important issues about analogy remain unsolved. Most notably, the model of mapping needs to be incorporated into a broader theory of all phases of analogical reasoning (Holyoak & Thagard, 1989). Of particular interest is the link between the initial spontaneous retrieval of plausibly useful analogs and the subsequent mapping process. There is evidence that retrieval is more heavily influenced by semantic similarity of predicates than is mapping (Gentner & Landers, 1985; Holyoak & Koh, 1987), although retrieval also seems to be influenced by deeper forms of structural similarity (Holyoak & Koh, 1987; Schank, 1982). Complementary to ACME, a program called ARCS (Analog Retrieval by Constraint Satisfaction) (Thagard, Holyoak, Nelson, & Gochfeld, 1989) has also been developed. ARCS is a constraint-satisfaction model of retrieval that uses semantic, structural, and pragmatic constraints to help find relevant analogs stored in memory. In contrast to ACME, semantic constraints take precedence in ARCS, with the retrieval of analogs being initiated through associations of semantically similar concepts. However, the retrieval process is also guided by structural correspondences and pragmatic import. ARCS represents an advance over ACME in that it is able to compute both semantic similarity and pragmatic centrality from more basic knowledge, rather than requiring semantic and pragmatic weights to be specified directly. ARCS computes semantic similarity from relations such as superordination and meronymy encoded in an automated thesaurus, WordNet, which is organized as a semantic network (Miller, Fellbaum, Kegl, & Miller, 1988). Pragmatic importance is computed by an analysis of the structure of problems and explanations. The output of ARCS provides a partial mapping of the target to retrieved source analogs; it should be possible to pass the output of ARCS to ACME so that ACME can simply continue the mapping process in greater detail.

The major issue not addressed here by the theories of mapping and retrieval is re-representation. To find useful analogies between complex analogs, it will often be necessary to interweave the mapping component with strategic manipulation of the representations of the source and target. In order to find homomorphic correspondences involving many elements, for example, it is important to be able to group tentatively elements of each analog into sets, which could then be treated as unitary objects.

More generally, it may often be advantageous to attempt mappings at different levels of abstraction, with mappings found at higher levels then being used to constrain lower level mappings (Holyoak, 1985). The part-correspondence restriction is a first approximation to a more serial and hierarchical component of the mapping process, in which decisions about mappings at a more global level subsequently restrict the possible mappings at a more detailed level of representation. This hierarchical aspect of mapping is analogous to Marr's (1982) model of stereoscopic vision, in which correspondences between images based upon low spatial frequencies are used to constrain correspondences between images based upon higher spatial frequencies. The overall mapping process, in this extended conception, is serial across major representational levels, but more parallel within each level.

The availability of mechanisms for re-representation will make possible more flexible constraints on mapping. For example, ACME's implementation of structural constraints employs a rigid type restriction, requiring that n-place predicates map only to n-place predicates. A richer semantic representation would enable ACME to map predicates with different numbers of arguments so long as the available arguments fall into appropriate semantic categories. Similarly, a richer semantics would allow appropriate mappings between propositions involving converse relations, such as *surround* (x, y) and *enclosed-by* (y, x), which the present model cannot handle.

Finally, it is noted that the general form of the theory proposed here for analogical mapping—a set of constraints satisfiable via a cooperative algorithm—may well be applicable to other high-level cognitive processes. Lehnert (1987), for example, describes a sentence analyzer that uses a constraint network to parse sentences into case-frame meaning relationships. Similiarly, Kintsch (1988) proposes a model of discourse comprehension that illustrates a constraint-satisfaction approach. Thagard (1989) and Thagard and Nowak (1988) show how scientific theories can be evaluated on the basis of principles of explanatory coherence that are implemented in a program that overlaps with ACME. These parallel constraint-satisfaction models belie the widespread interpretation of connectionism as a straightforward revival of associationism. Connectionism has a number of important aspects, which are conceptually quite separable. In particular, whereas connectionist learning theory indeed has a strongly behaviorist flavor, parallel constraint-satisfaction models, which depend upon an analysis of the structure of problems rather than on simple associations, are much more redolent of Gestalt psychology. An abstract isomorphism, which can be computed by constraint satisfaction, is a striking example of a whole that goes beyond the sum of its parts. The parallelism of human information processing, which is so evident in lower level perception and memory retrieval, may extend to important aspects of reasoning and problem solving as well.

Notes

The research reported in this article was supported by Contract MDA903–86–K–0297 from the Army Research Institute. The Connection Machine implementation of the program was supported by NSF Biological Facilities Award BBS 87–1420, and by a grant from the Keck Foundation.

We are grateful to Greg Nelson for graphics programming. David Gochfeld and Greg Nelson developed examples used to test the Connection Machine implementation, and Eric Melz reimplemented the program in *LISP. We thank John Bransford, Dedre Gentner, Jim Greeno, Doug Hofstadter, Greg Nelson, Laura Novick and David Rumelhart for helpful comments on earlier drafts, and Jay McClelland for useful advice on activation functions.

1. Throughout this article the term "structural" is used to refer to "structural consistency" *between* two analogs, following the terminology of Falkenhainer et al. (1986). This sense of "structural" is to be distinguished from that used by Holyoak (1985) and Holyoak and Koh (1987), who defined "structural" properties as the goal-relevant aspects *within* a single analog. Structural properties in the latter sense will be termed "pragmatically central" or simply "important" properties in the present paper. A pragmatically useful analogy is one in which structural consistency holds between the important properties of the source and target. Use of different senses of the term "structural" in the analogy literature has contributed to some theoretical misunderstandings (e.g., Gentner, 1989; Holyoak, 1985).

2. Note that Falkenhainer et al. (1986) allow mappings between nonidentical one-place predicates and objects; they only impose the identity restriction on multiplace relations. Since Falkenhainer et al. represent functions as one-place predicates, SME can map nonidentical functions.

3. ACME does not distinguish between object constants and variables representing classes of objects; hence the type restriction does not preclude mapping an object to a variable. Also note that mapping units may sometimes be formed for propositions with unequal numbers of predicates if such a mapping is suggested by a mapping of higher-order relations. For example, if *cause* (*T1, T2*) were mapped to *cause* (*S3, S2*), then the mapping unit *T1 = S3* would be formed even if T1 has one argument and S3 has two arguments. In this case, however, the type restriction would preclude forming a mapping unit linking the predicates of T1 and S1.

4. In an earlier version of ACME, propositions were not mapped directly using proposition identifiers; rather, mapping units were based solely upon correspondences between predicates and between their arguments. Structural consistency was enforced by placing excitatory connections from $predicate_T = predicate_S$ units to $object_T = object_S$ units. In many instances this simpler architecture is satisfactory. However, it leads to error in certain cases. For example, consider the following fragments from target and source analogs:

   T1: D(a, b)   S1: M(x, y)

   S2: N(x, z)

   S3: N(w, y).

   Suppose that other evidence provides high activation to the object-mapping units $a = x$ and $b = y$. Intuitively, this information should suffice to establish that predicate D maps to M rather than to N. However, without mapping units for the proposition identifiers (e.g., $T1 = S1$), ACME erroneously would provide slightly higher activation to $D = N$ than to $D = M$. The reason is that although excitatory links will be formed from $a = x$ and $b = y$ to $D = M$ (based upon the possible mapping of T1 and S1), these winning object-mapping units will also each have excitatory links to $D = N$. A link from $a = x$ to $D = N$ will be formed on the basis of the possible correspondence of T1 with S2, and a link from $b = y$ to $D = N$ will be formed on the basis of the possible correspondences of T1 with S3. Since, in addition, two possible proposition correspondences favor $D = N$ whereas only one favors $D = M$, the overall result is a preference for linking D to N rather than to the intuitively correct choice, M.

Such errors arise because the mapping network fails to capture a crucial aspect of structural consistency, which depends upon mapping propositions as integral units. The present architecture of ACME avoids errors of this sort by introducing proposition-mapping units which have excitatory connections both to the corresponding predicate-mapping units and to the object-mapping units, in addition to forming direct excitatory connections between the latter types of units. In the above example, the proposition-mapping unit $T1 = S1$ will be favored over its two competitors, which in turn ensures that $D = M$ is preferred to $D = N$. We thank Dawn Cohen for identifying a chemistry analogy that first brought this problem with the earlier architecture to out attention.

5. ACME represents objects by semantically empty constants; similarity of objects is represented indirectly by similarity of the mapped predicates that apply to the objects. It is possible, however, that people arrive at judgments of object–object similarity prior to the mapping stage, perhaps using additional information besides predicates available to the mapping process. The program could easily be extended to allow similarity weights to directly reflect object–object as well as predicate–predicate similarities.

6. Various alternative variants of the updating procedure were explored. Performance is improved for some examples if the minimum and maximum activation values are made asymmetric ($min = -.3$), as advocated by Grossberg (1978). The formula employed in McClelland and Rumelhart's (1981) model of word recognition was also used, in which the activation level of unit j on cycle t is given by

$$a_j(t+1) = a_j(t)(1-d) + \begin{cases} net_j(max - a_j(t)) & \text{if } net_j > 0 \\ net_j(a_j(t) - min) & \text{otherwise,} \end{cases}$$

where $min = -1$ and $max = 1$. The net input to unit j, net_j, is equal to $\Sigma_i w_{ij} o_i(t)$; $o_i(t)$ is the output on cycle t of a unit with activation a_i, with $o_i(t) = max(a_i(t), 0)$. The Grossberg rule considers excitatory and inhibitory inputs separately in adjusting activations, whereas the McClelland and Rumelhart rule sums all inputs before making the adjustment. Although both rules yield similar results for most of the examples, the Grossberg rule proved more effective in some of the more complex cases.

For both rules, it proved important to impose a zero threshold on the outputs of units, so that units with negative activations do not influence the units to which they are connected. Without this restriction, two units with negative activation levels that have an inhibitory weight on the connection between them will excite each other, yielding counterintuitive results for some examples.

7. The formula for G used in ACME is a variant of that used by Rumelhart et al. (1986). The present algorithm operates only on internal weights, and does not involve any external inputs. In addition, outputs rather than activation values are used because of the introduction of a threshold on outputs. Links between units that both have negative activations thus do not affect the value of G. Although there is not a proof that the activation-updating procedure finds a local maximum of G, the measure has been found to be heuristically useful in interpreting the behavior of the program.

References

Anderson, J. R., & Thompson, R. (1989). Use of analogy in a production system architecture. In S. Vosniadou & A. Ortony (Eds.), *Similarity and analogical reasoning*. London: Cambridge University Press.

Black, M. (1962). *Models and metaphors*. Ithaca, NY: Cornell University Press.

Brown, A. L., Kane, M. J., & Echols, K. (1986). Young children's mental models determine transfer across problems with a common goal structure. *Cognitive Development, 1*, 103–122.

Burstein, M. H. (1986). A model of learning by incremental analogical reasoning and debugging. In R. Michalski, J. G. Carbonell & T. M. Mitchell (Eds.), *Machine learning: An artificial intelligence approach* (Vol. 2). Los Altos, CA: Kaufmann.

Carbonell, J. G. (1983). Learning by analogy: Formulating and generalizing plans from past experience. In R. Michalski, J. G. Carbonell & T. M. Mitchell (Eds.), *Machine learning: An artificial intelligence approach*. Palo Alto, CA: Tioga Press.

Carbonell, J. G. (1986). Derivational analogy: A theory of reconstructive problem solving and expertise acquisition. In R. Michalski, J. G. Carbonell & T. M. Mitchell (Eds.), *Machine learning: An artificial intelligence approach* (Vol. 2). Los Altos, CA: Kaufmann.

Coombs, C. H., Dawes, R. M., & Tversky, A. (1970). *Mathematical psychology*. Englewood Cliffs, NJ: Prentice-Hall.

Darden, L. (1983). Artificial intelligence and philosophy of science: Reasoning by analogy in theory construction. In P. Asquith & T. Nickles (Eds.), *PSA 1982* (Vol. 2). East Lansing, MI: Philosophy of Science Society.

Duncker, K. (1945). On problem solving. *Psychological Monographs, 58* (Whole No. 270).

Falkenhainer, B., Forbus, K. D., & Gentner, D. (1986). The structure-mapping engine. In *Proceedings of the Fifth National Conference on Artificial Intelligence*. Los Altos, CA: Morgan Kaufmann.

Falkenhainer, B., Forbus, K. D., & Gentner, D. (1989). The structure-mapping engine: Algorithm and examples. *Artificial Intelligence, 41*, 1–63.

Gentner, D. (1982). Are scientific analogies metaphors? In D. S. Miall (Ed.), *Metaphor: Problems and perspectives*. Brighton, England: Harvester Press.

Gentner, D. (1983). Structure-mapping: A theoretical framework for analogy. *Cognitive Science, 7*, 155–170.

Gentner, D. (1989). The mechanisms of analogical reasoning. In S. Vosniadou & A. Ortony (Eds.), *Similarity and analogical reasoning*. London: Cambridge University Press.

Gentner, D., & Landers, R. (1985). Analogical reminding: A good match is hard to find. In *Proceedings of the International Conference on Systems, Man and Cybernetics*. Tuscon, AZ.

Gentner, D., & Toupin, C. (1986). Systematicity and surface similarity in the development of analogy. *Cognitive Science, 10*, 277–300.

Gholson, B., Eymard, L. A., Long, D., Morgan, D., & Leeming, F. C. (1988). Problem solving, recall, isomorphic transfer, and non-isomorphic transfer among third-grade and fourth-grade children. *Cognitive Development, 3*, 37–53.

Gick, M. L., & Holyoak, K. J. (1980). Analogical problem solving. *Cognitive Psychology, 12*, 306–355.

Gick, M. L., & Holyoak, K. J. (1983). Schema induction and analogical transfer. *Cognitive Psychology, 15*, 1–38.

Grossberg, S. (1978). A theory of visual coding, memory, and development. In E. L. J. Leeuwenberg & H. F. J. Buffart (Eds.), *Formal theories of visual perception*. New York: Wiley.

Halford, G. S. (1987). A structure-mapping approach to cognitive development. *International Journal of Psychology, 22*, 609–642.

Halford, G. S., & Wilson, W. H. (1980). A category theory approach to cognitive development. *Cognitive Psychology, 12*, 356–411.

Hall, R. (1989). Computational approaches to analogical reasoning: A comparative analysis. *Artificial Intelligence, 39*, 39–120.

Hammond, K. J. (1986). *Case-based planning: An integrated theory of planning, learning, and memory*. Unpublished doctoral dissertation, Department of Computer Science, Yale University, New Haven, CT.

Hesse, M. B. (1966). *Models and analogies in science*. Notre Dame, IN: Notre Dame University Press.

Hofstadter, D. R. (1984). The Copycat project: An experiment in nondeterministic and creative analogies. A.I. Laboratory Memo 755). Cambridge, MA: MIT.

Hofstadter, D. R., & Mitchell, M. (1988). Conceptual slippage and mapping: A report on the Copycat project. In *Proceedings of the Tenth Annual Conference of the Cognitive Science Society*. Hillsdale, NJ: Erlbaum.

Holland, J. H., Holyoak, K. J., Nisbett, R. E., & Thagard, P. (1986). *Induction: Processes of inference, learning, and discovery*. Cambridge, MA: Bradford Books/MIT Press.

Holyoak, K. J. (1982). An analogical framework for literary interpretation. *Poetics, 11,* 105–126.

Holyoak, K. J. (1984). Mental models in problem solving. In J. R. Anderson & S. M. Kosslyn (Eds.), *Tutorials in learning and memory: Essays in honor of Gordon Bower*. San Francisco: Freeman.

Holyoak, K. J. (1985). The pragmatics of analogical transfer. In G. H. Bower (Ed.), *The psychology of learning and motivation* (Vol. 19). New York: Academic.

Holyoak, K. J., & Koh, K. (1987). Surface and structural similarity in analogical transfer. *Memory & Cognition, 15,* 332–340.

Holyoak, K. J., & Thagard, P. (1989). A computational model of analogical problem solving. In S. Vosniadou & A. Ortony (Eds.), *Similarity and analogical reasoning*. London: Cambridge University Press.

Indurkhya, B. (1987). Approximate semantic transference: A computational theory of metaphors and analogies. *Cognitive Science, 11,* 445–480.

Kedar-Cabelli, S. (1985). Purpose-directed analogy. *Proceedings of the Seventh Annual Conference of the Cognitive Science Society*. Irvine, CA: Cognitive Science Society.

Kintsch, W. (1988). The role of knowledge in discourse comprehension: A construction–integration model. *Psychological Review, 95,* 163–182.

Kittay, E. (1987). *Metaphor: Its cognitive force and linguistic structure*. Oxford: Clarendon Press.

Kolodner, J. L., & Simpson, R. L. (1988). *The MEDIATOR: A case study of a case-based problem solver* (Tech. Rep. No. GIT–ICS–88/11). Atlanta: Georgia Institute of Technology, School of Information and Computer Science.

Kolodner, J. L., Simpson, R. L., & Sycara, E. (1985). A process model of case-based reasoning in problem solving. In *Proceedings of the Ninth International Joint Conference on Artificial Intelligence* (Vol. 1). San Mateo, CA: Kaufmann.

Kunda, Z. (1987). Motivation and inference: Self-serving generation and evaluation of causal theories. *Journal of Personality and Social Psychology, 53,* 636–647.

Lehnert, W. (1987). Learning to integrate syntax and semantics. In P. Langley (Ed.), *Proceedings of the Fourth International Workshop on Machine Learning*. Los Altos, CA: Kaufmann.

Maclane, S. (1971). *Categories for the working mathematician*. New York: Springer-Verlag.

Marr, D. (1982). *Vision*. New York: Freeman.

Marr, D., & Poggio, T. (1976). Cooperative computation of stereo disparity. *Science, 194,* 283–287.

McClelland, J. L., & Rumelhart, D. E. (1981). An interactive activation model of context effects in letter perception: Part 1. An account of basic findings. *Psychological Review, 88,* 375–407.

Miller, G. A. (1979). Images and models, similes and metaphors. In A. Ortony (Ed.), *Metaphor and thought*. Cambridge, England: Cambridge University Press.

Miller, G. A., Fellbaum, C., Kegl, J., & Miller, K. (1988). WordNet: An electronic lexical reference system based on theories of lexical memory (Tech. Rep. No. 11). Princeton, NJ: Princeton University, Cognitive Science Laboratory.

Newell, A., & Simon, H. A. (1972). *Human problem solving*. Englewood Cliffs, NJ: Prentice-Hall.

Novick, L. R. (1988). Analogical transfer, problem similarity, and expertise. *Journal of Experimental Psychology: Learning, Memory, and Cognition, 14,* 510–520.

Palmer, S. E. (1978). Fundamental aspects of cognitive representation. In E. Rosch & B. H. Lloyd (Eds.), *Cognition and categorization*. Hillsdale, NJ: Erlbaum.

Palmer, S. E. (1989). Levels of description in information processing theories of analogy. In S. Vosniadou & A. Ortony (Eds.), *Similarity and analogical reasoning*. London: Cambridge University Press.

Polya, G. (1973). *Mathematics and plausible reasoning* (Vol. 1). Princeton, NJ: Princeton University Press.

Reed, S. K., Ernst, G. W., & Banerji, R. (1974). The role of analogy in transfer between similar problem states. *Cognitive Psychology, 6,* 436–440.

Ross, B. J. (1987). This is like that: The use of earlier problems and the separation of similarity effects. *Journal of Experimental Psychology: Learning, Memory, and Cognition, 13,* 629–639.

Rumelhart, D. E., Smolensky, P., McClelland, J. L., & Hinton, G. E. (1986). Schemata and sequential thought processes in PDP models. In J. L. McCelland, D. E. Rumelhart & the PDP Research Group (Eds.), *Parallel distributed processing: Explorations in the micro-structure of cognition* (Vol. 2). Cambridge, MA: Bradford Books / MIT Press.

Schank, R. C. (1982). *Dynamic memory.* Cambridge, MA: Cambridge University Press.

Suppes, P., & Zinnes, J. L. (1963). Basic measurement theory. In R. D. Luce, R. R. Bush & E. Galanter (Eds.), *Handbook of mathematical psychology.* New York: Wiley.

Tarski, A. (1954). Contributions to the theory of models. *Indigationes Mathematicae, 16,* 572–588.

Thagard, P. (1984). Frames, knowledge, and inference. *Synthese, 61,* 301–318.

Thagard, P. (1986). Parallel computation and the mind–body problem. *Cognitive Science, 10,* 301–318.

Thagard, P. (1988a). *Computational philosophy of science.* Cambridge, MA: Bradford Books / MIT Press.

Thagard, P. (1988b). Dimensions of analogy. In D. Helman (Ed.), *Analogical reasoning.* Dordrecht, Holland: Kluwer.

Thagard, P. (1989). Explanatory coherence. *Behavioral and Brain Sciences, 12,* 435–467.

Thagard, P., Cohen, D., & Holyoak, K. J. (1989). Chemical analogies. In *Proceedings of the Eleventh International Joint Conference on Artificial Intelligence.* San Mateo, CA: Kaufmann.

Thagard, P., Holyoak, K. J., Nelson, G., & Gochfeld, D. (1989). *Analog retrieval by constraint satisfation.* Unpublished manuscript, Princeton University, Cognitive Science Laboratory.

Thagard, P., & Nowak, G. (1988). The explanatory coherence of continental drift. In A. Fine & J. Leplin, (Eds.), *PSA 1988* (Vol. 1, pp. 118–126). East Lansing, MI: Philosophy of Science Association.

Tourangeau, R., & Sternberg, R. J. (1982). Understanding and appreciating metaphors. *Cognition, 11,* 203–204.

Tversky, A. (1977). Features of similarity. *Psychological Review, 84,* 327–352.

Winston, P. H. (1980). Learning and reasoning by analogy. *Communications of the ACM, 23,* 689–703.

Ziegler, W. P. (1976). *Theory of modelling and simulation.* New York: Wiley.

Retrieving Analogies

Chapter 28

MAC/FAC: A Model of Similarity-Based Retrieval

Kenneth D. Forbus, Dedre Gentner, and Keith Law

1 Introduction

Similarity-based remindings range from the sublime to the stupid. At one extreme, seeing the periodic table of elements reminds one of octaves in music. At the other, a bicycle reminds one of a pair of eyeglasses. Often, remindings are neither brilliant nor superficial but simply mundane, as when a bicycle reminds one of another bicycle. Theoretical attention is inevitably drawn to spontaneous analogy: i.e., to structural similarity unsupported by surface similarity, as in the octave/periodic table comparison. Such remindings seem clearly insightful and seem linked to the creative process, and should be included in any model of retrieval. But as we review below, research on the psychology of memory retrieval points to a preponderance of the latter two types of similarity—(mundane) literal similarity, based on both structural and superficial commonalities—and (dumb) superficial similarity, based on surface commonalities. A major challenge for research on similarity-based reminding is to devise a model that will produce chiefly literal-similarity and superficial remindings, but still produce occasional analogical remindings.

A further constraint on models of access comes from considering the role of similarity in transfer and inference. The large number of superficial remindings indicates that retrieval is not very sensitive to structural soundness. But appropriate transfer requires structural soundness, so that knowledge can be exported from one description into another. And psychological evidence (also discussed below) indicates that the mapping process involved in transfer is actually very sensitive to structural soundness. Hence our memories often give us information we don't want, which at first seems somewhat paradoxical. Any model of retrieval should explain this paradox.

This chapter presents MAC/FAC, a model of similarity-based reminding that attempts to capture these phenomena. MAC/FAC models similarity-based retrieval as a two-stage process. The first stage (MAC) uses a cheap, non-structural matcher to quickly filter potentially relevant items from a pool of such items. These potential matches are then processed in the FAC stage by a more powerful (but more expensive) structural matcher, based on the structure-mapping notion of literal similarity (Gentner, 1983).

2 Framework

Similarity-based transfer can be decomposed into subprocesses. Given that a person has some current *target* situation in working memory, transfer from prior knowledge requires at least

1. *Accessing* a similar (*base*) situation in long-term memory,
2. *Creating a mapping* from the base to the target, and
3. *Evaluating* the mapping.

In this case the base is an item from memory, and the target is the probe; that is, we think of the retrieved memory items as mapped to the probe. Other processes may also occur—*verifying new inferences* about the target (Clement, 1986), *elaborating* the base and target (Ross, 1987; Falkenhainer, 1988), *adapting* or *tweaking* the domain representations to improve the match (Falkenhainer, 1990; Holyoak & Barnden, 1994), and *abstracting* the common structure from base and target (Gick & Holyoak, 1983; Skorstad, Gentner & Medin, 1988; Winston, 1982)—but our focus is on the first three processes.

2.1 Structure-Mapping and the Typology of Similarity

The process of *mapping* aligns two representations and uses this alignment to generate analogical inferences (Gentner, 1983, 1989). Alignment occurs via matching, which creates correspondences between items in the two representations. Analogical inferences are generated by using the correspondences to import knowledge from the base representation into the target. The mapping process is assumed to be governed by the constraints of *structural consistency: one-to-one mapping* and *parallel connectivity. One-to-one mapping* means that an interpretation of a comparison cannot align (e.g., place into correspondence) the same item in the base with multiple items in the target, or vice-versa. *Parallel connectivity* means that if an interpretation of a comparison aligns two statements, their arguments must also be placed into correspondence. In this account, similarity is defined in terms of correspondences between structured representations (Gentner 1983; Goldstone, Medin & Gentner, 1991; Markman & Gentner, 1997). Matches can be distinguished according to the kinds of commonalities present. An *analogy* is a match based on a common system of relations, especially one involving higher-order relations.[1] A *literal similarity* match includes both common relational structure and common object descriptions. A *surface similarity* or *mere-appearance* match is based primarily on common object descriptions, with perhaps a few shared first-order relations.

Considerable evidence shows that the mapping process is sensitive to structural commonalities. People can readily align two situations, preserving structurally important commonalties, making the appropriate lower-order substitutions, and mapping additional predicates into the target as *candidate inferences*. For example, Clement and Gentner (1991) showed people analogies and asked which of two lower-order assertions, both shared by base and target, was most important to the match. Subjects chose assertions that were connected to matching causal antecedents: that is, their choice was based not only on the goodness of the local match but on whether it was connected to a larger matching system. In a second study, subjects were asked to make a new prediction about the target based on the analogy with the base story. They again showed sensitivity to connectivity and systematicity in choosing which predicates to map as candidate inferences from base to target. (See also Spellman & Holyoak, 1992.)

The degree of relational match is also important in determining people's evaluations of comparisons. People rate metaphors as more apt when they are based on relational commonalities than when they are based on common object-descriptions (Gentner & Clement, 1988). Gentner, Rattermann, and Forbus (1993) asked subjects to rate the soundness and similarity of story pairs that varied in which kinds of commonalities they shared. Subjects' soundness and similarity ratings were substantially greater for pairs that shared higher-order relational structure than for those that did not (Gentner & Landers, 1985; Gentner, Rattermann & Forbus, 1993). Common relational structure also contributes strongly to judgments of perceptual similarity (Goldstone, Medin & Gentner, 1991) as well as to the way in which people align pairs of pictures in a mapping task (Markman & Gentner, 1993b) and determine common and distinctive features (Markman & Gentner, 1993a).

Any model of human similarity and analogy must capture this sensitivity to structural commonality. To do so, it must involve structural representations and processes that operate to align them (Goldstone, Medin & Gentner, 1991; Markman & Gentner, 1993a,b; Reed, 1987; Reeves & Weisberg, 1994). This would seem to require abandoning some highly influential models of similarity: e.g., modeling similarity as the intersection of independent feature sets or as the dot product of feature vectors. However, we show below that a variant of these nonstructural models can be useful in describing memory retrieval.

2.1.1 Similarity-Based Access from Long-Term Memory   There is considerable evidence that access to long-term memory relies more on surface commonalities and less on structural commonalities than does mapping. For example, people often fail to access potentially useful analogs (Gick & Holyoak, 1980, 1983). Research has shown that, although people in a problem-solving task are often reminded of prior problems, these remindings are often based on surface similarity rather than on structural similarities between the solution principles (Holyoak & Koh, 1987; Keane, 1987, 1988b; Novick 1988a,b; Reed, Ernst & Banerji, 1974; Ross, 1984, 1987, 1989; see also Reeves & Weisberg, 1994).

The experiments we will model here investigated which kinds of similarities led to the best retrieval from long-term memory (Gentner & Landers, 1985; Gentner, Rattermann & Forbus, 1993). Subjects were first given a relatively large memory set (the "Karla the Hawk" stories). About a week later, subjects were given new stories that resembled the original stories in various ways and were asked to write out any remindings they experienced to the prior stories while reading the new stories. Finally, they rated all the pairs for soundness— i.e., how well inferences could be carried from one story to the other. The results showed a marked disassociation between retrieval and subjective soundness and similarity. Surface similarity was the best predictor of memory access, and structural similarity was the best predictor of subjective soundness. This dissociation held not only between subjects, but also within subjects. That is, subjects given the soundness task immediately after the cued retrieval task judged that the very matches that had come to their minds most easily (the surface matches) were highly unsound (i.e., unlikely to be useful in inference). This suggests that similarity-based access may be based on qualitatively distinct processes from analogical inferencing.

It is not the case that higher-order relations contribute nothing to retrieval. Adding higher-order relations led to nonsignificantly more retrieval in two studies and to a small but significant benefit in the third. Other research has shown positive effects of higher-order relational matches on retrieval, especially in cases where subjects have been brought to do intensive encoding of the original materials or are expert in the domain (Novick, 1988). But higher-order commonalities have a much bigger effect on mapping once the two analogs are present than they do on similarity-based retrieval, and the reverse is true for surface commonalities.

These results place several constraints on a computational model of similarity-based retrieval. The first two criteria are driven by the phenomena of mapping and inference and the last four summarize the pattern of retrieval results:

> *Structured representation criterion:* The model must be able to store structured representations.
> *Structured mappings criterion:* The model must incorporate processes of structural mapping (i.e., alignment and transfer) over its representations.
> *Primacy of the mundane criterion:* The majority of retrievals should be literal similarity matches (i.e., matches high in both structural and surface commonalties).
> *Surface superiority criterion:* Retrievals based on surface similarity are frequent.
> *Rare insights criterion:* Relational remindings must occur at least occasionally, with lower frequency than literal similarity or surface remindings.
> *Scalability criterion:* The model must be plausibly capable of being extended to large memory sizes.

Most case-based reasoning models (Birnbaum & Collins, 1989; Kolodner, 1984, 1988; Schank, 1982) use structured representations and focus on the process of adapting and applying old cases to new situations. Such models satisfy the structured representation and structured mappings criteria. However, such models also typically presume a highly indexed memory in which the vocabulary used for indexing captures significant higher-order abstractions such as themes and principles. Viewed as psychological accounts, these models would predict that people should typically access the best structural match. That prediction fails to match the pattern of psychological results summarized by the primacy of the mundane and surface superiority criteria. Scalability is also an open question at this time, since no one has yet accumulated and indexed a large (1,000 to 10^6) corpus of structured representations.

The reverse set of advantages and disadvantages holds for approaches that model similarity as the result of a dot product (or some other simple operation) over feature vectors, as in many mathematical models of human memory (e.g., Gillund & Shiffrin, 1984; Hintzman, 1986, 1988; Medin & Schaffer, 1978; Stanfill & Waltz, 1986; but see Murphy & Medin, 1985) as well as in many connectionist models of learning (e.g., Smolensky, 1988; see also reviews by Humphreys, Bain & Pike [1989] and Ratcliff [1990].). These models typically utilize nonstructured knowledge representations and relatively simple match processes and hence do not allow for structural matching and inference. Such models also tend to utilize a unitary notion of similarity, an assumption that is called into question by the disassociation described above (see also Gentner & Markman, 1993; Medin, et al., 1993; Markman & Gentner, 1993b).

3 The MAC/FAC Model

The MAC/FAC model seeks to combine the advantages of both approaches. MAC/FAC is a two-stage model. There are good arguments for a two-stage process. In the initial stages of memory retrieval, the large number of cases in memory and the speed of human access suggests a computationally cheap process. But aligning representations and judging soundness require an expensive match process. MAC/FAC therefore uses a two-stage process, in which a cheap filter is used to pick out a subset of likely candidates for more expensive processing (c.f. Bareiss & King, 1989). The disassociation noted previously can be understood in terms of the interactions of its two stages.

Figure 28.1 illustrates the components of the MAC/FAC model. The inputs are a pool of memory items and a *probe*, i.e., a description for which a match is to be found. The output is an item from memory (i.e., a structured description) and a comparison of this item with the probe. (Section 3.1 describes exactly what a comparison is.) Internally there are two stages. The MAC stage provides a cheap but non-structural filter, which only passes on a handful of items. The FAC stage uses a more expensive but more accurate structural match, to select the most similar item(s) from the MAC output and produce a full structural alignment. Each stage consists of *matchers*, which are applied to every input description, and a *selector*, which uses the evaluation of the matchers to select

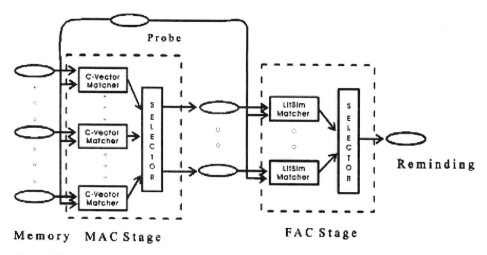

Figure 28.1
The MAC/FAC model.

which comparisons are produced as the output of that stage. Conceptually, matchers are applied in parallel within each stage.[2]

3.1 The FAC Stage and SME

The FAC stage takes as input the descriptions selected by the MAC stage and computes a full structural match between each item and the probe. We model the FAC stage by using SME, the *Structure-Mapping Engine* (Falkenhainer, Forbus & Gentner, 1986, 1989; Forbus, Ferguson & Gentner, 1994).

SME is an analogical matcher designed as a simulation of structure-mapping theory. It takes two inputs, a base description, and a target description. (For simplicity we speak of these descriptions as being made up of items, meaning both objects and statements about these objects.) It computes a set of *global interpretations* of the comparison between base and target. Each global interpretation includes

• A set of *correspondences*, which pair specific items in the base representation to specific items in the target.
• A *structural evaluation* reflecting the estimated soundness of the match. In subsequent processing, the structural evaluation provides one source of information about how seriously to take the match.
• A set of *candidate inferences*, potential new knowledge about the target which are suggested by the correspondences between the base and target. Candidate inferences are what give analogy its generative power, since they represent the importation of new knowledge into the target description. However, they are only conjectures; they must be tested and evaluated by other means.

For SME to play a major role in a model of similarity-based retrieval, it should be consistent with psychological evidence. We have tested the psychological validity of SME as a simulation of analogical processing in several ways. For instance, we compared SME's structural evaluation scores with human soundness ratings for the "Karla the Hawk" stories discussed later (Gentner & Landers, 1985) Like human subjects, SME rated analogical matches higher than surface matches (Skorstad, Falkenhainer & Gentner, 1987). The patterns of preference were similar across story sets: there was a significant positive correlation between the difference scores for SME and those for human subjects, where the difference score is the rating for analogy minus the rating for surface match within a given story set (Gentner, Rattermann & Forbus, 1993).

Because retrievals occur frequently, components in a model of retrieval must be efficient. SME is quite efficient. The generation of match hypotheses is $O(n^2)$ on a serial machine, where n is the number of items in base or target, and should typically be better than $O(\log(n))$ on data-parallel machines.[3] The generation of global interpretations is roughly $O(\log(n))$ on a serial machine, using the greedy merge algorithm of Forbus and Oblinger (1990),[4] and even faster parallel merge algorithms seem feasible.

3.2 The FAC Stage

The FAC stage is essentially a bank of SME matchers, all running in parallel.[5] These take as input the memory descriptions that are passed forward by the MAC stage and compute a structural alignment between each of these descriptions and the probe. The other component of the FAC stage is a *selector* —currently a numerical threshold—which chooses some subset of these comparisons to be available as the output of the retrieval system. (See Figure 28.1).

The FAC stage acts as a structural filter. It captures the human sensitivity to structural alignment and inferential potential (subject to the limited and possibly surface-heavy set of candidates provided by the MAC stage, as described below). Several remarks on this algorithm's role in retrieval are in order. SME is sensitive to both attributes and relations,[6] which models people's ability respond to and identify different kinds of similarity in reminding. (Recall that the literal similarity computation can compute relational similarity or object similarity as well as overall similarity). This choice seems ecologically sound because mundane matches are often reasonable guides to action; riding a new bicycle, for instance, is like riding other bicycles (Gentner, 1989; Medin & Ortony, 1989; Medin & Ross, 1989). Finally, this choice is necessary to model the high observed frequency of surface remindings. These surface remindings would mostly be rejected if FAC ignored attributes. The selector for the FAC stage must choose a small set of matches for subsequent processing. The selector outputs the best match, based on its structural evaluation, and up to *Max* other matches that are very close to it. The choice of *Max* represents assumed capacity limits and is typically set to three. The closeness criteria is a percentage of the maximum, usually 90%.

3.3 *The MAC Stage*

The MAC stage collects the initial set of matches between the probe and memory. Like the FAC stage, the MAC stage conceptually consists of a set of matchers and a selector that simply returns all items whose MAC score is within 10% of the best score given that probe. The challenge of the MAC stage is in the design of its matcher. It must allow quickly comparing, in parallel, the probe to a large pool of descriptions and passing only a few on to the more expensive FAC stage.

Ideally, the MAC matcher should find the most similar memory item for the given probe. Clearly running SME on the probe and every item in memory would provide the most accurate result. Unfortunately, even though SME is very efficient, it isn't efficient enough to take on all of memory. SME operates by building an intermediate structure, in the form of the network of local matches. The idea of building such networks for a small number of pairs is psychologically plausible because the size of the match hypothesis network is polynomial in the size of the descriptions being matched. This means, depending on one's implementation assumptions, that a fixed-size piece of hardware could be built which could be dynamically reconfigured to represent any local match network for input descriptions of some bounded size. What is not plausible is that such networks could be built between a probe and every item in a large memory pool, and especially that this could happen quickly enough in neural architectures to account for observed retrieval times.

This architectural argument suggests that, while SME is fine for FAC, MAC must be made of simpler stuff. To escape having to suffer the complexity of the most accurate matcher in the "innermost loop" if retrieval, we must trade accuracy for efficiency. The MAC matcher must provide a crude, computationally cheap match process to pare down the vast set of memory items into a small set of candidates for more expensive processing. Ideally, MAC's computations should be simple enough to admit plausible parallel and/or connectionist implementations for large-scale memory pools.

What is the appropriate crude estimator of similarity? We have developed a novel technique for estimating the degree of match in which structured representations are encoded as *content vectors*. Content vectors are flat summaries of the knowledge contained in complex relational structures. The content vector for a given description specifies which functors (i.e., relations, connectives, object attributes, functions, etc.) were used in that description and the number of times they occurred. Content vectors are assumed to arise automatically from structured representations and to remain associated with them. Content vectors are a special form of feature vectors.

More precisely, let Π be the set of functors used in the descriptions that constitute memory items and probes. We define the *content vector* of a structured description as follows. A content vector is an n-tuple of numbers, each component corresponding to a particular element of Π. Given a description ϕ, the value of each component of its content vector indicates how many times the corresponding element of Π occurs in ϕ. Components corresponding to elements of Π which do not appear in statements of ϕ have the value zero. One simple algorithm for computing content vectors is simply to count the number of occurrences of each functor in the description. Thus if there were four occurrences of IMPLIES in a story, the value for the IMPLIES component of its content vector would be four. (Figure 28.2 illustrates.) Thus, content vectors are easy to compute from a structured representation and can be stored economically (using sparse encoding, for instance, on serial machines). We normalize content vectors to unit vectors, both to reduce the sensitivity to overall size of the descriptions and because we assume that psychologically plausible implementation substrates for MAC/FAC (e.g., neural systems) will involve processing units of limited dynamic range.

The dot product of content vectors provides exactly the computational basis the MAC stage needs. It could be implemented efficiently for large memories using a variety of massively parallel computation schemes. For instance, connectionist memories can be built which find the closest feature vector to a probe (Hinton & Anderson, 1989). Therefore the MAC stage can scale up.

To summarize, the MAC matcher works as follows: Each memory item has a content vector stored with it. When a probe enters, its content vectors is computed. A score is computed for each item in the memory pool by taking the dot product of its content vector with the probe's content vector. The MAC selector then produces as output the best match and everything within 10% of it, as described above. (As for the FAC stage, variants that could be considered include implementing a threshold on the MAC selector so that if every match is too low MAC returns nothing).

Like other feature-vector schemes, the dot product of content vectors does not take the actual relational structure into account. It only calculates a numerical score, and hence doesn't produce the correspondences and candidate inferences that provide the power of analogical reasoning and learning. But items that pass MAC are fed to the FAC stage, which operates on structured representations. Thus it is the FAC stage which both filters out structurally unsound remindings and produces the desired correspondences and candidate inferences. We claim that the interplay of the cheap but dumb computations of the MAC stage and the more expensive but structurally sensitive computations of the FAC stage explains the psychological phenomena of Section 2. As the first step in supporting this claim, we next demonstrate that MAC/FAC's behavior provides a good approximation of psychological data.

4 Cognitive Simulation Experiments

In this section we compare the performance of MAC/FAC with that of human subjects, using the "Karla the Hawk" stories (Gentner, Rattermann & Forbus,

Solar System: Structured representation

```
(CAUSE
  (GRAVITY (MASS SUN) (MASS PLANET))
  (ATTRACTS SUN PLANET))
(GREATER (TEMPERATURE SUN)
         (TEMPERATURE PLANET))
(CAUSE (AND (GREATER (MASS SUN)
                     (MASS PLANET))
            (ATTRACTS SUN PLANET))
       (REVOLVE-AROUND PLANET SUN))
```

Solar System: Content Vector

```
(AND . 1)
(ATTRACTS . 1)
(CAUSE . 2)
(GRAVITY . 1)
(GREATER . 2)
(MASS . 2)
(OBJECTS . 2)
(REVOLVE-AROUND . 1)
(TEMPERATURE . 2)
```

Rutherford Atom: Structured representation

```
(CAUSE (OPPOSITE-SIGN (CHARGE NUCLEUS)
                      (CHARGE ELECTRON))
       (ATTRACTS NUCLEUS ELECTRON))
(REVOLVE-AROUND ELECTRON
                NUCLEUS)
(GREATER (MASS NUCLEUS)
         (MASS ELECTRON))
```

Rutherford Atom: Content Vector

```
(ATTRACTS . 1)
(CAUSE . 1)
(CHARGE . 2)
(GREATER . 1)
(MASS . 2)
(OBJECTS . 2)
(OPPOSITE-SIGN . 1)
(REVOLVE-AROUND . 1)
```

Figure 28.2
Sample representations with content vectors.

Table 28.1
Types of stories used in the "Karla the Hawk" experiments

| Probe type | Kinds of commonalities shared by probe and base | | |
	1st o. relations	H.o. relations	Object attributes
LS:	Yes	Yes	Yes
SF:	Yes	No	Yes
AN:	Yes	Yes	No
FOR:	Yes	No	No

Table 28.2
Proportion of correct base remindings for different probe types for human subjects (from Gentner, Rattermann, and Forbus, 1993)

Condition	Proportion
LS	0.56
SF	0.53
AN	0.12
FOR	0.09

1993, Experiment 2). For these studies, we wrote sets of stories consisting of base stories plus four variants, created by systematically varying the kind of commonalities. All variants shared first-order relations (primarily events) with their bases, but varied in which other commonalities were present, as shown in Table 28.1. The LS (literal similarity) stories shared both higher-order relational structure and object attributes. The AN (analogy) stories shared higher-order relational structure but contained different attributes, while the SF (surface similarity) stories shared attributes but contained different higher-order relational structure. The FOR (common first-order relations, primarily events) stories differed both in attributes and higher-order relational structure.

The subjects were first given 32 stories to remember, of which 20 were base stories and 12 were distractors. They were later presented with 20 probe stories: five LS matches, five AN matches, five SF matches, and five FOR matches. (Which stories were in each similarity condition was varied across subjects.) They were told to write down any prior stories of which they were reminded. As shown in Table 28.2, the proportions of remindings of the base stories for different match types were .56 for LS, .53 for SF, .12 for AN and .09 for FOR. This retrievability order was stable across three variations of this study: LS $\geq$ SF $>$ AN $\geq$ FOR.[7]

As discussed above, this retrievability order differs strikingly from the soundness ordering. When subjects were asked to rate how *sound* the matches were—how well the inferences from one story would apply to the other—they

Table 28.3
Proportion of correct retrievals given different kinds of probes

Probes	MAC	FAC
LS	1.0	1.0
SF	0.89	0.89
AN	0.67	0.67

Notes.
1. Memory contains 9 base stories and 9 FOR matches; probes were the 9 LS, 9 SF, and 9 AN stories.
2. The rows show proportion of times the correct base story was retrieved for different probe types.

rated AN and LS as significantly more sound than SF and FOR matches. SME running in analogy mode on SF and AN matches correctly reflected human soundness rankings (Forbus & Gentner, 1989; Gentner et al., 1995; Skorstad et al., 1987). Here we seek to capture human retrieval patterns: Does MAC/FAC duplicate the human propensity for retrieving SF and LS matches rather than AN and FOR matches? The idea is to give MAC/FAC a memory set of stories, then probe with various new stories. To count as a retrieval, a story must make it through both MAC and FAC. We use replication of the ordering found in the psychological data, rather than the exact percentages, as our criterion for success because this measure is more robust, being less sensitive to the detailed properties of the databases.

For the computational experiments, we encoded predicate calculus representations for 9 of the 20 story sets (45 stories). These stories are used in all three experiments described below.

4.1 Cognitive Simulation Experiment 1

In our first study, we put the 9 base stories in memory, along with the 9 FOR stories which served as distractors. We then used each of the variants—LS, SF, and AN—as probes. This roughly resembles the original task, but MAC/FAC's job is easier in that (1) it has only 18 stories in memory, while subjects had 32, in addition to their vast background knowledge; (2) subjects were tested after a week's delay, so that there could have been some degradation of the memory representations.

Table 28.3 shows the proportion of times the base story made it through MAC and (then) through FAC. The FAC output is what corresponds to human retrievals. MAC/FAC's performance is much better than that of the human subjects, perhaps partly because of the differences noted above. However, the key point is that its results show the same ordering as those of human subjects: LS > SF > AN.

4.2 Cognitive Simulation Experiment 2

To give MAC/FAC a harder challenge, we put the four variants of each base story into memory. This made a larger memory set (36 stories) and also one

Table 28.4
Mean numbers of different match types retrieved per probe when base stories are used as probes

Retrievals	MAC	FAC
LS	0.78	0.78
SF	0.78	0.44
TA	0.33	0.22
FOR	0.22	0.0
Other	1.33	0.22

Notes.
1. Memory contains 36 stories (LS, SF, AN, and FOR for 9 story sets); the 9 base stories used as probes
2. Other = any retrieval from a story set different from the one to which the base belongs.

with many competing similar choices. Each base story in turn was used as a probe. This is almost the reverse of the task subjects faced, and is more difficult.

Table 28.4 shows the mean number of matches of different similarity types that succeed in getting through MAC and (then) through FAC. There are several interesting points to note here. First, the retrieval results (i.e., the number that make it through both stages) ordinally match the results for human subjects: LS > SF > AN > FOR. This degree of fit is encouraging, given the difference in task. Second, as expected, MAC produces some matches that are rejected by FAC. This number depends partly on the criteria for the two stages. Here, with MAC and FAC both set at 10%, the mean number of memory items produced by MAC for a given probe is 3.4, and the mean number accepted by FAC is 1.6. Third, as expected, FAC succeeds in acting as a structural filter on the MAC matches. It accepts all of the LS matches MAC proposes and some of the partial matches (i.e., SF and AN), while rejecting most of the inappropriate matches (i.e., FOR and matches with stories from other sets).

4.3 Cognitive Simulation Experiment 3
In the prior simulations, LS matches were the resounding winner. While this is reassuring, it is also interesting to know which matches would be retrieved if there were no perfect overall matches. Therefore we removed the LS variants from memory and repeated the second simulation experiment, again probing with the base stories. SF matches were the clear winners in both the MAC and FAC stages. Again, the ordinal results match well with those of subjects: SF > AN > FOR.

4.4 Summary of Cognitive Simulation Experiments
The results are encouraging. First, MAC/FAC's retrieval results (i.e., the number that make it through both stages) ordinally match the results for human subjects: LS > SF > AN > FOR. Second, as expected, MAC produces some

matches that are rejected by FAC. The mean number of memory items produced by MAC is 3.4 and the mean number accepted by FAC is 1.6. Third, FAC succeeds in its job as a structural filter on the MAC matches. It accepts all of the LS matches proposed by MAC and some of the partial matches (the SF, AN, and FOR matches) and rejects most of the inappropriate matches (the "other" matches from different story sets). It might seem puzzling that FAC accepts more SF matches than AN matches, when it normally would prefer AN over SF. The reason is that it is not generally being offered this choice. Rather, it must choose the best from the matches passed on by MAC for a given probe (which might be AN and LS, or SF and LS, for example).

It is useful to compare MAC/FAC's performance with that of Thagard, Holyoak, Nelson and Gochfeld's (1990) ARCS model of similarity-based retrieval, the most comparable alternate model. Thagard et al. gave ARCS the "Karla the Hawk" story in memory along with 100 fables as distractors. When given the four similarity variants as probes, ARCS produced asymptotic activations as follows: LS (.67), FOR (−.11), SF (−.17), AN (−.27). ARCS thus exhibits at least two violations of the LS ≥ SF > AN ≥ FOR order found for human remindings. First, SF remindings, which should be about as likely as LS remindings, are quite infrequent in ARCS—less frequent than even the FOR matches. Second, AN matches are less frequent than FOR matches in ARCS, whereas for humans AN was always ordinally greater than FOR and (in Experiment 1) significantly so. Thus MAC/FAC explains the data better than ARCS. This is especially interesting because Thagard et al. argue that a complex localist connectionist network which integrates semantic, structural, and pragmatic constraints is required to model similarity-based reminding. While such models are intriguing, MAC/FAC shows that a simpler model can provide a better account of the data. Section 6 outlines experiments comparing MAC/FAC with ARCS.

Finally, and most importantly, MAC/FAC's overall pattern of behavior captures the motivating phenomena. It allows for structured representations and for processes of structural alignment and mapping over these representations thus satisfying the *structural representation* and *structured mappings* criteria. It produces fewer analogical matches than literal similarity or surface matches, thus satisfying the *existence of rare insights* criterion. The majority of its retrievals are LS matches, thus satisfying the *primacy of the mundane* criterion. It also produces a fairly large number of SF matches, thus satisfying the *surface superiority* criterion. Finally, its algorithms are simple enough to apply over large-scale memories, thus satisfying the *scalability* criterion.

5 Sensitivity Analyses

The experiments of the previous section show that the MAC/FAC model can account for psychological retrieval data. This section looks more closely into *why* it does, by seeing how sensitive the results are to different factors in the model. These analyses are similar in spirit to those carried out by VanLehn (1989) in his SIERRA project. VanLehn used his model to generate different possible learning sequences to see if these variations covered the space of observed mistakes made by human learners in subtraction problems. Thus variations in the model were used to generate hypotheses about the space of individual differences. Our methodology is quite similar, in that we vary aspects of our model in order to better understand how it accounts for data. The key difference is that we are not attempting to model individual differences, but instead are investigating how our results depend on different aspects of the theory. Such *sensitivity analyses* are routinely used in other areas of science and engineering; we believe they are also an important tool for cognitive modeling.

Sensitivity analyses can provide insight into why a simulation works. Any working cognitive simulation rests on a large number of design choices. Examples of design choices include the setting of parameters, the kinds of data provided as input, and even the particular algorithms used. Some of these design choices are forced by the theory being tested, some choices are only weakly constrained by the theory, and others are irrelevant to the theory being tested, but are necessary to create a working artifact. Sensitivity analyses can help verify that the source of a simulation's performance rests with the theoretically important design choices. Varying theoretically forced choices should lead to a degradation of the simulation's ability to replicate human performance. Otherwise, the source of the performance lies elsewhere. On the other hand, varying theoretically irrelevant choices should not affect the results, and if they do, it suggests that something other than the motivating theory is responsible for the simulator's performance. Finally, seeing how the ability to match human performance varies with parameters that are only weakly constrained by theory can lead to insights about why the model works.

The original paper (Forbus, Gentner & Law, 1995) details the method, data, and results of the sensitivity analyses. Here we briefly summarize the results:

- MAC/FAC's ability to model the data is robust with respect to choice of parameters. That is, varying the selector widths shows that there is a reasonably wide range of widths that fits the data, and extreme values fail to fit for reasons that fit the theoretical claims
- The results are not sensitive to the particular details of the normalization algorithm chosen for content vectors. This is important because the normalization algorithm is not a theoretically constrained choice, so our results should not rely critically on it.
- Content vectors need to include both attribute and relational information. Using attribute information alone leads to a violation of the *rare insights* criterion, and using relational information alone leads to a violation of the *scalability criterion*.

6 Comparing MAC/FAC and ARCS on ARCS Datasets

As mentioned earlier, the model of similarity-based retrieval that is closest to MAC/FAC is ARCS (Thagard, et al., 1990). ARCS uses a localist connectionist network to apply semantic, structural, and pragmatic constraints to selecting items from memory. Most of the work in ARCS is carried out by the constraint satisfaction network, which provides an elegant mechanism for integrating the disparate constraints that Thagard et al. postulates as important to retrieval. The use of competition in retrieval is designed to reduce the number of candidates retrieved. Using pragmatic information provides a means for the system's goals to affect the retrieval process. After the network settles, an ordering can be placed on nodes representing retrieval hypotheses based on their activation. Unfortunately, no formal criterion was ever specified by which a subset of these retrieval hypotheses is selected to be considered as what is retrieved by ARCS. Consequently, in our experiments we mainly focused on the subset of retrieval nodes mentioned by Thagard et al. (1990) in their article.

6.1 Theoretical Tradeoffs

Both models have their appeals and drawbacks. Here we briefly examine several of each.

- *Pragmatic effects:* In MAC/FAC it is assumed that pragmatics and context affect retrieval by influencing what is encoded in the probe. That is, we assume that plans and goals are important enough to be explicitly represented, and hence will affect retrieval. In ARCS, additional influence can be placed on particular subsets of such information by the user marking it as important.
- *Utility of results:* Because MAC/FAC uses SME in the FAC stage, the result of retrieval can include novel candidate inferences. Because the purpose of retrieval is to find new knowledge to apply to the probe, this is a substantial advantage. ARCS could close this gap somewhat by using ACME (Holyoak & Thagard, 1989) as a postprocessor.
- *Initial filtering:* MAC/FAC's content vectors represent the overall pattern of predicates occurring in a structured description, so that the dot product cheaply estimates overlap. ARCS' commitment to creating a network if there is any predicate overlap places more of the retrieval burden on the expensive process of setting up networks. The inclusive rather than exclusive nature of ARCS' initial stage leads to the paradoxical fact that a system in which pragmatic constraints are central must ignore CAUSE, IF, and other inferentially important predicates to be tractable.
- *Modeling inter-item effects:* Wharton et al. (1994) have shown that ARCS can model effects of competition between memory items in heightening the relative effect of structural similarity to the probe.

Perhaps the most important issue is the notion of *semantic similarity* (Holyoak & Thagard, 1989). A key issue in analogical processing is what criterion should be used to decide if two elements can be placed into correspondence. The FAC stage of MAC/FAC follows the standard structure-mapping position that *analogy is concerned with discovering identical relational systems*. Thus, other elements can be matched flexibly in service of relational matching: any two entities can be placed in correspondence, and functions can be matched non-identically if doing so enables a larger structure to match. But relations have only three choices: they can match identically, as in (a); they can fail to match, as in (b); or, if the surrounding structural match warrants it, they can be re-represented in such a way that part of their representation now matches identically, as in the shift from (c) to (d).

(a)   HEAVIER [camel, cow]——HEAVIER [giraffe, donkey]

(b)   HEAVIER [camel, cow]——BITE [dromedary, calf]

(c)   HEAVIER [camel, cow]——TALLER [giraffe, donkey]

(d)   GREATER [WEIGHT(camel), WEIGHT(cow)]——GREATER [HEIGHT(camel), HEIGHT(cow)].

The question is, how to formalize the requirement of common relational content. Structure-mapping uses the idea of *tiered identicality*. The default criterion of identical relational predicates, which we call the *simple identicality* criterion, is a very strict semantic similarity constraint. Simple identicality of conceptual relations is an excellent first-pass criterion because it is computationally cheap. However, there are circumstances where criteria requiring more processing are worthwhile (e.g., when placing two items in correspondence would allow a larger, or very relevant, structure to be mapped, as in Falkenhainer's [1990] work). One such test is *minimal ascension* (Falkenhainer, 1990) which allows two items to be placed into correspondence if their predicates have close common superordinates. Another technique is *decomposition*: Two concepts that are similar but not identical (such as "bestow" and "bequeath") are decomposed into a canonical representation language so that their similarity is expressed as partial identity (here, roughly, "give"). Decomposition is the simplest form of *re-representation* (Gentner, 1989; Gentner & Rattermann, 1991), where additional knowledge is used to reformulate a description in order to achieve a better match.

ACME and ARCS also share the intuition that analogy is a kind of compromise between similarity of larger structures and similarity of individual elements. But their local similarity metric is different. Their systems use graded similarity at all levels and for all kinds of predicates; relations have no special status. Thus ARCS and ACME might find pair (b) above more similar than pair (a) because of the object similarity. This would not be true for SME and MAC/FAC.

In ACME, semantic similarity was operationalized using similarity tables. For any potential matching term, a similarity table was used to assign a similarity rating, which was then combined with other evidence to decide whether the two predicates could match. Thus, in the examples above, both pair (b) and pair (c) stand a good chance of being matched, depending on the stored similarities between TALLER, HEAVIER, and BITE, camel, dromedary and giraffe, and so on. ARCS used a subset of WordNet (Miller, Fellbaum, Kegl & Miller, 1988) to calculate semantic similarity, identifying predicates with corresponding lexical concepts and using links in the lexical database to suggest what predicates could be placed into correspondence.

We prefer our tiered identicality account, which uses inexpensive inference techniques to suggest ways to re-represent non-identical relations into a canonical representation language. Such canonicalization has many advantages for complex, rich knowledge systems, where meaning arises from the axioms that predicates participate in. When mismatches occur in a context where it is desirable to make the match, we assume that people make use of techniques of re-representation. An example of an inexpensive inference technique to suggest re-representation is Falkenhainer's (1990) *minimal ascension* method, which looks for common superordinates when context suggested that two predicates should match. The use of pure identicality augmented by minimal ascension allowed Falkenhainer's PHINEAS system to model the discovery of a variety of physical theories by analogy.

Holyoak and Thagard (1989) have argued that broader (i.e., weaker) notions of semantic similarity are crucial in retrieval, for otherwise we would suffer from too many missed retrievals. Although this at first sounds reasonable, there is a counterargument based on memory size. Human memories are far larger than any cognitive simulation yet constructed. In such a case, the problem of false positives (i.e., too many irrelevant retrievals) becomes critical. False negatives are of course a problem, but they can be overcome to some extent by reformulating and re-representing the probe, treating memory access as an iterative process interleaved with other forms of reasoning. Thus it could be argued that strong semantic similarity constraints, combined with re-representation, are crucial in retrieval as well as in mapping.

How do these different accounts of semantic similarity fare in predicting patterns of retrieval? Forbus, Gentner, and Law (1995) describe a series of computational experiments on MAC/FAC and ARCS that investigate this issue. For brevity, we summarize the results here:

- MAC/FAC operates well on stimuli developed for testing ARCS. On the other hand, ARCS cannot successfully operate on the stimuli developed for testing MAC/FAC, failing to converge after thousands of iterations and 12 hours of CPU time.
- MAC/FAC produces similar results to ARCS on ARCS datasets.

- Combining ARCS datasets, to yield larger memory sets, causes ARCS' behavior to degrade. Specifically, it retrieves items based on size more than overlap. MAC/FAC's behavior with additional distractors remains unchanged.
- Thagard et al. used relative activation strengths as an estimate of relative retrieval frequencies, to argue that ARCS modeled the "Karla the Hawk" results. Unfortunately, ARCS' relative activation strengths vary strongly with the particular memory distractors used and sometimes include reversals of the ordinal relationships found in humans.
- Replacing the ARCS notion of semantic similarity with our stronger pure identicality constraint improved ARCS' ability to model the data, but it still fell short of MAC/FAC in this regard.

Our experiments provide evidence that structure-mapping's identicality constraint better fits retrieval patterns than Thagard et al.'s notion of semantic similarity. In retrieval, the special demands of large memories argue for simpler algorithms, simply because the cost of false positives is much higher. If retrieval were a one-shot, all-or-nothing operation, the cost of false negatives would be higher. But that is not the case. In normal situations, retrieval is an iterative process, interleaved with the construction of the representations being used. Thus the cost of false negatives is reduced by the chance that reformulation of the probe, due to re-representation and inference, will subsequently catch a relevant memory that slipped by once.

Finally, we note that while ARCS' use of a localist connectionist network to implement constraint satisfaction is in many ways intuitively appealing, it is by no means clear that such implementations are neurally plausible. The evidence suggests that MAC/FAC captures similarity-based retrieval phenomena better than ARCS does.

7 Discussion

To understand the role of similarity in transfer requires making fine distinctions both about similarity and about transfer. The psychological evidence indicates that the accessibility of matches from memory is strongly influenced by surface commonalities and weakly influenced by structural commonalities, while the rated inferential soundness of comparisons is strongly influenced by structural commonalities and little, if at all, influenced by surface commonalities. An account of similarity in transfer must deal with this disassociation between retrieval and structural alignment: between the matches people *get* from memory and the matches they *want*.

The MAC/FAC model of similarity-based retrieval captures both the fact that humans successfully store and retrieve intricate relational structures and the fact that access to these stored structures is heavily (though not entirely) surface-driven. The first stage is attentive to content and blind to structure and the second stage is attentive to both content and structure. The MAC stage uses content vectors, a novel summary of structured representations, to provide an inexpensive "wide net" search of memory, whose results are pruned by the more expensive literal similarity matcher of the FAC stage to arrive at useful, structurally sound matches.

The simulation results presented here demonstrate that MAC/FAC can simulate the patterns of access exhibited by human subjects. It displays the appropriate preponderance of literal similarity and surface matches, and it occasionally retrieves purely relational matches (Section 4). Our sensitivity studies suggest that these results are a consequence of our theory and are not hostage to non-theoretically motivated parameters or algorithmic choices (Section 5). Our computational experiments comparing MAC/FAC and ARCS (Section 6) suggest that MAC/FAC both accounts for the psychological results more accurately and more robustly than ARCS. In addition to the experiments reported here, we have tested MAC/FAC on a variety of other data sets, including relational metaphors (30 descriptions, averaging 12 propositions each) and attribute-rich descriptions of physical situations as might be found in common-sense reasoning (12 descriptions, averaging 42 propositions each). We have also tried various combinations of these databases with the "Karla the Hawk" data set (45 descriptions, averaging 67 propositions each). In all cases to date MAC/FAC's performance has been satisfactory and consistent with the overall pattern of findings regarding human retrieval. We conclude that MAC/FAC's two-stage retrieval process is a promising model of human retrieval.

7.1 Limitations and Open Questions

7.1.1 Retrieval Failure   Sometimes a probe reminds us of nothing. Currently the only way this can happen in the MAC/FAC model is for FAC to reject every candidate provided by MAC. This can happen if no structurally sound match hypotheses can be generated between the probe and the descriptions output by MAC. (Without any local correspondences there can be no interpretation of the comparison.) This can happen, albeit rarely. A variant of MAC/FAC with thresholds on the output of either or the both MAC and FAC stages—so that the system would return nothing if the best match were below criterion— would show more non-remindings.

7.1.2 Focused Remindings and Penetrability   Many AI retrieval programs and cognitive simulations elevate the reasoner's current goals to a central role in their theoretical accounts (e.g., Burstein, 1989; Hammond, 1986, 1989; Keane, 1988a,b; Riesbeck & Schank, 1989; Thagard, Holyoak, Nelson & Gochfeld, 1990). Although we agree with the claim that goal structures are important, MAC/FAC does not give goals a separate status in retrieval. Rather, we assume that the person's current goals are represented as part of the higher-order structure of the probe. The assumption is that goals are embedded in a relational structure linking them to the rest of the situation; they play a role in retrieval, but the rest of the situational factors must participate as well. When one is hungry, for instance, presumably the ways of getting food that come to mind are different if one is standing in a restaurant, a supermarket, or the middle of a forest. The inclusion of current goals as part of the representation of the probe is consistent with the finding of Read and Cesa (1991) that asking subjects for explanations of current scenarios leads to a relatively high rate of analogical reminding. However, we see no reason to elevate goals above other kinds of higher-order structure. By treating goals as just one of many kinds of higher-order structures, we escape making the erroneous prediction of many case-based reasoning systems: that retrieval requires common goals. People can retrieve information that was originally stored under different goal structures. (See Goldstein, Kedar & Bareiss, 1993, for a discussion of this point.)

A related question concerns the degree to which the results of each stage are inspectable and tunable. We assume that the results of the FAC stage are inspectable, but that explicit awareness of the results of the MAC stage is lacking. We conjecture that one can get a sense that there are possible matches in the MAC output, and perhaps some impression of how strong the matches are, but not what those items are. The feeling of being reminded without being able to remember the actual item might correspond to having candidates generated by MAC which are all either too weak to pass on or are rejected by the FAC stage. Some support for this two-stage account comes from Metcalfe's (1993) findings on feeling-of-knowing. She found that subjects report a general sense of feeling-of-knowing *before* they can report a particular retrieval. Reder (1988) suggests that this preretrieval sense of feeling-of-knowing might provide the basis for deciding whether to pursue and expect retrieval.

The idea that FAC, though not MAC, is tunable is consistent with evidence that people can be selective in similarity matching once both members of a pair are present. For example, in a triads task, matching XX to OO or XO, subjects can readily choose either only relational matches (XX–OO) or only surface matches (XX–XO) (Goldstone et al., 1991; Medin et al., 1993). This kind of structural selectivity in the similarity processor is readily modeled in SME (by assuming that we select the interpretation that fits the task constraints), but not in ACME (Holyoak & Thagard, 1989). ACME produces one best output that is its best compromise among the current constraints. It can be induced to produce different preferred mappings by inputting different pragmatic activations, but not by inviting different structural preferences (Spellman & Holyoak, 1992).

7.1.3 Size of Content Vectors   One potential problem with scaling up MAC/FAC is the potential growth in the size of content vectors. Our current descriptions use a vocabulary of only a few hundred distinct predicates. We implement content vectors via sparse encoding techniques, analogous to those used in computational matrix algebra, for efficiency. However, a psychologically plausible representation vocabulary may have hundreds of thousands of predicates. It is not obvious that our sparse encoding techniques will suffice for vocabularies that large, nor does this implementation address the question of how systems with limited "hardware bandwidth," such as connectionist implementations, could serve as a substrate for this model. Two possible solutions, semantic compression and factorization, are discussed in Forbus, Gentner, and Law (1995).

7.1.4 Combining Similarity Effects Across Items   MAC/FAC is currently a purely exemplar-based memory system. The memory items can be highly situation-specific encodings of perceptual stimuli, abstract mathematical descriptions, causal scenarios, etc. Regardless of the content, MAC/FAC lacks the capacity to average across several items at retrieval (Medin & Schaffer, 1978) or to derive a global sense of familiarity by combining the activations of multiple retrievals (Gillund & Shiffrin, 1984; Hintzman, 1986, 1988). An interesting extension of MAC/FAC would be to include this kind of between-item processing upon retrieval. If such inter-item averaging occurs, it could provide a route to the incremental construction of abstractions and indexing information in memory.

7.1.5 Iterative Access   Keane (1988) and Burstein (1983) have proposed incremental mapping processes, and we suggest that similarity-based retrieval may also be an iterative process. In particular, in active retrieval (as opposed to spontaneous remindings) we conjecture that MAC/FAC may be used iteratively, each time modifying the probe in response to the previous match (c.f. Falkenhainer, 1990; Gentner, 1989). Suppose, for example, a probe yielded several partial remindings. The system of matches could provide clues as to which aspects of the probe are more or less relevant, and thus should be highlighted or suppressed on the next iteration. MAC should respond to this altered vector by returning more relevant items, and FAC can then select the best of these.

Another advantage of such incremental reminding is that it might help explain how we derive new relational categories. Barsalou's (1982, 1987) *ad hoc* categories, such as "things to take on a picnic" and Glucksberg and Keysar's (1990) metaphorically based categories, such as "jail" as a prototypical confining institution, are examples of the kinds of abstract relational commonalities that might be highlighted during a process of incremental retrieval and mapping.

7.1.6 Embedding in Performance-Oriented Models   MAC/FAC is not itself a complete analogical processing system. For example, both constructing a model from multiple analogs (e.g., Burstein, 1983) and learning a domain theory by analogy (e.g., Falkenhainer, 1990) require multiple iterations of accessing, mapping, and evaluating descriptions. Several psychological questions about access cannot be studied without embedding MAC/FAC in a more comprehensive model of analogical processing. First, as discussed above, there is ample evidence that subjects can choose to focus on different kinds of similarity when the items being compared are both already in working memory. Embedding MAC/FAC in a larger system should help make clear whether this penetrability should be modeled as applying to the FAC system or to a separate similarity engine. (Order effects in analogical problem solving [Keane, 1990] suggest the latter.)

A second issue that requires a larger, performance-oriented model to explore via simulation is when and how pragmatic constraints should be incorporated (cf. Holyoak & Thagard, 1989; Thagard et al., 1990). Since we assume that goals, plans, and similar control knowledge are explicitly represented in working memory, the MAC stage will include such predicates in the content vector for the probe and, hence, will be influenced by pragmatic concerns. There are two ways to model the effects of pragmatics on the FAC stage. The first is to use the SME *pragmatic marking algorithm* (Forbus & Oblinger, 1990) as a relevance filter. The second is to use incremental mapping, as in Keane and Brayshaw's (1988) Incremental Analogy Machine (IAM).

7.1.7 Expertise and Relational Access Despite the gloomy picture of surface-based retrieval painted in the present research and in most of the problem-solving research, there is evidence of considerable relational access (a) for experts in a domain and (b) when initial encoding of the study set is relatively intensive. Novick (1988) studied remindings for mathematics problems using novice and expert mathematics students. She found that experts were more likely than novices to retrieve a structurally similar prior problem, and when they did retrieve a surface-similar problem, they were quicker to reject it than were novices.

The second contributor to relational retrieval is intensive encoding (Seifert, 1994). Gick and Holyoak (1988) and Catrambone and Holyoak (1987) found that subjects exhibited increased relational retrieval when they were required to compare two prior analogs, but not when they were simply given two prior analogs. Seifert, McKoon, Abelson, and Ratcliff (1986) investigated priming effects in a sentence verification task between thematically similar (analogical) stories. They obtained priming when subjects first studied a list of themes and then judged the thematic similarity of pairs of stories, but not when subjects simply read the stories.

The increase of relational reminding with expertise and with intensive encoding can be accommodated in the MAC/FAC model. First, we assume that experts have richer and better structured representations of the relations in the content domain than do novices (Carey, 1985; Chi, 1978). This fits with developmental evidence that as children come to notice and encode higher-order relations such as *symmetry* and *monotonicity*, their appreciation of abstract similarity increases (Gentner & Rattermann, 1991). Second, we speculate that experts may have a more uniform internal relational vocabulary within the domain of expertise than do novices (Clement, Mawby & Giles, 1994; Gentner & Rattermann, 1991). The idea is that experts tend to have relatively comprehensive theories in a domain and that this promotes canonical relational encodings within the domain.

To the extent that a given higher-order relational pattern is used to encode a given situation, it will be automatically incorporated into MAC/FAC's content vector. This means that any higher-order relational concept that is widely used in a domain will tend to increase the uniformity of the representations in memory. This increased uniformity should increase the mutual accessibility of situations within the domain. Thus, as experts come to encode a domain according to a uniform set of principles, the likelihood of appropriate relational remindings increases. That is, under the MAC/FAC model, the differences in retrieval patterns for novices and experts are explained in terms of differences in knowledge, rather than by the construction of explicit indices.

Bassok has made an interesting argument that indirectly supports this claim of greater relational uniformity for experts than for novices (Bassok, Wu & Olseth, 1995). Noting prior findings that in forming representations of novel texts people's interpretations of verbs depend on the nouns attached to them (Gentner, 1981; Gentner & France, 1988), Bassok suggests that particular representations of the relational structure may thus be idiosyncratically related to the surface content, and that this is one contributor to the poor relational access. If this is true, and if we are correct in our supposition that experts tend to have a relatively uniform relational vocabulary, then an advantage for experts in relational access would be predicted.

As domain expertise increases, MAC/FAC's activity may come to resemble a multi-goal, case-based reasoning model with complex indices (e.g., Birnbaum & Collins, 1989; King & Bareiss, 1989; Martin, 1989; Pazzani, 1989; Porter, 1989). We can think of its content vectors as indices with the property that they change automatically with any change in the representation of domain exemplars. Thus as domain knowledge—particularly the higher-order relational vocabulary—increases, MAC/FAC may come to have sufficiently elaborated representations to permit a fairly high proportion of relational remindings. The case-based reasoning emphasis on retrieving prior examples and generalizations that are inferentially useful may thus be a reasonable approximation to the way experts retrieve knowledge.

7.2 The Decomposition of Similarity

The dissociation between surface similarity and structural similarity across different processes has broader implications for cognition. It is consistent with arguments that similarity is pluralistic (Medin et al., 1993; Gentner, 1989) and that there is a dissociation between (surface) similarity, typicality, and categorization (Rips, 1989). Further, consistent with SME's local-to-global matching algorithm, local object matches appear to be processed faster by adults than structural commonalities (Goldstone & Medin, 1994).

These kinds of results render less plausible the notion of a unitary similarity that governs retrieval, evaluation, and inference. Instead, they suggest a more complex view of similarity. MAC/FAC provides an architecture that demonstrates how such a pluralistic notion of similarity can be organized to account for psychological data on retrieval.

Acknowledgments

This research was supported by the Office of Naval Research (Contract No. N00014-89-J-1272). We thank Ray Bareiss, Mark Burstein, Gregg Collins, Ron Ferguson, Brian Falkenhainer, Rob Goldstone, Art Markman, Doug Medin, and Mary Jo Rattermann for discussions of these issues. We thank Paul Thagard for providing us with ARCS and its associated databases.

Notes

1. We define the order of an item in a representation as follows: Objects and constants are order 0. The order of a statement is one plus the maximum of the order of its arguments.
2. We make minimal assumptions concerning the global structure of long-term memory. We assume here only that there is a large pool of descriptions from which we must select one or a few that are most similar to a probe. We are uncommitted as to whether the pool is the whole of long-term memory or a subset selected via some other method, e.g., spreading activation.
3. The worst case parallel time would be $O(n)$, in degenerate cases where all but one of the local matches is proposed by matching arguments.
4. The original exhaustive merge algorithm was worst-case factorial in the number of "clumps" of match hypotheses (kernels), but in practice was often quite efficient. See Falkenhainer, Forbus, and Gentner (1989) for details.
5. In our current implementation SME is run sequentially on each candidate item in turn, but this is an artifact of the implementation.
6. Our original version of SME had distinct modes for analogy, literal similarity, and appearance matches. We eliminated modes in favor of always being sensitive to both attributes and relations (i.e., what was called literal similarity mode) on psychological grounds, since the kind of comparison will arise from the descriptions being compared.
7. LS and SF did not differ significantly in retrievability. In Experiment 2, AN and FOR did not differ significantly, although in Experiment 1 AN matches were better retrieved than FOR matches.

References

Bareiss, R., & King, J. A. (1989). Similarity assessment in case-based reasoning. *Proceedings: Case-Based Reasoning Workshop* (pp. 67–71). San Mateo, CA: Kaufmann.

Barsalou, L. W. (1982). Context-independent and context-dependent information in concepts. *Memory and Cognition, 10*, 82–93.

Barsalou, L. W. (1987). The instability of graded structure: Implications for the nature of concepts. In U. Neisser (Ed.), *Concepts and conceptual development: Ecological and intellectual factors in categorization*. Cambridge, England: Cambridge University Press.

Bassok, M., Wu, L., & Olseth, K. L. (1995). Judging a book by its cover: Interpretative effects of content on problem solving transfer. *Memory & Cognition, 23*(3), 354–367.

Becker, L., & Jazayeri, K. (1989). A connectionist approach to case-based reasoning. *Proceedings: Case-Based Reasoning Workshop* (pp. 213–217). San Mateo, CA: Morgan Kaufmann.

Birnbaum, L., & Collins, G. (1989). Remindings and engineering design themes: A case study in indexing vocabulary. *Proceedings: Case-Based Reasoning Workshop* (pp. 47–51). San Mateo, CA: Morgan Kaufmann.

Brown, A. L. (1989). Analogical learning and transfer: What develops? In S. Vosniadou & A. Ortony (Eds.), *Similarity and analogical reasoning* (pp. 369–412). Cambridge, England: Cambridge University Press.

Burstein, M. H. (1983a). Concept formation by incremental analogical reasoning and debugging. *Proceedings of the International Machine Learning Workshop* (pp. 19–25), Monticello, IL. Urbana: University of Illinois.

Burstein, M. H. (1983b). A model of learning by incremental analogical reasoning and debugging. *Proceedings of the National Conference on Artificial Intelligence* (pp. 45–48), Washington, DC. Los Altos, CA: Morgan Kaufmann.

Burstein, M. (1989). Analogy vs. CBR: The purpose of mapping. *Proceedings: Case-Based Reasoning Workshop* (pp. 133–136). San Mateo, CA: Morgan Kaufmann.

Carey, S. (1985). *Conceptual change in childhood.* Cambridge, MA: MIT Press.

Catrambone, R., & Holyoak, K. J. (May, 1987). *Do novices have schemas?* Paper presented at the Fifty-Second Annual Meeting of the Midwestern Psychological Association, Chicago, IL.

Chi, M. T. H. (1978). Knowledge structures and memory development. In R. S. Siegler (Ed.), *Children's thinking: What develops?* (pp. 73–96). Hillsdale, NJ: Erlbaum.

Clement, J. (1986). Methods for evaluating the validity of hypothesized analogies. *Proceedings of the Eighth Annual Conference of the Cognitive Science Society,* (pp. 223–234), Amherst, MA. Hillsdale, NJ: Erlbaum.

Clement, C. A., & Gentner, D. (1991). Systematicity as a selection constraint in analogical mapping. *Cognitive Science, 15,* 89–132.

Clement, C. A., Mawby, R., & Giles, D. E. (1994). The effects of manifest relational similarity on analog retrieval. *Journal of Memory and Language, 33,* 396–420.

Elio, R., & Anderson, J. R. (1981). The effects of category generalizations and instance similarity on schema abstraction. *Journal of Experimental Psychology: Human Learning and Memory, 7,* 397–417.

Elio, R., & Anderson, J. R. (1984). The effects of information order and learning mode on schema abstraction. *Memory & Cognition, 12,* 20–30.

Falkenhainer, B. (1988). *Learning from physical analogies: A study of analogy and the explanation process* (Tech. Rep. No. UIUCDCS-R-88-1479). Urbana: University of Illinois, Department of Computer Science.

Falkenhainer, B. (1990). A unified approach to explanation and theory formation. In Shrager, J. and Langley, P. (Eds.) *Computational models of scientific discovery and theory formation* (pp. 157–196). Los Altos, CA. Morgan Kaufmann.

Falkenhainer, B., Forbus, K. D., & Gentner, D. (1986). The structure-mapping engine. *Proceedings of the Fifth National Conference on Artificial Intelligence* (pp. 272–277). Los Altos, CA: Morgan Kaufmann.

Falkenhainer, B., Forbus, K., & Gentner, D. (1989). The structure-mapping engine: Algorithm and examples. *Artificial Intelligence, 41,* 1–63.

Forbus, K., & Gentner, D. (1986). Learning physical domains: Towards a theoretical framework. In R. S. Michalski, J. G. Carbonell, & T. M. Mitchell (Eds.), *Machine learning: An artificial intelligence approach* (Vol. 2, pp. 311–348). Los Altos, CA: Morgan Kaufmann.

Forbus, K., & Gentner, D. (1989). Structural evaluation of analogies: What counts? *Proceedings of the Eleventh Annual Conference of the Cognitive Science Society* (pp. 341–348), Ann Arbor, MI. Hillsdale, NJ: Erlbaum.

Forbus, K., Gentner, D., & Law, K. (1995). MAC/FAC: A model of similarity-based retrieval. *Cognitive Science*, 19(2), April–June, pp. 141–205.

Forbus, K. D., & Oblinger, D. (1990). Making SME greedy and pragmatic. *Proceedings of the Twelfth Annual Conference of the Cognitive Science Society* (pp. 61–68), Cambridge, MA. Hillsdale, NJ: Erlbaum.

Gentner, D. (1981). Some interesting differences between nouns and verbs. *Cognition and Brain Theory*, 4(2), 161–178.

Gentner, D. (1983). Structure-mapping: A theoretical framework for analogy. *Cognitive Science, 7*, 155–170.

Gentner, D. (1989). The mechanisms of analogical learning. In S. Vosniadou & A. Ortony (Eds.), *Similarity and analogical reasoning* (pp. 199–241). New York: Cambridge University Press.

Gentner, D., & Clement, C. (1988). Evidence for relational selectivity in the interpretation of analogy and metaphor. In G. H. Bower (Ed.), *The psychology of learning and motivation* (Vol. 22, pp. 307–358).

Gentner, D., & France, I. M. (1988). The verb mutability effect: Studies of the combinatorial semantics of nouns and verbs. In S. L. Small, G. W. Cottrell, & M. K. Tanenhaus (Eds.), *Lexical ambiguity resolution: Perspective from psycholinguistics, neuropsychology, and artificial intelligence* (pp. 343–382). San Mateo, CA: Morgan Kaufmann.

Gentner, D., & Landers, R. (1985). Analogical reminding: A good match is hard to find. *Proceedings of the International Conference on Cybernetics and Society* (pp. 607–613), Tucson, AZ.

Gentner, D., & Markman, A. B. (1993). Analogy: Watershed or Waterloo: Structural alignment and the development of connectionist models of cognition. In S. J. Hanson, J. D. Cowan, & C. L. Giles (Eds.), *Advances in neural information processing systems 5* (pp. 855–862). San Mateo, CA: Morgan Kaufmann.

Gentner, D., & Markman, A. B. (1995). Similarity is like analogy: Structural alignment in comparison. In C. Cacciari (Ed.), *Similarity in language, thought and perception* (pp. 111–147). Brussels: BREPOLS.

Gentner, D., & Rattermann, M. J. (1991). Language and the career of similarity. In S. A. Gelman & J. P. Brynes (Eds.), *Perspectives on language and thought: Interrelations in development* (pp. 225–277).

Gentner, D., Rattermann, M. J., & Forbus, K. D. (1993). The roles of similarity in transfer: Separating retrievability from inferential soundness. *Cognitive Psychology* 25, 524–575.

Gentner, D., Rattermann, M. J., Kotovsky, L., & Markman, A. B. (1995). The development of relational similarity. In G. Halford & T. Simon (Eds.), *Developing cognitive competence: New approaches to process modeling*. Hillsdale, NJ: Erlbaum.

Gick, M. L., & Holyoak, K. J. (1980). Analogical problem solving. *Cognitive Psychology, 12*, 306–355.

Gick, M. L., & Holyoak, K. J. (1983). Schema induction and analogical transfer. *Cognitive Psychology, 15*, 1–38.

Gillund, G., & Shiffrin, R. M. (1984). A retrieval model for both recognition and recall. *Psychology Review, 91*, 1–67.

Glucksberg, S., & Keysar, B. (1990). Understanding metaphorical comparisons: Beyond similarity. *Psychological Review, 97*, 3–18.

Goldstein, E., Kedar, S., & Bareiss, R. (1993). Easing the creation of a multi-purpose case library. *Proceedings of the AAAI-93 Workshop on Case-Based Reasoning* (pp. 12–18), Washington, DC. Menlo Park, CA: AAAI Press.

Goldstone, R. L., & Medin, D. L. (1994). Similarity, interactive-activation and mapping: In K. J. Holyoak & J. A. Barnden (Eds.), *Advances in connectionist and neural computation theory, vol. 2: Connectionist approaches to analogy, metaphor, and case-based reasoning*. Norwood, NJ: Ablex.

Goldstone, R. L., Medin, D., & Gentner, D. (1991). Relational similarity and the non-independence of features in similarity judgments. *Cognitive Psychology, 23*, 222–264.

Gronlund, S. D., & Ratcliff, R. (1989). The time-course of item and associative information: implications for global memory models. *Journal of Experimental Psychology: Learning, Memory, & Cognition, 15,* 846–858.

Halford, G. S. (1992). Analogical reasoning and conceptual complexity in cognitive development. *Human Development, 35,* 193–217.

Hammond, K. J. (1986). CHEF: A model of case-based planning. *Proceedings of the Fifth National Conference on Artificial Intelligence* (pp. 267–271). Philadelphia, PA. Los Altos, CA: Morgan Kaufmann.

Hammond, K. (1989). On functionally motivated vocabularies: An apologia. In *Proceedings: Case-Based Reasoning Workshop,* (pp. 52–56). San Mateo, CA: Morgan Kaufmann.

Hammond, K. J., Seifert, C. M., & Gray, K. C. (1991). Functionality in analogical transfer: A hard match is good to find. *The Journal of the Learning Sciences, 1*(2), 111–152.

Hinton, G. E., & Anderson, J. A. (1989). *Parallel models of associative memory.* Hillsdale, NJ: Erlbaum.

Hintzman, D. L. (1984). MINERVA 2: A simulation model of human memory. *Behavior Research Methods, Instruments, & Computers, 16,* 96–101.

Hintzman, D. (1986). "Schema abstraction" in a multiple-trace memory model. *Psychological Review, 93,* 411–428.

Hintzman, D. L. (1988). Judgments of frequency and recognition memory in a multiple-trace memory model. *Psychological Review, 95,* 528–551.

Holyoak, K. J., & Koh, K. (1987). Surface and structural similarity in analogical transfer. *Memory & Cognition, 15,* 32–340.

Holyoak, K. J., & Barnden, J. A. (1994) *Analogical Connections.* Norwood, NJ: Ablex.

Holyoak, K. J., & Thagard, P. (1989). Analogical mapping by constraint satisfaction. *Cognitive Science, 13,* 295–355.

Humphreys, M. S., Bain, J. D., & Pike, R. (1989). Different ways to cue a coherent memory system: A theory for episodic, semantic, and procedural tasks. *Psychological Review, 2,* 208–233.

Keane, M. (1987a). On retrieving analogues when solving problems. *Quarterly Journal of Experimental Psychology, 39A,* 29–41.

Keane, M. (1987b). Why is analogical thinking fundamental. *AIAI Newsletter, 2,* 19–23.

Keane, M. (1988a). Analogical mechanisms. *Artificial Intelligence Review, 2,* 229–250.

Keane, M. T. (1988b). *Analogical problem solving.* Chichester: Ellis Horwood; New York: Wiley.

Keane, M., & Brayshaw, M. (1988). The incremental analogy machine: A computational model of analogy. *European Session on Machine Learning.* London, England: Pitman.

Keil, F. C. (1989). *Concepts, kinds, and cognitive development.* Cambridge, MA: MIT Press.

King, J., & Bareiss, R. (1989). Similarity assessment in case-based reasoning. *Proceedings: Case-Based Reasoning Workshop* (pp. 67–71). San Mateo: Morgan Kaufmann.

Kolodner, J. L. (1984). *Retrieval and organizational structures in conceptual memory: A computer model.* Hillsdale, NJ: Erlbaum.

Kolodner, J. L. (1988). *Proceedings of the First Case-Based Reasoning Workshop.* Los Altos, CA: Morgan Kaufmann.

Kotovsky, L., & Gentner, D. (1996). Comparison and categorization in the development of relational similarity. *Child Development, 67,* 2797–2822.

Markman, A. B., & Gentner, D. (1993a). Splitting the differences: A structural alignment view of similarity. *Journal of Memory and Language, 32,* 517–535.

Markman, A. B., & Gentner, D. (1993b). Structural alignment during similarity comparisons. *Cognitive Psychology, 25,* 431–467.

Martin, C. (1989, May). Indexing using complex features. In *Proceedings of the Case-Based Reasoning Workshop* (pp. 26–30). San Mateo, CA: Morgan Kaufman.

Medin, D. L., Goldstone, R. L., & Gentner, D. (1993). Respects for similarity. *Psychological Review, 100*(2), 254–278.

Medin, D., & Ortony, A. (1989). Psychological essentialism. In S. Vosniadou & A. Ortony (Eds.), *Similarity and analogical reasoning* (pp. 179–195). New York: Cambridge Univ. Press.

Medin, D. L., & Ross, B. H. (1989). The specific character of abstract thought: Categorization, problem-solving, and induction. In R. J. Sternberg (Ed.), *Advances in the psychology of human intelligence* (Vol. 5, pp. 189–223). Hillsdale, NJ: Erlbaum.

Medin, D. L., & Schaffer, M. M. (1978). Context theory of classification learning. *Psychological Review, 85*, 207–238.

Metcalfe, J. (1993). Novelty monitoring, metacognition, and control in a composite holographic associative recall model: Implications for Korsakoff amnesia. *Psychological Review, 100*(1), 3–22.

Minsky, M. (1981). A framework for representing knowledge. In J. Haugland (Ed.), *Mind design* (pp. 95–128). Cambridge, MA: MIT Press.

Murphy, G. L., & Medin, D. L. (1985). The role of theories in conceptual coherence. *Psychological Review, 92*, 289–316.

Novick, L. R. (1988a). Analogical transfer: Processes and individual differences. In D. H. Helman (Ed.), *Analogical reasoning: Perspectives of artificial intelligence, cognitive science, and philosophy* (pp. 125–145). Dordrecht, The Netherlands: Kluwer.

Novick, L. R. (1988b). Analogical transfer, problem similarity, and expertise. *Journal of Experimental Psychology: Learning, Memory, and Cognition, 14*, 510–520.

Pazzani, M. (1989). Indexing strategies for goal-specific retrieval of cases. *Proceedings: Case-Based Reasoning Workshop* (pp. 31–35). San Mateo, CA: Morgan Kaufmann.

Porter, B. W. (1989, May). Similarity assessment: Computation vs. representation. In *Proceedings: Case-Based Reasoning Workshop* (pp. 82–84). San Mateo, CA: Morgan Kaufmann.

Ratcliff, R. (1990). Connectionist models of recognition memory: Constraints imposed by learning and forgetting functions. *Psychological Review, 97*, 285–308.

Ratcliff, R., & McKoon, G. (1989). Similarity information versus relational information: Differences in the time course of retrieval. *Cognitive Psychology, 21*, 139–155.

Read, S. J., & Cesa, I. L. (1991). This reminds me of the time when ...: Expectation failures in reminding and explanation. *Journal of Experimental Social Psychology, 27*, 1–25.

Reder, L. M. (1988). Strategic control of retrieval strategies. *The Psychology of Learning and Motivation, 22*, 227–259.

Reed, S. K. (1987). A structure-mapping model for word problems. *Journal of Experimental Psychology: Learning, Memory, and Cognition, 13*, 124–139.

Reed, S. K., Ackinclose, C. C., & Voss, A. A. (1990). Selecting analogous problems: similarity versus inclusiveness. *Memory & Cognition, 18*(1), 83–98.

Reed, S. K., Ernst, G. W., & Banerji, R. (1974). The role of analogy in transfer between similar problem states. *Cognitive Psychology, 6*, 436–450.

Reeves, L. M., & Weisberg, R. W. (1994). The role of content and abstract information in analogical transfer. *Psychological Bulletin, 115*(3), 381–400.

Riesbeck, C. K., & Schank, R. C. (1989). *Inside case-based reasoning.* Hillsdale, NJ: Erlbaum.

Rips, L. J. (1989). Similarity, typicality, and categorization. In S. Vosniadou & A. Ortony (Eds.), *Similarity and analogical reasoning* (pp. 21–59). New York: Cambridge University Press.

Rosch, E., Mervis, C. B., Gray, W. D., Johnson, D. M., & Boyes-Braem, P. (1976). Basic objects in natural categories. *Cognitive Psychology, 8*, 382–439.

Ross, B. H. (1984). Remindings and their effects in learning a cognitive skill. *Cognitive Psychology, 16*, 371–416.

Ross, B. H. (1987). This is like that: The use of earlier problems and the separation of similarity effects. *Journal of Experimental Psychology: Learning, Memory and Cognition, 13*, 629–639.

Ross, B. H. (1989). Remindings in learning and instruction. In S. Vosniadou & A. Ortony (Eds.), *Similarity and analogical reasoning* (pp. 438–469). New York: Cambridge University Press.

Schank, R. (1982). *Dynamic Memory.* New York: Cambridge University Press.

Schumacher, R., & Gentner, D. (1987, May). *Similarity-based remindings: The effects of similarity and interitem distance*. Paper presented at the Midwestern Psychological Association, Chicago, IL.

Seifert, C. M. (1994). The role of goals in retrieving analogical cases. In J. A. Barnden & K. J. Holyoak (Eds.), *Advances in connectionist and neural computation theory, vol. 3: Analogy, metaphor, and reminding* (pp. 95–125). Norwood, NJ: Ablex Publishing Company.

Seifert, C. M., McKoon, G., Abelson, R. P., & Ratcliff, R. (1986). Memory connections between thematically similar episodes. *Journal of Experimental Psychology: Learning, Memory, and Cognition, 12*, 220–231.

Skorstad, J., Falkenhainer, B., & Gentner, D. (1987). Analogical processing: A simulation and empirical corroboration. *Proceedings of the Sixth National Conference on Artificial Intelligence* (pp. 322–326), Seattle, WA. Los Altos, CA: Morgan Kaufmann.

Skorstad, J., Gentner, D., & Medin, D. (1988). Abstraction processes during concept learning: A structural view. *Proceedings of the Tenth Annual Conference of the Cognitive Science Society* (pp. 419–425), Montreal, Canada. Hillsdale, NJ: Erlbaum.

Smith, L. B. (1984). Young children's understanding of attributes and dimensions: A comparison of conceptual and linguistic measures. *Child Development, 55*, 363–380.

Smolensky, P. (1988). On the proper treatment of connectionism. *Behavior and Brain Sciences, 11*, 1–74.

Spellman, B. A., & Holyoak, K. J. (1992). If Saddam is Hitler then who is George Bush? Analogical mapping between systems of social roles. *Journal of Personality and Social Psychology, 62*(9), 913–933.

Stanfill, C., & Waltz, D. (1986). Toward memory-based reasoning. *Transactions of the ACM, 29*(12), 1213–1228.

Thagard, P., & Holyoak, K. J. (1989). Why indexing is the wrong way to think about analog retrieval. *Proceedings: Case-Based Reasoning Workshop* (pp. 36–40). San Mateo, CA: Morgan Kaufmann.

Thagard, P., Holyoak, K. J., Nelson, G., & Gochfeld, D. (1990). Analog retrieval by constraint satisfaction. *Artificial Intelligence, 46*, 259–310.

Van Lehn, K. (1989). *Mind bugs: The Origins of procedural misconceptions*. Cambridge, MA: MIT Press.

Waltz, D. (1989, May). Panel discussion on "Indexing Algorithms." *Proceedings: Case-Based Reasoning Workshop* (pp. 25–44). San Mateo, CA: Morgan Kaufmann.

Wharton, C. M., Holyoak, K. J., Downing, P. E., Lange, T. E., & Wickens T. D. (1991). Retrieval competition in memory for analogies. In *Proceedings of the Thirteenth Annual Conference of the Cognitive Science Society* (pp. 528–533). Hillsdale, NJ: Erlbaum.

Winston, P. H. (1982). Learning new principles from precedents and exercises. *Artificial Intelligence, 19*, 321–350.

Representing Structure

Chapter 29

Distributed Representations of Structure: A Theory of Analogical Access and Mapping

John E. Hummel and Keith J. Holyoak

A fundamental challenge for cognitive science is to understand the architecture that underlies human thinking. Two general properties of thinking jointly present extremely challenging design requirements. First, thinking is *structure sensitive*. Reasoning, problem solving, and learning (as well as language and vision) depend on a capacity to code and manipulate relational knowledge, with complex structures emerging from the systematic recombination of more primitive elements (Fodor & Pylyshyn, 1988). Second, thinking is *flexible* in the way in which knowledge is accessed and used. People apply old knowledge to new situations that are similar but by no means identical, somehow recognizing and exploiting useful partial matches. Both of these properties, structure sensitivity and flexibility, are apparent in the use of analogies (Gentner, 1983), schemas (Rumelhart, 1980), and rules (Anderson, 1983).

The first steps in analogical thinking are *access* and *mapping*. Access is the process of retrieving a familiar *source* analog (or schema, or rule) from memory given a novel *target* problem as a cue. Mapping is the process of discovering which elements in the target correspond to which in the source. For example, in the analogy between the atom and the solar system, the sun maps to the nucleus of the atom rather than to the electrons (Gentner, 1983). Once a source has been retrieved from memory and mapped onto the target, the former can be used to generate inferences about the latter; jointly, the two can be used to induce a more general schema that captures the essential properties they have in common (Gick & Holyoak, 1983; Ross & Kennedy, 1990). Analogical access and mapping are both structure sensitive (guided by relational correspondences) and highly flexible (able to tolerate partial matches), although access is less structure sensitive than mapping (Gentner, Rattermann, & Forbus, 1993; Wharton et al., 1994).

This article presents a theory of analogical access and mapping motivated by the problem of simultaneously achieving both structure sensitivity and flexibility. Although our current focus is on problems surrounding analogical thought, our aim is to lay the groundwork for a more general theory of human thinking.

Structure Sensitivity and Flexibility in Computational Models of Cognition

The twin design requirements of structure sensitivity and flexibility have figured prominently in discussions of the contrast between symbolic and connectionist approaches to modeling human cognition. These approaches have a strikingly complementary pattern of apparent strengths and weaknesses (Barnden, 1994; Holyoak, 1991; Norman, 1986). Roughly, symbolic systems readily model structure sensitivity but often fail to demonstrate humanlike flexibility, whereas connectionist systems exhibit flexibility in pattern matching and generalization but have great difficulty in forming or manipulating structured representations. One approach to capitalizing on the strengths of both symbolic and connectionist models has been to develop hybrid models. For example, Holyoak and Thagard (1989) proposed a hybrid model of analogical mapping. Most hybrids combine symbolic knowledge representations with connectioniststyle constraint satisfaction. However, although hybrid models have had considerable success in simulating important aspects of analogical processing, their architectures seem to represent a "marriage of convenience" between their symbolic and connectionist components, lacking a natural interface between the two. An alternative line of theoretical effort has focused on the development of more sophisticated connectionist representations that can code and manipulate structured knowledge (e.g., Elman, 1990; Hummel & Biederman, 1992; Pollack, 1990; Shastri & Ajjanagadde, 1993; Smolensky, 1990; Touretzky & Hinton, 1988).

The theory introduced in this article is based on the latter approach and takes the form of a structure-sensitive connectionist model. The model, embodied in a computer simulation called *LISA* (*Learning and Inference with Schemas and Analogies*), represents propositions (predicates and their arguments) as distributed patterns of activation over units representing semantic primitives. These representations have the flexibility and automatic generalization capacities associated with connectionist models. However, LISA departs from traditional connectionist models in that it actively (i.e., dynamically) binds these representations into propositional structures. The result is a system with the structure sensitivity of a symbolic system and the flexibility of a connectionist system. These representations—and the processes that act on them—naturally capture much of the flexibility and structure sensitivity of human cognition. However, this combination of strengths comes with costs: LISA has a number of inherent limitations, including capacity limits, sensitivity to the manner in which a problem is represented, and sensitivity to strategic factors such as the order in which elements of a problem are processed. A key theoretical claim is that similar limitations arise in human reasoning. LISA thus provides a computational account of many strengths and weaknesses of the human cognitive architecture.

Analogical Access and Mapping

A great deal is now known about how adults access and use analogies and how analogical abilities develop over the course of childhood (for reviews, see Gentner, 1989; Goswami, 1992; Holyoak & Thagard, 1995; Keane, 1988; Reeves & Weisberg, 1994). These findings have motivated the development of a number of theories and computational models of analogical access and mapping (e.g., Falkenhainer, Forbus, & Gentner, 1989; Forbus, Gentner, & Law, 1995; Halford et al., 1994; Hofstadter & Mitchell, 1994; Holyoak & Thagard, 1989; Keane, Ledgeway, & Duff, 1994; Kokinov, 1994; Thagard, Holyoak, Nelson, & Gochfeld, 1990). These models differ in important ways, but they have converged in positing a few basic constraints that guide human intuitions about natural correspondences between the elements of source and target analogs. We describe these constraints in the terminology of Holyoak and Thagard's (1989, 1995) *multiconstraint* theory of analogical mapping.

Three broad classes of constraints, which overlap with those identified by other theorists (e.g., Gentner, 1983, 1989), form the basis of the multiconstraint theory.

> 1. The structural constraint of *isomorphism* has two components:
> (a) *structural consistency* implies that source and target elements that correspond in one context should do so in all others, and
> (b) *one-to-one mapping* implies that each element of one analog should have a unique correspondent in the other.
> 2. The constraint of *semantic similarity* implies that elements with some prior semantic similarity (e.g., joint membership in a taxonomic category) should tend to map to each other.
> 3. *Pragmatic centrality* implies that mapping should give preference to elements that are deemed especially important to goal attainment and should try to maintain correspondences that can be presumed on the basis of prior knowledge.

Each of these constraints is inherent in the operation of LISA. However, the design of LISA differs from that of previous models based on the multiconstraint theory in that it also honors additional cognitive constraints on representation and processing.

Table 29.1 summarizes 12 interrelated empirical phenomena concerning analogical access and mapping. For convenience we divide these phenomena into three broad classes, which concern the relationship between access and mapping, detailed aspects of mapping, and phylogenetic and ontogenetic change in mapping ability.

Access and Its Relationship to Mapping
In general, analogical access (the process of retrieving one analog, usually a source, from memory when given another analog as a cue) appears to be sensitive

Table 29.1
Empirical phenomena for evaluation of models of analogical access and mapping

---

Access and its relationship to mapping

1. Semantic similarity has greater impact than in mapping
2. Isomorphism has less impact than in mapping
3. Close analog and schema easier to access than far analog
4. Access is competitive
5. Familiar analog accessed more readily

Analogical mapping

6. Isomorphism
7. Semantic similarity
8. Pragmatic centrality
9. Multiple possible mappings for one analogy
10. Correct initial correspondence facilitates finding subsequent mappings
11. Difficulty finding mapping for "unnatural" analogy problems[a]
12. Possible to map predicates with different numbers of arguments[a]

---

a. These criteria are considered plausible but lack direct empirical evidence.

to the same basic constraints as analogical mapping (the process of discovering the specific correspondences between the source and target). However, semantic similarity appears to have relatively greater impact on access than on mapping (Phenomenon 1), whereas isomorphism has a greater impact on mapping than access (Phenomenon 2; Gentner et al., 1993; Holyoak & Koh, 1987; Ross, 1987, 1989). When analogs must be cued from long-term memory (rather than simply being stated as part of an explicit mapping problem), then cases from a domain similar to that of the cue are retrieved much more readily than cases from remote domains (Keane, 1986; Seifert, McKoon, Abelson, & Ratcliff, 1986). For example, Keane (1986, Experiment 1) measured retrieval of a *convergence* analog to Duncker's (1945) radiation problem (for which the key solution is for a doctor to apply multiple low-intensity rays simultaneously to a stomach tumor from different directions). The source analog was studied 1–3 days before presentation of the target radiation problem. Keane found that 88% of participants retrieved a source analog from the same domain (a story about a surgeon treating a brain tumor), whereas only 12% retrieved a source from a remote domain (a story about a general capturing a fortress). This difference in ease of access was dissociable from the ease of post-access mapping and transfer, as the frequency of generating the convergence solution to the radiation problem once the source analog was cued was high and equal (about 86%) regardless of whether the source analog was from the same or a different domain.

Access is also facilitated by learning conditions that encourage induction of an abstract schema from remote analogs (Brown, Kane, & Echols, 1986; Catrambone & Holyoak, 1989; Gick & Holyoak, 1983). For example, Catrambone and

Holyoak (1989, Experiment 5) had college students read three convergence problems drawn from three distinct domains and then answer questions that highlighted the abstract structural commonalities among them (e.g., use of multiple small forces from different directions to achieve the effect of a single large force). After a 1-week delay, 74% of participants spontaneously generated an analogous convergence solution to the radiation problem. The overall pattern of findings concerning analogical access suggests that close analogs and schemas are accessed relatively easily, whereas access is considerably more difficult for remote analogs (Phenomenon 3).

Factors other than similarity and isomorphism also influence access. It has been shown that analogical access is inherently competitive (Phenomenon 4). For any cue, people are more likely to retrieve a case from long-term memory if it is the best match available (based on both structural and semantic constraints) than if some other stored case provides a better match (Wharton, et al., 1994; Wharton, Holyoak, & Lange, 1996). In addition (Phenomenon 5), highly familiar cases tend be preferentially retrieved (even when the familiar case is less similar to the cue than are some alternative stored cases). A particularly well-established example is the prevalent use of the person analog by children to make inferences about other animals and plants (Inagaki & Hatano, 1987). It has also been shown that people understand new individuals by spontaneously relating them to significant others, such as a parent or close friend (Andersen, Glassman, Chen, & Cole, 1995).

Mapping
The role of isomorphism in mapping (Phenomenon 6) is apparent when people are able to find sensible relational correspondences in the absence of substantial similarity between mapped objects (e.g., Gick & Holyoak, 1980; Gentner & Gentner, 1983), or even when relational correspondences conflict with object similarity (Gentner & Toupin, 1986). Recent work has established that human similarity judgments are also sensitive to isomorphism, in that perceived similarity is increased by consistent role correspondences (Goldstone, 1994; Goldstone, Medin, & Gentner, 1991; Markman & Gentner, 1993a, 1993b; Medin, Goldstone, & Gentner, 1993). For example, common features contribute more to the perceived similarity of two patterns when they participate in similar relations in the patterns ("matches in place") than when they participate in different relations across the patterns ("matches out of place"; Goldstone & Medin, 1994). Semantic similarity (Phenomenon 7) reveals its influence in the greater ease of mapping when similar objects fill parallel roles than when objects and roles are "cross mapped" (Gentner & Toupin, 1986; Ross, 1987, 1989). It has also been shown that increasing predicate similarity (when it converges with structural parallels) decreases the latency of finding structurally consistent mappings (Keane et al., 1994). The impact of pragmatic centrality (Phenomenon 8) is evident when mappings are ambiguous on the basis of structural and semantic

constraints. In such cases, people tend to preferentially map objects and relations they deem important to their goal (Spellman & Holyoak, 1996).

It has also been established that different people will produce different, internally consistent mappings for the same analogy (Phenomenon 9; Burns, 1996; Spellman & Holyoak, 1992, 1996). That is, it is often the case that there is not just one correct mapping between two analogs. Much like the two incompatible visual interpretations of a Necker cube, people typically arrive at one interpretation of an ambiguous analogy (although they may be able to shift from one interpretation to another).

Analogical mapping is sensitive to order of processing. When people are led to map analogs incrementally (e.g., by mapping as they read the two analogs), then the overall accuracy of their object mappings is influenced by the order in which mappings are made. Keane and colleagues (Keane, 1995; Keane et al., 1994) have shown that for purely structural analogies, mapping is more accurate when the order in which the analogs are processed encourages a correct initial mapping, which can then constrain subsequent mappings (Phenomenon 10).

Phenomena 11 and 12 have a less firm empirical basis than the other entries in Table 29.1; however, each can be supported by informal observations and "thought experiments."

Distributing Structure Over Time

Representing a proposition entails binding the argument roles of the proposition to their fillers (Fodor & Pylyshyn, 1988). For example, to represent the statement "John loves Mary," John must be bound to the role of lover while Mary is bound to the role of beloved. Traditional distributed representations are illsuited to representing such structures because they do not make these bindings explicit: Simply jointly activating patterns representing "John," "Mary," and "loves" cannot distinguish "John loves Mary" from "Mary loves John" (or even from a description of a narcissistic hermaphrodite).

A number of distributed approaches to representing role bindings have been proposed (e.g., Elman, 1990; Pollack, 1990; Shastri & Ajjanagadde, 1993; Smolensky, 1990; Touretzky & Hinton, 1988). One general approach is to introduce units or vectors that code conjunctions of roles and fillers. Models based on tensor products (Smolensky, 1990) and holographic reduced representations (Plate, 1991) are particularly sophisticated variants of this conjunctive coding approach. Models based on conjunctive coding can provide some of the advantages of distributed representations while preserving structure, but they also have limitations (Hummel & Biederman, 1992). In general, the capacity of a distributed conjunctive code to represent binding information declines in proportion to its capacity to preserve similarity across different bindings: In a conjunctive code, these capacities are fundamentally in conflict (Hummel & Holyoak, 1993).

Dynamic Binding

An alternative to conjunctive coding is *dynamic binding*, in which units representing case roles are temporarily bound to units representing the fillers of those roles. Dynamic binding is difficult in neural networks because it requires an explicit tag with which units can represent group membership. This tag must be independent of a unit's activation (because activation expresses information that is independent of binding; Hummel & Biederman, 1992). One possible dynamic binding tag is based on synchronized oscillations in activity, in which units fire in synchrony if they are bound together and fire out of synchrony if they are not (Milner, 1974; von der Malsburg, 1981, 1985; see Gray, 1994, for a review). Although controversial (see Tovee & Rolls, 1992), there is some neurophysiological evidence for binding by synchrony in visual perception (e.g., in striate cortex; Eckhorn et al., 1988; Gray & Singer, 1989; König & Engel, 1995) and in higher level processing dependent on frontal cortex (Desmedt & Tomberg, 1994; Vaadia et al., 1995).

Numerous connectionist models use synchrony for binding. This mechanism has been applied in models of perceptual grouping (e.g., Eckhorn, Reitboeck, Arndt, & Dicke, 1990; von der Malsburg & Buhmann, 1992), object recognition (Hummel & Biederman, 1990, 1992; Hummel & Saiki, 1993; Hummel & Stankiewicz, 1996), and rule-based reasoning (Shastri & Ajjanaggade, 1993). LISA (like its predecessor, the Indirect Mapping Model, IMM; Hummel, Burns, & Holyoak, 1994; Hummel & Holyoak, 1992; Hummel, Melz, Thompson, & Holyoak, 1994) uses synchrony to represent role-filler bindings in propositions. For example, "John loves Mary" would be represented by units for John firing in synchrony with units for the agent role of "loves," whereas units for Mary fire in synchrony with units for the patient role. The John–agent units must fire out of synchrony with the Mary–patient units.

Dynamic binding permits a small set of units to be reused in an unlimited number of specific bindings. This capacity to reuse units allows the representation of case roles and objects to be completely independent of one another, thereby preserving similarity across different bindings. For example, all propositions in which John serves as a role filler are similar by virtue of their sharing the units that represent John; likewise, all propositions involving the predicate "love" employ the same "love" units. Accordingly, the representation of two propositions overlap to the extent that their meanings overlap. Analogous benefits accrue from the use of dynamic binding to represent structure in models of perception (see Hummel & Biederman, 1992). The common role of dynamic binding in perception and reasoning, although not surprising, suggests additional linkages between perception and cognition: Because both require a capacity to represent structure, both are subject to the computational constraints imposed by the need for dynamic binding.

Constraints on Dynamic Binding in the Representation of Structure

Although it is useful, dynamic binding is nonetheless subject to important limitations. One is a capacity limit. Dynamic binding (by synchrony or any other means; see Hummel & Stankiewicz, 1996) does not permit unlimited parallel processing over distributed representations. Rather, the number of dynamic bindings that can be represented at any given time is limited to the number of distinct tags in the binding scheme. For example, in the case of synchrony, the number of binding tags is given by the number of groups of units that can be simultaneously active and mutually desynchronized. Let us refer to a collection of mutually synchronized units as a *group*, and to a collection of mutually desynchronized groups as a *phase set*. The capacity limit of binding by synchrony is equivalent to the size of the phase set: How many groups is it possible to have simultaneously active but mutually out of synchrony?[1] This number is necessarily limited, and its value is proportional to the length of time between successive peaks in a given group's output (the period of the oscillation) divided by the duration of each peak. Single unit recording studies with monkey and cat suggest that, at least in the visual systems of these animals, a reasonable estimate of the size of a phase set is between four and six phases (e.g., Gray & Singer, 1989; see also Hummel & Biederman, 1992).

A second and less obvious limitation of dynamic binding is the *one-level restriction*, which concerns the number of levels of embedding that can be represented simultaneously at the level of semantic primitives. Dynamic binding can only operate at one level of abstraction or hierarchy at a time (Hummel & Holyoak, 1993; Hummel et al., 1994). Consider the higher order proposition "Sam believes that John loves Mary," in which an entire proposition is bound to the patient role of the "believe" predicate. To represent the internal structure of "John loves Mary," the bindings "John-lover" and "Mary-beloved" must be desynchronized; however, to represent "John loves Mary" as the unitary filler of "what is believed," the representation of the entire proposition must be synchronized with the patient role of the "believes" predicate. Simply binding "what is believed" to both case roles of "John loves Mary" creates ambiguity at the level of semantic binding (see Hummel & Holyoak, 1993). Synchrony can only dynamically represent role bindings at one hierarchical level at a time. For the same reason, it can only represent the structure of one proposition at a time. If John loves Mary and also is hated by Sam, then simultaneously representing "John-lover" and "John-hated" would (given distributed representations of predicate meaning) blend the "lover/hated" roles.

In summary, LISA translates the computational constraints imposed by the similarity–structure trade-off into an architecture that combines distributed representations with a capacity for dynamic binding. The benefit of this approach is that LISA can represent structure without sacrificing similarity. The cost is that, in contrast to models such as ACME and SME, LISA must operate within inherent capacity limits (given by the size of the phase set). As a result, LISA lacks the ability to solve analogical mappings by massively parallel constraint satisfaction. Rather, mapping in LISA requires systematic serial processing combined with limited parallel constraint satisfaction. The theoretical claim is that the human cognitive architecture represents a similar algorithmic solution to the same computational problem. The surprising result is that for a wide range of suitably structured problems, the serial mapping algorithm yields outputs that closely mimic those that would be produced by unlimited parallel constraint satisfaction. However, analogies that make excessive demands on working memory, or that have an "unnatural" structure, reveal LISA's limitations—which appear to be shared with people.

The Architecture and Operation of LISA

Overview

LISA is designed to represent propositional knowledge both dynamically in working memory and statically in LTM. Based on these representations, it performs structured comparisons during both access and mapping as a form of guided pattern matching. When a proposition becomes active, the units representing it in LTM generate distributed, synchronized patterns of activation (one for each case role) on a collection of *semantic units*. These patterns, which serve as the model's working-memory representation of the proposition, capture both the semantic content of the proposition (by virtue of the distributed representation) and the structure of its case role-argument bindings (via dynamic binding by synchrony). The semantic primitive units are shared by all propositions in LTM, so the pattern generated by one proposition will tend to activate one or more similar propositions in other analogs. This process is a form of memory access. Mapping is performed by augmenting access with the capacity to learn which propositions responded to which patterns, that is, to learn the correspondence between the generating proposition and the responding (recipient) proposition or propositions. These correspondences, which are stored as connection weights, then serve to constrain subsequent memory access. Over the course of several propositions, the result is a representation of the correspondences between the elements of two or more analogs.

Architecture and Representation of Propositions

The core of LISA's architecture is a system for representing dynamic role-filler bindings and encoding those bindings in LTM. In working memory, role-filler bindings are represented as activation patterns distributed over the semantic units. These semantic units are linked to *structure units* that store, recreate, and respond to patterns on the semantic units. Structure units serve the purely structural function of encoding the binding relations among the components of a proposition into LTM. This function is enhanced by their strictly localist implementation (Hummel & Holyoak, 1993).

Every proposition is encoded in LTM by a hierarchy of three types of structure units (see Figure 29.1). At the bottom of the hierarchy are *predicate* and *object* units. (Predicate and object units are functionally equivalent; we distinguish them only for conceptual clarity.) Each predicate unit locally codes the semantic primitives of one case role of one predicate. For example, the predicate unit *loves1* represents the first (agent) role of the predicate "loves" and has bidirectional excitatory connections to all of the semantic units representing that role (e.g., *actor, emotion1, positive1, strong1,* etc.); *loves2* represents the second role of "loves" and is connected to the semantic units representing that role (e.g., *patient, emotion2, positive2, strong2,* etc.). Different instantiations of a predicate may have different shades of meaning (e.g., *loves* in "John loves Mary" differs from *loves* in "John loves winning an argument"), but much of this difference can be captured in the semantics attached to the arguments filling the roles. In the current implementation, shades of meaning that cannot be captured in this fashion are captured by coding the different shades as distinct semantic units. We generally distinguish semantic primitives for predicates by place: *emotion1*, representing emotion in the first role of an emotion predicate, and *emotion2*, representing emotion in the second role, are separate units. However, this separation is not strictly necessary, and different roles of the same predicate may share semantic units. Similar predicates will tend to share units in corresponding roles (e.g., the predicate units *loves1* and *likes1* will be connected to many of the same semantic units). However, some predicates will share units in different roles (e.g., converses such as *parent of* and *child of*, which have reversed roles). In this way, the structural and semantic similarity of different predicates is made explicit.

Object units are just like predicate units except that they are connected to semantic units describing things rather than roles. For example, the object unit *Mary* might be connected to semantic units such as *human, adult, female,* and so on, whereas *John* might be connected to *human, adult,* and *male.*

Subproposition (SP) units are structure units that bind case roles to their fillers (objects or propositions) in LTM. For example, "John loves Mary" would be represented by two SP units: one representing John as agent of loving, and the other representing Mary as patient of loving. The John-agent SP would share bidirectional excitatory connections with *John* and *loves1*, and the Mary-patient SP would share connections with *Mary* and *loves2*.

Proposition (P) units reside at the top of the hierarchy. Each P units shares bidirectional excitatory connections with the corresponding SP units. P units serve a dual role for the purposes of representing hierarchical structures, such as "Sam knows John loves Mary" (see Figure 29.1b). In their role as binding units for a proposition, they are connected to SPs representing their constituent

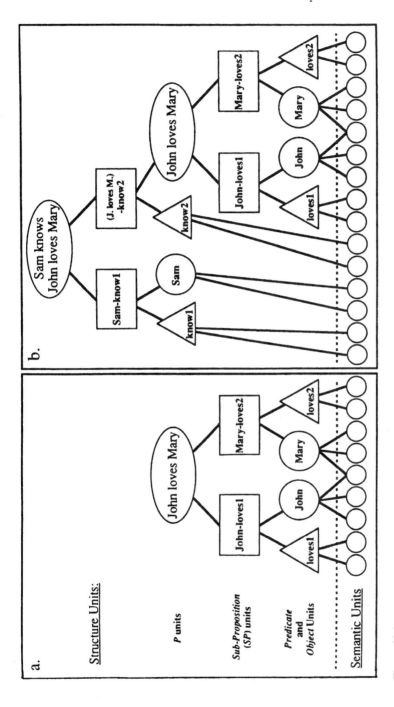

Figure 29.1
(a) Illustration of the LISA representation of the proposition *loves (John Mary)*. (b) LISA representation of the hierarchical proposition *knows (Sam loves (John Mary))*. (J = John; M = Mary).

role-filler bindings (Figure 29.1a). When a proposition serves as the filler of a role in another proposition, the lower level P unit serves in the place of an object unit under the appropriate SP. For example, the P unit for "John loves Mary" is connected (in the place of an object) to the second SP of the proposition "Sam knows [X]." In this way, the binding of "John loves Mary" to the patient role of "knows" is made explicit in LTM.

Every analog is represented by a hierarchy of this type for each proposition it contains. Object and predicate units are not repeated within analogs. For example, if John serves as an argument to multiple propositions in a given analog, the same *John* unit will be connected to multiple SP units. Each type of structure unit plays an important role in LISA's operation. Having separate units for roles, objects, and propositions allows the model to treat each such entity as an entity, a capacity that is critical for mapping analog elements onto one another. At the same time, it is important to emphasize that the structure units do not directly encode meaning. Rather, they work together to impose (and respond to) particular patterns of synchrony on the semantic units; it is only the latter that encode meaning.

The final component of LISA's architecture is a set of *mapping connections* between structure units of the same type in different analogs. Every P unit in one analog shares a mapping connection with every P unit in every other analog; likewise, SPs share connections across analogs, as do object and predicate units. These connections are assumed to reside in working memory and to be established when the analogs are called into working memory for mapping. At the beginning of a simulation run, the weights on these connections are initialized to zero. A mapping weight grows larger (taking larger positive values) whenever the units it links are active simultaneously and grows more negative whenever one unit is active and the other is inactive. In this way, LISA keeps track of what-corresponds-to-what across the analogs. By the end of a simulation run, corresponding units will have large positive weights on their mapping connections, and noncorresponding units will large negative weights.

The mapping connections play an important role in the model's operation. LISA treats analogical mapping as a form of learning. By allowing structure units in one analog to directly activate structure units in other analogs, mapping connections permit learned mappings to constrain future mappings. We will see that by treating mapping as a kind of learning, LISA provides a unified account of analogical access and mapping with a single assumption: Mapping connections can only be learned when the analogs reside in working memory.

Operation

For clarity, the model's operation is described here only in broad strokes.

For the purposes of mapping, analogs are divided into two mutually exclusive sets: a *driver*, and one or more *recipients*. The driver and all recipients are assumed to reside in working memory. For the purposes of memory retrieval, there is a third class of *dormant* analogs, which are assumed to reside in LTM but not working memory. Dormant analogs are candidates for retrieval from memory but cannot participate in analogical mapping (i.e., no mapping connections are established for dormant analogs). The only differences between the operation of recipient and dormant analogs are that (a) the former, but not the latter, update their mapping connections with the driver; and (b) the activations of units in dormant analogs decay faster than the activations of units in recipient analogs. The theoretical assumption motivating (a) is that the mapping connections reside in working memory; the assumption motivating (b) is that activation consumes attentional resources, so unattended (dormant) elements decay more rapidly than attended (recipient) elements. As in systems such as ARCS and MAC/FAC, retrieval in LISA is an inexpensive process that consumes fewer working memory resources than mapping. However, in contrast to ARCS and MAC/FAC, access in LISA operates in the same fundamental way—and on the same knowledge representations—as analogical mapping. As a result, access in LISA is sensitive to role-arguments bindings. Except when it is necessary to distinguish mapping from memory retrieval, we refer to both active recipient analogs and dormant analogs as recipients.

There is a strong asymmetry between the activity of driver and recipient analogs, in that mapping and retrieval are controlled by the driver. Note that there is no necessary linkage between the driver–recipient distinction and the more familiar source–target distinction. However, a canonical flow of control would involve initially using a target analog (the unfamiliar, novel situation) as the driver to access a source analog stored in long-term memory. Once a source is in working memory, mapping can be performed in either direction (including successive switches of driver assignment from one analog to the other). After a stable mapping is established, the source will be used to drive inference generation and schema induction in the target (processes beyond the scope of this article; however, see Hummel & Holyoak, 1996).

Driver Operation   As a default, propositions in the driver are selected one at a time to become active in the phase set. (We discuss the possible selection of multiple propositions shortly). The protocol specifying the order in which propositions are selected is given as input. We assume that the order in which propositions are selected is based, in part, on factors that determine text coherence, such as argument overlap (Kintsch & van Dijk, 1978) and causal connections (Keenan, Baillet, & Brown, 1984; Trabasso & van den Broek, 1985). That is, successive propositions entering the phase set will tend to overlap in the objects that fill their slots or will themselves be related by a higher order proposition expressing a causal or other functional dependency. Although we have yet to implement a specific algorithm by which LISA would determine its own selection order, it is possible to take advantage of the fact that normal text is ordered so as to maintain coherence. Therefore, as a general default for verbal analogies, we simply select propositions in the order in which they appear in a sequential propositional representation of the text describing the driver analog. In addition, we assume that propositions that are deemed to be especially important (e.g., because of their apparent relevance for achieving a goal) will tend to be selected earlier and more frequently than less important propositions. Such factors (e.g., goal relevance and causal-chain status) also serve as top-down constraints on strategic processing (e.g., allocation of attention) in human text and event comprehension (Fletcher, 1986; Fletcher & Bloom, 1988; van den Broek, 1988). For example, readers allocate more attention to statements following causal antecedents than to statements following causal consequents (Fletcher, Hummel, & Marsolek, 1990). As we will demonstrate, variations in selection priority allow LISA to simulate the influence of pragmatic centrality on mapping.

A proposition is selected by setting the activation of its P unit to 1.0 and allowing that unit to excite the SP units below itself. SPs under the same P unit represent the separate rolefiller bindings of that proposition, so they must fire out of synchrony with one another. To this end, SPs inhibit one another, competing to respond to input from the P unit. Due to random noise in their excitatory inputs, one SP will win the initial competition, becoming highly active and inhibiting all others to inactivity. Active SPs excite the predicate and object units under them, which in turn excite the semantic units to which they are connected. The result is a pattern of activity on the semantic units representing the semantic primitives of the object and case role connected to the winning SP (see Figure 29.2a). SPs "take turns" firing because of the operation of an inhibitory unit (von der Malsburg & Buhmann, 1992) associated with each SP. As detailed in Appendix A, an SP's inhibitor allows the SP to remain active for a short time and then temporarily inhibits it to inactivity. The result is that, with a constant input from a P unit, an SP's activation will oscillate between zero and one. In combination with SP-to-SP inhibition (and SP-to-predicate and SP-to-object excitation), this arrangement causes SPs, predicates, and objects to oscillate in SP-based groups. For example, when "John loves Mary" is selected, the John-as-lover group fires out of synchrony with the Mary-as-beloved group, alternating between the patterns depicted in Figures 29.2a and 29.2b, respectively.

So far, we have illustrated the driver's operation with a simple, nonhierarchical proposition. Hierarchical propositions work in the same way except that they are subject to two additional constraints (dictated by the one-level restriction). The first is that only one level of hierarchy is selected to be active at a time. For example, consider the hierarchical proposition "Sam knows John loves Mary" (Figure 29.3). This proposition will be activated (selected) in two sets: the parent set, "Sam knows [X]" (Figures 29.3a and 29.3b), and the daughter set, [X] = "John loves Mary" (Figures 29.3c and 29.3d). When "John loves Mary" is selected, LISA operates exactly as described previously. When

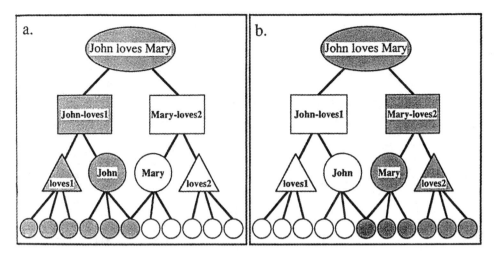

Figure 29.2
Proposition (P) units impose the working-memory representation of a proposition onto the semantic units via subproposition (*SP*), predicate, and object units. Case roles of a proposition fire out of synchrony with one another. Shaded areas depict active units, and unshaded (white) areas depict inactive units.

"Sam knows [X]" is selected, LISA also runs as described previously: Its SPs and their associated role and filler units fire out of synchrony. However, now, one filler is a P unit rather than an object unit. The second constraint on hierarchical propositions is that P units activated as fillers (i.e., via SPs above themselves, in the way that "John loves Mary" is activated when "Sam knows [X]" is selected) are not allowed to excite their constituent SPs. When the SP for "[X]-as-known" fires (Figure 29.3b), the P unit for "John loves Mary" will become active, but it will not activate its own SPs (John-as-lover and Mary-as-beloved). We refer to these two modes of operation as the "parent" and "daughter" modes, respectively. Selected P units enter parent mode, exciting their constituent SPs ("Sam knows [X]" is selected in Figures 29.3a and 29.3b. "John loves Mary" is selected in Figures 29.3c and 29.3d); however, when a P unit is activated by an SP above itself, it enters daughter mode and does not excite its constituent SPs (e.g., "John loves Mary" in Figure 29.3b). As elaborated in Appendix A, this mode distinction is straightforward to implement on the basis of signals that are completely local to the P units. Parent propositions and their daughters are selected at separate times, just like any other pair of propositions, but they will typically be selected in close temporal proximity (usually with the daughter immediately following the parent).

Recipient Operation and Learning a Driver–Recipient Mapping   Distributed patterns of activation are produced on the semantic units in response to the

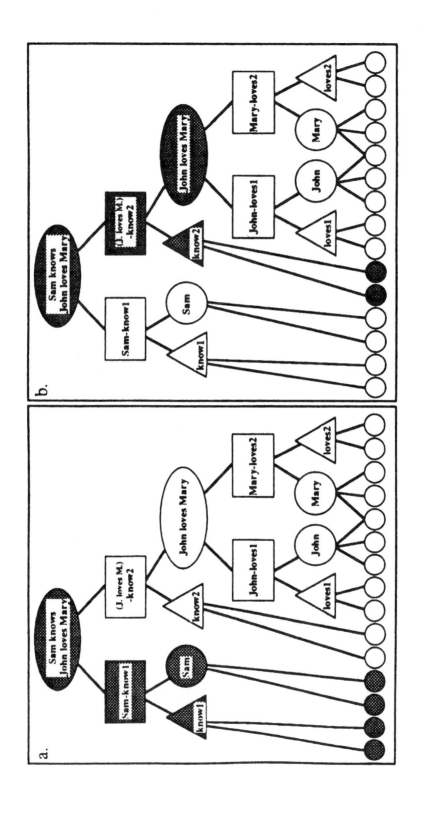

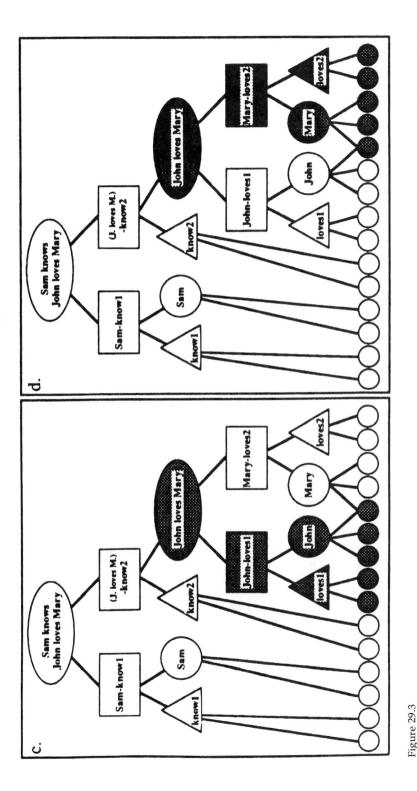

Figure 29.3

Illustration of parent and daughter propositions. Parent propositions and their daughters (argument propositions) are constrained by the one-level restriction to be selected (active) at different times. Shaded areas depict active units, and unshaded (white) areas depict inactive units. (a) The higher-level proposition (P) *know (Sam X)* is active. (J = John; M = Mary). (b) The higher-level proposition *X-know2 know (Sam X)* is selected, and its first subproposition (SP) *Sam-know1* is selected and its first subproposition (SP) *Sam-know1* is selected and its second SP is active. When it receives input from *X-know2*, the P unit for *loves (John Mary)* goes into daughter mode and passes no excitation to its constituent SPs. (c) The lower-level proposition is selected (and therefore in parent mode) and its first SP, *John-loves1*, is active. (d) The lower-level proposition is selected and its second SP, *Mary-loves2*, is active.

sequential selection of propositions in the driver. These patterns are arranged hierarchically in time. On a coarse time scale, patterns correspond to propositions: One proposition is selected to fire, followed by another. At a finer time scale, patterns correspond to role-filler bindings: The SPs under a common P unit fire out of synchrony with one another.

The job of a recipient analog is to respond to these patterns. Object, predicate, and SP units in the recipient compete to respond to patterns varying over the fine time scale, and P units compete to respond to patterns varying over the coarse time scale. That is, the recipient analog treats patterns on the semantic units as inputs to be classified—a task for which connectionist networks are extremely well-suited. Important to note is that the recipient is initially completely blind to the driver producing the patterns; its only source of information is the patterns themselves. Thus, unlike virtually all current analogy models in which mapping is treated as an explicit comparison between analogs (based on symbols representing hypothesized correspondences), mapping in LISA is a much more implicit process in which the recipient reacts to semantic patterns created by the driver.

In the recipient, units of the same type are competitive (mutually inhibiting one another) and units within a proposition are cooperative (mutually exciting one another). (The competitive rule takes precedence such that SPs in the same proposition inhibit one another.) Consider mapping "John loves Mary" in the driver onto "Bill likes Susan" versus "Peter fears Beth" in the recipient (see Figure 29.4). When the SP for John-as-lover (*John loves1*) fires in the driver, it will activate *John* and *loves1*, which will activate their semantic units (e.g., *human, male, adult,* and *emotion1, positive1, strong1*). This pattern will excite object and predicate units in the recipient, which will compete to become active. *Human, male,* and *adult* will excite *Bill* and *Peter; human* and *adult* will excite *Susan* and *Beth.* In this competition, *Bill* and *Peter* will become equally active, inhibiting *Susan* and *Beth.* Based on their semantic overlap alone, LISA begins to act as if *John* corresponds to either *Bill* or *Peter.* At the same time, *emotion1,* and *positive1* will excite the predicate unit *likes1,* but only *emotion1* will excite *fears1. Likes1* will inhibit *fears1:* LISA begins to act as if *loves1* corresponds to *likes1.* Because *likes1* is more active than *fears1,* the SP *Bill-likes1* will receive more bottom-up input—and therefore become more active—than the SP *Peter-fears1.* SPs excite the P units to which they belong, so the unit for "Bill likes Susan" will become more active than the unit for "Peter fears Beth." Hence, LISA concludes that "John loves Mary" corresponds to "Bill likes Susan" rather than "Peter fears Beth." The SP mappings also allow LISA to resolve the semantically ambiguous *John-to-Bill* versus *John-to-Peter* mappings. SPs feed activation back to their predicate and object units, giving *Bill* an edge over *Peter.* Now, LISA concludes that *John* corresponds to *Bill* rather than to *Peter.* Analogous operations will cause LISA to conclude that *Mary* corresponds to *Susan* rather than to *Beth,* and that *loves2* corresponds to *likes2.* Selected P units in the driver remain active

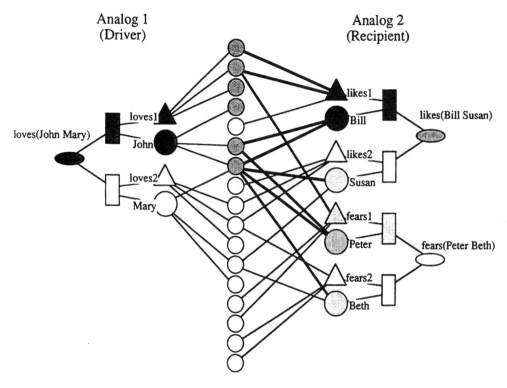

Figure 29.4
Illustration of mapping *loves (John Mary)* (Analog 1) onto *likes (Bill Susan)* versus *fears (Peter Beth)* (Analog 2). The subproposition (SP) encoding the binding of *John* to *love1* (the agent role of "love") is active in the driver (Analog 1). For both the driver and the recipient, black units are very active and white units are inactive. In the recipient, moderately active units are depicted in gray. *Loves1* shares more semantic primitives with *likes1* (the agent role of "like") than with *fears1* (the agent role of "fear"), so the pattern generated by *loves1* will activate *likes1* rather than *fears1*. As a result, *John* will map to *Bill* rather than *Peter*, even though *John* shares just as much semantic content with *Peter* as with *Bill*.

for a fixed number of iterations. At the end of this time, the activations of all units in the recipient are initialized to zero in preparation for the next driver proposition.

As these operations run, the cross-analog mapping connections keep track of which structure units are coactive across the analogs. When structure unit i is active at the same time as structure unit j (where i and j are units of the same type in different analogs), a *buffer* on the connection from j to i is incremented; when i is active while j is inactive, the buffer from j to i is decremented. After all propositions in the phase set have been selected (and run), the values accumulated on the mapping connection buffers are used to set the weights on those connections: A connection weight is incremented or decremented in proportion to the value of the corresponding buffer, with the result that structure units develop positive mapping weights to the extent that they are active simultaneously, and negative weights to the extent that one is active while the other is inactive. The mapping weights are then normalized to enforce the constraint of one-to-one mapping: Whenever the weight from j to i increases by some value, $\Delta w_{ij} > 0$, all other mapping weights leading *into* unit i are decremented by $\Delta w_{ij}/n_i$, (where n_i is the number of other weights leading into i), and all other weights leading *out of* unit j are decremented by $\Delta w_{ij}/n_j$, (where n_j is the number of other weights leading out of j). In the preceding example, the mapping weights from *John* to *Bill*, *Mary* to *Susan*, *loves1* to *likes1*, and *loves2* to *likes2* (as well as the associated SP and P weights) will all develop positive values. All other mapping weights will develop negative values. The resulting weights serve as LISA's representation of the mapping, with positive weights between corresponding elements.

These mapping weights serve to enforce structural consistency, both with hierarchical propostions and with multiple nonhierarchical propositions. First consider the nonhierarchical case. Imagine that LISA learns to map *John* to *Bill* and *Mary* to *Susan*, and let us add some additional propositions to the driver and recipient analogs: "Mary gave John flowers" in the driver, and "Susan gave Bill candy" and "Beth gave Peter a watch" in the recipient. If we assume that *flowers* shares just as much semantic content with *watch* as it does with *candy*, then in isolation the "give" mapping would be ambiguous: "Mary gave John flowers" would map equally well to both "Susan gave Bill candy" and "Beth gave Peter a watch." However, if "John loves Mary" has already mapped to "Bill loves Susan," then "Mary gave John flowers" will tend to map to "Susan gave Bill candy" because of the positive weights from *Mary* to *Susan* and from *John* to *Bill*. As a result, LISA will also map *flowers* to *candy* rather than to *watch*. This kind of biasing works with analogies of any size, serving both to implement structure sensitivity in mapping and to produce an interesting order sensitivity: LISA can resolve the mapping of *flowers* to *candy* in the context of the *gave* propositions only after it has mapped *Mary* to *Susan* in the context of the *loves–likes* propositions. Additional implications of this order sensitivity are discussed in the report of simulation results.

The same biasing allows LISA to map hierarchical propositions in spite of the one-level restriction. Let the driver consist of the proposition "Sam knows John loves Mary," and let the recipient consist of "Joe knows Bill likes Susan," and "Robert likes Beth." At the lowest level of hierarchy, the mapping of *John* to *Bill* versus to *Robert* is completely ambiguous: "John loves Mary" maps equally well to both "Bill likes Susan" and "Robert likes Beth." However, in the context of the higher-level propositions, "Sam knows [X]" and "Joe knows [Y]", the mapping is unambiguous. "John loves Mary" and "Bill likes Susan" serve as arguments of corresponding higher level propositions and therefore correspond to one another. Hence, the correct mapping places *John* into correspondence with *Bill* rather than with *Robert*. LISA discovers this mapping as follows. When "Sam knows [X]" is selected in the driver, "Joe knows [Y]" will become active in the recipient, establishing the correspondence between *Sam* and *Joe* and—more importantly—between [X] ("John loves Mary") and [Y] ("Bill likes Susan"). This latter mapping will be stored as a positive weight on the connection from the P unit for "John loves Mary" to the P unit for "Bill likes Susan." When "John loves Mary" is selected, this positive weight will give "Bill likes Susan" an advantage over "Robert likes Beth." As a result, *John* will map to *Bill* rather than to *Robert*.

Simulation Results

We now describe a series of simulations of analogical access and mapping using the LISA model. The program used in these simulations is written in TurboPascal (Version 7, Borland International, Inc., Scotts Valley, CA) and runs on an IBM-compatible 486 microcomputer. Our aim in this article is not to test the capacity of the model to scale up to large examples[2] but rather to demonstrate its ability to account for the qualitative phenomena listed in Table 29.1. Accordingly, the simulations are based on small examples that illuminate specific phenomena. Most of the examples are based on simplified versions of materials used in empirical studies of human processing of analogies. Unlike most previous analogy models (with the exception of the Copycat system of Hofstadter & Mitchell, 1994), the performance of LISA is stochastic, potentially yielding different outputs for multiple runs on the same inputs. In addition, LISA is sensitive to the order in which propositions in the driver enter the phase set. Each simulation we report is based on a number of runs sufficient to establish a stable pattern of results. Unless otherwise indicated, simulations involved placing one proposition (with from one to three arguments) at a time in the phase set, so that the mapping weights were updated after each proposition.

It is necessary to specify dependent measures that can be used to relate the performance of LISA to that of people. For mapping, the most common dependent measure used in human studies is some form of accuracy measure. For LISA, the accuracy of specific mappings can be identified with the learned weights on the relevant mapping connections. Accordingly, we use the mean advantage of the learned weight for the correct correspondence relative to the strongest competitor as an index of LISA's mapping accuracy. To model experiments in which latency is the primary dependent measure, we use the number of cycles and/or propositions required for LISA to generate the correct set of correspondences.

To provide a measure of analogical access, we use a retrieval index based on the fit between the driver (i.e., retrieval cue) and each analog in LTM. Two retrieval indices—a raw index and a Luce index—are computed for each recipient or dormant analog. The raw retrieval index, R_i, for analog i in LTM is computed as a Weber function of the sum of maximum P unit activations, j, in i:

$$R_i = 100 \left(\frac{\sum_{j=1}^{N_i} \alpha_j}{(0.5 + N_i)} \right)^2, \tag{1}$$

where α_j is the maximum activation obtained (during the run) by P unit j in analog i, and N_j is the number of propositions in analog i. (The scaling constant, 100, was chosen simply to keep retrieval indices roughly in the range of 0.01 to 2.00.) R_i is proportional to the number of propositions in i that become active in response to the driver and the degree to which each becomes active. The Weber fraction (Marshall, 1995) allows analogs that have few propositions to compete on an equal footing with analogs that have many; it is superior in this regard both to a raw sum of activations (which would favor retrieval of large analogs over small ones) and to a raw proportion (which would favor small analogs over large ones). The squaring serves to enhance small differences between the Weber fractions of different analogs. This retrieval index can be computed even if only a single analog at a time is stored in LISA's LTM and is directly proportional to the degree of fit between the driver and the recipient analog.

We assume that during retrieval, analogs compete through shunting (divisive) inhibition. The effect of such inhibition is captured by the Luce retrieval index, L:

$$L_i = \frac{R_i}{\sum_j R_j}, \tag{2}$$

which is mathematically equivalent to subjecting each R_i to Luce's (1959) choice axiom. Wharton, Holyoak, Downing, Lange, & Wickens (1991) have shown that human analog retrieval fits well to the predictions of the Luce choice model.

Relationship Between Analogical Access and Mapping
We begin by reporting simulations of phenomena that bear on the relationship between analogical access and mapping (Table 29.1).

Similarity and Role Binding in Access and Mapping   Ross (1987, 1989) has investigated the influence of two types of similarity—general domain similarity (i.e., similarity of objects and predicates), and consistency of role bindings (i.e., whether or not similar objects played similar roles)—on both analogical access and mapping. His results highlight both similarities and differences between access and mapping. The pattern Ross observed is complex and, to the best of our knowledge, has never been simulated by any computational model of analogy. This set of simulations therefore provides a challenging test of the psychological adequacy of LISA, particularly with respect to our claim that the model provides a unified account of access and mapping.

Ross gave college students word problems illustrating the use of equations to solve probability problems (e.g., permutation and combination problems). He then gave them new word problems that differed in their semantic and structural relationships to the studied source problem. For example, the source might involve assigning cars to mechanics at the IBM motor pool (e.g., for repair). In the illustrated equation for permutations, the number of cars instantiated a variable n representing the total number of items from which an ordered subset of a fixed size is selected. The subsequent target problem varied whether the basic story line was similar (e.g., another car assignment problem at the motor pool vs. a formally equivalent problem involving assignment of students at a high school). A second dimension of variation involved bindings of objects into roles, that is, which objects (humans or artifacts) served as n in the equation. Recall that in the source problem the two major types of objects were humans (mechanics) and artifacts (cars), and the artifacts filled the role of n in the permutation equation. The test problem could either be consistent with the source (humans and artifacts, with the artifacts as n), inconsistent (cross mapped) with the source (humans and artifacts, with the humans as n), or neutral (two categories of humans, one of which served as n).

Ross tested both access (participants' ability to retrieve the source problem given the cue) and mapping (their ability to use the source as a basis for solving the target) as a function of the semantic and structural relations between source and target. Table 29.2 (adapted from Table 3 in Ross, 1989, p. 464) summarizes his major qualitative findings. Following the notation used by Ross, each condition is denoted by an expression in the form $\{+,0\}/\{+,0,-\}$, with one symbol selected from within each set of brackets. The first symbol represents similarity of story line ($+$ for *close*, 0 for *far*). The second symbol represents the similarity of objects in matching roles ($+$ for *similar*, 0 for *neutral*, $-$ for *dissimilar*). For example, the condition $+/-$ represents a target problem with a similar story line as the source problem (e.g., both involving car repairs at a motor pool) but with similar objects playing dissimilar roles (e.g., mechanics instead of cars as n).

Table 29.2 shows four sets of ordinal comparisons between conditions, for both access and mapping. The data provided by Ross (1989) for the first comparison, $(+/+) - (+/-)$, reveal that when the overall story line is similar, assigning similar objects to dissimilar rather than similar roles impairs both access and mapping. That is, the difference $(+/+) - (+/-)$ evaluates to a positive number. The second comparison, $(0/+) - (0/-)$, indicates that when the story line is dissimilar, assigning similar objects to dissimilar roles impairs mapping but has little impact on access. The third comparison, $(0/0) - (0/-)$,

Table 29.2
Associations and dissociations between access and mapping as observed in humans and simulated by LISA

Condition[e]	Access		Mapping	
	Humans[a]	LISA[b]	Humans[c]	LISA[d]
$(+/+) - (+/-)$	.22	.58	.19	1.98
$(0/+) - (0/-)$	.04	.17	.14	1.82
$(0/0) - (0/-)$	.01	.09	.11	0.94
$(0/0) - (+/-)$	−.22	−1.3	.16	0.94

Note. Human data from Ross (1989, Table 3). Adapted from "Distinguishing Types of Superficial Similarities: Different Effects on the Access and Use of Earlier Problems," by B. Ross, 1989, *Journal of Experimental Psychology: Learning, Memory, and Cognition, 15,* p. 464. Copyright 1989 by the American Psychological Association. Adapted with permission of the author.
a. Human access score based on proportion of cases in which appropriate formula was recalled.
b. LISA's score based on the raw retrieval index, *R*.
c. Human mapping score based on proportion of cases in which variables were correctly instantiated in formula.
d. LISA's score based on value of correct mapping minus value of highest incorrect mapping.
e. All scores are based on differences between the two indicated conditions, expressed as story line similarity–object correspondence similarity.

shows a similar dissociation between mapping and access when the cross-mapped condition is compared to the neutral condition. Finally, the fourth comparison, $(0/0) - (+/-)$, pits the two factors in opposition to each other: a neutral assignment of objects to roles in the absence of a similar story line $(0/0)$ versus a similar story line with a cross-mapping of objects to roles $(+/-)$. This comparison yielded a dramatic reversal of difficulty between access and mapping, with the similar, crossmapped condition $(+/-)$ yielding easier access but less accurate mapping than the dissimilar, neutral condition $(0/0)$.

Table 29.3 shows the representations of simplified versions of the problems in one of Ross's item sets that were provided to LISA. These consist of (a) a list of propositions for each analog; and (b) for each object and predicate used in the propositions, a list of semantic features. The features are given descriptive labels to aid readability; however, these labels have no import to LISA (nor do the labels for predicates, objects, and propositions). Each predicate is defined to have a certain number of arguments slots; by default, each slot is represented by a distinct set of semantic features. The critical properties of these representations for the purposes of simulating Ross's results are the following:

1. The predicates and objects in the source and target problems with similar story lines have greater semantic overlap than do those in problems with dissimilar story lines, and
2. The object filling the first role of "assigned to" plays the role of *n* in the relevant equation to be instantiated.[3]

Table 29.3
LISA representations of problems used to simulate access and mapping results of Ross (1989)

A. Propositional representations of analogs

Source analog ("cars assigned to mechanics"; cars $\rightarrow n$)

   P1 (work-at mechanics motor-pool)

   P2 (belong cars executives)

   P3 (assigned-to cars mechanics)

Target analogs

   $+/+$ ("cars assigned to mechanics"; cars $\rightarrow n$)

     P1 (work-at mechanics motor-pool)

     P2 (belong cars salespeople)

     P3 (assigned-to cars mechanics)

   $+/-$ ("mechanics assigned to cars"; mechanics $\rightarrow n$)

     P1 (work-at mechanics motor-pool)

     P2 (belong cars salespeople)

     P3 (assigned-to mechanics cars)

   $0/+$ ("computers assigned to students"; computers $\rightarrow n$)

     P1 (enrolled-at students high-school)

     P2 (assigned-to computers students)

   $0/0$ ("students assigned to counselors"; students $\rightarrow n$)

     P1 (work-at counselors high-school)

     P2 (enrolled-at students high-school)

     P3 (assigned-to students counselors)

   $0/-$ ("students assigned to computers"; students $\rightarrow n$)

     P1 (enrolled-at students high-school)

     P2 (assigned-to students computers)

B. Semantic features

Objects

   motor-pool: location company workplace IBM

   executives: animate person job business exec1

   salespeople: animate person job business sales1

   cars: inanimate machine transport cars1

   mechanics: animate person job mechanic1

   high-school: location school workplace high1

   students: animate person unpaid student1

   counselors: animate person job teaching counsel1

   computers: inanimate machine info device computer1

Predicates

   work-at: locative activity work1

   enrolled-at: locative state enroll1

   belong: state posses belong1

   assigned-to: trans passive alter-poss assign1

These representations were used to simulate the four comparisons summarized in Table 29.2, for both access and mapping. In each simulation, the source analog (which was constant across all runs) was the recipient, and the target was the driver. Propositions in the driver entered the phase set one at a time, in the order listed in Table 29.3. The "assigned to" proposition in the target was selected twice as often as any other proposition, reflecting its greater pragmatic importance. The sole difference between LISA's operation in simulating access versus mapping was that learning of mapping connections was disabled during access runs. We report the raw retrieval index, R (Equation 1), as a measure of access. (There was only one analog—namely, the source—in LTM during any simulation, so the Luce fit was always 1.0.) As a measure of mapping, we recorded the mapping weights from the driver (target) objects to the critical source (recipient) object, "cars" ("cars" in the source analog corresponds to n in the equation). We treated a mapping as correct if it would yield the correct answer in the target problem: Does the participant (or LISA) treat the correct object as n in the equation? The specific measure of mapping accuracy (in this and all subsequent simulation reports) was taken as the weight of the mapping connection for the correct mapping minus the weight of the strongest connection for an incorrect mapping (with the latter truncated to zero if it was negative). For both access and mapping, difference scores were calculated for each of the four comparisons of conditions provided by Ross (1989).

The dependent measures derived from the simulations with LISA (mean values over three runs) are presented in Table 29.2, along with the comparable data for human problem solvers as reported by Ross (1989). LISA captures the major qualitative associations and dissociations between the influence of the two similarity factors on access and mapping. When story lines are similar, assigning similar objects to dissimilar roles impairs both access and mapping (comparison 1). However, when story lines are dissimilar, assigning similar objects to dissimilar roles continues to impair mapping but has little or no impact on access (comparisons 2 and 3). Moreover, the relative impact of the two types of similarity is reversed for access and mapping: For access, it is better to have a similar story line even if objects are cross-mapped, but for mapping it is better to have a dissimilar story line with a neutral assignment of objects to roles than to have a similar story line with cross-mapped objects (comparison 4).

LISA's ability to simulate the patterns of access and mapping observed by Ross (1989) follows directly from its basic principles of operation. During both access and mapping, structured comparisons are initially driven by semantic features (of both predicates and objects) shared by the driver and recipient. The only major difference between access and mapping is that the latter process, which operates on information in active memory, is able to exploit the mapping connections, thereby encouraging subsequent mappings that are structurally consistent with initial mappings. (Recall that the only other difference is that activation decays faster for access than for mapping.) Prior to access, however, the recipient or recipients are in a passive state in LTM, and hence mapping connections cannot be updated. Access must depend solely on preexisting connections (i.e., shared semantic features), whereas mapping can create new structural connections. Similarity of story line (which LISA models as overlapping of semantic features) is therefore more critical to access than to mapping.

The benefit of having similar objects in similar roles (i.e., the benefit of consistent mappings over cross-mappings) follows from the fact that SP units integrate inputs from both predicates and objects. If both the object and predicate components of a driver SP pattern converge in activating a single SP in the recipient, then that SP (and the P unit to which it is connected) will clearly win the inhibitory competition in the recipient: The SP and associated P units will become highly active. Conversely, if the object pattern activates one SP while the predicate pattern activates another, then the lateral inhibition between SP and P units will result in no SP or P units becoming highly active. Together, these tendencies produce overadditivity for recipient SPs that match on both the object and predicate patterns relative to SPs that match on only one or the other. This tendency operates in both recipient and dormant analogs (i.e., in both working and long-term memory), but its effects are compounded in working memory as mapping connections are learned. If the driver and recipient have little semantic overlap in the first place (i.e., when the story lines are dissimilar), then the influence of similarity at the level of role bindings will be minimal due to the low baseline activation of the recipient.

The simulations of the results of Ross (1989) demonstrate that LISA can stimulate Phenomena 1 and 2 as well as Phenomena 6 and 7 (see Table 29.1).

Access and Mapping for Close Analogs, Far Analogs, and Schemas   Phenomenon 3 in Table 29.1 involves the ordering of ease of access: Close analogs and schemas are accessed relatively easily, whereas far analogs are much more difficult to access. We applied LISA to simulate this finding by using a set of materials based on convergence problems, which have been used in several relevant empirical studies (Catrambone & Holyoak, 1989; Gick & Holyoak, 1980, 1983; Keane, 1986). The results of these studies reveal differences in ease of access and also suggest a dissociation between access and mapping. Once a hint to use the source problem or problems is given, the frequency with which college students generate the convergence solution to the radiation problem is high and roughly comparable (generally over 80%), regardless of whether the source is a close analog, a far analog, or a schema induced from comparisons between multiple analogs.

Three sets of runs were performed, one for each source analog. In each run, the radiation problem served as driver, with its propositions entering into the phase set in order. The retrieval runs (with learning of mapping connections disabled) yielded mean Luce retrieval indices of .43 for the close analog, .34 for the schema, and .23 for the far analog, matching the empirical ordering. The mapping runs yielded roughly comparable results for all three sets. The representation of the target problem includes seven objects (the doctor, the tumor, the stomach, the tissue, the ray source, the high-intensity rays, and the low-intensity rays). For both the close analog and the schema, all seven objects were mapped correctly (weights on correct mapping connections ranging from .65 to 1.00, with negative weights on all incorrect mapping connections); for the far analog, six of the seven objects mapped correctly (weights on correct mapping connections ranging from .51 to 1.00, with negative weights on all but one incorrect mapping connection).

In terms of LISA's operation, the greater ease of accessing the close than the far analog is a direct consequence of the greater number of semantic features that a close analog shares with the target. The ease of accessing the schema relative to the far analog has a more subtle basis. Like R, the raw analog retrieval index, LISA's predicate and object units use a Weberlaw input rule (see Appendix A), favoring recipients that have a greater proportion of their units activated by the driver.[4] Relative to objects and predicates in a far analog, objects and predicates in a schema share about the same number of semantic features with objects and predicates in the target, but they include fewer unshared features. (Objects and predicates in a schema represent general classes rather than specific instances.) A target analog will therefore tend to activate a small abstraction based on a subset of its features (i.e., a schema) much more readily than it will activate a remote analog that includes the same subset of the target's features embedded among many additional mismatching features (as the remote analog will have larger denominator terms in the Weber law input rule). In response to the objects and predicates in any given target, the objects and predicates in a schema will tend to become more active than the objects and predicates in any distant analog. This same property of a schema will tend to extend to the level of propositions: A distant analog is likely to contain propositions that do not fit (i.e., are not structurally consistent with) a target, whereas a schema, which is an abstraction containing only the relevant propositions, will tend to contain fewer such nonmatching propositions. This difference will also tend to result in a higher retrieval index from any particular target to a schema than to a distant analog. At the same time, however, a near analog will tend to become more active than a schema: Due to the non-zero constant (0.5) in the denominator of the Weber law, additional propositions in an analog only "penalize" that analog when they do not fit with the driver (target). A near analog with, say, ten propositions, all of which fit the driver, will become somewhat more active than a schema with only five propositions, all of which fit the driver.

Competition and Role Binding in Access   Wharton et al. (1994) have demonstrated that analogical access is inherently competitive (Phenomenon 4). These

Table 29.4
LISA's Luce retrieval index (nonitalic) and observed retrieval proportions (italic)

| | Cue condition | | | |
Source analog	Singleton		Competition	
Consistent	.37	*.80*	.31	*.54*
Inconsistent	.28	*.67*	.20	*.42*

Note. Observed retrieval proportions (data) are from Wharton et al. (1994, Experiment 2).

investigators showed both that retrieval is sensitive to role binding (greater access to analogs in which similar objects play similar roles as in the retrieval cue; cf. Ross, 1989) and that access to any individual analog is decreased by the presence of a strong competing case stored in LTM. LISA was used to simulate a simplified version of Experiment 2 as reported by Wharton et al. (1994). Each analog was a single proposition. A sample set consisted of three interrelated analogs, such as:

1. The judge was alerted by the rescue worker. (cue)
2. The lawyer was warned by the paramedic. (consistent role assignments)
3. The attorney cautioned the firefighter. (inconsistent role assignments)

In the original experiment, participants first studied a series of such sentences. After a brief delay, they saw a series of cue sentences and were asked to write down any sentence of which they were reminded. Wharton et al. varied two factors. First, relative to the cue (e.g., sentence 1), a studied sentence either had consistent role assignments (similar objects in similar roles, as in sentence 2), or inconsistent assignments (cross-mapped, as in sentence 3). Second, for a given cue, the study set included either one related sentence (e.g., either 2 or 3), or both.

Table 29.4 summarizes the results from Wharton et al. (1994), which revealed that access was more likely when (a) the role bindings were consistent rather than inconsistent, and (b) only one related sentence (singleton condition) rather than two (competition condition) had been studied. To simulate this pattern of results, we gave LISA the eight sentences used by Wharton et al. to serve as the contents of LTM, including sentences 2 and 3 above. Sentence 1 always served as the retrieval cue (i.e., the driver). Three runs were performed: (a) singleton consistent condition, in which sentence 2 but not 3 was in LTM; (b) singleton inconsistent condition, in which sentence 3 but not 2 was in LTM (with the missing sentence being replaced in each of the above by an unrelated filler item); and (c) competitor condition, in which both sentences 2 and 3 were in LTM. Table 29.4 presents the Luce retrieval index in each condition. (Recall that the Luce index, L in Equation 2, is an index of competition.) The simulation results capture the major ordinal relations of the human recall data. In particular, in both the singleton and competition conditions, the Luce index is higher for consistent than inconsistent sentences; moreover, for both consistent and inconsistent sentences, the index is higher in the singleton than in the competition condition. For LISA, the advantage for consistent over inconsistent sentences is slightly greater in the competition condition than in the singleton condition. Although such an interaction was not observed in the particular experiment we simulated, it has been obtained in three similar experiments (Wharton et al., 1994, 1996).

The access advantage that LISA exhibits for the consistent over the inconsistent cases has the same basis as the model's fit to the comparable finding from Ross (1989; the advantage of the $+/+$ over the $+/-$ conditions). The competition effect arises directly from LISA's use of lateral inhibition between stored cases (as reflected in the Luce retrieval index).

Familiarity and Access   The final access phenomenon in Table 29.1, Phenomenon 5, is that highly familiar source analogs (e.g., people as an analog for other living things, or the Vietnam War as an analog of a new foreign crisis facing the United States) are especially likely to be retrieved (more likely than can be explained on the basis of similarity to the target). In its current state, LISA does not simulate this finding, but it is straightforward to understand how such an effect might obtain in terms of LISA's operation and architecture. Consider how LISA would learn a new analog. Encoding an analog into memory would entail establishing a new set of within-analog connections (e.g., from semantic units to object and predicate units, and from objects and predicates to SPs, etc.) to encode the analog's propositional content (see Hummel & Holyoak, 1996, in press). If this learning is assumed to be incremental (like virtually all learning in connectionist systems), then highly familiar analogs (i.e., analogs that have been encountered many times) would be expected to have higher within-analog connection weights than unfamiliar analogs. These higher weights would manifest themselves in higher activation values for structure units (most important, proposition units) in familiar analogs than in less familiar analogs, so the former would be more readily retrieved from memory than the latter (see Equation 1).

Analogical Mapping
We now present a series of simulations that focus specifically on phenomena involving analogical mapping (Table 29.1). The impact of isomorphism (Phenomenon 6) and semantic similarity (Phenomenon 7), as well as the manner in which they interact, have already been illustrated in the simulations of the mapping results of Ross (1989), described earlier. We will now consider pragmatic centrality (Phenomenon 8) and multiple mappings (Phenomenon 9).

Pragmatic Centrality and the Resolution of Ambiguous Mappings   Spellman and Holyoak (1996) reported a series of experiments that investigated the impact of processing goals on the mappings generated for inherently ambiguous analogies. In Experiment 2, participants read two science-fiction stories about countries on two planets. These countries were interrelated by various economic and military alliances. Participants first made judgments about individual countries based on either economic or military relationships and were then asked mapping questions about which countries on one planet corresponded to which on the other. Schematically, Planet 1 included three countries, such that "Afflu" was economically richer than "Barebrute," whereas the latter was militarily stronger than "Compak." Planet 2 included four countries, with "Grainwell" being richer than "Hungerall" and "Millpower" being stronger than "Mightless." These relationships can be summarized in simple two-proposition representations, which were used as input to LISA:

Planet 1
    P1 (richer Afflu Barebrute)
    P2 (stronger Barebrute Compak)
Planet 2
    P1 (richer Grainwell Hungerall)
    P2 (stronger Millpower Mightless).

The critical aspect of this analogy problem is that Barebrute (Planet 1) is both economically weak (like Hungerall on Planet 2) and militarily strong (like Millpower) and therefore has two competing mappings that are equally supported by structural and similarity constraints. Spellman and Holyoak found that participants whose processing goal led them to focus on economic relationships tended to map Barebrute to Hungerall rather than to Millpower (43% vs. 35%, respectively), whereas those whose processing goal led them to focus on military relationships had the opposite preferred mapping (29% versus 65%). The variation in pragmatic centrality of the information thus served to decide between the competing mappings.

Spellman and Holyoak (1996) simulated the impact of pragmatic centrality using the ACME model, under the assumption that information about the analogs that is relatively less important to the active processing goal is inhibited. LISA's architecture provides a similar mechanism that makes mapping sensitive to the relative importance of information in active memory. As noted earlier, we assume that people tend to think about information they regard as important more often and earlier than information they regard as unimportant. We simulate this in LISA by selecting important propositions in the driver earlier and more often than less important propositions. We tested the impact of pragmatic centrality in LISA using the above propositional representations of the two analogs, with semantic representations in which all planets were equally similar in terms of feature overlap. Planet 1 served as the driver. Five levels of pragmatic focus were defined. In the Econ-hi condition, the economic proposition P1 was selected three times, after which the military proposition P2 was selected once; in Econ-lo, P1 was selected once followed by P2 once. Two

Table 29.5
LISA's mappings for ambiguous country ("Barebrute") as a function of emphasis on economic versus military propositions

Emphasis	Weight on mapping connection[a]		Difference
	"Hungerall" (economic)	"Millpower" (military)	
Econ-hi	.63	.05	.58
Econ-lo	.79	.71	.08
Neutral	.68	.64	.04
Mil-lo	.74	.77	−.03
Mil-hi	.08	.65	−.57

Note. Econ-hi = high emphasis on the economic relation; Econ-lo = low emphasis on the economic relation; Neutral = emphasis on neither the economic nor the military relation; Mil-lo = low emphasis on the military relation; Mil-hi = high emphasis on the military relation.
a. Means over two simulation runs.

conditions favoring the military proposition (P2) over the economic proposition (P1) to varying degrees (Mil-hi, Mil-lo) were defined by reversing the above biases. In all four of these conditions, the mapping connections were updated after each proposition was selected (i.e., there was always only one proposition in the phase set), so that earlier propositions were able to influence the mapping weights before the latter propositions were selected. In the Neutral condition, P1 and P2 were both selected once in a single phase set, thus eliminating any variation in either frequency or order of selection.

Table 29.5 presents the mean weights on the two competing connections for the ambiguous country, Barebrute, based on two sets of runs for the seven conditions. These simulations reveal an orderly shift in the difference between the strength of the economic-based mapping (Hungerall) and the military-based mapping (Millpower) with the frequency and order of selection of the two driver propositions. These results show both that LISA is sensitive to pragmatic centrality and that it can resolve an inherently ambiguous mapping.

We also simulated the schematic design of Spellman and Holyoak's (1996) Experiment 3, which is presented in Table 29.6. In this experiment, participants read plot summaries for two elaborate soap operas. Each plot involved various characters interconnected by professional relations (one person was the boss of another), romantic relations (one person loved another), and cheating relations (one person cheated another out of an inheritance). Each of the three relations appears once in Plot 1 and twice in Plot 2. Based solely on the *bosses* and *loves* relations, Peter and Mary in Plot 1 are four-ways ambiguous in their mapping to characters in Plot 2: Peter could be mapped to any of Nancy, John, David, or Lisa; Mary could be mapped to any of those same characters. If the *bosses* propositions are made more important than the *loves* propositions (i.e., if a

Table 29.6
LISA's schematic propositional representations of the relations between characters in the "Soap Opera" experiment of Spellman and Holyoak (1996)

Plot 1		Plot 2
Bosses (Peter, Mary)	Bosses (Nancy, John)	Bosses (David, Lisa)
Loves (Peter, Mary)	Loves (John, Nancy)	Loves (Lisa, David)
Cheats (Peter, Bill)	Cheats (Nancy, David)	Cheats (Lisa, John)

processing goal provided a strong reason to map *bosses* to *bosses* and hence the characters in the *bosses* propositions to each other), then Peter should map to either Nancy or David and Mary would correspondingly map to either John or Lisa. There would be no way to choose between these two alternative mappings (ignoring gender, which in the experiment was controlled by counterbalancing). However, if the *cheats* propositions are considered, then they provide a basis for selecting unique mappings for Peter and Mary: Peter maps to Nancy so Mary maps to John. In a similar manner, if the *loves* propositions are made important (absent *cheats* propositions), then Peter should map to John or Lisa and Mary would correspondingly map to Nancy or David; if the *cheats* propositions are also considered, then Peter should map to Lisa and, hence, Mary to David.

Spellman and Holyoak (1996) manipulated participants' processing goals by having them produce an analogical extension of Plot 2 based on Plot 1, where the extension involved either professional or romantic relations; the cheating relations were always irrelevant. Participants' preferred mappings were revealed on this plot-extension task by their choice of Plot 2 characters to play roles analogous to those played by Peter and Mary in Plot 1. Afterwards, participants were asked directly to provide mappings of Plot 1 characters onto those in Plot 1.

The results are presented in Figure 29.5a, which depicts the percentage of mappings for the pair Peter–Mary that were consistent with respect to the processing goal (collapsing across focus on professional vs. romantic relations), inconsistent with the processing goal, or some other response (e.g., a mixed mapping). The goal-consistent and goal-inconsistent mappings are further divided into those consistent versus inconsistent with the irrelevant cheating relation. The plot-extension and mapping tasks both proved sensitive to the processing goal, as participants' preferred mappings in both tasks tended to be consistent with the goal-relevant relation; however, this effect was more pronounced in the plot-extension than the mapping task. In contrast, consistency with the cheating relation was more pronounced in the mapping than the plot-extension task. Spellman and Holyoak (1996) modeled this qualitative pattern using ACME by assuming that goal-irrelevant relations were inhibited to a greater degree in the plot-extension task (where the goal focused directly on

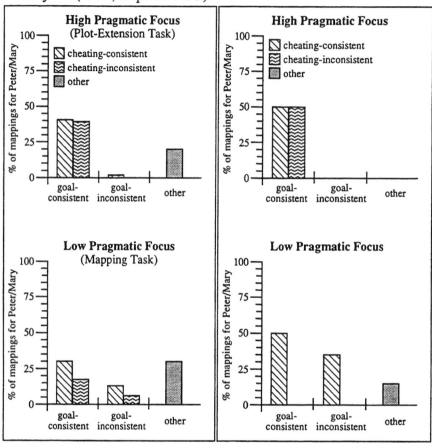

Figure 29.5
A: Summary of the results of Spellman and Holyoak (1996), Experiment 3. B: LISA's simulation results under different levels of pragmatic focus.

one type of relation, either professional or romantic) than in the mapping task (which was only indirectly influenced by the goal in the preceding plot-extension task).

To simulate the results of Spellman and Holyoak's (1996) Experiment 3, LISA was given schematic representations of the two plots on the basis of the propositions in Table 29.6. Plot 1 always served as driver. Four levels of pragmatic focus were generated. To counterbalance the order in which the low-focus propositions were selected, we ran two different selection orders at each level of focus. For clarity, we denote the proposition (in the driver) stating the professional relationship (the proposition listed first in Plot 1; see Table 29.6) as P, the proposition stating the romantic relationship as R, and the proposition stating the cheating relation as C. High focus on the professional relationships (P-hi) was simulated by selecting P four times for every one time R and C were selected. The orders used were [P P R P C P] and [P P C P R P]. Low focus on the professional relationships (P-lo) was simulated by selecting P three times for every two that R or C were selected, giving the orders [P R C P C R P] and [P C R P R C P]. Note that, in addition to being selected more often, P (the proposition stating the professional relationship, which was the relationship of focus) was also the first and last to be selected in both the P-hi and P-lo orders. High and low focus on the romantic relationships (R-hi and R-lo) were defined by switching the selection of R and P in the P-hi and P-lo conditions, respectively; thus R-hi was [R R P R C R] and [R R C R P R], and R-lo was [R P C R C P R] and [R C P R P C R]. Each order was run 10 times, for a total of 20 runs in each condition (P-hi, P-lo, R-hi, and R-lo), and a total of 40 high-focus and 40 low-focus runs. On each run, we recorded whether the dominant mappings (as given by the strongest mapping weights for Peter and Mary in Plot 1) were jointly consistent with the professional relationship, the romantic relationship, or neither, and whether or not they were also consistent with the cheating relation.

The results of the LISA simulations are summarized in Figure 5b, using a format that matches the data from Spellman and Holyoak's (1996) Experiment 3 (presented in Figure 29.5a). The simulations were based on the assumption that low pragmatic focus corresponded to Spellman and Holyoak's mapping task and that high focus corresponded to their plot-extension task. The simulations thus simplified the situation posed to participants in Spellman and Holyoak's experiment by replacing an inference task (plot extension) with a mapping task. However, given that analogical inference necessarily depends on the correspondences computed in the mapping stage, this simplification appears reasonable.

We did not attempt to produce a detailed quantitative fit between the simulation results and human data; nonetheless, a close qualitative correspondence is apparent, with LISA generally yielding a cleaner form of the pattern obtained with people. In the high pragmatic-focus simulations (collapsing across the P-hi and R-hi conditions), LISA's Peter–Mary mappings were invariably consistent with the goal-relevant relation (either professional or romantic) but were entirely independent of the irrelevant cheating relation. LISA effectively ignored the constraint imposed by the cheating relation, instead producing, with equal probability, one of the two Peter–Mary mappings consistent with the goal-relevant relationship. In the low pragmatic-focus simulations (collapsing across the P-lo and R-lo conditions), LISA was again more likely to produce mappings that were goal-consistent rather than goal-inconsistent, but this preference was much weaker than in the high pragmatic-focus simulations. On the other hand, in the low-pragmatic focus simulations, LISA reliably selected mappings that were consistent with the cheating relation. Thus LISA, like people, produced mappings that were dominated by the goal-relevant relation alone when pragmatic focus was high but that were also influenced by goal-irrelevant relations when pragmatic focus was low.

These results illustrate two important properties of LISA's mapping algorithm. First, as illustrated by the results of the high pragmatic-focus simulations, LISA will stochastically produce different mappings, each consistent with the goal-relevant relation but independent of goal-irrelevant relations, when the latter are only given a limited opportunity to influence mapping. Second, as illustrated by the low pragmatic-focus simulations, small differences in selection priority (i.e., order and frequency) are sufficient (when no single relation is highly dominant) to bias LISA in one direction or another in resolving ambiguous mappings. More generally, the simulations of the Spellman and Holyoak (1996) results demonstrate that LISA is sensitive to the constraint of pragmatic centrality (Phenomenon 8) and that it can successfully find alternative mappings for a single ambiguous analogy (Phenomenon 9).

Mapping Performance With an "Unnatural" Analogy Problem   We now examine LISA's ability to map variants of an "unnatural" analogy, illustrating how it deals with Phenomena 10 and 11 in Table 29.1. As noted earlier, LISA operates in parallel (or semi-parallel) with respect to the proposition or propositions that fire together within a single phase set (i.e., prior to updating the mapping connections). However, in so far as working-memory limits restrict the number and complexity of propositions that can fit into a phase set, LISA must necessarily build mappings incrementally (in a similar manner to such systems as IAM; Keane et al., 1994).

These properties cause major variations in the model's performance as a function of the structure of the analogy. LISA's performance with the convergence analogs indicates that its incremental approach to mapping can successfully mimic the results of parallel constraint satisfaction under some circumstances, even when the analogs are relatively large and semantically dissimilar. Despite their size and complexity, the convergence analogs are natural in that (a) they contain semantically similar predicates that aid in finding an approximately isomorphic structure, and (b) each analog exhibits a high degree of textual coherence, with propositions interconnected by role-filler relationships. The first property plays a critical role in LISA's ability to bootstrap the mapping (that is, to find at least a few correspondences early in mapping), and the second plays a critical role in its ability to use those established mappings to constrain otherwise ambiguous future mappings.

General Discussion

Analogical Processing With Distributed Representations
Analogy plays an important role in many aspects of human cognition, and the processes of analogical access and mapping are fundamental to analogical thinking. Previous models of analogical access and mapping have made important contributions to our understanding of the constraints on human analogical reasoning. However, these models are limited in that they fail to capture both some of the strengths of human analogical thought (such as our ability to discover correspondences between predicates that take different numbers of arguments) and some of its limitations (such as the difficulty we have solving "unnatural" analogies). More important, it is unclear how the representations and processes these models use for analogical mapping could be adapted for other cognitive operations, such as schema induction, in which analogy plays an important role. In large part, this limitation reflects a failure to represent knowledge in a way that captures both the flexibility and structure sensitivity of human knowledge representation.

We have presented a theory of analogical access and mapping that exhibits both sensitivity to structural relations (the hallmark of symbolic cognition) and flexibility in the face of imperfect matches (a strength of distributed representations). LISA's performance hinges on five assumptions that form the core of the theory:

1. Propositions are represented in active memory as distributed patterns that specify the semantic content of predicates and objects, with case roles dynamically bound to their fillers.
2. These structures are encoded in LTM in a way that statically binds semantic primitives into predicates and objects, and role-filler conjunctions into propositions.
3. Analog retrieval is a process of guided pattern classification, in which units representing stored propositions compete to respond to the distributed patterns generated by an active driver analog.
4. Analogical mapping is performed by augmenting analog retrieval with a capacity to *learn* the correspondences generated during the process of pattern classification.
5. Dynamically binding roles and objects into propositions and learning analogical correspondences consume (finite) working-memory resources.

A number of properties follow from these assumptions. The most apparent are a variety of properties related to the limitations of working memory. The upper bound on the complexity of the mappings that can be computed is determined by limits on the capacity of working memory (as given by the size of the phase set). In particular, performance on analogies that require attention to interlocking structural constraints is limited by the size of the phase set and the associated buffers that control changes in mapping connection weights. LISA is also sensitive to the semantic content of an analogy and strategic variables, such as the order in which propositions are selected to fire, and the grouping of propositions into phase sets. As a result, LISA's mapping capacity is not tied strictly to the formal complexity of the mapping problem. For example, LISA can solve complex, semantically rich analogies with greater ease than it can solve formally simpler but semantically impoverished analogies. It is important to note that the meaning of *semantically rich* is intimately tied to what LISA "knows": Depending on how an analog is represented, LISA can be made to perform like either an expert or a novice.

Capacity limits, sensitivity to semantics, and sensitivity to strategic variables constitute formal disadvantages of LISA's approach to analogical mapping (in the sense that LISA is weaker than mapping engines based on massively parallel constraint satisfaction and related algorithms), but they also constitute a source of behavioral predictions. Human reasoners are subject to some of these limitations (e.g., order effects; Keane et al., 1994), and it is very plausible that they are sensitive to others. In addition to formal disadvantages, LISA's approach to mapping also affords formal and theoretical advantages, including freedom from the *n*-ary restriction, the unification of access and mapping, and a form of knowledge representation that is useful for other processes, such as inference and schema induction (Hummel & Holyoak, 1996). Together, these properties make LISA both weaker and more powerful than other models of analogical access and mapping.

LISA, like any model that integrates distributed representations of concepts with dynamic binding, is subject to the one-level restriction: At the level of semantic primitives, activating more than one level of a hierarchical structure in a single group (i.e., time slice) creates ambiguity about the role-filler bindings. Accordingly, LISA activates only one level of hierarchy at a time at the semantic level. LISA can nonetheless exploit hierarchical structure to map propositions based on higher-order relations. Central to this capacity is the ability of a P unit to act both as an object filling a role in one proposition (daughter mode) and as a pointer to its constituent role-filler bindings (parent mode). Augmented with this duality of processing modes, the single degree of freedom that synchrony (or alternative dynamic binding codes) provides for binding suffices to capture structural relations within multilevel propositions.

More generally, LISA exploits both local and distributed representations and both serial and parallel processing. The units that encode structural relations are strictly localist, but the meanings of individual concepts are distributed over multiple semantic units. During mapping, driver propositions are activated serially; at a finer time scale, the firing of elements associated with distinct roles are desynchronized and, hence, serial. This serial processing is crucial in representing the bindings of objects to roles. At the same time, recipient propositions respond in parallel to the semantic patterns generated by the role-filler bindings of an active driver proposition. The integrated system provides distributed representations of propositional meaning while maintaining systematicity of knowledge, thus solving the core problem for distributed representations posed by Fodor and Pylyshyn (1988).

Conclusion

Although a great deal of additional work remains to be done, LISA's success in simulating core phenomena associated with human analogical access and mapping is encouraging. By introducing mechanisms to perform dynamic binding, it is possible to achieve the flexibility afforded by distributed representations while maintaining the structure sensitivity so critical to propositional reasoning. The cognitive architecture embodied in LISA may help us to understand how human thinking can, at its best, appear to transcend the constraints imposed by a limited-capacity working memory.

Notes

John E. Hummel and Keith J. Holyoak, Department of Psychology, University of California, Los Angeles.

Preparation of this article was supported by National Science Foundation Grant SBR-9511504.

We thank Graeme Halford, Art Markman, and an anonymous reviewer for their helpful comments on a previous draft.

1. Although this discussion is couched in terms of phase, it is not necessary to assume that the units outputs are strictly phased-locked (i.e., oscillating with regular and equal periods). The analysis operates in the same way if one simply assumes that the units are synchronized.
2. Our microcomputer is running under Microsoft DOS (Version 5.0, Microsoft Corp., USA, Redmond, WA), the memory limitations of which severely limit the size of the simulations we can run.
3. The predicate *assign* was used in all of the representations because it allows reversals of object roles (i.e., whether people or artifacts serve as the assigned set versus the assignee set). Bassok, Wu, and Olseth (1995) have shown that mapping performance on transfer problems similar to those studied by Ross (1989) is also guided by people's knowledge about the schematic roles that the specified objects tend to play with respect to each other (e.g., prizes are typically assigned to students rather than vice versa). Our simulations do not address such interpretive effects. We thank Miriam Bassok for advice on the representations used in these simulations.
4. The use of a Weber-fraction input rule (Marshall, 1995) as in LISA eliminates various retrieval biases. For example, ARCS (Thagard et al., 1990), which does not normalize analog activation in proportion to analog size, tends to be biased toward retrieving large rather than small analogs, even when the larger analogs are less isomorphic (Forbus et al., 1995). This bias is removed when the ARCS algorithm is modified by adding the Weber-fraction computation (Eric Melz, personal communication, June 1995).

References

Andersen, S. M., Glassman, N. S., Chen, S., & Cole, S. W. (1995). Transference in social perception: The role of chronic accessibility in significant-other representations. *Journal of Personality and Social Psychology, 69*, 41–57.

Anderson, J. R. (1983). *The architecture of cognition*. Cambridge, MA: Harvard University Press.

Barnden, J. A. (1994). On the connectionist implementation of analogy and working memory matching. In J. A. Barnden & K. J. Holyoak (Eds.), *Advances in connectionist and neural computation theory: Vol. 3. Analogy, metaphor, and reminding* (pp. 327–374). Norwood, NJ: Ablex.

Bassok, M., Wu, L. L., & Olseth, K. L. (1995). Judging a book by its cover: Interpretative effects of content on problem-solving transfer. *Memory & Cognition, 23*, 354–367.

Brown, A. L., Kane, M. J., & Echols, C. H. (1986). Young children's mental models determine analogical transfer across problems with a common goal structure. *Cognitive Development, 1*, 103–121.

Burns, B. D. (1996). Meta-analogical transfer: Transfer between episodes of analogical reasoning. *Journal of Experimental Psychology: Learning, Memory, and Cognition, 22*, 1032–1048.

Catrambone, R., & Holyoak, K. J. (1989). Overcoming contextual limitations on problem-solving transfer. *Journal of Experimental Psychology: Learning, Memory, and Cognition, 15*, 1147–1156.

Desmedt, J., & Tomberg, C. (1994). Transient phase-locking of 40 Hz electrical oscillations in prefrontal and parietal human cortex reflects the process of conscious somatic perception. *Neuroscience Letters, 168*, 126–129.

Duncker, K. (1945). On problem solving. *Psychological Monographs, 58* (Whole No. 270).

Eckhorn, R., Bauer, R., Jordan, W., Brish, M., Kruse, W., Munk, M., & Reitboeck, H. J. (1988). Coherent oscillations: A mechanism of feature linking in the visual cortex? Multiple electrode and correlation analysis in the cat. *Biological Cybernetics, 60*, 121–130.

Eckhorn, R., Reitboeck, H., Arndt, M., & Dicke, P. (1990). Feature linking via synchronization among distributed assemblies: Simulations of results from cat visual cortex. *Neural Computation, 2*, 293–307.

Elman, J. L. (1990). Finding structure in time. *Cognitive Science, 14*, 179–212.

Falkenhainer, B., Forbus, K. D., & Gentner, D. (1989). The structure-mapping engine: Algorithm and examples. *Artificial Intelligence, 41*, 1–63.

Fletcher, C. R. (1986). Strategies for the allocation of short-term memory during comprehension. *Journal of Memory and Language, 25*, 43–58.

Fletcher, C. R., & Bloom, C. P. (1988). Causal reasoning in the comprehension of simple narrative texts. *Journal of Memory and Language, 27*, 235–244.

Fletcher, C. R., Hummel, J. E., & Marsolek, C. (1990). Causality and the allocation of attention during comprehension. *Journal of Experimental Psychology: Learning, Memory, and Cognition, 16*, 233–240.

Fodor, J. A., & Pylyshyn, Z. W. (1988). Connectionism and cognitive architecture: A critical analysis. In S. Pinker & J. Mehler (Eds.), *Connections and symbols* (pp. 3–71). Cambridge, MA: MIT Press.

Forbus, K. D., Gentner, D., & Law, K. (1995). MAC/FAC: A model of similarity-based retrieval. *Cognitive Science, 19*, 141–205.

Gentner, D. (1983). Structure-mapping: A theoretical framework for analogy. *Cognitive Science, 7*, 155–170.

Gentner, D. (1988). Metaphor as structure-mapping: The relational shift. *Child Development, 59*, 47–59.

Gentner, D. (1989). The mechanisms of analogical learning. In S. Vosniadou & A. Ortony (Eds.), *Similarity and analogical reasoning* (pp. 199–241). New York: Cambridge University Press.

Gentner, D., & Gentner, D. R. (1983). Flowing waters or teeming crowds: Mental models of electricity. In D. Gentner & A. L. Stevens (Eds.), *Mental models* (pp. 99–129). Hillsdale, NJ: Erlbaum.

Gentner, D., Rattermann, M., & Forbus, K. (1993). The roles of similarity in transfer: Separating retrievability from inferential soundness. *Cognitive Psychology, 25*, 524–575.

Gentner, D., & Toupin, C. (1986). Systematicity and surface similarity in the development of analogy. *Cognitive Science, 10*, 277–300.

Gick, M. L., & Holyoak, K. J. (1980). Analogical problem solving. *Cognitive Psychology, 12*, 306–355.

Gick, M. L., & Holyoak, K. J. (1983). Schema induction and analogical transfer. *Cognitive Psychology, 15*, 1–38.

Goldstone, R. L. (1994). Similarity, interactive activation, and mapping. *Journal of Experimental Psychology: Learning, Memory, and Cognition, 20*, 227–247.

Goldstone, R. L., Medin, D. L., & Gentner, D. (1991). Relational similarity and the nonindependence of features. *Cognitive Psychology, 23*, 222–262.

Goswami, U. (1992). *Analogical reasoning in children*. Hillsdale, NJ: Erlbaum.

Gray, C. M. (1994). Synchronous oscillations in neuronal systems: Mechanisms and functions. *Journal of Computational Neuroscience, 1*, 11–38.

Gray, C. M., & Singer, W. (1989). Stimulus specific neuronal oscillations in orientation columns of cat visual cortex. *Proceedings of the National Academy of Sciences, USA, 86*, 1698–1702.

Halford, G. S., Wilson, W. H., Guo, J., Gayler, R. W., Wiles, J., & Stewart, J. E. M. (1994). Connectionist implications for processing capacity limitations in analogies. In K. J. Holyoak & J. A. Barnden (Eds.), *Advances in connectionist and neural computation theory: Vol. 2. Analogical connections* (pp. 363–415). Norwood, NJ: Ablex.

Hofstadter, D. R., & Mitchell, M. (1994). An overview of the Copycat project. In K. J. Holyoak & J. A. Barnden (Eds.), *Advances in connectionist and neural computation theory: Vol. 2. Analogical connections* (pp. 31–112). Norwood, NJ: Erlbaum.

Holland, J. H., Holyoak, K. J., Nisbett, R. E., & Thagard, P. (1986). *Induction: Processes of inference, learning, and discovery*. Cambridge, MA: MIT Press.

Holyoak, K. J. (1991). Symbolic connectionism: Toward third-generation theories of expertise. In K. A. Ericsson & J. Smith (Eds.), *Toward a general theory of expertise: Prospects and limits* (pp. 301–335). Cambridge, England: Cambridge University Press.

Holyoak, K. J., & Koh, K. (1987). Surface and structural similarity in analogical transfer. *Memory & Cognition, 15*, 332–340.

Holyoak, K. J., & Thagard, P. (1989). Analogical mapping by constraint satisfaction. *Cognitive Science, 13*, 295–355.

Holyoak, K. J., & Thagard, P. (1995). *Mental leaps: Analogy in creative thought*. Cambridge, MA: MIT Press.

Hummel, J. E., & Biederman, I. (1990). Dynamic binding: A basis for the representation of shape by neural networks. In *Program of the Twelfth Annual Conference of the Cognitive Science Society* (Vol. 32, pp. 614–621). Hillsdale, NJ: Erlbaum.

Hummel, J. E., & Biederman, I. (1992). Dynamic binding in a neural network for shape recognition. *Psychological Review, 99*, 480–517.

Hummel, J. E., Burns, B., & Holyoak, K. J. (1994). Analogical mapping by dynamic binding: Preliminary investigations. In K. J. Holyoak & J. A. Barnden (Eds.), *Advances in connectionist and neural computation theory: Vol. 2. Analogical connections* (pp. 416–445). Norwood, NJ: Ablex.

Hummel, J. E., & Holyoak, K. J. (1992). Indirect analogical mapping. In *Proceedings of the Fourteenth Annual Conference of the Cognitive Science Society* (pp. 516–521). Hillsdale, NJ: Erlbaum.

Hummel, J. E., & Holyoak, K. J. (1993). Distributing structure over time. *Behavioral and Brain Sciences, 16*, 464.

Hummel, J. E., & Holyoak, K. J. (1996). LISA: A computational model of analogical inference and schema induction. In *Proceedings of the Eighteenth Annual Conference of the Cognitive Science Society* (pp. 352–357). Hillsdale, NJ: Erlbaum.

Hummel, J. E., Melz, E. R., Thompson, J., & Holyoak, K. J. (1994). Mapping hierarchical structures with synchrony for binding: Preliminary investigations. In A. Ram & K. Eiselt (Eds.),

Proceedings of the Sixteenth Annual Conference of the Cognitive Science Society (pp. 433–438). Hillsdale, NJ: Erlbaum.

Hummel, J. E., & Saiki, J. (1993). Rapid unsupervised learning of object structural descriptions. *Proceedings of the Fifteenth Annual Conference of the Cognitive Science Society* (pp. 569–574). Hillsdale, NJ: Erlbaum.

Hummel, J. E., & Stankiewicz, B. J. (1996). An architecture for rapid, hierarchical structural description. In T. Inui & J. McClelland (Eds.), *Attention and performance XVI: Information integration in perception and communication* (pp. 93–121). Cambridge, MA: MIT Press.

Huttenlocher, J. (1968). Constructing spatial images: A strategy in reasoning. *Psychological Review, 75,* 286–298.

Inagaki, K., & Hatano, G. (1987). Young children's spontaneous personification as analogy. *Child Development, 58,* 1013–1020.

Keane, M. T. (1986). On retrieving analogues when solving problems. *Quarterly Journal of Experimental Psychology, 39A,* 29–41.

Keane, M. T. (1988). *Analogical problem solving.* Chichester, UK: Ellis Horwood.

Keane, M. T. (1995). On order effects in analogical mapping: Predicting human error using IAM. In J. D. Moore & J. F. Lehman (Eds.), *Proceedings of the Seventeenth Annual Conference of the Cognitive Science Society* (pp. 449–454). Hillsdale, NJ: Erlbaum.

Keane, M. T., Ledgeway, T., & Duff, S. (1994). Constraints on analogical mapping: A comparison of three models. *Cognitive Science, 18,* 387–438.

Keenan, J. M., Baillet, S. D., & Brown, P. (1984). The effects of causal cohesion on comprehension and memory. *Journal of Verbal Learning and Verbal Behavior, 23,* 115–126.

Kintsch, W., & van Dijk, T. A. (1978). Toward a model of text comprehension and production. *Psychological Review, 85,* 363–394.

König, P., & Engel, A. K. (1995). Correlated firing in sensory-motor systems. *Current Opinion in Neurobiology, 5,* 511–519.

Luce, R. D. (1959). *Individual choice behavior: A theoretical analysis.* New York: Wiley.

Markman, A. B., & Gentner, D. (1993a). Structural alignment during similarity comparisons. *Cognitive Psychology, 23,* 431–467.

Markman, A. B., & Gentner, D. (1993b). Splitting the differences: A structural alignment view of similarity. *Journal of Memory and Language, 32,* 517–535.

Marshall, J. A. (1995). Adaptive pattern recognition by self-organizing neural networks: Context, uncertainty, multiplicity, and scale. *Neural Networks, 8,* 335–362.

Medin, D. L., Goldstone, R. L., & Gentner, D. (1993). Respects for similarity. *Psychological Review, 100,* 254–278.

Milner, P. M. (1974). A model for visual shape recognition. *Psychological Review, 81,* 521–535.

Norman, D. A. (1986). Reflections on cognition and parallel distributed processing. In J. L. McClelland, D. E. Rumelhart, & the PDP Research Group (Eds.), *Parallel distributed processing: Explorations in the microstructure of cognition* (Vol. 2; pp. 531–546). Cambridge, MA: MIT Press.

Plate, T. (1991). Holographic reduced representations: Convolution algebra for compositional distributed representations. In J. Mylopoulos & R. Reiter (Eds.), *Proceedings of the 12th International Joint Conference on Artificial Intelligence* (pp. 30–35). San Mateo, CA: Morgan Kaufmann.

Pollack, J. B. (1990). Recursive distributed representations. *Artificial Intelligence, 46,* 77–106.

Reeves, L. M., & Weisberg, R. W. (1994). The role of content and abstract information in analogical transfer. *Psychological Bulletin, 115,* 381–400.

Ross, B. (1987). This is like that: The use of earlier problems and the separation of similarity effects. *Journal of Experimental Psychology; Learning, Memory, and Cognition, 13,* 629–639.

Ross, B. (1989). Distinguishing types of superficial similarities: Different effects on the access and use of earlier problems. *Journal of Experimental Psychology: Learning, Memory, and Cognition, 15,* 456–468.

Ross, B. H., & Kennedy, P. T. (1990). Generalizing from the use of earlier examples in problem solving. *Journal of Experimental Psychology: Learning, Memory, and Cognition, 16,* 42–55.

Rumelhart, D. (1980). Schemata: The building blocks of cognition. In R. Spiro, B. Bruce, & W. Brewer (Eds.), *Theoretical issues in reading comprehension* (pp. 33–58). Hillsdale, NJ: Erlbaum.

Seifert, C. M., McKoon, G., Abelson, R. P., & Ratcliff, R. (1986). Memory connections between thematically similar episodes. *Journal of Experimental Psychology: Learning, Memory, and Cognition, 12,* 220–231.

Shastri, L., & Ajjanagadde, V. (1993). From simple associations to systematic reasoning: A connectionist representation of rules, variables and dynamic bindings using temporal synchrony. *Behavior and Brain Sciences, 16,* 417–494.

Smolensky, P. (1990). Tensor product variable binding and the representation of symbolic structures in connectionist systems. *Artificial Intelligence, 46,* 159–216.

Spellman, B. A., & Holyoak, K. J. (1992). If Saddam is Hitler then who is George Bush?: Analogical mapping between systems of social roles. *Journal of Personality and Social Psychology, 62,* 913–933.

Spellman, B. A., & Holyoak, K. J. (1996). Pragmatics in analogical mapping. *Cognitive Psychology, 31,* 307–346.

Thagard, P., Holyoak, K. J., Nelson, G., & Gochfeld, D. (1990). Analog retrieval by constraint satisfaction. *Artificial Intelligence, 46,* 259–310.

Touretzky, D., & Hinton, G. (1988). A distributed production system. *Cognitive Science, 12,* 423–466.

Tovee, M., & Rolls, E. (1992). Oscillatory activity is not evident in the primate temporal visual cortex with static stimuli. *Neuroreport, 3,* 369–372.

Trabasso, T., & van den Broek, P. (1985). Causal thinking and the representation of narrative events. *Journal of Memory and Language, 24,* 612–630.

Vaadia, E., Haalman, I., Abeles, M., Bergman, H., Prut, Y., Slovin, H., & Aertsen, A. (1995). Dynamics of neuronal interactions in monkey cortex in relation to behavioural events. *Nature, 373,* 515–518.

van den Broek, P. (1988). The effects of causal relations and hierarchical position on the importance of story statements. *Journal of Memory and Language, 27,* 1–22.

von der Malsburg, C. (1981). The correlation theory of brain function. (Internal Rep. 81–2). Göttinger, Germany: Max-Planck-Institute for Biophysical Chemistry, Department of Neurobiology.

von der Malsburg, C. (1985). Nervous structures with dynamical links. *Ber. Bunsenges, Phys. Chem., 89,* 703–710.

von der Malsburg, C., & Buhmann, J. (1992). Sensory segmentation with coupled neural oscillators. *Biological Cybernetics, 67,* 233–242.

Wharton, C. M., Holyoak, K. J., Downing, P. E., Lange, T. E., & Wickens, T. D. (1991). Retrieval competition in memory for analogies. In *Proceedings of the Thirteenth Annual Conference of the Cognitive Science Society* (pp. 528–533). Hillsdale, NJ: Erlbaum.

Wharton, C. M., Holyoak, K. J., Downing, P. E., Lange, T. E., Wickens, T. D., & Melz, E. R. (1994). Below the surface: Analogical similarity and retrieval competition in reminding. *Cognitive Psychology, 26,* 64–101.

Wharton, C. M., Holyoak, K. J., & Lange, T. E. (1996). Remote analogical reminding. *Memory & Cognition, 24,* 629–643.

Retrieving Structure

Chapter 30

Case-Based Learning: Predictive Features in Indexing

Colleen M. Seifert, Kristian J. Hammond,
Hollyn M. Johnson, Timothy M. Converse,
Thomas F. McDougal, and Scott W. VanderStoep

1 Learning in Humans and Machines

In many machine models of learning, the goal seems be the *mimicking* of human learning at the level of input and output behavior. However, I/O matching is problematic because human and machine behaviors are fundamentally different in their environments and background knowledge. Even in novel domains, it is nearly impossible to achieve access to large quantities of background knowledge (as humans do with problem-solving strategies, analogical remindings, prior processing contexts, and episodic traces of similar events) in machine learners. How can humans and machines be performing the same processing given such different knowledge bases? One possible fix to this comparison problem is to equate background knowledge by choosing tasks where little or no knowledge is involved. This strategy was used in the development of EPAM (Feigenbaum, 1990) as a computer model of human verbal learning, where the input stimuli (nonsense syllables) are designed to provide little connection to past knowledge. However, EPAM involved a part of human behavior that is, by experimental design, far outside of the normal learning circumstances that an individual encounters in the world. When do people learn in the absence of *any* knowledge?

Another alternative is to attempt to provide the machine with background knowledge for some task comparable to that of human subjects. When the domain is very restricted (*e.g.*, inflating balloons (Pazzani, 1991)), this approach may be successful. However, in most domains (for example, in commonsense planning), there is no limited set of rules that can be considered sufficient. Without comparable knowledge bases, a machine learning model should be dissimilar to a human learner for the same reasons that a water plant near the Great Lakes is unlike one at the edge of the Gobi desert: they must produce the same product under extremely different operating circumstances. We face great difficulty in trying to "test" machine and human learners under similar conditions of environment, experience, and background knowledge.

Therefore, we argue for the importance of testing not I/O performance, but *paradigms*. What needs "testing" is the underlying assumptions of any machine learning model—the specific processing claims of its approach that should obtain across other tasks and learning situations, and that distinguish the approach from other competing theories. Newell (1991) argues for this approach, suggesting that one should first determine whether one has the basics of the class of models that will work before worrying about exactly matching detailed behavior. By examining the assumptions of a computational model, we can determine its psychological plausibility while avoiding the temptation of repeatedly adjusting it in order to exactly match human behavior in a specific test task.

In the following paper, we present an example of this approach to models of learning. We start with a problem: how does a case-based learner find relevant information in memory? We begin with a hypothesis that the indices with predictive utility in the planning domain are those structural features that distinctively indicate when particular plans are appropriate. A series of studies with human learners is then presented, contributing an explanation of what role predictive features play in retrieval. We then examine one case-based learning model in particular, RUNNER, and describe the implementation of the predictive features hypothesis for plan execution called "appropriateness conditions." Finally, we present experiments designed to examine whether appropriateness conditions are effective in human learning.

2 Predictive Features Hypothesis: What Indices are Learned?

Previous research has demonstrated the utility of learning by analogy (Carbonell, 1983; Gick & Holyoak, 1983; Gick & Holyoak, 1980; Hammond, 1989; Pirolli & Anderson, 1985; Ross, 1989). However, one must first *retrieve* a relevant candidate case from memory. Given that memory is full of past experiences, only a small number of which may be relevant, successful access requires identifying a past case with important similarities to the current situation, while distinguishing among other cases with similar features. How experiences are encoded into memory, and what types of cues may provide access to them, is called the *indexing* problem. How to find a relevant analog in memory is a central issue in research on analogical learning in psychology (Anderson, 1986; Gentner, 1983; Gentner & Landers, 1985; Gick & Holyoak, 1980; Holyoak, 1985; Pirolli & Anderson, 1985; Rattermann & Gentner, 1987; Ross, 1987; Ross, 1989; Seifert, McKoon, Abelson, & Ratcliff, 1986). While most computational approaches have ignored the problem of retrieving past experiences, one approach—case-based learning (Hammond, 1989; Kolodner, 1985; Riesbeck & Schank, 1989)—has attempted to determine the type and source of features used to index cases in episodic memory during learning.

2.1 Types of Indices: Surface vs. Structural

By most psychological accounts, retrieval depends on how similar the new problem is to a target example stored in memory, given a context of other related competing cases (Anderson, 1986; Gentner & Landers, 1985; Tversky, 1977). However, previous psychological research on indices has focused on a single factor in explaining when access occurs: the abstractness of the features (Gentner, 1983; Holyoak, 1985). Specifically, features that are more superficially (surface) related to the intended analogical meaning are contrasted with features that involve more deep, thematic (structural) relations among pattern elements (Gentner, 1983; Ross, 1987). Gentner (Gentner & Landers, 1985; Rattermann & Gentner, 1987) has found that surface features result in more frequent access in a memory retrieval task, and Ross (1987) has demonstrated that different kinds of surface similarity (story line versus object correspondence) lead to different rates of access. One possible explanation for these results is that the ability to make use of structural features is limited even when they are available; however, this does not appear to be the case. In these same studies, more abstract, relational features also reliably produced access to past cases based on structural features alone (Gentner & Landers, 1985; Rattermann & Gentner, 1987; Ross, 1987). Other studies have also shown activation of prior cases in memory based solely on abstract, thematic cues, particularly if subjects are instructed to attend to them (Seifert et al., 1986).

Why, then, do superficial features appear to promote better case access compared to abstract features? Surface features may be more readily available (require less inference) than structural features, playing a role in memory access before any abstract features are even available (Hammond & Seifert, 1992). Surface features may also serve to identify prior examples when individual cases are unique in content within the memory set (as in Rattermann and Gentner, 1987, where there was only one base "squirrel" story in memory). Unfortunately, in many real-world domains, there is substantial overlap of surface features between cases, so that abstract features are particularly important. For example, access based on structural features alone may be necessary when learning in a new domain, where past experiences won't share many surface features with new problems. In these cross-contextual remindings (Schank, 1982), abstract strategies from one domain are applied in another, such as taking the "fork" strategy from chess and developing it as the "option" play in football (Collins, 1987). Access to past information based on abstract features is particularly important when the common features are incomplete or ambiguous (Seifert, 1992).

The capacity to learn a general principle in one setting and transfer it to other, nonsuperficially related settings, is the essence of intelligent behavior. Even if people are only rarely able to make use of structural features, it is critical that we determine *when* such transfer does occur, and how we might accomplish this process in machine learners.

2.2 Useful Indices: Causal vs. Correlated

Our research on planning suggests that structural indices—those representing the abstract relationships among goals and plans—serve to constrain plan choices in a given situation (Hammond, 1989; Hammond & Seifert, 1992). Because this causal information serves to distinctly identify types of planning problems, the types of solution strategies that can be applied, and potential failures to avoid, it also provides useful indices to past plans. Thus, our claim is that among all possible features in a planning situation, only a limited set of these features—those that are relevant to the way in which the current causal interaction of goals and plans can be changed—are predictive of planning constraints, and therefore most useful as indices.

Two examples illustrate features most useful in predicting when plan knowledge is appropriate:

Flight of the Phoenix

X was working late on a project that was due in a matter of days. As he saw the deadline approach, he considered the following two plans: either continue to work straight through the night (and the next day) or get a good night's sleep and come back to the office refreshed. The first plan allows the use of all of the time for work on the project. The second provides less time, but the time it does provide is of a better quality.

While thinking about his problem, X was reminded of a scene from the movie "Flight of the Phoenix" in which a character played by Jimmy Stewart had to start a damaged plane in the desert. The plane's ignition needed explosive cartridges, and Stewart had only seven left. The plane's exhaust tubes were also filled with sand, which has to be blasted out using the same explosive cartridges. Stewart's character was faced with a choice: either try to start the plane using all the cartridges directly, or use some of them to clear the exhaust tubes to enhance the overall utility of the other cartridges. Stewart decided to use some of the cartridges to clear the lines, thus optimizing the likelihood of success for the remaining cartridges in starting the engine.

This situation involves a specific type of resource conflict, and the reminding carries with it information about how to make the decision. In the next example, the reminding is much more concretely related to the task at hand:

Missed Exit

Y was driving along an expressway in the left lane, because traffic was moving faster there. He spotted the exit where he wanted to get off. Unfortunately, by the time he worked his way into the right-hand lane, he had missed the exit.

The next time Y was driving on the same expressway in the left lane, intending to get off at the same exit, he again remembered the exit too late to make the exit, but noticed it had been preceded by a large billboard advertising "Webber's Inn."

The third time, Y noticed the billboard, remembered the exit, and got into the right lane in time to make the exit.

In the Flight of the Phoenix example, the movie situation shares no surface features with the write-or-sleep decision, but on the structural level the two situations match exactly: Each protagonist has a goal and a limited resource and must decide between two plans for using the resource; one plan uses the resource directly in service of the goal, while the other splits the resource between an optimization step and a direct-use step. These features suggest the solution of focusing attention on the question of whether sleeping would leave enough time to complete the project.

In the Missed Exit example, the features used in indexing are much more concretely related to the task at hand. Rather than predicting a causal relationship, the billboard simply serves as a correlated feature that is easier to notice. Structurally, the problem is to optimize over two goals: drive fast (hence drive in the left lane), and get off at the right place; however, a structure-level "solution" would look like "Move into the right-hand lane only when you need to," which does not provide detectable features. By recalling the earlier failures, Y is able to modify the features used to retrieve the exit goal from memory so as to make optimal use of observable surface features that are correlated with the presence of the exit. Through experience, non-causally related features that predict the desired choice point can also be learned.

These two examples represent opposite ends of the causal spectrum—in one, the features are predictive because they are causally related; in the other, the features are predictive because they happen to be correlated with the desired event. Thus, predictiveness is not an inherent feature of the indices themselves, such as "surface" or "structural" properties, but of the *relative* role played in characterizing episodes within a domain (Seifert, 1988). In some situations, surface features alone may be sufficient to predict what past knowledge should be accessed. For example, in learning several rules of statistics, retrieving past examples based on surface features like "the smaller set being mapped onto the larger one" may be sufficient for the learner's purposes (Ross, 1989). In other situations, structural features may be the only constants available across a variety of planning situations. Together, these examples present challenges that any model of learning must be capable of answering.

The point of these examples is that indexing of information will occur based on any and all predictive features within the task context. Structural feature remindings may be more likely to carry information needed to solve complex problems, while surface-level remindings may be more likely to help us react quickly to our environment. In both cases, the indexing features can be expected to consist of those that reliably predict the utility of the retrieved information. This suggests that indexing should be based on any features that are apparent to the planner at the time when retrieval would be useful.

3 Predictive Features in Human Learning

In human learning, is memory access possible through a subset of structural features that help to select plans? From a functional perspective, prior cases must be indexed using features that will be readily apparent to the processor at the time when retrieval is desired. In planning situations, this point may be defined as when conditions and constraints are known, but a decision has not yet been made. That way, the retrieved plan can suggest possible solutions or warn of potential dangers while the situation outcome is yet undetermined. Features that predict when prior cases might be useful could be better retrieval cues because they more specifically describe relevant planning constraints in the current processing context. If human memory is indeed operating under the predictive features hypothesis, features related to *when* plans are relevant should lead to better access to past experiences in memory than other, equally associated features.

For example, consider this story:

> A chemist was trying to create a new compound designed to allow preservation of dairy products stored at room temperature. The chemist was so confident that his experiments would succeed that he went ahead and ordered several truckloads of fresh dairy products to be delivered to demonstrate the utility of the new compound.

This story contains features with *predictive utility*; that is, the features present in the story allow the retrieval of past experience and predict a possible planning failure *before* the complete structural analog (namely, *counting your chickens before they're hatched*) is even available.

In order to examine the issue of predictive features in indexing, we conducted several experiments (as reported in Johnson & Seifert, 1992) comparing the retrieval of prior cases based on structural cues. The critical question is, are some subsets (cues predictive of planning failures) better than other (equally similar) cue subsets in retrieving prior cases? A set of common structural features was determined within narrative stories based on common cultural adages such as "closing the barn door after the horse is gone" (Seifert, McKoon, Abelson, & Ratcliff, 1986). These themes are based on knowledge about problems in planning that can occur, and how to avoid or solve them (Lehnert, 1980; Dyer, 1983), and so are also likely to be familiar patterns to subjects.

According to the predictive features hypothesis, structural features involving planning errors should form a privileged subset that leads to more successful case access than would be attained using other sets of features. Other shared

Table 30.1
Example feature sets for the Chemist story.

Theme: Counting your chickens before they're hatched.

Base story elements:

1) X desires A.

2) X assumes A.

3) X does not act to ensure A.

4) X invests resources based on A.

5) A does not occur.

6) X has wasted resources.

Story elements contained in each cue story type:

Complete: 1–6

Predictive: 1–3

Outcome: 4–6

---

structural features should be less useful as indices. To test this claim, we used a reminding paradigm based on Gentner and Landers (1985). Previous studies established that this retrieval task paradigm produces results similar to problem-solving tasks (Ross, 1989). In the current experiments, retrieval alone served as the dependent measure, but the stories all involved planning content. In a single experimental session, subjects were given a set of base stories to read. After a ten minute distractor task, subjects were given a set of cue stories and asked to write down any base stories that came to mind. The cues used in the experiments were of three types: a complete-theme cue, a predict-theme cue, and an outcome-theme cue. Table 30.1 shows the abstract features for one of the themes used, and which of those features each cue story type contained.

The critical decision point precedes the action of going ahead and investing resources based on anticipated success. It is *before* taking this action that one can make a choice of pursuing a different plan. Once made, one has committed to "counting the chickens," whether or not they hatch as planned. Therefore, the failure itself is not considered a predictive feature, since its presence already determines the set of outcomes. The predictive features set contained thematically-matching information up to the point of a planning decision; the other, conclusion features set included the thematically matching information from the point of decision through the outcome of the story. Examples of the stories used in the experiments are given in table 30.2.

Each of the cue stories was followed by instructions taken from Gentner and Landers (1985): "If this story reminds you of a story from the first part of the experiment, please write out the matching story as completely as you can. Try to include the names of characters, their motives, and what happened." The

Table 30.2
Example study and cue stories in the experiments.

Sample study story:
Judy was overjoyed about the fact that she was pregnant. She looked forward to having a baby boy, and wanted one so badly she felt absolutely certain it would be male. As a result, she bought all kinds of toy cars, trucks, miniature army soldiers, and even arranged an extravagant "It's a boy" party. Finally, the big moment came, and she was rushed to the hospital. Everything went smoothly in the delivery room, and at last she knew. Judy's lively bouncing baby was actually a girl.

Complete-theme test cue:
Harrison disliked his small apartment and shabby furniture. His rich aunt Agatha was near death, and although he hadn't seen or spoken to her in 15 years, he felt assured of inheriting a great fortune very shortly because he was her only living relative. He had already thought of plenty of ways to spend a lot of money fixing his place up. Confident of his inheritance, Harrison began charging everything from color televisions to cars to gourmet groceries. When Aunt Agatha finally died and her will was read, she had left all her millions to the butler and now Harrison was in debt.

Predict-theme test cue:
Harrison disliked his small apartment and shabby furniture. His rich aunt Agatha was near death, and although he hadn't seen or spoken to her in 15 years, he felt assured of inheriting a great fortune very shortly because he was her only living relative. He had already thought of plenty of ways to spend a lot of money fixing his place up.

Outcome-theme test cue:
Confident of his inheritance, Harrison began charging everything from color televisions to cars to gourmet groceries. When Aunt Agatha finally died and her will was read, she had left all her millions to the butler and now Harrison was in debt.

---

responses were scored based on whether they matched the intended base story, matched a different study story, matched no study stories, or was left blank. The rate of remindings was compared to chance estimates, one of which measured the probability of access given demonstrated availability in free recall for each subject.

The results showed that, while both subsets of cues resulted in reliable retrieval of study stories, the cue set that included features predictive of a planning decision proved to contain better cues than the set including the planning decisions themselves and their outcomes. The main findings were that there were no differences in the number of *matches* for predictive and outcome cues. However, only predictive cues were matched at a higher-tan-chance level because the predict-theme cues led to significantly fewer responses involving *mismatched* stories than did outcome features. Therefore, the stories containing predictive features led to more *reliable* access to matching stories in memory.

In follow-up experiments, we asked subjects to directly compare each type of partial cue to the base stories used in the experiments to determine whether the cues were differentially distinguishing the base stories, based on a) an overall similarity judgment not biased towards themes and b) thematic similarity (using thematic similarity instructions for the rating task from Gentner and Landers (1985)). The results showed that subjects rated the sets of pre-decision (predictive) cues and the sets of decision and post-decision (outcome) cues as equally similar to the base stories, whether using just thematic or overall similarity as a standard; thus, the reminding results are not due to any differences in length of cue or amount of information in the two types of cues.

In a final experiment, we asked subjects to match pre-decision stories and post-decision stories to the base stories, as in the second experiment, except that the subjects *directly* compared the stories rather than using the partial cue stories to retrieve base stories from memory. The results showed that the pre-decision cues produced more reliable matches than the decision and post-decision cues. Predictive features thus appear to more *distinctively* characterize relevant planning situations, leading to remindings appropriately specific to the planning decision, and few other remindings. The predictive features better characterize individual themes as distinct from other themes. While both the predict-theme and the theme-outcome cues were found to provide reliable access to matching cases, the predictive features showed an advantage in terms of the *selectivity* of reminding. This indicates that the elements in the predict-theme stories distinguished the themes more clearly, and thus subjects tended either to find the right story or to retrieve nothing. The theme-outcomes, however, tended to evoke a wider range of intrusion responses, indicating that the features available in them were also shared by other potentially retrievable episodes. Causal features involving goal and plan interactions will, when encoded, distinguish among situations where different plans will be appropriately applied.

4 Predictive Features in Case-Based Models

In the following section, we describe current research on a specific model of indexing in case-based learning, RUNNER, which incorporates this notion of the predictive features needed for successful indexing. Like other case-based systems (Alterman, 1985; Hammond, 1989; Kolodner, 1985; Kolodner & Simpson, 1989; Simpson, 1985; Riesbeck & Schank, 1989), RUNNER makes the following basic claims:

- New solutions are built from old solutions.
- Intelligent learning arises from anticipation of difficulties and optimizations based on prior experience.
- Prior experiences are selected from memory through matching indices.
- Useful indices in the planning domain involve features of goals, features associated with past successes, and features predicting problems to avoid.

A distinctive thrust of this case-based approach to learning (as opposed to other types of AI systems) is the incorporation of "lessons learned" into memory so that past errors can be retrieved and avoided appropriately. Case-based learners accomplish this through a specific strategy: *anticipate and avoid* problems. To do this, case-based learners keep track of the features in their domains that are *predictive* of particular problems, so those problems can be anticipated in future situations where they are likely to arise. As a result, the use of predictive features in indexing allows a case-based learner to find relevant past experiences in memory, thereby providing the chance to bootstrap from experience. Thus, learning is supported by the ability to store and access *actual* past problems, rather than attempting to anticipate all *possible* ones (as in search models such as SOAR (Newell, 1991)).

In case-based learning, experiences encoded into the memory base reflect the structure of a domain (*e.g.*, more examples of the goals that tend to arise in conjunction, the interactions between steps that tend to occur, and successful solutions) and are built up incrementally through learning. This approach involves the study of the actual *content* of features used in the organization of memory. In particular, we are interested in the type of features that may be predictive within a particular knowledge domain and task. A processor would benefit from retrieving related past cases at any time that they can provide information that is helpful in the current situation.

4.1 Predictive Features in Planning: Appropriateness Conditions

Our argument has been that it is not possible to characterize the utility of indices on the basis of inherent type (*e.g.* surface vs. structural). Rather, the types of indices that turn out to be predictive depend strongly on the domain, the task, and the type of processing normally performed for the task.

The RUNNER project focuses on questions of retrieval in the context of routine plan execution. In this task, predictive features are those indices that signal that a particular plan may be used with success, and should be attempted. The problem of plan use is somewhat different than the more general problem of planning—in particular, retrieval of standard plans in routine situations can often be more directly tied to perceptually available features, and this is advantageous if it can increase the efficiency of a frequently-used plan.

It might seem that the indices appropriate for plan retrieval are simply the preconditions of the plan, since a plan can be executed when its preconditions are satisfied, and not otherwise. However, some preconditions are not at all predictive of plan relevance; for example, "having money" is a precondition for many plans, yet having this precondition met does not necessarily predict a prime occasion for executing any of these plans. Instead, it would be useful to learn those features that should be explicitly considered when deciding whether to embark on a given plan. These *appropriateness conditions* provide memory access to the plan itself when circumstances are favorable to plan execution.

The plan then serves both as a memory organization point for annotations about the current progress and problems of the use of the plan, and as a hook on which to hang past experiences of its use. Its appropriateness conditions determine whether it is relevant to selecting current actions to be executed.

4.2 *Appropriateness Conditions in* RUNNER

Learning in many domains can be characterized as the acquisition and refinement of a library of plans. "Plan" refers to the collection of explicitly represented knowledge that is specifically relevant to repeated satisfaction of a given set of goals, and which influences action only when a decision has been made to use it. The plans in the library that are used will be incrementally debugged and optimized for the sets of conjunctive goals that typically recur (Hammond, 1989). The RUNNER project centers around plan use in a commonsense domain. By examining case-based learning within a planning task, we have uncovered a specific indexing vocabulary related to the control of action in the world.

The representational system for RUNNER's memory, as well as the bulk of the algorithm for marker-passing and activation, is based on Charles Martin's work on the DMAP parser (see Martin, 1990). The memory of RUNNER's agent is encoded in semantic nets representing its plans, goals, and current beliefs. Each node in RUNNER's plan net has associated with it a (disjunctive) set of *concept sequences*, which are a (conjunctive) listing of states that should be detected before that plan node can be suggested.

In the plan network, this amounts to a nonlinear hierarchical plan net, where the activation of plan steps (that are not ordered with respect to each other) can be dependent on environmental cues that indicate a particularly good time to perform that step.

Nodes in the plan net become activated in the following ways:

> • "Top-level" (the basic level instantiating different action sequences) plans become activated when the goal they serve is activated, and a concept sequence indicating appropriate conditions is completed.
> • Specializations of plans are activated by receiving a *permission marker* from the abstract plan, in addition to the activation of a concept sequence.
> • Parts (or steps) of plans are also activated by completion of a concept sequence, and by receiving a permission marker from their parent.

Once activated, many plans have early explicit verification steps which check if other conditions necessary for success are fulfilled, and abort the plan if not. Passing of permission markers is not recursive, so that the state information indicating an opportunity to perform a sub-plan must be recognized for execution to proceed further. This means that individual sub-plans must have associated with them concept sequences that indicate opportunities to be performed. (For a more complete explication, see Hammond, Converse, & Martin, 1990.)

As an example, RUNNER's plan for making coffee involves a number of steps, many of which are independent in terms of ordering. Among these is a step for taking a filter from a box of filters and installing it in the coffeemaker. When the coffee plan becomes active, this step and others receive permission markers from the plan, which means that they can now be activated if they "see" one of their concept sequences completed. One of the sequences for the filter-installing step is simply the conjunction of seeing the filter box and being close to it. This activates the plan to install the filter. After doing one perceptual check (that there are indeed filters in the box), the step is performed. This style of sub-plan activation has the advantage that opportunities to perform steps can be taken without having explicitly planned the opportunity.

Appropriateness conditions in RUNNER, then, are the union of the concept sequences of plan nodes and any initial verification steps required. Recognizing situations under which it is appropriate to invoke a plan is handled by testing the set of preconditions for the plan. Under assumptions of perfect knowledge and a closed world, there is little divergence between preconditions and the appropriateness conditions. When these assumptions are relaxed, however, there are several different ways in which the divergence can become important in plan execution and reuse:

- A precondition can effectively be "always true." This means that the plan may depend upon it for correctness, but an executor will never run into trouble by not worrying about its truth value. This sort of fact should not be an "appropriateness condition" since consideration of it cannot help in the decision whether to use the plan.
- A precondition may be almost always true, and it may be difficult to know or check in advance. If the consequences of an abortive attempt at performing the plan are not too severe, then this sort of fact should not be an appropriateness condition since the utility of knowing its truth is outweighed by the cost of acquiring the knowledge.
- A precondition may be intermittently true, but may be easily "subgoaled on" in execution, and achieved if false. (This of course depends strongly on representation of plans, and how flexible the execution is.) To the extent this can be handled in "execution," the condition should not be an appropriateness condition since whether or not the condition holds, the plan is likely to succeed.
- A particular condition may not be a precondition *per se*, but may be evidence that the plan will be particularly easy to perform, or will produce results that are preferable to the usual default plan for the relevant goals. This *should* be an appropriateness condition, even though it is not a precondition.

The power of appropriateness conditions is that they help to select the set of features that an agent should consider before deciding on a given plan.[1] This predictive features set is interestingly different from both the (possibly infinite) set of facts that need to be true for the plan to work, and also the set of facts explicitly used in the plan's construction. Even if an agent is assumed to have immutable plans in memory that will determine its competence, there is still room for learning the particular appropriateness conditions that govern when to invoke particular plans. The set of predictive features for indexing in RUNNER, then, is the set of appropriateness conditions needed to identify *when* a potential plan may be relevant.

4.3 The Predictive Utility of Appropriateness Conditions

Predictive yet only probabilistic conditions are included as appropriateness conditions even though they are not true preconditions because they are a concern of the agent in deciding on the viability of a plan. Here, as with the indexing of plans and repairs (Hammond, 1991), actions need to be indexed by the conditions that favor their applicability. As new conditions are learned and others are found to be unreliable, this set of predictive features changes.

Part of the process of refining appropriateness conditions can be taken care of by relatively simple "recategorization" of various conditions in the taxonomy sketched above, in response to both failure and unexpected success. Here are some ways in which this sort of recategorization can be applied:

> • Drop appropriateness conditions that turn out to be always true. At its simplest, this is merely a matter of keeping statistics on verification steps at the beginning of plans.
> • If a plan fails because some sup-plan of it fails, and that sub-plan failed because some appropriateness condition didn't hold, then *promote* that condition to the status of an appropriateness condition for the super-ordinate plan. That is, make the use of the larger plan contingent on finding the condition to be true.
> • If a plan is frequently found to have false appropriateness conditions in situations where the plan is needed, and the conditions are under the agent's control, consider including the conditions in an *enforcement* plan that maintains them, so that the conditions can then be assumed true for that plan.

At present, the RUNNER program reliably handles the first two types of learning listed above, and both of them are entirely empirical. That is, RUNNER starts to omit particular sensory verification steps when they turn out to be always true, and, when possible, RUNNER verifies conditions that have turned out to determine failure of a plan before undertaking the body of the plan. Continuing research on the problem of recognizing opportunities for enforcing conditions will focus on prioritizing learning for goals considered most important.

A major part of learning to plan effectively, then, is the development of a library of conjunctive goal plans, and the simultaneous tuning of the plans, their appropriateness conditions, and the environment itself to maximize the effectiveness of the plans. This approach requires:

1. having a plan library with optimized plans for the different sets of goals that typically recur;

2. for each plan, using indices consisting of appropriateness conditions, which are easily detectable and indicate the conditions under which the plan is appropriate;

3. *enforcing* standard preconditions so that they can be assumed true.

Thus, in RUNNER, predictive features are determined by separating preconditions that define the plan structure from the conditions that signal *appropriate use* of the plans. This separation allows tuning the conditions under which an agent will consider a given plan independent of its defined structure. This learning process improves the match between an environment and use and reuse of a library of plans in memory. Vocabularies for indexing (the appropriateness conditions in RUNNER) are thus designed to index actions in terms of the circumstances that favor their utility.

This type of utility assessment is distinguished from the type of consideration done in systems such as PRODIGY (Minton, 1988) in two ways. First, the assessment done in RUNNER concerns the utility of the features used to control the access of plans rather than the utility of the plans themselves. This allows RUNNER to actually store and reuse plans that might not be useful *in general* but are highly applicable in specific situations. Second, RUNNER's assessment is incremental and does not depend on the existence of a complete domain model. As such, it also allows the system to both remove and promote features to *appropriateness* status.

5 Indexing Plans in Human Learning

Predictive features were found to show an advantage in terms of the selectivity of reminding, producing more reliable recall of related information. This predictive features hypothesis was then implemented in the case-based model RUNNER. These "appropriateness conditions" identified structural planning features that indicate when a relevant plan should be selected. Because of the variation in surface content in planning problems, the features one must recognize to access past plans will often be ones that relate to the causal structure of the planning situation. These appropriateness conditions should include the same features a planner needs to detect and monitor anyway during the planning process.

Two experiments were conducted to explore the effect of explicitly teaching the appropriateness conditions for two plans within a complex lesson (see Vanderstoep & Seifert, 1992). Rather than using specific examples from the RUNNER project, which require a lot of interaction with the environment during planning, we chose stimuli that had the same critical properties: a variety of features could be used to index the plans in memory; a set of structural features are present; and

Table 30.3
Examples of the two similar probability problems.

Permutations problem: An art contest has 10 artists who have entered a painting. Two awards will be given: one to the first-place artist and one to the second-place artist. How many different ways can the artists win the awards?

Combinations problem: An art contest gives away three awards each year for "Outstanding Young Artist." All of the awards are identical—a $100 cash prize. There are 15 artists who are eligible for this award. How many different ways can the eligible artists win the three awards?

---

a subset of these features could be identified as "appropriateness conditions" that predict when a particular plan is appropriate for execution. Our domain involved elementary probability theory, which has been shown to produce learning of a variety of indexing features to retrieve relevant probability principles (Ross, 1989). These prior studies demonstrated that human learners can and do attend to both structural features and surface features in order to select a relevant principle. However, the paradigm also provides a testbed for the role of appropriateness conditions in plan selection: Will the presence of structural features predicting when a plan may be used facilitate human learning?

In these experiments, subjects studied either a similar pair of principles (combinations and permutations) or a dissimilar pair of principles (combinations and conditional probability) through example problems and formulas. Examples of the similar principles are given in table 30.3.

The primary manipulation was whether or not learners received information regarding the appropriateness conditions that indicate *when* to apply each principle. For these plans, the appropriateness conditions were defined as whether the order of the set is considered when counting the number of possibilities. Half of the subjects received appropriateness condition information that identified what aspects of the problem (whether the order of the objects in the sets being counted was important) determined when each of the principles should be used. The other half of the subjects received no instructions on appropriateness conditions, but were asked to review the study information for an equal time interval. It is hypothesized that when people are learning principles that are very similar to each other (i.e., easily confused), knowledge of the appropriateness conditions of the principles will be very important for learning to apply the principles. Will instructing learners about the appropriateness conditions of these problem-solving principles improve later performance?

The answers to the test problems were scored for correctness using a system similar to Ross (1989). The two groups showed no differences in the number of problems completed accurately. However, subjects instructed about the appropriateness conditions made fewer confusion errors than subjects in the review-only condition whenever a similar problem pair was used; however, this instructional manipulation had no effect when a dissimilar problem pair was used.

Why did the appropriateness conditions group make fewer errors than the review-only group? Consider that performance on this problem-solving task is a function of 1) recognizing the appropriate principle, and 2) remembering the specific content of the procedure (*e.g.*, in a mathematical problem-solving task, the particular variables and how they are arranged in the formula), and 3) using the principle correctly in the new problem. Because the appropriateness conditions subjects made fewer errors, but they did not solve more problems correctly, the instructions may have improved just the ability to identify *when* to apply a procedure, but may not improve memory for the formula, or the ability to implement it.

A second experiment examined this notion by testing subjects' *selection* of a principle for a new problem separate from their ability to execute the plan correctly. Subjects learned two of three principles of probability theory using the same materials as in the first experiment. However, instead of asking subjects to solve the test problems (as in Experiment 1), in this experiment they were told simply to select the formula (by name) among four response choices: the names of the two principles the subjects studied, along with the formulas, "neither formula" and "don't know (can't remember)." Finally, they were asked to provide an explanation for their answer.

The subjects informed about the appropriateness conditions did in fact perform better at the more specific task of selecting when to use each formula. No difference was found between the appropriateness conditions group and the review-only condition for low-similarity problems. However, subjects informed about appropriateness conditions did better than subjects in the review-only condition at selecting the correct planning principle to use. The results also suggest that subjects informed about the appropriateness conditions provided significantly better explanations for their answers than subjects in the review-only condition. In both the high-similarity and low-similarity pairs, no differences were found between the review-only and the appropriateness conditions groups for memory of any of the formulas.

These studies support the notion that instructions on appropriateness conditions facilitate the *selection* of appropriate solution procedures in solving probability problems. With the appropriateness conditions instructions, subjects received information about the importance of the order of the objects, how to identify when order is or is not important, and when each principle should be applied. When learners were provided with this information, they were more likely to correctly detect situations when each formula should be used. These experiments show that when plans are similar, providing appropriateness conditions instructions does improve selection performance while not affecting memory for the formula or the ability to instantiate the formula correctly in a target problem.

Although it may seem intuitively obvious that teaching appropriateness conditions would be helpful, instruction is not often designed like this. Consider how these same principles might be presented in a probability textbook. Permutations might be taught in one section, followed by combinations taught in the next section. Students could become proficient at solving each of the two different types of problems; however, without explicit instruction on what makes a certain problem a permutations problem and what makes another problem a combinations problem, learners may have inadequate knowledge of when each formula should be applied.

These results confirm the predictive features hypothesis, and illustrate the need for appropriateness conditions when learning in a domain with similar plans. Much of the previous work on memory retrieval of analogies and cases has focused on the features that determine similarity; however, these results suggest distinctiveness, as well as similarity, is very important for recognizing when to apply prior knowledge.

6 Implications for Indexing in Learning Models

Our computational and empirical results have shown that plans are indexed in memory based on the features that predict their applicability. These results confirm the predictive features hypothesis as developed in the RUNNER model, and serve as strong verification of the case-based learning approach as a psychological model. When indexing cases in memory, appropriateness conditions —indices related to when to consider a particular plan—are more useful than equally related information that is not helpful in distinguishing among plan options. Thus, from a functional perspective, the most useful features would be those that let one predict and access potential problems and solutions whenever they are relevant to current processing. This definition of predictive features constrains the set of indices one might propose for a computational model using past experiences, and also serves as a hypothesis for the features expected to be evident in human learning.

Past approaches have suggested that the level of abstraction of indexing features, in terms of the surface versus structural dichotomy, predicts what features will be helpful in learning by analogy (Gentner & Landers, 1985; Rattermann & Gentner, 1987; Ross, 1987). However, the evidence from the experiments using structural features presented here, and from the performance based on structural features in RUNNER, suggests that all structural features are not the same; instead, the distinctiveness—the ability to select among related plans—of a subset of structural features, and not the overall similarity or abstractness, determines valuable indices in memory.

Specifying predictive features in a task domain requires establishing the causality inherent in the domain for characterizing plan examples, and identifying both surface and structural features that are predictive of important decisions within the task context. By using a causal analysis of the goal interactions as indices for storing planning information in memory, it is possible to access plan strategies applicable to the problem (Hammond & Seifert, 1992). These strategies provide the planner with alteration techniques and information as to what parts of the initial causal configuration are appropriate targets of change, leading to specific plans for the current situation. This type of causal feature vocabulary has been incorporated into models that design tools for programs (Birnbaum & Collins, 1988), plan in the cooking domain (Hammond, 1989; Kolodner, 1987), plan radiation treatments (Berger & Hammond, 1991), schedule deliveries (Hammond, Marks, & Converse, 1988), run errands (Hammond, Converse, & Martin, 1990), and learn geometry (McDougal & Hammond, 1992).

In some domains, knowledge of the causal factors in goal and plan interactions will be needed in order to characterize when to use particular plans. For example, natural categories reflect learning the features "animate" and "inanimate" as critical concepts (Smith & Medin, 1981; Mandler, 1991). This is not simply because it is *possible* to divide the natural world into living and nonliving things; certainly, many other such criteria are possible (such as, external versus internal gestation) and are correlated with desirable information. Rather, recognizing the class of objects that are animate, and therefore capable of self-initiation, allows one to make plans that take into account possible actions on the part of those objects. The "animate" feature serves to activate expectations about how these actions may affect one's own goals. Thus, it is an important predictive feature in the natural world when making decisions about how to deal with objects in the environment. Within planning domains, then, we propose that the commonalities in the features that serve as useful indices are likely to be based on those features that predict successful pursuit of one's goals.

Other, equally related surface and structural features may be present in a domain, such as preconditions necessary for plan execution. However, unless these features are capable of distinguishing one goal pursuit situation from another, learning them is in a sense "academic": only distinctive features, whether surface or structural, provide predictive indices. A purely correlational learner such as Anderson's rational analysis model (Anderson, 1991) could find some predictive features, if the world is kind enough to isolate them in different types of causal problems. For example, correlated features may be used to signal problem types (e.g., "incline plane" problems in physics) (Chi, 1988). While this approach is often successful, it will be unable to learn the types of nonobservable structural features predictive of goal satisfaction in RUNNER. Unless these causal features are computed and encoded into memory, a model will be unable to learn the important features needed to distinguish appropriate plans across problem contexts. Of course, correlational models could be adapted to incorporate this ability to attend to structural and predictive features; however, exactly how to accomplish this, and a theory of what those features are likely to be in the planning domain, is what our predictive features model provides.

7 Conclusion

Our approach to learning predictive features not only describes what people *do* learn, it also suggests what people *should* learn in a functional sense, and therefore what knowledge learning programs must be capable of acquiring. In this collaborative enterprise, the psychological experiments confirm that human memory access to prior cases can be facilitated by cues that contain particular predictive structural features. This evidence lends support to case-based models as potential models of human reasoning and memory; more specifically, our results have shown that human behavior is consistent with the case-based learning tenant that cases are indexed by the features that predict their applicability. The empirical studies in this collaboration confirm the *ideas* behind our computational models, rather than the specific *behaviors* of a particular implementation.

Acknowledgments

This work was supported by the Office of Naval Research under contract N0014-85-K-010 to the University of Chicago and contract N0014-91-J-1128 to the University of Michigan. Support was also provided by the Defense Advanced Research Projects Agency under contact F49620-88-C-0058 to the University of Chicago, DARPA contract number N00014-91-J-4092 monitored by the Office of Naval Research, and Office of Naval Research grant number N00014-91-J-1185. Thanks to Michael Pazzani and anonymous reviewers for comments on an earlier manuscript.

Note

1. One alternative approach is to design the agent so that it considers only relevant conditions, either by hand-crafting the decision procedure, or by a mixture of hand-crafting and clever compilation of declarative specifications (Rosenschein, 1986).

References

Alterman, R. (1985). Adaptive planning: Refitting old plans to new situations. *Cognitive Science*.

Anderson, J. R. (1990). The *adaptive character of thought*. Hillsdale, NJ: Lawrence Erlbaum.

Berger, J., and Hammond, K. (1990). ROENTGEN: A case-based approach to radiation therapy planning. In *The Proceedings of the 32nd Annual Scientific Meeting of the American Society of Therapeutic Radiology and Oncology*.

Berger, J., and Hammond, K. J. (1991). ROENTGEN: A memory-based approach to radiation therapy treatment design. In (R. Bareiss, Ed.), *Proceedings of the 1991 DARPA Workshop on Case-Based Reasoning*. Los Altos, CA: Morgan Kaufmann, Associates.

Birnbaum, L., and Collins, G. (1988). The transfer of the experience across planning domains through the acquisition of abstract strategies. In J. Kolodner (Ed.), *Proceedings of a Workshop on Case-based Reasoning*. Los Altos, CA: Morgan Kauffmann, p. 61–79.

Carbonell, J. G. (1983). Learning by analogy: Formulating and generalizing plans from past experience. In R. S. Michalski, J. G. Carbonell, and T. M. Mitchell (Eds.), *Machine Learning: An Artificial Intelligence Approach*. Los Altos, CA: Morgan Kaufman.

Dyer, M. G. (1983). *In-depth understanding: A computer model of integrated processing for narrative comprehension.* Cambridge, MA: MIT Press.

Feigenbaum, E. (1990). The simulation of verbal learning behavior. In J. Shavlik, and T. Dietterick (Eds.), *Readings in machine learning.* New York: Morgan Kauffmann.

Gentner, D. (1983). Structure-mapping: A theoretical framework for analogy. *Cognitive Science, 7,* 155–170.

Gentner, D., and Landers, R. (1985). Analogical reminding; A good match is hard to find. In *Proceedings of the International Conference on Systems, Man, and Cybernetics.* Tucson, AZ.

Gick, M. L., and Holyoak, K. J. (1980). Analogical problem solving. *Cognitive Psychology, 12,* 306–355.

Gick, M. L., and Holyoak, K. J. (1983). Schema induction and analogical transfer. *Cognitive Psychology, 15,* 1–38.

Hammond, K. J., Marks, M., and Converse, T. (1992). Planning, opportunism and memory. In D. Atkinson, and D. Miller (Eds.), *Planning systems for autonomous mobile robots.*

Hammond, K. J., Converse, T., and Martin, C. (1990). Integrating planning and acting in a case-based framework. In *The Proceedings of the 1990 National Conference of Artificial Intelligence.*

Hammond, K. (1989). *Case-based planning: Viewing planning as a memory task.* San Diego: Academic Press, Inc.

Hammond, K. J., and Seifert, C. M. (1992). Indexing plans in memory. *Proceedings of the Fourteenth Annual Cognitive Science Society Conference,* Bloomington, IN.

Hammond, K. J., and Seifert, C. M. (1993). A cognitive science approach to case-based planning. In S. Chipman and A. L. Meyrowitz (Eds.), *Foundations of knowledge acquisition: Cognitive models of complex learning.* Norwell, MA: Kluwer Academic Publishers, 245–267.

Hammond, K. J., Seifert, C. M., and Gray, K. C. (1991). Functionality in analogical transfer: A hard match is good to find. *Journal of the Learning Sciences, 1:2,* 111–152.

Johnson, H. M., and Seifert, C. M. (1992). The role of predictive features in retrieving analogical cases. *Journal of Memory and Language, 31,* 648–667.

Johnson, H. K., and Seifert, C. M. (1990). Predictive utility in case-based memory retrieval. In *Proceedings of the Twelfth Annual Cognitive Science Society,* Boston, Massachusetts.

Kolodner, J. L., and Simpson, R. L. (1989). The mediator: Analysis of an early case-based problem. *Cognitive Science.*

Kolodner, J. L. (1984). *Retrieval and organizational strategies in conceptual memory: A computer model.* Hillsdale, NJ: Lawrence Erlbaum Associates.

Kolodner, J. L., Simpson, R. L., and Sycara, K. (1985). A process model of case-based reasoning in problem-solving. In *The Proceedings of the Ninth International Joint Conference on Artificial Intelligence,* Los Angeles, CA: IJCAI.

Kolodner, J. (1987). Extending Problem Solver Capabilities Through Case-Based Inference. In *Proceedings of the Fourth International Workshop on Machine Learning.* Los Altos, CA: Morgan Kaufman Publishers, Inc., p. 167–178.

Kolodner, J. L. (1983). Reconstructive memory: A computer model. *Cognitive Science, 7,* 281–328.

Lehnert, W. (1980). Plot units and narrative summarization. *Cognitive Science, 5,* 293–331.

Martin, C. E. (1990). Direct Memory Access Parsing. Ph.D. Thesis, Yale University.

Martin, C. E., and Reisbeck, C. (1986). Uniform parsing and inferencing for learning. In *Proceedings of the Fifth Annual Conference on Artificial Intelligence,* Philadelphia, PA: AAAI.

McDougal, T., Hammond, K. J., and Seifert, C. M. (1991). A functional perspective on reminding. *Proceedings of the Thirteenth Annual Cognitive Science Society,* Chicago, Illinois.

McDougal, T. and Hammond, K. (1992). A recognition model of geometry theorem-proving. *Proceedings of the Fourteenth Annual Conference of the Cognitive Science Society,* Bloomington, Indiana.

Minton, S. (1988). Learning effective search-control knowledge: An explanation-based approach. Technical Report #133, Carnegie-Mellon University, Department of Computer Science.

Newell, A. (1991). *Unified theories of cognition.* Cambridge: Harvard University Press.

Owens, C. (1990). Functional criteria for indices and labels. *Working Notes of the AAAI Spring Symposium Series.* Palo Alto, CA.

Pazzani, M. J. (1989). Indexing Strategies for goal specific retrieval of cases. *Proceedings of the Case-Based Reasoning Workshop,* Pensacola Beach, FL.

Pazzani, M. J. (1991). *Learning causal relationships: An integration of empirical and explanation-based learning methods.* Hillsdale, NJ: Lawrence Erlbaum Associates.

Pirolli, P. L., and Anderson, J. R. (1985). The role of learning from examples in the acquisition of recursive programming skills. *Canadian Journal of Psychology, 39,* 240–272.

Ratterman, M. J., and Gentner, D. (1987). Analogy and similarity: Determinants of accessibility and inferential soundness. In J. Anderson (Ed.), *Proceedings of the Ninth Annual Meeting of the Cognitive Science Society.* Hillsdale, NJ; Lawrence Erlbaum Associates, Inc.

Riesbeck, C. K., and Schank, R. C. (1989). *Inside Case-based Reasoning.* Hillsdale, NJ: Erlbaum.

Rosenschein, S. J., and Kaelbling, L. P. (1986). The synthesis of digital machines with provable epistemic properties. In *Proceedings of 1986 Conference on Theoretical Aspects of Reasoning About Knowledge.*

Ross, R. H. (1987). This is like that: The use of earlier problems and the separation of similarity effects. *Journal of Experimental Psychology: Learning, Memory, and Cognition, 13,* 629–639.

Ross, B. H. (1989). Distinguishing types of superficial similarities: Different effects on the access and use of earlier problems. *Journal of Experimental Psychology: Learning, Memory, and Cognition, 15,* 456–468.

Ross, B. H. (1989). Remindings in learning and instruction. In S. Vosniadou and A. Ortony (Eds.), *Similarity and analogical reasoning.* Cambridge: Cambridge University Press.

Schank, R. C. (1982). *Dynamic memory: A theory of reminding and learning in computers and people.* New York: Cambridge University Press.

Schank, R. C., and Abelson, R. P. (1977). *Scripts, plans, goals, and understanding.* Hillsdale, NJ: Lawrence Erlbaum Associates.

Schank, R. C., and Riesbeck, C. (1990). *Inside case-based reasoning.* Hillsdale, NJ: Erlbaum.

Seifert, C. M. (1988). Goals in reminding. *Proceedings of the DARPA Work on Case-based Reasoning in AI,* Clearwater Beach, Florida.

Seifert, C. M. (1993) "The role of goals in analogical retrieval." K. J. Holyoak and J. A. Barnden (Eds), *Advances in connectionist and neural computation theory, vol. 2: Analogical connections.* Norwood, NJ: Ablex Publishing Company.

Seifert, C. M. McKoon, G., Abelson, R. P., and Ratcliff, R. (1986). Memory connections between thematically similar episodes. *Journal of Experimental Psychology: Learning, Memory, and Cognition, 12,* 220–231.

Simpson, R. L. (1985). A computer model of case-based reasoning in problem-solving: An investigation in the domain of dispute mediation. Ph.D. Thesis, School of Information and Computer Science, Georgia Institute of Technology.

Smith, E. E., and Medin, D. L. (1981). *Categories and concepts.* Cambridge, MA: Harvard University Press.

VanderStoep, S. W., and Seifert, C. M. (1993). "Learning 'how' vs. learning 'when:' Improving problem solving transformer." *Journal of the Learning Sciences.*

VanderStoep, S. W., and Seifert, C. M. (1993). "Learning WHEN: Predictive features in analogical transfer." P. Pintrich, D. Brown, C. Weinstein (Eds.), *Perspectives on Student Motivation, Cognition, and Learning: Essays in Honor of Wilbert J. McKeachie.* Hillsdale, NJ: Erlbaum Associates.

Inductive Reasoning

Chapter 31

Feature-Based Induction

Steven A. Sloman

Feature-Based Induction

One way we learn about and function in the world is by inducing properties of one category from another. Our knowledge that leopards can be dangerous leads us to keep a safe distance from jaguars. Osherson, Smith, Wilkie, Lopez, and Shafir (1990) examine the conditions under which a property that is asserted of one or more categories will also be asserted of another category by asking about the judged strength of *categorical* arguments such as

> Elephants love onions.
> Mustangs love onions.
> ―――――――――――――――――
> Therefore, Zebras love onions.

(a)

What degree of belief in the conclusion of such an argument is attributable to the premises and what is the nature of the inductive inference?

Osherson et al. (1990) propose that the psychological strength of categorical arguments depends on "(i) the degree to which the premise categories are similar to the conclusion category and (ii) the degree to which the premise categories are similar to members of the lowest level category that includes both the premise and the conclusion categories" (p. 185). Their model accounts for 13 qualitative phenomena and provides good quantitative fits to the results of several experiments (corroborative data are presented in Osherson, Stern, Wilkie, Stob, & Smith, 1991, and Smith, Lopez, & Osherson, 1992).

This paper proposes an alternative, feature-based, model of this inductive task. The model is expressed using some simple connectionist tools, similar to those that have been used to model learning processes (e.g., Gluck & Bower, 1988). The main idea is that an argument whose conclusion claims a relation between category C (e.g., Zebras) and predicate P (e.g., love onions) is judged strong to the extent that the features of C have already been associated with P in the premises. The automatic generalization property of distributed representations is exploited in order to model the induction of predicates from one category to another (cf. Hinton, McClelland, & Rumelhart, 1986). The model accounts for 10 of the phenomena described by Osherson et al. (1990) and provides a more accurate account of one of the remaining phenomena. A generalization of the model, discussed near the end of the paper, is shown to be compatible with the remaining 2 phenomena. The model also motivated 2 new phenomena. Finally, the model is shown to provide good fits to argument strength ratings.

Osherson et al.'s model is *category-based* in that it assumes that judgments of argument strength depend on a stable hierarchical category structure that is describable without reference to the attributes or features of either category, such as the superset–subset relation that exists between Mammals and Elephants. Indeed, the primitive elements in Osherson et al.'s (1990) model are pairwise similarities between categories at the same hierarchical level. In Osherson et al. (1991), pairwise similarities are derived from feature vectors. Nevertheless, their model remains category-based in that features are used only to derive similarities between categories at the same hierarchical level.

The present model is *feature-based* in that it assumes that argument strength judgments depend on connection strengths between features of the conclusion category and the property of interest without regard to any fixed structural relations that may exist between whole categories. All categories are represented as vectors of numerical values over a set of features. The existence of a stable category-structure is not assumed by the model because it is not necessary; all inductive processes depend strictly on the features of premise and conclusion categories. Obviously, people do have some knowledge about the hierarchical organization among some categories. Many people know that Elephants are Mammals. The assumption being made here is that this knowledge is represented in a way distinct from the structures that normally support judgments of categorical argument strength. Knowledge about category structure is not generally used when engaging in the kind of inductive task under consideration, although surely it is used some of the time.

The foregoing assumes a distinction between what might be called *intuitive* and *logical* modes of inference (cf. Rips, 1990, for a parallel distinction between the loose and strict views of reasoning). The feature-based model is intended to capture an aspect of only the "looser," intuitive form of reasoning. As a model of argument strength, it presupposes that, given a fixed featural representation of each category, category hierarchies are needed to describe only the logical reasoning process, not the intuitive one. The similarity-coverage model can be construed as a model of intuition only if one is willing to ascribe categorical reasoning to an intuitive process.

A second difference between the two models is that only the category-based model assumes that subjects explicitly compute similarity. The feature-based model does assume a feature-matching process, but not one that computes any empirically valid measure of similarity per se.

The Similarity-Coverage Model of Argument Strength
Both the category and feature-based models of argument strength apply to arguments, such as (a) above, that can be written schematically as a list of sentences, $P_1 \ldots P_n/C$, in which the P_i are the premises of an argument and C is the conclusion, each with an associated category (cat). Osherson et al.'s (1990) model consists of a linear combination of two variables defined in terms of SIM_S. The first variable, similarity, expresses the degree of resemblance between premise categories and the conclusion category. The second variable, coverage, reflects the degree of resemblance between premise categories and members of the lowest-level category that properly includes both the premise and conclusion categories. Therefore, they refer to their model as the similarity-coverage model of argument strength.

The arguments examined by Osherson et al. (1990) were all categorical in that premises and conclusion all had the form "all members of Y have property X" where Y was a simple category (like Feline or Reptile) and X remained fixed across the premises and conclusion within each argument (cf. Rips, 1975). Categories all involved natural kinds, in particular the hierarchy of living things. Predicates were chosen so that subjects would have few prior beliefs about them, for instance "secretes uric acid crystals." Osherson et al. (1990) dub these *blank* predicates, and point out that their use permits theorists to focus on the role of categories in the transmission of belief from premises to conclusion, minimizing the extent to which subjects reason about the particular properties employed. Some comments and speculation about modeling nonblank predicates can be found in this paper's concluding section. Otherwise, my discussion is limited to blank predicates whose identity is irrelevant and therefore will be generically referred to as "predicate X."

The Feature-Based Model

Overview
We start with a set of input units to encode feature values and an output unit to encode the blank predicate X. Consider the argument

> Robins have X.
> ———————————
> Falcons have X.

(b)

The process by which the feature-based model determines the strength of this argument is diagramed in fig. 31.1. The state of the network before presentation of the argument is illustrated in fig. 31.1a. Because the argument's predicate is blank, the unit representing it is initially not connected to any featural units. Premises are then encoded by connecting the units representing the features of each premise category to the predicate unit allowing the category units to activate the predicate unit (fig. 31.1b). To encode the premise of Argument (b) for

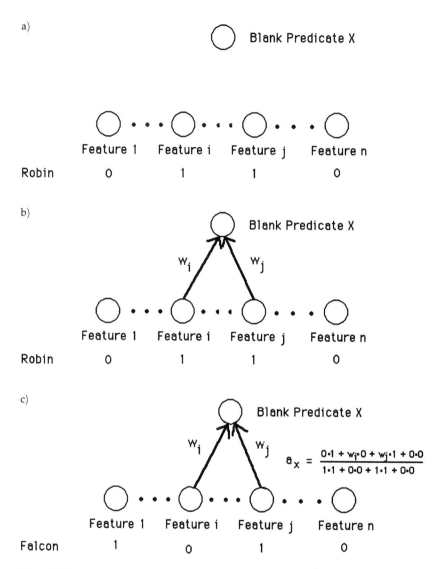

Figure 31.1
Illustration of the feature-based model for the argument "Robins have property X, therefore, Falcons have property X." (a) Before encoding premise "Robins have property X." (b) After encoding premise "Robins have property X." (c) Testing conclusion "Falcons have property X."

instance, the units encoding features of Robins (a small number of binary features are used for expository purposes only) are connected to the blank predicate unit X. Had there been more than one premise in Argument (b), the features of each additional premise's category would have been connected to unit X in identical fashion. Second, conclusions are tested by determining the extent to which unit X becomes "activated" upon presentation of the features of the conclusion category (fig. 31.1c). In the example, this would be accomplished by observing the activation value of unit X upon presentation of the features of Falcons which would be 0.5 because the predicate unit is connected to one-half of the active category units.

I posit two rules, an encoding rule and an activation rule, which, along with a set of feature vectors, completely determine the model's predictions. The encoding rule, Eq. 1 below, defines how connections are established. The activation rule, Eq. 3 below, determines the value of unit X (denoted a_x). Because connection strengths depend on the values of premise features, a_x increases with the extent of shared features between premise and conclusion categories. a_x is defined to decrease with the extent of features in the conclusion category alone.

Throughout the paper, vectors will be represented by capital letters (e.g., vector B) and their scalar elements will be represented by corresponding lower-case letters subscripted by their ordinal position (e.g., b_1 or b_i).

Categories and Predicates

Every category, such as Robins, Mammals, or Animals, is identified with a vector F of n real numbers from the closed $[0, 1]$ interval. For instance, F(Robins) = $[f_1(\text{Robins}), \ldots, f_n(\text{Robins})]$, where $F(\text{Robins})$ is a vector encoding the feature values of Robins. The f_i are variables which represent a basis set of atomic features and are assigned individual feature values, in this case those corresponding to Robins. Both the vector F and the scalar f_i's could be subscripted by S, to indicate that F refers to a given subject S's representation of a category, because a category's representation presumably varies from subject to subject. We could also index representations by time. Such indices will be left implicit in what follows.

Feature values used for modeling can be derived by having subjects list or rate features or attributes for each category. I do not assume that vectors represent sets of necessary or sufficient features, nor that features are independent of each other. I rather assume that they represent a large number of interdependent perceptual and abstract attributes. In general, these values may depend on the context in which categories are presented. I will assume however that category representations are fairly constant within each of the experiments to be discussed. Notice that no distinction is made between the nature of the representations of general categories like Animals and specific categories like Robins.

Network Architecture and Dynamics
The model of any single argument uses a network of n input units and a single output unit. Each input unit is assigned value a_i equal to f_i, the value of feature i of the category under consideration. So, upon presentation of category Y, activation vector $A(Y) = [a_1(Y), \ldots, a_n(Y)] = F(Y)$; the current stimulus $A(Y)$ is set equal to the stored representation $F(Y)$. The activation of the output unit, a_x, represents the willingness to confirm predicate X of the input category. Upon presentation of a conclusion category, if the value of a_x is high, then the argument is judged strong; if low, then it is judged weak. Finally, connecting input units to predicate unit X is a vector of weights, $W = [w_1, \ldots, w_n]$. All weight values are restricted to the closed interval $[0, 1]$.

A, a_x, and W are dynamic variables and should somehow be indexed by their history. A is already indexed by the current input. W depends only on encoded premises P_1 to P_j. It will be indexed as $W(P_1, \ldots, P_j)$. When encoding the jth premise in a multiple-premise argument, a_x depends on encoded premises P_1 to P_{j-1} and input premise P_j, in which case I will write $a_x(P_j/P_1, \ldots, P_{j-1})$. When testing a conclusion, a_x depends on encoded premises P_1 to P_j and conclusion C, and I will write $a_x(C/P_1, \ldots, P_j)$. I will compress the notation by not writing out predicates because they are blank and therefore uninformative. For example, the strength of Argument (a) would be written a_x(Zebras/Elephants, Mustangs). If no premises have previously been encoded, the value of a_x given premise P as input will be denoted $a_x(P)$.

Encoding a Premise (Learning Rule)
To encode the category in a premise P, input units are set equal to the feature values of the category in P, so that $A(P) = F(P)$, and then weights are changed according to the following delta rule (cf., Sutton & Barto, 1981) in which the network is learning to turn on unit X in the presence of input from the category of P. Let the weight vector have some value $W(P_0)$ where P_0 represents zero or more premises, then after encoding premise P,

$$w_i(P_0, P) = w_i(P_0) + \lambda_i[1 - a_x(P/P_0)]a_i(P), \tag{1}$$

where each λ_i is a scalar coefficient. To keep each weight between 0 and 1, I assume that a_x does not exceed 1 and set

$$\lambda_i = 1 - w_i(P_0). \tag{2}$$

This removes the one free parameter we otherwise would have had. It also ensures that weights never decrease.

An important property of this encoding rule is that it depends on the activation of unit X. The extent to which each premise category activates unit X is established before that premise is encoded. Encoding a premise involves updating connection strengths. The amount of change that connection strengths undergo is proportional to the premise's *surprise* value $[1 - a_x(P/P_0)]$, or the extent to which the premise category does not activate unit X given the premises already encoded.

Activation Rule for Unit X
The activation of unit X depends on the premises P_1 to P_j that have already been encoded in the weights as well as the current input category I which comes either from another premise or from the conclusion. The activation rule is

$$a_x(I/P_1, \ldots, P_j) = \frac{W(P_1, \ldots, P_j) \cdot A(I)}{|A(I)|^2},$$
(3)

where $\cdot$ means the dot or inner product, defined as $U \cdot V = \sum_{i=1}^{n} u_i v_i$, which is a measure of the two vectors' overlap. The vertical bars represent the length of a vector. By "magnitude," I refer to the denominator of (3), or length squared: $|U|^2 = \sum_{i=1}^{n} u_i^2$. In words, the activation of unit X is proportional to the overlap between values of corresponding weights and input elements and inversely proportional to the number and size of input elements. When I is a conclusion category, $a_x(I/P_1, \ldots, P_j)$ is a model of argument strength.

Psychological Interpretation of Activation Rule
Equation 3 states that the activation value of unit X increases with the dot product of the current input and previous inputs as they are encoded in the weights by the learning rule. The interpretation is that a novel predicate is affirmed of the current input category to the extent that it shares features with other categories which are known to have the relevant property. If we know that Robins have some property X, then to the extent that Robins and Falcons have other properties in common, we will judge that Falcons also have property X.

Equation 3 also states that the activation value of unit X is inversely proportional to the magnitude of the current input. Magnitude is a measure of the number and size of the features in a category's representation. It is meant to capture the richness of a representation by indicating the extent of salient features in the category. The magnitude of a representation would be determined by the category's familiarity and complexity. The claim is that our willingness to affirm a property of a category decreases with the amount we already know about that category, given that the number of features the category shares with other categories that possess that property is held constant.

The most straightforward test of the conclusion magnitude prediction requires a specification of the features of some set of categories so that we can measure their common features and magnitudes directly. Throughout this paper, I will make use of feature ratings collected by Osherson et al. (1991), who obtained ratings of "the relative strength of association" between a set of properties and a set of mammals.[1]

I constructed pairs of one-premise arguments by choosing triples of Mammal categories such that one Mammal shared an equal number of features with both of the other categories but the two other categories differed in their magnitudes. For example, according to Osherson's feature-ratings, Collies and Horses have about as many features in common as Collies and Persian cats; i.e., F(Collies) · F(Horses) $\approx$ F(Collies) · F(Persian cats). But the representation of Horses is of greater magnitude than that of Persian cats. $|F(Horses)|^2 > |F(Persian\ cats)|^2$. Consider the pair of arguments

> All Collies produce phagocytes.
> ───────────────────────────
> All Persian cats produce phagocytes.

(c)

and

> All Collies produce phagocytes.
> ───────────────────────────
> All Horses produce phagocytes.

(d)

According to the feature-based model, the weight vectors obtained by encoding the premises of each argument will be identical because the premises themselves are identical. The premise and conclusion categories in the two arguments have the same measure of common features, so any difference in strength between the two arguments must be attributable to the difference in magnitude of their conclusion categories (this is further explicated below, by Eq. 5). In particular, people should find Argument (c) stronger than Argument (d) because it has a lower magnitude conclusion category.

I asked 34 University of Michigan undergraduates to rate the convincingness of each of 20 arguments, 10 pairs of arguments that conformed to this structure. Within a pair, premises were identical and shared an equal measure of common features with the two conclusion categories. But conclusions had different magnitudes. Subjects rated each argument on an interval scale in which 0 meant very unconvincing and 10 meant very convincing.

For each pair, the argument with the smaller magnitude conclusion category was rated as stronger (mean rating was 2.17) than that with the larger magnitude conclusion category (mean of 1.65). This difference was highly significant for these 10 argument pairs across subjects, $t(33) = 2.75$, $p < .01$. The feature-based model has successfully predicted a rather nonintuitive result: The strength of an argument can be increased by choosing a conclusion category which has fewer features associated with it, even when a measure of features common to the premise and conclusion categories is held constant.

The magnitude prediction also finds support in people's tendency to generalize less from a member of an in-group to other in-group members than from a member of an out-group to other out-group members (Quattrone & Jones, 1980). For example, Rutgers sophomores who were told that another Rutgers student had chosen to listen to classical music over rock music gave lower percentage estimates that other Rutgers students would also choose classical music relative to estimates they gave that Princeton students would choose classical music after observing a Princeton student do so. This tendency supports the current hypothesis since people presumably know more about the category of people in their in-group than in an out-group.

Feature Coverage
According to the model, argument strength is, roughly, the proportion of features in the conclusion category that are also in the premise categories. For single-premise arguments in which features are all either 0 or 1, this statement is exact. An exact formulation for the general case is provided by the geometric interpretation below. Intuitively, an argument seems strong to the extent that premise category features "cover" the features of the conclusion category, although the present notion of coverage is substantially different from that embodied by the similarity–coverage model.

Single-Premise Arguments
Before encountering an argument, weights are all equal to 0, indicating that the network has no prior knowledge relevant to the property; i.e., the property is blank. In other words, $w_i(\ ) = 0$ for all i, where the empty parentheses indicate that nothing has been encoded. Therefore, using Eq. 3, the value of a_x as the first premise is encoded is

$$a_x(P_1) = \frac{W(\ ) \cdot A(P_1)}{|A(P_1)|^2}$$

$$= \frac{\Sigma w_i(\ ) a_i(P_1)}{\Sigma a_i(P_1)^2}$$

$$= 0,$$

and the value of each weight after encoding a single premise is

$$w_i(P_1) = w_i(\ ) + [1 - w_i(\ )][1 - a_x(P_1)]a_i(P_1)$$

$$= 0 + (1 - 0)(1 - 0)a_i(P_1)$$

$$= a_i(P_1)$$

$$= f_i(P_1). \tag{4}$$

Therefore, the weight vector after encoding a single premise is identical to the vector representing the category in the premise, $W(P_1) = F(P_1)$. Furthermore, the strength of an argument consisting of a single premise and a conclusion is, using first (3) and then (4):

$$a_x(C/P_1) = \frac{W(P_1) \cdot F(C)}{|F(C)|^2}$$

$$= \frac{F(P_1) \cdot F(C)}{|F(C)|^2}. \tag{5}$$

In sum, single-premise arguments depend only on the dot product of the vectors representing premise and conclusion categories and, inversely, on the magnitude of the conclusion category vector.

Geometric Interpretation

By considering a geometric representation of the feature-based model, we can state precisely the sense in which it posits that the strength of an argument is equal to the proportion of the conclusion category's features that it shares with the premise categories.

In words, the strength of an argument is equal to the proportion of the length of the conclusion category vector that is spanned by the length of the projection of the weight vector onto the conclusion category vector. In this sense, argument strength is the proportion of features in a conclusion category that are also in the premise categories.

In the previous section, we saw that the weight vector used to determine the strength of a single-premise argument is identical to the vector representing the premise category. Therefore, the strength of a single-premise argument is simply the proportion of the length of the conclusion category vector that is spanned by the length of the projection of the premise category vector onto the conclusion category vector. One interpretation is that an argument is strong to the extent its conclusion can be "justified" or "explained" by its premises relative to the total amount that must be justified or explained, i.e., relative to the number of features that the conclusion category is known to possess.

Definition of Similarity

As mentioned above, the feature-based model does not assume that similarity is computed in the course of making argument strength judgments. Nevertheless, in order to make contact with the phenomena to be described, a theoretical measure of the similarity between two category vectors is required. This model of similarity does not reflect any of the computations performed by the feature-based model. It functions only to represent phenomena described in terms of similarity in a language compatible with the feature-based model.

Perhaps the simplest measure of similarity would be the dot product between the two category vectors, an indicator of the categories' common features. One disadvantage of the dot product is its sensitivity to the magnitudes of its operands. Consequently, I define the *similarity* (sim) of two categories D and E using a measure of correlation between the vectors $F(D)$ and $F(E)$, specifically the cosine of the angle between them:

$$\text{sim}(D, E) = \frac{F(D) \cdot F(E)}{|F(D)| \, |F(E)|}.$$ (6)

The virtues of this measure are that it captures most of the properties normally attributed to similarity judgments and its relation to the feature-based model is simple mathematically. This will facilitate many of the demonstrations below concerning phenomena involving similarity judgments.

Phenomena Consistent with Both Models

Osherson et al. (1990) and Smith et al. (1992) review, propose, and provide empirical support for several phenomena concerning the variables that influence argument strength. Since the phenomena are intended to describe tendencies, as opposed to laws, we should expect counterexamples to exist, as both models predict. In fact, the phenomena themselves can generate opposing expectations for certain arguments (e.g., phenomenon *i* below, similarity, versus phenomena *ii* and *iii*, premise diversity). Because of this fuzziness in the sets of arguments to which they apply, the phenomena are presented by example, and I demonstrate how the feature-based model accounts for each of these examples. Each phenomenon is illustrated with one or more contrasting pairs of arguments in which the first argument is stronger than the second.

i. Premise–Conclusion Similarity (Specific)   Arguments are strong to the extent that categories in the premises are similar to the conclusion category (Rips, 1975). The following exemplifies the phenomenon for single-premise arguments:

A.		B.
German shepherds have X.		German shepherds have X.
$\overline{\rule{3cm}{0pt}}$ is stronger than		$\overline{\rule{3cm}{0pt}}$.
Collies have X.		Chihuahuas have X.

Sixty-one of 64 University of Michigan undergraduates chose the first argument as more convincing ($p < .0001$).[2] Similarity ratings were also collected from 63 of these subjects. The mean similarity rating between German shepherds and Collies was 5.30, significantly higher than that between German shepherds and Chihuahuas (3.88), $t(62) = 7.38$, $p < .0001$. The feature-based model attributes this phenomenon to feature coverage: Due to their greater similarity, German shepherds cover more features of Collies than they do of Chihuahuas. A more formal analysis follows.

To obtain argument strengths, the first step is to encode the premise German shepherds (GS) have X. From (4), $W(GS) = F(GS)$. The second step is to test the conclusion. From Eq. 5, the strength of Argument A is

$$a_x(\text{Collies}/\text{GS}) = \frac{F(GS) \cdot F(\text{Collies})}{|F(\text{Collies})|^2}.$$

The strength of Argument B is derived similarly with the result that

$$a_x(\text{Chihuahuas}/\text{GS}) = \frac{F(\text{GS}) \cdot F(\text{Chihuahuas})}{|F(\text{Chihuahuas})|^2}.$$

One way that we can determine whether the feature-based model makes the right prediction is to compute argument strengths from empirically determined estimates of category features and then compare these strengths to the obtained ones. I used Osherson et al.'s (1991) ratings to estimate F(GS), F(Collies), and F(Chihuahuas), and computed that $F(\text{GS}) \cdot F(\text{Collies}) = 7.5$ and $F(\text{GS}) \cdot F(\text{Chihuahuas}) = 6.8$; the former pair of categories have more common features. Furthermore, $|F(\text{Collies})| = 7.7$, slightly less than $|F(\text{Chihuahuas})|^2 = 8.0$. Mainly because German shepherds and Collies have more common features than do German shep herds and Chihuahuas, the feature-based model correctly predicts that $a_x(\text{Collies}/\text{GS}) > a_x(\text{Chihuahuas}/\text{GS})$.

A more general formulation of the model's predictions can be obtained by examining its relation to Eq. 6, our model of similarity. Consider categories A, B, and C such that $\text{sim}(A, B) > \text{sim}(A, C)$ or, from Eq. 6,

$$\frac{F(A) \cdot F(B)}{|F(A)| \, |F(B)|} > \frac{F(A) \cdot F(C)}{|F(A)| \, |F(C)|},$$

which implies

$$\frac{F(A) \cdot F(B)}{|F(B)|} > \frac{F(A) \cdot F(C)}{|F(C)|}. \tag{7}$$

What are the implications of this inequality for the relative strength of the arguments "A have X, therefore B have X," and "A have X, therefore C have X"? The strength of the former argument is

$$a_x(B/A) = \frac{F(A) \cdot F(B)}{|F(B)|^2} \qquad \text{by Eq. 5,}$$

$$> \frac{F(A) \cdot F(C)}{|F(C)| \, |F(B)|} \qquad \text{by substitution with Eq. 7,}$$

$$\geq \frac{F(A) \cdot F(C)}{|F(C)|^2} \qquad \text{if } |F(C)| \geq |F(B)|$$

$$= a_x(C/A) \qquad \text{by Eq. 5.}$$

$a_x(C/A)$ is the strength of the second argument. So as long as $|F(C)| \geq |F(B)|$, the argument involving the more similar pair of categories will b stronger. In most cases, this argument will be stronger even if $|F(B)| > |F(C)|$. To see this, observe that rearranging Eq. 7 gives

$$F(A) \cdot F(B) > \frac{|F(B)|}{|F(C)|} F(A) \cdot F(C).$$

In words, A and B have more common features than A and C relative to the ratio of the magnitudes of B and C. If A and B have sufficiently many more common features than A and C, if $F(A) \cdot F(B)$ is sufficiently greater than $F(A) \cdot F(C)$, then the right-hand side of this inequality will remain smaller even if we square the coefficient $|F(B)|/|F(C)|$. In this case, we have that

$$F(A) \cdot F(B) > \left[\frac{|F(B)|}{|F(C)|}\right]^2 F(A) \cdot F(C).$$

If this condition does hold, then by dividing both sides by $|F(B)|^2$, we have that $a_x(B/A) > a_x(C/A)$, or the first argument is stronger, even if $|F(B)| > |F(C)|$. The critical condition for the similarity phenomenon to hold is that the features of the more similar conclusion category are better covered by the premise category. If the features of the two more similar categories have enough overlap, they will produce a stronger argument regardless of the magnitude of the conclusion category.

As an illustration of the power of this analysis, I now provide a counterexample to the similarity phenomenon that is consistent with both the feature-based model and Eq. 6, the model of similarity. Consider the pair of arguments

Fact: Bobcats have sesamoid bones.
_____   (e)
Conclusion: Moles have sesamoid bones.

Fact: Bobcats have sesamoid bones.
_____   (f)
Conclusion: Rats have sesamoid bones.

According to the judgments of 40 University of Michigan students, the similarity of Bobcats and Moles, which averaged 3.10, was not significantly different from the mean similarity rating of Bobcats and Rats (2.95), $t(39) = 1.03$, ns. Equation 6 expresses this fact as

$$\frac{F(\text{Bobcats}) \cdot F(\text{Moles})}{|F(\text{Bobcats})|\,|F(\text{Moles})|} = \frac{F(\text{Bobcats}) \cdot F(\text{Rats})}{|F(\text{Bobcats})|\,|F(\text{Rats})|},$$

which implies

$$\frac{F(\text{Bobcats}) \cdot F(\text{Moles})}{|F(\text{Moles})|} = \frac{F(\text{Bobcats}) \cdot F(\text{Rats})}{|F(\text{Rats})|}.$$

According to Osherson et al.'s (1991) feature ratings, more properties were rated as having a higher strength of association to Rats than to Moles, $|F(\text{Rats})| > |F(\text{Moles})|$, which is consistent with the claim that people's representation of Rats is, on average, richer than that of Moles. In conjunction with the equality immediately above, this implies

$$\frac{F(\text{Bobcats}) \cdot F(\text{Moles})}{|F(\text{Moles})|^2} > \frac{F(\text{Bobcats}) \cdot F(\text{Rats})}{|F(\text{Rats})|^2},$$

or that, according to the feature-based model, Argument e should be stronger than Argument f, and 26 of 40 of the students chose it the stronger ($p < .05$ by a binomial test of the probability of achieving a value of 26 or greater).[3] This pattern of data was replicated with a separate group of subjects. In short, the feature-based model was able to predict a case in which one argument was stronger than another, despite apparently equal category similarity, by virtue of the relative magnitudes of their conclusions.

The problem is more complicated with two-premise argument pairs such as

A.	B.
German shepherds have X.	German shepherds have X.
Dalmatians have X.	Dalmatians have X.

A. German shepherds have X. Dalmatians have X. ———————— is stronger than German shepherds have X. Dalmatians have X. ———————— , Collies have X. Chihuahuas have X.

in which both German shepherds and Dalmatians are more similar to Collies than to Chihuahuas (60 of 64 students chose Argument A as the stronger one. The mean similarity of Dalmatians and Collies was judged to be 4.94, significantly greater than that of Dalmatians and Chihuahuas of 3.86, $t(63) = 6.08$, $p < .0001$). The explanation for the premise–conclusion similarity phenomenon with multiple premises is conceptually identical to that for the single-premise case. Argument strength is proportional to the dot product of the conclusion category vector and the weight vector encoding the premises. The more features shared by the conclusion and premise categories, the greater will be this dot product.

Analytic derivations are too complicated to detail for two or more premise arguments. Their patterns, however, show a clear generalization of the one- and two-premise cases and the same intuitions hold. Although this increase in derivational complexity with the number of premises may be considered a drawback of the feature-based model, note that the computational complexity of the model is only linearly related to the number of premises. The same encoding rule, Eq. 1, is applied iteratively to each premise. Perhaps more important, the conceptual complexity of the model is unrelated to the number of premises. The same rules are applied for the same reasons to any argument, whether it has one or many premises. Arguments are deemed strong in all cases if the weights obtained after encoding the premises cover the features of the conclusion category.

ii and iii. Premise Diversity (General and Specific)   The less similar premises are to each other, the stronger the argument tends to be. An example of a pair of general arguments satisfying premise diversity is

A.
Hippos have X.
Hamsters have X.

──────────────── is stronger than

Mammals have X.

B.
Hippos have X.
Rhinos have X.

─────────────── .

Mammals have X.

For an example of a pair of specific arguments, substitute Giraffes for Mammals (cf. Osherson et al., 1990). The account of the specific case follows from that of the general one. The feature-based model attributes the diversity phenomenon, again, to feature coverage. More diverse premises cover the space of features better than more similar premises because their features are not redundant, and therefore are more likely to overlap with features of the conclusion category and more likely to be encoded. More precisely, (i) featural overlap between dissimilar premise categories and a conclusion category will tend to be less redundant than the overlap between similar premise categories and a conclusion category; and (ii) weight changes are greater during encoding of a dissimilar premise than a similar premise (dissimilar premises have more surprise value). A more formal analysis follows.

The similarity of Hippos and Rhinos is greater than that of Hippos and Hamsters. In the discussion of Phenomenon i, similarity, I showed that this leads us to expect

$$a_x(\text{Rhinos}/\text{Hippos}) > a_x(\text{Hamsters}/\text{Hippos}). \tag{8}$$

Let Hi stand for Hippos, Ha for Hamsters, M for Mammals, and R for Rhinos. As shown in Appendix B, we can write the strength of Argument A as

$a_x(\text{M}/\text{Hi}, \text{Ha})$

$$= \frac{\text{F}(\text{Hi}) \cdot \text{F}(\text{M}) + [1 - a_x(\text{Ha}/\text{Hi})][\text{F}(\text{Ha}) \cdot \text{F}(\text{M}) - \Sigma f_i(\text{Hi}) f_i(\text{Ha}) f_i(\text{M})]}{|\text{F}(\text{M})|^2}$$

and the strength of Argument B as

$a_x(\text{M}/\text{Hi}, \text{R})$

$$= \frac{\text{F}(\text{Hi}) \cdot \text{F}(\text{M}) + [1 - a_x(\text{R}/\text{Hi})][\text{F}(\text{R}) \cdot \text{F}(\text{M}) - \Sigma f_i(\text{Hi}) f_i(\text{R}) f_i(\text{M})]}{|\text{F}(\text{M})|^2}.$$

Cancelling like terms, we see that Argument A is stronger than Argument B if and only if

$$[1 - a_x(\text{Ha}/\text{Hi})][\text{F}(\text{Ha}) \cdot \text{F}(\text{M}) - \Sigma f_i(\text{Hi}) f_i(\text{Ha}) f_i(\text{M})]$$
$$> [1 - a_x(\text{R}/\text{Hi})][\text{F}(\text{R}) \cdot \text{F}(\text{M}) - \Sigma f_i(\text{Hi}) f_i(\text{R}) f_i(\text{M})]. \tag{9}$$

Inequality 8 states that $[1 - a_x(\text{Ha}/\text{Hi})] > [1 - a_x(\text{R}/\text{Hi})]$, so the first term on the left hand side of Condition 9 is greater than the first term on the right. $F(R) \cdot F(M)$ is a measure of the features that Rhinos have in common with the mental representation—the prototype perhaps—of the Mammal category. Most of us comparing these arguments do not know substantially more about Rhinos than about Hamsters, which is consistent with Osherson et al.'s feature ratings, $|F(R)| = 2.6 < |F(H)| = 3.0$. Moreover, Rhinos are not more typical Mammals than are Hamsters, as evidenced by both the rarity of horned mammals with plated skin, and typicality judgments showing that in fact Hamsters are more typical.[5] We can expect, therefore, that for most of us $F(R) \cdot F(M)$ is not substantially greater, and probably less, than $F(\text{Ha}) \cdot F(M)$. The only remaining difference between the two sides of the inequality lies in the three-way product terms $\Sigma f_i(\text{Hi}) f_i(\text{Ha}) f_i(M)$ and $\Sigma f_i(\text{Hi}) f_i(R) f_i(M)$. The value of these terms would tend to be proportional to premise similarity because the more features two-premise categories share, the more likely that features will be shared by all of the premise and conclusion categories. Because the premises of Argument B are more similar, $\Sigma f_i(\text{Hi}) f_i(R) f_i(M)$ is likely to be greater than $\Sigma f_i(\text{Hi}) f_i(\text{Ha}) f_i(M)$. So a bigger quantity is being subtracted on the right-hand side and Condition 9 is therefore likely to hold. More precisely, Argument A will be stronger than Argument B for every subject for whom it does hold.

Feature Exclusion (New Phenomenon)
The feature-based model predicts a boundary condition on the diversity phenomenon. A premise category that has no overlap with the conclusion category should have no effect on argument strength even if it leads to a more diverse set of premises. Consider the arguments

> Foxes require trace amounts of magnesium for reproduction.
> Deer require trace amounts of magnesium for reproduction.
> ———————————————————————————————
> Weasels require trace amounts of magnesium for reproduction.

(g)

and

> Foxes require trace amounts of magnesium for reproduction.
> Rhinos require trace amounts of magnesium for reproduction.
> ———————————————————————————————
> Weasels require trace amounts of magnesium for reproduction.

(h)

The second argument indeed has a more diverse set of premises than the first; the similarity between Foxes and Rhinos was rated significantly lower than the similarity between Foxes and Deer (2.02 and 4.00, respectively, $t(45) = 10.00$; $p < .001$). Nevertheless, the feature-based model predicts that Argument g will be stronger than Argument h because Rhinos and Weasels have so few features in common, the dot product of their feature vectors was only 3.0 in the feature ratings collected by Osherson et al. (1991), relative to Deer and Weasels (dot product of 5.5). Let F be Foxes, R be Rhinos, and W be Weasels. The derivation in Appendix B tells us that the argument strength of h is

$$a_x(W/F, R) = \frac{F(F) \cdot F(W) + [1 - a_x(R/F)][F(R) \cdot F(W) - \Sigma f_i(F) f_i(R) f_i(W)]}{|F(W)|^2}.$$

If $F(R) \cdot F(W)$ is negligible, then so is $\Sigma f_i(F) f_i(R) f_i(W)$ since it is always positive but less than $F(R) \cdot F(W)$ which implies that

$$a_x(W/F, R) \approx \frac{F(F) \cdot F(W)}{|F(W)|^2}$$

$$= a_x(W/F).$$

In other words, Rhinos contribute little strength to the argument, even though Foxes and Rhinos compose a diverse set. To test this analysis, I asked 46 University of Michigan undergraduates to choose the stronger of Arguments g and h. As predicted, 41 of them chose g ($p < .0001$).

The similarity–coverage model can explain this result by assuming that, even though the premises in h had greater diversity, they had less coverage. If Rhinos have few similar neighbors, they may not add much to the coverage of the lowest-level category that includes both premises and conclusion.[6] To derive the prediction from the similarity–coverage model, we need first to define the lowest-level category both with and without Rhinos as a premise (presumably Mammals in both cases) and then compute coverage using similarity ratings between every member of this lowest-level category and each premise category. To derive the prediction from the feature-based model, we need to know that the feature overlap between the premise and conclusion categories is small.

iv. Premise Typicality (General) The more typical premise categories are of the conclusion category, the stronger is the argument (Rothbart & Lewis, 1988). For example,

A.
Wolves have X.
———————— is stronger than
Mammals have X.

B.
Oxen have X.
————————,
Mammals have X.

where Wolves are more typical of the category Mammals than are Oxen.[7] By virtue of the typicality of Wolves, their similarity to Mammals is greater than the similarity of Oxen to Mammals. Therefore, from Eq. 6,

$$\mathrm{sim}(\mathrm{Wolves}, \mathrm{Mammals}) = \frac{F(\mathrm{Wolves}) \cdot F(\mathrm{Mammals})}{|F(\mathrm{Wolves})| \, |F(\mathrm{Mammals})|}$$

$$> \frac{F(\mathrm{Oxen}) \cdot F(\mathrm{Mammals})}{|F(\mathrm{Oxen})| \, |F(\mathrm{Mammals})|}$$

$$= \mathrm{sim}(\mathrm{Oxen}, \mathrm{Mammals}).$$

Tversky (1977) proposed that the features of more typical items are more salient or prominent. The typicality phenomenon can be derived directly from the difference in similarity for those pairs of categories that satisfy a weaker condition, namely that the representation of the more typical category is at least as rich as that of the more atypical category. This condition will hold for most readers for this example because Wolves tend to be more familiar than Oxen. Osherson et al.'s (1991) feature ratings also provide support, $|F(\text{Wolves})| = 3.4 > |F(\text{Oxen})| = 3.2$. This condition, along with the inequality above, implies that

$$\frac{F(\text{Wolves}) \cdot F(\text{Mammals})}{|F(\text{Mammals})|^2} > \frac{F(\text{Oxen}) \cdot F(\text{Mammals})}{|F(\text{Mammals})|^2}. \tag{10}$$

Notice that Eq. 10 will hold as long as Wolves have more features in common with Mammals than Oxen do, regardless of their respective magnitudes. Taken generally, condition 10 will obtain whenever a typical category has more in common with its superordinate than does an atypical category. To derive the strength of Argument A, we use Eq. 5:

$$a_x(\text{Mammals/Wolves}) = \frac{F(\text{Wolves}) \cdot F(\text{Mammals})}{|F(\text{Mammals})|^2}.$$

The strength of Argument B is

$$a_x(\text{Mammals/Oxen}) = \frac{F(\text{Oxen}) \cdot F(\text{Mammals})}{|F(\text{Mammals})|^2}.$$

The inequality in Eq. 10 dictates that $a_x(\text{Mammals/Wolves}) > a_x(\text{Mammals/Oxen})$ or that Argument A is stronger than Argument B.

As an illustration of this analysis, I provide an example in which argument strength is derived using categories which are equally similar to a superordinate, but which differ in their magnitudes.

v and vi. Premise Monotonicity (General and Specific)   Adding a premise whose category is new and chosen from the lowest level category that includes both the categories of the old premises and the conclusion will increase the strength of an argument. A pair of general arguments that satisfy premise monotonicity is

A.   B.

Sparrows have X.   Sparrows have X.

Eagles have X.   Eagles have X.

Hawks have x.

———————————— is stronger than ————————.

Birds have X.   Birds have X.

An example of a pair of specific arguments satisfying premise monotonicity would be obtained by substituting "Ravens" for "Birds" in both arguments. The analysis below would apply equally well. Premise monotonicity holds whenever the conclusion category shares values on one or more features with the additional premise category that it does not share with the other premise categories. Specifically, the new premise category must include features of the conclusion category whose corresponding weights are not already at their maximum value after encoding the old premise categories.

More formally, the strength of Argument A is

$$a_x(\text{Birds}/\text{Hawks}, \text{Sparrows}, \text{Eagles})$$

$$= \frac{\text{W(Hawks, Sparrows, Eagles)} \cdot \text{F(Birds)}}{|\text{F(Birds)}|^2},$$

and the strength of Argument B is

$$a_x(\text{Birds}/\text{Sparrows}, \text{Eagles}) = \frac{\text{W(Sparrows, Eagles)} \cdot \text{F(Birds)}}{|\text{F(Birds)}|^2}.$$

Recall that weights are never decreased (assuming $a_x \leq 1$). Adding a new premise will always increase weights connected to features of its category that are not already at their maximum value. Therefore, for each i,

$$w_i(\text{Hawks}, \text{Sparrows}, \text{Eagles}) \geq w_i(\text{Sparrows}, \text{Eagles}),$$

which implies that

$$\frac{\text{W(Hawks, Sparrows, Eagles)} \cdot \text{F(Birds)}}{|\text{F(Birds)}|^2} \geq \frac{\text{W(Sparrows, Eagles)} \cdot \text{F(Birds)}}{|\text{F(Birds)}|^2}.$$

In terms of a_x, or argument strength,

$$a_x(\text{Birds}/\text{Hawks}, \text{Sparrows}, \text{Eagles}) \geq a_x(\text{Birds}/\text{Sparrows}, \text{Eagles})$$

and strictly greater whenever

$$[\text{W(Hawks, Sparrows, Eagles)} - \text{W(Sparrows, Eagles)}] \cdot \text{F(Birds)} > 0.$$

Although the contribution to argument strength provided by the new premise may be small, it is necessarily nonnegative. The model therefore predicts that when the monotonicity phenomenon is evaluated over a large number of subjects, some tendency to prefer the argument with the larger number of premises should be observed.

vii. Inclusion Fallacy (One Specific and One General Argument) Shafir, Smith, and Osherson (1990) demonstrate that, counter to normative prescription, arguments with more general conclusions can sometimes seem stronger than arguments with identical premises but specific conclusions:

A.   B.
Robins have X.   Robins have X.
————————————— is stronger than ————————————.
Birds have X.   Ostriches have X.

The feature-based model explains this phenomenon by appealing to greater coverage by the premise category of the features of the general category (Birds) than of the specific category (Ostriches). The account follows directly from that of phenomenon *i*, similarity, on the assumption that Robins are more similar to Birds than they are to Ostriches. This is precisely the assumption made by Osherson et al. (1990). The feature-based model makes no distinction between the representation of general and specific categories; both are represented as feature vectors. Therefore, any of the model's logic that applies to one kind of category will apply equally to the other.

viii. Conclusion Specificity (General) When premise categories are properly included in the conclusion category, arguments tend to be stronger the more specific is the conclusion category. Corroborating data can be found in Rothbart and Lewis (1988). This is illustrated by the following example because Birds is more specific than Animals, and because Sparrows and Eagles are Birds which are in turn Animals

A.   B.
Sparrows have X.   Sparrows have X.
Eagles have X.   Eagles have X.
————————————— is stronger than ————————————.
Birds have X.   Animals have X.

This phenomenon follows from *i*, premise–conclusion similarity, whenever the more specific category is more similar than the more general category to the premise categories. Instances of Birds tend to be more similar to the category of Birds than to the more general category of Animals (cf. Smith, Shoben, & Rips, 1974), implying that Birds are more similar to Sparrows and Eagles than Animals are so that Argument A will be stronger than Argument B.

However, categories *k* levels apart are not always more similar than categories more than *k* levels apart (Smith et al., 1974). If a premise category is more similar to a more general category, the feature-based model expects the conclusion specificity phenomenon to reverse as long as the magnitude of the vector corresponding to the more general category is not too large. For instance, Chickens are more similar to Animals than to Birds for some people. The model predicts that the Argument "Chickens have X, therefore Animals have X" will be stronger for these people than "Chickens have X, therefore Birds have X." Evidence for just this type of event is provided by the inclusion fallacy. Gelman (1988) has offered an alternative explanation for conclusion specificity which appeals to the relative homogeneity of categories at different levels.

ix. Premise–Conclusion Asymmetry (Specific) This phenomenon, first discussed by Rips (1975), involves single-premise arguments. Switching premise and conclusion categories can lead to asymmetric arguments, in the sense that the strength of P/C will differ from that of C/P. An example is provided by Osherson et al. (1990):

A.

Mice have X.

————————— is stronger than

Bats have X.

B.

Bats have X.

—————————.

Mice have X.

Those authors, along with Rips (1975), attribute the phenomenon to differences in typicality. People are assumed to be more willing to generalize from a typical instance to an atypical instance than from an atypical instance to a typical instance. According to the similarity–coverage model, this is because typical instances provide greater coverage of the lowest-level category that includes both the premise and conclusion categories. The phenomenon follows if Mice are assumed more typical than Bats of some common category, such as Mammals.

The feature-based model attributes the phenomenon to differential richness of category representations (which is likely to be correlated with typicality). From Eq. 5, we write the strength of Argument A as

$$a_x(\text{Bats/Mice}) = \frac{F(\text{Mice}) \cdot F(\text{Bats})}{|F(\text{Bats})|^2},$$

and the strength of Argument B as

$$a_x(\text{Mice/Bats}) = \frac{F(\text{Bats}) \cdot F(\text{Mice})}{|F(\text{Mice})|^2}.$$

Because their numerators are identical, the relative strength of the two arguments depends entirely on the relative magnitudes of their conclusion categories. On the one hand, Bats have distinctive properties that would tend to increase the richness of their representations, like having wings, being nocturnal, and living in caves. On the other hand, we know a lot about Mice because they are so familiar (e.g., they have long tails, they eat cheese, we have a more precise idea of their appearance) and this gives us confidence that they possess common mammalian properties that we know about (e.g., they probably have normal sensory and motor systems). In any case, the relative magnitudes of the two categories' representations are an open (and difficult) empirical question, the complexity of which cannot be addressed with simple feature ratings.

However, categories do exist which will let us both make reasonable guesses as to the relative magnitude of their representations and also pit the two explanations for the asymmetry phenomenon against each other. Given a pair of categories D and E in which the representation of D is richer than that of E but E is more typical than D of the lowest-level category that properly includes them both, the argument D/E should be stronger than E/D. The similarity–coverage model predicts the opposite.

I chose six such pairs of categories (Killer whales and Weasels, Kangaroos and Wolverines, Chickens and Orioles, Penguins and Finches, Tomatoes and Papayas, and Cucumbers and Guavas). In each case, the first category is less typical of the lowest-level inclusive category than the second (Mammals, Mammals, Birds, Birds, Fruit, and Fruit, respectively), but it is more familiar and subjects are likely to have more detailed knowledge of it.[8] I constructed two arguments from each pair of categories by having each category serve as both premise and conclusion category and asked subjects to rate the convincingness of each argument on a scale from 0 to 10.

For five of the six pairs, the argument with the less typical premise and lower magnitude conclusion category (e.g., Chickens have X, therefore Orioles have X) was judged more convincing (mean of 3.12) than the argument with the more typical premise and greater magnitude conclusion category (e.g., Orioles have X, therefore Chickens have X; mean of 2.93). The sole exception was the pair involving Killer whales and Weasels. Although the judgments were in a direction that supported the feature-based model, the overall difference was not statistically significant for these item–pairs across subjects, $t(33) = 1.54$, ns.

x. Premise–Conclusion Identity   Phenomena x and xi were dubbed "limiting-case phenomena" and posited by Osherson et al. (1990, 1991) without experimental evidence. Premise–conclusion identity states that arguments with identical premises and conclusions are perfectly strong, i.e., they have maximum argument strength:

$$\frac{\text{Pelicans have } X.}{\text{Pelicans have } X.} \text{ is perfectly strong.}$$

According to the feature-based account, the strength of this argument is

$$a_x(\text{Pelicans/Pelicans}) = \frac{F(\text{Pelicans}) \cdot F(\text{Pelicans})}{|F(\text{Pelicans})|^2}$$

$$= \frac{\Sigma f_i(\text{Pelicans}) f_i(\text{Pelicans})}{|F(\text{Pelicans})|^2}$$

$$= \frac{|F(\text{Pelicans})|^2}{|F(\text{Pelicans})|^2}$$

$$= 1.$$

Certain unusual conditions exist which could cause a_x to take on values greater than 1. This will occur if the weight vector has the same or a similar direction as the input vector and a greater magnitude. An example of an argument leading to such a situation would be

Pelicans have X.
Flamingoes have X.
_____
Pelicans have X.

The psychological strength of such an argument is not obvious, and may require detailed analysis. We can either ignore these degenerate cases or, as suggested earlier, extend the definition of a_x so that its maximum value is 1, with the result that no argument can be stronger than one with identical premises and conclusions.

Phenomena That Distinguish the Two Models

The category-based and feature-based models differ with respect to three of the phenomena described by Osherson et al. (1990) as well as a new one.

xi. Premise–Conclusion Inclusion   The second limiting-case phenomenon stipulated by Osherson et al. (1990), and predicted by their model, states that arguments in which the conclusion category is subordinate to the premise category are perfectly strong:

$$\frac{\text{Animals have } X.}{\text{Mammals have } X.} \text{ is perfectly strong.} \tag{m}$$

This phenomenon has an obvious logical justification. To the extent one knows and applies the category-inclusion rule, such arguments *are* perfectly strong. As phenomenon *vii*, the inclusion fallacy, suggests however, rules consistent with the logic of argument are not always applied. The feature-based account predicts that, to the extent that use of such rules is not overriding the postulated associative process, such arguments will not always be perfectly strong. Rather, they will depend on the featural overlap between premise and conclusion categories and the richness of the conclusion category representation. The strength of Argument m is

$$a_x(\text{Mammals}/\text{Animals}) = \frac{F(\text{Animals}) \cdot F(\text{Mammals})}{|F(\text{Mammals})|^2}$$

$$\neq 1.$$

The numerator will increase as the extent of common features between the premise and conclusion categories increases, and therefore so will argument strength. The feature-based model predicts that, given most models of similarity, premise–conclusion inclusion arguments should vary with the similarity of premise and conclusion categories. The category-based model predicts that, since all such arguments are perfectly strong, no such variation should take place. A test of these different predictions is embodied in the experiments described in support of the next phenomenon.

Inclusion Similarity (New Phenomenon)
The strength of an argument in which the conclusion category is properly included in the premise category varies with the similarity of the two categories. I asked subjects to select the stronger of the following arguments:

1A.
Animals use norepinephrine as a neurotransmitter.
_____

Mammals use norepinephrine as a neurotransmitter.

1B.
Animals use norepinephrine as a neurotransmitter.
_____

Reptiles use norepinephrine as a neurotransmitter.

Forty-four of 50 subjects chose Argument A ($p < .001$). Also, Animals were judged significantly more similar to Mammals (mean similarity judgment was 5.7 on a 7-point scale) than to Reptiles (4.5 out of 7), $t(49) = 5.24$, $p < .001$. Subjects did not find these choices overwhelmingly difficult to make. The mean rating of confidence in choice of argument was 4.5 on a 7-point scale. I also asked subjects to choose between

2A.
Birds have an ulnar artery.
_____

Robins have an ulnar artery.

2B.
Birds have an ulnar artery.
_____

Penguins have an ulnar artery.

Again, the consistency in choice behavior was remarkable. Thirty-eight of 40 subjects chose A ($p < .001$). Also, Birds were judged significantly more similar to Robins (6.5) than to Penguins (4.6), $t(38) = 6.46$, $p < .001$. Again, subjects did not, on average, find the task extremely difficult. Mean confidence ratings in their choice were 4.6. Finally, and toward an examination of the phenomena in a different domain, I asked subjects which of the following they found stronger;

3A.
Furniture cannot be imported into Zimbabwe.
_____

Tables cannot be imported into Zimbabwe.

3B.

Furniture cannot be imported into Zimbabwe.

Bookshelves cannot be imported into Zimbabwe.

Thirty-three of 39 subjects chose A ($p < .001$). Similarity judgments between Furniture and Tables (6.2) were significantly higher than those between Furniture and Bookshelves (5.3), $t(38) = 3.69$, $p < .001$. Again subjects were not overly strained by the choices they were asked to make; mean confidence was 3.9.

The preceding demonstrations suffer from a limitation imposed by the forced-choice task. The task required subjects to choose one or the other argument. Subjects could have based their choice on similarity, even though both arguments seemed perfectly strong, only to satisfy the task requirements. I therefore tried to replicate the inclusion similarity phenomenon using a rating task which did not make the task demands of the forced-choice procedure.

I gave 60 undergraduates at the University of Michigan the same six arguments as above (1A, 1B, 2A, 2B, 3A, and 3B) and asked them how convincing they found each one. To make their rating, subjects circled one of the integers from 1 (not at all convincing) to 10 (very convincing). In general, we would expect the strength of arguments satisfying premise–conclusion inclusion to be relatively high because categories usually share many features with their subordinates.

The mean convincingness rating for Argument 1A (Animals therefore Mammals) was 7.50, significantly greater than the mean rating for Argument 1B (Animals therefore Reptiles) of 5.88, $t(59) = 5.07$; $p < .001$. The same pattern held for the second pair of arguments (Birds therefore Robins versus Birds therefore Penguins). Mean convincingness ratings were 9.45 and 6.73, respectively, $t(59) = 7.35$; $p < .001$. The third pair also showed the phenomenon. The mean for 3A (Furniture therefore Tables) of 9.32 was significantly higher than the mean for 3B (Furniture therefore Bookshelves) of 8.53, $t(59) = 2.86$; $p < .01$. The argument with the more similar categories was judged significantly more convincing in all three cases. Similarity judgments replicated the patterns reported above.

Perhaps subjects failed to realize that each category was meant to subsume all members of that category. For example, they might have interpreted "Mammals have X" as "*some* Mammals have X." So I clarified the meaning of each statement by preceding each premise and conclusion category by the quantifier "all," for example "All animals use norepinephrine as a neurotransmitter." I asked a new group of 46 students to rate the convincingness of the six modified arguments.

I obtained an identical pattern of judgments. The mean convincingness ratings for the first two arguments (all Animals therefore all Mammals and all Animals therefore all Reptiles) slightly increased to 7.54 and 6.00, respectively,

$t(45) = 3.02$; $p < .01$. For the second pair of arguments (all Birds therefore all Robins versus all Birds therefore all Penguins), corresponding means were 9.59 and 6.41, $t(45) = 6.76$; $p < .001$. Finally, the mean for 3A (all Furniture therefore all Tables) was 8.35, whereas the mean for 3B (all Furniture therefore all Bookshelves) was 7.91, $t(45) = 3.24$; $p < .001$. Even when categories were explicitly quantified to include all category members, convincingness ratings were consistent with the model in all three cases.

These demonstrations support the feature-based model which predicts the strength of arguments satisfying premise–conclusion inclusion to be proportional to coverage of the conclusion category's features by the premise category, and therefore correlated with similarity, and refute the category-based model which cannot explain these data without auxilliary assumptions. One such auxilliary assumption[9] is to suppose that, in decomposing the premise category, subjects sample some of its subcategories and these tend to be the more typical. Upon incorporating this assumption, the category-based model will no longer predict premise–conclusion inclusion and will no longer always predict premise–conclusion identity.

xii and xiii. Nonmonotonicity (General and Specific)   As described with respect to the premise monotonicity phenomena (*v* and *vi*), the feature-based model never expects additional premises to decrease the strength of an argument. Osherson et al. (1990) show that this can happen however. Adding a premise that converts either a general or a specific argument to a mixed argument can decrease the strength of that argument. For example,

A.		B.
Crows have X.		Crows have X.
Peacocks have X.		Peacocks have X.
		Rabbits have X.
――――――――――	is stronger than	――――――――――
Birds have X.		Birds have X.

Similarly,

A.		B.
Flies have X.		Flies have X.
		Orangutans have X.
―――――――	is stronger than	――――――――.
Bees have X.		Bees have X.

Osherson et al. (1990) explain these effects by invoking their concept of coverage. Flies cover the lowest-level category including Flies and Bees, namely Insects, better than Flies and Orangutans cover the lowest-level category including Flies, Orangutans, and Bees, namely Animals. A similar analysis applies to the other nonmonotonicity example. The feature-based model cannot explain the result.

One possible explanation for nonmonotonicities, consistent with a variant of the feature-based model, is that the features of the unrelated category compete with the features of the other premise categories. Features may be weighted by the number of premise categories that they are consistent with so that features shared by all categories would have the most influence on belief in the conclusion. Features appearing in only one premise category of a multiple-premise argument could reduce argument strength if this category shared few features with (i) the other premise categories, for it would reduce the influence of their features, and (ii) the conclusion category, because it would then provide little additional feature coverage itself. Both of these conditions are met in the examples of nonmonotonicity above in that, for instance, Orangutans share few features with either Flies or Bees.

One implication of this hypothesis is that examples of nonmonotonicities should be observable in which the lowest-level inclusive category for both arguments is the same but the two feature-overlap conditions just described are met nevertheless. The similarity–coverage model could not explain such cases because it assumes that the lowest-level superordinate for the argument with the greater number of premises is at a higher level than the superordinate for the other argument. Preliminary data directed at this issue were collected by asking subjects to rate the convincingness of five pairs of arguments. Each pair consisted of a single-premise specific argument such as

> All crocodiles have acidic saliva.
> _____
> All alligators have acidic saliva.

and a two-premise argument constructed by adding a premise category that, in the experimenters' judgment, had relatively few features in common with the other premise or the conclusion categories but came from the same lowest-level superordinate category as both the other categories (Reptiles in this example). For instance,

> All crocodiles have acidic saliva.
> All king snakes have acidic saliva.
> _____
> All alligators have acidic saliva.

In each of the five cases nonmonotonicities were observed. The convincingness of the single-premise argument was rated as significantly higher (mean of 5.62) than that of the two-premise argument (mean of 4.98), $t(33) = 2.87$; $p < .01$. Nonmonotonicities were obtained using arguments whose categories apparently have the same lowest-level superordinate. To argue that subjects did use different (and nonobvious) superordinates for the arguments within each pair is to assume that category hierarchies are much less rigid and more idiosyncratic than the similarity–coverage model would suggest, at least in its simplest, most elegant form. If the hierarchies that subjects use are highly variable, and especially if they are context-dependent, then they may not provide any explanatory power beyond that of a featural description.

Quantitative Tests of the Model

To provide further empirical tests of the feature-based model, numerical predictions generated by the model were correlated with subjects' judgments of argument strength. Because the feature-based model has no free parameters, all we need to derive predictions is a set of categories, each with an associated feature list. Again, I used the ratings of strength of association between 85 properties and 48 mammals that Osherson et al. (1991) collected. These strength ratings can encourage subjects to judge a category as associated to properties that are not salient aspects of the subjects' conception of the category, as exemplified by the positive judgments between Sheep and *has tail* or *is weak*. Judgments of relative strength of association in this sense lead to some overestimation of the value of features that are only weakly represented. I therefore applied a varying cutoff to the feature ratings, setting all values to 0 that were below a specified cutoff value.

Predictions of the feature-based model were calculated from the feature ratings using Eqs. 1, 2, and 3. Judgments of argument strength were obtained from data published in Osherson et al. (1990) and Smith et al. (1992). Five data sets were used, all involving arguments of the form described above. Categories were from the set of Mammals. The first set involved 15 two-premise-specific arguments, each with a different blank property (Smith et al., 1992, Table 4). The conclusion category was always Fox. Premise categories consisted of all possible pairs from the set (Dog, Hamster, Hippo, Mouse, Rhino, and Wolf). Because I did not have feature ratings for Dog, I used the ratings for German shepherd, on the assumption that a German shepherd is a highly typical dog. Smith et al. asked 30 University of Michigan undergraduates to estimate the probability of the conclusion on the assumption that the premises were true.

Cutoff values were varied from 0 to 1 in increments of 0.01. However, cutoff values close to 1 eliminated all or most of the data thereby rendering the feature ratings meaningless. I therefore did not consider cutoff values sufficiently close to 1 that category representations were all identical. Correlations were calculated between the model's predictions using feature ratings calculated for each cutoff value and subjects' probability estimates.

Feature ratings were obtained by averaging over subjects at one university (MIT) and argument strength ratings by averaging over subjects at a different university (Michigan). The only parameter varied was the cutoff value. Nevertheless, the mean correlation was 0.91 between the model's predictions and mean probability judgments, taken over all cutoff values less than 0.71. The maximum correlation was 0.96, achieved at cutoffs of 0.58 and 0.59. The magnitude of these correlations bodes well for the feature-based model.

Discussion

I have described a simple model that accounts for a variety of phenomena regarding people's willingness to affirm a property of some category given confirmation of the property in one or more categories. The model implements the principle that one's willingness is given by the proportion of the category's features that are associated with the property; i.e., the proportion of features that are covered by the categories known to possess the property. The model accounts for 10 phenomena described by Osherson et al. (1990). It motivated empirical work suggesting that another one of their phenomena, premise–conclusion inclusion, does not hold in general although a related phenomenon predicted by the current model only, inclusion similarity, does. An experiment was reported to suggest that a generalization of the feature-based model may provide a more direct account of the two remaining phenomena, the non-monotonicities. The model successfully predicted two new phenomena: feature exclusion, a reversal of the diversity phenomenon in which one of the more diverse premises fails to contribute to feature coverage, and category richness, in which an argument with a lower magnitude conclusion category is judged stronger than one with a higher magnitude. Preliminary data were also reported that were in a direction supporting the feature-based model's explanation for the asymmetry phenomenon. Finally, the feature-based model showed high correlations between its predictions and ratings of argument strength.

The feature-based model has two primary components that are probably not equally important in determining argument strength. Feature overlap, the dot product term in the feature-based model, seems to be generally more influential than representational richness, the magnitude term. Feature overlap played a role in all but one of the demonstrations of the various phenomena, premise–conclusion asymmetry. On the other hand, only four of the phenomena depended on vector magnitude, namely, category richness, typicality, asymmetry, and premise–conclusion identity. The relative weight of the dot product and magnitude terms in determining argument strength is related to the ratio of their variabilities. If, for instance, the magnitude of every representation were the same, then magnitude would play no role in determining argument strength. The variability in feature overlap among arguments may well be substantially greater than the variability in representational richness. The range of magnitude variation could be restricted by limited attention which may act to constrain the number of salient features of a category.

The Feature-Based View versus the Category-Based View

Broadly construed, the category-based view of induction is not necessarily inconsistent with the feature-based view. Even if a feature-based model were consistent with a wide variety of data under many different conditions, a category-based model might still capture, in an easy-tounderstand way, some large and important set of phenomena. Categories surely provide a useful level of abstraction. The category-based view has the distinct advantage of requiring only pairwise similarity ratings to generate quantitative predictions. The feature-based view is limited by the difficulties inherent in gathering reliable and complete sets of feature values for individual categories. On the other hand, the category-based view, by virtue of its abstractness, may be unable to capture all the subtleties of induction. A category-based model which appeals to relations among categories is not necessarily derivable from a feature-based model which appeals to relations among category attributes.

In terms of the specific models of concern here, the category-based and feature-based models differ in several respects. First, they suggest different ways of classifying the phenomena. The similarity–coverage model motivates a distinction between phenomena whose explanation relies on similarity—the prototype being the similarity phenomenon—versus phenomena whose explanation is premised on differences in coverage—the prototype being diversity. The feature-based model attributes both of these phenomena to a single factor, the degree of match between the premise categories as encoded in the weights and the conclusion category. A distinction more compatible with the feature-based model would separate phenomena explained in terms of the relative degree of match between weights and conclusion categories, the term in the numerator of Equation 3, with phenomena explained in terms of the relative degree of richness of the conclusion category, the denominator of the argument strength model. The asymmetry phenomenon is the prototype of the latter class.

Second, the two models differ with respect to their toleration of flexibility in our representations of categories. The feature-based model allows for extreme flexibility; the set of features representing a category could be highly context-dependent. By assuming a stable category hierarchy, the category-based model expects some rigidity. To the extent that new categories must be identified to explain new data, the usefulness of the similarity–coverage model is suspect. For example, what is the lowest-level category that includes ducks, geese, and swans? Is it birds, water-birds, web-footed birds? How do we deal with categories that are not natural kinds such as ad hoc categories (Barsalou, 1985), like birds found in national parks? The feature-based model requires only a set of features for each category. On the other hand, to the extent we can appeal to an established category hierarchy, the featural description of individual categories might become unnecessarily tedious.

The models also differ with respect to the explanatory burden they put on different parts of an argument. Both models emphasize the relation between premise and conclusion categories. However, whereas the feature-based model puts some weight on characteristics of the conclusion category in isolation (by computing its magnitude), the similarity–coverage model gives weight to characteristics of the premise categories (by computing their coverage of a category that includes them).

Finally, the feature-based model has a computational advantage. All the model needs in order to derive argument strengths for a new category are its features. The similarity–coverage model requires similarity ratings (possibly derived from features) between the new category and each old one at the same hierarchical level, and the re-calculation of coverage values for all categories that include the new one.

In sum, we may be mistaken to interpret the success of Osherson et al.'s (1990) similarity–coverage model as implying the existence of two psychological processes which operate on pairwise similarity judgments, one of which computes overall similarity and the other coverage. Their pair of theoretical constructs may be only approximate abstract descriptions of more microlevel processing mechanisms.

The Problem of Nonblank Predicates
Some nonblank predicates do not seem fundamentally different from blank ones. Sloman and Wisniewski (1992) show that familiar predicates behave like blank ones when subjects cannot explain their relation to the categories of an argument. But cases of this sort are probably rare. The most important advantage of the feature-based view, and of the model proposed here in particular, is the direction it suggests for generalizing to arguments involving a range of nonblank predicates. One such direction would be to model some nonblank predicates as consisting of features, some of which have preexisting connections to features of premise and conclusion categories. One implication of this move would be that premises would influence argument strength only to the extent that they are surprising in relation to prior knowledge; that they inform people of links between features of conclusion categories and predicates that they do not already know.

A second implication of this type of feature-based model for nonblank predicates is that arguments will tend to be judged strong given a strong prior belief in their conclusion (for supporting evidence, see Lord, Ross, & Lepper, 1979). The model expects argument strength to be high whenever the weight vector is highly correlated with the conclusion category vector, whether those weights come from the premises of the argument or from prior knowledge. The model predicts, therefore, that people will have trouble ignoring prior knowledge. (This is irrelevant when predicates are blank because, by definition, no prior beliefs exist.) However, practiced subjects may be able to evaluate a conclusion before and after encoding premises, and use the difference between the two outcomes as their measure of argument strength. Moreover, arguments like

Tables have legs.
_____

Therefore, people have legs.

may be judged weak despite prior belief in the conclusion because the meager amount of overlap between the features of tables and those of people is so obvious.

A second direction involves generalizing the notion of feature coverage. Some nonblank predicates may have the effect of selecting those features of a category that are particularly relevant. Consider the argument

> Tolstoy novels make good paperweights.
> _____
> Michener novels make good paperweights.

Whatever your feelings and knowledge about literature, the only features of both kinds of novels that are relevant to this argument have to do with size, shape, and weight. An important and unanswered question is how those features become available to us so effortlessly. Indeed, some feature selection of this sort may be going on even with the "blank" predicates of this paper. The predicates are just about all biological in kind, not really entirely blank after all, and so other biological properties of the categories may have greater weight than nonbiological properties. This may be why we seem, sometimes, to respond to these arguments on the basis of taxonomic knowledge. Animal taxonomies are certainly informative about biological properties. But once the relevant features for each category of an argument are selected, feature coverage may become the principle determining argument strength. (The example argument is a strong one because the relevant features of Michener novels are covered by Tolstoy novels.) And the feature-based model would still be a contender as a way to implement that principle. These issues will have to be clarified before we can expect a feature-based model for nonblank properties to offer much insight.

Conclusion

The feature-based model provides for a new perspective on argument strength. By using rules normally associated with models of learning (the delta rule and activation rule), it gives substance to the view that the process of confirming an argument is intimately related to concept learning. Encoding a premise is viewed as a process of linking new properties with old concepts. Testing a conclusion is described as a process of examining the extent to which the new links transfer to other concepts. The study of confirmation, for better or for worse, becomes an aspect of the study of generalization.

Notes

This research was conducted while the author held a postdoctoral fellowship from the Natural Sciences and Engineering Research Council of Canada. I thank James Morgan for assisting with data collection and Ed Wisniewski, Keith Holyoak, Dan Osherson, Doug Medin, John Kruschke, two anonymous reviewers, and especially Ed Smith for helpful comments and ideas. Correspondence should be addressed to the author who is now at the Department of Cognitive and Linguistic Sciencies, Box 1978, Brown University, Providence, RI 02912.

1. I thank Daniel Osherson and Tony Wilkie for making these feature ratings available. Subjects rated 48 mammals for 85 properties on a scale that started from 0 and had no upperbound. Ratings were provided by 8 or 9 M.I.T. students for each mammal. The ratings were linearly transformed to values in the $[0, 1]$ interval and then averaged.

2. The blank predicate used for both this argument and the multiple-premise example was "produce THS by their pituitary." Unless noted otherwise, the data reported were gathered from students who were given questionnaires which asked them to either choose between pairs of arguments or rate single arguments according to their convincingness. A pair of arguments bearing no relation to any tested argument was provided as an example and briefly discussed to clarify the meaning of "convincingness." Subjects were asked to consider each argument on its own merit, ignoring all information other than the facts presented. Following the argument strength task, similarity ratings were collected from the same students on a 7-point scale were 1 was "not at all" and 7 was "very" similar. Students went through the questionnaire at their own pace and were given as much time as they desired.

3. All p values reported below corresponding to choice proportions will refer to binomial tests.

4. $F(GS) \cdot F(C) = 7.5 > F(GS) \cdot F(Ch) = 6.8$, $F(D) \cdot F(C) = 6.2 > F(D) \cdot F(Ch) = 5.6$, $\Sigma f_i(GS) f_i(D) f_i(C) = 3.3 > \Sigma f_i(GS) f_i(D) f_i(Ch) = 3.1$. $|F(C)|^2 = 7.7 < |F(Ch)|^2 = 8.5$.

5. Unpublished data collected by Tony Wilkie.

6. Supporters of the similarity–coverage model cannot appeal to greater similarity between the premises and conclusion of Argument g relative to Argument h to explain this result. According to that model, overall similarity is given by the maximum of the pairwise similarities between each premise category and the conclusion category. Yet, only 1 of 46 subjects rated Deer more similar to Weasels than Foxes to Weasels. With regard to the following demonstration, only 7 of 39 subjects rated Beavers more similar to Chihuahuas than Foxes to Chihuahuas. Excluding these subjects from the analysis has no effect on the pattern of data.

7. The blank predicate was "use serotonin as a neurotransmitter." Twenty-nine of 39 students chose the first argument ($p < .01$). The mean typicality judgment for Wolves as Mammals was 5.23, for Oxen it was only 4.85, $t(38) = 2.84$, $p < .01$.

8. The Wolverine is the University of Michigan mascot and therefore could be more familiar to our subjects than the Kangaroo. However, informal questioning of the participants suggested otherwise.

9. Suggested by Ed Smith.

References

Barsalou, L. W. (1985). Ideals, central tendency, and frequency of instantiation as determinants of graded structure in categories. *Journal of Experimental Psychology: Learning, Memory, and Cognition*, 11, 629–654.

Gelman, S. (1988). The development of induction within natural kind and artefact categories. *Cognitive Psychology*, 20, 65–95.

Gluck, M. A., & Bower, G. H. (1988). From conditioning to category learning: An adaptive network model. *Journal of Experimental Psychology: General*, 117, 227–247.

Hinton, G. E., McClelland, J. L., & Rumelhart, D. E. (1986). Distributed representations. In D. E. Rumelhart, J. L. McClelland, & The PDP Research Group (Eds.) *Parallel distributed processing* (Vol. 1). Cambridge, MA: The MIT Press.

Kahneman, D., & Tversky, A. (1973). The psychology of prediction. *Psychological Review*, 80, 237–251.

Krogh, A., & Hertz, J. A. (1992). A simple weight decay can improve generalization. In J. E. Moody, S. J. Hanson, & R. P. Lippmann, (Eds.) *Advances in neural information processing systems* (Vol. 4). San Mateo, CA: Morgan Kauffmann.

Lord, C., Ross, L., & Lepper, M. R. (1979). Biased assimilation and attitude polarization: The effects of prior theories on subsequently considered evidence. *Journal of Personality and Social Psychology*, 37, 2098–2109.

Osherson, D., Smith, E. E., Wilkie, O., Lopez, A., & Shafir, E. (1990). Category-based induction. *Psychological Review*, 97, 185–200.

Osherson, D., Stern, J., Wilkie, O., Stob, M., & Smith, E. E. (1991). Default probability. *Cognitive Science*, 15, 251–269.

Quattrone, G. A., & Jones, E. E. (1980). The perception of variability within in-groups and out-groups: Implications for the Law of Small Numbers. *Journal of Personality and Social Psychology*, 38, 141–152.

Rips, L. (1990). Reasoning. *Annual Review of Psychology*, 41, 321–353.

Rips, L. (1975). Inductive judgments about natural categories. *Journal of Verbal Learning and Verbal Behavior*, 14, 665–681.

Rothbart, M., & Lewis, S. (1988). Inferring category attributes from exemplar attributes: Geometric shapes and social categories. *Journal of Personality and Social Psychology*, 55, 861–872.

Shafir, E., Smith, E. E., & Osherson, D. (1990). Typicality and reasoning fallacies. *Memory & Cognition*, 18, 229–239.

Sloman, S. A., & Wisniewski, E. (1992). Extending the domain of a feature-based model of property induction. In *Proceedings of the Fourteenth Annual Conference of the Cognitive Science Society*, Hillsdale, NJ: Erlbaum.

Smith, E. E., Lopez, A., & Osherson, D. (1992). Category membership, similarity, and naive induction. In A. Healy, S. Kosslyn, & R. Shiffrin (Eds.) *From learning processes to cognitive processes: Essays in honor of W. K. Estes* (Vol. 2), Hillsdale, NJ: Erlbaum.

Smith, E. E., Shoben, E. J., & Rips, L. (1974). Structure and process in semantic memory: A featural model for semantic decisions. *Psychological Review*, 81, 214–241.

Sutton, R. S., & Barto, A. G. (1981). Towards a modern theory of adaptive networks: Expectation and prediction. *Psychological Review*, 88, 135–170.

Tversky, A. (1977). Features of similarity. *Psychological Review*, 84, 327–352.

Tversky, A., & Kahneman, D. (1983). Extensional versus intuitive reasoning: The conjunction fallacy in probability judgment. *Psychological Review*, 90, 293–315.

Deductive Reasoning

Chapter 32

Deduction as Verbal Reasoning

Thad A. Polk and Allen Newell

Human beings are constantly faced with the need to reason, to infer something novel from available information. If John's friend tells him that she will be either at home or at work and he cannot reach her at work, John fully expects her to pick up the phone when he calls her house. John comes to this conclusion so quickly and easily that it hardly seems like reasoning. Yet John could reach it only by combining the information from at least two separate assumptions: (a) His friend is either at home or at work and (b) his friend is not at work (not to mention the assumptions that his friend told the truth, that the phones are working, and so forth). Neither assumption alone would lead John to the conviction that his friend is at home, so he must have put them together in some way. How did he do it? More specifically, what cognitive processes did he apply so effortlessly to reach that conclusion?

A particularly pure form of reasoning is deduction: determining logically valid consequences from information. A number of different hypotheses have been proposed concerning the nature of the cognitive processes that people use when reasoning deductively. Braine (1978) and Rips (1983), among others, have argued that human deduction can best be characterized as the application of logical inference rules. According to this view, the cognitive architecture implements a set of syntactic rules that can be used to draw inferences. For example, one such rule that is commonly proposed is *modus ponens*: If *A* and if *A* implies *B*, conclude *B*. Given a set of such rules, reasoning consists of encoding the problem into a form against which these rules can match (some kind of logical proposition), applying some of these rules to generate new propositions, and decoding the results into a form appropriate for the task (e.g., natural language). By assuming that the rule set is incorrect or incomplete in some way (e.g., missing a rule for *modus tollens*: If not *B* and if *A* implies *B*, conclude not *A*) and that some rules are more likely to be used than others, it is possible account for correct performance on some problems while explaining errors on others. Problem difficulty is accounted for in terms of the number of rules that must be applied. Problems that require long "proofs" are predicted to be harder than those that require shorter ones.

Cheng and Holyoak (1985) have proposed a different type of rule theory to account for deduction. They hypothesized that participants sometimes solve deductive reasoning problems by using *pragmatic reasoning schemas*. Pragmatic reasoning schemas are "generalized sets of rules defined in relation to classes of goals" (Cheng & Holyoak, 1985, p. 391). The idea is that a reasoning problem might trigger the retrieval of a schema from memory and that inference rules are associated with this schema; these inference rules can then be used to make deductions. For example, a problem that involves determining who is allowed to drink alcoholic beverages is hypothesized to evoke the use of a permission schema. Associated with such a schema are a number of content-specific inference rules such as the following: If the action is to be taken, then the precondition must be satisfied. Errors can arise when these rules are incomplete or not strictly valid.

Johnson-Laird and his colleagues (Johnson-Laird, 1983; Johnson-Laird & Bara, 1984; Johnson-Laird & Byrne, 1991) have argued against rule theories of deduction in favor of a mental model theory. This theory proposes that deductive reasoning consists of three stages: comprehension, description, and validation. Comprehension corresponds to encoding the problem into an internal representation. Unlike rule theories, this representation is assumed to take the form of a mental model rather than a set of logical propositions or a schema. A mental model represents a scenario consistent with the problem statement. For example, if the problem states that all dogs have four legs, the corresponding mental model would contain a set of tokens corresponding to dogs, and all of them would be represented as having four legs. In contrast, rule theories would posit a single logical proposition containing a universal quantifier [e.g., $\forall x Dog(x) \rightarrow Four Legs(x)$]. The second stage of deduction, according to mental model theory, involves generating a putative conclusion. This stage requires formulating a description of some aspect of the mental model that was not explicit in the problem statement. Finally, in the validation stage, participants are hypothesized to search for alternative mental models that falsify the conclusion just generated in an attempt to ensure its validity. Mental model theory accounts for errors in terms of a failure to consider falsifying models. Problems that are consistent with more models are thus predicted to be harder than those that are consistent with fewer.

Despite their differences, these approaches have all been based on what we call a *transduction paradigm*: Participants encode the problem into an internal representation (be it logical propositions, schemas, or mental models), reason using operations that are specifically devoted to inference (applying formal rules or searching for alternative models), and decode or describe the result to produce a response. The only role played by the operations of encoding and decoding is transduction: translating the problem into a form that the reasoning-specific mechanisms can operate on and then translating back the results. Although these transduction operations are sometimes assumed to lead to errors in reasoning (e.g., through the construction of invalid encodings; see Henle, 1962), they are assumed to play only a peripheral role in reasoning.

The heart of deduction, according to these theories, is in the application of reasoning-specific processes. As Johnson-Laird and Byrne (1991) have stated, for example, "only in the third stage [searching for alternative models] is any essential deductive work carried out: the first two stages are merely normal processes of comprehension and description" (p. 36).

We have come to believe that the linguistic processes of encoding and re-encoding actually play a central role in deduction itself and that processes that are devoted exclusively to reasoning (applying inference rules and searching for alternative models) play a smaller role in comparison. We propose that the behavior of most untrained participants on standard deduction tasks can best be characterized as *verbal reasoning*, that is, the deployment of linguistic processes according to and so as to satisfy the demands of a reasoning task.

Verbal Reasoning

Newell (1990) argued that cognitive science can and should work toward unified theories of cognition, that is, "theories that gain their power by positing a single system of mechanisms that operate together to produce the full range of human cognition" (p. 1). He proposed a computer system called Soar as an exemplar unified theory of cognition and, with John Laird and Paul Rosenbloom, began an effort to apply Soar in as many domains as possible (Laird, Newell, & Rosenbloom, 1987; Newell, 1990).

The idea of verbal reasoning arose out of one such attempt, namely to model human syllogistic reasoning behavior within the Soar architecture (Newell, 1990; Polk, 1992; Polk & Newell, 1988; Polk, Newell, & Lewis, 1989). Implementing a theory based on the transduction paradigm is unnatural within Soar, because Soar does not contain any processes or mechanisms that are devoted to reasoning (or to encoding and decoding for that matter). Indeed, the mechanisms in Soar (e.g., searching in problem spaces, subgoaling to other problem spaces, and learning by summarizing previous problem-solving experience in new production rules) were specifically designed to be general-purpose rather than task-specific mechanisms. We were thus forced to ask whether the processes used in reasoning could be acquired. And although it was clear that people can and do acquire the verbal operations of encoding from and decoding into language, it was much less clear whether people acquire processes devoted exclusively to reasoning without any training. Consequently, we began to explore the idea that verbal processes might be more central to the deduction of naive participants than are sophisticated reasoning-specific mechanisms. Given that all standard tests of deduction are presented verbally and require a verbal conclusion, the task clearly calls for linguistic processes to encode the premises and to produce a response. And although participants' linguistic processes are extremely sophisticated, we assume that their reasoning-specific processes are much less well developed (or perhaps, in some cases, even missing entirely). If one is faced with a deductive reasoning task, then, a natural approach would be to attempt to adapt one's well-developed linguistic skills to the demands of the task. For example, if a conclusion is not obvious after the initial encoding of the problem statement, then participants could use their linguistic skills to reencode the problem repeatedly in an attempt to elaborate their internal representation until it makes a conclusion explicit (or until they give up). Note that if this explanation of participants' behavior is correct, the operations of encoding and reencoding are not just playing the role of transduction; they are at the very heart of reasoning itself. It is this kind of behavior that we refer to as verbal reasoning.

Although verbal reasoning is a natural strategy for solving deductive reasoning problems, it can often lead to errors. The problem is that linguistic processes cannot be adapted to a deductive reasoning task instantaneously. Like most highly skilled processes, encoding, reencoding, and decoding processes are undoubtedly largely automatic; people do not have deliberate control over their internal workings. We assume that individuals can organize the flow of control through these processes to meet the demands of the task (e.g., first encode, then go back and reencode, and then decode) but that they have to take what they get whenever one is evoked. And although these outputs serve the needs of communication extremely well, they are less well suited to the demands of deductive reasoning. For example, in standard communication people often expect listeners to make plausible (if invalid) assumptions without being told explicitly. If someone asks you if you know what time it is, it goes without saying that that person wants you to tell him or her (rather than just to answer yes or no). Conversely, listeners expect speakers to make important information explicit even if it is logically implied by what they have already said. The demands of deductive reasoning are quite different. Making unwarranted assumptions, however plausible, is precluded by correct deduction. Similarly, deduction requires appreciating the validity of certain information even if it was not made explicit. According to this view, the reason untrained participants make mistakes is that they are using linguistic processes that are adapted to the needs of communication rather than those of deduction. Although mistakes make these participants appear irrational, the errors arise from the decidedly rational strategy of applying the only available processes to a task for which they are poorly adapted (this argument is similar to a rational analysis as proposed by Anderson, 1990).

The verbal reasoning hypothesis does not imply that deduction is simply a special case of language processing. The demands of deductive tasks could lead participants to use their linguistic processes in very different ways than they are used in communication (e.g., repeatedly reencoding the problem statement and generating responses that relate specific terms from the problem). Although the verbal reasoning hypothesis proposes that the central processes in deduction are linguistic, these processes are assumed to be used in a way that reflects the demands of deduction rather than communication. Also, this hypothesis claims that the processes that are central to deduction are linguistic, not the representational structures. In particular, verbal reasoning does not preclude visuo-spatial representations or imagery (indeed, we follow Johnson-Laird, 1983, in assuming that people use a mental model representation). The claim is simply that the most important cognitive processes in deduction are the same ones that are used in language comprehension and generation. Furthermore, although the verbal reasoning hypothesis claims that high-level verbal processes (encoding, reencoding, and generation) play a central role in deduction, this does not imply that the detailed mechanisms underlying these processes are all linguistic. For example, these processes undoubtedly rely on underlying mechanisms (e.g., memory retrieval) that are used in a variety of nonlinguistic tasks. Rather, the hypothesis is that the same high-level processes, as a whole, that are used to transform verbal representations into semantic representations and back again also play a central role in deduction. Thus, *verbal* simply refers to transforming between verbal and semantic representations. Finally, the verbal reasoning hypothesis does not rule out reasoning-specific mechanisms, especially in participants who have had training in logic. People can certainly learn to use specific strategies (e.g., Venn diagrams and Euler circles) or even to change how they interpret specific words in deduction tasks (e.g., learning that "Some x" can refer to a set of xs that are distinct from any other xs in the problem; Lehman, Newell, Polk, & Lewis, 1993). But without such training, this hypothesis predicts that the major processes used in deduction will be linguistic rather than reasoning specific.

It is important to point out that the verbal reasoning hypothesis does not apply to tasks that require information beyond that presented verbally in the problem statement. The hypothesis is that on tasks in which all of the relevant information is provided verbally, the verbal processes of encoding and reencoding play a central role in reasoning itself (they are not simply transduction operators), at least for untrained participants. If this claim is true, then it is fair to say that deduction can usually be characterized as verbal reasoning, because almost all deductive tasks satisfy this criterion. There are exceptions, however. For example, tasks that require metadeduction, such as the Wason (1966) selection task, are not amenable to a pure verbal reasoning account. Linguistic processes may still play an important role in these tasks; however, because they require knowledge that cannot be extracted from the problem statement, linguistic processes will necessarily be insufficient. Similarly, a verbal reasoning explanation would presumably not apply to reasoning tasks that involve nonverbal materials. In particular, verbal reasoning does not predict that participants must translate nonverbal materials into a linguistic format to solve such problems.

In this chapter, we present evidence in favor of this view of deduction as verbal reasoning. We begin by showing that a computational model—VR—

based on verbal reasoning can account for the detailed behavior of participants on a specific task, namely categorical syllogisms. VR handles all of the major syllogism variants, models all of the standard phenomena, and makes a number of novel predictions that have been empirically confirmed. Furthermore, it fits the behavior of individual participants with an accuracy that rivals the test–retest reliability of the participants themselves.[1] We then turn to previous explanations of the major phenomena of other deductive reasoning tasks and show either that they can be reinterpreted as verbal reasoning accounts or that verbal reasoning provides a more parsimonious explanation.

Verbal Reasoning on Categorical Syllogisms

Categorical syllogisms are reasoning problems consisting of two premises and a conclusion (Figure 32.1, left). There are four different premise types, called *moods*, each of which relates two of the terms and contains a quantifier (Figure 32.1, middle). The two premises always share a single term, called the *middle term* (*bowlers* on the left of the figure). A conclusion is legal if it relates the two noncommon terms (the *end terms: archers* and *chefs*) using one of the four moods. Sometimes there is no legal conclusion that is deductively valid. In that case, the correct response is that there is no valid conclusion (NVC). The first premise has two possible orders (relating x to y or relating y to x), as does the second premise (relating y to z or relating z to y); thus, together there are four possible orders, or *figures* (Figure 32.1, right). The four figures, together with the four moods for the first premise and the four moods for the second premise, combine to form 64 possible premise pairs. Different versions of the task require determining the validity of each member of a set of conclusions (Sells, 1936; Wilkins, 1928), choosing a valid conclusion from a set of alternatives (Ceraso & Provitera, 1971; Chapman & Chapman, 1959; Dickstein 1975; Revlis, 1975b), evaluating the validity of a given conclusion (Janis & Frick, 1943), and generating a valid conclusion given only the premises (Johnson-Laird & Bara, 1984).

Categorical syllogisms are relatively straightforward to understand and simple to administer. When responses are aggregated over groups of participants, some striking regularities emerge[2]:

Premise 1: No archers are bowlers.	A: All x are y.	P1: Axy / P2: Iyz | P1: Oyx / P2: Ayz
Premise 2: Some bowlers are chefs.	I: Some x are y.	
Conclusion: Some chefs are not archers.	E: No x are y.	P1: Exy / P2: Ezy | P1: Iyx / P2: Ozy
	O: Some x are not y.	

Figure 32.1
Categorical syllogism task (A = all, I = some, E = no, O = some not).

1. The difficulty effect: The average participant makes many errors (often making errors on approximately half the tasks; Dickstein, 1975; Wilkins, 1928).

2. The validity effect: The average participant performs better than chance (Johnson-Laird & Steedman, 1978; Revlis, 1975b).

3. The atmosphere effect: Excluding NVC responses, (a) if either premise is negative (*No x are y* or *Some x are not y*), most responses are negative, and otherwise most are positive, and (b) if either premise is particular (referring to a subset: *Some x are y* or *Some x are not y*), most responses are particular, and otherwise most are universal (*All x are z* or *No x are z*; Sells, 1936; Woodworth & Sells, 1935).

4. The conversion effect: Excluding NVC responses, many erroneous responses would be correct if the converse of one or both premises were assumed to be true (Chapman & Chapman, 1959; Revlis, 1975b).

5. The figural effect: Excluding NVC responses, if only one end term (*x* or *z*) appears as the subject of a premise, that term tends to appear as the subject of the conclusion (Johnson-Laird & Bara, 1984; Johnson-Laird & Steedman, 1978).

6. The belief bias effect: Participants are more likely to generate and accept as valid a conclusion that they believe to be true in comparison with one they believe to be false, independent of its true logical status (Evans, Barston, & Pollard, 1983; Janis & Frick, 1943; Morgan & Morton, 1944; Oakhill & Johnson-Laird, 1985; Oakhill, Johnson-Laird, & Garnham, 1989; Wilkins, 1928).

7. The elaboration effect: Participants are more accurate if the premises are elaborated to be unambiguous (e.g., *All A are B, but Some B are not A;* Ceraso & Provitera, 1971).

VR: A Computational Model for Categorical Syllogisms

VR is a computational model of behavior on categorical syllogisms that is based on the idea of verbal reasoning. Figure 32.2 presents the general control structure of VR when generating a conclusion from a pair of premises, as well as the major assumptions of the model.[3]

In keeping with verbal reasoning, the central processes in VR are linguistic: initial encoding, conclusion generation, and reencoding. In contrast, VR's control structure reflects the basic demands of the reasoning task. At the very least, the task requires encoding the premises (initial encoding) and producing a response (generating a conclusion). If VR fails in generating a conclusion, then it repeatedly reencodes the premises until generation succeeds or until it gives up. Reencoding in this context is a natural response to the task demand of producing a conclusion: The system lacks the knowledge to relate the end terms, the main source of knowledge for the problem is the premises, and encoding is the most natural way of extracting knowledge from a premise. If

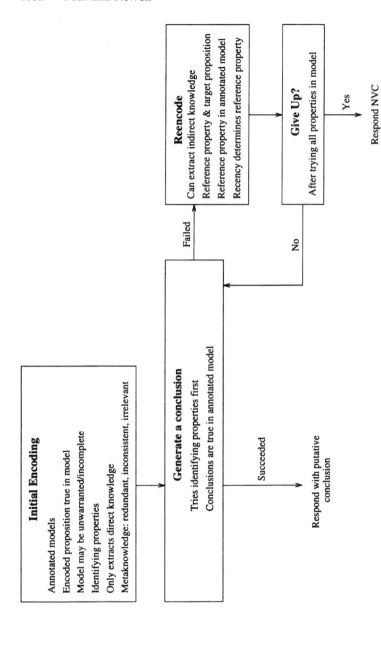

Figure 32.2
Summary of VR (NVC = no valid conclusion).

repeated reencoding fails to lead to a conclusion, then VR gives up and responds NVC. We now turn to specifying each of the processes in Figure 32.2: initial encoding, conclusion generation, reencoding, and giving up.

Initial Encoding   Following Johnson-Laird (Johnson-Laird, 1983; Johnson-Laird & Bara, 1984; Johnson-Laird & Byrne, 1991), VR first constructs a mental model of a situation in which the premises are true (as previously discussed, VR assumes the same data structure as mental model theory, but the central processes proposed by the theories—reencoding vs. searching for alternative models—are different). Mental models consist of a set of model objects with properties and relations among them. Objects, properties, and relations in a mental model are representational constructs that correspond to objects, properties, and relations in the situation being represented (the referent). Indeed, the defining characteristic of mental models is that they satisfy the structure-correspondence principle: All objects, properties, and relations in the mental model must map one to one into objects, properties, and relations in the referent. VR uses an annotated model representation in which properties can be annotated with two additional pieces of information: a *not* flag (represented by the − symbol) indicating that the object does not have the specified property and (b) an *identifying* flag (represented by the prime ['] symbol) indicating that the object is identified by the specified property (e.g., VR distinguishes a painter [identifying] who is a sculptor from a sculptor [identifying] who is a painter). Identifying properties are distinguished from other, secondary properties by being more easily accessible. Specifically, when VR generates conclusions based on its annotated models, it produces conclusions about identifying properties before trying conclusions about secondary properties. For syllogisms, the identifying properties simply correspond to the topics of the propositions being encoded (i.e., their grammatical subjects).

After encoding a proposition, the resulting annotated model is guaranteed to represent a situation in which that proposition is true. But, in general, there are an infinite variety of such situations, and most of them are unwarranted or incomplete with respect to the initial proposition. That is, an annotated model may encode information that is not inherent in a proposition (and be unwarranted) or may fail to encode information that is inherent (and be incomplete). Figure 32.3 gives examples of each. On the left is an annotated model that is unwarranted with respect to the proposition *Some archers are bowlers*. The annotated model consists of two model objects represented as a set of properties enclosed in parentheses. The first object corresponds to a person who is an archer and bowler, but the second is an archer and explicitly not a bowler. The proposition *Some archers are bowlers* is true in this annotated model, but the model also encodes information that is unwarranted given only that proposition: the fact that some archers are not bowlers. On the right is an example of an incomplete annotated model. Once again, the model supports the initial

Unwarranted Annotated Model

```
┌─────────────────────────────────────────┐
│ Proposition: Some archers are bowlers.   │
│                                          │
│ Annotated Model:    (archer bowler)      │
│                     (archer -bowler)     │
│                                          │
└─────────────────────────────────────────┘
```

Incomplete Annotated Model

```
┌─────────────────────────────────────────┐
│ Proposition: No archers are bowlers.     │
│                                          │
│ Annotated Model:    (archer -bowler)     │
│                     (bowler)             │
│                                          │
└─────────────────────────────────────────┘
```

Figure 32.3
Examples of unwarranted and incomplete annotated models.

proposition (*No archers are bowlers* in this case), but now it fails to reflect the fact that the second object (the bowler) cannot be an archer. In this case, then, the annotated model is incomplete with respect to the initial proposition.

During initial encoding, VR encodes only direct knowledge, that is, information about the topic of each proposition. For example, suppose encoding the first premise of a syllogism leads to an annotated model with a single object $(A'\ B)$. Then an initial encoding of *No C are B* will not affect that object because the direct knowledge is about C and that model object does not have property C. Only if this direct knowledge is insufficient to produce a conclusion will VR try to extract indirect knowledge (i.e., knowledge about nontopic properties) via reencoding.

Finally, when encoding a proposition into an annotated model, VR encodes metaknowledge representing whether the proposition was redundant, inconsistent, or irrelevant with respect to the annotated model. The choice of flag is based on how the annotated model was affected during encoding: If it was unchanged, then the proposition was redundant; if an existing property was removed or replaced, then the proposition was inconsistent; and if the existing objects were unchanged but new unrelated objects were created that share no properties with the old objects, then the proposition was irrelevant.

Figure 32.4 shows default encodings consistent with these assumptions for each of the four syllogism premise moods. For each premise type, the figure shows how the model would be augmented, both when there are no objects in the model that relate to the topic of the proposition (left) and when there are (right). We assume that there is substantial individual variation in these encodings, and later we address this diversity.

Conclusion generation   Once VR has encoded the premises, it attempts to produce a conclusion based on its annotated model. It does so using a simple generate-and-test procedure. First, it proposes simple propositions that it considers to be true based on the annotated model, and then it tests each proposed proposition to determine whether it is a legal syllogism conclusion (i.e., whether it relates the end terms using one of the four standard moods [*All, Some, No,* or *Some not*]). The simple propositions that VR may propose

	No object (X ...)	An object (X ...) exists
All x are y	(X' Y)	all (X ...) ⟶ (X' ... Y)
Some x are y	(X' Y) (X')	MR (X ...) ⟶ (X' ... Y) (X' ...)
No x are y	(X' -Y)	all (X ...) ⟶ (X' ... -Y)
Some x are not y	(X' -Y) (X')	MR (X ...) ⟶ (X' ... -Y) (X' ...)

Figure 32.4

Default encodings for VR. At left are the model objects that would be added to the annotated model if no existing model objects relate to the topic of the proposition (X). If the annotated model already contains model objects with property X, shown at right are how those objects would be changed (e.g., augmenting all such objects with property Y or augmenting the most recently accessed such object with property Y). (' = identifying property; MR = most recently accessed; ··· = other properties)

include the legal syllogism conclusions but may also involve the middle term, other quantifiers, or both. As previously mentioned, VR proposes propositions about identifying properties first. The proposal phase is based on templates that are associated with each simple proposition. Each such template specifies the conditions under which the associated proposition should be considered true (and hence proposed) in the annotated model. When the annotated model matches the template, the associated simple proposition is proposed. If none of the proposed propositions are legal syllogism conclusions, generation fails and reencoding is evoked. If at least one is legal, generation succeeds. In practice, there is rarely more than one proposed conclusion that is legal. When there is, VR produces the set of conclusions it considers equally probable. It could obviously choose randomly among the alternatives, but having the entire set makes it possible to compute the exact expected value of accurate predictions.

As a default, we assume that *All x are y/No x are y* will be proposed when there is an object with X as an identifying property and all objects with property X also have property $Y/-Y$. *Some x are y/Some x are not y* will be proposed when there is an object with X as an identifying property and there is at least one object with properties X and $Y/-Y$. Again, we address individual differences later.

Reencoding   If generation fails to produce a legal conclusion, VR tries to extract additional knowledge from the premises by reencoding. Unlike initial encoding, reencoding can extract indirect knowledge about nontopic properties. It first chooses a property based on the annotated model (the reference property) and then tries to extract additional knowledge about that property from any premise that mentions it (the target proposition). If the reference property is the topic of the target proposition, then reencoding works just like initial encoding (extracting only direct knowledge). If, however, the reference property is not the target proposition's topic, then VR will try to extract indirect knowledge about that property from the proposition. For example, in trying to extract more knowledge about property B, VR might reencode the premise *No A are B* (assuming that generation has failed so far). This premise does contain valid knowledge about B (that objects with property B in the model do not have property A), and VR may or may not be able to extract it. VR selects reference properties on the basis of how recently the corresponding model objects were accessed by the system. It starts with the most recently accessed objects because they are less likely to reflect information from older propositions. Reencoding with respect to these properties is more likely to augment the annotated model and lead to progress.

Giving Up   We assume that most participants give up only as a last resort, when they feel confident that repeated attempts to extract more knowledge will not lead anywhere. VR reaches such a point after it has tried extracting more knowledge about every property in the annotated model. This is when it quits and responds "NVC."

An Example of VR's Behavior   Figure 32.5 illustrates VR's default behavior on the following syllogism: *Some B are A. All B are C. Therefore, what necessarily follow?* As a means of illustrating reencoding, this version of VR has been given the ability to extract some indirect knowledge: When reencoding *Some x are y* with respect to property y, it augments the model in the same way that it would when encoding *Some y are x*.

VR's behavior on this syllogism follows the structure presented in Figure 32.2. After initially encoding the premises (Step 1 in Figure 32.5), it repeatedly reencodes them with respect to different reference properties until it is able to generate a legal conclusion *Some A are C* as its response (Steps 2–4).

Consider the initial encoding in more detail (Step 1). VR begins by encoding the first premise *Some B are A* into an annotated model. In keeping with the default encoding for *Some x are y*, VR creates two new objects: (B') and $(B' A)$. (Throughout this example, the model objects in Figure 5 are ordered from the least recently accessed [at the top] to the most recently accessed [at the bottom].) VR then encodes the second premise *All B are C*. It marks property B as identifying in all objects (a null operation in this case) and augments all objects having property B with property C. In this example, both objects are augmented. The result is an annotated model with two model objects $(B' C)$ and $(B' A C)$. This annotated model satisfies the default generation templates for *Some B are A* and *All B are C*, and so these conclusions are proposed. Because neither is a legal

Initial Encoding   **Generation**

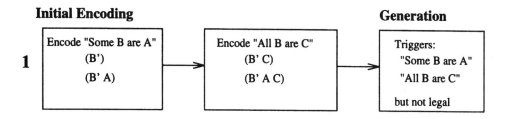

Reencode: extract information about C   **Generation**

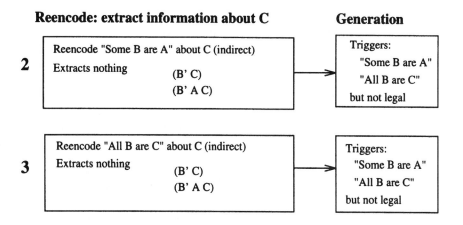

Reencode: extract information about A   **Generation**

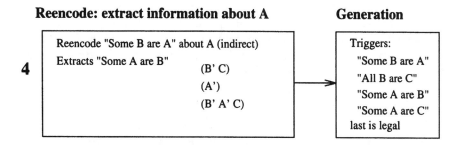

5 Respond "Some A are C"

Figure 32.5
VR on "Some B are A, All B are C." (′ = identifying property)

syllogism conclusion (they do not relate the end terms), VR must resort to reencoding. The most recently accessed model object is the recently augmented (B' A C), and C is its most recent property, so VR will begin reencoding using C as the reference property. Property A is the next most recent, and so it will be tried next, followed by B.

Steps 2 and 3 illustrate VR's reencoding when the reference property is C. Reencoding *Some B are A* extracts nothing about C (Step 2). There is no way it could, because the premise does not even mention that property. The annotated model therefore remains unchanged, and the same (illegal) conclusions are proposed. *All B are C* does mention property C, and so there is a possibility that reencoding will extract new indirect information from this premise. In this example, however, VR does not realize it can extract anything about C from the premise, and so once again the model is unchanged and generation fails (Step 3).

VR then turns to reencoding the premises using reference property A (Step 4). Unlike the previous attempts, reencoding *Some B are A* does extract some indirect knowledge, as previously mentioned. In this context, VR extracts the knowledge *Some A are B*. More precisely, it augments the annotated model in the same way it would when encoding that proposition. It marks property A as identifying and creates a new object (A'). Because A has now become an identifying property, generation finally proposes conclusions about A in addition to those about B. One of these new conclusions (*Some A are C*) is legal, and so generation succeeds and reencoding stops.

In keeping with verbal reasoning, the central processes in VR are linguistic: encoding, reencoding, and generation. VR does not have any processes devoted specifically to deduction (e.g., applying inference rules or searching for alternative models). Can such a model accurately capture the behavior of real participants? We now analyze VR's ability to fit aggregate and individual data as well as to make accurate novel predictions.

Aggregate Data

Analysis 1: Phenomena Using Standard Content and Form   Table 1 presents aggregate data from six experiments and results using three default versions of VR as well as their average. Standard syllogism variants were used in which effects of content (belief bias) and form (elaboration effect) did not play a role. At the far right are the values that would be expected in purely random data. The top row in the table presents the percentage of legal responses that were correct (of 6,592 total participant responses, 159 [2.4%] were either illegible or did not correspond to one of the nine legal responses [many involved the middle term], and these were not included). The other three rows present measures of the atmosphere, conversion, and figural effects. Because the atmosphere effect does not apply to NVC responses, these were not included. Instead, the numbers represent the percentage of legal responses other than

NVC that followed the atmosphere effect. The conversion effect also does not apply to NVC responses, and, in addition, it is restricted to errors. Consequently, the numbers in the third row represent the legal but erroneous non-NVC responses that would be valid if the converse of one or both premises were true. Finally, the figural effect is relevant only to 32 of the 64 tasks (those in the xy–yz and yx–zy figures), and it too does not apply to NVC responses. The numbers in the bottom row therefore represent the percentage of legal non-NVC responses on relevant tasks that followed the figural effect.

The first three data sets were collected from students at the University of Milan (Johnson-Laird & Bara, 1984). In the first (unlimited), participants were given an unlimited amount of time to write down a response. In the second (timed), participants were asked to respond within 10 s. Afterward, they were given the same tasks along with the responses they provided in the timed condition and were given 1 min to revise their answers if desired. These data are recorded in the fourth column (revised). The next two data sets (Week 1 and Week 2) were collected a week apart from the same group of students at Teachers College, Columbia University. The last data set (Inder) was collected from 3 undergraduates at the University of Edinburgh (Inder, 1986, 1987). None of the participants had training in logic.

The three columns labeled VR1, VR2, and VR3 present predictions from three versions of VR, and column VR1–3 presents their average. These three systems were intended to be very direct implementations of the defaults described previously. VR1 is the simplest possible such system, and so it is very streamlined. In particular, it does not extract any indirect knowledge when reencoding and often fails to relate the end terms, producing a large number of NVC responses (52 of 64). As a result, the measures of the atmosphere, conversion, and figural effects for VR1 may not be reliable because they are based on a small sample of non-NVC responses (12 of 64 [19%]). To overcome this problem, we built two other versions of VR that do extract indirect knowledge and that, consequently, produce fewer NVC responses. VR2 is identical to VR1 except that it can extract two pieces of (correct) indirect knowledge: (a) When the target proposition is *Some x are y* and the reference property is y, it augments the model in the same way that encoding the proposition *Some y are x* would augment it, and (b) when the target proposition is *No x are y* and the reference property is y, it augments the model in the same way that *No y are x* would.[4] This version of VR produces significantly more non-NVC responses (25 of 64) than VR1. VR3 is an extreme case that always extracts indirect knowledge and therefore produces relatively few NVC responses (8 of 64). The specific indirect knowledge extracted was chosen to be consistent with the target proposition, to relate the same two terms, and to share the same quantity (universal or particular).

The numbers in the far right column of Table 32.1 (random) correspond to percentages that would be expected by chance alone. There are 576 legal task–response pairs (64 tasks × 9 legal responses each). Of these, 85 (15%) represent a

Table 32.1
Percentages of correct, atmospheric, conversion, and figural responses from humans, VR, and random data

| Response type | Human data | | | | | | | | VR's predictions | | | | |
	Unlimited ($n = 20$)	Timed ($n = 20$)	Revised ($n = 20$)	Week 1 ($n = 20$)	Week 2 ($n = 20$)	Inder ($n = 3$)	Total ($n = 103$)		VR1–3	VR1	VR2	VR3	Random
Correct	40	49	45	59	69	61	53		58	64	75	38	15
Atmospheric	69	72	76	81	84	84	77		89	100	100	83	25
Conversion	28	38	38	38	51	54	37		40	50	29	41	9
Figural	90	81	83	90	86	70	86		89	100	86	86	50

Note. VR = verbal reasoning model.

correct response to the associated task. This number is higher than the total number of tasks (64) because some tasks have more than a single correct response. If all 64 NVC responses are removed, 512 task–response pairs remain that do not involve NVC. Of these, 128 (25%) are consistent with the atmosphere effect. Similarly, there are 464 task–response pairs that both represent errors and do not involve NVC. Forty of these (9%) would be valid if the converse of one or both premises were true. Finally, the figural effect does not apply to 256 of the 512 non-NVC task–response pairs (those in the yx–yz and xy–zy figures). Of the remaining 256, 128 (50%) follow the figural effect.

The human data in Table 32.1 reflect the first five of the seven regularities listed earlier. The difficulty of the task is reflected in the low percentage of correct responses (53% on average). Nevertheless, participants performed far better than would be expected by chance alone (15% in the column on the far right), demonstrating a validity effect. In keeping with the atmosphere effect, 77% of the legal non-NVC responses were consistent with atmosphere (25% would be expected by chance). A conversion effect is also apparent because 37% of the legal, erroneous non-NVC responses would have been valid with conversion, in comparison with only 9% in random data. Finally, the data also reflect a strong figural effect; the percentage of relevant, legal non-NVC responses that followed the figure of the premises in the human data (86%) was much higher than what would be expected in random data (50%). Note that these five regularities are reflected in all six data sets, indicating their robustness.

Table 32.1 also demonstrates that all three default versions of VR produce these five regularities. They solve only between 38% and 75% of the syllogisms correctly (difficulty effect), but this is much better than would be expected at random (validity effect). Also, far more of their responses follow the atmosphere (83%–100% of non-NVC responses), conversion (29%–50% of non-NVC errors), and figural effects (86%–100% of relevant non-NVC responses) than would be expected in random data (25%, 9%, and 50%, respectively). The crucial point is that computational models based on the verbal reasoning hypothesis do account for these empirical phenomena.

These versions of VR not only produce the regularities, but the qualitative size of the effects is similar to that in the human data. The mean percentages correct in the human data sets from Table 32.1 range from 40% to 69%, with a mean of 53%; for the three VR systems, they range from 38% to 75%, with a mean of 58%. Similarly, the size of the atmosphere effect in these data sets (ranges from 69% to 84%, with a mean of 77%) is similar to that produced by the VR systems (83% to 100%, with a mean of 89%), as is the size of the conversion effect (28% to 54% [$M = 37\%$] in human data and 29% to 50% [$M = 40\%$] for the VR systems) and the figural effect (70% to 90% [$M = 86\%$] in human data and 86% to 100% [$M = 89\%$] for the VR systems).

Because VR predicts these regularities, analyzing how it does so will suggest explanations for why they occur. First consider the question of why syllogisms are so difficult. VR suggests that the main reason is that language comprehension is not guaranteed to deliver a necessary and sufficient representation of what the premises are about. VR simply constructs a model of a situation that is consistent with the premises (i.e., the premises will be true in the model). Such a model can both support conclusions that are not strictly valid (and be unwarranted) and fail to support conclusions that are (and be incomplete). Figure 32.3 gave examples of each.

The assumption that annotated models are always consistent, if not always necessary and sufficient, also provides an explanation of the validity effect (the fact that people perform better than chance). If an annotated model is consistent with the premises, then it follows that no entailments of the premises can be false in the model (this does not mean that the entailments must be true in the model). Otherwise one (or both) of the premises would have to be false. Equivalently, a consistent annotated model never supports conclusions that contradict an entailment of the premises. So if people base their conclusions on an annotated model that is consistent with the premises, their responses will always be possible (although not necessary); people will not consider (invalid) conclusions that contradict an entailment of the premises. Consequently, they do better than just randomly selecting from all possible conclusions.

The reason that VR produces the atmosphere effect and, hence, the suggested explanation is that the standard semantics of the premises rule out most non-atmospheric conclusions. Assuming that *some* is typically interpreted as *some but not necessarily all* (or just *some but not all*) explains why particular responses are so common for syllogisms that involve a particular premise (but not for those that do not). When a *some* premise is read, it creates additional model objects that do not satisfy the predicate of the premise. These additional model objects rule out universal conclusions and lead to particular responses. For example, the default encodings lead to the following annotated model for the premise *Some A are B*:

(A')

$(A'B)$

where the upper model object encodes the *not all* information. Augmenting this model based on *All B are C* leads to

(A')

$(A'B'C)$

and the upper model object refutes the universal conclusion *All A are C*, leading to a *some* response instead. If both premises are universal, these additional objects are not created, and universal conclusions can be drawn. If the interpretation of *some* during generation is similar to that during comprehension (*some but not [necessarily] all*), then particular conclusions will be drawn only if universals cannot. Consequently, two universal premises tend to produce a universal conclusion.

In a similar way, negative premises tend to refute positive conclusions because they create negative rather than positive associations between properties. For example, consider reading *All A are B* and *No B are C* using the default encodings. *All A are B* leads to the single model object $(A'B)$, and then *No B are C* augments it with $-C$—$(A'B' - C)$—creating a negative rather than positive association. Because negative premises tend to produce negative associations, the resulting conclusions are also negative. Conversely, if both premises are positive, then positive rather than negative associations among properties are created, and conclusions tend to be positive.

There are two main reasons VR produces a conversion effect. The first is straightforward: VR often extracts indirect knowledge that is equivalent to the converse of a premise (even if that converse is invalid). For example, when VR3 tries to extract knowledge about y from a premise that relates x to y, the knowledge it encodes is always equivalent to the converse of the premise. In two of the four cases, the converse is invalid and can lead to errors consistent with the conversion effect. Consider the processing that VR3 goes through while working on the following premise pair: *Some A are B, All C are B*. Initial encoding leads to the following annotated model:

(A')

$(A'B)$

$(C'B)$

and B is chosen as the first reference property. Reencoding the first premise with respect to B changes only the recency of some of the objects, but reencoding *All C are B* with respect to B augments the model in the same way encoding *All B are C* would:

(A')

$(C'B')$

$(A'B'C)$

which supports both *Some A are C* and *Some C are A*. Both responses are consistent with the conversion effect (i.e., they are invalid but would be correct if the converse of one or both premises were true).

This explanation is reminiscent of previous theories of syllogistic reasoning that assumed illicit conversion (Chapman & Chapman, 1959; Revlis, 1975b), but there are important differences. For one, those theories attempted to explain most non-NVC errors in terms of illicit conversion, but we assume that there are a variety of other sources of error. Indeed, as shown in Table 32.1, only 40% of non-NVC errors produced by VR1, VR2, and VR3 can be explained in terms of illicit conversion, but this simulates the human data very well (in which only 37% of non-NVC errors were consistent with the conversion effect). The fact that approximately 60% of non-NVC errors cannot be explained in terms of illicit conversion poses problems for the Chapman and Chapman (1959) and Revlis (1975b) theories but not for VR. Furthermore, Revlis intentionally implemented the strongest version of the conversion hypothesis, namely, that both premises are always explicitly converted and that both they and their converses are encoded at the same time (as Revlis pointed out, Chapman and Chapman were vague on this point). VR makes no such assumptions. In VR, indirect knowledge is extracted only if direct knowledge fails to lead to a conclusion. And although indirect knowledge is assumed to augment the annotated model in the same way encoding a corresponding explicit proposition would, VR does not assume that the indirect knowledge is available as an explicit proposition. It may or may not be; VR does not take a stand on the issue.

VR1 and VR2 both produce conversion effects (Table 32.1), and yet neither extracts invalid indirect knowledge (VR2 extracts only valid indirect knowledge, and VR1 does not extract any at all). According to VR, then, there must be at least one other factor that contributes to errors consistent with the conversion effect. The source of most of these other errors is the traditional fallacy of the undistributed middle term, which shows up in the interpretation of particular premises. Consider the premise pair *All A are B, Some B are C*. Both VR1 and VR2 behave the same way on this problem. Encoding the first premise creates a single model object $(A'B)$, and the second premise augments it and creates a new one as well:

$$(A'B)$$

$$(A'B'C)$$

This annotated model leads to the invalid conclusion *Some A are C*. Furthermore, this conclusion is consistent with the conversion effect because it would be valid if the converse of *All A are B* (i.e., *All B are A*) were true. But no knowledge corresponding to the converse of either premise has been extracted (indeed, no indirect knowledge has been extracted at all). The problem is that *Some B* was interpreted as referring to a subset of the objects mentioned in the first premise, and this interpretation is invalid (to see this, consider the syllogism *All cats are animals, Some animals are dogs. Therefore, some cats are dogs*). So some errors consistent with the conversion effect can be explained in terms of the erroneous interpretation of particular premises, without any reference to illicit conversion.

VR's explanation of the figural effect is based on the special availability of proposition topics in the annotated model. After encoding, properties in the annotated model that correspond to premise topics are more available than

Table 32.2
Percentages of believed and disbelieved conclusions accepted as valid

Experiment	Humans		VR1–3 average		VR1		VR2		VR3	
	B (%)	D (%)	B (%)	D (%)	B (%)	D (%)	B (%)	D (%)	B (%)	D (%)
Evans et al. (1983)										
Experiment 1	92	50	67	33	50	0	75	50	75	50
Experiment 2	76	38	63	25	50	0	75	50	63	25
Experiment 3	79	30	65	29	50	0	75	50	69	38
Oakhill et al. (1989)										
Experiment 3	58	52	75	50	75	50	75	50	75	50

Note. B (%) indicates the percentage of believed conclusions that were accepted as valid; D (%) indicates the same percentage for disbelieved conclusions. VR = verbal reasoning model.

other properties (they are marked as identifying properties). During generation, conclusions about those properties are tried first. If only one end term appeared as the topic of a premise, then the corresponding property will be marked as identifying, and generation will tend to produce conclusions about it. In the xy–yz and yx–zy figures, this leads to xz and zx conclusions, respectively, as predicted by the figural effect.

Analysis 2: Effects of Belief   Tables 32.2 and 32.3 present percentages of trials on which the provided or suggested conclusion was considered valid, both when that conclusion was consistent with beliefs [column B (%) in the tables] and when it was inconsistent with beliefs [column D (%) in the tables]. In most cases, believability ratings were collected from an independent set of participants. Table 32.2 presents four experimental paradigms involving testing conclusions, and the four in Table 32.3 involve generating conclusions.[5]

The second and third columns in Table 32.2 present the human data from four belief bias experiments in which provided conclusions had to be evaluated. The other columns present the predictions of three versions of VR, as well as their average. These systems are the same as those described previously but have been modified to respond to the new experimental paradigm. In particular, they test rather than generate conclusions. They do so by encoding the premises followed by the conclusion and basing their responses on metaknowledge. If the conclusion is found to be inconsistent with the annotated model of the premises, they consider it invalid. If it is redundant, they consider it valid. If neither of these outcomes occurs, then they repeatedly reencode until they can decide or until they give up. We simulated the belief effects by having VR choose randomly between "invalid" and the response suggested by belief whenever it gave up (i.e., encoding and reencoding were inconclusive). We did not incorporate any belief effects when the results of reasoning were conclusive.

Table 32.3

Percentages of generated conclusions that matched believed and disbelieved suggested conclusions

Experiment	Humans		VR1–3 average		VR1		VR2		VR3	
	B (%)	D (%)	B (%)	D (%)	B (%)	D (%)	B (%)	D (%)	B (%)	D (%)
Oakhill & Johnson-Laird (1985)										
Experiment 1	46	30	0	0	0	0	0	0	0	0
Experiment 2	49	43	50	25	0	0	100	50	50	25
Oakhill et al. (1989)										
Experiment 1	66	37	50	17	50	25	50	17	50	8
Experiment 2	74	28	50	15	50	25	50	13	50	6

Note. B (%) indicates the percentage of generated conclusions that matched a believed suggested conclusion; D (%) indicates the same percentage when the suggested conclusion was disbelieved. The suggested conclusion is what would be predicted by Johnson-Laird and Bara (1984) if the participant considered only one mental model. VR = verbal reasoning model.

The four experiments presented in Table 32.3 investigated belief bias effects involved in generating a conclusion rather than determining the validity of one that was given. In these studies, participants were presented with premise pairs and the experimenters manipulated the believability of the conclusion "suggested" by the premises. The suggested conclusions were selected on the basis of Johnson-Laird's theories of syllogistic reasoning (Johnson-Laird, 1983; Johnson-Laird & Bara, 1984)—they corresponded to conclusions that are true in one mental model of the premises (the specific mental model that Johnson-Laird & Bara, 1984, assumed to be built first)—and were confirmed to be common responses in the data he collected. Table 32.3 shows the percentage of generated conclusions that matched the suggested conclusion when that conclusion was both believable (46%) and unbelievable (30%).

The second and third columns in Table 32.3 present the human data from these four experiments. The other columns present the predictions from the three versions of VR and their average. Once again, the systems are the same as before but have been adapted to the demands of the task; they generate conclusions just like the original versions, but they incorporate a belief bias. Specifically, whenever the systems generate a conclusion that is unbelievable, they go back and try to generate a different conclusion by repeatedly reencoding the premises. If that fails, they choose randomly between their original conclusion and NVC.

Tables 32.2 and 32.3 demonstrate a belief bias in both testing and generating conclusions. In all four experiments in Table 32.2, the percentage of believed conclusions that were accepted as valid was consistently larger than the percentage for disbelieved conclusions (92% vs. 50%, 76% vs. 38%, 79% vs. 30%, and 58% vs. 52%). This same effect can be seen in the four experiments that required generating rather than testing conclusions (Table 32.3).

Furthermore, Tables 32.2 and 32.3 show that the three VR systems are more likely as well to accept and generate a conclusion if it is believed rather than is disbelieved, demonstrating that the model also produces a belief bias. In the one experiment in which the systems failed to show an effect of beliefs (Oakhill & Johnson-Laird, 1985, Experiment 1), only two premise pairs were used. In both cases, VR1 and VR2 produced NVC and VR3 produced *Some C are not A*. These responses did not correspond to the suggested conclusion *Some A are not C*, and, as a result, VR did not consider them either believable or unbelievable. Consequently, there was no opportunity for an effect of belief to show up. Similarly, the second experiment involved only two syllogisms, and VR1 produced NVC on both; thus, it did not produce a belief bias. In all other cases (and in all cases involving testing given conclusions), however, all three systems did produce a belief bias effect.

At the most general level, there are two reasons VR is biased by beliefs. First, its reasoning attempts are often inconclusive, so it looks for other knowledge sources on which to base a decision. Beliefs are such a knowledge source. More specifically, beliefs can influence how VR responds after giving up (by responding on the basis of beliefs rather than in keeping with a default). Second, because VR's reasoning attempts can be faulty, it will reconsider results it would normally accept as valid if they contradict beliefs. For example, beliefs can influence the criteria under which conclusion generation is considered successful (the "succeeded" test for conclusion generation in Figure 32.2). If VR generates a conclusion that contradicts beliefs, then it will go back and try to generate a different one, even if the original conclusion was legal.

It is important to point out that these explanations depend on assumptions beyond the verbal reasoning hypothesis. The reason is that the effect depends on information that is not provided in the problem statement (participants' beliefs). Consequently, verbal processes will necessarily be insufficient to produce these effects. Of course, verbal reasoning is still apparent in the behavior of these systems (e.g., they repeatedly reencode propositions both to test conclusions and to generate new ones). But verbal reasoning provides only part of an explanation. Additional assumptions are necessary for a complete explanation.

Analysis 3: Elaboration Effect   Table 32.4 presents data relevant to the elaboration effect. The top row presents the percentage of responses that were correct for a set of 13 standard syllogisms used by Ceraso and Provitera (1971). The bottom row presents the percentage of correct responses for the same syllogisms when their premises were elaborated to be unambiguous. The elaborated and unelaborated forms of the premises are shown in Figure 32.6. In the

Table 32.4
Percentage correct for elaborated and unelaborated premises in humans and VR

Premise type	Humans	VR1–3 average	VR1	VR2	VR3
Unelaborated	58	59	62	69	46
Elaborated	80	95	100	100	85

Note. VR = verbal reasoning model.

unelaborated condition, only the premises in boldface were presented. In the elaborated condition, the others were included as well. Each syllogism was presented with four alternatives: (a) *All A are C*, (b) *Some A are C*, (c) *No A are C*, and (d) *Can't say*. The participants were asked to choose the valid response from among these four.

The human data (second column in Table 32.4) were collected from 80 students at the Newark campus of Rutgers University (Ceraso & Provitera, 1971). The other columns present predictions from the three default versions of VR and their average. For this analysis, the VR systems were unchanged. The only difference between the conditions was whether the systems were given only the unelaborated premises or the entire set of elaborated premises (Figure 32.6).

Table 32.4 illustrates the elaboration effect. The percentage of responses that were correct rose significantly when the premises were elaborated to be unambiguous (58% vs. 80%). Table 32.4 demonstrates that the VR systems exhibited an elaboration effect as well. All three systems produced a higher percentage of correct responses when the premises were elaborated to be unambiguous (between 85% and 100%) than when they were left unelaborated (46% to 69%). Furthermore, the percentage of elaborated and unelaborated syllogisms that the three VR systems solved correctly was also quite similar to the human data (59% vs. 58% for unelaborated premises and 95% vs. 80% for elaborated premises). The bottom line is that systems based on the verbal reasoning hypothesis do account for the elaboration effect.

VR's behavior on the premises in Figure 32.6 suggests that part of the elaboration effect on these tasks is due to artifacts in the experiment. Specifically, there are two main problems with the Ceraso and Provitera (1971) study that could account for part of the elaboration effect they observed: It presented only four responses from which to choose, and the valid conclusions were sometimes different for the elaborated and unelaborated premises. Consider Tasks 8 and 12 in Figure 32.6. The VR systems produce the erroneous response *Some A are C* to the unelaborated forms of both tasks but give the correct response (NVC) in the elaborated forms. These systems do generate one conclusion (*Some C are not A*) while working on the elaborated premises; however, because this conclusion is not one of the alternatives and because they cannot produce any others, they respond with NVC. In a different version of the task (that included

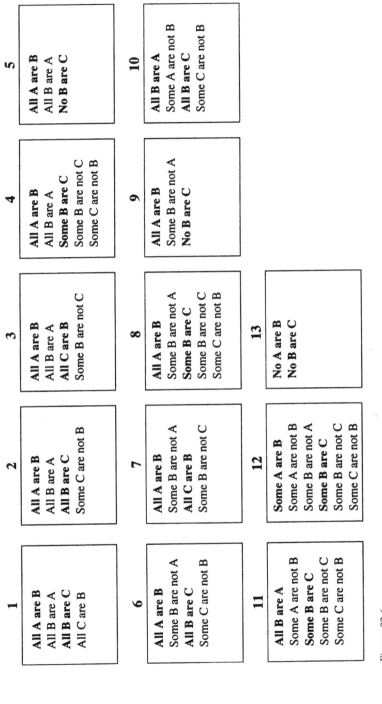

Figure 32.6
Elaborated and unelaborated (boldface) premises used by Ceraso and Provitera (1971).

Table 32.5
Percentage correct for elaborated and unelaborated premises in humans and VR with four tasks excluded

Premise type	Humans	VR1–3 average	VR1	VR2	VR3
Unelaborated	70	78	78	89	67
Elaborated	80	96	100	100	89

Note. VR = verbal reasoning model.

this conclusion as a legal choice), these systems would also have solved the elaborated tasks incorrectly. Task 4 (Figure 32.6) demonstrates a different problem with the experiment. In the unelaborated form the correct response to this task is NVC, but in the elaborated form it is *Some A are C*. In both formats, all three VR systems respond *Some A are C*, and they appear to exhibit an elaboration effect. The problem is that it is impossible to determine whether elaboration has had any effect. Even a theory that assumed that elaborations would have no impact on performance could exhibit an elaboration effect on this task as long as it responded *Some A are C*.

An obvious question is whether there really is an elaboration effect at all or whether it can be completely explained by these kinds of artifacts. Table 32.5 presents data relevant to this question. These data are the same as those in Table 32.4 except that the three tasks discussed earlier have not been included. Task 3 has also been excluded because the correct response changes between the unelaborated and elaborated forms (like Task 4). Note that although these tasks have been removed, both the human data and VR's predictions still show an elaboration effect (although it is smaller than before).

VR suggests two explanations for why this effect continues to show up. First, elaborated premises can constrain the annotated model to represent objects that fail to relate the end terms (so that invalid universal conclusions are not generated). Premise elaborations often refer to objects that are not referred to in the premises themselves and that do not associate the end term properties. Because the annotated model is constrained to be consistent with the propositions it encodes (i.e., the propositions are true in the model), it must represent these objects explicitly when given elaborated premises. Because these objects do not relate the end terms, invalid universal conclusions (that would otherwise be generated) are not proposed.

A second reason VR produces an elaboration effect is that elaborations can make certain properties more available (by marking them as identifying), causing conclusions to be generated that might otherwise be overlooked. In some cases, VR will produce an annotated model that relates the end terms but still be unable to generate a legal conclusion because the property that should be the topic does not appear as an identifying property. But if that property appears as the topic of a premise elaboration, it will be marked as identifying, and the appropriate conclusion can be drawn.[6]

Both of these effects can be seen in VR1's behavior on Task 10 in Figure 32.6. After initial encoding and reencoding (VR1 does none) of the unelaborated premises, *All B are A*, *All B are C*, VR1 constructs the following annotated model:

$$(B'AC)$$

Although this model relates properties *A* and *C*, VR1 cannot draw a conclusion because neither of these properties is marked as identifying. Consequently, it responds with NVC. Note that even if property C had, in fact, been an identifying property, VR1 would have responded with *All C are A*, which is still incorrect (this is the response given by VR3 to this premise pair). In contrast, if the original premises had been elaborated to include the additional premises *Some A are not B* and *Some C are not B*, then the annotated model would have been

$$(A')$$

$$(A' - B)$$

$$(B'AC)$$

$$(C')$$

$$(C' - B)$$

The premise elaborations have caused two significant changes to the annotated model: (a) Properties *A* and *C* now appear as identifying properties, and (b) additional objects that do not relate the end terms have been included. As a result, VR1 produces the valid conclusions *Some A are C* and *Some C are A* (and only those conclusions). *Some A are C* is one of the four legal alternatives, and so it is selected.

The main point of all of these analyses is that simple but different VR systems all produce the seven major regularities. This result demonstrates that the verbal reasoning hypothesis can account for the major phenomena of syllogistic reasoning (although, as discussed, belief bias effects depend on additional assumptions).

Individual Data
Data from individual participants provide an even more stringent test for a theory than do aggregate data. Nevertheless, essentially no work in the reasoning literature has attempted to analyze and predict such data. A computational system like VR, however, provides a natural approach to attacking this issue. The first step is to identify the aspects of VR that could most plausibly

differ across participants and to formulate those aspects as a set of explicit parameters. Then VR can be run with different parameter settings to tailor its performance to that of individual participants. Such an analysis can provide insight into the ability of the verbal reasoning hypothesis to account for individual data.

Individual-Differences Parameters for VR   Figure 32.7 presents such a set of individual-differences parameters. The first six parameters affect how VR encodes propositions. The next three (7–9) influence VR's conclusion generation process. Parameters 10 through 21 control what indirect knowledge VR extracts during reencoding. Finally, Parameter 22 controls whether or not VR attempts to falsify its putative conclusion by searching for alternative models (in keeping with mental model theory; Johnson-Laird & Bara, 1984; Johnson-Laird & Byrne, 1991). According to the verbal reasoning hypothesis, such a falsification strategy should be much less important in explaining behavior than are the verbal processes or encoding and reencoding. We included the parameter to allow us to test whether searching for alternative models would help VR's fits.

To reduce the size of this parameter space, we performed some preliminary analyses to identify parameter values that were most and least important in fitting the individual data. We divided the 64 premise pairs into four sets of 16 tasks such that each set contained the same number of tasks from each figure and of each premise type[7] and randomly selected 20 participants from the 103 in Table 32.1.[8] We then computed the best-fit parameter settings for each participant on all four task subsets, that is, the parameter settings that caused VR to produce the most correct predictions on those tasks. This and all subsequent fits were computed with the ASPM system, a suite of computational tools that makes it possible to fit and analyze symbolic parameter models with as many as 10 billion parameter settings (Polk, Newell, & VanLehn, 1995; Polk, VanLehn, & Kalp, 1995). On the basis of these results, we computed two subsets of parameter space, one large and one small. The large space excluded parameter values that the preceding analysis suggested could be safely removed and whose absence we intuitively thought would not be important. Those values are indicated by a minus sign in Figure 32.7. The analysis also suggested removing Value b for Parameter 22, which causes VR to attempt to falsify its putative conclusions by searching for alternative models (only 2% of our best-fitting settings contained that value). But because falsification is central to other theories of deduction, we wanted to investigate it further and did not remove it. The small space includes only parameter values that were critical in achieving good fits for the 20 participants in the preceding analysis. These values are indicated by a plus sign in Figure 32.7.

In the course of these analyses, we noticed that VR was fitting tasks that did not involve *All* much better than it was fitting those that did. Specifically, VR responded with NVC to these tasks more often than did the participants. This phenomenon is reminiscent of Lee's (1983) *A-effect:* Premise pairs involving

Compound semantics of premises

1. Some X are Y and ...
+ a. other x may or may not be y
+ b. different x may or may not be y
   c. different x are not y
− d. other x are not y and
      other x may or may not be y
− e. nothing

2. Some X are not Y and ...
+ a. other x may or may not be y
+ b. different x may or may not be y
   c. different x are y
− d. other x are y and
      other x may or may not be y
− e. nothing

Atomic semantics of premises

3. All X are Y
+ a. all (x) → (x' y)

− b. all (x) → (x' y) and
     new (x' y)

4. Some X are Y
− a. MR (x y) → (x' y) else
     MR (x [not -y]) → (x' y) else
     new (x' y)

+ b. MR (x [not -y]) → (x' y) else
     new (x' y)

+ c. MR (x y) → (x' y) else
     new (x' y)

   d. new (x' y)

5. No X are Y
+ a. all (x) → (x' -y)

− b. all (x) → (x' -y) and
     new (x' -y)

6. Some X are not Y
− a. MR (x -y) → (x' -y) else
     MR (x [not y]) → (x' -y) else
     new (x' -y)

+ b. MR (x [not y]) → (x' -y) else
     new (x' -y)

+ c. MR (x -y) → (x' -y) else
     new (x' -y)

   d. new (x' -y)

Generation templates

7. Some X are Y
+ a. (x') (x [not y])
   b. (x' y)

8. Some X are not Y
+ a. (x' -y) (x [not -y])
   b. (x' -y)

Topics to try

9. Generation topics
+ a. only identifying properties
   b. identifying and then secondary properties

Indirect knowledge extracted about Y from ...

10. All X are Y
+ a. none
+ b. All y are x
   c. Some y are not x
− d. There exists a different y

11. Some X are Y
+ a. none
+ b. Some y are x

12. No X are Y
+ a. none
+ b. No y are x

13. Some X are not Y
+ a. none
− b. Some y are x
+ c. Some y are not x

Indirect knowledge extracted about -X from ...

14. All X are Y
+ a. none
   b. No non-x are y
− c. All non-x are y

15. Some X are Y
+ a. none
   b. Some non-x are not y
   c. Some non-x are y

16. No X are Y
+ a. none
− b. All non-x are y
   c. No non-x are y

17. Some X are not Y
+ a. none
− b. Some non-x are y
   c. Some non-x are not y

Indirect knowledge extracted about -Y from ...

18. All X are Y
+ a. none
   b. No non-y are x

19. Some X are Y
+ a. none
   b. Some non-y are not x
   c. Some non-y are x

20. No X are Y
+ a. none
   b. All non-y are x

21. Some X are not Y
+ a. none
− b. Some non-y are x
   c. Some non-y are not x

22. How to falsify
+ a. don't
   b. do, if succeed then NVC

Figure 32.7
Individual-differences parameters for VR. + = most useful values; − = least useful values; MR = most recently accessed; ' = identifying property)

All seem to facilitate the generation of conclusions. Inder (1987) argued that the effect could be explained in terms of a syntactic generation strategy for premise pairs involving *All* (Ford, 1995, recently made a similar proposal). The basic idea is that, given the premise *All y are x*, participants may simply respond with the other premise after having replaced the *y* in it with *x*. For example, given the premise pair *All y are x, Some z are not y*, this strategy would replace the *y* in the second premise with *x* and produce the response *Some z are not x*. Note that this strategy applies only if the middle term (*y* in this case) appears as the topic of an *All* premise. A more extreme version of this strategy would perform the replacement even if the middle term appeared only as the predicate of an *All* premise. We augmented the small space with a parameter that allowed for both strategies, as well the absence of either:

23. All substitution strategy
a. do not apply it
b. apply if middle term appears as topic of "All"
c. apply for any "All" premise

VR's Fits to Individual Data   Figure 32.8 presents VR;s average fits to the 103 participants for both the large parameter subspace (without the all-substitution strategy) and the small parameter subspace (with it). We used complementary tasks for setting the parameters and evaluating the fit. Specifically, we chose four task subsets that contained 16 tasks, four that contained 32 tasks, and four

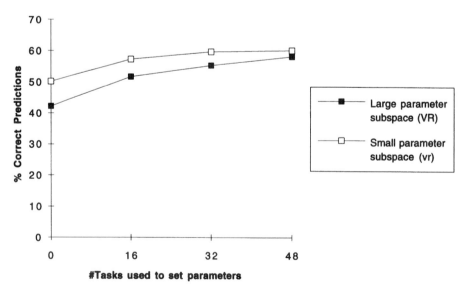

Figure 32.8
VR's fits to individual data.

that contained 48 tasks. Each of the 64 tasks was equally represented across the subsets of tasks. This is important because it means that all 64 tasks were also equally weighted in the evaluation (described later).[9] We also included the null set (no tasks). Then, for each participant, we computed all of the best-fitting parameter settings for each subset of tasks. In the case of the null set, no parameter settings could fit better than any other, so all were included.

Given such a set of best-fitting settings, we then computed their average fit (i.e., the average proportion of tasks for which VR and the participant gave the same response) over all of the other tasks (those that were not used to set the parameters) for which the participant gave a legal response. If VR predicted N responses for a task, one of which was the observed response, then the fit for that task would be $1/N$ (usually N was 1). The overall fit was the sum of these task fits divided by the number of tasks. For the large parameter space, it was not feasible to average over all best-fitting parameter settings in the no-task case because this constituted searching the entire space. Instead, we took a random sample of 1,000 parameter settings and averaged their fits on the 64 tasks. Figure 32.8 presents the average of all of these mean fits for each space and set of fitting tasks.

One interesting aspect of these results is that the smaller parameter space performs better than the larger space. In the four sets of fitting tasks in Figure 32.8, the smaller space produces fits that are between 2% (48 fitting tasks) and 8% (no fitting tasks) better than the larger space. We believe that two main factors contributed to this unexpected result. First, the small space, but not the large space, included the all-substitution strategy. Consequently, the small space had an advantage in fitting participants who applied this strategy despite the greater flexibility of the large space. Second, the added flexibility of the larger space could reduce the fit's quality because of overfitting (by including parameter settings that lead to rarely observed behaviors). For example, suppose we were using 16 tasks to set the parameters and the optimal fit on those tasks was 15 correct predictions. Then all and only the settings that produced that level of fit would be included in the analysis, regardless of how common or uncommon we might consider those settings a priori. Thus, plausible settings that produce a slightly lower fit (e.g., 14 of 16) would not be included, but implausible settings that just happened to do well on the set of fitting tasks would be. These implausible settings would presumably not do very well in fitting the evaluation tasks, and the average fit would go down. This problem is not nearly as severe for the smaller space because it includes only plausible settings. Furthermore, adding fitting tasks alleviates the problem because it becomes less and less likely that the implausible settings will fortuitously produce optimal fits on the fitting tasks. This explains why the disparity in fits between the large and small spaces is largest in the no-task case (in which none of the implausible settings are ruled out in the fit) and smallest in the 48-task case (in which almost all of them are).

As expected, the fits improve as additional tasks are used to set the parameters. When no tasks are used, the fit indicates only how well the settings in the space do on average. As more fitting tasks are added, VR can fine-tune its behavior to model the individual participants more closely. Also note that the first few fitting tasks lead to much larger improvements than do the last few; the difference between using 0 and 16 tasks is much larger than the difference between using 32 and 48. Apparently, the first few tasks rule out portions of parameter space that are way off the mark, whereas the last few can lead only to small refinements in the predictions, not major improvements. Indeed, the smaller space appears to level off at approximately 60% correct predictions. Adding fitting tasks would probably not help much. Thus, 60% correct predictions is a stable estimate of how well the smaller space can do in predicting individual behavior. It is important to note that, in one sense, these are zero-parameter fits; none of the data used to evaluate the fits contributed to the setting of the parameters (because different tasks were used for each purpose). Consequently, the fit qualities are not artificially high as a result of overfitting.

Comparisons with Reference Theories Figure 32.9 presents several additional analyses that provide useful reference theories for comparison. On the far left is the expected percentage of accurate predictions for a completely random theory. Because there are nine legal conclusions, the probability of such a theory predicting any particular response is 11% (1 in 9). We also computed the number of identical responses between pairs of participants and averaged over all such pairs. On average, 44% of responses were consistent across pairs of participants (other-subjects in Figure 32.9). The correct theory predicts correct performance on every task. For tasks in which there are multiple correct responses, this theory chooses randomly. Such a theory predicts 49% of the observed responses from the individuals in our data sets. Test–retest is the average proportion of responses given by a specific participant during one session that exactly match his or her responses to the same tasks a week later (on average, 58% of responses are identical). This is based on the one data set (Johnson-Laird & Steedman, 1978) that retested the same 20 participants a week later. VR's average fits to this same subset of participants are labeled in Figure 32.9 as Test—retest (VR) (59%; the large parameter space) and Test–retest (vr) (62%; the small parameter space). The model case (59%) is a post hoc analysis in which the most common response over all of the participants is treated as the prediction. Finally, VR and vr correspond to the model's average fit to all 103 participants for the large and small parameter spaces, respectively. All of VR's fits in this figure were computed using the four sets of 48 tasks to set the parameters and the other tasks to evaluate the fit.

The reference theories in Figure 32.9 provide a baseline against which to compare VR's fits. As one would expect, VR's predictions are significantly better than those that would be produced by predicting randomly or assuming that responses were always correct. What is much more impressive is that VR's

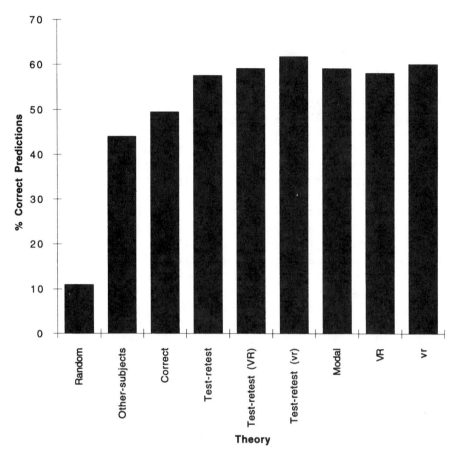

Figure 32.9
Comparison of VR's fits with various reference theories. (VR = large parameter space; vr = small parameter space)

fits are at or beyond the test–retest reliability of the participants themselves. Test–retest reliability gives a pessimistic estimate of the stability and systematicity of the participants and thus provides an estimate of how well a fixed deterministic theory could possibly do without overfitting the data. (The estimate is pessimistic because the two tests occurred a week apart. If they had been administered together, the test–retest reliability estimate would probably be a little higher, although such a measure would also confound reliability with memory of the responses.) Consequently, one could hardly ask for more from VR without attempting to capture the instability of the participants' performance over time (e.g., learning). Modeling instability in participant behavior is a natural next step for our approach but one that we have not yet undertaken.

The other-subjects and modal cases in Figure 32.9 provide insight into how much of VR's fit could be due to capturing group trends versus individual differences. The other-subjects result gives an estimate of how well a theory without any parameters could do if it had access only to 1 participant's data. Such a theory could be tailored to predict that 1 participant perfectly, but, without any parameters to allow for individual differences, only 44% of its predictions would be accurate on average. Clearly, VR is capturing significantly more of the behavior than this.

The best that any fixed theory (i.e., one without parameters) could possibly do would be to behave like the modal theory (i.e., to predict the most commonly observed response for every task). This theory's success (59% correct predictions) demonstrates what a large proportion of behavior could, in principle, be explained without reference to any individual differences. Of course, the theory provides an upper bound that is unlikely to be attained in practice. Nevertheless, it is worth pointing out that the modal theory's accuracy is comparable to the test–retest reliability of the participants. That is, the most common response is as good a predictor of performance as is a specific participant's own behavior a week earlier. In any case, the fact that VR's predictions are as good or better than the modal theory shows that VR can predict behavior more accurately than can any fixed theory.

It is also interesting to compare the modal theory's performance with VR when the number of tasks used to set the parameters is zero (VR is being treated as a fixed theory or a set of fixed theories). In the case of the small parameter space (which was designed to include only the most common parameter settings), the quality of VR's predictions is within 10% of optimality.

Because the smaller space produces such good fits, the few parameters that it allows to vary account for many of the individual differences. One can identify these parameters in Figure 32.7 because they have more than one plus sign beside them (the others have a fixed value and cannot vary). These parameters can be grouped into two major classes: those involving the interpretation of particular premises (*Some* and *Some not* [Parameters 1, 2, 4, and 6]) and those involving the extraction of indirect knowledge about a proposition's predicate (Parameters 10–13). In addition to these two, the all-substitution strategy (the new parameter) is another important source of individual differences; including more than one of its values (especially Values a and c) was important in obtaining good fits for different participants. This results agrees with data from Ford (1995) indicating that the use of a syntactic substitution strategy is an important source of individual differences. According to VR, then, the three most important sources of individual differences in syllogistic reasoning are (a) the interpretation of the quantifier *Some*, (b) what indirect knowledge participants can extract from propositions about their predicates, and (c) whether or not participants apply the all-substitution strategy. Of course, the crucial point from this analysis is that the verbal reasoning hypothesis, as manifested in VR, can and does account for the detailed behavior of individual participants solving categorical syllogisms.

Discussion

VR's behavior exemplifies verbal reasoning. After initial encoding, VR repeatedly reencodes the premises until it can generate a legal conclusion (see Figure 32.2). And all of these processes (initial encoding, reencoding, and conclusion generation) are fundamentally linguistic; that is, they transform verbal information into a semantic representation and back again. Far from being devoted exclusively to deduction, their main role is presumably language processing. Other tasks (e.g., reading) might also require giving up on reencoding to avoid excessive delays, although one could argue that VR's exhaustive reencoding would be unique to reasoning. In any case, giving up is certainly much less central to VR's behavior than are reencoding and conclusion generation. Falsification is the one process we explored that is clearly designed specifically for reasoning. Its purpose is to ensure deductive validity, and so it would presumably not be relevant in other domains. And unlike linguistic processes, it does not map between verbal and semantic representations; rather, it transforms one semantic representation into another. If used, falsification could be as important as the other processes, especially if a sequence of putative conclusions is successively falsified, leading to a completely different response. Falsification proved to be an unnecessary assumption in achieving the fits we did with VR, however. Only 1 participant's fit (out of 103) improved significantly when VR falsified as opposed to when it did not.

Conclusion

Previous theories of deduction have shared the same basic structure at the most general level: Participants encode the problem statement into some internal representation, apply certain reasoning-specific processes to that representation (e.g., searching for alternative models or applying formal or content-specific rules of inference), and then decode the result. We propose that the central processes in deductive reasoning are linguistic (encoding, reencoding, and generation) rather than reasoning-specific skills.

This verbal reasoning hypothesis provides a parsimonious and accurate account of deductive reasoning. It explains behavior in terms of standard linguistic processes without the need to posit reasoning-specific mechanisms. When implemented in the form of a computational model of syllogistic reasoning, it provides the most detailed and accurate account to date of behavior on the task; it explains all of the major phenomena, it makes accurate novel predictions, and it models the behavior of individual participants with an accuracy that rivals their own test–retest reliability.

Notes

This research was supported in part by a fellowship from the Eastman Kodak Company, by the James S. McDonnell Foundation under Grant 91-34, by the Office of Naval Research under Contract N00013-91-J-1527, and by the Avionics Laboratory, U.S. Air Force, under Contract F33615-90-C-1465. This article formed the basis of an unpublished doctoral dissertation (Polk, 1992). A summary of the argument that the mental model theory accounts of behavior on most deductive reasoning tasks correspond to verbal reasoning explanations can be found in Polk (1993).

We gratefully acknowledge Philip Johnson-Laird, members of the Carnegie Mellon University Soar group (especially Richard Lewis and Richard Young), and Graeme Halford for helpful comments on this research and article.

1. Thanks to Phil Johnson-Laird for graciously providing us with the raw data from his experiments with Bruno Bara and Mark Steedman that we used in these analyses.
2. Wilkins (1928) and Sells (1936) have also claimed evidence for a concreteness effect: Participants are more accurate on syllogisms involving concrete (*archer, bowler*) rather than abstract (*A, B, C*) terms. The effect is not well established, however (attempted replications have failed; Gonzalez-Marques, 1985), and it may disappear when believability effects are controlled (Revlis, 1975a; Revlis, Ammerman, Petersen, & Leirer, 1978).
3. Variants of this model have been built that handle all of the standard task variants (e.g., testing conclusions and multiple choice). For more information, contact Thad A. Polk.
4. Encoding indirect knowledge could work either by generating an intermediate proposition (e.g., *Some y are x* and *No y are x* in these cases) and then encoding that proposition (an inner speech strategy) or by encoding the indirect knowledge directly without an intermediate proposition. VR is consistent with either mechanism.
5. Wilkins (1928), Janis and Frick (1943), and Morgan and Morton (1944) also collected data relevant to belief bias, but these studies did not include the critical comparisons between believed and disbelieved conclusions for syllogisms with the same logical form.
6. There are at least two other factors that could also lead to elaboration effects but that VR has not simulated. First, premise elaborations could improve performance by blocking the extraction of contradictory indirect knowledge. Second, elaborated premises could influence whether existing model objects are augmented or new objects are created. For example, VR would predict that using elaborated particular premises such as *Some other B are C* instead of just *Some B are C* could significantly improve performance by helping participants avoid the fallacy of the undistributed middle term (see earlier discussion).
7. The specific tasks in each set were as follows (in terms of the notation from the middle of Figure 32.1): (a) {ObaEcb, EbaEcb, AbaOcb, AbaIcb, ObaEbc, ObaAbc, IbaObc, AbaEbc, EabIcb, IabAcb, AabEcb, AabAcb, OabObc, OabIbc, IabEbc, IabIbc}, (b) {AabIbc, EabOcb, EbaAbc, ObaAcb, IabOcb, IbaEbc, EabEbc, ObaOcb, IabIcb, AbaAbc, ObaIcb, OabAbc, AabIcb, EbaOcb, EbaIbc, EabAbc}, (c) {ObaIbc, OabAcb, AbaEcb, EabIbc, IbaAcb, EabObc, IbaIbc, EabEcb, ObaObc, AbaAcb, IabObc, OabEcb, IabAbc, EbaIcb, EabAcb, AbaObc}, and (d) {AbaEbc, Oableb, EbaObc, IbaEcb, IbaAbc, AabObc, OabOcb, IbaIcb, EbaEbc, AabAbc, IbaOcb, IabEcb, AbaIbc, OabEbc, AabOcb, EbaAcb}.
8. Participants 2 and 11 from unlimited; 4, 13, and 18 from timed; 3, 5, 6, 11, 15, and 16 from revised; 5, 7, 8, and 13 from Week 1; 2, 6, 13, and 20 from Week 2; and 1 from Inder (1986, 1987).
9. The sets of 16 tasks are specified in note 7. The sets of 32 tasks were formed by combining pairs of those 16 tasks (specifically, Sets 1 and 2, 3 and 4, 1 and 4, and 2 and 3). Similarly, the sets of 48 tasks were formed by combining sets: {2, 3, 4}, {1, 3, 4}, {1, 2, 4}, and {1, 2, 3}.

References

Anderson, J. R. (1990). *The adaptive character of thought*. Hillsdale, NJ: Erlbaum.

Braine, M. D. S. (1978). On the relation between the natural logic of reasoning and standard logic. *Psychological Review, 85*, 1–21.

Ceraso, J., & Provitera, A. (1971). Sources of error in syllogistic reasoning. *Cognitive Psychology, 2,* 400–410.

Chapman, L. J., & Chapman, J. P. (1959). Atmosphere effect re-examined. *Journal of Experimental Psychology, 58,* 220–226.

Cheng, P. W., & Holyoak, K. J. (1985). Pragmatic reasoning schemas. *Cognitive Psychology, 17,* 391–416.

Dickstein, L. S. (1975). Effects of instruction and premise order on errors in syllogistic reasoning. *Journal of Experimental Psychology: Human Learning and Memory, 104,* 376–384.

Evans, J. S. B. T., Barston, J. L., & Pollard, P. (1983). On the conflict between logic and belief in syllogistic reasoning. *Memory & Cognition, 11,* 295–306.

Ford, M. (1995). Two modes of mental representation and problem solution in syllogistic reasoning. *Cognition, 54,* 1–71.

Gonzalez-Marques, J. (1985). La influencia de materials no emocionales en la solution de silogismos categoricos [The effects of nonemotional stimulus materials on the solution of categorical syllogisms]. *Informes-de-Psicologia, 4,* 183–198.

Henle, M. (1962). On the relation between logic and thinking. *Psychological Review, 69,* 366–378.

Inder, R. (1986). Modeling syllogistic reasoning using simple mental models. In A. G. Cohn & J. R. Thomas (Eds.), *Artificial intelligence and its applications* (pp. 211–225). New York: Wiley.

Inder, R. (1987). *The computer simulation of syllogism solving using restricted mental models.* Unpublished doctoral dissertation, University of Edinburgh, Edinburgh, Scotland.

Janis, I. L., & Frick, F. (1943). The relationship between attitudes towards conclusions and errors in judging logical validity of syllogisms. *Journal of Experimental Psychology, 33,* 73–77.

Johnson-Laird, P. N. (1983). *Mental models: Towards a cognitive science of language, inference, and consciousness.* Cambridge, MA: Harvard University Press.

Johnson-Laird, P. N., & Bara, B. G. (1984). Syllogistic inference. *Cognition, 16,* 1–61.

Johnson-Laird, P. N., & Byrne, R. M. J. (1989). *Only* reasoning. *Journal of Memory and Language, 28,* 313–330.

Johnson-Laird, P. N., & Byrne, R. M. J. (1991). *Deduction.* Hillsdale, NJ: Erlbaum.

Johnson-Laird, P. N., & Steedman, M. (1978). The psychology of syllogisms. *Cognitive Psychology, 10,* 64–99.

Laird, J. E., Newell, A., & Rosenbloom, P. S. (1987). Soar: An architecture for general intelligence. *Artificial Intelligence, 33,* 1–64.

Lee, J. R. (1983). *Johnson-Laird's mental models: Two problems.* Unpublished manuscript, School of Epistemics, University of Edinburgh.

Morgan, J. I. B., & Morton, J. T. (1944). The distortions of syllogistic reasoning produced by personal connections. *Journal of Social Psychology, 20,* 39–59.

Newell, A. (1990). *Unified theories of cognition.* Cambridge, MA: Harvard University Press.

Oakhill, J. V., & Johnson-Laird, P. N. (1985). The effects of belief on the spontaneous production of syllogistic conclusions. *Quarterly Journal of Experimental Psychology, 37A,* 553–569.

Oakhill, J. V., Johnson-Laird, P. N., & Garnham, A. (1989). Believability and syllogistic reasoning. *Cognition, 31,* 117–140.

Polk, T. A. (1992). *Verbal reasoning.* Unpublished doctoral dissertation, Carnegie-Mellon University, Pittsburgh, PA.

Polk, T. A. (1993). Mental models: More or less. *Behavioral and Brain Sciences, 16,* 362–363.

Polk, T. A., & Newell, A. (1988). Modeling human syllogistic reasoning in Soar. In *Proceedings of the Annual Conference of the Cognitive Science Society* (pp. 181–187). Hillsdale, NJ: Erlbaum.

Polk, T. A., Newell, A., & Lewis, R. L. (1989). Toward a unified theory of immediate reasoning in Soar. In *Proceedings of the Annual Conference of the Cognitive Science Society* (pp. 506–513). Hillsdale, NJ: Erlbaum.

Polk, T. A., Newell, A., & VanLehn, K. (1995). *Analysis of symbolic parameter models (ASPM): A new model-fitting technique for the cognitive sciences.* Unpublished manuscript.

Polk, T. A., VanLehn, K., & Kalp, D. (1995). ASPM2: Progress toward the analysis of symbolic parameter models. In P. Nichols, S. Chipman, & R. Brennan (Eds.), *Cognitively diagnostic assessment* (pp. 127–139). Hillsdale, NJ: Erlbaum.

Revlis, R. (1975a). Syllogistic reasoning: Logical decisions from a complex data base. In R. J. Falmagne (Ed.), *Reasoning: Representation and process* (pp. 93–133). Hillsdale, NJ: Erlbaum.

Revlis, R. (1975b). Two models of syllogistic reasoning: Feature selection and conversion. *Journal of Verbal Learning and Verbal Behavior, 14,* 180–195.

Revlis, R., Ammerman, K., Peterson, K., & Leirer, V. (1978). Category relations and syllogistic reasoning. *Journal of Educational Psychology, 70,* 613–625.

Rips, L. J. (1983). Cognitive processes in propositional reasoning. *Psychological Review, 90,* 38–71.

Sells, S. B. (1936). The atmosphere effect: An experimental study of reasoning. *Archives of Psychology, No. 200.*

Wason, P. C. (1966). Reasoning. In B. M. Foss (Ed.), *New horizons in psychology* (pp. 135–151). New York: Penguin Books.

Wilkins, M. C. (1928). The effect of changed material on the ability to do formal syllogistic reasoning. *Archives of Psychology, No. 102.*

Woodworth, R. S., & Sells, S. B. (1935). An atmosphere effect in formal syllogistic reasoning. *Journal of Experimental Psychology, 18,* 451–460.

Task Performance

Chapter 33

Project Ernestine: Validating a GOMS Analysis for Predicting and Explaining Real-World Task Performance

Wayne D. Gray, Bonnie E. John, and Michael E. Atwood

1 Introduction

"Design is where the action is," argued Newell and Card (1985, p. 214); to affect the field of human–computer interaction significantly, a theory or methodology must apply to design of a system, not merely to after-the-fact evaluation. Newell and Card argued further that to facilitate their application to design, psychological theories must quantitatively predict user performance from specifications of the task and of a proposed system, without relying on observations of human behavior with a working system or prototype.

One such theory is GOMS (Card, Moran, & Newell, 1983; John & Kieras, 1996a, b), which analyzes behavior in terms of the user's Goals; the Operators available for accomplishing those goals; frequently used sequences of operators and subgoals (Methods); and, if there is more than one method to accomplish a goal, Selection rules to choose between them. GOMS is a family of analysis techniques composed of goals, operators, methods, and selection rules; these components, however, are expressed in different ways, such as goal hierarchies (Card et al., 1980a, 1983), lists of operators (Card et al., 1980b), production systems (Bovair, Kieras, & Polson, 1990), working memory loads (Lerch, Mantei, & Olson, 1989), and schedule charts (Gray, John, & Atwood, 1993; John, 1990, 1996). The different expressions have different strengths and weaknesses and predict different measures of performance (e.g., operator sequences, performance time, learning, errors). Variants of GOMS have been used successfully to predict user behavior with computer systems in the laboratory (see Olson & Olson, 1990, for a review). In this study, we go outside the laboratory to assess a GOMS model's ability to quantitatively predict expert performance on a real-world task, to provide explanations for the predictions, and to direct future design activity.

1.1 Appropriateness of Project Ernestine for the Evaluation of GOMS

New England Telephone was considering replacing the workstations currently used by toll and assistance operators (TAOs) with new workstations. A TAO is the person you get when you dial "0." A TAO's job is to assist a customer in completing calls and to record the correct billing. Among others, TAOs handle person-to-person calls, collect calls, calling-card calls, and calls billed to a third number. (TAOs do not handle directory assistance calls.) We evaluated two workstations, which we called *current* and *proposed*. The current workstation uses a 300-baud, character-oriented display and a keyboard on which keys are color coded and grouped by function. Information is presented on the display as it becomes available, often as alphanumeric codes, with the same category of information always presented at the same screen location (e.g., the calling number is always on the third line of the display). In contrast, the proposed workstation uses a high-resolution display operating at 1,200 baud, uses icons and windows, and in general is a good example of a graphical user interface whose designers paid attention to human–computer interaction issues. Similar care went into the keyboard, where an effort was made to minimize travel distance among the most frequent key sequences. In addition, the proposed workstation also reduces keystrokes by replacing common, two-key sequences with a single key.

A major factor in making a buy/no-buy decision was how quickly the expected decrease in average worktime per call would offset the capital cost of making the purchase. Given the number of TAOs employed by NYNEX (the parent company of New England Telephone) and the number of calls it processes each year, a ballpark estimate is that an average decrease of 1 sec in worktime per call saves $3 million per year. Thus, differences in expert performance time attributable to workstation differences are economically important to NYNEX. Project Ernestine was initiated to provide a reliable estimate of these differences.

1.2 The Structure of This Chapter

Our top-level goal for this chapter is to assess the validity of GOMS models for predicting and explaining performance on real-world tasks. In the next section, we discuss the model building effort. Models for the current workstation were based on observational data. In contrast, models for the proposed workstation were based on specifications supplied by the manufacturer.

In Section 3 we discuss the field trial and the empirical results of the workstation comparison. This provides data against which to compare the quantitative predictions of the GOMS analysis and a baseline of information against which to argue the usefulness of GOMS.

In Section 4, we first evaluate the representativeness of the benchmark tasks on which we based the model building effort (4.1). We then compare our predictions to the field-trial data to determine the quantitative accuracy of our models (4.2), and to compare our predictions with an alternative, noncognitive, basis for prediction (4.3). We then go beyond the data and provide explanations of the results (4.4).

In the original paper (Gray et al., 1993), we went beyond this discussion of results to show how such calculational models (Newell & Card, 1985) could be used as tools in the design of future workstations.

Before continuing, it is important to emphasize that the two major parts of Project Ernestine, the field trial and the GOMS analyses, were done separately and during the same time period. It is NOT the case that the GOMS models were built with knowledge of the empirical data. (Also, to this day, we have not observed a single TAO using the new workstation.)

2 Building CPM–GOMS Models

[Note from the authors: We limit our abridged version of this section to an analysis of the activity-level goal structure of the TAO's task. In the original, we presented two less-detailed GOMS models, one at the unit-task level and one at the functional level. These models permitted us to build up to the activity level by successive approximation. We also omit from this section a detailed discussion of the issues and process of model building.]

The unit task for TAOs is the individual call. This corresponds to the individual edit discussed in Card et al.'s (1983) analysis of text editing. For example, consider the situation in which a person directly dials a number and has the TAO bill the call to his or her calling card. The dialog is sparse but typical:

Workstation:	[Beep]
TAO:	New England Telephone, may I help you?
Customer:	Operator, bill this to 412–555–1212–1234.
TAO:	Thank you.

Figure 33.1 shows an activity-level analysis of the TAO's task. The conditionality on operators starts to be unwieldy at the activity level, so for illustrative purposes this figure shows only the sequence of goals and operators for the specific credit-card call described before. In addition, the observable activities that the TAO engages in to handle this call are shown next to the operators that represent them in the model.

The activity level may be sufficient to identify the skills that TAOs need to have or need to be trained in to do the job (e.g., training in using standard greetings). It may also help to guide design questions. For example, the first RECEIVE-INFORMATION goal has two operators: LISTEN-FOR-BEEP, which alerts the TAO that a call is arriving, and READ-SCREEN, which provides information about the source of the call so the TAO can choose the appropriate greeting. Can one of these operators be eliminated? Can the beep both signal the arrival of a call and indicate the source of the call (e.g., with a small number of different-pitched tones)? At the activity level, differences between call categories would be mirrored in differences between the patterns of goals, subgoals, and operators.

GOMS Model	Observed Activities
GOAL: HANDLE-CALLS	
. GOAL: HANDLE-CALL	
. . GOAL: INITIATE-CALL	
. . . GOAL: RECEIVE-INFORMATION	
. . . . LISTEN-FOR-BEEP	Workstation: Beep
. . . . READ-SCREEN(2)	Workstation: Displays information
. . . GOAL: REQUEST-INFORMATION	
. . . . GREET-CUSTOMER	TAO: "New England Telephone, may I help you?"
. . . GOAL: ENTER-WHO-PAYS	
. . . GOAL: RECEIVE-INFORMATION	
. . . . LISTEN-TO-CUSTOMER	Customer: "Operator, bill this to 412–555–1212–1234."
. . . GOAL: ENTER-INFORMATION	
. . . . ENTER-COMMAND	TAO: Hit F1 key
. . . . ENTER-CALLING-CARD-NUMBER	TAO: Hit 14 numeric keys
. . . GOAL: ENTER-BILLING-RATE	
. . . GOAL: RECEIVE-INFORMATION	
. . . . READ-SCREEN(1)	
. . . GOAL: ENTER-INFORMATION	
. . . . ENTER-COMMAND	TAO: Hit F2 key
. . GOAL: COMPLETE-CALL	
. . . GOAL: REQUEST-INFORMATION	
. . . . ENTER-COMMAND	TAO: Hit F3 key
. . . GOAL: RECEIVE-INFORMATION	
. . . . READ-SCREEN(3)	Workstation: Displays credit-card authorization
. . . GOAL: RELEASE-CALL	
. . . . THANK-CUSTOMER	TAO: "Thank you"
. . . . ENTER-COMMAND	TAO: Hit F4 key

Figure 33.1
Activity-level GOMS analysis of the TAO's task.

Despite its uses, the activity level is not appropriate for predicting time differences either between workstations or between call categories. For workstations, the problem is obvious. At the activity level, the proposed and current workstations have exactly the same goal-subgoal-operator structure.[1] Hence, they would be predicted to have exactly the same duration.

For call categories, the situation is only slightly more subtle. Any operator is given the same estimated duration regardless of the variety of circumstances that it may encompass. For example, LISTEN-TO-CUSTOMER would have the same duration for the "Operator, bill this to 412–555–1212–1234" example as for "Operator, I want to make this collect to my Grandmother Stewart, who has been feeling ill lately, from her grandson Wayne" as for "Bill this to 1234." Hence, at the activity level, differences in the type and number of operators for each call category would tend to be overwhelmed by the range and variability of individual operators.

The activity level also highlights a problem with the sequential nature of the original GOMS models. As an illustration, suppose the durations of the observable operators (LISTEN-TO-BEEP, GREET-CUSTOMER, ENTER-COMMAND, ENTER-CALLING-CARD-NUMBER, and THANK-CUSTOMER) and system response time were set from a videotape of this sample call and an estimate of READ-SCREEN came from previous work reading short words from a CRT screen (John & Newell, 1989, 1990). Then the sum of these operators and system response times predicts that the call would take almost 17.85 sec (see Figure 33.2). In reality, this sample call takes 13 sec to complete. The reason for this is obvious from a time line of actual events recorded in the videotape (Figure 33.3). The TAO is clearly performing activities concurrently, and the GOMS analysis does not capture this dominant feature of the task. The assumption of strictly sequenced operators substantially overpredicts performance time for this task, even when using measured values for most of the operator durations. Therefore, to make quantitative predictions of TAOs' performance requires a more powerful representation for parallel activities—that of the CPM–GOMS analysis technique.

2.1 The CPM–GOMS Analysis

The CPM–GOMS extension to classic GOMS is linked closely to the cognitive architecture underlying GOMS: the MHP (Card et al., 1983). The MHP has three processors: a cognitive processor, a perceptual processor, and a motor processor. In general, these processors work sequentially within themselves and in parallel with each other, subject to information-flow dependencies. To display parallel activities and information-flow dependencies and to calculate total task times, we use the critical path method, a common tool used in project management. Thus the CPM–GOMS analysis technique gets its name from expressing Cognitive, Perceptual, and Motor operators in a GOMS analysis using the Critical Path Method.

GOMS Model	Duration Estimates	Operator Source of Estimate
GOAL: HANDLE-CALLS		
. GOAL: HANDLE-CALL		
. . GOAL: INITIATE-CALL		
. . . GOAL: RECEIVE-INFORMATION		
. . . . LISTEN-T0-BEEP	100 msec	Videotaped call
(SYSTEM-RESPONSE-TIME)	730 msec	Videotaped call
. . . READ-SCREEN(2)	340 msec	John and Newell (1987, 1989a)
. . GOAL: REQUEST-INFORMATION		
. . . . GREET-CUSTOMER	1,570 msec	Videotaped call
. . GOAL: ENTER-WHO-PAYS		
. . . GOAL: RECEIVE-INFORMATION		
. . . . LISTEN-TO-CUSTOMER	6,280 msec	Videotaped call
. . GOAL: ENTER-INFORMATION		
. . . . ENTER-COMMAND	320 msec	Videotaped call (average)
. . . . ENTER-CALLING-CARD-NUMBER	4,470 msec	Videotaped call
. . GOAL: ENTER-BILLING-RATE		
. . . GOAL: RECEIVE-INFORMATION		
. . . . READ-SCREEN(1)	340 msec	John and Newell (1987, 1989a)
. . GOAL: ENTER-INFORMATION		
. . . . ENTER-COMMAND	320 msec	Videotaped call (average)
. . GOAL: COMPLETE CALL		
. . . GOAL: REQUEST-INFORMATION		
. . . . ENTER-COMMAND	320 msec	Videotaped call (average)
. . . GOAL: RECEIVE-INFORMATION		
(SYSTEM-RESPONSE-TIME)	2,000 msec	Videotaped call
. . . READ-SCREEN(3)	340 msec	John and Newell (1987, 1989a)
. . GOAL: RELEASE-CALL		
. . . . THANK-CUSTOMER	360 msec	Videotaped call
. . . . ENTER-COMMAND	320 msec	Videotaped call (average)

Figure 33.2
Activity-level prediction of task performance time (total predicted = 17,850 msec; total observed = 13,000 msec; percent error = 37%). Notes: We include observed system response time when it does not overlap with user behavior as per Card, Moran, and Newell (1983). Operators corresponding to observed behavior with more than one occurrence (only the ENTER COMMAND operator) are assigned a duration equal to the average of all observed occurrences; operators with only one occurrence are assigned a duration identical to that occurrence (all other operators set from the videotape). Unobservable operators (only the READ-SCREEN operator) are assigned a duration based on prior research, as noted.

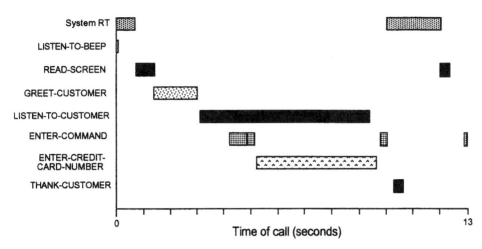

Figure 33.3
Time line of activities in the sample call. Note: The durations of the observable operators are the actual durations in the videotape, not the averaged durations used in the GOMS analysis in Figure 33.2. The unobservable operator, READ-SCREEN, is shown with the duration estimated from the literature (340 msec) and is positioned just after the relevant information appears on the TAO's screen.

To model the TAOs' tasks, perceptual operators are divided into two categories: visual and auditory operators. Motor operators are divided into four categories: right-hand, left-hand, verbal, and eye-movement operators. Cognitive operators are not further divided into categories. These operators are at a finer grain than the operators of the previously mentioned activity-level analysis; that is, the activity-level operators become CPM-level goals, with the MHP-level operators combining to accomplish these goals. The details of where MHP-level operators come from in general, estimates for their duration, and how they combine to accomplish activity-level goals are presented elsewhere (John, 1990; John & Gray, 1992, 1994, 1995), but we discuss building TAO task-specific models in more detail in the next section.

Other processors exist in this human-computer system (e.g., the call-switching processor, the databases of credit card numbers, and the workstation itself). The operators of these processors are represented by two categories of system response time: workstation display time and other systems-rt (where *rt* means response time). Although system-rt is not a true GOMS operator, we refer to it as an operator for simplicity of exposition.

Only one operator in each category can be performed at a time; that is, operators are serial within category. However, they can be performed in parallel with operators in other categories.

Schedule Charts: A Notation for Representing Parallelism   In CPM–GOMS, the parallelism of the TAOs' task is represented in a *schedule chart* (Figure 33.4).

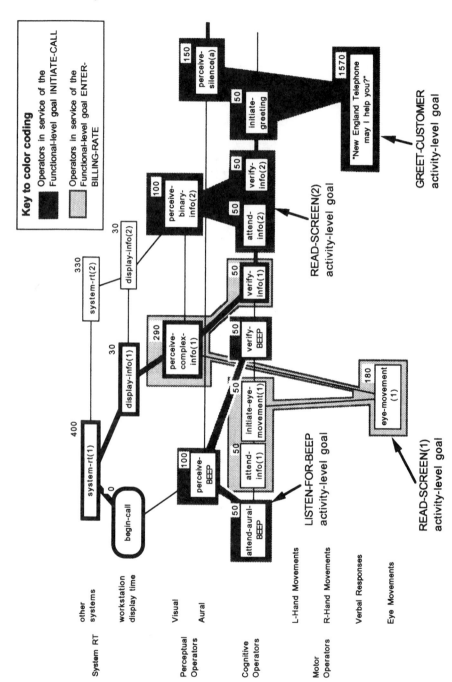

Figure 33.4
Example CPM-GOMS schedule chart. To illustrate the higher level goal structure common to classic GOMS but not explicit in CPM-GOMS, for this sample the higher level goals are indicated by groups of operators and the background color of the groups (light vs. medium gray). Each group indicates a different activity-level goal; each background color indicates a different functional-level goal.

Each MHP-level operator is represented as a box with a name centered inside it and an associated duration above the top-right corner (in msec). Lines connecting the boxes represent information-flow dependencies; that is, when a line joins two operators, the operator to the left produces information required by the operator to the right. For visual clarity, we place operators of the same category along a horizontal line.

The goal hierarchy of the classic GOMS analysis is not explicitly represented in the schedule chart, but it is implicit in the operators that are represented. For example, an activity-level operator READ-SCREEN(1) in Figure 33.1 represents the TAO reading the screen to find information about the billing rate (about halfway down the figure). This becomes an activity-level goal in the CPM–GOMS model, READ-SCREEN(1), and is accomplished by five MHP-level operators explicitly represented in Figure 33.4 (backed by light gray shading): attend-info(1), a cognitive operator that decides to look for this information; initiate-eye-movement(1), a cognitive operator that initiates an eye movement to where that information will appear on the screen; eye-movement(1), a motor operator that positions the eyes; perceive-complex-info(1), a visual perception operator that takes in and comprehends the information when it is displayed; and finally verify-info(1), another cognitive operator that confirms that the information is as expected (i.e., not something unexpected like a workstation failure producing an error message).

We represent the information-flow dependencies between these operators by drawing lines between them. There is a line from attend-info(1) to initiate-eye-movement(1) because the TAO must first decide to find this information before determining that an eye movement is necessary. There is a line from initiate-eye-movement(2) to eye-movement(1) because the eyes cannot move until a cognitive operator instructs them to do so. Eye-movement(1) is connected to perceive-complex-info(1) because the information cannot be perceived until the eyes are in the right place. Finally, there is a line between perceive-complex-info(1) and verify-info(1) because the information must be perceived and comprehended before a cognitive operator can verify that it is indeed the information that was expected. The rationale for these dependencies is based both on common sense and on the control structure of the MHP (Card et al., 1983).

In addition to the previously described MHP-level operators that represent the actions of the TAO, the actions of the workstation also play a part in this example. The information that the TAO needs to determine the billing rate is not displayed instantaneously at the beginning of the call. Rather, the other systems take 400 msec to deliver that information to the workstation, represented by system-rt(1), and the workstation itself takes 30 msec to display that information, display-info(1). The TAO cannot perceive the information until it is displayed on the screen, so there is an additional dependency line from display-info(1) to perceive-complex-info(1).

This pattern of five MHP-level operators, linked to the display of information on the screen, implicitly represents that the READ-SCREEN activity-level goal is being served.

Altogether, Figure 33.4 shows four patterns of MHP-level operators that implicitly represent four activity-level goals: LISTEN-FOR-BEEP, READ-SCREEN(1), READ-SCREEN(2), and GREET-CUSTOMER. Note that the pattern of MHP-level operators that achieves similar goals is not identical. For example, in Figure 33.4, READ-SCREEN(1) requires an eye movement that is not needed for READ-SCREEN(2) because the TAO's eyes are already in the right place in the course of the task. Likewise, READ-SCREEN(1) has a perceive-complex-info MHP-level operator whereas READ-SCREEN(2) has a perceive-binary-info MHP-level operator because the information needed for billing, display-info(1), is a complex code that must be comprehended whereas the information needed to initiate the call, display-info(2), is simply whether any information is displayed in a particular place on the screen or whether it remains blank.

The patterns of operators in Figure 33.4 are backed in either light or medium gray. The background shading indicates that these operators accomplish activity-level goals that are in service of different functional-level goals found in Figures 33.1 and 33.2. The operators backed in light gray accomplish READ-INFO(1), which is in service of RECEIVE-INFORMATION, which is, in turn, in service of ENTER-BILLING-RATE. The operators in medium gray accomplish LISTEN-FOR-BEEP, READ-SCREEN(2), and GREET-CUSTOMER, which are in service of RECEIVE-INFORMATION and REQUEST-INFORMATION, which serve the functional-level goal of INITIATE-CALL. Thus, the goal hierarchy of the classic GOMS analyses is implicitly represented in patterns of MHP-level operators in the CPM–GOMS schedule chart.

The Critical Path   An important concept in analyzing the total time for tasks involving the complex interaction of parallel activities is the *critical path*. The critical path is the sequence of operators that, because of their durations and dependency relationship to other operators, determines the total time of the task. In CPM–GOMS models, the critical path is indicated by a bold outline of the operators' boxes and bold dependency lines between them. The sum of the durations of the operators on the critical path is the total time for the task.

For example, before deciding on a particular greeting for this customer, the TAO perceives the first piece of information displayed on the screen (perceive-complex-info(1); see Figure 33.4) and then the presence or absence of the second piece of information (perceive-binary-info(2)). The perception, comprehension, and verification of this information (perceive-complex-info(1) and verify-info(1)) plus turning attention to the presence of the second piece of information (attend-info(2)) take longer than the system response times to deliver and display information (system-rt(2) and display-info(2)). Therefore, the critical path goes through the human activity rather than through the system response times, and the path is lined in bold. In this case, the systems' response times are said to have *slack time*, are not on the critical path, and are not lined in bold. Human activity that has slack time has also been observed in videotapes of TAOs handling calls. For example, TAOs move to specific function keys then hover over them while waiting for the customer or the workstation to give information that will dictate which key to press.

Comparison of the GOMS and CPM–GOMS Analyses   The classic GOMS models of the TAO's task (Figure 33.4) and the CPM–GOMS model (Figure 33.7) look very different. Although CPM–GOMS is an extension to classic GOMS, its graphic representation of operators and dependencies can obscure the theoretical roots common to both analysis techniques as well as the theoretical differences between them.

Both techniques start with a decomposition of the task into a hierarchy of goals and subgoals that determines which operators are performed. However, since durations are only assigned to operators, not to the manipulation of goals (Card et al., 1983), only operators contribute to the total task duration. CPM–GOMS schedule charts are a representation of task duration and thus do not include any explicit representation of goals. The fact that goals are explicitly represented in the classic GOMS goal-operator lists but only implicitly represented in the CPM–GOMS schedule charts is a superficial difference between the two techniques.

However, there are two important theoretical differences between classic GOMS and CPM–GOMS: parallelism of operators and relaxing the hierarchical goal structure. CPM–GOMS does not assume sequential application of operators to accomplish a goal as does classic GOMS. The MHP-level operators are performed in parallel with those of other categories, subject to resource limitations and task-specific information-flow dependencies described before.

In addition, CPM–GOMS does not enforce the stack discipline of classic GOMS, in which only one goal can be active at a time. In CPM–GOMS, different goals can exist concurrently. In Figure 33.4, for example, the TAO reads the first two pieces of information that are displayed on the screen at the very beginning of the call (perceive-complex-info(1) and perceive-binary-info(2), respectively). As it happens, the second piece of information displayed is the information required to choose the appropriate greeting in service of the first functional-level goal in the classic GOMS analysis, INITIATE-CALL. The first piece of information displayed is part of the information required to determine the appropriate rate in service of a later functional-level goal, ENTER-BILLING-RATE. The ENTER-BILLING-RATE goal cannot be completed until the customer supplies more information later in the call, but the TAO assimilates this information opportunistically as it appears on the screen. Thus, this CPM–GOMS model has two functional-level goals active at the same time: INITIATE-CALL (represented by the three operator patterns backed by medium gray in Figure 33.4) and ENTER-BILLING-RATE (backed by light gray).

A second example occurs at a lower level with activity-level goals in Figure 33.4. Concurrent activity-level goals are evident in how the MHP-level operators that accomplish the LISTEN-FOR-BEEP activity-level goal (backed by medium gray) are interleaved with the operators that accomplish the READ-SCREEN(1) goal (backed by light gray). These situations would have been impossible to represent in classic GOMS, but they more accurately reflect observed behavior in the TAO's task.

The four previously presented analyses are a basis for understanding the TAO's task in general and its representation in CPM–GOMS. The next section explains the specific model-building procedure we used to model TAOs' performance with the current workstation and to predict their performance with the proposed workstation.

2.2 The Benchmark Method

The *benchmark method*, which compares two or more systems constructed to accomplish the same task, is a well-established technique in engineering disciplines. The method involves choosing a set of *benchmarks* that typify the tasks, running the systems on those benchmarks, and (for each benchmark) comparing performance across systems.

To perform the CPM–GOMS analysis with the benchmark method, first we selected appropriate benchmarks. We then determined the CPM–GOMS operators necessary to perform these benchmark tasks on the current workstation, dependencies between them, and estimates of their durations. Finally, we built CPM–GOMS models for all the benchmark tasks using the proposed workstation and made quantitative predictions of performance.

Twenty call categories were selected because of either their high frequency or their particular interest to NYNEX Operator Services. Benchmark tasks were developed for each of these 20 call categories. For a variety of reasons, however, five of the call categories were dropped from the empirical analysis and are not considered further in this chapter.

2.3 Observation-Based CPM–GOMS Models for the Current Workstation

The next step in constructing CPM–GOMS models to predict TAO performance is to build observation-based models of the benchmark tasks performed on the current workstation. We used the videotaped behavior on the current workstation to determined MHP-level operators necessary to perform these tasks, dependencies between them, and estimates of their durations.

First, we transcribed the videotape for the 15 selected benchmark calls. Each transcript included the actual start and stop times for each verbal communication, for each keystroke, and for each change on the workstation display (to the accuracy of a video frame, 32 msec).

After the transcript was made, we created a CPM–GOMS schedule chart reflecting the procedures observed in the videotapes, observable operators, and (using the classic GOMS models as a guide) our best guess for both the unobservable operators and the dependencies (details can be found in John, 1990, and John & Gray, 1992, 1994, 1995). Because we were modeling a single benchmark for each call, there was no opportunity for us to observe different methods for accomplishing a call or to infer selection rules if different methods existed. However, because the TAO's task is so constrained that often only a single correct method corresponds to a particular script, this simplification seems reasonable. Note that, in a few of the videotapes we analyzed, we observed inefficient keying strategies, typically extra keystrokes. NYNEX Operator Services personnel tell us that some of these inefficient strategies are holdovers from older, now obsolete, procedures. Others may reflect a mis-understanding of procedures on the part of the videotaped TAOs, whereas others may simply be slips. We chose to model the inefficiencies as observed, rather than model the most efficient procedures possible on the current work-stations. Because all of the videotaped TAOs were experts with at least 2 years of experience, we felt that our observations were representative of the actual behavior of expert TAOs on the current workstations.

We then made estimates of the operator durations. For observed operators, we used the actual durations, which we call *benchmark durations*. For the unob-served operators, we used *normative estimates* set from the literature.

2.4 Specification-Based CPM–GOMS Models of the Proposed Workstation
In contrast to modeling the current workstation based on videotaped calls, we modeled the proposed workstation without ever observing TAOs using that workstation. Our primary goal in this part of Project Ernestine was to validate the use of CPM–GOMS as an evaluation tool at the specification stage of design, in the absence of a working system. Thus, we treated the proposed workstation as if it did not yet exist.

For each call category, we modeled the proposed workstation as if this par-ticular customer (in the videotaped call) called with these particular requests and were handled by this particular TAO using the proposed workstation. Therefore, things related to the customer-TAO dialog (e.g., wording, pauses, and duration of phrases) are the same for the models of the proposed workstation as for the models of the current workstation. Likewise, things related to individual TAO performance (e.g, typing speed) are the same for both sets of models. Things specific to the workstation do vary: layout of the proposed display, keyboard arrangement, manufacturer-specified procedures, and manufacturer-supplied estimates of system response time.

2.5 Summary of CPM–GOMS Model Building
The modeling process resulted in 30 CPM–GOMS models in schedule chart form. Fifteen of these are the CPM–GOMS models for the benchmark tasks as executed on the current workstation, and 15 are the CPM–GOMS models for

the benchmark tasks as executed on the proposed workstation. Each schedule chart gives a prediction of the length of its benchmark call, which is an estimate of the length of that type of call as it occurs in the field. (NYNEX considers the absolute time in seconds to be proprietary knowledge; therefore, we cannot report the detailed quantitative predictions of these models. We do, however, report summary statistics in Section 4.) These predictions of the length of benchmark calls can be combined with information about the frequency of call categories to predict the differences in average worktime between the two workstations. We work through the quantitative predictions of the models and compare them to empirical field data in Section 4.

3 The Field Trial and Data

The field trial was conducted in a working telephone company office, with experienced TAOs, with an unobtrusive data-collection technique. The data are very rich and can be used to address many issues. In this report, we use the data to highlight three issues most important for validating GOMS. First, are there reliable differences in TAO worktime between the two workstations? This difference also has practical significance, as each second of worktime is typically cited as being worth $3 million per year in operating costs. Second, if there are differences between workstations, are these due to workstation design per se or are they affected by the TAOs' unfamiliarity with a new device? That is, do the differences diminish over the 4 months of the trial? Third, are these differences constant or do they interact with the type of call? If they are constant, then there may exist some basic design or technological flaw that could be simply fixed. If they interact with call category, then there may be as many fixes required as there are call categories. Understanding how to fix any given call category would require an in-depth analysis of the human–human and human–computer interactions for that call category.

There were 24 TAOs on each workstation. All participants had at least 2 years of job experience, were scheduled to work continuously for the next 6 months, and had a "satisfactory" or "outstanding" job appraisal. Training for the proposed workstation group was conducted before the trial started and followed standard New England Telephone procedures. During the 4-month trial, all normal phone company procedures and management practices were followed. No new procedures or practices were introduced. Except for the new workstation, everything about their work remained the same; both groups worked their normal shifts, with their normal days off, throughout the trial. Data collection involved tapping into a pre-existing database and required no experimenter intervention or on-site presence.

The analyses of the empirical data yielded three conclusions. First, performance with the proposed workstation is slower than with the current workstation. When worktime differences are weighted by call category frequency, the proposed workstation is 3.4% (0.65 s) slower than the current one. At $3 million per second, these calculations represent a difference in annual cost of almost $2 million.

Second, this difference is due to the workstation rather than to learning to use a new machine. Although performance on the proposed workstation improves during the first month of the trial, it remains slower than the current workstation, and this difference does not diminish over the last 3 months. Third, whatever causes the difference in worktime is not a simple constant. That is, for some call categories there is a slight advantage (0.1% for cc04) whereas for others the worktime disadvantage is quite large (13.5% for cc06) (see Figure 33.9).

4 Comparing the CPM–GOMS Models to the Data

The CPM–GOMS models of the 15 benchmark tasks provide both quantitative and qualitative predictions about real-world performance on the current and proposed workstations. In this section, after evaluating the representativeness of our selected benchmarks (Section 4.1), we examine the quantitative predictions of the models and compare them to the data in the field trial (Section 4.2). In Section 4.3, we compare the CPM–GOMS predictions with those derived from a "reasonable alternative" calculation. We then look for qualitative explanations for the quantitative results (Section 4.4).

4.1 Evaluating Benchmark Tasks

An important step in using the benchmark method for comparing systems is to confirm that the benchmarks are indeed representative of the tasks for which the systems will be used. This is particularly important for our benchmarks because we used only a single script, performed by a single TAO, for each call category, and we did not deliberately design the scripts to approximate the median-duration call of each call type. For each call category, if this single instance was far from an average duration for that category, it would produce an abnormally long or short call duration for both workstations, with unknown effects on the predicted relative efficiency of the two workstations. Therefore, we compared performance time on the scripted calls to calls handled by TAOs on the current workstation during the trial. (Recall that NYNEX routinely collects average worktime by call category, so the ability to compare the benchmark times to real times was not dependent on the performance of a field trial.)

In terms of absolute worktime predictions, the average percent difference (see Figure 33.5) between trial times and videotape times over all call categories was 8.24%, with the benchmarks averaging slightly faster times than the real calls. When we weight the benchmark calls by the observed call frequencies, the prediction of worktime is even better: 2.08% less than the observed worktime.

Call Category	Percent Differences
cc01	− 6.67%
cc02	− 32.44%
cc03	20.45%
cc04	18.17%
cc05	7.07%
cc06	49.46%
cc07	− 8.30%
cc08	45.71%
cc09	29.67%
cc10	− 74.79%
cc11	18.88%
cc12	41.27%
cc13	8.30%
cc16	8.68%
cc18	− 1.81%
Mean difference	8.24%

Figure 33.5
Percent difference between the 3-month current workstation trial data and the benchmark calls: (Current − Benchmark)/Current.

Simple linear regression shows that the correlation of call category times between the videotapes and trial data on the current workstation is significant ($r^2 = .70$; see Figure 33.6).

We also computed the standard score (z score) for each call category. The standard score expresses the difference between the videotape and trial means as a function of the variability of the trial data (difference/SD),[2] so that a z score between +1.00 and −1.00 indicates that the benchmark is within 1 SD of the mean of the trial calls. The standard scores showed that the benchmarks for 14 of the 15 call categories are within 1 SD.[3] These analyses support the conclusion that the set of benchmarks are representative of the calls TAOs handle in the real world.

Although in the aggregate, the set of benchmarks is representative of the set of real calls a TAO handles, the individual benchmarks varied widely in how well they matched their respective call types. The percent differences between times for the individual benchmarks and the trial data ranged from −74.79% to +49.46%, and 6 of the 15 call categories differed from the trial data by more than 20%. In retrospect, it might have been better to collect baseline performance data on the current workstation prior to modeling and use it to help design benchmark scripts. Depending on the observed distribution of a call category, a single benchmark could be designed to be close to the median, or several benchmarks could be designed to reflect a nonnormal distribution.

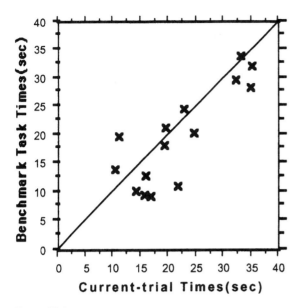

Figure 33.6
Compares the times of the benchmark tasks calls with current trial data. Note that the 45° diagonal illustrates where the points would fall if the benchmarks predicted the trial data perfectly.

4.2 Predicting Duration: Quantitative Validity

The CPM–GOMS models predicted durations for each of the benchmark calls for each of the workstations. Here we examine these predictions and compare them to the data from the field trial. First, we look at the relative difference between workstations. Does CPM–GOMS predict the 0.65-sec difference between current and proposed workstations when weighted by call frequency? Second, we look at the absolute worktimes for each workstation. How well do the models predict the absolute time for each of the two workstations? Third, for each workstation we look at the absolute difference between prediction and field data for each of the 15 call categories. Finally, for each call category, we look at the relative difference between workstations.

Predicting the Difference Between the Two Workstations   When each model is weighted by the frequency of occurrence of its call category, CPM–GOMS predicts that the proposed workstation will be 0.63 sec slower than the current workstation. For comparison, when the empirical data are weighted by the frequency of call occurrence, the proposed workstation is 0.65 seconds slower than the current.

This overall prediction is the one that is most important to NYNEX. Pragmatically, at $3 million in operating costs per second of average worktime per year, the ability to predict performance on the mixture of calls that NYNEX

TAOs handle is the most prized prediction. An analytic model of a proposed workstation, which was built without direct observation and based only on knowledge of the task and specifications obtained from the manufacturer, predicted, a priori, performance on that workstation in a real-world setting. Contrary to everyones expectation that the new technology would be significantly faster than the old technology, the models predicted a small difference favoring the old technology. This small difference in worktime meant that the proposed workstation would cost NYNEX an estimated $2 million per year more than the current workstation in operating costs. The CPM–GOMS models predicted the overall outcome of the trial with remarkable accuracy.

Predicting the Absolute Worktime for Each Workstation   For the current workstation, the CPM–GOMS models, when weighted by call category frequency, underpredict the trial data by an average of 4.35%. This underprediction is continued by the models of the proposed workstation, with these models predicting a weighted worktime 4.31% faster than the trial data. These weighted predictions are well within the 20% error limit that previous work (John & Newell, 1989) has argued is the useful range of an engineering model.

Because these underpredictions are very consistent at about 4%, the relative prediction of the two sets of CPM–GOMS models (0.63 sec predicted vs. 0.65 sec found in the empirical data) is more accurate than the absolute predictions themselves. It is possible that this underprediction represents factors that are consistently missed by CPM–GOMS modeling. If further research also shows this consistent underprediction, then future analysts might consider adding a 4% adjustment to make more accurate absolute predictions of performance time.

Predicting Absolute Worktime by Call Category   Across call categories, the average percent difference between the CPM–GOMS models and the observed calls was 11.30% for the current workstation and 11.87% for the proposed workstation. The regression scatterplots of predicted versus actual times (Figure 33.7) show that the correlation between the CPM–GOMS predictions and the trial data was significant for the current workstation ($r^2 = .71$) and for the proposed workstation ($r^2 = .69$). For each workstation and call category, the standard z scores show that for 14 of the 15 call categories the CPM–GOMS prediction is within 1 *SD* of the trial mean for both current and proposed. These data support the conclusion that the CPM–GOMS models predict the trial data in the aggregate.

As with the benchmark tasks, the individual predictions of worktime per call category were less accurate. The percent difference per call category for the current workstation ranged from −63% to +49%, with eight call categories more than 20% away from their observed times (see Figure 33.8). Likewise, the percent difference for the proposed workstation ranged from −54% to +49%, with the same eight call categories being more than 20% away from the observed times.

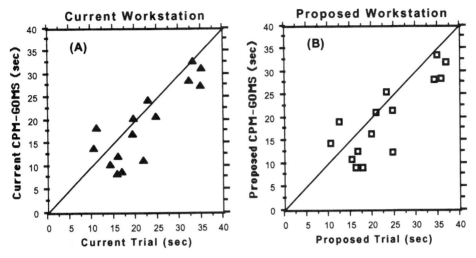

Figure 33.7
Regression scatterplots for call categories in seconds. (A) For the current workstation, comparisons of CPM-GOMS predictions with the trial data. (B) Comparison for the proposed workstation. Note that the 45° diagonal illustrates where the points would fall if the predictions were prefect.

Call Category	Current	Proposed
cc01	– 6.06%	– 9.57%
cc02	– 32.92%	– 36.96%
cc03	24.71%	23.27%
cc04	16.46%	12.16%
cc05	12.14%	16.60%
cc06	48.63%	49.17%
cc07	– 2.61%	– 0.38%
cc08	49.24%	49.23%
cc09	29.04%	29.00%
cc10	– 62.86%	– 54.45%
cc11	21.73%	20.63%
cc12	47.76%	44.39%
cc13	11.93%	17.94%
cc16	11.10%	12.98%
cc18	1.26%	4.10%
Mean difference	11.30%	11.87%

Figure 33.8
For the current and proposed workstations, the percent difference between CPM-GOMS predictions and the 3-month trial data: (Trial – GOMS)/Trial.

The scatterplots in Figure 33.7 are extremely similar to the scatterplot of the measured times for the benchmark tasks versus trial data shown in Figure 33.6. This is not at all surprising for the current workstation because, in that the models predicted the benchmarks very well, their prediction of the trial data should be similar to the benchmarks' representativeness. Likewise, because there is much more variability between call categories than between work-stations, the scatterplot for the proposed workstation (Figure 33.7b) also looks similar to that of the benchmarks (Figure 33.6).

These general results, that overall prediction of worktime (both weighted by call frequency and unweighted) is very good whereas the individual pre-dictions of call category is not as good, is a statistical fact of life. If the individual predictions vary more or less randomly around the actual call times, some being too short and some being too long, aggregate measures will involve some canceling out of these predictions. Because the aggregate measures are of primary importance to NYNEX, this fluctuation at the level of individual call types is interesting to examine but not too important to the results of the modeling effort.

Predicting the Workstation Difference by Call Category   As can be seen in Figure 33.9, CPM–GOMS predicted the direction of the difference for all but three call categories (cc04, cc05, and cc13). We view the predictions as somewhat akin to EPA mileage ratings. Few drivers get the exact mileage predicted by EPA. However, the ratings are meaningful in that they tend to predict the direction of the differences between cars and the general size of those differences.

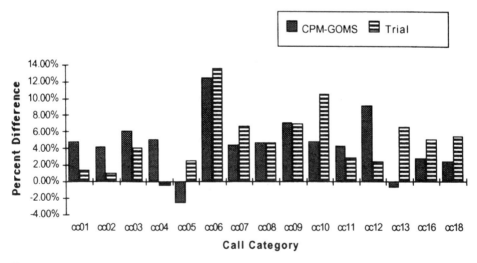

Figure 33.9
Predicted percent difference in the Workstations × Call Category.

Summary: Quantitative Validity of CPM–GOMS Models   The CPM–GOMS models of benchmark calls predicted that the proposed workstation would be 0.63 sec slower than the current whereas the field trial found a real difference of 0.65 sec. For each workstation, the 15 CPM–GOMS models predicted worktimes that correlated highly with the empirical data ($r^2 = .71$ for current and .69 for proposed). Additionally, for 12 of the 15 call categories, the models predicted the direction of the current versus proposed difference.

In the next section, we compare the quantitative validity of the CPM–GOMS predictions with those derived from a reasonable alternative calculation. In Section 4.4, we use the CPM–GOMS models to do something that the data do not do (viz., provide a qualitative explanation of the differences between the current and proposed workstations).

4.3 Value Added of CPM–GOMS Models

As mentioned in the introduction, a simple, seemingly reasonable calculation can be done to predict worktime differences between the current and proposed workstations without cognitive modeling. Such a calculation was made before Project Ernestine, which raised NYNEX's initial expectations of improved performance with the proposed workstation and justified the expense of the field trial. Here we work through such a calculation and compare its accuracy to the CPM–GOMS predictions to evaluate the value added of cognitive modeling in the form of CPM–GOMS.

The benchmark tests can be used to make seemingly reasonable predictions of worktime differences between the current and proposed workstations without cognitive modeling. The proposed workstations displays a screenful of information faster than the current workstation and changes the keying procedure to eliminate keystrokes for several call categories. For each call category, we work through these changes to predict overall differences in worktime.

From Card et al. (1983, Figure 9.1, p. 264) we get an estimate of 280 msec per keystroke for an average, 40 words/minute, nonsecretary typist. For each call category, this time was substracted for each keystroke that the manufacturer's procedures eliminated. Four keystrokes were eliminated from one benchmark call; two keystrokes from two calls; one keystroke from each of seven calls; zero keystrokes from four calls; and one keystroke was added to one call.

The manufacturer estimated that the proposed workstation would be 880 msec faster than the current workstation to display a screenful of information. We subtracted this estimate from every benchmark call.

By this benchmark-based, noncognitive procedure, we would predict an average advantage for the proposed workstation of 5.2%. When call categories are weighted by their frequency of occurrence, the predicted advantage becomes 18.6% (4.1 sec), for an estimated savings in annual operating costs of $12.2 million.

In contrast, the CPM–GOMS models predicted, and the field trial confirmed, that the proposed workstation would actually be about 3% slower than the current workstation. Thus, the seemingly reasonable calculation based on the benchmarks and the manufacturer's procedures and response-time estimates is wrong in both magnitude and sign. It is important to remember that the non-cognitive prediction is more than just a straw man. Large-scale empirical trials such as Project Ernestine are expensive to conduct. Expectations based on such a calculation led NYNEX to commit to the time and expense required to conduct an empirical trial.

Why were the CPM–GOMS predictions so much more accurate than the noncognitive predictions? Two reasons are apparent: (a) Building CPM–GOMS models requires that the analyst understand the details of information flow between the workstation and the TAO, which were overlooked by the non-cognitive predictions, and (b) CPM–GOMS models incorporate the complex effects of parallel activities.

For example, the noncognitive model assumed that each time a screenful of information was displayed, the proposed workstation's faster system response time would reduce the time of the call. However, the more detailed analysis required to build CPM–GOMS models revealed that the TAO does not have to see the entire screen to initiate the greeting (i.e., just the first line is needed). Hence, comparisons of how fast the two workstations display an entire screen of information are largely irrelevant. Likewise, the noncognitive model assumes that every keystroke contributes to the length of the call. However, CPM–GOMS shows that removing a keystroke only speeds the task if that keystroke is on the critical path.

Thus, CPM–GOMS disciplines the analyst to incorporate the right level of detail to evaluate such tasks and correctly calculates the effects of parallel activities to produce accurate quantitative predictions. A noncognitive approach based on benchmarks and design changes alone does not work as well. In addition to producing more accurate quantitative predictions, CPM–GOMS models can provide qualitative explanations for the quantitative results (see next section) and can also be used as a tool in workstation design (as discussed in Gray et al., 1993). Clearly, CPM–GOMS adds value over noncognitive predictions.

4.4 Explaining Differences: Qualitative Validity

Beyond predicting performance time, the CPM–GOMS models provide explanations for their predictions and, thus, explanations for the empirical data. Here, we inspect the models to find what causes their differences in worktime and why these difference are not constant but vary with call category.

Why Do the Workstations Differ?   Despite its improved technology and ergonomically superior design, performance with the proposed workstation was slower than with the current workstation. A high-order look at the critical paths shows the task to be dominated by conversation and system response time. Seldom is the TAO's interaction with the workstation on the critical path. This pattern is so strong that it was found in our initial model of just one call category (Gray, John, Lawrence, Stuart, & Atwood, 1989) and so consistent that we declared it confirmed (Gray, John, Stuart, Lawrence, & Atwood, 1990) after modeling five call categories. Thus, the top-order prediction of the CPM–GOMS analyses is that the design of the workstation should have little, if any, effect on the length of calls.

We can look at the details of the models to understand why the proposed workstation is actually slower than the current workstation. The workstations differ in their keyboard layout, screen layout, keying procedures, and system response time, each of which may affect call duration.

KEYBOARD LAYOUT   Compared to the current workstation, the keys necessary for the TAO's task are more closely grouped on the proposed workstation, with the most common keys clustered around the numeric keypad. Although this arrangement tends to reduce keying time, most keystrokes are not on the critical path, so this advantage disappears into slack time for most of the calls.

Opposing this advantage, the new arrangement of keys introduces procedural changes that increase the length of many calls. For example, for the current workstation, the key pressed when a call is complete (POS–RLS) is on the far left of the keyboard and is typically pressed with the left index finger. Because most other keys are pressed with the right index finger, the TAO can move to the POS–RLS key with the left hand while other keys are being pressed with the right hand. The proposed workstation locates the POS–RLS key near the numeric keypad, with the other function keys, on the right side of the keyboard. Because of the POL–RLS key's proximity to the right hand, when we modeled this keystroke we assumed that, rather than making an awkward cross-body movement with the left hand, the TAO would press this key with the right index finger. This means that the horizontal movement to the POS–RLS key can no longer be done in the slack time while other keys are being pressed but must wait until the last function keypress is finished. This procedural change puts the movement to the POS–RLS key onto the critical path of several call types, increasing the overall length of those calls.

SCREEN LAYOUT   Getting information from the screen involves moving the eyes to the correct location, waiting for information to appear if it is not already present, and perceiving and understanding the information. The need to wait for information to appear is a property of the system response time and is discussed later. The CPM–GOMS models assume that the TAOs are experts at finding the information they need from the screen; they can move their eyes to the next correct location in anticipation of getting the necessary information. Therefore, eye movements never appear on the critical path for either workstation. Likewise, the assumption of expertise means that the time to perceive and comprehend the information on both workstations can be estimated with either a complex visual-perception operator of approximately 290 msec or a binary visual-perception operator of approximately 100 msec (John, 1990). Although these operators are often on the critical path of both sets of models, because they are the same for both workstations, they do not produce a difference in the call-length predictions.

KEYING PROCEDURES   For several calls, the keying procedures for the proposed workstation eliminated keystrokes. In some of these calls, this decrease in keystrokes was an advantage for the proposed workstation. However, because of the complex interaction of parallel activities in the TAO's task, merely eliminating keystrokes is not necessarily an advantage. For example, Figures 33.10 and 33.11 show the first and last segments of a CPM–GOMS analysis for a calling-card call in which new procedures eliminated two keystrokes from the beginning of the call and added one keystroke to the end of the call, for a net decrease of one keystroke. For each figure, the top chart represents the call using the current workstation and the bottom shows the CPM–GOMS analysis for the same call using the proposed workstation.

Figure 33.10 has two striking features. First, the model for the proposed workstation has 10 fewer boxes than the model for the current workstation, representing two fewer keystrokes. Second, none of the deleted boxes is on the critical path; all are performed in slack time. At this point in the task, the critical path is determined by the TAO greeting and getting information from the customer. The CPM–GOMS model predicts that removing keystrokes from this part of the call will not affect the TAO's worktime. Worktime is controlled by the conversation, not by the keystrokes, and not by the ergonomics of the keyboard.

The middle of the model, not shown (the activities between those shown in Figures 33.10 and 33.11), is identical for both workstations and essentially shows the critical path being driven by how fast the customer says the 14-digit number to which the call should be billed. TAOs are taught to "key along" with the customer. Although a rapidly speaking customer could force the critical path to be determined by the TAO's keying speed, both workstations use the standard numeric keypad, so the critical path (and resulting speed of keying in numbers) would be the same for both workstations.

If the proposed keying procedures simply eliminated the two keystrokes required by the current workstation in the beginning of the call, then CPM–GOMS would predict equivalent performance. For the proposed workstation, however, the procedure was changed so that one of the keystrokes eliminated at the beginning of the call would occur later in the call (see the four extra boxes in the bottom of Figure 33.11). In this model, this keystroke goes from being performed during slack time to being performed on the critical path. The cognitive and motor time required for this keystroke now adds to the time required

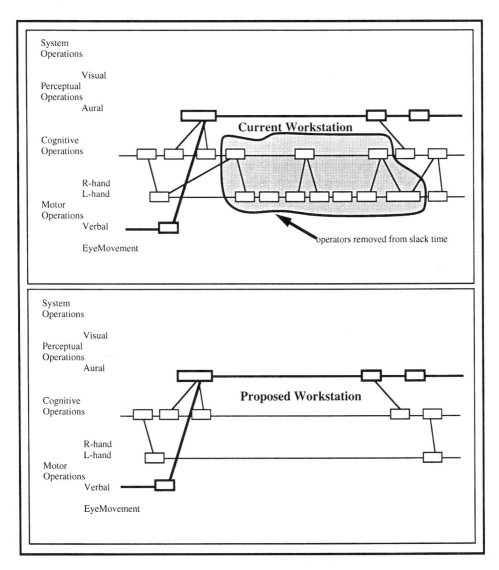

Figure 33.10
Section of CPM-GOMS analysis from near the beginning of the call. Notice that the proposed workstation (bottom) has removed two keystrokes (which required seven motor and three cognitive operations) from this part of the call. However, none of the 10 operators removed was along the critical path (shown in bold).

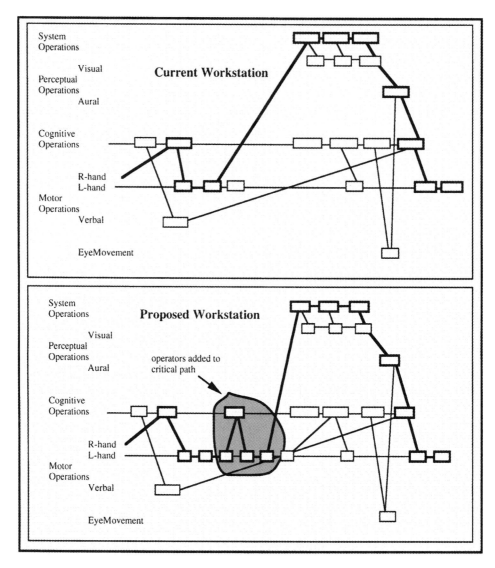

Figure 33.11
Section of CPM-GOMS analysis from the end of the call. Notice that the proposed workstation (bottom) has added one keystroke to this part of the call, which results in four operators (three motor and one cognitive) being added to the critical path (shown in bold).

to process this call. Thus, the net elimination of one keystroke actually increases call time because of the complex interaction between parallel activities shown in the critical-path analysis.

SYSTEM RESPONSE TIME   Time to display information to the screen as well as time to output keystrokes vary between workstations and generally contribute to the slowness of the proposed workstation. For example, the proposed workstation is slower than the current workstation in displaying the first line of information but faster to display an entire screenful of information. In some call types, the information displayed at the bottom of the screen is on the critical path, and this speed-up in display time provides an advantage for the proposed workstation. However, the very first line of information is necessary for the TAO to decide which greeting to use to initiate the call, and waiting for this information to be displayed is on the critical path of every call. The manufacturer's estimate of the latency to display that first line of information is 0.57 sec longer for the proposed than for the current workstation. This half second is added to the duration of every benchmark call.

A less straightforward factor is the outpulsing of keystrokes. The proposed workstation is faster in outpulsing large numbers of keystrokes (e.g., a 14-digit calling-card number) but slower to outpulse single function keys. Whether this factor, number of keystrokes, favors, hurts, or is neutral to the worktime of the proposed compared to the current workstation depends only partly on how many keystrokes are being outpulsed. More important than number is what else is going on in the call while the numbers are being outpulsed. If the outpulsing is on the critical path, then number is an important factor; if it is not on the critical path, then number of outpulsed keystrokes does not matter.

SUMMARY: EFFECT OF DESIGN CHANGES   The complex interactions among all these changes produced critical paths that were longer for the proposed than for the current workstation. The predominant reason was an increase in initial system response time, but time to outpulse single function keys, keying procedures, and keyboard changes also contributed to the performance deficit.

5 Conclusions

This study validates the use of CPM–GOMS in predicting performance time for routine cognitive tasks accomplished through complex interaction among a user, a workstation and associated computer systems, and another human. In addition to quantitatively predicting the outcome of the field trial, the CPM–GOMS models provided explanations for the results. Indeed, the CPM–GOMS models saved the field trial from a potential disaster. Faster display times and the elimination of keystrokes from most calls were expected to result in faster worktimes. The data from the trial were so counterintuitive that, in the absence of a compelling explanation as to why the proposed workstation was slower than the current one, the tendency was to blame the trial instead of the workstation (Atwood, Gray, & John, 1996). On the basis of these analyses, NYNEX decided not to buy the proposed workstation.

The accurate prediction of workstation performance challenges the efficacy of conducting large, empirical field trials. In many cases, the time and expense required for empirical trials might be eliminated and replaced by the much shorter and less disruptive time required for model building. In other cases, the models can be used to sort among competing devices and procedures. For example, if there were five workstations to the evaluated, CPM–GOMS might predict that two of these were better than the others, with small differences between the two best. An empirical trial could then be conducted to evaluate factors such as hardware quality and maintenance. In this way, CPM–GOMS would allow us to thoroughly consider more workstations in less time than is currently possible.

The explanations provided by the CPM–GOMS models far surpass any information given by empirical trials alone. These explanations led to an understanding of why old technology can outperform new technology, why this difference was not constant but varied with call category, and why learning over the course of the trial did not affect worktime. The CPM–GOMS models allow us to see the forest for the trees, evaluating all components of the task as an integrated whole with complex interactions. This holistic approach, dictated by the CPM–GOMS analysis methodology, is of value in understanding the complex effects of any design decision.

We believe that the biggest benefit will be to use the explanatory and predictive powers of CPM–GOMS in the design process to focus design effort and to provide a quantitative test-bed for design ideas. Such an approach is currently being used at NYNEX (Stuart & Gabrys, 1993), and it represents the early fruits of the decade-long struggle to "harden the science" of human-computer interaction (Newell & Card, 1985, p. 237).

Notes

The first two authors contributed equally to this article. The order of their names reflects alphabetical order and not seniority of authorship.

The work on the abridgment of Gray, John, and Atwood (1993) was supported by grants from the National Science Foundation to Wayne D. Gray (IRI-9618833) and Bonnie E. John work (IRI-9457628).

1. Although this statement is true for the two workstations that were compared in Project Ernestine, it may not be true in general. For Project Ernestine, the proposed workstation did not change the nature of the job being performed. For situations in which a change in workstation was also accompanied by a change in the job, say from the use of a drafting table to the use of a CAD/CAM system, then analysis at the activity or functional level may be sufficient to bring out critical differences.

2. Because we were dealing with such a large amount of data (78,240 calls), we typically left the individual call data on the mainframe and downloaded the summary data that we used in our statistics. For part of the last month of the trial, however, we did download data on every call for

every TAO for every call category. This database resulted in 16,059 calls: 8,125 for the current workstation and 7,934 for the proposed. Calls per call category ranged from 154 to 1,795. We use this database to supply estimates of worktime variability within call category.

3. The benchmark used for cc10 had the customer giving much more information than the TAO needed to complete the call. The TAO politely waited until the customer had finished talking before answering her and completing the call. This procedure satisfied the constraint of serving the customer politely, but it produced a call time almost twice what was found in the trial in which, presumably, the average customer was less verbose.

References

Atwood, M. E., Gray, W. D., & John, B. E. (1996). Project Ernestine: Analytic and empirical methods applied to a real-world CHI problem. In M. Rudisill, C. Lewis, P. B. Polson, & T. D. McKay (Eds.), *Human-Computer interface design: Success stories, emerging methods, and real world context* (pp. 101–121). San Francisco: Morgan-Kaufmann.

Bovair, S., Kieras, D. E., & Polson, P. G. (1990). The acquisition and performance of text-editing skill: A cognitive complexity analysis. *Human–Computer Interaction, 5*(1), 1–48.

Card, S. K., Moran, T. P., & Newell, A. (1983). *The psychology of human–computer interaction*. Hillsdale, NJ: Lawrence Erlbaum Associates.

Gray, W. D., John, B. E., & Atwood, M. E. (1992). The précis of Project Ernestine or an overview of a validation of GOMS. In *Proceedings of the ACM CHI '92 Conference on Human Factors in Computing Systems* (pp. 307–312). New York: ACM Press.

Gray, W. D., John, B. E., & Atwood, M. E. (1993). Project Ernestine: Validating a GOMS analysis for predicting and explaining real-world performance. *Human–Computer Interaction, 8*(3), 237–309.

Gray, W. D., John, B. E., Lawrence, D., Stuart, R., & Atwood, M. (1989, April). *GOMS meets the phone company, or, Can 8,400,000 unit-tasks be wrong*. Poster presented at the CHI '89 Conference on Human Factors in Computing Systems, Austin, TX.

Gray, W. D., John, B. E., Stuart, R., Lawrence, D., & Atwood, M. E. (1990). GOMS meets the phone company: Analytic modeling applied to real-world problems, *Proceedings of IFIP INTERACT '90: Human-Computer Interaction* (pp. 29–34).

John, B. E. (1990). Extensions of GOMS Analyses to Expert Performance Requiring Perception of Dynamic Visual and Auditory Information. In *Proceedings of the ACM CHI '90 Conference on Human Factors in Computing Systems* (pp. 107–115). New York: ACM Press.

John, B. E. (1996). TYPIST: A theory of performance in skilled typing. *Human–Computer Interaction, 11*(4), 321–355.

John, B. E., & Gray, W. D. (1992). GOMS analysis for parallel activities, *Tutorial presented at the ACM CHI '92 Conference on Human Factors in Computing Systems*, Monterey, CA.

John, B. E., & Gray, W. D. (1994). GOMS Analysis for Parallel Activities, *Tutorial presented at the ACM CHI '94 Conference on Human Factors in Computing Systems* (Vol. 2, pp. 395–396).

John, B. E., & Gray, W. D. (1995). GOMS Analysis for Parallel Activities, *Tutorial presented at the ACM CHI '95 Conference on Human Factors in Computing Systems* (Vol. 2, pp. 395–396).

John, B. E., & Kieras, D. E. (1996a). The GOMS family of user interface analysis techniques: Comparison and contrast. *ACM Transactions on Computer–Human Interaction, 3*(4), 320–351.

John, B. E., & Kieras, D. E. (1996b). Using GOMS for user interface design and evaluation: Which technique? *ACM Transactions on Computer–Human Interaction, 3*(4), 287–319.

John, B. E., & Newell, A. (1987). Predicting the Time to Recall Computer Command Abbreviations, *Proceedings of ACM CHI + GI '87 Conference on Human Factors in Computing Systems and Graphics Interface* (pp. 33–40). New York: ACM.

John, B. E., & Newell, A. (1989). Cumulating the Science of HCI: From S-R Compatibility to Transcription Typing. In *Proceedings of the ACM CHI '89 Conference on Human Factors in Computing Systems* (pp. 109–114). New York: ACM Press.

John, B. E., & Newell, A. (1990). Toward an engineering model of stimulus-response compatibility. In R. W. Proctor & T. G. Reeve (Eds.), *Stimulus-Response Compatibility: An Integrated Perspective* (pp. 427–479). North-Holland: Elevier Science Publishers B.V.

Lerch, F. J., Mantei, M. M., & Olson, J. R. (1989). Skilled financial planning: The cost of translating ideas into action. In *Proceedings of the ACM CHI '89 Conference on Human Factors in Computing Systems* (pp. 121–126). New York: ACM Press.

Newell, A., & Card, S. K. (1985). The prospects for psychological science in human–computer interaction. *Human–Computer Interaction, 1*(3), 209–242.

Olson, J. R., & Olson, G. M. (1990). The growth of cognitive modeling in human–computer interaction since GOMS. *Human–Computer Interaction, 5* (2–3), 221–265.

Stuart, R., & Gabrys, G. (1993, April). *Analytic modeling of Directory Assistance: An extension of CPM–GOMS*. Short paper presented at the ACM InterCHI '93 Conference on Human Factors in Computing Systems.

Part III

Issues in Cognitive Modeling

Connectionist vs. Symbolic Models

Chapter 34

Connectionism and the Problem of Systematicity (Continued): Why Smolensky's Solution *Still* Doesn't Work

Jerry Fodor

Paul Smolensky has recently announced that the problem of explaining the compositionality of concepts within a connectionist framework is solved in principle. Mental representations are vectors over the activity states of connectionist "units," but the vectors encode classical trees, whose structural properties in turn "acausally" explain the facts of compositionality. This sounds suspiciously like the offer of a free lunch, and it turns out, upon examination, that there is nothing to it.

Human cognition exhibits a complex of closely related properties—including systematicity, productivity, and compositionality—which a theory of cognitive architecture ignores at its peril.[1] If you are struck with a theory that denies that cognition has these properties, you are dead and gone. If you are stuck with a theory that is compatible with cognition having these properties but is unable to explain why it has them, you are, though arguably still breathing, clearly in deep trouble. There are, to be sure, cognitive scientists who do not play by these rules, but I propose to ignore them in what follows. Paul Smolensky, to his credit, is not among them.

Smolensky has recently been spending a lot of his time trying to show that, vivid first impressions to the contrary notwithstanding, some sort of connectionist cognitive architecture can indeed account for compositionality, productivity, systematicity, and the like. It turns out to be rather a long story how this is supposed to work; 185 pages of a recent collection of papers on connectionism (Macdonald and Macdonald, 1995) are devoted to Smolensky's telling of it, and there appears still to be no end in sight. It seems it takes a lot of squeezing to get this stone to bleed.

Still, Smolensky's account of compositional phenomena has had a good press in some quarters; the Churchlands tell us, for example, that "Smolensky (1990) has shown that [his sort of cognitive architecture is] at least adequate to embody ... the systematic linguistic structures and transformations deemed essential by Fodorean accounts of cognition" (McCauley, 1995, 234). It would certainly be big news if that were true. But, in fact, Smolensky's account doesn't work, and the formal details, though they are daunting and take up a lot of pages in Smolensky's papers, are largely inessential to understanding what's gone wrong.

To begin, I want to sketch an area of consensus. Unlike the kind of cognitive theory that Smolensky calls "local" connectionism, and quite like what have come to be called "classical" or "language of thought"[2] cognitive architectures, Smolensky architectures[3] invoke a structural relation between concepts (mutatis mutandis, between mental representations)[4] to explain compositional phenomena. The accounts of compositionality that S-architectures and classical theories propose are thus of the same general form. Both turn essentially on postulating an (asymmetric) structural relation (call it R) that holds between concepts and constrains their possession conditions and their semantics. In particular, according to both S-architectures and classical architectures:

> (i) (possession conditions) If a concept C bears R to a concept C^*, then having C^* requires having C; and
>
> (ii) (semantics) If a concept C bears R to a concept C^*, then the content of C^* is determined (at least inter alia) by the content of C.

We'll see presently that what distinguishes S-architectures from classical architectures is *what relation they say R is*.

I can now tip my polemical hand: I'm going to argue that the account of R that S-theories give is entirely and hopelessly parasitic on the account of R that classical architectures give. That's the sense in which, even after all those pages, Smolensky *hasn't so much as made a start* on constructing an alternative to the classical account of compositional phenomena. I propose to take this in three stage: First, I want to remind you of what classical theories say about relation R. I'll then say how Smolensky's putative alternative is supposed to work. I'll then say why Smolensky's alternative is *merely* putative. Then I'll stop.

Stage 1: Classical Theories

According to classical architectures, R is the *constituency* relation: C bears R to C^* iff C is a constituent of C^*. It's worth getting clear on how the assumption that R is the constituency relation connects with assumptions (i) and (ii) and with the classical account of compositional phenomena.

The Connection with (i)
Roughly, the constituency relation is a *part/whole* relation: If C is a constituent of C^*, then a token of C is a part of every token of C^*. More precisely, constituency is a *co-tokening* relation; that is, if C is a constituent of C^*, then it is metaphysically necessary that for every tokening of C^* there is a corresponding tokening of C. (Part/whole isn't, of course, the only relation of co-tokening. For present

purposes, it doesn't matter which of these you choose as *R*.) Since on this construal of *R*, nobody can *token C** without tokening *C*, it follows that nobody can *have C** without having *C*.

The Connection with (ii)
Reading *R* as the constituency relation doesn't literally entail (ii) since presumably it's possible for a system of representations to exhibit syntactic constituency without exhibiting semantic compositionality (in effect, all the syntactically complex symbols in such a system would be idioms).[4] But taking *R* to be the constituency relation does provide for a natural explication of the informal idea that mental representations are compositional: what makes them compositional is that the content of structurally complex mental symbols is inherited from the contents of their less structurally complex parts.

To claim that this is a "natural" way to explicate compositionality is to put the case very mildly. If *R* is constituency, then (ii) says that the semantics of complex representations derives from the semantics *of their parts*. The effect is to make the connection between compositionality, systematicity, productivity, and the like immediately clear; an example may serve to give the flavor of the thing.

There seems to be a strong pretheoretic intuition that to think the content *brown cow* is ipso facto to think the content *brown*. This amounts to considerably more than a truism; for example, it isn't explained just by the *necessity* of the inference from *brown cow* to *brown*. (Notice that the inference from *two* to *prime* is necessary too, but it is *not* intuitively plausible that you can't think *two* without thinking *prime*.) Moreover, the intuition that thinking *brown cow* somehow requires thinking *brown* is pretty clearly connected with corresponding intuitions about the systematicity of the concepts involved. It's plausibly *because* thinking the content *brown cow* somehow invokes the *concept* BROWN that anybody who is able to think *brown cow* and *tree* is ipso facto able to think *brown tree*.

Assuming that (ii) holds and that *R* is the constituency relation (or some other co-tokening relation; see above) is a way to guarantee that thinking *brown cow* does indeed invoke the concept BROWN, so it provides an elegant solution to the galaxy of observations I just detailed. If the mental representation BROWN is *a part of* the mental representation BROWN COW, then *of course* you can't have a token of the former in your head without having a token of the latter in your head too. Systematicity likewise falls into place: If the mental representation BROWN is a part both of the mental representation BROWN COW and of the mental representation BROWN TREE, then if you're in a position to think the intentional (semantic) content that BROWN contributes to BROWN COW, you are *thereby* in a position to think the intentional (semantic) content that BROWN contributes to BROWN TREE. Constituency and compositionality, taken together, guarantee that all of this is so.

Very satisfactory, I would have thought; so I want to emphasize that none of this follows from (ii) alone (i.e., from (ii) *without* the identification of R with constituency). (ii) says only that if C bears R to C*, then C (partially) determines the intentional and semantic content of C*. But that doesn't come close to entailing that you can't think C* without thinking C; and, as we've been seeing, it's this latter constraint that the explanation of compositional phenomena appears to turn on. What accounts for compositionality, according to classical architectures, is (ii) *together with the assumption that if C bears R to C*, then C is co-tokened with C**; and this assumption is guaranteed, in turn, by the identification of R with constituency. (More on all this later in the discussion).

Stage 2: Smolensky Architectures

For present purposes, the briefest sketch will do.

According to Smolensky, mental representations are *vectors*: "[T]he import of distributed representation is precisely that ... a representation is not to be found at a unit but in an activity pattern. Mathematically, an activity pattern is ... a list of numbers ... giving the activity of all the units over which the pattern resides" (232). All you need to know about such representations, for present purposes, is that they do *not* decompose into constituents. Of course lists can have sublists, and every sublist of a vector specifies the activation level of some unit(s) or other. But there is, for example, no guarantee that the list of numbers that expresses the content *brown cow* and the list of numbers that expresses the content *brown tree* will have any of their sublists in common. (Quite generally, the fact that a certain vector has a semantic interpretation does not even guarantee that its subvectors have semantic interpretations too. This is because it's not guaranteed—in fact, it's not usually the case—that every "unit" has a semantic interpretation.) We're about to see that S-architectures do offer a relation R that makes (ii) true, but it isn't a part/whole relation; in fact, it isn't a co-tokening relation of any kind.

So, if R isn't constituency, what is it? Roughly, according to S-architectures, R is a *derivation* relation. We arrive at the core of Smolensky's theory. The core of Smolensky's theory is an algorithm for encoding constituent structure trees as vectors. Once again, the details don't matter (for a sketch, see Smolensky [1995a] circa 236), but for the sake of the argument, I'll suppose (with Smolensky) that the encoding algorithm is bi-unique: Given a tree, the algorithm yields a corresponding vector; given a vector derived from a tree, the algorithm yields the tree from which the vector is derived.

Here's how things stand so far: Vectors don't have constituents. But vectors can be derived from trees; and, of course, trees *do* have constituents. Smolensky's proposal (though he doesn't put it quite this way) is that we introduce a notion of *derived constituency* for vectors that works as follows: C is a *derived constituent of* vector V iff V (uniquely) encodes C* and C is a constituent of C*. That is, the *derived* constituents of a vector V are the constituents of that of the tree that V encodes. So, for example, the vector for *brown* needn't (and generally won't) be a part of the vector for *brown cow*. But if (by assumption) V encodes the tree ((brown) (cow)), then the subtree (brown) is a classical constituent of the tree that V encodes. So it follows from the definition that the subtree (brown) is a *derived* constituent of V. So, according to S-architectures, R is a sort of constituency relation after all, only it's, as it were, a constituency relation once removed: Though it's *not* a part/whole relation over vectors, it *is* a part/whole relation over what the vectors encode.

As you will probably have gathered, I don't actually care much whether this apparatus can be made to operate (e.g., whether there is an algorithm of the sort that S-architecture wants to use to encode vectors into trees and vice versa). But I am *very* interested in the question of whether, if the apparatus can be made to operate, then a connectionist architecture can explain the compositionality. So let's turn to that.

Stage 3: Why Smolensky's Solution Still Doesn't Work

The explanations of compositional phenomena that classical theories offer are, in general, quite naturally construed as *causal* explanations. That this is so follows from the classical construal of R as constituency. Constituency is, as previously remarked, a co-tokening relation; so if BROWN is a constituent of BROWN COW, it can hardly be surprising that whenever a token of the latter is available to play a causal role in a mental process, *so too is a token of the former*. This is the heart of the classical account of compositionality: If the effects of tokening BROWN COW partially overlap with the effects of tokening BROWN TREE, that's because, in a perfectly literal sense, the causes of these effects do too.

Now, patently, this pattern of explanation is not available to an S-architecture; remember, the tokening of the BROWN COW vector does *not* guarantee a co-tokening of the BROWN vector, so it can't be taken for granted that the effects of a tokening of BROWN COW will include the effects of a tokening of BROWN. Mental representations are, by definition, necessarily co-tokened with their *classical* constituents. But it is not the case that they are, by definition or otherwise, necessarily co-tokened with their *derived* constituents. In fact, it's perfectly possible that a vector should be tokened *even if none of its derived constituents ever was or ever will be*. Remember that *all* that connects the vector V with its derived constituents is that there is a bi-unique algorithm which, *if it were executed, would compute* a tree such that the *derived* constituents of the vector are the *real* constituents of the tree. But nothing in the notion of an S-architecture, or in the kind of explanations S-architectures provide, requires that such subjunctives ever get cashed. It is perfectly all right for C to be a derived constituent of vector token V, even though all the tokens of C are, and always will be, entirely counterfactual.

Now, I suppose it goes without saying that merely *counterfactual* causes don't have any actual effects. So explanations that invoke the *derived* constituents of a vector cannot, in general, be construed as *causal* explanations. So, if the explanation of compositionality that S-architectures offer isn't causal, *what sort of explanation is it?*

Smolensky has said a lot about this in his papers, but I honestly don't understand a word of it. For example: "Tensor product constituents [what I'm calling "derived" constituents] play absolutely indispensable roles in the description and explanation of cognitive behavior in ICS [integrated connectionist symbolic architectures]. But these constituents do not have a *causal* [*sic*] role in the sense of being the objects of operations in algorithms actually at work in the system. These constituents are in this sense *acausally explanatory* [*sic*]"[5] (249). If, like me, you don't know what sort of thing the acausally explanatory explanation of "cognitive behavior" would be, I don't expect you'll find that such passages help a lot, since though they tell you what acausal explanations *aren't* (viz., they aren't causal), they don't tell you what acausal explanations *are*. There are, notice, quite a lot—say, infinitely many—domains of "objects" that aren't ever tokened in anybody's head but which correspond bi-uniquely to the representations that mental processes work on; every scheme for Gödel numbering of mental representations provides one, as Smolensky himself observes. Do all these "objects" acausally explain cognitive behavior? If not, why not?

Digression on Singing and Sailing   In an enigmatic footnote to the passage I just quoted,[6] Smolensky asks rhetorically whether it is "so incomprehensible that Simon's and Garfunkel's voices each have causal consequences, despite the fact that neither are '*there*' [*sic*] when you look *naively* [*sic*] at the pressure wave realizing *The Sounds of Silence?*" (284)[7] What makes this puzzling is that the passage in the text wanted to *deny* what the footnote apparently wishes to *assert*; namely, that theories that appeal to derived constituents thereby invoke causes of the events that they explain. Smolensky himself appears to be having trouble figuring out which explanations are supposed to be the "acausal" ones. I do sympathize.

In any event, the answer to the rhetorical question about Simon and Garfunkel is "yes and no." That the several voices should have their several effects is *not* incomprehensible *so long as you assume that each of the voices makes its distinct, causal contribution to determining the character of the waveform to which the ear responds*. Alas, the corresponding assumption is *not true* of the contribution of trees and their constituents to the values of the vectors that encode them in S-architectures.

Perhaps a still homelier example will help to make things clear. One normally sails from *A* to *B* along a vector that corresponds (roughly) to the sum of the force that the wind exerts on the boat and the force that the current exerts on the boat. The wind and the current make their respective causal contributions to determining your track *jointly* and *simultaneously* in the ways the resultant vector expresses. The counterfactuals fall into place accordingly: Increase the force of the wind and, ceteris paribus, the value of the vector changes in the wind's direction; increase the force of the current and, ceteris paribus, the value of the vector changes in the current's direction. And likewise, mutatis mutandis, for Simon's and Garfunkel's respective contributions to determining the form of the sound wave your hi-fi set produces and your ear responds to. This is all fine, well understood, and not at all tendentious.

But notice that this story is quite *disanalogous* to the way in which, on to Smolensky's account, vector values vary with the constituent structures of the trees that they encode. For, to repeat, the wind and current determine the value of the vector that one sails along *by exerting their respective causal forces on the boat*. So, it goes without saying, there must *really be* winds and currents acting causally upon the hull, and there must be causal laws that control these interactions. Otherwise, that the boat sails along the vector that it does is an utter mystery. It's only because properties like *being a force four wind* are occasionally instantiated and locally causally active that the vectors one sails along ever have the values that they do. *If the wind and the current were just "imaginary"*— specifically, causally nugatory—boats without motors wouldn't move.

In contrast, remember, the trees that vectors encode need *never* be tokened, according to Smolensky's theory. A fortoiri, the theory does *not* countenance causal interactions that involve tree tokens, or causal laws to govern such interactions. The question that arises for Smolensky (but not for Simon or Garfunkel or for me out sailing) is *how*—by what causal mechanism—the values of the putative vectors in the brain come to accord with the values that the encoding algorithim computes. On the one hand, Smolensky agrees that explaining compositionality (etc.) requires tree-talk. But, on the other hand, he concedes that S-achitectures acknowledge no causal transactions involving trees. Smolensky really does need an explanation of how both of these claims could be true at the same time. But he hasn't got one.[8]

To return to the main thread: Let's grant, to keep the argument going, that there are indeed acausal explanations, and that derived constituents are sometimes invoked in giving them. Granting all that, can't we now stop the philosophy and get to the cognitive science? No, Smolensky is *still* not out of the woods. The problem resides in a truism that he appears to have overlooked: *Bi-uniqueness goes both ways.*

Apparently Smolensky is reasoning as follows: That vectors are bi-uniquely derivable from trees licenses an architecture according to which vectors causally explain some of the facts and trees acausally explain the rest. But then, by the very same reasoning, that trees are bi-uniquely derivable from vectors should license an architecture according to which trees causally explain some of the facts (compositional phenomena, as it might be) and vectors acausally explain the rest. Sauce for the goose, sauce for the gander, after all. If unique derivability in one direction suffices to transfer the explanatory power of a tree architecture to vectors, unique derivability in the other direction should correspondingly suffice to transfer the explanatory power of a vector architecture to trees; prima facie, the total of explanation achieved is the same in either direction.[9] I am not, please note, offering this observation either as an argument for tree architectures or as an argument against vector architectures; it's just a reductio of Smolensky's assumption—which is, anyhow wildly implausible on the face of it—that explanatory power is inherited under unique derivability.

The plot so far: Smolensky thinks the best account of compositionality is that it's causally explained by vectors and acausally explained by trees. But he explicitly supposes that trees and vectors are bi-uniquely derivable, and apparently he implicitly supposes that explanatory power is inherited under bi-unique derivation. So it looks like, on Smolensky's own principles, the account according to which compositionality is causally explained by trees and acausally explained by vectors *must* be as good as the one that Smolensky actually endorses. Smolensky needs, to speak crudely, to get some asymmetry into the situation somewhere. But there doesn't seem to be any place for him to put it.

Patently, Smolensky can't afford to give up the inheritance of explanation under biunique derivability. That would invite the question of why the derivability of vectors from trees should be *any reason at all* for supposing that vectors can explain what trees do. Likewise, he can't afford to give up the bi-uniqueness of the algorithm that encodes trees as vectors. For, on the one hand, if you can't derive a unique vector corresponding to each tree, then clearly the vector notation doesn't preserve the structural distinctions that the tree notation expresses; this is trivially true, since if trees map onto vectors many to one, the vectors *thereby* fail to preserve the structural properties that distinguish the trees. And, on the other hand, if you can't derive from each vector the unique tree that it encodes, then the concept of a "derived constituent" of a vector isn't well defined and the whole scheme collapses.

But even though Smolensky needs explanation to be inherited under derivability and "is *derivable* from," to be symmetric, "is (*actually*) *derived* from" needn't be. So why, you might wonder, doesn't Smolensky say this: "The reason vectors explain what trees do but trees don't explain what vectors do is that vectors are actually derived from trees in the course of mental processing, but not vice versa." This would have the added virtue of making "derived constituent of" a sort of co-tokening relation: to get a vector token for mental processes to operate upon, you would need first to token the tree that the vector derives from. And if derived constituency is a co-tokening relation after all, then maybe S-architectures could provide for *causal* explanations of compositionality phenomena after all—in which case, Smolensky could just scrap the puzzling talk about "acausal explanations"—a consummation devoutly to be wished.

In fact, however, Smolensky doesn't and mustn't say any of that. For the mind actually to derive vectors from trees—for it actually to execute the algorithm that takes trees onto vectors—would require a cognitive architecture that can support operations on trees. But, by general consensus, S-architectures can't do so; S-architectures work (only) on vectors. That, after all, is where we started. It was, as we saw, *because* S-architectures don't support operations on trees that they have trouble explaining compositionality in the first place.

To put the same point slightly differently: If Smolensky were to suppose that vector tokens come from tree tokens via some algorithm that the mind actually executes in the course of cognitive processing, he would then have to face the nasty question of where the tree tokens themselves come from. Answering that question would require him to give up his connectionism since, again by general consensus, connectionist architectures don't generate trees; what they generate instead is *vector encodings* of trees.

It's important, at this point in the discussion, to keep clear on what role the tree encoding algorithm actually plays in an S-architecture.[10] Strictly speaking, it isn't part of Smolensky's theory *about the mind* at all; strictly speaking, it's a part of his theory about *theories about the mind*. In particular, it's a device for exhibiting the comparability of classical architectures and S-architectures by translating from the tree vocabulary of the former into the vector vocabulary of the latter and vice versa. But there is no cognitive architecture that postulates mental processes that operate on *both* kinds of representation (at least there is none that is party to the present dispute);[11] a fortiori, there is no mental process in which the two kinds of representations are supposed to interact; and no mind ever executes Smolensky's encoding algorithm in the course of its quotidian operations (except, perhaps, the mind of a theorist who is professionally employed in comparing classical architectures with connectionist ones).

So if everybody, Smolensky included, agrees that the encoding algorithm isn't really part of Smolensky's theory of how the mind works, why does Smolensky keep making such a fuss about it? It's because, since he admits that the explanation of compositionality should be couched in terms of trees and their constituents, Smolensky needs somehow to make the vocabulary of tree-talk accessible to vector theories. The function of the encoding algorithm in Smolensky's overall picture is to permit him to do so, and hence to allow the connectionist explanation of compositionality to parasitize the classical explanation. That's all it does; it has no other motivation.

The sum and substance is this: Smolensky's argument is, for all intents and purposes, that since there is exactly one vector that is derivable from each tree, then, if the structure of a tree explains compositionality (or whatever else; the issue is completely general), so too does the structure of the corresponding vector. *Smolensky gives no grounds, other than their biunique derivability from trees, for claiming that vectors explain what trees do.* Put this way, however, the inference looks preposterous even at first blush; *explanation is not, in general, preserved under one-to-one correspondence;* not even if the correspondence happens to be computable by algorithm. Why on earth would anyone suppose that it would be?

In effect, Smolensky proposes that the classical theory should do the hard work of explaining compositionality, systematicity, etc., and then the connectionist theory will give the *same* explanation except for replacing "constituent" with "derived constituent" and "explain" with "acausally explain" throughout. Would you like to know why thinking *brown cow* requires thinking BROWN? Glad to oblige: It's because, since BROWN is a classical constituent of BROWN COW, it follows by definition that the BROWN vector is a derived constituent of the BROWN COW vector. And, by stipulation, if C is a derived constituent of C^*, then your thinking C^* *acausally explains* your thinking C. Smolensky's architecture offers no alternative to the classical story and adds nothing to it except the definition and the stipulation. This way of proceeding has, in Russell's famous phrase, all the virtues of theft over honest toil. Can't something be done about it?

What Smolensky really wants is to avail himself of tree explanations without having to acknowledge that there are trees; in effect, to co-opt the vocabulary of the classical theory but *without endorsing its ontology*. But that, alas, he is not permitted to do, unless he is prepared to recognize the resulting theory as merely heuristic. (It is, of course, perfectly all right to talk about the Sun's orbit around the Earth for purposes of doing navigation; but that's sailing, not science).

If, for an example that I hope is untendentious, you want rock-talk in your geological theory—if you want, that is, to frame your geological generalizations and explanations in terms of rocks and their doings—you will have to admit to rocks as part of the actual causal structure of the world. What you are *not* allowed to do is borrow rock-talk when you want to explain what it is that holds Manhattan up and *also endorse a rock-free ontology when you come to saying what the world is made of;* that would be cheating. After all, how *could* rocks explain what holds Manhattan up if there aren't any rocks? It is not, notice, a respectable way of avoiding this question to reply that they do hold it up, only acausally.

Likewise, you are not allowed to borrow the idea that the constituent structure of classical mental representations is what explains the compositionality of thought and also deny that there are mental representations that have classical constituent structure; that is cheating too. How *could* classical constituents explain why thought is compositional if thoughts don't have classical constituents?

Smolensky proceeds as though the choice of an explanatory vocabulary and the choice of an ontology were orthogonal parameters at the cognitive scientist's disposal. To the contrary: What kinds of things a theorist says there are sets an upper bound on what taxonomy his explanations and generalizations are allowed to invoke. And what taxonomy his explanations and generalizations invoke sets a lower bound on what kinds of things the theorist is required to say that there are. In this fashion, science goes back and forth between how it claims the world works and what it claims the world is made of, each kind of commitment constraining the other (to uniqueness if we're lucky).

Smolensky, it appears, would like a special dispensation for connectionist cognitive science to get the goodness out of classical constituents without actually admitting that there are any. In effect, he wants, just this once, to opt out of the duality of ontology and explanation; that's what his appeals to acausal explanation are intended to allow him to do. It's the special convenience of acausal explanations that, by definition, they carry no ontological burden; just as it's the special convenience of free lunches that, by definition, there is no charge for them. That's the good news. The bad news is that there aren't any.

Acknowledgment

I'm very grateful to Zenon Pylyshyn for his comments on an earlier draft of this chapter.

Notes

1. Just to have a label, I'll sometimes call whatever things belong to this bundle "compositional phenomena." It won't matter to my line of argument exactly which phenomena these are, or whether compositionality is indeed at the center of the cluster. Though I have strong views about both of these questions, for present purposes I don't need to prejudge them.

2. For this terminology, see Fodor and Pylyshyn (1987). What distinguishes classical architecture from local connectionism is that the former recognizes *two* sorts of primitive relations between mental representations, one causal and one structural. By contrast, local connectionist architectures recognize the former but not the latter. Fodor and Pylyshyn argue, correctly, that the problems that local connectionists have with compositional phenomena trace to this fact. Apparently Smolensky agrees with them.

3. More terminology: Smolensky calls his kind of theory an "integrated connectionist/symbolic cognitive architecture." That, however, is a mouthful that I'd rather not swallow. I'll call it a "Smolensky Architecture" or "Smolensky Theory" ("S-architecture" or "S-Theory" for short).

4. Still more terminology. (Sorry.) For present purposes, I'll use "concept" and "mental representation" pretty much interchangably; I'm supposing, in effect, that concepts are interpreted mental representations. I shall, however, want to distinguish between a concept (or mental representation) and its semantic value (e.g., the individual that it denotes or the property that it expresses). I'll write names for concepts in capitals (thus "RED" denotes the concept RED) and I'll write names for the semantic values of concepts in italics (thus, the concept RED expresses the property *red*.) These conventions tacitly assume a representational theory of mind; but that's common ground in the present discussion anyway.

   The reader should bear in mind that "RED," "BROWN COW," and the like are supposed to be *names* of concepts, not structural descriptions. The notation thus leaves open whether "BROWN COW" (or, for that matter, "RED") names a complex concept or an atomic one. It is also left open that mental representations are kinds of vectors and have no constituents.

5. This is concessive. If you think that, in the long run, even what passes as syntactic constituency must be semantically defined, so much the better for the line of argument I'm about to develop.

6. The next three paragraphs differ substantially from the original published version. Smolensky has often complained that the role vectors play in his theory is just like the role that they play in untendentious scientific explanations in (e.g.) mechanics. So why is everybody picking on Smolensky? This question deserves an answer; the discussion in the text provides it.

   The "normal decomposition" of a vector is, ipso facto, decomposition into factors the ontological and causal status of which the theory acknowledges. The sailor factors the vector he sails on into components for wind and tide because he believes (correctly) that both are causally implicated in determining his course.

   I am indebted to a discussion with Smolensky, Brian McLaughlin, and Bruce Tessor among others for these revisions.

7. I have made inquiries. It would appear that *The Sounds of Silence* is some popular song or other, of which Simon and Garfunkel are among the well-known expositors. I don't imagine that the details matter much.

8. Sometimes Smolensky writes as though S-architectures offer *reductions* of classical architectures (see, e.g., 1955b, 272: "the symbolic structure of [classical]) representations and the recursive character of the functions computed over these representations have been *reduced to* [my emphasis] tensor product structural properties of activation vectors...." See also 1995a, passim). But that can't really be what he intends. Causality is *preserved* under reduction; it couldn't be that water reduces to H_2O *and* that H_2O puts out fires *and* that water doesn't. But that vectors are causes *and trees aren't* is Smolensky's main claim.

9. To be sure, the two treatments would differ in the way they divide the burden between causal and acausal explanation; and in principle, that might allow one to choose between them. Perhaps, for example, some kinds of facts are intrinsically suited for causal explanations, while others are, by their nature, best acausally explained. But who knows which kinds of facts are which? In particular, what could justify Smolensky in assuming that facts about compositionality are of the latter sort?

10. I think, by the way, that Smolensky *is* clear on this; that is why he conceeds that "in the classical, but not the ICS architectures ... constituents have a causal role in processing" (236). I therefore regard this part of the discussion untendentious and expository. The polemics start again in the next paragraph.

11. Why not a "mixed" theory, as a matter of fact? Sure, why not. But the claim that *some* mental processes are vector transformations sounds like a lot less than the pardigm shift that connectionists keep announcing. I suppose, for example, Smolensky would agree that if a cognitive architecture allows tree operations *as well as* vector operations, it should be the former that its explanation of compositional phenomena appeals to. It is, after all, exactly because he admits that trees are the natural way to explain compositionality that Smolensky feels compelled to invoke explanations in which they figure acausally.

References

Fodor, J., and Pylyshyn, Z. 1998. "Connectionism and Cognitive Architecture: A Critical Analysis," *Cognition* 28: 3–71.

Macdonald, C., and Macdonald, G. (Eds.). 1995. *Connectionism*. Cambridge, MA: Blackwell.

McCauley, R. (Ed.) 1995. *The Churchlands and Their Critics*. Cambridge, MA: Harvard University Press.

Smolensky, P. 1990. "Tensor Product Variable Binding and the Representation of Structure in Connectionist Systems," *Artificial Intelligence* 46: 159–216.

Smolensky, P. 1995a. "Connectionism, Constituency, and the Language of Thought," in Macdonald and Macdonald, q.v.

Smolensky, P. 1995b. "Reply: Constituent Structure and Explanation in an Integrated Connectionist/Symbolic Cognitive Architecture," in Macdonald and Macdonald, q.v.

Theory vs. Modeling

Chapter 35

Networks and Theories: The Place of Connectionism in Cognitive Science

Michael McCloskey

It is no exaggeration to say that connectionism has exploded into prominence within cognitive science over the last several years. The enormous upsurge of interest is attested by conferences and symposia too numerous to list, new journals (e.g., *Neural Networks, Neural Computation*), special issues of existing journals (e.g., *Cognition, Journal of Memory and Language, The Southern Journal of Philosophy*), and a virtual avalanche of monographs and edited volumes (e.g., Anderson & Rosenfeld, 1988; Barnden & Pollack, 1991; Bechtel & Abrahamsen, 1991; Clark, 1990; McClelland & Rumelhart, 1986; Morris, 1989; Pinker & Mehler, 1988; Rumelhart & McClelland, 1986).

In this chapter I discuss an issue that has sparked considerable debate (Bechtel, 1987; Estes, 1988; Fodor & Pylyshyn, 1988; Massaro, 1988; McClelland, 1988; Minsky & Papert, 1988; Pinker & Prince, 1988; Smolensky, 1987, 1988): What is the proper role of connectionism in cognitive science? This issue is complex and multifaceted, and I will not endeavor to explore all of its ramifications (nor am I capable of doing so). Instead, I attempt to develop two specific points. First, I suggest that connectionist networks should not be viewed as theories of human cognitive functions, or as simulations of theories, or even as demonstrations of specific theoretical points. Second, I argue that these networks nevertheless hold considerable promise as tools for development of cognitive theories.

My remarks are directed specifically at the class of connectionist models that has generated the greatest interest among cognitive scientists: the class involving networks in which (1) concepts have distributed network representations; (2) the network includes hidden as well as visible units; and (3) the connection weights encoding the network's "knowledge" are not specified directly by the modeler but rather are established through application of a learning algorithm (e.g., back propagation, or the Boltzmann Machine algorithm). The most well-developed model of this class, and the one I will take as an example, is the Seidenberg and McClelland (1989) model of word recognition and naming (see also Seidenberg, 1989; Patterson, Seidenberg, & McClelland, 1989). This model addresses the ability of literate humans to categorize a letter string (e.g., *house, boke*) as a word or nonword, as well as the ability to read both words and non-words aloud.

Seidenberg and McClelland (1989) trained a three-layer network with the back-propagation learning algorithm. The network maps a distributed ortho-graphic representation of a word or nonword onto a distributed phonological representation, which is presumed to provide the basis for a spoken naming response. The network also generates an orthographic output representation, and the extent to which this representation duplicates the initial network input is taken as a basis for classifying the stimulus as a word or nonword (i.e., lexical decision). Seidenberg and McClelland (1989) argue that the network performs well at lexical decision and naming, and also exhibits several specific phenom-ena obtained in studies with human subjects (e.g., an interaction of word fre-quency and regularity in reaction time for naming words). The question to be considered here is the following: In what way can networks of this sort con-tribute to our understanding of human cognition?

Simulation versus Explanation

In exploring this question, it is worthwhile first to distinguish between simu-lating and explaining human cognitive performance. Suppose I present you with a black box connected to a keyboard and video monitor. When you enter a letter sequence at the keyboard, the device displays on the monitor a word/nonword classification, a sequence of phonetic symbols, and a reaction time for each of these outputs. Thus, imagine that given the input LAUGH, the device displayed the following output:

Word/Nonword Classification: word (487 msec)

Phonological Representation: /læf/ (654 msec)

Suppose further that you test the device extensively by presenting many word and nonword stimuli, and find that its performance matches reasonably well, although not perfectly, the performance of human subjects. That is, it usually though not always generates correct word/nonword classifications and pronunciations; it shows the interaction of frequency and regularity, and so forth.

Certainly this would be an interesting and impressive device. But would it, as a black box, constitute a theory of human word recognition and naming? Would it explain the ability of humans to recognize and name words, or spe-cific phenomena such as the frequency–regularity interaction? Obviously, the answer is no. Before you would credit me with having offered an explanatory theory, I would presumably have to describe how the black box worked, and what aspects of its structure and functioning were to be counted as relevant to modeling human performance. And, of course, this description would have to be in a form that made clear to you how the device was able to generate pronunciations and word/nonword decisions, and how its functioning gave rise to particular phenomena. You might then consider the description a theory of word recognition and naming, and the device a simulation of the theory.

The point here is simple and presumably obvious: Although the ability of a connectionist network (or other computational device) to reproduce certain aspects of human performance is interesting and impressive, this ability alone does not qualify the network as a theory, and does not amount to explaining the performance (see also Cummins & Schwarz, 1987; Humphreys, 1989).

Simulation in Search of Theory

Suppose I now tell you that the black box encloses a connectionist network of the form described by Seidenberg and McClelland (1989): 400 orthographic units that send activation to 200 hidden units, which in turn send activation to 460 phonological units, and also feed activation back to the orthographic units. Suppose further that I specify the activation rule for the units, the way in which letter strings and pronunciations are represented across the orthographic and phonological units, the learning algorithm used in training the network, and the training regimen (e.g., the corpus of words presented to the network, the procedures for determining frequency and order of presentation). Suppose finally that I specify how the pattern of activation generated by the network across the phonological and orthographic units in response to a stimulus is used to determine a word/nonword decision, a pronunciation, and a latency for each of these outputs.

Does this description of the network now constitute a specific theory of word recognition and naming, a theory simulated by the network itself? Certainly the temptation is to say yes. After all, I have provided (let us say) a precise and detailed description of network architecture, input and output representations, the functioning of individual units, and the learning procedures. Upon reflection, however, it becomes clear that my description falls short of being a theory in two critical respects.

Separating Wheat from Chaff
First, I have not specified what aspects of the network are to be considered relevant, and what aspects are to be considered irrelevant, for modeling human lexical processing. For example, is the specific form of orthographic representation implemented in the network integral to the theory, or is this representation an instance of a more general class of representations, such that any member of the class could be considered equivalent from the standpoint of the theory? And, if the latter, how is the class to be defined? In other words, what features of the representation are relevant to the theory, and what features are irrelevant?

Similarly, which aspects of network architecture are crucial to the theory, and which aspects are incidental features of the particular simulation? Is it significant, for instance, that the same set of hidden units is involved in generating the orthographic and phonological output? Further, what features of the learning procedures are relevant and irrelevant to the theory? Is it important that the network was trained with the back-propagation algorithm? Should any significance be attached to the particular settings of parameters such as the learning rate and momentum? And so forth and so on. A description of a particular network cannot provide answers to questions of this sort, and hence cannot be considered a theory. In describing the network, then, I have at best characterized a simulation, without specifying what theory it simulates.

Elucidating Cognitive Processes
My description of the network also falls short as a theory of human word recognition and naming in that it fails to provide a specific account of how word–nonword discrimination and orthography–phonology conversion are carried out. In describing network architecture, input and output representations, the functioning of individual units, and the learning procedures, I have presented important information. However, this information is not sufficient to explicate the structure and functioning of the network at a level relevant for understanding human word recognition and naming (Grossberg, 1987; see also Chandrasekaran, Goel, & Allemang, 1988). What knowledge is encoded in the network's connection weights? How is this knowledge distributed among the weights, and how is the knowledge used in converting inputs to outputs? For example, what transformation is accomplished in the mapping from orthographic to hidden units, or from hidden to phonological units? My description of the network does not answer these sorts of questions, and hence cannot be said to explain how the network (or a person) discriminates words from nonwords, or reads words and nonwords aloud.[1]

Theories and Simulations

If, then, one's goal is to present a connectionist theory of a human cognitive function, along with a network simulating the theory, one must offer more than a detailed description of a particular network.

Stating a Theory
First, one must formulate the theory at a level more abstract than that of a particular network simulation, identifying the theory's claims about how the cognitive function is carried out, and how specific phenomena arise. This is not to say that the theory must be stated in terms of rules operating on symbolic representations; the appropriate theoretical vocabulary for connectionist theories remains an open issue. What is critical, however, is that the formulation be adequate to fulfill the functions we expect a theory to fulfill. For example, a

theory should organize and make sense of the available observations concerning the cognitive process in question by allowing generalizations to be stated (e.g., because orthography–phonology conversion is accomplished in such-and-such a way, variable x should affect naming time and accuracy as follows, whereas variable y should be irrelevant). Similarly, a theory should support clear-cut credit and blame assignment. That is, when the theory successfully predicts some phenomenon, it should be possible to identify the aspects of the theory important for generating the prediction; and when the theory makes an incorrect prediction, it should be possible to relate the failure to specific assumptions of the theory, and hence to assess the extent to which the failure is fundamental. Further, the statement of a theory should provide a basis for discerning its important similarities to, and differences from, alternative theories in the same domain. Only if a theory fulfills these sorts of functions can it serve as a foundation for further theoretical and empirical progress.

Tying Simulation to Theory
In presenting a connectionist theory-plus-simulation, it is important not only to provide an appropriate statement of the theory, but also to establish that the network simulation is relevant to the theory. In particular, one must demonstrate that the network actually instantiates the theory's assumptions about the cognitive function in question. Further, the characterization of network structure and functioning should provide a basis for assessing the extent to which successes or failures in simulating particular phenomena reflect theory-relevant or theory-irrelevant features of the network.

Connectionist Theorizing and Simulation

If we now consider current connectionist work in light of the preceding discussion, two points become apparent. First, although explicit theories of human cognitive processes could conceivably be developed within the connectionist framework, this potential remains unrealized at present. Second, attempts to tie theoretical claims to network implementations face a serious obstacle in the form of limited understanding of complex connectionist networks.

Theoretical Proposals
Connectionist work on human cognition has led to some interesting and innovative theoretical proposals. However, these proposals (as distinguished from descriptions of particular networks) are in most instances rather vague and general, and do not amount to explicit theories of human cognitive functions.[2] This point may be illustrated by referring once again to the Seidenberg and McClelland (1989) model, widely regarded as one of the most fully developed connectionist cognitive models.

Seidenberg and McClelland offer several important theoretical claims. They assume that word recognition and naming involve distributed orthographic and phonological representations, such that orthographically similar words have overlapping orthographic representations, and phonologically similar words have overlapping phonological representations. Further, they argue that contrary to the claims of "dual-route" theories, a single mechanism suffices to map orthographic to phonological representations for regular words (e.g., *dog*), irregular words (e.g., *yacht*), and nonwords (e.g., *mave*). In particular, they argue that the mapping is accomplished without representations of specific lexical items, via connection weights encoding statistical regularities as well as idiosyncracies in relationships between the orthography and phonology of English words.

As these examples indicate, Seidenberg and McClelland's theoretical proposals are novel and substantive. However, these proposals do not add up to an explicit theory of human word recognition and naming. For one thing, Seidenberg and McClelland do not specify just what regularities and idiosyncracies are encoded through experience with words, how the acquired knowledge is distributed over a set of connection weights, or how the appropriate knowledge is brought into play in just the appropriate circumstances. For example, exactly what do people learn about the phonological correspondences of the letter *a* in various contexts? How is the knowledge represented in a network of simple processing units? And how does propagation of activation through the network compute the appropriate phonological instantiation of *a* in the case of regular words like *hat* or *hate*, regular inconsistent words like *gave*, exception words like *have*, and nonwords like *mab* or *mave*? The Seidenberg and McClelland theory is not sufficiently well-developed to provide specific answers. Similarly, at the level of theory (as opposed to simulation) Seidenberg and McClelland's claims about the form of orthographic and phonological representations are limited to the rather vague and general assumptions described above (i.e., representations are distributed, and similar words have similar representations).

Consult the Simulation?   It might be objected that Seidenberg and McClelland neither intended nor needed to offer a complete verbal formulation of their theory, because the details are provided by the implemented simulation. However, we cannot look to the network simulation to fill gaps in Seidenberg and McClelland's verbal statement of their theory. In the first place, any simulation includes theory-irrelevant as well as theory-relevant details; hence, the details of a simulation cannot be identified straightforwardly with the details of the corresponding theory. For example, Seidenberg and McClelland (1989, p. 563) are careful to emphasize that they are not committed at the level of theory to the specific orthographic and phonological representations implemented in the simulation.

A second reason we cannot use the simulation to flesh out the verbal formulation of the theory is that our understanding of the network's "knowledge" and functioning is quite limited. We do not know what regularities and idio-syncracies are captured in the network, how this information is reflected in the weights, and so forth. In other words, our understanding of how the network accomplishes word–nonword discrimination and orthography–phonology mapping is no more detailed than the description of these processes in Seiden-berg and McClelland's statement of their theory.

The difficulty is not simply that Seidenberg and McClelland failed to describe in sufficient detail the network's encoding of knowledge and its functioning as a whole. Rather, the problem is that connectionist networks of any significant size are complex nonlinear systems, the dynamics of which are extremely diffi-cult to analyze and apprehend (Dyer, 1988; Grossberg, 1987; Minsky & Papert, 1988; Pavel, 1990; Rager, 1990). At present, understanding of these systems is simply inadequate to support a detailed description of a network's knowledge and functioning. In several recent studies attempts have been made to analyze the internal representations established through training of a complex network —for example, by applying cluster analysis techniques to patterns of activation across hidden units elicited by different inputs (see, e.g., Gorman & Sejnowski, 1988; Hanson & Burr, 1990; Sejnowski & Rosenberg, 1987). These important studies reflect a recognition of the need to understand connectionist networks more thoroughly. In fact, in a later section I suggest that the promise of con-nectionism lies in work of this genre. For present purposes, however, the rele-vant point is that techniques for network analysis are currently rather crude. Although these techniques have yielded some interesting insights, they are not adequate to provide a detailed understanding of a network's knowledge or functioning.[3] Thus, although we may understand in detail the architecture, input and output representations, individual unit functioning, and learning procedures for the Seidenberg and McClelland (1989) network, we can achieve at best a vague and general understanding of how the network accomplishes word–nonword discrimination, or orthography–phonology conversion. This point may perhaps be brought home by noting that the Seidenberg and McClelland network incorporates more than 1,000 units, and more than 250,000 weighted connections between units. Seidenberg and McClelland's (1989) net-work simulation cannot, then, remedy the vagueness in the verbal formulation of their theory.

The Nature of Connectionist Simulations   It may seem odd or even obviously incorrect to describe the Seidenberg and McClelland (1989) theory as vague, given that the ability to instantiate a theory in a computer simulation is gener-ally taken to indicate that the theory has been specified explicitly. However, connectionist modeling is not simulation in the traditional sense. A modeler developing a traditional computer simulation must build in each of the crucial features of an independently specified theory. If the theory is not explicitly formulated, the simulation cannot be built. In connectionist modeling, on the other hand, the modeler may be able to proceed on the basis of vague and fragmentary theoretical notions, because much of the work is left to the learning algorithm. In a sense the modeler "grows" the network rather than building it. And, just as a gardener's ability to grow a plant from a seed does not imply that the gardener has an explicit theory of plant physiology, the ability to grow a network that mimics in some respects a human cognitive function does not demonstrate that the modeler has an explicit theory of that function. In essence, the learning algorithms constitute procedures for creating complex systems we do not adequately understand.[4]

Development of a connectionist simulation might be taken as evidence of an explicit theory if the modeler built the simulation by specifying the connection weights directly, rather than growing the simulation by delegating this work to the learning algorithm. However, neither the Seidenberg and McClelland theory nor our understanding of complex connectionist networks is sufficiently detailed to sustain such an endeavor.

Relating Simulations to Theories

Limited understanding of complex connectionist networks also represents a serious problem for attempts to establish that a network simulation is germane to a set of theoretical claims. Even given an explicit theory, it may be difficult or impossible to (1) determine whether a particular network actually instantiates the theory's assumptions, or (2) assess the extent to which theory-relevant as opposed to theory-irrelevant features of the network are responsible for its successes and failures in reproducing phenomena.

Does the Network Simulate the Theory?   Consider as an example Seidenberg and McClelland's (1989) theoretical claim that a single mechanism accomplishes orthography-to-phonology mapping for words and nonwords. Given this claim, it is important to consider whether the simulation actually performs orthography–phonology conversion for words and nonwords with a single mechanism. In one sense it certainly does, because processing of both words and nonwords is accomplished by a single network. However, one could argue by a similar logic that all human cognitive processes involve a single mechanism, because all are implemented by a single organ (i.e., the brain).

Thus, the issue is not whether there is some level of description at which the Seidenberg and McClelland (1989) network handles words and nonwords with a single mechanism. Rather, the question is whether the network, when characterized at levels relevant for cognitive theorizing (i.e., levels appropriate for stating generalizations about word recognition and naming, for establishing credit and blame, etc.), accomplishes orthography–phonology conversion in the same way for words and nonwords. As I have repeatedly emphasized, however, our understanding of the network at such levels is extremely limited. Hence, Seidenberg and McClelland's (1989) assertions notwithstanding (see, e.g., p. 549), it is unclear whether the network in any interesting sense employs a single mechanism for naming words and nonwords.

Evaluating Successes and Failures   Similar difficulties arise in assessing the implications of a simulation's successes and failures in reproducing specific phenomena. In developing any simulation one must make some choices that are arbitrary from the standpoint of the theory, and introduce some simplifications and idealizations. For example, in the Seidenberg and McClelland (1989) simulation some aspects of the orthographic and phonological representations were essentially arbitrary, as were the settings of several parameters. Further, the phonological representations collapsed some distinctions among phonemes (e.g., the initial sounds in *shin* and *chin* were not distinguished); the network was trained on only 2,897 words, all of which were monosyllabic and most of which were monomorphemic; the procedures for training the network greatly compressed the range of word frequencies actually experienced by a human reader; and so forth.

These arbitrary choices and simplifications do not in and of themselves constitute a weakness of the Seidenberg and McClelland simulation; decisions of this sort must be made in developing any simulation. The difficulties arise from the fact that the functioning of the network is not sufficiently well-understood to assess the consequences of the decisions (although see Seidenberg and McClelland, 1989, for some discussion). Did the network perform as well as it did only, for example, because it was trained on a constrained set of words, or because the frequency range was compressed (Bever, 1992; McCloskey & Cohen, 1989)? Similarly, do the network's shortcomings reflect incidental properties of the simulation, or fundamental problems with the Seidenberg and McClelland (1989) theory? Questions of this sort are difficult for any simulation, but they are made doubly difficult by our limited understanding of connectionist networks.

For example, Besner, Twilley, McCann, and Seergobin (1990) argue that the Seidenberg and McClelland network performs much more poorly than human subjects at lexical decision (i.e., word/nonword discrimination). But what are the implications of this deficiency? Does it reflect some arbitrary feature(s) of the network's representations, architecture, or parameter settings, such that theory-neutral modifications could remedy the problem? Or might the responsibility lie in the limited set of words to which the network was exposed, so that training with a larger set would improve its lexical decision performance? Or is the problem more fundamental, reflecting feature(s) of the simulation that are central to the underlying theory (e.g., the putative absence of lexical representations)? The unfortunate fact is that our understanding of the network is insufficient to answer these questions, or even to suggest systematic approaches toward finding answers. We might undertake an empirical exploration of various network modifications chosen on largely pretheoretical grounds—we could, for example, try more (or fewer) hidden units or a different form of orthographic representation. However, if we succeed thereby in improving the network's lexical decision performance the success will be largely due to chance, and if we fail we will not know how to interpret the failure.

Connectionist Networks As Demonstrations

In response to these arguments it might be suggested that connectionist networks, at least at present, are properly viewed not as simulations of fully developed theories, but rather as more limited demonstrations of specific theoretical points concerning human cognition. For example, even if Seidenberg and McClelland (1989) have not presented an explicit theory, perhaps their network at least demonstrates that naming of words and nonwords can be accomplished without lexical representations, and hence that a theory of human lexical processing need not necessarily postulate such representations.

Unfortunately, this view of connectionist modeling does not escape the above-noted problems of relating network to theory. For example, we do not know whether the Seidenberg and McClelland network, characterized at appropriate levels, in fact lacks lexical representations. Also, whatever the nature of the mechanism(s) implemented in the network, we do not know whether these mechanisms are capable of achieving word-naming performance comparable to that of human subjects under the conditions humans typically encounter (e.g., exposure to at least tens of thousands of different words with widely varying frequencies). Finally, we do not know whether the implemented mechanisms are adequate to reproduce other human phenomena that have been thought to require lexical representations. (Indeed, the current network's poor lexical decision performance provides some grounds for skepticism on this point.) Thus, the Seidenberg and McClelland results do not demonstrate (for lexical processing in general, or even for naming in particular) that performance comparable to that of humans can be achieved in the absence of lexical representations.

A Role for Connectionist Modeling

Am I suggesting, then, that connectionist modeling has no role to play in cognitive science? Definitely not. In my view connectionist models hold substantial promise as tools for developing cognitive theories, if viewed from an appropriate perspective. Specifically, it may prove fruitful to think of connectionist models as akin to animal models of human functions or disorders (e.g., an animal model of working memory, or an animal model of attention deficit disorder).

Animal Models

In work with an animal model, some animal system thought to share critical features with a human system of interest is studied with the aim of shedding light on the human system. By studying the animal model rather than working directly with the human system, one may be able to carry out manipulations that could not be performed on human subjects (e.g., lesions to particular brain structures, histological examination of brain tissue). The model system may also be somewhat simpler than the human system, and therefore more amenable to analysis.

Thus, an animal model is not a theory (or a simulation of a theory), but rather an object of study. In work with an animal model the goal is to elucidate the structure and functioning of the animal system, and on this basis to formulate a theory of the corresponding human system. Of course, one does not assume that insights gained through study of the animal system will necessarily apply without modification to the human system. Instead, it is simply assumed that because the animal system may be similar in relevant respects to the human system, studying the former may aid in developing a theory of the latter.

Connectionist Networks as Analogues to Animal Models

Connectionist networks should, I suggest, be viewed from a similar perspective. A network that exhibits some of the phenomena observed for a cognitive process such as naming may perhaps resemble in relevant respects the mechanisms underlying the process in humans. If by studying the network we can gain some understanding of its structure and functioning at a level relevant for cognitive theorizing, this understanding might aid in developing a theory of the human cognitive process (see Cummins & Schwarz, 1987, for a similar suggestion). For example, if one could determine how the Seidenberg and McClelland (1989) network accomplishes word–nonword discrimination and orthography–phonology mapping, this information might contribute to development of an explicit theory of human word recognition and naming.[5]

Connectionist networks share both the advantages and disadvantages of animal models. On the positive side, networks can be subjected to manipulations that are not possible with human subjects. For example, one can observe the effects of varying the network architecture while holding the training process constant; one can subject a network to several different forms of damage, and restore it to its "premorbid" state; one can inspect connection weights and activation patterns across hidden units; and so forth. On the other side of the ledger, a network that reproduces human phenomena in some cognitive domain may not actually resemble in critical respects the mechanisms mediating human performance (Hanson & Burr, 1990; Lamberts & d'Ydewalle, 1990). Perhaps, for example, the Seidenberg and McClelland (1989) network does not accomplish word recognition or naming in anything like the manner of humans. If this were the case, then analyses of the network might be uninformative or even misleading with respect to human lexical processing. Thus, careful attention must be paid to issues concerning the extent to which a network shares critical features with the human mechanisms of interest.[6]

It must also be emphasized that connectionist modeling does not represent an atheoretical procedure for discovering cognitive theories. In the absence of at least some general theoretical premises, a modeler would be reduced to random exploration of the huge model space defined by possible network architectures, representations, training procedures, and so forth. Similarly, analyses of network functioning taking the form of atheoretical fishing expeditions are unlikely to prove fruitful (Hanson & Burr, 1990). Modeling is an aid to, but not a substitute for, theoretical work (Olson & Caramazza, 1991).

The Practice of Connectionist Modeling

To a large extent, connectionist cognitive modeling efforts have focused on demonstrating that a network can recapitulate certain human phenomena in the domain of interest. Analysis of network functioning has been considered interesting, but perhaps not essential to the enterprise (although see Hanson & Burr, 1990). The analogy to animal models suggests that some refocusing of effort is needed. Demonstrations that a network reproduces human phenomena are certainly important, as such demonstrations may contribute to assessing whether a network is similar in relevant respects to the human cognitive mechanisms under investigation. However, attention must also be directed toward elucidating the structure and functioning of the network, and applying the insights gained thereby in developing an explicit theory of the human mechanisms. On this view, analyses of the network at levels relevant for cognitive theorizing are crucial. Further, the ultimate aim of the endeavor is not merely to understand the network, but rather to develop a theory that characterizes human cognitive mechanisms independent of any particular network.

Prospects for Connectionism

It remains to be seen how fruitful connectionist modeling will prove in advancing our understanding of human cognition. The capabilities of connectionist networks are impressive, and study of these networks appears to hold promise for shedding light on such features of human cognition as content-addressable memory, learning, categorization (Estes, 1988, 1991; Gluck & Bower, 1988), and effects of brain damage (Hinton & Shallice, 1991; McCloskey & Lindemann, 1992; Patterson et al., 1989). However, in assessing the prospects for connectionism there are at least two imponderables. First, it is not clear how fast and how far we will progress in attempting to analyze connectionist networks at levels relevant for cognitive theorizing. Indeed, Suppes (1990) offers the pessimistic conjecture that connectionist networks may be computationally irreducible, such that "no analysis in terms smaller than the nets themselves will give anything like a really detailed and accurate picture of how they work" (p. 508).

The second, and closely related, imponderable concerns the terms in which a connectionist theory should be stated. As we have seen, a description of network architecture, input and output representations, individual unit functioning, and training procedures does not suffice to delineate a network's functioning at a level relevant for cognitive theorizing, and certainly does not constitute a theory of a human cognitive process. Thus far, however, no alternative framework or vocabulary has emerged for characterizing networks or formulating connectionist cognitive theories. It may turn out that connectionist networks can be aptly characterized in terms of computations carried out on symbols (although perhaps symbols representing information at a level below that of whole concepts such as *dog* or *tree*; see, e.g., Fodor & Pylyshyn, 1988). In this case, connectionist modeling might lead to the development of detailed and explicit cognitive theories that were not, however, different in kind from traditional symbol-processing theories. Alternatively, connectionist work may eventuate in development of a new form of cognitive theory that does not employ symbols and rules as explanatory concepts. At present, however, this new form of theory is a possibility and not a reality.

The appeal of connectionism within cognitive science stems in part from a (not entirely unwarranted) dissatisfaction with traditional theoretical frameworks (see, e.g., Bechtel & Abrahamsen, 1991; McClelland, Rumelhart, & Hinton, 1986; Seidenberg, 1988; Smolensky, 1987, 1988). Hence, if connectionist modeling led either to more detailed, explicit, and widely applicable symbol-processing theories, or to a new form of theory that was more satisfactory for at least some purposes, the contribution of the connectionist approach would be important and positive. In any event, the coming years are certain to be interesting and productive for cognitive scientists, as we grapple with the fascinating and difficult questions raised by connectionism.

Acknowledgments

Preparation of this article was supported by NIH grant NS21047. I thank Bill Badecker, Alfonso Caramazza, Margrethe Lindemann, and Brenda Rapp for their helpful comments.

Notes

1. These difficulties cannot be resolved simply by providing more details about the network. Suppose that in addition to the above-mentioned information, I also present all of the connection weights established by the training procedure. Although I have now provided all of the information needed to duplicate the network exactly, my description would still not constitute a theory of word recognition and naming. First, a listing of connection weights would not identify the theory-relevant features of the network, and in fact would introduce additional problems of separating crucial from incidental properties. Presumably, the configuration of weights generated in a particular network training run is merely an exemplar of a more general class, any member of which would count as an implementation of the same theory of word recognition and

naming. However, a listing of weights does not specify what properties of a weight configuration are crucial for instantiating a theory, and what properties are irrelevant. Furthermore, merely listing the large number of weights would not illuminate how the network performed orthography–phonology conversion, or word/nonword discrimination.

2. Further, it is not clear to what extent the theoretical proposals are dependent upon the connectionist view that cognition involves propagation of activation within networks of simple processing units. That is, the contributions of connectionist theorists may have more to do with their insights into the abstract nature of cognitive processes (e.g., that many such processes involve satisfaction of multiple soft constraints) than with the specific connectionist conceptions of the computational machinery instantiating these processes.

3. Seidenberg and McClelland (1989, pp. 540–543) describe efforts to analyze their network's processing of a few specific words. However, these efforts were less formal and systematic than those of the above-cited researchers, and yielded little more than a few vague and fragmentary glimpses of internal network representations.

4. A related point may be made with respect to the learning process itself. The ability to grow a network that reproduces some human cognitive phenomena does not imply that the modeler has an explicit theory of how the cognitive function in question develops. Although we have procedures for training a network, we do not fully understand what the network has learned at the completion of, or at any time during, training. Hence, we can hardly be said to understand the learning process.

5. It is important to emphasize that in speaking here of theories, I have in mind functional as opposed to neural theories. It is not at all clear that connectionist networks resemble neural circuits in ways relevant to understanding the implementation of cognitive processes in the brain (e.g., Douglas & Martin, 1991; Olson & Caramazza, 1991).

6. It is worth noting that even a network exhibiting performance clearly discrepant from that of human subjects might nevertheless contribute to understanding of the human system. If the inability of a network to reproduce certain human phenomena could be tied to particular features of the network, then the failure might be interpreted as evidence that the human system differs from the network in these features. For example, if the poor lexical decision performance of the Seidenberg and McClelland (1989) network turned out to reflect the network's (putative) lack of lexical representations, the network's performance might be taken to suggest that an adequate theory of human lexical processing will need to postulate such representations (see Besner et al., 1990).

References

Anderson, J. A., & Rosenfeld, E. (Eds.). (1988). *Neurocomputing*. Cambridge, MA: MIT Press.

Barnden, J. A., & Pollack, J. B. (Eds.). (1991). *Advances in connectionist and neural computation theory. Vol. 1: High-level connectionist models*. Norwood, NJ: Ablex.

Bechtel, W. (1987). Connectionism and the philosophy of mind: An overview. *The Southern Journal of Philosophy, 26*(Suppl.), 17–41.

Bechtel, W., & Abrahamsen, A. (1991). *Connectionism and the mind*. Cambridge, MA: Basil Blackwell.

Besner, D., Twilley, L., McCann, R. S., & Seergobin, K. (1990). On the association between connectionism and data: Are a few words necessary? *Psychological Review, 97*, 432–446.

Bever, T. G. (1992). The demons and the beast—Modular and nodular kinds of knowledge. In R. Ronan & N. Sharkey (Eds.), *Connectionist approaches to natural language processing*. Hillsdale, NJ: Erlbaum.

Clark, A. (1990). *Microcognition: Philosophy, cognitive science, and parallel distributed processing*. Cambridge, MA: MIT Press.

Chandrasekaran, B., Goel, A., & Allemang, D. (1988). Information processing abstractions: The message still counts more than the medium. *Behavioral and Brain Sciences, 11*, 26–27.

Cummins, R., & Schwarz, G. (1987). Radical connectionism. *The Southern Journal of Philosophy,* *26*(Suppl.), 43–61.

Douglas, R. J., & Martin, K. A. C. (1991). Opening the grey box. *Trends in Neuroscience, 14,* 286–293.

Dyer, M. G. (1988). The promise and problems of connectionism. *Behavioral and Brain Sciences, 11,* 32–33.

Estes, W. K. (1988). Toward a framework for combining connectionist and symbol-processing models. *Journal of Memory and Language, 27,* 196–212.

Estes, W. K. (1991). Cognitive architectures from the standpoint of an experimental psychologist. *Annual Review of Psychology, 42,* 1–28.

Fodor, J. A., & Pylyshyn, Z. W. (1988). Connectionism and cognitive architecture: A critical analysis. *Cognition, 28,* 3–71.

Gluck, M. A., & Bower, G. H. (1988). From conditioning to category learning: An adaptive network model. *Journal of Experimental Psychology: General, 117,* 227–247.

Gorman, R. P., & Sejnowski, T. J. (1988). Analysis of hidden units in a layered network trained to classify sonar targets. *Neural Networks, 1,* 75–89.

Grossberg, S. (1987). Competitive learning: From interactive activation to adaptive resonance. *Cognitive Science, 11,* 23–63.

Hanson, S. J., & Burr, D. J. (1990). What connectionist models learn: Learning and representation in connectionist networks. *Behavioral and Brain Sciences, 13,* 471–518.

Hinton, G. E., & Shallice, T. (1991). Lesioning an attractor network: Investigations of acquired dyslexia. *Psychological Review, 98,* 74–95.

Humphreys, G. W. (1989). Introduction: Parallel distributed processing and psychology. In R. G. M. Morris (Ed.), *Parallel distributed processing: Implications for psychology and neurobiology* (pp. 65–75). Oxford: Clarendon Press.

Lamberts, K., & d'Ydewalle, G. (1990). What can psychologists learn from hidden-unit nets? *Behavioral and Brain Sciences, 13,* 499–500.

Massaro, D. W. (1988). Some criticisms of connectionist models of human performance. *Journal of Memory and Language, 27,* 213–234.

McClelland, J. L. (1988). Connectionist models and psychological evidence. *Journal of Memory and Language, 27,* 107–123.

McClelland, J. L., & Rumelhart, D. E. (Eds.). (1986). *Parallel distributed processing: Explorations in the microstructure of cognition. Vol. 2: Psychological and biological models.* Cambridge, MA: MIT Press.

McClelland, J. L., Rumelhart, D. E., & Hinton, G. E. (1986). The appeal of parallel distributed processing. In D. E. Rumelhart & J. L. McClelland (Eds.), *Parallel distributed processing: Explorations in the microstructure of cognition. Vol. 1: Foundations* (pp. 3–44). Cambridge, MA: MIT Press.

McCloskey, M., & Cohen, N. J. (1989). Catastrophic interference in connectionist networks: The sequential learning problem. In G. H. Bower (Ed.), *The psychology of learning and motivation: Advances in research and theory, 24* (pp. 109–165). San Diego: Academic Press.

McCloskey, M., & Lindemann, A. M. (1992). MATHNET: Preliminary results from a distributed model of arithmetic fact retrieval. In J. I. D. Campbell (Ed.), *The nature and origin of mathematical skills.* New York: Elsevier.

Minsky, M. L., & Papert, S. A. (1988). *Perceptrons: An introduction to computational geometry* (Expanded ed.). Cambridge, MA: MIT Press.

Morris, R. G. M. (Ed). (1989). *Parallel distributed processing: Implications for psychology and neurobiology.* Oxford: Clarendon Press.

Olson, A., & Caramazza, A. (1991). The role of cognitive theory in neuropsychological research. In S. Corkin, J. Grafman, & F. Boller (Eds.), *Handbook of neuropsychology* (pp. 287–309). Amsterdam: Elsevier.

Patterson, K., Seidenberg, M. S., & McClelland, J. L. (1989). Connections and disconnections: Acquired dyslexia in a computational model of reading processes. In R. G. M. Morris (Ed.),

Parallel distributed processing: Implications for psychology and neurobiology (pp. 132–181). Oxford: Clarendon Press.

Pavel, M. (1990). Learning from learned networks. *Behavioral and Brain Sciences, 13*, 503–504.

Pinker, S., & Mehler, J. (Eds.). (1988). *Connections and symbols.* Cambridge, MA: MIT Press.

Pinker, S., & Prince, A. (1988). On language and connectionism: Analysis of a parallel distributed processing model of language acquisition. *Cognition, 28*, 73–193.

Rager, J. E. (1990). The analysis of learning needs to be deeper. *Behavioral and Brain Sciences, 13*, 505–506.

Rumelhart, D. E., & McClelland, J. L. (Eds.). (1986). *Parallel distributed processing: Explorations in the microstructure of cognition. Vol. 1: Foundations.* Cambridge, MA: MIT Press.

Seidenberg, M. S. (1988). Cognitive neuropsychology and language: The state of the art. *Cognitive Neuropsychology, 5*, 403–426.

Seidenberg, M. S. (1989). Visual word recognition and pronunciation: A computational model and its implications. In W. Marslen-Wilson (Ed.), *Lexical representation and process* (pp. 25–74). Cambridge, MA: MIT Press.

Seidenberg, M. S., & McClelland, J. L. (1989). A distributed, developmental model of word recognition and naming. *Psychological Review, 96*, 523–568.

Sejnowski, T. J., & Rosenberg, C. R. (1987). Parallel networks that learn to pronounce English text. *Complex Systems, 1*, 145–168.

Smolensky, P. (1987). The constituent structure of connectionist mental states: A reply to Fodor and Pylyshyn. *The Southern Journal of Philosophy, 26*(Suppl.), 137–161.

Smolensky, P. (1988). On the proper treatment of connectionism. *Behavioral and Brain Sciences, 11*, 1–74.

Suppes, P. (1990). Problems of extension, representation, and computational irreducibility. *Behavioral and Brain Sciences, 13*, 507–508.

Computation in the Brain

Chapter 36

Neuropsychological Inference with an Interactive Brain: A Critique of the "Locality" Assumption

Martha J. Farah

The fact that the various parts of the encephalon, though anatomically distinct, are yet so intimately combined and related as to form a complex whole, makes it natural to suppose that lesions of greater or lesser extent in any one part should produce such general perturbation of the functions of the organ as a whole as to render it at least highly difficult to trace any uncomplicated connection between the symptoms produced and the lesion as such.
Ferrier (1886)

1 Introduction

Brain damage often has rather selective effects on cognitive functioning, impairing some abilities while sparing others. Psychologists interested in describing the "functional architecture" of the mind, that is, the set of relatively independent information-processing subsystems that underlies human intelligence, have recognized that patterns of cognitive deficit and sparing after brain damage are a potentially useful source of constraints on the functional architecture. In this chapter I wish to focus on one of the assumptions that frequently underlies the use of neuropsychological data in the development of cognitive theories.

1.1 The Locality Assumption
Cognitive neuropsychologists generally assume that damage to one component of the functional architecture will have exclusively "local" effects. In other words, the nondamaged components will continue to function normally and the patient's behavior will therefore manifest the underlying impairment in a relatively direct and straightforward way. This assumption follows from a view of the cognitive architecture as "modular," in the sense of being "informationally encapsulated" (Fodor, 1983; see also multiple book review, *BBS* 8(1) 1985).

According to this version of the modularity hypothesis, the different components of the functional architecture do not interact with one another except when one has completed its processing, at which point it makes the end product available to other components. Even these interactions are limited, so that a given component receives input from relatively few (perhaps just one) of the other components. Thus, a paradigm module takes its input from just one other component of the functional architecture (e.g., phonetic analysis would be hypothesized to take its input just from prephonetic acoustic analysis), carries out its computations without being affected by other information available in other components (even potentially relevant information, such as semantic context), and then presents its output to the next component in line, for which it might be the sole input (e.g., the auditory input lexicon, which would again be hypothesized to take only phonetic input).

In such an architecture, each component minds its own business and knows nothing about most of the other components. What follows for a damaged system is that most of the components will be oblivious to the loss of any one, carrying on precisely as before. If the components of the functional architecture were informationally encapsulated then the locality assumption would hold; the removal of one component would have only very local effects on the functioning of the system as a whole, affecting performance only in those tasks that directly call upon the damaged component. Indeed, one of Fodor's (1983) other criteria for modulehood, which he suggests will coincide with informational encapsulation, is that modules make use of dedicated hardware and can therefore be selectively impaired by local brain damage. In contrast, if the different components of the cognitive system were highly interactive, each one depending on input from many or most of the others, then damage to any one component could significantly modify the functioning of the others.

Several cognitive neuropsychologists have pointed out that informational encapsulation and the locality of the effects of brain damage are assumptions, and they have expressed varying degrees of confidence in them (Allport 1985; Caplan 1981; Humphreys & Riddoch 1987; Kinsbourne 1971; Kosslyn & Van Kleek 1990; Moscovitch & Umiltà 1990; Shallice 1988; von Klein 1977). For example, Shallice (1988, Ch. 2) endorses a weaker and more general version of modularity than Fodor's, according to which components of the functional architecture can be distinguished, (1) conceptually in terms of their specialized functions and (2) empirically by the relatively selective deficits that ensue upon damage to one of them. He likens this concept of modularity to Posner's (1978) "isolable subsystems" and offers the following criterion from Tulving (1983) for distinguishing modular systems with some mutual dependence among modules from fully interactive systems: components of a modular system in this weaker sense may not operate as efficiently when other components have been damaged but they will nevertheless continue to function roughly normally. According to this view, the locality assumption is not strictly true, but it is nevertheless roughly true: one would not expect *pronounced* changes in the functioning of nondamaged components.

Closely related to the locality assumption is the "transparency assumption" of Caramazza (1984; 1986). Although different statements of this assumption leave room for different interpretations, it is probably weaker than the locality assumption. Particularly in more recent statements (e.g., Caramazza 1992), it appears transparency requires only that the behavior of the damaged system be *understandable* in terms of the functional architecture of the normal system. Changes in the functioning of nondamaged components are not considered a violation of the transparency assumption so long as they are understandable. In particular, interactivity and consequent nonlocal effects are permitted; presumably only if the nonlocal interactions became unstable and chaotic would the transparency assumption be violated.

Unlike the weaker transparency assumption, the locality assumption licenses quite direct inferences from the manifest behavioral deficit to the identity of the underlying damaged cognitive component, inferences of the form "selective deficit in ability *A* implies a component of the functional architecture dedicated to *A*." Obviously such inferences can go awry if the selectivity of the deficit is not real, for example, if the tasks testing *A* are merely harder than the comparison tasks, if there are other abilities that are not tested but are also impaired, or if a combination of functional lesions is mistaken for a single one (see Shallice 1988, Ch. 10, for a thorough discussion of other possibilities for misinterpreting dissociations in a weakly modular theoretical framework). In addition, even simple tasks tap several components at once, and properly designed control tasks are needed to pinpoint the deficient component and absolve intact components downstream. However, assuming that the relevant ability has been experimentally isolated and that the deficit is truly selective, the locality assumption allows us to delineate and characterize the components of the functional architecture in a direct, almost algorithmic way.[1]

1.2 The Locality Assumption is Ubiquitous in Cognitive Neuropsychology
At this point the reader may think that the locality assumption is naive and that the direct inferences that it licenses constitute a mindless reification of deficits as components of the cognitive architecture, something "good" cognitive neuropsychologists would not do. Note, however, that the locality assumption is justifiable in terms of informational encapsulation. Furthermore, whether or not this seems an adequate justification, many of the best-known findings in neuropsychology fit this form of inference. A few examples will be given here and three more will be discussed in detail later (perusal of recent journals and textbooks in cognitive neuropsychology will reveal many more examples).

With the domain of reading, phonological dyslexics show a selective deficit in tasks that require grapheme-to-phoneme translation; they are able to read real words (which can be read by recognizing the word as a whole), they can copy and repeat nonwords (demonstrating intact graphemic and phonemic representation), but they cannot read nonwords, which must be read by grapheme-to-phoneme translation. This has been interpreted as an impairment in a grapheme-to-phoneme translation mechanism and hence as evidence for the existence of such a mechanism in the normal architecture (e.g., Coltheart 1985). Similarly, in surface dyslexia a selective deficit in reading irregular words with preserved regular word and nonword reading has been used to identify a deficit in whole-word recognition and hence to infer a whole-word reading mechanism distinct from the grapheme-to-phoneme route (e.g., Coltheart 1985).

In the production and understanding of spoken language, some patients are selectively impaired in processing closed class, or "function" words, leading to the conclusion that these lexical items are represented by a separate system, distinct from open class or "content" words (e.g., Zurif 1980).

In the domain of vision, some right hemisphere-damaged patients show an apparently selective impairment in the recognition of objects viewed from unusual perspectives. This has been taken to imply the existence of a stage or stages of visual information processing concerned specifically with shape constancy (e.g., Warrington 1985). Highly selective deficits in face recognition have been taken to support the existence of a specialized module for face recognition, distinct from more general-purpose recognition mechanisms (e.g., DeRenzi 1986).

In the domain of memory, the finding that patients can be severely impaired in learning facts and other so-called declarative or explicit knowledge while displaying normal learning of skills and other forms of implicit knowledge is interpreted as evidence for multiple learning systems, one of which is dedicated to the acquisition of declarative knowledge (e.g., Squire 1992).

Some of these inferences may well be proved wrong in the light of further research. For example, perhaps there is a confounding between the factor of interest and the true determinant of the deficit. In the case of aphasics who seem selectively impaired at processing closed class words, perhaps speech stress pattern, and not lexical class, determines the boundaries of the deficit. Critical thinkers may find reasons to question the inferences in any or all of the examples given above. However, note that in most cases the question will concern the empirical specifics of the case, such as stress pattern versus lexical class. In the course of scientific debate on these and other deficits, the *form* of the inference is rarely questioned. If we can truly establish a selective deficit in ability A then it seems reasonable to attribute the deficit to a lesion of some component of the functional architecture that is dedicated to A, that is, necessary for A and necessary only for A. We are, of course, thereby assuming that the effects of the lesion on the functioning of the system are local to the lesioned component.

1.3 Two Empirical Issues about the Locality Assumption
Although it is reasonable to assume that the effects of a lesion are confined to the operation of the lesioned components and the relatively small number of

components downstream in a system with informationally encapsulated modules, we do not yet know whether the brain is such a system. There is, in fact, some independent reason to believe it is not. Neurologists have long noted the highly interactive nature of brain organization and the consequent tendency for local damage to unleash new emergent organizations or modes of functioning in the remaining system (e.g., Ferrier 1886; Jackson 1873). Of course, the observations that led to these conclusions were not primarily of cognitive disorders. Therefore, whether or not the locality assumption holds in the domain of cognitive impairments, at least to a good approximation, is an open empirical question.

Note that we should be concerned more about "good approximations" than precise generalizations to neuropsychological methodology. As already mentioned, Shallice (1988) has pointed out that modularity versus interactionism is a matter of degree. From the point of view of neuropsychological methodology, if nonlocal interactions were to modulate weakly the behavior of patients after brain damage, this would not necessarily lead to wrong inferences using the locality assumption. In such a case, in which the remaining parts of the system act ever-so-slightly differently following damage, the cognitive neuropsychologist would simply fail to account for 100% of the variance in the data (not a novel experience for most of us) but would make the correct inference about functional architecture. If deviations from locality were a first-order effect, however, then the best-fitting theory of the data using the locality assumption would be false.

There is a second question concerning the locality assumption: Is it really indispensable to cognitive neuropsychology? Must we abandon all hope of relating patient behavior to theories of the normal functional architecture if lesions in one part of the system can change the functioning of other parts? Like the first question, this one too is a matter of empirical truth or falsehood.

Nevertheless, unlike many empirical questions, these two are not of the type that lend themselves to single critical experiments. They concern very general properties of the functional architecture of cognition and our ability to make scientific inferences about complex systems using all the formal and informal methods and types of evidence available to us. The most fruitful approach to answering these two questions would therefore involve an analysis of the body of cognitive neuropsychological research, or at least an extensive sample of it.

As a starting point, I will describe three different neuropsychological dissociations that have been used to make inferences about the functional architecture of the mind. The aspect of cognition under investigation in each case is different: semantic memory, visual attention, and the relation between visual recognition and awareness. What all three have in common is the use of the locality assumption. For each I will explore alternative inferences about the functional architecture that are not constrained by the locality assumption.

How will such explorations answer the questions posed above? We can assess the empirical basis for the locality assumption by comparing the conclusions about functional architecture that are arrived at with and without it. Specifically, we can determine which conclusions are preferable, in the sense of being simpler and according better with other, independent evidence about the functional architecture. If the locality assumption generally leads to preferable conclusions, this suggests that we are probably justified in using it. However, if it often leads to nonpreferable conclusions, this suggests we should not assume that the effects of brain damage on the functioning of the cognitive architecture are local. The question of whether it is possible to draw inferences about the functional architecture from neuropsychological dissociations without the locality assumption will also be addressed by the degree to which sensible conclusions can be reached without it.

1.4 An Architecture for Interactive Processing
Of course, comparisons between the results of inferences made with and without the locality assumption will be meaningful only if both types of inferences are constrained in principled ways. The locality assumption is one type of constraint on the kinds of functional architectures that can be inferred from a neuropsychological dissociation. It limits the elements in our explanation of a given neuropsychological deficit to just those in the normal functional architecture (minus the damaged component), operating in their normal fashion. If we simply eliminate that constraint without replacing it with other principled constraints on how local damage affects the remaining parts of the system then the comparison proposed above will not be fair to the locality assumption. We could, of course, pick the simplest, most appealing model of the normal functional architecture and say "the way in which the remaining parts of the system change their functioning after damage produces this deficit," without saying why we chose to hypothesize *that* particular change in functioning as opposed to some other that cannot explain the deficit.

The parallel distributed processing (PDP) framework will be used as a source of principled constraints on the ways in which the remaining parts of the system behave after local damage. Computer simulation will be used to test the sufficiency of the PDP hypotheses to account for the dissociations in question. Readers who would like a detailed introduction to PDP are referred to Rumelhart and McClelland's (1986) collection of readings. For present purposes, the relevant principles of PDP are:

Distributed representation of knowledge. In PDP systems, representations consist of patterns of activation distributed over a population of units. Different entities can therefore be represented using the same set of units, because the pattern of activation over the units will be distinctive. Long-term memory knowledge is encoded in the pattern of connection strengths distributed among a population of units.

Graded nature of information processing. In PDP systems, processing is not all or none: representations can be partially active; for example, through partial or subthreshold activation of some of those units that would normally be active. Partial knowledge can be embodied in connection strengths, either before learning has been completed or after partial damage.

Interactivity. The units in PDP models are highly interconnected and thus mutual influence among different parts of the system is the rule rather than the exception. This influence can be excitatory, as when one part of a distributed representation activates the remaining parts (pattern completion), or it can be inhibitory, as when different representations compete with one another to become active or to maintain their activation. Note that interactivity is the aspect of the PDP framework that is most directly incompatible with the locality assumption. If the normal operation of a given part of the system depends on the influence of some other part, it may not operate normally after that other part has been damaged.

The psychological plausibility of PDP is controversial but it need not be definitively established here before proceeding. Instead, just as locality is being identified as an assumption and evaluated, so PDP is to be evaluated as a specific alternative assumption. In addition, as will be discussed further in the "General Discussion" (sect. 3), much of the controversy surrounding PDP concerns its adequacy for language and reasoning. It is possible that the arguments advanced here will not generalize to these cognitive domains.

2 Reinterpreting Dissociations Without the Locality Assumption: Three Case Studies

2.1 The Functional Architecture of Semantic Memory: Category-Specific?

The existence of patients with apparent category-specific impairments in semantic memory knowledge has led to the inference that semantic memory has a categorical organization, with different components dedicated to representing knowledge from different categories. The best-documented forms of category-specific knowledge deficit (as opposed to pure naming or visual recognition deficits) are the deficits in knowledge of living and nonliving things.

2.1.1 Evidence for Selective Impairments in Knowledge of Living and Nonliving Things   Beginning in the 1980s, Warrington and her colleagues began to report the existence of patients with selective impairments in knowledge of either living or nonliving things (Warrington & McCarthy 1983; 1987; Warrington & Shallice 1984). Warrington and Shallice (1984) described four patients who were much worse at identifying living things (animals, plants) than nonliving things (inanimate objects); all four had recovered from herpes encephalitis and had sustained bilateral temporal lobe damage. Two of the patients were studied in detail and showed a selective impairment for living things across a range of tasks, both visual and verbal. Table 36.1 shows examples of their performance

Table 36.1
An impairment in knowledge of living things: Performance on two tasks assessing knowledge of living and nonliving things

Case	Task	
	Living (%)	Nonliving (%)
Picture identification		
JBR	6	90
SBY	0	75
Spoken word definition		
JBR	8	79
SBY	0	52

in a visual identification task (in which they were to identify by name or description the item shown in a colored picture) and in a verbal definition task (in which the names of these same items were presented auditorially and they were to define them). Examples of their definitions are shown in Table 36.2. Other cases of selective impairment in knowledge of living things include additional postencephalitic patients described by Pietrini et al. (1988), Sartori and Job (1988), and Silveri and Gianotti (1988), a patient with encephalitis and strokes described by Newcombe et al. (1994), two head injury patients described by Farah et al. (1991), and a patient with a focal degenerative disease described by Basso et al. (1988). In all these cases there was damage to the temporal regions, known to be bilateral except in Pietrini et al.'s case 1 and the case of Basso et al., where there was evidence only of left temporal damage.

The opposite dissociation, namely, impaired knowledge of nonliving things with relatively preserved knowledge of living things, has also been observed. Warrington and McCarthy (1983; 1987) described two cases of global dysphasia following large left-hemisphere strokes in which semantic knowledge was tested in a series of matching tasks. Table 36.3 shows the results of a matching task in which the subjects were asked to point to the picture in an array that corresponded to a spoken word. Their performance with animals and flowers was more reliable than with nonliving things. One subject was also tested with a completely nonverbal matching task in which different-looking depictions of objects or animals were to be matched to one another in an array; the same selective preservation of knowledge of animals relative to inanimate objects was found.

Although these patients are not entirely normal in their knowledge of the relatively spared category, they are markedly worse at recognizing, defining, or answering questions about items from the impaired category. The existence of a double dissociation makes it unlikely that a sheer difference in difficulty underlies the apparent selectivity of the deficits; some of the studies cited above

Table 36.2
Examples of definitions of living and nonliving things

Case	Definition
Living things	
JBR	Parrot: don't know
	Daffodil: plant
	Snail: an insect animal
	Eel: not well
	Ostrich: unusual
SBY	Duck: an animal
	Wasp: bird that flies
	Crocus: rubbish material
	Holly: what you drink
	Spider: a person looking for things, he was a spider for his nation or country
Nonliving things	
JBR	Tent: temporary outhouse, living home
	Briefcase: small case used by students to carry papers
	Compass: tools for telling direction you are going
	Torch: hand-held light
	Dustbin: bin for putting rubbish in
SBY	Wheelbarrow: object used by people to take material about
	Towel: material used to dry people
	Pram: used to carry people, with wheels and a thing to sit on
	Submarine: ship that goes underneath the sea
	Umbrella: object used to protect you from water that comes

Table 36.3
An impairment in knowledge of nonliving things: Performance on two tasks assessing knowledge of living and nonliving things

	Task		
Case	Animals (%)	Flowers (%)	Objects (%)
Spoken word/picture matching			
VER	86	96	63
YOT	86	86	67
Picture/picture matching			
YOT	100		69

tested several alternative explanations of the impairments in terms of factors other than semantic category (such as name frequency, familiarity, etc.) and failed to support them.

2.1.2 Interpretation of "Living Things" and "Nonliving Things" Deficits Relative to the Functional Architecture of Semantic Memory   Using the locality assumption, the most straightforward interpretation of the double dissociation between knowledge of living and nonliving things is that they are represented by two separate category-specific components of the functional architecture of semantic memory. A related interpretation is that semantic memory is represented using semantic features such as "animate," "domestic," and so on, and that the dissociations described here result from damage to these features (Hillis & Caramazza 1991). In either case, the dissociations seem to imply a functional architecture for semantic memory that is organized along rather abstract semantic or taxonomic lines. Figure 36.1 represents a category-specific model of semantic memory and its relation to visual perception and language.

Warrington and colleagues, however, have suggested an alternative interpretation, according to which semantic memory is fundamentally modality-specific. They argue that selective deficits in knowledge of living and nonliving things may reflect the differential weighting of information from different sensorimotor channels in representing knowledge about these two categories. They have pointed out that living things are distinguished primarily by their sensory attributes, whereas nonliving things are distinguished primarily by their func-

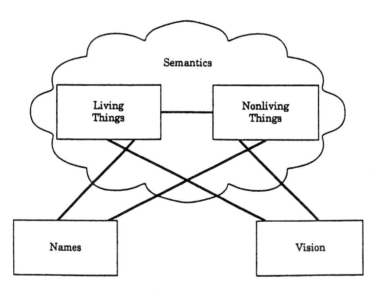

Figure 36.1
Category-specific functional architecture for semantic memory.

tional attributes. For example, our knowledge of an animal such as a leopard, by which we distinguish it from other similar creatures, is predominantly visual. In contrast, our knowledge of a desk, by which we distinguish it from other furniture, is predominantly functional (i.e., what it is used for). Thus, the distinctions between impaired and preserved knowledge in the cases reviewed earlier may not be living/nonliving distinctions per se but sensory/functional distinctions, as illustrated in Figure 36.2.

The modality-specific hypothesis seems preferable to a strict semantic hypothesis for two reasons. First, it is more consistent with what is already known about brain organization. It is well known that different brain areas are dedicated to representing information from specific sensory and motor channels. Functional knowledge could conceivably be tied to the motor system. A second reason for preferring the sensory/functional hypothesis to the living/nonliving hypothesis is that exceptions to the latter have been observed in certain cases. For example, Warrington and Shallice (1984) report that their patients, who were deficient in their knowledge of living things, also had impaired knowledge of gemstones and fabrics. Warrington and McCarthy's (1987) patient, whose knowledge of most nonliving things was impaired, seemed to have retained good knowledge of very large outdoor objects such as bridges or windmills. It is at least possible that our knowledge of these aberrant categories of nonliving things is primarily visual.

Unfortunately, there appears to be a problem with the hypothesis that "living-thing impairments" are just impairments in sensory knowledge, and

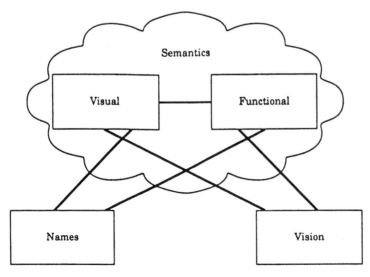

Figure 36.2
Modality-specific functional architecture for semantic memory.

"nonliving-thing impairments" are just impairments in functional knowledge. This hypothesis seems to predict that cases of living-thing impairment should show good knowledge of the functional attributes of living things and cases of nonliving-thing impairment should show good knowledge of the visual attributes of nonliving things. The evidence available in cases of nonliving-thing impairment is limited to performance in matching-to-sample tasks, which does not allow us to distinguish knowledge of visual or sensory attributes from knowledge of functional attributes. However, there does appear to be adequate evidence in cases of living-thing impairment, and in at least some cases it disconfirms these predictions (for review see Farah & McClelland 1991). For example, although the definitions of living things shown in Table 36.2 contain little visual detail, in keeping with the sensory/functional hypothesis, they are also skimpy on functional information. If these cases had lost just their visual semantic knowledge, then why could they not retrieve functional attributes of living things, for example, the fact that parrots are kept as pets and can talk, that daffodils are a spring flower, and so on? A more direct and striking demonstration of the apparently categorical nature of the impairment is provided by Newcombe et al. (1994), whose subject was impaired relative to normal subjects in his ability to sort living things according to such nonsensory attributes as whether or not they were generally found in the United Kingdom, in contrast to his normal performance when the task involved nonliving things.

In sum, the sensory/functional hypothesis seems preferable to the living/ nonliving hypothesis because it more in keeping with what we already know about brain organization. However, it is not able to account for the impaired ability of these patients to retrieve nonvisual information about living things.

2.1.3 Accounting for Category-Specific Impairments with an Interactive Modality-Specific Architecture   Jay McClelland and I have modeled the double dissociation between knowledge of living and nonliving things using a simple autoassociative memory architecture with modality-specific components (Farah & McClelland 1991). We found that a two-component semantic memory system, consisting of visual and functional components, could be lesioned to produce selective impairments in knowledge of living and nonliving things. More important, we found that such a model could account for the impairment of both visual and *functional* knowledge of living things.

The basic architecture of the model is shown in Figure 36.2. There are three pools of units, representing the names of items, the perceived appearances of items, and the semantic memory representations of items. The semantic memory pool is subdivided into visual semantic memory and functional semantic memory. An item, living or nonliving, is represented by a pattern of +1 and −1 activations over the name and visual units, and a pattern of +1 and −1 activations over a *subset* of the semantic units. The relative proportion of visual and functional information comprising the semantic memory representation of living and nonliving things was derived empirically. Normal subjects identified terms in dictionary definitions of the living and nonliving items used by Warrington and Shallice (1984) as referring to either visual or functional properties. This experiment confirmed that visual and functional information was differentially weighted in the definitions of living and nonliving things and the results were used to determine the average proportions of visual and functional units in semantic memory representations of living and nonliving items. For the living items, about seven times as many visual semantic units than functional ones participated in the semantic memory pattern; for nonliving items the proportions were closer to equal. Units of semantic memory not involved in a particular item's representation took the activation value of 0.

The model was trained using the delta rule (Rumelhart et al. 1986) to associate the correct semantic and name portions of its pattern when presented with the visual portion as input, and the correct semantic and visual portions when presented with the name portion as input. It was then damaged by eliminating different proportions of functional or visual semantic units and its performance was assessed in a simulated picture-name matching task. In this task, each item's visual input representation is presented to the network and the pattern activated in the name units is assessed, or each pattern's name is presented and the resultant visual pattern is assessed. The resultant pattern is scored as correct if it is more similar to the correct pattern than to any of the other 19 patterns.

Figure 36.3A shows the averaged picture-to-name and name-to-picture performance of the model for living and nonliving items under varying degrees of damage to visual semantics. With increased damage, the model's performance drops, and it drops more precipitously for living things, in effect showing an impairment for living things comparable in selectivity to that of the patients in the literature. Figure 36.3B shows that the opposite dissociation is obtained when functional semantics is damaged.

The critical challenge for a modality-specific model of semantic memory is to explain how damage could create an impairment in knowledge of living things that includes functional knowledge of living things. To evaluate the model's ability to access functional semantic knowledge, we presented either name or visual input patterns as before, but instead of assessing the match between the resulting output pattern and the correct output pattern, we assessed the match between the resulting pattern in functional semantics and the correct pattern in functional semantics. The normalized dot product of these two patterns, which provides a measure between 0 (completely dissimilar) and 1 (identical), served as the dependent measure.

Figure 36.4 shows the accuracy with which functional semantic memory information could be activated for living and nonliving things after different degrees of damage to visual semantics. At all levels of damage, the ability to retrieve functional semantic knowledge of living things is disproportionately impaired.

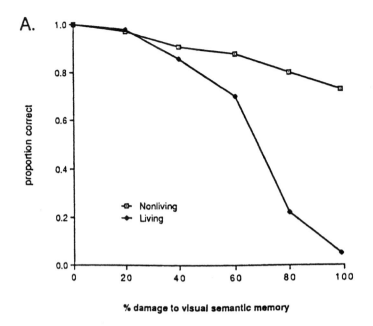

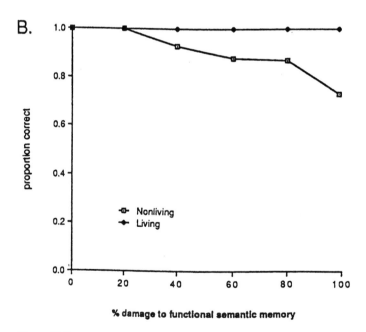

Figure 36.3
A: Effects of different degrees of damage to visual semantic memory units on ability of network to associate names and pictures of living things (diamonds) and non-living things (squares). B: Effects of different degrees of damage to functional semantic memory units on ability of network to associate names and pictures of living things (diamonds) and non-living things (squares).

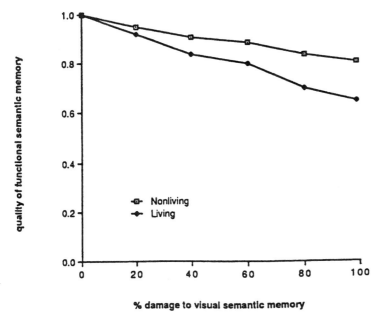

Figure 36.4
Effects of different degrees of damage to visual semantic memory units on ability of network to activate correct pattern in functional semantic memory units for living things (diamonds) and non-living things (squares).

These dissociations can be understood as follows. In the case of picture-name matching, the ability of a given output unit (e.g., a name unit, in the case of picture-to-name matching) to attain its correct activation value depends on the input it receives from the units to which it is connected. These consist of other name units (collateral connections) and both visual and functional semantic units. Hence the more semantic units that have been eliminated, the more the output units are deprived of the incoming activation they need to attain their correct activation values. Because most of the semantic input to the name units of living things is from visual semantics, whereas the same is not true for non-living things, damage to visual semantics will eliminate a greater portion of the activation needed to retrieve the name patterns for living things than nonliving things, and will therefore have a more severe impact on performance.

The same principle applies to the task of activating functional semantics, although in this case the units are being deprived of collateral activation from other semantic units. Thus, when visual semantic units are destroyed, one of the sources of input to the functional semantic units is eliminated. For living things, visual semantics comprises a proportionately larger source of input to functional semantic units than for nonliving things, hence the larger effect for these items.

2.1.4 Relevance of the Locality Assumption for Architecture of Semantic Memory
Contrary to the locality assumption, when visual semantics is damaged the remaining parts of the system do not continue to function as before. In particular, functional semantics, which is part of the nondamaged residual system, becomes impaired in its ability to achieve the correct patterns of activation when given input from vision or language. This is because of the loss of collateral support from visual semantics. The ability of this model to account for the impairment in accessing functional knowledge of living things depends critically upon this nonlocal aspect of its response to damage.

2.2 The Functional Architecture of Visual Attention: A "Disengage" Module?
One of the best-known findings in cognitive neuropsychology concerns the "disengage" deficit that follows unilateral parietal damage. In an elegant series of studies, Posner and his colleagues have shown that parietally damaged patients have a selective impairment in their ability to disengage attention from a location in the spared ipsilesional hemifield in order to move it to a location in the affected contralesional hemifield (e.g., Posner et al. 1984). From this they have inferred the existence of a disengage component in the functional architecture of visual attention.

2.2.1 Evidence for the Disengage Deficit   Posner and colleagues inferred the existence of a disengage operation from experiments using a cued simple reaction time task. The typical task consists of a display, as shown in Figure 36.5A,

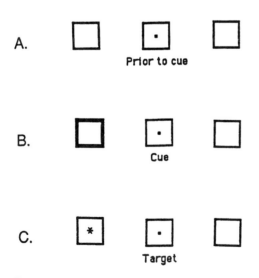

Figure 36.5
Sequence of trial events in the lateralized simple reaction time task: (A) fixation display; (B) cue; (C) target.

which the subject fixates centrally, and in which both "cues" and "targets" are presented. The cue is usually the brightening of one of the boxes, as depicted in Figure 36.5B. This causes attention to be allocated to the region of space around the bright box. The target, usually a simply character such as an asterisk, is then presented in one of the boxes, as shown in Figure 36.5C. The subject's task is to press a button as soon as possible after the appearance of the target, regardless of its location. When the target is "validly" cued, that is, when it occurs on the same side of the display as the cue, reaction times to it are faster than with no cue, because attention is already optimally allocated for perceiving the target. When the target is "invalidly" cued, reaction times are slower than with no cue because attention is focused on the wrong side of space.

When parietally damaged patients are tested in this paradigm, they perform roughly normally on validly cued trials when the target appears on the side of space ipsilateral to their lesion. However, their reaction times are greatly slowed to invalidly cued contralesional targets. It is as if once attention has been engaged on the ipsilesional, or "good," side it cannot be disengaged to be moved to a target occurring on the contralesional, or "bad," side.

2.2.2 Interpretation of the Disengage Deficit Relative to the Functional Architecture of Visual Attention The disproportionate difficulty that parietally damaged patients have in disengaging their attention from the good side to move it to the bad side has led Posner and colleagues to infer the existence of a separate component of the functional architecture of disengaging attention. The resulting model of attention therefore postulates distinct components for engaging and disengaging attention, as shown in Figure 36.6.

2.2.3 Accounting for the Disengage Deficit with an Interactive Architecture that has no "Disengage" Component Jonathan Cohen, Richard Romero, and I (Cohen et al., 1994) have modeled normal cuing effects and the disengage deficit using a simple model of visual attention that contains no "disengage" component.

The model is depicted in Figure 36.7. The first layer consists of visual transducer, or input, units, through which stimuli are presented to the network. These units send their output to visual perception units, which represent the visual percept of a stimulus at a particular location in space. In this simple model there are only two locations in visual space. The visual perception units are connected to two other kinds of units. One is the response unit, which issues the detection response when it has gathered sufficient activation from the perception units to reach its threshold. We will interpret the number of processing cycles that intervene between the presentation of a target to one of the visual transducer units and the attainment of threshold activation in the response unit as a direct correlate of reaction time.

The visual perception units are also connected to a set of spatial attention units corresponding to their spatial location. The spatial units are activated by the visual unit at the corresponding location and reciprocally activate that same

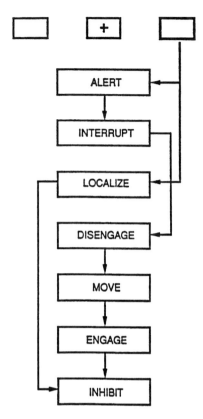

Figure 36.6
Functional architecture of visual attention system derived by Posner et al. (1984) from the study of brain-damaged patients.

unit, creating a resonance that reinforces its activation. These reciprocal connections are what allow the spatial attention units to facilitate perception.

The spatial attention units are also connected to each other. For units corresponding to a given location, these connections are excitatory, that is, they reinforce each other's activation. The connections between units corresponding to different locations are inhibitory. In other words, if the units at one location are more active, they will drive down the activation of the other location's units. These mutually inhibitory connections are what give rise to attentional limitations in the model, that is, the tendency to attend to just one location at a time.

Connection strengths in this model were set by hand. Units in the model can take on activation values between 0 and 1, have a resting value of 0.1, and do not pass on activation to other units until their activation reaches a threshold of 0.9.

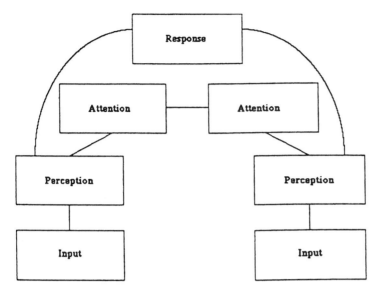

Figure 36.7
Functional architecture of visual attention system as modeled by Cohen et al. (1994).

Before the onset of a trial, all units are at resting level activation except for the attention units, which are set to 0.5 to simulate the subject's allocation of some attention to each of the two possible stimulus locations. The presentation of a cue is simulated by clamping the activation value of one of the visual input units to 1 for the duration of the cuing interval. Presentation of the target is then simulated by clamping the activation value of one of the visual input units to 1. The target is validly cued if the same input unit is activated by both cue and target and invalidly cued if different input units are activated. We also simulated a neutral cuing condition in which no cue preceded the target. The number of processing cycles needed for the perception unit to raise the activation value of the response unit to threshold after target onset is the measure of reaction time. By regressing these numbers of cycles onto the data from normal subjects, we were able to fit the empirical data with our model.

Figure 36.8 shows the data from normal subjects obtained by Posner et al. (1984) and the model's best fit to the data. Why does our model show effects of valid and invalid cuing? In our model, attentional facilitation due to valid cuing is the result of both residual activation from the cue and top-down activation that the attention units give the perception unit at its corresponding location. When the perception unit is activated by the cue, it activates the attention units on that side, which feed activation back to the perception unit, establishing a resonance that strengthens the activation of the target representation. Attentional inhibition due to invalid cuing is the result of the activated attention unit

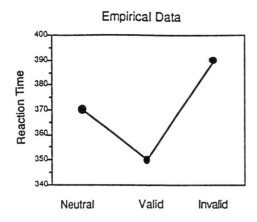

Empirical Data

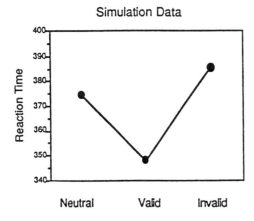

Simulation Data

Figure 36.8
Performance of normal subjects and network in lateralized cued simple reaction time task. Number of cycles needed for "response" unit to reach threshold has been regressed onto reaction times.

at the cued location suppressing the activation of the attention unit at the target location, leading to diminished top-down activation of the target perception unit. That is, the attention units on the cued side inhibit the attention units on the opposite side. As a result, when the target is presented to the opposite side, the attention unit on that side must first overcome the inhibition of the attention unit on the cued side before it can establish a resonance with its perception unit, and response time is therefore prolonged.

This very simple model of attention, which has no disengage component, captures the qualitative relations among the speeds of response in the three different conditions and can be fitted quantitatively to these average speeds with fairly good precision. In this regard, it seems preferable to a model that

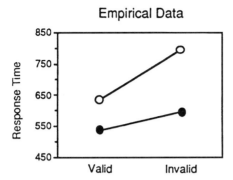

Empirical Data

O Damaged

● Undamaged

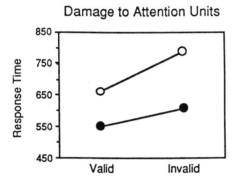

Figure 36.9
Performance of parietally damaged patients and damaged network in lateralized cued reaction time task. Number of cycles needed for "response" units to reach threshold has been regressed onto reaction times.

postulates separate components for orienting, engaging, and disengaging attention. The disengage component, however, was postulated on the basis of the behavior of parietally damaged subjects, not normal subjects. The critical test of this model, therefore, is whether it produces a disengage deficit when damaged.

A subset of the attention units on one side was eliminated and the model was run in the valid and invalid cuing conditions. (No patient data were available for the neutral condition). Figure 36.9 shows the data of Posner et al. (1984) from parietally damaged patients and the simulation results, fitted to the data in the same way as before. Both sets of results show a disengage deficit: a disproportionate slowing from invalid cuing when the target is on the damaged side.

Why does the model show a disengage deficit when its attention units are damaged? The answer lies in the competitive nature of attentional allocation in the model and the imbalance introduced into the competition by unilateral damage. Attentional allocation is competitive, in that once the attention units on one side have been activated, they inhibit attentional activation on the other side. When there are fewer attention units available on the newly stimulated side, the competition is no longer balanced and much more bottom-up activation will be needed on the damaged side before the remaining attention units can overcome the inhibition from the attention units on the intact side to establish a resonance with the perception unit.

One might wonder whether we have really succeeded in simulating the disengage deficit without a disengage component, or whether some part of the model with a different label, such as the attention units or the inhibitory connections between attention units, is actually the disengage component. To answer this question, consider some of the attributes that would define a disengage component. First, it should be brought into play by perception of the target, and not the cue, on a given trial. Second, it should be sued to disengage attention and not for any other function. By these criteria, there is no part of the model that is a disengager. The attention units as well as their inhibitory connections are brought into play by both cue and target presentations. In addition, the attention units are used as much for engaging attention as for disengaging it. We therefore conclude that the disengage deficit is an emergent property of imbalanced competitive interactions among remaining parts of the system that do not contain a distinct component for disengaging attention.

Humphreys and Riddoch (1993) have independently proposed an account of the disengage deficit that does not include a disengage component in the normal architecture. Instead, they suggest that the deficit could be secondary to an impairment in orienting attention or to an overly strong engagement of attention ipsilesionally.

2.2.4 Relevance of the Locality Assumption for Architecture of Visual Attention
After damage to the attention units on one side of the model, the nondamaged attention units on the other side function differently. Specifically, once activated they show a greater tendency to maintain their activation. This is because of the reduced ability of the attention units on the damaged side to recapture activation from the intact side, even when they are receiving bottom-up stimulus activation. The ability of this model to account for the disengage deficit depends critically upon this nonlocal aspect of its response to damage.

2.3 The Functional Architecture of Visual Face Recognition: Separate Components for Visual Processing and Awareness?
Prosopagnosia is an impairment of face recognition that can occur relatively independently of impairments in object recognition and is not caused by impairments in lower-level vision or memory. Prosopagnosic patients are

impaired in tests of face recognition such as naming faces or classifying them according to semantic information (such as occupation); they are also impaired in everyday life situations that call for face recognition. Furthermore, based on their own introspective reports, prosopagnosics do not feel as though they recognize faces; however, when tested using certain indirect techniques, some of these patients do show evidence of face recognition. This has been taken to imply that their impairment lies not in face recognition per se, but in the transfer of the products of their face-recognition system to another system required for conscious awareness. This in turn implies that different components of the functional architecture of the mind are needed to produce perception and awareness of perception.

2.3.1 Evidence for Dissociated Recognition and Awareness of Recognition   Three representative types of evidence will be summarized here. The most widely documented form of "covert" face recognition occurs when prosopagnosics are taught to associate names with photographs of faces. For faces and names that were familiar to the subjects prior to their prosopagnosia, correct pairings are learned faster than incorrect ones (e.g., de Haan et al. 1987b). An example of this type of finding is shown in Table 36.4. It seems to imply that, at some level, the subject must have preserved knowledge of the faces' identities. The other two types of evidence come from reaction time tasks. One measures speed of visual analysis of faces, in which subjects must respond as quickly as possible to whether two photographs depict the same face or different faces. Normal subjects perform this task faster with familiar than unfamiliar faces. Surprisingly, as shown in Table 36.5, a prosopagnosic subject showed the same pattern, again implying that he was able to recognize them (de Haan et al. 1987b). The last task to be reviewed is a kind of semantic priming task. Subjects must classify printed names as actors or politicians as quickly as possible, while on some trials photographs of faces are presented in the background. Even though the

Table 36.4
Performance on correct and incorrect face-name pairings in a face-name relearning task

Trial	1	2	3	4	5	6	7	8	9	10	11	12
Correct pairings	2	1	1	2	1	2	0	3	2	3	2	2
Incorrect pairings	0	0	0	1	1	0	0	0	1	1	0	0

Table 36.5
Speed of visual matching for familiar and unfamiliar (in msec)

	Familiar	Unfamiliar
Prosopagnosic subject	2,795	3,297
Normal subjects	1,228	1,253

Table 36.6
Priming of occupation judgments (in msec)

	Baseline	Unrelated	Related
Prosopagnosic subject	1,565	1,714	1,560
Normal subjects	821	875	815

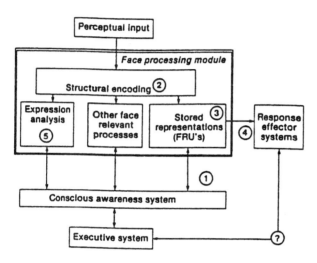

Figure 36.10
Functional architecture of perception and awareness, proposed by de Haan et al. (1992).

faces are irrelevant to the task subjects must perform, they influence reaction times to the names. Specifically, normal subjects are slowed in classifying the names when the faces come from the other occupation category. As shown in Table 36.6, the prosopagnosic patient who was tested in this task showed the same pattern of results, implying that he was unconsciously recognizing the faces fully enough to derive occupation information from them (de Haan et al. 1987a; 1987b).

2.3.2 Interpretation of Covert Recognition Relative to the Functional Architecture of Visual Recognition and Conscious Awareness The dissociation between performance on explicit tests of face recognition and patients' self-reporting of their conscious experience of looking at faces, on the one hand, and performance on implicit tests of face recognition on the other, has suggested to many authors that face recognition and the ability to make conscious use of it depend on different components of the functional architecture. For example, de Haan et al. (1992) interpret covert recognition in terms of the components shown in Figure 36.10, in which separate components of the functional architecture subserve

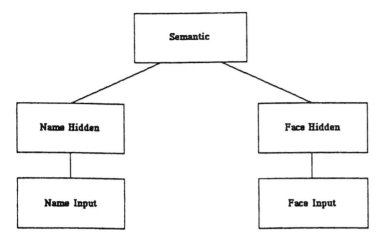

Figure 36.11
Functional architecture of face perception as modeled by Farah et al. (1993).

face recognition and conscious awareness thereof. According to their model, the face-specific visual and mnemonic processing of a face (carried out within the "face processing module") proceeds normally in covert recognition, but the results of this process cannot access the "conscious awareness system" because of a lesion at location number 1.

2.3.3 Accounting for Dissociated Covert and Overt Recognition with an Interactive Architecture   Randy O'Reilly, Shaun Vecera, and I (Farah et al. 1993) have modeled overt and covert recognition using the five-layer recurrent network shown in Figure 36.11, in which the same set of so-called face units subserves both overt and covert recognition. The face input units subserve the initial visual representation of faces, the "semantic" units represent the semantic knowledge of people that can be evoked either by the person's face or by the name, and the "name" units represent names. Hidden units were used to help the network learn the associations among patterns of activity in each of these three layers. These are located between the "face" and "semantic" units (called the "face" hidden units) and between the "name" and "semantic" units (the "name" hidden units). Thus, there are two pools of units that together comprise the visual face-recognition system in our model in that they represent visual information about faces: the "face input" units and the "face hidden" units.

The connectivity among the different pools of units was based on the assumption that in order to name a face, or to visualize a named person, one must access semantic knowledge of that person. Thus, face and name units are not directly connected but send activation to one another through hidden and semantic units. All connections shown in Figure 36.11 are bidirectional.

Faces and names are represented by random patterns of 5 active units out of the total of 16 in each pool. Semantic knowledge is represented by 6 active units out of the total of 18 in the semantic pool. The only units for which we have assigned an interpretation are the "occupation units" in the semantic pool: one represents the semantic feature "actor," and the other, "politician." The network was trained to associate an individual's face, semantics, and name whenever one of these was presented, using the Contrastive Hebbian Learning algorithm (Movellan 1990). After training, the network was damaged by removing units.

Figure 36.12 shows the performance of the model in a 10-alternative, forced-choice naming task for face patterns after different degrees of damage to the "face input" and "face hidden" units. At levels of damage corresponding to removal of 62.5% and 75% of the face units in a given layer, the model performs at or near chance on this overt-recognition task. This is consistent with the performance of prosopagnosic patients who manifest covert recognition. Such patients perform poorly, but not invariably at chance, on overt tests of face recognition.

In contrast, the damaged network showed faster learning of correct face-name associations. When retrained after damage, it consistently showed more learning for correct pairings than incorrect ones in the first 10 training epochs, as shown in Figure 36.13. The damaged network also completed visual analysis of familiar faces faster than unfamiliar ones. When presented with face patterns after damage, the face units completed their analysis of the input (i.e., the face units settled) faster for familiar than unfamiliar faces, as shown in Figure 36.14. And finally, the damaged network showed semantic interference from faces in a name classification task. Figure 36.15 shows that when the network was presented with name patterns and the time it took to classify them according to occupation (i.e., the number of processing cycles for the occupation units to reach threshold) was measured, classification time was slowed when a face from the incorrect category was shown, relative to faces from the correct category and, in some cases, to a no-face baseline.

Why does the network retain "covert recognition" of the faces at levels of damage that lead to poor or even chance levels of overt recognition? The general answer lies in the nature of knowledge representation in PDP networks. As already mentioned, knowledge is stored in the pattern of weights connecting units. The set of the weights in a network that cannot correctly associate patterns because it has never been trained (or has been trained on a different set of patterns) is different in an important way from the set of weights in a network that cannot correctly associate patterns because it has been trained on those patterns and then damaged. The first set of weights is random with respect to the associations in question, whereas the second is a subset of the necessary weights. Even if it is an inadequate subset for performing the overt association, it is not random; it has "embedded" in it some degree of knowledge of the

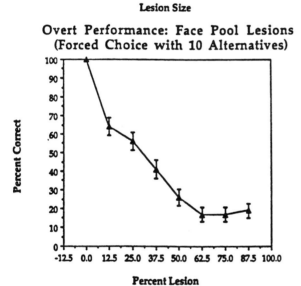

**Overt Performance: Hidden Unit Lesions
(Forced Choice with 10 Alternatives)**

**Overt Performance: Face Pool Lesions
(Forced Choice with 10 Alternatives)**

Figure 36.12
Effect of different amounts of damage to face units on the network's ability to perform 10-alternative
forced choice naming of faces, an overt face recognition task.

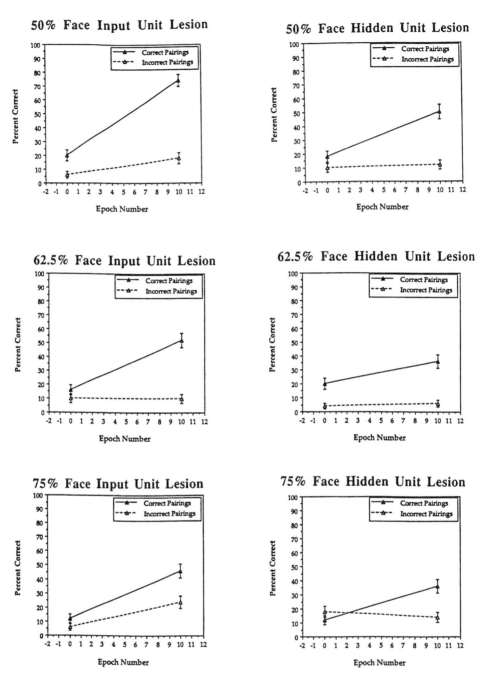

Figure 36.13
Ability of the network after different amounts of damage to face units to produce the name associated to a face (to within 2 bits), for correctly and incorrectly paired names and faces, immediately after damage and following 10 epochs of further training. Note that learning occurs more quickly for correctly paired names and faces.

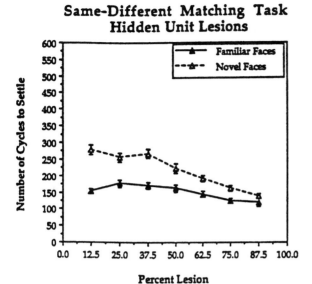

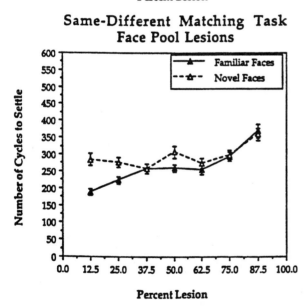

Figure 36.14
Effect of different amounts of damage to face units on the time needed for the face units to settle, for familiar input patterns (closed triangles) and for unfamiliar input patterns (open triangles). Note that familiar patterns tend to settle more quickly.

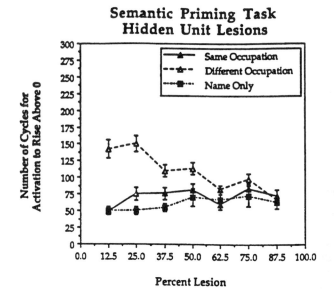

Figure 36.15
Effect of different amounts of damage to face units on the number of cycles needed for the "actor"
and "politician" units to reach threshold when presented with name and face input patterns. When
the face is from a different occupation category, it takes longer for the name to push the correct
occupation unit over threshold.

associations. Furthermore, consideration of the tasks used to measure covert recognition suggest that the covert measures should be sensitive to this embedded knowledge.

A damaged network would be expected to relearn associations that it originally knew faster than novel associations because of the nonrandom starting weights. The faster settling with previously learned inputs can be attributed to the fact that the residual weights come from a set designed to create a stable pattern from that input. Finally, to the extent that the weights continue to activate partial and subthreshold patterns over the nondamaged units in association with the input, these resultant patterns will contribute activation toward the appropriate units downstream, which are simultaneously being activated by intact name units.

2.3.4 Relevance of the Locality Assumption for Architecture of Perception and Awareness   The role of the locality assumption is less direct in the foregoing example than in the previous two, but it is nevertheless relevant. Many authors have reasoned according to the locality assumption that the selective loss of overt recognition and the preservation of covert recognition implies that there has been localized damage to a distinct component of the functional architecture needed for overt, but not covert, recognition. The alternative account, proposed here, suggests that partial damage to the visual face-recognition component changes the relative ability of the remaining parts of the system (i.e., the remaining parts of the face-recognition component along with the other components) to perform the overt and covert tasks. Specifically, the discrepancy between the difficulty of the overt and covert tasks is increased, as can be seen by comparing the steep drop in overt performance as a function of damage shown in Figure 36.12 with the relatively gentle fall-off in the magnitude of the covert recognition effects shown in Figures 36.13–15. According to the model, this is because the information processing required by the covert tasks can make use of partial knowledge encoded in the weights of the damaged network and is therefore more robust to damage than the information processing required by the overt task. In other words, with respect to the relative ability of the remaining system to perform overt and covert tasks, the effects of damage were nonlocal. The ability of the model to account for the dissociation between overt and covert recognition depends critically on this violation of the locality assumption.

3 General Discussion

3.1 Evaluating the Truth and Methodological Necessity of the Locality Assumption
The foregoing examples were intended as a small "data base" with which to test two empirical claims about the locality assumption. First, that it is true that after local brain damage the remaining parts of the system continue to function

as before. Second, that it is necessary that there is no other way to make principled inferences from the behavior of brain-damaged subjects to the functional architecture of the mind, and that the only alternative is therefore to abandon cognitive neuropsychology.

The examples allow us to assess the likely truth of the locality assumption by assessing the likely truth of the different inferences made with and without it. Of course, each such pair of inferences was made on the basis of the same data and fits those data equally well, so the choice between them rests on considerations of parsimony and consistency with other information about brain organization. On the basis of these considerations, the inferences made without the locality assumption seem preferable. In the case of semantic memory, the model obtained without the locality assumption is consistent with an abundance of other data implicating modality-specificity as a fundamental principle of brain organization and with the lack of any other example of a purely semantic distinction determining brain organization. In the case of visual attention, the model obtained without the locality assumption has fewer components: although the overviews of the models presented in Figures 36.6 and 36.7 are not strictly comparable, Figure 36.6 includes components postulated to account for other attentional phenomena, and Figure 36.7 includes separate depictions of the left and right hemispheres' attentional mechanisms as well as two different levels of stimulus representation. It can be seen that the same "attention" component shown in Figure 36.7 does the work of both the "engage" and "disengage" components in Figure 36.7. Similarly, setting aside the irrelevant differences in the complexity of Figures 36.10 and 36.11 arising from factors such as the greater range of phenomena to be explained by Figure 36.10, it is clear that the same visual "face" components in Figure 36.11 do the work of the visual "face" components and "conscious awareness system" in Figure 36.10, at least as far as explaining performance in overt and covert tasks is concerned.

It should be noted that the success of these models is a direct result of denying the locality assumption, as explained in subsections on the relevance of the locality assumption (sects. 2.1.4, 2.2.4, 2.3.4). In linking each neuropsychological dissociation to the more parsimonious functional architecture, a key explanatory role is played by the nonlocal effects that damage to one component of the architecture has on the functioning of other components. Hence the weight of evidence from the three cases discussed here suggests that the locality assumption is false. Finally, with respect to its necessity, the examples provide existence proofs that principled inferences can be made in cognitive neuropsychology without the locality assumption.

3.2 Possible Objections

In this section I consider some possible objections to these conclusions, with the hope of clarifying what has and has not been demonstrated here.

3.2.1 PDP and Box-and-Arrow: Apples and Oranges?   One kind of objection concerns the comparability of the hypotheses that were derived with and without the locality assumption. The two types of hypotheses do indeed differ in some fundamental ways, and comparing them may be a bit like comparing apples and oranges. Nevertheless, apples and oranges do share some dimensions that afford meaningful comparisons, and I argue that the hypotheses under consideration here are likewise comparable in the ways discussed above.

For example, one objection might be that the computer models denying the locality assumption can only demonstrate the sufficiency of a theory, not its empirical truth, whereas the alternative hypotheses are empirically grounded. It is true that the models presented here have only been shown to be sufficient to account for the available data, but this is also true of the alternative hypotheses, and indeed of *any* hypothesis. It is always possible that a hypothesis can fit all the data collected so far, but that some other, as yet undiscovered, data could falsify it. The reason this may seem more problematic for PDP models is that there is a research tradition in computer modeling that takes as its primary goal the accomplishment of a task rather than the fitting of psychological data (e.g., Rosenberg & Sejnowski 1986), relying exclusively on computational constraints rather than empirical constraints to inform the models. This is not a necessary feature of modeling, however, and the models presented here are constrained as much as the alternative hypotheses are by the empirical data.

Furthermore, the computational models presented here and the alternative hypotheses are on equal footing with respect to the distinction between prediction and retrodiction of data. In all three cases, the locality assumption has been used to derive a hypothesis, post hoc, from the observed neuropsychological dissociation. It was not the case that researchers had already formulated hypotheses to the effect that semantic memory was subdivided by taxonomic category or that there was a distinct component of the attention system for disengaging attention, or that awareness of face recognition depended on distinct parts of the mental architecture from face recognition; nor did they then go looking for the relevant dissociations to test those hypotheses. Rather, they began with the data and inferred their hypotheses just as we have done with the models presented earlier. Both the hypotheses derived using the locality assumption and the PDP models presented here await further testing with new data. An example of the way in which new data can be used to distinguish between the competing hypotheses comes from the work of Verfaellie et al. (1990) with a bilateral parietally damaged patient. They found that, contrary to their expectation of a bilateral disengage deficit, their subject showed diminished effects of attentional cuing. When attention units are removed bilaterally from the Cohen et al. (1994) model, which was developed before the authors knew of the Verfaellie et al. finding, the model also shows reduced attentional effects rather than a bilateral disengage deficit. This is because the disengage deficit in our model is caused by the imbalance in the number of attention units available to compete with one another after unilateral damage; bilateral damage does not lead to an imbalance but it does, of course, reduce the overall number of attention units and therefore the magnitude of the attentional effects.

Another way the comparisons presented above might seem mismatched is in their levels of description. The hypotheses derived using the locality assumption concern "macrostructure," that is, the level of description that identifies the components of the functional architecture, as shown in the so-called box-and-arrow models. In contrast, the hypotheses that deny the locality assumption appear to concern "microstructure," that is, the nature of the information processing that goes on within the architectural components. However, the latter hypotheses concern both microstructure and macrostructure, as should be clear from the macrostructures depicted in Figures 36.2, 36.7, and 36.11. We can therefore compare the two types of hypotheses at the level of macrostructure.

3.2.2 The Locality Assumption can be Saved with more Fine-Grained Empirical Analysis of the Deficit   Perhaps the prospects for the locality assumption look so dim because the types of data considered so far are unduly limited. The arguments and demonstrations presented above concern a relatively simple type of neuropsychological observation, namely, a selective deficit in some previously normal ability. I have focused on this type of observation for two reasons; the first is its very simplicity, and the seemingly straightforward nature of the inferences that follow from it. At first glance, a truly selective deficit in *A* does seem to demand the existence of an *A* component, and this inference is indeed sound under the assumption that the *A* component is informationally encapsulated. The second reason is that this is still the most common form of inference in cognitive neuropsychology, as argued earlier in the section on ubiquity (sect. 1.2).

Nevertheless, other, finer-grained ways of analyzing patient performance are used increasingly by cognitive neuropsychologists to pinpoint the underlying locus of impairment in a patient's functional architecture. The two most common are qualitative error analyses, and selective experimental manipulations of difficulty of particular processing stages. Can the use of the locality assumption be buttressed by the additional constraints offered by these methods? Several recent PDP simulations of patient performance suggest that these finer-grained analyses are just as vulnerable to nonlocal effects of brain damage as are the more brute-force observations of deficit per se.

For example, semantic errors in single-word reading (e.g., pear → "apple") have been considered diagnostic of an underlying impairment in the semantic representations used in reading, and visual errors (pear → "peer") are generally taken to imply a visual processing impairment (e.g., Coltheart 1985). Hinton and Shallice (1991) showed how a PDP simulation of reading could produce both kinds of errors when lesioned either in the visual or the semantic components of the model. Humphrey et al. (1992) make a similar point in the domain of visual search: error patterns suggestive of an impairment in gestalt-like grouping processes can arise either from direct damage to the parts of the system that accomplish grouping or by adding noise to earlier parts of the system. In both cases, the nondiagnosticity of error types results from the interactivity among the different components of the model.

Another well-known example of the use of error types to infer the locus of impairment is the occurrence of regularization errors in the reading performance of surface dyslexics (e.g., Coltheart, 1985). As mentioned earlier, surface dyslexics fail to read irregular words; this has been interpreted, using the locality assumption, as the loss of a whole-word reading route with preservation of the sublexical grapheme-phoneme translation route. The inference that these patients are relying on the latter route seems buttressed by a further analysis of the nature of their errors, which are typically regularizations (e.g., *pint* is pronounced like "lint"). Patterson et al. (1989), however, showed that a single-route architecture, comprised only of whole-word spelling-sound correspondences, produced, when partially damaged, both a selective impairment in the reading of irregular words and a tendency to regularize them. With the distributed representations used in their model, similar orthographies and phonologies have similar representations at each of these levels and there is consequently a tendency toward generalization. Although with training the system learns not to generalize the pronunciation of, say, *pint* to the pronunciation of most other *-int* words (such as *lint, mint, hint*), this tendency is unmasked at moderate levels of damage. The model's regularization errors are probably best understood as a result of the distributed nature of the word representations in their model. The principles of PDP are closely interrelated, however, and the regularization effects can also be viewed as the result of interactions among different word representations, with the less common pronunciations losing their "critical mass" and therefore being swamped by the remaining representations of more common pronunciations.

Analyses of selective deficits and of the nature of the errors produced have in common the use of a purely observational method. Perhaps experimental manipulations designed to tax the operation of specific components offer a more powerful way of pinpointing the locus of impairment. Two recent models speak to this possibility and show that direct manipulations of particular processing stages are no more immune to nonlocal effects than are the previous methods. Mozer and Behrmann's (1990) model of visual-spatial neglect shows how the manipulations of a stimulus property designed to affect postvisual processing, namely the lexicality of a letter string (word, pseudoword, nonword), can have pronounced effects on the performance of a model whose locus of damage is visual. Interactions between attended visual information and stored lexical representations allow letter strings to be reconstructed more efficiently the more they resemble familiar words. Tippett and Farah (1998) showed how apparently conflicting results in the literature on the determinants of naming difficulty in Alzheimer's disease can be accounted for with a single hypothesis. Although most researchers believe that the naming impairment in Alzheimer's disease results from an underlying impairment of semantic knowledge, manipulations of visual difficulty (degraded visual stimuli) and lexical access difficulty (word frequency) have pronounced effects on patients' likelihood of naming, leading to alternative hypotheses of visual agnosia or anomia (Nebes, 1989). When semantic representations were damaged, a PDP model of visual naming showed heightened sensitivity to visual degradation and word frequency. Thus, when one component of an interactive system is damaged, the system as a whole becomes more sensitive to manipulations of the difficulty of any of its components.

In sum, the problem of nonlocal effects of brain damage is not limited to inferences based on the range and boundaries of the impairment; it also affects inferences based on the qualitative mode of failure and the sensitivity of the system to manipulations designed to affect specific components directly.

3.2.3 PDP Could be False   A different type of objection concerns the assumptions of the PDP framework. As already acknowledged, PDP is controversial. How can one be convinced, through comparisons involving PDP models, that the locality assumption is false, if it has not been established first that PDP is a correct way of characterizing human information processing? First, it should be pointed out that much of the controversy concerning PDP involves the adequacy of PDP models of language and reasoning, which are not relevant here. Few vision researchers would deny that the basic principles of PDP are likely to apply to visual attention and pattern recognition (e.g., see the recent textbook overviews of these topics by Allport, 1989; Biederman, 1990; Hildreth & Ullman, 1989; Humphreys & Bruce, 1989; and even Pinker, 1985, who has been critical of PDP models of language). Semantic memory may be a more controversial case. Second, and perhaps more important, one can remain agnostic about PDP as a general framework for human information processing and still appreciate that the particular models presented here are credible alternatives to those derived using the locality assumption. PDP, like the locality assumption, is ultimately an empirical claim that will gain or lose support according to how well it helps explain psychological data. The ability of PDP to provide parsimonious accounts for neuropsychological dissociations such as the ones described here counts in its favor. Finally, even if PDP were false, there would remain other ways of conceptualizing human information processing that would provide explicit, mechanistic alternatives to modularity. For example, in production system architectures (see Klahr et al., 1987) working memory is highly non-encapsulated. Kimberg and Farah (1993) found that weakening association strengths in working memory produced an array of specific and characteristic frontal impairments that were in no transparent way related to working memory. Although interactive computation is at the heart of PDP, which makes PDP the natural architecture to contrast with the locality assumption, other architectures are also capable of accommodating high degrees of interactivity.

3.3 General Implications of Denying the Locality Assumption

3.3.1 Modularity The truth of the locality assumption has implications for issues in psychology beyond how best to infer functional architecture from the behavior of brain-damaged patients. As discussed at the outset, the locality assumption follows from a view of the mind and brain according to which the components of the functional architecture are informationally encapsulated, that is, their inputs and outputs are highly constrained. Components interact only when one has completed its processing, at which point it makes the end product available to a relatively small number of other components. If this were true, then the effects of damaging one component should be relatively local. Alternatively, if we judge that the best interpretation of various neuropsychological deficits (on the grounds of parsimony or consistency with other scientific knowledge, not on the grounds of a priori preferences for encapsulation or interactivity) involves denying the locality assumption, then this counts as evidence against modularity.

The term "modularity" is often used in a more general sense than I have used it so far, and this more general sense is not challenged by the failure of the locality assumption. Specialized representations are sometimes called "modules," so that the model in Figure 36.2 could be said to contain "visual knowledge" and "functional knowledge" modules. In this more general sense, the "modularity hypothesis" is simply that there is considerable division of labor among different parts of functional architecture with, for example, knowledge of language represented by a separate part of the system (functionally, and possibly anatomically), compared with other knowledge. Of course, if such a system is highly interactive, it may be difficult to delineate and characterize the different modules, but this is a problem of *how* you find something out, not of what it is or whether it exists.

3.3.2 Top-Down Versus Bottom-Up Research Strategies Denying the locality assumption also has a more general implication for research strategy in cognitive neuroscience. Most researchers in neuroscience and cognitive science acknowledge that there are multiple levels of description of the nervous system, from molecules to thoughts, and that one of the goals of science is a complete description of the nervous system at all of these levels. However, such researchers may differ in their opinions as to the most efficient way to arrive at this complete description. The bottom-up, or reductionist, approach is to begin with the most elementary levels of description, such as the biophysics of neurons, believing that it will be impossible to understand higher levels of organization if one does not know precisely *what* is being organized. This approach is anathema to cognitive neuroscience, which is, by definition, forging ahead with the effort to understand such higher-level properties of the brain as perception, memory, and so forth, while acknowledging that our understanding of the more elementary level of description is far from complete.

The main alternative, explicitly endorsed by many cognitive neuroscientists, is the top-down approach, according to which the most efficient way to understand the nervous system is by successive stages of analysis of systems at higher levels of description in terms of lower levels of description. It is argued that our understanding of lower levels will be facilitated if we know what higher-level function they serve. It is also argued that the complexity of the task of understanding the brain will be reduced by the "divide and conquer" aspect of this strategy, in which the system is analyzed into simpler components that can then be further analyzed individually (e.g., Kosslyn et al.'s 1990 "hierarchical decomposition constraint"). In the context of the three examples discussed earlier, this corresponds to first deriving the macrostructural hypotheses, in which the relevant components of the functional architecture are identified, and then investigating the microstructure of each component's internal operation. Unfortunately, to derive a macrostructure from neuropsychological data requires either making the locality assumption or considering the system's microstructure, as was done in the foregoing examples. If the locality assumption is false, the microstructure has implications for the macrostructure, and one cannot be assured of arriving at the correct macrostructural description without also considering hypotheses about microstructure.

Thus, even if one's only goal is to arrive at the correct macrostructural description of the functional architecture, as is the case for most cognitive neuropsychologists, the three examples presented here suggest that one must nevertheless consider hypotheses about microstructure. This points out a correspondence between theories of functional architecture and the methodologies for studying it. If one holds that the components of the functional architecture are informationally encapsulated, one can take a strictly top-down approach to the different levels of description, "encapsulating" one's investigations of the macrostructure from considerations of microstructure. In contrast, if one views the functional architecture as a highly interactive system, with each component responding directly or indirectly to the influences of many others, then one must adopt a more interactive mode of research, in which hypotheses about macrostructure are influenced by constraints imposed simultaneously at both the macrostructural and the microstructural levels.

3.3.3 Implications for Cognitive Neuropsychology   The conclusion that the locality assumption may be false is a disheartening one. It undercuts much of the special appeal of neuropsychological dissociations as evidence about the functional architecture. Although perhaps naive in hindsight, this special appeal came from the apparent directness of neuropsychological data. Conventional methods of cognitive psychology are limited to what Anderson (1978) has called "input-output" data: manipulation of stimuli and instructions on the input end and the measurement of responses and response latencies at output. From the relations between these, the nature of the intervening processing must be inferred. Such inferences are indirect, and as a result often underdetermine choices between competing hypotheses. In contrast, brain damage directly affects the intervening processing, constituting a direct manipulation of the "black box."

Unfortunately, the examples presented here suggest that even if the manipulation of the intervening processing is direct, the inferences by which the effects of the manipulations must be interpreted are not. In Ferrier's (1886) words, it may well be "at least highly difficult to trace any uncomplicated connection between the symptoms produced and the lesion as such." The locality assumption, which constitutes the most straightforward way of interpreting neuropsychological impairments, does not necessarily lead to the correct interpretation. If the locality assumption is indeed false, then dissociations lose their special status as particularly direct forms of evidence about the functional architecture.

Even for cognitive neuropsychologists who would not claim any special status for neuropsychological data, abandoning the locality assumption would make their work harder. The interpretation of dissociations without the locality assumption requires exploring a range of possible models that, when damaged, might be capable of producing that dissociation. What makes this difficult is that the relevant models would not necessarily have components corresponding to the distinctions between preserved and impaired abilities, and we therefore lack clear heuristics for selecting models to test.

The foregoing demonstrations and arguments are not intended to settle decisively the issue of whether the locality assumption is correct. As already acknowledged, this is not the type of issue that can be decided on the basis of a single study or even a small number of studies. Instead, my goal has been to call attention to the fact that we do not have any firm basis for an opinion one way or the other, despite the widespread use of the locality assumption. Furthermore, at least in a few cases, the best current interpretation seems to involve denying the locality assumption.

It is possible that some cognitive domains will conform more closely to the locality assumption than others; if so, this would have interesting theoretical as well as methodological implications concerning the degree of informational encapsulation in different subsystems of the functional architecture. However, until we have a broad enough empirical basis for deciding when the locality assumption can safely be used and when it will lead to incorrect inferences, we cannot simply assume it to be true, as has been done almost universally in the past.

Acknowledgments

The writing of this paper was supported by ONR grant N00014-91-J1546, NIMH grant R01 MH48274, NIH career development award K04-NS01405, and a grant from the McDonnell-Pew Program in Cognitive Neuroscience. I thank my coauthors on the projects described herein for their collaboration and tutelage in PDP modeling: Jonathan Cohen, Jay McClelland, Randy O'Reilly, Rick Romero, and Shaun Vecera. Special thanks to Jay McClelland for his encouragement and support. I thank several colleagues for discussions of the ideas in this paper: John Bruer, Alfonso Caramazza, Clark Glymour, Mike McCloskey, Morris Moscovitch, Edmund Rolls, and Larry Squire. I also thank Larry Weiskrantz for calling my attention to the passage from Ferrier quoted at the beginning. Finally, I thank the reviewers and editor of *BBS* for useful comments and criticisms of a previous draft: C. Allen, S. Harnad, G. Humphreys, M. McCloskey, M. Oaksford, T. Van Gelder, and four anonymous reviewers.

Note

1. There are, of course, many other ways to make a wrong inference using the locality assumption, even with the foregoing conditions satisfied, but these have to do with the particular content of the hypothesis being inferred and its relation to the data, not the use of the locality assumption per se. For example, Caramazza et al. (1990) have pointed out that selective impairments in modality-specific knowledge do not imply that knowledge of different modalities is represented in different formats; dissociability will not, in general, tell us about representational formats.

References

Allport, D. A. (1985) Distributed memory, modular subsystems, and dysphasia. In: *Current perspectives in dysphasia*, ed. S. K. Newman & R. Epstein. Churchill Livingstone.

Allport, D. A. (1989) Visual attention. In *Foundations of cognitive science*, ed. M. I. Posner. MIT Press.

Anderson, J. R. (1978) Arguments concerning representation for mental imagery. *Psychological Review* 85:249–77.

Basso, A., Capitani, E. & Laiacona, M. (1988) Progressive language impairment without dementia: A case with isolated category specific defect. *Journal of Neurology, Neurosurgery and Psychiatry* 51:1201–7.

Biederman, I. (1990) Higher-level vision. In: *Visual cognition and action*, ed. D. N. Osherson, S. M. Kosslyn & J. M. Hollerbach. MIT Press.

Caplan, D. (1981) On the cerebral localization of linguistic functions: Logical and empirical issues surrounding deficit analysis and functional localization. *Brain and Language* 14:120–37.

Caramazza, A. (1984) The logic of neuropsychological research and the problem of patient classification in aphasia. *Brain and Language* 21:9–20.

Caramazza, A. (1986) On drawing inferences about the structure of normal cognitive systems from the analysis of patterns of impaired performance: The case for single-patient studies. *Brain and Cognition* 5:41–66.

Caramazza, A. (1992) Is cognitive neuropsychology possible? *Journal of Cognitive Neuroscience* 4:80–95.

Caramazza, A., Hillis, A. E., Rapp, B. C. & Romani, C. (1990) The multiple semantics hypothesis: Multiple confusions? *Cognitive Neuropsychology* 7:161–90.

Cohen, J. D., Romero, R. D., Servan-Schreiber, D. & Farah, M. J. (1994) Disengaging from the disengage function: The relation of macrostructure to microstructure in parietal attentional deficits. *Journal of Cognitive Neuroscience* 6:377–87.

Coltheart, M. (1985) Cognitive neuropsychology and the study of reading. In: *Attention and Performance XI*, ed. M. I. Posner & O. S. M. Marin. Erlbaum.

de Haan, E. H. F., Bauer, R. M. & Greve, K. W. (1992) Behavioural and physiological evidence for covert face recognition in a prosopagnosic patient. *Cortex* 28:77–95.

de Haan, E. H. F., Young, A. & Newcombe, F. (1987a) Faces interfere with name classification in a prosopagnosic patient. *Cortex* 23:309–16.

de Haan, E. H. F., Young, A. & Newcombe, F. (1987b) Face recognition without awareness. *Cognitive Neuropsychology* 4:385–416.

DeRenzi, F. (1986) Current issues in prosopagnosia. In: *Aspects of face processing*, ed. H. D. Ellis, M. A. Jeeves, F. Newcombe & A. Young. Martinus Nijhoff.

Farah, M. J. & McClelland, J. L. (1991) A computational model of semantic memory impairment: Modality-specificity and emergent category-specificity. *Journal of Experimental Psychology: General* 120(4):339–57.

Farah, M. J., McMullen, P. A. & Meyer, M. M. (1991) Can recognition of living things be selectively impaired? *Neuropsychologia* 29:185–93.

Farah, M. J., O'Reilly, R. C. & Vecera, S. P. (1993) Dissociated overt and covert recognition as an emergent property of lesioned neural networks. *Psychological Review* 100:571–88.

Ferrier, D. (1886) *The functions of the brain.* Smith, Elder.

Fodor, J. A. (1983) *The modularity of mind.* Bradford Books / MIT Press.

Hildreth, E. C. & Ullman, S. (1989) The computational study of vision. In: *Foundations of cognitive science*, ed. M. I. Posner, MIT Press.

Hillis, A. E. & Caramazza, A. (1991) Category-specific naming and comprehension impairment: A double dissociation. *Brain* 114:2081–94.

Hinton, G. E. & Shallice, T. (1991) Lesioning an attractor network: Investigations of acquired dyslexia. *Phychological Review* 98(1):74–95.

Humphreys, G. W. & Bruce, V. (1989) *Visual cognition: Computational, experimental and neuropsychological perspectives.* Erlbaum.

Humphreys, G. W., Freeman, T. & Muller, H. J. (1992) Lesioning a connectionist model of visual search: Selective effects of distractor grouping. *Canadian Journal of Psychology* 46:417–60.

Humphreys, G. w. & Riddoch, M. J. (1987) *Visual object processing: A cognitive neuropsychological approach.* Erlbaum.

Humphreys, G. W. & Riddoch, M. J. (1993) Interactions between object- and space-vision revealed through neuropsychology. In: *Attention and performance XIV*, ed. D. E. Meyer & S. Kornblum. MIT Press.

Jackson, J. H. (1873) On the anatomical and physiological localization of movements in the brain. *Lancet* 1:84–85, 162–64, 232–34.

Kimberg, D. Y. & Farah, M. J. (1993) A unified account of cognitive impairments following frontal lobe damage: The role of working memory in complex, organized behavior. *Journal of Experimental Psychology: General* 122:411–28.

Kinsbourne, M. (1971) Cognitive deficit: Experimental analysis. In: *Psychobiology*, ed. J. L. McGaugh. Academic Press.

Klahr, D., Langley, P. & Neches, R. (1987) *Production system models of learning and development.* MIT Press.

Kosslyn, S. M. & Van Kleek, M. (1990) Broken brains and normal minds: Why Humpty Dumpty needs a skeleton. In: *Computational neuroscience*, ed. E. Schwartz. MIT Press.

Moscovitch, M. & Umiltà, C. (1990) Modularity and neuropsychology: Modules and central processes in attention and memory. In: *Modular deficits in Alzheimer-type dementia*, ed. M. F. Schwartz. MIT Press.

Movellan, J. R. (1990) Contrastive Hebbian learning in the continuous Hopfield model. In: *Proceedings of the 1989 Connectionist Models Summer School*, ed. D. S. Touretzky, G. E. Hinton & T. J. Sejnowski. Morgan Kaufmann.

Mozer, M. C. & Behrmann, M. (1990) On the interaction of selective attention and lexical knowledge: A connectionist account of neglect dyslexia. *Journal of Cognitive Neuroscience* 2(2):96–123.

Nebes, R. D. (1989) Semantic memory in Alzheimer's disease. *Psychological Bulletin* 106:377–94.

Newcombe, F., Mehta, Z. & de Haan, E. F. (1994) Category-specificity in visual recognition. In: *The neural bases of high-level vision: Collected tutorial essays*, ed. M. J. Farrah & G. Ratcliff. Erlbaum.

Patterson, K. E., Seidenberg, M. S. & McClelland, J. L. (1989) Connections and disconnections: Acquired dyslexia in a computational model of reading processes. In: *Parallel distributed processing: Implications for psychology and neurobiology*, ed. R. G. M. Morris. Oxford University Press.

Peitrini, V., Nertimpi, T., Vaglia, A., Revello, M. G., Pinna, V. & Ferro-Milone, F. (1988) Recovery from herpes simplex encephalitis: Selective impairment of specific semantic categories with neuroradiological correlation. *Journal of Neurology, Neurosurgery and Psychiatry* 51:1284–93.

Pinker, S. (1985) Visual cognition: An introduction. In: *Visual cognition*, ed. S. Pinker. MIT Press.

Posner, M. I. (1978) *Chronometric explorations of mind.* Erlbaum.

Posner, M. I., Walker, J. A., Friedrich, F. J. & Rafal, R. D. (1984) Effects of parietal lobe injury on covert orienting of visual attention. *Journal of Neuroscience* 4:1863–74.

Rosenberg, C. R. & Sejnowski, T. K. (1986) NETtalk: A parallel network that learns to read aloud. *EE & CS Technical Report #JHC-EECS-86/01.* Johns Hopkins University Press.

Rumelhart, D. E. & McClelland, J. L. (1986) *Parallel distributed processing: Explorations in the microstructure of cognition. Vol. I: Foundations.* MIT Press.

Sartori, G. & Job, R. (1988) The oyster with four legs: A neuropsychological study on the interaction of visual and semantic information. *Cognitive Neuropsychology* 5:105–32.

Silveri, M. C. & Gianotti, G. (1988) Interaction between vision and language in category-specific semantic impairment. *Cognitive Neuropsychology* 5:677–709.

Squire, L. R. (1992) Memory and the hippocampus: A synthesis from findings with rats, monkeys, and humans. *Psychological Review* 99:195–231.

Tulving, E. (1983) *Elements of episodic memory.* Oxford University Press.

Verfaellie, M., Paresak, S. Z. & Heilman, K. M. (1990) Impaired shifting of attention in Balint's syndrome. *Brain and Cognition* 12:195–204.

von Klein, B. E. (1977) Inferring functional localization from neurological evidence. In: *Explorations in the biology of language*, ed. E. Walker. Bradford Books/MIT Press.

Warrington, E. K. (1985) Agnosia: The impariment of object recognition. In: *Handbook of clinical neurology*, ed. P. J. Vinken, G. W. Bruyn & H. L. Klawans. Elsevier.

Warrington, E. K. & McCarthy, R. (1983) Category specific access dysphasia. *Brain* 106:859–78.

Warrington, E. K. & McCarthy, R. (1987) Categories of knowledge: Further fractionation and an attempted integration. *Brain* 110:1273–96.

Warrington, E. K. & Shallice, T. (1984) Category specific semantic impairments. *Brain* 107:829–54.

Zurif, E. B. (1980) Language mechanisms: A neuropsycholinguistic perspective. *American Scientist* 68:305–34.

Mind vs. World

Chapter 37

Is Human Cognition Adaptive?

John R. Anderson

1 A Rational Theory of Cognition

There has been a long tradition of trying to understand human cognition as an adaptation to its environment. The writings of Brunswik (1956) and Gibson (1966; 1979) represent classic examples of this approach. More recently, Marr (1982) and Shepard (1987) have provided rigorous developments of this perspective. I (Anderson 1990a) have tried to develop what I call "rational analyses" of several broad categories of human cognition. A *rational analysis* is an explanation of an aspect of human behavior based on the assumption that it is optimized somehow to the structure of the environment. The term comes from an analogy with the "rational man" hypothesis that plays such a major role in economic explanation. As in economics, the term does not imply any actual logical deduction in choosing the optimal behavior, only that the behavior will be optimized.

This rationality thesis has often been supported with evolutionary arguments, but from my perspective the evolutionary connections are as much of a hindrance as a help. The idea that any aspect of an organism has evolved to an optimal form is quite problematical (e.g., see the readings edited by Dupré 1987). I will discuss these problems shortly; first, I would like to state what draws me to the position in the absence of any strong encouragement from evolutionary considerations.

If there were some precise relationship between the structure of the environment and the structure of behavior, this would provide a much needed perspective in cognitive psychology. The principal goal of the field has been to find mental structures that explain behavior. This goal has been impeded by two related obstacles. First, there is a serious and perhaps intractable induction problem in inferring the structure of a black box from the structure of the behavior it produces. Second, there is a serious and intractable identifiability problem in that many different proposals about mental structure are equivalent in their behavioral consequences.

The rational approach helps rather directly with the induction problem. If we know that behavior is optimized to the structure of the environment and we also know what that optimal relationship is, then a constraint on mental mechanisms is that they must implement that optimal relationship. This helps suggest mechanisms, thus reducing the induction problem.

A rational theory can also provide help with the identifiability problem. It provides an explanation at a level of abstraction above specific mechanistic proposals. All mechanistic proposals which implement the same rational prescription are equivalent. The structure driving explanation in a rational theory is that of the environment, which is much easier to observe than the structure of the mind. One might take the view (and I have so argued in overenthusiastic moments, Anderson, in press) that we do not need a mechanistic theory, that a rational theory offers a more appropriate explanatory level for behavioral data. This creates an unnecessary dichotomy between alternative levels of explanation, however. It is more reasonable to adopt Marr's (1982) view that a rational theory (which he called the "computational level") helps define the issues in developing a mechanistic theory (which he called the level of "algorithm and representation"). In particular, a rational theory provides a precise characterization and justification of the behavior the mechanistic theory should achieve.

This chapter discusses the general issues surrounding a rational analysis and reviews its applications to memory, categorization, causal analysis, and problem solving. It closes with an example of how rational analysis might be related to a mechanistic implementation.

1.1 The Evolutionary Perspective

A rational theory should stand on its own in accounting for data; it need not be derived from evolutionary considerations. Still, its connections with evolution are undeniable and have influenced the formulation of the rationalist program. It is accordingly worth discussing these evolutionary considerations explicitly.

Here is the simple view of evolution adopted here: At any stable point in evolution a species should display a range of variability in its traits. The differences in this range are not important enough in their adaptive value for any to have been selected. There may be some change in the species during this stable stage because of such things as genetic drift, in which the distribution of nonsignificant variability alters. Optimization might get involved if some truly novel genetic variation is created by some random mutation. Optimization is more often evoked, however, when the environment undergoes some significant change, after which the former range of traits is no longer equivalent in adaptive value. According to this view, changes in the environment are more significant than random changes in genetic code in driving evolutionary change.

If this view is approximately correct, evolution is a local optimizer. This can be understood as a kind of hill-climbing in which the set of possible traits defines the space and the adaptive value defines altitude. At a stable point in time the species is at some point or plateau of a local maximum. When there is an environmental change, the contours of the space change and the species may no longer be at a maximum. It will climb along the slope of steepest ascent to a new maximum and reside there. Extinction occurs when it is not possible for a species to adapt to the environmental changes. New species appear when different members of one species evolve to adapt to different environments. This means that the local optimum that any species achieves is a function of the accidents of its past. Maybe humans would be better adapted if they had the social structure of insects, but given our mammalian origins, there is no path to this hypothetical global maximum.

According to the hill-climbing metaphor, there are two major constraints on the predictions of an optimization analysis. One comes from the proximity structure of the space of traits and the other comes from the species' current location in that space. Only certain variations are reachable from where it is right now. Consider the case of the moths of Manchester, a standard illustration of evolutionary optimization (Kettlewell 1973): When pollution became a major factor in Manchester, the former peppered gray moth was no longer optimal in avoiding predators and a mutant black moth largely replaced it. Other conceivable morphological responses to predators are just as effective as changing color or more so. For example, one could imagine the development of offensive weapons like those of other insects. Moth mutants with offensive weapons do not occur, however, whereas color mutants do. Thus, color was a direction open for hill-climbing but offensive weaponry was not.

This means that any species or any aspect of a species is subject to constraints which depend on evolutionary history and can be arbitrary and complex. The more arbitrary and complex these constraints, the less explanatory an appeal to optimization will be. The general lesson we can take from such considerations is that in some cases much explanatory power is achieved by appealing to optimization and in other cases little. In optimal foraging theory (e.g., Stephens & Krebs 1986) we see a full range of explanatory outcomes from an optimization analysis. [See also: Fantino & Abarca: "Choice, Optimal Foraging, and the Delay-Reduction Hypothesis" *BBS* 8(3) 1985; and Houston & McNamara: "A Framework for the Functional Analysis of Behaviour" *BBS* 11(2) 1988.] My work on rational analysis is intended to explore explanatory power in human cognition.

The idea that cognition is optimized to the environment should be taken as a scientific hypothesis and evaluated by how well it organizes the data. One should not be surprised to find it successful in explaining some aspects of cognition but not others. In particular, I have held that the strong regularities in basic cognitive functions such as memory or categorization reflect a statistical optimization to the structure of the environment. Shepard has been a strong proponent of the idea that deep regularities of the mind reflect deep regularities of the world. "In view of the extended time base of biological evolution, I suppose that it would have been the most persuasive and enduring features, invariants, or constraints of the world in which we have evolved that would have become most deeply and thoroughly entrenched" (Shepard, 1982, p. 50). It is interesting to ask whether these function-specific optimizations add up to an overall optimization of human cognition. I return to this question at the end of the paper.

As a final remark, it should be noted that developing a rational theory of an aspect of human cognition is a higher-risk, higher-gain enterprise than cognitive psychology's more normal endeavor of developing a mechanistic theory. It is high risk in that it may turn out that the given aspect of human cognition is not optimized in any interesting sense. In contrast, there is little doubt nowadays that human cognition is realized in a set of mechanisms. The rational approach is high gain in that we will have made a substantial discovery if we can show that certain aspects of human cognition are optimized in some interesting sense. This would be informative, whereas discovering that the mind is mechanistically realized is no longer news.

1.2 Applying the Principle of Rationality
So far the notion of a rational theory has been very general. I have followed a rather specific program for developing such a theory, one involving six steps (outlined in Table 37.1). Each step requires some discussion:

> *Step 1* The first step in developing a rational analysis is to specify the goals being optimized by the cognitive system. Any behavior can be seen as optimizing some imaginable goal. Thus, the mere fact that one can predict a behavior under the assumption of optimality is no evidence for a rational analysis. One must motivate the goals to be optimized. So far this has been easy because there is the strong constraint that these goals must be relevant to adaptation. If we were to analogize from other adaptionist applications, however, we would expect that, as the cognitive analyses advance, circumstances will arise in which it becomes a significant research problem to determine what needs to be optimized. A good example of such an issue comes from optimal foraging theory where the question arises whether caloric intake should always be maximized and how to trade off caloric intake with other goals (Stephens & Krebs 1986). [See also

Table 37.1
Steps in developing a rational theory

---

1. Specify precisely the goals of the cognitive system.
2. Develop a formal model of the environment to which the system is adapted.
3. Make the minimal assumptions about computational limitations.
4. Derive the optimal behavioral function given 1–3 above.
5. Examine the empirical literature to see whether the predictions of the behavioral function are confirmed.
6. Repeat, iteratively refining the theory.

Houston & MacNamara, 1988.] Although maximizing caloric intake is a good first-order rule of thumb, situations can arise which require more complicated formulations. Such considerations are a sign of maturity and success, indicating that we have reached a point where we can apply our theory to particular situations in such detail that we can raise very specific questions about what should be optimized.

Step 2 The second step is to specify the structure of the environment to which cognition is optimized. As in Step 1, any behavior can be seen as optimal in some possible environment. Thus, converging evidence is needed to support one's assumptions about the environment. It is here that the observability of the environment is a great potential strength of the rational analysis, although just how one capitalizes on this potential can vary. Sometimes one can appeal to existing scientific theory about the relevant environment, as in the rational analysis of categorization that is described later in this paper. Other times, one must resort to statistical studies of the environment, as in the rational analysis of memory. Occasionally, one must turn to plausibility arguments, as in the rational analysis of problem solving. The first approach yields the most compelling theory and the last the least compelling.

There are two problems in any attempt to characterize the environment. The first is that one's characterization is usually based on only a portion of the environment and it is uncertain whether this will generalize to other portions. The second problem concerns whether the environment that one has characterized is the right one. For example, if one takes an evolutionary perspective, one might argue that our current environment is quite different in its information-processing demands from the past environment that shaped our evolution. The solution to both of these problems should be to study the information-processing demands imposed by many aspects of the environment in many different cultures. To the extent that these studies tell the same story, generalization is justified. To the extent that different patterns appear, one must complicate one's environmental theory.

The theory of the environment that seems to arise in most situations is basically probabilistic. The information-processing implications of various environmental cues are not certain. This leads to the Bayesian character of the optimization analysis in Step 4. Many characterizations of human cognition as irrational make the error of treating the environment as being much more certain than it is. The worst and most common of these errors is to assume that the subject has a basis for knowing the information-processing demands of an experiment in as precise a way as the experimenter does. What is optimal in the microworld created in the laboratory can be far from optimal in the world at large.

An example is the matching law in operant conditioning (see Williams 1988, for a review). Choices between two alternative behaviors generally tend to be proportional to the reinforcement allocated to each behavior. This can be derived for a momentary maximizing model (Shimp, 1966) or a melioration model (Herrnstein & Vaughan, 1980) in which the organism chooses the behavior with the greatest local probability of reinforcement. It turns out that such local optimization can in some circumstances lead to behavior which is globally nonoptimal (Herrnstein, 1990). For example, there are experiments in which response A always is reinforced more than response B. However, the rate of reinforcement of both responses increases with the proportion of response B. The "optimal" behavior is to choose B often enough to keep the reinforcement level high but A often enough to enjoy its higher payoff. Organisms typically choose A too often to maximize this overall level of reinforcement. [See also Rachlin et al.: "Maximization Theory in Behavioral Psychology" BBS 4(3) 1981.]

It has been called into question (e.g., Staddon, 1987) whether organisms can be aware of such complex contingencies. It also seems inappropriate to call such behavior nonoptimal. It is nonoptimal in the experimenter's definition of the world but might actually be optimal in the organisms's definition (see Rachlin et al., 1981). To determine what is optimal from the organism's perspective, one must know the distribution of reinforcement contingencies in the organism's environment in general, the symptoms of these various contingencies, and what would be reasonable inferences about the current situation given these assumptions and the organism's current experience. In Bayesian terms, the distribution of contingencies is the prior probability, the symptoms given the contingencies are the conditional probabilities, and the inferences given the experience are the posterior probabilities. Characterizations of the organism as nonoptimal make the error of ignoring prior uncertainty and assume that the organism should have the same model of the situation as the experimenter. It is possible, given reasonable assumptions about priors, that local maximization has the highest expected value over possible contingencies in the environment. The hypothesis about the actual contingencies might have too low a posterior probability to influence behavior.

Step 3 The third step is to specify the computational constraints on achieving optimization. This is the true Achilles heel of the rationalist enterprise. It is here that we take into account the constraints that prevent the system from adopting a global optimum. As admitted earlier, these constraints could be complex and arbitrary. To the extent that this is the case, a rationalist theory would fail to achieve its goal, which is to predict behavior from the structure of the environment rather than the structure of the mind.

This potential danger has not caused problems in my own work on rational theory so far. It has only called for two global constraints on cognition. The first is that it costs the mind something to consider each alternative. A basic capacity limit on processing alternatives is quite reasonable given current conceptions of both cognition and computation. The second constraint is more uniquely human: There is a short-term memory limit on the number of things that can be simultaneously held in mind.

Step 4 The fourth step is to combine the assumptions in Steps 1–3 to determine what is optimal. Given the statistical characterization in Step 2, the optimization process becomes a Bayesian decision-making problem. Specifically, what behavior will maximize expected utility, defined as the expected goals from Step 1 minus the expected costs from Step 3? Expectations are defined in terms of the statistical structure of the environment from Step 2.

The major complication in this step is analytic tractability. While the idea of optimal behavior is precise enough, it is not always trivial to determine just what it is. In principle, it can always be determined by a Monte Carlo simulation in which we go through the consequences of different possible behavioral functions in the hypothesized environment. It would not be feasible to consider a full Monte Carlo simulation in practice, although we have done partial simulations (e.g., Anderson & Milson 1989). One consequence of the problem of analytic tractability is that many simplifying assumptions have to be made. This is a ubiquitous practice in science. Although I am fairly comfortable with the simplifying assumptions, the range of possible simplifying assumptions and their consequences should be explored. As will be noted in Step 6, most of my iterative theory construction activity has involved such exploration.

Step 5 The fifth step is to see whether subjects' behavior can be predicted from the optimal behavior. A noteworthy feature of my work to date is its reliance on existing experimental literature to test predictions of the rational theory. On the one hand, it is relatively impressive that such a scope of literature can be accommodated within the theory. On the other hand, this raises the question (worrisome to some) of whether the theory leads to novel predictions and experiments. There are many potential research directions. I have chosen to begin by using the wealth of the existing literature on human cognition. This paper will nonetheless describe a number of novel empirical tests (Phenomena 14, 16, and 21).

Step 6 The sixth step is to refine the theory iteratively. If one formulation does not work, we must be prepared to try another. Such iterations have often been seen as a sign that an adaptionist enterprise is fatally flawed (Gould & Lewontin, 1979). As Mayr (1983) notes in response to Gould and Lewontin, however, iterative theory construction is the way of all science.

In cognitive science we have certainly seen a long succession of mechanisms for explaining cognition. It is to be hoped that in cognitive science
we understand that a theory should be evaluated by how well it does in
organizing the data and not by whether it is the nth theory of that type
that has been tried. Let me also add that my own experience with theory
construction in the rationalist framework has been less iterative than my
experience with theory construction in the mechanistic framework. This is
what we would hope for—that rational considerations would provide
more guidance in theory construction. The major point of iteration has
been to play with approximating assumptions, trying to find a set that is
reasonable and which leads to a modicum of analytic tractability. Thus,
the iteration is being focused on trying alternative forms of the theory to
fit the data.

1.3 Pre-empirical Summary

The theory is created in Steps 1–3 in Table 37.1. The remaining points in that
table are concerned with deriving and testing predictions from the theory. I
refer to the theory created in Steps 1 through 3 as a *framing of the information-
processing problem*. So far I have attempted framings for four separate aspects
of cognition: memory, categorization, causal inference, and problem solving.
Given that the evidence for rational analysis is based on how well we can predict behavior from the structure of the environment and not on rhetoric about
the prior plausibility of an adaptionist analysis, this chapter reviews these four
subtheories and 21 nontrivial behavioral phenomena which have been explained
by rational analysis.[1] Table 37.2 provides a summary of these four subtheories
by specifying their assumptions about the goals, the environments, and the
costs. The following sections will review these subtheories.

Table 37.2
Summary of rational analyses of the four domains of cognition

Domain	Goal	Structure	Cost
Memory	Get access to needed experiences	Patterns by which need for information repeats	Retrieving a memory
Categorization	Predict features of new objects	How features of objects cluster together	Hypothesis formation
Causal inference	Predict future events	Statistical models of causal structure	Hypothesis formation
Problem solving	Achieve certain states in external world	How problems vary in dif-ficulty and how similarity to the goal is related to distance to the goal	Internal effort in generating plans and external effort in executing plans

2 A Rational Theory of Memory

The goal of memory is to get access to needed information from the past (e.g., remembering where the car is parked in the airport parking lot). The relevant structure of the environment has to do with how the need for information tends to repeat itself in various situations. The simple cost function is that it costs something to retrieve a memory. These considerations all fit into a basic decision theory. The system can use its model of the environment and experience with any memory A to estimate a probability $p(A)$ that the memory is relevant at the current moment. If G is the value of achieving the current goal and C is the cost of considering any single memory, the optimal retrieval algorithm can be specified. A rationally designed information-retrieval system would retrieve memory structures ordered by their probabilities $p(A)$ and would stop retrieving when

$$p(A)G < C \tag{1}$$

That is, the system would stop retrieving when the probabilities are so low that the expected gain from retrieving the target is less than its cost. This strategy guarantees retrieval episodes of maximum utility where this is defined as the probability of successful retrieval multiplied by G minus expected cost.

A basic assumption is that the probability of being needed, $p(A)$, is monotonically related to the latency and probability of recall, which are the two major dependent measures used in the memory literature. It is related to latency because memory structures are ordered according to $p(A)$, and it is related to accuracy because of the threshold on what items will be considered.

This means that a rational theory of memory is going to be a theory of how to estimate $p(A)$. It is assumed that, like computer information-retrieval systems (Salton & McGill 1983), human memory has two sources of information for deciding whether a memory A is going to be relevant in the current context. One is the past context-independent history of use of that memory. The other is the cues impinging on the person in the current context.[2]

Estimation can be characterized as a process of inferring a Bayesian posterior probability of being needed, conditional on these two sources of information. Formally, we are conditionalizing on a history H_A of being relevant in the past and a *set* of cues, denoted as Q. These cues will consist of a set of terms denoted by indices i. Characterized this way we can come up with the following Bayesian odds formula for estimating the conditional probability $P(A|H_A \& Q)$ which is $P(A)$ from Equation 1:

$$\frac{P(A|H_A \& Q)}{P(\bar{A}|H_A \& Q)} = \frac{P(A|H_A)}{P(\bar{A}|H_A)} \times \prod_{i \in Q} \frac{P(i|A)}{P(i|\bar{A})} \tag{2}$$

That is, the odds ratio for item A is the product of the odds ratio for item A given history H_A multiplied by the product of the ratio of the conditional probabilities for each cue in the context. This equation makes certain assumptions about conditional independence, namely, that the degree to which A affects the probability of i in the context does not depend on A's past history or the other cues in the context. This assumption is typically made in the computer information-retrieval literature for purposes of tractability.[3]

The first term on the right side of Equation 2, $P(A|H_A)/P(\bar{A}|H_A)$, is basically a prior odds ratio for the item given its past history. This is the *history factor*. H_A will be a record of all the times A has been needed. As such, it reflects, among other things, frequency of use and how recently it was last used. The other quantities, the $P(i|A)/P(i|\bar{A})$ are the odds ratios of the conditional probabilities of the cues given that the memory is needed versus not needed. These ratios can be thought of as associative strengths between cues and memories. They constitute the *context factor*. This history and context factors will be considered in the next two subsections.

2.1 The History Factor

To address the history factor, $P(A|H_A)$, we need to determine how the past history of a memory structure's use predicts its current use. To determine this in the most valid way, we would have to follow people about in their daily lives keeping a complete record of when they use various facts. Such an objective study of human information use is close to impossible. One possibility is to study records from nonhuman information-retrieval systems. Such studies have been done on borrowing books from libraries (Burrell, 1980; Burrell & Cane, 1982) and on accessing computer files (Satyanarayanan, 1981; Stritter, 1977). Both systems tend to yield rather similar statistics. It is also possible to look at various recorded subsets of the information-processing demands placed on human memory: Lael Schooler and I have examined the use of words in *New York Times* headlines and sources of messages in electronic mail. These display the same kinds of statistics as libraries or file systems. Thus, there appear to be certain universals in the structure of information presentation and use.

Burrell (1980; 1985) has developed a mathematical theory of usage for information-retrieval systems such as libraries (a similar model appears in Stritter, 1977, for file usage). His theory can be plausibly extended to human memory. It involves two layers of assumptions: First, the items (books, files, memory structures) in an information-retrieval system vary in terms of their desirability. These desirabilities vary as a gamma distribution. Second, desirabilities determine rate of use in a Poisson process. Burrell's model was augmented by Anderson and Milson (1989) with the assumption that there will be fluctuations in the desirability of items—an assumption that is true of books in libraries, words in the *New York Times*, or sources of electronic messages. The detailed application can be found in Anderson and Milson (1989) or Anderson (1990a), but, in summary, this augmented Burrell model predicts:

Phenomenon 1 Memory performance increases as a power function of the amount of practice (Newell & Rosenbloom, 1981). Basically, if we look at these various sources (libraries, headlines, etc.) we find that the probability that an item will be used in the next unit of time increases as a power function of the number of times it has been used. Thus, the memory function is a direct reflection of the environmental function.

Phenomenon 2 Memory performance decreases as a power function of delay between experience and test (Wickelgren, 1976). Basically, if we look at these various sources we find that the probability that an item will be used in the next unit of time decreases as a power function of the time since last use. Again, the memory function is a direct reflection of the environmental function.

Phenomenon 3 Holding constant the number of exposures (Phenomenon 1) and the time since last exposure (Phenomenon 2), there is an effect of the spacing between the exposures (e.g., Bahrick, 1979; Glenberg, 1976); If an item has been used at time t, its probability of use at time $t + \Delta t$ is approximately maximal if its previous use was at time $t - \Delta t$. Again the environment shows the same relationship.

There is no other theory that can fit all three of these phenomena simultaneously. It needs to be stressed that these predictions derive from the structure of the environment and the definition of optimal memory performance. These empirical relationships can be seen directly in library borrowings, file access, *New York Times* articles, or electronic mail messages. Any system faced with the same statistics of information use and optimized in the sense defined will produce the basic human memory functions. *No additional assumptions are required.*

2.2 The Context Factor

The analysis of the contextual factor focuses on the quantities $P(i|A)/P(i|\bar{A})$, which are the cue strengths. Note that $P(i)$ and $P(i|\bar{A})$ are going to be nearly identical because conditionalizing on the nonrelevance of one memory structure out of millions cannot change the probability of any cue much. Thus, this discussion of cue strength will focus on the simpler form of $P(i|A)/P(i)$. Note that $P(i|A)/P(i) = P(A|i)/P(A)$. The cue strength (the ratio) thus reflects either the degree to which the context element (i) is more or less probable when a memory trace (A) is needed, or, equivalently, the degree to which it is more or less probable that a trace (A) is needed when a context element (i) is present. Intuitively, these cue strengths reflect the degree of association between the terms i and the memory structures A.

A critical question is how to estimate these cue strengths. The assumption of a rational analysis is that whatever factors should influence the estimation of $P(A|i)/P(A)$ should also show corresponding influences on memory. Thus, the associative effects in memory reflect a rational effort to adjust the estimation of need probability on the basis of statistical factors relating cues in the context to the probability that the memory will be needed. There are two obvious factors. One is based on direct experience and the other on inference. The direct experiential factor is the proportion of times that A has been needed in the past when cue i was in the context. The inferential factor is the proportion of times that memories similar to A have been needed when cue i was in the context. A memory model like SAM (Gillund & Shiffrin, 1984) uses only the direct experiential factor but this is a poor basis when A is a recent memory and we have not had sufficient experience for estimating the true proportion. In that case we want to emphasize the inferential factor. In Bayesian terms, the inferential factor establishes a prior probability on the basis of similar memories which can be adjusted as the system gathers experience.

One question concerns how to measure similarity for the inferential factor. Following the lead of the work in information retrieval (Salton & McGill, 1983), which is also reflected by a strong tradition in psychology, we decompose the memory trace A into a number of elements. Thus, for example, my memory of Ronald Reagan defeating Jimmy Carter might be decomposed into the elements *Ronald Reagan, defeated,* and *Jimmy Carter.* The similarity between a cue i and memory A would be defined in terms of the similarity of cue i to every element of A. Thus, if cue i were *George Bush,* its similarity to the Ronald Reagan memory could be defined in terms of the individual similarity of *George Bush* to *Ronald Reagan,* to *defeat,* and to *Jimmy Carter.* These element-to-element similarities should reflect the frequency with which a memory trace involving one element is needed when the other element is in the context. Operationally, these element-to-element similarities can be tapped by free association norms or direct ratings.

To summarize, the analysis of the contextual factor identifies direct cooccurrence of the target cue and the memory and similarity between the cue and memory components as factors which should be related to $P(A|i)/P(A)$. Given that identification, a number of phenomena from the experimental literature can be predicted, including the following:

> *Phenomenon 4* Recognition memories are generally poorer when cued by more frequent words (Gillund & Shiffrin, 1984; Kintsch, 1970). The basis for this can be seen in the ratio $P(i|A)/P(i)$. If $P(i|A)$ is held constant, as it usually is in memory experiments, there will be a negative effect of the frequency of i, which increases $P(i)$.
>
> *Phenomenon 5* Memories are poorer the more memories are associated to a particular term (Anderson, 1983). The basis for this classic interferential effect is easy to see in the ratio $P(A|i)/P(A)$. If the probability of a particular memory is held constant as it usually is in a memory experiment, this ratio will vary with $P(A|i)$. The more things, A, associated with i, the lower $P(A|i)$ must be on average for any A.

Phenomenon 6 Memories are more accessible in the presence of related elements and less accessible in the presence of unrelated elements. This phenomenon occurs in many contexts but has been studied at great length in research on word priming, where words related to primes are processed more quickly than unprimed words, but words unrelated to primes are processed more slowly (e.g., Meyer & Schvaneveldt, 1971; Neely, 1977). Because of the similarity factor, $P(A|i)/P(A)$ is greater than 1 for primes i that are related to the word. Since, the $P(A|i)$ must average to $P(A)$ and the $P(A|i)$ are greater than $P(A)$ for related primes, they must be lower than $P(A)$ for unrelated words. Thus, for unrelated words, $P(A|i)/P(A)$ will be a ratio that will lesson the estimated odds of A.

Many other phenomena are addressed in Anderson (1990a) and Anderson and Milson (1989), but the three examples above establish that frequency, interference, and priming effects all reflect adaptive estimation strategies on the part of memory. This contrasts with their typical treatment, according to which they are idiosyncrasies of the memory system. Interference (Phenomenon 5) is typically seen as a weakness. These effects, as well as those associated with the history factor, however, reflect sensible procedures for estimating the potential relevance of a target memory rather than weaknesses or peculiarities of the memory system.

3 A Rational Theory of Categorization

The goal assumed for categorization is to predict features of objects (e.g., predicting whether a creature will be dangerous). A category label is just another feature to be predicted. On this view, predicting that a creature will be called a tiger is no different from predicting that it will be dangerous. There has been a tendency in the empirical literature to assume that category labeling is the raison d'etre of a category. A number of investigators (e.g., Kahneman & O'Curry, 1988; Mandler et al., 1988) have recently pointed out that the focus on predicting category labels may have distorted our understanding of categorization. Category formation is not equivalent to assigning labels, and it is possible to form categories in the absence of any labels (Brooks, 1978; Fried & Holyoak, 1984; Homa & Cultice, 1984). A label is just another feature.

Having specified the goal of categorization, the next step in a rational analysis is to specify the relevant structure of the environment. Our rational theory of categorization rests on the structure of living objects produced by the phenomenon of speciation. Species form a nearly disjoint partitioning of the natural objects because they cannot interbreed. Within a species there is a common genetic pool, which means that individual members will display particular feature values with probabilities that reflect the proportion of those phenotypes in the population. Another useful feature of species structure is that the display of features within a freely interbreeding species is largely independent.[4] For example, there is little relationship between size and color in species where those two dimensions vary. Thus, the critical aspect of speciation is the disjoint partitioning of the object set and the independent probabilistic display of features within a species.

An interesting question concerns whether other types of objects display these same properties. Another common type of object is the artifact. Artifacts approximate a disjoint partitioning but there are occasional exceptions—for example, mobile homes are both homes and vehicles. Other types of objects (stones, geological formations, heavenly bodies, etc.) seem to approximate a disjoint partitioning but here it is hard to know whether this is just how we perceive them or whether there is any objective sense in which they are disjoint. One can use the understanding of speciation in the case of living objects and the manufacturer's intended function in the case of artifacts to objectively test disjointness.

I have taken this disjoint, probabilistic model of categories as the approximate structure of the environment for predicting object features. As discussed in Anderson (1990), it would be too costly computationally to calculate the exact probabilities with this model. Based on considerations of controlling computational cost, an iterative categorization algorithm (much like those of Fisher, 1987 and Lebowitz, 1987) has been developed that calculates approximations to the exact probabilities. The following is a formal specification of the iterative algorithm:

1. Before seeing any objects, the category partitioning of the objects is initialized to be the empty set of no categories.

2. Given a partitioning for the first m objects, calculate for each category k the probability P_k that the $m + 1st$ object comes from category k. Let P_o be the probability that the object comes from a completely new category.

3. Create a partitioning of the $m + 1$ objects with the $m + 1st$ object assigned to the category with maximum probability calculated in Step 2.

4. To predict the probability of value j on dimension i for the $n + 1st$ object, calculate:

$$Pred_{ij} = \sum_k P_k P(ij|k) \tag{3}$$

where P_k is the probability the $n + 1st$ object comes from category k and $P(ij|k)$ is the probability of displaying value j on dimension i.

The basic algorithm is one in which the category structure is grown by assigning each incoming object to the category it is most likely to come from. Thus a specific partitioning of the objects is produced. Note, however, that the prediction for the new $n + 1st$ object is *not* calculated by determining its most likely category and the probability of j given that category. The calculation in

Equation 3 is performed over all categories. This gives a much more accurate approximation to $Pred_{ij}$ because it handles situations where the new object is ambiguous among multiple categories. It will weight these competing categories approximately equally.

It remains to come up with a formula for calculating P_k and $P(ij|k)$. Since $P(ij|k)$ turns out to be involved in the definition of $P_{k'}$ we will focus on P_k. In Bayesian terminology, P_k is a posterior probability $P(k|F)$ that the object belongs to category k given that it has feature structure F. Bayes' formula can be used to express this in terms of a prior probability $P(k)$ of coming from category k before the feature structure is inspected and a conditional probability $P(F|k)$ of displaying the feature structure F given that it comes from category k:

$$P_k = P(k|F) = \frac{P(k)P(F|k)}{\sum\limits_{k} P(k)P(F|k)} \tag{4}$$

where the summation in the denominator is over all categories k currently in the partitioning, including a potential new one. This then focuses our analysis on the derivation of a prior probability $P(k)$ and a conditional probability $P(F|k)$.[5]

3.1 The Prior Probability

The critical assumption with respect to the prior probability is that there is a fixed probability c that two objects come from the same category and this probability does not depend on the number of objects seen so far. This is called the *coupling probability*. If one takes this assumption about the coupling probability between two objects being independent of the other objects and generalizes it, one can derive a simple form for $P(k)$ (see Anderson, 1990a, for the derivation):

$$P(k) = \frac{cn_k}{(1-c) + cn} \tag{5}$$

where c is the coupling probability, n_k is the number of objects assigned to category k so far, and n is the total number of objects seen so far. Note that for large n this closely approximates n_k/n, which means that there is a strong base rate effect in these calculations with a bias to put new objects in large categories. The rational basis for this is presumably apparent.

We also need a formula for $P(0)$, which is the probability that the new object comes from an entirely new category. This is

$$P(0) = \frac{(1-c)}{(1-c) + cn} \tag{6}$$

For a large n this closely approximates $(1-c)/cn$, which is again a reasonable form—that is, the probability of a brand new category depends on the coupling probability and the number of objects seen. The greater the coupling probability and the more objects, the less likely it is that the new object comes from an entirely new category.

3.2 Conditional Probability

In the case of the conditional probability, the critical assumption, based on our analysis of speciation, is that the probability of displaying features on various dimensions given category membership is independent of the probabilities on other dimensions. Thus we can write

$$P(F|k) = \prod_i P(ij|k) \tag{7}$$

where $P(ij|k)$ is the probability of displaying value j on dimension i given that the object comes from category k. This is the same quantity that appeared in Equation 3. The importance of Equation 7 is that it allows us to analyze each dimension separately.

Standard Bayesian models (Berger, 1985) can be used to calculate a posterior density of probabilities and the mean of this density. There are different solutions for discrete and continuous dimensions. I will present the discrete case here. Anderson and Matessa (1990) can be consulted for the more complex continuous case. In the discrete case we have:

$$P(ij|k) = \frac{n_{ij} + \alpha_j}{n_k + \alpha_0} \tag{8}$$

where the α_j are parameters reflecting our priors, $\alpha_0 = \sum \alpha_j$, n_k is the number of objects in category k which have a known value on dimension i, and n_{ij} is the number of objects in category k with the value j. α_j/α_0 reflects the prior probability of the value j and α_0 reflects the strength of belief in these priors. For large $n_k P(ij|k)$ approximates n_{ij}/n_k which one frequently sees promoted as the rational probability. It has to have this more complicated form to deal with problems of small samples, however. For example, if one had just seen one object in a category and it had the color red, one would not want to guess that all objects were red. If there were seven colors with the α_j for each equal to 1.0, the above formula would given $\frac{1}{4}$ as the posterior probability of red and $\frac{1}{8}$ for the other unseen six colors.

Basically, Equations 7 and 8 define a basis for judging how similar an object is to the category's central tendency.

3.3 Empirical Phenomena

The algorithm and mathematical relationships just described have allowed us to simulate a large number of experimental results in the literature including:

> *Phenomenon 7* Subjects more reliably assign an object to a category the closer it is to the central tendency of the category (Hayes-Roth & Hayes-

Roth, 1977; Posner & Keele, 1968; Reed, 1972). This is in direct response to Equation 8 and variations on it which indicate that the conditional probabilities should be higher for closer objects.

Phenomenon 8 Although test objects tend to be more reliably categorized the closer they are to the central tendency of the category, there is also an effect of their distance from specific members of the category (Medin & Schaffer, 1978). This is demonstrated by having subjects study instances that are distant from the central tendency. Subjects will do well in categorizing test items that are similar to the distant instance. The way the model handles this is to create two categories—one for the instances that define the central tendency and one for the oddball instance. This is done because it maximizes the overall predictive structure of the object set.

Phenomenon 9 Lately, much has been made of the fact that the probability of categorization is an exponentially decaying function of the number of features on which the test instance mismatches the category (Russell, 1986; Shepard, 1989). This is produced in the rational model by Equation 8, which makes conditional probability a product (not a sum) of the probabilities on individual dimensions.

Phenomenon 10 Subjects' categorization is sensitive to the number of objects in a category such that they have a greater tendency to assign objects to categories with larger membership (e.g., Homa & Cultice, 1984). This sensible base rate effect is produced by Equation 5, which defines the prior probability of belonging to a category. It turns out that the model also predicts some of the subtle deviations from base rate effects reported by Medin and Edelson (1988).

Phenomenon 11 Subjects are sensitive to the correlation of features in an experimenter's category (Medin et al., 1982). The model predicts this despite the fact that it treats dimensions in its internal categories as independent. When there are correlated features it breaks out different categories to correspond to each combination of correlated values. This is just one example of many where the model does not observe the labeling conventions of the experimenter in deciding what category structure maximizes prediction.

Phenomenon 12 Subjects tend to identify a category structure in which the categories are sufficiently specific to pick up most of the predictive structure of the objects but are not unnecessarily narrow. Rosch (e.g., Rosch et al., 1976) called these the basic level categories. This model forms categories that correspond to the basic level categories subjects identify (Hoffman & Ziessler, 1983; Murphy & Smith, 1982) because this does maximize the predictive structure of the categories.

For details of these phenomena and others see Anderson (1990a; 1991). The evidence seems quite compelling that subjects' categorization behavior can be seen as an attempt to optimize their predictions about the features of objects.

Shepard (1987) also analyzes generalization phenomena as the consequence of trying to optimize prediction. Although his method of analysis is quite different, he comes to very similar conclusions. This is comforting, because an optimization analysis should not depend on the details of the optimization methodology. What is optimal for achieving a goal in a particular environment should be the same under all carefully reasoned analyses.

4 A Rational Analysis of Causal Inference

The analysis of causal inference is quite parallel to the analysis of categorical inference. In the case of causal inference, the assumed goal of the system is to maximize the accuracy of its predictions about future events (e.g., whether a light will go on when a switch is flipped). To do this, the system must extract the laws that govern the world's predictive structure and recognize the situations in which these laws are apt to apply. These laws are serving the same basic role in making predictions about events as categories were in making predictions about objects.

There are a number of ways causal inference is more complicated and the rational analysis correspondingly less complete. For one, it is not entirely clear what the best conception is of a "causal law." I have opted for such rather traditional situation-action rules as, "If the forest is dry and lightning strikes, there will be a fire." Such laws are necessarily probabilistic. Another complication is that generalizing these laws requires generalizing over relational structures and the problem of relational generalization is notably more difficult than categorical generalization.

A situation can be conceived as presenting a set of cues, C, that might be relevant to predicting that an event, E, will occur (Einhorn & Hogarth 1986). The prediction task is to come up with a probability $P(E|C)$ of an event E conditional on the cues C. The relevant intervening constructs are the set of causal rules, i, that we have inferred. $P(E|C)$ can be calculated by the following rule:

$$P(E|C) = \sum_i P(i|C)P(E|i) \tag{9}$$

where $P(i|C)$ is the probability of rule i applying in the presence of cues C and $P(E|i)$ is the probability of event E should rule i apply. This rule is the analog of Equation 3 for categorization.

Equation 9 focuses on $P(i|C)$, the probability of a causal law applying in a situation and $P(E|i)$, the probability of an event should a causal law apply. $P(E|i)$ will be basically derived from how often the event occurs when the rule is applicable. Analogous to Equation 3 the relevant equation for $P(i|C)$ is:

$$P(i|C) = \frac{Con(i)P(C|i)}{\sum_i Con(i)P(C|i)} \tag{10}$$

where $Con(i)$ denotes the confidence that i exists and $P(C|i)$ is the probability of cues C if rule i did apply. Note $Con(i)$ plays the role of a prior probability but it is not a prior probability. Rather than reflecting a probability that the rule will apply it reflects a confidence in the existence of the rule.

Before turning to the empirical phenomena, a brief comment is required on the treatment of causality as probabilistic. There is a long standing tradition in philosophy, extending back to Hume and Kant, of treating causality as deterministic. I am relatively naive with respect to the underlying philosophical issues, but I am inclined to agree with Suppes's (1984) characterization of nonprobabilistic treatments of causality as fundamentally incoherent. More to the point, however, our enterprise is not directly concerned with philosophical issues but rather with how to maximize predictions about events in the future. Whatever one's conception of the nature of causality, I assume one would be hard pressed not to take a statistical and hence a probabilistic approach to the prediction task.

4.1 Empirical Phenomena

This analysis identifies a number of quantities as relevant to causal inference—$Con(i)$, $P(C|i)$, and $P(E|i)$. $Con(i)$ is one's confidence in a causal rule such as "smoking causes lung cancer." $P(C|i)$ is the conditional probability of a cue C given that law i applies. An example might be the probability that one would see yellow teeth in someone to whom the law applies (i.e., a smoker). $P(E|i)$ is the probability of getting the effect when the law applies—that is, the probability that someone will have lung cancer because of smoking. We have been able to examine a number of empirical phenomena relevant to these quantities and to show their rational basis:

> *Phenomenon 13* With respect to $Con(i)$, there are a number of studies of human causal inference given 2×2 contingency data in which subjects experience an effect or the absence of an effect in the presence or absence of a purported cause (e.g., Arkes & Harkness, 1983; Crocker, 1981; Schustack & Sternberg, 1981). Human inference has often been characterized as nonoptimal in such situations because people are more influenced by changes in the joint cooccurence of cause and effect than changes in the joint nonoccurrence of cause and effect. It is assumed that subjects should be symmetrically sensitive. This assumption depends, however, on subjects' prior beliefs about the frequency of an effect in the presence of a cause compared with its absence. If subjects are much more certain about what the frequency is in the absence of a cause than in its presence, an asymmetry is predicted that corresponds to what is empirically observed. It seems reasonable to assume that subjects will assume that any particular event should have a probability near zero in the absence of a cause whereas they should be uncertain just how strong the relationship is in the presence.[6]

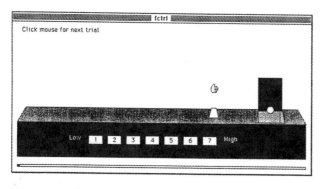

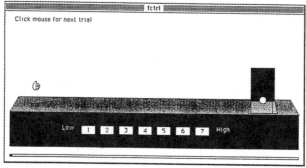

Figure 37.1
The stimulus situation for judging causality: (a) when a weight is dropped and a vibratory wave
model is invoked and (b) when a ball is dropped and a projectile model is invoked.

Anderson (1990a) reports very good data fits to human causal attributions
given these assumptions. Thus, what has been characterized as non-
rational may in fact be optimal given appropriate assumptions about
prior probabilities.

Phenomenon 14 With respect to $P(C|i)$, there has been a long history of
concern with the effect of cues about the temporal and spatial contiguity
between cause and effect. At least since Hume's writings there has been
the belief that humans reflexively see causality in cases of close spatial and
temporal proximity. In joint research with Mike Matessa and Ross
Thompson, however, we find that how subjects use these cues depends on
the particular prior model they bring to the situation.

Because contiguity has been so closely tied to thinking about causality and
since our research on this is not yet published, we will describe it in a little
detail. Figure 37.1 shows the two experimental situations we used with our
subjects: In all cases, the event to be explained is a trap door opening and a ball
rising out of the hole at the right of the box. Prior to this, an event occurs to the

left of the hole. The subject's task is to judge whether or not the first event appears to be the cause of the door opening and the ball coming out. In Figure 37.1a, a hand lets go of a weight and it drops onto the box. Subjects are told that it may have jarred loose a latch that opens the door and releases the ball. Subjects are asked to judge how likely it is that the weight is responsible. In Figure 37.1b, subjects see a hand drop a ball into a hole and are told that there might be a passage in the box through which it goes and comes out at the trap door. The time between the dropping of the weight or ball and the opening of the box is varied, as is the distance between where the weight or ball drops and the door.

Subjects were asked to rate on a 1–7 scale how strong a causal link they perceived between the two events (the dropping of either the weight or the ball and the ball rising from the hole). The first event occurred at various distances from the second and at various delays in time. Figure 37.2 shows how subjects' ratings varied as a function of these two dimensions. The results are in sharp contrast for the two conditions. In the case of the weight (Figure 37.2a), the results correspond approximately to the classical prescriptions. There is a large effect of temporal contiguity on the causal ascriptions. The effect of spatial contiguity is more complex. People ascribe more causality to the closer stimulus only in the case of short temporal contiguity. The effects of the two dimensions are not additive. This interaction is what would be predicted under the appropriate physical model: The weight dropped on the beam should set up a vibratory wave that travels through the beam nearly instantaneously (and presumably jars the mechanism that causes the door to open and the ball to spring forth). Any substantial delay between one event and the other should appear causally anomalous. In nonanomalous cases, distance becomes a valid cue because the force at a location should diminish with something between $1/d$ and $1/d^2$ where d is the distance from the source.

The case where the ball is dropped into the beam (Figure 37.2b) shows an even stronger interaction between time and distance. There is no favored time or distance. Rather, subjects are looking for a match between time and distance. The model they must be assuming is one in which the ball moves through the beam at a constant velocity and what they are looking for is cases where the ball would travel that distance in that time. Thus, in both parts a and b of Figure 37.2, we see that temporal and spatial contiguity are not used as mindless cues to causality, but rather are filtered through plausible models of the situation to make sensible inferences about causality. If closer temporal and spatial contiguity usually lead to causal ascriptions, it may reflect the fact that people tend to perceive situations in terms of something like the vibratory wave model. Schultz (1982) has emphasized the primacy of a prior model in people's causal attributions.

Phenomenon 15 People are also influenced by similarity between cause and effect in their causal attributions; there has been a long tradition of

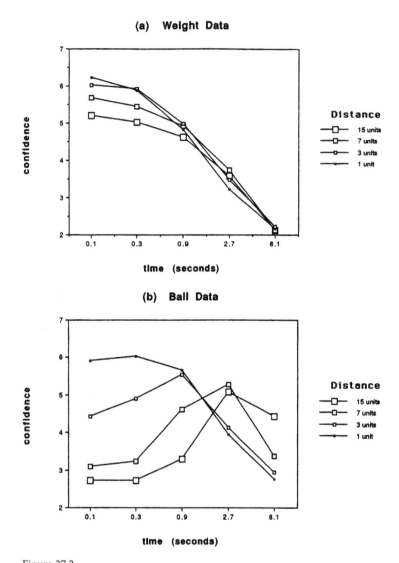

Figure 37.2
Strength of causal perception as a function of distance in space and time for (a) the weight and the vibratory wave model and (b) the ball and projectile model.

viewing this reliance on similarity as irrational (for a review, read Nisbett & Ross, 1980). We were able to show that under certain prior models similarity is a valid cue to causation—basically, when the cause transfers part of itself to the effect. For example, when all the wash turns out a brilliant purple it is reasonable to blame an item of clothing that has that color and people naturally use similarity in this case. On the other hand, they are very unlikely to blame a similarly colored wallpaper. Thus, similarity is not used mindlessly as a cue for causality but is within the framework of justifiable prior models. Such inferential use is statistical (or, in artificial intelligence terms, a heuristic) and may lead to incorrect conclusions on occasions. This does not make its use justified, however.

Phenomenon 16 When we see a causal law apply to an object it is reasonable to infer that it will apply again to that object, but what other objects will it also apply to? It is an implication of the rational analysis of categorization and the rational analysis of causal inference that subjects ought to use category boundaries to define the range of generalization of their causal inferences. We showed experimentally (Anderson 1990a, Chapter 4) that subjects' causal inferences do take place in the manner predicted by the conjunction of the two models.

Phenomena 13–15 have a status somewhat different from that of the earlier ones. In the case of these three, there were certain aspects of human causal inference that had been commonly described as irrational. In each case there was a failure to consider reasonable prior models one might bring to situations of causal inference. When reasonable prior models are factored in, there is evidence for a great deal of rationality in human causal inference.

5 A Rational Analysis of Problem Solving

With respect to problem solving it was assumed that the goal of the system was to achieve certain states of affairs (e.g., getting from one location to another). Achieving a state of affairs has some value, G. The problem solver is characterized as searching for some plan which will achieve this state of affairs. Any plan is characterized as having a certain cost, C, and probability of success, P. The rational behavior is one of choosing among plans to find one that maximizes $PG - C$ and executing it, provided its expected value is positive.

This characterization of problem solving is unlike the characterization that exists in the problem-solving literature in that it considers plans as probabilistic and concerns itself explicitly with the trade-off of gains and costs. This seems more like the actual problem solving that people face daily, however. This characterization of problem solving is clearly connected to the decision-making tasks that have been studied and indeed such decision-making tasks are special cases of problem solving under this characterization. This leads to the first rational phenomenon under problem solving:

Phenomenon 17 Subjects appear to make decisions in which they combine subjective probabilities and subjective utilities in accordance with a standard economic logic (for a review, Kahneman & Tversky, 1984). A rational analysis would predict the economic combination principle but it is often thought that rational subjects should combine the stated probabilities and utilities and not subjective quantities that systematically deviate from them. This only follows, however, if the stated quantities are the true values, and there is no justification for believing this is so. It is rare for probabilities that are stated to us to be accurate, particularly extreme probabilities (e.g., I don't know how many times programmers, students, friends, etc., said they were almost *certain* to have a task done by a particular date). Also, true adaptive utility (e.g., number of surviving offspring) could not be linearly related to money or other stated utilities over an unbounded region. Matching these discrepancies between stated and true quantities, subjective probability functions tend to discount extreme stated probabilities and subjective utility functions are nonlinear in money and wealth. Although there are still many second-order considerations (which would require a paper in themselves), it still appears to be more adaptive to use subjective probabilities and utilities than stated probabilities and utilities.

5.1 Combinatorial Structure

Problem-solving tasks often have a combinatorial structure that most experimental decision-making tasks do not. A typical decision-making task involves taking a single action. A typical problem-solving task involves taking a sequence of actions or steps to achieve a goal. Therefore, there is a sequence of decisions to be made. For example, in the Tower of Hanoi problem (see Anderson, 1990b, Chapter 8), no single allowable step will go from the start state to the goal state. There are logically more complex possibilities, but consider a pure serial step structure such as in an eight puzzle[7] or getting from an office to a new lecture hall.[8] In these cases each step causes a new state that "enables" the next step and finally results in the goal.

The probability that a sequence of steps intended to produce the goal will actually do so is the product of the probabilities' that the individual steps will have their intended effects.[9] The cost is the sum of the costs of all the steps. This suggests that such step combinations can be treated as single macro-steps with the derived probabilities and costs, and that one can choose among them with the same expected utility logic (discussed under Phenomenon 17) used for choosing single steps.

The major difficulty is in applying this logic to discovering such sequences for the first time. This is the traditional domain of problem-solving search. In the problem-solving literature, the steps are called operators. The difficulty is searching the exponentially expanding space of operators leading from the current state: If a operators can apply to each state, there are a^n chains of n operators extending from the start state.

The typical AI program searches through such sequences of steps using various heuristics, finds some sequence that leads to the goal state, and then executes that sequence. Thus, the typical scheme is to plan a complete solution and then act on it. There are two difficulties with this scheme. The first concerns the probabilistic nature of these steps. That is, the planned sequence of steps will lead to the goal only with a certain probability. With some probability they will fail and lead elsewhere. It would not always be rational to plan a long sequence of steps if the sequence is going to diverge from the intended path at an early point. The second difficulty is that limits on memory span results imply that one cannot hold a long sequence of such steps in mind, let alone compare a large number of such sequences.

Thus, one can at best plan a few steps before acting. This is in fact how human problem solving typically plays itself out. For example, when I put something in one side of the car I seldom consider whether it is the easier side to take it out from—only whether it is the easier side to put it in from. This can and does lead to overall problem-solving episodes that are nonoptimal. This iterative plan-and-act structure is an inevitable consequence, however, of the uncertainty of problem solving in these domains and the limitations of working memory.

The iterative plan-and-act structure in human problem solving is transparent in many situations. For example, people trying to solve the eight puzzle will plan short sequences of steps to get a piece in a desired position, execute them, plan, execute, and so forth. Their problem-solving episodes often consist of a pause when a plan of some sort is being hatched, a sequence of steps resulting in a piece in position, another pause, and so on.

The basic logic of such iterative plan-and-act schemes is to approximate optimality in global problem solving by achieving local optimality. This is reminiscent of the issues discussed with respect to the operant literature on the matching law. Just as local maximizing can lead to global nonoptimality, so too problem-solving sequences which are locally optimal might not be globally optimal. The argument here, as in the case of the matching law, is that such exceptions are too unpredictable statistically and too costly computationally to be considered. Such local optimization can have optimal expected value even if it produces a specific instance of behavior that is nonoptimal (ignoring computational cost) in a specific situation.

5.2 Rational Analysis of Partial Plans

I use the phrase *plan* or *partial plan* to refer to a plan for achieving a goal which involves a move (a sequence of one or more steps) followed by the intention to complete the achievement of the goal after this move. An interesting question is how one chooses the partial plan to execute. One cannot use the criterion that

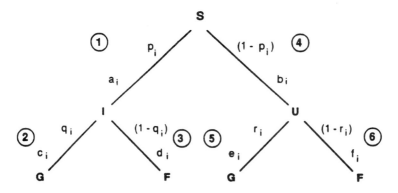

Figure 37.3
The state of affairs with respect to evaluating a move "I." The first level in the tree represents whether the move achieves its intended state (I) or some unintended state (U). The second level reflects whether it is possible to get from these states to the goal (G) or not (F).

the plan achieves the goal because the plan does not get one all the way to the goal.

Figure 37.3 is an objective analysis (i.e., not necessarily in the subject's head) of the state of affairs with respect to evaluating a plan i involving a move of one or more steps and then the intention to reach the goal. The diagram starts at state S and branches off from there. Each branch in that diagram is explained:

1. The move in plan i has some probability p_i of producing its intended state I and some cost a_i associated with that move.
2. Since I is not the goal state, there is some probability q_i that the goal state will be reached from I with a cost c_i.
3. With probability $(1 - q_i)$ the goal state cannot be reached from I. There will be some cost d_i associated with the moves before the goal is abandoned.
4. With probability $(1 - p_i)$ the move in plan i does not produce its intended state I but some unintended state U. There is a cost b_i associated with getting to U.
5. From state U there is still some probability r_i that the goal can be achieved with cost e_i.
6. Finally, there is a probability $(1 - r_i)$ that the goal cannot be reached from state U and a cost f_i before the goal is abandoned.

The overall probability of success and cost associated with plan i is

$$P_i = p_i q_i + (1 - p_i) r_i \tag{11}$$

$$C_i = p_i[a_i + q_i c_i + (1 - q_i)d_i] + (1 - p_i)[b_i + r_i e_i + (1 - r_i)f_i] \tag{12}$$

Given this definition of P_i and C_i for a plan i, the system should choose among the plans just as it chose when there was only one step to the goal. The logic for choosing among plans is one in which one considers them mutually exclusive and chooses the one that maximizes $P_iG - C_i$ provided that quantity is positive. Indeed, multimove plans can be put into competition with single-move plans and a choice can be made among all of the possible plans according to this economic logic. In some cases, a multimove plan might be chosen over a single-move plan because the multimove plan is cheaper or more probable.

Anderson (1990a) goes through a series of mathematical simplifications to reduce Equations 11 and 12 into the following more easily analyzable forms:

$$P_i = p_iq_i/[1 - (1 - p_i)f] \tag{13}$$

$$C_i = a_i + c_i \tag{14}$$

where f is a parameter reflecting how much a failure to achieve an intended intermediate state affects the prospects of finally achieving the goal.

The upshot of these simplifications is to reduce the estimation problems to that of estimating p_i, the probability of the move in the partial plan producing the intended state; q_i, the probability of getting from that state to the goal; a_i, the cost of the partial plan; and c_i, the remaining cost if it succeeds. The decision procedure becomes simply to choose i with maximum expected $P_iG - C_i$ (as defined by Equations 13 and 14) or to give up if there is no i such that $P_iG > C_i$.[10]

The terms a_i and p_i can be estimated directly from knowledge of the steps in the move associated with the partial plan. The question becomes how to estimate q_i and c_i, since they are associated with unknown steps after the intermediate state has been reached. There are a number of possible bases for their estimation, but two have been analyzed in detail. One is the similarity between the goal and the state the move is intended to result in. The second is the amount of effort expended so far.[11]

Bayesian techniques were used again to estimate q_i and c_i from similarity and effort. This involved developing prior models of how problems varied in the amount of effort they required for completion and how they varied in similarity. In the case of effort required for completion, the assumption was that problems varied according to a gamma distribution. With respect to similarity, a correlation was assumed between the number of differences between a state and a goal and the amount of effort required to reach the goal. If differences were independent there would be a perfect correlation—every difference would require an extra unit of effort to eliminate. Because of nonindependence of differences, this correlation is not perfect, and an exponential distribution of differences was assumed with the mean of the distribution proportional to the amount of effort.

A final issue that needs to be factored into the analysis of problem solving is an internal cost of generating moves. A satisficing model (Simon, 1955) was produced in which the problem solver stops generating moves when the expected improvement from considering another move is less than the cost of generating it.

5.3 Empirical Phenomena

Based on these assumptions a simulation of human problem solving was developed which reproduced the following phenomena (see Anderson, 1990a, Chapter 5, for details):

> *Phenomenon 18* The typical first attack on a problem in a novel domain is to do hill-climbing (e.g., Atwood & Polson, 1976; Kotovsky et al., 1985). This falls out of the correlation between difference and amount of effort.
>
> *Phenomenon 19* When subjects have difficulty with a novel problem they switch from hill-climbing to means-end analysis (Kotovsky et al., 1985). This turns out to be the result of the fact that hill-climbing promises to minimize effort whereas means-ends analysis promises to maximize probability of success. Early in a problem sequence the subject is justified to believe in a high probability of success because most problems are solvable by this means. If the subject fails to succeed for longer than expected, he will switch to a method that promises to maximize probability of success.
>
> *Phenomenon 20* This analysis predicts that subjects are variable in their behavior and do not always make the optimal moves. This follows from the analysis of "satisficing" in which students stop seeking moves when the expected value of search decreases below a threshold. Moreover, their variability and nonoptimality is a function of both the value of the goal and the cost of considering moves.

The phenomena listed above do not really test the sophisticated interactions implied by the rational model of problem solving. This basically reflects a mismatch between this theory and the literature on problem solving. No literature deals with problem solving under conditions of uncertainty, real costs and gains, and complex problem-solving structure. There are decision-making tasks that involve uncertainty and real costs and gains. Unfortunately, they focus on simple one-step problems. There are problem-solving tasks that have a complex combinatorial structure, but they involve steps whose outcome is certain with unclear costs and gains. The rational model applies to these two types of tasks in a rather degenerate way.

In the case of decision making, the problem of managing search does not arise. The problem concerns how gradations in subjects' choice behaviors vary with gradations in the choice sets. In contrast, the problem-solving literature tends to treat the subject as totally deterministic, making all-or-none choices. There is no way to conceptualize the fact that subjects make different choices except to put a random function in the simulation. As a consequence, the typical problem-solving theories (including previous theories of my own) have great difficulty dealing with the statistics of group behavior and are content to simulate single subjects.

> *Phenomenon 21* Most everyday problem solving has a structure that differs significantly from the one studied in the decision-making and problem-solving literature. A paradigmatic example is route finding, where the maze of potential paths creates a very concrete search space in which the uncertainties of passage cause real variability and time and money are real costs. Recently, we have been studying route finding in the laboratory (Anderson & Kushmerick, 1990), putting novel predictions of the theory to test. We show, for example, a linear relationship between decision time and the number of alternatives considered before our satisficing model selects an alternative. This is an example of a novel prediction of the rational model being put to test.

6 Implementation of a Rational Analysis

It is in the spirit of a rational analysis to prescribe what the behavior of a system should be rather than how to compute it. It is not our claim that the human system actually goes through the relatively complex Bayesian analysis used to establish what the optimal behavior was. Inevitably, however, the criticism is made that such rational models are unrealistic because they imply unrealistic mental computations. It is often quite easy to convert these rational prescriptions into plausible mechanisms, however. As one example, consider the following proposal for implementing the categorization prescription described earlier in a connectionist architecture.

Figure 37.4 shows a connectionist network designed to implement a category structure created by a rational model simulation of an experiment by Gluck and Bower (1988). Subjects in their experiment learned to associate two diseases, a rare and a common one, with the absence or presence of four symptoms (thus there are in effect eight symptoms). Our system in this simulation induced four categories to capture various patterns of symptom-disease correlation. It should be noted that the disease labels are features associated with the category and are no different from the symptoms. In the center of the figure are the four categories. Figure 37.4 illustrates associations from each of the 10 features (eight symptoms and two disease labels) to each category and from the category to each feature. Activation will spread from the input feature nodes to the category nodes and then to the output feature nodes.

We can use the rational analysis to prescribe the appropriate activation calculations. Let us first consider a calculation of the activation levels of the category nodes. This activation calculation should implement Equations 4–8. The two relevant probabilities in this equation are $P(k)$ for each category and

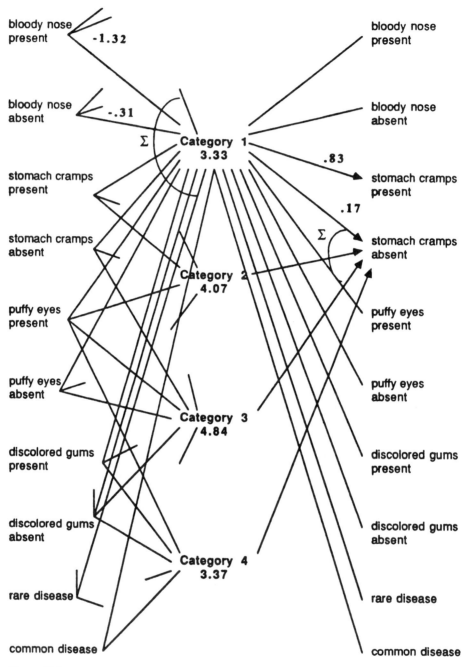

Figure 37.4
A schematic representation of how a category structure might be represented in an ACT declarative network.

$P(ij|k)$ for each link from feature j to category k. Actually, we do not have to calculate Equation 4; rather, we need only calculate a quantity proportional to $P(k)\prod P(ij|k)$ which is what the numerator in Equation 4 will become. Continuing this logic of proportionality, we can substitute the numerators of Equations 5 and 8 and make it our goal to calculate a quantity proportional to $n_k \prod[(n_{ij} + \alpha_j)/(n_k + \alpha_0)]$. This is a multiplicative relationship whereas it is typical to think of activations from various sources as adding. We therefore take logarithms and make $\ln n_k$ the activation level of the category nodes and $\ln(n_{ij} + \alpha_j) - \ln(n_k + \alpha_0)$ the strengths of the j to k links. For example, for category 1, $n_k = 28$ and $\ln n_k = 3.33$, which is what is shown in Figure 37.4. Similarly, for category 1 and bloody nose $n_{ij} = 7$ and, assuming $\alpha_j = 1$, $\ln(n_{ij} + \alpha_j) - \ln(n_k + \alpha_0) = -1.32$, which is what is shown in Figure 37.4. Activation spreading from the prescribed features would calculate

$$\ln(n_k) + \sum_j [\ln(n_{ij} + \alpha_j) - \ln(n_k + \alpha_0)],$$

which is the log of a quantity proportional to the probability of the object coming from the target category.

The real purpose of categorization is not to assign objects to categories but rather to make predictions. This requires the spreading of activation out of the category nodes to the feature nodes and the accumulation of activation there. According to the rational analyses, we want to calculate Equation 3. This requires converting the log quantities, which is what the node activation represents, to probability, which is what the output activation should represent. Therefore, we need the following formula, which relates a node's activation, A, to the amount of activation output, O.

$$O = e^{bA},$$

which makes the output activation proportional to the probability. This output activation is multiplied by $P(ij|k)$, which represents outgoing link strength, to determine the amount of activation arriving at features j from category k.

The activation-based scheme just described will deliver a level of activation to node j which is proportional to the probability $Pred_{ij}$. If we assume that the probability of making a prediction is a function of this level of activation, we have an architecture that produces the categorization results we reviewed. There are such architectures. For example, the probability of pattern-matching in the ACT* (Anderson, 1983) architecture is a function of level of activation.

Given this mapping of the categorization process into an architecture, one can specify the category learning algorithm. New category nodes have to be created every time an object cannot be assigned to an existing category (or, equivalently, each time it fails to get activation of a category node above threshold). Every time an object is assigned to an existing category the link strengths between the category and features have to be updated so that they are linearly related to $\ln(n_{ij} + \alpha_j) - \ln(n_k + \alpha_0)$ for incoming links and proportional to $n_{ij} + \alpha_j/(n_k + \alpha_0)$ for outgoing links. Also, the base level activation of the category node has to be updated to be linearly related to $\ln(n_k)$. Note that these are very trivial learning algorithms. We are not doing complex Bayesian mathematics; we are just updating strengths to reflect frequency.

There are striking similarities between this network and PDP networks with hidden units that are learned by the backprop algorithm (Rumelhart et al., 1986). The category nodes are like hidden units and the calculations in which they participate are similar if not identical. The real difference occurs in the learning algorithm. Whereas it takes huge numbers of iterations to get the backprop algorithm to learn a category structure, this algorithm basically gives asymptotic structure after each trial. The speed of learning of this procedure is gained by its strong priors concerning the structure of the environment whereas the backprop algorithm assumes, unrealistically I think, a much less structured environment.

Learning algorithms are not optimal in and of themselves. They are optimal with respect to environments. There are imaginable environments in which the backprop algorithm would do better. A rational approach encourages us to inquire about the structure of our actual environment and to design an algorithm optimal for it rather than designing algorithms which would only be optimal in some bizarre world.

7 Conclusions

This completes the review of the application of rational analysis. Although many details were necessarily omitted, I hope it is clear from this review that many of the major characteristics of human cognition can be explained as an optimal response, in a Bayesian sense, to the informational structure in the world. We also see in examples like the network implementation of categorization, the potential to advance to the second stage of the program outlined by Marr, which is to implement these rational prescriptions in a cognitive architecture.

I am not advocating rational analysis to the exclusion of other approaches to cognition. I think we see evidence, however, that other approaches to human cognition would be more profitable if we took seriously the idea that there is a reason for the way the mind is. We are not trying to understand an arbitrary black box built out of billions of neurons.

Finally, to return to the title of this target article, is human cognition adaptive? Despite the compelling evidence that various components of it are optimized to the structure of the environment, it is unclear that we can leave with as positive an opinion about the functioning of the cognitive system as a whole. Consider memory, for example. Our memory performance can be relatively insensitive to our knowledge about our memory needs. Therefore, we may know we will need to remember a telephone number in an hour's time and will then be able to forget it. Memory does not respond to this knowledge and provide a momentary surge in the availability of the number in an hour's time, however. Rather, it responds to the general statistics of the number's use, oblivious to our "knowledge" about its future use. It is possible that the various components of cognition are optimized within their narrow bounds but that they are unable to pass information which allows a global optimum to be achieved. Just as we achieve only local optima in problem solving over time, we may only achieve local optima over components. If so, such local-by-component optimization may or may not be explainable by considering computational constraints and uncertainty in defining the global optimum.

Acknowledgment

I would like to thank Albert Corbett, Melvin Reder, and Lynne Reder for their comments on this paper. This research is supported by Grant 8705811 from the National Science Foundation and Contract N00014-90-J-1489 from the Office of Naval Research.

Notes

1. This is not to imply that these are the only behavioral phenomena that can be explained or that there are contradictory phenomena. A fuller exposition of this approach can be found in Anderson (1990a).

2. Thus, for example, my memory for my locker combination has a history of being periodically useful and I may now be in context where the cues are those of the locker-room, such as lockers, showers, towels, etc.

3. Human memory may not be so constrained and it is interesting to ask which predictions might be upset by nonindependence.

4. This independence assumption is not perfect because more than one phenotypic feature can be controlled by the same gene. The most frequent form of nonindependence involves sex-linked characteristics. However, even here there is much less variation of most features (size) between sexes within a species than between species. As we will see (discussion of Phenomenon 11), in the presence of a strong set of sex-linked characteristics, the model would extract two categories—one for the male and one for the female members of the species.

5. A somewhat different Bayesian approach to categorization can be found in Cheeseman et al. (1988).

6. Consider one's confidence about the probability that a forest fire will start spontaneously at any moment when lightning does not strike versus the probability that it will start when lightning does strike. The probability in the former case is presumably near zero whereas I, at least, am very uncertain how to assign a probability in the latter case.

7. The eight puzzle is the tile-moving game (see Anderson, 1990b) where the problem solver is given a 3×3 matrix containing eight tiles and one open space. The problem solver can move the tiles into the free space. The goal is usually to achieve some target configuration of the tiles.

8. Presumably a "step" in going from the office to the lecture hall is not an actual physical step but such a well-learned fragment of a route as getting from the office to the hall.

9. Conditionalized on the success of prior steps.

10. That is, if giving up is a costless option. Otherwise, one must consider the cost of giving up in competition with the other options and choose the minimum cost option.
11. Another possible basis we are currently studying is the history of past success with a method. Therefore, if I have had a history of success with trying to repair things by hand, I will be more inclined to try to repair something myself rather than call a repair shop.

References

Anderson, J. R. (1978) Arguments concerning representations for mental imagery. *Psychological Review* 85:249–77.

Anderson, J. R. (1983) *The architecture of cognition.* Harvard University Press.

Anderson, J. R. (1990a) *The adaptive character of thought.* Erlbaum.

Anderson, J. R. (1990b) *Cognitive psychology and its implications, 3rd ed.* W.H. Freeman.

Anderson, J. R. (1991) The place of cognitive architectures in a rational analysis. In: *Architectures for intelligence,* ed. K. vanLehn. Erlbaum.

Anderson, J. R. & Kushmerick, N. (1990) A rational analysis of production system architecture. Paper presented at the 31st Annual Meeting of the Psychonomic Society, November 16–18.

Anderson, J. R. & Matessa, M. (1990) A rational analysis of categorization. In: Proceedings of the Seventh International Machine Learning Conference, Palo Alto, CA, ed. M. Kaufmann.

Anderson, J. R. & Milson, R. (1989) Human memory: An adaptive perspective. *Psychological Review* 96(4):703–19.

Arkes, H. R. & Harkness, A. R. (1983) Estimates of contingency between two dichotomous variables. *Journal of Experimental Psychology: General* 112:117–35.

Atwood, M. E. & Polson, P. G. (1976) A process model for water jug problems. *Cognitive Psychology* 8:191–216.

Bahrick, H. R. (1979) Maintenance of knowledge: Questions about memory we forget to ask. *Journal of Experimental Psychology: General* 108:296–308.

Berger, J. O. (1985) *Statistical decision theory and Bayesian analyses.* Springer-Verlag.

Brooks, L. (1978) Nonanalytic concept formation and memory for instances. In: *Cognition and categorization,* ed. E. Rosch & B. B. Lloyd. Erlbaum.

Brunswik, E. (1956) *Perception and the representative design of psychological experiments.* University of California Press.

Burrell, Q. L. (1980) A simple stochastic model for library loans. *Journal of Documentation* 36: 115–32.

Burrell, Q. L. & Cane, V. R. (1982) The analysis of library data. *Journal of the Royal Statistical Society Series* A(145):439–71.

Crocker, J. (1981) Judgment of covariation by social perceivers. *Psychological Bulletin* 90:272–92.

Dupré, J. (1987) *The latest on the best.* MIT Press.

Einhorn, H. J. & Hogarth, R. M. (1986) Judging probable cause. *Psychological Bulletin* 99:3–19.

Fantino, E. & Abarca, N. (1985) Choice, optimal foraging and the delay reduction hypothesis. *Behavioral and Brain Sciences* 8:315–30.

Fisher, D. H. (1987) Knowledge acquisition via incremental conceptual clustering. *Machine Learning* 2:139–72.

Fried, L. S. & Holyoak, K. J. (1984) Induction of category distributions: A framework for classification learning. *Journal of Experimental Psychology: Learning, Memory, and Cognition* 10:234–57.

Gibson, J. J. (1966) *The senses considered as perceptual systems.* Houghton Mifflin.

Gibson, J. J. (1979) *The ecological approach to visual perception.* Houghton Mifflin.

Gillund, G. & Shiffrin, R. M. (1984) A retrieval model for both recognition and recall. *Psychological Review* 91:1–67.

Glenberg, A. M. (1976) Monotonic and nonmonotonic lag effects in paired-associate and recognition memory paradigms. *Journal of Verbal Learning and Verbal Behavior* 15:1–16.

Gluck, M. A. & Bower, G. H. (1988) From conditioning to category learning: An adaptive network model. *Journal of Experimental Psychology: General* 8:37–50.

Gould, S. J. & Lewontin, R. C. (1979) The spandrels of San Marco and the Panglossian paradigm: A critique of the adaptionist program. Reprinted in: *Conceptual issues in evolutionary biology: An anthology*, ed. E. Sober. MIT Press. (1984)

Hayes-Roth, B. & Hayes-Roth, F. (1977) Concept learning and the recognition and classification of exemplars. *Journal of Verbal Learning and Verbal Behavior* 16:321–38.

Herrnstein, R. J. (1990) Rational choice theory: Necessary but not sufficient. *American Psychologist* 45(3):356–67.

Herrnstein, R. J. & Vaughan, W., Jr. (1980) Melioration and behavioral allocation. In: *Limits to action: The allocation of individual behavior*, ed. J. E. R. Staddon. Academic Press.

Hoffman, J. & Ziessler, C. (1983) Objectidentifikation in kunstlichen Begriffshierarchien. *Zeitschrift für Psychologie* 194:135–67.

Homa, D. & Cultice, J. (1984) Role of feedback, category size, and stimulus distortion in the acquisition and utilization of ill-defined categories. *Journal of Experimental Psychology: Learning, Memory, and Cognition* 10:83–94.

Houston, A. I. & McNamara, J. M. (1988) A framework for the functional analyses of behaviour. *Behavioral and Brain Sciences* 11:117–63.

Kahneman, D. & O'Curry, S. (1988) Surprise as an indication for spontaneous categorization. Presented at the 29th Annual Meeting of the Psychonomic Society, November 10–12.

Kahneman, D. & Tversky, A. (1984) Choices, values and frames. *American Psychologist* 39:341–50.

Kettlewell, P. (1973) *The evolution of melanism.* Oxford University Press (Oxford).

Kintsch, W. (1970) Models for free recall and recognition. In: *Models of human memory*, ed. D. A. Norman. Academic Press.

Kotovsky, K., Hayes, J. R. & Simon, H. A. (1985) Why are some problems hard? Evidence from Tower of Hanoi. *Cognitive Psychology* 17:248–94.

Lebowitz, M. (1987) Experiments with incremental concept formation: UNIMEM. *Machine Learning* 2:103–38.

Mandler, J. M., Bauer, P. J. & McDonough, L. (1988) Differentiating global categories. Presented at the 29th Annual Meeting of the Psychonomic Society, November 10–12.

Marr, D. (1982) *Vision.* W. H. Freeman.

Mayr, E. (1983) How to carry out the adaptionist program? *American Naturalist* 121:324–34.

Medin, D. L. & Edelson, S. M. (1988) Problem structure and the use of base-rate information from experience. *Journal of Experimental Psychology: General* 117:68–85.

Medin, D. L. & Schaffer, M. M. (1978) Context theory of classification learning. *Psychological Review* 85:207–38.

Medin, D. L., Altom, M. W., Edelson, S. M. & Freko, D. (1982) Correlated symptoms and simulated medical classification. *Journal of Experimental Psychology: Learning, Memory, and Cognition* 8:37–50.

Meyer, D. E. & Schvaneveldt, R. W. (1971) Facilitation in recognizing pairs of words: Evidence of a dependence between retrieval operations. *Journal of Experimental Psychology* 90:227–34.

Murphy, G. L. & Smith, E. E. (1982) Basic level superiority in picture categorization. *Journal of Verbal Learning and Verbal Behavior* 21:1–20.

Neely, J. H. (1977) Semantic priming and retrieval from lexical memory: Roles of inhibitionless spreading activation and limited-capacity attention. *Journal of Experimental Psychology: General* 106:226–54.

Newell, A. & Rosenbloom, P. (1981) Mechanisms of skill acquisition and the law of practice. In: *Cognitive skills and their acquisition*, ed. J. R. Anderson. Erlbaum.

Nisbett, R. E. & Ross, L. (1980) *Human inference: Strategies and shortcomings of social judgment.* Prentice-Hall.

Posner, M. I. & Keele, S. W. (1968) On the genesis of abstract ideas. *Journal of Experimental Psychology* 77:353–63.

Rachlin, H., Battalio, R. C., Kagel, J. H. & Green, L. (1981) Maximization theory in behavioral psychology. *Behavioral and Brain Sciences* 4:371–88.

Reed, S. K. (1972) Pattern recognition and categorization. *Cognitive Psychology* 3:382–407.

Rosch, E., Mervis, C. B., Gray, W., Johnson, D. & Boyes-Braem, P. (1976) Basic objects in natural categories. *Cognitive Psychology* 7:573–605.

Rumelhart, D. E., McClelland, J. L. & the PDP Research Group (1986) *Parallel distributed processing: Explorations in the microstructure of cognition*, vols. 1–2. MIT Press.

Russell, S. J. (1986) A quantitative analysis of analogy by similarity. In: *Proceedings of the National Conference on Artificial Intelligence*, Philadelphia, PA. American Association for Artificial Intelligence (AAAI).

Salton, G. & McGill, M. J. (1983) *Introduction to modern information retrieval.* McGraw-Hill.

Satyanarayanan, M. (1981) A study of file sizes and functional lifetimes. In: *Proceedings of the Eighth Symposium on Operating Systems Principles.* Asilomar, CA, December.

Schustack, M. W. & Sternberg, R. J. (1981) Evaluation of evidence in causal inference. *Journal of Experimental Psychology: General* 110: 101–20.

Shepard, R. N. (1987) Towards a universal law of generalization for psychological science. *Science* 237:1317–23.

Shepard, R. N. (1989) A law of generalization and connectionist learning. Plenary address to the Cognitive Science Society, Ann Arbor, MI, August 18.

Shimp, C. P. (1966) Probabilistically reinforced choice behavior in pigeons. *Journal of the Experimental Analysis of Behavior* 9:443–55.

Simon, H. A. (1955) A behavioral model of rational choice. *Quarterly Journal of Economics* 69:99–118.

Staddon, J. E. R. (1987) Optimality theory and behavior. In: *The latest on the best: Essays on evolution and optimality.* ed. J. Dupré. MIT Press.

Stephens, D. W. & Krebs, J. R. (1986) *Foraging theory.* Princeton University Press.

Stritter, E. (1977) File migration. Unpub. Ph.D. thesis (STAN-CS-77-594), Stanford University.

Suppes, P. (1984) *Probabilistic metaphysics.* Basil Blackwell.

Wickelgren, W. A. (1976) Memory storage dynamics. In: *Handbook of learning and cognitive processes*, ed. W. K. Estes. Erlbaum.

Williams, B. A. (1988) Reinforcement, choice, and response strength. In: *Stevens's handbook of experimental psychology*, ed. R. C. Atkinson, R. J. Herrnstein, G. Lindzey & R. D. Luce. Wiley.

Generality vs. Specificity of Models

Chapter 38

Précis of *Unified Theories of Cognition*
Allen Newell

The book begins by urging on psychology unified theories of cognition:

> Psychology has arrived at the possibility of unified theories of cognition—
> theories that gain their power by positing a single system of mechanisms
> that operate together to produce the full range of human cognition.

> I do not say they are here, but they are within reach and we should strive
> to attain them.

My goal is to convince the reader that unified theories of cognition are really
worth striving for—now, as we move into the nineties. This cannot be done just
by talking about it. An exemplar candidate is put forth to illustrate concretely
what a unified theory of cognition means and why it should be a goal for cognitive science. The candidate is a theory (and system) called SOAR (Laird et al.
1987).

The book is the written version of the *William James Lectures*, delivered at
Harvard University in spring 1987. Its stance is personal, reflecting the author's
thirty years of research in cognitive science, although this précis will be unable
to convey much of this flavor.

Chapter 1: Introduction

The first chapter describes the enterprise. It grounds the concerns for how cognitive science should proceed by reflecting on a well-known earlier paper entitled "You can't play 20 questions with nature and win" (Newell 1973a), which
even then fretted about the gap between the empirical and theoretical progress
in cognitive psychology and called for more integrative theories. This book may
be seen as a step toward answering that call.

The Nature of Theories

Chapter 1 discusses the notion of theory, to ground communication, building
on some concrete examples: Fitts's Law, the power law of practice, and a theory
of search in problem spaces. There is nothing special about a theory just because it deals with the human mind. It is important, however, that the theory

make predictions, not the theorist. Theories are always approximate, often deliberately so, in order to deliver useful answers. Theories cumulate, being refined and reformulated, corrected and expanded. This view is Lakatosian, rather than Popperian: A science has investments in its theories and it is better to correct one than to discard it.

What are Unified Theories of Cognition?
Unified theories of cognition are single sets of mechanisms that cover all of cognition—problem solving, decision making, routine action, memory, learning, skill, perception, motor activity, language, motivation, emotion, imagining, dreaming, daydreaming, and so on. Cognition must be taken broadly to include perception and motor activity. No unified theory of cognition will deal with the full list above all at once. What can be asked is a significant advance in its coverage.

As the title indicates, the book is focused on the plural, on many unified theories of cognition. This is not eclecticism, but a recognition of the state of the art. Cognitive science does not have a unified theory yet. Many candidates will arise, given the current practice of theorizing in cognitive science, where every scientist of note believes himself a major theorist. This point is important, since the book works with a single exemplar (SOAR). An exemplar is not *the* unified theory, and not necessarily even a candidate.

Why strive for unified theories, beyond the apple-pie desire of all sciences to be unified? The biggest reason is that a single system (the mind) produces behavior. There are other reasons, however. Cognitive theory is radically underdetermined by data, hence as many constraints as possible are needed and unification makes this possible. A unified theory is a vehicle of cumulation simply as a theoretically motivated repository. A unified theory increases identifiability and allows theoretical constructs to be amortized over a wide base of phenomena.

The human mind can be viewed as the solution to a set of multiple constraints. Exhibiting flexible behavior, exhibiting adaptive (goal-oriented) behavior, operating in real time, operating in terms of the four-dimensional environment of perceptual detail and a body with many degrees of freedom, operating in a world requiring immense knowledge to characterize, using symbols and abstractions, using language, learning from experience about the environment, acquiring abilities through development, operating autonomously but also within a social community, being self-aware with a sense of self are all essential functionalities of the mind. A system must satisfy these constraints to be mind-like. Humans also have known constraints on construction: a neural system, grown by embryological processes, and arising through evolution. How necessary these constructive processes are, so that only systems built that way can be minds, is currently an open question, but the major point is that the embodied minds we see satisfy all these constraints and any theory that ignores any appreciable number of them loses important sources of direction.

Is Psychology Ready for Unified Theories?

Cognitive science is well into its fourth decade; it is no longer a young child of a science. Indeed, behaviorism reached its own peak in fewer years. Cognitive science must take itself in hand and move forward. This exhortatory point is not made to suggest that cognitive science has made little progress. The strongest reason cognitive science should attempt unified theories now is that it has accumulated a vast and elegant body of regularities, highly robust and often parametric. This is especially the product of cognitive psychology and psycholinguistics, which have developed an amazing experimental engine for discovering, exploring, and confirming new regularities. Other sciences (e.g., biochemistry) have many more regularities, but they all fit within a theory that is integrated enough so that they never pose the challenge cognitive science now faces. If we do not begin integration now, we will find ourselves with an increasingly intractable task as the years go by while the engine of regularities works ever more industriously.

Though cognitive science does not yet have unified theories, there are harbingers: Many local theories make evident what cognitive mechanisms must be operating. But important attempts at unified theories have also been made. John Anderson's work on ACT* (Anderson, 1983) must be taken to have pride of place among such attempts. [See also Anderson: "Is Human Cognition Adaptive" *BBS* 14(3) 1991.] Other examples are the Model Human Processor (Card et al., 1983), the CAPS theory (Just & Carpenter, 1987), and a collection of efforts in perceptual decisions (Ratcliff, 1985).

The Task of the Book

The book endeavors to make the case for serious work on unified theories of cognition. It adopts a specific strategy, presenting an exemplar theory. Any other way seems to involve just talk and exhortation, guaranteed to have little effect. There are lots of risks to such a course—it will seem presumptuous and people will insist on subjecting the exemplar to a Popperian criticism to falsify it. But, on the positive side, one can hope the reader will follow a frequent plea of Warren McCulloch's, issued in similar circumstances: "Don't bite my finger, look where I'm pointing" (McCulloch, 1965).

Chapter 2: Foundations of Cognitive Science

Chapter 2 works through some basic cognitive-science concepts to provide a foundation for the remainder of the book. This is cast as a review, although some novel points arise.

Knowledge Systems

A particularly important way of describing the human is as a knowledge system. The human is viewed as having a body of knowledge and a set of goals, so that it takes actions in the environment that its knowledge indicates will attain its goals. The term *knowledge* is used, as it is throughout computer science and AI, as *belief* (it can be wrong and often is), not as the philosopher's *justified true belief*. Knowledge systems are one level in the hierarchy of systems that make up an intelligent agent. For current computers, this is physical devices, continuous circuits, logic circuits, register-transfer systems, symbol (or programming) systems, and knowledge-level systems, all of which are simply alternative descriptions of the same physical system. Knowledge-level systems do not give a set of mechanisms that determine behavior, the hallmark of all other descriptive levels. Rather, behavior is determined by a principle of rationality that knowledge is used in the service of the agent's goals. This is analogous to other teleological principles, such as Fermat's principle of least time for optics. Lower-level descriptions (the symbol level) describe how a knowledge-level system is realized in mechanism. The knowledge level is useful to capture the notion of a goal-oriented system and abstract away from all details of processing and representation. However, humans can only be described approximately as knowledge-level systems, and the departure can be striking.

Representation

Knowledge must be represented in order to be used. The concept of representation is captured by the representation law. In an external world, entity (X) is transformed (T) into entity (Y). A representation of X-T-Y occurs in a medium within some system when an encoding from X to an entity in the medium (x) and an encoding of T into an internal transformation in the medium (t) produces an internal entity (y), which can be decoded to the external world to correspond to Y. Actual representations are comprised of myriad instances of the representational law to cover all of the specific representational connections that actually occur.

Obtaining a representation for a given external situation seems to require discovering an internal medium with the appropriate natural transformations —this is the essence of analog representation. But as external situations become more diverse, complex, and abstract, discovering adequate analogs becomes increasingly difficult, and at last impossible. A radically different solution exists (the great move), however, where the internal medium becomes freely manipulable with combinatorially many states and all the representational work is done by being able to compose internal transformations to satisfy representational laws. Sufficiently composable schemes of transformations allow the formation of highly general representational systems that simultaneously satisfy many of the requisite representational laws.

Computation

Computational systems are exactly those that provide composability of transformations. The prime question about computational systems is what functions they can produce. The great move to composable transformations for representations occurs precisely because most machines do not admit much variety in their selectable transformations. This leads to the familiar, but incredible, results from computer science about *universal* computational systems that can attain the ultimate in flexibility. They can produce, by being instructed, all the functions that can be produced by any class of machines, however diverse. Thus, systems (universal computers) exist that provide the universal composability of transformations needed to produce systems that can universally represent whatever needs to be represented. This also shows that computation does not in itself represent. It provides the wherewithal for a system to represent if the appropriate representational laws are satisfied.

Symbols

The book takes the term *symbol* to refer to the parts of expressions that represent, for example, the "cat" in "The cat is on the mat." Symbols provide distal access to knowledge-bearing structures that are located physically elsewhere within the system. The requirement for distal access is a constraint on computing systems that arises from action always being physically local, coupled with only a finite amount of knowledge being encodable within a finite volume of space, coupled with the human mind's containing vast amounts of knowledge. Hence encoded knowledge must be spread out in space, whence it must be continually transported from where it is stored to where processing requires it (distribution does not gainsay this constraint). Symbols are the means that accomplish the required distal access.

Symbol systems are universal computational systems with the role of symbols made manifest. Symbol systems consist of (1) a *memory*, containing independently modifiable structures that contain symbols; (2) *symbols* (patterns in the structures), providing the distal access to other structures; (3) *operations*, taking symbol structures as input and producing symbol structures as output; and (4) *interpretation processes*, taking symbol structures as input and executing operations (the structures thereby representing these operations). There must be sufficient memory and symbols, complete composability of structures by the operators, and complete interpretability (any sequence of operations can be represented).

Within this cognitive-science framework, the great philosophical puzzle of intentionality (Brentano 1874)—how symbols can be *about* external things—has a straightforward solution. There are knowledge-level systems. The knowledge in them is *about* the external world. Symbol systems implement knowledge-level systems by using symbols, symbol structures, and so on. Therefore, these internal symbol structures are about (i.e., represent) the external world. They will only approximate such representation if the symbol system cannot realize the knowledge-level system adequately. Moreover, as the amount of knowledge and the diversity of goals increases, it is not possible, even theoretically, to realize faithfully the knowledge-level description of a system. How a given system comes to have its knowledge is a matter of the system's history, including the knowledge available to the processes that created the system. This appears to be a satisfactory resolution to the vexed question of intentionality.

Architectures

Unified theories of cognition will be formulated as architectures. The architecture of the mind is a major source of commonality of behavior, both within an individual and between individuals. The architecture is the fixed structure that realizes a symbol system. In the computer hierarchy this is the description at the registertransfer level; in biological systems it is the level of neural structure that is organized to provide symbols.

The important question about the architecture concerns what functions it provides. The architecture provides the boundary that separates structure from content, but all external tasks require both structure and content for their performance. So the division of function is what in the architecture *enables* the content to determine task performance. An obvious part of the answer is that the architecture provides the mechanisms for realizing a symbol system, but two additional types exist. One is the mechanisms to exploit implementation technology for power, memory, and reliability—such as caches and parallelism. The other is the mechanisms to obtain autonomy of operation—interrupts, dynamic-resource allocation, and protection. What is understood about the functions of the architecture comes entirely from engineered computers. Additional functions are surely involved in natural architectures for autonomous, intelligent creatures.

Architectures exhibit an immense variety. Universal computation might seem to require highly specialized systems for its realization. On the contrary, any specific symbol system can be realized in an indefinite variety of architectures, and any specific architecture can be implemented in an indefinite variety of technologies. Any technology that can implement one architecture can implement an indefinite variety of them. All these systems must perform the key functions of symbol systems, but these can be realized in an indefinite variety of ways. This potential for variety means that strong inferences are not possible from the structure of engineered digital computers to how architectures are realized in the brain.

Intelligence

The concept of intelligence is crucial for cognitive science. Unfortunately, its long, variegated history produced a multiplicity of notions that bear a family resemblance but serve different masters—often designed to block any unified concept of intelligence. Still, cognitive science (and any unified theory of cognition) must conceptualize the potential of a given task to cause difficulty to a person who attempts it and the potential of a given person for solving difficult tasks. *A system is intelligent to the degree that it approximates a knowledge-level system.* This is what emerges from the concept in the second chapter. The distinction between knowledge and intelligence is key. If a system does not have some knowledge, failure to use it cannot be a failure of intelligence, which can work only with the knowledge the system has. If a system uses *all* the knowledge it has and noting improves its performance, then there is no role left for intelligence. Thus intelligence is the ability to use the knowledge the system has in the service of the system's goals. This notion answers many requirements of a concept of intelligence, but it does not lead directly to a quantitative measure of intelligence, because knowledge per se is not quantifiable.

Search and Problem Spaces
What processing is required to obtain intelligent behavior? How does a system bring its knowledge to bear to attain its goals? For difficult tasks the general answer is that the system will *search*. Search is not just another cognitive process, occurring alongside other processes (the view prior to the cognitive revolution), but the fundamental process for attaining tasks that require intelligence. There are two fundamental reasons for this. First, a difficult task is one in which the system does not always know how to behave. But to make progress means to generate some behavior, and when an error arises and is detected, to attempt to correct it—a de facto search step. When errors occur within errors, combinatorial search emerges. Second, search provides a method of last resort. If no other methods are available to a system, it can always posit a space within which goal attainment lies, and then search that space. No matter how little it knows, it can always posit a bigger space, so this method of "generate and test" can always be formulated.

An intelligent system is always operating in a *problem space*, the space of the system's own creation that attempts to restrict the arena of action to what is relevant. The agent is at some current state in this space with a set of available operators. The system searches within this space to reach a desired state that represents task attainment. This search is combinatorial in character, just as all the experience in AI attests. Solving problems in problem spaces is not just an arbitrary search. Knowledge can be brought to bear to guide the search. Given enough knowledge, no search at all will occur: The appropriate operator will be selected at each state and the desired state will be reached forthwith. For general intelligent systems (and humans), life is a sequence of highly diverse tasks and the system has available a correspondingly large body of knowledge. Thus, besides the problem search in the problem space there is also at every current state a knowledge search to discover what knowledge can be brought to bear to guide the search fruitfully. Knowledge search is a major activity in general intelligent systems.

Summary
The concepts in this chapter constitute the cumulated yield of thirty years of attempting to understand the nature of computation, representation, and symbols. As cast here, all the concepts are not equally familiar. The knowledge level is still not common in theoretical treatments, although it permeates the practice of cognitive and computer sciences. The separation of representation from computation is not sufficiently appreciated. The concept of intelligence may even seem strange. Despite these traces of novelty, this chapter should be like a refresher course to the practicing cognitive scientist.

Chapter 3: Human Cognitive Architecture

The concepts of Chapter 2 apply to humans and computers alike, but a unified theory of human cognition will be expressed in a theory of human cognitive architecture. This chapter attempts to discover some generally applicable constraints on the human architecture. Any proposed specific theory of the architecture would take such constraints as given and not as part of its specific architectural proposal. The chapter is necessarily speculative, since general arguments are notoriously fragile.

The Human is a Symbol System
This chapter argues that human minds are symbol systems. The strongest argument is from the flexibility and diversity of human response functions (i.e., responses as a function of the environment)—the immense variety of ways that humans generate new response functions, from writing books to reading them, to creating recipes for cooking food, to going to school, to rapping, to dancing. Other organisms are also adaptive, and in fascinating ways, but the diversity and range of human adaptations exceeds these by all bounds, indeed it is beyond enumeration. Focusing on diversity of response functions links up directly with the defining property of symbol systems as systems that admit the extreme of flexible response functions. Any system that is sufficiently flexible in its response functions must be a symbol system (i.e., capable of universal computation). Actually, the argument holds only asymptotically: No one has the foggiest notion what a class of systems might be like that showed human-scale flexibility but weren't universal. In addition, the simplicity of the functional requirements for symbol systems makes it most unlikely that such systems exist. Thus, the human mind is taken to be a symbol system, establishing a high-level constraint on the human cognitive architecture. It must support a symbol system.

Systems Levels and the Time Scale of Human Action

Intelligent systems are built up in a hierarchy of system levels. Each system level consists of a more abstract way of describing the same physical system and its behavior, where the laws of behavior are a function only of the states as described at that level. In computers, engineers work hard to make the levels perfect, so that nothing from a lower level ever disturbs the given level. Nature is not so compulsive and levels are stronger or weaker depending on how complete is the sealing off from effect from lower levels. Higher system levels are spatially larger and run more slowly than do lower ones, because the higher levels are composed of multiple systems at the next lower level and their operation at a higher level comes from the operation of multiple interactive systems at the next lower level. Increase in size and slow-down in speed are geometric, although the factor between each level need not be constant. The concern in this chapter is with time, not space. In particular, the temporal factor for a minimal system level is about a factor of 10, that is, an order of magnitude. It could be somewhat less, but for convenience we will take ×10 as the minimal factor.

Ranging up the time scale of action for human systems, a new systems level appears just about every factor of 10, that is just about as soon as possible. Starting at organelles, they operate at time scales of about 100 μsecs. Neurons are definitely a distinct system level from organelles, and they operate at about 1 msec, ×10 slower. Neural circuits operate at about 10 msec, yet another ×10 slower. These three systems can be taken to constitute the *biological band*. Continuing upward reaches what can be called the *cognitive band*—the fastest deliberate acts (whether external or internal) take on the order of 100 msec, genuine cognitive operations take 1 sec, and above that, at the order of 10 sec is a region with no standard name, but consisting of the small sequences of action that humans compose to accomplish smallish tasks. Above the cognitive band lies the *rational band* where humans carry out long sequences of actions directed toward their goals. In time scale this ranges from minutes to hours. No fixed characteristic systems level occurs here, because the organization of human activity now depends on the task being attempted and not on the inner mechanisms. Above the rational band is the social band, dominated by the distributed activities of multiple individuals. As the scale proceeds upward, the boundaries become less distinct, due to the flexibility of human cognition and the dominance of task organization. The time scale of human action reflects both a theoretical view about minimal systems levels and an empirical fact that human activities, when ranged along such a scale, provide distinguishable system levels about every minimal factor.

The Real-Time Constraint on Cognition

That neurons are ∼1 msec devices and elementary neural circuits are ∼10 msec devices implies that human cognition is built up from ∼10 msec components.

But elementary cognitive behavior patently occurs by 1 sec. Fast arcs from stimulus to response occur five times faster (~ 200 msec), but their simplicity and degree of preparation make them suspect as cognition. Yet creative discourse happens in about one second. These two limits create the real-time constraint on cognition: Only about 100 operation times are available to attain cognitive behavior out of neural-circuit technology. This constraint is extremely binding. It provides almost no time at all for the cognitive system to operate. The constraint may also be expressed as follows: Elementary but genuine cognition must be produced in just two system levels. Neural circuits (at ~ 10 msec) can be assembled into some sorts of macrocircuits (one factor of 10) and these macrocircuits must then be assembled to produce cognitive behavior (the second factor of 10). This constraint is familiar (Feldman & Ballard, 1982; Fodor, 1983) and has been deployed mostly to deny the relevance of the algorithms developed in AI for vision and natural language processing because they take too long. But the constraint is much more binding than that and can be used to make a number of inferences about the human cognitive architecture.

The Cognitive Band

The human cognitive architecture must now be shaped to satisfy the real-time constraint. A particular style of argument is used to infer the system levels of the cognitive band. Functions are allocated to the lowest (fastest) possible system level by arguments that they could not be accomplished any faster, given other allocations (and starting at the bottom of ~ 10 msec). Whether they could be slower is undetermined. But as they stack up, the upper limit of cognitive behavior at ~ 1 sec is reached, clamping the system from the top, thereby determining absolutely the location of cognitive functions at specific system levels.

The upshot is that the distal accessing associated with symbols must occur at the level of neural circuits, about 10 msec. Above this, hence at ~ 100 msec, comes the level of elementary deliberations, the fastest level at which (coded) knowledge can be assembled and be brought to bear on a choice between operations. This level marks the distinction in cognition between automatic and controlled processing. What happens within an act of deliberation is automatic, and the level itself permits control over action.

A level up from elementary deliberations brings simple operations, composed of a sequence of deliberations with their associated microactions, hence taking of the order of 1 sec. This brings the system up against the real-time constraint. It must be able to generate genuine, if elementary, cognitive activity in the external world. Simple operations provide this: enough composition to permit a sequence of realizations of a situation and mental reactions to that realization, to produce a response adaptive to the situation. Thus, the real-time constraint is met.

With time, cognition can be indefinitely composed, though a processing organization is required to control it. Above the level of simple operations is the first level of composed operations, at ∼10 sec, characterized by its operations being decomposed into sequences of simple operations. An important bridge has been crossed with this level, namely, simple operations are a fixed repertoire of actions and now the operations themselves can be composed.

The Intendedly Rational Band

Composition is recursive and more complex operations can exist whose processing requires many sublevels of suboperations. What prevents the cognitive band from simply climbing into the sky? Cognition begins to succeed; as the seconds grow into minutes and hours, enough time exists for cognition to extract whatever knowledge exists and bring it to bear. The system can be described increasingly in knowledge-level terms and the internal cognitive mechanism need not be specified. This becomes the band of rational—goal and knowledge driven—behavior. It is better labeled *intendedly* rational behavior, since the shift toward the knowledge level takes hold only gradually and can never be complete.

Summary

This chapter has produced some general constraints on the nature of the human cognitive architecture. These must hold for all proposed architectures, becoming something an architecture satisfies rather than an architectural hypothesis per se. The gain to theorizing is substantial.

The different bands—biological, cognitive, and (intendedly) rational—correspond to different realms of law. The biological band is solidly the realm of natural law. The cognitive band, on the other hand, is the realm of representational law and computational mechanisms. The computational mechanisms are described by natural law, just as are biological mechanisms. But simultaneously, the computations are arranged to satisfy representational laws, so that the realm becomes about the external world. The rational band is the realm of reason. Causal mechanisms have disappeared and what determines behavior is goals and knowledge (within the physical constraints of the environment).

Chapter 4: Symbolic Processing for Intelligence

The chapter deals with the symbolic processing required for intelligence and introduces the SOAR architecture. The shift from general considerations to full details of an architecture and its performance reflects the cardinal principle that the only way a cognitive theory predicts intelligence is if the system designed according to that theory exhibits intelligent behavior. Intelligence is a functional capability.

The Central Architecture for Performance

In SOAR, all tasks, both difficult and routine, are cast as *problem spaces*. All long-term memory is realized as a production system in which the productions form a recognition memory, the conditions providing the access path, and the actions providing the memory contents. Unlike standard production systems, there is no conflict resolution, all satisfied productions put their contents into working memory. Thus SOAR is entirely problem-space structured, and the recognition of which productions fire constitutes the knowledge search.

Control over behavior in the problem space is exercised by the *decision cycle*. First, information flows freely from the long-term memory into working memory. New elements may trigger other productions to fire, adding more elements, until all the knowledge immediately available in long-term memory is retrieved. Included in this knowledge are preferences about which decisions are acceptable or better than others. Second, a decision procedure sorts through the preferences to determine the next step to take in the problem space: what operator to select, whether the task is accomplished, whether the problem space is to be abandoned, and so on. The step is taken, which initiates the next decision cycle.

The decision cycle suffices if the knowledge retrieved is sufficient to indicate what step to take next. But if not, an *impasse* occurs—the decision procedure cannot determine how to proceed given the preferences available to it. Impasses occur frequently, whenever knowledge cannot be found just by immediate pattern recognition. The architecture then sets up a subgoal to acquire the missing knowledge. Thus the architecture creates its own goals whenever it does not have what is needed to proceed. Within the subgoal, deciding what problem space to use and what operators to select occurs imply by continuing with decision cycles in the new context. Impasses can arise while working on a subgoal, giving rise to a hierarchy of goals and subgoals, in the manner familiar in complex intelligent systems.

Chunking

The organization of productions, problem spaces, decisions, and impasses produces performance, but it does not acquire new permanent knowledge. *Chunking* provides this function. This is a continuous, automatic, experience-based learning mechanism. It operates when impasses are resolved, preserving the knowledge that subgoals generated by creating productions that embody this knowledge. On later occasions this knowledge can be retrieved immediately, rather than again reaching an impasse and requiring problem solving. Chunking is a process that converts goal-based problem solving into long-term memory. Chunks are active processes, not declarative data structures to be interpreted. Chunking does not just reproduce past problem solving; it transfers to other analogous situations, and the transfer can be substantial. Chunking applies to all impasses, so learning can be of any kind whatever: what operators to select, how to implement an operator, how to create an operator, what test to use, what problem space to use, and so on. Chunking learns only what SOAR experiences (since it depends on the occurrence of impasses). Hence, what is learned depends not just on chunking but on SOAR's problem solving.

The Total Cognitive System

SOAR's cognitive system consists of the performance apparatus plus chunking. The *total cognitive system* adds to this mechanisms for perception and motor behavior. The working memory operates as a common bus and temporary store for perception, central cognition, and motor behavior. Perceptual systems generate elements in working memory, which are matched by the productions in long-term memory. Central cognition generates elements in working memory, which are interpreted as commands by the motor system. Perceptual processing occurs in two stages: the (sensory) mechanisms that deliver elements to working memory and the analysis and elaboration of these perceptual elements by encoding productions. Likewise on the motor side, decoding productions in long-term memory elaborate motor commands and produce whatever form is needed by the motor systems, followed by motor system proper that makes movements. The sensory and motor modules are cognitively impenetrable, but the encoding and decoding processes interact with other knowledge in working memory.

SOAR As an Intelligent System

Intelligence is only as intelligence does. The chapter describes the range of different tasks, types of learning, and modes of external interaction that SOAR has exhibited. Two large SOAR systems are described in some detail. One, R1-SOAR (Rosenbloom et al., 1985), does the task of R1, a classical expert system (McDermott, 1982), which configures VAX systems. R1-SOAR does the same task. It shows that a single system can mix general (knowledge-lean) problem solving and specialized (knowledge-intensive) operation as a function of what knowledge the system has available. R1-SOAR also shows that experiential learning can acquire the knowledge to move the system from knowledge-lean to knowledge-intensive operation. The second system, Designer-SOAR (Steier, 1989), designs algorithms, a difficult intellectual task that contrasts with the expertise-based task of R1. Designer-SOAR starts with a specification of an algorithm and attempts to discover an algorithm in terms of general actions such as generate, test, store, and retrieve, using symbolic execution and execution on test cases. Designer-SOAR learns within the span of doing a single task (within-task transfer), and also between tasks of the same basic domain (across-task transfer), but it shows little transfer between tasks of different domains.

Mapping SOAR onto Human Cognition
SOAR is an architecture capable of intelligent action. Next, one must show that it is an architecture of human cognition. Given the results about the cognitive band, deriving from the real-time constraint, there is only one way to interpret SOAR as the human cognitive architecture. Moreover, since these results have established absolute, though approximate, time scales for cognitive operations, this interpretation leads to an order-of-magnitude absolute temporal identification of the operations in SOAR as a theory of cognition. SOAR productions correspond to the basic symbol access and retrieval of human long-term memory, hence they take ~10 msec. The SOAR decision cycle corresponds to the level of elementary deliberation and hence takes ~100 msec. The problem-space organization corresponds to higher organization of human cognition in terms of operations. Operators that do not reach an impasse correspond to simple operations, hence they take ~1 sec. SOAR problem spaces within which only simple (nonimpassing) operators occur correspond to the first level of composed operations. This is the first level at which goal attainments occur and the first at which learning (impasse resolution) occurs. Problem spaces of any degree of complexity of their operators are possible and this provides the hierarchy of operations that stretches up into the intendedly rational level.

Summary
This chapter has a strong AI flavor, because the emphasis is on how a system can function intelligently, which implies constructing operational systems. A prime prediction of a theory of cognition is that humans are intelligent and the only way to make that prediction is to demonstrate it operationally. The prediction is limited, however, by the degree to which the SOAR system itself is capable of intelligence. SOAR is state of the art AI, but it cannot deliver more than that.

Chapter 5: Immediate Behavior

The book now turns to specific regions of human behavior to explore what a unified theory must provide. The first of these is behavior that occurs in a second or two in response to some evoking situation: immediate-response behavior. This includes most of the familiar chronometric experimentation that has played such a large role in creating modern cognitive psychology.

The Scientific Role of Immediate-Response Data
When you're down close to the architecture, you can see it, when you're far away you can't. The appropriate scale is temporal and behavior that takes 200 msec to about 3 sec sits close to the architecture. Thus, immediate-response performance is not just another area of behavior to illustrate a unified theory, it is the area that can give direct experimental evidence of the mechanisms of the

architecture. Furthermore, cognitive psychology has learned how to generate large numbers of regularities at this level, many of which are quantitative, parametric, and robust. Literally thousands of regularities have been discovered (the book estimates ~3000). Tim Salthouse (1986) provides an illustration by his listing of 29 regularities for just the tiny area of transcription typing (this and several other such listings are given and discussed throughout the remainder of the chapter and book). All of these regularities are constraints against the nature of the architecture. They provide the diverse data against which to identify the architecture. Thus, it is appropriate to start the consideration of SOAR as a unified cognitive theory by looking at immediate behavior.

Methodological Preliminaries

SOAR is a theory just like any other. It must explain and predict the regularities and relate them to each other; however, it need not necessarily produce entirely novel predictions: An important role is to incorporate what we now understand about the mechanisms of cognition, as captured in the microtheories of specific experimental paradigms. A scientist should be able to think in terms of the architecture and then explanations should flow naturally. SOAR should not be treated as a programming language. It is surely programmable—its behavior is determined by the content of its memory and stocking its memory with knowledge is required to get SOAR to behave. But SOAR is this way because humans are this way, hence programmability is central to the theory. That SOAR is not only programmable but universal in its computational capabilities does not mean it can explain anything. Important additional constraints block this popular but oversimple characterization. First, SOAR must exhibit the correct time patterns of behavior and do so against a fixed set of temporal primitives (the absolute times associated with the levels of the cognitive band). Second, it must exhibit the correct error patterns. Third, the knowledge in its memory— its program and data—must be learned. It cannot simply be placed there arbitrarily by the theorist, although as a matter of necessity it must be mostly posited by the theorist because the learning history is too obscure. Finally, SOAR as a theory is underspecified. The architecture continues to evolve, and aspects of the current architecture (SOAR 4 in the book, now SOAR 5) are known to be wrong. In this respect, a unified theory is more like a Lakatosian research programme than a Popperian theory.

Functional Analysis of Immediate Responses

The tasks of immediate responding comprise a family with many common characteristics, especially within the experimental paradigms used by cognitive psychologists. These common properties are extremely constraining, and make it possible to specialize SOAR to a theory that applies just to this class of tasks. Immediate responses occur in the base-level problem space, where the elements generated by perception arise and where commands are given to the motor system. This base-level space is also the one that does not arise from impassing. Other spaces arise from it when knowledge is lacking to handle the interaction with the world. Given that time is required by both the perceptual and the motor systems, immediate-response behavior can impasse only infrequently if it is to meet the temporal demands of the task.

The main structure of the system that performs the immediate-response task is the pipeline of processing that occurs in the top space—*Perceive (P), Encode (E), Attend (A), Comprehend (C), Task (T), Intend (I), Decode (D), Move (M)*. The order is highly constrained, but not invariant. Setting the task *(T)* usually occurs prior to the perception of the stimulus. Some processes need not occur, for example, attention *(A)*, which may already be focused on the appropriate object. This pipeline is a functional organization of SOAR operators given certain task constraints. The pipeline is not architectural, although some of its components, perception *(P)*, and move *(M)*, reflect architectural divisions. Each component can be identified with the execution of collections of productions or simple operators, and by assigning rough a priori durations to the times for productions (∼10 msec) and minimum simple operators (∼50 msec) it is possible to compute a priori durations for immediate-response tasks.

Immediate Response Tasks

The above functional scheme is applied to the classical simple reaction task (SRT) of pressing a button in response to a light and to the two-choice reaction task (2CRT) of pressing the button corresponding to whichever light goes on. In both cases the model follows directly from the pipeline, yielding a priori estimates of ∼220 msec and ∼380 msec respectively, which are close to typical experimental values.

The scheme is then applied to a more complex case, stimulus-response compatibility, in which the response depends in some nonstraightforward way on the stimulus (such as pressing the lower button to call the *Up* elevator). The basic empirical results are that the more involved the mapping between stimulus and response, the slower the response and the greater the likelihood of error. The predictions of SOAR about duration flow from executing a conditional sequence of simple operators to perform the mapping. The more complex the mapping, the longer the sequence. A particular example is worked through for a task of using compatible or incompatible abbreviations for computer commands where the a priori prediction of the model is ∼2140 msec and the observed experimental average is 2400 msec.

There is more to this story than just close predictions and the fact that they do not require fitting any parameters to the data at hand. The work is actually that of Bonnie John (John & Newell, 1987) and the theory she used is a version of the GOMS theory (Goal, Operators, Methods, and Selections rules), developed in HCI (human-computer interaction) to predict the time it takes expert users to do tasks that have become routine cognitive skills. This theory does an excellent job of predicting stimulus-response compatibility and the book exhibits a graph of predicted versus observed performance for some 20 different experiments, including many of the classical experiments on stimulus-response compatibility, showing better than 20% accuracy (all without fitting parameters). The GOMS theory is essentially identical to the specialization of SOAR to the *P-E-A-C-T-I-D-M* pipeline. Thus, SOAR *incorporates* the GOMS theory and with it inherits all the predictions it makes. This is not usurpation but the proper role for a unified theory of cognition, namely, to incorporate what is known throughout cognition, both regularities and mechanisms.

Item Recognition
The chapter examines another classical example of immediate behavior, the Sternberg item-recognition paradigm (Sternberg, 1975), where a subject is presented a set of items and then must say (as rapidly as possible) whether a presented probe is a member of the presented set. The main phenomenon is that response time is linear in the size of the presented set (suggesting a search process), but the time per item is very fast (~ 40 msec) and the data confute the obvious search process, where termination occurs after the target is found and appears instead to support an exhaustive search in which all items are always examined. An almost unimaginable number of variations on this paradigm have been run: A list of 32 regularities are presented, which provide another example of how rich the data from experimental cognition are for theory building. Some theories deal with half a dozen of these regularities; no theory comes close to explaining all 32.

SOAR is applied to the item recognition paradigm differently from the way it is applied to the reaction-time and stimulus-response compatibility paradigms to emphasize, in part, that a unified theory of cognition is to be applied in diverse ways depending on the situation. A qualitative theory is derived from SOAR in which essential regularities of the paradigm, such as exhaustiveness, are seen to some directly from characteristics of the architecture. Then it is shown why a fully detailed theory of the paradigm is not fruitfully constructed now: because it interacts with known places in the architecture that are uncertain and in flux.

Typing
The final immediate-response paradigm examined is that of transcription typing, using the list of 29 regularities developed by Salthouse (1986) presented earlier in the chapter. Typing introduces several additions: continuous behavior, even though the subject must respond to new stimulus information immediately; concurrent processing, because humans overlap processing in typing and discrete motor behavior.

As in the immediate-reaction tasks, a complete model is provided. This is also the work of John (1988) and extends the GOMS model used for stimulus-response compatibility to concurrent processors for perception, cognition, and motor action. The model is highly successful (again without estimating parameters from the data), accounting for three-quarters of the regularities and not clearly contradicting any. The model is silent about error regularities, which all depend on the analog and control aspects of the motor system working within the anatomy of the hands and arms, aspects not yet covered by the model. As earlier, the extension of GOMS to concurrent processing fits into the SOAR architecture, providing (or extending) the example of incorporating this theory into SOAR. SOAR makes the same predictions as the GOMS models.

Summary
This chapter provides basic confirmation that the detailed SOAR architecture is in reasonable accord with a range of experimental facts about immediate behavior. This is important, since it was already clear—by construction, so to speak—that gross aspects of SOAR were consonant with human data. Problem spaces, production systems, and chunking are all major theoretical constructs in cognitive psychology. Any reasonable way of composing an architecture from these elements will successfully cover large domains of behavior, especially higher-level behavior such as problem solving. But, in general, such architectural ideas have not been brought to bear on modelling the details of immediate behavior. The same architecture (and theory) that explains immediate behavior explains higher-level behavior.

A theme that was illustrated throughout the chapter was that SOAR moves toward making predictions that do not require estimating parameters from the data being predicted—so-called no-parameter predictions. No-parameter predictions almost never occur in current cognitive theorizing, mostly because the theories do not cover the entire arc from stimulus to response, so there are always unknown perceptual and motor processes coupled with the processes of interest. One advantage of a unified theory is to provide a complete enough set of mechanisms so no-parameter predictions can become the norm, not the exception.

Chapter 6: Memory, Learning and Skill

This chapter covers the SOAR theory of human memory, learning, and skill acquisition. Three fundamental assertions capture much of what the SOAR architecture implies for learning. First, according to the *functional unity of long-term memory*, all long-term memory consists of recognition-retrieval units at a fine grain of modularity (SOAR's productions being simply one instance). Second, according to the *chunking-learning hypothesis*, all long-term acquisition occurs by chunking, which is the automatic and continuous formation of recognition-retrieval units on the basis of immediate goal-oriented experience. Third, according to the *functionality of short-term memory*, short-term memory arises because of functional requirements of the architecture, not because of technological limits on the architecture that limit persistence.

An important aspect of the SOAR architecture is that it embodies the notion of chunking and hence provides a variety of evidence about what chunking can do. The chapter provides a thorough review of this, especially ways that chunking permits SOAR to learn from the eternal environment and ways chunking operates as a knowledge-transfer process from one part of SOAR to another.

The SOAR Qualitative Theory of Learning
A definite global qualitative theory of learning and memory can be read out of the SOAR architecture, much of it familiar in terms of what we know about human learning and memory. All learning arises from goal-oriented activity. Learning occurs at a constant average rate of about a chunk every 2 secs. Transfer is essentially by identical elements (although more general than Thorndike's [1903]) and will usually be highly specific. Rehearsal can help to learn, but only if some processing is done (as in depth-of-processing conceptions). Functional fixity and *Einstellung*, well attested memory biases in humans, will occur. The encoding specificity principle applies and the classical results about chunking, such as from chess, will hold. Some of these aspects are controversial, either theoretically or empirically, so the SOAR theory takes a stand at a general level.

A unified theory of cognition must yield answers to questions of interest, for instance the distinction between episodic and semantic memory (Tulving, 1983). Ultimately, what must be explained are the regularities and phenomena, but it is useful to see what global answers SOAR gives. First, in SOAR, episodic and semantic information are held in the same memory, because there is only one long-term memory in SOAR. This simply moves the question to how SOAR handles episodic and semantic knowledge. Basically, chunks are episodic recordings collecting this experience. The more specific that collection, the more episodic it is, to the point where the chunks that record the selection of operators provide in effect a reconstructable record of what operators were applied at the original time. This episodic record has a strong flavor of remembering what one did in the prior situation, rather than the objective sequence of (say) environmental states. There is some evidence of that, as well, however. Chunking being episodic, semantic memory arises by abstraction. Chunks are not conditional on all the specific features of the learning situation, only on those that entered into obtaining the goal. Thus, chunking can abstract from the conditions that tie the chunk to the episode and depend only on conditions on content; they hence provide semantic information. An example given in the book is how SOAR learns to solve little block-stacking problems in ways that become completely independent of the problems in which the learning took place. In sum, we see that SOAR contains both semantic and episodic knowledge but that it all happens within a single memory. It is important to note that this solution followed from the SOAR architecture, independently of the episodic/semantic issue.

Data Chunking

A theory must be right in its details as well as its global explanations. Chunking provides interesting and appropriate learning in many situations, but it fails when extended to certain tasks, producing what is called the data-chunking problem. A prominent example is paired-associate learning, where the non-sense pair (BAJ, GID) is presented and the subject must later say GID if presented with the cue BAJ. SOAR should obviously construct a production something like BAJ → GID. The problem is that any chunks built are conditional on both BAJ and GID, since they are both provided from the outside (indeed, the production must be conditional on GID: What if the pair (BAJ, DAK) were presented later?). There seems to be no way to get a production with only BAJ as a condition and GID as the action. This example reveals a deep difficulty, and the learning task involved (learning data) seems central. The difficulty was discovered empirically after many successful studies with chunking in SOAR. It provides a nice paradigm for what a unified theory of cognition should do.

A natural reaction is to modify the architecture but the chapter describes the successful result of staying with architecture in the belief that it will ultimately yield a solution. The solution seems quite technical, resting on the way problem spaces separate operator applications and the search control that guides them. Yet the solution carries with it some deep implications. For one, long-term memory for data is reconstructive, that is, SOAR has learned to reconstruct the past in response to the cues presented. For another, the theory of verbal learning that emerges is strongly EPAM-like (Simon & Feigenbaum, 1964).

Skill Acquisition

Skill acquisition flows naturally from chunking, which in many ways is procedural learning. In particular, there is a well-known law, the power law of practice (Newell & Rosenbloom, 1981), that relates the time taken to do a task to the number of times that task has been performed. The chunking mechanisms in SOAR were actually developed, in prior work, to explain the power law of practice, which might make it unsurprising that SOAR exhibits the power law. Such a sociological reaction does not gainsay that chunking is also the mechanism that supports episodic and semantic memory, so that a single memory and learning organization supports all the different types of memory that cognitive sciences distinguish.

Short-Term Memory

Structurally, SOAR seems like the perfect image of a 1960's psychological theory: a long-term memory, a short-term memory, and (perhaps) sensory buffers. But the story is not so simple. In particular, SOAR's working memory is entirely functionally defined. Its short-term time constants for replacement, access, and retention directly reflect the requirements of the operations it must perform. No limitation of retention or access arises simply from the technology in which the architecture is built—to create short-term memory problems for the system. Such technological limitations have been central to all short-term memory theories: decay, fixed-slot, interference. Thus, SOAR cannot provide simple explanations for standard short-term memory phenomena but must establish limitations out of the need for functionality elsewhere in the system. Technological limitations are certainly possible and SOAR could be so augmented. But strategically, this becomes a move of last resort.

An interesting conjecture about short-term memory does flow from the architecture, even as it stands. The current literature reveals a virtual zoo of different short-term memories—visual, auditory, articulatory, verbal (abstract?), tactile, and motor modalities; with different time constants and interference patterns. SOAR offers a conjecture about how such a zoo arises, based on the way the perceptual and motor systems integrate with cognition through an attention operator that permits perceptual and motor systems, with their varying forms of persistence, to be exploited by central cognition as short-term memories.

Summary

A unified theory of cognition must provide a theory that covers learning and memory as well as performance. One reason the current era is right for beginning to attempt unified theories is that we have just begun (throughout machine learning) to develop systems that effectively combine both.

Chapter 7: Intendedly Rational Behavior

This chapter treats how humans go about obtaining their goals—how they *intend* to be rational. As the time available for a task lengthens (relative to its demands), the human is able to bring more and more knowledge to bear and hence approaches being a knowledge-level system. In the time-scale of human action, the human passes out of the cognitive band into the rational band. This happens only gradually. If being describable purely in terms of knowledge is attaining the peaks of rationality, then this chapter deals with how humans explore the foothills of rationality, the region where problem solving is manifest. Three specific tasks are used to make some points about how unified theories of cognition deal with this region.

Cryptarithmetic

Cryptarithmetic played a key role in establishing that human problem solving could be modeled in extreme detail as search in a problem space (Newell & Simon, 1972). It is a puzzle in which an arithmetic sum is encoded as words: $SEND + MORE = MONEY$, where each letter is a digit and distinct letters are distinct digits. The original work posited a production-system architecture and developed manual simulations of the moment-by-moment behavior of humans attempting to solve the problem, based on think-aloud protocols of the subjects while working on the problem. This chapter provides a version of soar that simulates successfully a particularly difficult segment of a subject from Newell and Simon (1972).

Resimulating old situations, which were already more detailed than most psychologists appreciated, would seem not to have wide appeal in psychology, yet reasons exist for doing it within a unified theory of cognition. First, a unified theory must explain the entire corpus of regularities. Old data do not thereby become less valuable. An important activity in a unified theory is going back and showing that the theory covers classic results. Often it will be important to go behind the familiar results, which are statements of regularities, to explain the original data. Second, cognitive psychology needs to predict long stretches of free behavior to show that it can obtain enough knowledge about a human to predict all the zigs and zags. Cryptarithmetic, although an experimental laboratory task, is freely generated: Individual human subjects simply work away for half an hour, doing whatever they decide will advance solving the task. It is a good candidate for this endeavor at long-duration detailed prediction.

Syllogisms

Logical reasoning is epitomized in the task of categorical syllogisms: *Some bowlers are actors. All bowlers are chefs. What follows necessarily about actors and chefs?* Such tasks have been studied continuously by psychology, driven by the urge to understand whether humans have the capacity for logical thought. Syllogisms can be surprisingly difficult, even though they are easy to state and it is easy to understand what is wanted. This raises the possibility that humans somehow do not have the capacity for rational thought. Additional regularities have emerged and the chapter gives half a dozen.

A soar model of syllogistic reasoning is presented. A central question is whether the internal representation is in terms of propositions or models. The two types are analyzed, culminating in a definition of annotated models, the representation used in the soar theory of syllogisms, which is model-like but admits highly restricted types of propositions. (Mental) models versus propositions have been an important issue in cognitive science (Johnson-Laird, 1983). Annotative models do not flow from the architecture; hence they require an additional assumption about how humans encode tasks (though hints exist on how to ground them in the perceptual architecture). The soar model presented not only exhibits all the main known regularities of syllogistic reasoning, but it also fits very well the data on the (64 distinct) individual syllogisms. For unified theories of cognition, this shows how an important cognitive concept, mental models, which is not part of the theory's conceptual structure, is handled. A mental model is simply a type of problem space, with the model being the state representation. This identification is not superficial; it represents the solution to an existing cognitive-science issue.

Sentence Verification

Elementary sentence verification has been a paradigm task since the early 1970s to probe the nature of comprehension (Clark & Clark, 1977). In a typical task, the subject reads a sentence, *Plus is above star*, then sees a picture that shows a star sign above a plus sign, and answers (correctly) *No*. The task takes about 3 sec and by varying sentence and pictures it was discovered that different structural features produced different characteristic durations (e.g., using *below* rather than *above* adds 90 msec). These striking chronometric regularities in genuine, albeit simple, language behavior provided striking confirmation for the basic assumptions of cognitive science. A soar model is presented that performs sentence verification and shows the right pattern of regularities. Theorizing in the sentence-verification paradigm has occurred primarily by means of flowcharts (which are widely used in cognitive theory). Again, the question is how an important concept outside a unified theory is to be accommodated. The answer flows directly from the soar theory instantiated to this task. Flowcharts are inferred by the scientist from multiple temporal behavior traces. These traces are generated dynamically by the paths in the problem spaces that deal with the task. Hence flow charts do not exist in the human in static form and the human does not behave by interpreting or running a flowchart. Again, this solution is not superficial; it settles an important theoretical issue in cognitive science, though one that has seldom been raised.

The answer to the question of what flowcharts are raises the question of where flowcharts come from. This permits an excursion into the soar theory of how the human acquires the sentence verification task. This is cast as the problem of taking instructions: *Read the sentence. Then examine the picture. Press the T-button if the sentence is true of the picture. . . .* In both the syllogism task (reading the syllogisms) and the sentence-verification task (reading the sentence), soar produces a model of the situation it believes it is dealing with (respectively, actors and bowlers, and pictures with pluses and stars). It does the same for taking instruction, except that the situation comprises intentions for its own future behavior. As soar attempts to perform the task (and finds out it doesn't know how), it consults these intentions and behaves accordingly. As it does so, it builds chunks that capture that knowledge, so that on future attempts it knows how to do the task without being instructed. This answers the question of where the flowcharts come from. soar acquires from the instructions the problem spaces it uses to do the task and the traces of which produce the data from which the psychologist infers the flowchart. It also shows how a unified theory of cognition permits one and the same theory to be moved in entirely new directions (here, instruction taking).

Summary

These three tasks provide a sampling of the diverse issues that attend the foothills of rationality. They indicate that a unified theory of cognition must have the scope to cover a wide territory. A single theory should cover all these distinct tasks and phenomena. A side theme of Chapter 7 is to note that there are variations on simulation other than simply producing the full trace of behavior in a given task. In cryptarithmetic, the operators were controlled by the experimenter so as always to be correct; simulation was hence focused exclusively on the search control involved. In syllogisms, simulation was used to discover the basic form of the theory. In sentence verification, simulation was used to be sure simple processing was being accomplished exactly according to theory. The general lesson, already noted in an earlier chapter, is that unified theories are to be used in diverse ways depending on the scientific endeavor at hand.

Chapter 8: Along the Frontiers

The last chapter assesses where matters stand on the case for unified theories of cognition and their promise for cognitive science. To be concrete the book has used an exemplar unified theory (SOAR) but a point stressed throughout is that the concern is not to promote SOAR as *the* unified theory, or even as a candidate theory (hence the use of the term *exemplar*), but to get the construction of unified theories on the agenda of cognitive science. (SOAR is my candidate in the post-book period, but that is not the book.)

To restate basics: A unified theory of cognition is a theory of mind, but a theory of mind is not by definition computational. A computational unified theory of cognition must be a theory of the architecture. The hallmark of a unified theory is its coverage of cognitive phenomena, taken broadly to include perception and motor behavior. The last half of the book was devoted to coverage—intelligence, immediate chronometric behavior, discrete perceptual-motor behavior, verbal learning, skill acquisition, short-term memory, problem solving, logical reasoning, elementary sentence verification, and instructions and self-organization for new tasks. Listing all these varieties seems tedious, but it emphasizes that coverage is important. Coverage per se is a surrogate for dealing with the full detail of phenomena and regularities in every region. A long list of what SOAR covers does not gainsay an equally long list of what SOAR does not cover: A list of thirty is presented, among which are emotion and affect, imagery, perceptual decisions, and priming.

A unified theory of cognition cannot deal with everything at once and in depth; however, a unified theory does not have the luxury of declaring important aspects of human cognition out of bounds. Thus, the chapter considers, even more speculatively than in the main body of the book, several areas along the frontier of its current capabilities.

Language

Language is central to cognition, although it has not been central to the exemplar, because of SOAR's growth path through AI and cognitive psychology. Some general theoretical positions on language can be read out of SOAR. Language will be handled by the same architecture that handles all other cognitive activities. Language, being a form of skilled behavior, will be acquired as other skilled behaviors are, by chunking. Language is entirely functional in its role because an architecture is a device for producing functional behavior. It is possible to go further than these general statements. The fragment of language behavior presented in sentence verification made evident a basic principle: Comprehension occurs by applying comprehension operators to each word in the incoming utterance, where each comprehension operator brings to bear all the knowledge relevant to that word in context. One reason comprehension operators are the appropriate organization comes from the way chunking can grow the comprehension operators. To emphasis this possibility, a small example of language acquisition by SOAR is presented, making the further point that a unified theory of cognition should be able to approach all of cognition.

The nascent SOAR theory of language seems to be a highly specific one within the spectrum of active theories of the nature of human language. In particular, it seems at the opposite pole from ideas of modularity (Fodor, 1983), being the very epitome of using general cognitive mechanisms for language. An extended discussion of SOAR against the criteria of modularity aims to show that this view is mistaken—that SOAR is as modular or as nonmodular as various task domains make it. The essential ingredient is chunking, which is a mechanism for starting with generalized resources and creating highly specialized ones. Thus, language mechanisms grown by chunking may exhibit all the attributes of modular architectures. A general lesson from this discussion is that there are more possibilities in architectures than might be imagined, and that it is only in considering the details that the actual implications of an architecture can be discovered.

Development

Like language, the development of cognitive capabilities in children is an essential aspect of cognition. While a unified theory of cognition can be excused from dealing with developmental phenomena right off, it must be possible to see how development would be approached. This is accomplished by picking a specific example, namely, the balance-beam task. Children from age 5 upward watch as a balance beam is loaded with disks on pegs situated along the beam. They then predict whether the beam will tilt right or left or remain balanced when support is withdrawn. Siegler (1976) demonstrated experimentally the progress of children of increasing age through a series of theoretically defined processing stages. This work is a beautiful example of comparative statics, in which separate theories are defined for each stage, making possible theoretical comparisons of how processing capabilities advance. What is missing, both here and throughout developmental psychology, is any theory of the mechanisms of transition. A SOAR theory is presented of the first and second transitions (the third transition is of quite a different character). This is an operational SOAR system that actually moves up the levels as a function of its experience in doing the task (all by the occurrence of an appropriate pattern of chunking). This transition mechanism, though not extended to detailed explanations of all the regularities of the balance-beam paradigm, is still a viable suggestion for the nature of the transition mechanism—indeed, it is a singular suggestion, given the paucity of suggestions in the field.

The attempt to obtain a transition mechanism is dominated by a more pervasive problem in SOAR; namely, how to recover from error. Given successful adaptation to limited cases of the balance beam, what to do when the next level of complexity is introduced and the old program of response is inadequate? In SOAR, chunks are neither modified nor removed, hence, as in humans, much of the past remains available. Entrenched error is accordingly a problem. As in data chunking, SOAR's solution of this involves schemes for working within the existing architecture by creating new problem spaces to hold new correct chunks and permitting old incorrect chunks to be sequestered in old problem spaces whose access can usually be avoided. Chapter 8 lays out these recovery mechanisms in some detail, not only to make clear how transitions occur, but to illustrate how the SOAR architecture poses deep problems. The example also illustrates how the focus of analysis moves up from productions to operators to problem spaces and then to characteristic patterns of problem space activity.

The Biological Band

Brief consideration is given to how the SOAR architecture relates to the neurological substrate—the frontier below. Most basically, the SOAR architecture has been pinned down in absolute temporal terms, so that, for example, productions must occur at the level of simple neural circuits and the decision procedure must be of the order of 100 msec. Thus, the cognitive band no longer floats with respect to the biological band. This is in itself a genuine advance over the decades of declaring cognition to be autonomous from the brain.

Regarding connectionism, which mediates for cognitive science much of the orientation toward neural-based theory, the story is more complex. SOAR is equally committed to neural technology and the analysis and enforcement of time scales make that commitment realistic. With respect to the commitment to constraint-satisfaction computations, SOAR has an alternative orientation to simultaneous pattern matching as fundamental. SOAR is equally committed to continuous learning. Regarding the requirement that functional power reside in the instantaneous solutions of huge numbers of soft (graded) constraints (a view not held by all connectionists), SOAR relies on different principles of task organizations (problem spaces and impasses); but soar also responds strongly to meeting the constraints of performing a diversity of multiple higher-level tasks, a requirement that connectionism does not yet respond to. Many basic features attributed to connectionist systems, such as massive parallelism and continuous learning, are shared by soar. Any dichotomous view—with soar cast as the paradigm example of the physical symbol system—is simplistic.

The Social Band

Even briefer consideration is given to the social band, the frontier above. Basically, a unified theory of cognition can provide social theories with a model of the individual cognizing agent. A theory of cognition, unified or otherwise, is not a theory of social groups or organization, nascent or otherwise. Whether an improved agent would be useful is problematic in the current state of social science. The subarea of social cognition has been involved in moving the results of cognitive psychology into social psychology for almost two decades. Much has happened; there can now be free talk of retrieval, availability, and processing. Most social theories are still not cast in terms of cognitive mechanisms, however, but posit variables with values defined only up to their order. That an essential factor in the power of all cognitive theories (including soar) is their being cast in terms of mechanisms that actually determine the processing is still almost completely lost on the sciences of the social band. One other possibility to help the theories of the social band is to disentangle the social from nonsocial mechanisms. An example of how such an analysis might go is presented using Festinger's *Social comparison theory* (Festinger, 1954). The interesting result from this analysis is that to get some conclusions at the social level required Festinger to devote most of this theory to defining nonsocial factors. A cleaner standard notion of a cognitive agent, complete enough to be useful to the social scientist (i.e., unified) might actually help out.

The Role of Applications

Applications are an important part of the frontier of any science, though not the same as the scientific frontier. An important way unified theories of cognition contribute to applications is to permit all aspects of an application to be dealt with. The area of Human-Computer Interaction (HCI) provides good illustrations, where many aspects of perception, cognition, and motor performance all enter into each application situation (e.g., how computer browsers should be designed so as to be most useful). soar in fact already covers a wide proportion of the processes involved in interaction with computer interfaces, and HCI is a major area of application for soar. However, the most relevant aspect of applications is in the other direction—not what the unified theory does for applications but what applications do for the theory. This is of course not the direction usually emphasized, although everyone believes that application success convinces the polity to support the science. Much more is involved, however. Applications establish what accuracy is sufficient, when a regularity is worth remembering, and when a theory should not be discarded. Moreover, they provide a community that cares about relevant parts of a science and will cherish and nurture them, even when the theorist, following the will-o'-the-wisp of new exciting data, ignores them.

How to Move Toward Unified Theories of Cognition
The tour of the frontier is finished. What remain are not questions of science but of strategy. How are we to evolve unified theories of cognition: How to get from where we now are, with unified theories only in prospect, to where we want to be, with all of us working within their firm and friendly confines? Here are my suggestions. Have many unified theories: Unification cannot be forced, and exploration requires owning an architecture conceptually. Develop consortia and communities: Unified theories require many person-years of effort; they are not for the lone investigator. Be synthetic and cumulative: Incorporate, rather than replace, local theories. Modify unified theories, even in radical ways: Do not abandon them after they have received massive investments. Create data bases of results and adopt a benchmark philosophy: Each new version must predict all the benchmark tasks. Make models easy to use, easy to learn, and easy to make inferences from. Finally, acquire one or more application domains to provide support.

So the book ends where it began, but with understanding by the reader.

> Psychology has arrived at the possibility of unified theories of cognition—theories that gain their power by positing a single system of mechanisms that operate together to produce the full range of human cognition.

> I do not say they are here. But they are within reach and we should strive to attain them.

References

Brentano, F. (1874) *Psychology from an empirical standpoint*. Duncker & Humbolt. Reprinted 1973; Humanities Press.

Card, S., Moran, T. P. & Newell, A. (1983) *The psychology of human-computer interaction*. Erlbaum.

Clark, H. & Clark, E. (1977) *The psychology of language: An introduction to psycholinguistics*. Harcourt Brace Jovanovich.

Feldman, J. A. & Ballard, D. (1982) Connectionist models and their properties. *Cognitive Science* 6:205–54.

Festinger, L. (1954) A theory of social comparison processes. *Human Relations* 7:117–40.

Fodor, J. (1983) *The modularity of mind: An essay on faculty psychology*. MIT Press.

John, B. E. (1988) Contributions to engineering models of human-computer interaction. Ph.D. dissertation, Psychology Department, Carnegie-Mellon University.

John, B. E. & Newell, A. (1987) Predicting the time to recall computer command abbreviations. In: *Proceedings of CHI '87 Human Factors in Computing Systems*. Association for Computing Machinery.

Johnson-Laird, P. (1983) *Mental models*. Harvard University Press.

Johnson-Laird, P. N. & Byrne, R. M. J. (1991) *Deduction*. Erlbaum.

Just, M. A. & Carpenter, P. A. (1987) *The psychology of reading and language comprehension*. Allyn & Bacon.

Laird, J. E., Rosenbloom, P. S. & Newell, A. (1986) *Universal subgoaling and chunking*. Kluwer.

McCulloch, W. S. (1965) *Embodiments of mind*. MIT Press.

McDermott, J. (1982) R1: A rule-based configurer of computer systems. *Artificial Intelligence* 19:39–88.

Newell, A. (1973) You can't play 20 questions with nature and win. Projective comments on the papers of this symposium. In: *Visual information processing*, ed. W. G. Chase. Academic Press.

Newell, A. & Rosenbloom, P. (1981) Mechanisms of skill acquisition and the law of practice. In: *Cognitive skills and their acquisition*, ed. J. R. Anderson. Erlbaum.

Newell, A. & Simon, H. A. (1972) *Human problem solving*. Prentice-Hall.

Ratcliff, R. (1985) Theoretical interpretations of the speed and accuracy of positive and negative responses. *Psychological Review* 92:212–25.

Rosenbloom, R. S., Laird, J. E., McDermott, J., Newell, A. & Oreiuch, E. (1985) R1-Soar: An experiment in knowledge-intensive programming in a problem solving architecture. *Pattern Analysis and Machine Intelligence* 7:561–69.

Salthouse, T. (1986) Perceptual, cognitive, and motoric aspects of transcription typing. *Psychological Bulletin* 99:303–19.

Siegler, R. S. (1976) Three aspects of cognitive development. *Cognitive Psychology* 8:481–520.

Simon, H. A. & Feigenbaum, E. A. (1964) An information-processing theory of some effects of similarity, familiarization, and meaningfulness in verbal learning. *Journal of Verbal Learning and Verbal Behavior* 3:385–96.

Steier, D. M. (1989) Automating algorithm design within an architecture for general intelligence. Ph.D. dissertation. Computer Science, Carnegie-Mellon University.

Sternberg, S. (1975) Memory scanning: New findings and current controversies. *Quarterly Journal of Experimental Psychology* 27:1–32.

Thorndike, E. L. (1903) *Educational Psychology*. Lemke & Buechner.

Contributors

John R. Anderson
Carnegie Mellon University
Department of Psychology
Carnegie Mellon University
Pittsburgh, PA 15213
ja+@cmu.edu

Dana Apfelblat
Department of Psychology
University of Michigan
525 East University
Ann Arbor, MI 48109-1109

Michael E. Atwood
College of Information Science and
Technology
Drexel University
3141 Chestnut Street
Philadelphia, PA 19104
michael.atwood@cis.drexel.edu

Irving Biederman
Department of Psychology
Neuroscience HNB 316
Mail Code: 2520
University of Southern California
Los Angeles, CA 90089
bieder@usc.edu

Stephen B. Blessing
Department of Psychology
University of Florida
Gainesville, FL 32611-2250
blessing@psych.ufl.edu

Daniel J. Bothell
Department of Psychology
Carnegie Mellon University
Pittsburgh, PA 15213
db30@cmu.edu

Lisa K. Burger
University of Illinois, Urbana-
Champaign
833 Psychology Bldg., MC 716
603 E. Daniel
Champaign, IL 61820

Gail A. Carpenter
Cognitive and Neural Systems
Boston University
677 Beacon St.
Boston, MA 02215
gail@bu.edu

Patricia A. Carpenter
Department of Psychology
Carnegie Mellon University
Pittsburgh, PA 15213

Jonathan D. Cohen
Green Hall
Princeton University
Princeton, NJ 08544
jcohen@phoenix.princeton.edu

Timothy M. Converse
Department of Computer Science
University of Chicago
1100 East 58th St.
Chicago, IL 60637

Garrison W. Cottrell
Computer Science and Engineering
0114
University of California, San Diego
9500 Gilman Dr.
La Jolla, CA 92093-0114
gary@cs.ucsd.edu

Gary S. Dell
University of Illinois, Urbana-
Champaign
833 Psychology Bldg., MC 716
603 E. Daniel
Champaign, IL 61820
g_dell@uiuc.edu

Jeffrey L. Elman
Department of Cognitive Science 0515
University of California, San Diego
La Jolla, CA 92093-0515
elman@cogsci.ucsd.edu

Martha J. Farah
Psychology—3815 Walnut St.
University of Pennsylvania
Philadelphia, PA 19104-6196
mfarah@cattell.psych.upenn.edu

Jerry A. Fodor
Department of Philosophy
University of New Jersey, Rutgers
26 Nichol Ave.
New Brunswick, NJ 08901
fodor@ruccs.rutgers.edu

Kenneth D. Forbus
The Institute for the Learning
Sciences
Northwestern University
1890 Maple Avenue
Evanston, IL 60201
forbus@ils.nwu.edu

Dedre Gentner
Department of Psychology
Northwestern University
2029 Sheridan Rd.
Evanston, IL 60208-2710
gentner@nwu.edu

Jennifer Glass
Department of Psychology
University of Michigan
525 East University
Ann Arbor, MI 48109-1109
jglass@umich.edu

Leon Gmeidl
Department of Psychology
University of Michigan
525 East University
Ann Arbor, MI 48109-1109
gmeidl@umich.edu

Robert L. Goldstone
Psychology Department
Indiana University, Bloomington
Bloomington, IN 47405
rgoldsto@ucs.indiana.edu

Wayne D. Gray
George Mason University
MSN 3F5 4400 University Dr.
Fairfax, VA 22030-4444
gray@gmu.edu

Stephen Grossberg
Cognitive and Neural Systems
Boston University
677 Beacon St.
Boston, MA 02215
steve@cns.bu.edu

Peter W. Halligan
Department of Experimental
Psychology
Rivermead Rehabilitation Centre
South Parks Road
Oxford, OX1 3UD England
peter.halligan@psy.ox.ac.uk

Kristian J. Hammond
The Institute for the Learning
Sciences
Northwestern University
1890 Maple Avenue
Evanston, IL 60201
hammond@ils.nwu.edu

John Hertz
NORDITA (Nordic Institute for
Theoretical Physics)
Blegdamsvej 17
DK-2100 Copenhagen, Denmark
hertz@nordita.dk

Geoffrey E. Hinton
Gatsby Computational Neuroscience
Unit
University College London
Alexandra House, 17 Queen Square
London, WC1N 3AR England
g.hinton@ucl.ac.uk

Keith J. Holyoak
University of California, Los Angeles
Department of Psychology
UCLA
Los Angeles, CA 90095-1563
holyoak@lifesci.ucla.edu

John E. Hummel
University of California, Los Angeles
UCLA—Department of Psychology
405 Hilgard Ave.
Los Angeles, CA 90095-1563
jhummel@psych.ucla.edu

Bonnie E. John
Carnegie Mellon University
Human-Comp Interaction Institute
Carnegie Mellon University
Pittsburgh, PA 15213
bej@cs.cmu.edu

Hollyn M. Johnson
Psychology Department
University of Michigan
525 E. University Avenue
Ann Arbor, MI 48109-1109

Randy M. Jones
Electrical Engineering and Computer
Science
1101 Beal Ave.
University of Michigan
Ann Arbor, MI 48109-2110
rjones@eecs.umich.edu

Michael I. Jordan
Massachusetts Institute of Technology
77 Massachusetts Avenue
Cambridge, MA 02139-4307
jordan@psyche.mit.edu

Marcel A. Just
Department of Psychology
Carnegie Mellon University
Pittsburgh, PA 15213
just+@cmu.edu

David E. Kieras
Electrical Engineering and Computer
Science
University of Michigan
1101 Beal Ave.
Ann Arbor, MI 48109-2110
kieras@umich.edu

Walter A. Kintsch
Department of Psychology
University of Colorado, Boulder
Campus Box 345
Boulder, CO 80309-0345
wkintsch@psych.colorado.edu

Anders Krogh
Center for Biological Sequence
Analysis
The Technical University of Denmark
Building 208
2800 Lyngby, Denmark
krogh@cbs.dtu.dk

John K. Kruschke
Department of Psychology
Indiana University
Bloomington, IN 47405-1301
kruschke@indiana.edu

John E. Laird
Electrical Engineering and Computer
Science
University of Michigan
1101 Beal Ave.
Ann Arbor, MI 48109-2110
laird@umich.edu

Erick J. Lauber
0421 Psychology
University of Georgia
Athens, GA 30602-3013
elauber@egon.psy.uga.edu

Keith Law
The Institute for the Learning
Sciences
Northwestern University
1890 Maple Avenue
Evanston, IL 60201

Christian Lebiere
Psychology Department
Carnegie Mellon University
Pittsburgh, PA 15213
cl+@cmu.edu

Richard L. Lewis
Computer and Information Science
Ohio State University
Dreese Lab- 2015 Neil Ave.
Columbus, OH 43210
rick@cis.ohio-state.edu

Robert McCarl
Electrical Engineering and Computer
Science
University of Michigan
1101 Beal Ave.
Ann Arbor, MI 48109-2110
mccarl@umich.edu

Jay McClelland
Department of Psychology
Carnegie Mellon University
Pittsburgh, PA 15213
jlm@cnbc.cmu.edu

Mike McCloskey
Cognitive Science Department
Johns Hopkins University
Baltimore, MD 21218
michael.mccloskey@jhu.edu

Thomas F. McDougal
Department of Computer Science
University of Chicago
1100 East 58th St.
Chicago, IL 60637

Bruce McNaughton
Department of Psychology and
Physiology
University of Arizona
Tucson, AZ 85721
bruce@nsma.arizona.edu

Virginia A. Marchman
Department of Psychology
University of Wisconsin
1202 W. Johnson St.
Madison, WI 53706-1611
marchman@psy.uwisc.edu

John C. Marshall
The Radcliffe Infirmary
Oxford, OX2 6HE, England
john.marshall@clneuro.ox.ac.uk

Michael Matessa
Department of Psychology
Carnegie Mellon University
5000 Forbes Ave.
Pittsburgh, PA 15213
mm4b@andrew.cmu.edu

Douglas L. Medin
Psychology
Northwestern University
2029 Sheridan Rd.
Evanston, IL 60202
medin@nwu.edu

David E. Meyer
Department of Psychology
University of Michigan
525 East University
Ann Arbor, MI 48109-1109
demeyer@umich.edu

Michael C. Mozer
Department of Computer Science
University of Colorado, Boulder
Boulder, CO 80309-0430
mozer@cs.colorado.edu

Alan Newell
(deceased)

Randall O'Reilly
Department of Psychology
University of Colorado, Boulder
Campus Box 345
Boulder, CO 80309-0345
oreilly@psych.colorado.edu

Richard G. Palmer
Department of Physics
Duke University
Box 90305
Durham NC 27708
palmer@phy.duke.edu

Karalyn Patterson
MRC Cognition and Brain Sciences
Unit
15 Chaucer Road
Cambridge, England
CB2 2EF
karalyn.patterson@mrc-cbu.cam.ac.uk

David Plaut
Carnegie Mellon University
Mellon 115 CNBC CMU
4400 Fifth Ave.
Pittsburgh, PA 15213-2683
plaut@cmu.edu

Kim Plunkett
Experimental Psychology
Oxford University
South Parks Rd.
Oxford Oxfordshire
OX1 3UD United Kingdom
kim.plunkett@psy.ox.ac.uk

Thad Polk
Psychology Department
University of Michigan
525 E. University Ave.
Ann Arbor, MI 48109-1109
tpolk@umich.edu

Alan Prince
Linguistics
University of New Jersey, Rutgers
18 Seminary Pl.
Brunswick, NJ 08901
prince@ruccs.rutgers.edu

Paul S. Rosenbloom
Information Sciences Institute
University of Southern California
4676 Admiralty Way
Marina Del Rey, CA 90292-6695
rosenbloom@isi.edu

David E. Rumelhart
Department of Psychology
Stanford University
Palo Alto, CA 94305-2130

Eric H. Schumacher
Department of Psychology
University of Michigan
525 East University
Ann Arbor, MI 48109-1109
eschu@umich.edu

Mark S. Seidenberg
Psychology Department
University of Southern California
Neuroscience HNB 18B
Mail Code: 2520
Los Angeles, CA. 90089
marks@gizmo.usc.edu

Colleen M. Seifert
Psychology Department
University of Michigan
525 E. University Avenue
Ann Arbor, MI 48109-1109
seifert@umich.edu

David Servan-Schreiber
University of Pittsburgh
536A Scaife Hall, 624 0702
200 Terrace St.
Pittsburgh, PA 15213
ddss+@pitt.edu

Steven A. Sloman
Cognitive and Linguistic Sciences
Brown University
Box 1978—190 Thayer St.
Providence, RI 02912
steven_sloman@brown.edu

Paul Smolensky
Cognitive Science—Krieger
Johns Hopkins University
3400 N. Charles St.
Baltimore, MD 21218-2685
smolensky@mail.cog.jhu.edu

Willian R. Svec
Department of Psychology
Indiana University, Bloomington
Bloomington, IN 47405

Paul R. Thagard
Philosophy Department
University of Waterloo
Waterloo, Ontario N2L 3G1
Canada
pthagard@watarts.uwaterloo.ca

Scott W. VanderStoep
Psychology Department
Hope College
35 E. 12th St.
Holland, MI 49422-9000
vanderstoep@hope.edu

Kurt VanLehn
LRDC, Computer Science Department
University of Pittsburgh
Pittsburgh, PA 15260
vanlehn@pop.pitt.edu

Ronald J. Williams
Department of Cognitive Science—
0515
University of California, San Diego
LA Jolla, CA 92093-0515

Eileen Zurbriggen
Psychology Department
University of Michigan
525 E. University Ave.
Ann Arbor, MI 48109-1109

Index

ACME, 820, 842–843, 859–909, 926–929, 973
ACT Theory, 50–51, 112, 799
ACT-R, 50–66, 464–469, 577, 580, 606–611, 617–620
Activation
  of knowledge in memory, 16–19, 25–26, 133, 152–156, 164–168, 466–469, 874, 898, 964, 1015–1016
  in network models, 199–201, 217, 281–283, 324, 397, 543, 764–767, 788, 817–847, 1167, 1223
Adaptive Executive Control (AEC) models, 115–118
Adaptive Resonance Theory (ART), 296–314
Addition, 623–627, 637–642
Age-Related differences, 144
ALCOVE, 537–575
Algebra, 52–55, 581–583
Algorithms, 187–188, 191–195, 223, 225, 252
Alignment, 822–829, 833–834
Ambiguity, 145–148, 160–164, 406–410, 702, 806–809
Amnesia, 499–504
Analogy, 820, 849, 869–909, 911–934, 943–981, 988–1005
Animal models, 501–505, 1140–1142
Anticipatory effects, 749, 752–777
Aphasia, 783, 787, 786, 1152
Applications, 1083–1114, 1257–1258
Architectures, 71, 169, 943, 1117–1118, 1150, 1236, 1242
ARCS, 903, 926–929
Argumentation, 881–884
Arguments, 1009–1040
Arithmetic, 28–32, 623–645
Artificial Intelligence, 71
ARTMAP, 289–290, 293, 301–307
Associative networks, 7, 9–10, 669

Attention
  capacity theory of, 135, 170–171
  filter theory of, 20
  and neglect, 422–460
  processes of, 377–383, 398–406, 428–430, 544–553
  spatial, 1166
Attentional Mechanism (AM), 427, 455–457
Attractors, 198–199, 205, 722–737
Augmented Transition Network (ATN), 157

Backpropagation, 184–188, 213–220, 223, 232–233, 295, 555–561, 701, 713, 727–730, 1132, 1224
Beliefs, 1065–1067
Binding, 339–343, 369, 949–951, 970
BLIRNET, 425–427
Boltzman machine, 223
Brain damage, 423–457, 786–787, 1149–1152, 1162–1164

Capacity limitations, 751, 799, 809–811, 980
Capacity theory, 131, 171, 135–136
CAPS, 153–156
Case-Based Reasoning, 987–1005
Categorization, 61–63, 513–520, 537–555, 800–814, 1013–1040, 1050–1051, 1155–1164, 1205–1224
CCReader, 154
Chunks, 55, 79–80, 464, 579–580, 1242–1243
Cognitive modeling, 44, 411–412, 453–455, 488–490, 1135–1140
Compositionality, 1117, 1124
Concepts, 9, 621
Connectionism, 8, 10, 133, 259, 377, 392–395, 512–528, 706, 1120–1127, 1131–1143, 1221–1224. See also Parallel Distributed Processing
Constituency relations, 1118–1120

Constraint satisfaction, 851–859, 903
Constraints, 318–334, 819, 857, 1198–1199, 1232
Construction-integration theory, 5–45
Content-addressable memory, 197
Context effects, 38–40, 134, 138, 259–261, 280, 383, 700, 1203–1205
Continuous Performance Task (CPT), 381–382, 403–406
Contrast model, 821–822
COPYCAT, 869
CPM-GOMS, 1089–1112
Credit assignment, 635

Decisions, 77, 90, 1242
Declarative knowledge, 52, 76, 464
Deduction, 1045–1079
Default knowledge, 81–82
Deficits, 377–392, 499–512, 1155–1186
Design, 1083–1114
Development, 649–652, 654–656, 785–786, 1255–1256
Dissociations, 1155–1160
Distance effects, 151–152
Dopamine, 386–393, 395–398, 699
Dual route theories, 691–693, 719–720
Dynamic environments, 244–248, 1224, 1232
Dyslexia, 662, 692

Elaboration, 1067–1071
Energy function, 206–209
EPIC, 112–118
Error
  functions, 184, 204, 214, 265, 728
  in language use, 650–658, 666–668, 685–686, 718, 721, 725, 749–789
  learning from, 292, 543
  signals, 236–237
  types of, 265, 269, 749–789, 1183, 1185
Evolution, 1194–1196
Exclusive OR (XOR), 261–267, 545
Executive processes, 115, 124
Expertise, 933–934
Explanation, 884–889, 1132–1133
Eye movements, 6, 138–139, 192

Face recognition, 193–195, 1170–1179
Faithfulness constraints, 320–323
Feature-Based Model, 1011–1013, 1019–1040
Features, 817–847, 988–1005, 1009–1040
Feedforward networks, 220, 225–227, 235–236, 243–244, 255, 261, 285, 711–722
Free recall, 486–488

Fuzzy ART algorithms, 308–312
Fuzzy logic, 302–307

General Inductive Problem Solver (GIPS), 627–645
Generality, 610, 779–780
Generalized Content Model (GCM), 537–538
Geons, 343–358
Goals, 77–79, 90–91, 642–643, 990, 1093
GOMS, 1085–1089
Gradient descent, 220, 393, 573–575
GRAIN network, 696

Harmony function, 324, 456
Hidden units, 183, 191, 278, 566, 661
High threshold theory, 124
Hill-Climbing, 1220
Hippocampus, 499–504, 507–510
Hopfield model, 202
Human Associative Memory (HAM), 50
Human-Computer Interaction, 1085

Impasses, 81–82, 624–626
Indices, 989–992
Individual differences, 108–109, 120, 131, 135, 142–144, 778–779, 1071–1079
Induction, 1009–1040
Inference, 26–27, 32–38, 1045–1079, 1210–1215
Inhibition, 761–769
Integration, 15–19, 21, 87
Intelligence, 49–50, 73–74, 1236–1237
Intelligent tutors, 50
Interactivity, 722–738, 1155, 1160
Interference, 520–525, 557–560, 800–803
Inverse models, 229–232
Isomorphism, 860, 892
Iterative network, 219

JIM, 342–371

Keyboard design, 1106–1111
Knowledge
  acquisition, 55–57
  activation (see Activation)
  capacity, 57–58
  use, 57–58

Language
  comprehension of, 5–47, 132–175, 797–811
  context effects in, 383–386
  grammar, 317–323, 330–332
  morphology, 291, 662–686, 691–696

phonology, 1132
speech, 330, 747–794
structure of, 1255
syntax, 137–142, 157–164, 267–282, 801–814
vocabulary, 267–282, 649–658, 691–740
Learning
  associative, 223–255, 520–525
  brain mechanisms in, 504–511
  case-based, 987–1005
  chunks, 79–80, 93–94
  competitive learning, 191, 301
  cooperative learning, 819
  goal oriented, 242–243, 523, 1224
  in connectionist networks, 181–195, 223–255, 543–544, 768
  incremental, 330–332
  interactive, 223–224
  interleaved, 512–520
  language, 41, 328, 686–687
  rule-based, 561–565
  skill acquisition, 577–612, 649–658, 1249–1251
  supervised, 225–235, 565–567
  unsupervised, 191, 195, 213, 223, 296
Lesion, 424–425, 430–435, 441–443, 1152
Lexical access, 22, 156–157, 270–271, 692–671.
  See also Word recognition
Line bisection task, 424, 438–441
LISA, 944, 951–963
Locality assumption, 1149–1151, 1170–1186

MAC/FAC, 911–940
Mapping, 681–683, 817–846, 848–909, 919–940, 945–948, 964–979
Memory
  activation, 58–61
  associative, 197–199
  capacity, 41, 88–90, 135–136, 203–204, 280, 284, 797–812
  consolidation into, 510–511, 529–530
  load, 148–150
  long term, 75–77, 913–915, 963, 1201–1203
  organization, 89, 499–512
  recognition, 481–483, 1201–1205
  retrieval, 12, 930–931, 996–1007, 1200
  semantic, 159, 513–520, 1155–1164, 1178, 1249–1250
  serial order effects in, 258–286, 463, 470–490, 749–789
  for words, 463–492
  working, 55, 75, 131–132, 136, 144–145, 148–150, 797–814, 1250
Mental models, 1046

Metaphor, 895–899
Minima, 210, 220
Minimax learning rule, 294
Modality, 1159–1160
Model fitting, 488–490
Modularity, 136–138, 237, 1149, 1153, 1185
MORSEL, 425–455
Motor movements, 80–81, 94, 114–115, 257, 663
MultiDimensional Scaling (MDS), 820–823

Neocortical area, 506–507
NETTALK, 707
Neural networks, 181–184, 213, 323–328, 331–371, 861–865
Neurons, 181, 186, 195, 343, 695
NL-SOAR, 801
Nonconvexity problem, 239–242

Object recognition, 337–371
Ontology, 1126–1127
Operant conditioning, 1198
Operators, 76, 633, 1093
Optimality theory, 317–334
Optimization, 455, 1194–1196
Overgeneralization, 654–656, 668–669

Parallel Distributed Processing (PDP), 259, 268, 691–639, 691, 767–768, 1154–1155, 1184–1185. *See also* Connectionism
Parallelism, 76, 92, 111, 902, 1091–1094
Parameters, 478, 490–492, 604, 900
Perception, 20, 80–81, 94, 101, 113, 337–374, 818–819
Perceptrons, 213
PDP. *See* Parallel Distributed Processing
Planning, 635–637, 760–764, 997–1003, 1217–1220
Population codes, 191–195
Practice effects, 747–787
Pragmatics, 162–164, 855–857, 881–889, 926
Predictive, 986–1007
Preferences, 75
Prefrontal cortex, 386–392
Principal Components Analysis, 189–191, 295
Problem solving, 28–32, 63–65, 78, 91, 577, 630–633, 869–881, 1215–1220
Problem space, 70, 92, 854–855, 928, 1237–1238
Procedural knowledge, 52, 76, 464, 577–612
Production rules, 49, 51–55, 75–76, 113–114
Project Ernestine, 1085

Psychological refractory period (PRP), 103–105, 118
Pull-out networks, 427

Rational analysis, 1193–1200
Rationality, 1196–1200, 1251–1258
READER, 134
Reading, 6, 136–145, 691–740
Recurrent networks, 256–287, 661, 671, 728, 767
Regularities, 708
Reinforcement learning, 250–251, 566–567
Reminding, 930–931, 996–1007
Representations
    connectionist, 188, 257, 279–283, 338–343, 378–379, 706–711, 768–772, 852–854, 1014–1015, 1154–1155
    distributed, 284, 979
    localized, 560–561, 899, 1118, 1149
    multiple, 145–148
    production system, 75–79, 132–133, 627–630, 861, 872, 1234
    propositional, 5–15, 51–52, 951–954, 1234
    scene, 259, 843
    slot-based, 706
    symbolic, 1120–1121
Resource allocation, 172–173
Response selection bottleneck (RSB), 101–102
Retrieval, 988–1005
Retrieval status, 210
RUNNER, 997–1000

Schema, 89, 747, 946, 969
Schizophrenia, 377–392, 784
Semantics, 665–666, 683–685
Sentence processing, 5–40, 132–175, 271–278, 328, 797–811, 1253
SIAM, 834–846
Signal detection theory (SDT), 124, 883
Similarity, 543, 664–665, 677–681, 687, 797, 817–846, 854–855, 911–915, 934–935, 1018–1019
Similarity-Coverage Model, 1011, 1019–1040
Situation models, 43
SME, 820, 842–843, 867–869, 888, 916–940
Smolensky architectures, 1120–1127
Soar, 71–73, 82–86, 112, 802, 1243–1244
Sternberg item recognition task, 483–486, 1247
Strategic response deferment, 120–123
Strategies, 30–32, 621–645
Stroop task, 379–381, 398–403
Structural complexity, 162, 319–323, 337–338, 526–528, 943–951

Subgoals, 79
Syllogisms, 1050–1051, 1252–1253
Symbols, 279, 1235–1236, 1238
Syntax, 138–142

Task time, 1101–1105
Task types, 82–86, 1246–1248
Text comprehension, 5–47, 151–152
Theories, 168–169, 944, 1117, 1126, 1134–1135, 1231–1232, 1250–1257
Time, 71–72, 257–261, 283–285, 830, 948–951, 1239–1240
Tokens, 281, 652–653, 1123
Topdown processing, 6, 428
Training
    effects, 109–110, 120
    for networks, 186, 202, 243, 393, 408, 650, 675, 713, 727
Typing, 1247–1248

Unified theories, 1231–1233

Vectors, 1120–1121
Verbal reasoning, 1045–1079
Vision, 1164–1173

Weights, 182, 216, 218–219, 234, 303, 324, 701, 769, 822
Word recognition, 19–29, 267, 406–410, 425, 481–483, 691–740, 1133–1137. *See also* Lexical access